The **Vermont** Encyclopedia

editors **JOHN J. DUFFY, SAMUEL B. HAND, & RALPH H. ORTH**

mont
Encyclopedia

UNIVERSITY PRESS OF NEW ENGLAND   Hanover & London

University Press of New England,

37 Lafayette St., Lebanon, NH 03766

© 2003 by University Press of New England

All rights reserved

Printed in the United States of America

5   4   3   2   1

Library of Congress

Cataloging-in-Publication Data

The Vermont encyclopedia /

editors, John J. Duffy, Samuel B. Hand,

Ralph H. Orth

    p.   cm.

ISBN 1–58465–086–9 (alk. paper)

1. Vermont—Encyclopedias. I. Duffy,

John J. II. Hand, Samuel B., 1931–

III. Orth, Ralph H.

F47.V46 2003

974.3'003—dc21   2003010744

For

THOMAS DAY

SEYMOUR BASSETT

Collector and transmitter

of the story of Vermont

1912–2001

CONTENTS

CONTRIBUTORS

Jane Ambrose
James Barickman
Julie Becker
Dona Brown
Robert Buckeye
Lilian Baker Carlisle
Deborah P. Clifford
Ann E. Cooper
Robert V. Daniels
Prudence Doherty
Sarah L. Dopp
John Dumville
Hilari Farrington
Connell Gallagher
Hal Goldman
Barbara K. Hamblett
Mark Hazeltine
Carl Johnson
Karen Lane
Gary T. Lord
Winifred McCarthy-Don
Patricia Mardeusz
Addison Minott
D. Scott Newman
William E. Osgood
Anthony Paré
J. Tyler Resch
Ronald J. Salomon
Joseph-André Senécal
Michael Sherman
David M. Stameshkin
Fred Stetson
Winn L. Taplin
Gerald F. Vaughn
Edward J. Wildblood
Steve Wright

Glenn M. Andres
Andrew Barker
Michael A. Bellesiles
Herman Brown
Sylvia J. Bugbee
Paul A. Carnahan
Lawrence Coffin
Ann S. Cousins
Polly C. Darnell
Emmie Donadio
James H. Douglas
Janice B. Edwards
Vince Feeney
Nancy L. Gallagher
William W. Goss
Susan J. Harlow
Wesley Herwig
Donald B. Johnstone
Sarah B. Laughlin
John Lovejoy
John McClaughry
Jeffrey D. Marshall
Mariafranca Morselli
Reidun Nuquist
Anthony Otis
Kenneth A. Peck
Jason Roberts
Gregory Sanford
Gene Sessions
Tom Slayton
Peter J. Stanlis
Ernest Stires
Donald Tinney
Jane Vincent
Jane Williamson
John C. Wriston, Jr.

Donald Balch
T. D. Seymour Bassett
Marilyn Blackwell
David Bryan
Chris Burns
Edward J. Cashman
Arthur Cohn
Jay Craven
Forest Davis
David Donath
Virginia C. Downs
John S. Ellis
Harriet F. Fisher
Thomas H. Geno
J. Kevin Graffagnino
Kathleen McKinley Harris
Allen D. Hodgdon
Roy Korson
Richard Leyden
James Lowe
Marcus A. McCorison
Charlotte Mehrtens
H. Nicholas Muller III
Charles O'Brien
Candace Page
Ann Porter
Nancy Rucker
Mark Scott
Doris Severy
Frank Smallwood
Ann Stanton
Neil Stout
Robert Titterton
Lester Wallman
Kari J. Winter
Allen Yale

Betty Bandel
Jane C. Beck
David Blow
Frank Bryan
Karen Campbell
Richard T. Cassidy
Selene Colburn
Jere Daniell
Stephen Diehl
Erica H. Donnis
William Doyle
Paul Eschholz
Ann Lyons Fry
Paul Gillies
Edwin Granai
Richard Hathaway
Dee Dee Jameson
Madeleine M. Kunin
Mary G. Lighthall
Jerry McBride
Malcolm Macmillan
Addison Merrick
Gertrude Myrick
Ghita M. Orth
Lyssa Papazian
Hans Raum
Will Ryan
Paul Searls
Greg Sharrow
George E. Spear
William Steinhurst
Richard Sweterlitsch
Sherry Urie
Donald Wickman
Frederick Wiseman
Ray Zirblis

If you want to understand Vermont, take a walk through the halls of the Vermont State House. That elegant, slightly quirky granite building where much of the official life of the state has been conducted over the last 150 years mirrors our state character and experience in ways that are both obvious and surprising. In addition to being the building in which the Vermont legislature meets each winter, the State House is a shrine to Vermont's history, especially the state's heroic participation in the Civil War. Its contents and architecture also say much about this small state's determination to go its own way, its devotion to agriculture, its love of both independence and that form of interdependence we call community.

The State House is an ornate, mid-nineteenth-century building, and it is possible to feel a bit overwhelmed as you walk its high-ceilinged halls, flanked by paintings of past governors. But the decorative carpets and high ceilings simply add grace and elaboration to a fundamental Vermont principle: a belief in open, accessible government that is expressed in the building itself. There are very few private offices in the State House. Most legislators have a desk from which to do their business, a common sitting room in which to relax, and very little else. Committee rooms are almost always unlocked and open to the public. There is no place for legislators to hide (should they want to); the building forces them to do their business in the open.

Not that Vermont's legislature is an ideal governing body; it has its flaws. For example, Vermont's State House was, for much of its existence, home to one of the most poorly apportioned legislative bodies in the western world. Until it was forced by federal court order to reapportion itself according to the principle of one person, one vote, the Vermont House had one representative from every town in the state. There were 246 members in the House of Representatives in those days, and the city of Burlington had the same representation (one member) as did the tiny town of Victory.

That all changed in 1965, and today the House has 150 members, the Senate 30. Both bodies are apportioned, by law, on the basis of population. It may or may not be coincidental, but in the roughly forty years since reapportionment, the Legislature, like the state of Vermont itself, has become less politically conservative, more liberal, and at times, downright radical. The economic depletion that Vermont suffered in the nineteenth century, combined with the stronghold gained here by the Republican party in post–Civil War days, made the state one of the most conservative in the country for many years. But a modest economic prosperity, an influx of new residents from "down-country," and more widespread education in the latter half of the twentieth century combined to moderate that conservative stance. As the rest of the United States grew more conservative, Vermont maintained its strong attachment to the underdog and its social consciousness. By the turn of the millenium, the Green Mountains had become known as home to one of the most libertarian—some would say most liberal—states in the country.

Both perceptions of Vermont's political nature are probably mistaken, however, for conservative and liberal factions have existed here almost since the beginning. Vermont's strong environmental laws have been under nearly constant political attack since they were passed, and even the conservative farmers who dominated the legislature in the 1940s had no hesitancy about promptly declaring war on Nazi Germany when the time came. There has, in fact, been a constant ebb-and-rise for conservative and liberal factions in Vermont politics, and the Vermont State House has mirrored those dynamics. One faction may win the day for a time, but the other seems always to retain a vital base in the hearts of Vermonters and merely awaits the day of its revival when the times and the issues seem right.

The State House remains a surprisingly small building, emblematic of the small state it oversees. Further, the building sits on the edge of a forest in a tiny city—Montpelier—that has fewer than ten thousand inhabitants. It is the smallest, most rural capital city in

America; before sunrise, deer sometimes graze on the State House lawn. Members and staff of the legislature regularly complain of their cramped quarters, and plans are perennially made to enlarge it with more offices and amenities, but the elegant compactness of this small state capitol says much about the frugality and governmental vision of Vermonters.

Above the speaker's podium in the largest room in the building, the House of Representatives, hangs the original Vermont State Seal, complete with the motto: "Freedom and Unity." Vermont's first governor, Thomas Chittenden, coined the phrase when he declared that Vermont was "the home of freedom and unity," thus summing up succinctly our experience as a people and a state. That little phrase still epitomizes much of the Vermont experience, because it expresses perfectly the balance that has existed over the years between Vermont's well-known affection for personal independence and our equally strong respect for community values.

Vermont was an independent republic before it joined the United States in 1791. But it was also a frontier, where neighborly cooperation and mutual aid in times of distress—and other times as well—helped people survive a cold and often hostile environment. Barn raisings, wool shearings, harvest work parties, and work bees to help a sick or needy neighbor have been a fact of life in the Green Mountains for many, many years. The Catamount Tavern in Bennington, where Ethan Allen and his cronies met and held forth, was one of the places where Vermont independence was fomented and formed. Today, the values of community life still balance the well-known Vermont affection for personal independence. The emergence of a suburban lifestyle in many places in Vermont has tempered but not eliminated that aspect of Vermont's character. However much they love independence, Vermonters down through the years also have loved and practiced the mutual respect, care, and consideration that living in small towns in a small state demands. If "Freedom"—independence—is one pole of the Vermont compass, then "Unity"—interdependence—is the other. In Vermont, they are two sides of the same coin.

Atop the State House's gilded dome is a piece of genuine folk art, a representation of "Agriculture" hand-carved in 1938 under the direction of then Sergeant-at-Arms Dwight Dwinnell. It replaced an earlier version of the same goddess sculpted by Larkin Mead, which became too rotted to remain in place. Although agriculture is no longer the primary base of Vermont's economy (it is now exceeded in economic weight by both manufacturing and tourism), the presence of this lovely allegorical figure atop the State House is still appropriate, since much of Vermont's persona—our sense of humor, our independence and skepticism, even some of our everyday phrases—are a product of our long farming experience. And so is the incomparable Vermont countryside.

George Aiken, the horticulturist who became Vermont's longest-serving U.S. senator in the twentieth century and liked to refer to the wildflowers he learned to propagate as his friends, once said: "I believe that all human people need close association with Nature's people." And it was the nineteenth-century Vermont Congressman George Perkins Marsh who wrote in *Man and Nature*, the book that launched the American environmental movement: "Man has too long forgotten that the earth was given to him for usufruct [fruitful use] alone, not for consumption, still less for profligate waste."

Both viewpoints are based on the careful use of resources that farming in a cold place with a short growing season implies. The contemporary Vermont environmental movement, a bipartisan effort championed in the Vermont State House by Republicans and Democrats alike, takes much of its strength from the respect that Vermont farmers have traditionally shown their land.

Ever since the mid-nineteenth century, and even before, manufacturing has been an important part of the Vermont economic picture, and in the twentieth century, tourism has come to be a major player also. In fact, a higher percentage of the Vermont Gross State Product today comes from manufacturing than in the nation as a whole, and most Vermonters are not farmers, but jobholders. Especially in Chittenden County, around Burlington, the lifestyle has become largely suburban, and the experience of nature for many is recreational. Still, much of Vermont's appeal to residents, as well as outsiders, is directly linked to the remarkable beauty of a countryside that remains pastoral and forested in most of the state. Vermont today is more a home for chemical engineers, waitresses, office workers, garage mechanics, and teachers than it is a haven for hill farmers. But its rural past dictates much of its habits, speech, and folklore, even today.

Thriftiness in economics combined with a generosity

of spirit has characterized Vermonters down through the years, and those values can be seen in daily community life, and also in the State House, where some of the nation's most progressive legislation has been passed. Quite often that legislation has been based on Vermont's bedrock belief in equality. What may be the most controversial statute passed in recent memory, the Civil Unions law that allows homosexual couples most of the rights traditionally associated with marriage, stems directly from that firm conviction in the equality of all people. Like all advances in Civil Rights, that law encountered bitter opposition from many Vermonters and a strong backlash at the polls in the following election. But the law has of this writing not been repealed or significantly amended, and it stands today as a testament to the determination of Vermonters to treat their fellow citizens equally, despite differences that may exist among them.

Vermont's commitment to equality is not a recent idea. Vermont was the first state in the union to prohibit slavery, in its Constitution of 1777, and the state's belief in human equality was also expressed clearly by former President Calvin Coolidge in his *Autobiography*. There Coolidge wrote, describing his Plymouth neighbors: "They drew no class distinctions except toward those who assumed superior airs. Those they held in contempt. They held strongly to the doctrine of equality."

In all this, I'm speaking of the ideal. In Vermont, as in the larger world, people are people, and they can be as hateful, dishonest, elitist, and mean here as they can be anywhere else. Vermont, which banned slavery in its constitution, has had its racist interludes—the Ku Klux Klan appeared in the 1920s, the Eugenics Movement found advocates in the 1930s, and the Irasburg Affair of the 1960s was more recent. And there have been episodes of violence, bitter feuds, and grim, tawdry murders like that of Orville Gibson in the 1950s, throughout our history. Vermont is not Brigadoon; it is a real place with real people who try—and sometimes fail, but try pretty consistently—to be honest and decent.

One of the reasons that Vermonters seem generally to behave pretty well is not because their character is any better than anyone else's, but because Vermont is small and intimate in scale. There are still fewer than seven hundred thousand people here—about the population of a medium-sized city anywhere else. People know one another, and it is very difficult to be really

nasty to people you're going to run into on Main Street the next afternoon.

There can be no denying that Vermont is changing, that farming faces difficulty here, that suburban sprawl continues to gnaw away at our roadsides and open meadows and that trophy homes are cropping up on many hillsides and lakeshores. Public debate and legislative action have led to environmental regulations aimed at slowing the spread of mindless development and preventing and reversing the pollution of our air and streams. That very struggle is an expression of Vermont's traditional character, as Vermont fights to go its own way, against the immense pressures of an international economy that eats open farmland for breakfast and has no way to measure adequately the value of streams and lakes that are clean and clear, mountains that are wild and free, or a beautiful countryside that produces food.

Vermont's future depends upon maintaining our traditional values, even as our traditional way of life changes. Vermont can continue to go its own way and remain a place apart only if we maintain our long belief in the values of independence and equality before the law of every person, if we maintain our traditional ties to farming and the land, and if we work together as a community to realize those ideals. Fortunately, Vermont seems determined to remain itself, despite pressures to be otherwise.

As it has through much of its history, Vermont today still values the independent free thinker who follows his or her own guiding star. The state that Matthew Lyon and Abby Hemenway called home has elected and re-elected to Congress a feisty and independent self-proclaimed socialist, U.S. Representative Bernard Sanders, apparently because most Vermonters respect his populist beliefs and his outspoken independence despite his heavy Brooklyn accent.

The state that put a symbolic figure of "Agriculture" atop its gold State House dome is still the most extensively farmed state in New England. The home of George Perkins Marsh, a founder of the American environmental conservation movement, recently approved the largest conservation land purchase in its history to protect 130,000 acres of threatened forestland in Essex County. Even in a rapidly changing world, in Vermont, old values matter and the Green Mountain State remains, in many ways, "the home of Freedom and Unity."

PREFACE *John J. Duffy*

The Vermont Encyclopedia was prompted by remarks and advice from many Vermonters that a reliable, broad-based reference book was missing from the resources they consulted for information on the state. *The Vermont Encyclopedia* aims to fill that void. It will provide Vermonters and other readers who are interested in or attracted to this place a one-volume collection of information on some of Vermont's most noteworthy people, places, events, natural features, organizations, artifacts, flora, and fauna, and it will help them verify a name, date, or fact, enliven a discussion, strengthen an argument, write a report, proposal, or student paper, or just learn something interesting. The editors subscribe to the notion that knowing Vermont today is enhanced by knowing the who, why, and when of how it came to be as it is, so *The Vermont Encyclopedia* both looks back in time and attends to the present. It is an historical dictionary and a current report.

An early advisor whom we consulted urged us to produce a complete biographical dictionary of Vermonters. That was an attractive, though daunting, concept, for the long story of this place is full of interesting characters, many of them far less celebrated than they should be. Though not strictly the biographical dictionary first urged on us, *The Vermont Encyclopedia* contains many short biographies of people who in some way contributed to the shaping of Vermont or represent recognizable features of the community. Some were prominent, even heroic figures, others less so. Still others would qualify as scamps and villains, or at least as a bit eccentric, and a few are or were convicted felons.

Encyclopedias have been published about Vermont, most of them more than seventy years ago, but this one is clearly different from earlier productions in the genre. We found when our compiling was finished that this book contained far more material on women and minorities than earlier general reference books had included. Vermont places, as well as many of those events and organizations that shape the story of Vermont, are also recorded and described here. Additionally, some of Vermont's persistently appealing real and imaginary non-human critters who share this environment are presented in this book. Significant aspects of Vermont's built and natural environments are also detailed here.

The term "Vermonter" has been used several times already without a definition. Americans have been a mobile, transient people from the beginning, and any definition of "Vermonter" is shaped largely by that fact. We have employed neither birth nor residency requirements to qualify people for inclusion in this book.

The Vermont Encyclopedia is organized in a traditional alphabetical format. When the subject of an entry is mentioned in another entry for the first time, it is presented in small capital letters, indicating that it is the subject of an entry elsewhere in the book. The only entries not so cross-referenced are the frequently occurring names of cities, towns, and gores (and Warner's Grant).

Population figures are from the 2000 federal census.

More than 140 writers, including the three editors, have contributed entries to this book. They are teachers, librarians, archivists, college professors, constitutional officers of the state, physicians, museum workers, independent scholars, homemakers, police officers, and lawyers, mostly from Vermont but also from New York, New Hampshire, Massachusetts, Ohio, Illinois, Georgia, Arizona, and Australia. Entries without an author's name at the end were written by one of the editors.

Many Vermonters from across the state advised us on subjects for *The Vermont Encyclopedia*. When work on this book began in 1999, we knew we would depend heavily on T. D. Seymour Bassett for entries drawn from his long and deep research and knowledge of Vermont. Those entries display his full, special understanding of Vermont. One of our first advisors as well, Tom Bassett's contributions to this book were cut short by his death in 2001. This book is dedicated to him.

The glossary provided in Frederick Wiseman's *Voice of the Dawn* (University Press of New England, 2001) is the source for Abenaki place-names used here. For permission to publish photographs from their collections, we thank the University of Vermont's Special Collections in the Bailey Howe Library, Diane Konrady and the Vermont Department of Tourism and Marketing, John Hall in the Vermont Department of Fish and Wildlife, *Vermont Life*, Kurn Hattin Homes, Stephen Diehl, Nuna Teal, and Robert Titterton.

We are grateful to Phyllis Deutsch of the University Press of New England for her friendly and always encouraging support for this book. The A. D. Henderson Foundation has generously assisted the publication of *The Vermont Encyclopedia*, and we are very grateful to the Henderson family and Barbara Monz for their continued strong interest in Vermont and their support for this book.

VERMONT, THE GREEN MOUNTAIN STATE

The name "Vermont" was adopted on June 7, 1777, at a convention of delegates in Windsor who had been meeting there and earlier at Dorset and Westminster for the purpose of forming a state separate from New Hampshire and New York. At a previous session, they had named it New Connecticut, but Ira Allen circulated a letter from Dr. Thomas Young, a friend of many of the delegates, who urged the convention to call their new state Vermont. Not known to have been literate in French, Young claimed that the name Vermont was derived from French words. No evidence from when the region was part of New France suggests that the French ever called the place or the mountains Vermont. Place names acknowledging dominant colors in the landscape were familiar to settlers from the Red River and Green Pond Mountain districts of western Connecticut, and the mountain chain that dominated the region had been called the Green Mountains by the earliest settlers. In 1770, an irregular militia of settlers formed to resist New York authority took the name "Green Mountain Boys" to taunt the New York governor who threatened to drive them off their land and into the mountains.

VERMONT FACTS

Vermont became the fourteenth state on March 9, 1791.

The nickname of Vermont is the Green Mountain State.

The state motto is "Freedom and Unity."

Montpelier has been the permanent state capital since 1805.

Official state symbols:

  The state bird is the hermit thrush.

  The state tree is the sugar maple.

  The state animal is the Morgan horse.

  The state flower is red clover.

  The state soil is the Tunbridge Soil Series.

  The state insect is the honey bee.

  The state beverage is milk.

  The state fish are brook trout and walleye pike.

The Vermont state poet is currently Grace Paley.

The state song is *These Green Mountains*, composed by Diane Martin and arranged by Rita Buglass.

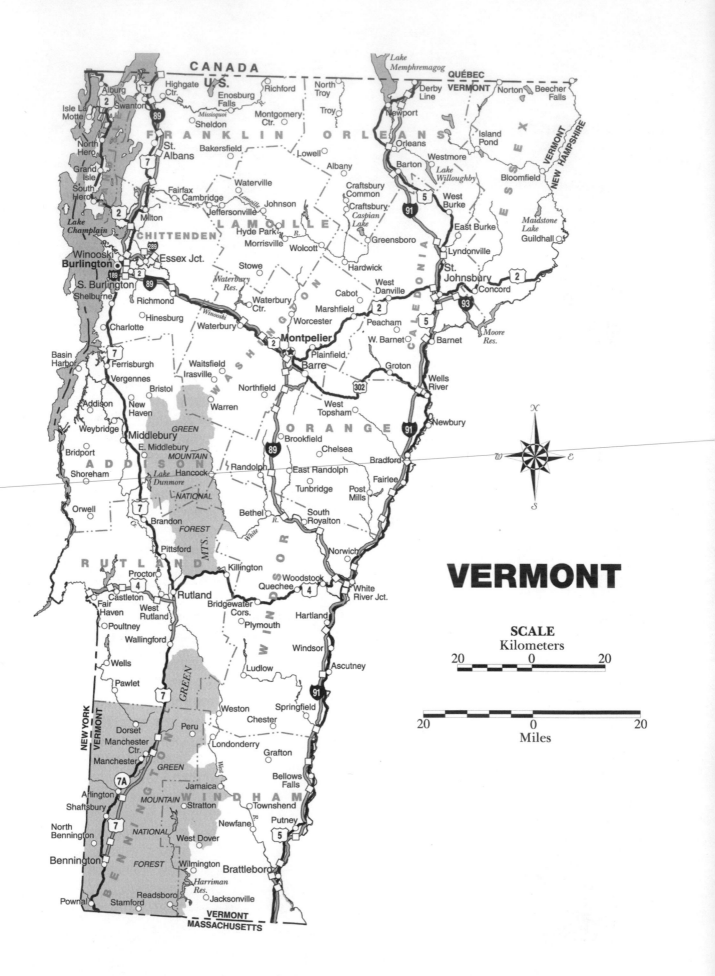

VERMONT

SCALE
Kilometers
20   0   20

20   0   20
Miles

introduction

VERMONT GEOGRAPHY, WEATHER, AND NATURAL HISTORY   *Ralph H. Orth*

The northwestern-most New England state and the only one without an Atlantic shoreline, Vermont, at 9,609 square miles, is the eighth-smallest state in the union. Its dominant physical feature is the Green Mountains, a part of the Appalachian range, which bisect the state from north to south. The west bank of the Connecticut River forms the eastern boundary, and the deep-water channel of Lake Champlain forms the upper two-thirds of the western. Its northern border with Canada is officially 45 degrees north latitude, which is halfway between the equator and the North Pole, but the actual border as determined by inaccurate nineteenth-century surveys is not exactly on the forty-fifth parallel.

What Mark Twain said about New England weather, that it has "sumptuous variety," certainly applies to Vermont. Situated as it is near the eastern edge of North America approximately halfway between the equator and the pole, the state is the continual battleground between weather systems from the northwest and the south, with an occasional storm from the Atlantic Ocean thrown in. Whatever the season, cool dry air masses from Canada alternate with cloudier, more humid systems that draw their moisture from as far away as the Gulf of Mexico. The result, at Vermont's latitude, is a temperately warm summer naturally air cooled every few days by winds from the north, and in winter, generally cold weather subject to occasional warming spells and even thaws of several days' duration. In the spring and fall, the battle between these two air masses increases in intensity as the region reacts to equinoctial transitions in global temperature. Spring usually arrives grudgingly and produces the period called "mud season," when thawing of the upper few inches of the ground traps layers of water, which liquefy the soil and make travel on dirt roads difficult. But in most years it also produces a favorable combination of warm days and cold nights that induce maple sap to flow and lead to the production of one of the state's prime agricultural products, maple syrup. Autumn, by contrast, usually lasts many weeks and is marked by a spectacular foliage season that draws hundreds of thousands of "leaf peepers" every year and is a vital component of Vermont's tourist industry.

At the summer solstice in June, we have fifteen hours and thirty-eight minutes of daylight, while at the winter solstice in December, the duration shrinks to eight hours and forty minutes, a difference of seven hours, enough to produce in some people the "wintertime blues," also known as seasonal affective disorder. The growing season (between killing frosts) in the warmest parts of Vermont (the Champlain Valley and the southern portion of the Connecticut River valley) ranges from 130 to 150 days, while in the Northeast Kingdom the season usually lasts between 100 and 130 days.

Precipitation in the form of rain in summer and snow in winter varies with location and elevation. The regions of greatest precipitation in Vermont are the higher altitudes of the Green Mountains and the southernmost portions of the state, while the Champlain Valley, in the rain shadow of the Adirondacks, receives the least rain and snow. There can also be great variation from year to year in the amount of precipitation or even in the same year, as in 2001, when record snow totals in the winter were followed by a prolonged drought in the summer and fall. For Vermont farmers who are dependent on the weather for their livelihood, a bad summer, either due to inadequate rain, windstorms, or other phenomena, can spell disaster. For others, such as ski area owners, it is possible to compensate for inadequate snowfall by snow-making operations, although nothing can alleviate a prolonged warm spell.

A not-unusual phenomenon of late fall, winter, and early spring in Vermont are storms called northeasters (colloquially nor'easters), caused by intense areas of low pressure rotating counterclockwise off the Atlantic coast that bring intense cold down from Canada, which, mixed with moisture-laden air, produces high winds, snow, sleet, or freezing rain. Many of the state's major winter storms have been northeasters.

The average high and low temperatures for July are

80 degrees and 59 degrees Fahrenheit, and for January 25 degrees and 8 degrees Fahrenheit. The coldest temperature ever recorded in Vermont (and a record for New England as well) was 50 degrees below zero Fahrenheit in Bloomfield, Essex County, on December 30, 1933. The warmest was 105 degrees Fahrenheit in Vernon, in the state's southeastern corner, on July 4, 1911. The greatest fall of snow from a single storm deposited 50 inches on Readsboro in Bennington County on March 2 through 5, 1947, and the greatest season snowfall total was 318.6 inches (26½ feet) on Mount Mansfield in 1970 to 1971.

Vermont history is replete with unusual weather events, among which are the "year without a summer," 1816, apparently caused by the dust cast into the atmosphere by the eruption of Mount Tambora (in today's Indonesia) in April 1815; the great flood of November 1927, the most disastrous event in the state's history; the hurricane of 1938, which on September 21 did enormous damage to the forests in the Connecticut River valley and on the eastern slopes of the Green Mountains; and the ice storm of 1998, when in early January freezing rain coated trees and power lines with several inches of ice, causing millions of dollars worth of damage and loss of power to thousands of people for up to several weeks.

What effects the phenomenon of global warming will have on Vermont is not entirely clear, but it seems certain not only to raise annual average temperatures in all seasons but also to affect the amount and kind of precipitation the state receives. It may also in the long term modify the kinds of vegetation found in the state, and affect such important parts of the Vermont economy as skiing, the foliage season, and maple sugar production. Coming decades will allow us to chart the possible changes in the weather in the Green Mountain State.

As delineated in *The Story of Vermont: A Natural and Cultural History*, by Christopher McGrory Klyza and Stephen C. Trombulak, Vermont consists of six distinct geographical regions based upon "broad patterns of geology, topography, climate, and species distributions." The main region is the Green Mountains, a highly eroded range 400 to 450 million years old composed mostly of granite whose tallest summits top out at 4,000 to 4,400 feet. To the east of them and also extending the length of the state is a piedmont region of low hills cut by watercourses flowing into the Connecticut River, a pattern reflected also on the New Hampshire side of the Con-

necticut. The extreme northeastern part of the state, roughly equivalent to the area known as the Northeast Kingdom, is a cold, snowy highland area that can be considered a foothills region of the White Mountains.

On the western side of the Green Mountains is the Champlain Valley, dominated by Lake Champlain, which at 435 square miles is the sixth-largest freshwater lake in the United States. Broad, fertile, and with a higher average temperature than any other part of the state, the valley extends northward into Canada toward the St. Lawrence River. The valley ends to the south at the Taconic Mountains, which form the boundary between Vermont and New York and extend southward into the Hudson Highlands. The Taconics are as old as the Green Mountains but geologically different, and their highest summits are two to six hundred feet lower.

Finally, the last and smallest geographical region is what is known as the Valley of Vermont, a lowland area only a mile to a few miles wide between the Taconics and Green Mountains extending northward until it merges into the Champlain Valley. Two rivers mark the valley, the Batten Kill in its central section flowing south and then westward, and Otter Creek, Vermont's longest river, which flows northward and empties into Lake Champlain. The state's topography precludes major watercourses. Otter Creek is just 102 miles long, and the other rivers of note emptying into Lake Champlain are the Missisquoi (96 miles), Winooski (88 miles), and Lamoille (85 miles). The Connecticut River tributaries, which include the West, the Williams, the White, and the Passumpsic, are all shorter than their western Vermont counterparts. Several short rivers, including the Barton and the Clyde, drain into Lake Memphremagog on the border with Canada and eventually join with the St. Francis on its way to the St. Lawrence, and the Batten Kill in the Valley of Vermont empties into the Hudson at Schuylerville, New York.

Despite its relatively small size, Vermont has a remarkably varied natural landscape. In *Wetland, Woodland, Wildland: A Guide to the Natural Communities of Vermont*, the authors, Elizabeth H. Thompson and Eric R. Sorenson, list eighty separate natural communities in the state. (A natural community is defined as "an interacting assemblage of organisms, their physical environment, and the natural processes that affect them.") These range from various types of bogs, marshes, and swamps through floodplain forests, shale and sand beaches, talus slopes, woodlands composed of various mixes of hardwoods and softwoods, upland meadows, and subalpine regions at the highest elevations of the Green Mountains. Relatively undisturbed in the thousands of years before the beginning of European settlement, this landscape has undergone dramatic changes since the middle of the eighteenth century. The forests have been cut over, the rivers have been dammed, the hills have been mined, the swamps have often been drained or filled in. Invasive plant or animal species have altered the original composition of the natural environment, and commercial and residential construction induced by economic expansion and human population growth steadily and subtly changes the appearance of the landscape. Nevertheless, given the inherent resilience of nature, much of that landscape remains healthy, and over the past few decades, efforts to protect and enhance it have grown exponentially. The actions of government and private citizens working together have made it possible to believe that Vermont's natural environment will survive and remain healthy in the face of inevitable future development.

POPULATION *Frederick Schmidt*

Although Vermont is the forty-ninth state in population in the union—with a 2000 census count of 608,827—it is actually near the median ranking in terms of population density. With 24.8 people per square kilometer, it ranks far below Alaska (0.4 people), Wyoming (1.9), and Montana (2.3), and is comfortably above the most crowded states, New Jersey (424) and Rhode Island (366).

Yet Vermont is also demonstrably the most rural state in the nation. This derives from the fact that in the United States the definition of "rural" depends upon the number of people who reside in places with fewer than twenty-five hundred inhabitants. Since Vermonters live in 246 cities and towns comprising "places" in Vermont, and most of these have fewer than twenty-five hundred inhabitants, the state is ipso facto rural. Services and elected representatives typically follow these local boundaries. Unlike most states, in which counties are the unit used to determine rural and urban populations, Vermont's fourteen counties are organized only to provide law enforcement (sheriff) and judicial (court houses) services; no other governmental apparatus exists at the county level. In most other states, "open country" rural residents have no local government and seek their representation from county officials. In Vermont (and in New England generally), town and city government prevails and allegiance to "place" is intense. The fact that the state's rural population is counted in this manner established Vermont's claim to being overwhelmingly rural. Simply put, different criteria are used to establish rural character in New England compared to other states, and true comparisons are not really possible.

Nevertheless, Vermont does have an officially recognized metropolitan area. Centered on Burlington and including numerous nearby cities and towns, this area has a population of 165,000 persons, which constitutes just under 30 percent of the state's total population. The balance of the population, the so-called non-metropolitan category, was calculated at 72.1 percent in 1999, and that figure supports the claim of being the most rural state in the nation. The state with the next-largest non-metropolitan population was Wyoming, at 70.4 percent.

Total number of inhabitants and comparisons to other states aside, the most important news is Vermont's sustained population growth over the past four decades. After 140 years of very slow growth, including two decades with actual numerical declines, Vermont has enjoyed a steady, albeit variable, rate of growth since 1960. The figures tell the tale: a 14.1 percent increase in the 1960s, 15 percent in the 1970s, 10 percent in the 1980s, and 8.2 percent in the 1990s. Altogether, the increase during this period was 56.2 percent, large enough by anyone's standards to require considerable structural and cultural adjustment, as is evident in the current public debate over "sprawl." To put these increases in perspective, it is important to note that they are below the national growth rate in the 1990s of 13.2 percent, and far below the rocket increases occurring in the southern and southwestern states.

Growth has been uneven throughout the state. Five of the nine cities lost population. The greatest increase occurred in Chittenden County and influenced the growth of Grand Isle, Lamoille, and Franklin counties. The northwestern corner of the state, in fact, accounted for half of the state's 8.2 percent population increase in the 1990s. Rutland, Bennington, and Essex counties had little growth, and in fact Essex County, in the heart of the Northeast Kingdom, replaced Grand Isle County as the least-populated area. Southern Vermont counties had moderate growth. Political struggles during redistricting are inevitable as northwestern Vermont gains clout at the expense of the rest of the state.

The racial and ethnic composition of Vermont's population has changed slightly over the decades, but the state remains one of the whitest in the nation—the second-whitest, in fact, behind Maine. Despite a marked self-consciousness among Vermonters regarding the lack of cultural diversity in the state, small changes over the past decade do indicate greater ethnic diversity. However, in the 2000 census we remained the second "whitest" state (at 96.8 percent white); only Maine at 96.9 percent is whiter. As one might suspect, the impact of urbanization and industrialization in New England is closely associated with the presence of peoples of color. One exception of course is the indigenous, Native Ameri-

POPULATION COMPARISONS

| Year | Population | | Electoral College | | |
	New England (1000)	United States (1000)	Vermont	New England	United States
1800	1,233	5,297	4	39	138
1812	1,472	7,244	8	51	218
1820	1,660	9,618	8	47	235
1832	1,955	12,901	7	50	288
1840	2,235	17,120	7	50	294
1852	2,728	23,261	5	41	296
1860	3,135	31,513	5	41	303
1872	3,488	39,905	5	40	366
1880	4,011	50,262	5	40	369
1892	4,701	63,056	4	39	444
1900	5,592	76,094	4	39	447
1912	6,553	92,407	4	44	531
1920	7,401	106,466	4	44	531
1932	8,126	123,188	3	41	531
1940	8,437	132,122	3	41	531
1952	9,313	151,683	3	40	531
1960	10,509	179,323	3	40	537
1972	11,847	203,235	3	37	538
1980	12,323	226,505	3	37	538
1996	13,312	265,562	3	37	538
2000	13,920	281,422	3	37	538

can population, which appears in greater percentages in the more sparsely populated Vermont (0.4 percent).

Demonstrating trends toward greater ethnic diversity in Vermont, the Vietnamese population has more than tripled in the past decade (from 236 in 1990 to 980 now). Also between 1990 and 2000, Vermont's African-American population grew from 1,951 to 3,063. The Asian population grew from 3,134 to 5,217 over the same period and the ethnic Latino population grew from 3,661 to 5,504. Smaller groups also grew. For example, Vermont's tiny Samoan population grew from 18 to 44. With a population of 1,374, there are more Puerto Ricans here than any other single group of Hispanics.

Two other dimensions of ethnicity are often discussed in this state: French-Canadian heritage and the decline of native-born Vermonters. French-speaking residents of direct French-Canadian descent are well represented in the communities of all the three northern New England states and until very recently the French-Canadians were the single largest ethnic group in each of Vermont's fourteen counties. Forthcoming data from Census 2000 may challenge this generalization. Preliminary figures from the last census show that despite continued inmigration, the majority of Vermont's population (55 percent) are Vermont natives. This figure has dropped just a few points in recent decades. Some of these natives, however, will be children of recent immigrants to Vermont.

HISTORY   *Samuel B. Hand*

Direct documentary evidence is scarce for the early historic period of what is today called Vermont, but scholars estimate that in the seventeenth century approximately ten thousand Native Americans occupied the region that was to become northwestern New England and southern Quebec. In 1609, when the French explorer Samuel de Champlain became the first recorded European to visit Vermont, its aboriginal inhabitants included Mohawks, Mohicans, and Abenaki. Hunters and gatherers, the Abenaki maintained settlements at present-day Swanton, in the Champlain islands and along the Winooski and Connecticut rivers.

Champlain initiated an alliance between the Abenaki and the French directed intermittently for 150 years against the Iroquois Confederacy and the British. Although Vermont attracted few European settlers, by 1675 a struggle between France and England for control of the North American continent propelled the region into periodic turmoil. The Abenaki, augmented by a southern New England Indian diaspora after King Philip's War (1675–1677), joined elements of the French army to raid New England settlements. A Woronoco from Massachusetts known to the English as Gray Lock settled with the Missisquoi Abenaki and was their war leader for nearly fifty years. During King William's War (1688–1697), the North American operations of the War of the League of Augsburg and Queen Anne's War (1702–1713), the North American counterpart to the War of the Spanish Succession, the French and Abenaki raided Deerfield, Massachusetts, and other Connecticut River villages. In response, Massachusetts colonists in 1724 established the first British settlement in Vermont at Fort Dummer on the Connecticut River near present-day Brattleboro to protect southern New England settlers from French and Indian attacks.

The French, meanwhile, moved south up Lake Champlain, building Fort Sainte-Anne on Isle La Motte (1666), Pointe à la Chevelure (1731; later Chimney Point), and Fort Carillon (1755; later Fort Ticonderoga). Despite control of the strategic and fertile Lake Champlain basin, the French, primarily involved in fur trade, gave less attention to colonizing than did the British. By 1755, New France contained 75,000 settlers, British America 1.5 million.

The French and Indian War (1754–1763), the North American campaigns of the Seven Years' War in Europe and the final British-French contest for North American empire, ended with a British victory that gave them sovereignty over what was to become Vermont, a lightly settled frontier region saddled with conflicting claims fueled by inaccurate maps supporting different royal charters. In 1741, a boundary dispute between Massachusetts and New Hampshire resolved by the crown in New Hampshire's favor had obligated New Hampshire to maintain Fort Dummer and emboldened New Hampshire Governor Benning Wentworth to assert that New Hampshire's western boundary extended to Lake Champlain. New York Province, relying in part on a 1664 grant by Charles II to his brother the Duke of York (later James II), rejected Wentworth's claims and maintained that its jurisdiction extended to the Connecticut River. Nonetheless, in 1750 Wentworth issued a grant for the town of Bennington, the westernmost point of his claim, and from then until 1754 when war erupted, chartered fifteen additional towns in what was soon referred to as the New Hampshire grants.

With the Crown Point Military Road crossing the Green Mountains from the Connecticut River to Lake Champlain and British victories removing the French and Indian threat from the north, land-hungry frontiersmen and speculators were drawn to the Green Mountains and their rich intervales. After the fall of Carillon, renamed Ticonderoga, and Quebec in 1759, Wentworth resumed dispensing grants, reaching a total of 138 by 1763, when the Treaty of Paris formally ended the war. By then, New York was issuing patents that were more remunerative to the crown's provincial officers than Wentworth's and that often overlapped New Hampshire grants. Equally significant, New York City served as a mustering-out point for military veterans who took their pensions in land titles. In 1764, a King's Order in Council ruled the border between New York and New Hampshire "to be the west bank of the Connecticut River." New Hampshire title holders interpreted "to be" as referring to jurisdiction from the date of the Order's issuance. Until 1764, they contended, the boundary was unsettled and governors of both New York and New Hampshire, as agents of the crown, possessed grant-issuing authority, Thus, they argued, New Hampshire grants issued prior to 1764, except where they overlapped pre-existing New York titles, were perfectly valid. New York took exception to this interpretation, contending that the ruling was retroactive, and continued to make grants overlapping New Hampshire's while pursuing ejectment suits against settlers with New Hampshire titles.

While the title issue continued unsettled, New York's jurisdiction had been affirmed by the 1764 Order in Council and the province responded by establishing its county government system upon the grants, dividing it into four counties, each with its own court and representatives to the provincial assembly. The southwesternmost region was situated in Albany County and in 1770 the title issue was contested in an Albany County court with Ethan Allen serving as agent for the Wentworth titleholders. The court rejected all New Hampshire claims. Wentworth titleholders responded with para-military units, called the Green Mountain Boys, which thwarted New York efforts at ejectment. Led by Ethan Allen, Seth Warner, Remember Baker, and others from west of the Green Mountains, the Green Mountain Boys, many with heavy investments in New Hampshire titles, used force to block New York settlements. East of the Green Mountains, where smaller land holders dominated, the title controversy was calmed by New Hampshire grantees paying reconfirmation fees to New York. However, court fees and seizures for debt fed discontent among eastern settlers and led to a March 1775 court house riot in Westminster, leaving two dead, the complete breakdown in New York jurisdiction, and increased popular support for the outlawed Green Mountain Boys.

The month after the "Westminster Massacre," while New York authorities were distracted by protests by the Sons of Liberty in New York City, the battles of Lexington and Concord sparked the American Revolution. And in May, Ethan Allen and his Green Mountain Boys along with Benedict Arnold captured the British Fort Ticonderoga in New York. The first American victory of the war, it succeeded in closing the Champlain-Hudson corridor against invasion from Canada for two years and in capturing sorely needed cannon for the Continental army. Immediately afterward, the Continental Congress authorized a Continental army regiment of Green Mountain Rangers who were to be paid by New York. When the troops chose Seth Warner as their colonel, Ethan Allen was left without a command. In September 1775, smarting from this rejection, Allen staged an ill-advised attack on Montreal and was captured.

In January 1777, following a series of conventions of town representatives from the New Hampshire grants, delegates declared their independence from New York and Great Britain, and in July met in Windsor to draft a constitution, schedule elections, and establish a government for the state of New Connecticut, later renamed Vermont.

The times were not auspicious. General John Burgoyne had mounted an invasion south along Lake Champlain from Canada as settler families fled to the southern reaches of Vermont. In July, as the delegates pondered the constitution, news of the British recapture of Fort Ticonderoga reached them. By fall, however, patriot prospects had brightened. In August, New Hampshire and Vermont troops under the command of General John Stark defeated a British force near Bennington, and in September, General Burgoyne surrendered his army to continental troops after the Battle of Saratoga.

As neither Congress nor New York recognized Vermont as a state until 1791, it was an anomaly, at times assuming the character of a sovereign nation. Its conduct of foreign policy involved the "Haldimand Negotiations" (1781), dealings with Great Britain that contemplated a restoration of Vermont to the Empire in return for a promise that the British army would not invade Vermont or New York. Whether the Vermont negotiators were sincere or engaged in a deception to enhance their military security is still debated. A strong Loyalist presence in Vermont was evidenced by Loyalist forces recruited principally from Vermonters that fought at Bennington under Justus Sherwood of New Haven and at Saratoga under the command of Royalton's John Peters. A second Vermont initiative was to annex amenable towns in western New Hampshire and eastern New York. These "east and west unions" attracted considerable New York, New Hampshire, and congressional displeasure, and Vermont complied with directives from Philadelphia to relinquish control of the towns in the hopes that submission would promote admission into the new United States. It was not until March 4, 1791, after Vermont "bought itself free" by paying New York $30,000 to settle disputed land titles, that Vermont was admitted as the fourteenth state.

The years between the Revolution and the War of 1812 were the period of the state's greatest growth. Both an example and a symbol of America's frontier, its population grew from 85,341 in 1791 to 217,895 in 1810. Such increases did not survive the second war with Great Britain. Lacking an ocean port (Vermont was the first state not to border on the Atlantic), western and particularly northwestern Vermont was dependent upon trade with Canada through Lake Champlain. The north-flowing lake carried potash, lumber, and grains. Hogs, horses, and beef cattle were often brought to market on the hoof. The suspension of trade with Canada in 1808 stimulated popular support for smuggling and political opposition to the party of Jefferson and to the ensuing war itself. Although the war was not popular in eastern Vermont either, the region was less dependent upon Canadian trade. With the Connecticut River serving as its principal commercial artery, economic interests east of the Green Mountains were more closely aligned with New Hampshire and southern New England.

While post-war prosperity helped Vermont recover from the devastating effects of the embargo, pre-war rates of population and economic growth failed to return after 1816. Not until the mid-1820s did modest prosperity and a quiet political atmosphere soothe the devastating effects of the embargo and war. The Napoleonic Wars in Europe, however, afforded the American Consul in Lisbon, Portugal, the opportunity to bring two hundred head of merino sheep to Vermont. By 1840, there were almost 1,690,000 merinos in the state, thrusting Vermont into the forefront among wool-producing states. Sheep grazing, less labor-intensive than most agricultural pursuits and possible even on rocky uplands, stimulated additional land clearing and depressed population growth. In areas of heavy merino density, population declined. After 1840, sheep farming itself declined, the victim of western competition and the lowering of protective tariffs. In contrast, dairying began a steady growth. This refocusing of agriculture lessened the inducement for large farm families and Vermont daughters frequently chose to leave their family homesteads to work for wages in textile mills, some as far from home as Lowell or Amoskeag before returning, if they ever did, to Vermont. After 1840, however, mills in Vermont as well as southern and central New England were increasingly staffed by immigrant labor.

Also reorienting the Vermont economy was the Champlain-Hudson cutoff to the Erie Canal, opened in 1823. Initially hailed for making access to a wider market possible for Vermont produce, it instead opened the state to western wheat and western land to ambitious Vermonters. The awareness that Vermont could not compete with western grain farmers helped direct Vermont agriculture into wool production, woolen mills, and ultimately dairy farming. Another consequence of the Erie Canal was to loosen the Champlain Basin's ties with Canada and bind it more tightly to eastern Vermont. Nonetheless, political conventions such as the Mountain Rule, designed to assure power sharing between the eastern and western sides of the state, persisted into the twentieth century.

During the late 1830s, relations with Canada were convulsed by the Patriot Rebellion in lower Canada, which sought reforms that included greater authority for the popularly elected assembly and the French-Canadian majority. Crushed by British army regulars and Canadian loyalists, many Patriots escaped to Vermont, where they enjoyed broad-based support. Only the intervention of President Martin Van Buren, who proclaimed neutrality and dispatched U.S. army forces to close the border, and Governor Silas Jenison's forceful support for Vermont's neutrality forestalled further violence.

The railroads influenced everything they touched. The first rail line in Vermont began operation in 1848, and by 1855 there were over 500 miles of track in the state. Designed to cross the state as a link between the Great Lakes Basin and Atlantic ports rather than handle Vermont freight, the roads nonetheless had a tremendous social, economic, and political impact. The largest Vermont enterprise into the twentieth century, they also brought thousands of Irish into the state as construction workers. These Irish, along with the French-Canadians who worked in the textile mills and on farms, made up almost the entire immigrant census, roughly equalling in numbers the native Vermonters who left for other states. Much to the dismay of many of the almost exclusively Protestant natives, the new arrivals were mostly

Catholic and posed a threat to the power structure of the time. Their growing influence was made clear in 1853 when a Burlington diocese was established under Bishop de Goesbriand.

These economic and demographic disruptions prompted both secular and religious ferment. Perceiving Free Masonry as an anti-democratic movement, Vermont became the most virulently anti-Masonic state in the nation, electing an Anti-Masonic party governor and in 1832 becoming the only state to cast its electoral votes for the Anti-Mason presidential candidate. By 1836, with Vermont Free Masonry no longer conceived as a threat, the Anti-Masons gave way to the newly founded Whig party. Other movements included early forms of labor unions known as Workingmen's Associations that thrived alongside religious revivals. These embraced the Millerites, founders of the Advent Church, whose original leader, sometime Poultney resident William Miller, prophesied the second coming of Christ in 1843, and the Perfectionist Society, a utopian commune founded in 1839 in Putney by John Humphrey Noyes and forced to relocate to Oneida, New York, because of its "complex marriage" practices. Mormon founders Joseph Smith and Brigham Young were other religious leaders with Vermont roots.

Such ferment attracted the attention of aspiring editors from elsewhere, most notably William Lloyd Garrison and Horace Greeley, who came to the state and set up reform periodicals. Among the social reform movements, temperance and anti-slavery, both initially church rooted, had the greatest appeal. Temperance societies dated from the 1820s and attempts to impose a state-wide ban on liquor dated from the 1840s. It wasn't until 1852, however, after Maine adopted a state-wide prohibition law, that the General Assembly, prodded by the enthusiastic endorsement of a Whig governor, narrowly passed a bill calling for a referendum prohibiting the manufacture and sale of liquor. The bill passed the House 91 to 90 with substantial abstentions from the smaller towns and solid support from the larger, suggesting that prohibition had become a goal of larger communities seeking social control over their newly arrived immigrant populations. In 1853, prohibition was approved by a vote of 22,215 to 21,045 at considerable political expense to its Whig sponsors. While not always rigidly enforced, it remained law until 1902, when a local option law was adopted.

Anti-slavery, a second movement stimulated by church activities, enjoyed even more widespread support. Vermonters celebrated the fact that their 1777 constitution prohibited slavery and granted universal male suffrage, and more recently they had championed anti-slavery resolutions in Congress and state legislation to annul federal fugitive slave laws. This anti-slavery sentiment fueled state politics giving rise to the Liberty and then the Free-Soil party which, along with the perennially feeble Democratic party, usually were able to deny the Whigs a popular majority and left the election of state-wide candidates to the General Assembly.

By 1854, the passage of the Kansas-Nebraska Act, along with the temperance issue, further complicated Vermont politics. The continued growth of splinter parties and the inability of any party to command a popular or legislative majority now threatened to paralyze state government. Whigs and Free-Soilers responded by banding together in a common slate and platform and, calling themselves Republicans, won an overwhelming victory. The party imposed a remarkable political stability upon the state, soon conceded to be the most Republican in the nation. It won every gubernatorial election until 1962 and every Republican presidential candidate carried the state until 1964.

Vermont's overwhelming support of Lincoln affirms that the vast majority of voters opposed the extension of slavery into the territories or opposed slavery itself, but this opposition accommodated a broad range of attitudes towards the "peculiar institution." What really united Vermonters was their determination to save the Union. After the firing on Fort Sumter in South Carolina, Vermont answered President Lincoln's call to arms with enthusiasm. Antipathy to the south, rooted in the slavery question, reached to other areas of public policy. The South, in addition to imposing such overtly pro-Southern measures as the annexation of Texas and the Kansas-Nebraska Act, had frustrated Vermont's ambitions for a higher tariff, national banking legislation, and other economic measures the state considered vital to its well being.

Almost thirty-five thousand Vermonters served in the Union army, suffering casualty rates that were among the highest of any Union state and leaving mourners in virtually every town and family. With one of four adult males in the service, the farm work and financial responsibility fell increasingly on women and in many instances remained so as war casualties drained some towns of almost their entire adult male population. The northernmost action of the war occurred in October 1864 in St. Albans, when Confederate soldiers crossed the Canadian border to rob the town banks and escaped with over $200,000. While the St. Albans Raid prompted extensive diplomatic negotiations between the United States, Great Britain, and Canada, it had no impact on the course of the war.

More significant for the state was the injection of money and military contracts that rescued Vermont from the economic doldrums. Farmers found a ready market for produce and livestock, and over ten thousand Morgan horses were sold to the military as calvary mounts. The men heading for the front created a labor shortage at home and wages rose. The struggling textile mills and the machine and firearms shops experienced full demand, and the railroads carried profitable cargoes of men and supplies. The mustering of troops in a large camp near Rutland provided the market that allowed the *Rutland Herald* to become, after the *Burlington Free Press*, the second daily newspaper in the state. Federal legislation that created the national banking system and the land-grant colleges (both with the key support of Vermont Congressman Justin Morrill) brought new institutions to the state.

No sooner had hostilities ceased than St. Albans was back in the news, this time as a military base for Fenians, Irish nationalists who hoped to advance their cause by freeing Canada from British rule. Just as the invasion of Canada by the Patriots in 1838 was thwarted at Alburg by U.S. and British troops at the border, U.S. and British troops suppressed the Fenians in 1866 and again in 1870. As in the past, many of the participants sought refuge in Vermont, but the leaders of the second invasion were arrested by the state's U.S. Marshal.

The most celebrated of Vermont's post-war adjustments was its embrace of the Republican party as a civic religion. The party dominated the state's politics and government, escaping effective challenge until the second half of the twentieth century. Exercising a virtual monopoly of national and state offices, it frequently claimed over 200 of the 246 Vermont house delegates and all thirty state senators. The factionalism that marked ante-bellum elections, when candidates seldom obtained a popular majority, gave way to elections in which Republican candidates regularly exceeded 70 per-

cent of the popular vote. Contributing further to the decline in political contentiousness were constitutional amendments converting state government from annual to biennial elections and legislative sessions. The adoption of the Fifteenth Amendment extending suffrage to black males, a civil right Vermont's small black population had possessed since 1777, sparked efforts to extend that right to women. In 1870, a women's suffrage amendment survived as far as a state constitutional convention, where it was defeated 233 to 1.

After the Civil War, agriculture, particularly dairy farming, remained a major pursuit, shaping the state's economy and its landscape. Shipping cream, cheese, and butter by railroad broadened Vermont farmers' marketing opportunities for perishable goods, and the development of the refrigerated railway car enabled them to convert to the even more lucrative marketing of fresh milk. The lumber industry was so major an activity that through the 1860s Burlington was one of the busiest inland ports in the nation. Kindled by duty-free provisions of the Canadian Reciprocity Act, timber cut and sawed near Ottawa was brought by water to Burlington, finished, and transhipped to markets throughout the world. The machine-tool industry, with a long history in the Connecticut River valley, experienced steady growth, and in 1850, Windsor's Robbins and Lawrence, a rifle manufacturer, produced Vermont's highest value product. The largest employer, however, was E. & T. Fairbanks and Company, inventor and marketer of the platform scale. Located in St. Johnsbury, it enjoyed extensive international sales. The extractive industries, with their activities expedited by the railroads, became major employers of immigrant craftsmen. Slate quarries were generally worked by Welsh while the granite industry, dominated by scores of small independent enterprises, attracted Scotch, Italian, and Spanish labor. The marble industry, consolidated as the Vermont Marble Company by Redfield Proctor, Sr., solicited Italian craftsmen and by the final quarter of the nineteenth century replaced Fairbanks as the largest employer in the state.

Also by the final quarter of the nineteenth century, Redfield Proctor had emerged as the state's most significant political figure. As a governor and senator, his name came to denote a political dynasty that, until long after his death, remained the dominant faction in the Republican party. Conservative and business oriented, it often exercised a keen strategic sense for compromise.

Fletcher Proctor, Redfield's son, presided in 1904 over one of the most progressive administrations in state history. Allen Fletcher, a distant cousin elected Republican governor in 1912 when Vermont was one of only two states to cast its electoral votes for the Republican presidential candidate, was the first gubernatorial candidate of either major party to solicit labor union support.

Yet despite the succession of affluent, business-oriented governors, the state's political image was best defined by the legislature. The combination of a house with one representative from each town irrespective of population and the dominant role of agriculture in the state resulted in a general assembly in which farmers were frequently a majority and always the largest occupational category.

Though governance reflected this rural dominance, Vermont farms were seldom prosperous enough to support or require the work force provided by traditionally large families, and from 1850 through 1940 the state's population grew by only forty-five thousand souls. Emigration was so common that by 1860, over 40 percent of native-born Vermonters had moved to some other state or territory. Unlike other states, newly arrived European immigrants barely kept the population constant. Aggregate figures fail to reflect internal changes. In 1920, while state population declined by thirty-five hundred, Burlington's population increased by twenty-five hundred. The larger communities gained population as the smaller declined. In 1850, the median size of a Vermont town was over twelve hundred, but by 1920 it was under nine hundred, a loss that was also manifested in a decline in material resources. While the smallest and poorest towns found it increasingly difficult to assemble the finances and personnel necessary to meet town obligations, the one-town one-vote House apportionment continued to assure them a General Assembly majority.

Rural poverty so dominated Vermont politics that soon after the Civil War the legislature began voting to shift expenditures from town to state government according to a need formula. From 1890 until 1931, when a state income tax was enacted, state levies on town grand lists were applied to bolster educational resources among poorer municipalities. Welfare and highway needs were also met through state programs. The Republican state committee countered protests over the resulting increase in state taxes by asserting the virtue of the redistribution formulas as meeting the proper demands of the

people. By 1902, it had become the settled policy of the state.

Tourism inspired recurring efforts to stimulate the state's economy. While Vermont's landscape lacked the ruggedness and grandeur associated with the Adirondack and White Mountains, its pastoral qualities were unmatched and became the focus of promotion, originally through railroad advertisements and then through other media. Eventually, as a government operation, Vermont's summer tourist promotion exceeded that of any other state. As the railroad gave way to the automobile, highways replaced rails as primary arteries. Yet with no significant new track laid after the turn of the century, and with few hard-surfaced roads, Vermont's transportation network was unable to accommodate its own internal needs, not to mention additional demands of the tourist industry.

In the fall of 1927, the transportation dilemma was compounded by the worst flood in state history. Eighty-four lives were lost and homes, farms, and industrial sites destroyed, along with much of the state's transportation and communication network. Within weeks, the state implemented a recovery effort planned and financed with state and federal resources that ushered in a motor age on hard-surfaced roads. After the reconstruction had been completed, however, the state rejected a New Deal program to build a parkway along the ridge of the Green Mountains, modeled on the Blue Ridge Parkway of Virginia, as too expensive and likely to desecrate the mountains while attracting the "wrong sort" of tourist. The popularity of skiing converted Vermont's recreation industry from a summer-long to a year-round activity. But though it sprouted in the 1930s, skiing did not blossom until after World War II and owed much of its success to the arrival of the interstate highway system.

Until 1958, Democratic party challenges to Republican management of state government were largely ceremonial, and even during the Great Depression and the New Deal there were few closely contested elections. Meaningful political contests took place in Republican primaries. While ardent conservatives were entrenched in the state organization, party candidates were less ideologically consistent and, with few exceptions, participated eagerly in New Deal largess. The first social security recipient was a Vermonter, Ida Fuller of Ludlow, and the state hosted a disproportionately large number of Civilian Conservation Corps camps. The corpsmen built mountain roads and state parks, carved out early ski trails, and helped construct dams.

The first signs of recovery from the Great Depression occurred in 1939 in the machine-tool industry. Preparations for war and then the war itself created a boom economy in the Springfield area that was never matched elsewhere in the state, although most sectors of the economy prospered. Meriting special attention was the increased prominence of organized labor and its organizing successes among machine-tool, textile, marble, and white-collar workers, particularly state employees and teachers.

On September 16, 1941, almost three months before Pearl Harbor, Vermont declared war on Germany. The rest of the world took little note of this event, but by then the state's National Guard unit had been activated and the military draft implemented. Ultimately, thirty-eight thousand Vermont men and women served on active duty, with twelve hundred killed or missing in action. Pre-eminent among the state's military heroes was Leonard Wing, a Rutland attorney and National Guard officer, who rose to the rank of general to become the only National Guard officer to command a division in combat.

Once the war ended, returning veterans reoriented Vermont politics. Former Colonel Ernest Gibson, Jr., mobilizing a cadre of World War II confederates, and allied with his friend and political ally Senator George Aiken, was able to dislodge Mortimer Proctor as governor in the 1946 Republican primary. This Aiken-Gibson wing of the Republican party, advocating an extensive agenda that included programs of federal and state aid to education and health as vital to the state's future, vied with the more traditional Proctor wing that urged less ambitious approaches emphasizing Vermont's limited fiscal resources. Governor Gibson succeeded in implementing large elements of his program, but after 1950, when he left office to become a federal judge, the Aiken-Gibson wing never again succeeded in nominating a governor. One reason for this failure was that after 1952 Democrats who had supported Gibson in Republican primaries were increasingly drawn to their own party's contests. Democratic strength ripened in 1958 when the state sent a Democrat, William Meyer, to the House of Representatives and came within a few hundred votes of electing a Democratic governor. The 1960 elections restored Republican fortunes, but in 1962 Philip Hoff became the first Democratic governor elected in over one hundred years. In 1964, he was re-elected along with the entire Democratic state slate and Vermont for the first time cast its electoral votes for a Democratic president, Lyndon Johnson. Hoff, re-elected in 1966 to a third term, served during what was up to then the longest period of uninterrupted prosperity in national history, an era that made the Great Society possible (eighty Great Society programs operated in Vermont) and brought more new settlers to Vermont than at any time during the previous 150 years.

Reapportionment was the most debated of all reforms occurring during the Hoff era. In 1965, Vermont's house and senate both convened under court reapportionment orders. The house, one of the nation's most malapportioned legislative bodies, consisted of one representative from each of Vermont's 246 organized cities and towns irrespective of population. By 1960, the twenty-two largest towns and cities housed over half the state's population, paid more than 64 percent of the state's income tax, 50 percent of the state's property tax, and elected fewer than 9 percent of the house members. The house was reapportioned down to 150 members (a number proposed as early as 1850) with smaller towns combined into single districts and the largest municipalities broken down into multiple districts, some with two representatives. The senate was kept at 30 members, but county lines were no longer sacrosanct.

Since Hoff, the governor's office has alternated between parties and in 1984 the Democrats elected Madeleine Kunin, the state's first female governor. Reapportionment facilitated Democratic gains in the legislature, but nowhere near as rapidly as anticipated. The first Democratic House Speaker, Timothy O'Connor, was elected in 1975 while the Republicans held a slight majority, a frequent situation until 1987, when the Democrats first gained a majority. The first Democratic senate was elected in 1984. Since then, both houses have been keenly contested. The state's apparent disdain for party regularity is best illustrated by the composition of its congressional delegation. In the year 2003, it consisted of an Independent and a Democratic senator and an Independent (self-styled socialist) representative.

This post–World War II reorientation of Vermont politics reflected contemporary demographics and economics. While in 1880 the locally owned Vermont Marble Company was the state's largest employer, in 1989 it was

International Business Machines. Furthermore, home-grown businesses were absorbed into national operations. The *Burlington Free Press* was absorbed into Gannett publications while native corporations such as Vermont Marble and Springfield's machine and tool mainstay Jones and Lamson passed under the control of international conglomerates. Even Ben and Jerry's, the state's signature premium ice cream phenomenon, was bought up by Unilever. International enterprises had become Vermont's principal employers and sources of revenue, but they deprived the state of the leadership and commitment that homegrown businesses had provided.

Tourism became a four-season economic activity, with more people employed in the ski industry in winter than were employed on farms in summer. The interstate highway system converted Vermont from a remote pastoral retreat to a three-hour drive for an estimated forty million urban dwellers. Mountain sides and roadside properties were converted into ski resorts and strip developments, often without regard for the environment or the capacity of local government to provide essential services. There was no single solution to this problem, but Governor Deane Davis took the lead by promoting legislation popularly known as Act 250 that in 1970 mandated permits for development, with the developer responsible for proof of the ecological soundness of the project. The statewide planning provision of the act was repealed, but in 1988 the legislature passed Act 200 to encourage towns to develop their own plans. Some critics argue that the permit process is too cumbersome and inhibits sound development. Others oppose land management legislation as an outright denial of property rights and local control.

A related effort has been to retain Vermont's pastoral landscape by encouraging the preservation of farmland. The much-heralded green pastures are the workscape of rapidly disappearing Vermont dairy farms. Between 1948 and 1990, almost eight thousand such farms (many now the sites of housing developments and shopping malls) disappeared. Yet despite the decline in the number of dairy farms and a decrease in cows and pasture acreage, milk production increased. A federal program to curb overproduction, the whole herd buy-out, was instituted in 1986, and some farmers who accepted the buy-out then sold their land to developers. Highlighting the potential for harmful development in Vermont, the National Trust for Historic Preservation designated the entire state an "endangered place" in 1993. But farmland preservation efforts, such as calculating a farmer's property tax on a lower rate based on agricultural use rather than market value, along with the intervention of conservation trusts that purchase land development rights from farmers, have stayed their decline.

Elections around the turn of the twenty-first century were marked by bitter political controversy sparked by legislation precipitated by Vermont Supreme Court decisions, *Brigham v. State* and *Baker v. State*. The first was an act directed toward equalizing educational resources statewide, known as Act 60; and the second, passed by the 2000 legislature as the Civil Union Act, provided same-sex couples with rights similar to those possessed by married couples. The 2000 general election was a deeply emotional contest sparked by controversy over the Civil Union Act that produced mixed results, but Republicans generally opposed to the Act won control of the house for the first time in fourteen years.

The Civil Union Act was the first of its kind in the nation and observers attributed its passage to the state's evolving demographic character, in particular emigration to Vermont from northeastern urban centers. The 1970 census was the first since 1810 to record more than a 10 percent rise in the state's population, and the 1980 census showed even more rapid growth. The 1990 census evidenced slower growth, which was attributed to a sluggish economy and the state's efforts to regulate development. The 2000 census still retains evidence of Vermont's special character. As the second-smallest state in the union with a population of just under 609,000, it boasts the smallest biggest city of any state, the smallest state capital, and the only state capital without a McDonald's.

GOVERNMENT *Samuel B. Hand*

CONSTITUTION

Vermont's constitution, the shortest and least amended of the fifty states, was promulgated in 1777. Modeled on a 1776 Pennsylvania constitution, the Vermont version was salted with variations (statewide elections and unlimited number of terms), that have served it well. Amended in 1786 and again in 1793 to reflect Vermont's admission into the union as the fourteenth state (holding federal and state offices simultaneously was barred and separation of powers were more rigidly imposed), the constitution was only infrequently amended thereafter until 1974. A 1994 amendment rendered the constitution gender neutral.

The 1777 constitution provided for a Council of Censors, popularly elected every seven years, to propose necessary amendments and to call a constitutional convention to vote on ratification. Amendments were permitted once every seven years until 1870 when the council was abolished and the time-lock was extended to ten years. Authority for proposing amendments was vested in the Vermont Senate. Following concurrence by the House and reconsideration the following session by both the House and Senate, any surviving proposed amendments were submitted for approval to the general electorate. Few proposed amendments survived. The ten-year time lock was replaced in 1974 by a four-year process.

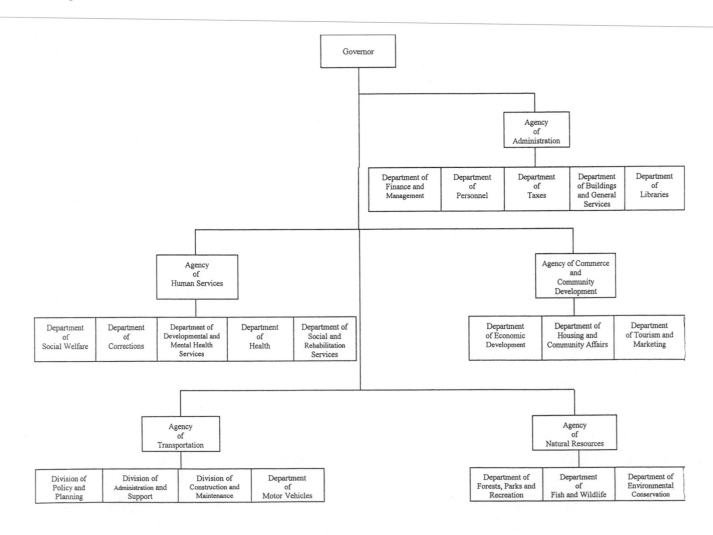

Seven Vermont governors meet in 1979 (left to right): Richard A. Snelling, Republican (1976–1984), Joseph B. Johnson, Republican (1954–1958), Thomas P. Salmon, Democrat (1972–1976), George D. Aiken, Republican (1936–1940), F. Ray Keyser, Jr., Republican (1960–1962), Robert T. Stafford, Republican (1958–1960), Philip H. Hoff, Democrat (1962–1968). Special Collections, Bailey/Howe Library, University of Vermont

Chapter 1 of the constitution, "Declaration of the Rights of the Inhabitants," in addition to the rights typically claimed in Revolutionary state constitutions, affirmed the prohibition of slavery, universal male suffrage, and compensation for private property taken for public use. More recently, Vermont courts have cited the state constitution to provide broader protection from search and seizure than the federal constitution. Chapter 2 establishes the frame of government, detailing political and judicial offices and delegating and assigning the distribution of powers. Section 47 requires a popular majority for election to statewide constitutional office and as a result elections are occasionally determined by joint ballot of the Senate and House of Representatives.

GOVERNOR

The constitutional powers of the governor are enumerated in Chapter 2 Article 20 of the constitution and have been basically unchanged since 1835. The governor is elected to a two-year term in even-numbered years, and recent efforts to extend the tenure of statewide constitutional officers to four years have failed. Vermont remains one of only two states with two-year terms. There are no term limits. The governor may commission officers and fill vacancies, represent the state outside Vermont, introduce business before the General Assembly, grant pardons, mitigate fines, and "take care that the laws be faithfully executed." The governor can also call special legislative sessions and serves as commander in chief of the state's National Guard but cannot command in person without the consent of the Senate.

In more recent years and almost always independently of constitutional amendment, administrative reor-

ganizations and the influx of federal dollars through such programs as the War on Poverty, Medicare, and Medicaid have enhanced the power and visibility of the governor's office, and helped transform it from a largely ceremonial position to an institution with unrivaled power. Some observers have suggested that the office has taken on the characteristics of a modern corporation with the governor serving as the chief operating officer.

In the absence of the governor, the lieutenant governor assumes the power of the governor. The offices are voted on separately and are often held by opposing party members.

OTHER STATEWIDE OFFICERS

In addition to the governor and lieutenant governor, the other popularly elected statewide officers are the treasurer, secretary of state, auditor of accounts, and attorney general. All serve two-year terms, but unless they win a popular majority their election is determined by the General Assembly. The attorney general, unlike the others, is not a constitutional officer but a creature of statute. From 1795 until 1904, the state operated without one. Currently, the attorney general's office represents the state in criminal and civil matters including consumer protection and civil rights. It is the attorney general's responsibility to defend the state's legal interests, and on occasion differences between the attorney general's interpretation of state interest and the governor's have precipitated political conflict.

The treasurer's principal responsibilities have been to disburse state funds, administer the municipal retirement system, and keep watch over the state's credit rating through counseling sound budget practices and dealing with Wall Street bond houses.

The secretary of state administers elections, registers corporations, maintains a state archive, and licenses professions and other occupations. The auditor of accounts, who until a government reorganization in 1961 was arguably more powerful than the governor, is currently responsible for auditing all state accounts and whatever additional duties are assigned it by the legislature. Critics of the system have recommended that all four offices be made appointive.

LEGISLATURE

Vermont operated under a unicameral legislature until 1836, when a Governor's Council of twelve men was replaced by a thirty-man senate with each of the four-teen counties allocated a minimum of one senator and the remaining sixteen apportioned by population. Vermont held annual elections and annual legislative sessions until 1870 when it adopted a biennial calendar. The 1777 constitution provided that for the first seven years every town with eighty taxable inhabitants would be allowed two representatives to the general assembly and all others one. After seven years, all towns would have one representative irrespective of population. This practice persisted until 1965, when the federal courts ruled it unconstitutional. The House was then reduced from 246 to 150 members and apportioned by population. The Senate retained 30 members, but it too was tied more closely to population and county boundaries are no longer inviolate.

The House is presided over by a Speaker, the most powerful of Vermont's legislators, who assigns committee chairpersons, committee members, and bills to committee. Since 1975, sessions with Republican majorities have occasionally elected Democratic Speakers. The Senate is presided over by the lieutenant governor in whose absence the president pro tempore, invariably elected by the majority party, presides. The lieutenant governor and the president pro tempore along with a second senator elected for the purpose constitute the committee on committees and share responsibilities exercised by the Speaker in the House. The General Assembly, nominally a part-time legislature, convenes in January and usually remains in session through April.

JUDICIARY

The Vermont Supreme Court, the state's final court of appeals, is the apex of a "unified" system that houses three major trial courts, the superior, district, and family, along with an environmental court and one to deal with traffic violations and misdemeanors. Probate courts operate in every county and are presided over by judges elected by the county to four-year terms.

All other judges are nominated by the governor from among candidates approved by a constitutionally mandated judicial nominating body and confirmed by the Senate. They serve six-year terms after which they may be retained by vote of the legislature.

The judiciary was reshaped by constitutional amendments adopted in 1974, which mandated legally trained jurists, altered the appointment process, lengthened

terms, and enhanced the supreme court's rule-making authority. The post-1980 supreme court has remained a five-person bench, but in addition to deciding appeals it promulgates rules of practice, procedure, and evidence, administers all courts, and enforces rules of judicial and lawyer ethics.

The superior court was established in 1906 as the state's general trial court and functioned until 1974 as the county court. The constitution then required a court to sit at least one week in every county. Presided over by a superior judge on circuit along with two popularly elected assistant judges, often called side judges, who were usually without legal training and could outvote the presiding judge on issues of fact, it was the last remaining bench of its kind in the nation. During the 1960s, however, the side judges' judicial power was eroded by supreme court decisions. Currently, the superior court deals almost exclusively with civil matters.

In 1965, the district court system was instituted to secure legally trained municipal court jurists and to expedite the appointment of fulltime jurists. Over time, the court's jurisdiction has expanded and personnel increased until, by 2000, as a practical matter district court judges exercise almost exclusive jurisdiction over criminal matters. Although district judges were initially regarded as of a lower professional caste than superior judges, receiving lower salaries, distinctions between them have become difficult to discern. The state also provides a family court and a single judge hearing environmental cases. Despite the Vermont system's specialized courts, judges are usually generalists. A 1980 law allowed district judges to be assigned to superior court and superior judges to district court when the business of the court warrants it. The practice has erased distinctions between classes of jurists as they work nearly equally in superior, district, and family courts. A recurring complaint is that under this system the family court dockets are frequently heard only after other dockets have been cleared.

Although the probate court seems least altered over time, it too has been subjected to change. Notably, most current probate judges are lawyers and the supreme court has attempted to modernize and standardize probate court procedure.

A restructured judicial career pattern has also emerged. Until 1975, superior judges were elected by the legislature and were usually from the legislature. Once on the court, they ascended a judicial ladder that, if they survived, would take them rung by rung to the chief justiceship of the supreme court. After elective power was taken from the legislature and appointive power given the governor, the judicial ladder was discarded and judges were less likely to be drawn from the legislature and more often from the executive branch or from outside government.

LOCAL GOVERNMENT

The 237 chartered towns and 9 cities that constitute all 246 primary units of local government were once popularly referred to as little republics. In more recent years, their relative autonomy dealing with schools, highways, welfare, and other once-local activities has shifted to the state, while the 1965 reapportionnent ended each town sending a single representative to the General Assembly.

Although there are fourteen counties, county government is limited to maintaining a sheriff's office and a court house. Only Franklin County continues to operate a jail. The county, however, remains the voting district for the state's attorney who prosecutes offenders of crimes committed within the district. The administrative units beyond the town and below the state are usually special districts fashioned to deal with specific activities such as water supplies, planning, and solid waste disposal.

Except for Vergennes, Vermont cities have all evolved from towns, usually as in the instance of Burlington, in which a densely populated section broke away as a city while the more rural region retained town status. On such occasions, the town retained and the city gained representation in the legislature. Towns and cities continue to exercise executive (selectboards or mayors), judicial (boards of civil authority for zoning issues), and administrative (clerks and treasurers) authority, and issue annual reports. All hold annual town meetings and school district meetings in the spring where they vote on budgets, tax rates and bond issues, and elect officers. Although the Australian ballot is reforming Norman Rockwell's image of town meeting by permitting absentee ballots and extended access to the polling place, measures criticized for limiting debate of the issues, the forum retains its place as a fixture of town government. Finally, most governing communities have planning, public works, and zoning commissions. The University of Vermont Center for Rural Studies maintains that at least nine thousand Vermonters serve in some official town capacity. State statutes mandate at least thirty town offices, and some towns chose to elect or appoint individuals to multiple offices.

ADMINISTRATIVE AGENCIES

In 1957, the legislature created a Little Hoover Commission, which recommended that the state consolidate its numerous agencies, departments, and boards into a manageable number of superagencies whose secretaries, appointed by the governor with the consent of the Senate, would report directly to the governor and serve as a cabinet. Over the years, the legislature responded piecemeal to the recommendations, and there are currently five superagencies: administration, transportation, human services, commerce and community development, and natural resources, which house departments with their own boards.

The secretary of administration has been described as "the governor's primary alter ego in matters of overall management." The agency houses the Departments of Budget and Management, Finance, Taxes, Purchases, State Buildings, and Public Archives. The Human Services Agency presides over the Departments of Rehabilitation, Health, Mental Health, Corrections, and Equal Opportunity. It is the superagency most often in the news and its departments are those most subject to public scrutiny.

The secretary of natural resources presides over the Fish and Wildlife Department, Department of Forests and Parks, Department of Water Resources, a Recreation Division, and a Natural Resources Conservation Council. The Agency of Commerce and Community Development currently hosts eight departments, the two largest being the Department of Housing and the Department of Economic Development, but also exercises responsibility for the state's Division for Historic Preservation and the magazine *Vermont Life*. In 1977, the last of the superagencies, the Agency of Transportation, was created by the legislature by combining the former highways, motor vehicles, aeronautics and bus/rail/waterways/ motor carrier services departments. In 1991, the agency was reorganized by creating a Division of Rail, Air, and Public Transportation (RAPT) which exercises responsibility for funding and improvements along with a Division of Planning.

PROTECTING THE ENVIRONMENT *Carl Reidel*

On January 8, 1970, Governor Deane Davis dedicated his entire state-of-the-state address before a joint assembly of the legislature to the topic of environmental protection. The government agenda he set forth was to be, in great part, the environmental agenda for Vermont into the twenty-first century. Davis's bold proposals were in tune with Vermont's venerable environmental heritage, recalling the writings of Woodstock native George Perkins Marsh, who had launched the American conservation movement a century before. Davis was building on the work of his predecessor, Governor Philip Hoff, who laid the institutional foundation for environmental protection in Vermont by guiding legislative reapportionment in 1965 and creating a dozen interagency and citizen task forces plus a central planning office. These actions set the stage for Davis's consolidation into five cabinet-level superagencies of over 150 boards, commissions, and agency heads who reported directly to the governor. Hoff's Interagency Committee on Natural Resources (1964) became the framework for creation of the Agency of Environmental Conservation in 1970, which brought together departments responsible for forestry, state parks, recreation, air and water pollution, and solid waste management. This agency, later renamed the Agency of Natural Resources, under the guidance of a streamlined and more representative General Assembly and a series of progressive governors, moved Vermont's modern environmental revolution forward. In his address, Governor Davis called for comprehensive land-development control legislation, which was enacted into law a few months later and popularly known as Act 250. This law included provisions for a statewide land capability plan, a development permit system directed by nine District Environmental Commissions with a State Environmental Board, and the adoption of a State Land Use Plan. Additional legislation that year strengthened regulations for water quality, and provided for purchase of scenic easements and pesticide regulation.

Although the General Assembly eventually rejected the State Land Use Plan in 1976 and removed its provision from Act 250 in 1984, the act became the cornerstone of Vermont's environmental protection efforts. In 1984, during the administration of Governor Richard Snelling, a significant amendment to Act 250 further strengthened the law by eliminating a loophole that allowed subdivisions of lots over 10 acres in size without a permit. By the mid-1990s, Act 250 had grown from nine pages in the Vermont statutes to over sixty-five pages, with important supporting case law and declaratory rulings. Legislation enacted earlier during the Hoff administration, known as the Municipal and Regional Planning and Development Act, had laid an important local foundation for the implementation of Act 250 by authorizing local planning and zoning. Subsequently, that early law was significantly modified by the Growth Management Act of 1988 during the administration of Governor Madeleine Kunin.

The administration of Governor Thomas Salmon saw enactment of a capital gains tax on land speculation sales, a move that further strengthened efforts to regulate unsound land development. Earlier, Governor Davis had also persuaded the 1970 General Assembly to enact another significant natural resources law, known as Act 252, which provided a comprehensive plan to reduce water pollution. Reinforced by a series of new federal water laws a few years later, Act 252 gave state government sweeping powers to control a wide range of pollutants, and included a permit system to control all discharges into state waters by individuals, businesses, or municipalities.

By the end of the 1970s, Vermont had also banned highway billboards and phosphates in detergents, required deposits on beverage containers and the screening of junk yards, and passed legislation controlling municipal dumps. The 1980s were a time of consolidation and refinement of both laws and institutions that produced major new controls on trash and garbage dumps and sanitary landfills in Act 78. The legislature also strengthened both executive agencies and the courts by shifting responsibility for the management of natural resources from legislative committees to professional commissions and agency staff, and by the designation of the nation's only state environmental judge.

Legislation in the 1990s limiting large-scale clearcutting and aerial herbicide spraying of forests further strengthened government authority over forest resources on private lands. The growing state environmental movement of the past several decades was led by a remarkable array of governors, legislative and agency leaders, and citizen activists in nongovernmental organizations (NGOs) working together. These environmental leaders forged both an effective organizational infrastructure and a new culture of respect for one another and for the environment. An example of this public-private cooperation was the Vermont Housing and Conservation Trust Fund, which provides investment capital to public agencies and NGOs for the acquisition of land and development rights for conservation and long-term affordable housing. Enacted in 1987 during Governor Kunin's administration, it became a major conservation theme for Governor Howard Dean. The success of this public-private effort to conserve land is due in great part to the efforts of the Vermont Land Trust (VLT), an NGO founded in 1977, which has conserved over 350,000 acres of farm and forest land, and to numerous local land trusts established in the 1980s and 1990s.

Along with over eighty town conservation commissions, the state's land trusts are a major force in land protection and conservation. In 2002, nearly 900,000 acres in local, state, and national holdings, almost 20 percent of the state's land area, is under conservation protection of some type. The role of conservation and environmental NGOs in Vermont is especially significant because of the state's strong tradition of town-meeting government and a citizen legislature in which individual legislators have neither offices nor staff and must run for re-election every two years, as must all other elected state officials. NGO staff persons and their citizen members serve both as special interest lobbyists and reliable sources of information to the legislature and government agencies. Early conservation organizations such as the Green Mountain Club (1910), Vermont Natural Resources Council (1963), Lake Champlain Committee (1963), and Vermont Public Interest Research Group (1972) work with newer organizations, including Forest Watch, Wild Earth, Preservation Trust of Vermont, and numerous local Audubon clubs, watershed associations, and town-

level conservation commissions and planning boards. State affiliates of regional and national organizations like the Conservation Law Foundation, National Wildlife Federation, Sierra Club, Friends of the Earth, the Nature Conservancy, Wilderness Society, and others provide a national context and expert assistance to the local groups and to government. These national groups also have played a pivotal role in strengthening the standing of NGOs and individuals before the courts and in government procedures, which has significantly enhanced the role of citizens in environmental protection cases. Both the state and federal governments engage these groups in a variety of cooperative efforts. Recent examples include the Lake Champlain Basin Program, a federally funded effort guided by a steering committee of citizens, NGO representatives, and agency personnel from Vermont, New York, and Quebec, and the Northern Forest Lands Council, with representatives from Vermont, New Hampshire, Maine, and New York.

Vital to the success of these accomplishments has been the strong support of Vermont's congressional delegation over the past few decades, which has included people with some of the best environmental records in Congress, notably Senators George Aiken (R), Robert Stafford (R), James Jeffords (I), and Patrick Leahy (D), and current Representative Bernard Sanders (I). All of the current delegation meet regularly with Vermont's NGO leaders, as did Governor Howard Dean with his Governor's Council of Environmental Advisors, a sort of "kitchen cabinet." Likewise, the General Assembly has always had numerous representatives and senators serving on key committees to craft some of the best environmental legislation of any state in the nation. The same is true of many people who serve as unpaid members of town select boards, planning commissions, conservation commissions, and other town boards. Also important are a cadre of environmental lawyers, consultants, and business leaders statewide.

Perhaps the most important long-term force for environmental protection in Vermont is education. Since the founding of the university-wide environmental program at the University of Vermont in 1971, several thousand graduates in environmental studies have found careers in public and private schools, NGOs, state and local government, and businesses, and as lawyers, farmers, physicians, and journalists. They staff important environmental education organizations such as Shelburne Farms, the Merck Forest and Farmland Center, the Montshire Museum, the Vermont Institute of Natural Science, and the Vermont Leadership Center. Several graduates (and a faculty member) of the program have served as members of the legislature, and on the staffs of the political leaders cited above. Likewise, UVM's School of Natural Resources has trained foresters, wildlife biologists, and recreation and water resources specialists who staff many state and federal agencies in Vermont. Along with UVM, Goddard College, Green Mountain College, Johnson State College, Marlboro College, Middlebury College, Sterling College, and Vermont Law School collectively offer more college-level environmental education courses than those of any other state of comparable size.

Many of Vermont's primary and secondary schools, public and private, offer environmental courses and field studies as well. Environmentally based research is critical to effective environmental protection in an era when many problems require advanced scientific and policy skills. Pollution that one could "see and smell" has been largely controlled, but complex toxic pollutants like endocrine disruptors, together with subtle but serious impacts on natural ecosystems, defy either simple detection or easy remediation. Again, UVM and other colleges play a key role, as do Vermont-based NGO organizations such as the Northeast Natural Resources Center of the National Wildlife Federation, the Environmental Law Center of the Vermont Law School, the Center for Northern Studies, and the New England Environmental Policy Center. Despite all that Vermont has done in the way of environmental protection, the future will likely bring unexpected and dramatic change.

Whereas past environmental problems have been the result primarily of conditions within Vermont's boundaries, future impacts will increasingly come from afar, and may be global in nature. These include the long-range effect of climate change from atmospheric pollution, and intercontinental transfer of organisms such as infectious viruses and fungi, exotic insects, and non-native plants and animals. The invasion of the European zebra mussel into Lake Champlain is one of many likely such invasions that may be impossible to control in the future.

Long-range transport of air-borne pollution will likely increase the deposition of mercury, dioxins, and other deadly toxic substances on Vermont, which will diminish water and air quality and threaten public health. These external threats will require that Vermont build coalitions with other states and continue to send an environmentally committed congressional delegation to Washington. The globalization of the state's economy will also present serious new challenges to Vermont's ability to protect the environment. With most of the state's major corporations, from ski areas to banks and food suppliers, now owned and controlled by national and multinational corporations, decisions about land use and industrial development may well be made by others outside the state with little regard for their impact on Vermont.

The collective effect of such economic changes on the Vermont landscape has been loosely labeled "sprawl" by environmental and political leaders. This involves much more than visual changes and congestion along major roads, because as a growing population spreads across the landscape farmland is lost, river and stream ecosystems are stressed, and critical terrestrial ecosystems and habitats are damaged. In addition, the traditional working landscape of rural Vermont will be lost, along with the community and environmental values rooted in a close relationship to the land. Town government may become ineffective, as will development controls based in local and regional institutions. Sprawl in all its manifestations is also exacerbated by the lack of a comprehensive control policy. Over time development control systems that rely on negative regulatory approaches, as does Act 250 to a great extent, will eventually fail as independent decisions by hundreds of public agencies, industries, and individuals overpower the regulatory process. Without a comprehensive development-control policy, every new road, sewer extension, housing or resort development will inevitably degrade the environment and slow economic growth. Governor Davis understood this in 1970 when he said in his state-of-the-state address that "One of the first essentials to planning future economic growth is the preparation of a comprehensive land use plan for the State of Vermont." Preparation of such a comprehensive plan as part of a strategic environmental policy remains at the top of Vermont's unfinished environmental agenda.

HISTORIC PRESERVATION   *Elsa Gilbertson*

Painted on the wall behind the pulpit of the Old West Church in Calais, built in 1823, are these words from Proverbs 22:28: "Remove not the ancient landmarks which thy fathers have set." Many people in Vermont, whether they are familiar with this verse or not, have come to cherish and take pride in both the natural environment and the physical record of ten thousand years of human habitation—from archeological evidence of the first Vermonters to the buildings and settlements of more recent generations—and actively pursue the preservation of these characteristic features of the state.

Historic buildings and their relation to the natural and built environment around them were recognized early as among Vermont's greatest assets. *Rural Vermont: A Program for the Future* (1931), the report of the Commission on Country Life, found that the state had a distinctive architectural heritage: "old-time meeting houses with steeples, colonial houses painted white with green blinds and other characteristic features associated with New England villages and farms." The commission stressed that it "is good business and a patriotic duty to preserve a distinctive type. We ought to preach this doctrine extensively." The Vermont Historic Sites Commission, established in 1947, concluded in its 1950 annual report that the state's historic resources "furnish an aesthetic value like no other factor . . . recognition and preservation of historic sites in Vermont has already had and will continue to have more and more economic value to the entire state."

The first known preservation project in Vermont was the 1906 restoration of the Rockingham Meeting House, built 1788 to 1800. It was funded by local taxes and private donations and led to the formation of a nonprofit association to support the building. In that same year, the National Antiquities Act, authorizing the President of the United States to designate "historic landmarks, historic and prehistoric structures, and other objects of historic or scientific interest" on federally owned land, reflected America's new awareness of its architectural and cultural landmarks. In 1947, in a similar vein, the Vermont legislature created the Historic Sites Commission (changed in 1959 to the Board of Historic Sites) to mark, acquire, and develop significant properties of the past. The commission created a historic roadside marker program and began acquiring such properties as those related to Calvin Coolidge in Plymouth, the Hyde Log Cabin in Grand Isle, the Hubbardton Battlefield, the Chester A. Arthur Memorial in Fairfield, the Bennington Battle Monument, and the Old Constitution House in Windsor.

By the 1960s, as historic buildings, residential and industrial districts, and archeological sites continued to age and as Vermont's growing population inevitably led to development pressures, it became clear that the state's heritage, like the nation's, was being destroyed bit by bit, either through adverse government action such as wholesale urban renewal or by general neglect, obsolescence, and lack of maintenance of endangered sites. In 1965, concerned citizens rallied to protest plans to tear down the historic Pavilion Hotel in Montpelier and replace it with a modern state-office building. In a compromise that gained national recognition, the hotel was demolished but the outer shell of the new building was designed to duplicate the façade of its predecessor. The United States Conference of Governors convened a commission, whose members included Vermont Governor Philip Hoff, to study the precarious situation of historic sites. Their far-reaching recommendations, set forth in a book titled *Heritage So Rich* (1966), led to the passage of the National Historic Preservation Act (1966), which established a partnership between the National Park Service and historic preservation offices in each state. A framework was created to address and resolve issues threatening historic resources affected by federally funded, licensed, or permitted projects, and also provided assistance to the public in protecting heritage sites. In Vermont, the Board of Historic Sites immediately began nominating such structures as the Justin Smith Morrill Homestead in Strafford, the Emma Willard House in Middlebury, and the steamboat *Ticon-*

deroga for designation as National Historic Landmarks. The board also worked to ensure that historic sites were considered in Act 250, Vermont's land use legislation passed in 1970. By 1971, the board was recommending significant properties to the National Register of Historic Places, an honor providing recognition and some preservation incentives but not prohibiting private owners from developing their own property with their own money. The board also began the Vermont Historic Sites and Structures Survey to inventory significant properties in every town.

In 1975, the state legislature passed the Vermont State Historic Preservation Act, which established the Vermont Division for Historic Preservation to further carry out provisions of the National Historic Preservation Act, provide technical assistance to property owners, and conduct reviews of state and federal projects that might impact historic resources. The division also began the Vermont Archeological Inventory and in 1976 implemented a new federal investment tax credit program encouraging substantial rehabilitation of National Register buildings that would be used for income-producing purposes. It also helped award and administer a large number of grants to historic buildings through the Economic Development Administration. These grants, intended to help celebrate the United States bicentennial, made possible the restoration of numerous historic buildings and the removal of many incompatible 1950s and 1960s façade alterations in historic districts in such places as Bellows Falls, Montpelier, Rutland, Bennington, Burlington, Brandon, and Vergennes. Later, other federal preservation grants were awarded for buildings offering a public benefit. Over the years, review of federal and state government projects has led, for example, to the preservation of historic truss bridges, mitigation of potentially adverse impacts of government projects on other historic resources, and the study of archeological sites revealing important aspects of the hundred centuries of Vermont's human history.

Despite the state and federal preservation legislation of 1966 and 1975, it was often difficult for private citizens to prevent destruction of local landmarks. Burlington residents rallied in 1969 to prevent the demolition of the Ethan Allen Fire House on Burlington's City Hall Park; and in 1971, when the old Windsor House hotel in Windsor was to be torn down, citizens formed Historic Windsor, Inc., to buy it and restore it for new purposes.

Historic Windsor, Inc., also became a force to revitalize Windsor village, and founded the Preservation Institute to provide educational programs for the public and to teach preservation techniques to those in the building trades.

In further recognition of the importance of educating the citizenry, the University of Vermont established a graduate program in historic preservation in 1975, with an emphasis on preservation advocacy and hands-on experience. The Preservation Trust of Vermont was founded in 1980 as a private nonprofit organization to foster and advocate preservation in ways that government agencies cannot. The trust has become an influential force, developing grant, technical assistance, and awards programs, and highlighting larger issues such as development pressures, sprawl, and threats to historic downtowns.

In 1985, the legislature, aware that the historic and scenic resources of the state were threatened, passed the Vermont Townscape Preservation Act, which gave towns the ability to designate local historic districts and landmarks and design control districts through zoning and public vote. Two years later, the legislature began funding a state historic preservation grant program for historic properties owned by nonprofit organizations and municipalities, in recognition of the ways these buildings benefit the public and add to the state's character. Later, a grant program for historic agricultural buildings was added, and in 1987 the Vermont Housing and Conservation Board was established, one of whose missions is to conserve historic properties.

When it became clear in the 1990s that large quantities of Vermont's open space were being developed and commerce was moving out of established historic downtowns, local and state interests worked together closely to begin a Vermont Downtown Program at the state level. In 1998, the Vermont Downtown Program legislation was passed to provide incentives to plan for and maintain historic downtowns, encourage old and new businesses, and keep the downtowns vibrant centers of community life.

In Vermont, the balance between saving and using historic resources while allowing for necessary new growth has often been difficult to achieve. Over the course of the twentieth century and now beyond, Vermonters from all walks of life, ranging from private citizens to local groups coming together for a cause to petition local, state, and federal governments, have been in the national forefront in working together to identify historic resources and find ways to preserve them. In so doing, they have paved the way for a future that gains strength and energy from the richness of Vermont's past.

THE ECONOMY *Malcolm F. Severance*

GROWTH

The 2000 census counted 608,827 Vermont residents, an increase of 8.2 percent since 1990, a growth rate that exceeded the average for the New England states (5.4 percent) if not the nation (13.2 percent). Except for New Hampshire and New Jersey, the percentage increase in Vermont's population in the decade exceeded all the other states in the Northeast.

Given the relative population growth in Vermont, has the state done well economically compared to the rest of New England and the nation as a whole? The unemployment rate is less than the national average, state government's rainy-day funds are full, taxes have been cut, and a sense of optimism prevails. Gross State Product (GSP) data produced by the Bureau of Economic Analysis (BEA) in the U.S. Commerce Department provides a perspective on the relative performance of the Vermont economy from 1990 through 1999, the last data available. GSP is the market value produced within the state by labor and productive resources and thus is a proxy for wage, salary, and property income.

GSP for the nation grew at a healthy annual rate of 5.6 percent over the nine-year span, New England grew at 5.3 percent and Vermont at 4.3 percent. New Hampshire led the region with an annual growth rate of 7.1 percent. Although these rates do not appear to vary greatly, considerable absolute variation results over the span of nine years. The GSP in Vermont grew 46 percent in the nine years. In New England as a whole, the increase was 60 percent, the national increase was 63 percent, and New Hampshire's GSP was up 85 percent. Of the ten sectors of the economy, Vermont grew at a rate below the New England rate in every category except government and below the national rates in every category except government, agriculture, and mining.

Using the U.S. Census Bureau data for 1997, government in Vermont absorbed 11.75 percent of income earned. Vermont was tenth highest in the nation and 12 percent above the national average of 10.5 percent. State and local taxes as a percent of income earned were higher in Maine and Connecticut than in Vermont, while New Hampshire had the lowest taxes in the region at 8.5 percent of personal income.

INCOME DATA

Per capita income in the United States in 2000 was $29,676, while in New England it was $35,983, and in Vermont $26,901. Historically, New England has led the nation in personal income statistics with the high incomes earned in Connecticut and Massachusetts, but increasingly New Hampshire has contributed significantly. All three states were well above the U.S. average in 2000, while Maine and Vermont were distinctly below. Massachusetts increased its rank order from fourth to second among the states over the decade. New Hampshire moved from eleventh to sixth. Vermont moved from twenty-sixth to thirty-second and Maine moved from thirty-first to thirty-sixth.

Statewide data masks the dramatic variation in income between regions within the state. Median family income in Vermont was $44,069 in 1999, the most recent data. In Chittenden County, median family income was $57,448, or 130.4 percent of the statewide average, while in Orleans and Essex counties, the heart of the Northeast Kingdom, it was slightly more than half that level. Even more dramatic contrasts exist when comparing median family income by towns. Norwich stands at $85,300, Shelburne at $79,000, and Charlotte at $76,300. The seventeen families that live in Searsburg had a median family income of $21,700, and the towns of Browning-ton, Lowell, and Wells River all were below $25,000. The data also show that over the last decade the more affluent counties in Vermont have grown faster than other counties, creating a widening income gap.

EMPLOYMENT OPPORTUNITIES

Department of Employment and Training (DET) data indicate that in the decade just passed, over 40,600 new nonfarm jobs were created in Vermont. Well over half of them (22,700) were in services and 90 percent of them were in three areas: services, wholesale and retail trade, and government. There is a misconception that the service sector is made up of chambermaids, clerks, janitors, and others earning modest incomes. In reality, while the service sector does include these groups, it also includes legal, health, and business services, engineering and management services, public relations, private educational services, and the like. Health services comprise almost one-third of the employment in the service sector and have been the fastest growing area of services in the past ten years. Business services, which include computers and data processing, personnel supply, and services to buildings, are the second-largest employment area under the "services" umbrella and have grown the fastest in percentage terms, more than doubling in ten years. In the DET data, the government sector includes public education at all levels from primary to post-secondary education. Growth in employment in the noneducation sector of government has been modest at 3.1 percent during the decade, while employment in education has increased 23.8 percent to over twenty-eight thousand employees.

Almost one-half of all the jobs created during the decade were in the Burlington labor market. At the end of the decade, 36 percent of all the nonfarm jobs in Vermont were in Chittenden County. This fact, coupled with the income data cited earlier, makes the Burlington area the economic engine for the state. In contrast, no nonfarm job growth occurred in the Rutland market from 1997 to 2000. Only marginal job growth occurred in Springfield, and in the Brattleboro and White River Junction markets the growth was actually across the river in New Hampshire.

AGRICULTURE

For many years, there has been a belief that the Vermont economy has three important sectors—agriculture, manufacturing, and tourism. In fact, the contribution of agriculture to the Gross State Product has been declining for years. According to BEA statistics, that contribution was only 2.2 percent in 2000. The dairy industry dominates the agriculture sector and continues to experience dramatic changes. The long decline in the number of producing farms and number of dairy animals continues. Just since 1993, the number of dairy farms decreased from twenty-five hundred to only sixteen hundred, with most of the decrease in farms of less than one hundred animals. The farms that remain have become ever larger.

In 2000, there were thirty farms with a herd size of five hundred or more, while in 1995 there were none. Those thirty farms are less than 2 percent of the total, but they have 13 percent of the cows and produce 6 percent of the milk. The farms with one hundred or more cows, 28 percent of all farms, have 60 percent of the cows and produce 65 percent of the milk. In the last thirty-five years, dairy farming has changed from being a "way of life" to a business requiring the use of sophisticated management techniques. Selective breeding, coupled with nutritionally dictated feeding, has resulted in persistent increases in milk production per cow. The herd average in Vermont in 2000 was nearly 17,000 pounds of milk per cow per year, with many herds exceeding 20,000 pounds per cow. Some cows produce as much as 40,000 pounds per lactation period. The increased production per cow has offset the declining number of cows, so total milk production in Vermont has increased over time. Cash receipts from milk marketing in 1999 totaled $413 million dollars.

TOURISM

Although it is generally understood that the travel and tourism industry is a significant part of the Vermont economy, consistent and reliable data to measure its contribution is not available. Ideally, data on the industry would tie in with the Gross State Product data produced by the Bureau of Economic Analysis. To date, the data that has been collected centers on estimates of the total amount of spending and levels of employment. The industry is composed of three broad areas—lodging, food and drink, and the ski areas—but the economic impact of tourism is also felt in retail, transportation, construction and services in second-home ownership, and the finance, insurance, and real estate sector.

According to data generated by the Vermont Tourism Data Center at the University of Vermont, the travel and tourism industry employs approximately fifty thousand people and total spending approached $2.5 billion in 1999, the latest data available. What part of the Gross State Product is generated by tourism awaits additional study and research.

MANUFACTURING

Vermont is not known as a state with any sizeable manufacturing base. In fact, a higher proportion of the GSP comes from manufacturing in Vermont than in the country as a whole—17.5 percent in Vermont and 16.1 percent natonally. Manufacturing firms in Vermont vary in size from those with just a few employees to the large IBM plant in Essex Junction with eight thousand employees and at least three thousand more who are contract workers at the plant or are located off site. IBM has a huge economic impact on the economy of the state and especially on Chittenden County. Consequently the area is vulnerable to variations in the dynamics of the computer and chip manufacturing industry and the intense worldwide competition that exists. Over the course of the last ten years, employment at the IBM plant has dropped from eight thousand to six thousand and then returned to the eight thousand level.

HIGHER EDUCATION

There were twenty-four institutions of higher education in Vermont in the fall of 1999 with a total enrollment of approximately 36,600 students. Over 20,500 were enrolled in public institutions, with 10,300 of those at the five Vermont State Colleges and 10,200 at the University of Vermont. A total of 16,100 were enrolled in private institutions, with Middlebury College, Norwich University, St. Michael's College, and Champlain College enrolling almost exactly 10,000 of them. Over 7,000 of the students came from out of state. Data collected in 1995 by the Vermont Higher Education Council indicated that out-of-state tuition and fees, room and board costs, and other living expenses totalled about $340 million. In addition, colleges and universities received federal and other out-of-state grants, appropriations, and gifts totalling $90 million. Thus over $430 millon were imported into Vermont by post-secondary institutions in 1995. Certainly these numbers were higher in 2000. With upwards of 70 percent of college and university budgets allocated for wage and salary compensation, a large percentage of the imported dollars remains in Vermont and contributes to the GSP. It is interesting to compare these numbers with the $413 million of cash receipts from milk marketing received in 1999.

THE BUSINESS ENVIRONMENT

The Vermont Department of Economic Development recently commissioned the O'Neal Group of Hartford, Connecticut, to conduct a study of the Vermont image. Over thirteen hundred leisure travellers were interviewed and they gave Vermont very high marks, characterizing it as a state with a strong "feeling of well-being—peaceful, beautiful, special, romantic."

Over three hundred business leaders were interviewed and agreed that quality of life is the greatest perceived advantage to having a business in Vermont. However, 63 percent of them said it is "somewhat" or "very" difficult to do business in Vermont. The greatest perceived disadvantage is the permitting process. High personal and property taxes ranked below difficulty in recruiting personnel, the inconvenience and inferior quality of access by air, defects in the communication infrastructure, and shortages of labor. The survey indicated that most small businesses with fewer than twenty employees would likely expand in Vermont, while companies with more than twenty employees are increasingly choosing to expand outside the state. Almost one-half of the companies surveyed viewed the state as "unfriendly to business."

Many factors shape Vermont's economy. It is tucked away in the northeast corner of the country, far from the growing market areas of the South and West. In addition, it has limited natural resources, long and cold winters, and a challenging terrain. It is not within the orbit of a large metropolitan area, as southern New Hampshire is, and its attitude toward business is less accommodating than that of its eastern neighbor. Yet as the nation grows in population and economic might, all of these qualities can be turned to advantage if properly handled. The future holds both peril and promise for a state that throughout its history has used hard work, native ingenuity, and the talents of its citizens to transform itself several times to meet the requirements of changing times.

The **Vermont**
Encyclopedia

A

Abenaki

A term used by the French meaning "Eastern Indians," *Abénaki* is probably derived from the seventeenth-century Innu or Montagnais term for people living in Northern New England and the Canadian Maritimes. It is cognate to the Western Abenaki term *Wôbanikiiak,* meaning "people of the Dawnland." Abenaki in a restricted sense refers to native people living in the region that stretches from Vermont to the Penobscot River drainage basin. Linguists consider the Penobscot Nation of Maine to be "Eastern Abenaki," while the Dawnland people of Vermont are *Alnôbak* or "Western Abenaki." *N'dakinna* (our land), the homeland of the *Alnôbak,* is bounded by *Bitawbagok* (lake between) or LAKE CHAMPLAIN, the Richelieu River, the St. Lawrence River, the Chaudière River (whose outlet is opposite Quebec City), the height of land between the Kennebec and Penobscot river drainage basins (where it abuts the lands of the Penobscots), the Atlantic Ocean, northern Massachusetts, and the area around the headwaters of OTTER CREEK (where it abuts the lands of the MAHICANS) and thence back to *Bitawbagok.* Three Abenaki communities continue to live in *N'dakinna*: the Missisquoi, the Cowass, and the Sokoki Abenaki. The Missisquoi Abenaki, the major Native American group in Vermont, are concentrated in Swanton and Highgate in the lower MISSISQUOI RIVER valley, the heart of a several-thousand-year-old settlement of Abenaki people and the site of an historic village that continues to be a scene of Abenaki communal activity. During a period of Native American ethnic renewal in the 1970s after nearly two centuries of a quiet and nearly invisible presence, the Abenaki of Missisquoi organized in general accordance with the provisions of the Indian Reorganization Act of 1924, which prescribes the organizational format for communities of indigenous people who seek to be recognized as tribes by the federal government. The Missisquoi Abenaki have adopted a written constitution to provide a tribal government that includes an executive, who is an appointed chief with life tenure. The annually elected tribal council advises the chief and establishes regulations, and a tribal judge resolves disputes. The tribal repatriation officer assures the general public's compliance with the articles of the Native American Graves and Repatriation Act of 1990 in the handling and re-interment of exhumed Abenaki burial remains. The director of the Abenaki Tribal Museum is charged with promoting cultural revitalization and educating other Vermonters about Abenaki culture and history. Tribal enrollment and franchise require supporting genealogical and cultural evidence. The Missisquoi Abenaki have also sanctioned the ethnohistorical Abenaki Research Project or Abenaki Archives, which documents and records genealogical and cultural information about the community and provides data used in relations with the state and federal government, such as the application for federal recognition of the tribe. The Abenaki Self Help Association, a tax-exempt nonprofit organization, applies for and distributes grants to provide assistance and training to Abenaki seeking social services and developing economic opportunities. The Abenaki Tribal Museum and Cultural Center educates Abenaki about their history and culture, including language, religion, decorative arts, and ceremonial and performing arts, and aims to communicate an accurate picture of the Abenaki experience to other Vermonters and visitors to the state. The Cowass Abenaki of eastern Vermont historically lived in an ancient settlement on the west bank of the CONNECTICUT RIVER near the modern settlement of Newbury. The term Cowass is anglicized from *Goasek,* "the place of the pines." The Cowass Abenaki were closely allied to the Sokokis, but also maintained close ties with the Champlain valley and more eastern Abenaki. Numerous descendants of this village still live in eastern Vermont, adjacent New Hampshire, and elsewhere in the Abenaki homeland. There are several Abenaki bands that consider themselves the political descendants of the Cowasucks. The Sokoki, "the people who separated," were historically located in the middle and upper Connecticut River valley, principally at settlements such as Squakheag (today's Northfield, Massachusetts), and further north at Fort Hill, New Hampshire. After the dispersion of native peoples from lower New England subsequent to King Philip's War in 1676, Sokoki Abenaki settled with Cowasucks at their settlement in today's Newbury and were reported among Abenaki on the eastern shore of Lake Champlain. Like the modern Cowasucks, Sokoki families today reside in several regions of Vermont and New Hampshire. The 2000 census reported that 2,450 native Americans live in Vermont today. About half of them are Abenaki.   *Frederick Wiseman*

Abenaki Heritage Days

First held in 1990 on the campus of JOHNSON STATE COLLEGE, the Abenaki Heritage Days event is an annual celebration and sharing of ABENAKI and Native American culture with other Vermonters and visitors. Organized and run by the Missisquoi Abenaki, the celebration began in the early 1990s at the former Sandy Point fish hatchery on LAKE CHAMPLAIN in West Swanton. From 1993 to 1999, it was held at the Franklin County Field Days grounds in Highgate. Since then, invited by the village of Swanton to make use of the village green, the Abenaki hold the event close to the site of their original settlement. The festival has three main parts. The first consists of numerous public activities. Lectures on native culture and art are given each morning of the celebration by Abenaki Tribal Museum personnel. Topics have included clothing, wampum, and ancient treaty rights. Prominent storytellers and authors such as Joseph Bruchac, Marge Bruchac, or Wolfsong narrate traditional and modern tales and stories. Abenaki artists, including woodcarver Frederick Watso of Odanak, canoe maker Aaron York of Lachine, Quebec, and Swanton basketmaker Jesse Larocque have shared their skill and knowledge with spectators. Dance groups from Kahnawake, the Mohawk reservation southwest of Montreal, as well as from the Abenaki settlement of Odanak on the St. Lawrence River and one from central Vermont, have performed. Musicians have played on the flute, drum, and the Australian didgeridoo. Craftspeople making canoes and other artifacts attract audiences to their exhibits throughout the day. The second part of the festival is the Pan-Indian "Pow-Wow." Although the pow-wow originated with native peoples of the western plains and the upper Midwest, it became an important cultural event for New England's native people in the late twentieth century. The pow-wow begins at noon on Saturday with the Grand Entry, when dignitaries, honored guests and dancers enter the dancing circle to the beat of the Host Drum group. This is followed by a ceremony to honor American armed forces veterans. Throughout the afternoon, the drum groups provide music for a variety of dances that spectators are invited to join. The third part of the celebration is a private social event held in the evening after the final public program of Heritage Days. The Abenaki and neighboring Nations gather with a few invited Euro-American friends for an evening meal, followed by impromptu drumming and dancing, as well as the recounting of stories and traditions.

Frederick Wiseman

Abolition of Slavery

Vermont's anti-slavery tradition is enshrined in its constitution, which forbade adult slavery. The first formally organized opposition to slavery occurred when the Vermont branch of the American Colonization Society was founded in 1817. The society believed in gradual, compensated emancipation of slaves and their repatriation to Africa. Other anti-slavery advocates scorned the society, which they saw as racist and too accommodating to slave owners. Most abolitionists supported immediate, uncompensated emancipation and urged the integration of freed slaves into society. In the early years of the nineteenth century, LEMUEL HAYNES, an African-American clergyman, spoke from several pulpits across Vermont of the sinfulness of slaveholding. The greatest influences on Vermont abolitionists were WILLIAM LLOYD GARRISON and the New England Anti-Slavery Society. An early advocate of colonization, Garrison altered his views after 1828 when he worked for the abolitionist *Journal of the Times* in Bennington and later, as publisher of *The Liberator*, espoused radical abolitionism. Garrison attracted many followers in Vermont, including OLIVER JOHNSON, ORSON S. MURRAY, and ROWLAND T. ROBINSON. WILLIAM SLADE, governor and congressman, was more moderate, but still an outspoken abolitionist. The Vermont Anti-Slavery Society was founded in 1833. During the 1830s, many towns formed anti-slavery societies, with concentrations in south-central Vermont, Addison County, and northeastern Caledonia and Orleans counties. The actual number of society members was not large.

Mirroring the contemporaneous religious revival meetings, abolition societies were often formed after particularly rousing speakers appeared in rural towns; though many joined, there is little evidence of sustained activity. In larger towns, notably Burlington, Montpelier, and Woodstock, abolitionist speakers addressed hostile audiences. Still, Vermont remained an active voice against slavery for several decades. The state legislature enacted personal liberty laws in defiance of the two federal Fugitive Slave Acts and petitioned Congress to end slavery in the District of Columbia and to prevent the expansion of slavery. The legislature never went far enough to satisfy the abolitionists, who called for an end to all inequality, particularly racism, and for full citizenship for African-Americans. By contrast, surviving private correspondence reveals a disconcerting streak of racism among many Vermonters. In response, Vermont's abolitionists, though not in the majority, often tried to set examples of acceptance in their own households and communities. Ex-slave and fervent abolitionist Frederick Douglass visited Vermont and commented that Vermonters were in great sympathy with "the slave power," but perhaps his judgment was no more accurate than the post–Civil War tradition that all Vermonters were abolitionists and devoted to notions of racial equality. For the most part it seems that Vermonters disapproved of slavery, feared its spread, and believed that the slave states should be left alone. In 1861, however, the threat of dissolution of the United States aroused Vermonters to action supporting the Union and, for the state's many convinced abolitionists, freeing the slaves.

Ronald J. Salomon

Act 60:
Funding Public Education

The Vermont General Assembly promulgated the Equal Educational Opportunity Act of 1997 as Act 60 of that session. The law, passed in response to a Vermont Supreme Court decision—*Brigham v. State* (S. Ct. 1997) 1997 Vt. Lexis 13, 166 Vt. 246, 692 A.2d 384—recognized substantially equal access to a quality public education as a political right under the Vermont Constitution. Following the supreme court's directions, the law attempts to ameliorate differences in quality among different educational districts by requiring that all local school districts meet

quality standards set and monitored by the State Education Board and its commissioner. The law also required substantially equal funding among all of the state's school districts. Local property taxes traditionally have funded public education in a manner that reflects the relative economic wealth of the different communities. The quality of education provided Vermont students in different school districts often reflected those tax-base differences. Communities with high property values provided higher quality and more educational options than those with smaller local tax bases. The law fixed a required statewide equal amount of funding per pupil without regard to school district. Communities could not provide less funding. Those that wished to provide funding greater than that set amount paid a percentage of that additional amount into a state education fund for distribution to less wealthy communities. These two provisions created substantial controversy within local communities that had enjoyed more discretion with setting school academic programs and funding levels and were contributing factors to the TAKE BACK VERMONT movement.

Edward J. Cashman

Act 250:
Regulated Development

In 1969, the Vermont General Assembly passed a State Land Use and Development Plan as Act 250 of that session. The law requires the creation of a statewide capability and development plan to set guidelines for the future growth within the state. These guidelines seek to promote in an efficient and coordinated manner only that development within the state that meets a number of economic, environmental, and public health goals. The law created a state environmental board to manage development within the state through nine district commissions spread throughout the state. The law defines "development" to include any change or improvement to real estate of more than 10 acres held by a single owner within a 5-mile radius in a rural setting and within 1 mile in a city. Developers must submit plans to the local commissions, participate in public hearings, and obtain detailed Act 250 permits prior to starting any development. The local commissions employ ten criteria addressing issues of pollution, availability of water and soils to permit development, highway congestion, availability of educational facilities and other municipal services, and impact on the aesthetics, scenic beauty, historical value, and wildlife of an area subject to the permit. Act 250, along with the Municipal and Regional Planning and Development Act of 1968, set up a comprehensive framework of state and local planning and zoning requirements to bring order to what the legislature perceived as unrestricted and detrimental development of Vermont. The two statutes require local zoning and planning boards to work in concert with regional planning commissions and the environmental commissions to manage growth that often crosses municipal boundaries.   *Edward J. Cashman*

Adams, Clarence (d. 1904)

Earning the title "The Gentleman Burglar," Clarence Adams of Chester conducted a series of fifty nighttime burglaries from September 1886 to July 1902. Houses, mills, farmers' supply stores, and other venues were victims. Despite a $500 reward offered by the selectmen, the criminal remained unapprehended. Finally, Charles H. Waterman, owner of a grist mill that had lost numerous bags of feed, boobytrapped a window in his mill with a shotgun. In his next break-in attempt, the thief was wounded, and turned out to be one of the leading citizens of the town, Clarence Adams, a member of the selectboard, founder of the local library, incorporator of the Chester Savings Bank, and former town representative to the Vermont General Assembly. Many reasons for his astonishing career were offered, including a love of adventure nurtured in childhood, a warped need to demonstrate qualities of genius, and a dual personality (confirmed for some neighbors when Robert Louis Stevenson's *Strange Case of Dr. Jekyll and Mr. Hyde* was found on his bookshelves). Adams was convicted and sentenced to a term in the state prison at Windsor, where he died (or, as some claimed, faked his death and escaped to Canada) in March 1904.

Addison

Addison, population 1,393, a town in Addison County, was granted by BENNING WENTWORTH in 1761 and named for Joseph Addison (1672–1719), the great English author and statesman who had been a patron of Wentworth's father John. Bordered on the west by LAKE CHAMPLAIN and bisected from north to south by the waters of Dead Creek (a popular spot for sighting migratory birds in the spring and fall), the town consists of broad flatlands devoted to DAIRY FARMING and apple orchards. Isolated Snake Mountain (elevation 1,287 feet) dominates its eastern border. The main settlement is Addison village, on Route 22A running from Vergennes to Fair Haven. CHIMNEY POINT, a promontory on Lake Champlain called POINTE À LA CHEVELURE (Scalp Point) by the French, was the site of an early-eighteenth century French stockade fort and settlement, counterparts of Fort St. Frédéric across the lake in New York State. Today, the Chimney Point Tavern, built in the 1780s and put into its present form in 1823, is a State Historic Site containing a museum of Native American and French history in the Champlain Valley. Nearby, the Champlain Bridge, built in 1928, spans the distance between the two shores. A marker notes the northern end of the CROWN POINT ROAD, built by troops under British general Jeffrey Amherst in 1759 to connect with Fort Number 4 (near present-day Charlestown, New Hampshire) on the CONNECTICUT RIVER. The prosperity of Addison in the nineteenth century, based on agriculture, sheep raising, and its strategic location on Lake Champlain, led to the construction of many imposing residences, numbers of which can still be seen along the town's roads.

African-American Vermonters

Though always less than 5 percent of the population, African-Americans have played a largely ignored part in Vermont history from colonial times to the present as settlers, soldiers, ministers and revivalists, educators, and activists. Slaves and servants of African descent arrived with the settlers of New England and New France. African-Americans traveled the CONNECTICUT RIVER and LAKE CHAMPLAIN basins, and appear in contemporary documents as soldiers, scouts, slaves, fugitives, and captives. With the close of the French and Indian Wars, freemen, slaves, and servants were among the early settlers of Vermont. Five African-American veterans of the Continental Army's GREEN MOUNTAIN REGIMENT appear on the pension lists. The 1791 census notes 271 black Vermonters, and the number increases to 903 by 1820. The 12 black citizens of Hyde Park in 1810 made 11 percent of the population. Larger communities had from 10 to 50 black citizens. Freed slaves ABIJIAH PRINCE (Sunderland), Cuff Bass (Pomfret), and Freeman Pearson (Rutland) were drawn by the same opportunities for inexpensive land and a premium labor market as white settlers. Racism enjoyed little legal sanction in Vermont. Universal male suffrage assured the vote to all races. However, African-American Vermonters lived with racial prejudice deeply rooted in social custom, as made plain by contemporary accounts of intimidation and harassment. The State Constitution of 1777 abolished adult slavery, and numerous fugitives from New York fled here. The comment, "Half a dozen rows of ebony faces" in attendance at an 1806 Middlebury hearing for a New York fugitive suggests a politically engaged African-American community, as does the 1835 petitioning of Woodstock by its black citizens, abolition debates by JAMES and JOSEPH HOLLY, and anti-slavery letters to the editor by Louden Langley and JOHN LEWIS. During the antebellum years, the Reverend LEMUEL HAYNES, Congregational minister, achieved international fame, as did educator, Haitian adviser, and early pan-Africanist PRINCE SAUNDERS. Free Will Baptist minister CHARLES BOWLES evangelized northern Vermont. ALEXANDER TWILIGHT, the first African-American graduate of MIDDLEBURY COLLEGE, ran the Brownington Academy and represented his community in the legislature. Census records from 1791 to 1870, however, indicate the lower economic status of African-Americans: more than half recorded are part of white households as servants, hired hands, and domestics. Throughout the nineteenth century, many more black than white females worked outside the home. Men were employed as farmers, laborers, cooks, barbers, teamsters, and musicians. They also show employment in taverns, hotels, and the steamship lines. Most telling is the high rate of mobility in black households, probably for economic reasons. Between 1830 and 1860, the UNDERGROUND RAILROAD brought a new influx of fugitives. Nationally known fugitives Shadrach Minkins and Moses Roper passed through Vermont, as did abolition speakers Frederick Douglass, Milton Clark, Sojourner Truth, John Lewis, Solomon Northrup, and Louis Hayden. During the Civil War, some 71 African-American Vermonters served in the Fifty-fourth Massachusetts infantry and some 60 more in other colored troops and the U.S. Navy. Ex-slaves, including GEORGE W. HENDERSON—who had a distinguished career in education—came to the state sponsored by returning white soldiers. The 1870 census notes 922 Vermont blacks, 222 listing an out-of-state birthplace. Following the Civil War, self-congratulatory and paternalistic views of the past fueled prejudice. Many Vermont blacks sought opportunity elsewhere. Literate black activists James T. Holly, MARTIN FREEMAN, and John Lewis emigrated to Haiti or Liberia. Irish and French-Canadian immigrants supplanted blacks as domestics and hired hands in middle and upper class white households. Census figures show a declining black population, partly caused by intermarriage and "passing." The tenth Colored Cavalry, famous as the BUFFALO SOLDIERS, was posted to FORT ETHAN ALLEN in Colchester, 1909 to 1913. Segregated CIVILIAN CONSERVATION CORPS units, composed of war veteran bonus marchers, helped construct the East Barre Dam in 1933. WILLIAM J. ANDERSON, son of a freed slave father and French-Canadian mother, represented Shoreham in the state legislature in 1944 to 1949 but was at first unable to find a Montpelier hotel to accept him in his first session. During the Civil Rights activism of the 1960s, Vermonters initiated the VERMONT–NEW YORK YOUTH PROJECT and formed the Burlington Community Relations Council to help African-Americans chronically turned down for apartments. Racism in Vermont remained visible in the IRASBURG AFFAIR. In recent decades, African-Americans have come to Vermont as part of a new wave of immigration, including a new trend of interracial child adoption. Two African-Americans have recently served in the legislature, though only doubling that racial group's presence since Alexander Twilight in the 1840s and William Anderson one hundred years later. Senator Julius Canns, a Republican, and Representative Francis Brooks, a Democrat, have found themselves on opposing sides of issues such as the CIVIL UNIONS law.   *Ray Zirblis*

African-American Vermonters in the Civil War

The 1860 census reported that seven hundred African-Americans lived in Vermont in 1861. Federal law initially prohibited their military service, but some men did act as servants to officers. When the Emancipation Proclamation went into effect on January 1, 1863, colored regiments could be raised in the northern states. When the Fifty-fourth Massachusetts Regiment was created in early 1863, three African-American Vermonters enlisted; others were drafted into the regiment in July of that year. When casualties warranted additional enlistments in late 1863, African-American Vermonters were counted toward each town's quota. Between enlistees and draftees, seventy-one African-Americans from Vermont served in the Fifty-fourth Massachusetts Regiment, fighting in the battles of Olustee and Honey Hill plus several skirmishes. The regiment mustered out in August 1865. Besides the African-American Vermonters serving in the Fifty-fourth Massachusetts, forty others from Vermont enlisted and served in the United States Colored Troops in regiments heavily involved in the fighting around Richmond and Petersburg. Seven African-American Vermonters were in the Forty-third U.S. Colored Troops who were trained to lead the assault in the disastrous Battle of the Crater before Petersburg. The night before the attack, General Grant substituted an untrained and under-strength white unit for the Forty-third, reasoning that if the attack failed, he would be accused of uncaringly sending black men to their deaths. Given a new objective, the Forty-third captured rifle pits and routed the rebel force that had been decimating the untrained white force sent into the Crater in their place. Of the 152 African-American Vermonters to serve in the Civil War, 13 died in service, 3 of them killed in action.

Donald Wickman

Agriculture

Vermont had 6,700 farms in 1999. While 1,600 of those were dairy, the main type of agriculture throughout the twentieth century, the rest represented a variety of products. Vermont's terrain, climate, and geographic location favor small farms, and small farms are having a difficult time everywhere competing economically with agricultural enterprises in other parts of the world. More often, nondairy farms are owned by part-timers who hold other jobs off the farm. However, some small enterprises have been able to thrive by adding value to raw commodities and selling them retail. Farmers can pickles, milk sheep and make cheese, or spin wool into yarn. Or they find a unique niche to exploit, such as a demand for kosher goat kids in New York City. Organic farms grew steadily in number and size throughout the 1980s and 1990s. Vermont has been a source of fresh market apples since 1900, especially of the McIntosh variety, which grows well in the Northeast. The 1960s saw growth in apples, and by the end of the century, the state produced 1.4 million bushels. But the industry was threatened by competitive imports from Washington State, China, and Southern Hemisphere countries, and many orchards have gone out of business. Vermont grows few vegetables for processing, but fresh market vegetables have gained in popularity. Customers want healthier food, so they buy more fresh vegetables grown locally or regionally. Farmers who grow sweet corn, tomatoes, pumpkins, cabbages, and other produce benefit from that demand. The production of bedding plants and flowers saw phenomenal growth in the last quarter of the twentieth century. Sales that had been stagnant at less than $1 million annually until the mid-1980s suddenly boomed to $27 million in 1993, thanks to greater suburbanization and more landscaping. Apart from cattle, livestock production rises and falls, depending on the species. Most beef cattle are raised by small, part-time farmers. Sheep and goats for dairy have become more popular, but sheep raised for wool and meat, which had been Vermont's agricultural mainstay in the mid-1850s, have made little headway. The state had 18,000 sheep in 1999. Turkeys had a renaissance later in the twentieth century as consumers bought more fresh birds. Vermont raised 943,000 turkeys in 1999. Chicken egg production declined, until there were just four farms in 1999, with production of 65 million eggs. Some exotic livestock industries enjoyed brief financial success in the 1990s, then declined as the market for their products became saturated. These included llamas, emus, and fallow deer.   *Susan J. Harlow*

Aiken, George David (1892–1984)

Governor of Vermont (1937–1941) and United States senator (1941–1975), George Aiken was born in Dummerston, educated in the common schools of Putney, and graduated from Brattleboro High School in 1909. He married twice: to Beatrice Howard, who died in 1966, and to his long-time administrative assistant, LOLA PIEROTTI AIKEN, in 1967. A horticulturalist and nurseryman, Aiken was master of the Putney Grange at age eighteen, helped

Governor George D. Aiken, 1937. Special Collections, Bailey/Howe Library, University of Vermont

organize the Windham County Farm Bureau in 1913, the second to be founded in Vermont, and served as bureau president in 1935 and 1936. A Putney school director from 1920 to 1937, Aiken was elected to the Vermont House of Representatives in 1931, and became famous for his opposition to the private power companies over the issue of flood control. This popularity helped him in 1933 to win the Speaker's post in the Vermont House. He was elected lieutenant governor the following year and governor in 1936 and 1938. A moderate Republican who championed the New Deal programs that helped working-class Vermonters, Aiken attacked programs that required deficit spending or created executive aggrandizement. In a 1938 Lincoln Day Address, he castigated "old guard" Republicans who were too wedded to corporate and monied interests. Although the speech increased his popularity generally, it made enemies of national and Vermont Republican party regulars who hoped to block an Aiken third-term candidacy. Upon the death of U.S. Senator ERNEST W. GIBSON, SR., in 1940, Aiken appointed ERNEST W. GIBSON, JR., to fill out the term vacated by the death of his father. When Gibson declined to seek election the following year, Aiken declared his own candidacy, beat RALPH FLANDERS in the Republican primary, and went on to win the election and serve the next thirty-four years in the U.S. Senate. His first speech on the Senate floor was against lend lease to Great Britain. He saw the bill as strengthening the

power of the executive branch, and he felt also that U.S. interests lay in the western hemisphere, particularly with Canada. In 1943, he introduced a bill to build the St. Lawrence Seaway. He and Vermont politicians before him saw Vermont's future to the north; the seaway, with a short CHAMPLAIN WATERWAY canal link, would break the monopoly of the railroads and bring grain prices down, while helping with the industrial development of Vermont. The seaway would also provide cheap public electricity and thwart the interests of the greedy power companies who showed little interest in helping rural America. Aiken supported the Rural Electrification Administration (REA) in opposition to his own party, because it directly improved people's lives. Aiken requested and was granted a seat on the Senate Committee on Agriculture and Forestry, and retired as ranking member of that committee in 1975 after serving two short periods as chair in 1947 to 1948 and 1953 to 1954. As a freshman he was appointed to the Committees on Pensions, Civil Service, Expenditures in the Executive Department, and Education and Labor, and he bided his time and waited for an opening on Foreign Relations. Aiken was a loyal Republican for all of the years he served in the senate, but he was a maverick within his party. Though opposed to the Taft-Hartley Act (1947), for instance, he voted for it and for the subsequent override of the President's veto because it was a Republican initiative, but maintained that he would work within his party to amend it. Aiken signed Margaret Chase Smith's "Declaration of Conscience" (1950), a controversial document that many felt was directed at Senator Joseph McCarthy, and in 1954 he joined colleagues to censure the Wisconsin Republican. In 1954, Aiken gave up his seniority on Labor to take a seat on the Foreign Relations Committee to put together the powerful combination of Agriculture and Foreign Affairs that was to result in the passage of the St. Lawrence Seaway Act (1954) and the famous "Food for Peace" legislation that was part of the U.S. attempt to fight communism through foreign aid. Rather than artificial support of agricultural prices, Aiken wanted to expand the markets for American agricultural products. Aiken had established his reputation as a pragmatist, party loyalist, executive branch watchdog, and supporter of middle-class, mainstream values by the end of the Eisenhower administra-

tion. By then, he had begun his famous breakfasts with Democratic Senator Mike Mansfield. In 1958, Aiken became chair of the Subcommittee on Canada, and with bipartisan support, he retained this position until he left the Senate in 1975. A year later, he was appointed to the Joint Committee on Atomic Energy, and helped place the Vermont Yankee Nuclear Power Plant in Vernon. Aiken opposed the ascendancy of Senator Barry Goldwater in the 1960s, and made his position known by placing Margaret Chase Smith's name into nomination for president against him at the 1964 Republican National Convention. President Johnson turned to Aiken in 1964 to help develop a compromise for the landmark Civil Rights Bill. He helped draft an exception for "Mrs. Murphy's boarding house" in the public accommodations section of the bill, exempting persons who rented four or fewer rooms from the law, and broke a legislative logjam. Mansfield christened Aiken "the wise old owl" during the Vietnam War for his proposal to declare victory and get out, as a balance between "hawks" who wanted victory and "doves" who wanted to withdraw at any cost. Aiken was ambivalent throughout the war, voting against his better judgement for the Gulf of Tonkin Resolution (1964), which gave more power to the President, voting for increases in troops, and later supporting the Cooper-Church Amendment for a phased withdrawal of American forces. Aiken had great confidence in President Nixon, backed his plans to bomb Hanoi as a way to end the war quickly, and supported him throughout the Watergate investigations, urging Congress to impeach or get off the President's back. Aiken was seventy-five years old when he ran for his last term in the Senate in 1968, but he was still so popular that, according to legend, he spent only $17 on his campaign. He finished out his Senate career as an environmentalist. He had a passionate desire to open the NORTHEAST KINGDOM—a name he applied to the northeastern counties of Vermont in a 1948 speech in Lyndonville—for recreational use, and in 1974 he sponsored the Eastern Wilderness Areas Act to create such a place in the heart of the Kingdom. Throughout his career, and in the books he wrote, Aiken expressed a vision of a "Vermont with a heritage of ideals that included the principles of loving liberty, of self-reliance, of thrift and liberalism."

Connell Gallagher

Aiken, Lola Pierotti

Lola Pierotti Aiken was born in Montpelier. After graduating from Montpelier High School as valedictorian in 1930, she secured a position in the Vermont Secretary of State's office. During Governor GEORGE AIKEN'S 1940 U.S. Senate campaign, she served as a volunteer in his election headquarters and after his victory was invited to join his staff in Washington. Starting as the lowest paid member, she worked her way up to administrative assistant and manager of the senator's staff. Their close professional association ripened into a deep personal relationship and in 1967, after the first Mrs. Aiken (Beatrice Howard Aiken) died, the senator and Lola married. Their wedding day, June 30, the last day of the fiscal year, was chosen to simplify bookkeeping; Lola Aiken retained her professional responsibilities until the senator retired in 1975, but worked without pay. Upon the Aikens's return to Vermont, Mrs. Aiken participated with the senator in teaching at the UNIVERSITY OF VERMONT and in establishing the Aiken Lecture Series. After George's death in 1984, Lola Aiken sold their Putney home and relocated in Montpelier. She has remained active in numerous causes, including the Aiken Lecture Series, and is involved with CHAMPLAIN COLLEGE, the VERMONT HISTORICAL SOCIETY, the ETHAN ALLEN HOMESTEAD, and the Friends of the State House.

Albany

Albany, population 840, a town in Orleans County, was granted by the Vermont legislature in 1782 as Lutterloh after the first grantee, Colonel Henry Lutterloh, and changed to Albany (for reasons unknown) by petition of the inhabitants in 1815. Solidly rural, the town consists of a series of low, forested hills flanking broad river valleys, the most prominent of which is that of the northern Black River. The largest of the widely scattered settlements is the village of Albany, on Route 14 in the western part of town.

Alburg

Alburg, population 1,952, a town in Grand Isle County, was granted by the Vermont legislature in 1781 to IRA ALLEN and sixty-four associates. The name (spelled Alburgh in the charter, a form preferred by the town's historical society and some residents) is a contraction of Allenburg. It is the only town in Grand Isle County that is not an island in LAKE CHAMPLAIN, being comprised of a tongue of land that reaches down from Canada between Missisquoi Bay and the Richelieu River. Four bridges connect Alburg with the towns of Swanton, North Hero, Isle La Motte, and the New York town of Rouses Point. The landscape is uniformly flat and dotted with marshes. DAIRY FARMING remains economically important, although the days when Alburg village was an important railroad junction (where the Rutland Railroad and the Central Vermont met) are long past. Smuggling, as during PROHIBITION, has occasionally been carried on across the Canadian border. The United States and Canadian governments have collaborated to build a common customs house astride the U.S.-Canada boundary line in Alburg. It is the only customs house operated and maintained by both countries on the entire international border.

Allen, Ebenezer (1743–1806)

The grandfather of Ebenezer Allen was the brother of ETHAN and IRA ALLEN'S grandfather, making them second cousins. Born in Northampton, Massachusetts, and raised in New Marlboro, Massachusetts, Ebenezer Allen had little education and only a brief apprenticeship to a blacksmith when he was quite young. He moved to Bennington in 1768, living there three years, and then to Poultney, where he became active in the dispute between New Hampshire grantees and the Province of New York. He was with Ethan at TICONDEROGA on May 10, 1775, and moved to Tinmouth soon after. In late 1775, he joined SETH WARNER'S regiment of GREEN MOUNTAIN CONTINENTAL RANGERS as a lieutenant, and was a captain in SAMUEL HERRICK'S ranger regiment of the Vermont militia at the BATTLE OF BENNINGTON. Ebenezer Allen was a delegate to the conventions of 1776 and to the convention at Windsor that wrote the first Vermont constitution in 1777, leaving there to join Herrick's rangers at Bennington in August, where he distinguished himself. Under cover of a natural breastwork of rocks, Ebenezer led only thirty men in driving back the main body of Brunswickers under Colonel Baum. Allen at Bennington is not to be confused with the Pennsylvania Ebenezer Allen (1753–1813), who was also at that battle with Colonel Pfister's American Loyalists and to whom the New York legislature presented a bill for more than $1,000 in damages to New York property by his Loyalist company during that battle. After BURGOYNE'S defeat at Saratoga, Ebenezer was a sub-commander in a militia attack against British-held Ticonderoga, capturing the vantage point of Mount Defiance and the British guns overlooking the fort. JOHN BROWN, commander of the attacking Americans, decided against an attempt to take Ticonderoga. But when the British abandoned the fort two months later, Ebenezer Allen cut off their rear guard and captured forty-nine British regulars. From among the captives taken then, he freed Dinah Mathis and her son, black slaves of a British officer, thus extending the freedom of the new Vermont constitution into New York State. After 1778, he commanded militia at forts on the western side of Vermont at Vergennes and Pittsford. In May 1780, he led three hundred men to MOUNT INDEPENDENCE on the request of New York's Governor George Clinton in an effort to intercept Sir John Johnson's withdrawal into Canada after a raid into the Mohawk Valley. Johnson escaped by way of Crown Point when Clinton failed to provide boats to ferry Ebenezer's force, but the New York governor favorably reported to Congress on the Vermonters' punctuality. In 1783, Ebenezer Allen settled on the south end of South Hero Island, where he ran a ferry service and kept public rooms in his house. Cousin Ethan spent the last night of his life at Ebenezer's home on Allen's Point in February 1789. In 1792, Ebenezer Allen of Vermont met the Loyalist Ebenezer Allen when the Vermonter made a tour guided by the Loyalist Allen through the sparsely settled regions of western New York and the Niagara country to investigate opportunities for land speculations with his cousin Ira Allen. In February 1793, a party of British travellers from Canada, led by Edward Augustus, duke of Kent, son of George III and father of Queen Victoria, accompanied by his current mistress, stayed at Ebenezer Allen's inn on South Hero en route to New York. Allen represented South Hero in the legislature from 1788 to 1792 and was a member of the convention that voted for admission to the Union in 1791. He moved to Burlington in 1800, where he opened a tavern near the south wharf that he conducted until his death in 1806. Unlike his cousins Ethan the Deist, Ira the Jeffersonian Democrat, and Levi the slave owner, Ebenezer Allen was a Calvinist, a Hamilton Federalist, and an emancipator.

Allen, Ethan (1738–1789)

Aggressively opposing New York's claim to jurisdiction over the New Hampshire Grants in the early 1770s, and a forceful defender of the new state of Vermont against Britain and New York during and after the American Revolution, Ethan Allen was perhaps the most colorful and notable figure in the formative years of Vermont. He served briefly in the last French and Indian War (1754–1760), and in 1762 began operating a productive iron forge in Salisbury, Connecticut. His religious opinions and outrageous personal conduct ruined this early promise, as Ethan was warned out of Salisbury in 1765 and out of Northampton, Massachusetts, in 1767. Ethan turned next to hunting for deer, at which he excelled, but never profited as the market for deer skins was weak at the time. In 1770, he tramped through the GREEN MOUNTAINS and began investing in nearly worthless New Hampshire titles to lands then also claimed by New York. Within a year, he had become the leader and chief propagandist of the resistance to New York's jurisdiction. In 1771, he assumed leadership of the GREEN MOUNTAIN BOYS, an irregular militia whose violent actions against New York title holders and law officers led New York to offer a £100 reward offered for his capture. In his many newspaper articles and books, Ethan argued that the land belonged to those who worked it, with or without proper legal title. The settlers were therefore entirely justified in resisting those with other claims to the land. After four years of successfully nullifying New York's rule in the Green Mountains, Ethan extended his reasoning to justify the people's right to create their own state. Meanwhile, he and his extended family of brothers and cousins, doing business as the ONION RIVER LAND COMPANY, acquired New Hampshire titles to over 200,000 acres in the contested region between the CONNECTICUT RIVER and LAKE CHAMPLAIN. The royal government of New York unsuccessfully sought troops from Quebec to quell this frontier uprising in early 1775. Allen and others with New Hampshire grants had in the same months collaborated with PHILIP SKENE of Skenesborough, New York, to petition the Crown to establish a new royal province separate from New York and New Hampshire to include parts of the Green Mountain region and to stretch west to Lake Ontario, with Skene

Ethan Allen's statue on the porch of the Vermont State House. Vermont Department of Tourism and Marketing

as governor. Skene was on his way back from London with permission to conduct a poll to learn if residents of the region wished to establish a new government. Prompted by events at Lexington and Concord and supported by funds from the Connecticut Provincial Assembly, on May 10, 1775, Ethan Allen grudgingly allied with BENEDICT ARNOLD, who had been sent from Massachusetts, to lead the Green Mountain Boys and some Connecticut men in a bold surprise attack on FORT TICONDEROGA. Within two days, Ethan's forces had taken control of Lake Champlain without a single casualty. News of this first offensive victory made Ethan an instant national hero and Congress awarded him a lieutenant colonelcy and command of the Green Mountain regiment of the Continental Army. Returning from New York City, where he had persuaded the revolutionary government there to pay for the Green Mountain regiment, Ethan Allen arrived back on the grants to learn that the men of the new regiment had elected his cousin SETH WARNER as colonel commandant. "The old men of the grants," as Ethan called

them, did not trust his leadership. While three of Ethan's brothers were chosen as subalterns in the unit, he was left to seek an appointment to the staff of General Philip Schuyler, commander of the new American Northern Army occupying the Champlain Valley in late 1775 in preparation for the invasion of Canada. Undeterred, Ethan went into Quebec's Richelieu River valley as a recruiter. Ignoring orders from Schuyler, Allen attempted to capture a weakly defended Montreal and was taken prisoner. Over the next two years, he suffered a brutal captivity in British prisons, aboard prison ships, and in the Halifax and New York City jails. Thanks to the efforts of his family, Ethan Allen's cruel treatment at the hands of the British became a *cause célèbre*. Finally exchanged in May 1778 for Lieutenant-Colonel Archibald Campbell, Ethan wrote a narrative of his captivity that lacerated the British as vindictive monsters while calling on Americans to forsake any thought of compromise. Allen's *Narrative* was an enormous success, going through eight reprints in two years, and is rated the second-best-selling book of the Revolutionary period after Thomas Paine's *Common Sense*. Between 1778 and 1781, Ethan operated as commander-in-chief of Vermont's military forces, unofficial member of its legislature, chief diplomat, advisor to Governor THOMAS CHITTENDEN, ex officio judge of Vermont's court of confiscation, and prosecutor in the trial of DAVID REDDING, a New York Tory, who had stolen horses in New York but committed no crime in Vermont, who nonetheless suffered the state's first death by hanging in 1778. Allen devoted his energies in these years to defending his state, but adopted policies that tarnished his fame as a patriot among his contemporaries. After Congress twice reneged on promises to admit Vermont into the union, Ethan opened negotiations with the British commander in Canada, General FREDERICK HALDIMAND. For three years, Allen and Haldimand discussed the possibility of Vermont joining the British Empire as an autonomous province. Their conversations led nowhere, but did keep any sizeable British force out of Vermont after 1780. Though lacking a formal education, Ethan Allen had aspirations to be accepted as an Enlightenment philosopher. From 1781 to 1785, he worked to reach these ambitions in a book, *Reason the Only Oracle of Man*. This first American deistic work quickly faded from sight, though not before destroying Ethan's reputation. Ethan Allen was twice married, first to Mary Brownson of Woodbury, Connecticut (1732–1783), in 1762, with whom he had five children; and then to Frances Montresor Buchanan (1760–1834), in 1784, with whom he had three children. Ethan Allen died on February 12, 1789, at his home overlooking the Winooski River in the Burlington intervale.   *Michael A. Bellesiles*

Allen, Frances Margaret (1784–1819)

A daughter of ETHAN ALLEN and his second wife, Frances "Fanny" Allen was born in Sunderland. She was educated by her stepfather, Dr. JABEZ PENNIMAN. In 1807, after studying French with the sisters of the Congregation of Notre Dame in Montreal, Fanny joined the Roman Catholic Church. Despite family opposition, she returned to Montreal in 1808, where she entered the Congregation of the Religious Hospitalers of St. Joseph, a seventeenth-century nursing order founded in France that was instrumental in settling Montreal. During the remaining years of her life she worked in the apothecary of the Hotel Dieu, the order's hospital, spent much time as an interpreter and in visiting patients, and came to be known as the "beautiful American nun." Like many of the Allens in her father's generation, she died of a lung disease while still in her early thirties. In 1894, the sisters of St. Joseph came to Vermont to establish a hospital in Colchester, naming it the Fanny Allen Hospital in her honor.

Deborah P. Clifford

Allen, Frances Montresor Buchanan

See PENNIMAN, FRANCES MONTRESOR BUCHANAN ALLEN.

Allen, Heber (1743–1782)

Heber Allen was the third son and fourth child of Joseph and Mary Baker Allen and the brother of ETHAN ALLEN. He was the first of the Allens to settle on the New Hampshire grants in 1771, but was not an organizer of the ONION RIVER LAND COMPANY with his brothers. He was Poultney's first town clerk and served as assistant judge of the Rutland shire of the CUMBERLAND COUNTY COURT in 1778 to 1779. Heber participated in the capture of FORT TICONDEROGA in 1775 and was a major in the Vermont militia under MOSES ROBINSON when the Americans evacuated the fort in 1777. He died in

Poultney from long-term complications, probably due to tuberculosis, brought on from exposure during the march from Ticonderoga and the rainstorm during the BATTLE OF BENNINGTON.

Allen, Heman (1740–1778)

The next younger brother to ETHAN ALLEN, Heman Allen was first a storekeeper in Salisbury, Connecticut, and then an original member of the ONION RIVER LAND COMPANY. Though never a permanent settler of the New Hampshire grants, he acquired large tracts of land there and presented Vermont's statehood petition to Congress in 1777. Ethan Allen's first wife, Mary Brownson (1732–1783), and their five children lived with Heman during Ethan's many absences. Heman served with the GREEN MOUNTAIN CONTINENTAL RANGERS in the Canadian expedition of 1775 to 1776, including the five-month siege of Quebec and at the BATTLE OF BENNINGTON, where, like his brother HEBER ALLEN, he suffered from exposure to the rain and cold, complications from which caused his death in May 1778, one week before Ethan's return to Vermont from British imprisonment in New York City.

Allen, Heman "Chili" (1779–1852)

A congressman and minister to Chile, and the son of HEBER ALLEN, a brother of ETHAN and IRA ALLEN, Heman "Chili" Allen was so called to distinguish him from his distant cousin HEMAN "MILTON" ALLEN of Milton, who was also elected to the United States Congress. He was born in Poultney, and after his father's death in 1782 his mother, Sarah Owen, took her five children, of whom Heman was the youngest, to live with her brother-in-law Ira Allen. He moved the household and family to the falls of the Onion River at Colchester in 1784, where Sarah kept house for this extended family. She died in 1786, and Ira assumed responsibility for the children. He adopted Heman, sent him to Dartmouth College (class of 1795), and provided for his law studies. Firmly loyal to his Uncle Ira, Heman supervised his business affairs during nearly six years that Ira was in England and France and after he fled Vermont for the last time to evade imprisonment for debt in 1803. An attorney who seems not to have practiced law except in his Uncle Ira's affairs, Heman was sheriff of Chittenden County (1808–1809), chief judge of Chittenden

County (1811–1814), elected to the Vermont General Assembly (1812–1817) and the United States Congress (1817–1818), resigning to accept an appointment as United States marshal (1818–1823) and as minister to Chile (1823–1828). In 1830, he was appointed president of the Bank of the United States's Vermont branch in Burlington, moving to Highgate in 1837 after the expiration of the bank's charter, where he died.

Allen, Heman "Milton" (1777–1844)

Called "Milton" for his town to distinguish him from his distant cousin HEMAN "CHILI" ALLEN, Heman "Milton" Allen was born in Ashfield, Massachusetts, studied at Chesterfield Academy in New Hampshire and, after joining his family in Vermont, in Grand Isle with the Reverend ASA LYON. He read law with Elnathan Keyes in Burlington and Judge Bates Turner of Fairfax, and became the town of Milton's first resident lawyer, where he developed a very respected reputation as the best real estate lawyer in the circuit. He represented that town in the legislature from 1810 to 1822, and was elected to Congress as a Federalist/Whig in 1826 and again from 1832 to 1838. Milton Allen voted for President Van Buren's neutrality bill during the Canadian PATRIOTS uprising of 1837, which cost him the next election, as the town of Milton and much of western Vermont was a hotbed of Patriot partisans in 1837 to 1838.

Allen, Ira (1751–1816)

An early Vermont political leader and entrepreneur in the land business with his five brothers, ETHAN, LEVI, HEBER, HEMAN, and Zimri, Ira Allen was born in Cornwall, Connecticut, the youngest child of Joseph and Mary Baker Allen. He received a rudimentary education and in 1770 followed four elder brothers north to the New Hampshire grants region. There he joined brother Ethan in the Yankee versus Yorker struggle for control of the grants, but in the early 1770s Ira concentrated more of his time and attention on land speculation than politics. He surveyed much of the Champlain and Winooski valleys and persuaded his brothers Ethan, Heman, and Zimri, together with cousin REMEMBER BAKER, to form the ONION RIVER LAND COMPANY to buy New Hampshire-granted lands in the region. Within two years the partnership held title to 65,000 acres, cementing a

Ira Allen. Special Collections, Bailey/Howe Library, University of Vermont

family geographic focus that would dominate Ira's plans for the next forty years. Ira served as a lieutenant in the 1775 American invasion of Canada, returning to the grants early in 1776. Ethan Allen was a British prisoner until May 1778, and in his absence Ira rose to a leadership role in the faction living west of the GREEN MOUNTAINS. From Vermont's declaration of independence in January 1777 through the early 1780s, Ira served simultaneously as state treasurer, secretary to Governor THOMAS CHITTENDEN, surveyor-general, and member of the Governor's Council. He wrote propaganda proclaiming Vermont's right to freedom from New York, traveled extensively in search of outside support for Vermont's independence, and played a key role in the clandestine 1780 to 1783 HALDIMAND NEGOTIATIONS that discussed returning Vermont to British allegiance. The October 1781 news of Cornwallis's surrender at Yorktown saved the Vermont leaders from having to choose between England and the United States, but for Ira Allen it was clear that strong ties to Canada were essential to the Champlain Valley's post-war prosperity. Ira's political power in Vermont eroded after the Revolution, and he moved to Colchester to concentrate on developing his real estate holdings of 200,000 acres. With brother Levi situated as a merchant trader at St. Johns on the Richelieu River, Ira planned to ship Green Mountain lumber and agricultural products north and import European manufactured goods for sale in Vermont. On paper this plan looked sound, but success proved elusive, and by the mid-1790s the Allen brothers were deeply in debt. In December 1795, Ira mortgaged his best lands, sailed to England, and sought permission to build a canal from St. Johns to the St. Lawrence River to give the Champlain Valley access to transatlantic trade. When the Pitt government hesitated, Allen went to France in search of backing for a democratic revolution in British Canada. In November 1796, he sailed from Ostend aboard the ship *Olive Branch* with fifteen thousand muskets for French-Canadian and American recruits, but his plans unraveled when a British warship captured the *Olive Branch*. Eighteen months of litigation followed, during which time Ira published several books and pamphlets claiming that the arms were meant for sale to American state militias. When he returned to France to gather documentation, authorities there imprisoned him for nearly a year on suspicion of being a British spy. Ira returned to Vermont in May 1801 to find his Champlain Valley empire in ruins. Unable to salvage anything from the wreckage, he fled south in April 1803 to avoid imprisonment for debt. He spent the last decade of his life in Philadelphia, estranged from his Green Mountain family and associates, unsuccessfully petitioning England for compensation of his *Olive Branch* losses, and dreaming of a triumphant return to Vermont. A final chance at success came in 1813 to 1814, when he helped a group of Spanish-American revolutionaries plan an invasion of Mexico that collapsed soon after it began. Ira Allen died a pauper in Philadelphia in 1814, and his body went to an unmarked grave in that city's Free Quaker Cemetery. Although his grand plans of empire through frontier intrigue and rebellion ultimately failed, between 1775 and 1795 Ira Allen was a powerful force in Vermont political and economic affairs and a leading example of the American frontier entrepreneur-adventurers of his generation. His most lasting contribution to Vermont was his personal funding for the establishment of the UNIVERSITY OF VERMONT.

J. Kevin Graffagnino

Allen, Levi (1746–1801)

The brother of ETHAN and IRA ALLEN, Levi Allen was born in Cornwall, Connecticut. He was among the first European-Americans to trade in the Miami country in the 1760s, becoming a life-long defender of the Native Americans. After a competitor in Detroit tried to kill Levi, he joined his family in the GREEN MOUNTAINS in 1771, becoming a member of the GREEN MOUNTAIN BOYS. Like every other member of his large family, Levi Allen rushed to support the patriot cause in the days after Lexington and served as Ethan Allen's adjutant and courier during the capture of FORT TICONDEROGA from the British on May 10, 1775. Levi abandoned military duty after Ethan Allen was taken prisoner during an attack on Montreal and devoted himself for two years to obtaining his brother's release from British captivity. In New York City attempting to arrange his brother's release in 1776, Levi made a great deal of money supplying goods to the British Army, and adopted a qualified loyalism. He argued that everyone would benefit if the Americans and British ended the war and devoted themselves to business. Patriot officials felt otherwise, jailing Levi Allen for six months in 1778 at New London, Connecticut, for passing counterfeit money and trading with the British. While Levi was in jail, his brothers charged him with loyalism and arranged for the Vermont Court of Confiscation to seize most of his property. After his release in 1779, Levi married Anna Allen of New Milford, Connecticut, with whom he had one daughter. Joining the British Army in the south as a supplier, Levi opened a store on the St. Johns River in East Florida, where the British government planned a refuge for southern Loyalists. But in 1783, Britain abandoned the Loyalists, ceding East Florida to Spain. Levi Allen returned to Vermont, where, despite challenging Ethan to a duel over the confiscation of his property in 1779, he was welcomed back by his family and played a role in the last phase of the HALDIMAND NEGOTIATIONS, which almost brought Vermont into the British Empire as an autonomous province. With the failure of those efforts in 1784, Levi opened a store in St. Johns, Quebec, traded British goods to his brothers and other merchants in the Champlain Valley, worked to keep Vermont out of the American Union, and successfully negotiated a free trade treaty between Vermont and Canada. As Vermont's unofficial representative in Canada, Levi Allen won a number of significant trade concessions from the British. After three years in London (1789–1791) unsuccessfully attempting to negotiate a contract for Vermont lumber with the British Navy and failing to get license for a canal from the St. Lawrence River to permit sea-going vessels into LAKE CHAMPLAIN, Levi Allen returned to America, where he turned his efforts to reconciling the United States and Britain on the principles of Adam Smith and free trade, all the while speculating in frontier land titles in Vermont, New York, Quebec, Pennsylvania, and Georgia. Levi's former allies on both sides of the Revolution remained suspicious of him. In 1797, the government of Quebec, convinced that his brother Ira Allen was behind a plot to overthrow British rule in Canada, imprisoned Levi Allen for two months in Fort St. Louis on suspicion of high treason in the David McLean affair. After his release, Levi's complicated business deals began to unravel. He died in the Burlington jail while imprisoned for unpaid debts. Well-read in a variety of popular writers and periodicals of his time, Levi Allen was an articulate and fluently expressive, even volatile, character whose modern, pragmatic sensibility distinguished him in a family of notable early Vermonters.

Michael A. Bellesiles

Alvarez, Julia (b. 1950)

The author of twelve books, including four novels, four books of poetry, two children's books, and one collection of essays, Julia Alvarez wrote all of them in Weybridge, where she lives with her husband. She is best known for her fiction about the Dominican experience both in the United States and the Dominican Republic, where she was born and lived until the age of ten. *In the Time of the Butterflies* (1994) and *In the Name of Salome* (2000) are historical novels of the Dominican Republic and Cuba (with a Dominican protagonist). *How the Garcia Girls Lost Their Accents* (1991) and *¡Yo!* (1997) are about a Dominican family in the United States. Her fiction has been translated into nine languages, and she has been honored by the borough of Manhattan, the New York Historical Society, and *Latina* magazine (as its woman of the year in 2000). After graduating from MIDDLEBURY COLLEGE in 1971 and receiving a master's degree in creative writing from Syracuse University, she returned to Vermont in 1981 as visiting assistant professor at the UNIVERSITY OF VERMONT for two years. She began teaching at Middlebury College in 1988, where she is currently Writer-in-Residence. *Robert Buckeye*

American Fork & Hoe Company

Lyman Batcheller (1795–1858), a native of Stratton, moved to Arlington in 1817 to work as a blacksmith. Here he started forging quality pitchforks for local farmers. In 1835, he shifted his business to Wallingford, where he focused on the production of pitchforks, gradually improving their design and reducing their weight. As Batcheller & Sons after his sons entered the trade, the company gained a national and soon international reputation for its product. The sons assumed management of the company after Batcheller's death. With increased production, they purchased a larger building on OTTER CREEK, into which the company moved in 1865. Further expansion proved necessary in 1884. In 1902, the Cleveland-based American Fork & Hoe Company absorbed Batcheller & Sons as the Batcheller Works, but management remained local. A severe fire in 1924 destroyed most of the company buildings, greatly reducing tool production. Thereafter, the company switched its emphasis to the manufacturing of high-quality tool handles. The American Fork & Hoe Company was renamed True Temper Tool Company in 1949. Today it is a division of the Ames True Temper Tool Company. *Donald Wickman*

American Museum of Fly Fishing

Founded in 1968 by a group of anglers concerned about the need for preserving the heritage of fly fishing, the American Museum of Fly Fishing in Manchester is an independent nonprofit institution that supports education and research into fly fishing and its related fields, social history and conservation. The museum serves as a repository for and conservator to the world's largest collection of angling and angling-related objects, including over 1,200 rods, 1,100 reels, 20,000 flies, and a library of over 300 volumes. Since 1974, the museum has published *The American Fly Fisher*, a quarterly journal of articles that illustrate fly fishing's history. Thousands of people have learned about the sport from travelling exhibits organized by the museum and by its publications.

American Society of Dowsers

The American Society of Dowsers (ASD) originated at a National Dowsing Convention held in Danville in 1958 and was formally organized in 1961. The term "dowsing" involves searching for information, and can involve the use of a forked stick or pendulum. Dowsers are historically known for their ability to find sources of underground water, but the art of dowsing can also be used to find lost items, track criminals, locate missing persons, and seek guidance of a more spiritual nature. Since its founding, the society's focus has expanded from simply seeking water to include many uses and practices of dowsing. The Latin motto of the ASD is *Indigo Felix* or "successful search." Still headquartered in Danville, with a bookstore in St. Johnsbury, the society holds an annual meeting in Vermont in August, and regional conferences around the United States. These meetings draw dowsers from around the world, and include informational sessions on dowsing topics as well as guided lessons in dowsing technique.

Chris Burns

Anderson, Mary Perle (1864–1945)

A highly trained naturalist and pioneer in teaching nature study, East Berkshire native Mary Perle Anderson helped lay the foundation of modern environmental education. An 1890 graduate of Mount Holyoke College's scientific course, she pursued graduate study at MIT, Woods Hole, the University of Chicago, and Columbia University. Decades before Aldo Leopold and Rachel Carson sought to raise modern ecological consciousness, Anderson understood and taught the principles of ecology in schools, colleges, and nature-study camps in Missouri, Massachusetts, Illinois, New York, and Vermont. She won first prize for her essay "The Protection of Our Native Plants" (1904) in a competition sponsored by the New York Botanical Gardens and the Wildflower Preservation Society of America. She assisted her brother WILBERT LEE ANDERSON in writing his book *The Country Town* (1906). Tours of the Kew Botanical Gardens in London and the Jardin des Plantes in Paris preceded Anderson's appointment to supervise nature-study education at Columbia University's experimental Horace Mann Elementary School, where she worked from 1908 to 1917. In 1909 her essay "The Passing of the Wild Flowers" won another competition first prize. Beginning in 1912, Anderson ran a summer nature-study camp for children called The Bluebird in East Berkshire, where she returned to live in 1917. An early proponent of training teachers for nature-study education in Vermont, Anderson joined the Vermont Department of Education in promoting school gardens as aids for children to study nature, agriculture, and beautification.   *Gerald F. Vaughn*

Anderson, Wilbert Lee (1857–1915)

A Congregational minister who urged an enlarged role for churches in preventing the decline of rural life during the late nineteenth century, Wilbert Lee Anderson was born and grew up in Berkshire. He attended St. Albans Academy and the preparatory department of Oberlin College before earning a bachelor's degree from that college in 1879. In 1882, he was awarded a bachelor of divinity degree from Yale, was ordained in Stowe, and became minister to the town's Congregational church, serving until 1890. Deeply concerned by population losses in many of Vermont's rural towns in the 1890s (half of Vermont's counties lost population or saw no growth), Anderson wrote *The Country Town: A Study of Rural Evolution* (1906) in which he argued "that more depends upon the vitality and the activity of the church than upon the fortune of the town in keeping or losing its people. . . . [the church] must take account of spiritual forces—the social tradition, the theological interest, the missionary enthusiasm." Anderson went on to lead congregations in Michigan, New Hampshire, and Massachusetts, and served as a consultant to national church bodies on the role of religion and churches in rural life.

Gerald F. Vaughn

Anderson, William J. (1876–1959)

A state legislator, orchardist, and equal rights advocate, William J. Anderson was the son of an ex-slave from Virginia who was befriended by Vermont soldiers during the Civil War and settled in Shoreham about 1864. Anderson was reared in Vermont, but lived in Massachusetts from 1900 to 1920, excepting military service during World War I. He was a delegate to the Republican State Convention that nominated CALVIN COOLIDGE as governor. He started the Diamond A Orchard in Shoreham in 1920—probably the first commercial apple orchard in the town—and made it into a successful business. When asked why he went into the orchard business, he responded that he wished to get into work that would afford him equal opportunity. When World War II began, he lobbied Senator WARREN AUSTIN, a close friend and member of the Senate Armed Services Committee, to help end segrega-

tion and discrimination in the armed forces. Anderson was particularly interested in improving the training of black officers. His efforts led to the establishment of R.O.T.C. training at Tuskegee Institute and the graduation of the first African-American pilots from the Tuskegee Advanced Flying School in 1942. Anderson served in various town offices and represented Shoreham in the state legislature from 1944 to 1949. He was also a musician, singer, writer of horticultural articles, and much sought-after public speaker.   *Ray Zirblis*

Andover

Andover, population 496, a town in Windsor County, was granted by BENNING WENTWORTH in 1761 and originally included the area that in 1799 became the town of Weston. Andover is probably named after the town of that name in Connecticut, the home colony of many of the grantees, rather than the better-known town in Massachusetts. The landscape is a mixture of forested hills and upland pastures cut by small watercourses and culminates in two summits, 2,882-foot Terrible Mountain and 2,509-foot Markham Mountain, on the border with Weston. After attaining a population of 1,000 in the census of 1820, Andover declined steadily for the next 130 years, finally achieving a modest increase in the period after World War II. There are three tiny settlements, Middletown, Simonsville, and Andover village.

Andrus, Charles Hardin (1851–1924)

Charles Hardin Andrus of Enosburg Falls specialized in designing and painting theater curtains, panoramas, and other large-scale works from the 1880s to the 1920s. Many Vermont towns used their public meeting spaces for local or travelling theater productions before the advent of movie houses. It was an expression of local pride to commission a stage curtain to serve as a backdrop or permanent decoration for these spaces. Painted theatre curtains and backdrops by Charles Andrus now hang in the Enosburg Opera House, the Hyde Park Opera House, Burlington City Hall, and Irasburg Town Hall. The Bakersfield Town Hall curtain is on exhibit at the VERMONT HISTORICAL SOCIETY Museum in Montpelier's Pavilion Building. His large-format historical paintings can be seen at the Vermont Veterans Museum (*Sheridan's Ride*) and the Ver-

mont Historical Society (*General George Stannard* and *Grand Panorama of the Civil War*). He also painted murals (St. John the Baptist Church, Enosburg Falls) and commercial signs, and designed commercial stationery, trade cards, and business forms at his studio in Richford. He died in the Waterbury State Hospital.

Michael Sherman

Anti-Masonic Movement

The mysterious disappearance of William Morgan in western New York in 1826 after he threatened an exposé of FREEMASONRY triggered a reaction against secret societies that spread throughout the nation but was particularly virulent in Vermont. The state's Masonic Grand Lodge was pressured to dissolve itself but rejected the proposal and agreed to accept charters from those lodges desiring to surrender them and to provide that the funds from such lodges would go to the state public school fund. The movement also spawned a national political party (anti-Jackson) that for a short time dominated Vermont politics. In 1832, Vermont was the only state to cast its votes for William Wirt, the Anti-Mason presidential candidate. From 1829 through 1835, the party won nine congressional contests and elected Vermont's governor annually from 1831. SILAS H. JENISON, elected governor as an Anti-Mason/Whig in 1836, was re-elected as a Whig in 1837, formally conceding the absorption of the Anti-Masons into the WHIG PARTY.

Arlington

Arlington, population 2,397, a town in Bennington County, was granted by BENNING WENTWORTH in 1761 and probably named for Augustus Henry Fitzroy (1735–1811), fourth earl of Arlington. Settlement is concentrated in the VALLEY OF VERMONT in the eastern quarter of the town, where the main village of Arlington lies along Route 7A, the major north-south artery. East Arlington is a short distance away on the border with Sunderland, and West Arlington is on Route 313 in the valley of the BATTEN KILL as it heads toward New York State. Most of the town lies in the heavily forested TACONIC MOUNTAINS, rising to 3,109 feet at Grass Mountain. Arlington was home at one time or another to a number of the GREEN MOUNTAIN BOYS, including ETHAN and IRA ALLEN, SETH WARNER, REMEMBER BAKER, and THOMAS CHITTENDEN, and also to a substantial body of Tories during the Revolution, when the town was derisively called Tory Hollow. AGRICULTURE and later lumbering were the town's economic mainstay in the early years, while the Batten Kill provided power for mills and small industries, including furniture making. A major employer today is the Mack Molding Company, a custom molder of plastic products. In recent decades, Arlington has developed a modest tourist industry linked to neighboring Manchester to the north. CARL RUGGLES, the composer, lived in Arlington from the 1920s to 1966, and NORMAN ROCKWELL made his home here from 1939 to 1953, using many of the local people as models in his paintings. Other prominent residents were Rockwell Kent, the artist, and DOROTHY CANFIELD FISHER, the novelist and short-story writer, who lived in Arlington for over fifty years until her death in 1958.

Arlington Junto

A modern term that refers to the tightly knit coterie who guided Vermont's affairs in the early years of the republic, the Arlington Junto got its name because it often gathered to discuss strategy in the Arlington house of THOMAS CHITTENDEN. The eight men aware of the HALDIMAND NEGOTIATIONS—Chittenden, ETHAN and IRA ALLEN, JOHN FASSETT, JR., JOSEPH FAY, MOSES ROBINSON, SAMUEL SAFFORD, and Timothy Brownson—formed its core. Others closely allied to it included MATTHEW LYON, JONAS FAY, and Nathan Clark. These men, many related through marriage and other family ties, worked together as a kitchen cabinet. They also held various offices, often for unbroken tenures, including governor, council member, secretary of state, judge of the supreme and lower courts, council of safety member, and member of the legislature. They espoused an independent Vermont and sought to establish rules for entitling land ownership and to keep trade open with Canada. The Arlington Junto gradually lost its influence by the mid-1780s as Vermont's population grew and diversified and its institutions began to mature.   *H. Nicholas Muller III*

Arnold, Benedict (1741–1801)

A real American hero on LAKE CHAMPLAIN and in the Canadian campaign of the Revolutionary War, as well as in the great American victory at Saratoga, Benedict Arnold was arguably the Continental Army's most effective field commander, though his contributions to the American struggle during the years 1775 to 1777 are overshadowed by his treason in 1780. His first exploit on Lake Champlain occurred when he and ETHAN ALLEN shared command of the irregular force that took FORT TICONDEROGA from the British on May 10, 1775. "Bred a mariner" on the Connecticut coast, Arnold then led a sortie against Fort St. Johns in June 1775 and captured the largest armed vessel on Champlain, giving the Americans control of the entire lake until October 1776. George Washington approved Arnold's plan for a late 1775 invasion of Canada, which sent Arnold and several militia regiments across the roadless wilds of northern Maine to join General Richard Montgomery's small army before the walls of Quebec, but the midnight assault on December 31, 1775, failed with Montgomery's death and Arnold wounded. Arnold then blockaded the walled city until it was relieved by reinforcements from England the following May, after which he withdrew to Lake Champlain and hastily built a small group of gunboats to face a British fleet constructed at St. Johns in 1776. On October 11, a powerful British fleet met Arnold's flotilla near Valcour Island and drove it from the lake, but the Americans' fierce resistance in the BATTLE OF VALCOUR ISLAND upset British plans to attack the American forces based at Ticonderoga and MOUNT INDEPENDENCE. Arnold's tactics stalled the British on the lake in 1776 and gave the Americans another year to gather forces from New England and the south that eventually met and defeated JOHN BURGOYNE's troops at the BATTLE OF BENNINGTON in August 1777 and, with Arnold displaying extraordinary courage and again wounded, in the victory at Saratoga in September.   *Arthur Cohn*

Arnold, Jonathan (1741–1793)

A self-taught physician and political leader of the Revolutionary period, Jonathan Arnold was born in Providence, Rhode Island. During the Revolution, he commanded a grenadier company, served in the Rhode Island Assembly, wrote the statute repealing the oath of allegiance to Britain, and was chief surgeon of the Revolutionary Hospital of Rhode Island. As a delegate to the Continental Congress in the 1780s, Arnold led the opposition to every effort to strengthen the Articles of Confederation. He also acted as Vermont's chief advocate in Congress, probably because of his heavy investment in Vermont land titles. In late 1784, Arnold abruptly quit Rhode Island and moved to St. Johnsbury. Moving quickly to the center of Vermont politics, Arnold served as Vermont's agent to Congress, a member of the governor's council, and a trustee of the planned UNIVERSITY OF VERMONT. He was selected by the General Assembly as one of the special councilors to negotiate Vermont's admission to the Union. Despite previous opposition to increased federal powers, Arnold supported the ratification of the United States Constitution at Vermont's 1791 ratifying convention. Arnold died at home shortly after being elected to the Orange County Court.

Michael A. Bellesiles

Arthur, Chester Alan (1830–1886)

The twenty-first president of the United States, Chester Alan Arthur was born in Fairfield, the son of a well-educated but impecunious Irish immigrant Baptist minister. Reverend William Arthur's brick church on a nearby hillside is open to visitors. Chester A. Arthur graduated from Union College in Schenectady, New York, in 1848 and began studying law at home while earning his living as a teacher at North Pownal and as principal of the academy at Cohoes, New York. He received his final training in New York City at the law office of Culver and Parker and was admitted to the bar in 1854, opening his law practice in 1856. An early member of the new REPUBLICAN PARTY, Arthur worked diligently for the re-election of New York's Governor Edwin D. Morgan, and received several political appointments in return. His support of the party and its boss, Senator Roscoe Conkling, led President Grant to appoint Arthur as collector of the Port of New York with many patronage jobs attendant to that office. Arthur's party loyalty led to his nomination and election to the vice-presidency in 1880. When President James Garfield was assassinated in 1881, Arthur assumed the presidency. His three years in the White House were noted for his independence and integrity. But his support for civil service reform and attempts to revise the tariff code alienated his party's leaders, who refused to renominate him in 1884. He suffered from Bright's disease, a fatal kidney condition, and died less than nine months after leaving the presidency. The President Chester A. Arthur State Historic Site is located off

Route 36 or 108 in Fairfield. The present structure, built by the State of Vermont, is a replica of the parsonage the Arthur family moved to in 1830. Rather than being furnished as the cramped living quarters must have been, it offers instead a pictorial exhibit on Chester A. Arthur's life and career. Arthur's ancestral home in Culleybackey, county Antrim, Northern Ireland, is open to visitors. *John Dumville*

Arthur, Harold (1904–1971)

An attorney, a long-time clerk in the Vermont legislature, and lieutenant governor (1948–1950) when he succeeded to the governor's office to complete the unexpired term of Governor ERNEST W. GIBSON, JR., Harold Arthur was a native of Whitehall, New York. He graduated from Albany Business College and received a law degree from La Salle Extension University (1932). Associated with Senator WARREN R. AUSTIN as a student and an attorney, he was admitted to the Vermont bar in 1932 and served as a longtime clerk to the Vermont legislature. An inveterate joiner, he was master of the Vermont Grange and president of the Vermont Elks. A member of the Vermont National Guard since 1928, he was called into active service during World War II to serve as assistant judge advocate general of the Army Air Corps with the rank of major. During his brief term as governor, Arthur was a caretaker filling out Gibson's term and did not seek his own election to the office in 1950. In a surprise move, he decided to run for Congress, but lost the primary to WINSTON PROUTY. In 1952, he lost the lieutenant governor primary race to CONSUELO NORTHRUP BAILEY. In 1958, he won a six-person race for the Republican nomination for Congress with only 30.2 percent of the vote, but was defeated in the general election by a Democratic unknown, WILLIAM H. MEYER, who was the first Democrat in more than one hundred years to defeat a Republican for a major public office in Vermont. Arthur retired from public life after his unsuccessful congressional campaign.

Aschenbach, Paul (1921–1994)

A sculptor, Paul Aschenbach, a native of Poughkeepsie, New York, joined the faculty of the UNIVERSITY OF VERMONT in 1958. With a deep commitment to sculpture in public places, he conceived and directed three international symposia (1969, 1971, and 1990) devoted to the pro-

duction of public sculpture. The eighteen massive *Sculptures on the Highway* standing at rest stops between the Canadian border and the Massachusetts line on INTERSTATE HIGHWAYS 89 and 91 in Vermont were designed and fabricated by sculptors from nine countries. Other symposium sculptures stand in Burlington's waterfront Sculpture Garden and along the walkway from College Street to Battery Park. In a nationwide competition, Paul Aschenbach won the commission to produce the sculpture honoring Mother Elizabeth Ann Seton, the first American woman canonized by the Catholic church. He also produced the 14-foot-high untitled sheet bronze sculpture standing beside the Bailey-Howe Library at the University of Vermont. *Lilian Baker Carlisle*

Athens

Athens ("a" as in "pay"), population 340, a town in Windham County, was granted by the Vermont legislature in 1780 and named after the city in Greece in keeping with the contemporary enthusiasm for classical place names. The hilly, heavily wooded land, cut from north to south by the narrow valley of Bull Creek, a tributary of Saxtons River, has always resisted settlement and, except for a modest population boom around 1830 to 1840 from the raising of sheep, the town has always been sparsely settled. The single village of Athens lies in the northern part of town near the border with Grafton.

Atkinson, John (1742–1823)

A wealthy merchant whose successful businesses allowed him to retire to Bellows Falls in 1819, John Atkinson was the principal financier of the Bellows Falls canal around the falls of the CONNECTICUT RIVER in 1792. Born in Kirby Moorside, Kent, England, Atkinson retained business relations in London. Before retiring to Bellows Falls, he had for some years maintained a summer residence and engaged in various business activities there. The Bellows Falls canal became the foundation of the industries developed at that crucial place on the river. Among his business interests was a partnership with BILL BLAKE, a papermaker and bookseller of the town. Atkinson died at Bellows Falls. *Marcus A. McCorison*

Austin, Warren R. (1877–1962)

A native of Highgate Center, UNIVERSITY OF VERMONT class of 1899, Warren R.

Austin was an attorney, United States senator, and the first United States ambassador to the United Nations. Austin read the law in his father's St. Albans law office, where he practiced after admission to the Vermont bar in 1902. He worked his way up the REPUBLICAN PARTY ladder, but lost his bid for Congress in 1912. Four years later, he accepted a position to represent the American International Corporation in Peking (now Beijing), China, where he negotiated loans with the Chinese government for railroad and canal-engineering projects. In 1931, he was elected to the United States Senate to fill the balance of the term of FRANK LESTER GREENE, who died in December 1930. Austin served in the Senate for fifteen years. He was a staunch conservative on domestic issues and an unwavering opponent of the New Deal, voting, for example, against the Social Security Act, which he claimed would destroy frugality and traditional individual responsibilities. In foreign affairs, his experiences in China led him to the conviction that America had a democratic, moralistic, and capitalistic mission in world affairs, and he urged his party to adopt a flexible foreign policy that shunned isolationism. His position put him at odds with most of his Republican colleagues in the Senate, but opened doors for him to a larger bipartisan group in Congress and the Roosevelt and Truman administrations, leading to his appointment by President Harry Truman as ambassador to the new United Nations in 1947. Austin was an eloquent and effective spokesman for the administration's internationalist positions, but after the start of the Korean War he became increasingly skeptical, then antagonistic toward the Soviet Union and its allies. While he never lost faith in the importance and goals of the United Nations, he became increasingly anti-Communist. Austin returned to Burlington after his service at the United Nations, and continued his involvement in the national effort to keep the People's Republic of China out of the United Nations. *Michael Sherman*

Averill

Averill, population eight, an unorganized township in Essex County, was granted by BENNING WENTWORTH in 1762 to Samuel Averill and others. One of the most remote locations in the state, it is totally forested and has never had more than forty-eight residents (in 1880). Three mountains,

Black, Green, and Sable, in the 2,700- to 2,800-foot range, dominate the southern section. The settlement of Averill on Route 114, which passes through the northern tip of the town just south of the Canadian border, is actually in the neighboring town of Norton. Resort activity on Great Averill Pond (812 acres), Little Averill Pond (483 acres), and Forest Lake (62 acres) supplements the traditional economic activity of lumbering. In 1999, most of the township became part of the CHAMPION LANDS, a public-private project devoted to conservation and sustainable forest harvesting.

Avery's Gore

Avery's Gore, population zero, in Essex County, was granted by the Vermont legislature in 1791 to Samuel Avery of Westminster. Completely forested, it has never had any settlements or public roads, and lumbering has been the sole economic activity. Three peaks in the northern part of the gore, Round, Middle, and Gore mountains, rise to approximately three thousand feet. Its one body of water is called simply Unknown Pond. In 1999, most of the gore became part of the CHAMPION LANDS, a public-private project devoted to conservation and sustainable forest harvesting.

B

Babcock, Robert S. (1915–1985)

A professor of political science at the UNIVERSITY OF VERMONT, Robert S. Babcock blended his interests in the academic study and the practical activities of politics by serving in the Vermont House and Senate and as lieutenant governor, by running for governor, and by serving as the first chief executive (provost) of the VERMONT STATE COLLEGES. Born in Evanston, Illinois, Babcock graduated from Evanston High School and in 1937 from the University of Rochester. An outstanding student and football player, he was awarded a Rhodes Scholarship and received an M.A. from Oxford University in 1939. During World War II, Babcock served as a lieutenant junior grade in the United States Navy. He came to the University of Vermont to teach political science in 1946. He received a Ph.D. from Northwestern University in 1949. Developing a passion for Vermont state politics, in 1950 Babcock won a Senate seat as a Republican from Chittenden County and was re-elected in 1952. Defeated in 1954, he served as Governor JOSEPH B. JOHNSON's secretary of civil and military affairs. In 1956, he regained his Senate seat and was elected unopposed to president pro tem of that body. In 1958, he won an easy race for lieutenant governor. In 1960, he sought the Republican nomination for governor and, although the early favorite, lost in a four-man race to F. RAY KEYSER, JR., by only 729 votes. In 1964, he lost in a second attempt to capture the Republican gubernatorial nomination. In 1965, he was named provost of the Vermont State Colleges, where he oversaw a large building program, directed the transformation of three teacher training schools into comprehensive undergraduate colleges, and initiated the formation of the COMMUNITY COLLEGE OF VERMONT. After retiring as provost in 1974, Babcock returned to the state legislature where he represented South Burlington from 1976 through 1980.

Back-to-the-Landers

In a widespread turnaround from a long trend in national life, many Americans migrated to the countryside from suburban and urban centers beginning in the 1960s. The most rural areas of Vermont began to attract them in this back-to-the-land movement as a place to find freedom to realize specific social ideals. They came as separate individuals, as recounted in Ray Mungo's *Total Loss Farm* (1970), or as a group, calling themselves communes for their professed ethic of sharing work and its benefits, which in practice could vary from group to group. Some of nearly one hundred communes had special purposes, such as the artistic community of Madbrook Farm, while others, such as EARTH PEOPLE'S PARK in Norton, seemed rough settlements with plenty of drugs. The 1970 census registered an in-migration of working age adults, precisely the age group that for a century had been leaving rural America, including Vermont, for employment in more industrialized urban areas. With only modest increases in urban population in the first half of the twentieth century, the state's overall population had increased by 42,000 or 12 percent from 1900 to 1960. But by 1970 the rural population had increased by 25.6 percent, double the rate of the overall population increase for that decade. The most rural areas of the state saw dramatic increases of as much as 31.1 percent. Concerns about urban crime, race and racism, environmental pollution, corporate conformity, suburban monotony, and the war in Vietnam contributed to a sense of disorientation among a generation of post-war baby boomers whose expectations seemed to exceed society's ability to provide expanded standards of living or achieve higher standards of democratic government. Vermont's attraction to these immigrants was captured in historian Arnold Toynbee's description of the northeastern section of the United States as a museum piece of early American yeoman farming that tourists love because it seems to preserve "what [America] was when . . . cities had not yet begun to arise out of the wilderness." Vermont's pre-industrial infrastructure—ancient farmsteads, weathered barns, stone walls, and sugarhouses—promised a release from the destructive aspects of urban civilization. Sensitive to environmental issues, the new settlers frequently transformed those relics and installed modern nonpolluting technologies. During the 1970s, President Carter's tax credits and government grants supporting environmentally friendly technologies and the use of renewable resources helped to produce a Vermont countryside where new technologies for wind and water power supported organic farming and conservation forestry. New settlers restored farm houses, barns, and other structures. Craftspeople and artists often found commercial value in the old structures, the cheap land, and easy transportation to urban centers by the new INTERSTATE HIGHWAYS and improved airway connections. Professionals—teachers, doctors, and lawyers in particular—found a job market in need of their training. Vermont's reputation for tolerance and respect for individual privacy and freedom also attracted less organized bohemians, hippies, uncertain youths, and other adults in between jobs or otherwise disaffected by urban life. HELEN AND SCOTT NEARING's *Living the Good Life* (1954) was studied for practical help on living in rural Vermont. For each group among the back-to-the-landers, rural Vermont's modest economic resources provided a visually satisfying landscape, expansive space, and environmentally clean surroundings that were difficult to obtain in metropolitan areas for any but the very rich. The national recognition that Vermont offered a return to a simpler life was reflected in the words of a young dancer in the popular 1970s musical *A Chorus Line* who prays that she will marry a dentist, move to Vermont, and raise a lot of kids. By the mid-1970s, however, back-to-the-landers were aging into their mid-thirties and forties. The original impulse to "drop out, tune in, and turn on in Vermont" had begun to cool. A mismanaged rock festival at Earth People's Park in Norton saw thirty thousand attendees crash the gates, leaving tons of trash for volunteers to haul away. With age, a generation that came to Vermont in the 1960s and early 1970s were prominent participants in the broader Vermont communities by the 1980s. Some had already done so as school teachers, physicians, and other professionals. The new VERMONT LAW SCHOOL's emphasis on environmental law drew some back to formal studies that led to positions of local and state leadership. Others helped form new political parties and eventually elect a candidate, BERNARD SANDERS, to mayor of Burlington and Vermont's seat in the U.S. House of Representatives.

Winifred McCarthy-Don

Bagley, Edwin Eugene (1857–1922)

A musician and composer of popular marches, E. E. Bagley was born in Craftsbury and later lived in Randolph. From age nine on, however, he was frequently on the road, singing and playing cornet in shows with touring groups of bellringers. By 1880, he held principal cornet positions in several Boston orchestras and bands, including the early Boston Symphony Orchestra. In addition, he played trombone and baritone horn. In 1893, he moved to Keene, New Hampshire, where he taught music, composed, performed, and conducted. Although his ties to Randolph were strong—two brothers lived there—it is likely that he composed most of his marches in Keene, including his first and most famous one, *The National Emblem* (1906), which appeared in eleven editions and has been performed throughout the world. Tuneful and patriotic, with its quotation of *The Star Spangled Banner*, the march also contains a section inspired, according to Bagley, by the pounding hoofs of prairie buffalo. John Philip Sousa considered *National Emblem*—along with four of his own marches—among the most effective street marches. Bagley also composed *The Ambassador, America Victorious*, and *Knights Templar March*. Despite its enduring popularity, *National Emblem* did not make Bagley a wealthy man, as he sold the copyright for $25. Indeed, he had very little to leave his widow and daughter. *James Barickman*

Bailey, Consuelo Northrup (1899–1976)

A native of Fairfield, UNIVERSITY OF VERMONT class of 1921, and Boston University School of Law class of 1925, Consuelo Northrup Bailey was the first woman lieutenant governor in the United States (Vermont 1954–1956) and the first Vermont woman to acquire status in national political affairs. She was appointed Burlington city prosecutor in 1925, elected first woman state's attorney for Chittenden County in 1926, and re-elected in 1928. From 1931 to 1937, Consuelo Bailey was secretary to United States Senator ERNEST GIBSON, SR., and from 1936 to 1976 represented Vermont on the Republican National Committee. She married Henry A. Bailey (1893–1961), also a Republican attorney. Consuelo Bailey served in the Vermont House of Representatives from 1950 to 1954, where she was the first woman speaker in 1953. She was elected lieutenant governor in 1954, but after serving one term stepped aside to care for her dying husband. From 1952 to 1956, she was vice-chair of the Republican National Committee. For nearly forty years she was one of the most influential politicians in Vermont. She achieved TV personality status when she called the roll of the states at the Republican National Convention in 1968. The first woman to practice before the United States Supreme Court, Consuelo Bailey was keenly aware of her position as a role model for younger women in the political and legal arenas, often speaking on that topic at schools and youth organizations in Vermont.

Sylvia J. Bugbee

Bailey, Guy Winfred (1876–1940)

A native of Hardwick and a graduate of the UNIVERSITY OF VERMONT class of 1900, Guy Bailey read for the law with attorney Allen Martin in Essex Junction. In 1904, he was admitted to the Vermont bar and elected to the Vermont House. In 1908, he was elected secretary of state. Bailey joined UVM's board of trustees in 1917 and was appointed president of the university in 1919, an office he held until his death twenty-one years later. During the 1920s, when UVM, MIDDLEBURY COLLEGE, and NORWICH UNIVERSITY were all receiving small legislative appropriations, Guy Bailey successfully cultivated a network of support for the university within Vermont's political and public education leadership, as well as generous contributions from benefactors both in and out of the state. The single largest contribution ever to UVM came in 1929 when trustee JAMES B. WILBUR provided in his will for a gift of $3 million to endow scholarships for Vermonters. The Great Depression of the 1930s restrained donations to the university, and enrollments hovered around five hundred students. Although less than 5 percent of Vermont's high school graduates went on to college, Bailey continued to proclaim an elitist mission for the University of Vermont: to provide an Ivy League education at Vermont's public university. The final years of his presidency at UVM were marked by poor financial health and soon after his death the university appeared to be headed for bankruptcy. Yet alumni admired him, and Edward Crane, editor of the *BURLINGTON FREE PRESS*, remarked on Guy Bailey's death: "Few men in Vermont had a wider circle of friends."

Baker, Remember (1737–1775)

First cousin to ETHAN and IRA ALLEN through their mother, Mary Baker Allen, Remember Baker distinguished himself for courage and ferocity at hand-to-hand combat during General James Abercrombie's fruitless attack in July 1758 on Carillon, the French fortress on LAKE CHAMPLAIN renamed FORT TICONDEROGA by the British. Baker moved to a New Hampshire grant in Arlington in 1768 and was active in the New York land controversy as an officer of the GREEN MOUNTAIN BOYS. He was an original partner in the ONION RIVER LAND COMPANY. While scouting near Lacolle, Quebec, in July 1775 at the opening of the Revolutionary War, Baker was killed by Mohawks, who severed his head and took his remains to the fort at St. Johns, where he was buried until the Americans took the fort and disinterred him for an Arlington burial. Remember Baker was described in a wanted notice in the *Hartford Courant* as "about 5 feet 9 or 10 inches high, pretty well sett, something freckled in his face . . . notorious for blasphemous expressions."

Bakersfield

Bakersfield, population 1,215, a town in Franklin County, was granted by the Vermont legislature in 1787 to LUKE KNOULTON of Newfane, who sold it a year or two later to Joseph Baker of Westboro, Massachusetts, after whom the town is named. The landscape, a series of rolling hills and fertile valleys, rises to 3,000 feet at the Cold Hollow Mountains along the border with Montgomery and Belvidere. The single settlement of Bakersfield village lies at the junction of Routes 108 and 36 in the approximate center of town. A regional educational center in the nineteenth century, Bakersfield was home to Bakersfield Academy and Brigham Academy, the latter founded by Peter Bent Brigham in 1879 (it lasted until 1967), who was born in Bakersfield and created the Boston hospital that bears his name. Once primarily agricultural, Bakersfield today has fewer than ten dairy farms, although the number of smaller specialized farms is growing. In recent years it has become one of the bedroom communities for workers in the cities and towns of Franklin and Chittenden counties.

Balch, Frank A. (b. 1926)

A radio executive and public servant, Frank Balch has been one of Burlington's most influential citizens for many decades. A native of Lynn, Massachusetts, Balch moved to the Burlington area in 1951. He was named station manager of WJOY-AM and WQCR-FM in 1961, and became president of those stations in 1967. Among the public institutions on which he has served are the Burlington Rotary, the Burlington Planning Commission, the state Highway Board, and the Greater Burlington Industrial Corporation. Balch has been active with many philanthropic organizations in Vermont, and served on the board of trustees of both the UNIVERSITY OF VERMONT and the Medical Center Hospital. Balch was a leading figure in the state DEMOCRATIC PARTY in the 1960s and 1970s, serving for a time as the chairman of the Vermont Democratic party executive committee and running for the state senate in 1968. In 1978, the BURLINGTON FREE PRESS named Balch one of Burlington's "ten most powerful citizens."

Paul Searls

Baldwin, Jeduthan (1732–1788)

A veteran of the Seven Years War, Jeduthan Baldwin was the Continental Army's engineer responsible for the major defensive features on MOUNT INDEPENDENCE and those constructed at FORT TICONDEROGA (1776–1777). He was also responsible for constructing works around Boston and later at West Point, New York. Baldwin commanded a regiment of Artificers until 1781 and retired from the army in 1782.

Donald Wickman

Ballou, Hosea (1771–1852)

A leader of the Universalist Church during its early development in America, Hosea Ballou was born in Richmond, New Hampshire, to an impoverished Baptist minister who could not afford to send his children to school. Young Ballou became a Baptist in 1789, but developed doubts about Baptist doctrine and, after acquiring an education in his early twenties, turned to Universalism. Becoming a preacher of Universalist doctrine, he served as pastor to a Universalist congregation in Massachusetts, leaving there in 1802 to officiate in Universalist societies in Barnard, Woodstock, Hartland, and Bethel, where in 1805 he engaged in a theological debate by pamphlet over the doctrine of eternal life with the Reverend LEMUEL HAYNES of West Rutland. After a brief pastorate in Portsmouth, New Hampshire, in 1817 he returned to Massachusetts to become pas-

tor of the second Universalist society of Boston. For the next thirty-five years, Ballou contributed to the denomination he had already done so much to establish in America. Joined by his grandnephew, Hosea Ballou (1796–1861) of Halifax, he founded the *Universalist Magazine*, later the *Universalist Expositor*, and still later the *Universalist Quarterly Review*, for which he composed hymns and wrote sermons, essays, and controversial articles. Most of his writings, including the book-length *Examination of the Doctrine of Future Retribution* (1834), appear in the multi-volume *Universalist Collection*. Hosea Ballou the younger was also an ordained Universalist clergyman, author, and editor of the magazines his great-uncle founded. In 1853, he was named the first president of Tufts University, which he was largely instrumental in founding.

Baltimore

Baltimore, population 250, in Windsor County, is the second-smallest town in area (3,008 acres) in Vermont (only St. George is smaller at 2,304 acres). It was originally the southeastern corner of the town of Cavendish but was completely cut off from it by the long ridge of 2,092-foot Hawk's Mountain, so in 1793 the Vermont legislature made it a separate town. Why it was named Baltimore is not known, since there is no obvious connection with the city in Maryland. The town has always been sparsely populated, reaching only two hundred souls in the 1830s and 1840s when starch-making was the town's chief industry, and has never had a village, post office, school, church, store, or paved road.

Bandel, Betty (b. 1912)

Awarded the Legion of Merit for her distinguished service as a lieutenant colonel in the Women's Army Corp during World War II, Betty Bandel is also a scholar who has researched and written on early Vermont hymnody and on JUSTIN MORGAN and his work as a hymnist. She was born in Washington, D.C., and moved with her parents and sister to Tucson, Arizona, in 1918. Attending Tucson High School and graduating from the University of Arizona as a music major in 1933, she worked for the *Arizona Daily Star* as a reporter and women's-page editor until June of 1942, when she became one of the first women to enlist in the Women's Auxiliary Army Corps (WAAC), subsequently renamed Women's Army Corps (WAC). Soon after

graduating second in her officer training class, she was chosen by WAAC Director Colonel Oveta Culp Hobby to serve as her aide. Serving at times as acting deputy director of the corps, she rose quickly through the ranks, eventually attaining the rank of lieutenant colonel. In 1943, she was designated as "Air WAC Officer" with staff supervision over the WAC program in the Army Air Corps. She received the Legion of Merit and was demobilized in November 1945. After her discharge, Bandel enrolled in Columbia University, where she received an M.A. in English in 1947 and a Ph.D. in 1951. She was recruited to teach English at the UNIVERSITY OF VERMONT in 1947, where she remained until her retirement from teaching in 1975. An immensely popular lecturer, she was particularly noted for her course on Shakespeare, about whom she also published several articles in scholarly journals. Since retirement, she has continued her research and publishing with emphasis on Vermont history. Her works include *Vermont Harmony*, a collection of fuguing tunes, anthems, and secular pieces by Vermont composers of the period 1790 to 1810, including the complete works of JUSTIN MORGAN (1972), *Sing the Lord's Song in a Strange Land: The Life of Justin Morgan* (1981), and *Vermont Harmony* (1973), a sound recording. A collection of her wartime letters is scheduled for publication in the near future. *Sylvia J. Bugbee*

Banyar, Goldsbrow (1724–1815)

Deputy secretary of the Province of New York and a large speculator in New York patents lying between the CONNECTICUT RIVER and LAKE CHAMPLAIN, Goldsbrow Banyar lost 114,600 acres of New York–granted land when in 1775 a convention of New Hampshire grants' settlers in Manchester ordered his seizure with fellow New York lawyer-land speculator John Kelly if they appeared in the grants. In 1778, Vermont's Commissioners of Confiscation seized his New York–titled land in Royalton. He continued to hold title to 150,000 acres in Vermont during the Revolutionary War. After the war, in 1788, Banyar and Kelly purchased grants from the state of Vermont. On April 3, 1791, Goldsbrow Banyar was awarded $7,218.94 in the division of $30,000 paid by Vermont to New York claimants for the loss of lands previously entitled by New York authority in the contested New Hampshire grants.

Barnard

Barnard, population 958, a town in Windsor county, was granted by BENNING WENTWORTH in 1761 and originally spelled Bernard, after Sir Francis Bernard, the governor of the Massachusetts Bay Colony and one of the grantees of the town. The landscape of forested hills and gentle valleys culminates on the western border in the long ridge of Delectable Mountain (named for a locale in John Bunyan's *Pilgrim's Progress*), the highest summit of which is 2,403-foot Mount Hunger. The village of Barnard lies in the center of town on the shores of Silver Lake, which is dotted with summer cottages. SINCLAIR LEWIS and his wife DOROTHY THOMPSON lived in Barnard for a number of years at a property called Twin Farms; she is buried in the Barnard cemetery next to her third husband, Maxim Kopf, a Czech artist. During World War II, the German dramatist CARL ZUCKMAYER lived with his family on a farm in Barnard. The last CATAMOUNT killed in Vermont was shot in Barnard in 1881 and is now on display at the VERMONT HISTORICAL SOCIETY's museum in Montpelier.

Barnes, Lawrence (1815–1886)

A businessman noted for his indomitable cheerfulness and good luck, Lawrence Barnes, a native of Hillsboro, New Hampshire, arrived in Burlington in 1855 looking for new opportunities. He went to Trois Rivières, Quebec, that same year and purchased rough lumber and began shipping it by canal boat to Burlington for distribution by railroad to different points in New England. Little lumber business was transacted at that time in Burlington, a small town of four thousand people. Railroads charged high freight rates, so Barnes conceived the idea of dressing the lumber at Burlington prior to shipping it, thereby saving 12½ percent of the freight expense due to reduced tonnage. These economies encouraged the lumber trade, and when Barnes established his own lumber yard in Burlington in 1856, his initiative helped stimulate economic vitality in the town. By 1860, Barnes' inventory included 8 million feet of lumber worth $140,000. A decade later, his business exceeded $4 million annually. In the 1870s, Burlington became the third-largest inland lumber port in the United States, for which Barnes deserved much credit. Only Chicago and Albany exceeded Burlington in lumber

importation. Barnes's company expanded dramatically and by 1880 it had branches in Montreal, Boston, Detroit, and Whitehall, Ogdensburg, and Albany, New York.

David Blow

Barnet

Barnet, population 1,690, a town in Caledonia County, was granted by BENNING WENTWORTH in 1763 and probably named for the town of Barnet in England. Many of the early settlers, starting in 1774, were Scots from the Company of Farmers of Perth and Stirling in Scotland, making it one of two Vermont towns settled from "across the water" (the neighboring town of Ryegate was the other). Much of the landscape is composed of low, wooded mountains cut by watercourses and farms. The PASSUMPSIC RIVER flows through the northeastern section of town and joins the CONNECTICUT RIVER a few miles below Comerford Dam at Fifteen-Mile Falls, from which a reservoir extends eastward along the Vermont-New Hampshire border. It was at the junction of the two rivers that in 1759 ROBERT ROGERS and his rangers emerged from the wilderness after their attack on the settlement of the St. Francis Indians in Quebec, only to find that no provisions had been left for them. The town has five villages: Barnet, East Barnet, West Barnet, Passumpsic, and McIndoe Falls. HENRY STEVENS, SR., and HENRY STEVENS, JR.—the elder the principal founder of the VERMONT HISTORICAL SOCIETY, the younger one of London's best-known nineteenth-century

booksellers—were born in Barnet. Chogyam Trungpa Rimpoche (1940–1987), a Tibetan meditation master, founded KARME-CHOLING, a meditation center, in Barnet in 1970.

Barre City

Barre, population 9,291, a city in Washington County, was incorporated out of the west central part of the town of Barre by the Vermont legislature in 1894. By that time, the settlement along the banks of the Stevens Branch of the WINOOSKI RIVER had become the industrial center of the granite industry, with long sheds for cutting and polishing the stone, which was quarried in the hills to the south. By 1910, Barre had become the third largest city in the state, after Burlington and Rutland. (Today it is the tenth largest population center.) Uniquely for Vermont, its working population was made up primarily of European immigrants, including many quarry workers from Scotland and stone cutters from Italy. The city was also the most heavily unionized area in the state. Most workers were socialist, although anarchist and syndicalist groups also existed, especially in the period before the First World War. Disputes over wages and working conditions resulted in major strikes in 1922 and 1933. Gradually, beginning in the late 1930s (when the Vermont Department of Public Health noted that 73 percent of granite workers died of silicosis), the introduction of safety and health measures such as suction devices to remove dust greatly improved the health

Granite quarry in Barre. *Special Collections, Bailey/Howe Library, University of Vermont*

of the workers. Although the granite industry still dominates the city (and Barre town), employing well over a thousand people, the number of firms has been reduced drastically, so that the sixty or so that existed in 1900 have been reduced, essentially, to the giant Rock of Ages Company and some much smaller firms. In recent years, other corporations, such as the Canadian Bombardier Company (maker of railroad cars), have established facilities in Barre, providing relatively high wages in skilled trades such as fabrication and metal work. Physically, the city includes not only workers' neighborhoods but also many imposing public buildings and churches, in addition to tree-lined streets of substantial turn-of-the-twentieth-century homes. Two recently restored structures are the Barre Opera House (1866, rebuilt 1889), one of the most sumptuous theaters in the state, and the SOCIALIST LABOR PARTY HALL (1900), built as a political and social center for the granite workers. Both are on the National Register of Historic Places. Three monumental sculptures dot the city: the Robert Burns statue (1899), whose pedestal depicts scenes from three of Burns's poems; the *Youth Triumphant* war memorial in City Park; and the Italian-American Stonecutters' Monument (1985), depicting a typical aproned stone worker with the tools of his trade in his hands. HOPE CEMETERY, off Maple Avenue, is nationally known for its granite memorials, some of which include life-size figures of the deceased and other unusual examples of the carver's art.

Barre Town

Barre, population 7,602, a town in Washington County, originally included the area that became the city of Barre, which was incorporated by the Vermont legislature in 1894. The town was granted by the legislature in 1781 and named Wildersburgh to commemorate the town of the same name in Massachusetts where some of the grantees lived. In 1793, the name sounding "uncouthly" to the inhabitants, it was changed to Barre after Barre, Massachusetts, which in its turn had been named for Isaac Barré, an Irishman of Huguenot descent who was a staunch friend of the colonies during the Revolution. (An apocryphal story says that the renaming was done by the winner of a wrestling match who contended for the honor.) Much of the town, in a region of

low hills cut by tributaries of the WINOOSKI RIVER, remained pastoral for many years, even after a substantial granite industry began to grow in the southern part of town and led to the creation of such settlements as Graniteville and Websterville. In the early years the granite was used for millstones, lintels, and doorsteps, but by 1859 it was being used for buildings, including the VERMONT STATE HOUSE, rebuilt after a fire two years earlier. Eventually the industry supplied granite for buildings, monuments, tombstones, and other uses nationally and even internationally. Today the town of Barre also serves as a bedroom community for the cities of Montpelier and Barre. The massive East Barre Dam, finished in 1935 as part of the Winooski Flood Control Project, is a key factor in reducing the flood danger in the Winooski River valley.

Richard Hathaway

Barton

Barton, population 2,780, a town in Orleans County, was granted by the Vermont legislature in 1781 to Colonel WILLIAM BARTON and, among others, IRA ALLEN and John Paul Jones. Except for Barton Mountain and May Hill, both about two thousand feet high, the landscape is generally rolling and suited for AGRICULTURE. In the southern part of town is 778-acre Crystal Lake, a glacier-gouged body of water similar to considerably larger LAKE WILLOUGHBY in the neighboring town of Westmore. At the northern end of the pond is the village of Barton, formerly an industrial center severely damaged during the FLOOD OF 1927, from which the village has never fully recovered. The remains of some of the village's destroyed factories, now partly hidden by trees and being restored by the Crystal Lake Falls Historical Association and Pierce House Museum of Industry and Education, are among the state's more unusual sites to visit. In the northwesternmost part of town is the village of Orleans (settled in 1829 and known as Barton's Landing until 1909), home of the Orleans Manufacturing Company, maker of Ethan Allen Furniture.

Barton, William (1747–1831)

A resident of Providence, Rhode Island, William Barton captured the British general Richard Prescott, ETHAN ALLEN's cruel captor at Montreal, in a courageous night raid across Narragansett Bay in 1777.

The Vermont legislature in 1781 granted him the town of Providence, doubtless through Allen's influence. Failing to perfect the original grant by timely paying of the required fees, Barton petitioned the General Assembly, which re-granted the town in 1789, naming it after him. Much embarrassed with debt, Barton spent many years in debtors' jail until the Marquis de Lafayette on his 1825 visit to Vermont intervened for his liberation by paying off Barton's obligations.

Baseball

See NORTHERN LEAGUE.

Bassett, Thomas Day Seymour

(1913–2000)

Born at home in Burlington, T. D. Seymour Bassett attended Burlington schools and in 1931 graduated from the Choate School in Wallingford, Connecticut. In 1935, he received his bachelor's degree from Yale University, where he was a member of Phi Beta Kappa. He subsequently received a Ph.D. in history from Harvard University. In 1943, he began alternate service as a conscientious objector in a CIVILIAN PUBLIC SERVICE Camp in Elmira, New York, where he worked until the end of the war. Between 1946 and 1958, Bassett taught at Princeton University, Earlham College, and the University of California at Riverside. In 1958, he returned to Burlington as associate professor of history at the UNIVERSITY OF VERMONT, and was subsequently appointed university archivist and curator of the Wilbur Collection. A member of the Society of Friends since 1950, he helped to found the Burlington Friends Meeting in 1958, and represented the meeting as a travelling Friend throughout the United States. Following his retirement, he expanded his range to include visits to Honduras, Wales, and Cuba as a member of the Friends World Committee for Consultation. His doctoral dissertation at Harvard was an exhaustive study of the urban impact on nineteenth-century Vermont villages. His subsequent research into Vermont's history produced numerous articles published in such journals as *Vermont History*, *The New England Quarterly*, and *The Emerson Society Quarterly*. He was the compiler of *Outsiders Inside Vermont* (1967), an anthology of observations on Vermont by visitors over three hundred years. His contributions to *The New England Bibliography* (1981–1983) are the most complete bibliographies of New

Hampshire's and Vermont's history yet produced. The VERMONT HISTORICAL SOCIETY published a revised version of his doctoral dissertation as *The Growing Edge* (1992). His history of religion in Vermont, *The Gods of the Hills*, was published in 2000. He had commenced work on a history of the Quakers in Vermont in his last year. In August 2000, he received the Governor's Award for Vermont History from the Vermont Historical Society. As an archivist, Tom Bassett's early policy of collecting the surviving records of ordinary Vermonters, not just the state's historical elites, is now recognized as a standard practice in the field.

Bates, Joshua (1776–1854)

The third president of MIDDLEBURY COLLEGE, Joshua Bates, a native of Cohasset, Massachusetts, entered Harvard College as a sophomore and graduated in 1800 with highest honors. The following year, he taught at Phillips Andover Academy and, after studying theology under Reverend Jonathan French, was ordained and installed at the First Church in Dedham, Massachusetts, in 1803, serving as pastor for fifteen years. On March 18, 1818, he was inaugurated as president of Middlebury College. The college was in serious financial trouble, but under his administration was freed from its debt. Enrollment grew, a chapel building was completed, and the faculty ranks were strengthened. During President Bates's second decade in office, the Second Great Awakening, a religious revival movement allied to significant broad social movements in the 1830s, came to Middlebury in the form of the New Measure Revivals conducted by the Reverend Jedidiah Burchard, a colleague of Charles Grandison Finney, the Awakening's most fiery preacher and founder of Oberlin College. President Bates accepted the Reverend Burchard's unusual, sometimes acrobatic, methods of preaching, despite criticism from the town's leaders and conservative faculty. Students and other young people of the Middlebury region, however, were drawn to Burchard's meetings, where his preaching relieved their anxieties for their souls, after which they joined the church as testimony to their conversions, just as the young and disaffected did in other Vermont towns Burchard visited. The college did not fare well after Burchard's visit. Faculty continued to split over Burchard's effects on the young. The Panic of 1837 made college education unaffordable to many and enrollment had declined from 168 students to 46 when Bates resigned in 1839. He was subsequently elected as chaplain of the U.S. House of Representatives for the twenty-sixth Congress. In 1843, he was installed as minister in Dudley, Massachusetts, and served until his death at the age of seventy-seven.

Hans Raum

Battell, Joseph (1839–1915)

An eccentric conservationist, lover of MORGAN HORSES, wealthy town philanthropist, amateur scientist, innkeeper, and newspaper editor, Joseph Battell was born in Middlebury. He attended MIDDLEBURY COLLEGE from 1856 to 1859 but dropped out because of "weak lungs." His health restored by hunting and fishing in the mountains around Ripton, in 1866 he bought a farm there that he later turned into the Bread Loaf Inn, which he operated for over fifty years. He willed the property to Middlebury College, and it is now the home of the BREAD LOAF SCHOOL OF ENGLISH and the BREAD LOAF WRITERS' CONFERENCE. A lifelong bachelor, he purchased mountain land and forests —everything he could see from the Bread Loaf Inn between Brandon and Waterbury. Hoping to preserve the wilderness and pass it on to future generations, in 1910 he gave CAMEL'S HUMP to the state as a public park, and also willed more than 30,000 acres of forest land to Middlebury College (most of it sold by the College in 1936 to establish a section of the GREEN MOUNTAIN NATIONAL FOREST). He loved horses, particularly Morgans, and painstakingly researched and published two important and massive horse registers, *The Morgan Horse and Register* and *The American Stallion Register*. He despised automobiles, refusing to register at the Inn any guests who arrived by car, and filling pages of his *Middlebury Register* (which he edited from 1884 until his death) with accounts of car accidents. His religious, philosophical, political, and scientific ideas (such as his advocacy of the corpuscular theory of sound) were often unusual, and the form in which he presented them—two enormous volumes of dialogues between a teenage girl and a pine tree on top of a mountain, entitled *Ellen, or Whisperings of an Old Pine*—did little to enhance his reputation. He served four terms in the state legislature and ran unsuccessfully for governor. A local aristocrat and patron in outlook, he beautified the town of Middlebury by helping to erect the stone bridge over OTTER CREEK, the modern Battell Block downtown, and other public works projects. A strong advocate of women's education, he bought town land and deeded it to Middlebury College for a women's campus.

David Stameshkin

Batten Kill

The Batten Kill begins on the side of Mount Aeolus in the town of Dorset and runs through Manchester, Sunderland, and Arlington before crossing into New York State. Despite the fact that its Vermont journey is not much more than twenty miles, the Batten Kill is renowned as one of the best trout streams in New England. Maintained by the state as a wild trout stream, it attracts anglers for both brook and brown trout as soon as the season opens in April and remains popular until the season ends in October. Because of an unexplained 81 percent decline in the number of brown trout taken in the river between 1988 and 1998, the Vermont Fish and Wildlife Department declared a 20-mile stretch of the Batten Kill a no-kill, catch-and-release zone for brown trout from 2000 to 2005.

Baxter, Portus (1806–1868)

A Congressman known as "the soldier's friend" during the Civil War, Portus Baxter was born in Brownington and attended Norwich Military Academy and the UNIVERSITY OF VERMONT, which he left after his junior year in 1823. In 1828, he moved to Derby Line, where he gained a reputation as a merchant and farmer. He served as an assistant judge of Orleans County in 1846 to 1847. His marriage to Ellen Janette Harris in 1832 wedded him to a prominent Vermont family, with ties to JUSTIN SMITH MORRILL. In addition to his mercantile and agricultural pursuits, Baxter was involved in the development and promotion of the Connecticut River-Passumpsic Railroad. Though he repeatedly declined elective office, Baxter, a Henry Clay Whig, became politically influential in Orleans County and in neighboring Stanstead County, Quebec. In 1848, Baxter was the only New England Whig at the National Convention initially supporting Zachary Taylor. As presidential elector in 1852, Baxter supported Winfield Scott. Joining the REPUBLICAN PARTY, he attended the informal Republican National

Convention in 1856 and was a presidential elector in that year supporting John C. Frémont. Having twice previously declined nominations for Congress, Baxter successfully ran in 1860. Preferring behind-the-scenes maneuvering to speechmaking, Baxter was a close friend of Secretary of War Stanton and was associated with the Radical Republicans. As "the soldier's friend," his special concern for Vermont's wounded was exemplified in 1864 when he went to Fredericksburg to take personal care of Vermont casualties. Baxter failed to obtain the required majority for re-election in 1866 and withdrew from the contest, remaining in Washington, where he died two years later.

Bayley, Jacob (1728–1816)

A principal settler of the Coos country of the CONNECTICUT RIVER valley and the town of Newbury in 1764, Jacob Bayley was a native of Newbury, Massachusetts. A veteran of the Seven Years' War, he was a brigadier general in the New York militia for New York's CUMBERLAND AND GLOUCESTER COUNTIES before the Revolution and a commissioned general in the Continental Army at the beginning of the Revolutionary War. He joined with MOSES HAZEN to construct a military road from Newbury to St. Johns in Quebec which, if completed, would have permitted the American army's retreat from Canada to the Connecticut River and eventually to Boston in 1776. Construction of the road halted when it was realized that the British could easily follow the Americans to Boston. Loyal to New York until he learned that its new constitution ensured the same political structures of the previous Crown government, he accepted Vermont's constitution in 1777 with little objection. In 1780 to 1781, George Washington ordered Bayley to prepare for a second invasion of Canada, but it was never launched. Almost simultaneously, during the negotiations conducted between some of Vermont's political leaders and the Brititish government in Canada known as the HALDIMAND NEGOTIATIONS, Bayley suspected THOMAS CHITTENDEN and the Allens of plotting to realign Vermont with Great Britain. To silence Bayley, Governor Haldimand sent a raiding party to Newbury to capture Bayley and several others who had expressed similar opposition to the negotiations, but the raid failed. Bayley escaped the British with the aid of his friend, the Loyalist spy JOHN TAPLIN.

Though Bayley took the field against the British only once, commanding a division at Saratoga, his contribution to the war effort was substantial. As commissary general for the Connecticut River valley, Bayley had spent his own funds to buy supplies for and pay wages to soldiers mustered in that region, to construct the military road, and to support dependent Indians. Though zealous for American independence, he also exploited his authority to drive the prominent Loyalist JOHN PETERS from his land and seize it for his own benefit. Jacob Bayley died a poor man, never compensated by Congress for his service or expenses. A monument to Bayley, dedicated in 1912, stands on the Newbury common.

Bayley-Hazen Military Road

In 1776, in the early years of the American Revolution, JACOB BAYLEY began to open a road from Newbury to St. Johns, Quebec, over which the American army retreating from Canada could have moved to safety in southern New England. Bayley's road was marked by surveyors aided by JOSEPH SUSAP and other ABENAKI familiar with the region, but work was halted 6 miles above Peacham when the American command realized that a pursuing British army would also have easy access to southern New England over the same road. The retreating American army stayed in the Champlain Valley, taking quarters at FORT TICONDEROGA in New York and MOUNT INDEPENDENCE in Shoreham. In 1779, MOSES HAZEN was ordered to Peacham with part of a Continental regiment to complete Bayley's road for an American invasion of Canada. Hazen continued the road above Peacham for 50 miles to a mountain notch in Westfield today known as Hazen's Notch, where the project was halted after the Continental Congress cancelled the planned invasion of Canada. Later the Bayley-Hazen Military Road served to funnel settlers into the region. Signs placed by the Vermont Division of Historic Preservation mark the route of the Bayley-Hazen Military Road.

Beard, Edna Louisa (1877–1928)

Edna Beard of Orange was the first woman elected to the Vermont House of Representatives, only two months after ratification of the WOMEN'S SUFFRAGE amendment to the United States Constitution in 1920. Born in Chenoa, Illinois,

Edna Beard moved with her parents back to their family home in Orange in 1883. She had a common school education and graduated from Barre's Spaulding High School in 1896. After teaching in Orange's schools, in 1906 she was elected for the first of four years as town school superintendent. Besides serving as clerk of the Congregational Church, teaching Sunday School, singing in the choir, and directing church plays, Edna Beard served as Orange's town treasurer for sixteen years (1912–1928). In the 1920 REPUBLICAN PARTY primary election, she was narrowly defeated for town representative by Bert L. Richardson. In late October, forty newly enfranchised women registered to vote in Orange, and Beard, running as the Citizens party candidate, won the November election by a thirty-eight-vote margin. In 1921, the *Barre Times* featured her brief maiden speech in the House of Representatives seconding, "with hearty applause," the nomination of Stanley C. Wilson for judge. She served on the House Institutions Committee and was interested in the Vergennes Industrial School, the BRANDON TRAINING SCHOOL, and the Waterbury Mental Hospital. She also participated in suffrage issues, especially the amendment of the Vermont Constitution to assure women's suffrage under state law and to help achieve Vermont's delayed ratification of the suffrage amendment. In 1922, she was elected Senator from Orange County, serving as chair of the Library Committee and on the Institutions and Suffrage and Elections Committees. Urged to run for lieutenant governor, Edna Beard declined, reportedly because of ill health, nor did she run for a third term in the General Assembly. She died of a heart attack in 1928.

T. D. Seymour Bassett

Beaudoin, Louis Alfred (1920–1980)

A native of Lowell, Massachusetts, Louis Beaudoin settled in Burlington in 1937 and became one of New England's finest old-time French-Canadian fiddlers. *La famille Beaudoin*—Louis on fiddle, his brother Wilfred on guitar, and daughter Lisa on the piano—played at the Festival of American Folklife at the Smithsonian Institution in Washington for President Jimmy Carter's inauguration-eve square dance in 1977 and later at the National Folk Festival at Wolf Trap Farm in Virginia. Beaudoin was chairman of the board of the Northeast Fiddlers and also gave performances under the auspices of the Council of the Arts all over the eastern United States and Canada. His 1973 recording *Louis Beaudoin* was well received. Beaudoin's music was dance music composed primarily of reels, jigs, and waltzes derived from material that his father had taught him and other pieces that he learned from the tight-knit family and neighborhood structures that characterized French-Canadian life. Beaudoin was also a Burlington policeman (1953–1964).

David Blow

Beauharnois de la Boische, Marquis de Beauharnois, Charles de (1671–1749)

The governor of New France (1726–1747), the Marquis de Beauharnois persuaded Louis XV to build a new line of defense against English encroachments at the southern end of LAKE CHAMPLAIN. Beauharnois's line of defense included a wooden stockade fort constructed at POINT À LA CHEVELURE (today's CHIMNEY POINT in Addison County) in 1731 and a stone fortress, Fort Saint Frederic (1735–1739) on the west shore of the lake at today's Crown Point.

Joseph-André Senécal

Beaumont, William (1785–1853)

The first American physiologist to publish direct observations of human digestion, William Beaumont, a native of Lebanon, Connecticut, came to Vermont in 1810 in order to study medicine as an apprentice to Dr. Benjamin Chandler. The two-year apprenticeship qualified him for membership in the Medical Society of Vermont. He joined the army as a surgeon during the War of 1812 and, while stationed at Fort Mackinac, Michigan, in 1822, attended a young Canadian fur trader, Alexis St. Martin, who had incurred a perforating gunshot wound through his lung and stomach. The healed wound left an opening in the abdominal wall communicating with the stomach, through which Beaumont was able to examine the stomach, its secretions, and its temperature under various conditions. He also inserted particles of food tied with string and withdrew them at intervals for examination. Beaumont's experience with St. Martin's wound and stomach opening led to his book *Experiments and Observations on the Gastric Juice and the Physiology of Digestion* (1833). Beaumont's experimental insertions and observations of food particles in St. Martin's stomach allowed him to report that food in the stomach is digested when it comes in contact with a clear, odorless, acidic liquid secreted by the stomach, composed in part of hydrochloric acid. The presence of food stimulates and initiates the secretion, which is the only agent of digestion. The process, he also learned, is influenced by exercise, emotion, and general health. Beaumont's book was a popular and scientific success, was translated into several languages, and his observations were adopted by textbook writers. Beaumont retired from the army to a private medical practice in St. Louis, where he was awarded an honorary degree of doctor of medicine and appointed professor at St. Louis University.

Lester Wallman

Beaver

According to nineteenth-century naturalist ZADOCK THOMPSON, beaver were generally exterminated in Vermont by 1841. But by the last quarter of the twentieth century, with protective rules for trapping furbearers, increased new forest growth, and a declining demand for fur coats, Vermont's previously small beaver population had exploded. Their domed houses could be seen in ponds and wetlands across the state. Complaints about the beaver and cries for help geometrically multiplied from the beavers' human neighbors who flooded inadequately staffed state wildlife managers with requests that they trap and move beavers away from residential areas when their dams backed up brooks into domestic septic fields. Beaver intrusion into settled areas, like deer and moose wandering in shopping mall parking lots or bears feeding from suburban bird feeders, is a fact of life in Vermont.

Bellows, Benjamin (1740–1802)

The son of the founder of Walpole, New Hampshire, Benjamin Bellows commanded a militia company at FORT TICONDEROGA in 1775 and 1776 and at Saratoga in 1777. When a crowd threatened to burn the Westminster Court House on March 13, 1775, Bellows led a New Hampshire militia company whose presence helped calm the moment. Tensions finally burst later that night after Bellows left, when CUMBERLAND COUNTY's New York–appointed Sheriff William Patterson ordered his men to fire on the crowd, killing two and wounding ten, an event quickly named the WESTMINISTER MASSACRE. In 1780, Bellows chaired a convention at Walpole where delegates from New Hampshire towns along the CONNECTICUT RIVER recommended union with Vermont in a second attempt at an EAST UNION. But by 1781, he turned against union with Vermont and complained to New Hampshire's Governor Meshech Weare about Vermont's efforts to enforce jurisdiction in New Hampshire.

Bellows Falls

See ROCKINGHAM.

Belvidere

Belvidere, population 294, a town in Lamoille County, was granted by the Vermont legislature in 1791 to John Kelly, a New York City lawyer. The name, which means "beautiful view" in Italian, was probably meant to be descriptive of the landscape. Lying just to the west of the main spine of the GREEN MOUNTAINS, Belvidere is wooded and mountainous, rising to a height of 2,780 feet at Laraway Mountain on the southern border of the town. The main settlement of Belvidere Center is on Route 119, which follows the route of the North Branch of the LAMOILLE RIVER bisecting the town from east to west.

Ben & Jerry's Homemade Ice Cream

First produced in 1978 by Ben Cohen and Jerry Greenfield in a former gas station converted to an ice cream store in downtown Burlington, Ben & Jerry's Homemade Ice Cream is sold as a "premium" ice cream. This rich and creamy product comes in a variety of unusual fruit and other flavors with names to match: White Russian (vodka flavored), Cherry Garcia (the Grateful Dead's deceased guitarist), and Doonesberry (playing on the comic strip). Professing a social conscience, Ben & Jerry's has directed a portion of the company's profits to social and environmental issues. The company's headquarters factory in Waterbury is a major tourist attraction. A second ice cream factory in St. Albans buys a major portion of Franklin County's milk production. When Ben & Jerry's was purchased in early 2000 by Unilever, a Dutch-British conglomerate, critics of the sale warned that the company's special Vermont character and social conscience would be lost in the giant international corporation. Ben Cohen, Jerry Greenfield, and spokesmen for Unilever assured the ice cream's fans that there would be no noticeable change in the product or the company's social conscience.

Benedict, George Grenville (1826–1907)

Owner and editor of the BURLINGTON FREE PRESS, George G. Benedict was his era's chief historian of Vermont's contributions to the Civil War. After graduation from the UNIVERSITY OF VERMONT in 1847, Benedict directed the construction of telegraph lines for the Boston and Vermont Telegraph Company and became the company's president. With his father GEORGE WYLLYS BENEDICT, he became a proprietor and associate editor of the *Free Press* in 1853, and soon after served as postmaster of Burlington. He left his editorship of the newspaper and as head of the telegraph company in 1862 to enlist as a private in the Union Army. Benedict rose to the rank of lieutenant and was an aide-de-camp to General GEORGE J. STANNARD at the time of the BATTLE OF GETTYSBURG. Upon his father's retirement in 1866, Benedict became the sole owner and editor of the *Free Press*; he sold the paper in 1897, but remained editor until 1907. His tenure as editor was distinguished by aggressive modernization of the newspaper's facilities and the ardent promotion of such progressive causes as temperance and WOMEN'S SUFFRAGE. A secretary and chairman of Vermont's REPUBLICAN PARTY, Benedict served two terms as a state senator and was a delegate to his party's 1880 national convention. Benedict was president of the VERMONT HISTORICAL SOCIETY, and was appointed state military historian by Governor REDFIELD PROCTOR, SR. In that capacity, he wrote extensively on the Civil War, most notably in the two-volume *Vermont in the Civil War*. There is a memorial tablet to Benedict on the wall of the College Street Church in Burlington, of which he was the clerk for forty years.   *Paul Searls*

Benedict, George Wyllys (1798–1871)

George Wyllys Benedict led distinguished careers in education, commerce, and publishing. He was born in North Stamford, Connecticut, and graduated from Williams College in 1818. In 1825, he was hired by the UNIVERSITY OF VERMONT as professor of mathematics and natural philosophy. Arriving at a time when the university was deeply troubled (its only building had burned down the previous year), Benedict was appointed president pro tem in 1826 and energetically worked to re-

store the university's economic and academic vitality. A man of broad academic interests, Benedict was the primary force behind the creation of a College of Natural History, which he then directed for two decades. A lack of institutional support for the college led Benedict to resign from the university in 1847, three years before the college itself was terminated. In 1849, Benedict joined a number of investors in founding the Boston and Vermont Telegraph Company, the lines of which followed the Vermont Central Railroad. Benedict purchased the BURLINGTON FREE PRESS from DE WITT CLINTON CLARKE four years later and served as editor until 1866, when he was succeeded by his son GEORGE GRENVILLE BENEDICT. Active in public affairs, Benedict served as a state senator for one term and was a member of the committee in 1865 that recommended that Burlington incorporate as a city. Benedict's house on Prospect Street in Burlington now houses UVM's sociology department.   *Paul Searls*

Benjamin, Asher (1773–1845)

An architect whose designs in the classical style influenced the Greek Revival in New England, Asher Benjamin was born in Greenfield, Massachusetts, and practiced there and in Windsor from about 1800 to 1810. Benjamin owned several houses in Windsor and designed several other buildings, including the Old South Congregational Meeting House. In 1802, he proposed, but failed to establish a school of architecture in Windsor. He also designed the First Congregational Church in Bennington (1806). He wrote several books, including *The Country Builder's Assistant* (1797), *The Rudiments of Architecture* (1814), and *The Practical House Carpenter* (1830).

Bennington

Bennington, population 15,737, a half-SHIRE TOWN (with Manchester) in Bennington County, was the first town granted by Governor BENNING WENTWORTH of New Hampshire after that colony was made independent of Massachusetts. The date was January 3, 1749, and the grantees included Wentworth himself and friends of his who lived around Portsmouth, New Hampshire. The name honors not only Wentworth but also his mother, whose family name was Benning. Settlement was delayed until 1761, after the conclusion of the last French and Indian War, at which

time a group of Congregational Separatists from Hardwick, Massachusetts, and Norwich, Connecticut, arrived in the area. Pioneering families settled near the geographic center of town, today's Old Bennington. ETHAN ALLEN arrived from Connecticut about 1769 and commanded the GREEN MOUNTAIN BOYS as informal militia units who, by harassment and intimidation, challenged New York's attempts to exert jurisdiction under its patents. (In New York, the group was known as the Bennington Mob.) The Boys' meeting place was the CATAMOUNT TAVERN, so named for the stuffed CATAMOUNT above its entrance. During the Revolution, in the BATTLE OF BENNINGTON, fought on August 16, 1777, Hessian forces attempting to capture military supplies and provisions stored in the town were defeated by colonial units under the leadership of General JOHN STARK of New Hampshire. (The battle was actually fought just across the border in New York.) During the fourteen years (1777–1791) that Vermont was an independent state, Bennington was its virtual capital. United States statehood followed a 1791 convention held in Bennington that ratified the federal Constitution. Printer ANTHONY HASWELL, who in 1783 founded the weekly *Vermont Gazette*, was a book publisher and Vermont's first postmaster. U.S. Secretary of State Thomas Jefferson and Congressman James Madison visited the town in June 1791 and stayed at Elijah Dewey's Tavern, now the Walloomsac Inn. Bennington held the state's political focus in early decades, and produced several governors, four of whom —MOSES ROBINSON, ISAAC TICHENOR, JOHN S. ROBINSON, and HILAND HALL —are buried in the cemetery near the OLD FIRST CHURCH. Present-day Bennington village, which replaced what is today called Old Bennington as the town's population center, developed in the 1830s and 1840s along the Roaring Branch and Walloomsac River, whose waters were used to power mostly textile mills. North Bennington, near the border with Shaftsbury, developed as a separate community, with more water-powered manufacturing plants. The first railroad arrived in 1852, with North Bennington as a junction linking Rutland and points north with a line that went to Mechanicville, New York, and points west and south. Two local businessmen became town benefactors. Henry W. Putnam, a manufacturer of hardware, glass "lightning jars," and barbed wire, gave funds to build a hospital, now Southwestern Vermont Medical Center. TRENOR WILLIAM PARK, lawyer and businessman, built a mansion (today's PARK-MCCULLOUGH HOUSE, site of musical and cultural events), and he and Seth Hunt founded the Bennington Free Library. With Park's money, Hunt's home in turn became an institution for widows and orphans, later the Vermont Veterans Home. Hiland Hall of North Bennington served a decade in the U.S. House of Representatives (1833–1843), was federal land commissioner in California in 1851, and Vermont's governor in 1858 to 1860. Hall founded the Bennington Historical Society, which erected the 306-foot BENNINGTON BATTLE MONUMENT, dedicated in 1891 in ceremonies that marked Vermont's centennial. The Historical Society in 1928 opened the BENNINGTON MUSEUM, dedicated to regional history; it has gained renown for its collection of paintings by Anna Mary "Grandma" Moses, who lived nearby in the New York village of Eagle Bridge. The castle-like retirement mansion of Edward H. Everett, Henry W. Putnam's stepson, who made a turn-of-the-century fortune in bottle glass, became SOUTHERN VERMONT COLLEGE in the late twentieth century. The town is also the home of BENNINGTON COLLEGE, which began in 1932 as a small progressive college for women and has been co-educational since 1969. Culture thrives today with the Oldcastle Theater and Bennington Center for the Arts. The town's manufacturing base is diverse, and includes such large firms as Energizer Battery, Hemmings Motor News, NASTECH (automotive steering columns), and Tansitor Electronics (tantalum capacitors). Bennington Potters carries on a tradition of nineteenth-century decorative pottery production. Bennington's location in the VALLEY OF VERMONT between the TACONIC MOUNTAINS and the western slope of the GREEN MOUNTAINS contributes to its attractiveness to tourists, as does its history and noteworthy buildings. The burying ground of the Old First Church contains the graves of British, American, and Hessian dead from the Battle of Bennington, and also those of ROBERT FROST and his family, who resided nearby in Shaftsbury in the 1920s and 1930s. Award-winning author JAMAICA KINCAID, a long-time contributor of nonfiction articles and stories to *New Yorker* magazine and author of several novels, resides in Bennington

and has taught at Bennington College and Harvard. For many decades the state's third-largest population center, after Burlington and Rutland, Bennington is now its sixth, after Burlington, Essex, Rutland, Colchester, and South Burlington.

J. Tyler Resch

Bennington Banner

The *Bennington Banner* newspaper began in April 1841 as the weekly *State Banner* and was originally financed by a group of Whigs who wanted a political voice to counteract the *Vermont Gazette*, which had a Democratic orientation. Chief among these was HILAND HALL of North Bennington, then the veteran of a decade in the U.S. House at a time when Vermont had five Congressional districts. Eventually the *State Banner* became the *Bennington Banner* and snuffed out the *Gazette*, which was one of the state's earliest newspapers, founded in 1783 by ANTHONY HASWELL. The *Banner* has been in many hands through several ownerships, the longest being that of Frank E. "Ginger" Howe, who acquired it soon after 1900 and converted it from weekly to daily in 1903. Howe ran it as editor and publisher until his death in 1956. The *Banner* was purchased in December 1960 by brothers Lawrence K. and Donald B. Miller, who owned the *Berkshire Eagle* in Pittsfield, Massachusetts. The Millers made it a showcase for photographic reproduction by installing, in 1962, the first offset press at any daily in New England, and the paper won national awards for presswork and appearance. In 1995, a national chain headed by W. Dean Singleton, known regionally as New England Newspapers Inc., acquired the *Banner*, along with other Vermont papers in Brattleboro and Manchester, as well as in Pittsfield and North Adams, Massachusetts.

J. Tyler Resch

Bennington Battle Monument

The 306-foot obelisk that can be seen from many points in Bennington County resulted from efforts of the Bennington Historical Society, which formed in 1875. The original goal was to construct a suitable monument to commemorate the BATTLE OF BENNINGTON of August 16, 1777, on its centennial. Though a massive parade was held in 1877, construction of the monument did not begin until a decade later. The monument's location is the site of a storehouse that British Gen-

Bennington Battle Monument. Vermont Department of Tourism and Marketing

eral JOHN BURGOYNE intended to plunder. By virtue of a temporary rail line, and using steam-operated pulleys, the monument was completed in November 1889. Material for the obelisk, a blue dolomite, was quarried from Sandy Hill, New York, near the Hudson River. Formal dedication of the monument was delayed to coincide with a ceremony marking the centennial of the state of Vermont in 1891, an event attended by President Benjamin Harrison and most of his cabinet. First-time visitors are always awed by the monument's enormous size, which results from a vision of the political figure HILAND HALL. A former congressman and governor of Vermont, Hall thought that the Battle of Bennington played such an important role in achieving American victory in the Revolution that its commemorative symbol deserved to be "massive and lofty." In pressing for this design, Hall, at age ninety, overrode his own handpicked committee that included his grandson-in-law, the future Governor JOHN G. MCCULLOUGH. By the early 1950s, the monument was deteriorating and there was talk of tearing it down. But after a visit from Governor ROBERT T. STAFFORD, who personally climbed an interior ladder to the summit, the State of Vermont took it over, installed an elevator to the 200-foot observation lookout room, and did some expensive pointing of the masonry. In recent years, the state Division for Historic Preservation has made more repairs and upgraded the gift shop and visitor facilities. The monument now welcomes about fifty thousand visitors per year who pay a small fee to ride the elevator, see the view, and hear about that important battle.

J. Tyler Resch

Bennington, Battle of

After a night of heavy rain, the morning of August 16, 1777, found a British force of 800 men, including Colonel Frederick Baum's veteran Brunswick dragoons, Scots marksmen, American (including Vermont) Loyalists, Canadian volunteers, and 100 Indians holding an entrenched position on the west bank of the Walloomsac, a branch of the Hoosac River, less than 10 miles from stored provisions in the Continental army depot at Bennington. Over 600 Brunswick mercenaries were also en route to support Baum from General JOHN BURGOYNE's main column in the west. At three in the afternoon, 1,600 opposing Americans under JOHN STARK's command swept around the British flanks and broke Baum's frontal defenses with the weight of the New Hampshire, Massachusetts, and Vermont militia in a 2-hour battle. When it seemed that a relief column of 600 Brunswickers were coming in time to take back the victory from the Americans, SAMUEL SAFFORD arrived with 140 men from SETH WARNER's Continental regiment, who helped Stark's various militias organize a stand against the Germans and repeat their flank sweeps and frontal attack in the second part of a battle that carried past sundown. The British lost 207 dead, including Baum and the Loyalist Colonel Pfister. The Americans lost 30 dead and 40 wounded. Although fought in New York, the American victory has been celebrated as the Battle of Bennington.

Bennington College

After a nine-year gestation period that was slowed by the Great Depression, Bennington College opened to a freshmen class of eighty-five young women in September 1932, and that first class graduated in 1936. It was an alternative, or "progressive" experiment from the beginning, which adhered to "learning while doing" precepts of Vermonter JOHN DEWEY, and integrated visual and per-forming arts into a liberal-arts curriculum. In its early days Bennington gained a reputation as the college with the longest winter off campus work term (launched originally to save money on heat) and the most relaxed parietal rules. The spark of an idea for the college is attributed to the Reverend Vincent Ravi-Booth, pastor of the First Congregational Church, who thought that a women's college would enliven long boring winters in Old Bennington. Credit for the educational energy must be given to Mrs. HALL PARK McCULLOUGH, who had connections at several Eastern colleges, and her husband, who had the financial wherewithal to follow through. An original gift of land in that village had to be withdrawn because of Depression reversals, but the Jennings family, closely related to the McCulloughs, donated its estate in North Bennington in two stages. After the college moved to co-educational status in 1969, its enrollment nearly doubled to six hundred. News media reports also gave it persistent notoriety as the American liberal-arts college with the highest tuition, though the college has always been quick to explain that its comprehensive fee covered many amenities such as private music or art lessons and lab fees, for which others charged extra. Unlike most colleges, Bennington has no school colors, songs, or yearbooks. There are no required courses, and faculty comments take the place of grades. Each student has a faculty counselor, and inventive senior projects are encouraged instead of "majors." Extracurricular activities abound but are usually regarded as extensions of academic work. Bennington College has sometimes emitted an aura of insouciant arrogance, such as during the episode in the early 1990s when, simultaneously, some twenty-nine members of the faculty were dismissed, traditional academic divisions were abolished, and the concept of "presumptive tenure" was abolished. Resulting litigation lingered for several years but did little or no long-term damage. In recent years, the learning-while-doing precept has been extended to faculty members, who frequently work on a part-time basis and are encouraged to involve themselves in professional endeavors elsewhere; they act, publish, dance, edit, write, paint, sculpt, or perform music. These faculty contacts, in addition to those picked up during the winter field-work term, are almost guaranteed to lead students directly into either graduate schools or the business world.

J. Tyler Resch

Bennington Museum

The Bennington Museum traces its origins to 1875 and the formation of a Bennington Historical Society, whose priority was to erect a monument to mark the centennial of the BATTLE OF BENNINGTON of August 16, 1777, a goal that was achieved with the completion of the BENNINGTON BATTLE MONUMENT in 1889. A secondary mission, to create a museum in which to display "relics" of that battle and other regional memorabilia, had to wait several more years. Writer JOHN SPARGO, who had gained a reputation for his socialist activities, founded the Bennington Museum in 1928 after persuading the town's Catholic priest, Father Carty, to allow his abandoned St. Francis de Sales Church building to be deconsecrated and used for the purpose. The old fieldstone edifice had been built in 1855, one of the oldest Catholic churches in Vermont. Many older artifacts are still exhibited in the "church gallery." The museum itself has been enlarged several times and attracts thousands of visitors annually. The museum contains the largest public collection of the primitive paintings of Grandma Moses, who lived nearby in Eagle Bridge, New York, and the actual one-room schoolhouse she attended has become an integral part of the museum. Other permanent exhibits include an elegant car, the WASP, manufactured in Bennington in 1923, and an interpretive look at the strong tradition of nineteenth-century Bennington pottery. The museum's history-genealogy library draws many patrons who research their ancestry and Vermont's history.

J. Tyler Resch

Benoit, Larry (b. 1924)

A famously successful hunter of large white-tailed deer in Vermont, New Hampshire, and Maine, Larry Benoit of Duxbury is the author of a book and video on hunting and taking exceptionally large deer. He has also been a frequent lecturer on deer hunting at sporting shows around New England. In his hunting career since 1933, Benoit has employed hunting techniques derived from his Native American heritage in taking over sixty deer weighing on average around two hundred pounds and carrying about eight points on their antlers.

Benson

Benson, population 1,039, a town in Rutland County, was granted by the Vermont legislature in 1780 and probably named for Egbert Benson, a New York lawyer and Revolutionary patriot who had land interests in Vermont and was instrumental in settling the land title disputes between New York and Vermont. The town is located at the point where LAKE CHAMPLAIN narrows to the width of a river, and the landscape has the open, gently rolling character of the Champlain lowlands. AGRICULTURE, including the raising of merino sheep, was the economic base of the town for many years, but with the decline in the number of farms it has acquired an additional role as a bedroom community for Fair Haven and even Rutland. The only significant settlement is Benson village, located on the old stage road that led north up the Champlain Valley. RUFUS WILMOT GRISWOLD, the biographer and literary executor of Edgar Allan Poe, was born in Benson.

Bentley, Wilson Alwyn "Snowflake" (1865–1931)

A close student of the weather that forms snow crystals, the photographer and meteorologist Wilson "Snowflake" Bentley lived his entire life on the family farm at the base of Bolton Mountain in Jericho. When he was twelve years old, his mother gave him a microscope and encouraged him to study the natural world. After three years trying to draw the figures of snow crystals seen through his microscope, Bentley bought photographic equipment adequate to the tasks of making images of snowflakes. He spent the rest of his life tending to the farm, studying weather and the conditions required to form snow and ice crystals, raindrops and dew, and photographing thousands of snowflakes, each specimen different from all the others. In 1898, he began publishing his photomicrographs and analyses of crystal formations in the *Monthly Weather Review*. After 1910, university meteorologists, the United States Weather Service, and the American Meteorological Society recognized that Snowflake Bentley's photographs were important contributions to the science of meteorology. His photographic slides were added to the collections of museums and scientific institutions. In addition to articles in the *Weather Review*, Bentley wrote many articles for such magazines as *Country Life*, *National Geographic*, *Popular Mechanics*, and *The New York Times Magazine*. William J. Humphreys, the chief physicist for the United States Weather Bureau, in 1931 raised the money for Bentley to publish *Snow Crystals*, a collection of nearly 2,500 photomicrographs of ice crystals, frost, and dew. Many of his theories about the atmospheric conditions that form different types of ice and snow crystals and raindrops are today fully accepted by meteorological scientists.

Berkshire

Berkshire, population 1,388, a town in Franklin County, was granted by the Vermont legislature in 1780 to Major William Goodrich and others and named after Berkshire County in Massachusetts, the home county of most of the grantees. Bordered on the north by Canada, the town consists of a series of gentle hills and placid valleys devoted largely to DAIRY FARMING. The main settlement is East Berkshire, on the MISSISQUOI RIVER in the southeastern part of the town halfway between the larger regional centers of Enosburg Falls to the south and Richford to the north.

Berlin

Berlin (accented on the first syllable), population 2,864, a town in Washington County, was granted by BENNING WENTWORTH in 1763. The name probably derives from Berlin, Massachusetts, not the German city. Berlin's proximity to Montpelier on the north and Barre on the east has made it in modern times an adjunct to those two cities; it is the site not only of the long shopping strip called the Barre-Montpelier Road but also of the Berlin Mall and the regional airport and hospital. The eastern section of town, which lies on a plateau above the WINOOSKI RIVER, is bisected from north to south by Interstate 89 and its access roads. The western section, hilly and wooded, is bisected from north to south by Route 12, which follows the course of the Dog River.

Bethel

Bethel (accented on the first syllable), population 1,968, a town in Windsor County, was in 1779 the first town granted by the independent state of Vermont, and named after the biblical locale. The landscape consists of forested hills cut by narrow valleys and rises to 2,480-foot Mount Olympus in the southwestern corner of the town. The Third Branch of the WHITE RIVER flows north to south in the eastern section and joins the White River itself at the village of Bethel, the major settlement. For many years in the early part of the twentieth century, the town's quarries supplied a granite known as "Bethel White" for structures such as Washington's Union Station and New York's Western Union Building. Bethel was also the home of Mary E. Waller, whose novel *The Woodcarver of 'Lympus*, published in 1904, was a best seller of the day. The town is the site of the White River National Fish Hatchery, which each year produces about four hundred thousand salmon fry as part of an Atlantic Salmon Restoration Program administered by the U.S. Fish and Wildlife Service in the CONNECTICUT RIVER and its major tributaries in Vermont and New Hampshire.

Bigwood, Jessie (1874–1953)

Vermont's first woman lawyer was born Jessie LaFountain in Plattsburgh, New York, graduated high school at sixteen, and then attended Burlington Business College. There she learned stenography and accounting and became a government "reporter" at FORT ETHAN ALLEN. She married Frederick H. Bigwood of Winooski in 1898 and studied law in the office of V.A. Bullard of Burlington and in a special course at Boston University. On October 4, 1902, she passed the bar exam and was admitted to the Vermont bar. It would be another ten years before a second woman was admitted. Mrs. Bigwood maintained a law office in Burlington for several years. When she won her first case in Chittenden Superior Court, the local press reported her success indicated that she "was not in the business for fun." In 1908, she and her husband moved to Toronto.

Billings, Franklin Swift, Jr. (b. 1922)

Chief justice of the Vermont Supreme Court (1984–1988) and U.S. District Court judge (1988–1994), Franklin Swift Billings, Jr., was born in Woodstock and is the son of Franklin Swift Billings, Sr., governor from 1925 to 1927. Franklin Jr. was educated in the Woodstock public schools and Milton Academy, graduating from Harvard College in 1943. During World War II, he served as a lieutenant with the British Eighth Army and was wounded in action. He graduated from the University of Virginia Law School in 1949, the same year he was appointed assistant secretary of the

Vermont Senate. During the next decade he served as secretary of the Senate, municipal court judge, executive clerk, and secretary of civil and military affairs. In 1960, after an unsuccessful bid for a superior court judgeship, he was elected to the General Assembly as Woodstock town representative and appointed judiciary committee chairman that year. A Republican, Billings participated in a bipartisan study group of like-minded freshmen House members called the YOUNG TURKS that included PHILIP HOFF and RICHARD MALLARY, and which by 1963 had assumed leadership of state government. Billings, elected Speaker, was able to work comfortably with Democratic Governor Hoff and presided over the 1965 court-ordered REAPPORTIONMENT of the Vermont legislature. After reapportionment, he chose not to seek re-election and pursued private law practice. In 1966, he supported Hoff for governor rather than RICHARD SNELLING, the Republican candidate. He was appointed to the superior court by Governor Hoff; in 1975 to the state supreme court by Governor THOMAS SALMON, and in January 1983 was elevated to chief justice by Governor Snelling. In September 1984, he resigned to accept appointment as U.S. District Court judge, becoming chief district judge in 1988. In June 1994, he retired to senior status.

Billings, Frederick (1823–1890)

An attorney, railroad magnate, and philanthropist, Frederick Billings was born in Royalton and moved with his family to Woodstock in 1835. He attended the grammar school in that town, prepared for college at Kimball Union Academy in Meredith, New Hampshire, and graduated from the UNIVERSITY OF VERMONT in 1844. He read the law in the office of O. P. Chandler, and served as secretary to Governor Horace Eaton (1846–1848). After qualifying to practice law in 1849, he joined the Gold Rush to California, where he immediately opened the first law office in San Francisco at Portsmouth Square. The firm grew to include partners Archibald Peachy, Henry Halleck (a commander of the Union Army later during the Civil War), and TRENOR PARK, and was recognized as the leading law firm in San Francisco. In the meantime, Billings was also involved in establishing the University of California at Berkeley, which he served as a founding trustee. In 1860, Billings gave speeches in support of the government in Washington, an effort recognized as helping to keep California in the Union. He served as attorney general of California in 1861 to 1862. After the war, Billings sold out his own California interests and returned first to New York and then to Woodstock, where he became president of the Woodstock Bank and purchased the CHARLES MARSH estate, renovating and expanding its residential and farm buildings and developing a model dairy farm using the most advanced agricultural equipment and practices. In 1869, Billings also purchased a half interest in the Northern Pacific Railroad, soon joining the board of directors. During the financial panic of 1873, he kept the railroad running by reducing the workforce, cutting expenses, and borrowing necessary capital. The great cost of bridging the Missouri River, however, contributed to the railroad declaring bankruptcy in 1875. Billings and other bondholders formed a committee that reorganized, refinanced, and bought the railroad, leading it into a period of prosperity with Billings as president. Financier Henry Villard acquired controlling interest in the railroad in 1881 and Billings withdrew from active direction of the enterprise. Focusing on Vermont affairs, Billings bought the library of GEORGE PERKINS MARSH in 1882 and paid for a building to hold it at the University of Vermont. He also established a Billings endowment at the University of Vermont with $50,000, and made similar gifts to Amherst College, one to endow a professorship in memory of his son Parmly (Amherst class of 1884), and to the Moody School at Mount Hermon in memory of his son Ehrick. His home in Woodstock today is part of the MARSH-BILLINGS-ROCKEFELLER NATIONAL HISTORICAL PARK. Billings, Montana is named for him.   T. D. Seymour Bassett

Billings Farm & Museum

An operating dairy farm in Woodstock that invites visitors to explore and learn about the farm heritage of Vermont, the Billings Farm & Museum preserves and interprets the historic model farm of FREDERICK BILLINGS (1823–1890) and the lives and work of Vermont farm families a century ago. The historic Billings Farm (established in 1871) milks a herd of registered Jersey cows and maintains a flock of Southdown sheep as well as draft horses, oxen, and other farm animals. The farm raises its feed on about two hundred acres of Ottauquechee Valley farmland, emphasizing sustainable agricultural practices in an environmentally sensitive watershed. The museum includes extensive exhibits depicting farm life around 1890, as well as the farm's restored 1890 creamery and manager's residence. In addition, the museum offers a half-hour documentary film about GEORGE PERKINS MARSH, Frederick Billings, and MARY AND LAURANCE ROCKEFELLER and their legacy of conservation stewardship. The Farm & Museum opened to the public in 1983. Each year, over sixty thousand people visit, including more than six thousand schoolchildren who participate in educational programs that support established curriculum standards while they provide engaging experiences. The Farm & Museum operates in partnership with MARSH-BILLINGS-ROCKEFELLER NATIONAL HISTORICAL PARK, sharing the park's mission of furthering appreciation of the values of conservation stewardship. It is owned and operated by The Woodstock Foundation, Inc., which is a private foundation.   David Donath

Birds and Nongame Wildlife

Vermont's diverse forests, fields, streams, lakes, and wetlands provide a home for 15,000 to 20,000 species of insects, 23 species of amphibians, 19 species of reptiles, 88 species of fish, 247 species of birds, and 58 species of mammals. Nearly three in four of all Vermont's vertebrates fall under the heading of nongame species. In a single day, an experienced birder can see more than 100 species anywhere in Vermont. Common yellowthroats sing in shrubby wetlands. Northern waterthrushes patrol the shores of forested ponds. The hermit thrush, Vermont's state bird, and the melancholy wood thrush stake out their territories in the mixed coniferous and deciduous forest. But these species are just a start. Vermont's canopy hides bright, diminutive songbirds through the summer months, and most birdwatchers find late April through the second week of May to be peak viewing for American redstarts, red-eyed vireos, ruby-crowned kinglets, ovenbirds, scarlet tanagers, and warblers such as black-throated blues, yellow-rumps, yellows, and black-and-whites. Fields and forest edges remain the most likely spot to see these and other returning songbirds, the most popular of which is probably the eastern bluebird. Once considered rare in Vermont, bluebirds continue to increase in number, raising their young in nest boxes or tree cavities. The state's tallest and gangliest bird species, the heron, appears as the little green heron and the black-crowned night heron, especially in the LAKE CHAMPLAIN wetlands, as well as the American bittern and least bittern. The great blue heron is probably the most memorable. Of Vermont's birds of prey, the most abundant includes the broad-winged hawk and the most visible from roadways is the red-tailed hawk as it patrols field edges. Some thirteen other birds of prey, including the turkey vulture, golden eagle, and bald eagle can be seen in Vermont. The ridges and mountaintops on the edges of the Champlain Valley, such as Mount Philo, make ideal sites for watching these birds on their fall migration. Vermont's common barred owl, with its characteristic "who cooks for you, who cook for you all" hoot can be heard almost any evening or early morning in mature forest stands. Vermont's largest hooting owl, the great-horned, frequents suburban edges, with sightings in Rutland, Montpelier, and St. Johnsbury. So resonant is this owl's deep, five-note rhythmic hoot, that it is frequently attributed to a black bear.   *Will Ryan and Mark Scott*

Bishop, Harriet E. (1817–1883)

A missionary teacher in the earliest wave of Vermont women who went to serve on the western frontier, Harriet E. Bishop was a native of Panton. Educated in Vergennes and the Fort Edward Institute (New York), she taught for a time in Essex County, New York, common schools. In 1847, she went as a missionary to St. Paul on the Minnesota frontier. There she opened the first permanent school, which became a model for others. Bishop also introduced Sunday schools into Minnesota, out of which grew the first Baptist, Presbyterian, and Methodist churches. She was a promoter as well of temperance and WOMEN'S SUFFRAGE.   *Deborah P. Clifford*

Black Snake Affair

An incident of smuggling, murder, and a public hanging in Burlington, the *Black Snake* affair has become symbolic of Vermont's strong resistance to the EMBARGO ACT OF 1808. Despite the federal embargo, smuggling of goods and produce, especially lumber and potash on LAKE CHAMPLAIN, was carried on extensively

between Vermont and Canada. The *Black Snake*, a 40-foot, single-masted, seven-oar cutter, was the most notorious smuggling boat on Lake Champlain in the early months of the embargo. Formerly a ferry between Charlotte and Essex, New York, the tarred-hull boat was bought by the Taylor brothers of Caldwell Manor (today's Noyan), Quebec, to smuggle embargoed goods into Canada. Learning that the smugglers' boat was beached about 3 miles up the WINOOSKI RIVER, officers on the revenue cutter *Fly* attempted to take the boat as it slipped down the river loaded with potash intended for Canada on August 3, 1808. The smugglers resisted, firing a long gun from their boat that wounded senior officer Lieutenant Daniel Farrington and killed two militiamen, Asa Marsh of Rutland and Ellis Drake of Clarendon, plus the boat's tillerman and Jonathan Ormsby, a bystander on shore. The trial for the murders created a sensation; anti-embargo Federalists reviled the national government's harsh trade restrictions, while Jeffersonian Democrats reproached the opposition party for their lack of patriotism. Called for jury duty, Ethan Allen, Jr., said the smugglers were heroes. Only after the Vermont Supreme Court sitting as a grand jury handed down indictments could a trial proceed. Convicted of capital murder, smuggler Cyrus Dean of Swanton was given a legislative reprieve of two weeks, and was hanged in Burlington on November 11 at high noon before a crowd of ten thousand, probably the largest crowd ever to gather for any public event in the history of Chittenden County until well into the twentieth century. Though Samuel Mott of Alburg was shown to have fired the big gun at the crew of the *Fly*, his murder conviction was set aside. At his second trial in January 1809, Mott was found guilty of manslaughter, and with three others was sentenced to one hour in the pillory, fifty lashes, and ten years in the WINDSOR STATE PRISON, the first inmates to reside there. All were pardoned three years later. In 1810, Captain Truman Mudgett of Highgate was discharged after the prosecutor withdrew the charges against him.

Karen Campbell and John Lovejoy

Blake, Bill (1774–1856)

In 1802, Bill Blake of Alstead, New Hampshire, formed a partnership with Seth and Ruxby B. Kingsbury to purchase land and water rights from JOHN ATKINSON and

Dr. William Page of Charlestown, New Hampshire, at the falls of the CONNECTICUT RIVER at Bellows Falls, where they built a paper mill. Atkinson bought out the Kingsburys' shares in 1804. Again with Atkinson's financing, Bill Blake & Company established a printing and bookselling business in 1817, and published the *Vermont Intelligencer*, with THOMAS GREEN FESSENDEN as editor. After 1821, when Atkinson and his assigns withdrew from the business, Blake continued under various partnerships until 1825. He was also engaged in papermaking at Wells River and at Saxtons River, at which place he died. The Bellows Falls paper-mill business that Blake founded went through a series of ownerships during the nineteenth century, leading to the operations of the plant in the 1890s by the International Paper Company as the Fall Mountain Mills, which produced 100 tons of newsprint daily.   *Marcus A. McCorison*

Blodget, William (1754–1809)

A native of Stonington, Connecticut, who moved to Vermont after the Revolution, William Blodget was an ironmonger and mapmaker whose large *Topographical Map of the State of Vermont* (New Haven, Connecticut, 1789) provided substantial detail on independent Vermont. Blodget served in the American army during the Revolution, achieving the rank of major, and also spent four years as chaplain aboard the frigate *Duane*. In 1786, he settled in Bennington, where he ran a store, advertised as a land agent, and operated an iron forge. Unsuccessful in Vermont, he relocated to New Haven, Connecticut, in 1789.   *J. Kevin Graffagnino*

Blodgett Ovens

Blodgett Ovens was founded by Jericho native Gardner Spring Blodgett, who in 1848 designed a more efficient wood-fired stove, set up a Burlington plant, and mass produced the stove for homemakers during the nineteenth century. In 1892, Gardner Blodgett sold out to new management and the company changed ownership on a number of occasions since. In 1997, it became a division of the Maytag conglomerate. Blodgett Ovens also operates plants in New Hampshire and Pennsylvania, and over time has converted its ovens to gas and electricity, expanding them in size and complexity for commercial use. By the year 2000, Blodgett Ovens was manufacturing commercial ovens large enough to roast forty chickens in less than an hour, selling its products in forty-six countries, and serving restaurant chains such as McDonald's and Pizza Hut from Vermont manufacturing sites currently situated in Williston, Shelburne, and Burlington. The firm has plans to consolidate its 385-person workforce and Vermont manufacturing operations into a single facility on the Burlington lakefront.

Bloody Act

See GREEN MOUNTAIN BOYS.

Bloomfield

Bloomfield, population 261, a town in Essex County, was granted (as the town of Minehead, after Minehead in England) by BENNING WENTWORTH in 1762 to Samuel Averill and others. At the request of the residents, the name was changed to Bloomfield in 1830, probably to replace an unattractive name with an attractive one. Bounded by the CONNECTICUT RIVER on the east, the town is almost completely forested; lumbering has always been the main industry. In 1999, the western half of the town became part of the CHAMPION LANDS, a public-private project devoted to conservation and sustainable forest harvesting. The only settlement is Bloomfield village at the junction of Routes 102 and 105 in the extreme southern part of the town, where the Nulhegan River flows into the Connecticut. New England's lowest recorded temperature, fifty degrees below zero Fahrenheit, was recorded in Bloomfield on December 30, 1933.

Bohjalian, Chris (b. 1961)

A novelist and newspaper columnist, Chris Bohjalian of Lincoln is the author of eight novels. His two best sellers, *Past the Bleachers* (1992) and *Midwives* (1997) were subsequently produced as made-for-television movies. *Midwives* achieved wide popular success with a fifty-thousand-copy first printing after it was selected for the Oprah Winfrey Book Club and Bohjalian appeared on Winfrey's television show. His fiction is set in imagined Vermont places, exploring individual and community experiences in graceful and transparent prose. Since 1992, he has written a weekly column for the *BURLINGTON FREE PRESS*. He has had articles featured in the *Boston Globe*, *New York Times*, and national magazines. His latest novel, *The Buffalo Soldier* (2002), is about an African-American foster chid who comes to live in a small town in Vermont.

Bolton

Bolton, population 971, a town in Chittenden County, was granted by BENNING WENTWORTH in 1763 and probably named for Bolton, Massachusetts. The town lies directly on the main spine of the GREEN MOUNTAINS and is cut from east to west by the deep valley of the WINOOSKI RIVER. Except for the meadows along the river, the town is unsuitable for farming and has always been sparsely settled. A portion of its northern section is taken up by the government-owned Ethan Allen Firing Range, which extends into the neighboring towns of Underhill and Jericho. The Bolton Valley ski area, the only significant nonagricultural enterprise, has fifty trails, six lifts, and a vertical drop of 1,625 feet.

Bombers Crash In Vermont

Two U.S. Army Air Corps bombers crashed in Vermont during World War II. On June 27, 1943, a bright, sunny Memorial Day, a new B-17 Flying Fortress bomber en route from Nebraska to Maine and then to Europe crashed into Fish Hill in Randolph. Seven of the crew bailed out and three died in the crash on the Seymour farm. The descending plane and parachutes were clearly visible to people on the ground, especially a group at a local swimming hole. Nearly fifty years later, a group of World War II veterans from Randolph erected a memorial near the crash site. Survivors of the 1943 crash attended, as did some family members of those who died in that event. Memorial Day services are now regularly held at the memorial to the crash of the B-17. The second bomber crash occurred on October 16, 1944, when an Army Air Corps B-24 Liberator bomber on a training mission from Westover Field in Chicopee, Massachusetts, crashed into the side of CAMEL'S HUMP. The state's worst aviation disaster at the time killed nine of ten crewmen. Almost sixty years later, remains of the plane are still visible at the site of the crash.   *Wesley Herwig*

Bomoseen, Lake

Castleton's Lake Bomoseen is the largest lake (seven miles long covering 2,360 acres) entirely within Vermont's borders. From the 1870s to the 1950s, it was a noted tourist resort with hotels, cottages, dance halls, and recreational beaches. Its shores today are developed mostly with seasonal and year-round homes. NESHOBE ISLAND, the lake's largest island, was the summer home of author and drama critic Alexander Woollcott from 1924 to 1943.

Donald Wickman

Boorn Murder Trial

In 1812, following a quarrel and a fight with his brother-in-law Stephen Boorn, Russell Colvin disappeared while clearing stones from a field in East Manchester. Seven years passed, and Russell's wife, Sally, became pregnant, refocusing attention on her husband's disappearance. Not wanting to "go on the town" for child support, Sally thought to name the child's father. Her brother Stephen Boorn advised her she was free to "swear her child to its father" and not suffer a charge of adultery, since her husband was legally dead after seven years' absence. People in East Manchester started to wonder after Amos Boorn, another brother and a man of unimpeachable character, had a dream in which Russell said he had been murdered and showed him an old cellar hole, where searchers later found a jackknife and a button. A little dog barked until her master investigated a tree stump and discovered a thumb nail. Others had dreams of Russell Colvin walking the streets of Manchester village. Growing suspicions and rumors pointed to Stephen and his brother Jesse Boorn as Colvin's murderers. The state's attorney convened the grand jury, which indicted the Boorns, who were promptly arrested. Both brothers were convicted of murder and sentenced to be hanged, although later the legislature changed Jesse's sentence to life imprisonment. But before Stephen's day for hanging, Russell Colvin returned from New Jersey where he had been living, his mental capacity seriously diminished. When Stephen met Russell at the jailhouse door, he told Russell, "They say I murdered you." Simple-minded Russell answered, "You never hurt me. Jesse struck me with a briar once, but it did not hurt me." The Boorns were released, and Russell returned to New Jersey, leaving many Vermonters shaken at the thought that the state had nearly hanged an innocent man. The story of the Boorn murder trial circulated throughout Vermont, and was often cited by those in the state who sought to abolish the death penalty. Today, treason against the state of Vermont is the only crime with a death penalty. Capital punishment was repealed by the legislature for the crime of murder in 1965.

Paul Gillies

Borgmann, Carl W. (1905–1998)

As president of the UNIVERSITY OF VERMONT, Carl W. Borgmann was responsible for negotiating a new relationship between the university and the state. Born in Mt. Washington, Missouri, Borgmann graduated from the University of Colorado (B.S., M.S., chemical engineering, 1931); and Cambridge University, England (Ph.D., 1934). He served as chair of the Department of Chemical Engineering, University of Colorado (1938–1946); dean of faculties, University of Nebraska (1947–1951); and was appointed president of the University of Vermont in 1952. When Borgmann became president, UVM consisted of three separate legal entities: the University of Vermont, a private corporation chartered in 1791; the Vermont Agricultural College, chartered as a public corporation under the Morrill Act by the state legislature in 1865; and the University of Vermont and State Agricultural College, an amalgam of the previous two corporations charted by the state in 1865. Borgmann negotiated a new charter in 1955, which integrated the three corporations into "an instrumentality of the state," and provided increased state financial support for the university. During Borgmann's tenure as president of UVM, the Graduate College was organized to coordinate advanced degree programs and numerous construction projects were completed. In 1958, Borgmann left UVM to become program director of science and engineering at the Ford Foundation.

Frank Smallwood

Boston Canes

In an effort to promote circulation throughout New England, *The Boston Post* in 1909 sent ebony canes with 14-karat gold crowns to communities throughout the region with instructions that a cane was to be presented to the oldest resident of the town and passed on to the next oldest upon the death of the current cane holder. Although the newspaper stopped publication in 1957 and towns have mostly either lost their canes or put them on display in a town museum, Fairlee continues the tradition of passing the Boston cane on to each successive oldest resident.

Larry Coffin

Botta, Anne Charlotte Lynch (1815–1891)

Author and literary hostess, Anne Charlotte Lynch was born in Bennington. She left Vermont as a child, settling eventually in New York City. In 1855, she married Vincenzo Botta, a professor of Italian literature. Best remembered for presiding over the first important literary salon in America, her receptions were attended by prominent men and women of the day, including William Cullen Bryant, Ralph Waldo Emerson, Julia Ward Howe, and Margaret Fuller. Botta's published writings include poetry, critical essays, and a once-popular textbook, *A Hand-book of Universal Literature* (1860).

Deborah P. Clifford

Bowker, Joseph (1725–1784)

A highly respected leader of the Vermont independence movement and early government, Joseph Bowker settled on a New Hampshire–entitled grant of 100 acres in Rutland in 1773. Born in Hopkinton, Massachusetts, he served from 1755 to 1757 in a Massachusetts militia company on garrison duty at FORT TICONDEROGA. In Rutland, Bowker moderated a Proprietors' meeting, took part in the opposition to New York's competing claim named Socialborough, helped lay out the town's center, and served as selectman, town treasurer, magistrate, and, during the Revolution, on the Committee of Safety. He joined with other New Light settlers to found the first church in Rutland in 1773, and with three partners erected a sawmill there in 1780. In January 1776, at the convention held in Cephas Kent's tavern in Dorset, the third in a series that led to Vermont's independence, Bowker was elected chairman. He presided over all the subsequent conventions in Dorset, Westminster, and Windsor, where independence was first mentioned, the name "Vermont" was chosen, and the Constitution of 1777 was adopted. After Vermont declared independence, Bowker served on the Board of War, as a commissioner of sequestration, commissary of purchases, judge of probate, and as chief judge of a special legislative court. He was elected to represent Rutland at the first session of the Vermont General Assembly at Windsor in March 1778 and there was elected Speaker of the House. A member of the committee to tally the votes for governor and other statewide officers, Bowker received the most votes to sit on the council. He resigned his seat in the General Assembly

and served on the council until his death on July 11, 1784.   *H. Nicholas Muller III*

Bowles, Charles (1761–1843)

The grandson of Revolutionary War leader Daniel Morgan of Virginia, Charles Bowles was also the grandson of three African-Americans. He served for more than twenty years in Vermont as an itinerant Free Will Baptist evangelist. Raised by foster parents, he served in the Revolution first as an officer's servant boy and then as a private in the infantry. After the war, he farmed and went to sea as a ship's cook until, in about 1808, he bought a farm in Huntington, started preaching, organized a church there, and was ordained. Bowles covered the Champlain Valley and beyond, organizing the Huntington and Enosburg Free Will Baptist quarterly meetings, and facing down racist rowdies with the courage of a veteran infantryman.

T. D. Seymour Bassett

Boy Scouts

The Boy Scout movement began in England in 1908 under the leadership of Sir Robert Baden-Powell and was officially organized in this country as the Boy Scouts of America on February 8, 1910. The idea of scouting had been in the minds of a number of men in different parts of the country for several years before that, however, and a Barre group (known as the "Boy Scouts Club") was organized on October 29, 1909, some three months before the national club, with most evidence suggesting that it was the first in the country. William P. Milne, a young Scottish stone-cutter recently arrived in this country, helped form the Barre group, having seen the program in action back home. Milne obtained copies of the *Scout's Manual* from England and enlisted the enthusiastic cooperation of James Grearson, a Sunday-school teacher at the Barre Baptist Church. Soon after the manuals arrived, they formed the first troop in America from this group of boys. Over ten thousand Scouts meet in Vermont now, in some three hundred packs, troops and posts. A Green Mountain Council, which also operates two permanent Scout camps, Camp Sunrise in Benson and Mt. Norris in Eden, coordinates their activities.   *John C. Wriston, Jr.*

Brace, Jeffrey (1742–ca. 1820)

A West African slave who earned his freedom in the Continental Army and settled in Vermont, Boyrereau Brinch was captured by English slave traders in 1758, transported to Barbados, and sold to an English ship captain who renamed him "Jeffrey Brace." In 1761, he was brought to Connecticut, where he was held in slavery until 1775, when he enlisted in the Revolutionary Army. In 1783, in recognition of his military service, he was emancipated and given a pension. Brace moved to southwestern Vermont in 1784, where he met and married Susannah Dublin, an African-born woman who shared his abolitionist politics. Around 1795, they purchased land in Poultney, which they farmed for seven years, until the persecutions of a neighbor who coveted their land and a townswoman who coveted their children as servants drove them to the St. Albans area, where they purchased a 60-acre farm and prospered. Susannah died in 1807. In 1810, with the help of an amanuensis, Benjamin Prentiss, a blind, elderly Brace published what is perhaps the rarest of all extant slave narratives, *The Blind African Slave, or Memoirs of Boyrereau Brinch, Nicknamed Jeffrey Brace*. Brace's descendants still live in St. Albans and vicinity. His great-grandson Jeffrey S. Brace (1844–1895), who is buried along with nine other Braces in St. Albans' Greenwood Cemetery, served in Company E, Fifty-fourth Massachussetts regiment, the first African-American volunteers to engage in Civil War combat.   *Kari J. Winter*

Bradford

Bradford, population 2,619, a town in Orange County, was established by a New York patent in 1770 and originally called Mooretown after Sir Henry Moore, the royal governor of New York. Settlers who had arrived before the town was patented had called the area Waitstown after Joseph Wait, who had fought with Rogers' Rangers. In 1788, the name was changed from Mooretown to Bradford, probably after Bradford, Massachusetts. The town rises from the meadows of the CONNECTICUT RIVER, which forms its eastern boundary, through a series of low hills and river valleys to culminate in 1,822-foot Wright's Mountain near the northern border with Newbury. The Waits River cuts through the town in a southeasterly direction and enters the Connecticut just below the main village of Bradford, which has always been an industrial and commercial center for the surrounding rural towns and villages. JAMES WILSON, a local

farmer and self-taught engraver, who in the early nineteenth century created America's first geographical globes, lived in Bradford.

Bradley, Stephen Rowe (1754–1830)

Jurist, state legislator, and United States senator, Stephen Rowe Bradley was born in Wallingford, Connecticut, and graduated from Yale College in 1775. In 1776, he was commissioned a captain of volunteers in the American army. He served in a variety of capacities and retired with the rank of colonel. He studied law with Tapping Reeve in Litchfield, Connecticut, and then moved to Vermont, where in 1778 he and NOAH SMITH were the first two lawyers admitted to the Vermont bar. Within a year after opening a law office in Westminster, Bradley assumed positions of leadership in Vermont's struggle for independence from New York. He served with IRA ALLEN as an agent to present Vermont's case for statehood to Congress and was the author of the pamphlet *Vermont's Appeal to the Candid and Impartial World*, an influential and militant argument for Vermont's right to statehood. He served in the state legislature as speaker as well as on the state supreme court and was an active participant in the negotiations with New York that culminated in Vermont becoming the fourteenth state. Elected one of the state's first United States senators (he drew the four-year term), he was defeated for re-election in 1794 but was selected to fill a vacancy in 1801 and served continuously until 1813. He served as president pro tempore 1802 to 1803 and 1808. Although a Republican, he presided over the congressional caucus that nominated James Madison for president; he was not an ardent partisan. He supported Chief Justice John Marshall rather than Thomas Jefferson in the president's efforts to impeach judges, and his opposition to war against Great Britain before an American army was organized has been suggested as his reason for resigning from the Senate in 1813.

Bradley, William Czar (1782–1867)

The son of STEPHEN ROWE BRADLEY, one of Vermont's first two United States senators, William Czar Bradley of Westminster was one of the most successful lawyers and political figures of mid-nineteenth-century Vermont. Largely self-taught after his expulsion from Yale University for a prank, he read law in Massachusetts and

Vermont and was admitted to the bar at age twenty. He was appointed state's attorney for Windham County in 1804 and used that post both as a way to practice law before the state supreme court, from which he was barred because he was underage, and as a stepping stone for a long career in law and politics in Vermont. He served as representative from Westminster in the Vermont General Assembly (1806–1809 and 1852) and congressional representative from Vermont (1813–1815 and 1823–1827). Following the conclusion of the War of 1812, Bradley was appointed agent for the United States under the Treaty of Ghent to survey and fix the northeastern border with Canada (1817–1822; accepted under the Webster-Ashburton Treaty, 1842). This work he considered his greatest public service. At first a staunch Jacksonian Democrat (he was nominated five times for governor by the Democrats), Bradley joined the anti-slavery wing of the party, then abandoned it for the FREE-SOIL PARTY, and finally became one of the early members of the new REPUBLICAN PARTY. He was a presidential elector from Vermont in 1856 and cast his vote for John Frémont, the first presidential candidate of the party. Bradley had a long and deep interest in theology—he was considered a "free thinker" in his day—and had a good reputation as an orator and poet, although most of his work remained in manuscript and only a few poems were published posthumously.

Michael Sherman

Bradwell, Myra Colby (1831–1894)

A lawyer and native of Manchester, Myra Colby moved to Illinois with her family as a young woman where, in 1852, she married James Bolesworth Bradwell, a prominent Chicago lawyer and judge. In 1868, she began publishing the *Chicago Legal News*. The most influential legal newspaper in the Midwest, it successfully promoted important reforms, from regulation of the RAILROADS to the removal of women's legal disabilities. In 1869, Bradwell was denied admission to the Illinois bar because of her sex, although she was finally admitted in 1890. At the time of her death, the *American Law Review* called her "one of the most remarkable women of her generation."   *Deborah P. Clifford*

Brady, Matthew Francis (1893–1959)

Fourth Bishop of the Diocese of Burlington (1938–1944), Matthew Francis Brady was a firm supporter of labor's right to unionize and collectively bargain for a living wage. He was ordained in 1916 and prepared for the priesthood at St. Thomas Seminary in Bloomfield, Connecticut; The American College of Louvain, Belgium; and St. Bernard Seminary in Rochester, New York. Bishop Brady was a leader in the movement to gain living wages for workers. During World War II, local business leaders urged Bell Aircraft Corporation to offer low wages when the company opened a plant in Burlington to build airplane engines, fearing the defense industry would raise Vermonters' wages. When Bell announced a wage scale starting at 50 cents per hour, labor unions protested, causing the War Labor Relations Board to hold hearings in Burlington. In August 1943, Monsignor WILLIAM TENNIEN presented Bishop Brady's testimony to the labor board that the church was on the side of labor in Vermont and argued for higher wages generally across the state. The public pressure of the national attention given to Vermont's workers and Bishop Brady's pro-labor statement led to Bell Aircraft's offering wages considerably higher than planned. Brady continued to work for Vermont's labor force in 1944, when he convened a meeting of the Catholic Conference on Industrial Problems in Burlington, an event that led in 1945 to ST. MICHAEL'S COLLEGE opening a labor school that offered courses in parliamentary procedure, collective bargaining, social principles, and labor law. With Bishop Brady's prompting, the 1944 Conference and St. Michael's Labor School helped clear the way for the AFL-CIO to come to Vermont. By 1946, eleven labor unions were organized in the Burlington area alone, where previously there had been five. Bishop Brady was appointed Bishop of Manchester, New Hampshire, in late 1944, another diocese where labor issues drew his attention. He died in 1959 while attending a conference in Burlington.

David Blow

Brainerd, Lawrence (1794–1870)

Senator, railroad promoter, and founder of the Vermont REPUBLICAN PARTY, Lawrence Brainerd was born in East Hartford, Connecticut, the fourth of twelve children. In 1802, he moved with an uncle to Troy, New York, and in 1808 to St. Albans, where he attended St. Albans Academy for two years and clerked in a local store. After establishing a successful mercantile business, he was able to indulge his passion for agriculture by purchasing a tract of swampland on LAKE CHAMPLAIN and developing it into a 1,200-acre farm. In 1826, he helped found the Bank of St. Albans, which he served as director and president. His business activities expanded beyond St. Albans and included steamboat construction and navigation on Lake Champlain and RAILROAD construction and management, particularly of the Vermont and Canada Railroad, which he managed in association with his son-in-law, JOHN GREGORY SMITH, until his death. Elected to the state legislature as a Whig in 1834, Brainerd had ardent anti-slavery convictions that propelled him into leadership positions in the Liberty party and then the FREE-SOIL PARTY, serving as its candidate for governor in 1846, 1847, 1852, and 1853. In 1853, his candidacy denied Whig incumbent ERASTUS FAIRBANKS a popular majority and threw the election to the legislature, which chose Democrat JOHN S. ROBINSON. In July 1854, Franklin County Whigs retaliated by denying Brainerd election to the state senate, but in October he was elected to the United States Senate as a Republican and served until March 1855. His political efforts during this period were directed toward the formation of the Vermont Republican party. Successful in electing a state ticket in 1854 and again in 1855, Brainerd was selected to represent Vermont at a preliminary Republican convention to plan the first Republican National Convention that met in 1856 in Philadelphia. He also called the national convention to order.

Braintree

Braintree, population 1,194, a town in Orange County, was granted by the Vermont legislature to sixty-five associates, many of whom were from Braintree, Massachusetts. Settlement in the hilly, heavily forested town is concentrated in its eastern section. West of Route 12A, which cuts through the town in a southeasterly direction and follows the course of the Third Branch of the WHITE RIVER, the land rises to 3,030 feet at the summit of Braintree Mountain, a southern extension of the Northfield Mountains, which are themselves the first range east of the GREEN MOUNTAINS. Logging, agriculture, and the quarrying of green marble have at various times been part of the economic base in Braintree.

Brandon

Brandon, population 3,917, a town in Rutland County, was granted by BENNING WENTWORTH in 1761 and originally named Neshobe after a section of Littleton, Massachusetts, the birthplace of Captain Joseph Powers, one of the grantees. For reasons unknown, the name was changed to Brandon in 1784, nor has the origin of the name been established with certainty. The town's landscape is quite varied. Its eastern section is dominated by the foothills of the GREEN MOUNTAINS, rising to approximately 2,000 feet; the central section marks the point where the VALLEY OF VERMONT joins the Champlain lowlands; and the western section is part of Vermont's largest swamp, which extends through five other towns to the outskirts of Middlebury village. There are two significant settlements, Brandon village (the core of which is on the National Register of Historic Places) and FOREST DALE, a nineteenth-century ironworking center, where THOMAS DAVENPORT invented the first electric motor. STEPHEN A. DOUGLAS, the "Little Giant" and adversary of Lincoln, was born in Brandon village in 1813. The village was also the home of James Conant, who began manufacturing his cast-iron Conant cooking stoves, now much prized by collectors, here in 1810. From 1915 to 1993, Brandon was the home of the state facility for Vermonters with mental retardation and developmental disabilities, best known as the BRANDON TRAINING SCHOOL. At its peak in 1968, the campus included over thirty buildings and 400 acres and served over 650 persons. The school closed after a gradual decline in its census as more and more people were treated in community-based programs.

Brandon Training School

In 1912 the Vermont State Legislature authorized the construction of a school for "the care and training of feebleminded children aged five to twenty-one years." Called the Vermont State School for the Feebleminded when it opened in Brandon in 1915, it soon assumed the eugenic function of segregating from society "feebleminded women of childbearing age." The institution soon became over-crowded with women and children, many placed there for reasons of poverty, neglect, illiteracy, or failure in school. In 1918, destitute children could no longer be placed in poorhouses or on POOR FARMS, and child welfare agents often placed children at the State School in Brandon. In 1919, the age for women committed to Brandon was raised to forty-five years. Dr. Truman J. Allen, superintendent (1918–1937), urged the state to expand the institution and enlarge its authority over Vermont's "feebleminded" population. In 1925, a women's colony was started in Rutland, where women received training as domestics and were hired out to local families to help make the institution self-supporting. The "farm program" provided meat, produce, and dairy products for the institution. In 1929, the State School for the Feebleminded was renamed Brandon Training School. The Brandon Training School assumed an important role in Vermont's eugenics movement. Records of inmates provided data for the EUGENICS SURVEY OF VERMONT's "pedigrees of degenerate families" (1925–1928) and for reports of the Subcommittee on the Handicapped for the VERMONT COMMISSION ON COUNTRY LIFE. Superintendent Truman Allen promoted the passage of the 1931 sterilization law as "one tool" in a comprehensive state program to control the mentally deficient population. Dr. Frederick Thorne, Allen's successor, expanded the Brandon campus to accommodate over six hundred men, women, and children and supervised the state psychiatric clinics instituted in 1939. Initiatives to provide community-based support and special education services for mentally handicapped persons instead of institutional care began in the late 1960s, and in the early 1990s political and financial support enabled community placement of all Brandon residents. From 1915 until it closed in 1993, Brandon Training School was home to 2,324 Vermonters.   *Nancy L. Gallagher*

Brattleboro

Brattleboro, population 12,005, a town in Windham County, is the seventh-largest population center in the state. BENNING WENTWORTH issued a royal grant for Brattleborough (so spelled) in 1753, the name deriving from Colonel William Brattle of Boston, the first named grantee. The first settlement in the 1760s was located away from the river, but the town's commercial focus grew up around the confluence of Whetstone Brook and the CONNECTICUT RIVER. John Holbrook, who in the early 1800s began using flatboats to transport goods on the river, in the 1820s founded the firm of Holbrook & Fessen-

den to print Bibles, establishing Brattleboro as a printing center. In 1835, Jacob Estey purchased a lead pipe and pump shop that he developed into the ESTEY ORGAN COMPANY, the world's largest manufacturer of reed organs. In 1849, the first RAILROAD came to Brattleboro, stimulating business and bringing visitors. In the 1850s, the town was known as a center for water cures, attracting famous literary figures and others. The BRATTLEBORO RETREAT opened in 1836 as the Vermont Lunatic Asylum and became one of the largest private psychiatric hospitals in the country. During the Civil War, Brattleboro was the site of the state's most important mustering center, with 10,200 volunteers mustered into service and 4,666 mustered out. A U.S. military hospital was established in 1863 through the work of Vermont Governor FREDERICK HOLBROOK, who came from Brattleboro. The town has had a long association with the arts. LARKIN G. MEAD was the sculptor of the statue of ETHAN ALLEN in the U.S. capitol and of the Lincoln tomb in Springfield, Illinois, and his brother WILLIAM RUTHERFORD MEAD was a partner in the important architectural firm of McKim, Mead & White. Also from Brattleboro was another pair of brothers, WILLIAM MORRIS HUNT, a painter, and Richard Morris Hunt, architect for the Vanderbilt family in Newport, Rhode Island, and Asheville, North Carolina. Brattleboro had its own native-son robber baron, Colonel JAMES "JUBILEE JIM" FISK, JR., a railroad tycoon and competitor of the Vanderbilts. Fisk was murdered in New York City and buried in Brattleboro under a memorial designed by Larkin Mead. RUDYARD KIPLING, the British author, moved to Dummerston on the Brattleboro town line in 1892 and built a house he called "Naulakha," where he wrote the two *Jungle Books*, leaving in 1896 after a falling out with his brother-in-law. The Brooks Memorial Library, opened in 1887 in an attractive Victorian brick building on Main Street, has since been demolished and replaced at a different location by a building completed in 1967. The Brattleboro Memorial Hospital was founded in 1902 under a bequest left by Boston millionaire Thomas Thompson. The Austine School, a private school for the deaf, was established in 1912 with a bequest from Colonel William Austine. In the middle of the twentieth century, Brattleboro was the center of the Gibson-Aiken progressive wing of the REPUBLI-

CAN PARTY, with Governor ERNEST W. GIBSON, JR., coming from Brattleboro and U.S. Senator GEORGE D. AIKEN coming from nearby Putney. When the INTERSTATE HIGHWAY system came to Vermont via Brattleboro starting in 1958, its three local exits made the town a stop for tourists and businesses coming from the south, as well as for BACK-TO-THE-LANDERS seeking a rural lifestyle. Brattleboro has long been a recreation and cultural center for southeastern Vermont. In 1921, Fred H. Harris built a ski jump in Brattleboro, and Harris Hill remains one of the few Olympic-sized ski jumps in the eastern United States. LOUIS MOYSE AND BLANCHE HONEGGER MOYSE, who had helped organize the nearby MARLBORO MUSIC FESTIVAL in 1951, founded the Brattleboro Music Center in 1952. The visual arts were advanced by the Brattleboro Museum & Art Center, founded in 1972 in the town's former Union Station. Brattleboro and the surrounding area had a strong counterculture community in the late 1960s and 1970s, giving rise to natural food stores and restaurants as well as other services and activities. In 1980, Brattleboro gained its and the state's second largest employer when C&S Wholesale Grocers, which today employs 4,300 people, moved its grocery distribution business to Brattleboro.   *Paul A. Carnahan*

Brattleboro Reformer

A daily newspaper with a circulation of eleven thousand, the *Reformer* was founded by C. N. Davenport and his son, Charles Davenport, in 1876 as the *Windham County Reformer*, a Democratic weekly. When the elder Davenport died, ownership passed to Charles, who published and edited the paper until 1901, when it was sold to G. Ullery. In 1903, the Vermont Printing Company bought the newspaper, and in 1913 began publishing daily. In 1918, HOWARD CROSBY RICE became publisher and editor, a position he retained into the 1960s as a vigorous political participant and commentator. Since then the *Reformer* has had a number of owners and since 1995 it has been held along with the *Bennington Banner* by New England Newspapers Inc., a subsidiary of MediaNews Group. Priding itself as an "independent newspaper," in 1990 the *Reformer* endorsed a Democrat for governor and a Republican for lieutenant governor, in 1994 backed neither candidate for governor, and in 1998 characterized the impeachment proceedings of President Clinton as "cynical politicking."

Brattleboro Retreat

Founded in 1834 by a bequest from the estate of Anna Marsh of New Hampshire, the Brattleboro Retreat was the first hospital for the mentally ill in Vermont and among the first ten psychiatric hospitals in the United States. With treatment based in a Quaker theory known as moral treatment, the hospital's therapeutic regimen included meaningful work, daily exercise, and sound nutrition. To provide these services, the Retreat became the first American psychiatric hospital with a working dairy farm, newspaper, gymnasium, swimming pool, bowling alley, and golf course. The hospital also offered the first training course in the country for attendants. The original and continued purpose of these activities is to emphasize and enhance patients' physical well being during treatment for mental illness. Today, a full range of diagnostic, therapeutic, and rehabilitation services are offered for children and adults. The Retreat is affiliated with Dartmouth Medical School and operates an accredited school and vocational center for patients.

Bread and Puppet Theater

Founded in New York City by Peter Schumann (b. 1934), a German-born puppeteer and conceptual artist, the Bread and Puppet Theater moved to GODDARD COLLEGE in Plainfield and performed its first

Our Domestic Resurrection Circus in 1970. Originating in anti-Vietnam war protests and street theater during the 1960s, Schumann's giant puppets acted out his views of how politics, leadership, and the military had gone badly awry. In 1974, Bread and Puppet established a museum and summer performance venue on a farm in Glover that belonged to Elka Schumann's father, who was the son of SCOTT NEARING, the original Vermont BACK-TO-THE-LANDER. Our Domestic Resurrection Circus, a summer weekend event, was held annually until 1998. Audiences as large as thirty thousand gathered on the Glover circus grounds, an outdoor amphitheater created from an old gravel pit. Large papier-mâché puppets propelled by stilt-walking circus members roamed the field with the help of multiple puppeteers, while sideshows featured smaller puppets and masked performers. The puppetry pageants displayed a rich mix of political commentary and playfulness. Schumann baked and distributed dozens of loaves of bread. In the late 1990s, as the circus drew ever larger crowds, drugs and alcohol abuse in the audience began to spoil the event for both performers and visitors. When a young man was fatally assaulted in 1998, the group considered disbanding. But in July and August of 2000, a schedule of seven Sunday afternoon performances with special themes drawn from contemporary political and social issues restored the full season of puppetry in Glover. One performance of the circus in July, for

instance, featured brief one-act skits in which puppets satirized the World Bank and opponents of Vermont's new CIVIL UNIONS law.

Bread Loaf School of English

The Bread Loaf School of English, founded in 1920, provides courses of study at four campuses leading toward the master of arts or master of letters degree in English from MIDDLEBURY COLLEGE. The central location, at the Bread Loaf Campus of Middlebury College in Ripton, was given to the college in 1915 by JOSEPH BATTELL. Beginning in 1866, Battell had purchased thousands of acres of land in the GREEN MOUNTAINS, and in a beautiful setting in the midst of his holdings he constructed the Bread Loaf Inn and other buildings to house his summer guests. After his death, because the inn was losing money and becoming rather shabby, the Middlebury trustees voted in 1919 to sell it. However, the success of the new and innovative MIDDLEBURY COLLEGE SUMMER LANGUAGE SCHOOLS that had been inaugurated in 1915 encouraged the college's president, JOHN MARTIN THOMAS, to consider opening a summer school that would be limited to the study of English language and literature. Since there would not be enough space on campus to house students for the English school, and because Bread Loaf suddenly appeared to be a perfect site for the new program, the decision to sell the Bread Loaf properties was quickly rescinded. The Bread Loaf School of English was an immediate success, and over the years has attracted distinguished faculty such as George K. Anderson, Carlos Baker, Harold Bloom, Cleanth Brooks, Elizabeth Drew, Perry Miller, and John Crowe Ransom, to name only a few. In 1921, ROBERT FROST was invited to the school, and he returned every summer but three for forty-two years. Each summer, approximately 250 students attend the School of English and enroll in courses in literature, literary theory, creative writing, the teaching of writing, and theater. The school is also the home for the Bread Loaf Acting Ensemble, which visits classrooms and appears in theatrical productions during the summer. Although Battell's original buildings have been modernized and several buildings have been added, the charm of the nineteenth-century inn and the surrounding cottages has been maintained, and, surrounded by the Green Mountains,

Bread and Puppet Theater. Special Collections, Bailey/Howe Library, University of Vermont

Bread Loaf is one of the most remarkable and beautiful campuses in the United States. *David M. Stameshkin*

Bread Loaf Writers' Conference

Since its founding in 1926, the MIDDLE-BURY COLLEGE Bread Loaf Writers' Conference, the oldest such institution in the United States, has brought together established and aspiring authors for an intensive two-week course of study in late August at the Bread Loaf Campus of Middlebury College in Ripton. At the core of the curriculum are workshops in fiction, poetry, and nonfiction. Each faculty member conducts a small workshop, most often of ten students, meeting for five two-hour sessions over the course of the conference. All participants—two hundred are usually in attendance—also meet individually with their workshop leader. In addition, students can attend lectures and special classes, and obtain helpful information on publishing. Theodore Morrison, who served as director of the conference from 1932 to 1955, held that the Writers' Conference always had a dual philosophy, with the emphasis subtly shifting between the two purposes of encouraging the study of writing as an art and the more practical objective of assisting students in finding publishers for their work. The conference's outstanding reputation was established early on when it attracted outstanding faculty such as Bernard DeVoto, ROBERT FROST, Archibald McLeish, James T. Farrell, WALLACE STEGNER, John Marquand, Catherine Drinker Bowen, and John Crowe Ransom, to name only a few. The quality of the faculty has not diminished over the years, and the conference has retained its position as one of the most respected summer writing conferences in the world.

David M. Stameshkin

Bridges, Covered

Vermont has 106 covered bridges remaining out of the hundreds that dotted the state in the nineteenth century. (Over thirty once spanned the CONNECTICUT RIVER, of which three are left.) The main purpose of the roof and walls was simple: to protect the wooden trusses from rain and thus rot. Bridges were of various design. The oldest types used a kingpost, that is, a vertical beam shored up by two diagonal beams, which was appropriate for short bridges, or a queenpost, an extension of the kingpost idea using more

The Coburn covered bridge, East Montpelier. Vermont Department of Tourism and Marketing

than one vertical beam. Both of these types, either in basic form or modified in various ways, were the method of construction of forty of the state's surviving bridges. Another forty were of the Town lattice variety, named after their inventor, Ithiel Town, a Connecticut architect. As its name indicates, this design consists of a series of crossed beams forming a network that extends from one end of the bridge to the other. Other bridges were constructed in a variety of techniques named after their designers, who included Theodore Burr, William Howe, and Peter Paddleford, or were made using a variety of elements drawn from different designs. Able to bear any load put upon them in the nineteenth century, covered bridges in the twentieth century became increasingly vulnerable as vehicle weights increased. This, with the arrival of new bridge-construction techniques relying upon steel and concrete, and increasing neglect by town authorities, reduced the number of bridges rapidly. In the last half-century, their reliability when properly cared for and posted for weight has been recognized, and many, especially those on secondary roads, continue to serve the function for which they were intended. Their value as tourist attractions has also been made clear. The oldest surviving covered bridge in Vermont is the two-lane Pulp Mill Bridge spanning OTTER CREEK on the Middlebury-Weybridge town line, built about 1820. The most famous is the one across the Connecticut River between

Windsor and Cornish, New Hampshire, the longest covered bridge in the United States. (Since the boundary between the two states is the Vermont bank of the river, the bridge is technically in New Hampshire until it reaches the west bank.) Two covered railroad bridges, now disused, in Shoreham (1897) and Wolcott (1908), are a tribute to the strength of this form of bridge architecture.

Bridges, Lake Champlain

The first bridge over LAKE CHAMPLAIN connected Addison county at CHIMNEY POINT with Crown Point, New York. Opened with great fanfare as a toll bridge in 1929, the Champlain Bridge's high, fixed span permitted passage of tall-masted sailboats and other large craft. This successful joint venture between the two states was followed by a second toll bridge over the lake that connected Alburg with Rouses Point, New York, in 1932. The original swinging-span drawbridge at Alburg was replaced in 1987 by the Korean War Veterans Bridge, a 55-five-foot-high fixed-span bridge that permits the passage of large and tall-masted vessels. The bridges opened up the Champlain Valley region to the ever-growing tourist industry. They are now toll free.

Donald Wickman

Bridges, Metal Truss

In the first half of the nineteenth century, bridges were built with Vermont's ample supply of timber and stone, as evidenced today by an exceptional collection of wooden COVERED BRIDGES and some fine examples of masonry arch bridges. In the late 1860s, however, iron works began supplying prefabricated cast- and wrought-iron bridge members according to the designs of the emerging profession of structural engineering. New York's Groton Bridge Company and Connecticut's Berlin Bridge Company supplied many of the approximately three hundred nineteenth-century metal truss bridges in Vermont. Metal truss bridges consist of one or more spans constructed from prefabricated iron or steel members connected in a series of triangles between top and bottom members called chords. They vary in how they distribute forces of tension and compression, the specific pattern of vertical and diagonal members, and the shape of the chords. Three types of truss bridges can be seen in Vermont: through truss, pony truss, and deck truss. Designed for the heaviest loads, the through truss has lateral bracing between the two top chords; when in use, a vehicle passes "through" the structure, hence its name. For lighter traffic, the pony truss has shorter trusses and no bracing between the top chords. The deck truss carries its traffic load at the top chord, with vehicles passing over the structural members of the bridge. Because of their versatility in configuration and member size, truss bridges were adaptable to a wide variety of sites. Two truss designs, the Pratt and the Warren, dominated, offering simplified fabrication and the ability to fully describe the distribution of stresses through mathematical analysis. Pin-connected iron bridge structures noted for their ease of field assembly eventually gave way to bridges with stiffer riveted connections. Fabricating shops bought rolled wrought iron in the shapes of channels, plates, and angles, then cut the pieces to the required length and shape, drilled or punched the holes for rivets that connected the pieces, and shipped the entire disassembled bridge to the construction site by rail. The FLOOD OF 1927 destroyed more than twelve hundred bridges. Most of the approximately 120 truss bridges standing today were constructed in 1928 and 1929. Standardized steel trusses, mostly Warren and Pratt truss designs with heavier members to accommodate motorized traffic, replaced trusses lost to the flood. One noted exception is the "Pennsylvania Truss" in Richmond, the longest bridge constructed in the post-flood program.   *D. Scott Newman*

Bridgewater

Bridgewater, population 980, a town in Windsor County, was granted by BENNING WENTWORTH in 1761 and most likely named for Francis Egerton (1736–1803), the third duke of Bridgewater. Because of the town's situation in the eastern foothills of the GREEN MOUNTAINS, it contains numerous summits over two thousand feet, the highest of which is 2,618-foot Morgan Peak in the extreme southwestern corner. The North Branch of the Ottauquechee River cuts through the town from north to south and joins the Ottauquechee itself at the village of Bridgewater Corners. Farming has always been limited because of the terrain. In the early 1850s, gold was discovered in the town, but the ore proved of low quality and investors lost most of the money they had put into mining operations. Also in the 1800s, Bridgewater produced the popular "Vermont Tweeds" in the vast, rambling woolen-mill buildings (now the home of shops) that can still be seen in Bridgewater village. ZADOCK THOMPSON (1796–1856), historian and author of numerous invaluable works on early Vermont, was born in Bridgewater.

Bridport

Bridport, population 1,235, a town in Addison County, was granted by BENNING WENTWORTH in 1761 and named for Bridport, England, on the English Channel. Bordered on the west by LAKE CHAMPLAIN, the town consists largely of broad flatlands cut by the east and west branches of Dead Creek, a prime migratory fowl viewing area, and marked by a range of low hills along the eastern border. AGRICULTURE and DAIRY FARMING are the town's economic mainstays. The main settlement is Bridport village, on Route 22A running from Vergennes to Fair Haven. The initial section of the CROWN POINT ROAD, built by troops under British General Jeffrey Amherst in 1759 to connect with Fort Number 4 (near present-day Charlestown, New Hampshire) on the CONNECTICUT RIVER, ran through Bridport. In the nineteenth century, prosperity resulting from the raising of merino sheep and MORGAN horses led to the construction of imposing residences, examples of which can still be seen throughout the town.

Brighton

Brighton, population 1,260, a town in Essex County, was granted (as the town of Gilead, after the biblical locale) by the Vermont legislature to a group of Connecticut men in 1780. When they did not pay the requisite fees, the town was re-granted to a group of Rhode Island men, who called it Random because they chose it at random from among several towns offered for sale. It acquired its more presentable current name, taken from the English resort city, in 1832. The land is hilly and forested, and lumbering has always been an important industry. Located in the middle of the town is Island Pond, a 608-acre body of water that lies at the height of land dividing the Clyde and Nulhagen rivers, which flow west (to LAKE MEMPHREMAGOG) and east (to the CONNECTICUT RIVER) respectively. The village of Island Pond on its shores played an important role in the nineteenth century as division headquarters of the Canadian National Railway due to its strategic location on the Grand Trunk railway halfway between Montreal and Portland, Maine. The resultant prosperity lasted well into the twentieth century, and even today the village services the operations of the St. Lawrence and Atlantic Railroad. Island Pond—where the singer and band leader RUDY VALLEE was born in 1901—contains almost four-fifths of Brighton's population, and is a gateway to the CHAMPION LANDS, 133,000 forested acres conserved by federal, state, and private entities. It is also the center for snowmobiling in the vast empty stretches of the NORTHEAST KINGDOM in the wintertime. A controversial event, the so-called "Island Pond Raid," in which state police and social workers raided a communal sect known as the NORTHEAST KINGDOM COMMUNITY CHURCH in response to reports of child abuse, occurred in June 1984.

Brink, Jeanne A. (b. 1944)

An ABENAKI artist and activist who seeks to raise the awareness of both Vermont Abenaki and the general public of Abenaki culture and language, Jeanne A. Brink of Barre was born in Montpelier and earned a bachelor's degree from VERMONT COLLEGE and a master's degree in Native American Studies from NORWICH UNIVERSITY. She has served as the cultural awareness director of the Dawnland Center in Montpelier and as project director for the exhibit Shamanism, Magic, and the

Busy Spider that toured the United States in 2000 to 2001. Since 1987, she has been a presenter and consultant on Western Abenaki culture and experience for schools, colleges, libraries, teacher groups, elder hostels, and other organizations throughout New England and New York. She is the coordinator and a performing member of the Wabanaki Dancers, as well as coordinator of People of the Dawn, the Abenaki Heritage Tour Group. A member of the Obomsawin family of Thompson's Point in Charlotte and Odanak, Quebec, well-known Abenaki basketmakers who practiced their craft until 1959, she served a two-year apprenticeship in traditional Abenaki ash-splint and sweetgrass basketry through the Vermont Folklife Center's Traditional Arts Program and continues the Obomsawin tradition of fine craftwork as a master basketmaker with two apprentices. Her work has been exhibited throughout New England and New York. Jeanne Brink and GORDON DAY published *Alnobaodwa! A Western Abenaki Language Guide* (1990).

Bristol

Bristol, population 3,788, a town in Addison County, was granted by BENNING WENTWORTH in 1762 and originally named Pocock, after Admiral Sir George Pocock, then engaged in the successful siege of Havana during Britain's recent war with Spain. In 1789, the Vermont legislature changed the name to Bristol, probably after the manufacturing city in Rhode Island. The town lies at the point where the New Haven River flows out of the GREEN MOUNTAINS and enters the broad Champlain Valley, creating a landscape that contains both steep hillsides and fertile farmlands. About half the town is in the GREEN MOUNTAIN NATIONAL FOREST, including the 3,740-acre Bristol Cliffs Wilderness. The only significant settlement is Bristol village, on a plain above mill sites on the river. Begun as a market and milling center for the surrounding farm community, the village gradually became one of the most important wood-products manufacturing centers in the state. The resulting prosperity led to the creation of an imposing main street, which is today on the National Register of Historic Places, and the building of many comfortable homes in a variety of styles from Federal to Queen Anne. Today the town has two lumber mills and a number of small businesses, while numerous resi-

Brookfield Floating Bridge. Vermont Department of Tourism and Marketing

dents commute to jobs in Middlebury, Vergennes, or the Burlington area. On Route 17 in the eastern part of Bristol is the curious Lord's Prayer Rock, inscribed by Buffalo physician, Quaker, and former Bristol resident Dr. Joseph Greene in 1891. His motivation (the story has it) was to discourage swearing by teamsters urging their horses up the steep roadway leading to the village.

Bristol Silver Mine

In the later part of the eighteenth century, folk history contends, a prospector named DeGrau, a Spaniard, and his young son located a vein of silver on the slopes of Bristol's South Mountain. What they mined and smelted that summer they stowed away in a cave, which they walled shut with mud and rocks for safe keeping. The elder DeGrau's plans to return and recover the silver bars never materialized, but several decades later, in the early years of the nineteenth century, his son returned seeking the treasure. He never was able to locate it, and the cave with its wealth remains lost. Over ensuing years, local folk and outsiders poked about South Mountain seeking the silver treasure. Some of them claimed to have learned about the lost silver mine from clairvoyants; others heard tales from DeGrau himself, and still others had a scrap of a map with an "X" marking the spot of untold wealth. Over the last two centuries, tales about the Bristol treasure and the money diggers who sought its

secrets proliferated to include accounts of curses and of the discovery of smelting crucibles and other clues to the cave's existence. The legend of the Bristol silver mine with its enriching motifs possesses all the accoutrements of a finely honed local folk tradition and makes a good pair of such stories when told with the legend of JEAN PIERRE MALLETT's lost treasure in Colchester.   *Richard Sweterlitsch*

Brookfield

Brookfield, population 1,222, a town in Orange County, was granted by the Vermont legislature in 1781 to several individuals who had received an earlier New York patent for a town called Wickham, which included the area that is now Brookfield. The name probably derives from Brookfield, Massachusetts. Much of the town lies at an elevation of a thousand feet or more, rising to 1,940 feet at Bear Hill in Allis State Park in the western part of town, resulting in a landscape of forested hills and upland meadows. The long, deep valley of the Second Branch of the WHITE RIVER cuts southward through the town's easternmost part. The main village of Brookfield lies on the shore of Sunset Pond, which is crossed by the 320-foot Floating Bridge, built in 1820 and replaced several times since. The bridge, made of planks resting on a series of pontoons, has ramps at either end to allow for the rise and fall of the pond, and is closed in winter. One of New England's last ice harvest festivals takes place at Sunset Pond every

January. The oldest library in continuous operation in Vermont was established in Brookfield in 1791.

Brookline

Brookline, population 467, the smallest town in area in Windham County, was created by the Vermont legislature in 1794 out of parts of Athens and Putney. The reason presumably was the difficulty the residents had in getting to their respective town centers from the narrow valley of Grassy Brook, which flows through the town from north to south and enters the WEST RIVER on the border with Newfane. The town's name is a description of its physical situation. The hilly, heavily wooded land has always limited settlement, which reached its highest level of approximately 480 people in the early nineteenth century. The village of Brookline lies on the single road that passes through the town northward from Newfane.

Brouilette, C. Bader (1914–1988)

For twenty years president of CHAMPLAIN COLLEGE in Burlington, Bader Brouilette was born in Easthampton, Massachusetts. He graduated from the Northampton Junior College teachers' training program, was a student at Columbia Teachers College, and held instructional and administrative positions at various teaching institutions. In 1937, he helped found a Hartford, Connecticut, acoustical tile business, which in 1955 he transferred to Burlington. In 1956, he and Albert Jensen bought Burlington Business College, a two-year school that operated in five rooms over a pharmacy in downtown Burlington. Jensen died within eight months and Brouilette reorganized the school. Renaming it Champlain College, he expanded its curriculum, enrollment, and physical plant. In 1958, the college moved to a 1902 carriage house in the hill section of Burlington off South Willard Street. A growing student population led President Brouilette to purchase an 1880 brick Victorian house and an 1872 Italianate-style house. He continued to expand the college until his retirement in 1977, when the college boasted a campus of over a dozen buildings, housing for 450 students, and more than forty faculty members. An inveterate joiner and civic booster, Brouilette's memberships included president of the Hartford, Connecticut, Conservatory of Music; president of the Vermont Higher Education Council; president of the Burlington Industrial Corporation; president of the Burlington YMCA; and director of the New England Board of Higher Education. He was a Mason and a Rotarian. In 1977, Brouilette retired to Kennebunkport, Maine, where he died eleven years later.

Brown, John (1744–1780)

A Yale graduate and a lawyer in Pittsfield, Massachusetts, John Brown went to Montreal on a spy mission in April 1775 to prepare for an attack on FORT TICONDEROGA. On a commission from the Boston Committee of Correspondence in February 1775, Brown went to discover Canadian and Indian sentiments toward the revolutionary cause. WINTHROP HOYT, who spoke Mohawk, and PELEG SUNDERLAND, who spoke ABENAKI, accompanied him. Brown's report to the committee urged the strategic importance of Ticonderoga: The fort "must be seized as soon as possible, should hostilities [break out]." People of the New Hampshire grants, he added, were "ready for the job." Brown later carried reports to the Continental Congress from ETHAN ALLEN and BENEDICT ARNOLD of the success at Ticonderoga. In September 1775, Brown commanded a detachment of men as a part of General Montgomery's invasion of Canada. Later that month, for unknown reasons, Brown failed to cross the St. Lawrence River and join his force with Allen's in the Vermonter's unsuccessful attack on Montreal. A month later, Brown and James Livingston of Montreal captured Fort Chambly. In November, they tricked a British relief fleet into retreating from Montreal. Brown was killed in an ambush in the Mohawk Valley in 1780.

Brown, Thomas Storrow (1803–1888)

An incompetent, if not cowardly, leader of a Canadian PATRIOTS force in battles with British regulars in the Richelieu River valley during 1837, Thomas Storrow Brown was the son of a Loyalist who had fled to New Brunswick in 1776 but returned to settle in Woodstock in 1811. At age fifteen, Brown left Vermont for Montreal to work for an ironmonger. In the 1820s, he went into the hardware business, failed at it, and turned to land speculation. By the mid-1830s, he was a bank director and allied with radical members of the Patriots, some of them anglophones who were receptive to American democratic ideas. After preaching revolution in 1837 in the *Vindicator*, a Patriots newspaper for which he had written several articles, Brown was wounded in the eye during an attack by government supporters on the paper's offices. He immediately joined the Patriots at St. Charles and St. Denis in the Richelieu valley, where he was received as a wounded hero and appointed general with Patriot leader Louis-Joseph Papineau's approval. When British regulars marched against his army, however, Brown fled to Vermont, arriving in Berkshire in early December. Imprisoned for a month in a Vermont jail for debts in Canada, Brown failed to integrate with refugee Patriots, even after playing a prominent role in a large rally in Middlebury supporting the Canadians' cause. He published a long article on the rebellion in the Vergennes *Vermonter* (April 1838) and went soon thereafter to Key West, Florida, where he edited the *Florida Herald*, finally returning to Canada in 1844 after amnesty was declared. Brown eventually took a government job in 1864, which he held for fourteen years until he became blind.

Brown, William Eustis (1887–1968)

Physician, decorated World War II colonel, and medical school dean, Dr. William E. Brown inaugurated changes that elevated the quality of medical education and hospital care in northern New England. Born in Jersey City, New Jersey, he received his bachelor's degree from Lafayette College in 1909, a Certificate of Public Health from Harvard-MIT School of Public Health in 1915, and his M.D. degree from Harvard in 1920. In 1942, after twenty years as professor of preventive medicine at the University of Cincinnati, Brown accepted an appointment in the United States Public Health Service and was sent to the Army Training School for Military Government and a refresher course in tropical medicine. Sent to Cairo, Egypt, in charge of the United Nations Relief and Rehabilitation Administration (UNRRA) in the Middle East and Balkans, Brown directed his principal efforts to securing sanitary conditions in the refugee camps. Soon after the liberation of Greece from German occupation, Brown's deputy in Greece suffered a coronary and the situation there was so desperate that Brown had himself reassigned to Athens. Despite having to negotiate among competing British, royalist, and communist factions, and needing to function during active warfare among them, Brown was able to restore a functioning medical structure under UNRRA auspices. He was decorated by the Greek government with its highest order for service to the people of Greece. After being discharged in 1945, Brown was named dean of the UNIVERSITY OF VERMONT Medical School, serving from 1945 until 1952. Under his leadership, the school and its associated hospitals were able to attract greater numbers and varieties of medical specialists, increasingly emphasize research, and upgrade their facilities, evolving from a local resource into a major medical center. After retirement, Dean Brown remained active in civic activities.

Brownington

Brownington, population 885, a town in Orleans County, was granted by the Vermont legislature in 1790 to Daniel and Timothy Brown and others. Solidly rural, much of the town consists of an upland plateau devoted to farming. The main settlement of Brownington village, in the nineteenth century a thriving community, is the site of the Old Stone House Museum, a remarkable four-story granite structure built in 1836 by ALEXANDER TWILIGHT to serve as both dormitory and classrooms for his academy. Today it houses the Orleans County Historical Society.

Brownson, Gideon (1739–1786)

Brother to Mary Brownson Allen, the first wife of ETHAN ALLEN, Gideon Brownson of Sunderland was a captain and then major in the GREEN MOUNTAIN CONTINENTAL RANGERS under SETH WARNER. He was wounded and captured at Montreal with Ethan Allen on September 25, 1775, but not sent to England with Allen and other prisoners taken in that incident. Released when the Americans took Montreal in November, Brownson continued in the Continental service. Brownson was also wounded at the BATTLE OF BENNINGTON, August 16, 1777, and again wounded and taken prisoner at Lake George in 1779. He received a total of thirteen gunshot wounds in battle. Suspicious of Vermont's dealings with the British during the HALDIMAND NEGOTIATIONS, George Washington denied a request from Ethan Allen on August 30, 1780, to negotiate Brownson's release from imprisonment in Canada. When Eli Brownson, Gideon's brother, personally requested that Washington arrange an exchange for Gideon in 1781, Washington again refused because of rumors that Vermont was conspiring to unite with Britain. Washington threatened to "destroy it entirely" if the rumors were true. Believing Washington, Eli Brownson returned to Vermont accusing Allen of treason. According to a report from Loyalist spy Lemuel Bottum in Vermont to British Major Robert Mathews in Quebec, Eli Brownson acted "like a madman and is doing everything in his power to set the people against [Ethan] Allen." Gideon Brownson was eventually exchanged, and retired from the Continental army in 1781.

Brownson, Orestes Augustus (1803–1876)

An editor and writer on philosophy and religion, Orestes Brownson was born in Stockbridge, the youngest son of a farm family of five children, one of whom was his twin sister. His father died when Brownson was young and his mother, unable to support all of her children, gave Orestes to be raised by an elderly couple of nearby Royalton, who brought him up in the strict Puritan tradition. In 1817, his mother with all of her children moved to Ballston Spa, New York, ending Brownson's direct connection with Vermont. He became a Presbyterian, then a Universalist minister, and later a Unitarian one, converting, finally, to Roman Catholicism in 1844. His social and political views were also varied: He was a socialist, then a Democrat, and finally a believer in guidance by a spiritual elite (the hierarchy of the Catholic Church) that would restrain the excesses of American individualism. He established the *Boston Quarterly Review* in 1838, which later became *Brownson's Quarterly Review*, a journal largely written by Brownson and reflecting his views on religion, politics, and society. Controversial in his own time, in the twentieth century Brownson has been recognized for his contribution to American intellectual conservatism.

Brunswick

Brunswick, population 107, a town in Essex County, was granted by BENNING WENTWORTH in 1761 and, like the nearby towns of Ferdinand and Lunenburg, derived its name from Prince Karl Wilhelm Ferdinand of Brunswick-Lüneburg (1735–1806), a German hero of the Seven Years' War with family connections to the British royal house of Hanover. Bounded by the CONNECTICUT RIVER on the east, Brunswick is almost completely forested and lumbering has always been the main industry. In 1999, much of the town became part of the CHAMPION LANDS, a public-private project devoted to conservation and sustainable forest harvesting. The former settlement of Brunswick Springs, on Route 102 along the Connecticut, derived its name from the mineral springs that once gave the village a brief period of fame as a summer resort.

Brush, Crean (1725–1778)

Son of a loyal Anglo-Irish Ascendancy family of county Tyrone, Ireland, Crean Brush came to New York in 1762 and worked for GOLDSBROW BANYAR, deputy secretary of the New York provincial assembly and a large speculator in New York and New Hampshire land grants. By New York grants Brush acquired 20,000 acres in the vicinity of Westminister in the region on the CONNECTICUT RIVER that New York claimed as CUMBERLAND COUNTY. Settling in Westminster in 1771, Brush continued to acquire land by New York grant, was appointed registrar of New York deeds and clerk of the Cumberland County court, and was elected from Westminster to the New York Provincial Assembly, where he vigorously opposed New Hampshire's jurisdiction west of the Connecticut River and the movement for American independence from Britain. He chaired the New York legislative committee reporting in February 1774 on riotous conduct by "the Bennington Mob" and was subsequently in March the principal draftsman of the infamous Bloody Act that set a reward for the capture of ETHAN ALLEN and several of the GREEN MOUNTAIN BOYS. Unable to return to Westminster from New York City in 1775 because of his loyalist sympathies, he went to Boston, where he was authorized to seize American property. In 1776, Brush joined the British retreat to Halifax, Nova Scotia, with a boatload of goods, but was taken at sea by an American privateer and returned to Boston. Found innocent of counter-revolutionary crime by the Patriot court, he was nonetheless held nineteen months in jail. He escaped to British-occupied New York in his wife's clothes and was given British military pay, but died there in May 1778. When he married Margaret Schoolcraft in 1766, she brought to their marriage six-year-old Frances Montresor, her sister Anna's illegitimate daughter by John Montresor, a British army engineer. Frances Montresor married Ethan Allen in 1784.

Buck, Pearl S. (1892–1973)

A native of Hillsboro, West Virginia, Pearl S. Buck was a Pulitzer Prize– and Nobel Prize–winning novelist who purchased a large parcel of land in Jamaica, Vermont, in 1950 and established her residence in Danby in 1969. The daughter of Presbyterian missionaries to China, Pearl Sydenstricker had for nearly forty years lived mainly in China, except for her college years at Randolph-Macon Woman's College, class of 1914. She married an agricultural missionary, John Lossing Buck, in 1917, and taught in Nanking from 1921 to 1931. Her best-known novel, *The Good Earth*, was written in 1931 and won the Pulitzer Prize for fiction in 1932, the same year that the Bucks returned to the United States. Divorced in 1934, she married her publisher, Richard Walsh, one year later. She won the Nobel Prize for literature in 1938, only the third American so honored. After their land purchases in Jamaica in 1950 and 1954, where they built a stone house, the Walsh family used Mountain and Forest Haunt as a summer retreat. Richard Walsh died in 1960. By 1969, Pearl was living in Vermont permanently and embarking on her ultimately unfinished project, the revitalization of Danby village. Under the (some claimed exploitative) influence of Ted Harris, Buck established Creativity, Inc., to transform Danby into a tourist mecca of antiques, arts, crafts, and dining. A week in September 1972 was proclaimed by the State as "Pearl S. Buck Week." After two hospitalizations in Rutland and Burlington in 1972, she died on March 6, 1973, in Danby House. After her death, a Rutland judge found in favor of the family who contested the 1968 will that had left most of Buck's assets to entities then controlled by Harris.

Sarah L. Dopp

Buckham, Matthew Henry (1832–1910)

Matthew Henry Buckham was the longest-serving president of the UNIVERSITY OF VERMONT. Born in Hinckley, England, he emigrated to Chelsea in 1834, where his father served as a preacher. Graduated as valedictorian, UVM class of 1851, Buckham completed further graduate study at University College, London. He was appointed professor of Greek, rhetoric, and English literature at UVM in 1856 and

became president in 1871. UVM experienced numerous innovations during his long tenure: The first two women students graduated in 1875, and the first African-American in 1877; also the first woman faculty member was appointed in 1909. Buckham made substantial efforts to integrate the State Agricultural College into the university. He also presided over a massive building program that included the Old Mill renovations (1883), Billings Library (1885), Williams Science Hall (1886), the gymnasium (1901), the College of Medicine building (1901), and Morrill Hall (1907). An energetic fund-raiser, he secured support to increase library and museum collections and to establish five endowed faculty chairs in chemistry, natural history, mathematics, economics, and anatomy. When President Buckham died in 1910 at the age of seventy-eight, he had served the University of Vermont for fifty-four years and had played a critical role in shaping the university's growth.

Frank Smallwood

Budbill, David (b. 1940)

A poet, novelist, and playwright, David Budbill is a native of Cleveland, Ohio, and has lived in Hardwick since 1970. He earned a B.A. from Muskingum College and a master of divinity from Union Theological Seminary. His books of poems include *Barking Dog* (1968), *The Chain Saw Dance* (1977), *From Down to the Village* (1981), *Why I Came to Judevine* (1987), *Judevine: The Complete Poems* (1991, revised and expanded 1999), and *Moment to Moment* (1999). His fiction has been published as a collection of short stories, *Snowshoe Trek to Otter River* (1976), and a novel sequel to the short stories, *Bones on Black Spruce Mountain* (1978). His play *Judevine* (1984) has been well received and enjoys repeated production by professional and amateur companies. Additional plays include *Thingy World* (1991), *Little Acts of Kindness* (1993), and *Two for Christmas* (1996). Budbill won the DOROTHY CANFIELD FISHER Award for *Bones on Black Spruce Mountain*, received a Guggenheim Fellowship in Poetry in 1981, and a National Endowment for the Arts Play Writing Fellowship in 1991.

Buel, Elias (1737–1824)

A native of Coventry, Connecticut, Elias Buel settled in Rutland about 1780 and acquired the town of Coventry, named after his birthplace, by a "flying grant" in

1784 from the Vermont legislature to himself and fifty-nine associates, including IRA ALLEN, who in turn acquired most of the township at a tax vendue or sale. Allen eventually lost his land holdings in Coventry in an 1801 tax sale while he was in Paris. In 1788, Buel petitioned the General Assembly for a small tract of land in Chittenden County as part of his original "flying grant" of 1784 and received 4,273 acres, Buel's Gore. He finally settled in Huntington in 1798.

Buel's Gore

Buel's Gore, population 12, in Chittenden County, was granted by the Vermont legislature in 1788 to ELIAS BUEL and others as part of a "flying grant" (one for which no territory was specified), leading to a complicated transaction that also included land now in the towns of Coventry and Newport in Orleans County. The heavily forested, triangularly shaped gore lies directly on the western slope of the main spine of the GREEN MOUNTAINS, rising to 2,863 feet at Baby Stark Mountain and to 2,967 feet at Molly Stark Mountain (on the border with Huntington to the north). It is crossed by one road, the winding McCullough Highway, which passes eastward through the Appalachian Gap to Fayston.

Buffalo Soldiers

Members of the United States Army's Tenth Cavalry regiment, the Buffalo Soldiers were an all-black unit that was assigned to FORT ETHAN ALLEN in Colchester from 1909 to 1913. This strictly segregated unit of "U.S. Colored troops" was renowned for its discipline, bravery, and fighting skills. Organized after the Civil War, its duty assignments had been primarily on the western frontier participating in the last of the "Indian Wars." The unit was assigned to Fort Ethan Allen partly as a response by the War Department to public criticism that the regiment—and the Army's other all-black units—were habitually given only the military's worst duty stations, at posts west of the Mississippi River and in the Philippines. While at Fort Ethan Allen, the soldiers made many contacts with the citizens of the surrounding communities of Colchester, Winooski, and Burlington through participation in town parades, regimental band performances, rodeos, and polo matches staged by the soldiers, and baseball games against local teams. Although good relations prevailed, racial altercations occasionally occurred off the base. When Burlington citizens protested that African-American soldiers were observed in the presence of local white women, white officers issued orders forbidding such color-line breaches. In December 1913, the War Department transferred the Tenth Cavalry regiment to Fort Apache and Fort Huachuca, Arizona.

Gene Sessions

Bull, Gerald (1928–1990)

Canadian aeronautics engineer Gerald Bull in 1962 to 1964 developed methods of launching space satellites by firing them from an oversized artillery gun. After the Canadian government shut off his research funds in 1967, Bull developed an association with NORWICH UNIVERSITY and as the Space Research Institute (SRI), purchased 4,000 acres of land in the border town of North Troy adjacent to 6,000 acres in Highwater, Quebec, where he established a laboratory. The Vermont Agency for Development assisted in constructing research facilities in North Troy. Inside a fence surrounding the 10,000 acres astride the Vermont-Quebec border, Bull conducted research on big-gun ballistics under contract to the United States Navy. In 1968, Bull reorganized and incorporated Space Research Corporation-Vermont and Space Research-Quebec as commercial ventures and acquired several large contracts for SRC-Vermont with the U.S. Air Force and Navy in the early 1970s. Through a private bill in Congress sponsored by Senators Barry Goldwater and GEORGE AIKEN, Bull acquired United States citizenship in order to work on a super gun with an 800-foot-long barrel for the United States government. Though never tested, the super gun was rumored to be intended to launch nuclear weapons into space. In 1973, under the corporate umbrella of SRC-Vermont, Bull developed and tested a very-long-range 155-millimeter artillery projectile that increased the 155-millimeter gun's range from 30 to 45 kilometers. With CIA and army cooperation, Bull sold over fifty thousand super-long-range 155-millimeter artillery projectiles to the Israeli army in 1973. In 1976, Bull's SRC-Vermont secured a $19 million contract with ARMSCOR, the South African armaments agency. Rough shells were manufactured at the army's arsenal in Scranton, Pennsylvania, trucked to SRC-Vermont's site in North Troy, and then moved across the border into SRC-Quebec's buildings in Highwater, Quebec,

unknown to Canadian or United States customs. The shells were shipped from New Brunswick to Antigua, and were then transhipped to South Africa in 1977 to be used against Angola and Namibia in their war with South Africa, in violation of a United Nations embargo. Using Bull's long-range 155-millimeter G-5 gun and his aeroballistic projectiles, the South African army destroyed efforts to establish independence for Namibia and crushed Cuban and Russian military support in Angola. Bull was convicted in 1980 in the U.S. District Court at Rutland for the unlicensed exportation of thirty thousand 155-millimeter projectiles, two guns, and a radar system through SRC-Vermont. He paid a $45 thousand fine and spent six months in the federal prison in Allenwood, Pennsylvania. In 1988, Bull began working on a new super gun for Iraq while that country was at war with Iran. With a 27.5-meter barrel and a 350-millimeter projectile, Bull's last big gun could hit a target several hundred kilometers away. Iraq also ordered a 155-millimeter gun to fire a projectile from a location in the Saudi desert that would achieve a polar orbit. A few prototypes were delivered to Iraq, but were never fully produced. British, Canadian, and U.S. investigations into Bull's exportation of gun parts to Iraq had just begun in March 1990 when an unknown assailant shot and killed Gerald Bull in Brussels. SRC continued the development of big guns in Canada under the direction of Gerald Bull's son Michael, but the laboratory and other buildings in North Troy were abandoned and SRC-Vermont was dissolved.

Burgoyne, John (1723–1792)

A major general and Tory member of Parliament, John Burgoyne was ordered to Canada in 1776. In the summer of 1777, he led an army of eight thousand British regulars, Canadian militia, American Loyalists, and Mohawk Indians up the Champlain Valley to join an army sent from New York to Albany, aiming to cut off New England from mid-Atlantic and southern colonies. By July 6, Burgoyne had taken Crown Point, MOUNT INDEPENDENCE, and FORT TICONDEROGA without resistance. Burgoyne, however, had recognized the nature of his enemies on the east side of the valley: "The district of the New Hampshire grants, a wilderness little known in the last war, abounds with the most hardy, active, and rebellious race of

men on the continent, who hang like a gathering storm, ready to burst on my left." Under SETH WARNER's command, an American rear guard action at the BATTLE OF HUBBARDTON inflicted nearly 30 percent casualties on British and German troops diverted from Burgoyne's main march. Then, on August 16, Burgoyne's army lost 207 men and two senior officers in the BATTLE OF BENNINGTON. By the time Burgoyne's full force faced a strong American army near Saratoga, he had lost nearly one thousand men on the excursions to Hubbardton and Bennington. After the American victory at Saratoga, "to Burgoyne" quickly became an American catch-phrase meaning to cut off, choke, or crush.

Burke

Burke, population 1,571, a town in Caledonia County, was granted by the Vermont legislature in 1782 and possibly named for Edmund Burke, the British statesman. The town is composed mostly of low, wooded hills dotted with farms in the lowlands and cut by the East and West branches of the PASSUMPSIC RIVER. The most noteworthy physical feature is 3,267-foot Burke Mountain on the town's eastern border, site of Darling State Park and also of Burke Mountain Ski Area, which has forty-three trails and a vertical drop of 2,000 feet. A steep paved road gives access to the summit in summertime. Burke Mountain Academy has trained many ski students who have qualified for the Olympics. The town's villages are East Burke, West Burke, and Burke Hollow.

Burke, James Edmund (1848–1943)

The first Democratic mayor of Burlington, James Edward Burke was born of Irish parents in Williston and received his education at the Williston Academy. In 1873, he settled in Burlington and learned the blacksmith trade. His neighborhood, the Third Ward, was an ethnic enclave of Irish, French-Canadians, Jews, and Italians. After a bitterly fought campaign, Burke in 1903 became the first Democratic mayor in the city's history. Burke was a progressive and supported laws to alleviate the hardships of poor people, positions making him so popular with the working class that they elected him mayor for most of the next thirty years. His power base produced six more Irish-American mayors of Burlington. He was a principal figure in projects to build a water filtration plant, a municipal electricity-generating plant, fire and police stations, and Union Station on the waterfront at the west end of Main Street. *Vince Feeney*

Burling, William (fl. 1745–1780)

A wealthy Quaker living in New York City, William Burling acquired large holdings in the original New Hampshire grants in the 1760s. The Burlings had extensive property holdings in New York City, including the valuable Burling slip on the waterfront. The Allen brothers purchased some of Burling's New Hampshire grants in the first years of the ONION RIVER LAND COMPANY, including land he and other family members owned in Burlington and several other nearby towns. New Hampshire's Governor BENNING WENTWORTH did not name the New Hampshire grants town of Burlington after the New York Burling family, as is commonly assumed.

Burlington

Burlington, population 39,824, the largest city in Vermont and the SHIRE TOWN of Chittenden County, was granted by BENNING WENTWORTH in 1763 and originally included what is today the city of South Burlington, from which it was separated at its own request by the Vermont legislature in 1864. The name presumably derives from the earldom of Burlington, held by the influential Boyle family, specifically at the time of the town's naming by John Boyle (1707–1763), fourth earl of Burlington. The "Queen City of Vermont" rises from LAKE CHAMPLAIN at its widest point to a long ridge with a maximum elevation of 400 feet along its eastern border. The WINOOSKI RIVER, which here forms a broad intervale, is the city's northern border and empties into Lake Champlain 4 miles north of the downtown area. Burlington is Vermont's commercial, financial, and banking center, the home of the UNIVERSITY OF VERMONT and the state's largest hospital, enjoys a thriving cultural life, and is a prime summertime tourist destination. Its early history is tied to the ONION RIVER LAND COMPANY, an association of Allen family members, who foresaw the potential of the Winooski River, including the falls of the river on Burlington's northern edge, where IRA ALLEN built an early fort and mill. The lake provided transport northward to Canada and, after the opening of the Champlain Canal in 1823 (which linked the southern extremity of Lake Champlain

Church Street Marketplace, Burlington. Marketplace District Commission

with the Hudson River), southward toward New York City. The Erie Canal, completed in 1825, enhanced Burlington's status as an entrepôt sending goods north, south, and west, and it became one of the largest inland ports in the United States. By 1830, it was the state's largest population center, a position it lost only once thereafter, in the 1880 census, to Rutland. The RAILROADS, which arrived in 1849, solidified Burlington's status as Vermont's commercial, manufacturing, and transshipment hub. One result of its continual growth was a need for workers that drew many Irish and French-Canadian immigrants and their families, and by 1850 Burlington was the most heterogeneous town in the state. It became a city at the time of its split into two entities in 1864. Prosperity lined some of its streets with impressive mansions for the well to do, while worker and middle-class housing of a more humble character was erected in many sections of the city. By the end of the nineteenth century, with the depletion of Quebec's forests, the lumber boom was over and commercial lake traffic declined drastically, although passenger traffic in the form of ferries and steamboats continued for some decades. The waterfront was largely abandoned as a manufacturing and commercial district, while Burlington continued to consolidate its position in business, banking, the law, and finance. After the Second World War, industrial and population growth in the towns adjacent to the city was rapid, so that today 73 percent of Chittenden County's population lies outside the city as opposed to 47 percent in 1950. With income and education levels higher than those enjoyed by

most Vermonters, the Burlington area's business, financial, legal, academic, and medical professionals, plus the students at its several institutions of higher learning, provide the basis of the city's sophisticated urban atmosphere, with its upscale shops and restaurants, while leaving untouched many of the city's workaday neighborhoods. Urban renewal in the 1960s eventually replaced five blocks of the downtown area with stores and a hotel, while transformation of Church Street, the city's four-block main shopping street, into a pedestrian mall called the Marketplace, has been highly successful in drawing locals and visitors. The once derelict waterfront has been transformed into a park with amenities such as a boathouse, waterfront science center, docking area for private craft, and skateboarding facility. A bike path that largely follows an old waterside railroad track runs the length of the city. Since 1981, when BERNARD SANDERS, a self-styled socialist, was elected mayor, the city has had (except for a two-year period) independent chief executives and a city council that includes Democratic, Republican, and Progressive members.

Burlington, Bombardment of

On July 31, 1813, a British force under Lieutenant Colonel John Murray raided settlements in the Champlain Valley. Also known as Murray's Raid, the attack was intended to delay an American march against Montreal by striking at the army encampments at Plattsburgh and Burlington. Murray's force first landed at Plattsburgh, where they destroyed the arsenal, barracks, and storehouses, then looted a number of private houses. Proceeding to Burlington Bay, the British flotilla kept its distance to avoid fire from Captain THOMAS MACDONOUGH's ships protecting the battery. The bombardment lasted about twenty minutes, causing only minor damage. The raiders continued south to Shelburne and Charlotte, and captured several private vessels before returning to Canada.

Karen Campbell

Burlington College

Founded in 1972 as the Vermont Institute of Community Involvement, Burlington College, in Burlington's Old North End, offers a progressive liberal arts curriculum with a non-graded evaluation system. Degree programs are available in cinema studies/film production, human services, transpersonal psychology, interdisciplinary humanities, writing and literature, and fine arts. Enrollment is about 240 students, equally divided between male and female, and the average student age is twenty-eight. The film studies program has become one of the college's most popular, and regularly hosts a speakers series and panels on cinema.

Burlington Daily News

An afternoon newspaper published from 1894 to 1961, the *Burlington Daily News* was distinguished by the degree to which it reflected the will of its various owners. The *Daily News* was founded by Joseph Auld, previously an editor of the RUTLAND HERALD and general manager of the BURLINGTON FREE PRESS. Auld's newspaper, like its competitor the *Free Press*, was strongly Republican. Upon Auld's death in 1921, the *Daily News* was purchased by Dr. HORATIO NELSON JACKSON, a colorful figure who frequently endorsed Democratic candidates, though he ran for governor as a Republican in 1936. Jackson sold the *Daily News* to Charles Hasbrook in 1939. Always a distant second to the *Free Press* in circulation, the *Daily News* was sold in 1942 to WILLIAM LOEB, whose tenure as

publisher was distinguished by his vitriolic conservative front-page editorials. After a time, the *Daily News* was kept alive only through infusions of capital from Loeb's profitable New Hampshire daily, the *Manchester Union Leader*, and Loeb finally terminated publication on May 19, 1961.

Paul Searls

Burlington Free Press

With a daily morning circulation of fifty thousand and a Sunday circulation of sixty-one thousand the *Burlington Free Press* is Vermont's largest daily newspaper. Since 1971, the newspaper has been owned by the Gannett Co. Inc., one of the nation's largest newspaper firms. Two Burlington lawyers, Seneca Austin and Luman Foote, founded the weekly *Free Press* in 1827. Foote served as editor from offices on Court House Square. DE WITT CLINTON CLARKE owned and edited the *Burlington Free Press* from 1846 to 1853. GEORGE WYLLYS BENEDICT purchased the *Free Press* from Clarke in 1857 and served as editor until 1866, when he was succeeded by his son GEORGE GRENVILLE BENEDICT. The *Free Press* began publishing daily editions in 1848, two months after telegraph service reached Burlington, but it would be October 26, 1975, before the newspaper launched a Sunday edition. (It published a special Sunday edition during the Spanish-American War to keep its readers informed of war news.) The Howe family bought the paper in 1897 from George G. Benedict, though he remained editor until 1907. J. Warren McClure and other *Free Press* personnel bought the paper in 1961 and controlled it until it was sold to Gannett. Usually hewing to the Republican point of view, the *Free Press* has nonetheless been known to crusade for progressive causes and support candidates or issues at odds with the GOP. When United States senators were first chosen by a direct election in 1914, the *Free Press*'s editor pointed out that a popular referendum of Vermont voters had

approved a direct primary election, so the Republicans should nominate their senatorial candidate by a direct primary. When Vermont's Republican Senator WILLIAM PAUL DILLINGHAM and the Republican state organization refused, the *Free Press* withdrew its support of the Republican candidate. It also supported child labor laws. In more recent times, the *Free Press* has endorsed Democrats and Independents for public office.

Candace Page

Burt, Craig O. (1882–1965)

The principal leader in developing Stowe as a ski center, Craig Burt was born in Waterbury Center. He enrolled in NORWICH UNIVERSITY's Class of 1904, but left in his sophomore year when his father died. An owner of Stowe's largest lumber enterprise, he made skis in 1912 to cruise his timberlands and was Stowe's first competent skier. He was responsible for the introduction of the ski business in Stowe. In 1921, Burt helped to plan Stowe's first winter carnival, after which winter sports in Stowe evolved into a new source of income for the community and state. He worked with the Central Vermont and B & M Railroads to bring snowtrains to Vermont. His former logging camp, Ranch Camp, provided lodging for hundreds of pioneer skiers. Called "Father of Stowe Skiing" and "Maharaja of Stowe" by radio broadcaster Lowell Thomas, Burt was a founding member and first president of Stowe Ski Club in 1932. In 1933, he and CHARLES LORD laid out Bruce Ski Trail and later other trails crossing "Burtland." In 1936, he and Lord assumed leadership of the Ski Patrol and formulated rescue procedures. In 1939, Norwich conferred the degree of B.S. in civil engineering retroactively to 1904 because of his civic contributions. A prime mover in the Lake Mansfield Trout Club and the MOUNT MANSFIELD Electric Railroad, Burt converted Mount Mansfield Toll Road from a carriage to an automobile road.

Kathleen McKinley Harris

Cabot

Cabot, population 1,213, a town in Washington County, was granted by the Vermont legislature in 1781 largely to members of the Continental army. It is named for Sophia Cabot, the bride of one of the town's settlers, Lyman Hitchcock. Its gently rolling countryside has been devoted mainly to DAIRY FARMING. The incorporated village of Cabot, which lies on Route 215 almost exactly in the middle of the town, is the site of the Cabot Farmers Co-op Creamery, the state's major producer of cheese and a popular tourist attraction. The WINOOSKI RIVER begins in Cabot, rising in several bodies of water in the town including Molly's Pond, probably named for Mali Susap, the ABENAKI wife of JOSEPH SUSAP who, according to tradition, was friendly to the settlers.

Cady, Daniel L. (1861–1934)

Born in West Windsor, Daniel L. Cady prepared for college at Kimball Union Academy and the Montpelier Seminary, and graduated from the UNIVERSITY OF VERMONT in the class of 1886. He studied law and established a practice in New York City in 1894, retiring in 1912 to Burlington. Thereafter, Cady gained fame in Vermont for three volumes of sentimental local dialect verse, *Rhymes of Vermont Rural Life*, which both UVM and NORWICH UNIVERSITY recognized by awarding him the honorary degree of doctor of letters.

Calais

Calais (rhymes with "palace"), population 1,529, a town in Washington County, was granted by the Vermont legislature in 1780 to Colonel Jacob Davis and others. Its name derives, as does that of Montpelier directly to its south, from the enthusiasm for France inspired by that country's help during the American Revolution. Calais is on a high fertile plateau dotted with many small lakes and is primarily agricultural. The principal village is East Calais, on Route 14 as it passes through town from north to south, while North Calais, Kents Corner, Maple Corner, Pekin, and Ada-

mant (formerly Sodom) are crossroads settlements.

Caldwell, Henry (1735–1810)

A famously handsome soldier prominent in the defense of Quebec against Richard Montgomery's American army in 1775, Henry Caldwell leased an original French grant, the Foucault Seigneury, a 30,000-acre tract straddling the forty-fifth parallel on the eastern shore of LAKE CHAMPLAIN and the Richelieu River, from Quebec's former Governor James Murray in 1774, ten years after Murray bought the grant from the Foucaults. Caldwell subsequently bought it from Murray's heirs in 1801. Caldwell repaired the French mill on Windmill Point, rebuilt a church, and raised a manor house, renaming the seigneury Caldwell's Manor. He moved settlers to his land in the 1780s, including onto land below the forty-fifth parallel that Vermont claimed. In 1781, the Vermont General Assembly granted a township to IRA ALLEN, including a portion of Caldwell's Manor lying south of the forty-fifth parallel, and renamed it Alburgh. The ensuing ownership dispute between Caldwell and Allen was ultimately settled in the 1830s when HEMAN "CHILI" ALLEN, Ira's nephew, paid $30,000 to Caldwell's heirs. Drawn into expensive disputes with Alburgh's long-established residents over the validity of their titles, Heman Allen ultimately failed to realize any profit from the settlement with Caldwell's heirs.

Cambridge

Cambridge, population 3,186, a town in Lamoille County, was granted by the Vermont legislature in 1781 to a number of individuals prominent in Vermont's early history, including THOMAS CHITTENDEN, JONAS FAY, SAMUEL ROBINSON, SR., and members of their families. The name almost certainly derives from Cambridge, Massachusetts, the home colony of a number of the grantees. The landscape is quite varied, ranging from the broad, fertile valley of the LAMOILLE RIVER, which cuts across the town from east to west, to the rugged, uninhabited northern slopes of MOUNT MANSFIELD, the state's highest peak. The deepest and most dramatic cut in the GREEN MOUNTAINS, Smugglers' Notch, lies in the town's southeasternmost corner. Its remote location made the Notch an ideal spot for the illegal transport of goods during the EMBARGO PERIOD (1808–1809) and later during PROHIBI-

TION. A road, closed in winter, goes through the narrow defile. Nearby is Smugglers' Notch ski area (sixty-seven trails, seven lifts, and a vertical drop of 2,610 feet), which is on the other side of a mountain ridge from the Spruce Peak ski area in the town of Stowe. Cambridge's main settlements are Cambridge village and Jeffersonville, both along the Lamoille. While each serves the needs of local residents, Jeffersonville, because of its location at the beginning of the road into the mountains, also provides some services for skiers. Its collection of craft shops and art galleries reflects its continuing role as a regional creative center.

Camel's Hump

Vermont's fourth-highest peak at 4,083 feet, Camel's Hump was called by the French *le lion couchant*, the resting lion, because of its distinctive shape. (The ABENAKI name for it was *Dowabodiwadzo*, "saddle mountain.") English settlers renamed it "Camel's Rump," a term that was changed to Camel's Hump after 1800, presumably to spare delicate sensibilities. The mountain is the centerpiece of 18,000-acre Camel's Hump State Park, and is preserved above 2,500 feet as a natural area. Numerous hiking trails, as well as the LONG TRAIL, lead to the summit. The boreal summit environment includes 10 acres of Arctic tundra, a remnant of the Ice Age and one of only two examples of Arctic tundra in the state (a larger one is on MOUNT MANSFIELD). Like many other high peaks in the GREEN MOUNTAINS, Camel's Hump is severely affected by acid rain and has seen substantial die-off of vegetation, especially red spruce. On the night of October 16, 1944, one of the worst airplane crashes in the state's history occurred when an Army Air Corps B-24 Liberator bomber on a training run crashed into the sheer face of Camel's Hump 100 feet below the summit, killing nine of the ten crewmembers on board.

Canaan

Canaan, population 1,078, a town in Essex County, was granted by the Vermont legislature in 1782 to a group of investors from Connecticut and takes its name from Canaan in that state. Hilly and heavily forested, the town occupies the extreme northeastern tip of Vermont, bounded on the east by the CONNECTICUT RIVER and on the north by the Canadian border. The earliest settlers were attracted by the wide and fertile meadows along the river, but only a few farms remain today and the town has a primarily forest-based economy. The major employer is the Ethan Allen Company, makers of fine furniture, whose plant is in the hamlet of Beecher Falls, which, along with Canaan village, lies along the Connecticut in the northern part of town. Residents do most of their shopping in the nearby towns of Colebrook, New Hampshire, or Coaticook, Quebec. East of Beecher Falls is the only land boundary (about 1 mile long) between Vermont and New Hampshire, established by federal court action in 1934 after a long period of dispute between the two states.

Canfield, Thomas Hawley (1822–1897)

An ante-bellum operator of steamboats on LAKE CHAMPLAIN and the Great Lakes, an extensive RAILROAD builder in Vermont, and organizer of the project to build the Northern Pacific Railway after the Civil War, Thomas H. Canfield was born in Arlington of a family settled there since 1768. Educated in his town common school, Burr Seminary in Manchester, the Troy Episcopal Institute, and Union College, Canfield moved to Williston in 1844 to work as a storekeeper. He married Elizabeth A. Chittenden, great-granddaughter of THOMAS CHITTENDEN, Vermont's first governor. She died in 1848 and he then married Caroline Hopkins, the daughter of the Reverend JOHN HENRY HOPKINS, the first Episcopal bishop of Vermont. In 1847, Canfield moved to Burlington, formed the mercantile house of Bradley & Canfield, and operated wholesale stores and warehouses on the Burlington wharf, as well as a steamboat line to New York and Montreal. At the same time, he organized a telegraph company with a line between Troy, New York, Burlington, and Montreal that completed connections in February 1848. In 1850, Bradley & Canfield, with other parties, built a railroad from Bellows Falls to Burlington by way of Rutland. Much interested in the efforts to connect Boston and Burlington by railway, he strongly favored the Rutland and Fitchburg route, while CHARLES PAINE of Northfield fought for the Montpelier and Concord route. Both railroads were built, but the Rutland line ended at Burlington, thereby lacking a connection to Ogdensburg, New York, or Montreal. Bradley & Canfield built a steamer and barges in ninety days sufficient to carry twelve

thousand barrels of flour between Rouses Point, New York, and Burlington to compete with the Vermont Central. He next opened a route for products of the West to be carried by steamboat from the Great Lakes to Ogdensburg on the St. Lawrence River, then connecting with the railroad to Boston. Working on this project with Edwin F. Johnson, one of the most experienced engineers in America, and from his own tours to the Great Lakes, Canfield saw the significance of a railroad to the Pacific coast by a northern route. As a first step, he contracted with others to build the Chicago & Northwestern Railroad from Chicago to St. Paul, Minnesota, and Fond du Lac, Wisconsin, even before a railroad from the east ran into Chicago. When Canfield proposed the northern route for a Pacific railroad to President Franklin Pierce, Secretary of War Jefferson Davis attempted to block the project by proposing transcontinental explorations for three different routes. When the Civil War broke out in 1861, Canfield was enlisted by Assistant Secretary of War Thomas Scott to manage rail transportation about Washington. Canfield and SOLOMON FOOT raised, armed, equipped, and provided mounts in sixty days for the First Regiment of Vermont Cavalry. Canfield returned to Lake Champlain after the war as superintendent of steamers. Resuming his interest in a northern railway to the Pacific, which had been chartered in 1864 as the Northern Pacific Railway, Canfield joined with other backers, including FREDERICK BILLINGS, to construct by 1870 a line that extended from Duluth to Seattle and Portland. He also advocated the St. Lawrence, Lake Champlain, and Hudson River freight route between the Great Lakes and the Atlantic, partly because Vermont would have benefitted by the traffic. An Episcopalian since childhood, in 1854 Canfield was an original incorporator and trustee of the Vermont Episcopal Institute in Burlington. He contributed to the founding of several Episcopal churchs in the upper midwest and maintained a home in Lake Park, Minnesota, where he died in 1897.

Cannon, Le Grand (1815–1906)

A New York City native who spent six months of each year after 1865 at Overlake, his 60-acre Burlington estate overlooking LAKE CHAMPLAIN, Le Grand Cannon graduated from Rensselaer Polytechnic Institute at Troy, New York, in

1834, and was initially employed there at his father's extensive iron-rolling mills. In 1838, Cannon served as an aide to General John E. Wool, the U.S. Army commander responsible for enforcing neutrality along Vermont's border with Canada during the Canadian PATRIOTS War of 1837 to 1838. Moving to New York City in 1850, Cannon embarked upon a business career that came to include major interests in the RAILROAD and steamship companies that served the Champlain Valley in the second half of the nineteenth century. In the late 1850s, he became principal owner and manager of the Saratoga and Whitehall rail line and, through that enterprise, acquired a major interest in the CHAMPLAIN TRANSPORTATION COMPANY, serving as president of the company during the forty years it dominated steamboat service on Lake Champlain. When the Delaware & Hudson Canal Company acquired the Champlain Transportation Company and its subsidiary railroad companies, Cannon became vice president of the D&H and was its chief manager during the great strike of 1888. He went on active military service at the outbreak of the Civil War, again serving on General Wool's staff, first in organizing troops in New York and then as Wool's aide-de-camp and chief of staff as colonel at Fortress Monroe in Virginia. He wrote a report on the condition of slaves who fled to the Federal lines that was adopted and carried out in orders effectively emancipating former slaves employed by the army nine months before the Emancipation Proclamation. As a witness of the battle between the ironclads *Monitor* and *Merrimac,* Cannon wrote a report of the event at the request of the Navy Department. His annual six-month retreat from New York City to Overlake led to the purchase of a large farm in Shelburne where he employed the latest agricultural methods and worked to improve horse and cattle breeds. He was a trustee of the UNIVERSITY OF VERMONT for many years. His heirs had the main house at Overlake demolished in 1925, leaving only estate outbuildings, among which was the carriage house, later restored and now a private residence. His son, Henry Le Grand Cannon (1856–1895), was an artist and traveler who at his death bequeathed to UVM "my collection of East India curios and bric a brac . . . including furniture, carpets, rugs, and hangings on condition that the collection be placed in a separate room attached to or connected with the museum of said university." The first Cannon Room was constructed in Torrey Hall, and when the FLEMING MUSEUM opened in 1931 a second Cannon Room was set up using the original Cannon collection and additional objects donated by surviving family members. The room remained intact until the mid-1980s, when the Fleming Museum was renovated. At present, small objects from the collection are on exhibit at the museum, and other objects may be seen upon request.

Carignan-Salieres Regiment

Raised in Savoy by the Prince of Carignan in 1644, and tough fighters in the Turkish wars, the Carignans were incorporated into the French army under the command of Colonel de Salieres and brought to New France in 1664. They quickly suppressed hostile activities by the Iroquois and in 1665 to 1666 built forts at Sorel on the St. Lawrence River and Chambly on the Richelieu River to block Iroquois and British movement against Montreal and Quebec. In the spring of 1666, PIERRE DE ST. PAUL, SIEUR DE LA MOTTE led a company from the Carignan-Salieres and laborers totalling three hundred men to a sandy point on the first large island at the foot of LAKE CHAMPLAIN, where they built FORT SAINTE-ANNE, which was dedicated to the patron saint of Quebec on her feast day, July 26, 1666, with a mass celebrated by Jean Baptiste du Bois-d'Esgriselles, chaplain of the Carignan regiment. Several companies of the Carignan-Salieres were stationed at Fort Sainte-Anne, a presence that initially seemed to pacify the Iroquois. But in the summer of 1666, while hunting and fishing on the western shore of the lake in sight of the fort, a small party of French officers and soldiers were attacked by a band of Mohawks who killed captains de Traversy and de Chasy and took several prisoners. In 1669, the Carignan-Salieres withdrew to Montreal. In subsequent years, the northernmost island in Lake Champlain came to be known as Isle La Motte.

Carleton, Christopher (b. 1749)

An Irish major in the British Twenty-ninth Regiment of Foot stationed in Quebec during the years 1775 to 1781, Christopher Carleton was the nephew of GUY CARLETON, governor of Canada at several times between 1767 and 1796. Young Carleton had earlier been to North America and lived with Indians, accepting their tattoos and taking an Indian wife. In October 1778, he led a force of 115 British regulars and 97 Indians of various tribes on a mission of destruction into the Champlain Valley. He returned in 1780 with a larger force, burned several settlements in New York, and opened communications with the leaders of Vermont, which led to a truce between Vermont and the British, arrangements to exchange prisoners, and the HALDIMAND NEGOTIATIONS.

Carleton, Guy (1724–1808)

Born at Strabane, county Tyrone, Ireland, Guy Carleton, Lord Dorchester, served as governor of Quebec from 1767 to 1770, 1775 to 1777, 1786 to 1791, and 1793 to 1796. He first suggested the Quebec Act of 1774, which established a legislative council and provided tolerance of Catholicism. The act's provision of religious tolerance in French Canada contributed to American opposition to Parliament's policy, especially in New England, and eventually to the Revolution. In the American invasion of Canada in late 1775, SETH WARNER and his GREEN MOUNTAIN CONTINENTAL RANGERS thwarted Carleton's attempt to lift the American siege of Fort St. Johns on the Richelieu. A month later in December, Carleton escaped the American capture of Montreal, fleeing down the St. Lawrence disguised as a riverman in a whale boat. After successfully resisting the American siege of Quebec in 1775 to 1776, he led a heavily armed fleet into LAKE CHAMPLAIN and engaged an American fleet led by BENEDICT ARNOLD in the BATTLE OF VALCOUR ISLAND on October 11 to 13, 1776. Too powerful for Arnold's boats, the British fleet swept the lake to Crown Point, but prospects of a drawn-out siege of FORT TICONDEROGA led Carleton to withdraw his forces to winter quarters at St. Johns. Disagreeing with London's decision in 1777 to send General JOHN BURGOYNE to lead an offensive campaign up Lake Champlain, Carleton returned to England in 1778. FREDERICK HALDIMAND succeeded him as governor of Quebec. After the cessation of hostilities, Carleton went to New York in 1782 as commander-in-chief to oversee the evacuation of British forces and civilian Loyalists. For his services he was created Baron Dorchester and returned to Quebec as governor in 1786. During the last years of the 1780s Carleton permitted easy relations to develop between Vermont and Quebec. ETHAN, IRA, and LEVI ALLEN visited Quebec several times between 1786 and 1790 on their own business affairs and as official emissaries of Vermont and successfully negotiated free access to sell Vermont lumber and agricultural products in Quebec markets and to purchase manufactured British products. During Carleton's final term of service as governor general, from 1793 to 1796, Britain's relations with the United States had so deteriorated over the British army's support of their native allies in the northwestern Indian war of 1794, that a larger war between Britain and the United States seemed imminent. Addressing three thousand Indians convened in Quebec in February 1794, Carleton urged them to wreak revenge on the Americans, assuring them that war between Britain and the United States was certain. Vermont's official public and individual private relations with the government of Canada under direct British rule were probably never more complex than during Guy Carleton's terms of service as governor general.

Carlisle, Lilian Baker (b. 1912)

A writer, historian, and antiques connoisseur, Lilian Baker Carlisle was born in Meridian, Mississippi, and raised in suburban Philadelphia. She dropped out of college during the Depression, trained as a legal secretary, and married Grafton Carlisle in 1933. They moved to Burlington in 1946. In 1950, she was hired as "social secretary" to ELECTRA HAVEMEYER WEBB, founder of the SHELBURNE MUSEUM, but her secretarial role was short-lived. As the museum developed, Carlisle organized and catalogued Mrs. Webb's eclectic collection of folk art, creating the museum's filing system from scratch. During the accession process, she wrote booklets on quilts, carriages, and hatboxes, absorbing knowledge of antiques through the "journeyman's approach." She left the museum in 1961, a year after Mrs. Webb's death. For many years, she has written scores of magazine articles focusing on ladies' crafts, silver, history, and antiques. She also lectured at many major museums. She co-founded the Chittenden County Historical Society in 1965, with the goal of making history accessible. She compiled the "Look Around" series of booklets on Chittenden County towns, always telling stories about the city's buildings and the people who built and lived or worked in them. She also led walking tours of Burlington for more than twenty years and edited two volumes of the *Historic Guide to Burlington Neighborhoods* (1991 and 1997). She returned to college later in life, earning her B.A. from the UNIVERSITY OF VERMONT in 1981 and her masters in history and geography in 1986. That same year, she established an Heirloom Appraisal Day at the FLEMING MUSEUM at UVM, where she served on the board of advisors.   *Julie Becker*

Carlson, L. Wayne (b. 1942)

A legend of the early 1970s for his many escapes from Vermont jails and prisons, L. Wayne Carlson, a resident of Sturgis, Saskatchewan, was arrested in Burlington in May 1973 for entering the United States illegally from Canada, where he was wanted on a variety of criminal charges. Between May 1973 and March 1974, Carlson escaped from Vermont authorities five times: once from jail in Burlington, once from district court in Burlington, and three times from the aging WINDSOR STATE PRISON. He was convicted on escape charges in April 1974 and sent to a federal penitentiary. In January 1976, Governor THOMAS P. SALMON pardoned Carlson on condition that he be handed over to Canadian authorities, a transfer that was completed without incident at the end of the month. Possessing intelligence, charisma, and good looks, Wayne Carlson appealed to the popular imagination in an era of heightened interest in fugitives, outlaws, and anti-heroes. After his return to Canada, Carlson spent most of the next twenty years in prison. In 1996, he went to work in a prison suicide-prevention program sponsored by the Samaritans of Southern Alberta, and soon became a driving force for the program. He also began writing on prison issues for local and national journals. He was paroled in August 1999 and now drives a cab in Lethbridge, Alberta. His thirteen escapes from jails and prisons in Canada and the United States are probably a record for North America.

Jeffrey D. Marshall

Carter, Alan (1904–1975)

Founder of the VERMONT SYMPHONY ORCHESTRA and its director for forty years, Alan Carter was born in Greenwich, Connecticut, and began violin studies at the age of six. He continued his studies in violin and conducting in New York and then throughout Europe. After playing for one year in the Cologne Symphony, he returned to the United States in 1929 where he taught violin in Chicago. In the early 1930s, he founded and toured with the Cremona String Quartet. He founded the Vermont State Symphony Orchestra in 1934 and remained its director until 1974. During his tenure, the orchestra started as a semi-amateur ensemble and became a fully professional orchestra supported in part with funds from the state. Under his direction, the orchestra played numerous works by American composers. Carter was a professor of music at MIDDLEBURY COLLEGE from 1939 to 1969 and was chair of the music department for ten years. As a captain in World War II, he organized the First Service Command Symphony Orchestra in Boston comprised of professional musicians serving in the Army. While at Middlebury in 1946, he founded the COMPOSERS' CONFERENCE AND CHAMBER MUSIC CENTER, a summer program where composers could write music and hear it played. He founded the Vermont String Association (better known as the GREEN MOUNTAIN FIDDLERS) for the education of young string players in 1961. A trustee and president of the Vermont Council on the Arts, Carter was given the Vermont Governor's Award for Excellence in the Arts and an honorary degree from the UNIVERSITY OF VERMONT among other awards.

Jerry McBride

Carter, Robert McCrillis, Jr. (1902–1955)

An agricultural economist and rural sociologist whose post–World War II research influenced public policy during the late 1940s, Robert McCrillis Carter, Jr., was born in Sheffield and earned a bachelor's degree in economics from the University of Wisconsin in 1926. After college, he worked first as an accountant and statistician, and from 1932 to 1938 operated a dairy farm in Sutton. His first book, *Studies in Vermont History, Geography and Government* (1937), a long-time teaching aid in Vermont schools, was revised by his widow Helen Spinney Carter and reprinted in 1960 with "A Message to the Boys and Girls of Vermont" by DOROTHY CANFIELD FISHER. Carter earned a master's degree in agricultural economics from the UNIVERSITY OF VERMONT in 1939 and served as an assistant economist on the University's agricultural experiment station staff until 1943, when he earned a Ph.D. from Cornell and was appointed to UVM's faculty as an agricultural economist and rural sociologist specializing in public issues. The results of his research into long-neglected rural living conditions and trends in land use, the economics of farming, and issues of local control were published as *The Farm Business and Farm Family Living as Related to Land Class in Nine Vermont Towns* (1945), *The Development and Financing of Local Governmental Institutions in Nine Vermont Towns* (1946), *The People and their Use of Land in Nine Vermont Towns* (1947), and *Rural Non-Farm Family Living in Nine Vermont Towns* (1947). Utilizing data gathered by JOHN ALLEN HITCHCOCK, Carter's studies in deteriorating rural life and work during a post-war economic expansion contributed significant information to a public debate over issues of education, welfare, health, and safety that became part of the progressive budget and legislative proposals of Governor ERNEST W. GIBSON, JR.   *Gerald F. Vaughn*

Castleton

Castleton, population 4,367, a town in Rutland County, was granted by BENNING WENTWORTH in 1761 and may derive its name from places in England, Ireland, or the Isle of Man. The town lies in the northern TACONIC MOUNTAINS, rising to 2,216-foot Bird Mountain in its extreme southeastern corner, and is cut from east to west by the Castleton River, a tributary of the Poultney River. Castleton's most noteworthy physical feature is 2,360-acre LAKE BOMOSEEN, the largest body of water entirely within the borders of Vermont. The lake is a favorite summer destination and is lined with both permanent homes and vacation cottages; in its center is NESHOBE ISLAND, once the summer home of drama critic Alexander Woollcott, who entertained the rich and famous there from 1924 to 1943. SLATE is still mined profitably in Castleton, and large slate piles still dot the town. The main settlements are Castleton village, Castleton Corners, Hydeville, and Bomoseen. In Castleton village ETHAN and IRA ALLEN, SETH WARNER, BENEDICT ARNOLD, and others plotted the attack on FORT TICONDEROGA in May, 1775. A few years later Fort Warren was built outside the village to defend the northern frontier. Edwin L. Drake, who in 1859 drilled the first oil well in the world at Titusville, Pennsylvania, was born in Castleton. The Smith-Putnam generator, the first wind-powered, alternating-current electric turbine in the

United States, functioned atop Grandpa's Knob on Castleton's border with West Rutland from 1941 to 1945. CASTLETON STATE COLLEGE was founded as the Rutland County Grammar School in 1787.

Castleton State College

Founded in 1787, Castleton State College is the oldest institution now organized as one of the VERMONT STATE COLLEGES. The Vermont General Assembly granted a charter to the Rutland County Grammar School that was then established in a house located on Main Street in Castleton. In 1829, the cornerstone of the "Old Seminary" building was laid by NOAH LEE, who had served in the Revolutionary War, and SOLOMON FOOT, then principal of the grammar school and later a distinguished United States senator. This building was a landmark in the field of education in the state for nearly a century, as the Grammar School evolved to become, in turn, the Vermont Classical High School, the Castleton Academy, the Castleton Seminary, and the Castleton Normal School. It was destroyed by fire on January 3, 1924. In the following year, Castleton alumni, the citizens of Vermont, and the efforts of Dr. CAROLINE WOODRUFF, principal of the Castleton Normal School from 1921 to 1940, produced a new building, now known as Woodruff Hall. The VERMONT ACADEMY OF MEDICINE also played an important role in the histories of both the college and the town. Founded in 1818, it was the first such institution in Vermont, and for a time was the largest in New England. The Old Chapel-Medical College building has been a part of the college since 1865. When the Vermont legislature established normal, or teacher, training at Castleton in 1867, these courses were first held in this building, making it the original home of the Castleton Normal School. The Normal School had supplanted the seminary by the late 1870s. In 1881, Captain Abel E. Leavenworth became its principal and purchased the property. He was succeeded in 1897 by his son, Philip R. Leavenworth. In 1912, the State of Vermont purchased the Normal School. Since that time, Castleton State College has grown into a comprehensive institution of higher education offering a wide range of programs in the sciences, the arts, the humanities, and career and professional fields, leading to bachelors degrees in the arts, science, and social work, and associate degrees in science

and general studies. One of the Vermont State Colleges, Castleton enrolls nineteen hundred full- and part-time students. The majority are Vermonters, but over half of the fifty states are represented in the student body.

Catamount

The catamount (*Felis concolor*) is a large, rarely observed wild cat, usually tan colored but sometimes black, which can grow to 120 to 150 pounds. A skillful predator in North and Central America, the catamount is capable of taking down deer larger than itself and carrying them away. Known also as the cougar, puma, mountain lion, and panther, the catamount has adapted to every type of climatic zone from Southwestern deserts, where they seem to be flourishing, to the Florida subtropics, where a small population has been restored, though with little natural increase as yet observed. The last catamount taken in Vermont was shot on Thanksgiving day in 1881 in the town of Barnard; its stuffed and taxidermy-mounted pelt is on display at the VERMONT HISTORICAL SOCIETY's interpretive center in Montpelier. Claims of sightings of the catamount have increased in recent years, and DNA analysis of scat has revealed the presence of cougars in Vermont, but it has not been determined if they are released pets, escapees from private zoos or collections, solitary wandering individuals from the west, or from a resident breeding population. Historically, the catamount was known to range widely in this region before Vermont was first settled in the 1760s. STEPHEN FAY's Green Mountain Tavern in Bennington displayed a stuffed and mounted catamount pelt during the 1770s. Subsequent owners of the building named it the CATAMOUNT TAVERN and today a bronze statue of a catamount commemorates the site and its role as a gathering place for Vermont's early political leaders. A team mascot name for both the UNIVERSITY OF VERMONT (Catamounts) and MIDDLEBURY COLLEGE (Panthers), catamounts range most widely in Vermont today as images on college sweatshirts and signs for retail outlets of various products, as well as in the name of five manufacturing firms.

Catamount Film and Arts Center

JAY CRAVEN founded the Catamount Film and Arts Center in St. Johnsbury in

1975 to present contemporary American and foreign films, live performing arts programs, and visual arts exhibitions. The 16-millimeter film series also ran at various locations throughout the NORTHEAST KINGDOM. Summer arts programs for children are conducted in the center and a gallery shows the works of area artists. The Northeast Kingdom Classical Series of music performances is housed at the center. Plays, puppetry, and dance concerts by regional and visiting companies and individual artists are offered throughout the year.   *Virginia C. Downs*

Catamount Tavern

STEPHEN FAY's public house in Bennington, known as the Green Mountain Tavern in its own time, was called the Catamount Tavern many years after the building stopped functioning as a public house. ETHAN ALLEN and the GREEN MOUNTAIN BOYS met in the original tavern and were said to have planned the assault on FORT TICONDEROGA there in 1775. The tavern burned down in 1871. Today the statue of a catamount on a pedestal marks the approximate location of landlord Fay's public house.

Cathedral Fires of 1971 and 1972

The cathedrals of the Episcopal and Roman Catholic dioceses in Burlington were destroyed by arsonists in 1971 and 1972. The first fire, on February 15, 1971, demolished St. Paul's Episcopal Cathedral, which had been built as a parish church in 1832 and named cathedral of the Diocese of Vermont in 1966. The Roman Catholic Cathedral of the Immaculate Conception, built in 1862 to 1867 to be the cathedral of the Diocese of Burlington, was burned to the ground on March 13 and 14, 1972. The gothic churches had been viewed by some as impediments to the large urban renewal project in the surrounding area, so the design of replacement buildings on non-project sites prompted considerable public interest. The two cathedrals were replaced by buildings of contemporary design. A new Cathedral Church of St. Paul, by Burlington architects Thomas Cullins and William Henderson, was consecrated November 10, 1973. New York City architect Edward Larabee Barnes was selected from fifty-four competitors to design the new Cathedral of the Immaculate Conception, which was consecrated May 26, 1977.

David Blow

Catlin, Moses (1770–1842)

The son-in-law of the elder HEMAN ALLEN, Moses Catlin of Litchfield, Connecticut, in 1795 successfully sued Heman's brother IRA ALLEN in behalf of his wife, Lucinda Allen Catlin, for the maladministration of her late father's estate, which consisted of Heman's share in the ONION RIVER LAND COMPANY's land holdings in the Champlain Valley, as well as uncollected debts from his Connecticut mercantile business. The judgment in the federal court in Rutland gave the Catlins $46,847.80, which they immediately levied against Ira's property along the WINOOSKI RIVER in Colchester and Burlington, including saw and grist mills, forges, Allen's residence, and other buildings and adjoining land. The Catlins moved to Burlington to make full use of Lucinda's inheritance. With his brother Guy, who followed him to Burlington, Catlin developed a mercantile business, often as agent for merchants trading along the Champlain-Richelieu route from New York to Montreal. They represented John Jacob Astor of New York, Horatio Gates & Company of Montreal, and Benjamin Pell & Son of Albany. They also organized large lumber rafts in the spring to move Champlain Valley timber and produce to market in Canada in exchange for cash and imported goods. Catlin and Samuel Hickcock acquired an exclusive twenty-five-year franchise from the state to build a dock and storehouse at Burlington Bay. Moses and Guy Catlin took advantage of large profits generated by the illegal trade with Canada during the War of 1812. During the war, they joined others to charter the LAKE CHAMPLAIN Steamboat Company, which launched the *Phoenix* in 1815. The Catlins invested their commercial profits in developing waterpower on the Burlington side of the Winooski River, where they ground grain and plaster and sawed lumber, some of it from timber acquired in the judgment against Ira Allen.   *H. Nicholas Muller III*

Cavendish

Cavendish, population 1,470, a town in Windsor county, was granted by BENNING WENTWORTH in 1761 and originally included the area that later became the town of Baltimore. It was probably named for William Cavendish (1720–1764), fourth duke of Devonshire, an influential peer who held many offices including that of prime minister. The landscape consists of numerous hills in the 1,500- to 2,000-foot range; the tallest is 2,092-foot Hawk's Mountain, the long ridge of which cuts across the southeastern corner of the town and completely cut off contact with the isolated area that the legislature in 1793 formed into the town of Baltimore. The main settlements of Cavendish village and Proctorsville lie on the banks of the southern Black River, which flows across the lower part of the town from west to east. Proctorsville is named for the prominent Vermont family that included REDFIELD PROCTOR, SR., founder of the VERMONT MARBLE COMPANY and governor of the state. In 1847, the strange accident of PHINEAS GAGE, occurred in Cavendish. Gage had part of his brain blown away during an explosion but survived sufficiently unaffected to become a medical curiosity. For a number of years after his exile from the Soviet Union, ALEXANDER SOLZHENITSIN lived in Cavendish.

Caverly, Charles Solomon (1856–1918)

A Rutland physician whose concern with public health issues led him into pioneering studies of infantile paralysis, Charles Caverly was born in Troy, New Hampshire, attended high schools in Pittsford and Brandon and Kimball Union Academy and graduated Phi Beta Kappa from Dartmouth College in 1878. He received the doctor of medicine degree from the UNIVERSITY OF VERMONT in 1881 and subsequently studied for eighteen months at the College of Physicians and Surgeons in New York, settling into private practice in Rutland in 1883. Along with his successful practice, Caverly developed an early interest in the public health movement. He was appointed to the State Board of Health in 1890, served as president from 1891 until his death, and was also professor of hygiene and preventive medicine at the University of Vermont. His 1894 article on polio describing an epidemic that had occurred in Vermont that year has been regarded as the best contribution in America to the study of the disease up to that time. His subsequent biennial reports of polio in the state were also of great value. After 1914, when an epidemic of 306 cases occurred—a very high incidence for a state with so comparatively few inhabitants as Vermont—Caverly gave even greater attention and amounts of his time to the care and prevention of polio. Also deeply interested in the care and prevention of tuberculosis, Caverly was instrumental in the acquisition by the state of the private Proctor Hospital in Pittsford, and of its transformation it into the VERMONT SANATORIUM, which was additionally named the Caverly Preventorium in his honor after his death from influenza during the 1918 epidemic.

Donald Wickman

Cedar Creek, Battle of

Early on the morning of October 19, 1864, Confederate General Jubal Early launched a surprise attack on General Philip Sheridan's Union Army of the Shenandoah, which was camped along the north side of Cedar Creek near Middletown, Virginia. Early's men quickly overran the camps of the Union Eighth Corps and much of the Nineteenth Corps, capturing artillery, supplies, and men. Stephen Thomas, formerly colonel of the Eighth Vermont Infantry regiment but now commanding a Nineteenth Corps brigade that included his old regiment, marched his men into the fray. The Vermonters and their comrades fought heroically but were hopelessly outnumbered and were soon swept away. Thomas's forlorn stand cost the Eighth Vermont casualties in excess of 50 percent, but bought the remainder of the Union army precious time to prepare. As the sky lightened, just two divisions of the Sixth Corps and two divisions of cavalry remained intact before the rebel onslaught. These, however, were the best Union troops in Virginia, and they included the hardened veterans of the Old Vermont Brigade. Forming a line well behind the overrun camps, the Sixth Corps met the Confederate advance, then gradually fell back to the north. General Early halted the advance at mid-morning, having achieved a brilliant but incomplete victory. General Sheridan, meanwhile, missed the entire morning's fight. He had spent the night at Winchester, twelve miles north of Middletown, on his return from a meeting in Washington. When he heard the cannon booming to the south, Sheridan mounted his black charger, Rienzi, and commenced his celebrated ride to Cedar Creek. He found the remainder of his dispirited army dug in on a line to the north and west of Middletown, while the cavalry skirmished with the enemy on both flanks. Sheridan's arrival electrified the troops, and many who had taken flight now rejoined the ranks. After repositioning his forces, Sheridan launched a counter-attack in the late afternoon. Early's men held on tenaciously, but before long Union infantry, including the remnant of the Eighth Vermont, broke through on the right. Slowly at first, then in growing panic, the Confederate line collapsed. The First Vermont and Fifth New York Cavalry regiments, led by Vermont General WILLIAM WELLS, rushed forward in an attempt to cut off the retreat. When it was all over, Early had lost all of his artillery, large quantities of supplies, and hundreds of men taken prisoner. The Battle of Cedar Creek ended the Confederate threat in the Shenandoah Valley, and deprived Robert E. Lee of his ability to keep the Union armies off balance. A Confederate victory would have threatened Abraham Lincoln's re-election in November, but the Union victory sealed it. No major Union victory owed more to the efforts of Vermonters than Cedar Creek. All together, the Vermonters comprised more than 10 percent of the Army of the Shenandoah, serving in one cavalry and eight infantry regiments. JULIAN SCOTT's large painting of the Battle of Cedar Creek hangs in the ceremonial reception room of the VERMONT STATE HOUSE in Montpelier.   *Jeffrey D. Marshall*

Center for Northern Studies

Founded in 1971 in Wolcott, the Center for Northern Studies is a distinctive Vermont higher-education institution, focusing its attention on the Arctic, a unique area important as a barometer of environmental and social change. In the Arctic North, as by implication in the Antarctic South, ancient natural processes seem more evident than in warmer climates. The center from its beginning has concentrated on opening the North to students of all ages. North-central Vermont, where the Center is located, displays many characteristics of the Arctic in climate and life forms. Undergraduate and graduate students pursue courses of study in Arctic natural history, geology, anthropology, oceanography, ice and snow, environmental processes, and social sciences both at the center and in the field in the Arctic. Students may attend for residential terms of a semester or a full year and combine scientific fundamentals with seasonal travel studies, which allow them to extend the depth and breadth of their learning. Students completing courses at the center apply this specialized study to their concentrations at other colleges or universities or to a variety of field and job placements.

Forest Davis

Chambers, William (d. 1829)

Commander of the British fleet on LAKE CHAMPLAIN during the American Revolution, William Chambers was born in 1748 at Studley, England. He entered the Royal Navy as a midshipman in 1758, serving in Canada during the French and Indian War and rising to acting lieutenant by the start of the American Revolution. In 1777, Chambers returned to Canada and became "Master and Commander" of the British fleet on Lake Champlain in the summer of 1778, maintaining England's control of the Champlain-Richelieu waterway for the rest of the war. In the summers of 1779 and 1780, he created a detailed nautical atlas of the lake, a manuscript copy of which is at the VERMONT HISTORICAL SOCIETY. Chambers supported the British raids from Canada against American settlements in northeastern New York and northwestern Vermont and, as FREDERICK HALDIMAND's military representative in the Champlain Valley, served as Haldimand's first line of contact with IRA ALLEN and other agents who came north in 1780 and 1781 to discuss terms for Vermont's reunion with Canada in the HALDIMAND NEGOTIATIONS. With peace in 1783, Chambers returned to England and retired from active service.

J. Kevin Graffagnino

Champ

A distant relative of Nessie in Scotland and Chessie in Delaware, Champ, a gigantic aquatic serpent that supposedly inhabits its LAKE CHAMPLAIN, has captured the imagination of tourists and residents on both sides of the lake since the beginning of the nineteenth century. Reports of annual sightings reaffirm the conviction of believers in its existence, while nonbelievers discount such tales and are not swayed by photographs. This slippery phantom of the deep and of local folklore gained its popular following through such sighting accounts, dutifully recounted in the popular media, and through tall tales, local songs, patriotic orations, and promotional stunts such as having Champ serve as a mascot for a New York bank and a Burlington minor league baseball team. So broad has been the appeal of Champ that the New York and Vermont legislatures have both passed resolutions (though not laws) protecting it from extinction. For more than 180 years, Champ has avoided verification but nevertheless continues to fascinate Ver-

monters and visitors if only by its elusiveness.   *Richard Sweterlitsch*

Champion Lands Project

The largest conservation project in the history of Vermont, the Champion Lands Project conserves 132,000 forested acres in fourteen towns and one gore in the NORTHEAST KINGDOM, almost one-third of Essex County. The land was formerly the property of the Champion Paper Company, which was divesting itself of substantial holdings not only in Vermont but also in New Hampshire and New York. Fearful that the land would be sold piecemeal to speculators, the three states plus a number of foundations, public agencies, and nonprofit conservation groups including the Conservation Fund, the Nature Conservancy, the Richard King Mellon Foundation, and the VERMONT LAND TRUST purchased approximately 300,000 acres of land overall. In the summer of 1999, the Vermont portion was transferred to a number of federal, state, and private entities. These include the U.S. Fish and Wildlife Service (26,000 acres to become part of the Silvio O. Conte National Wildlife Refuge), the Vermont Agency of Natural Resources (22,000 acres), and the Essex Timber Company of Ipswich, Massachusetts, a group of private investors committed to sustainable forestry (84,000 acres). The Nature Conservancy and the Vermont Land Trust were also involved in various conservation easements that will maintain the land for recreation, habitat protection, and sustainable timber harvesting, thus also stabilizing the local economy for many years to come.   *Steve E. Wright*

Champlain, Lake

Lake Champlain, on Vermont's western border, is 120 miles long and 12 miles wide at its widest point. It covers an area of 435 square miles and reaches a depth of 400 feet in the narrows off the town of Ferrisburgh. Its drainage basin covers 8,234 square miles in the states of New York and Vermont and in the province of Quebec. The average elevation above sea level is 95.5 feet, although it has reached extremes of 92.4 (1908) and 101.89 (1993). The lake, which receives the waters of four of the state's major rivers—the MISSISQUOI, LAMOILLE, WINOOSKI, and OTTER CREEK—drains northward into Quebec's Richelieu River, a tributary of the St. Lawrence. The deep-water channel of the lake marks the Vermont–New York boundary from the Canadian border south to the east bank of the Poultney River at its mouth in East Bay. Missisquoi Bay, the lake's northernmost extension, lies partly in the province of Quebec. A home to Native Americans for thousands of years, the lake, called *Biawbagok* ("the waters in between") by the ABENAKI, was first visited by a European in June 1609, when SAMUEL DE CHAMPLAIN, accompanying an Algonquin war party, saw its broad expanse and supposedly named the body of water for himself. The French established the first European settlement on the lake, FORT SAINTE-ANNE on Isle La Motte, in 1666, although this was not long maintained. The French considered the lake part of their dominions but made no significant effort to colonize it. They began to realize its strategic importance only in the 1730s, when they became alarmed at the expansion of British control in the region north of Albany, New York. This resulted in the construction of Fort St. Frederic at Crown Point in 1731 and Fort Carillon at the later site of FORT TICONDEROGA in 1755, both on the west (now New York) side of the lake, but both fell into British hands with the loss of Canada by the French in 1759. With the advent of peace, from 1761 to 1763 Governor BENNING WENTWORTH of New Hampshire granted charters for fifteen towns covering almost the entire length of the east side of the lake, and settlement began in earnest. The Revolution brought a temporary halt to settlement as the lake once again became a scene of conflict, the most significant events of which were the capture of Fort Ticonderoga by ETHAN ALLEN and the GREEN MOUNTAIN BOYS in May 1775 and the BATTLE OF VALCOUR ISLAND in October 1776, which, although a defeat for the Americans, delayed the British recapture of Ticonderoga until July 1777. The defeat of the British under General JOHN BURGOYNE at Saratoga in October 1777 effectively ended hostilities in the region for the duration of the war. With rapid post-war settlement of the fertile lowlands of the Champlain Valley in Vermont and the exploitation of the state's natural resources, trade began to flourish. The natural direction of this trade followed the lake's flow northward into Canada, not primarily southward toward Albany and New York City, with which there was no water connection. Even during the period of the EMBARGO

ACTS of 1807 to 1809 and the War of 1812, products continued to flow to the traditional northern markets. But with the completion in 1823 of a canal linking the southern extremity of Lake Champlain with the Hudson River, goods began to flow southward and (after the opening of the Erie Canal in 1825) also westward. Burlington became a great lumber port, its waterfront piled high with logs and dense with numerous mills processing not only Vermont timber but also (after the opening of the Chambly Canal on the Richelieu River in 1843 to complete the HUDSON-CHAMPLAIN-RICHELIEU WATERWAY) logs from the endless forests of Canada. By the 1870s, the city was one of the busiest ports in the nation, processing 170 million board feet of lumber per year and seeing up to a thousand boat dockings per year. During the nineteenth century, watercraft on Lake Champlain included not only commercial freight boats but, starting with the steamboat *Vermont* in 1809, numerous passenger vessels. The CHAMPLAIN TRANSPORTATION COMPANY, founded in 1826, had a virtual monopoly on the construction and operation of steamboats on the lake from its shipyard in Shelburne Bay. The vessels eventually attained impressive size, up to 260 feet in length with a displacement of over one thousand tons, and were renowned for their elegance and comfort. The advent of the RAILROADS diminished the importance of steamboats, but integration of their timetables in some instances worked to the benefit of both. The automobile age, however, finally spelled the end of steamboats on the lake. The last survivor, the *TICONDEROGA*, built in 1906 and capable of carrying 1,137 passsengers, made its final run in 1953 and was eventually hauled overland to be exhibited at the SHELBURNE MUSEUM. Its role as a working waterway having ceased, Lake Champlain today is used primarily for recreation. In Vermont, twelve state parks, twelve marinas, and over thirty-five public boat-launch areas dot the lakeshore, in addition to private and municipal lake access sites. Post–World War II plans to reconstruct the CHAMPLAIN WATERWAY so that ocean-going vessels could enter the lake came to naught, as did plans to regulate the lake's natural rise and fall by the construction of dams on the same river. Pollution control has restrained the degradation of the lake's water quality from agricultural runoff and industrial discharge, but

it has also suffered from the invasion of non-native animal and plant species, including ZEBRA MUSSELS and Eurasian watermilfoil. The Lake Champlain Basin Program, a partnership between the states of Vermont and New York, the province of Quebec, and the U.S. Environmental Protection Agency, was created in 1990 to protect and enhance the environmental integrity and social and economic benefits of the Lake Champlain basin. The LAKE CHAMPLAIN MARITIME MUSEUM in Ferrisburgh has exhibits chronicling the military, commercial, and recreational history of the lake, and conserves artifacts brought up from the lake bottom. It also has a modern replica of BENEDICT ARNOLD's gunboat *Philadelphia*, sunk during the Battle of Valcour Island. The remains of the original *Philadelphia*, raised from the lake bottom in 1935, are on display at the Smithsonian Institution in Washington, D.C. The Center for Lake Champlain on the Burlington waterfront contains a Discovery and Learning Center and an Ecosystem Science Laboratory.

Champlain, Samuel de (ca. 1567–1635)

The explorer known as the father of New France, the French colonial empire in North America, Samuel de Champlain established a trading post on the St.

Samuel de Champlain's statue on Isle La Motte.
Vermont Department of Tourism and Marketing

Lawrence River at the present site of the city of Quebec in 1608 and governed it until his death. French settlements grew slowly under Champlain's guidance during the first quarter of the seventeenth century. Interested mainly in exploration to enlarge the fur trade with native people, he resisted colonization plans that might have competed with the fur trade. Attempting to form an alliance with the Algonquin tribes, in June 1609 Champlain and two of his men joined a party of Montagnais and ABENAKI to invade the territory of the Iroquois, their long-time enemy, in the region to the south visible from the peak of the mountain above the French settlement at Hochelaga, today's Montreal. They met two hundred Iroquois near the later site of FORT TICONDEROGA by the lake now known as LAKE CHAMPLAIN, killing several of them. This marked the beginning of warfare between the French and the Iroquois that lasted off and on for ninety years, repeatedly threatening to destroy New France.

Champlain College

Founded in downtown Burlington in 1878, the Burlington Business School was acquired by C. BADER BROUILETTE and Al Jensen in 1956, who changed its name to Champlain College and moved it to the city's "Hill Section," an area of large older homes once the domain of the city's elite. A vigorous campaign of academic expansion, building acquisition, and new construction followed, until today the college is Burlington's premier institution of career education. It offers both four-year and two-year degrees in a variety of majors, and has a co-educational student body of fourteen hundred drawn from thirty-three states and twenty countries. Majors include a range of business, management, computer, media, and education specialties. Average class size is twenty-three, with a sixteen-to-one student-faculty ratio. Most students live in restored Victorian-era mansions acquired in the neighborhood by the college, with the result that the look and feel of the Hill Section has been substantially retained.

Champlain Transportation Company

Founded in October 1826 in Burlington by Luther Loomis and other investors, the Champlain Transportation Company (CTC) entered into active competition with various other LAKE CHAMPLAIN ferry and steamboat organizations the fol-

lowing summer with the launching of the *Franklin*. The CTC proved more successful than its competitors at attracting business, and by 1835 had absorbed or bought up the equipment of the other Lake Champlain steamboat companies. The company grew steadily thereafter, and despite occasional competition from rival groups or individuals, dominated transportation of the lake throughout the nineteenth century. In 1858, the CTC bought control of the Lake George Steamboat Company, and two years later the Delaware and Hudson Railroad acquired ownership of the CTC. The Delaware and Hudson retained control of the CTC until 1937 when, after several years of declining revenues, the railroad sold the company to HORACE W. CORBIN, SR. Service on Lake George ceased in 1939, and steamboat runs on Lake Champlain also decreased throughout the 1940s. In 1948, the CTC ended its steamboat service on Lake Champlain (although a Burlington group acquired and ran the *TICONDEROGA* until she was moved to the SHELBURNE MUSEUM in 1954), replacing steamboats with steel ferries under the control of the new Lake Champlain Transportation Company, which presently operates year-round ferry service on the lake under the ownership of RAY PECOR.

Champlain Valley Exposition

In 1922, after the Essex Center Grange discontinued its eight-year-old agricultural fair, a group of business leaders in Chittenden County organized as the Champlain Valley Exposition, Inc. Known popularly as the Champlain Valley Fair, Vermont's largest fair runs for a week in August at its fair grounds on Pearl Street in Essex Junction, where it continues its original purpose of promoting and celebrating the progress of the Champlain Valley in agriculture, industry, commerce, culture, and education. Not only are agricultural products exhibited for juries to judge their qualities, but vendors of related agricultural machinery display their wares, and carnival rides and musical entertainment are provided. Prize monies of approximately $65,000 are paid to exhibitors and contestants. The buildings and facilities of the Champlain Valley Fair are utilized at other times for concerts by nationally recognized popular artists and specialized exhibitions, such as the annual spring Home Show, when the latest products for home construction and furnishings are exhibited.

Champlain Waterway

A proposed commercial link between LAKE CHAMPLAIN and the ocean via the Richelieu and St. Lawrence rivers, the Champlain Waterway was a dream of many Vermonters from IRA ALLEN to GEORGE AIKEN. In Quebec, a shallow-draft (about 6 feet) canal around the St. Jean rapids on the Richelieu was completed in 1843. Despite few serious engineering obstacles, this channel was never deepened because neither the United States nor Canada wished to facilitate the possible north-south movement of armed forces. In the early part of the twentieth century, economic considerations weighed against the project. For example, despite several lengthy studies, the Army Corps of Engineers never found a positive cost-benefit relation in such a waterway. Other sources of opposition came from Montreal, where business interests feared that a canal terminating at Sorel would effectively draw commerce from Montreal. Southern Vermonters believed that the state as a whole would not benefit. HOWARD C. RICE, for instance, an influential newspaperman from Brattleboro, told the International Joint Commission in 1938: "Burlington might look like a seaport, in fact it might even smell like a seaport at times, but I do not think as a matter of actual fact it would ever be a seaport." The completion of the St. Lawrence Seaway in 1959 brought new life to the concept. The prospect of adding Lake Champlain to the system was very appealing to many Vermonters, especially Senator George Aiken, who worked tirelessly on behalf of what was termed the "Champlain Cut-off" or Champlain Waterway. By this time, however, a strong environmental movement in the Champlain Valley and public recognition of the value of the lake for tourism generated effective opposition. Significant water pollution was deemed an inevitable result of large freighters plying the waterway. By the 1970s, the value of Lake Champlain for recreational purposes far exceeded any economic benefits that might have resulted from a Champlain Waterway. The completion in 1987 of a fixed-span bridge with a clearance of only 55 feet between Rouses Point, New York, and Alburg ended the possibility of ocean-going commerce in Lake Champlain.   *Charles O'Brien*

Chaousarou

This fabulous creature appears in SAMUEL DE CHAMPLAIN's journal account of his journey up LAKE CHAMPLAIN in 1609. His Algonquin guides told Champlain that a large fish lived in the lake: "The longest, as these people told me, is eight or ten feet." Further, they reported it drives off all other fish and has a wonderfully cunning method of catching birds: "It goes into the rushs or weeds which border the lake in several places, and puts its snout out of the water without moving at all, so that when the birds come to light on its snout, thinking that it is the trunk of a tree, the fish is so skillful in closing its snout, which had been half open, that it draws the bird under water by the feet." A cunning fish, indeed, as the native storyteller led Champlain to believe and record in this marvelous first Vermont fish story.

Charleston

Charleston, population 895, a town in Orleans County, was granted by the Vermont legislature in 1780 to Commodore Abraham Whipple of Rhode Island and others. Originally named Navy (by Whipple), the town changed its name to Charleston in 1825, probably for Whipple's defense of Charleston, South Carolina, during the Revolution. Solidly rural, the town is bisected from east to west by the broad, swampy valley of the Clyde River. The largest body of water is 544-acre Echo Lake, which is connected by a short watercourse with much larger Seymour Lake in the neighboring town of Morgan. The two settlements of West Charleston and East Charleston are both on Route 105 as it follows the course of the Clyde.

Charlotte

Charlotte (pronounced shar-LOT), population 3,569, a town in Chittenden County, was granted by BENNING WENTWORTH in 1762 and named for Charlotte Sophia of Mecklenburg-Strelitz, the wife of George III. The town lies entirely within the fertile Champlain lowlands and is extensively farmed, although its proximity to the Burlington metropolitan area has resulted in recent large-lot residential development. The villages of West Charlotte and East Charlotte are the major settlements, although Thompson's Point and Cedar Beach on LAKE CHAMPLAIN have long been the site of exclusive summer colonies. Nearby, a toll ferry (not operating in winter), founded in 1791 by John McNeil, runs from McNeil's Cove to Essex, New York. The highest point in town is 980-foot Mount Philo, site of Vermont's first STATE PARK, which affords an extensive view of the Champlain Valley, the Adirondacks, and the GREEN MOUNTAINS. In 1849, during the building of the Rutland Railroad, the skeleton of a beluga whale was found near Thompson's Point Road. This skeleton is now in the Perkins Museum of Geology at the UNIVERSITY OF VERMONT.

Charterhouse of the Transfiguration

Located in Sandgate, the Charterhouse of the Transfiguration is the only monastery of the cloistered Carthusian Order in North America and one of only twenty-six Carthusian monasteries in the world. The first American charterhouse monastery was founded in 1950 at a farmhouse (Sky Farm) in Whitingham, near the Vermont-Massachusetts border. Ten years later, the monks moved to the slopes of Mount Equinox. The late Dr. Joseph C. Davidson, former vice president of Union Carbide Corporation, and his wife, gave 7,000 acres on the mountain to the monks. The Carthusians sold their other property and began making plans for a permanent building, which was begun in 1967. The architect was Victor Christ-Janer of New Canaan, Connecticut, who designed the windowless structure to last nine hundred years. The large edifice is made of twenty-four hundred 3-ton blocks of Barre granite. One wing is for monks and the other for brothers, with the chapel, chapter house, and refectory in the center. The Vermont Charterhouse was completed and canonically closed to the world in 1971. The monastery is a quiet, austere, monolithic building, set among the seclusion and tranquility of the heavily wooded southwest shoulder of Mount Equinox. The remote location of the monastery underlines the strict, austere life of the inhabitants. Here about twenty monks lead solitary lives in individual cells.

David Blow

Chelsea

Chelsea, population 1,250, a town in Orange County, was granted by the Vermont legislature in 1781 as Turnersburgh, after Bela Turner, one of the grantees, and changed to Chelsea in 1788, probably after Chelsea, Connecticut. It has been the county SHIRE TOWN since 1796. The landscape is hilly and cut by many watercourses, of which the main one is the First Branch of the WHITE RIVER, which crosses the town from north to south. The summits of Holt Hill, 1,780 feet, and Beacon Hill, 1,747 feet, rise on either side of the river and loom over the town's single village, Chelsea, which is unique in Vermont for having two commons. One, the North Common, was established by the town in 1795, and the other, the South Common, was given by a local citizen in 1802 as part of a plan to build a courthouse and jail. The central part of the village is on the National Register of Historic Places. The town has always had a farm-based economy, although the number of dairy farms has in recent years shrunk to about a dozen.

Chester

Chester, population 3,044, a town in Windsor County, was granted by BENNING WENTWORTH in 1754 as the town of Flamstead (after the town of that name in England) and, the grantees not taking up their land, regranted to a separate group of grantees in 1761 as New Flamstead. But in 1766 it was patented by New York State as Chester to settlers who had moved there, the name deriving from the eldest son of King George III (who was almost four years old at the time), one of whose hereditary titles was Earl of Chester. Eventually the grant and the patent were reconciled and the New York name permanently adopted. The town, which contains several peaks in the 1,700- to 2,000-foot range in its western section, is cut from north to south by the Williams River, which is joined at Chester village and Chester Depot by its Middle and South branches. Chester village is filled with an exceptional array of well-maintained Victorian buildings (over 150 are on the National Register of Historic Places) and has become a tourist destination, as the antique stores, gift shops, inns, and restaurants attest. Chester Depot is the turn-around point for the *Green Mountain Flyer*, a vintage excursion train that makes four 26-mile round trips daily from Bellows Falls between June and October. North of Chester Depot is what is called the Stone Village, an unusual collection of early nineteenth-century houses faced in large blocks of gneiss quarried from nearby Mount Flamstead. Chester was the home of the notorious CLARENCE ADAMS, the "gentleman burglar" whose nighttime exploits baffled the community for sixteen years.

Children, Care and Advocacy of

In recent years, Vermont has become well known as a state that in public policy and in community programs takes very good care of its children, achieving top ratings from social scientists and the popular press. Today's children's advocacy and services are built on a forty-year-old foundation. During the 1960s, a sub-committee of the Governor's Commission on Children and Youth was formed to create what became Vermont's first set of regulations for early childhood programs. Chaired by Julie Lepeschkin (1915–1980), this subcommittee met in communities throughout the state to design regulations that would set high standards for the health, safety, and education of young children in non-public school settings. Dee Dee Jameson served with this group and also worked with Lepeschkin to develop the UNIVERSITY OF VERMONT's Laboratory Preschool, which served as a model of quality education for young children. In 1964, Jameson founded Saxon Hill School in Jericho, today Vermont's oldest parent cooperative preschool. Corinne Weil Mattuck (1909–1995) of GODDARD COLLEGE's faculty in early childhood and psychology developed and directed the Clockhouse, a model campus nursery school described by a grateful parent as "a mecca." She was a contributor to *Parent's Magazine* from 1942 to 1962 and was a national consultant to Headstart and an evaluator for the National Project on Followthrough, contributing to quality programming for young children. The Visiting Nurses' Association opened one of Vermont's early on-site, business-supported child-care centers in Burlington. Jeanne Simon (d. 1980), artist and early childhood educator, designed this center and served as consultant to the staff for several years. In 1983, several Vermont professionals, including Cheryl Mitchell, then director of the Addison County Parent Child Center; Amy Davenport, Esq.; Lee Lauber, child care director; Ken Libertoff, executive director of the Vermont Association of Mental Health; and Dee Dee Jameson joined with others to found the Vermont Children's Forum, an advocacy group whose members continue to represent a variety of programs for children and families and speak with one voice, promoting public support for all of Vermont's children and their families. Today's programs such as Success by Six ensure that Vermont's children and families will continue to benefit from Vermont's historic commitment to their well being.

Dee Dee Jameson

Chimney Point

Located in Addison County at the narrows of LAKE CHAMPLAIN, opposite Crown Point, New York, Chimney Point was called POINT À LA CHEVELURE, "Scalp Point," by French settlers in the 1730s. The French withdrew from the Champlain Valley at the conclusion of the Seven Years' or French and Indian Wars (1754–1763), burning their buildings, so the story goes, so that only the chimneys remained when the British moved in, giving the place its English name. Licensed ferries began to run across the lake from this point in 1785, and it is now the site of the first bridge over Lake Champlain, built in 1929. The eighteenth-century tavern at Chimney Point, visited by Thomas Jefferson and James Madison in 1791, has been restored and enlarged into a museum celebrating the Native American and French heritage of Vermont from prehistoric times to the present.

Ann E. Cooper

Chiott, Henry (1841–1907)

A Burlington native and owner of the Chiott Boat Works at the foot of King Street, Henry Chiott bought a gasoline internal combustion engine from the Sine Motor Company in Detroit in 1894 and installed it in a 25-foot runabout built for it. Chiott's boat was the first gasoline engine to operate on LAKE CHAMPLAIN. The two-cycle, four-horsepower engine with no muffler allowed the boat to cruise at 8 to 10 miles per hour. Lakeside dwellers claimed they could hear it from miles away over the lake. This noisy craft was also the first registered inboard motorboat in Vermont.

David Blow

Chipman, Nathaniel (1752–1843)

A jurist and conservative political leader, Nathaniel Chipman was born in Salisbury, Connecticut. A Yale graduate, he served in the Continental Army at Valley Forge and the Battle of Monmouth. In 1779, Chipman moved to Tinmouth with the intention of becoming the oracle of law in that state. Few people dominated the legal development of a state to the extent that Chipman did in Vermont. Instrumental in moving Vermont into the Union in 1791, he held numerous positions, from state's attorney to U.S. senator, from assemblyman to chief justice of the state supreme court. Three times he served on the committee revising the state's statute law, was a member of the COUNCIL OF CENSORS and a United States district court judge,

compiled the key decisions of the state's supreme court in one of the first collections of case law, and wrote a landmark legal treatise defending the sanctity of property. In the assembly, Chipman led the opposition to the THOMAS CHITTENDEN– ETHAN ALLEN faction, which he saw as dangerously radical. He also attempted to terminate Vermont's unicameral legislature. Chipman regularly resigned from influential positions in order to make more money in private practice, repeatedly returning to public service once his coffers were restored. Chipman ended his career as professor of law at MIDDLEBURY COLLEGE.

Michael A. Bellesiles

Chittenden

Chittenden, population 1,182, a town in Rutland County, was granted by the Vermont legislature in 1780 and named for THOMAS CHITTENDEN, who had been elected Vermont's first governor two years earlier. The state's second-largest town in area (only Stowe is larger), Chittenden lies directly on the main spine of the GREEN MOUNTAINS and, except for a ribbon of settlement along the western border, is completely within the GREEN MOUNTAIN NATIONAL FOREST. Six summits top three thousand feet, of which the tallest is Farr Peak (3,522 feet). Chittenden Reservoir (674 acres) lies in the hills above tiny Chittenden village. Although production of iron occurred in the early part of the nineteenth century, the main activity in Chittenden has historically been logging. Today many of the residents commute to jobs in the Rutland area.

Chittenden, Lucius Eugene (1824–1900)

Born in Williston, Lucius E. Chittenden, a great-grandson of Governor THOMAS CHITTENDEN, was a lawyer and public official. He studied law with his uncle Norman Whitmore, the corporation lawyer Corydon Beckworth, and the lawyer-poet JOHN GODFREY SAXE, and attended the lectures on law given by Supreme Court Judge Bates Turner in St. Albans before opening a law office in Burlington in 1845. Though early a Democrat, Chittenden rapidly gained prominence in the anti-slavery movement, editing *The Free-Soil Courier* and chairing the FREE-SOIL state committee. He served as Chittenden County senator (1856–1860) and headed a group of young legislators who met in the evenings and called themselves the Third House, passing mock legislation reflecting the comic nature of the law-making process. At a peace conference in Washington in 1861, he met Salmon P. Chase, who later became secretary of the treasury and appointed Chittenden to the office of register of the treasury during President Lincoln's first term. At the outset of the Civil War, Chittenden signed bonds and other official papers nonstop for nearly a week, ensuring that money was available for the war effort, and shortly left federal service on account of health problems brought on by the effort. After the war, Chittenden moved to New York City, where he practiced law for the rest of his life. He wrote a memoir of Abraham Lincoln and his autobiography, *Personal Reminiscences* (1893), which includes a discussion of his part in the founding of the REPUBLICAN PARTY. His writings on national and Vermont history reveal "a fondness for the dramatic as well as a bias for Vermont," covering subjects such as medical jurisprudence, RAILROADS, deer, and science fiction. Catching bibliomania in his twenties, he collected a valuable library of rare books relating to early Vermont that the UNIVERSITY OF VERMONT purchased through subscription. He died in Burlington.   *Paul Gillies*

Chittenden, Martin (1769–1840)

Son of THOMAS CHITTENDEN, Vermont's first governor, Martin Chittenden served ten years in Congress and two terms as governor. Born in Salisbury, Connecticut, he moved with his family to Vermont in 1774. After graduating from Dartmouth College in 1789, he farmed and speculated in land while active in town politics. Prominent in the Jericho militia, he rose to major general of the state militia in 1799, and represented Jericho in the state assembly for eight terms between 1790 and 1802. From 1803 until 1813, he served in Congress, and as a Federalist opposed Republican diplomacy and voted against the War of 1812. The state's voters, however, were divided on the war issue, as was shown in the 1813 gubernatorial election that pitted Chittenden against JONAS GALUSHA. This was Chittenden's third try against Galusha, and although Galusha managed almost a three-hundred-vote plurality, he lacked a popular majority, and Chittenden was elected governor by the Governor's Council and the General Assembly. He was re-elected in 1814 under similar circumstances. One of Chittenden's first official acts as governor was to order back to Vermont units of the state

militia that were stationed in Plattsburgh to defend against an imminent British invasion. The officers of the brigade refused to obey. The subsequent naval victory by Commodore THOMAS MACDONOUGH in the BATTLE OF PLATTSBURGH BAY and the celebration of the war as a triumph of American arms discredited the Federalists, and Chittenden was defeated in 1815, becoming the last Federalist governor of Vermont. Except for 1818 and 1821, when he served as town representative from Williston, and 1821 to 1823 when he served as probate judge, he held no further office.

Chittenden, Thomas (1730–1797)

The first governor of Vermont, Thomas Chittenden was born in East Guilford (now Madison), Connecticut, where he attended the common school. He married Elizabeth Meigs and moved to Salisbury, Connecticut, in 1749, where he prospered as a farmer. He was elected to many local government positions in Salisbury and served as an officer in the Connecticut militia from 1763 to 1770, reaching the rank of lieutenant colonel. Chittenden served in the Connecticut General Assembly (1764–1772) and was appointed justice of the peace for Litchfield County in 1773. In the spring of 1774, he and Elizabeth moved with their ten children to a new farmstead at Williston in the New Hampshire grants on land he bought from the ONION RIVER LAND COMPANY, the land-speculating business of his old Salisbury friends, the Allen brothers. Following the outbreak of the Revolutionary War, the Chittendens withdrew south from the threat of a British invasion of the northern sector of the grants and became active in the Vermont "New State" movement, attending the Dorset conventions in 1776. Chittenden helped to draft the first Vermont constitution in the spring of 1777. Following its adoption at the Windsor convention in July, 1777, he was appointed to serve on a statewide Council of Safety, which acted as an interim government during the British invasion of the Champlain Valley. Chittenden was elected chairman of the Council of Safety on July 11, 1777, and subsequently was elected to serve as Vermont's first governor in March 1778. He was elected governor for nineteen terms, until his death in 1797. His only political defeat took place in the 1789 to 1790 term when the legislature refused to elect him because of unfounded rumors involving an IRA ALLEN land grant that

Thomas Chittenden, Vermont's first governor. Vermont Department of Tourism and Marketing

Chittenden had approved. A shrewd and intuitive leader, Chittenden played a critically important role in early Vermont. During the Revolutionary War, he helped to hold the new state together by controlling domestic unrest and by directing such actions as the allocation of key resources and the sale of of state lands. He participated in the HALDIMAND NEGOTIATIONS with the British in Canada in an effort to forestall further military invasions from the north. After the war ended, he presided over Vermont's affairs as an independent republic until it became the fourteenth state in 1791. He was principally responsible in the 1780s for initiating the Betterment Acts to protect settlers who had improved their land from the conflicts of title disputes. Thereafter, serving as a transitional leader to a younger generation of state politicians while Vermont became the nation's fastest-growing state with a population of 155,000 by 1800, Chittenden's final years in office were less dramatic than the years of war with Britain and conflict with New York. In addition to serving as Vermont's governor, Thomas Chittenden was an extremely successful farmer and an astute land speculator. He died in Williston. One son, MARTIN CHITTENDEN, served as a controversial Federalist governor of Vermont from 1813 to 1814.   *Frank Smallwood*

Chivaree

The chivaree was a common neighborhood event during the late nineteenth and early twentieth centuries that marked a newly married couple's entry into the life of the community. On a night shortly after a couple's marriage when their house was dark and they were presumably long asleep, a group of adult neighbors would quietly assemble under the bedroom windows. On a signal, they fired guns, clattered cowbells, banged on saw blades, using whatever was available to make a startling amount of noise. Eventually the newlyweds would dress and come to the door. In some instances the group demanded that the couple participate in a form of ritual humiliation, such as bringing them to a village center where the husband would push his wife down the main street in a wheelbarrow. Whatever the course the evening followed, it ended with hospitality at the newlyweds' home. Vermonters who settled the upper Midwest brought this social custom with them, where it became known as a "belling."

Greg Sharrow

Church of God in Christ
The first African-American church established in Vermont, the Church of God in Christ began holding services in 1946 at 142 Archibald Street, Burlington. A Pentacostalist church, the Church of God in Christ was affiliated with the national church of the same name. In August 1951, the Burlington church's members hosted the week-long seventh annual convention of the national Church of God in Christ. The Burlington church disbanded about 1960.

David Blow

Circus Smirkus
Rob Mermin founded Circus Smirkus in 1987 in Greensboro in cooperation with JAY CRAVEN and CATAMOUNT FILM AND ARTS CENTER to provide a venue for children and adults to collaborate in learning and performing the traditional arts of the circus. Kids and adults work as performers and roustabouts for no cherry pie (circus lingo for overtime pay). Today's program consists of school workshops and residencies around Vermont and elsewhere, a summer camp for two hundred beginners, and constant rehearsals, leading to a six-week New England tour with ten shows weekly by a company of fifty performers aged eight to nineteen. Since 1989, Circus Smirkus has hosted children from Latvia, Ukraine, Mongolia, and eight other countries, as well as ten Native American tribes and fourteen states. Alla Youdin, a graduate of the Moscow Theatre Institute, for-

Governor George Aiken (center) reviewing Civilian Conservation Corps Company 1141 in Bellows Falls, April 1940. Special Collections, Bailey/Howe Library, University of Vermont

mer member of the Moscow Circus, and a performer with the Ringling Brothers, Barnum and Bailey Circus, is currently head coach and artistic director of Circus Smirkus.

Civilian Conservation Corps
The Civilian Conservation Corps, or CCC, one of President Franklin D. Roosevelt's most popular New Deal programs, was organized in Vermont as a section of the Second CCC District of the First Corps or New England area on May 18, 1933, with FORT ETHAN ALLEN in Colchester as district headquarters. The CCC program assisted economically disadvantaged young men, often from cities in Rhode Island, Massachusetts, and New York. They earned thirty dollars per month, with a large share sent home to their families. Organized as military-style companies, CCC crews lived in small barracks at campsites scattered throughout the length of the state. Despite a fair share of Vermonters expressing skepticism of federal work and relief programs, as well as some initial administrative confusion, the CCC accomplished much in Vermont. PERRY MERRILL, commissioner of forestry and state director of the CCC in Vermont, aggressively used the CCC to implement his already formulated plans for flood control, forestry conservation, and recreation developments on state land. Allotted 750 places to fill four camps, Vermont eventually claimed thirty camps that employed a total of 40,868 men. Merrill directed over

ninety CCC projects. Crews built bridges, dams, roads, power lines, guard rails, stone walls, fireplaces, springs, reservoirs, trails, channels, levees, and latrines. They improved 38,083 acres of forest, constructed 119,227 square yards of parking areas and parking overlooks, and stocked ponds and waterways with 214,500 fish. The 1135th Company in Underhill managed the region's first soil conservation project. Under the direction of CHARLES LORD of Stowe, CCC crews constructed the first ski trails on MOUNT MANSFIELD, Ascutney Mountain, and Burke Mountain. Major projects included the Winooski Valley flood control plan (the largest single CCC project in the nation) that built dams and channels in Barre, Wrightsville, Montpelier, and Waterbury; and construction of 105 miles of forest roads, ten fire towers, and eight lookout cabins. CCC projects improved management of the GREEN MOUNTAIN NATIONAL FOREST, state and municipal forests, and forest parks. Large blocks of evergreens planted in neat rows, steep, winding ski trails, backcountry roads, and grassy parks with fieldstone lodges or camps are a few of the still-evident accomplishments of the Civilian Conservaton Corps. Their work from 1933 to 1942 helped lay the foundation for Vermont's valuable tourism industry.

Michael Sherman and Fred Stetson

Civilian Public Service
Conscientious objectors (COs) during World War II had three options under the

Selective Service and Training Act of 1940: non-combat duty in the armed forces; imprisonment (several Vermonters chose this option); and civilian public service, a commitment to perform "work of national importance under civilian direction" by the historic "peace churches"—Church of the Brethren, Mennonites, and the Society of Friends (Quakers). Initially, men enrolled in CPS were assigned to conservation and forestry work, based at abandoned CIVILIAN CONSERVATION CORPS camps. Manpower shortages produced by the draft, and complaints that the COs were being hidden away from public view, led to expansions of CPS: assignment to hospitals, dairies and dairy testing services, training schools, public health services, medical research activities (in which COs served as "guinea pigs" for experiments in lice control, diet, dehydration, and the like), administrative services, the U.S. Weather Bureau, and Coast and Geodetic Surveys in thirty-seven states, Alaska, Hawaii, Puerto Rico, and the Virgin Islands. CPS 87, a "detached unit" from CPS 32 at West Campton, New Hampshire, operated at the BRATTLEBORO RETREAT from February 1943 to March 1946. Sponsored by the American Friends Service Committee, a total of forty-three men (some with wives) from seven states, and fifteen different religious denominations (or none), performed ward work, housekeeping duties, agricultural labor on the retreat's farm, and other non-medical or paramedical duties. The unit consisted of twelve to twenty-five men at any one time and had its own organization. An assistant director served as a liaison with Dr. George A. Elliott, chief of the medical staff of the retreat, and with the AFSC. An education director coordinated training, educational, and social activities of the unit. CPS men and their wives—with a few exceptions—lived on the grounds of the retreat, served without pay, were allowed limited time off, and were required to work for the duration of the war plus six months. CPS units assigned to mental hospitals around the nation have been credited with initiating reforms and techniques in the humane handling of mental patients that permanently changed the standards for patient care in the mental health profession. CPS 100.13 was assigned to testing dairy herds for certain diseases and recording milk productivity. A total of fifteen men—three to five at any one time working throughout the state—performed this duty from September 1943 to the end of the war. Members of the milk-testing unit lived and traveled on their own, reporting to agricultural agents of the Extension Service and members of the Dairy Herd Improvement Association.

Michael Sherman

Civil Unions

Responding to a decision by the Vermont Supreme Court in *Baker v. State*, 170 Vt. 194, 1999 Vt. Lexis 405 (S. Ct. 1999), the 1999 session of the Vermont General Assembly promulgated an act relating to civil unions. The Supreme Court held that under the Common Benefits Clause of the Vermont Constitution, which, in pertinent part, reads, "That government is, or ought to be, instituted for the common benefit, protection, and security of the people, nation, or community, and not for the particular emolument or advantage of any single person, family, or set of persons, who are a part only of that community . . ." (chapter I, article 7), the state is therefore constitutionally required to extend to couples of the same sex the common benefits and protections that flow from the marriages of heterosexual couples under Vermont law. The court advised the legislature to either include same-sex couples within the current marriage laws or provide a parallel "domestic partnership" system or some equivalent statutory alternative. The legislature elected the latter system, creating the status of civil union that mirrored the process, prohibitions, rights, and responsibilities concerning the marriage and divorce of heterosexual couples. As with marriage, same-sex couples must file a certificate of civil union with the town clerk in the community where an official who is also authorized to officiate at a marriage has legally certified the ceremony of civil union. Termination of the union, as with the termination of a marriage, requires a decree from a Vermont family court. The grounds for such dissolution, as well as the criteria used for resolution of property or custody disputes, follow those employed in the dissolution of traditional marriages. The civil unions law was one of the contributing causes of the protest movement known as TAKE BACK VERMONT.

Edward J. Cashman

Civil War Flags

Vermont's Civil War volunteer regiments were typically presented a pair of colors, one national flag and one regimental flag. As flags became worn from service and required replacement, the retired flags were displayed in the VERMONT STATE HOUSE. At war's end, all flags were returned to the adjutant general and exhibited in legislative chambers. In 1872, the colors were placed in glass cabinets in the House vestibule. In the 1980s, half of the sixty-eight colors were conserved. The remainder still await the process.

Donald Wickman

Civil War Hospitals

The U.S. Army operated 192 general hospitals during the Civil War, 16 of them in the Department of the East, 3 of those in Vermont. Governor Frederick Holbrook took credit for convincing President Lincoln and Secretary of War Stanton to establish general hospitals under army control far from battlefields to speed recuperation and rehabilitation of Union soldiers. Brattleboro General Hospital opened June 1, 1863, on the mustering grounds for the Vermont First and Second Brigades, using refurbished barracks. Under the command of EDWARD J. PHELPS, it treated 4,402 soldiers before closing on October 5, 1865. The hospital was auctioned off to the Agricultural Society of Brattleboro and is currently the site of Brattleboro High School. The Marine Hospital in Burlington began receiving sick and wounded soldiers in May 1862. Built in 1856 to 1858 two miles south of the business district, it was commissioned as an army general hospital in April 1863 and renamed Baxter General Hospital in September 1864. Commanded by Dr. S. W. Thayer, surgeon general of Vermont, it treated 2,406 patients before closing in July 1865. The building was sold to the Home for Destitute Children and was later razed to make room for a shopping center on Shelburne Road. Sloan General Hospital opened April 25, 1864. Located on a plateau above downtown Montpelier, its twenty-four hospital buildings were arranged in a circle, connected by covered pavilions—a prototype of the military hospital plan developed during the Civil War. Surgeon in charge was HENRY JANES, chief medical officer at Gettysburg, noted for his preference for "excision" over amputation. Sloan treated 1,670 patients and was noted for a high recovery rate. After closing December 12, 1865, the buildings were converted to use as dormitories and classrooms for the Montpelier Methodist Seminary. Several are still in use as private residences in the College Street area of Montpelier.

Michael Sherman

Clarendon

Clarendon, population 2,811, a town in Rutland County, was granted by BENNING WENTWORTH in 1761 and is thought to have been named for one or another of the four men who successively held the title of earl of Clarendon, although the title had been vacant for eight years when the town was created. Conceivably the name came from Clarendon in Wiltshire, or Clarendon House at Oxford University. The town lies in the northern reaches of the TACONIC MOUNTAINS and the VALLEY OF VERMONT, which here moderate into a series of low hills bisected by OTTER CREEK and the Castleton River. Although only a few miles from the city of Rutland to the north, Clarendon is still primarily rural. The main settlements are North Clarendon, near the Rutland city line and so to a degree suburbanized, Clarendon village, and Clarendon Springs, a fashionable watering place in the mid-nineteenth century.

Clark, Charles Edgar (1843–1922)

Naval officer and commander of the battleship *Oregon* during the Spanish-American War, Charles Clark was born in Bradford and attended the district school and Bradford Academy. In 1860, through the influence of Senator JUSTIN MORRILL, he received an appointment to the United States Naval Academy, graduating in 1863. During the Civil War he served under the command of Admiral David Farragut in engagements on the Mississippi River and the coast of Texas and at the war's conclusion was on duty at the Pacific and West India stations. In March 1898, having achieved the rank of captain after serving commendably in a wide range of postings, he was given command of the battleship *Oregon* and took the ship on a 14,000-mile voyage from San Francisco through the Straits of Magellan to join the Atlantic Squadron under the command of Admiral William Sampson. Joining the blockade of Santiago de Cuba, the *Oregon* participated in the destruction of the Spanish Atlantic fleet and Clark was particularly commended for his part in the beaching of the *Cristóbal Colón*, the pride of the Spanish fleet. As "Clark of the Oregon," he became, along with fellow Vermonter

GEORGE DEWEY, one of the best known and most admired officers of the United States Navy. With the removal of any Spanish threat to the Atlantic coast, Clark was assigned command of a "Flying Squadron" of battleships to proceed to the coast of Spain. The squadron proved unnecessary and never went to sea. Clark was promoted to rear admiral in 1902 and retired for age in 1905. A portrait of Clark in his Navy whites posed on the bridge of the *Oregon* hangs in the VERMONT STATE HOUSE at Montpelier.

Clark, Isaac (1749–1822)

Best known for his leadership of Vermont's troops during the War of 1812, Castleton's Isaac Clark had a public and military career that spanned more than a half century and involved many of the major events of Vermont's formative decades. As a militia man during the American Revolution, Clark fought at the BATTLE OF BENNINGTON and participated in the 1777 recapture of FORT TICONDEROGA. Clark took part in the HALDIMAND NEGOTIATIONS with the British to discuss Vermont's possible return to the British Empire. Intelligence agents sent into Vermont in 1782 to learn about Vermont's participation in the negotiations reported him "a man of low character." After the Revolution, he represented Castleton in the Vermont General Assembly (1784, 1787, and 1796–1799), served as judge of the Rutland County court (1806–1811), and was elected to the COUNCIL OF CENSORS (1806–1813). Clark married twice, first in 1779 to Governor THOMAS CHITTENDEN's daughter, Hannah (1755–1789), and, following her death, to a woman known only as Annie. At the onset of the War of 1812, Clark was appointed colonel and commander of the U.S. Eleventh Infantry Regiment, Champlain District. He established the army's headquarters in Burlington at present-day Battery Park. Clark's regiment patrolled the Vermont border to thwart British raiders and American smugglers. He led the attack on St.-Armand, Quebec, on October 12, 1813, and joined the attack on Lacolle, Quebec, on March 30, 1814. Colonel Clark's command ended with his arrest on July 12, 1814, for an alleged recruiting infraction. He was never formally charged and received an honorable discharge. Clark retired to a quiet life on his farm in Castleton after 1814 until his death at the age of 73.

Karen Campbell

Clarke, De Witt Clinton (1811–1870)

A newspaper editor, railroad booster, and behind-the-scenes political figure for the state's WHIG and REPUBLICAN PARTIES, De Witt Clinton Clarke was born in Granville, New York. A lawyer by training, he owned and edited the *BURLINGTON FREE PRESS* from 1848 to 1853 (introducing its first daily edition in 1848), and the *Burlington Times* from 1858 to 1861, earning a reputation as a gifted, combative, and partisan editorial stylist. He served as secretary of the Vermont senate from 1840 to 1853, and as Vermont quartermaster general from 1842 to 1851, under Whig patronage. In the late 1840s, a time when Vermont was strongly influenced by antiCatholic and "KNOW-NOTHING" sentiment, Clarke and his wife Caroline, a painter and novelist, became notable converts to the Catholic faith. Clarke became executive clerk of the United States Senate in 1861, a position he held until his retirement in 1868. He died in Burlington two years later.

Gene Sessions

Cleghorn, Sarah (1876–1959)

A Virginian, Sarah Cleghorn and her family moved to Manchester when she was a child. She graduated from Burr and Burton Seminary and attended Radcliffe College. A suffragist, pacifist, and humanitarian, she joined the Socialist party at the age of thirty-five. Her *Portraits and Protests*, a volume of what she called "burning poems," included "The Golf Links": they "lie so near the mill / That almost every day / The laboring children can look out / And see the men at play." Her "sunbonnet poems," on the other hand, rendered a portrait of an idyllic rural Vermont. She published hundreds of poems in periodicals, plus two novels—*The Turnpike Lady* (1907) and *The Spinster* (1916)—and an autobiography, *Threescore* (1936).

Richard Sweterlitsch

Clement, John P. (1893–1968)

A leader in twentieth-century efforts to preserve and interpret Vermont's history, John P. Clement was born in Rutland into a prominent family with ties to the city's MARBLE, RAILROAD, and banking interests. After serving as a soldier in France during World War I, he attended the Sorbonne in Paris, where he took a law degree and became an acquaintance of several American expatriate writers of the so-called Lost Generation. Back in Vermont in the early 1930s, he led efforts in the state for the repeal of the Eighteenth Amendment, serving as secretary of the Vermont Association Against the Prohibition Amendment. He took a leading role in the VERMONT HISTORICAL SOCIETY as editor of its *Proceedings* from 1930 to 1932 and as acting director in 1936, the year in which he also became the first director of the federal Historic Records Survey of Vermont, a program of the Works Progress Administration. He was a founding member of the American Association for State and Local History and of the Society of American Archivists, and encouraged historical preservation projects at FORT TICONDEROGA, MOUNT INDEPENDENCE, and the HUBBARDTON BATTLEfield. From 1959 to 1965 he served as president of the Vermont Historical Society. He was a director of the *RUTLAND HERALD*, and also worked full time for that newspaper beginning in 1961 as a copy editor, headline writer, and author of a weekly column entitled "One Hundred Years Ago this Week in Rutland."   *Gene Sessions*

Clement, Percival W. (1846–1927)

Born in Rutland into substantial wealth from his father's mercantile and MARBLE manufacturing businesses, Percival Clement served one term as governor (1919–1921) that was notable for his opposition to WOMEN'S SUFFRAGE and to the state's prohibition of the sale of alcoholic beverages. He was educated by private tutors, and graduated from St. Paul's School in Concord, New Hampshire, and Trinity College in Hartford, Connecticut. In 1868, he joined his father's marble firm, becoming a partner in 1871. He was also president of the Clement National Bank and the Rutland Board of Trade. His business interests expanded to include the Rutland Railroad, the Bristol Railroad, the *RUTLAND HERALD*, and several New York City hotels. In 1892, he was elected Rutland house representative as a Republican and in 1897, 1898, 1911, and 1912 served as mayor of Rutland. In 1900, he was elected senator from Rutland County. Denied the Republican nomination for governor in 1902, he bolted the party to run on a Local Option ticket advocating the repeal of state prohibition and allowing towns to vote independently on the question of permitting the sale of alcoholic beverages. Although the Republican gubernatorial candidate was denied an electoral majority for the first time since the organization of the REPUBLICAN PARTY, the candi-

date, JOHN GRIFFITH MCCULLOUGH, captured a plurality and was elected by the legislature. Local option, Clement's cause, triumphed. In 1908, he sought election as a Democrat but failed to match his 1902 totals. Returning to the Republican party, he served as Rutland mayor and was appointed to state boards and commissions. In 1918, he won a four-man gubernatorial primary by eight hundred votes and coasted to victory in the general election. As governor, Clement refused to call a special session of the legislature to allow Vermont to become the deciding state to ratify the women's suffrage amendment to the United States Constitution, witnessed the nation undo his local-option efforts by adopting prohibition, and promoted bonuses for those drafted into World War I military service. After his term expired in 1921, he returned to his business interests.

Coast Guard on Lake Champlain

First seasonally based on LAKE CHAMPLAIN in 1937, the U.S. Coast Guard station on the Burlington waterfront operated a 50-foot rescue boat that motored each summer to Vermont from its home base on Staten Island, New York. The boat and crew tended 143 short-range aids to navigation, including 103 buoys on the lake. Previously lighthouse keepers and buoy tenders had been hired from lakeshore communities by the U.S. Department of Commerce. In 1941, the Burlington Coast Guard station was upgraded to a year-round base. In 1949, an additional 63-foot craft was sent to the Burlington station during the boating season to aid in search, rescue, and lake patrol operations. In 1993, a new million-dollar Coast Guard station was erected on the Burlington lakefront.   *David Blow*

Coates, John Walter (1880–1941)

A poet and bibliographer, John Walter Coates was born near Lowville, New York. After operating GENERAL STORES in East Calais and North Montpelier, in 1926 he founded *Driftwind*, a journal specializing in contemporary and historical Vermont poetry, and established the Driftwind Press to publish limited editions of literary works. Coates published several volumes of his own work and also edited *Vermont Verse: An Anthology* (1931). He served on the VERMONT COMMISSION ON COUNTRY LIFE and compiled an extensive *Bibliography of Vermont Poetry* that the VER-

mont HISTORICAL SOCIETY published in part after his death. The UNIVERSITY OF VERMONT awarded him an honorary LL.D. in 1938.   *J. Kevin Graffagnino*

Cochran Family of Skiers

The only American family to have four children on the U.S. Ski Team, the Cochrans have operated a small ski area in Richmond since 1960. Patriarch Gordon S. "Mickey" Cochran played football and baseball at the UNIVERSITY OF VERMONT before serving in World War II, and managed the Ascutney Ski Area in the late 1950s. After moving to Richmond in 1960 to work as an engineer, Mickey and wife Ginny installed a small rope tow on the slope behind the family's house. In 1961, Ginny offered her first lessons to area children on the slope, and the Cochrans expanded the facility significantly in 1966. All four of the Cochran's children went on to become champion skiers. Barbara Ann was the 1972 Olympic gold medalist in slalom and U.S. national champion in the slalom and giant slalom. Robert and Marilyn also competed in the 1972 Olympics. Linda was the top American finisher in the 1976 Olympic slalom and giant slalom. The four children altogether amassed seven World Cup wins and fifteen national championships. Mickey was the alpine director of the U.S. Ski Team during the 1973 to 1974 ski season, and coach of the University of Vermont ski team throughout the 1970s. In 1999, the Cochran's Ski Area became a non-profit organization. After Barbara Ann's Olympic victory, a granite monument was placed on the Richmond town green honoring the Cochran family. At its dedication, GEORGE AIKEN likened the Cochran children to maple syrup and MORGAN HORSES, calling them "Vermont's finest products."

Paul Searles

Colburn, Francis (1909–1984)

Though perhaps best remembered as a Vermont humorist and raconteur, Francis Colburn was also a prolific artist and educator. He was born in Fairfax to John E. and Florence Reed Colburn and attended schools in Burlington and the UNIVERSITY OF VERMONT. After additional training at the Art Students League in New York, he returned to Vermont, where landscapes and people served as the subjects of his most successful paintings. His stylized and sometimes introspective works were exhibited at venues such as the

Corcoran Gallery, the Whitney Museum of Modern Art, the Boston Institute of Contemporary Art, the Chicago Art Institute, and numerous colleges and galleries throughout Vermont. He married Gladys LaFlamme, a poet and teacher, and the two briefly lived in Barton, where Francis taught in local schools, until 1942, when Colburn accepted the post of artist in residence at the University of Vermont. Over his years at UVM, Colburn taught art to hundreds of students, serving as the Arts Department chair for many years until his retirement in 1974, at which point the University conferred an honorary degree on him. In 1968, the Vermont Council on the Arts presented him with a Distinguished Service to the Arts Award. The Francis Colburn Gallery at UVM was established in 1977. Although affected by illness in his later years, Colburn's vivacity and sense of humor were legendary. His stories and jokes commemorated the tight lips and dry wit of Vermont "old-timers," and were so popular that many of them were eventually immortalized on recordings, including *A Graduation Address, Barn Talk,* and *That Campaign Speech.* He was also the author of *Letters Home and Further Indiscretions,* which captured more of his observations in the form of published letters and speeches. In 1984, the year of his death, he was the subject of a retrospective entitled *Francis Colburn: This I Remember,* at the Robert Hull FLEMING MUSEUM.   *Selene Colburn*

Colburn, Zerah (1804–1839)

In 1810, Abiah Colburn of Cabot found that his six-year-old son Zerah had the extraordinary mathematical skill of performing large-number multiplications in his head. Though Zerah was very young, his father led the boy through a tour of Vermont to exhibit his amazing skills. Young Colburn appeared before the annual town meeting in Cabot, executed complex multiplications for normally skeptical lawyers at the Caledonia court sitting in Danville, and then at Montpelier, where a trick question from a legislator—"How many black beans would it take to make five white ones?"—brought the quick response, "Five, if you skin them." Zerah and his father completed the Vermont circuit with a mathematical display in Burlington, returning home by way of Hanover, New Hampshire, where he was tested on finding squares and cubes, mathematical concepts about which Zerah had previously

shown no knowledge. The child's mathematical skills earned the offer of a scholarship from Dartmouth College. Suspecting that more than college tuition could be made from Zerah's skills, Colburn took his son to Boston, where he refused a speculator's offer of three thousand dollars to be allowed to tour the country with Zerah exhibiting his mathematical genius. After visits to New York, Philadelphia, and Washington, with fewer financial rewards for his son's displays than he expected, Colburn took Zerah to England in 1812 in the midst of embargo and war. In England and France, university mathematicians were intrigued by his performances, and in 1813, Zerah was paid by a curio exhibitor in Dublin, Ireland, to appear with a giant and an albino in a freak show to exhibit his polydactylic feet and hands— he had six digits on all four extremities— and demonstrate his mathematical skills. The earl of Bristol took an interest in Zerah, supporting him in school for five years, where he suffered from harsh treatment by his schoolmates. When his father died in 1824, Zerah went back to Vermont, but his mathematical skills had become less prominent as he took an interest in theology. Treated like a stranger by his family, Zerah left Cabot, became a Methodist preacher, and married. His mathematical skills seemed to decline through lack of use, but having acquired French in Europe, he taught it in Burlington, where he also attended the UNIVERSITY OF VERMONT. He taught briefly at Norwich Military College, but died of tuberculosis at the age of thirty-four. His extraordinary computational abilities were never fully explained or understood in his lifetime: Some contemporary commentators thought him a psychic; others believed he conspired with his father in an elaborate fraud; more recently some have thought that in his early life when his mathematical abilities were sharpest he might have also suffered from an autistic disorder. Yet at the age of eleven he and his father visited John Quincy Adams and William Crawford, the United States minister to France, in Paris where, Adams noted in his diary, Zerah gave a toast to Crawford "with the assurance of a man full grown but without offensive boldness."

J. Kevin Graffagnino

Colchester

A town in Chittenden County, Colchester was granted by BENNING WENTWORTH

in 1763 and named in honor of William Henry Nassau du Zuylestein (1717–1781), Baron Colchester, an influential member of the British establishment. With a population of 16,986, it is the fourth-largest population center in the state after Burlington, Essex, and Rutland. A town of the ONION RIVER COMPANY, Colchester was settled by IRA ALLEN and his cousin REMEMBER BAKER at the falls of the WINOOSKI RIVER in the section of town that in 1921 was incorporated as the city of Winooski. (The history of the falls area is dealt with in the entry on Winooski.) Despite its nearness to Burlington directly to its south, the town was until quite recent times primarily rural, with its major settlement at Colchester village. Today its largest population center is located in the Malletts Bay–Porter's Point section closest to Burlington. Its western border is LAKE CHAMPLAIN, marked, in order from south to north, by the intervale and delta of the Winooski River, a long peninsula leading to Colchester Point, cottage-lined Malletts Bay guarded by the exclusive peninsula known as Marble Island, and the delta of the LAMOILLE RIVER, which it shares with the neighboring town of Milton. The largest body of fresh water completely inside the town is Colchester Pond, which serves as a reservoir. On the border with Winooski is the area known as Winooski Park, home to ST. MICHAEL'S COLLEGE, a Catholic seat of learning established in 1904, and north of that is Camp Johnson, home of the Vermont National Guard. The camp is a remnant of FORT ETHAN ALLEN, a cavalry post founded in the 1890s, which from the end of the Second World War until the early 1960s was part of the air defense system centered on Plattsburgh Air Force Base across Lake Champlain in New York State. The fort has been completely rehabilitated and is now a residential and commercial community. In recent decades, because of its proximity to Burlington and its location along the Interstate 89 corridor, Colchester has become an important center for commerce and industry, including firms involved in cellular communications, computer services, clean-room building, and the production of metal strip-casting machinery.

Colchester Reef Lighthouse

Built in 1871 on the reef lying off Colchester Point on LAKE CHAMPLAIN, Colchester Reef Lighthouse now stands on

Colchester Reef Lighthouse at the Shelburne Museum. Vermont Department of Tourism and Marketing

the grounds of the SHELBURNE MUSEUM several miles inland from the lake. The U.S. Lighthouse Service selected the design for the lighthouse submitted by Albert R. Dow, a graduate engineer from the UNIVERSITY OF VERMONT, in a national design competition. Herman Melaney was the first of the nine keepers at Colchester Reef and remained for eleven years. The lighthouse has four bedrooms on its second floor, a kitchen and living room on the first. The beacon's fixed red light was visible for 11 miles, and its original sixth-order Fresnel lens is intact. The fog bell was sounded by winding a clockwork mechanism, and it was struck every twenty seconds when fog limited the light's visibility to less than three miles. August Lorenz was keeper at Colchester Reef from 1909 to 1931, the longest stint of any keeper. From 1933, when it was deactivated, until 1952, the Colchester Reef Lighthouse fell into disrepair. In July 1952, ELECTRA HAVEMEYER WEBB, founder of the Shelburne Museum, purchased the lighthouse from Paul and Lorraine Bessette, who had bought it from the Coast Guard. Before the building was dismantled, every part was photographed and numbered for identification, then the lighthouse parts were taken by barge to Shelburne and reassembled on a new foundation at the Museum. Inside the lighthouse are exhibits on Lake Champlain history, steamboats, and lighthouse life.

Collamer, Jacob (1791–1865)

One of two Vermonters (with ETHAN ALLEN) memorialized in the National Statuary Hall of the United States Congress, Jacob Collamer moved with his family from Troy, New York, to Burlington in 1795. Graduating from the UNIVERSITY OF VERMONT in 1810 in a class of seventeen, twelve of whom (including Collamer) became lawyers, he went to St. Albans to read the law. When war with England broke out in 1812, he was drafted for brief border duty, serving as lieutenant of artillery. Admitted to the bar in 1813, he moved to Randolph, where he was named collector of the federal war tax and appointed register of probate for Windsor County. Elected state's attorney in 1820, Collamer was never long without public office. In the 1820s, he represented Royalton four terms in the Vermont House, but during the early 1830s devoted himself to the law. His wide circles of friends and personal ability to avoid making enemies won him WHIG and ANTI-MASONIC endorsements for election to the Vermont Supreme Court. Settling in Woodstock in 1836, he also served VERMONT MEDICAL COLLEGE for twenty years as lecturer on medical jurisprudence, vice president, trustee, and president of the college. In 1842, he was elected to the first of three terms in Congress, where he supported FREE-SOIL Whig positions against the annexation of Texas and the Mexican War, and spoke for protective tariffs, internal

improvements, and sound banking. He was at the time also a trustee of UVM (1835–1849), presiding at its semi-centennial celebration in 1854. He declined to run for Congress in 1848 and returned to Vermont to serve as circuit judge. When the coalition that formed the REPUBLICAN PARTY emerged in 1854, Collamer was elected to fill a vacant Vermont seat in the United States Senate. In 1860, elected to his second term, he received Vermont's first ballot for presidential nominee at the Republican National Convention. Though hampered by ill health, he spoke several times from the Committee on Territories for free-state Kansas, anticipated Lincoln's emancipation policy when on April 24, 1862, he advocated freeing the slaves of rebels, and spoke for equalizing the pay of white and black Union soldiers. His last speech in February 1865 argued for congressional rather than presidential reconstruction. Senators JUSTIN MORRILL and GEORGE EDMUNDS nominated Collamer and Ethan Allen to represent Vermont in Congress's National Statuary Hall. Collamer's statue was made by Preston Powers, son of HIRAM POWERS, and installed in 1881.   *T. D. Seymour Bassett*

College of St. Joseph

Founded in 1950 by the Sisters of St. Joseph, the College of St. Joseph is located on a 90-acre wooded campus in Rutland. A career-oriented liberal arts college that awards associate, bachelor's, and master's degrees, St. Joseph has an enrollment of approximately 550 students, of which 70 percent are female. The student-faculty ratio is twelve to one, and average class size is sixteen. Favorite majors include psychology, business management, and elementary education. The college celebrates the Feast of St. Joseph every March 19, known as "Founder's Day," with speeches, awards, and a dinner.

Collins, Ray (1887–1970)

Often called the best left-handed pitcher in the American League from 1912 to 1914, Ray Collins of Colchester played major league baseball for seven years with the Boston Red Sox. A descendant of one of Burlington's original settlers, Collins liked to be known as "a Vermont Yankee." He threw the first pitch at Centennial Field when the UNIVERSITY OF VERMONT opened its new baseball stadium on April 16, 1907, and graduated in 1909 before joining the Red Sox. At the end of the 1914 season, Collins earned his nineteenth and twentieth victories of the season by pitching both ends of a double header against the Detroit Tigers, a team he always had great success against because of his idiosyncratic wind up and delivery. His pitching suffered mysteriously in the very next season and he was replaced in the starting rotation by young Babe Ruth. Collins started his second career in 1915 on his family's farm in Colchester, where poor soil, fires and diseased livestock made for a hard life. He served as UVM's baseball coach in 1925 to 1926, in the Vermont House for Colchester from 1943 to 1947, and on the UVM Board of Trustees in the 1950s. In 1969, he was one of the seven original inductees into UVM's Athletics Hall of Fame.   *Richard Leyden*

Community College of Vermont

The Community College of Vermont (CCV) was founded in 1970 by PETER SMITH and became one of the VERMONT STATE COLLEGES in 1975. A public, two-year, open-admissions institution providing degree, transfer, occupational, and continuing-education opportunities, CCV's mission is to deliver quality, affordable, post-secondary education in local Vermont communities and in innovative, flexible ways. Special emphasis is given to Vermonters who would otherwise have limited access to college because of a number of barriers, including low income, lack of academic preparation, family obligations, time constraints, or geographic remoteness. To fulfill its mission, CCV offers classes in twelve communities throughout Vermont, selects instructors from within those communities, and draws upon local resources and facilities. For thousands of Vermonters, the Community College of Vermont offers the opportunity to pursue an associate degree, improve professional skills, or enrich personal development. Instructors are knowledgeable practitioners in their fields as well as skilled teachers. The college serves nearly five thousand students each semester, making it the second largest college in the state in terms of enrollment. CCV's central administration is in the Government Office Complex in Waterbury. Its learning centers are located in Bennington, Brattleboro, Burlington, Middlebury, Montpelier, Morrisville, Newport, Rutland, Springfield, St. Albans, St. Johnsbury, and White River Junction.

Community Ski Hills

As general interest in SKIING started to spread across Vermont in the 1930s, informal groups of skiers in several regions began to use nearby hillside locations with good vertical drops and plenty of lasting snow as community ski hills. Some individual skiers who owned such hills also began to offer the opportunity to ski on their land for a nominal charge. Amenities at both community and private ski hills were usually limited to a warming hut heated by a wood or kerosene stove and a rope tow powered off a blocked-up car's wheel or a tractor's PTO to pull skiers to the top of the hill. Grooming might be one or two crops of hay laid on long before the first snowflake fell. Organized in 1937, the LYNDON OUTING CLUB is Vermont's oldest continuously operating volunteer group with its own ski hill. By the 1950s, Vermonters had at least fifty-six easily accessible, inexpensive community ski hills in almost every region of the state. But nearly twenty years with decreasing amounts of snowfall after 1980 and the increasing costs of operation have left fewer than ten private or community ski hills still offering an inexpensive opportunity to ski. Among the still-operating ski hills, Hard'ack in St. Albans is free but accepts donations. It offers night skiing four times weekly. Cochran's in Richmond, where the COCHRAN FAMILY OF SKIERS began their development into U.S. Ski Team members in the 1960s and early 1970s, is open five times weekly. The Lyndon Outing Club is open five days and three nights. Northeast Ski Slopes in East Corinth, open daily, may be the oldest privately owned ski hill in Vermont.

Composers' Conference and Chamber Music Center

In 1955, ALAN CARTER, founder and music director of the VERMONT SYMPHONY ORCHESTRA, organized the Vermont Composer's Conference. For two weeks each August the conference provided opportunity for young composers to hear performances and receive edited recordings of their music by the Conference's staff of instrumentalists and singers. Distinguished composers on the staff included Otto Leuning, Ezra Laderman, Hall Overton, Donald Erb, Charles Worn, Mario Davidowsky, and David Raskin. Selected compositions were performed in concerts held during the conference, at which traditional masterworks were also performed by the Composers' Conference Orchestra under the direction of Dr. Carter and the distinguished concertmaster Max Polikoff. Frequently, compositions performed at the conference were selected for performance by Polikoff's *Music In Our Time* series held each winter in New York City at the Ninety-second Street YWHA Theater. The Vermont Chamber Music Center also ran concurrently with the Composers' Conference each August under Carter's direction, bringing amateur chamber musicians from across the country and abroad to play and study traditional chamber music under the tutelage of the conference's instrumentalists. Tuition fees to attend the Chamber Music Center and grants to the Conference provided scholarships for young composers to attend the conference. The Composers' Conference and Chamber Music Center was held at MIDDLEBURY COLLEGE (1955–1962), BENNINGTON COLLEGE (1963–1970) and JOHNSON STATE COLLEGE (1971–1976). During its existence, college and university music departments rarely assembled staff capable of serving young composers with professional readings and performances of their work. For twenty years the Composers' Conference's annual event influenced and encouraged through its example universities that today assemble music staffs capable of serving young composers.   *Ernest Stires*

Concord

Concord, population 1,196, a town in Essex County, was granted by the Vermont legislature in 1780 to Dr. Reuben James and others and named for Concord, Massachusetts. Hilly and forested, the town has as its southern boundary the CONNECTICUT RIVER, here backed up behind Moore Dam into Moore Reservoir. Its main settlements are Concord village, on Route 2 along the Moose River, and North Concord, at the foot of 2,690-foot Miles Mountain in the town's northern section. Two small bodies of water, Shadow Lake and Miles Pond, are lined with summer camps. The first teacher-training school in America was founded at the tiny settlement of Concord Corner by the Reverend SAMUEL READ HALL in 1823 to 1825.

Congdon, Herbert Wheaton (1876–1965)

An influential student of Vermont's architectural heritage, Herbert Wheaton Congdon was born in West Brighton, New York.

He studied architecture at Columbia University and collaborated for a quarter-century with his father, Henry Martyn Congdon, on Gothic designs for Episcopal churches. After moving to Arlington in 1923, Congdon helped map the LONG TRAIL, served in the legislature and as president of the GREEN MOUNTAIN CLUB, and filled a seat on the VERMONT COMMISSION ON COUNTRY LIFE. In 1936, he became official photographer of the UNIVERSITY OF VERMONT's Old Buildings Project and spent three years touring the state to document outstanding examples of early Vermont architecture. In 1940, Congdon published *Old Vermont Houses: The Architecture of a Resourceful People*, which went through several editions. The following year, he collaborated with photographer Edmund H. Royce on *The Covered Bridge*. He devoted much of the last twenty-five years of his life to continuing the work of the Old Buildings Project, and in 1963 published *Early American Homes for Today* based largely on his Vermont research. His papers and voluminous photograph files at the University of Vermont library are a valuable resource for research on Vermont's pre-1850 architecture.   *J. Kevin Graffagnino*

Connecticut River

The Connecticut River, which forms Vermont's eastern boundary, rises in the Connecticut lakes of northern New Hampshire and, after a winding journey of 410 miles (270 as the crow flies), empties into Long Island Sound. The vertical drop from source to mouth is 2,650 feet. Its major tributaries in Vermont are, in order from north to south, the Nulhegan, PASSUMPSIC, Wells, Waits, Ompompanoosuc, WHITE, Ottauquechee, southern Black, Williams, Saxtons, and WEST rivers. In a 1934 ruling, the U.S. Supreme Court declared that the New Hampshire–Vermont border was the west bank of the river at low-water mark, confirming a 1764 decision of the British Privy Council that ceded jurisdiction over all of the river to New Hampshire. For Native Americans, the Connecticut was a favorite route through the wilderness, as well as a source of food, especially with its annual runs of Atlantic salmon, eel, and shad. In the seventeenth century, it was one of the prime sources of furs for traders from the English coastal towns. The first permanent European settlement on the Vermont side of the river was FORT DUMMER, near pres-

ent-day Brattleboro, built in 1724 to protect the farmers who had begun to move northward from Massachusetts. Between 1752 and 1763, BENNING WENTWORTH granted a total of twenty-three towns on the west bank of the Connecticut, starting an influx of settlers that was only temporarily slowed by the Revolutionary War. The suitability of the river for industry and commerce was soon exploited, especially at Bellows Falls, where one of the earliest canals in the United States was in operation by 1802, followed later by canals at Hartland and Wilder. Dams on the Connecticut and its tributaries provided the water power to run numerous early industries, including those producing machine tools in Windsor and Springfield, but the unregulated discharge of industrial effluent all along the river, as well as agricultural runoff from farmland and topsoil loss due to logging, led to serious degradation of water quality and the disappearance of a number of aquatic plant and animal species. In 1927, the greatest flood in Vermont history inundated the Connecticut River Valley and led to calls for flood control, resulting in the eventual construction of a total of five dams on four of the Connecticut's tributaries, plus an increase in the height of the Wilder Dam on the Connecticut itself. Hydroelectric dams were also constructed in Vernon and on the upper Connecticut in the towns of Barnet and Waterford, resulting in miles-long reservoirs that drowned both farmland and settlements. Cleanup of the polluted Connecticut became a serious concern with the passage of the state Water Pollution Control Act in 1972 and the similar federal act two years later, and in the next thirty years point-source control and the construction of sewage disposal facilities restored the river to something approaching its original state. Fish ladders built at Vernon, Bellows Falls, and Wilder in 1981, 1984, and 1987 respectively have permitted some sea-run salmon to return to the middle Connecticut, while Atlantic shad in large numbers have supported a lively sport fishery above the Vernon dam since the 1980s. Since 1991, the Connecticut's New England watershed of seven million acres has been the site of the Silvio O. Conte National Wildlife Refuge, which consists of hundreds of habitat-protection tracts under the control of public or private property owners. Among the refuge's eight "Special Focus Areas" in Vermont are the Nulhegan and Victory basins in the

NORTHEAST KINGDOM and the White and West rivers with their tributaries.

Coolidge, Calvin (1872–1933)

The thirtieth president of the United States (1923–1929), Calvin Coolidge was the only son of a storekeeper, John Calvin Coolidge, and his wife, Victoria Josephine Moor Coolidge. He was born in the family's living section at the rear of his father's combined general store and post office in Plymouth Notch. Schooled at Plymouth Notch and Black River Academy in Ludlow, he graduated from Amherst College in 1895, studied law in Northampton, Massachusetts, where he was admitted to the practice of law in 1897 and maintained a legal practice until 1919. In 1905, Coolidge married Grace Anna Goodhue of Burlington, who taught at the Clarke Institute for the Deaf in Northampton. Active in REPUBLICAN PARTY politics early in his legal career, he was elected city councilman of Northampton in 1898. His campaigning style—simply saying, "I want your vote. I need it. I shall appreciate it"—won elections for him between 1900 and 1911 as city solicitor, clerk of courts, representative in the Massachusetts legislature, and mayor of Northampton. He served as senator in the state legislature from 1912 to 1915, serving as its in president 1914 to 1915, and as lieutenant governor from 1916 to 1918. Loyal to the Massachusetts Republican party and its conservative principles, Coolidge earned the support of the party's leaders, including the financial support of the wealthy Boston department store owner Frank W. Stearns. Coolidge won the governorship by fewer than twenty thousand votes in 1918, but soon became nationally known in 1919, when he broke the Boston police strike by ordering Massachusetts national guard troops into the city and asked for federal soldiers as backup. Coolidge refused to allow striking policemen to return to their jobs, saying, "There is no right to strike against the public safety by anybody, anywhere, anytime," a statement that gained him wide popularity and led to a movement to nominate him for the presidency at the Republican National Convention in 1920. At the convention, Coolidge received all twenty-eight Massachusetts votes, but only six from other states. The convention nominated Ohio conservative Warren G. Harding, and Coolidge was later chosen to be his running mate. Harding and Coolidge achieved a popular victory of seven million

The room in the Coolidge home in Plymouth where Calvin Coolidge was administered the oath of office as president by his father on August 3, 1923. Vermont Department of Tourism and Marketing

votes over James Cox and Franklin Delano Roosevelt. Little was expected of the vice president, and Coolidge was not very active. By 1923, however, the nation experienced an economic slump, followed by revelations of gross corruption in Harding's administration. The secretaries of the Interior Department and the Navy were deeply involved in what became known as the Teapot Dome scandal, a scheme in which the Navy's oil reserves at Teapot Dome, Wyoming, were transferred to the secretary of the interior, who then leased them to private oil companies in return for more than $400,000. Harding died suddenly in San Francisco on August 2, 1923, and Coolidge, who was visiting his father in Plymouth Notch, received the news of the president's death early on August 3. The vice-president's father, John Coolidge, a justice of the peace, administered the oath of office to his son in the parlor by the light of kerosene lamps. Since his father's authority applied only to Vermont offices, however, Calvin Coolidge repeated the oath in Washington, D.C., on the twenty-first. The remainder of the Harding-Coolidge presidency was not marked by any great demands on the presidency, but in the summer of 1924, Coolidge suffered a great blow when his son Calvin Jr. died of an infection. "The power and the glory of the presidency went with him," Coolidge wrote in his autobiography. Coolidge was easily nominated for president in 1924. The Democrats went into the contest badly divided

because of a fierce convention fight, while the Republicans were unified and strong, campaigning with the slogan "Keep Cool With Coolidge." The economy had greatly improved in 1924 and Coolidge easily defeated Democrat John Davis, collecting 15,725,016 popular votes to Davis's 8,385,586 and the Progressive party's Robert La Follette's 4,822,856 popular votes. Coolidge maintained conservative policies during his second term. He disagreed with the Republican-controlled Congress on price supports for agriculture, vetoing the McNary-Haugen Farm Relief Bill in 1927 and 1928. His plans for reduction of higher income tax brackets were greatly modified by Congress. In 1927, Coolidge vetoed a bill to provide extra payments to World War I servicemen and allowed a bill providing for government operation of the hydroelectric plant on the Tennessee River at Muscle Shoals, Alabama, to expire without his signature. His diplomats achieved the Kellogg-Briand Treaty, which effectively established the international legal principle that war was a criminal act, averted war with Mexico over that country's expropriation of American-owned oil fields, and sent five thousand Marines into Nicaragua to suppress an insurrection and protect American citizens. In August 1927, as Coolidge vacationed in the Black Hills of South Dakota, he released a statement to the newspapers that said, "I do not choose to run for president in 1928." Though no subsequent explanation was forthcoming, it is thought

that the death of his son, the strain on his grieving wife, and his own exhaustion were the reasons for his withdrawal from public life. He returned to Northampton in 1930, wrote magazine articles advocating laissez-faire economic policy, served as a trustee for Amherst College, on the board of New York Life Insurance Company, and as president of the American Antiquarian Society. He died in Northampton in 1933 and is buried in the family plot in Plymouth Notch, where the state of Vermont maintains his birthplace and the immediately surrounding buildings as the President COOLIDGE STATE HISTORIC SITE.

Coolidge, Grace Goodhue (1879–1957)

The wife of CALVIN COOLIDGE, thirtieth president of the United States, Grace Goodhue Coolidge was born in Burlington. Her parents, Andrew Goodhue and Lemira Barrett, lived at 315–317 St. Paul Street, close to her father's work at the Gates Cotton Mill. In a few years the family moved up to 123 Maple Street and, by the time Grace was a student at the UNIVERSITY OF VERMONT, to 312 Maple Street. Sorority meetings of the fledgling chapter of Pi Beta Phi were often held there. She grew up a Methodist but at sixteen joined the College Street Congregational Church. Upon graduation, Grace moved to Northampton, Massachusetts, to teach at the Clarke School for the Deaf. After three years of teaching, she married Calvin Coolidge in 1905 at her parents' home and soon had two sons, Calvin Jr. (1906–1924) and John (1908–2000). Her husband, a lawyer, was already active in Northampton politics at the time of the marriage and progressed through mayoral, state senatorial, and gubernatorial offices in Massachusetts prior to becoming vice president of the United States in 1920. In August 1923, the death of President Harding propelled Calvin and Grace into the White House. Essentially kind and unassuming, the First Lady carried out her hostess responsibilites graciously and oversaw a major renovation of the White House. Returning to private life in Northampton in 1928, the couple purchased the Beeches, where Grace continued to live after the President's death in 1933. She was granted two honorary degrees by Smith and UVM, and held board positions at the Clarke School and other educational institutions. She worked in her church and community, travelled, enjoyed baseball on the radio, and was devoted to her family. She planned the transfer of the Coolidge Homestead in Plymouth to the State of Vermont, where she is buried in the Coolidge lot.   *Sarah L. Dopp*

Coolidge State Historic Site

The rural Vermont village of Plymouth Notch in the town of Plymouth was the birthplace and boyhood home of President CALVIN COOLIDGE, and remains virtually unchanged since the turn of the twentieth century. The homes of Coolidge's family and neighbors, the community church, cheese factory, one-room schoolhouse, and general store have been carefully preserved, and many have their original furnishings. The president is buried in the town cemetery. Listed on the National Register of Historic Places, the village has been designated as the Plymouth Notch Historic District and is owned and operated by the Vermont Division for Historic Preservation. Included in the village's preserved buildings are Coolidge's birthplace and childhood home. The birthplace is attached to the general store (built 1850) that his father, Colonel John Coolidge, owned from 1868 to 1917 and operated until 1877. Calvin Coolidge was born in the downstairs bedroom on July 4, 1872. The family lived in this modest house until 1876, when they moved across the road to what is now called the Coolidge Homestead, purchased by the state in 1968 and restored to its 1872 appearance. Original furnishings were donated by the Coolidge family. It was while vacationing here that Vice President Coolidge received word of the death of President Warren Harding and was administered the presidential oath of office by his father, a justice of the peace, at 2:47 A.M. on August 3, 1923. John Coolidge lived in this house until his death in 1926. His housekeeper, Aurora Pierce, stayed on for another thirty years. A tiny lady of steely will, Aurora never accepted the easy life of electricity and "newfangled" plumbing, and so the house remained much as it was in 1923, and is so preserved today.   *John Dumville*

Copper mine

See VERMONT COPPER COMPANY.

Coral Reefs of Isle La Motte

First called the world's oldest coral reefs by Percy Raymond in 1924, the coral reefs of Isle La Motte are fossilized coral and other organisms found in the Chazy Group of rock formations deposited 480 million years ago during the Middle Ordovician era. Appearing as small mounds of individual bryozoa (a taxonomic group present today), they preserve the oldest example of an ecological succession in the fossil record as they evolved over time from twig-like to encrusting species. These organic structures are best viewed on the south tip of Isle La Motte where it is also possible to see channels cutting through the reef and oriented generally east-west, which represent the passages for ocean water flushing in and out of the lagoon once located landward (west) of the reefs. These deposits are most accessible to view in a field north of the Isle La Motte Historical Society, and may be visited with permission of the landowner. These structures reveal reef tracts forming in less than 60 meters of warm (+68 degrees Fahrenheit or 20 Celsius) marine water. Thus, during the Middle Ordovician, Vermont was located on a shallow continental shelf much further south than Vermont is today, and facing the open ocean. In fact, configurations of ancient world geography place it approximately 30 degrees south of the equator. Western Vermont was the eastern edge of the ancient North American continent of Laurentia, bordered on the east by the Iapetus Ocean. The continental crust of Laurentia was forced under that of the Iapetus Ocean, forming an ocean trench with volcanic islands in what geologists term a "subduction zone." The collision between Laurentia and the Iapetus Ocean is called the Taconic Orogeny, a mountain-building event responsible for creating the GREEN MOUNTAINS. Reefs of Middle Ordovician age are found along the trend of the Appalachian Mountains from Newfoundland to Tennessee. The Chazy reefs are significant because they are part of a record of an important event in evolutionary history, the diversification of organisms capable of building rigid, wave-resistant structures in shallow water. The organisms that evolved to occupy this niche have changed over geologic time and are today represented by stony coral. Their ancestors' fossilized remains rest in the Middle Ordovician Chazy Group limestones of the Champlain Valley.   *Charlotte Mehrtens*

Corbin, Horace W., Sr. (1889–1951)

Horace W. Corbin of Grand Isle and Shelburne was the investor who merged LAKE CHAMPLAIN's several independent ferry companies into the CHAMPLAIN TRANSPORTATION COMPANY during the 1920s and 1930s when the automobile began to increase in popularity. A native of Dundee, Michigan, and a grand-nephew of George Armstrong Custer, Corbin attended the University of Michigan. He formed the Roosevelt Ferry Company in 1918, then gained control of the Grand Isle to Cumberland Head ferry and in 1924 merged the two companies. He also operated the large steel ferries *City of Burlington* and *City of Plattsburgh* out of Burlington under the banner of the Green Mountain-Adirondack Ferry Company. As ferries lost business to new BRIDGES OVER LAKE CHAMPLAIN to New York, Corbin oversaw the design and construction of the "streamlined ferries," so-called for design features similar to new train and automobile designs of that era. In 1937, he purchased all the property of the Champlain Transportation Company, including its boats, docks on both sides of the lake, shipyard in Shelburne, and charter from the Delaware & Hudson Railroad for $100,000. With the exception of the steamer *TICONDEROGA*, he redesigned, refitted, or sold the company's vessels. Because the shortage of gasoline during World War II severely limited the use of automobiles, Corbin pressed the *Ticonderoga* into extended ferry service between Burlington, Essex, Port Kent, Plattsburgh, and Grand Isle. The war also led Corbin to lease the company's Shelburne Shipyard to a firm that built PT and SUBCHASER boats for the Navy. In 1948, Corbin sold the Champlain Transportation Company to Lewis P. Evans, Jr., Richard H. Wadhams, and James G. Wolcott, who renamed it the Lake Champlain Transportation Company.

Corinth

A town in Orange County, Corinth (accented on the second syllable), population 1,461, was granted by BENNING WENTWORTH in 1764 and named after the ancient city in Greece, probably by way of the New Testament. Much of the town lies at an elevation of a thousand feet or more, rising to 2,148 feet at Garden Hill in the southwestern part of town, resulting in a landscape of forested hills and upland meadows. Two river valleys cut through the town, that of the Waits River in the northeastern section and the South Branch of the same river in the southeastern section. Despite its modest population, the town has seven settlements, of which the two main ones are Cookville and East Corinth. A Revolutionary War fort site, built in 1781, lies on Fort Hill just outside of Cookville. At one time, copper was mined at Pike Hill in the northern part of town.

Cornwall

Cornwall, population 1,136, a town in Addison County, was granted by BENNING WENTWORTH in 1761 and named for either Cornwall, Connecticut, or the county of the same name in England. A long, low rise, known in its northern section as the Ledges, runs north-south through the town, bordered on the southeast by an extensive swamp formed by OTTER CREEK and reaching into six other towns from Middlebury to Brandon. Much of Cornwall's section is a state wildlife management area. The main settlement is Cornwall village, at the junction of Routes 30 and 74. Despite its nearness to Middlebury just beyond the town's northeastern border, Cornwall remains primarily agricultural. In the nineteenth century, prosperity was derived from the raising of merino sheep and MORGAN HORSES, resulting in the building of numerous imposing residences, examples of which can still be seen along the town's roads today. The small dairy farms and apple orchards of the early and middle twentieth century have been consolidated into larger operations.

Cornwall, Ellsworth B. (1884–1964)

Founder of the Vermont FARM BUREAU, Vermont public service commissioner, and MIDDLEBURY COLLEGE professor, Ellsworth B. Cornwall was a controversial figure throughout much of his career. Born in Princeton, New Jersey, he graduated from Princeton University and attended New York Law School, settling in Middlebury in 1908. A lawyer and poultry farmer, in 1915 he became the first president of the Addison County Farm Bureau and a founder of the national and Vermont State Farm Bureau Federation, serving as the first president of the latter organization from 1919. During his tenure, the Bureau intensified its commercial and lobbying activities, but unlike his successor, ARTHUR PACKARD, Cornwall discouraged organization support for any political party or individual candidate. In 1928, Cornwall resigned as president to become professor of political science at

Middlebury College, a position he held until 1941. In 1938, he was appointed to the Public Service Commission by Governor GEORGE AIKEN and proved an ardent consumer advocate while serving as chairman and public service commissioner. Stripped of his chairmanship by Governor William Wills, he was denied reappointment to the commission by Governor MORTIMER PROCTOR. Proctor later maintained that this so angered Packard that he mobilized the Farm Bureau in support of ERNEST W. GIBSON, JR., to assure Proctor's defeat in the 1946 Republican primary. Gibson subsequently appointed Cornwall to the State Unemployment Commission, where he served until he retired in 1960.

Corti, Elia (1869–1903)

A native of Viggiu, Italy, Elia Corti came to Barre in 1892. One of Barre's finest stone carvers, he was first employed at Barclay Brothers Granite Company, then formed a partnership with Samuel Novelli. He is best remembered for having carved the panels on the base of Barre's Robert Burns Monument. His accidental death occurred tragically at a gathering for the socialist leader, Giacinto M. Serrati of New York. Anarchists who derided Serrati's views preceded him to the SOCIALIST LABOR PARTY HALL on Granite Street, where Serrati, who was the editor of the Socialist Labor party weekly *Il Proletario*, was to lecture. His late arrival at the Labor Hall caused the waiting crowd to grow unruly, and Alexander Garetto, a thirty-nine-year-old tool sharpener and a leader of the Barre socialists, became agitated, firing his pistol wildly and fatally wounding Elia Corti in the stomach. Corti died the following day, leaving his wife Maria and daughters Lelia, Mary, and Emma. Corti's death shocked the community, and the townspeople drew together to erect a monument in his memory at Barre's HOPE CEMETERY. In style, the monument conforms to the late nineteenth-century Italian sculpture movement of *verismo*, depicting the artist in realistic dress and traditional melancholy pose, his arm resting on a broken column symbolizing his life cut short. The pensive figure of Corti was carved by his brother-in-law John Comi and his brother William Corti from the model by the noted Italian sculptor Abramo Ghigli of Carrara, who had opened a studio in Barre in 1902. Grieving stonecarvers from throughout Vermont helped to carve the

base, where lie Corti's carving tools: calipers, square, hammer, chisel, and pneumatic carving tool, and a palm branch, the symbol of peace.   *Karen Lane*

Côté, Cyrille-Hector-Octave (1809–1850)

A Quebec physician who prepared for his profession at the UNIVERSITY OF VERMONT and later became a leader of the Canadian PATRIOTS in the uprising of 1837 to 1838, Cyrille Côté came from a family of British-dispossessed Acadians who emigrated to Canada in 1756. Familial anti-British sentiments inclined him to follow the developments in Quebec during the late 1820s that arose from an awakened French nationalism and increasing demands for a representative form of government. He associated with several Montreal lawyers and intellectuals at the printing shop of LUDGER DUVERNAY, where they developed their demands for a democratic government and relief from the British colonial regime. After a few months studying medicine at McGill College, Côté enrolled in the medical course at the University of Vermont, receiving a certificate of medical studies in October 1831 and a license to practice in Quebec in 1832. Settling in the Richelieu Valley, he first worked at L'Acadie during the cholera epidemic of 1832, but in 1833 moved to Napierville, where he became a prominent community figure, supported the region's farmers in their criticisms of the seigneurial fees system, and was elected to the Lower Canadian House of Assembly in 1834. A member of the revolutionary Fils de la Liberté by 1837, he organized farmers and took money by force from the presbyteries of Napierville and St-Valentin to buy arms for the Patriots uprising in late 1837. But when British regulars and Canadian militia defeated the Patriots at St-Charles-sur-Richelieu, Côté fled to Vermont. At large public meetings in Swanton and Middlebury during January 1838, Côté assumed leadership of the Patriot movement. He marshalled three to four hundred Patriots at Alburg in February 1838 who invaded Canada, but were easily driven back into Vermont. Charged with violating Governor SILAS JENISON's neutrality order, they were quickly discharged by a sympathetic Vermont court. Through the following nine months, Côté worked to organize the Association des Frères-Chasseurs, a secret military organization in Quebec and the United States. On

November 3, 1838, Côté and Robert Nelson led five hundred Patriots from Vermont and New York into Napierville, but Canadian militia crushed the insurgents on November 9 and Côté again fled to the United States. In 1839, he settled at Swanton, began to practice medicine again, and wrote several articles for the *North American* magazine in Boston attacking Louis-Joseph Papineau and other leaders of the failed Patriot movement. In 1841, he moved to Chazy, New York, and became a Baptist minister. By late 1849, he was back in Canada as minister for Marieville. Côté died in October 1850 in Hinesburg of a heart attack on his way to a meeting of the American Baptist Home Missionary Society.

Council of Censors

The 1777 Vermont constitution provided for a Council of Censors, thirteen men elected at large every seven years, whose most important duty was to propose constitutional amendments once during the septennial and call a convention to consider their adoption. The Council had additional powers: principally the authority to censure officers of government and to inquire whether public taxes had been fairly laid. Normally, a convention consisted of one delegate from each town. As it required a council majority to propose amendments and a two-thirds majority to call a convention, the council would on occasion propose amendments that a majority did not support to secure votes for a convention. Such was the case in 1870 when, despite majority support for maintaining the council, it proposed an amendment for its abolishment that the convention adopted. The new system of amendment provided that once every ten years two-thirds of the Senate might propose amendments and those with which a majority of the House agreed would be resubmitted the following session. Any receiving a majority vote in both houses were then presented to the general electorate for ratification. In 1974, the "ten-year time lock" was shortened to four years with the other provisions retained.

Coventry

Coventry, population 1,014, a town in Orleans County, was granted by the Vermont legislature in 1780 to Major ELIAS BUEL and others, and named for Major Buel's home town of Coventry, Connecticut. (From November 1841 to November 1843 the town was legally known as Orleans on petition of the residents in the fruitless hope that it would become the county seat.) The landscape is made up of low hills and farmland bisected by the northern Black River, which flows north into LAKE MEMPHREMAGOG just over the town line in Newport. The Barton River, in the eastern section of town, forms the extensive Barton River Marsh as it flows into the same lake. The single village of Coventry is on Route 5 as it follows the course of the Black River.

Crafts, Samuel C. (1763–1853)

The fourteenth governor of Vermont and a United States congressman, Samuel C. Crafts was born in Leicester, Massachusetts. In 1781, he and his father Ebenezer were grantees of Minden, which was later renamed Craftsbury. The Crafts came to settle Minden/Craftsbury in 1791. Samuel was Craftsbury's town clerk and by 1799 was a member of the Vermont House and served as clerk. From 1818 to 1824, he served in the U.S. House of Representatives and in 1828 as a National Republican candidate broke the Jeffersonian Democratic Republicans' hold on the governor's office, a position he held for three terms until 1831. A respected and prosperous farmer, he was also noted for his mathematical skills.

Craftsbury

Craftsbury, population 1,136, a town in Orleans County, was granted by the Vermont legislature in 1781 to Colonel Ebenezer Crafts and others. At first it was called Minden, perhaps to commemorate an English-German victory over France in the Seven Years War or to honor veterans of that event among the grantees, although why the legislature would honor an English victory during the Revolution is not known. The name was changed to Craftsbury in 1790 to honor its principal grantee. The landscape is a mixture of low hills and farmland, bisected by the northern Black River, which flows through the town from south to north. Of the four settlements, Craftsbury village, East Craftsbury, Mill Village, and Craftsbury Common, the last—called by some the loveliest village in the state—sits on a gentle ridge with views in nearly every direction. Its unusually large green is surrounded by pristine white buildings that include the United Church, the Craftsbury Public Library, Craftsbury Academy, and STER-LING COLLEGE, which specializes in environmental curricula. The 1955 Alfred Hitchcock film *The Trouble with Harry* was filmed in Craftsbury.

Craftsbury Chamber Players

A string quartet whose four original players were Allan and Ann Birney, Mary Lou Rylands, and music director Mary Anthony Cox, the Craftsbury Chamber Players began performing in Craftsbury Common in 1966. The quartet travels about Vermont performing its hallmark eclectic repertoire representing all periods of chamber music. Rylands and Cox continue to perform with the group in Hardwick and Burlington, their regular venues. Many guest performers in the six-week July-August season are associated with the Juilliard School of Music, where Mary Anthony Cox is a string instructor, and Yale University. Regulars and newcomers combine talents and volunteers perform many production tasks. The Chamber Players regularly perform free children's concerts.

Sarah L. Dopp

Craig, William (b. 1914)

The first chancellor of the VERMONT STATE COLLEGES (1973–1976) and a long-time administrator of higher education institutions in the United States and Europe, William Craig was born in West Hebron, New York, attended school there and in Middlebury, and received an academic scholarship to MIDDLEBURY COLLEGE. He graduated in the class of 1937 after playing as both offensive and defensive end and captain of the football team during one of the two undefeated seasons in the college's history. In 1963, President John F. Kennedy presented him with the Silver Goalposts Award from *Sports Illustrated*. After graduating from Middlebury, Craig earned a master's in education from the University of Minnesota (1939) and a doctorate in education from Harvard University (1955). Craig was an administrator and teacher in higher education for nearly fifty years. From 1939 to 1941, he was director of admissions for men at Middlebury College. During World War II, he served in the U.S. Navy. He was subsequently appointed dean of students and instructor in educational psychology at Washington State University (1946–1951); dean of students and professor of education at Kansas State University (1951–1955); admissions assistant, Harvard Graduate School of Business Administration (1953–

1955); dean of men and associate dean of students at Stanford University (1955–1962); vice-president for academic affairs, University of Montana (1969–1970); president of JOHNSON STATE COLLEGE (1970–1974); chancellor of the Vermont State Colleges; chancellor of the California Community Colleges (1977–1980); president of the Monterey Institute of International Studies (1980–1987); and president of International University-Europe in London, England (1987–1988). He was also headmaster of the John Burroughs School in St. Louis from 1964 to 1966. In addition to his years in higher education, Craig served in the federal government as special assistant to the director and director of training for the Peace Corps (1962–1964), deputy assistant secretary of health, education, and welfare and deputy associate commissioner for higher education (1966–1969). In 1976, William Craig unsuccessfully opposed RICHARD SNELLING in the Vermont Republican gubernatorial primary election. He has lived in La Jolla, California, since retirement in 1988.

Crane, Charles E. (1884–1960)

A journalist and publicity director, Charles E. Crane moved from Illinois to Ludlow as a boy when his father bought the *Vermont Tribune* newspaper. Following education at Black River Academy and Dartmouth College, Crane joined the Associated Press and worked as a journalist in Boston, New York, Pittsburgh, and London. He returned to Vermont as owner and editor of the *Middlebury Register*, later relocating to the *BRATTLEBORO REFORMER*. While in Brattleboro, he began doing publicity for Vermont businesses, as well as fund raising, and in 1931 Crane was hired as the first publicity director for National Life Insurance Company. The company's well-known series of illustrated historical advertisements were his work. Crane is author of the books *Pen-Drift: Amenities of Column Conducting* (1931), *Let me Show You Vermont* (1937), *Life Along the Connecticut* (1939), and *Winter in Vermont* (1941), as well as numerous articles and columns on Vermont topics. He was an honorary trustee of the VERMONT HISTORICAL SOCIETY and was awarded an honorary degree from NORWICH UNIVERSITY.   *Reidun Nuquist*

Craven, Jay (b. 1950)

Best known for his film adaptations of the HOWARD FRANK MOSHER stories *High Water* (1989), *Where the Rivers Flow North* (1994), and *A Stranger in the Kingdom* (1998), Pennsylvania native Jay Craven attended Boston University (1968–1971) and the School of Visual Arts, New York (1973). He earned a GODDARD COLLEGE M.A. in media arts education in 1977 and attended seminars at the American Film Institute and the Maine Photographic Workshops. He began his Vermont film career in 1975 by founding St. Johnsbury's CATAMOUNT FILM AND ARTS CENTER as a traveling 16-millimeter film series, which he built into a dynamic arts-producing organization that presented Merce Cunningham, Miles Davis, the San Francisco Mime Troupe, and other nationally prominent performers. At Catamount, Craven also co-founded the CIRCUS SMIRKUS (with artistic director Rob Mermin) and produced films including *Dawn of the People* (with Doreen Kraft), about the Nicaraguan Literacy Crusade, and *Gayleen* (with Don Sunseri), a portrait of Vermont grass-roots artist Gayleen Aiken. Today, Craven and partner Bess O'Brien oversee KINGDOM COUNTY PRODUCTIONS and its Fledgling Films education program. Craven also teaches at MARLBORO COLLEGE and is the recipient of the 1998 Vermont Governor's Award for Artistic Excellence, the Producers Guild of America's 1995 NOVA Award for Most Promising Theatrical Motion Picture Producer of the Year, and 1991 and 2000 National Endowment for the Arts Film Production Grants.   *Kenneth A. Peck*

Cree, Albert (1898–1976)

Albert Cree came to Vermont in 1935 as vice president of Central Vermont Public Service and president of Twin State Gas and Electric, becoming president of CVPS in 1936. In 1943, he directed the merger of the two companies. Cree remained the CEO of the CVPS for thirty-three years and played a major role in the Vermont and New England utility industry. As Vermont's most powerful and resourceful advocate of private power interests he led the defeat of efforts by Governor ERNEST GIBSON, JR., to create a Vermont Power Authority in 1949. In 1955, when the legislature authorized the Public Service Commission to negotiate for power with the New York State Power Authority, Cree responded by organizing a consortium of thirty-three companies into Vermont Electric Company (Velco) with Cree elected president. In 1959, after the Vermont senate defeated a bill endorsed by Vermont's U.S. Senator GEORGE AIKEN for state transmission of St. Lawrence power, the state signed a contract for Velco to deliver the power. Opposition to state transmission, defeated sixteen to fourteen, was organized by Cree and hailed as the most important victory ever achieved by private power companies in the general assembly. Despite Cree and Aiken's clashes over private utilities, they forged a working relationship through their mutual belief in the future of atomic energy. By then, Cree had suffered a coronary that restricted his activities but could not keep him from continuing to direct the state's largest utility operations. In 1966, during the PHILIP HOFF gubernatorial administration, Cree was instrumental in defeating a proposal to form a state power authority to import Canadian power from Churchill Falls. A dedicated believer in nuclear power, his alternative was to establish a Vermont Yankee nuclear plant at Vernon. Although possessing great influence until his final days, any personal ambitions he may have harbored for elective office were shattered in 1947, even before his coronary, when his public image was tarnished by the collapse of the CVPS's East Pittsford dam. An active promoter, he was deeply involved in state and particularly Rutland civic affairs.   *Donald Wickman*

Crockett, Walter Hill (1870–1931)

Newspaperman, teacher, and historian, Walter Hill Crockett was born in Colchester and attended local schools and Mount Hermon School in Massachusetts. He taught briefly in his home town before joining the staff of the *BURLINGTON FREE PRESS* in 1895. After six years with the *Free Press*, Crockett moved to the *St. Albans Messenger*, followed by a stint as managing editor of the *Montpelier Journal* from 1909 until 1913. He then became director of the new Vermont State Publicity Bureau, a job he retained when appointed editor of publications at the UNIVERSITY OF VERMONT in 1915. Crockett worked for UVM the rest of his life, lecturing in journalism and Vermont history in addition to his editorial duties. Other activities included service on the Vermont Tercentenary Commission, six years as a Burlington alderman, membership on the Vermont Sesquicentennial Commission, two terms in the Vermont senate, and service as secretary of the Vermont Society of the Sons of the American Revolution. Best known as a Vermont historian, he wrote two works, *A History of Lake Champlain* (1909, revised and reprinted 1937) and *Vermont: The Green Mountain State* (1921–1923, 5 volumes), which remain important sources for the study of the state's past.

J. Kevin Graffagnino

Crown Point Road

After the capture by the British of French forts Carillon and St. Frédéric in late July and early August 1759, General Jeffrey Amherst, commander of the British forces, determined to build a road through the Vermont wilderness to Fort Number 4 on the CONNECTICUT RIVER, near present-day Charlestown, New Hampshire. This road would provide a supply line to the New England colonies and supplement the one that led to New York via Lake George and the Hudson River. Captain JOHN STARK and two hundred rangers marked and cut the road between August 8th and September 8th in an almost straight line of 77 miles. In October and November, the road was improved with bridges and widened to a width of 20 feet by a body of men under the command of Major Hawks of the Massachusetts militia. After Canada fell to the British and peace returned to the area, the road provided a convenient route for settlers across Vermont and into the Champlain Valley. It was once again used for military purposes during the Revolution, when troops and supplies were sent over it to support the Americans after their capture of TICONDEROGA. As the eighteenth century ended and the nineteenth century began, the road gradually became abandoned, except for those stretches that were incorporated into town roads. Its path can today be followed by a series of seventy-seven markers erected over many years and described in a booklet distributed by the Crown Point Road Association.

Cumberland and Gloucester Counties

The British colonial province of New York gave the names of Cumberland and Gloucester to two counties formed from land grants made by New Hampshire and New York governors in the region between the CONNECTICUT RIVER and the spine of the GREEN MOUNTAINS. Cumberland County, established 1768, was bounded on the south by the Massachusetts Bay Colony and ended on the north in the area of present-day Norwich. Gloucester County, set off in 1770, stretched north to the forty-fifth parallel, the boundary line established by the Treaty of Paris in 1763 between New York and Quebec. A New York census of 1771 recorded Cumberland's population as 3,935 whites and 12 blacks. Gloucester's population was recorded as 715 whites and 7 blacks. After Vermont declared independence from the British Crown and opposed New York's jurisdiction, the Vermont General Assembly combined Cumberland and Gloucester into Unity County, then renamed the entire region Cumberland County and finally, in 1781, divided Cumberland County into four smaller counties. Today, the seven counties east of the Green Mountains comprise the original Cumberland and Gloucester counties.

Dairy Farming

The largest share of Vermont's farm income comes from dairy: more than 70 percent in 2000, the biggest percentage of any state. When the sheep industry declined in the second quarter of the nineteenth century, farmers turned to dairy cows. Butter had become profitable with the invention of the factory cream separator, the Babcock tester to measure butterfat content of milk, and refrigerated rail cars. Butter production rose to 40 million pounds in 1900, leading the United States, partially due to the world's largest butter manufacturer, St. Albans Cooperative Creamery. By 1920, however, Vermont's butter production had declined as Western farmers increasingly shipped butter to Boston. Farmers then shifted to fluid milk, as technology and health codes improved milk quality and nutritionists declared milk a healthy food. On the farm, larger silos stored better winter feed to boost year-round milk production. More than half of Vermont's milk was shipped as fluid by 1920. Market demands also brought changes in the choice of cattle breeds. The Ayrshire, the most popular breed until butter production became important, was superseded by the Jersey for its butterfat-rich milk. As more milk was sold for drinking, the high-volume Holstein grew in importance. Since 1920, Holsteins have been the dominant breed. By the end of World War II, Vermont produced 1.3 billion pounds of dairy products a year. With a growing surplus of milk and cheap transportation in the East Coast market, less-perishable cheese became the largest dairy product. By 1956, Vermont supplied 40 percent of New England's milk. Dairy expanded greatly with new government price supports and research programs, increase in demand for milk, and new technology, such as balers, milking machines, artificial insemination, cattle genetics, pesticides, and plant hybrids. Productivity increased when tractors replaced horses and milking methods changed from buckets to pipelines to reduce labor costs. Bulk tanks, introduced in the early 1950s, quickly replaced cans. Increased production per cow made up for the decline in the total number of milk cows in the state, but the average number of cows per farm increased in order to reach an economy of scale that could pay for the new equipment. Formerly diversified farms specialized in dairy. The price of milk did not keep pace with inflation, and a growing post-war population bought up land and raised land prices. In the post-war years, Vermont lost more than 85% of its dairies as small farms, with heavier debt and low profits, went out of business. In the last half of the century, fluid milk consumption slipped while demand for yogurt, ice cream, and especially cheese escalated. By 2000, Vermont was processing half of its milk into various dairy products. Dairy farms grew bigger in size and became concentrated in good agricultural counties such as Franklin, Addison, and Orleans. The average herd grew from twenty-five cows in 1953 to ninety-nine in 2000. Production per cow rose from 5,000 pounds in 1945 to 17,500 in 2000. Milk production in the state grew from 1.28 billion pounds in 1947 to 2.79 billion pounds in 2000. Higher production contributed to a persistent national surplus of milk that overwhelmed any rise in demand. So the price of milk to farmers has been chronically low, taking a toll on the number of Vermont dairy farms, which dropped from 10,500 in 1954 to 1,600 in 2000. The Northeast Dairy Compact, a consumer-funded income-support program, propped up farm income for a few years until its demise in 2001. But innovative Vermont farmers also found new ways to survive. Adapting to changing markets and technology, some have become organic, others make their own products, such as cheese, to sell from the farm, others have welcomed tourism or have consolidated with other farms. And the dairy cow grazing a green pasture remains the emblem of a rural Vermont.   *Susan J. Harlow*

Dake, Thomas Royal (1786–1852)

A joiner or house builder, Thomas R. Dake was born in Windsor, where he seems to have been an apprentice joiner under ASHER BENJAMIN, and arrived in Castleton about 1807. At that time he appears to have been well trained in building designs. He worked for Jonathan Deming and married his daughter Sally in 1809. By 1810, he had built a house for himself on South Street that was remarkable for its unusual but charming placement of the entrance on the building's front corner. In 1810, he built a house for John Meacham that in some ways resembles a work by Benjamin, though they both could have used the same design books. His houses are notable for their stairways. A fine spiral staircase by Dake survives in the Ransom house, a Greek Revival mansion with seventeen Ionic columns, built in 1846 from English plans. Dake built several houses in Castleton that survive from the period 1812 to 1823 to support Castleton's designation as an Historic District. Dake's masterpiece, the Castleton Federated Church (1832), is also in the Greek Revival style, with a colonnade of six Doric columns and an austere interior, except for the beautiful pulpit that Dake completed by hand.

Dale, Porter H. (1867–1933)

Born in Island Pond, Porter H. Dale represented Vermont in the United States House of Representatives from 1914 to 1923 and in the Senate from 1923 to 1933. Dale attended Washington County Grammar School and Eastman Business College in Poughkeepsie, New York. In 1889, he graduated from James E. Murdoch's National School of Elocution and Oratory in Philadelphia and spent two years studying elocution with a Shakespearian scholar in Boston. After teaching elocution at Green Mountain Seminary and Bates College (1890–1892), he studied law and was admitted to the Vermont bar in 1896. The following year he became deputy collector of customs at Island Pond, a position he held until 1910. He failed in an attempt to secure the Republican nomination for Congress in 1900, but in 1910 was appointed municipal court judge and elected to the Vermont Senate from Essex County. He served two terms and in 1914 ran successfully for a seat in the U.S. House of Representatives, where he remained until 1923 when he was elected to the U.S. Senate to fill the vacancy caused by the death of WILLIAM DILLINGHAM. He remained in the Senate for the rest of his life, winning re-election in 1926 and 1932. His principal legislative service was as chairman of the Committee on Civil Service. He died in Westmore.

Daly, John B. (d. 1872)

An Irish Franciscan priest assigned by the Bishop of Boston in 1837 to assist Burlington's Father JEREMIAH O'CALLAGHAN, the sole Roman Catholic priest in Vermont, Father Daly served the southern half of Vermont, with headquarters in Middlebury and Castleton. He also ventured into eastern New Hampshire and northern Massachusetts. The area of his service was so wide and his congregations so dispersed that, in true Franciscan spirit, he seldom spent two nights in a row under the same roof. Father Daly retired from Vermont in 1854 to New York City to spend the remaining eighteen years of his life as chaplain of the Female Orphan Asylum on the corner of Prince and Mott streets.

William W. Goss

Danby

Danby, population 1,292, a town in Rutland County, was granted by BENNING WENTWORTH in 1761 to a group of men from Dutchess County, New York, and most likely was named after Thomas Osborne (1713–1789), fourth earl of Danby and Leeds. The town's eastern boundary approximates the course of OTTER CREEK at one of the narrowest spots in the VALLEY OF VERMONT, while the rest of the town lies in the crumpled terrain of the TACONIC MOUNTAINS, rising to 3,804 feet at Dorset Peak on the town's southern border. MARBLE from the massive underground quarry near Dorset Peak has been used in a number of famous buildings, including the U.S. Supreme Court building in Washington, D.C. The main settlement is Danby village, directly on the Danby–Mount Tabor line on U.S. Route 7, which follows the course of Otter Creek. THOMAS ROWLEY, the doggerel "poet of the GREEN MOUNTAIN BOYS," lived in Danby, as did PEARL BUCK, the novelist, who won the Nobel Prize for literature in 1938.

Danforth, Clarissa (1761–ca. 1855)

The first woman evangelist in Vermont, Clarissa Danforth was born in Weathersfield Bow on the CONNECTICUT RIVER. Her father, Joseph Danforth, kept a tavern, an ashery, a wharf, and a fleet of river flat boats. Converted about 1809 by Free Will Baptist John Colby of Sutton, she began preaching in her neighborhood after the War of 1812. Tall and poised, with a good education, she could be heard in the largest house. By 1818, she moved on to New Hampshire and then for four years preached mainly in Rhode Island. After her marriage to Danford Richmond, a Baptist minister from Connecticut, they

moved to western New York where she preached only occasionally.

T. D. Seymour Bassett

Daniels, Philomene Ostiguy
(1843–1929)

A native of St.-Mathias, Quebec, Philomene Ostiguy Daniels of Vergennes at the age of forty-three had a good claim to being the first woman in the United States to secure a license as pilot and master of a steam vessel. She began working as a steamboat pilot in 1877, assisting her husband Louis in their Vergennes-based steamboat line. The Daniels Boat Line ran a regular route on LAKE CHAMPLAIN from the Vergennes Basin to the Westport Landing in New York, and provided excursion and moonlight cruises for over thirty years. They also towed freight-laden canal boats from the Fort Cassin dock at the mouth of OTTER CREEK to industries located at the Vergennes Falls. Always very feminine and stylish, Philomene dressed in elaborate hats, fancy dresses, and jangling gold jewelry while at the helm. Though of small stature, her bluff, vivacious, and aggressive manner, as well as a zest for adventure, helped her to hold her own against any "old salt." "Captain Phil," as she was called, piloted the *Water Lily*, the *Little Nellie*, the *Victor*, and the *Alexander* on Otter Creek and Lake Champlain. After the death of her husband in 1903, she headed the business until turning it over to her family a short time after her marriage in 1908 to C. E. M. Caisse of Vergennes. A pioneer of her time, Captain Philomene Daniels has been called "one of the most picturesque and colorful figures in the history of steamboating on Otter Creek."

Jane Vincent

Danville

Danville, population 2,211, a town in Caledonia County, was granted by the Vermont legislature in 1786 and named for Jean Baptiste Bourguignon d'Anville (1697–1782), France's royal cartographer, at the suggestion of Michel Guillaume St. Jean de Crèvecoeur, author of *Letters from an American Farmer* and a friend of ETHAN ALLEN. One of Vermont's highest towns, Danville consists largely of wooded hills, widely scattered farms, and several settlements, the largest of which is Danville village. The only substantial body of water is 396-acre Joe's Pond, which the town shares with Cabot to the west. The annual meeting of the AMERICAN SOCIETY OF

DOWSERS takes place in Danville every August. The town was the birthplace of THADDEUS STEVENS, leader of the abolitionist Radical Republicans during the Civil War and leader in the fight to impeach President Andrew Johnson.

Darling, Alfred Burbank (1821–1896)

A native of Burke, Alfred Burbank Darling went to work in 1844 for Paran Stevens, a Boston hotelier, rising in 1852 to manager and subsequently partner in the Battle House in Mobile, Alabama. Having fled north during the Civil War, Darling, on hearing of Robert E. Lee's surrender to Ulysses S. Grant at Appomattox Courthouse, Virginia, in April 1865, was anxious to learn the condition of his hotel in Mobile. Darling appealed to President Abraham Lincoln for a pass permitting him to travel to Mobile and inspect his property. Lincoln, on his way to dinner, picked up a scrap of paper from his desk and wrote: "Allow the bearer, A. B. Darling, to pass to, and visit Mobile, if, and when that City shall be in our possession. A. Lincoln, April 13, 1865." The next night, Abraham Lincoln was shot at Ford's Theater in Washington, D.C. Darling's descendants have given the original Lincoln pass to the VERMONT HISTORICAL SOCIETY. A benefactor to his hometown, in 1865 Alfred Darling bought the Baptist Church in East Burke, leased the building to the Congregational Society, and contributed to the building's maintenance. He also aided the restoration of the historic Union Meeting House in Burke Hollow in 1895.

Harriet F. Fisher

Darling, Elmer A. (1848–1931)

After studying architecture at the Massachusetts Institute of Technology, Elmer A. Darling of East Burke went to work in 1872 for Hitchcock, Darling & Company in the management of the Fifth Avenue Hotel in New York City. By 1890, he was an officer of the company. The Fifth Avenue Hotel was completed in the late 1850s by his uncle ALFRED BURBANK DARLING (1821–1896), an accomplished restaurateur and hotelier. In the 1890s, Elmer Darling bought up farms and property on Bemis Hill (now Darling Hill) in East Burke until he had the largest farm in Vermont, the Mountain View Farm. In 1904, Darling began construction of an elegant mansion, Burklyn Hall, situated on the Burke-Lyndon town line. The Fifth Avenue Hotel served dairy products and other produce shipped from Darling's Mountain View Farm, where he maintained a prize herd of Jerseys to supply the hotel in New York until it closed in 1908. Unmarried, Elmer Darling then settled permanently at Burklyn Hall, where his unmarried sister Louise (1854–1925) served as Mountain View Farm's bookkeeper and his brother Lucius (1857–1937) superintended farm operations. A community supporter, Elmer Darling founded the Burke Mountain Club and built a clubhouse that became the town's social center and housed the East Burke Library. After a large fire destroyed Lyndonville's only hotel (and several commercial blocks) in 1924, Darling headed a group of subscribers who built a replacement that he designed, furnishing the dining room himself. The Darling Inn no longer serves as a hotel, although the dining room, complete with Darling's original furnishings, serves as a seniors meal site. Elmer Darling served as a bank and a railroad director, a trustee of St. Johnsbury Academy, and president of Lyndon Institute. His estate contributed generously to the town of Burke and to Lyndon Institute.   *Harriet F. Fisher*

Davenport, Thomas (1802–1851)

Generally credited with devising the first electric motor, Thomas Davenport was born in Williamstown. He apprenticed as a blacksmith in his home town until, completing his service, he moved to Brandon at age twenty-one and settled in Forest Dale, the site of an iron works and mine, where he married and plied the blacksmith's trade. Fascinated by the action of a large magnet on display in Crown Point, New York, Davenport bought the device from its exhibitors and took it back to Brandon where he studied it at length. He learned that its power came from a current of electricity supplied by two wires running from two cups of mercury and wrapped around an iron bar, which weighed only 3 pounds but could suspend a 150-pound anvil simply by contact between the surfaces of the magnet and the bar. Davenport built larger magnets and learned how to cut off and restart currents with a switch. Experimenting with current fields and iron in the mid-1830s, Davenport eventually devised a method of inducing rotary motion to a wheel by charging an electric current through a coil wrapping on an iron bar. In 1837, Thomas Davenport was granted a patent for an electric induction motor. He also constructed a model railway car run by an electric motor at a time when not a single mile of steam railway ran through Vermont.

Davis, Deane C. (1900–1990)

Attorney Deane C. Davis of East Barre was the governor of Vermont whose efforts to protect land and water from damaging real estate and other developments produced landmark environmental legislation in Act 250, which regulates land use, and Act 252, a comprehensive water regulation program. After Boston University Law School and admission to the Vermont bar in 1922, Davis opened a law office in Barre and in 1936 joined the law firm of Wilson, Carver, Davis, and Keyser. In 1940, he was appointed general counsel to the National Life Insurance Company, beginning a career that led in 1965 to his election as chairman of the board and president. In the public sector, he served as state's attorney for Washington County (1926–1928) and superior court judge (1931–1936), before resigning from the bench to return to private practice. Active in Republican political circles, he participated in state and national conventions and was frequently mentioned for elective office. He was the appointed chairman of the legislative committee to study Vermont state government known as the "Little Hoover Commission," which proposed the Department of Administration later established by Governor Robert Stafford. In 1968, Davis was elected governor as a Republican. In addition to his legislative initiatives resulting in Acts 250 and 252, he reorganized the administrative functions of government and installed the cabinet system by which government agencies reported to him. He ran state government for four years with a balanced budget, a result in good part of a sales tax he initiated. Deficits inherited from past administrations were also eradicated. He retired from public life in 1973 but was remembered for many years thereafter for a television advertisement in his 1968 campaign in which gubernatorial candidate Davis in shirtsleeves was presented bailing out a sinking rowboat dubbed "Vermont."

Day, Gordon Malcolm (1911–1973)

An ethnohistorian who pioneered the modern study of the Abenaki and their language, Gordon Day was born in Albany and was employed by the Vermont Forest Service while attending the School of Forestry at Syracuse University. He earned a bachelor's degree in 1938 and a master of forestry the following year. In 1940–1941, he served as a junior forester for the U.S. Forest Service and shortly thereafter began work on a Ph.D. in forestry at Rutgers University that he completed in 1949. He taught intermittently at Rutgers from 1941 until 1952, rising from instructor to associate professor. His study of forest ecology heightened his interest in the Eastern Woodland's early Abenaki inhabitants and earned him an appointment as a research associate in anthropology at Dartmouth College and then appointment as ethnohistorian for the National Museum of Man in Ottawa, Canada. His works in forest ecology and linguistic studies have provided the foundation for subsequent research on the Abenaki and other Algonkians. His final contribution was a dictionary of the western Abenaki language that he compiled with Jeanne Brink.

Dean, Howard (b. 1948)

The longest-serving governor of modern times, Howard Dean was born in New York City and grew up in East Hampton, New York. He attended St. George's School in Newport, Rhode Island, graduated from Yale University in 1971, and received his M.D. degree from Albert Einstein College of Medicine in 1978. After a residency at the Medical Center Hospital in Burlington, he remained in the area and established a practice in internal medicine in Shelburne. Infected with a passion for politics at a young age, he joined the state Democratic party and in 1982 and 1984 was elected to the Vermont House of Representatives, where he served on the Rules Committee and as assistant minority leader. In 1986, he was elected lieutenant governor and re-elected in 1988 and 1990. He became governor upon the death of Richard Snelling in 1991, and committed himself to maintaining Snelling's fiscal program. In 1992, he was elected to a full term and re-elected biennially through 2000. Among his legislative accomplishments were the institution of the Success by Six and Dr. Dynosaur programs, the first a preschool program for four- and five-year-olds and the second a Medicaid program for children under eighteen. As a medical man, he opposed the growing of hemp as possibly contributing to a rise in marijuana use, and opposed the introduction of methadone clinics into Vermont to combat a growing heroin problem. A fiscal conservative but a social moderate, Dean signed into law two of the most controversial measures of recent times, the Equal Educational Opportunity Act of 1999 (ACT 60) and An Act Relating to CIVIL UNIONS in 2000. As a result of public reaction to both measures, he was limited to a narrow victory over Ruth Dwyer, a conservative Republican, and Anthony Pollina, a Progressive, in the 2000 gubernatorial election. He decided not to run for reelection in 2002 and was succeeded by James H. Douglas.

Dean, Leon W. (1889–1982)

Author, editor, professor, and inveterate joiner, Leon Dean pioneered in the dissemination of Vermont history and folklore through his writings and organizational skills. Born in Bristol, he graduated from Mount Hermon Academy in 1911 and the UNIVERSITY OF VERMONT, Phi Beta Kappa, in 1915. After graduation, he set up in New York as part-owner and editor of the *Lake Placid News* and wrote for juvenile publications. Returning to Burlington in 1923, he joined the University of Vermont faculty, taught journalism, short-story writing, and Vermont history, and for a time edited the alumni magazine, served as an Agricultural Extension editor, and as the first announcer for radio station WCAX-AM when it was located at the University. He retired in 1956. His articles and books were Vermont-based and, apart from *The Admission of Vermont into the Union* celebrating the state's sesquicentennial, were historical fiction for juveniles. Founder of the Green Mountain Folklore Society, the VERMONT OLD CEMETERY ASSOCIATION, and the Genealogical Society of Vermont, he was the first president of the Chittenden County Historical Society, a prominent member and officer of the VERMONT HISTORICAL SOCIETY, and participated actively in numerous other organizations, including patriotic societies such as the Sons of the American Revolution.

Dean, Reuben (d. ca. 1800)

A silversmith of Windsor, Reuben Dean lived "between the gristmill and the meeting house" on the east side of the highway along the CONNECTICUT RIVER when he cut the Vermont State Seal designed by IRA ALLEN. Allen charged the State on October 26, 1778, for "two days at Windsor drawing a plan for a state seal and getting

Mr. R. Dean to make it." Allen and Dean were both paid ten shillings for their work. Dean later billed the General Assembly on June 5, 1779, for "a screw for the State Seal."   *Lilian Baker Carlisle*

Deere, John (1804–1886)

Developer and manufacturer of the plow that broke the plains, John Deere was born in Rutland, where he attended the local common schools. At seventeen, he was apprenticed to a blacksmith in Middlebury, and after four years sufficiently mastered the trade to ply it successfully for the next twelve years in his native state. Seeking greener pastures, in 1837 he migrated to Grand Detour, Illinois, where he opened a blacksmith shop. He soon discovered that the plows brought from the east were unsatisfactory for working western prairie soil. Deere experimented with new plows that incorporated iron and steel parts in place of standard wooden ones, and along with a partner began manufacturing and selling these plows with some success. In 1846, their annual output approximated one thousand plows. At that time, Deere, who had continued experimenting, sold out his Grand Detour interest and moved to Moline, where he organized Deere and Company. By 1857, in large part due to improved steel plates, the annual output of Deere plows had risen to ten thousand. Subsequently the company took on the manufacture of cultivators and allied products. John Deere served actively as company president until his final illness, when the reins of leadership passed to his son.

Dellinger, David (b. 1915)

A peace activist and author of the autobiography *From Yale to Jail*, David Dellinger was raised in Connecticut in a comfortable upper-middleclass household, graduated from Yale University, attended Oxford on a graduate fellowship, and repudiated capitalism. After a short association with the U.S. Communist party, he left, rejecting both its ideology and discipline in favor of socialism. He also enrolled in the Union Theological Seminary in New York City but left after a year. When the United States entered World War II, Dellinger was living in a Newark, New Jersey, commune with his wife, Elizabeth Peterson, whom he had met at a National Conference of the Christian Student Movement. Dellinger refused to serve in the military or provide alternate service and

was sentenced to prison. Released at war's end after serving almost three years, he immediately resumed pacifist protests by participating in ban-the-bomb events, and later figured prominently in civil rights demonstrations. As an older radical, Dellinger attempted to bridge the gap between the old left molded by the Depression and the new left fueled by the Vietnam War. In the mid-1960s, he co-founded and became chairman of the National Mobilization and End the War in Vietnam (MOBE) and sparked civil disobedience protests in New York, San Francisco, and at the Pentagon. In 1968, Dellinger and younger radicals, some of whom he had recruited, participated in the Chicago riots that accompanied the Democratic National Convention. Eight of the protesters including Dellinger were subsequently brought to a five-month trial. Dubbed the Chicago Eight, they received daily national press and television coverage. Two were acquitted and Dellinger, five associates, and their lawyers were given jail terms. All convictions were overthrown on appeal. The Dellingers vacationed in Vermont during the 1970s and moved to Peacham after Dellinger had taught two years at GODDARD COLLEGE and VERMONT COLLEGE. Vermont living did not temper their activism. The couple was arrested at a Vermont sit-in opposing General Electric's production of military weapons and then-Representative JAMES JEFFORDS' support of U.S. aid to the Contras in Nicaragua. In April 2001, Dellinger traveled to Quebec City to protest corporate globalization at an international trade conference.

DeMar, Clarence (1888–1958)

Seven-time winner of the Boston Marathon, Clarence DeMar was born in Madeira, Ohio, and first came to Vermont at the age of sixteen to work on the Kinney fruit farm in South Hero. Entering the UNIVERSITY OF VERMONT in 1907, his first thought of running a marathon came to him while he was delivering milk samples from the experiment station to the State Hygiene Laboratory, DeMar electing to cover the distance by running. In his third year at UVM, he began running competitively with the cross-country team, but left UVM in 1910 to return to Melrose, Massachusetts, to help support his mother. In that same year, he ran his first Boston Marathon, remarkably finishing in second place. In 1911, he won the Boston Marathon for the first time. Eventually, DeMar ran in thirty-four Boston Marathons, finishing in the top ten fifteen times and winning his seventh victory in 1930 at the age of forty-two. He competed in the Olympics in 1912, 1924, and 1928, finishing in third place in 1924. In addition to running, DeMar worked as a printer and educator, taught Bible school, was a Boy Scout leader, and wrote his autobiography, *Marathon* (1937, reprinted 1981). Several running events held annually around New England memorialize his achievements, including the Clarence DeMar Annual Road Race (10K and 5K), sponsored by the South Hero Rescue Squad and the Green Mountain Athletic Association each July in South Hero.   *Chris Burns*

Democratic Party

In 1828, supporters of Andrew Jackson campaigning as Jacksonians and fielding a slate of candidates for state and local offices founded the immediate antecedent of the modern Vermont Democratic party. By 1832, they had appropriated the designation Democrats, but despite contesting every major Vermont and national election since their founding, they achieved few electoral victories until the second half of the twentieth century. Their most frequent ante-bellum successes were in congressional races, where they won seven of the thirty-one contested seats between 1836 and 1848, and none again until 1958. Only two of their candidates, Isaac Fletcher and PAUL DILLINGHAM, were ever reelected. The most celebrated pre–Civil War Democratic victory occurred in 1853 when the WHIG incumbent gubernatorial candidate won a plurality but ran short of a popular majority. The election was thrown to the legislature, where a coalition of Democrats and FREE-SOILERS elected Democrat JOHN S. ROBINSON in what proved a Pyrrhic victory. Reasons for the Democrats not gaining wide popular acceptance included their opposition to a protective tariff, their opposition to the principle of non-extension of slavery into the territories, and Democratic appeals to the Catholic population, all of which ran contrary to mainstream Vermont sentiment. At the outbreak of the Civil War, the failure of the party to unite in support of the Union cause led to additional defections and the transfer of some of the party's most popular leaders to REPUBLICAN PARTY leadership ranks. After the war, Democrats courted continued opprobrium by resisting Republican reconstruction. A unanimous vote against adoption of the fifteenth amendment by Democratic delegates to the Vermont house was particularly damaging. Toward the end of the nineteenth century, as Republican support for the freedmen diminished, Democrats alienated potential Vermont supporters by advocating inflationary monetary policies. After 1884, the election of Democratic national administrations provided greater patronage opportunities. The biggest prize, Vermont's then only federal district court judgeship, was held by a Democrat from 1915 (President Woodrow Wilson's first administration) until 1950 (President Harry Truman's second administration), yet despite temporarily narrowing the electoral gap during the New Deal, Vermont Democrats failed to win any important offices. In 1949, in an unprecedented repudiation of the state party and its longtime national committeeman, FRANK DUFFY, Harry Truman nominated Republican Governor ERNEST W. GIBSON, JR., as Vermont's federal district court judge. Duffy died the following year. With the party denied a traditional patronage source and dependent upon younger leadership, candidates campaigned more vigorously and emerged as competitive in non-presidential election years. In 1958, they broke through to elect WILLIAM MEYER as Vermont's congressman for a single term. In 1962, capitalizing on Republican disaffection and nominating PHILIP HOFF, the first non-Catholic Democratic gubernatorial candidate in decades, they captured the governor's office by a narrow popular majority made possible by splinter parties. In 1964, for the first time in history, Vermonters voted for Democratic presidential electors and put the entire state Democratic slate into office. Since then, Democrats have held the governor's office more often than not. It would not be until after REAPPORTIONMENT in 1965 that the party would win legislative majorities. By 1975, with the support of independent Republicans, house Democrats were able to elect Democratic speakers. In 1975, when GEORGE AIKEN retired from the U.S. Senate, he was replaced by Democrat PATRICK LEAHY, who has served into the twenty-first century. Democrats captured Vermont's house in 1983 and the senate in 1985. Since 1992, the state has been regarded as "safely Democratic" in presidential elections. Vermont's conversion to a two-party, Democratic-leaning state may be attributable to a large influx of newcomers since the 1960s who tend to bring liberal Democratic views with them. While this has contributed to the most-recent voting phenomena, the initial Democratic successes were due to attracting traditional Republican voters.

Derby

Derby, population 4,604, a town in Orleans County, was granted by the Vermont legislature in 1779 to Timothy Andrews and others and named after Derby, Connecticut. Still primarily rural despite its proximity to Newport city just to the west, Derby is bordered on the northwest by LAKE MEMPHREMAGOG and bisected east to west by the Clyde River, along which lie four lakes, the largest of which is 788-acre Lake Salem. Of the two major settlements, Derby Center and Derby Line, the latter is directly on the Canadian border and merges with its slightly larger neighbor, Rock Island, Quebec. Derby Line's Haskell Opera House, built in the nineteenth century, straddles the border, so that the audience sits in the United States while the stage is in Canada. A smaller border settlement, Beebe Plain, similarly merges with its Canadian counterpart, Beebe, Quebec.

DeWees, Rusty (b. 1960)

A hard-working actor who lives part-time in New York City, Stowe's Rusty DeWees had a popular success across Vermont in 1999 and 2000 with his one-man stage show *The Logger*. The hit comedy performance gave birth to spin-off videos, a compact disc, and a calendar. In the traditional stage character of the witty, sly, and heavily ironic Yankee rustic, DeWees portrays his Logger as the quintessential Vermont "WOODCHUCK." He is a Chestnut Hill, Pennsylvania, native who grew up in Stowe. DeWees' acting career in New York City has included jobs on the popular television show *Law and Order* and in films with Liam Neeson, Patrick Swayze, Harrison Ford, and Brad Pitt. Locally, he has appeared in features by JAY CRAVEN, David Giancola, and Nora Jacobson. Prior to his film success, DeWees' stage portrait of Antoine in DAVID BUDBILL's *Judevine* earned appreciation throughout Vermont. In *Mud Season*, an out-of-state independent film shot in Vermont in 1998, DeWees plays a softer, more sensitive character than the rough and sometimes hard-edged Logger and Antoine.   *Kenneth A. Peck*

Dewey, George (1837–1917)

A naval officer who became a hero during the Spanish-American War when the U.S. fleet he commanded destroyed the Spanish fleet at Manila in the Philippines, George Dewey was born in Montpelier and graduated from the U.S. Naval Academy in 1858. As a lieutenant in the U.S. Navy, he commanded the sloop *Mississippi* when Admiral David Farragut captured New Orleans in 1862. He remained in the navy after the Civil War and had attained the rank of commodore by 1897, commanding the navy's Asiatic Squadron. Prompted partly by a report to Congress on conditions in Cuba under Spanish rule by fellow Vermonter Senator REDFIELD PROCTOR, SR., the United States declared war on Spain in April 1898. Dewey's squadron was immediately ordered from Hong Kong to "capture or destroy the Spanish squadron" based in Manila. On May 1, he engaged the Spanish fleet in Manila Bay after giving his famous command to the captain of his flagship: "You may fire when you are ready, Gridley." Dewey's squadron completely destroyed the Spanish fleet without the loss of a single American and with only eight men wounded. The American victory thrust the United States into worldwide competition as a colonial power and helped heal the lingering wounds of the Civil War by creating a new symbol of national pride. Within a few days, Dewey was promoted to rear admiral. A year later he was promoted to the special rank of

Admiral George Dewey. Special Collections, Bailey/Howe Library, University of Vermont

Admiral of the Navy, and Congress passed a special act to enable Dewey to continue in active service past the legal retirement age. He also served as president of the General Board of the U.S. Navy from 1900 until his death.

Dewey, Jedediah (1714–1778)

A Bennington settler of the early 1760s, the Reverend Jedediah Dewey came from Westfield, Massachusetts, to become the first minister and first school teacher in the New Hampshire grants. He was a prominent figure in the disputes concerning the validity of land titles issued by both New York and New Hampshire for the same tracts of land in the Bennington region. He corresponded with New York's Governor William Tryon on the matter and worked to end the disputes by peaceful negotiation. The Reverend Dewey preached a thanksgiving sermon upon the capture of FORT TICONDEROGA in May 1775, giving the Lord full credit for the quick victory until, according to tradition, ETHAN ALLEN interrupted him to claim some credit for his own role in the event. Parson Dewey promptly ordered Allen to sit down, "thou bold blasphemer, and listen to the word of God." The Reverend Dewey also preached the war sermon previous to the BATTLE OF BENNINGTON in 1777, an event in which his son Elijah Dewey honorably led a Vermont militia company.

Dewey, John (1859–1952)

Philosopher, psychologist, and educator John Dewey was born in Burlington. He received a UNIVERSITY OF VERMONT bachelor of arts in 1879 and a Ph.D. degree from Johns Hopkins University in 1884. Dewey's long and influential career in education began on the faculty of the University of Michigan (1884–1894). He went on to the University of Chicago (1894–1904) and then Columbia University until his retirement in 1931. While at Chicago, Dewey became interested in the reform of educational theory and practice. He tested his educational principles at the University of Chicago's experimental Laboratory School. Dewey emphasized learning through varied activities rather than formal curricula, and opposed authoritarian methods as inadequate to prepare citizens for life in a democratic society. Dewey was largely responsible for the educational reforms in the United States during the early twentieth century that

John Dewey. Special Collections, Bailey/Howe Library, University of Vermont

shifted the focus of teaching to the student. Often misinterpreted by progressive educators, especially on the question of discipline, Dewey's opposition to authoritarian teaching methods did not surrender guidance and control. Education that simply amused or kept students busy and pure vocational training were also both alien to Dewey's vision. His philosophy, called either instrumentalism or experimentalism, stems from the pragmatism of William James. In 1924, he returned to UVM to help celebrate the one hundredth anniversary of the first American publication at Burlington of Samuel Taylor Coleridge's *Aids to Reflection* in an edition by UVM's President JAMES MARSH. Dewey said at the time that Coleridge's book, an influential text in the development of American philosophy, had also helped shape his thinking. His voluminous writings include *Psychology* (1887), *The School and Society* (1899), *Democracy and Education* (1916), *Reconstruction in Philosophy* (1920), *Human Nature and Conduct* (1922), *The Quest for Certainty* (1929), *Art as Experience* (1934), *Logic: The Theory of Inquiry* (1938), and *Problems of Men* (1946). He is buried beside the Ira Allen Chapel at UVM.

Dewey, Julius Y. (1799–1866)

Julius Y. Dewey was a practicing physician in 1848 when the State of Vermont issued a charter for the National Life Insurance Company to conduct business in Montpelier. Dewey became the company's first medical officer. In 1849, he succeeded William C. Kittredge as president, an office he held for twenty-six years. His son Charles succeeded him, serving another twenty-six years. Admiral GEORGE DEWEY, hero of the battle of Manila Bay in the Spanish-American war of 1898, was also a son of Dr. Dewey.

Dewey Day

On October 12, 1899, Vermonters converged on Montpelier to stage an historic welcome home for native son Admiral GEORGE DEWEY, whose success in destroying the Spanish fleet at Manila Bay during the Spanish-American War made him the nation's foremost naval hero and shed glory on his native state. Upon his return to the United States in September 1899, Dewey was greeted with nearly hysterical acclaim. Children nationwide contributed dimes for a magnificent trophy (now on exhibit at the Chicago Historical Society), private funds were contributed to purchase a house for him in Washington, D.C., and Congress made him a rear admiral, and then created for him the rank of Admiral of the Navy. Songs and poems were written about him. Vermont writer ROBERT L. DUFFUS recalled that in Vermont "children . . . were named Dewey. So were dogs, streets, and schools." Following a national tour, Dewey finally returned home, arriving in Bennington on October 10, 1899, where he was met by Governor Edward C. Smith and provided a special train by Dr. WILLIAM S. WEBB of Shelburne. He made a slow progress north and arrived in Montpelier the evening of October 11. The next day, forty thousand people converged on the state capital. The Central Vermont Railroad built thirteen special tracks and a temporary station to handle the trains bringing Vermonters from throughout the state. The VERMONT STATE HOUSE and other public buildings were draped in red, white, and blue bunting, and a huge portrait of the admiral hung from the State House portico, illuminated by 1,555 electric lights. A parade, fireworks, and an enormous bonfire punctuated the day's wild celebration. It was a triumph of nationalism, combining the pomp, romanticism, and extravagance of the Victorian era in America.

Michael Sherman

Dillingham, Paul (1799–1891)

Congressman, governor, and father of governor and U.S. Senator WILLIAM PAUL DILLINGHAM, Paul Dillingham ranked among the state's very ablest attorneys, and was credited with having drawn "tears and verdicts from juries" for over fifty years. His family migrated from Shutesbury, Massachusetts, to Waterbury in 1805 and Paul attended Waterbury district school and the Washington County Grammar School in Montpelier. He studied law in Montpelier with Dan Carpenter and after admission to the bar in 1823 formed a partnership with his mentor. A prolific officeholder, he served as Waterbury town clerk (1829–1844); representative from Waterbury to the state legislature (1833, 1834, 1837, 1838, and 1840); member of the constitutional conventions of 1836, 1857, and 1870; Washington County state senator (1841, 1842, 1861); and in 1842 and 1844 was elected as a Democrat to Congress. The only Democrat in Vermont's delegation, he supported the admission of Texas as a state and President Polk's policies leading to the Mexican War. The war, immensely unpopular in Vermont, contributed further to the decline of the state's DEMOCRATIC PARTY. Dillingham nonetheless retained his leadership role in the party until the outbreak of the Civil War, when his ardent support for the union led him to decline the 1860 Democratic nomination for governor and gain election to the 1861 state senate as a Republican. Accepted eagerly into REPUBLICAN PARTY ranks (a son was killed in the war), he was elected to three terms as lieutenant governor (1862, 1863, and 1864), and two terms as governor (1865 and 1866). The establishment of the state's first reform school was his proudest gubernatorial achievement. After leaving office, he served as a delegate to the 1870 constitutional convention and returned to a law practice, entering into a partnership with his son William Paul from which he retired in 1875.

Dillingham, William Paul (1843–1923)

Governor and U.S. senator, William Dillingham's national reputation rests on his influence over immigration policies. As chairman of the Joint Senate-House Immigration Commission, popularly known as the Dillingham Commission, his forty-one-volume report helped popularize the concept that race predetermined ability and spearheaded the movement for national origin quotas. Dillingham's own advocacy of Anglo-Saxon supremacy reflected a widely held belief in Vermont. Highly conscious of roots tracing back to service under General Wolfe on the Plains of Abraham and with an older brother killed during the Civil War, William was a strong proponent of tradition and encouraged societies such as the Sons of the American Revolution. A native of Waterbury, he attended the local schools and then Newbury Academy in Newbury and Kimball Union Academy in Meriden, New Hampshire. Disqualified for military service in the Civil War by bad health, he began study at Albany Law School and then apprenticed at his brother-in-law's office in Milwaukee, Wisconsin. He returned to Vermont where he was admitted to the bar in 1867 and formed a partnership with his father, former Governor PAUL DILLINGHAM. After his father retired, he practiced alone for a time and then formed a practice with Hiram Huse and Fred Howland, later president of National Life Insurance. The year William was admitted to the bar, he also served as secretary of civil and military affairs for his father, a post he also held from 1874 to 1876 during Governor Asahel's administration. He was state's attorney for Washington County 1872 to 1876, represented Waterbury in the state legislature in 1876 and 1884, and was state tax commissioner from 1882 to 1888. In the latter year, he was elected governor. In 1900, despite the opposition of Senator REDFIELD PROCTOR, SR., the most powerful politician in Vermont, the legislature chose Dillingham to fill the vacancy caused by the death of JUSTIN MORRILL. Two years later, he was elected to a full term and re-elected in 1908, 1914, and 1920. The state's first popular election for a Senate seat in 1914 was Dillingham's greatest challenge. As a strict party-line Republican who wore the label "reactionary" without protest and had seldom strayed from Washington, D.C., he returned to Vermont to preach the rural virtues and demonstrate consummate strength as a campaign orator. He won almost 60 percent of the vote and, in 1920, captured almost 80 percent. He died in office.

Dorr, Julia (1825–1913)

Born in Charleston, South Carolina, Julia Ripley Dorr grew up in Middlebury and spent most of her adult life in Rutland. She wrote stories, novels, travel sketches, and poetry, which were published in the major magazines of the nineteenth century and usually collected in books. Although highly conventional in subject and style, her poems found favor with contemporaries including Ralph Waldo Emerson, Oliver Wendell Holmes, and Henry Wadsworth Longfellow. Emerson wrote of her poetry that she had "extraordinary facility of versifying, good taste, and easy command of poetic material."

Dorset

Dorset, population 2,036, a town in Bennington County, was granted by BENNING WENTWORTH in 1761 and probably named after Lionel Cranfield Sackville (1688–1765), the first duke of Dorset. Its eastern section lies in the narrowest part of the VALLEY OF VERMONT, straddling the headwaters of OTTER CREEK, which flows north into LAKE CHAMPLAIN, and BATTEN KILL, which flows south and then west into the Hudson River. The western section of the town consists of another, shallower valley where the northward-flowing Mettawee River begins. In between the two valleys lie several peaks of the TACONIC MOUNTAINS, the highest of which is 3,185-foot Mount Aeolus, site of Vermont's largest and best-known bat cave. With Westminster and Windsor, Dorset can be said to be the place where Vermont began as a political entity. Twice in 1776 the leaders of the New Hampshire grants, including IRA ALLEN and THOMAS CHITTENDEN, met in Cephas Kent's tavern in Dorset village to proclaim independence from first New York and then New Hampshire as a "separate district"; in January of 1777 at Westminster the settlers called for "a new and separate state" and in July of the same year the Vermont constitution was adopted at Windsor. The first commercial MARBLE quarry in the United States was opened in South Dorset in 1785, and for many years supplied material for public buildings throughout the country. The major settlement is attractive, well-maintained Dorset village, which is on the National Register of Historic Places. The town, which has drawn affluent summer visitors for more than a century, is part of the string of upscale tourist destinations in southwestern Vermont that also includes the towns of Bennington, Arlington, and Manchester.

Douglas, Stephen Arnold (1813–1861)

A Democratic leader from Illinois noted for his debates with Abraham Lincoln, Stephen A. Douglas was born in Brandon and educated in schools there and in Canandaigua, New York. He practiced law in Illinois, where he rose through various state offices until he was elected to the U.S. House of Representatives in 1842. He became an outstanding spokesman for a policy of national expansion. Nicknamed the Little Giant for his small stature but great ability as an orator and legislator, he was elected to the U.S. Senate in 1846 by the state legislature. He set back the antislavery cause by leading the repeal of the Missouri Compromise in 1854 by incorporating in the bill to establish the territories of Kansas and Nebraska a provision that the inhabitants of these territories might decide whether slavery should be permitted within their borders. Vermont and other northern states formed anti-Nebraska groups. The *Montpelier Watchman* called the Kansas-Nebraska Act "a Deed of Darkness . . . Every vote in the affirmative we regard as a stain upon the personal integrity of the man who casts it. Let no such man be trusted." In 1851, Douglas visited Brandon and Middlebury, and at MIDDLEBURY COLLEGE was awarded a doctorate in legal letters *in honoris causa*. In his following remarks he observed that "Vermont was a good state to be born in provided one migrated early." Later, when he was the Democrats' candidate for president in 1860, Douglas campaigned in Vermont. He marched in a parade for him in Brandon and with Democratic gubernatorial candidate JOHN GODFREY SAXE addressed a large audience at Burlington town hall before going on to Montpelier to address a crowd in State Street from the balcony of the Pavilion Hotel. Douglas lost the presidential election to Abraham Lincoln, but when the Civil War broke out, he gave Lincoln loyal support. He contracted typhoid fever and died in Chicago while on a mission in the midwestern and border states to rally popular support for the Union cause.

Dover

Dover, population 1,410, a town in Windham County, was created in response to residents' petition by the Vermont legislature in 1810 out of the southern district of Wardsboro and named for Dover in either New Hampshire or England. The hilly, heavily wooded land rises to 3,556 feet at Mount Snow on the western border with Somerset, and more than half the town lies within the GREEN MOUNTAIN NATIONAL FOREST. The high hills were settled first by Revolutionary War veterans in 1779 and later by families from Massachusetts who fled to Vermont because of their involvement in SHAYS' REBELLION. A major settlement developed at Dover Center (now Dover Common), and subsequent population growth occurred in the valleys: East Dover was established on the Rock River and West Dover on the North Branch of the Deerfield. The number of inhabitants peaked just prior to 1816 and was not matched again until the 1990s. With the opening of the Mount Snow ski area in 1954, the town slowly evolved from an area dependent on subsistence dairy farming and logging into today's year-round resort. In addition to SKIING and SNOWBOARDING (130 trails and a vertical drop of 1,700 feet) in the winter months, summer attractions include mountain biking, hiking, golfing, and tennis. Lodging and dining facilities are available along Route 100, the major north-south artery.

Dowsers

See AMERICAN SOCIETY OF DOWSERS.

Dresden Press

The printing press that ALDEN SPOONER brought with him from Connecticut to Hanover, New Hampshire, in 1778 was used in the pamphlet wars over the first EAST UNION of sixteen New Hampshire towns with Vermont and later for official State of Vermont printing. The press, later known as the Dresden Press for the section of Hanover where it was first installed, apparently was purchased by Dartmouth College from Timothy Green III in Connecticut by means of a subscription, following which it passed into Spooner's hands. Now in the VERMONT HISTORICAL SOCIETY, it was once declared to be the press brought from England to Cambridge, Massachusetts, in 1638 by José Glover. That has not been proven, but it is accepted as the press used by Thomas Short, Connecticut's first printer, and was the first official press of the state of Vermont.

Marcus A. McCorison

Duane, James (1733–1797)

The New York attorney most persistently obnoxious to ETHAN ALLEN, James Duane of New York City was a large land speculator in the Province of New York, including those lands also granted by New Hampshire's Governor BENNING WENTWORTH. A conservative, he nonetheless supported the revolutionary cause from the beginning and was elected to the Continental Congress in 1774 and served almost continuously until 1783. From 1784 until 1789, he was mayor of New York City and in 1798 was appointed the first federal judge for the district of New York. As the largest holder of New York land grants in Vermont and a person of great influence, he resisted New Hampshire grant claimants, brought ejectment actions against several of them in the court at Albany, and came to personify the forces of oppression. "The GODS OF THE HILLS ARE NOT THE GODS OF THE VALLEY," Allen's defiant affirmation of resistance to New York authority, was given in response to an admonition that Allen abide by an Albany county court ruling that invalidated New Hampshire titles in Duane's favor.

Duffus, Robert Luther (1888–1972)

Waterbury native Robert Luther Duffus earned A.B. and M.A. degrees from Stanford University and went on to work as a reporter and editorial writer for newspapers in the San Francisco Bay area until 1937, when he joined the *New York Times*. An author of twenty books, including novels and observations on contemporary mores and customs, his works include two recollections of life in Vermont: *The Williamstown Branch* (1958) and *The Waterbury Record: More Vermont Memories* (1958).

Duffy, Frank H. (1871–1950)

Born and educated in East Dorset, Frank Duffy was a long-time leader of the DEMOCRATIC PARTY in Vermont, Democratic national committeeman from 1920 until his death, and personal friend of presidents and other national officials. A Rutland resident by 1890 where he began his business career, he started as a hardware store clerk and later worked for a wholesale beer business. He also managed hotels in Rutland and New York City. In 1914, he left hotels for the real estate business. He remained a realtor, and was president of the Rutland Building and Loan Association at the time of his death. During World War I, he managed the Rutland employment office for the U.S. Department of Labor. Duffy entered politics in 1896 when he became a Democratic city committeeman in Rutland. He was elected Democratic national committeeman from Vermont at the party's national convention in San Francisco in 1920 and held this post until his death, serving as the party's oldest national committeeman in terms of years of service. While never a candidate for elective office, Duffy served on city, county, state, and Democratic commit-

tees. A loyal Democrat in Republican Vermont, Duffy held that his party represented the "common folk," but despite Duffy's dispensing of patronage throughout the New Deal, the Democratic party never made a breakthrough in Vermont. In the 1936 presidential election, Franklin Roosevelt carried all states except Vermont and Maine. Duffy demonstrated a strong influence in framing the policies of his party both in the state and nationally. He was invited to the Wilson White House, and was a long-time and personal friend of both President Roosevelt and Cordell Hull, former secretary of state. Duffy played a role in Harry Truman's selection as vice president, but he lost influence when Truman became president. At the state convention in 1948, there was an unsuccessful attempt by Rutland Mayor Dan J. Healy and others to unseat Duffy as party leader. Healy charged that the party in Vermont concerned itself more with patronage and intra-party politics than winning elections or educating voters. Duffy's death left Vermont with only national committeewoman Beatrice P. Schurman of Newport to represent the state at the party's national assemblies, as his four-year term as committeeman was slated to expire in 1952. His death also signaled the reopening of the struggle for Democratic party control in which Healy had been one of the leaders since the state convention in 1948.   *Patricia Mardeusz*

Dummer, Fort

In 1723, the General Court of the Province of Massachusetts Bay resolved to build a blockhouse on the CONNECTICUT RIVER above Northfield, Massachusetts, in present-day Vernon. (The construction of the Vernon Dam backed up the river to inundate the site of Fort Dummer, thus locating it in the state of New Hampshire, since the border between New Hampshire and Vermont is the west bank of the Connecticut River.) Lieutenant Timothy Dwight with four carpenters and twelve soldiers began work in February 1724. Ready for occupancy in early summer, this first structure erected in the region later to be called the New Hampshire grants and then Vermont was named Fort Dummer after the lieutenant governor of Massachusetts. Built of hewn logs laid horizontally in a 180-foot square, the fort was surrounded on the outside by an 8-foot-high stockade of squared timbers set upright in the ground. The garrison force of Massa-

chusetts militia were armed with small arms, four swivel guns, and a "Great Gun," probably used mostly for signals. Shortly after the fort's completion in the fall, seventy hostile Indians attacked it and killed four men. In July 1725, a scouting party of sixty English volunteers trekked from the fort up the Connecticut River to the Wells River and then upstream to the WINOOSKI RIVER, following it to where they sighted LAKE CHAMPLAIN. The first English to cross the mountains and view the lake, they lacked provisions for further exploration and returned to Fort Dummer. A "truck house" to trade with the Indians was established at the fort in 1728. Massachusetts continued to maintain the fort into the 1740s even after New Hampshire began granting townships on the west bank of the Connecticut River.

Dummer, William (1677–1761)

William Dummer was appointed lieutenant governor of Massachusetts in 1716 and twice served as acting governor and commander in chief of the military. He retired in 1730 after acquiring substantial wealth, a portion of which he used to endow Dummer Academy, the earliest academy in New England. Dummer's link to Vermont dates from 1715, when in association with others he purchased land then on the northern Massachusetts border auctioned off by Connecticut as equivalents to lands previously granted by Massachusetts in Connecticut. The lands Dummer purchased are now the Vermont towns of Dummerston and Brattleboro, which is named after another purchaser. In 1724, while acting governor, Dummer ordered the construction of FORT DUMMER to protect against the French and Indian threat to northern Massachusetts.

Dummerston

Dummerston, population 1,915, a town in Windham County, was granted by BENNING WENTWORTH in 1753 as the town of Fullum (presumably after the town of Fulham in England, now part of greater London). From its settlement, however, it was unofficially called Dummerston, after WILLIAM DUMMER, chief magistrate of Massachusetts, who owned land in the CONNECTICUT RIVER valley in the early eighteenth century and after whom FORT DUMMER was named. (The change from Fullum to Dummerston was finally made by the legislature in 1937.) The town has the Connecticut River as its eastern boundary and is cut in its western section by the winding WEST RIVER, on whose banks lies the principal village of West Dummerston. In addition to AGRICULTURE, the town's economic base once included a granite quarry on 1,289-foot Black Mountain. The town's long population decline has been reversed in recent decades by economic and residential growth associated with nearby Brattleboro. RUDYARD KIPLING made his home in Dummerston from 1892 to 1896.

Dunham, Josiah (1769–1844)

A publisher and politician, Josiah Dunham was born in Lebanon Crank (Columbia), Connecticut. A 1789 graduate of Dartmouth College, he moved to Windsor in 1808 after nine years' service in the U.S. Army. Dunham published *The Washingtonian*, a Federalist newspaper, at Windsor from 1810 to 1814 and served as Vermont secretary of state from 1813 to 1815. He acted as clerk of the General Assembly's ballot to decide the gubernatorial contest of 1813, and was accused of palming a vote to ensure the election of Federalist candidate MARTIN CHITTENDEN over JONAS GALUSHA by a vote of 112 to 111. Principal of a female academy in Windsor from 1816 to 1821, Dunham moved to Lexington, Kentucky, where he founded and ran a school for girls. He died in Lexington.
J. Kevin Graffagnino and Marcus A. McCorison

Dutton, Ira (1843–1931)

Known as Brother Joseph during his years of working in the leper colony on the Hawaiian Island of Molokai, Ira Dutton was born in Stowe and migrated with his family to Janesville, Wisconsin, in 1847. He was home-educated until 1857, when he attended Milwaukee Academy, working during school recesses in a printing shop and bookstore. He joined Company B, Thirteenth Wisconsin Infantry at the outbreak of the Civil War and rose to captain by 1865. He stayed in Virginia after the war for two years gathering the remains of Federal dead into the national cemeteries at Shiloh and Corinth. From 1868 to 1883, he worked with little success at a variety of employments. In 1883, he converted to Catholicism, took Joseph as his baptismal name, and spent twenty months in the Trappist Monastery in Kentucky prepar-

ing himself to join Father Damien in his mission to the leper colonies on Molokai. Brother Joseph arrived in 1886 and remained working as a lay brother with the lepers until blindness from cataracts in 1930 forced him to leave the mission for the first time in forty-four years. He died in Honolulu. A mural on the outside wall of Blessed Sacrament Church on the Mountain Road in Stowe depicts Brother Joseph standing on the shore of Molokai watching the U.S. Navy's Pacific fleet cruising past as a tribute to him as "a brave man and a brave soldier."

Duvernay, Ludger (1799–1852)

The publisher of Vermont's first French language newspaper, Ludger Duvernay was a native of Vercheres, Lower Canada (Quebec), apprenticed as a printer in Montreal, leaving there in 1817 to launch several short-lived newspapers in Trois-Rivières. He purchased the French language *La Minerve* at Montreal in 1828, soon one of the most politically influential newspapers in the province. Duvernay's newspaper became the voice of the PATRIOTS movement as it developed in the late 1830s. When the Patriot insurrection broke out in 1837, Duvernay joined the rebel army as an officer, leading his troops in the battle at Saint-Armand on December 6, 1837. Defeated at Saint-Armand, Duvernay escaped to Swanton and finally to Burlington, where he established *Le Patriote Canadien*, the first Franco-American newspaper in the United States. In June 1839, Duvernay's press in Burlington issued the first North American edition of Patriot leader Louis-Joseph Papineau's *Histoire de l'insurrection du Canada. En refutation du rapport de Lord Durham*. The tract had been published a month earlier in Paris where Papineau was in exile. Duvernay's Burlington newspaper appeared from August 7, 1839 to February 5, 1840, and he took an active part in the French-Canadian community of Burlington until 1842. He organized the first St. John the Baptist celebration in Vermont. Duvernay and his friend Robert Shores Miles worked for nearly three years to convince church leaders in Montreal and France to send a priest to minister to the growing French community of Burlington and Winooski. In 1842, the year Duvernay returned to Montreal from exile in Vermont, the bishop

of Nancy, France, sent Père Ance to serve Catholics of northern Vermont. Duvernay again published *La Minerve* after his return to Montreal, but the newspaper no longer supported the Patriot cause. He denounced Papineau as the "Great Agitator" for his continued zealous opposition to the British government and called for French-Canadian accommodation with the British colonial regime in Canada.
Joseph-André Senécal

Duxbury

Duxbury, population 1,289, a town in Washington County, was granted by BENNING WENTWORTH in 1763 and derives its name from Duxbury, Massachusetts. Lying directly on the eastern slope of the main spine of the GREEN MOUNTAINS, the town is mountainous and densely wooded, with almost half of its territory lying within Camel's Hump State Park. (The summit of 4,083-foot CAMEL'S HUMP, Vermont's third-highest mountain, lies on the border with neighboring Huntington.) On the north, Duxbury borders the WINOOSKI RIVER, whose valley here is too narrow for all but the smallest farms. Route 100 bisects the town from north to south along its eastern border, connecting the town of Waterbury with the towns of the Mad River Valley.

Dwight, Timothy (1732–1817)

The president of Yale College, Timothy Dwight was one of the most important political and cultural conservatives of Revolutionary New England. He wrote *Travels in New-England and New-York* (1821) as a defense against a series of travel books by foreigners that attacked American manners and institutions. Dwight argued that New England, if not all the new United States, could boast a culture superior to Europe's in its piety, sobriety, enterprise, and education. But in Dwight's view, Vermont was not really part of New England. Vermont at the beginning of the nineteenth century was, in Dwight's view, a sort of anti–New England, a place where those who were impatient of the restraints of law, religion, and morality could escape. Dwight had in mind ETHAN ALLEN who, though dead for over a decade, he saw as the symbol of everything New England conservatives detested in Jeffersonian America.
Dona Brown

E

Eagle Square Company

The Stanley Works Eagle Square factory in Shaftsbury is the oldest continually operating factory in Vermont. A Stanley division since the 1930s, the Eagle Square factory was built in 1823 by Stephen Whipple, a South Shaftsbury blacksmith, and leased to Silas Hawes, a manufacturer of carpenter's squares, for which he had a patent. Through various ownership permutations, the original Eagle Square Company was organized by about 1846. Competing smaller shops in the region made carpenter's squares, but Eagle Square eventually dominated the market by perfecting and patenting an efficient method of marking gradations on the square. In the 1860s, the firm diversified into wood products, including bedsteads, doors, sashes, blinds, and other house-building materials, continuing production until their hardwood supply was exhausted in the 1880s, when the factory concentrated on metal tools. Both Vermont and out-of-state investors owned the company into the twentieth century, when banker JAMES B. WILBUR of Manchester bought most of the stock and gave the company to his son, J. B. Wilbur, Jr., who sold the company to Stanley Rule & Level Company of New Britain, Connecticut, in 1916 and became treasurer of Stanley, a position he held until his death in 1930. Eagle Square has been a division of Stanley Works since 1935. In recent years it has gone through significant changes in production methods. In the mid-1990s, the company invested heavily in automation, but productivity rates failed to justify automation's growing costs by the late 1990s, so Stanley began to return to more direct labor in production. Productivity rates improved and employment increased in the later years of the decade. Employee numbers levelled off as the new century progressed, however, and even declined recently as product demand slowed with a contracting national economy. Finally, Stanley Works closed its operations at Eagle Square and gave the building to the National Community Development Foundation, which now seeks to find new uses for the structure.

E. & T. Fairbanks and Company

Manufacturers of the nineteenth century's commercially most successful platform scales, E. & T. Fairbanks and Company was founded in St. Johnsbury in 1824 when ERASTUS FAIRBANKS, a struggling storekeeper, joined his brother THADDEUS FAIRBANKS in the operation of an iron foundry and machine shop making stoves, plows, and custom machinery. At that time, the company employed about a dozen workers. In 1830, the company became involved in the construction and operation of a hemp-processing facility. To weigh the raw hemp, Thaddeus devised a crude platform scale. The success of the scale caused the company to add platform scales to the products it made, and eventually, with the growing demand for scales, the company focused solely on this product. By the mid-nineteenth century, E. & T. Fairbanks was one of the largest industries in Vermont and the nation's leading manufacturer of scales. The company's success was due to a combination of product innovation and aggressive marketing. During the nineteenth century, over one hundred and twenty patents relating to scale design were attributed to individuals connected to the scale works. Fairbanks agents moved west as America expanded. Fairbanks scales were on sale in California the year it became a state in 1850. From the beginning, Fairbanks scales found a market outside the United States, first in Canada and Great Britain. By the end of the nineteenth century, Fairbanks was the world's leading scale manufacturer, with markets in Europe, Asia, Africa, and South America as well as North America. For example, the Japanese postal service used Fairbanks scales in the late nineteenth century. The company's motto "Weighing the World" had become a reality. In 1916, Fairbanks, Morse and Company of Chicago purchased control of E. & T. Fairbanks. In the twentieth century, the company experienced several changes of ownership, yet Fairbanks Scales are still manufactured today in St. Johnsbury as well as Meridian, Mississippi, although company headquarters are now located in Kansas City.   *Allen Yale*

Earl, Ralph (1751–1801)

One of Vermont's best-known eighteenth-century itinerant portrait artists, Ralph Earl pursued a career that was both peripatetic and checkered. He was born in Shrewsbury, Massachusetts, and raised in the nearby Worcester County town of Leicester. By 1774, he was in New Haven, Connecticut, married to Sarah Gates, and first demonstrated his talent by painting a portrait of Roger Sherman, a Connecticut shoemaker who had signed the Declaration of Independence. With a friend, engraver Amos Doolittle, Earl painted landscapes that depicted the conflagrations at Lexington and Concord that launched the American Revolution. Nonetheless, Earl's pro-Tory feelings were evidently strong enough for Connecticut authorities to threaten to deport him and, disguised as a servant to a British captain, he sailed to England in April 1778. While there, he became acquainted with other portraitists and improved his technique. He also married Ann Whiteside, having not divorced his wife in Connecticut. Earl returned to America in 1785 and moved from Boston to New York. A more skilled artist than businessman, he was thrown into debtor's prison for a year and a half. While in jail, he continued to paint until friends helped to release him. When he emerged, he renewed his work as an itinerant artist, though he was troubled by alcoholism. He travelled throughout New York, Massachusetts, Connecticut, and Vermont, working on portraits that often depicted the subject's face and body accurately but with lavishly inventive backgrounds, examples of which include imaginative apparel, red-fringed drapery, and patterned carpets. Among his better-known works in Vermont is a detailed 1798 landscape of Old Bennington, showing several buildings that still stand; this view, arguably the first American landscape painting, includes a small portrait of the artist and his son in one corner. He painted elaborate portraits of Elijah and Mary Dewey, whose tavern, now known as the Walloomsac Inn, had given him hospitality. These are on permanent exhibit at the BENNINGTON MUSEUM. Earl and his family settled for a time in Troy, New York, and he continued to paint from town to town, sometimes accompanied by his son, who was learning the trade. But after the turn of the nineteenth century his alcoholism worsened, and he died in Bolton, Massachusetts.

J. Tyler Resch

Earth People's Park

In the summer of 1970, Wavy Gravy, master of ceremonies at the Woodstock Festival, and a group of friends bought a 590-acre parcel of land on the Canadian border in the town of Norton. Naming the place "Earth People's Park," the group declared the land free and open to anyone who wanted to come live there. Norton's selectboard was soon concerned about the Park's residents' behavior, especially their nudity, drug use, and apparent disregard for personal hygiene. People with criminal records began to take up residence and drugs became easily available and obviously heavily used. Townspeople reported burglaries and threats. Governor DEANE DAVIS visited the Park in 1970 and concluded that a cold Vermont winter would drive residents of the Park to warmer climates, but they stayed. In 1975, police raided the Park after a resident was stabbed to death there. A mismanaged rock festival saw thirty thousand music fans and others crash the gates, leaving tons of trash to be hauled away by volunteers. The next day, Governor THOMAS SALMON viewed the wreckage and protested that such a disaster must not happen again in Vermont. Into the 1980s, arrests were made in the Park for welfare fraud, drug charges, and prison escapes. In 1990, the federal government seized the Park after marijuana was found growing there, and gave the land to the state as a public conservation area.

East Haven

East Haven, population 301, a town in Essex County, was granted by the Vermont legislature in 1790 to a group of Connecticut men headed by Timothy Andrews of East Haven in that state. The eastern three-quarters of the town is mountainous and heavily forested, with two peaks rising above three thousand feet, and is one of the few places in Vermont with patches of virgin woodland. In 1999, much of the town became part of the CHAMPION LANDS, a public-private project devoted to conservation and sustainable forest harvesting. The only significant settlement is East Haven village on Route 114, which follows the course of the East Branch of the PASSUMPSIC RIVER in the extreme western corner of the town.

East Montpelier

East Montpelier, population 2,578, a town in Washington County, was created by the Vermont legislature in 1848 by dividing the original town of Montpelier in two, East Montpelier getting by far the larger portion but Montpelier getting the state government, the majority of the people, and the choice river valley location. The gently rolling landscape of East Montpelier is suited for AGRICULTURE and the raising of sheep, horses, and cattle, all of which have at various times been part of the town's economic base. Today the town has six dairy farms and several diversified farms. There are two villages: East Montpelier, which was for long the town's trading center and a stop on the Montpelier and Wells River Railroad; and North Montpelier, a manufacturing locale where large woolen mills produced yardage well into the twentieth century. In recent decades the town has seen residential growth as a result of its proximity to the urban centers of Montpelier and Barre.

East Union

In 1778, many inhabitants of western New Hampshire, led by ELEAZAR WHEELOCK (1711–1779), the founder and president of Dartmouth College, and his son-in-law BEZALEEL WOODWARD, correctly felt that New Hampshire's government and its constitution perpetuated control by seaboard interests in Exeter and Portsmouth. The Wheelock or College camp actually wanted a union with Vermont towns in the CONNECTICUT RIVER Valley to form a new state with a capital at Hanover, specifically in that part of the town owned by Dartmouth College called Dresden. Separatist/Union propagandists argued that the war had revoked the Crown's sovereignty and negated its boundary decision of 1764; thus the towns along the Connecticut River were now in a state of nature and could form their own government. In March 1778, sixteen New Hampshire towns petitioned the Vermont Assembly for annexation to Vermont. Vermont town meetings by large majorities approved the annexation, compelling the assembly to accept the sixteen towns on June 11. Four days later, having admitted Dresden to the East Union with Vermont, the assembly appointed President Wheelock justice of the peace for the college corporation and gave the corporation power to appoint an assistant justice. When New Hampshire's government objected because the Vermont General Assembly had extended its jurisdiction across the Connecticut, Vermont sent ETHAN ALLEN—who opposed the union as a threat to western Vermont's political supremacy—to the Congress in Philadelphia, where he gained from New Hampshire a promise to support congressional recognition of Vermont in return for Allen's promise to influence the General Assembly to disconnect the sixteen New Hampshire towns from Vermont. He fulfilled that promise upon his return by in part exaggerating the extent of support for Vermont statehood that he had raised on his mission. The question of an East Union, however, arose again when delegates from towns on the east and west sides of the Connecticut River convened at Walpole, New Hampshire, in November 1780; at Charlestown, New Hampshire, on January 16, 1781; and again on February 10 at Cornish, New Hampshire, three miles from where the Vermont General Assembly was convened, and proposed uniting to the state of Vermont. This time towns on both sides of the river were speaking with one voice and it was clear they would either join with Vermont or attempt a political union on their own. The Vermont General Assembly on February 14, 1781, "resolved that this state have and do hereby lay a jurisdictional claim" to the lands requesting union, and on February 22, the General Assembly formally annexed the New Hampshire towns. Meanwhile, anticipating the loss of their political supremacy to a wealthier and more heavily populated east, the ARLINGTON JUNTO persuaded the General Assembly to set up a WEST UNION by annexing New York towns. Both New Hampshire and New York protested and threatened military action. In late February 1782, New Hampshire's Governor Meshach Weare ordered a thousand militia men to prepare for battle with Vermont in the East Union and an armed confrontation occurred in eastern New York. An even greater incentive for Vermont to dissolve the unions was General George Washington's advice to Governor THOMAS CHITTENDEN that, since Vermont's boundary disputes with New York and New Hampshire were an obstacle to Vermont's admission to the federal union, Vermont should withdraw its claims to towns in those states. With the British surrender at Yorktown and the Vermont legislature currying favor with Congress, in late February the General Assembly formally gave up its claim to territory in both states.   *H. Nicholas Muller III*

Eastman, Charles Gamage (1813–1860)

A newspaper man, politician, and poet, Charles Gamage Eastman was a native of Fryeburg, Maine, who grew up in Barnard and attended the UNIVERSITY OF VERMONT, where he founded the Lambda Iota Society. He worked for various newspapers in Vermont, beginning with his own publication in Woodstock of *The Spirit of the Age*, a Democrat paper, and was from 1845 to his death editor and co-owner of *The Vermont Patriot and State Gazette* in Montpelier. He served in the Vermont senate in 1852 and 1853. His verses, self-published as *Poems by Charles G. Eastman* (1848), gained some recognition beyond Vermont, a British review calling Eastman "The Burns of New England." A posthumous second edition with twenty-three additional poems was published in 1880.

Eaton, Ebenezer (1777–1859)

A printer, publisher, and bookseller in Rome, Geneva, and Scipio, New York, from 1799 to 1801 before settling permanently in Danville in the fall of 1806, Ebenezer Eaton published the *North Star* (1807–1840), an influential Jeffersonian Democratic, and later ANTI-MASONIC, newspaper. He was also an active printer of books and pamphlets. A Connecticut native, like many early Vermont printers, Eaton was occasionally appointed state printer.   *Marcus A. McCorison*

Eddy, Isaac (1777–1847)

An early printer and engraver of primitive but varied talents, Isaac Eddy, a native of Weathersfield, plied his crafts on the DRESDEN PRESS, so called because it was first established in Dresden, a section of Hanover, New Hampshire, in 1778 during the first, aborted EAST UNION of sixteen New Hampshire towns with Vermont. In 1812, the earliest known of Eddy's engravings on copper appeared in the first printing of the Bible in Vermont by Preston Merrifield and James Cochran of Windsor. In the same year, Eddy illustrated John Russell's *Authentic History of the Vermont State Prison*, an institution then barely three years old. Russell wrote the book to help pay for his education at MIDDLEBURY COLLEGE. Eddy bought the Dresden Press in 1814 and moved it to the hamlet of Greenbush in Weathersfield. In 1817 to 1818, he issued a large broadside (43 by 62 centimeters), *The Hypocrite's Looking Glass*, a radical political attack on the established power of the Congregational Church and the church's tithe collector or "tything man." Eddy's cartoon-like images of the tything man, his horse, and the Devil, as well as the fiercely critical tone of

the text, present a very nonconventional treatment of commonplace figures of the time. In 1817 to 1818, Jesse Cochran of Windsor printed John Cleveland's *Fanny Hill*, a classic of eighteenth-century erotica illustrated by Eddy and today much sought by Vermont bibliophiles. Isaac Eddy is also known to have experimented with a perpetual-motion machine, the nineteenth century's equivalent of the alchemist's philosopher's stone.

Marcus A. McCorison

Eden

Eden, population 1,152, a town in Lamoille County, was granted by the Vermont legislature in 1781 to SETH WARNER and seventy-one Vermonters serving in the GREEN MOUNTAIN CONTINENTAL RANGERS, a New York regiment of the Continental Army that Warner had commanded. The grant was to compensate them for the depreciation of the Continental dollars in their New York military pay. The name is presumably descriptive of the landscape. The main spine of the GREEN MOUNTAINS runs along the western border of the town, which is largely wooded and mountainous and rises to 3,360 feet at Belvidere Mountain on the northern border with Lowell. The small settlement of Eden Mills is on Route 100, which follows the course of the Gihon River as it bisects the town from northeast to southwest. The Gihon has its source just north of Eden Mills in 136-acre Lake Eden, a picturesque body of water lined with summer residences.

Edgewood Studios

Rutland filmmaker David Giancola began shooting his movies in the backyard of his parents' home on Edgewood Drive when he was still in high school. Businessman Peter Beckwith joined with Giancola in the late 1980s, helping Edgewood Studios in Rutland turn out profitable action adventure films in the early 1990s. During the late 1990s, Edgewood expanded its focus to include comedy, family, and disaster films. Giancola continues to make action pictures (*Icebreaker* with Stacy Keach and *Peril* with Morgan Fairchild, both 1999) assisted by commercial foreign and domestic financing.   *Kenneth A. Peck*

Ed Larkin Dancers

Contradancing, partly based on the quadrille, was a popular activity in the social life of nineteenth- and early twentieth-

century Vermont. A regular feature of KITCHEN JUNKETS, all-night parties fueled by home cooking and three-piece bands, contradancing entertained and exercised Vermonters until dance bands broadcasting on the radio drew the young to ballroom dancing (round dancing) in the 1920s and 1930s. Edward Loyal Larkin (1870–1954), a Chelsea sawyer, farmer, and long-time fiddler in a three-piece band, had developed a local reputation for his group's contradance music when in 1932 he was invited to perform a program of contradances at the Tunbridge Fair. He enlisted some of the area's best contradancers, dressed them in fanciful costumes as George Washington, Abraham Lincoln, and an Indian chief, got himself up as a Vermont farmer, and presented the newly formed Ed Larkin Dancers before the fair's grandstand. After eight years performing at Tunbridge, the Larkin Contra Dancers were invited to perform at the World's Fair in New York City in 1940. Larkin's group continued their popular public performances at the Tunbridge Fair under his direction until his death in 1954. Today dressed in more sober nineteenth-century styles, the group continues to perform Larkin's arrangements and to be known as the Ed Larkin Dancers, featuring his daughter Gertrude Larkin Roberts at the piano and fiddler Harold Luce, who joined the group in 1933. Larkin's Contra Dancers performed again at the New York World's Fair in 1960 and can still be seen annually at the Tunbridge World's Fair and at the Royalton Academy on the third Saturday of every month from January to April.

Edmunds, George Franklin (1828–1919)

A United States senator, constitutional lawyer, and REPUBLICAN PARTY leader, George Edmunds was born in Richmond and received his early education locally, often from private tutors. Regarded as too sickly to attend college, at seventeen he began the study of law at his brother-in-law's Burlington office, but in fear for his health he escaped Vermont during the winter of 1845 to 1846 for the milder climate of Washington, D.C. He valued that winter, studying in the great law libraries and observing proceedings before the United States Supreme Court, as one of his most valuable learning experiences. Returning to Vermont, he was admitted to the bar in 1849 and opened a practice in Richmond, but within two years moved to

Burlington, where he found greater professional opportunities and where he prospered. In 1852, he married Susan Marsh, a niece of GEORGE PERKINS MARSH (who was then minister to Turkey), who had an important influence on her husband's career. From 1855 through 1862, Edmunds was elected to the Vermont House, in which he served as Speaker, and the Senate, where he was president pro tempore. His first national (though unsuccessful) assignment to which he was appointed by Secretary of State Seward was as special counsel to secure the extradition of the ST. ALBANS RAIDERS from Canada. The death of Senator SOLOMON FOOT in 1866 occurred at a time when the Republicans needed every Senate vote they could muster to override President Johnson's veto of the Civil Rights Bill, and Governor PAUL DILLINGHAM had allegedly intended to appoint JOHN GREGORY SMITH to fill the vacancy. When Smith could not leave immediately for Washington, Edmunds was appointed in his stead. He left immediately for Washington, and his first vote provided the margin necessary to override the President's veto. JUSTIN MORRILL joined him in the Senate a few months later and they constituted the most powerful state delegation until 1891, when Edmunds resigned. Edmunds enjoyed a rapid rise to legislative prominence, devoting his major efforts to domestic matters, particularly those involving constitutional issues. From 1872, except for two years when the Democrats controlled the Senate, he chaired the Judiciary Committee. Regarded for most of his career as the ablest constitutional lawyer in Congress, he simultaneously pursued a lucrative federal law practice, something that was then neither illegal nor regarded as unethical. His most famous accomplishment was the design and adoption of the electoral commission, on which he served when the commission settled the disputed election of 1876. Although the principal force behind much major legislation, his name is attached only to an act prohibiting polygamy in the territories. He has been credited as the author of most of the Sherman Anti-Trust Act, collaborator with Senator Thurman on the Thurman Act that compelled transcontinental RAILROADS to fund their government debt, and bills to promote resumption acts. He turned down a Supreme Court opportunity, and he was disappointed by the court's ruling on the KU KLUX KLAN and

Civil Rights Acts that invalidated provisions that he had fought to have included in the act to protect former slaves. Edmunds was never reconciled to these court decisions. Henry Watterson, a former Congressman and Kentucky editor, "despaired of reasoning with such a man as Edmunds who in 1913 still believed radical reconstruction had been enlightened, justifiable, and beneficial." His resignation in 1891 surprised and displeased many of his colleagues. Ruthless in debate, Edmunds was so suspicious of genial behavior that he purposefully avoided it. Nonetheless, during CHESTER ALAN ARTHUR's administration, he was elected Senate president pro tempore, placing him next in the line of presidential succession, and in both 1880 and 1884 he collected support in the national convention. After leaving the Senate, Edmunds continued with his law practice, first in Philadelphia and then in Pasadena, California. His most famous legal triumph was in 1895, when he successfully argued the unconstitutionality of the income tax before the Supreme Court in *Pollack v. Farmers Loan and Trust Company*. Some years before his death, he sold his Burlington estate on generous terms to the city, which erected a school on the property. Edmunds died in Pasadena but his remains are interred in Burlington.

Edson, Merritt Austin (1897–1955)

Known as "Red Mike," Merritt Austin Edson, a native of Rutland, was one of the most decorated and celebrated Marines of the twentieth century. Dropping out of the UNIVERSITY OF VERMONT at twenty to serve briefly in World War I, Edson first qualified as a naval aviator but soon found himself leading a six-months patrol on the Cocos River in Nicaragua, where he won his first Navy Cross for bravery under fire. Following that service, Edson threw himself into improving Marine Corps marksmanship, and captained the Marine Corps national championship rifle and pistol teams in 1935 and 1936. He then organized the first Marine Raider Battalion, known as "Edson's Raiders," and in August 1942 won a quick and skillful victory on the island of Tulagi in the Pacific. For this first U.S. counterstroke against the Japanese in the South Pacific he was awarded a second Navy Cross. A month later, Edson won worldwide fame and a Medal of Honor when his battalion held "Bloody Ridge" on Guadalcanal against waves of Japanese attackers. Had Edson's heavily outnum-

bered battalion failed to hold the ridge line, the Japanese would almost certainly have retaken Henderson Field and annihilated the remaining Marine defenders, whose transport ships had withdrawn from the area. In August 1943, Edson was chief of staff for the Second Marine Division in its assault of Tarawa. His command of the division from the fire-swept beach won him a Legion of Merit and a battlefield promotion to brigadier general. He later won a Silver Star for combat service on Saipan. At the end of the war, General Edson returned to Marine Corps Headquarters, where he used his war hero prestige to fight the battle in Congress against disbanding the Marine Corps. That battle won, Edson retired from the Corps and in 1947 came home to Vermont to become the state's first commissioner of public safety and leader of the newly formed Vermont State Police. In 1951, he left that post to become executive director of the National Rifle Association, where he launched a major initiative for improved marksmanship. He died in Washington in 1955 and was buried at Arlington National Cemetery. Marine General Lewis Walt said, "He was a man of vision and resourcefulness. He was a man of extreme loyalty to his high ideals and to this country. He was one of the Marine Corps' greatest officers and leaders of all times."

John McClaughry

Elmer, Rachel Robinson (1878–1919)

An accomplished artist and illustrator, Rachel Robinson Elmer, the daughter of ROWLAND EVANS ROBINSON, was born at Rokeby (now the ROKEBY MUSEUM), her family home in Ferrisburgh. Rachel displayed a high degree of artistic talent from a very young age, drawing people and animals in remarkable detail long before any youngster should have been able to. Her parents' commitment to nurturing her talent was exemplified by the summer she spent studying art in New York City when she was only fourteen. After graduating from Goddard Seminary in Barre, she moved repeatedly between Vermont and New York, where she studied at the Art Students League, finally settling in New York in 1906. She became a successful illustrator of children's books, teaming up repeatedly with author Caroline Hofman, and is best known for her contribution to the development of the fine art post card. She painted a series of watercolor views of New York for the

Volland Art-Lovers' Post Card series in 1914, and in 1916 she produced another set of New York scenes from linoleum block prints. Rachel Robinson married Robert Elmer in 1911; they had no children. Her death in 1919 during the INFLUENZA EPIDEMIC cut short a successful, but still unfinished career.   *Jane Williamson*

Elmore

Elmore, population 849, a town in Lamoille County, was granted by the Vermont legislature in 1781 to a group of Connecticut Revolutionary War veterans including Colonel Samuel Elmore. The town, which lies between the Worcester and Woodbury ranges, is bisected from north to south by Route 12. The main settlement, Lake Elmore, lies on a 224-acre lake popular as a summer destination, and at the foot of Elmore Mountain, which rises to 2,608 feet.

Embargo Act of 1808

In an effort to resolve U.S.-British hostilities through economic sanctions, President Thomas Jefferson imposed a series of embargoes. The Embargo Act of 1808 made inland trade with the British colony in Canada illegal. Residents of the Champlain Valley had developed an economic dependence on Canada for both the export and import trade. Vermonters shipped lumber, potash, and produce to Montreal and Quebec City in exchange for manufactured goods. The embargo created economic hardships for northern Vermont and New York, which had no access to other markets. Commerce continued and even prospered by smuggling. Vermonters traded livestock and lumber for staples such as salt, coffee, and cloth, often within sight of the British army stationed near the border. Contemporary reports suggest that the British army received as much as one-third of its beef smuggled from Vermont. When smugglers were arrested in the notorious *BLACK SNAKE* AFFAIR of 1808, they initially resisted the revenue officers and killed two militia men and an innocent bystander. Despite the efforts of the U.S. Army and militia that patrolled the border, smuggling continued nearly unabated until the close of the War of 1812.   *Karen Campbell*

Emerson, Lee (1898–1976)

An attorney and native of Hardwick, Lee Emerson was elected to the Vermont House (1938 and 1940) and Senate (1942),

and was elected lieutenant governor (1944 and 1946) and governor (1950–1954) as a Republican and a close ally of the Proctor wing of the party. After service in World War I, graduation from Syracuse University (1921) and George Washington University Law School (1926), and admission to the Vermont bar in 1927, Emerson opened a law office in Barton, where he was elected school director and served as moderator of Barton town meetings for forty-eight years. In 1932 and 1936, he was elected Orleans County state's attorney. A Proctor stalwart as lieutenant governor, in his second term he led the opposition to several of Governor ERNEST W. GIBSON, JR.'s programs, and cast a tie-breaking vote in the senate that defeated Gibson's bill for a mobile public health unit. In 1948, Emerson lost a gubernatorial bid in a primary contest with Gibson, but in 1950 captured the nomination and won the general election with 74 percent of the vote. An ardent anti-communist, Emerson attacked President Harry Truman for relieving General Douglas MacArthur of his command during the Korean War and was later critical of President Dwight Eisenhower's budget. He believed the war required both the nation and Vermont to curtail domestic spending. Emerson convinced the legislature to raise taxes and tried to roll back his predecessor Gibson's initiatives as too expensive. When his first administration concluded with a large surplus, which his critics attributed to unnecessary tax increases, he suffered a decline in popularity. He barely won the 1952 Republican primary despite facing a last-minute opponent from the Aiken-Gibson wing of the party who almost beat him and went on to run against Emerson again in the general election. Emerson won the three-candidate gubernatorial election in 1952, but the event also marked the rise of the DEMOCRATIC PARTY when he captured less than 52 percent of the votes. As governor, Emerson proposed paying a bonus to Vermonters serving in the Korean War. He also proposed that the state conduct studies on the feasibility of building a natural gas pipeline in Vermont and to discover if racial discrimination existed in the state. When he left the governor's office after two terms, the state budget carried a substantial surplus. An able attorney, Emerson returned to his law practice in Barton. He lost primary races for the U.S. Senate in 1958 and the U.S. House in 1960.

Endangered Species

The passage of Vermont's Endangered Species Law in 1986 authorized the secretary of the Agency of Environmental Conservation (now Natural Resources) to list species as endangered or threatened, paving the way for protection of imperiled wildlife. Today, species listed as threatened or endangered in Vermont include five mammals, twelve birds, one amphibian, four reptiles, six fish, one amphipod, three insects, and ten mollusks. Two highly visible birds of prey, ospreys and peregrine falcons, have rebounded in recent years thanks to public awareness and conservation efforts. The now-banned insecticide DDT devastated both of these birds in the 1950s and 1960s. The move to help ospreys began in the 1980s, when the Fish and Wildlife Department, working with Vermont electric power companies, private citizens, and a number of other governmental agencies, placed nesting platforms in the LAKE CHAMPLAIN Valley and the NORTHEAST KINGDOM. In 1988, the first osprey in more than ten years nested in Vermont, using a platform erected in Porter's Bay in Ferrisburgh. Since then, the results have been remarkable. During 2000, forty-four osprey pairs built nests, and thirty-three successfully raised sixty young. Peregrine falcons were reintroduced in the 1980s after a twenty-year absence, with chicks hacked (stocked) on three Vermont cliffs. Release efforts continued through 1987, involving ninety-three peregrine chicks. Many of the young peregrines survived and returned in later years to nest on their own. In 2000, a record number of twenty-three pairs of adult peregrines fledged forty young.

Will Ryan and Mark Scott

Engels, John (b. 1931)

Poet John Engels of Burlington has published twelve collections of his poems, many of them appearing first in major publications such as the *New Yorker* and the *Nation*. Engels was born in South Bend, Indiana, and graduated from Notre Dame University in 1952. After three years in the Navy and several years studying in Dublin and London, he attended the University of Iowa's M.F.A. in writing program. Five years of teaching writing at St. Norbert's College in Wisconsin led to a position at ST. MICHAEL'S COLLEGE in 1962, where he continues to teach writing today. Many of Engels's poems are very much rooted in his experience of Vermont, especially those in *The Homer Mitchell Place* (1968), *Seasons in Vermont* (1982), and *Walking to Cootehill* (1993). His two most recent collections are *Sinking Creek* (1998) and *House and Garden* (2001). Engels has earned several awards and prizes, including a Fulbright Fellowship in the former Yugoslavia, a ROBERT FROST Fellowship (1974), two Vermont Council on the Arts Writing Fellowships (1977, 1979), and a nomination for the Pulitzer Prize in Poetry (1983). He is also an avid fly fisherman and amateur autoharp performer.

Enos, Roger (1729–1808)

Roger Enos of Windsor, Connecticut, joined the Continental Army in 1775 and commanded the rear guard of BENEDICT ARNOLD's trek through Maine to Canada. When the campaign to Quebec appeared to fail in the Maine forest, Enos led his men back home. At first censured, Enos was ultimately found faultless in the circumstances. He moved to Hartland, and by 1781 had risen to commanding general of the Vermont militia. A close associate of the ARLINGTON JUNTO, he was privy to the HALDIMAND NEGOTIATIONS. The Governor's Council granted him and fifty-nine associates the town of Enosburgh in 1780. His daughter Jerusha married IRA ALLEN in 1789.

Enosburgh

Enosburgh, population 2,788, a town in Franklin County, was granted by the Vermont legislature in 1780 to General ROGER ENOS, IRA ALLEN's father-in-law, and a number of others. The gently rolling landscape, cut by numerous watercourses and well suited to AGRICULTURE, reaches its highest elevation of about two thousand feet at the Cold Hollow Mountains in the town's southeastern corner. The Vermont Dairy Festival is held in the town on the first weekend of June every year. The substantial village of Enosburg (not Enosburgh) Falls lies along the MISSISQUOI RIVER as it cuts across the town from east to west. In the late nineteenth and early twentieth centuries, Enosburgh was known for its patent medicine manufactories, the most important of which produced Kendall's Spavin Cure, formulated by Dr. BURNEY JAMES KENDALL. The medicine, which treated an equine disease of the bone of the hind hock, or ankle bone, was so successful that it brought enormous prosperity to the town. Enosburg Falls, where the factory was located,

boasted a library, sewer system, concrete sidewalks, and OPERA HOUSE (recently refurbished). SUSAN MILLS, founder of Mills College in California, was born in Enosburgh, as was WILLIAM "LARRY" GARDNER, whose baseball career in 1908 to 1924 included four World Series.

Essex

A town in Chittenden County with a population of 18,626, Essex was granted by BENNING WENTWORTH in 1763 and probably named for William Anne Holles Capel, fourth earl of Essex. The town, whose southern boundary is the WINOOSKI RIVER, consists of the incorporated village of Essex Junction, which owes its existence to its location at the point where the Vermont Central Railroad met the Vermont and Canada Railroad in 1852, and the rural hinterland centered on the village of Essex Center three miles to the north. Each entity has a population of approximately nine thousand, and, despite periodic attempts at a merger, the two remain steadfastly separate. In addition to being an important RAILROAD center, with a spur line to Burlington, Essex Junction utilized the falls of the Winooski River for power generation and grew into a regionally important manufacturing and commercial locale. It became also the home of the CHAMPLAIN VALLEY EXPOSITION, a fair held annually in the week before Labor Day that draws thousands of visitors daily. A new era in the village's history began in 1957 when IBM (see entry) opened a plant on its outskirts, an operation that grew to employ thousands in a facility that eventually expanded into the neighboring town of Williston. Some other industries in town are involved in food services and direct mail, and the production of high temperature cable and sports bodywear. The growing congestion at the Five Corners intersection in the heart of the village was a contributing cause to the construction of the Circumferential Highway (Route 289), a partially completed bypass that has enhanced the residential and commercial growth of Essex until, in the 2000 census, the town surpassed Rutland as the second-largest population center in the state. Continued growth seems assured as the Burlington metropolitan region expands to include all the towns in Chittenden County.

Estey Organ Company

In 1846, the Brattleboro firm of S. H. Jones manufactured its first melodeon and by

1850 the firm employed ten men and produced seventy-five instruments per year. About that time, Jacob Estey accepted a share of the organ company in lieu of rent payments from tenants in a building he owned. In 1853, he purchased the firm along with two partners who formed I. Hines and Co. After a series of business reorganizations and factory fires, J. Estey and Company emerged from the former I. Hines and Co. with Jacob, his son Julius, and son-in-law and future governor Levi K. Fuller as partners. The new company made significant improvements in reed organ design, expanded greatly, and enjoyed financial success. Jacob Estey was actively involved in directing the company until his death in 1890, and Estey Organ continued to prosper under Julius and Levi Fuller. In the twentieth century, a new generation of leadership expanded the company's product line of reed organs to pipe organs. The early 1900s marked the reed organ's decline in popularity as the piano, player piano, and phonograph became the preferred home musical instruments. The company stayed in business by adopting new ideas in reed construction and developing innovative styles of organs. In the 1930s, the fourth generation of Esteys were in the business, and by the 1950s, the fifth. By then, Estey Organ had made almost five hundred thousand reed organs and about thirty-five hundred pipe organs. One hundred and thirty people were employed in twelve factory buildings in Brattleboro. During the 1950s, the company began to manufacture electronic organs, and eventually moved from Brattleboro to California. In 1961, the firm, then Estey Electronics, merged with the Organ Corporation of America, to be directed from West Hempstead, New York.

Ethan Allen, Fort

When REDFIELD PROCTOR, SR., former governor of Vermont, became President Benjamin Harrison's secretary of war in 1889, he began pressing immediately for a military base in northern Vermont, despite the lack of a perceived threat from Canada. On August 5, 1892, Congress authorized the construction of a post "near the northern frontier . . . provided that suitable land . . . is donated free of cost to the U.S." Leading citizens in the Burlington area were enthusiastic, the necessary funds were raised (partly at a fund-raiser at the Burlington YMCA on September 18), and a 60-acre tract, later expanded, was acquired in Essex Junction near the Colchester boundary. Construction was begun on March 13, 1893, and on September 28, 1894, four troops of the Third U.S. Cavalry arrived by train at the new fort. Although it was never used to help repel an invasion, Fort Ethan Allen did serve a variety of useful purposes in the next sixty years or so. Various military units rotated through the post, including the famous African-American cavalry regiment known as the BUFFALO SOLDIERS, and thousands of soldiers trained there for World War I. The post served as headquarters for the Vermont District of the CIVILIAN CONSERVATION CORPS in the 1930s, and the Vermont National Guard made use of various facilities. Fort Ethan Allen was declared inactive in 1944, and although it served for a brief period as an Air Force facility in the 1950s, the post was decommissioned and most of the buildings have been converted to civilian uses. Some barracks were turned into living quarters for married faculty and students from the UNIVERSITY OF VERMONT and ST. MICHAEL'S COLLEGE, and other barracks were rehabilitated to serve as private residences. The studios of Vermont Public Television and Vermont Public Radio operate in facilities at the old fort, along with many commercial enterprises that are located in former stables and other large buildings on the property. The tree-shaded campus-like appearance of the fort's former parade ground has been retained.   *John C. Wriston, Jr.*

Ethan Allen Club

An Act of Legislation in April 1857 granted a charter to the Ethan Allen Fire Engine Company Number 4 of Burlington, Vermont, "for the purpose of protecting property from fires and maintaining an association for the promotion of social intercourse and mutual improvement." The firefighters requesting that charter consisted of a group of young men "with a sprinkling of older heads to ensure a proper conservation in its management." Their new fire engine, called the *Ethan Allen*, first saw service at a fire on February 23, 1858, and helped fight a much larger blaze when the Pioneer Work Shops burned on April 3 of that year. The company's meetings, held in rented rooms on Church Street, sometimes included "fun and frolic, especially after making a successful run to a fire." Burlington's volunteer fire departments operated until 1895

when on January 9, the fire station on Colchester Avenue burned to the ground while rival volunteer companies obstructed each other in a competition to be the first to get a stream of water on the fire. The city responded by organizing a paid fire department that was located in the Ethan Allen fire station that had been built by the company on Church Street in 1889. The several volunteer companies disbanded and the "Ethans," at that time known as the "silk stocking crowd" because its members were bankers, merchants, and businessmen, moved to new quarters and continued as one of the more prestigious social clubs in the city. An all-male association, the members changed their name to the Ethan Allen Club and in 1905 purchased the Peck mansion on College Street, which they renovated and in which they installed a banquet hall, pool and billiard rooms, and a bowling alley. After the building burned in 1971, the club built a modern facilty on the property, which continued to serve as a social center and site for business deals. During the 1980s, the club's social and business status brought it into serious controversy when area businesswomen demanded that they be allowed to join. Up to then, women could be admitted as luncheon guests but were not permitted to enter through the front door. Charging sex discrimination and supported by the state bar association, which was pledged to fight against all-male clubs, in January 1989 women set up and dined at a luncheon table, complete with candles and flowers, on the snow-covered front lawn of the clubhouse. After a vote that retained the males-only charter, some members resigned and the Burlington City Council debated whether sex discrimination warranted nonrenewal of the club's liquor license. In 1990, a second vote produced the two-thirds majority required to change the charter and allow women to join. Once the right of membership was achieved, however, few women accepted invitations to join and the club seemed not to have fully recovered from the discrimination controversy. By the turn of the twenty-first century, the club remained among the state's most prestigious social organizations though its membership had declined significantly.

Lillian Baker Carlisle

Ethan Allen Homestead

From 1787 until his death in 1789, ETHAN ALLEN lived with his second wife, Frances,

and their three children as well as at least five other people who worked for him, including two African-Americans, in a simple wooden house overlooking the WINOOSKI RIVER in Burlington. It had a board exterior, wooden floors, and two stories plus a cellar. The house, with surrounding farmland, was sold out of the family in the 1790s. Directed by the research of RALPH NADING HILL, a group interested in local history identified the old farm house overlooking the river as Allen's last home. It was bought in 1976 in honor of the United States Bicentennial and given to the WINOOSKI VALLEY PARK DISTRICT. In 1982, a legislative grant assisted the restoration activities. Now managed by the Ethan Allen Homestead Trust, the house was opened to the public in 1989 after extensive restoration. Ethan Allen's final home is furnished in much the same manner as it would have been when the Allens lived there. The garden and the simple wooden fence that surrounds the property have also been restored. The trust conducts an extensive education program to familiarize the public with details not only of Ethan Allen's role in the founding of Vermont but also of early American life on the northeastern frontier. An important pre-European colonial archaeological site has been uncovered on the homestead property. A Native American campsite found there contains charred remains of corn, carbon-dated to the year 1450 and estimated to be the earliest evidence of AGRICULTURE in Vermont.

Ann E. Cooper

Ethan Allen Institute

Located in Concord and named after early Vermont's most famous figure, the ETHAN ALLEN Institute, Vermont's first independent public policy think tank, was founded in 1993 with an eleven-member board. Today, five hundred paid memberships support the institute's mission to educate Vermonters on the fundamentals of a free society, including individual liberty, private property, limited government, competitive enterprise, strong communities, and personal responsibility. The institute's activities include commentaries in Vermont newspapers and on Vermont Public Radio, issue luncheons and dinners and public programs, legislative seminars, and a wide range of publications, including a monthly newsletter. Current president John McClaughry is a former member of the Vermont House (1969–1972) and Senate (1989–1992) and a former senior policy advisor in the Reagan administration (1981–1982).   *John McClaughry*

Ethan Allen Tower

Erected as a memorial to the most famous of Vermont's founders, this Norman-style tower was designed by former Burlington mayor WILLIAM VAN PATTEN on land he donated. Standing on Indian Rock, one hundred feet above LAKE CHAMPLAIN, the Ethan Allen Tower commands an unparalleled view of the lake on land that was originally part of ETHAN ALLEN's farm. The tower was funded by the Vermont Sons of the American Revolution and dedicated on Bennington Battle Day in 1905. Originally a popular destination for Burlingtonians, the tower, suffering from time and vandalism, closed in 1974. In 1982, Save the Tower, Inc., led by Lana Jarvis and other citizens, raised $25,000 for restoration, a sum matched by the city, plus $14,000 for maintenance. The tower reopened in June 1984, and is open to the public on summer weekends.

Sarah L. Dopp

Eugenics Survey of Vermont

In 1925, HENRY F. PERKINS, professor of zoology at the UNIVERSITY OF VERMONT, organized the Eugenics Survey of Vermont as an adjunct to his heredity course. The mission of the survey was threefold: research, public education on its findings, and support for social legislation that would reduce the apparent growing population of Vermont's "social problem group." Most notorious of these reforms was Vermont's 1931 eugenic sterilization law, "A Law for Human Betterment by Voluntary Sterilization." With the financial support and endorsement of social reformers, government agencies, and private philanthropies, the Eugenics Survey acted as the official agency of the American eugenics movement in Vermont. From 1925 to 1928, the Eugenics Survey's research consisted of gathering evidence from social case records, town officials, and various "informants" of "bad heredity" in over sixty Vermont families to support campaigns for negative eugenics measures: sexual sterilization, expansion of colonies for the feebleminded, and mandatory use of mental testing in social work with dependent families, in public schools, and in the criminal justice system. In 1927, Professor Perkins briefed the state legislature using the findings of

these studies in a campaign to enact a sterilization law, and social workers and charity agencies were encouraged to use the survey's "pedigrees of degenerate families" in their case work. The Eugenics Survey targeted families of mixed racial ancestry, particularly French-Canadian and ABENAKI, and poor white families living in isolated rural districts. In 1927, Professor Perkins obtained funds to organize a comprehensive rural survey, which became the VERMONT COMMISSION ON COUNTRY LIFE. Its findings and recommendations, published as *Rural Vermont: A Program for the Future* (1931), became a model for state planning and rural development. The Eugenics Survey served as the VCCL "Committee on the Human Factor." Vermont's "dependent, delinquent, and deficient" families, whose problems Perkins had attributed to "bad heredity," were recast by the VCCL as "the handicapped" and studied by a special sub-committee of the Committee on the Human Factor. The Human Factor Committee studied the social forces that had contributed to rural depopulation and decline in family size among the "good old Vermont stock." The Eugenics Survey's Key Family Study and Migration Study celebrated the achievements, community spirit, and endurance of Vermonters in the face of a changing economy. Their recommendations, cast in eugenic terms, encouraged Vermonters to "study their own family records with a view to arousing their pride in the achievements and high qualities of their ancestral stock so that this pride may in turn stimulate their better efforts and guide them in their choice of mates," and "that the doctrine be spread that it is the patriotic duty of every normal couple to have children in sufficient number to keep up to par the 'good old Vermont stock.'" For so-called "handicapped" Vermonters, whose family records and ancestral stock had already been studied and stigmatized by the Eugenics Survey, the commission advocated an expansion of state programs in child health, education and welfare, and prevention of marriage and reproduction of "feebleminded" persons. In 1931, Vermont became the twenty-seventh state to enact a sterilization law. As secretary of the commission until 1931 and executive vice president after 1931, Henry Perkins launched an education campaign through study groups, libraries, and schools to promote eugenic objectives in Vermont communities using

Rural Vermont as a guidebook. As president of the American Eugenics Society, Perkins promoted the Vermont Commission on Country Life program as a model eugenics program for America. From 1932 to 1936, Elin Anderson, assistant director of the Eugenics Survey, conducted a sociological study of ethnic communities in Burlington. Anderson's sociological approach offered an alternative view of eugenics to the one Professor Perkins had advocated for a decade. Her study, *WE AMERICANS: A Study of Cleavage in an American City* (Harvard University Press, 1937), endures as an important statement on the value of cultural diversity in America and an indictment of those social forces that sought to suppress it. The Eugenics Survey closed in 1936 at the conclusion of benefactor Shirley Farr's ten-year commitment of funding. Yet eugenics education continued at the University of Vermont and other colleges and high schools in the state. Vermont's eugenic solutions—in the form of identification, registration, intervention in families with problem or backward children, and sterilization of those deemed unfit to conceive future Vermonters—were carried out under the supervision of the Department of Public Welfare. The archives of the Eugenics Survey and the Vermont Commission of Country Life in the Vermont Public Records Division, Middlesex, provide a detailed record of its studies and campaigns to shape public opinion and social policy in Vermont.

Nancy L. Gallagher

Eureka Schoolhouse

An historic site on Route 11 east of Springfield and west of U.S. Route 5 and exit 7 of Interstate 91, the Eureka Schoolhouse was probably constructed in the 1780s and is one of the few surviving eighteenth-century public buildings in the state. Its unusual exterior is of pine board cut to simulate stone block. Restored in 1968, the schoolhouse is furnished with memorabilia, including several desks dating from about 1800 and books used by school children of another century. Also on the grounds is the Town lattice truss Baltimore COVERED BRIDGE, built in 1870. A significant site-improvement project completed by forestry students at the Springfield Vocational Center has restored scenic views of the southern Black River and provides enhanced riverside picnic locations.

John Dumville

Evarts, Jeremiah (1781–1831)

Lawyer, editor, religious activist, and humanitarian, Jeremiah Evarts was born in Sunderland and moved with his family to the town of Georgia where he attended the local school until 1798, when he was sent to the old family home in East Guilford, Connecticut, to prepare for Yale College. Upon graduation from Yale in 1802, he returned to Vermont, where he served as principal of Caledonia County Grammar School in Peacham. A year later, he began to study law, clerked in the New Haven, Connecticut, office of Judge Charles Chauncey, and in 1806 was admitted to the Connecticut bar. An unsuccessful practice (contemporaries alleged he had too much unbending integrity to be a popular lawyer) led him to abandon his practice and assume editorship of the *Panoplist*, a monthly magazine of the orthodox Congregationalists published in Charleston, Massachusetts, where Evarts made his permanent home. As editor, Evarts dealt with a broad range of religious issues while advocating temperance legislation and the curtailment of Sunday mail delivery. He was a founder and officer of the American Board of Commissioners for Foreign Missions, a manager of the American Bible Society, and vice president of the American Education Society. By 1821, his missionary work became so consuming that he relinquished the editorship of the *Panoplist* while continuing work on missionary publications. He was distressed by the condition of the southeastern Indian tribes, particularly the Cherokees, and his *Essays on the Present Crisis in the Condition of the American Indians*, first published in 1821, remains a powerful indictment of federal and state government Native American policies. His son William Maxwell Evarts was a nationally known lawyer and U.S. secretary of state.

F

Fahnestock, Zephine Humphrey
(1874–1956)

A Philadelphian and Smith College graduate, class of 1896, Zephine Humphrey Fahnestock lived for fifty years in Dorset. Active in Vermont literary circles, in 1919 she was a member of the Committee on Traditions and Ideals under the VERMONT COMMISSION ON COUNTRY LIFE. Her impressionistic and appreciative essays were published in eighteen collections that included *The Story of Dorset* (1924), *The Beloved Community* (1930), *Green Mountains to Sierras* (1936), and *A Book of New England* (1954).

Fairbanks, Erastus (1792–1864)

Governor of Vermont from 1852 to 1853 and 1860 to 1861, Erastus Fairbanks was a native of Brimfield, Massachusetts, who settled in St. Johnsbury in 1813. He entered business with his brother THADDEUS FAIRBANKS in the manufacture of stoves and farm implements. By the 1830s, the company was concentrating on scale manufacturing. Erastus managed the business while Thaddeus focused on the manufacturing of scales. In 1836, Erastus was elected from St. Johnsbury to the Vermont

Erastus Fairbanks. Special Collections, Bailey/Howe Library, University of Vermont

House of Representatives and for the next two decades was among the most influential Vermont Whigs, serving as presidential elector in 1844 and again in 1848. In the latter year, he declined nomination to the United States Congress, presumably because of his responsibilities for the construction of the Connecticut and Passumpsic Rivers Railroad, which ran from White River Junction to the Canadian border in Derby and would provide major transportation facilities for E. & T. FAIRBANKS AND COMPANY. He ran for governor as a Whig in 1852, failed to win the majority in the popular vote but was elected governor by the legislature. After he signed into law a liquor prohibition act in 1853, voters gave him a plurality, though the legislature rejected him for a second term. Nonetheless, the liquor prohibition remained in effect until 1902. In 1861, as a Republican, he was elected governor over the Democratic candidate, poet JOHN GODFREY SAXE. Eight days after the assault on Fort Sumter in April 1861, Governor Fairbanks called a special session of the General Assembly, which appropriated $1 million for the war effort and gave Fairbanks full scope to spend the fund as he deemed best. The first six regiments of volunteers and a company of sharpshooters were mustered into service under Fairbanks's administration. He drew no salary as governor. Erastus and Thaddeus Fairbanks founded ST. JOHNSBURY ACADEMY in 1843.

Allen Yale

Fairbanks, Franklin (1827–1895)

The sixth child and fourth son of ERASTUS FAIRBANKS, Franklin Fairbanks became a partner in E. & T. FAIRBANKS AND COMPANY in 1856. Active in the company for fifty years, he served as its president from 1888 to 1895. An inveterate collector of natural history, Franklin founded the FAIRBANKS MUSEUM in 1891 to house his collection.

Allen Yale

Fairbanks, Horace (1820–1888)

The thirty-sixth governor of Vermont (1876–1878) and son of Governor ERASTUS FAIRBANKS, Horace Fairbanks was born in Barnet. In 1843, he was made partner in the Fairbanks Company. In 1865, he assumed his father's role as senior partner of E. & T. FAIRBANKS AND COMPANY. After the company incorporated in 1874, he served as its president until his death. During Horace's leadership, the company grew to annual sales of $2 million and

employed over five hundred men. During his one term as governor, Horace Fairbanks initiated some prison reforms and expressed modest opposition to the death penalty, for which he was harshly criticized. In 1871, he founded the ST. JOHNSBURY ATHENAEUM with eight thousand volumes as the community's library. An art gallery designed to house Albert Bierstadt's painting *Domes of the Yosemite* was attached to the Athenaeum in 1873.

Allen Yale

Fairbanks, Thaddeus (1796–1886)

Born in Brimfield, Massachusetts, Thaddeus Fairbanks settled in St. Johnsbury in 1815, setting up a wheelwright's shop above his father's gristmill. In 1824, he entered business with his brother ERASTUS FAIRBANKS in the manufacturing of stoves and farm implements. Finding currently available scales inaccurate for weighing hemp for market, Thaddeus developed a platform scale. Soon the firm of E. & T. FAIRBANKS AND COMPANY was specializing in scales. Thaddeus, the mechanic, concentrated on manufacturing for fifty-five years while Erastus managed the business. During the course of his life, Thaddeus was issued over forty patents. While most of these were related to scales, they also included an icebox, stoves, ploughs, radiators, and feed-water heaters. With Erastus he founded ST. JOHNSBURY ACADEMY in 1843. In recognition of the contributions to commerce of the Fairbanks platform scale, Thaddeus was knighted by the emperor of Austria and received honors from the King of Siam and the Bey of Tunis. *Allen Yale*

Fairbanks and Company

See E. & T. FAIRBANKS AND COMPANY.

Fairbanks Museum and Planetarium

The Fairbanks Museum and Planetarium, located in St. Johnsbury, was founded in 1889 by local industrialist FRANKLIN FAIRBANKS to house his substantial collections of natural science specimens and related artifacts. The building, listed on the National Register of Historic Places, was designed by LAMBERT PACKARD and opened to the public in 1891. The Museum continues to educate visitors about natural sciences and regional history through programs and exhibits and is home to the Northern New England Weather Center and Vermont's only public planetarium.

Selene Colburn

Fairfax

Fairfax, population 3,765, a town in Franklin County, was granted by BENNING WENTWORTH in 1763 to New York businessman Edward Burling and others and probably named for Thomas Fairfax (1693–1781), sixth baron Fairfax, a prominent nobleman who had moved to Virginia in 1747 and owned extensive estates there. The landscape, which consists of a series of low hills and gentle valleys, is cut in the southern part of town from east to west by the LAMOILLE RIVER, which at the generating plant at Fairfax Falls supplies electricity to the surrounding region. The chief settlement is Fairfax village, two miles downstream from the falls. Once a manufacturing center of some importance, the town is today chiefly devoted to DAIRY FARMING. Letter tiles for the game of Scrabble were made here for many years until the factory moved to China in 1998.

Fairfield

Fairfield, population 1,800, a town in Franklin County, was granted by BENNING WENTWORTH in 1763 to Samuel Hungerford and others and named for Fairfield, Connecticut, Hungerford's home town and that of some of the other grantees. Its rolling countryside is devoted to DAIRY FARMING and maple sugar production. The main settlements are Fairfield village and East Fairfield, both on Route 36 as it crosses the town from east to west. The only substantial body of water is 464-acre FAIRFIELD POND, also known as Dream Lake, in the town's northwestern corner. A replica of the small frame house on a remote dirt road in which CHESTER ALAN ARTHUR, twenty-first president of the United States, was supposedly born was erected by the Vermont Board of Historic Sites in 1954 and is open to visitors from late May to mid-October.

Fairfield Pond

Fairfield Pond in the town of Fairfield is sometimes referred to as Dream Lake for an event in 1842 when a crime was solved by a dream revealing the location of an important clue. Eugene Clifford, rumored to be a deserter from the British army in Canada, was married to the widow Elizabeth Gilmore, who owned a small farm in Fairfield, when on Sunday, October 16, Clifford took his wife and her daughter for a canoe ride on Fairfield Pond. He returned to the village later, announcing that his wife had fallen in the pond while adjusting a shawl around her child, but that he had been unable to rescue them. Their bodies, but not the shawl, were soon found by searchers. In a few days, a friend of Elizabeth told the sheriff that she had been having a recurring dream of where the shawl could be found and took officers to where it was hidden on the shore. Other neighbors came forward to say that Clifford had spoken of his expectation of outliving his wife and inheriting her farm. He was arrested, tried, and hanged in St. Albans in April 1843.   *Carl Johnson*

Fair Haven

Fair Haven, population 2,928, a town in Rutland County, was granted by the Vermont legislature in 1779 to a group of sixty people including IRA ALLEN, his cousin EBENEZER ALLEN, and THOMAS CHITTENDEN. If the town's name has a specific source it is not known; it may be simply a description of the aspect of the land. Originally, the town included all the territory which in 1792 became the town of West Haven, the separation of which reduced the area of Fair Haven by three-fifths. The town lies on the New York State border, which is here formed by the Poultney River, and is a mix of meadows and low hills, the northern extremity of the TACONIC MOUNTAINS. The only settlement is Fair Haven village, on the Castleton River just before it joins the Poultney. The town is one of the state's largest producers of SLATE, from a quarry on Scotch Hill. The most famous individual in the history of Fair Haven was MATTHEW LYON, one of the grantees, who arrived in 1783 and became the town's leading businessman before he began a tumultuous state and national political career.

Fairlee

Fairlee, population 967, the smallest town in area in Orange County, was granted by BENNING WENTWORTH in 1761 and originally also encompassed West Fairlee before the latter was made a separate town in 1797. The source of the name has not been established, but it may be Fairlee on the Isle of Wight in England. The town rises abruptly from the fertile meadows of the CONNECTICUT RIVER, which forms its eastern boundary, to a long ridge of summits running the length of the town from north to south, effectively limiting inland settlement. There are two villages, Fairlee, squeezed between the Connecticut and the Palisades, which rise six hundred feet behind it, and Ely, a riverside railroad stop that once served the copper mines in nearby Vershire. Two lakes, which serve as summer resort areas, are the town's economic mainstay: 538-acre Lake Morey and 463-acre Lake Fairlee, which lies partly in the neighboring towns of West Fairlee and Thetford. Lake Morey is named for SAMUEL MOREY, who as early as 1793 experimented with a steam-driven boat on the Connecticut and later sold his invention to Robert Fulton, who made the first long-range steamboat journey from New York to Albany in 1807.

Fairs, Field Days, and Festivals

A still vital tradition dating from the days when Vermont was primarily an agricultural state, fairs, field days, and festivals attract tens of thousands of visitors every

Harness racing at the Orleans County Fair in Barton. Vermont Department of Tourism and Marketing

year. The large ones, such as the CHAM-PLAIN VALLEY EXPOSITION in Essex Junction and the RUTLAND FAIR, both of which take place in late August and early September, feature agricultural and animal exhibits, judging contests, craft displays, live music performances, midway rides and games of chance, food booths, horse and tractor pulls, demolition derbies, and other popular attractions. Others focus more narrowly on special areas of interest: the Vermont Flower Show (early March), the Vermont Maple Festival (late April), the Vermont Dairy Festival (early June), the Vermont Sheep and Wool Festival (October), and the South Hero Applefest (October). The Vermont Agricultural Fair Association lists twenty-four separate fairs for 2001, including ones for Addison, Caledonia, Franklin, Orleans, Lamoille, Washington, and Windsor counties, as well as what many consider the most authentic fair of all, the Tunbridge World's Fair, held in Tunbridge every September.

Farm Bureau

The Vermont Farm Bureau, with ELLSWORTH B. CORNWALL as its first president, emerged, as had similar organizations in other states, from the activities of county agents, who as representatives of the University Extension Service organized farmers into county bureaus. Recognizing that they could never function as a strong political pressure group under Extension Service auspices, activist farmers pushed for an independent organization, and on February 12, 1919, twelve states sent representativees to a meeting in Ithaca, New York. Cornwall, as Vermont's representative, returned determined to mold the county bureaus into a state association and work toward a national organization. To that end he, along with W. ARTHUR SIMPSON and other Vermont representatives, participated in a Chicago meeting at which the American Farm Bureau Federation was born. Some county bureaus opposed the new organization's plan to be more independent of the Extension Service and to focus on national and state lobbying rather than remaining an educational institution. Fear that the national farm bureau would be dominated by midwestern interests was another issue, and membership did not stabilize until 1928, when ARTHUR PACKARD succeeded Cornwall as president. The Vermont Farm Bureau reached its heyday under Packard's leadership. Attaining its maximum

membership of 10,519 in 1946, it exercised a major influence on legislative affairs and state politics. Packard, a former legislator, allied with the liberal Aiken-Gibson faction of the REPUBLICAN PARTY and directed the bureau in the promotion of electric and buying-and-selling cooperatives, in regulating freight charges, and in imposing an income tax to relieve the personal property tax burden, among other farmer-interest programs. The bureau also entered into agreements with insurance companies that provided low-cost benefits to its membership and income for its treasury. By 1953, when Packard was succeeded by Keith Wallace, Vermont AGRICULTURE was in decline. Although the size of farms grew, the number of farms and farmers dereased substantially while REAPPORTIONMENT of the legislature had diminished agricultural representation in the General Assembly. Nonetheless, efforts to preserve Vermont's pastoral landscape have produced major supportive legislation. The bottle deposit law, a sales tax exemption for the purchase of farm machinery, and a land-use tax that taxes farm land at a lower rate than other real property were all objectives the Farm Bureau has helped to see through enactment into law.

Farnham, Roswell (1827–1903)

Lawyer, soldier, and governor, Roswell Farnham of Bradford struggled for nearly thirty years to keep the VERMONT COPPER COMPANY alive and its mines producing. Farnham was born in Boston and moved with his family to Bradford in 1840, attended the Bradford Academy, and graduated from the UNIVERSITY OF VERMONT in 1849. He read the law and taught school until gaining admission to the Orange County bar. A member of the Bradford Guards militia, he enlisted with that unit in the First Vermont Volunteer Regiment in 1861 as a second lieutenant and served also in the Twelfth Vermont, leaving the army in 1863 as a lieutenant colonel. He became general counsel for the Vermont Copper Company after the war and continued with the company as lawyer and administrator for the rest of his life. He was a member of the Republican State Committee (1865–1868), state senator (1868–1869), delegate to the 1876 Republican National Convention and presidential elector that same year. In 1880, he defeated Democrat EDWARD JOHN PHELPS for the governorship of Vermont. After one term as governor, Farnham re-

turned to his law practice, concentrating largely on the affairs of the financially ailing Vermont Copper Company. In 1889, he became president of a group of northern investors calling themselves the New England Company who sought to develop coal and iron deposits in northern Georgia. The coal and iron venture in Georgia was never a success, and Farnham spent most of the last decade of the nineteenth century keeping the copper company from bankruptcy. He died at his home in Bradford.

Fassett, John, Jr. (1743–ca. 1825)

A native of Hardwick, Massachusetts, and son of one of the first settlers to arrive in Bennington in 1761, John Fassett ran an inn and was captain of the town's first militia company and Bennington's representative to the first Vermont legislature. He was a lieutenant in SETH WARNER's Continental regiment of rangers in 1775 and a captain in 1776. A commissioner of sequestration in 1777 with THOMAS CHITTENDEN and MATTHEW LYON, Fassett was successful in subduing the Loyalists of Arlington. He represented Arlington in the General Assembly in 1778 and 1779, and Cambridge in 1787, 1788, 1789, and 1790. Fassett was also a member of the Governor's Council for fifteen years between 1779 and 1795, except for 1786. Judge of the superior court from 1778 to 1786, he moved to Cambridge in 1784 and then served also as chief judge of Chittenden County court from 1787 to 1794. His place of death is unknown, as he moved in his eighties from Cambridge to somewhere in the west.

Fausett, William Dean (1913–1998)

A portrait and landscape artist, William Dean Fausett settled in Dorset after World War II. His portrait subjects included, among others, the Duke and Duchess of Windsor, Grandma Moses on her one-hundredth birthday, and Ronald Reagan. His "Derby View" hung in President Eisenhower's White House study. Dean Fausett lived in the Cephas Kent house, site of four Vermont conventions in 1775 and 1776. Many of his works feature a five-hundred-year-old sugar maple, perhaps the oldest in New England, that stood in front of his house.

Fay, Jonas (1737–1818)

The chief author of of Vermont's declaration of independence, Jonas Fay was born in Hardwick, Massachusetts, where he taught himself medicine. In 1766, Fay moved with his family to Bennington, where his father STEPHEN FAY opened the CATAMOUNT TAVERN, a famous center for radical political action. Jonas Fay quickly became a key participant in the movement seeking to separate the New Hampshire grants from New York, generally serving as secretary of the extra-legal conventions that eventually created the state of Vermont. A member of the GREEN MOUNTAIN BOYS, Fay was present at the capture of FORT TICONDEROGA and served as a surgeon in SETH WARNER'S GREEN MOUNTAIN CONTINENTAL RANGERS during the invasion of Canada in 1775 and 1776. He attended his brother John's death at the BATTLE OF BENNINGTON, the first man killed there. Widely respected for his intelligence and confidentiality, Fay filled a number of key positions in the fluid revolutionary government of frontier Vermont. The chief author of Vermont's 1777 declaration of independence, Fay was also secretary of Vermont's constitutional convention and vice-president of Vermont's first government, served on the Governor's Council, the Board of War, and the Committee of Sequestration, and represented Vermont at the Continental Congress. He co-authored with ETHAN ALLEN *A Concise Refutation of the Claims of New-Hampshire and Massachusetts Bay, to the Territory of Vermont* (1780). Despite a complete absence of legal training, Fay held positions as justice of the peace, probate judge, and member of Vermont's Supreme Court. In 1787, Fay retired from public life and devoted himself largely to the Vermont Medical Society, which he co-founded.

Michael A. Bellesiles and Robert V. Daniels

Fay, Joseph (1752–1803)

Son of STEPHEN FAY of Bennington, the owner of the CATAMOUNT TAVERN, Joseph Fay was secretary of the Governor's Council from 1778 to 1795 and Vermont secretary of state from 1778 to 1781. After 1795, he worked as an import merchant in New York City. A close friend and political ally of ETHAN and IRA ALLEN, Fay was Ira Allen's associate in effecting the exchange of prisoners with the British in 1781 and 1782 at Skenesborough (later renamed Whitehall), New York, and treating with the British during the HALDIMAND NEGOTIATIONS.

Fay, Stephen (1715–1781)

Innkeeper and a leader of the GREEN MOUNTAIN BOYS, Stephen Fay was born in Westboro, Massachusetts, and settled in Bennington in 1766, where he lived with his wife Ruth Child until his death. He was the proprietor of the CATAMOUNT TAVERN, which from 1770 on served as the headquarters of the Green Mountain Boys, first in their struggle against the authority of the state of New York, and later in the Revolutionary War with Britain. Fay held the rank of captain. In 1772, he and his son JONAS FAY were the emissaries of the Bennington Convention to Governor William Tryon of New York to attempt to negotiate their land disputes. Five of his seven sons fought in the BATTLE OF BENNINGTON, and the eldest, John, was the first man killed there. His son Jonas was a leader in the creation of the state of Vermont, and his daughter Mary married MOSES ROBINSON, second governor of Vermont. His grandson John Fay was the first postmaster in Burlington, and another grandson, TIMOTHY FOLLETT, founded the Rutland Railroad.   *Robert V. Daniels*

Fay, William (1780–1840)

A native of Hardwick, Massachusetts, William Fay apprenticed as a printer to his brother Josiah, with whom he moved to Rutland in 1797 and formed a partnership with the Reverend SAMUEL WILLIAMS in publishing the *RUTLAND HERALD* starting in 1802. He continued in various other partnerships until 1840. In addition to maintaining an active printing business (he was appointed Vermont state printer for several years), Fay was sheriff of Rutland County from 1817–1818, and was town clerk of Rutland from 1835 to 1839.

Marcus A. McCorison

Fayston

Fayston, population 1,141, a town in Washington County, was granted by the Vermont legislature in 1782 and named for the Fay family of Bennington, among the most noted of Vermont's founders. Lying directly on the eastern slope of the main spine of the GREEN MOUNTAINS, the town is densely wooded and mountainous, rising to 3,662 feet at the summit of Stark Mountain. The only major road is Route 17, which crosses the town from east to west and passes through Appalachian Gap just over the western border in Buel's Gore. Directly before the Gap is the Mad River Glen ski area (forty-four trails and a

vertical drop of 2,037 feet). Because of the ski area and the nearby tourist towns of Waitsfield and Warren (the latter of which contains the Sugarbush ski area), Fayston has not only a number of inns and restaurants but also numerous private homes on the dirt roads that wind across its forested hillsides.

Fenian Raids

Twice in the 1860s the Fenian Brotherhood, an Irish-American society founded in 1858 and devoted to the liberation of Ireland from British rule, attempted an invasion of Canada from Vermont. Their ranks filled with Civil War veterans of Irish extraction, they hoped to establish a base for raids against British shipping and eventually attacks against England itself. The first of the two raids took place in early June 1866. Inspired by a recent foray across the Niagara River into Upper Canada by a force of six hundred Fenians who fought three skirmishes with Canadian militia before retreating, a band of a thousand men marched 6 miles across the border from the town of Franklin into the township of St.-Armand. Here they camped in anticipation of a battle, but learning that their reinforcements had been cut off by U.S. troops and that their Canadian opponents would be more numerous than previously thought, they retreated across the border, where they were disarmed and dispersed. The second and more ambitious raid took place in late May 1870. Led by General John O'Neill, a Union officer who had been in charge of the Niagara raid, an advance guard of 176 men of a larger force that numbered approximately 700 gathered at the border in Franklin. The purpose of their incursion was to cut the railroad line at St. Jean, 22 miles north on the Richelieu River, as a prelude to further hostilities. Warned by George P. Foster, U.S. Marshal for Vermont, to disperse, and impatient at the delay in receiving reinforcements, O'Neill sent his advance guard across the border only to have them run into determined resistance from Canadian militia on Eccles Hill, a steep boulder-strewn slope. Stymied, O'Neill rushed to the rear to find troops to bolster his men but was arrested at gun point by Marshal Foster and his deputy and taken away. Although the fighting lasted for a while longer, the Fenians were eventually repulsed, with two men killed and nine wounded. No Canadians were killed or injured. One innocent bystander, a servant girl, was killed by Canadian fire. O'Neill was imprisoned in Windsor but pardoned by President Grant in October. A final small Fenian assault in Manitoba in 1871 was frustrated by U.S. troops, and the organization disbanded in 1877.

Ferdinand

Ferdinand, population thirty-three, an unorganized township in Essex County, was granted by BENNING WENTWORTH in 1761 to Samuel Averill and others. Like the nearby towns of Brunswick and Lunenburg, it derived its name from Prince Karl Wilhelm Ferdinand of Brunswick-Lüneburg (1735–1806), a German hero of the Seven Years' War with family connections to the British royal house of Hanover. The southern two-thirds of the township is hilly and heavily forested, rising to 3,120 feet at Seneca Mountain along the border with East Haven. The only significant industry has always been lumbering. In 1999, most of Ferdinand became part of the CHAMPION LANDS, a public-private project devoted to conservation and sustainable forest harvesting. There is no village, and such settlement as has occurred is along Route 105, which follows the course of the Nulhegan River as it cuts across the northern section of the town from west to east.

Ferris, Hiram (1792–1876)

A native of Panton, Hiram Ferris was the first steamboat pilot on LAKE CHAMPLAIN. He took the helm of the *Vermont I* when she was launched in 1809, and served as a pilot on the lake until 1859. He discovered the rocky reef opposite Port Kent that bears his name. Ferris fathered twenty-five children, sixteen of them sons, all of whom were called "Ed": Edwin, Edward, Edmund, and variations thereof until the last one was named Edenough. Sometime between 1825 and 1830, Ferris settled in Chazy, New York, residing there until 1874 when he went west to live with one of his sons in Fond du Lac, Wisconsin, where he died. *David Blow*

Ferris, Peter (1725–1816)

After the French and Indian War, Peter Ferris of the town of Nine Partners in Dutchess County, New York, was one of the first settlers to move to Vermont. In 1765, he and his family settled on the shore of LAKE CHAMPLAIN at what became known as Ferris Bay in Panton, where his nearest neighbor was some twelve miles away in the British fortress at Crown Point. The location of his new home along the strategic waterway of Lake Champlain drew him into the American Revolutionary conflict. His sympathies were with those fighting for independence, and in the spring of 1776 his home was an overnight stopping place for a congressional delegation headed for Montreal that included Benjamin Franklin. On October 13, 1776, BENEDICT ARNOLD, fleeing a superior British fleet, intentionally destroyed five vessels in Ferris Bay and with the Ferris family retreated overland to FORT TICONDEROGA. In 1777, General JOHN BURGOYNE's advancing British army destroyed Ferris's crops and in 1778, a British raiding party took Peter and his sixteen-year old son Squire prisoners. The Ferrises made several attempts at escape, but were always recaptured, spending a total of three years, seven months, and fourteen days in captivity. After they were exchanged, the Ferrises returned to their home on the shore of Lake Champlain, where Peter established one of the first ferries across the lake and several sons and grandsons became lake captains. Peter died at the age of ninety-one, and his gravestone overlooks the bay he settled more than half a century earlier. Over time, his descendants moved away, Peter Ferris was forgotten, and Ferris Bay took on the name Arnold's Bay for the event of October 13, 1776. *Arthur Cohn*

Ferrisburgh

Ferrisburgh, population 2,657, a town in Addison County, was granted by BENNING WENTWORTH in 1762 to Benjamin Ferris, a prominent New York Quaker, and a number of others. Its gently rolling, fertile landscape is bordered on the west by LAKE CHAMPLAIN and cut deeply by the waters of OTTER CREEK, Little Otter Creek, Dead Creek, and Lewis Creek, which form extensive wetlands favored by wildfowl. The two main settlements are Ferrisburgh village and North Ferrisburgh, the first the main service center for the town's farms. Along Lake Champlain, in addition to numerous summer homes and camps, are two state parks (Kingsland Bay and Button Bay), the popular Basin Harbor Club, and the LAKE CHAMPLAIN MARITIME MUSEUM, devoted to the history of lake traffic in war and peace. On U.S. Route 7 north of Ferrisburgh village is ROKEBY, the home of the nineteenth-century writer Row-

LAND T. ROBINSON and his abolitionist father, ROWLAND E. ROBINSON, which is open to visitors.

Fessenden, Thomas Green (1771–1837)

Thomas Green Fessenden was editor of the influential agricultural magazine the *New England Farmer* (1822–1837) and author of the popular poem, "The Country Lover; or Jonathan's Courtship" (1796), a prototype of the humorous genre portraying New England country bumpkins. Born in Walpole, New Hampshire, he was a brother of WILLIAM FESSENDEN. After graduating from Dartmouth College in 1796, Fessenden went to Rutland to read law in the office of NATHANIEL CHIPMAN. Here he amused his neighbors with clever verse and took an interest in Barnabas Langdon's hydraulic pump, which Langdon claimed could raise a column of water up to 45 feet. Rutland backers raised money to send Fessenden to London to exploit the device but the pump was unequal to its claims. While in England, Fessenden issued his most famous work, *Terrible Tractoration!! A poetical petition against Galvinizing trumpery, and the Perkinistic Institution* (London, 1803). The volume was the result of another disastrous business alliance, this time with an American charlatan, Dr. Elisha Perkins. Returning to the United States, Fessenden began a long career as editor and author, gaining fame as a vitriolic Federalist apologist during the press wars of the Jeffersonian period. He came back to Vermont as editor of the *Vermont Intelligencer, and Bellows' Falls Advertiser* for BILL BLAKE, but his most lasting contribution to American life was his editorship at Boston of the *New England Farmer*, which became the most widely circulated agricultural journal of its day. Fessenden died at his home in Boston and was memorialized by Nathaniel Hawthorne. *Marcus A. McCorison*

Fessenden, William (1779–1815)

William Fessenden, brother to THOMAS GREEN FESSENDEN, was a printer and newspaperman in Brattleboro who developed a local newspaper printing house into a large book-printing business with customers as distant as Philadelphia. Fessenden apprenticed in ISAIAH THOMAS's printing house in his hometown of Walpole, New Hampshire. Following a brief stint in Vergennes from 1800 to 1801, Fessenden moved to Brattleboro, where he established the *Reporter* in February 1803.

In addition to printing his newspaper, Fessenden formed a partnership with his father-in-law, Deacon JOHN HOLBROOK, and David Porter as Holbrook, Fessenden & Porter (1808–1810), a firm that printed and distributed large quantities of school books and other publications on contract for publishers. In 1813, Fessenden had eight presses at work in his office, most of them engaged in the printing of Noah Webster's spellers. In that same year, he became principal owner of the paper mill built in 1811 on Whetstone Brook in Brattleboro. Fessenden died suddenly in Northampton, Massachusetts, while on a business trip at the age of only thirty-six. His business affairs were taken up by Holbrook, a successful merchant who was then living in Connecticut.   *Marcus A. McCorison*

Field, Sabra (b. 1935)

A well-known printmaker and Vermont's most popular contemporary artist, Sabra Field was born in Tulsa, Oklahoma, and grew up in the metropolitan New York area. She earned a B.A. with honors in the arts from MIDDLEBURY COLLEGE and an M.A.T. from Wesleyan University, where she studied printmaking with Russell T. Limbach. She taught high school art for seven years in public and private schools, then in 1969, divorced and with two children, moved to East Barnard and opened a studio to publish her hand-pulled woodblock prints. Most of them depict the Vermont countryside in simple, flowing forms with rich and finely delineated colors. Field has also executed numerous commissions in other media such as stained glass and collage, and was the designer of the 1991 Vermont Bicentennial stamp. In the same year, she was named an Extraordinary Vermonter by Governor MADELEINE KUNIN, and in 1999 she received the Governor's Award for Excellence in the Arts from Governor HOWARD DEAN. She is married to Spencer Field, a wildlife painter, who is her partner and business manager.

Fillmore, Lavius (1767–ca. 1850)

Designer and builder of two of Vermont's finest early churches in Bennington and Middlebury, Lavius Fillmore was born in Norwich, Connecticut, where he is known to have designed churches at East Haddam (1794) and Norwich (1801). He moved to Middlebury in 1796. From 1804 to 1805, he designed and built the First Congregational Church of Bennington, now known as OLD FIRST CHURCH, a high-styled church influenced by Charles Bulfinch of Boston and ASHER BENJAMIN. He told the church committee it was designed on the concept of "The Cross of Christ Embracing the World." It was generally approved by the congregation for its serene beauty and its practical fulfillment of their needs. Fillmore's fourth church came when GAMALIEL PAINTER engaged him in 1806 to build a new church for the Congregational society of Middlebury. Taking longer to complete than planned, it served temporarily to house the state legislature while still under construction. The interior design resembles the Bennington church. It is beautifully sited and displays a noble exterior, especially in its tower, clock, spire, and many decorative features. In 1807, Fillmore and David Page, Jr., of Jaffrey, New Hampshire, purchased Gamaliel Painter's mills and waterpower on the east side of the falls of the OTTER CREEK, tore down Painter's buildings, and constructed a six-story factory large enough to grind 80,000 bushels of grain annually. Almost nothing is known about Fillmore's later life, though he might have designed Middlebury's St. Stephen's Episcopal Church.

Films and Filmmakers

Film critic Barry Snyder believes that a Vermont film "would be any film which actively and intentionally addresses the political, historical, environmental and cultural realities of Vermont, past and present." As well as showing their films at movie theaters and town halls throughout Vermont, where they have also enjoyed substantial video sales, Vermont filmmakers have established international reputations for their filmmaking. During the early 1990s, independently produced Vermont narrative films included David Giancola's *Time Chasers* (1991), John O'Brien's *Vermont Is for Lovers* (1992), and JAY CRAVEN's *Where the Rivers Flow North* (1993), the last of which played in 212 U.S. cities and 43 countries. In 1996, John O'Brien's second feature, *Man with a Plan*, generated nearly thirty thousand video sales and launched a political career for the film's star, retired Tunbridge dairy farmer FRED TUTTLE. Jay Craven's *A Stranger in the Kingdom* (1998) explored the 1968 "IRASBURG AFFAIR," in which a black minister's home was attacked by night riders. David Giancola's action adventures, led by *Icebreaker* (1999), continued to carve out a niche in video and foreign markets. Alan Dater and Lisa Merton have been quietly turning out award-winning documentaries from Marlboro for many years. Their most celebrated work to date is *Home to Tibet* (1997), about a Tibetan refugee returning after many years to see his family. Mary Arbuckle (*Birth Stories*) in Lincoln, Dorothy Tod (*Warriors' Women*) in Warren, and Robin Lloyd (*Peace Train to Beijing*) in Burlington have made socially conscious documentaries for several decades. Jim Taylor of Burlington, whose late-1970s mock-documentary short *Deer Hunting in Vermont* is considered a local classic, has been producing award-winning, multi-hour cable television documentaries for Resolution Productions, Inc., for the last ten years. Cinematographer/director Jeff Farber of Middlesex, working with Taylor on second camera, created *Brother Bread, Sister Puppet* (1994), a portrait of the BREAD AND PUPPET THEATER in Glover. Fred Levine developed a series of popular children's videos, the best-known of which is *Road Construction Ahead* (1991). Michael Sacca of Tunbridge is respected for his cinematography and editing on the work of Lloyd, Levine, and others. His film *Gabriel Women: Passamaquoddy Basketweavers* (1998) is a study of Maine Native-American craftswomen. Experimental filmmaking may not attract mainstream attention but Ted Lyman of Richmond, Walter Ungerer of Montpelier, and Norman Bloom of Middlebury are well known in national film and video arts communities. Similarly, David Ehrlich of Randolph is a respected animator whose short hand-drawn works are featured at many foreign film festivals. John Douglas of Charlotte, a former political documentary filmmaker, established (with former partner Robert Kramer and others) the Newsreel Collective in New York in the late 1960s, and is now a computer graphic imaging (CGI) artist with internationally known avant-garde works (*The Whitehouse*, 1997–2001). Other Vermont animators of note are Anne Barrett and the CGI wizard Matt Strauss. Two bold films, *Where's Stephanie?* (Mary Arbuckle and Bess O'Brien), a cinéma vérité documentary about a rape-murder and its aftermath, and *My Mother's Early Lovers* (Nora Jacobson of Norwich), a narrative about a rape-in-marriage that is uncovered years later, had their 1998 premières at the Vermont International Film Festival to widespread acclaim. The Burlington-based festival, founded in 1985, provides an annual venue for Vermont film and video makers. Among the festival prizes is the JAMES GOLDSTONE Vermont Filmmaker Award, which was presented by the Vermont Film Commission to Peter Miller of Grand Isle in 1999 and to Michael Fisher of Montpelier in 2000.

Kenneth A. Peck and Jay Craven

Films of Vermont

With a few notable exceptions, Vermont has not figured largely in motion pictures made for general distribution, and historically little actual shooting has taken place in the state. If it played a role at all, Vermont was presented as a representative example of an unsophisticated rural locale, and its natives portrayed as either innocent, cranky, or comically backward. The true nature of the Vermont character and landscape has only been dealt with by filmmakers who live in the state and are dedicated to portraying it with honesty and affection. They are delineated in the entry on FILMS AND FILMMAKERS. The earliest known film featuring Vermont is a short made at FORT ETHAN ALLEN in Colchester in May 1897 showing cavalry horses being put through various maneuvers such as charging and jumping hurdles. Like many films of the pre-1900 era, no print is known to exist. In the early twentieth century, up until the advent of sound, films with Vermont characters or locales include *The Apostle of Vengeance*, 1916, with William S. Hart (a minister living in Vermont returns to his home in Kentucky to reconcile his family with their neighbors), *Why I Would Not Marry*, 1918 (a young woman opens a store in Vermont and eventually marries a young salesman), *The Street of Tears*, 1924 (a family involved with a gang of crooks is rescued by being sent to a Vermont farm), and *Which Shall It Be?* 1924 (a Vermont couple give up their child to a wealthy relative, then think better of it). It is unlikely that any of these were actually filmed in Vermont, since movie-making was centered in New York and Hollywood. Only three films of the silent era were actually made wholly or partly in Vermont. The most important of these is D. W. Griffith's *Way Down East*, 1920, the climax of which was filmed in White River Junction. Lillian Gish, as the heroine, was forced to flee across the ice of the CONNECTICUT RIVER in midwinter until rescued by Richard Barthelmess. The other two films, both

released in 1922, were made and starred in by Margery Wilson, who had had a prominent role in Griffith's *Intolerance* and was one of America's earliest woman directors. Shot in Randolph, both films deal with a young woman mistakenly accused of a crime: in *Insinuation* that of embezzling funds and in *The Offenders* that of murder. In the first twenty-five years of the sound era, up until about 1955, a number of films involved Vermont characters or locales, although none of them were made in the state. *Mr. Deeds Goes to Town*, 1936, featured Gary Cooper as Longfellow Deeds of Mandrake Falls, Vermont, who inherits twenty million dollars and wants to give it all away to needy people. In *Nothing Sacred*, 1937, Fredric March played a reporter who exploits the supposedly imminent death of a young woman (Carole Lombard) from Warsaw, Vermont, for big-city headline value. In *Young People*, 1940, Shirley Temple was a member of a vaudeville family who are finally accepted by their neighbors in the town of Stonefield. In *Moonlight in Vermont*, 1943 (the only commercial film ever made with "Vermont" in the title), Gloria Jean was a girl singer who returns to Vermont when her plans for a New York singing career do not work out. *White Christmas*, 1954, an Irving Berlin musical, dealt with two army buddies (Bing Crosby and Danny Kaye) who boost the popularity of a winter resort run by their former commander. Two films dealt with historical incidents in this region. *Northwest Passage*, 1940, starred Spencer Tracy as the leader of Rogers' Rangers as they trekked through the New England wilderness in 1759 to attack the ABENAKI settlement at St. Francis, Quebec. The film, in Technicolor, was shot on location in Idaho. *The Raid*, 1954, with Van Heflin, was about the Confederate ST. ALBANS RAID in 1864. It was filmed in Hollywood. Undoubtedly the most famous film ever shot in Vermont is Alfred Hitchcock's *The Trouble with Harry*, 1955, a comic mystery filmed at the height of the foliage season in Craftsbury. It concerned a bothersome corpse that causes all sorts of problems for the citizens of a peaceful rural community. The world premiere of the film took place in Barre on September 30, 1955, with Hitchcock and Shirley MacLaine, one of the players, in attendance. Other films with Vermont associations were *The Young Lions*, 1958, in which Montgomery Clift leaves his wife in her Vermont hometown while he goes

off to fight in World War II, and *Those Calloways*, 1965, with Brian Keith as the head of a rural family fighting to preserve a nearby lake. One film *not* made in Vermont was *Peyton Place*, 1957, an adaptation of Grace Metalious's novel about scandalous doings in a New Hampshire village, which was scheduled for shooting in Woodstock but was transferred to Maine locations after townspeople objected. Two foreign-made films have Vermont locales. *Die Trapp-Familie in Amerika*, 1958, a German-language film directed by Wolfgang Liebeneiner, follows the famous Austrian singing family as it establishes a following in America and eventually settles in Stowe. *Pittsville—Ein Safe voll Blut* ("a safe full of blood"), 1974, in German and Polish, was filmed in Vermont by Polish director Krzysztof Zanussi and told the story of two small-towners who try to pull off a bank heist. Since 1980, films made in Vermont, with their locations, include the following: *A Change of Seasons*, 1980 (Bennington, Wilmington), *Terror Train*, 1980 (Bellows Falls), *The Four Seasons*, 1981 (Stowe), *Ghost Story*, 1981 (Woodstock), *Exposed*, 1983 (Burlington), *I Am the Cheese*, 1983 (Montpelier, Berlin, Plainfield, Marshfield, Northfield), *Something Wicked This Way Comes*, 1983 (Montpelier, Jeffersonville), *The Survivors*, 1983 (unspecified locations), *A Return to Salem's Lot*, 1987 (Peacham, Newbury, St. Johnsbury), *Baby Boom*, 1987 (Peru), *Batman & Robin*, 1987 (Barre), *Beetlejuice*, 1988 (East Corinth), *Funny Farm*, 1988 (unspecified locations), *Sweet Hearts Dance*, 1988 (Hyde Park and other, unspecified locations), *The Wizard of Loneliness*, 1988 (Bristol), *Welcome Home*, 1989 (Bennington), *Ethan Frome*, 1993 (Peacham, Morrisville, Danville, Groton, West Barnet, Chester), *Forrest Gump*, 1994 (Woodstock, Reading), *Wolf*, 1994 (Roxbury), *The Spitfire Grill*, 1996 (Peacham, St. Johnsbury), *The Cider House Rules*, 1999 (Brattleboro, Bellows Falls, Dummerston), *Me, Myself and Irene*, 2000 (Burlington, Williston, Essex, Colchester, Milton, Addison, Middlebury, South Hero, Jeffersonville), and *What Lies Beneath*, 2000 (Burlington, Charlotte, Addison, Vergennes, Waterbury). Few of these films do anything to emphasize the particular qualities of Vermont, nor are the locations necessarily identified as being in Vermont or, indeed, in any particular state. But the continuing search by filmmakers for fresh (and often cheaper) places to shoot and the convenience of filming in a state where outsiders are routinely made welcome give promise that Vermont will continue to be a presence on the movie screen for some time to come.

Fisher, Dorothy Canfield (1879–1958)

A native of Lawrence, Kansas, Dorothy Canfield Fisher graduated from Ohio State University and pursued graduate studies at the Sorbonne and Columbia University. In 1907, she and John Fisher established residence on Canfield family land in Arlington where for the next fifty years she produced a large body of fiction and nonfiction. Her books include *Gunhild* (1907), *The Squirrel-Cage* (1912), *The Montessori Mother* (1912), *The Bent Twig* (1915), *Home Fires in France* (1918), *The Brimming Cup* (1921), *The Deepening Stream* (1930), *Rough-Hewn* (1922), *Made-to-Order Stories* (1925), and *Why Stop Learning?* (1927). She served for many years on the Vermont State Board of Education and on the editorial board of the Book-of-the Month Club. Fisher's short-story collection *Hillsboro People* (1915) and her last novel *Seasoned Timber* (1937) are her works of fiction most directly influenced by her experiences in Vermont. Her last book, *The Vermont Tradition* (1953), remains readable for its appreciation of Vermonters and the communities they created.

Fisher, Ray Lyle (1887–1982)

A MIDDLEBURY COLLEGE graduate, class of 1910, who pitched for the New York Yankees from 1910 to 1917, Ray Fisher had a 100-94 career record and a 2.82 earned run average, a remarkable accomplishment on a team noted for its weak hitting. Fisher was a spitball specialist in an era when that pitch was legal. While still an undergraduate, he began his professional career with Hartford of the Connecticut League in 1908, where he was dubbed "The Vermont Schoolteacher." His major league career was interrupted by service in the army during the First World War and ended in 1921 after he had helped the Cincinnati Reds capture their first National League pennant. Fisher became involved in a contract dispute with Cincinnati after the University of Michigan offered him a job teaching and coaching in their athletic department. For accepting the Michigan job, Fisher was blacklisted from organized baseball as a "contract jumper." He spent the next thirty-eight years as baseball coach and director of athletics at the University of Michigan, racially integrating the team in 1923 and winning fifteen Big Ten titles, as well as an NCAA championship in 1953. Ray Fisher never lost his ties to Vermont, coming back every summer to fish at his home in North Ferrisburgh and to manage the Burlington Cardinals and Twin City Trojans of Barre-Montpelier in the second NORTHERN LEAGUE. When Fisher died at the age of ninety-five, he was the oldest living alumnus of both the New York Yankees and the Cincinnati Reds.   *Richard Leyden*

Fisk, James "Jubilee Jim," Jr. (1834–1872)

A New England peddler who went on to larger money schemes and manipulations that led to financial panic and a depression in 1869, James Fisk was born in Bennington. His early career as a peddler selling shoddy goods across Vermont and other New England states led to his acquiring a dry goods firm in Boston by 1860. After making a fortune in government contracts and running cotton from the South through the blockade during the Civil War, Fisk joined Daniel Drew to found a brokerage house in New York City and then allied with Drew and Jay Gould to deprive Cornelius Vanderbilt of his holdings in the Erie Railroad, of which Fisk became vice president and Gould president. Together they carried out various financial and speculative operations that involved the bribery of government officials on city, state, and national levels, schemes that culminated in the so-called gold conspiracy of 1868 and 1869 in which their efforts to corner the market in gold produced the financial panic of Black Friday on September 24, 1869, and a subsequent financial depression. President Ulysses S. Grant's decision to sell government gold finally blocked Fisk and Gould's manipulations.

Fisk, Nelson W. (1854–1923)

Quarry owner, lieutenant governor, and friend of presidents, Nelson W. Fisk of Isle La Motte on the death of his father in 1884 succeeded to the ownership of the Fisk MARBLE quarries, the oldest in Vermont, which were originally opened in 1664 to supply a limestone kiln for FORT SAINTE-ANNE. The Fisk family had worked the quarries since the 1780s. In addition to the highly profitable marble business, Nelson Fisk shipped freight, including agricultural products, on LAKE CHAMPLAIN from the Fisk Dock and Landing, from which in 1887 and 1888 he sent boatloads of ice to New York City to fill a summer demand created by the Hudson River failing to freeze in two previous winters. Fisk represented Isle La Motte in the Vermont house 1883 to 1885, and Grand Isle County in the senate from 1889 to 1891. He was chair of the board of trustees of the Vermont Industrial School in 1894, trustee of Johnson State Normal School in 1895 to 1896 and the UNIVERSITY OF VERMONT from 1896 to 1918. In 1892, he was appointed postmaster for a new, second post office on Isle La Motte named Fisk Post Office. Located in his company store, Fisk P.O. continued in service until 1928. Fisk was a Vermont commissioner for the American Exposition of 1900. He was a delegate to the Republican National Conventions of 1888 and 1892, and in 1896 was elected lieutenant governor for one term. President William McKinley visited Fisk's home in 1897, as did Vice-President Theodore Roosevelt in 1901, and on those occasions they spoke to audiences of nearly a thousand delegates and guests attending the annual meeting of the Vermont Fish and Game League, of which Fisk was president. During Theodore Roosevelt's visit, Fisk relayed to the vice president the message reporting the assassination attempt on President McKinley. Within six weeks of Fisk's unexpected death in 1923, the large stone house built and expanded by three generations of Fisks since 1802 was destroyed by fire. The main Fisk marble quarry on Isle La Motte's West Shore Road is now an environmental interpretive site open to the public.

Flagg, George W. (fl. 1839–1925)

George W. Flagg of Braintree served in the Civil War as sergeant in the Second Regiment of Vermont Volunteers, seeing action in every engagement the Vermont Brigade fought from Bull Run to Appomattox. Serving from May 1, 1861, to July 25, 1865, he participated in twenty-five battles and missed only one month on duty from a wound received at the Wilderness. Entering as a private, Flagg rose to brevet captain, bringing home to Montpelier in 1865 the only company organized in the capital during the war. Flagg was the acknowledged collar and elbow wrestling champion of the Army of the Potomac. After the war, he prospered as a Cotswolds sheep farmer and orchardist. At the advanced age of thirty-five, he launched a career of two hundred wrestling matches that took him each summer throughout New England and New York to Ohio and Michigan, where he defeated the renowned Indian wrestler Chief Tipsico. No match lasted longer than five minutes. Outdoor wrestling matches were a prominent feature of public gatherings in the nineteenth century, and for fifteen years George Flagg of Vermont was a regular participant in matches held throughout the northern states at agricultural society meetings, fairs, and Fourth of July celebrations.

Flanders, Helen Hartness (1890–1972)

An avid collector and editor of Vermont folk music, Helen Hartness Flanders of Springfield was the wife of Senator RALPH FLANDERS and daughter of Governor JAMES HARTNESS. In 1930, she began recording early New England songs and music for the VERMONT COMMISSION ON COUNTRY LIFE. Over the years, her collection of recordings grew, and in 1941 she established the Helen Hartness Flanders Folk Music Collection at MIDDLEBURY COLLEGE, which contains recordings and typescripts of New England folksongs, ballads, and folk tunes. By the early 1950s, she had recorded over four thousand songs. Her publications include *Vermont Folk Songs and Ballads* (1931) and *The New Green Mountain Songster* (1939), the first scholarly treatment of the folk music in her collection.   *Deborah P. Clifford*

Flanders, Ralph E. (1880–1970)

Republican U.S. Senator, inventor, and nationally prominent engineer and businessman, Ralph Flanders was born in Barnet and moved with his parents to Pawtucket, Rhode Island, where he attended the public schools in Lincoln and Central Falls. In 1897, he began an apprenticeship at Brown and Sharp Manufacturing in Providence, Rhode Island. Moving from there to positions at other firms where he acquired experience as a draftsman, machinist, and electrical engineer, Flanders returned to Vermont in 1910 as sales engineer for Fellows Gear Shaper Company in Springfield. Within the next two decades, he emerged as a leader of the MACHINE TOOL INDUSTRY, in 1933 assuming the presidencies of Jones and Lamson Machine Company and Bryant Chucking Grinder Company after the retirement of his father-in-law, JAMES HARTNESS. Affiliated with major corporations and national councils, he served on the industrial advisory board to the National Recovery Administration, was president of the Federal

Reserve Bank of Boston, president of the New England Council, and a member of the national Economic Stabilization Board and the War Production Board. In 1946, when WARREN AUSTIN resigned from the Senate to accept nomination as ambassador to the United Nations, Flanders was appointed in his stead. Elected to a full term in November, he was reelected in 1952 and chose not to run in 1958. His voting record, more popular with conservative constituents than that of his colleague GEORGE AIKEN, reflected his business orientation. Flanders' Senate career, however, is most noted for having defied his party's leadership by setting into motion the machinery that led to the censure of Senator Joseph McCarthy. In 1961, while in retirement, Flanders produced his autobiography, *Senator from Vermont*.

Fleischmann, Isaac (b. 1910)

The first Lifetime Achievement Award recipient from the National Inventors Hall of Fame, Isaac Fleischmann was born in Burlington, attended the local schools, and graduated from the UNIVERSITY OF VERMONT in 1932, where he earn a master's degree in history the following year. He was an instructor with the CIVILIAN CONSERVATION CORPS in Vermont and New Hampshire before moving to Washington, D.C., in 1942 to join the Lend Lease Administration and the United States Patent and Trademark Office in 1946. As head of training of patent examiners and special assistant to the commissioner of patents, Isaac was distressed by public indifference to intellectual property and its importance, and in 1959 was appointed the first director of the Office of Information Services, now Public Affairs. He worked to build alliances with the intellectual property community and to support intellectual property institutions around the country. Formally retiring in 1983, he remained active in his profession garnering numerous awards from both the private and public sector. In 1995, the Patent and Trademark Museum in Washington was dedicated in his honor and in 2000 he received the Lifetime Achievement Award from the National Inventors Hall of Fame in Ohio.

Fleming Museum

The Robert Hull Fleming Museum of the UNIVERSITY OF VERMONT opened in 1931 to house the University's diverse collections and to serve as a cultural center

for the community. The museum's collection of over twenty thousand objects span the history of civilization from early Mesopotamia to contemporary America. The breadth of the collections supports the museum's mission of promoting understanding and appreciation of our worldwide cultural heritage through the exhibition and interpretation of works of art and artifacts. Vermont artists of the nineteenth and twentieth centuries are well represented in the collection. A year-round calendar of special exhibitions of both contemporary and historic art as well as permanent galleries highlighting European, American, Asian, African, Ancient Egyptian, and Vermont art attracts a diverse audience from UVM, area colleges, and the general public. The museum's educational programs reach thousands of school-age children annually through gallery tours, art classes, and outreach programs to schools and libraries throughout Vermont. The museum is housed in a Georgian Revival building designed by the distinguished architectural firm of McKim, Mead and White, located on the edge of the University campus on Colchester Avenue in Burlington. It is named after Robert Hull Fleming, a University of Vermont alumnus in the class of 1862, as stipulated by the major benefactor, Fleming's niece Katherine Wolcott.   *Ann Porter*

Fletcher

Fletcher, population 1,179, a town in Franklin County, was granted by the Vermont legislature in 1781 to, among others, General Samuel Fletcher, who had fought at the BATTLES OF TICONDEROGA, HUBBARDTON, and BENNINGTON, and for whom the town was named. Much of the landscape is taken up by mountains between a thousand and two thousand feet high, culminating in 2,140-foot Fletcher Mountain in the extreme eastern part of the town. DAIRY FARMING takes place in the lowland meadows. The two main settlements are Fletcher village and Binghamville, both in the southern part of town.

Fletcher, Mary Martha (1830–1885)

A generous benefactor of Burlington, Mary Martha Fletcher was born in Jericho. Her father, a merchant in Essex and Jericho, made his fortune in "wise investments out west." He reported to the 1870 census at least $300,000 in personal property and $70,000 in real estate and mortgages. Mary Martha remained unmarried and after her father's death she and her mother led reclusive lives, depending heavily on Michael Kelley, their coachman and household handyman. In 1873, mother and daughter Fletcher made their first joint gift to the city of Burlington, $10,000 for books and another $10,000 conditioned on the city erecting a suitable library building. Later, they paid $4,000 for printing a catalog of the books in the Fletcher Free Library. The mother, Mary Lawrence Peaslee Fletcher, died in 1876, leaving her daughter Mary sole heir to the family's $400,000 fortune. The bulk of this fortune was left to finance a state-sponsored, nonprofit public hospital in Burlington. Mary lived long enough to establish the Mary Fletcher Training School for Nurses, also in Burlington. Early in February 1885, she caught a severe cold. Told by Dr. Walter Carpenter that she had only a few hours to live, she asked to die in the hospital. Bundled into blankets and carried there in a sleigh, she died two hours later, surrounded by the ministries she had generously helped to create. Mary Martha Fletcher's gift to the hospital, honoring her father and mother, was the largest public beneficence recorded up to that time in Vermont. The hospital was subsequently named in her honor and continues to memorialize her as Fletcher Allen Health Care.   *Lilian Baker Carlisle*

Flood of 1927

The most celebrated natural disaster in state history, the flood of 1927 raged on November 2, 3, and 4, after a heavy rainfall coupled with an already abnormally wet autumn. The major losses were along the WINOOSKI and WHITE RIVERS, although damage occurred along virtually all of Vermont's rivers. Eighty-four deaths, including that of Lieutenant Governor Hollister Jackson, were recorded. The final report of the Advisory Committee of Engineers estimated losses in excess of $21 million; but this figure sorely underestimated damage to RAILROADS and did not encompass income lost through shutdowns, the loss of tillable farmlands, or crops lost because damage to the transportation system prevented them from reaching market. To meet the crisis, Governor JOHN WEEKS convened a special legislative session that enacted legislation to facilitate recovery and authorized an $8.5 million bond issue. Vermont's congressional delegation secured a $2,654,000 appropriation to help support reconstruc-

The flood of 1927, State Street, Montpelier. Special Collections, Bailey/Howe Library, University of Vermont

tion of its federal aid highway system, and the Red Cross contributed $600,000 for flood victims. The magnitude of the disaster also propelled significant changes in state governance toward greater executive continuity, highlighted by Weeks's election to a second term, which made him the first governor to serve more than two years since 1841 and the first in the modern two-term tradition.

Flower, J. Howard (1883–1967)

An important contributor to the vitality of Vermont literature in the first half of the twentieth century, J. Howard Flower was born in Hartland. He trained for the ministry, but took up the life of an itinerant poet, printer, publisher, school teacher, and odd-jobs man. His Solitarian Press, at Hartland, began publishing *Free Soul*, a small literary magazine, in 1917, which irregularly published poetry, essays, and books by Vermont authors from 1907 through the 1950s. In early years, Flower bound most of his publications himself. An ardent individualist, he dressed unconventionally, wore his hair long past his shoulders, and used his publications to advocate in behalf of pacifism, rights for women, vegetarianism, and the views of socialist Eugene V. Debs.   *Gene Sessions*

Flynn, John J. (1854–1940)

A Burlington financier and developer of public utilities and services, John Flynn was born in Dorset and educated there in the district schools. His early career in Burlington included work as a tenant farmer, retail grocer, and, after 1890, real estate dealer. He was a large owner of Vermont forest lands and organized and financed electric railways in several regions of Vermont, including the Burlington-Essex Junction route, the Barre-Montpelier system, the St. Albans-Swanton electric line, the Bellows Falls and Saxtons River electric lines, as well as an extensive electric street railway in New Jersey. He was a principal investor and organizer of the Vergennes Water Power Company, the Barre gas plant, and the Chittenden Trust Company, and was a major investor in the Burlington Traction Company. He also owned Vermont's last toll turnpike, the Peru Turnpike between Manchester and Peru. He owned and developed Starr Farm Beach on LAKE CHAMPLAIN north of Burlington as a summer community and in 1930 built Burlington's FLYNN THEATER, Vermont's finest example of art deco interior ornamentation and arguably his most lasting contribution to the public life of Vermont.

Flynn Theater

Burlington's classic art deco movie palace was built in 1930 by JOHN J. FLYNN, local banker and real estate speculator. Designed by Neveu and Rand of Boston, it was the first movie house in New England built primarily for sound pictures. Today it is the home for the Lyric Theater for the Performing Arts, founded in 1974 by Howard Delano, and has functioned solely as a performing arts theater since 1979.

David Blow

Follett, Timothy (1793–1857)

A lawyer and merchant, Timothy Follett was born in Bennington, graduated from the UNIVERSITY OF VERMONT in the class of 1810, studied law and was admitted to the Chittenden county bar in 1814. Five years later, he was appointed state's attorney and elected to that office in 1820. He was judge of Chittenden County Court (1824) and represented Burlington in the Vermont legislature from 1830 to 1832. In 1823, however, the year that the canal connecting LAKE CHAMPLAIN and the Hudson River opened, Follett became a partner with Henry Mayo in a mercantile business operating from the OLD STONE STORE warehouse and wharf at the foot of Maple Street in Burlington. They bought, sold, and shipped farm produce from surrounding towns, initially employing the *Vermont*, the second sailing canal boat to take the newly opened canal on the New York City run. In 1824, Follett abandoned his law practice and quickly developed Mayo & Follett into one of the largest import-export and forwarding houses in northern New England and neighboring New York. A director of the recently founded Lake Champlain Steamboat Company after 1818, Follett was also appointed trustee in 1832 to settle the affairs of the large Montreal wholesale firm of Horatio Gates & Co. Almost simultaneously, Follett formed a new partnership with John and Harry Bradley as general agents and commission merchants. Follett & Bradley revolutionized the freighting business on the lake in 1841 when they began running the "Merchants Line," which ran on regular schedules. The line consisted of twenty canal boats with sloop lines and frames strong enough to withstand rough water on the lake. They were rigged with a removable mast and sail to allow passage through the canal from Whitehall to Troy and towing to New York City by a steamer. In 1841, Follett built a magnificent Greek Revival mansion in Burlington designed by AMMI B. YOUNG, architect of the VERMONT STATE HOUSE. The ionic west portico is today a Burlington waterfront landmark. Follett was the chief promoter of the Burlington and Rutland Railroad in 1845,

becoming the superintendent of its construction and its first president when it opened for business in 1849. He was forced to resign by his enemies in 1852, ending his public career. One of the original incorporators of the Protestant Episcopal Church, he was also the founding president of Burlington's Merchants Bank in 1849.

David Blow

Foot, Solomon (1802–1866)

As a United States congressman, Solomon Foot of Cornwall pushed through the completion of the United States Capitol despite the onset of the Civil War. Foot graduated from MIDDLEBURY COLLEGE in 1826 and subsequently served as a teacher and principal at Castleton Seminary and an instructor at the UNIVERSITY OF VERMONT while reading law. Admitted to the Vermont bar in 1831, he was attracted more to political than trial work, winning election to the Vermont legislature as representative from Rutland in 1833, 1835, 1837, and 1838. During the 1837 and 1838 terms, he served as house speaker and in 1836 attended the state's constitutional convention. From 1836 until 1842, he also served as state's attorney for Rutland County. In the latter year, he was elected to Congress as a Whig, serving two terms before declining renomination. His service in the House was most notable for his opposition to the Mexican War. Returning to the Vermont legislature in 1847, Foot immediately reassumed the speaker's post. In 1850, he was elected to the United States Senate. An ardent anti-slavery advocate, he was twice re-elected as a Republican. Though his continuous sixteen years in office at the time of his death on March 28, 1866, made him senior member in point of service, he did not achieve national distinction. A popular platform speaker, though relatively ineffective as a debater, Foot's personal preference was to serve as presiding officer, a function he exercised frequently and well. He received praise from his peers for his ability as president pro tempore during the thirty-sixth and thirty-seventh congresses. As chairman of the committee on public buildings and grounds, Foot oversaw the completion of the Capitol.

Forest Dale Ironworks (1823–ca.1869)

The ironworks located in the Forest Dale section of Brandon did business as the Green Mountain Iron Company. A blast furnace and several forges were located at

the facility. Hematite ore was mined in the vicinity to feed the operation. Numerous cast implements were manufactured, but parlor stoves became the main product after 1840. The industrial site is now under the management of the Vermont Division for Historic Preservation.

Donald Wickman

Foucault, François (1690–1766)

A Quebec merchant, François Foucault was in charge of finances of the royal shipbuilding industry at Quebec in 1743 when he was granted a seigneury on LAKE CHAMPLAIN that included today's Alburg, Vermont, and parts of Noyan and Clarenceville, Quebec. The seigneur's domain was erected on Point Detour, subsequently renamed Windmill Point, on Lake Champlain in the present town of Alburg. Foucault's windmill drove a stone gristmill. Several houses were built, including one for a resident priest. English attacks and burnings drove the settlers north in the mid-1750s, effectively stopping negotiations for a church and a parish. After the peace of 1763 and the end of French dominion in the Champlain Valley, François Foucault sold his seigneury to James Murray, the British governor of Quebec. Failing to settle the land with immigrants from Scotland, Murray leased the Foucault seigneury both north and south of the province line at the forty-fifth parallel to HENRY CALDWELL in 1774.

Joseph-André Senécal

Fox, George (1901–1943)

A resident of Gilman in the town of Lunenburg in 1942 when he joined the army, George Fox was one of the four "Immortal Chaplains" who were killed when a German submarine sank the USS *Dorchester* on February 3, 1943. An army troopship carrying nine hundred men, the *Dorchester* went down 100 miles off the coast of Greenland as it steamed in a convoy toward England through a section of the north Atlantic known as Torpedo Alley. Born on Staten Island, New York, Fox had ministered to Methodist churches in West Berkshire, Waits River, Union Village, and Gilman before joining the army in the early months of World War II. He had enlisted in the First World War at the age of seventeen and had served at the front as a "First Aid Ambulance Man," participating in every major battle of the American Expeditionary Force in France, for which he was awarded the Purple Heart, the

Silver Star, and the Croix de Guerre. His wife, Isadore H. Fox, who was born in Hyde Park, memorialized him in her book *Immortal Chaplain*, and the U.S. Postal Service issued a postage stamp entitled "Immortal Chaplains" to honor all the chaplains who died on the *Dorchester*.

Franklin

Franklin, population 1,268, a town in Franklin County, was granted by the Vermont legislature in 1789 to Jonathan Hunt and others and first named Huntsburg. The name was changed to Franklin in 1817 after the county, which had been named in honor of Benjamin Franklin upon its creation in 1792. (An alternative theory is that it was named for Franklin, New Hampshire, home town of an early prominent settler.) Situated on the Canadian border, with a landscape composed of meadows and low hills, the town is primarily agricultural, with some diversified farming. The main settlement is Franklin village, much of which was rebuilt after a great fire in 1925. In the town's center is 1,375-acre Lake Carmi (formerly Silver Lake and Franklin Pond), lined by vacation cottages and, on its southeastern edge, by a state park. In 1866 and 1870, the town was a staging area for the FENIAN RAIDS into neighboring Canada, an attempt to advance the cause of Irish independence from Great Britain.

Frederick, Fort

A blockhouse erected in the spring of 1773 by IRA ALLEN and REMEMBER BAKER at the Lower Falls of the Onion or WINOOSKI RIVER in a section of the town of Colchester that is now the city of Winooski, Fort Frederick was a stronghold for the men working for the ONION RIVER LAND COMPANY on the Allens' land business in northern Vermont. Only a small fraction of the size and strength of the old French Fort St. Frédéric at Crown Point, New York, Fort Frederick might have been given its secularized name as an ironic snipe at New York by Allen and Baker. This blockhouse was the most northerly outpost in the part of the New Hampshire grants west of the GREEN MOUNTAINS. It was located on the north bank of the river close to the water, on high ground about 100 to 125 feet east of the present highway bridge between Winooski and Burlington. The greater part of the site on which it stood slid off the bank and washed away early in the nineteenth century. The fort

was unused after the American retreat from Canada in 1776, and Baker and some of the men working for him were probably its last occupants in the spring of 1775.

David Blow

Freeman, Martin (1826–1889)

Scholar, educator, champion of black nationalism and colonization, Martin Freeman, a native of Rutland and a MIDDLEBURY COLLEGE graduate, became the first African-American to serve as a college professor and president. A third-generation Vermonter, Freeman grew up in the house built on Rutland's Main Street by his grandfather, Pearson Freeman, a former slave who earned his freedom serving in the GREEN MOUNTAIN CONTINENTAL RANGERS during the American Revolution. Salutatorian of his Middlebury class of 1849, Martin Freeman went on to teach mathematics and sciences at Allegheny Institute in Pittsburgh, which later became Avery College. Freeman became president of the college in 1856. He married Lovinia Peck in 1857 and they had five children. Freeman was among the African-American intellectuals of his generation who concluded that racial equality in the United States was impossible. Along with colleagues Henry Highland Garnet, George B. Vashon, and David J. Peck, he saw colonization as the only course open to protect his family and people. During the late fifties, Freeman and other African-American leaders considered Ontario, Haiti, South America, and West Africa as settlement areas. He moved with his family to Liberia in 1864, taught at and administered Liberia College in the capital, Monrovia, and became president of the college shortly before his death in 1889. As a young man, Freeman had developed a warm, lifelong friendship with the Reuben Thrall family in Rutland, which produced a lengthy correspondence that records his career as an educator in America and Liberia.

Ray Zirblis

Freeman's Oath

The oath to be taken by all residents of Vermont as a qualification for voting is set forth in Chapter 2, Section 42 of the state constitution and reads as follows:

> You solemnly swear (or affirm) that whenever you give your vote or suffrage, touching any matter that concerns the State of Vermont, you will do it so as in your conscience you

shall judge will most conduce to the best good of the same, as established by the Constitution, without fear or favor of any person.

The oath derives from the Massachusetts Freeman's Oath of 1631, which in turn formed the basis of Connecticut's Freeman's Charge, both of which were known to the framers of the Vermont Constitution who met in Windsor in July 1777. Since adult slavery was forbidden by Chapter I, Article I, of the Constitution, in effect all males twenty-one years or older were entitled to the franchise, a situation unique in the colonies. All three oaths originally included a reference to the deity, Vermont's reading "I solemnly swear by the everliving God (or affirm in the Presence of Almighty God) . . . ," phrasing that was removed in 1786. The concluding word of the original oath, "man," was changed to "person" in 1924 after passage of the Nineteenth Amendment to the U.S. Constitution legalizing female suffrage.

Freemasonry

The Grand Lodge of Free and Accepted Masons of Vermont was formed on October 14, 1794, at a meeting of five lodges that had been earlier chartered in Massachusetts, Connecticut, and Canada. The five original lodges—Temple Lodge of Bennington, Union Lodge of Middlebury, Dorchester Lodge of Vergennes, North Star Lodge of Manchester, and Vermont Lodge of Springfield—have grown to ninety lodges and eight thousand Masons. The oldest fraternal organization in the world, the Masons also serve humanitarian purposes in such national activities as the Shrine Hospitals and Burn Centers. In Vermont, the primary charity supported by the Masons is the Vermont CARE Program, which provides seminars to teachers and other school employees to recognize and refer children at risk of substance abuse and similar problems. The Masons' fraternal activities seek to motivate and inspire members to become better citizens of their communities, state, and nation.

Edward J. Wildblood

Free-Soil Party

A national political party born out of rising opposition to the extension of slavery into new territories in the west acquired from Mexico, in Vermont the Free-Soil party succeeded the Liberty party. Drawing its members from among the opponents of slavery, its candidates were able to deny popular majorities to major party candidates and force state elections into the legislature. Led in Vermont by LAW-RENCE BRAINERD, from 1846 to 1853 Free-Soil candidates ran for governor, lieutenant governor, and in the state's four Congressional districts. In 1850, Thomas A. Bartlett, Jr., of Lyndon won a single Congressional term as a Free-Soil–Democrat coalition candidate. In governor and lieutenant governor races, Free-Soil candidates seldom won more than 29 percent of the vote, and then only when running as Free-Soil Democrats. *The Free-Soil Courier and Liberty Gazette*, published in Burlington under the editorship of LUCIUS CHITTENDEN, reported the Free-Soil platform to be congressional prohibition of slavery in new territories, especially California, Oregon, and New Mexico, repeal of the Missouri Compromise, free land grants, and reduction in the size of government. The Free-Soil party began to splinter in 1850, with many returning to the DEMO-CRATIC PARTY. In 1853, former Free-Soil Democrat JOHN S. ROBINSON, running as a regular Democrat, was elected governor by the legislature with Free-Soil votes. With enactment of the Kansas-Nebraska Act in 1854, however, Democrats were thoroughly discredited among Vermont's anti-slavery advocates, and the Free-Soilers, led by Brainerd, joined with Whigs and disillusioned Democrats to form the new REPUBLICAN PARTY.

Fresh Air Program

Started in 1944 by the Reverend A. RITCHIE LOW, who was the pastor of the United Church in Johnson, as part of his "Vermont Plan" to allow people to develop mutual respect and friendships and improve race relations, the Fresh Air Program brought 150 African-American children from the Abyssinian Baptist Church in New York City to Vermont for two weeks or longer to stay with local families. The Abyssinian Church selected the children, saw that they were outfitted, and paid the train fares, while Low found Vermont homes for the children. Groups of Vermonters made return visits to the Abyssinian Church in Harlem. Deeply concerned over the problem of race relations, Low spent the last year of his life traveling in the deep South pleading the effectiveness of his "Vermont Plan." The Fresh Air Program continues each summer to bring African-American children to Vermont. A plaque in the United Church

of Johnson commemorates Low's endeavors.   *David Blow*

Frost, Frances (1905–1959)

A native of St. Albans, Frances Frost graduated from MIDDLEBURY COLLEGE. She taught creative writing at the UNIVERSITY OF VERMONT while writing the poems that made up her first book, *Hemlock Wall*, published in 1929 in the Yale Series of Younger Poets. Other books of her poems include *Blue Harvest* (1931), *These Acres* (1932), and *This Rowdy Heart* (1954). Her poetry and other writings appeared in twenty-nine books, including a number of children's books and novels. After 1932, she lived in Charleston, South Carolina, and finally in New York City.

Frost, Robert (1874–1963)

Although Robert Frost was born in San Francisco, spent his high school years in Lawrence, Massachusetts, and his young manhood in Derry and Plymouth, New Hampshire, he came to be identified very closely with Vermont. His first experience of the state began in the summer of 1909, when he camped with his young family at LAKE WILLOUGHBY. In 1920, after his reputation as a poet was firmly established, he bought a farm in South Shaftsbury and lived in the "Stone Cottage" there even during the years he taught at Amherst College and was poet-in-residence at the University of Michigan. In 1929, he purchased Gully Farm in South Shaftsbury and moved his family there. Eventually he claimed Vermont as his chief state of residence. Frost received honorary degrees from the UNIVERSITY OF VERMONT in 1923 and from MIDDLE-BURY COLLEGE in 1924. After several decades in Vermont, he once referred to himself as "a Vermonter," only to have a native-born Vermonter deny his claim, saying to him "You are only a bastard Vermonter." Frost shot back, "And you are a Vermont bastard." Buying farms in Vermont became an obsession with Frost, and in 1941 he advised his friend Louis Untermeyer, "save your money and buy a farm in Vermont." The culmination of his passion for rural living came in 1939, when Frost bought the Homer Noble farm in Ripton. For the last twenty-four years of his life Frost spent about half of each year, from early May to late October, in Ripton, where he received as guests many famous national and world visitors, who admired his poetry and enjoyed his skills as a great

Robert Frost. Special Collections, Bailey/Howe Library, University of Vermont

conversationalist. The close proximity of his farm to the BREAD LOAF SCHOOL OF ENGLISH AND WRITERS' CONFERENCE was a great asset in Frost's literary and social life. He had given his first poetry reading at the newly founded school in July, 1921, and this began his forty-two years of close association with Middlebury College. Frost had long dreamed of having "a sort of summer literary camp" where aspiring young writers could talk about their work, so he was delighted when the Bread Loaf Writers' Conference was founded in 1926. His early and constant association with the Conference soon made him the tutelary reigning deity at Bread Loaf. He had much to do with its national recognition as the model for many other writers' conferences. Louis Untermeyer noted that Bread Loaf was "the most Frost-bitten place in America." In 1961, the state legislature named Frost the Poet Laureate of Vermont. Route 125 running between the village of Middlebury and the Bread Load campus has been designated the Robert Frost Memorial Highway, and an interpretive trail and picnic area named for the poet are near Frost's cabin on the Homer Noble farm. Robert Frost and his immediate family are buried in the Bennington Center cemetery in Old Bennington.   *Peter J. Stanlis*

Fur-bearing Trout

Vermonters are drawn each spring to fish in the icy depths of LAKE CHAMPLAIN or LAKE MEMPHREMAGOG, and sometimes glacial Lake Seymour, for these "runt beaver trout," as they are sometimes also called. With a fine covering of fur and a very delicate mouth, these prized trout can only be caught using the rare ice worm, a bait so brittle and gelid that it must be heated before attaching it to a hook, a process that makes the worm nearly invisible to the human eye. For reasons unknown, exposure to air usually evaporates the much sought after, but elusive, furred fish.   *Lilian Baker Carlisle*

Fur Trade

The desire of French and later British entrepreneurs for furs and skins was one of the early motivations for contacting the ABENAKI and MAHICAN people living in the region that became the state of Vermont. By the early 1600s, a variety of pelts were being taken from animals of this region, including deer hides, moose hides, mink, martin, and beaver. At first the exchange generally took place in native villages, and each "side" served as cultural and in some cases political ambassadors for their nations. Furs were traded for European materials such as brass kettles, knives, fish hooks, and articles of clothing. As a growing felt-hat industry in Europe during the seventeenth century enlarged the demand for beaver skins, from which curly inner hairs were taken to produce intertwined matted felt panels, Vermont's natives began travelling to nearby forts or trading posts such as Chambly, Quebec, or Springfield, Massachussetts, to exchange their furs for manufactured goods. During several years of trading with the Abenaki at Springfield, fur traders from Boston acquired as much as £4,000, or about half a million dollars in today's money, in pelts each year. Soon after 1660, when fur trading began to decline from a decreasing supply of animals and warfare between the Abenaki and the League of the Iroquois, a whole galaxy of products were being made specifically for the fur trade, including textiles, knives, axes, and glass bead jewelry. Although the fur trade era was over in Vermont before specialized items such as Indian trade silver, pipe tomahawks, and the "Northwest Trade Gun" were developed, these artifacts are nevertheless sometimes seen. These were more likely instruments of diplomatic exchange used in negotiations for political and military loyalty between the native Vermonters and European colonial powers during a series of wars in the eighteenth century between France and Britain after the fur trading business had moved to the west.   *Frederick Wiseman*

G

Gage, Phineas (1823–1860)
On September 13, 1848, Phineas Gage, of Lebanon, New Hampshire, was the foreman of a railway construction gang preparing the bed for the Rutland and Burlington Rail Road near Cavendish when an accidental explosion of a charge he had set blew his 13½-pound, 3-foot-7-inch long tapered tamping iron through his head. The iron went in point first under his left cheek bone and completely out through the top of his head, landing about 25 to 30 yards behind him. Gage was knocked over and may not have lost consciousness, even though most of the front part of the left side of his brain was destroyed. Dr. John Martyn Harlow, the young physician of Cavendish, treated him with such success that he returned home ten weeks later. Sometime in the second half of 1849, Gage felt strong enough to resume work but, because his personality had changed, the contractors who had employed him would not give him his place again. Before the accident, he had been their most capable and efficient foreman, one with a well-balanced mind who was looked on as a shrewd business man. He was now fitful, irreverent, and grossly profane, showing little respect for his fellows. He was also impatient and obstinate, yet capricious and vacillating, unable to settle on any of the plans he devised for future action. His friends said he was "no longer Gage." Although Gage seems not to have worked as a foreman again, he did not drift around as is often claimed. After about a year exhibiting himself in the larger towns of New England and Barnum's Museum in New York, he worked for about eighteen months in the livery stable of the Dartmouth Inn in Hanover, New Hampshire. He then went to Chile, where he drove coaches and cared for horses for about seven years. Sometime in 1859, his health began to fail and he went to live with his mother in San Francisco. On regaining his health, he worked on farms south of San Francisco but began having epileptic seizures in February 1860, from which he died on May 21. Late in 1867, his body was exhumed and his skull and tamping iron sent to Dr. Harlow, who reported the medical history and the changes to Gage's personality, and estimated the brain damage. Harlow gave the skull and tamping iron to the Warren Museum of the Medical School of Harvard University, where they were on display until 2000, when they were transferred to the Warren Museum Exhibition Gallery of the nearby Francis A. Countway Library of Medicine. No post mortem studies of Gage's brain were conducted and later studies have not resolved the uncertainty of the damage it suffered. In any case, not enough detail is known about Phineas Gage's pre- and post-accident behavior to establish precisely the relation between the damage to his brain and the changes to his personality. His accident is commemorated by a plaque on Cavendish town green unveiled in 1998.

Malcolm Macmillan

Gale, Samuel (1747–1826)
Clerk of the Court Samuel Gale, whose pistol waving helped incite the court riot that produced the WESTMINSTER MASSACRE in April 1775, was born in Kimpton, Hampshire, England. He came to America around 1770 as a paymaster in the English army and in 1772 was appointed to the lucrative office of deputy surveyor general of the province of New York. Gale moved to the Brattleboro area in 1773, married Rebecca, the eldest daughter of SAMUEL WELLS, and ran surveys of New York grants in the upper WINOOSKI RIVER Valley in the summer of 1773 until forced to flee from harm by IRA ALLEN and his own team of surveyors. In 1774, Gale purchased the clerkship of the CUMBERLAND COUNTY court from the incumbent CREAN BRUSH. A staunch loyalist, Gale was imprisoned for several weeks after the Westminster Massacre and on his release went to New York City. For a time in the late 1770s, he was a paymaster general of the British army as it waged war with the American colonies. After the war, he returned to London to claim compensation for the New York and Vermont land confiscated from him during the Revolution. Without records of the Vermont confiscation court's sale of his land, Gale's claim was denied by the Crown. A three-volume treatise Gale wrote while serving as army paymaster in Florida, *An essay on the nature and principles of public credit* (1784–1787), which proposed a means of extinguishing Britain's public debt, earned a £100 annuity from the Crown in 1788. In 1791, Gale moved to Quebec, where he served in the provincial government for twenty years. After 1800 he settled among other former Vermonters, including his brother-in-law and MICAH TOWNSEND, in the loyalist town of Farnham, Quebec, where he presided as a notary, though he insisted on the title of judge, and country squire.

J. Kevin Graffagnino

Galleani, Luigi (1861–1931)
The dominant figure of the Italian anarchist movement in the United States, Luigi Galleani edited and published the anarchist journal *Cronaca Sovversiva* in Barre from June 1903 until May 1919. A Piedmontese born in Vercelli, Italy, into a middle-class monarchist family, Galleani studied law at the University of Turin, where he was drawn into socialist circles in the 1880s. By the early 1890s, his activities as a writer, public speaker, and labor organizer brought him to prominence in the radical movement of northern Italy, as well as to the attention of the police. He was frequently arrested, imprisoned, and in the late 1890s exiled to the island of Pantelleria, from which he escaped in 1901. Fleeing to America, he became editor of *La Questione Sociale* of Paterson, New Jersey, but again fled to Canada to escape arrest for his role in a violent silk-workers' strike. In 1903, he arrived in Barre as Luigi Pimpino and began publication of *Cronaca Sovversiva*. The newspaper had a circulation of five thousand in Europe and both Americas. Though Galleani published such notables as the Russian anarchist Prince Peter Kropotkin, most of *Cronaca*'s articles were of his own writing. He frequently republished them in books or pamphlets with tracts by other leading anarchists. Galleani toured the country propounding the anarchist doctrine and its emphasis on the value of the individual in free association with others, for which he suffered frequent arrest and jailing. Groups of "Galleanisti" formed in his wake. Anti-militarist, he opposed the First World War, publishing anti-war tracts in which he sought to dissuade immigrants from returning to Italy for military service. After the United States entered the war in 1916, Galleani condemned American military conscription in the May 26, 1917, issue of *Cronaca* as a form of slavery

and thus contrary to the Constitution. Galleani and hundreds of his subscribers were arrested and *Cronaca* appeared again only in two clandestinely published issues in 1919. He was deported to Italy one month later, but resumed publication of *Cronaca* at Turin in 1920 with a special American edition. Finally silenced by repeated imprisonment in the 1920s by the Fascist regime, Galleani died alone in Tuscany in 1931 after several years of ill health and destitution. American "Galleanisti," meanwhile, continued to propagate his ideas in a new publication after he returned to Italy, *L'Adunata dei Reffratari*, which appeared from 1922 to 1971.

Richard Hathaway

Gallup, Joseph A. (1769–1849)

A physician, medical educator, and early epidemiologist, Joseph Gallup was born in Stonington, Connecticut, and moved with his family to Hartland in 1775. After studying medicine privately, he established a medical practice at Bethel about 1790, then returned to school, graduating in 1798 with Dartmouth Medical College's first class. In 1799, he established a practice in Woodstock, which became his principal residence for the rest of his life. Gallup took a leading role in building the institutions of his profession in the state. He was a founding member in 1812 of both the Windsor County Medical Society and of the Vermont Medical Society and served as president of the state society from 1818 to 1828. A man of independent temperament, Gallup often engaged in disputes with medical colleagues. After three years on the faculty of the VERMONT ACADEMY OF MEDICINE at Castleton, including one year as its president, he resigned in 1824 after a quarrel with other physicians on the staff. In another dispute a year later at the UNIVERSITY OF VERMONT, he withdrew from the faculty of the medical department after one academic term. In 1827, at Woodstock, he established the VERMONT MEDICAL COLLEGE, a clinical school of medicine, as a rival of the Burlington and Castleton institutions, but left the school in 1834 in yet another dispute. For a number of years after 1835 he resided in Boston, eventually returning to Woodstock, where he died on October 12, 1849. The author of several books on medical subjects, Gallup produced the first survey and statistics on an epidemic in Vermont in his report on the devastating LUNG FEVER EPIDEMIC of 1812.   *Gene Sessions*

Galusha, Jonas (1753–1834)

Elected to nine terms as Vermont governor, the last two with virtually no opposition, Jonas Galusha was born in Norwich, Connecticut, where he attended the common schools. In 1769, he moved with his family to Salisbury, Connecticut, and in 1775 to Shaftsbury, where he farmed, manufactured nails, and helped maintain an inn. Rising to the rank of captain in the local militia, he served in SETH WARNER'S GREEN MOUNTAIN CONTINENTAL RANGERS and fought at the BATTLE OF BENNINGTON. The following year he married Mary Chittenden, daughter of THOMAS CHITTENDEN. Mary died after giving birth to nine children, and though Jonas subsequently remarried twice he produced no additional heirs. Active in town and county politics, he served as Bennington County sheriff from 1781 to 1787 and was noted for suppressing an attempt by veterans of SHAYS' REBELLION to establish Vermont as a base of operations. A member of the Governor's Council from 1793 to 1798 and again from 1801 to 1805, he was elected a judge of the Bennington County court and in 1807 and 1808 a judge of the Vermont Supreme Court, a singular honor since Galusha lacked legal training and the supreme court had by then evolved into a lawyers' bench. In 1809, as the state's most prominent Jeffersonian Republican, he defeated incumbent Federalist governor ISAAC TICHENOR and was re-elected annually until 1813. That year, after approving of President Madison's diplomatic policies and supporting economic measures that many Vermonters found oppressive, he was unable to muster a majority vote in the gubernatorial contest. Galusha won a larger vote than Federalist MARTIN CHITTENDEN, his chief rival, but the legislature chose Chittenden governor by a vote of 112 to 111. A similar scenario was repeated the following year. By 1815, however, the Federalist Party was discredited by international events and party excesses, and Galusha was re-elected every year until 1820, after which he retired except for service as a presidential elector and delegate to state constitutional conventions. His efforts to prohibit the arrest and imprisonment of debtors for small amounts enhanced his popularity but did not result in a change of the law during his administrations.

García Lorca, Federico (1899–1936)

From August 16 to 29, 1929, the Spanish poet and playwright Federico García Lorca, while spending the summer at Columbia University in New York, took time off to stay at a cabin on Lake Eden with his friend Philip Cummings of Woodstock and his family. Besides taking walks in the woods and visiting with some of the local people, García Lorca wrote at least three poems at Lake Eden: "*Poema doble del lago Eden*" ("Double Poem of Lake Eden"), "*Cielo vivo*" ("Live Sky"), and "*Tierra y luna*" ("Earth and Moon"). He also wrote letters. One was written to his sister on birch bark. In another, to a Spanish friend, perhaps remembering his native Andalusia, he said that "the landscape is marvelous, but infinitely melancholy. . . . It never stops raining. This family is very nice, full of gentle charm, but the woods and lakes immerse me in a hardly bearable state of poetic desperation." Seven years later, also in August, García Lorca was executed by the fascists at the beginning of the Spanish Civil War.

Gardner, John (1933–1982)

A novelist and professor of literature who lived in Bennington and taught at BENNINGTON COLLEGE, John Gardner wrote books of literary criticism as well as novels, including *Grendel* (1971), *The Sunlight Dialogues* (1972), *Nickel Mountain* (1973), *October Light* (1977)—which won the National Book Critics Circle Award—*Freddy's Book* (1980), and *Mickelsson's Ghost* (1982). He authored two books on the craft of writing, *On Becoming a Novelist* (1983) and *The Art of Fiction* (1984). In a critical study entitled *Moral Fiction* (1978), Gardner deplored a pessimistic trend in modern fiction. He was also a gifted poet and published several books on Old and Middle English poetry and taught literature and fiction writing at Bennington College and the BREAD LOAF WRITERS CONFERENCE. He was killed in a motorcycle accident near Susquehanna, Pennsylvania.

Gardner, William Lawrence "Larry" (1886–1976)

Considered Vermont's greatest major league baseball player by many fans, Larry Gardner of Enosburg Falls spent seventeen years in major league baseball (1908–1925), first with the Boston Red Sox and later with the Cleveland Indians. In his twelve years as a regular third baseman, Gardner was named to *Baseball Magazine*'s All-American first team four times, and to the second team five times. He was the hero of Boston's 1912 World Series win and also led the Cleveland Indians to the pennant and World Series victory in 1920. The much-despised Red Sox owner Harry Frazee, who traded Babe Ruth away from Boston, also gave up Larry Gardner before the Vermonter enjoyed his best years. As a teenager, Gardner played in the first NORTHERN LEAGUE in 1906 and later served as the commissioner of the second Northern League (1935–1952). After his professional career ended, Gardner returned to the UNIVERSITY OF VERMONT, where he had co-starred with RAY COLLINS, and coached UVM's baseball team until 1952, also serving as athletic director after 1942. He valued sportsmanship above winning and preferred self-effacement to fame, about which he once told his sons, "If you boys ever get involved with the campaigning, [and] the politics of getting me into the Baseball Hall of Fame, I'll be upset and angry." He died at the home of his son Larry Jr. in St. George in 1976.

Richard Leyden

Garrison, William Lloyd (1805–1879)

The antislavery reformer William Lloyd Garrison was born in Newburyport, Massachusetts. In 1828, he became editor of Bennington's *Journal of the Times*, a weekly supporting the re-election of President John Quincy Adams. After six months with the *Journal*, Garrison moved to Boston where, in 1831, he began publishing the *Liberator*, a radical abolitionist weekly that demanded "immediate and complete emancipation." A founder and leader of the American Antislavery Society, Garrison saw his abolitionist crusade ended with the adoption of the thirteenth Amendment in 1865.

Deborah P. Clifford

General Stores

The general store is a time-honored institution in Vermont that saw its heyday in the last quarter of the nineteenth and the early decades of the twentieth centuries. At first, peddlers brought goods to rural areas, but before long they found it advantageous to establish at prominent crossroads or in the center of towns stores that carried the goods a community found most vital: foodstuffs, yard goods, hardware, patent medicines, and later, grain. There was not a lot of cash on hand, and much business was accomplished by barter and exchange. Hence the expression, "I am going down street to do my trading." An excellent example of folk architecture,

the general store was usually a rectangular building of post-and-beam (later stud) construction over a cellar with a dry-stone foundation. Built around its function, the store had a façade that frequently had only two windows in front with the door between. This left the back and sides free for long counters and for the goods on shelving behind the counters. Outside, four posts in front created a porch on which there was usually a "liars bench" for "settin'," and an overhanging storage area with a huge bow wheel to lift heavy goods, since all goods came in bulk. General stores were not self-service. The clerk collected the items the customer requested and put up orders to be delivered. Usually a pot-bellied stove along with spittoon or sandbox toward the back served as a gathering place for the male customers, who would draw up the odd chair, crate, or barrel to sit on while they played checkers or cribbage, passed the time of day, swapped the latest news, or played a practical joke. There was the opportunity for fun, one-upmanship, and general hilarity, which in turn helped shape Vermont humor. The store also provided important local services such as a post office, bank, court of law, or sometimes even a barber shop. The storekeeper himself was often a leading local citizen. Frequently he introduced the newest items of technology into his store—a telephone, gramophone, or radio, for instance. In the twentieth century, a number of innovations caused major changes for the general store. The first was the introduction of self-service in modern supermarkets. The general stores followed suit. This changed the internal layout of the store, with shelving now occupying every free space. In most cases the stove was removed and a central heating system installed, eliminating the comfortable gathering space conducive to extensive "visiting." But then the pace of life had quickened and the complexion of towns had changed. Many inhabitants now worked elsewhere. New roads and better transportation provided access to supermarkets and shopping malls. Today, the role of the general store (with some exceptions) is one of convenience store to the small rural towns, and along with convenience are those services that are important locally. A few maintain the post office; others house a deli or a snack bar, perhaps some catering services, or a gift shop. Many offer video rentals. While transformed from the old general store, the

new country stores still resemble their older predecessors in that they reflect the character of their community.

Jane C. Beck

Georgia

Georgia, population 4,375, a town in Franklin County, was granted by BENNING WENTWORTH in 1763 and named for King George III. Its gently rolling countryside is bordered on the west by LAKE CHAMPLAIN, whose shores are dotted with both seasonal and year-round homes. Once primarily agricultural, the town now has only twenty active dairy farms and is steadily gaining industry and housing as it becomes part of the outermost fringe of the Burlington metropolitan area. The main settlement is Georgia Center, on U.S. Route 7 as it crosses the town from north to south. In the town's southernmost section, the LAMOILLE RIVER opens into picturesque Arrowhead Mountain Lake, formed by a dam in the town of Milton. General GEORGE STANNARD, who led the Second Vermont Brigade at Gettysburg during the Civil War and was later honored by having the town of Stannard in Caledonia County named after him, was born in the town of Georgia.

Gettysburg, Battle of

In the three-day Battle of Gettysburg (July 1 to 3, 1863), Vermont troops played important roles on the second and third days. The Second Vermont Brigade, composed of the Twelfth, Thirteenth, Fourteenth, Fifteenth, and Sixteenth Vermont Infantry regiments—five thousand men mustered for nine-month terms—had served on picket and guard duty in the defenses of Washington since October 1862. When Confederate commander Robert E. Lee began his second campaign into the North late in June 1863, the Second Vermont received orders to join the First Army Corps. Brigade commander General GEORGE STANNARD was to report to the First Corps' General John Reynolds, who was now leading the long columns of troops northward to catch up with Lee. Stannard marched the men hard, and arrived at Gettysburg late on July 1. He found that Reynolds had been killed in fierce fighting earlier that day, and the remnants of his embattled corps, along with other units, clung to Cemetery Ridge, to the south and east of Gettysburg. This position, rapidly reinforced as the remainder of the army came up, would be the focal point of the conflict over the next two days. On the afternoon of July 2, Confederate General James Longstreet attacked the southern end of the Union-held ridge, beginning near its southern terminus at a hill called Little Round Top. Longstreet's assault continued northward in waves, inflicting heavy casualties on the Northern troops but failing to break through. Near the end of the afternoon, in the final wave, the Confederates found a gap in the Union line. A breakthrough at this point would have split the Union forces in two, and threatened catastrophe. One of the units rushed forward to fill the gap was the Second Vermont Brigade (lacking the Twelfth and Fifteenth regiments, which were assigned to guard wagons several miles from the front). The Vermonters helped to repulse this final assault, then camped for the night nearby, in the midst of the dead and wounded. On July 3, the Second Brigade found itself in the center of the Cemetery Ridge line, facing the Confederates across a mile-wide field. The battle resumed in the early afternoon with a tremendous Confederate bombardment. Most of the artillery fire passed over the Vermonters' heads, but their coolness under fire impressed nearby veterans, none of whom had ever seen such a massive barrage. When the cannon ceased firing, a force of some thirteen thousand rebel soldiers, including a division led by General George Pickett, began marching across the field, its right wing heading straight for the Second Vermont Brigade. As they drew near, however, the Confederates shifted their line of march northward. While leading elements of the rebel force reached the line and fought hand-to-hand with the defenders north of the Vermonters, the right flank of the attackers lay exposed. Seizing the opportunity, General Stannard swung his infantry around to face north against the rebel flank, and the Vermonters fired volley after volley into their ranks. Pickett's charge soon collapsed and the Confederates began a disorganized retreat across the field. Confederate reinforcements approaching belatedly from the southwest briefly threatened Stannard's line, which extended perilously far into the field, but these were soon repulsed. At the southern end of the Union line near Little Round Top, Major WILLIAM WELLS led the First Vermont Cavalry on a foolhardy charge under explicit orders from General Judson Kilpatrick. Riding over rocky and wooded ter-

rain, the cavalry were soon boxed in by enemy infantry, who fired from behind trees and stone walls. Wells eventually led most of the men to safety, but scores were killed, wounded, or captured. Stannard's flank attack, along with a similar attack on Pickett's left flank and the stiff resistance of the Union line on Cemetery Ridge, doomed Pickett's assault, and left Lee with no choice but to retreat. Although Lee's army remained formidable after Gettysburg, the rebel leader's ability to choose his own ground became increasingly limited. Vermonters at Gettysburg proved that Southern troops had no monopoly on valor, and that Union officers could match their Confederate counterparts in leadership and tactics.

Jeffrey D. Marshall

Gibson, Ernest Willard, Jr. (1901–1969)

A native of Brattleboro and the son of a United States senator, Ernest W. Gibson, Jr., was a decorated combat officer in World War II, a governor of Vermont (1947–1950), a United States senator (1940), and a United States district court judge (1950–1969). Gibson graduated from NORWICH UNIVERSITY (class of 1923) and attended George Washington University Law School (1924–1927). Admitted to the Vermont bar in 1927, he opened a law practice in Brattleboro, was elected Windham County state's attorney (1929–1933) and appointed assistant secretary and then secretary of the Vermont Senate (1931–1940). Upon the death of his father, United States Senator ERNEST WILLARD GIBSON, SR., in 1940, he was appointed as a Republican to fill the vacant senate seat, but did not run for that office in the November election. Gibson's friend, GEORGE AIKEN, ran for the senate seat instead, winning an office he held until 1975. Upon leaving the senate, Gibson assumed chairmanship of the Committee to Defend America by Aiding the Allies, an organization promoting the adoption of lend lease. After Congress enacted a lend lease bill, Gibson joined his Vermont National Guard unit that had been activated in February 1941. Gibson rose to colonel and received the Silver Star, the Legion of Merit, and the Purple Heart for wounds taken in the assault on Rendova Island in the New Georgia campaign of the Pacific theater. Transferred to the Pentagon in Washington, he served as deputy directory of Army intelligence. In 1946, he returned to Vermont and challenged MORTIMER PROCTOR in the Re-

Governor Ernest W. Gibson, Jr., in 1948. Special Collections, Bailey/Howe Library, University of Vermont

publican gubernatorial primary. With support from veterans and Democrats, he managed to deny the conservative faction's leader a customary second term. Gibson's subsequent election gave rise to a Gibson-Aiken Republican faction committing larger appropriations for expanded education, welfare, and health services. Gibson led the revision of the state's tax structure and established a state police force. Less aggresssively reformist in his second term, Gibson failed to persuade the legislature to establish a Vermont Power Authority. Shortly thereafter, President Harry S. Truman appointed him to the Federal bench as United States district court judge for the district of Vermont, where he served until his death nineteen years later.

Gibson, Ernest Willard, Sr. (1872–1940)

United States representative and senator, Ernest Gibson was born in Londonderry and attended Black River Academy (where CALVIN COOLIDGE was a classmate), NORWICH UNIVERSITY, and the University of Michigan Law School. In 1899, he located his law practice in Brattleboro. In 1906, he was elected to the Vermont House, and in 1908 to the Vermont Senate, where he was associated with progressive causes and was particularly active in support of the direct primary. In 1912, while attending the Republican National Convention, he bolted the party to support Theodore Roosevelt, but returned after the 1912 elections. As a captain of the Vermont National Guard, Gibson served as a company commander in Mexico and overseas during World War I. From 1921 to 1923, he was colonel of the 172nd Vermont National Guard Regiment. In 1924, after holding a variety of state offices that included municipal court judge, state's attorney, and secretary of civil and military affairs, Gibson was elected to the U.S. House of Representatives, serving until 1933. In November of that year, Governor Stanley Wilson appointed him to complete a U.S. Senate term of office upon the death of PORTER DALE. Elected in 1934 and re-elected in 1938, Gibson had a career in Washington that was highlighted by his successful efforts to secure federal funds to assist Vermont's recovery from the FLOOD OF 1927 and to gain benefits for veterans, though the latter seems an anomaly in light of his opposition to early payment of a veterans' bonus and his opposition to the 1932 bonus marchers. His most visionary proposal was the St. Lawrence Seaway, which he anticipated would promote Vermont's prosperity by further integrating the state into the nation's economic network. After his death in office in 1940, Governor GEORGE AIKEN appointed his son, ERNEST W. GIBSON, JR., interim senator.

Gibson, Orville (d. 1957)

Early on the morning of December 31, 1957, Newbury farmer Orville Gibson left his house to do chores. Three months later, state police troopers found his bound body in the CONNECTICUT RIVER about seven miles south of the village. Thus began one of Vermont's most infamous murder mysteries, one which remains unsolved to this day. The state of Vermont staked a reward and the *BURLINGTON FREE PRESS* doubled the offer, sending a reporter to live in Newbury to cover the story full time. The murder was labeled a "vigilante slaying" in revenge for Gibson's alleged beating of his hired man on Christmas Eve. According to this scenario, "everyone" in town knew who did it but engaged in a conspiracy of silence. This Gothic picture of dark and sinister forces beneath the postcard innocence of a typical little Yankee village proved irresistible to the media and propelled Newbury into the national spotlight. (Another theory holds that the crime was "a prank gone sour" and that relatively few people in Newbury knew what really happened.) On November 5, 1958, Robert "Ozzie" Welch, custodian of Newbury's school, was arrested on a charge of

first-degree murder, along with his alleged accomplice, farmer John Carpenter. Welch was acquitted in October 1959 on a directed verdict from the bench and died of cancer two months later still maintaining his innocence. Carpenter was later acquitted on a lesser charge of kidnapping and manslaughter. The Gibson slaying has been the inspiration for two novels, Gerald Jay Goldberg's *The Lynching of Orin Newfield* (1970) and Merle Drown's *Plowing Up a Snake* (1982).   *Frank Bryan*

Gilman, James Franklin (1850–1929)

An itinerant artist born in Massachusetts, James Franklin Gilman came to Vermont in 1872 as an itinerant painter and, apart from teaching "painting and drawing" at Barre's Goddard Seminary from 1875 to 1877, made his living in Vermont for two decades as a popular artist. Working principally in Washington County, Gilman produced numerous family portraits and many paintings and sketches of local farms and village scenes, occasionally issuing some of them as limited-edition etchings. Gilman's Vermont career ended in 1891, when he moved back to Massachusetts to work for the Church of Christian Science. He remained active as an artist, with declining success in his later years, and died in Westboro, Massachusetts.

J. Kevin Graffagnino

Gilman, Marcus Davis (1820–1889)

Vermont bibliographer Marcus Gilman was born in Calais and apprenticed in the Montpelier general store of Baldwin & Scott. At the age of twenty-one years, he co-founded the mercantile firm of White, Gilman and Company in Northfield. In 1845, Gilman moved to Chicago, where he prospered as a merchant, retiring from business and relocating to Newton, Massachusetts, in 1868. Three years later, he returned to Montpelier, where he won election to the legislature, served as a director of the state prison, and headed the Vermont delegation to the Democratic National Convention in 1876. In 1874, Gilman became librarian of the VERMONT HISTORICAL SOCIETY and began compiling an exhaustive bibliography of Vermont books and pamphlets. Serialized in the Montpelier *Argus and Patriot* in 1879 to 1880 and edited by GEORGE G. BENEDICT, *The Bibliography of Vermont*, published posthumously in 1897 with a subsidy from the Vermont legislature, listed nearly seven thousand Vermont titles and

provided extensive annotations on many of them. Superseded in part by THOMAS DAY SEYMOUR BASSETT's *Vermont: A Bibliography* (1981), Gilman's work remains an essential reference tool for collectors of antiquarian Vermontiana.

J. Kevin Graffagnino and
Marcus A. McCorison

Glastenbury

Glastenbury, population sixteen, in Bennington county, is one of only two towns ever disincorporated by the Vermont legislature (neighboring Somerset is the other). The population had dropped to seven, prompting the move in 1937. Since then, a supervisor appointed by the governor has exercised most government functions. Originally granted by BENNING WENTWORTH in 1761, the town was named either for Glastonbury in England or for a suburb of Hartford, Connecticut. The town's location directly on the spine of the GREEN MOUNTAINS, which here rise to 3,748 feet at Glastenbury Mountain, retarded early settlement, and incorporation did not occur until 1834. The maximum population of 241 in 1880 coincided with the flourishing of a logging settlement near the southern border, where charcoal kilns devoured the extensive forests of the time. A more enduring settlement was Fayville, now abandoned, in the town's northwest corner. The only significant road in the town is U.S. Route 7, which nicks the extreme northwestern corner but provides no access, all of which is through Shaftsbury. Approximately 90 percent of the town is owned by the National Forest Service as part of the GREEN MOUNTAIN NATIONAL FOREST.

Glover

Glover, population 966, a town in Orleans County, was granted by the Vermont legislature in 1783 to General John Glover and others. The landscape is hilly and wooded, with several substantial lakes. Its history resembles that of many Vermont towns, going from early subsistence farming to sheep raising in the mid-nineteenth century to DAIRY FARMING in the twentieth. Today, the dairy farms are few in number, and Glover has become a vacation and retirement site, with many lake camps and individual homes. In the southeastern corner of town along Route 16 is a marsh that was the scene of the 1810 "RUNAWAY POND" catastrophe. Nearby on Route 122 is the BREAD AND PUPPET THEATER

Museum, which commemorates a counterculture theater company that has staged pageants in Glover and elsewhere for many years.

Glück, Louise (b. 1943)

Poet Louise Glück presented images from her life and garden in Plainfield in her book *The Wild Iris* (1992), for which she won the Pulitzer Prize and the Poetry Society of America's William Carlos Williams Award in 1993. A New York City native, Glück came to Vermont in 1971 to head the M.F.A. in creative writing program at GODDARD COLLEGE and was VERMONT STATE POET from 1994 to 1998. She is the author of numerous books of poetry and criticism, including several prize winners besides *The Wild Iris. The Triumph of Achilles* (1985) received the National Book Critics Circle Award; *Ararat* (1990) was awarded the Rebekah Johnson Bobbitt National Prize for Poetry, the *Boston Globe* Literary Press Award, and the Poetry Society of America's Melville Kane Award. *Vita Nova* (1999) won the *Boston Book Review*'s Bingham Poetry Prize, and *Proofs and Theories: Essays on Poetry* (1994) won the PEN/Martha Albrand Award for Nonfiction. Glück's other honors include the Bollingen Prize in Poetry and fellowships from the Guggenheim and Rockefeller foundations and the National Endowment for the Arts. She teaches writing at Williams College.

Goddard College

Founded in 1863 as a private secondary school or seminary, the Green Mountain Central Institute was later renamed Goddard Seminary to honor Thomas A. Goddard and his family for their generous gifts to the school in its early years. With the growth of public high schools after 1900, private seminaries declined and, in an effort to avoid closure, Goddard Seminary operated as a school for girls for several years in the 1930s. ROYCE PITKIN took over as president in 1935, reorganized the school as a junior college and admitted men. In 1938, he moved the school to the Willard S. Martin estate in Plainfield and reorganized it as a progressive, experimental college based on the educational theories made famous at Columbia University's Teachers College by JOHN DEWEY and William H. Kilpatrick. Pitkin adapted Dewey's central idea that learning was best accomplished in practical activities rather than formal

classes. The school quickly became known for student-centered programs on and off campus, for its involvement in the surrounding communities, and for a governance by participatory democracy of students, faculty, and staff together. The college operated during the 1930s as a two-year school and after World War II expanded to four years. Financial difficulties were surmounted in the 1950s with the assistance of the Ford Foundation. In the 1960s, two additional campuses—Greatwood and Northwood—were developed in Plainfield as an educational experiment of a multi-campus college in which each unit developed uniquely and independently. Similarly, a curriculum based in educational experimentation provided students an almost unlimited range of studies to select from. Royce Pitkin retired in 1969 after nearly thirty-five years of leading the college. He was succeeded by twelve presidents or chief executives who led the college for an average of two and one-half years each, the longest tenure being eight years. In 1980 to 1981, Goddard sold its Northwood campus and some of its strongest programs to other institutions, including NORWICH UNIVERSITY. Goddard College today offers off-campus degree programs, in which students spend one week each semester at Goddard and the remainder of each term following a personal study program planned with a faculty mentor. Goddard confers bachelor's degrees in the arts and sciences, feminist and multicultural studies, business and community organization, education, and media studies. It awards master's degrees in education, psychology and counseling, social ecology, and writing.   *Forest Davis*

"Gods of the hills are not the gods of the valley"

"The gods of the hills" were invoked by ETHAN ALLEN against New York lawyers in an ejectment suit against Josiah Carpenter in Shaftsbury in 1770. Major John Small, a British army veteran with a military patent for land granted by New York, brought the suit in the Albany County court. Recognizing that it would test the validity of their New Hampshire titles, nonresident proprietors of New Hampshire land grants formed a defense fund for Carpenter and other settler defendants and appointed Allen to manage the defense. On the recommendation of New Hampshire Governor John Wentworth,

Allen engaged New Haven lawyer Jared Ingersoll to represent the Shaftsbury squatters and the nonresident proprietors in the trial at Albany on June 28, 1770. Ignoring their own conflicting ownership interests in similar New York–granted land in the contested region, the New York court found for plaintiff Small that New Hampshire titles were worthless, for the land was actually in New York and beyond New Hampshire's authority to grant. The court, Allen concluded, served only the interests of a "junto of land thieves." The day after the trial, Small's attorney JAMES DUANE and New York's Attorney General John Taber Kempe offered Allen money and land to join their side of the dispute. Kempe warned Allen that might would overpower right in this controversy. Allen replied: "The gods of the hills are not the gods of the valley." In explanation, he invited Kempe and Duane to join him on "the hill of Bennington, [where] the sense will be made clear." A Loyalist during the Revolution, Small returned to live in England.

Goesbriand, Louis Joseph Marie Theodore de (1816–1899)

The first Roman Catholic bishop of the Diocese of Burlington, Bishop Louis de Goesbriand was born in St. Urbain, Finisterre, Brittany, France. Educated in the local seminary and the Seminaire de St. Sulpice in Paris, he was ordained there in 1840. Father de Goesbriand emigrated to Ohio, where he was engaged in missionary work until 1847, when he was appointed vicar general, rector of the cathedral, and director of the regional seminary in the newly established Diocese of Cleveland. When Vermont's statewide Diocese of Burlington was created in 1853, Father de Goesbriand was named its bishop. The diocese then consisted of five priests, ten churches, and a Catholic population of roughly twenty thousand. De Goesbriand quickly arranged for an order of nuns from Montreal to administer the new Providence Orphan Asylum and Hospital. Shortly thereafter he went to Ireland and France to recruit priests for the diocese. Parishes were established and a school was encouraged for each parish. Additional communities of religious women opened houses around the state. Bishop de Goesbriand commenced construction of a cathedral in 1862, and the Cathedral of the Immaculate Conception in Burlington was dedicated in 1867, the first church in New England erected as a cathedral. Responding to increased immigration from French Canada in the 1860s, he encouraged the creation of "national parishes" to serve non-English speaking Catholics and lobbied the bishops of French Canada to send "missionary priests" to New England. At the First Vatican Council (1869–1870), Bishop de Goesbriand was a staunch supporter of the declaration of papal infallibility, and at the Third Plenary Council of Baltimore in 1884 he served on the committee that produced the long influential Baltimore Catechism. On the fiftieth anniversary of his ordination, he requested Rome to grant him an assistant. Father John Michaud, a Burlington native, was appointed co-adjutor bishop of Burlington in 1892, with right of succession. Bishop de Goesbriand retired to chambers in the Providence Orphanage in 1895. In his tenure as bishop of the Diocese of Burlington, de Goesbriand saw the number of priests increase from five in 1853 to fifty-two, and the number of churches grow from ten to seventy-eight. The Catholic population more than doubled from twenty to forty-six thousand. De Goesbriand died quietly at the orphanage in 1899.   *William W. Goss*

Goldstone, James (1931–1999)

A director of feature films and television shows, James Goldstone was a resident of Shaftsbury and a graduate of Dartmouth College. He earned a master of arts in drama from BENNINGTON COLLEGE, and became a film and television director. Goldstone's directing credits included *Red Sky at Morning*, *Winning*, and *The Gang That Couldn't Shoot Straight*. He won an Emmy in 1981 for directing the television movie *Kent State* and was nominated for another Emmy in 1970 for the television movie *A Clear and Present Danger*. He directed the pilot episode of *Star Trek*. In Vermont, Goldstone served as head of the Vermont Film Commission and directed plays for the Oldcastle Theatre Company in Bennington.

Goodrich, Chauncey (1798–1858)

A Burlington publisher and bookseller from the 1820s on, Chauncey Goodrich was also the "Johnny Appleseed" of the Champlain Valley, distributing apple cuttings in Vermont and New York, encouraging orchard plantings, and publishing pamphlets on the care and cultivation of apple trees.

Gore, Danny

"Danny Gore" is the stage name of Norman Lewis (b. 1928) of Lunenburg. A monologist specializing in Vermont humor, Lewis taught kindergarten through college for thirty years, retiring in 1983 as superintendent of schools in Essex North Supervisory Union. From 1962 to 1994, he performed for Vermont audiences as legislator or gubernatorial candidate from unpopulated Avery's Gore. In the mid-1960s, as small-town Vermonters began to experience the first stages of the late twentieth century's population boom and a legislative REAPPORTIONMENT shifted political power from rural to urban districts, Representative Danny Gore told his audiences, "We've got to hold back the tide against Vermont's rural character." Soon even recent Vermont immigrants, especially including BACK TO THE LANDERS, clapped and whistled for Danny Gore when he appeared at community celebrations, graduations, and local historical society events. Lewis/Gore recounted folksy comic tales in *Representative Danny Gore's Woodchuck Eggs* and *Representative Danny Gore's Choice: An Outsider's Manual to Good Hard Cider*. He also produced a video, *Representative Gore's Farm Family Values*.   *Virginia C. Downs*

Gores and Unorganized Towns

Vermont has 237 towns, 9 cities, 5 unorganized towns, 3 gores, and 1 grant. The five unorganized towns are Glastenbury in Bennington County, Somerset in Windham County, and Ferdinand, Averill, and Lewis in Essex County. Glastenbury and Somerset were disorganized by the general assembly in 1937 for insufficient population. The other unorganized towns (more accurately townships) never gained enough population to become towns. A gore is a small, usually triangular parcel of land formed by the failures of boundaries to be closed in town surveys. Vermont's gores are Avery's Gore and Warren Gore in Essex County and Buel's Gore in Chittenden County. Gores and unorganized towns are governed by supervisors. The governor appoints one supervisor in each county except for Essex County, where the county clerk is supervisor. The supervisor performs all the duties of selectboard, board of civil authority, school director, truant officer, constable, treasurer, collection of taxes, and town clerk. The supervisor in Essex County and the commissioner of taxes everywhere else appoint three

appraisers per county to perform the role of listers, appraising property and creating the grand list. The one grant is Warner's Grant in Essex County. For governance purposes, Warner's Grant is run in the same manner as the gores of Essex County by a supervisor appointed by the governor.   *Paul Gillies*

Goshen

Goshen, population 227, a town in Addison County, was granted by the Vermont legislature in 1782 as a "flying grant," that is, one for which no specific territory was established; it was not until 1798 that its boundaries were defined, and those boundaries were later adjusted still further. The name derives either from Goshen, Connecticut, or the original biblical locale. The town's eastern border approximates the spine of the GREEN MOUNTAINS, and most of its wooded, mountainous terrain lies in the GREEN MOUNTAIN NATIONAL FOREST. The one major road, Route 73, connects its neighboring towns, Brandon on the west and Rochester on the east, through picturesque Brandon Gap, dominated by the "Great Cliff" of 3,216-foot Mount Horrid. Tiny Goshen village is the only settlement.

Goss, Samuel (1776–1866)

A printer, paper maker, and publisher of the Montpelier newspaper *The Watchman*, Samuel Goss of Hollis, New Hampshire, served as printer's apprentice with Leonard Worcester, of Worcester, Massachusetts, and moved to Peacham where he established *The Green Mountain Patriot* in February 1798 and served as postmaster for nine years. He moved to Montpelier to take on the publication of the *Vermont Precursor* in July 1807, renaming it *The Watchman* in November. In 1810, Goss gave up printing for papermaking at his mill situated across the WINOOSKI RIVER in Berlin. He continued so until his death at the age of ninety in Montpelier. A major legacy to the state was his training of his apprentice and journeyman printer, EZEKIEL P. WALTON.

Marcus A. McCorison

GRACE:
Grass Roots Art and Community Effort

Founded in 1975 by Don Sunseri (1939–2001), a New York artist who settled in Glover, GRACE has served the NORTHEAST KINGDOM for twenty five years. GRACE's mission is to discover, develop, and promote visual art produced primarily, but not exclusively, by elderly self-taught artists in rural Vermont. Located in the Old Firehouse on Mill Street in Hardwick, with a staff of about seven artist-facilitators, GRACE offers workshops in various techniques and media, organizes shows of its participants' art in the gallery and on the road, and provides space for participants to produce their art. Staff artists offer workshops at regional sites in the Greensboro Town Hall, the Brooklyn Street Center in Morrisville, the St. Johnsbury Health and Rehabilitation Center, Howard Community Services in Burlington, and several nursing homes. Since 1999, GRACE artists have exhibited in the Bodell Gallery and the Outsider Art Fair in New York City, as well as in several Vermont galleries, including the Vermont Folklife Center in Middlebury, the T. W. Wood Gallery & Art Center in Montpelier, and For Art's Sake in Stowe. A recently featured GRACE artist is Dot Kibbee, an eighty-five-year-old former nurse who has lived most of her life in Hardwick and participated in GRACE's community workshops at Greensboro Town Hall since the mid-1980s. Her style of painting features heavily patterned renderings of imaginary landscapes inhabited by snakes, butterflies, turtles, and tiny people. Her paintings have been exhibited throughout the region as well as nationally and internationally. Dot says that when she paints, "I don't really know what I'm doing but I know it is good when my heart starts beating fast and my face gets all hot and red."

Grafton

Grafton, population 649, a town in Windham County, was granted by Benning Wentworth in 1754 as Thomlinson after two of the grantees, but when that name proved unpopular with residents, it was changed to Grafton in 1792—although why that particular name (which also occurs in Massachusetts) was chosen is not known. Much of the land is hilly and heavily wooded (there are at least seven peaks between 1,500 and 2,300 feet) and divided by the north and south branches of the Saxtons River. In the first half of the nineteenth century, the town was a prosperous agricultural, sheep-raising, and soapstone-quarrying center. A century-long decline that began in the 1840s was halted in the 1960s when the nonprofit Windham Foundation began to restore houses in and revitalize the economy of the main

village of Grafton, making it an idealized archetype of an early Vermont settlement. The foundation owns the Old Tavern, an inn built in 1801, and the Grafton Village Cheese Company, which produces over one million pounds of award-winning cheddar each year. One of the prettiest villages in Vermont, Grafton also boasts two museums, the Nature Museum and the Grafton History Museum.

Graham, Horace F. (1862–1941)

A native of Brooklyn, New York, Horace F. Graham was Vermont auditor of accounts for fourteen years (1902–1916) and was elected governor, but after leaving the governorship he was tried and convicted for irregularities in his accounts as state auditor. After graduating from the City College of New York and Columbia University Law School, he set up a law practice in Craftsbury in 1888 and served two terms as state's attorney for Orleans County. As state auditor of accounts, he was acclaimed for applying modern accounting practices to state systems. In 1916, he ran unopposed in the Republican gubernatorial primary and won the general election with over 70 percent of the vote. Before the end of his administration, most noted for granting women municipal suffrage and for his efforts promoting America's participation in World War I, irregularities were disclosed in Graham's accounts as state auditor. After leaving office, he was tried for malfeasance and found guilty of larceny of state funds while auditor of accounts and given a five-to-eight-year jail sentence. The afternoon of the sentencing, however, Governor Percival Clement gave him an unconditional pardon because of the distinguished service he had rendered the state. In 1922, Graham received both Republican and Democratic nominations from Craftsbury and served in the house as town representative.

Granai, Cornelius O. "Kio" (1897–1988)

An attorney, member of the Vermont house, and mayor of Barre, Cornelius "Kio" Granai was born in New York City. One of eleven children in an Italian immigrant family from Carrara, Italy, that moved to Vermont in 1902, Granai graduated from Syracuse University and its Law School in 1925. He was Vermont's first Italian-American state's attorney, serving Washington County from 1929 to 1933 and was mayor of Barre from 1956 to 1958 and 1964 to 1966. A Republican, he represented Barre

for six terms in the Vermont House of Representatives in 1947, 1951, 1953, 1955, 1957 and 1963. While serving in the Vermont House, "Kio" Granai was noted for his voluntary and inspirational instruction of visiting student delegations in the legislative processes of state and city governments, earning him the reputation among Vermont's school children as the "'Mayor' of Vermont." A professional baseball player, he was a pitcher with the Detroit Tigers and semi-professional leagues in Vermont and Canada. Throughout his adult life, he was a much sought-after commencement speaker in Vermont schools. As a certified lay preacher in the Methodist Church, he also supplied church pulpits throughout Vermont. His themes as a public speaker and orator centered on his passionate belief in individual freedom, human integrity, and love of others. He served terms as a trustee of Vermont College and the University of Vermont. He was a veteran of World War I, serving as a Merchant Marine seaman on the U.S. Army transport *Hercules* carrying troops between Newport News, Virginia, and France; and in World War II was a judge advocate major of the Allied military government in Italy. His commitment to the community of central Vermont was marked by a lifelong involvement in youth activities and veterans affairs.   *Edwin Granai*

Granby

Granby, population eighty-six, a town in Essex County, was granted by Benning Wentworth in 1761 and named for John Manners, the marquis of Granby (1721–1770), a British military hero during the Seven Years' War. Hilly and heavily forested, with six peaks rising to over two thousand feet, the town has always had lumbering as its only significant industry. The tiny village of Granby lies along a dirt road that cuts across the southern section of the town from east to west. Granby, along with neighboring Victory, was one of the last two towns in Vermont to get electricity, in 1963. The first General Store in the town opened on August 26, 2000.

Grand Isle

Grand Isle, population 1,955, a town in Grand Isle County, was granted by the Vermont legislature in 1779 as part of the grant of Two Heroes to Ethan Allen and 364 others, many of them Revolutionary War veterans. The Two Heroes grant covered the two largest islands in Lake

CHAMPLAIN and in 1798 was divided into the town of North Hero on the smaller island and the semi-independent towns of South Hero and Middle Hero on the larger island; in 1810, Middle Hero was made fully independent and renamed Grand Isle, a translation from an earlier French name for the whole island. A widely held belief assumes that the heroes honored were Ethan and IRA ALLEN, although it is more likely that all the Revolutionary War veterans were meant—that is, the grant bestowed on the grantees "two towns for the heroes." Grand Isle town occupies the upper half of twelve-mile-long South Hero island and is connected to North Hero island by a bridge; a ferry on the western shore provides a fifteen-minute crossing to Cumberland Head in New York State throughout the year. The landscape of the town is mostly flat and supports four dairy farms. The HYDE LOG CABIN STATE HISTORIC SITE preserves what is claimed to be the oldest surviving log cabin in the United States.

Grange, The

Also known as the Patrons of Husbandry, the Grange was founded in 1867 by Oliver Hudson (O. H.) Kelley as a national agricultural association to give farmers a collective voice. Some of the reasons for the formation of the Grange included the high price paid for RAILROAD freight, the large cut taken by various middlemen, and the high cost for farming implements and supplies. From its inception, women have been eligible for membership. Jonathan Lawrence formed the first Grange in New England, Green Mountain 1, in St. Johnsbury in 1871. The Vermont State Grange was organized on July 4, 1872, in St. Johnsbury, with O. H. Kelley attending the event. The first county Grange in Vermont, Chittenden County Pomona 1, was founded January 3, 1876. The Grange grew rapidly at first, adding numerous subordinate Granges and members. Cooperative buying and selling ventures were initially the main attraction for the Grange, and when the majority of these ventures failed by the end of the nineteenth century, membership dropped significantly. In Vermont, cooperative buying began in late 1872 and early 1873, and the State Grange appointed a purchasing agent in 1874. The Grange had greater success in its work on railroad rates. The main result was the federal government's establishment of the Interstate Commerce Commission (ICC)

in 1886. The Grange has also established various insurance ventures over the years, including the Patron's Fire Insurance Company. One issue that has always been central to the mission of the Grange is education. It has worked to improve rural schools, and has established scholarships for students to attend college. There are currently seventy-four Granges and twenty Pomona or County Granges in Vermont.

Chris Burns

Granite

See BARRE CITY.

Granville

Granville, population 303, a town in Addison County, was granted by the Vermont legislature in 1781 to Reuben King and his family and originally named Kingston. The name was changed to Granville in 1834 after the similarly named town in either New York or Massachusetts. The landscape consists of three main sections. On the west is the rugged, wooded eastern slope of the main spine of the GREEN MOUNTAINS, all within the GREEN MOUNTAIN NATIONAL FOREST; on the east is the lower but still imposing ridge of the Northfield Mountains, outriders of the Greens; and in between is a slender valley that narrows to Granville Gulf, out of which flows the Mad River heading north and Alder Meadow Brook, a tributary of the WHITE RIVER, heading south. The villages of Granville and Lower Granville are in the southern end of the valley along Route 100; the village of East Granville, on Route 12A in the extreme northeastern section of town, lies in the entirely separate valley of the Third Branch of the White River.

Grau, Charles William (d. 1861)

A hydropathic physician and co-founder of Brattleboro's Lawrence Water-Cure, Charles William Grau emigrated to America from Germany after participating in the European revolutions of 1848 and settled in Brattleboro, where he joined the staff of ROBERT WESSELHOEFT's water-cure establishment. Following Wesselhoeft's death in 1852, Grau helped found the Lawrence Water-Cure, which prospered in Brattleboro for a few years, during which time Grau edited *The Brattleboro Hydropathic Messenger* and published a detailed map of the vicinity for his patients to use on their long daily walks. The Lawrence Water-Cure closed in 1859,

but Grau continued to practice in Brattleboro until his death two years later.

J. Kevin Graffagnino

Gray Lock (fl. 1674–1740)

A leader of native warriors resisting English settlement pressures in western Massachusetts and the CONNECTICUT RIVER valley during the 1720s with bands of MAHICANS from Schagticoke, New York, and ABENAKI from MISSISQUOI VILLAGE, Gray Lock (also called Whitehead or *le Tête Blanche*, for a streak of prematurely white hair) belonged to the Waranoke tribe of Massachusetts who were driven as refugees to Schagticoke in 1676 by King Philip's War. So many war and other exploits are attributed to him over such a long span of time that a father and son might have carried that name. Though a Gray Lock is reported to have led a raid in 1712 against Northampton, Massachusetts, the Abenaki name, *wawánolewát*, meaning "he who fools the others," first appears in English records during Governor Dummer's War (1722–1727), when he became notorious for swift and elusive raids against Massachusetts settlements along the Connecticut River. Known to be living with the Abenaki at Missisquoi village in 1723, Gray Lock fell upon Northfield and Rutland, Massachusetts, taking captives back to Canada. His second attack on Northfield in October caused Massachusetts to build FORT DUMMER near present-day Brattleboro. After a winter at Missisquoi, Gray Lock headed for Massachusetts in 1724, eluding English forces sent out to capture him at OTTER CREEK. He raided Deerfield, Northampton, and Westfield, returning to Missisquoi in early November. In 1725, he again escaped English forces sent to take him and harassed Fort Dummer and Northfield, skirmishing with the English several times during that summer. The Penobscot Abenaki negotiated a peace with the English in 1725, but the agreement did not include Gray Lock or his twenty to fifty Abenaki warriors. New York authorities sent his brother *malalamet* from Schagticoke to invite the war chief to Albany for negotiations, but nothing came of the effort. No mention of Gray Lock's party appears in records of the negotiations that finally established peace between the English and the Penobscot and Canadian Abenaki at Portland, Maine, in July 1727. In 1740, Jean-Baptiste, son of Pierre-Jean, *dit* La Tête Blanche and his wife Hélène, was baptized, according to the records of Fort Saint-Fréderic at Crown Point. A possible grandson was Captain Louis Wahawanulet, one of the party that killed General Braddock at Fort du Quesne in 1754. Gray Lock's burial place is unknown, but the descendants of his English enemies named the highest peak of the Berkshire Hills in Massachusetts Greylock for him.

Great Cow War of 1779

Governor THOMAS CHITTENDEN and the Board of War on April 2, 1779, ordered a militia draft to defend Vermont's northern frontier against British and Indian attacks. In Putney, which New York continued to treat as part of its CUMBERLAND COUNTY, James Clay and Benjamin Willson, who held commissions as officers in New York's Cumberland County militia company, refused to serve in the Vermont militia. Vermont's Sergeant William McWain seized a cow from each draft resister to be sold at public vendue on April 28. Colonel Eleazar Patterson and one hundred men of Cumberland County's militia appeared at the cattle sale and seized them in turn. Under secret orders from Governor Chittenden, ETHAN ALLEN, commanding general of the Vermont militia, led one hundred of his militiamen on May 24 into Cumberland County, arrested Patterson and forty-four others on charges of riotous and other illegal behavior, and marched them back to Bennington. In a grand gesture of beneficence and good will intended to gain support for the still-young Vermont, on June 3, 1779, Chittenden issued a proclamation of pardon "of all public Offences, Crimes, and Misdemeanors heretofore committed within the limits of this State . . . since the 15th of January 1777," which included the rioters whom Allen's armed force had arrested.

Greeley, Horace (1811–1872)

One of the most noteworthy political journalists in American history, Horace Greeley, a native of Amherst, New Hampshire, was apprenticed to a printer in East Poultney at the age of fourteen and worked briefly as an itinerant printer in Vermont and elsewhere between 1825 and 1831 until settling in New York City. In 1841 he founded the *New York Tribune*, one of the most influential newspapers of the nineteenth century.

Green, Hetty (1834–1916)

A Quaker from New Bedford, Massachusetts, Hetty Green inherited a large fortune from her parents. Drawn to business by her father's tutoring, she was able to read and understand business and stock reports at the age of six and invested the $6 million of her inheritance very profitably after 1860. At age thirty-three, she sued to break an aunt's will so as to gain the entire estate of $2 million, but she was forced to flee to London with her husband and financial advisor Edward H. Green of Bellows Falls to avoid criminal charges for forging a second version of her aunt's will. Returning to America in 1875, she became a major figure on Wall Street, investing heavily in railroad stocks, government bonds, and urban real estate, at one point owning eight thousand parcels of real estate in New York, Chicago, St. Louis, and San Francisco. She maintained a simple lifestyle, owning no houses for herself and her family, instead living in cheap rental properties in New Jersey, New York, and Vermont. Her clothing was shabby and she munched graham crackers from her purse rather than spend money in New York restaurants. Her life was simple because, she said, "I am a Quaker." When her son Ned lost his leg to an infection because she would not pay for proper medical treatment and refused to lend money to her bankrupt husband, newspapers scolded her and named her "The Witch of Wall Street." Leaving her husband's funeral in Bellows Falls in 1902, she is reported to have said, "Well, gentlemen, don't you think we've wasted enough time? Let's get down to business." Late in life she carried a pistol to protect herself "against lawyers." She died alone in Hoboken, New Jersey, was buried in Bellows Falls, and left her $150 million estate to her son Ned and daughter Sylvia Ann. When Sylvia Ann died in 1951, much of Hetty Green's remaining fortune went for taxes and to heirs of the cousins she had fought over her aunt's will eighty years earlier.

Greene, Frank Lester (1870–1930)

A United States Representative and Senator, Frank Lester Greene was born in St. Albans where he attended the local schools and was employed from age thirteen by the Central Vermont Railway in various capacities, leaving in 1891 to become a reporter for the St. Albans *Daily Messenger*. Having in the interim joined the Vermont National Guard as a private, he recruited an infantry regiment during the Spanish-American War and was commissioned captain. Returning to the *Messenger* soon after the war, he rose to editor and in July 1912, as a Republican, was elected to Congress to complete the unexpired term of the deceased incumbent, David Foster of Burlington. Greene served continuously until he was elected to the Senate in 1922. In February 1924, while walking with his wife in Washington, he was trapped in the crossfire between prohibition agents and bootleggers and caught a bullet in the head. He never fully recovered from his wounds and was permanently paralyzed in his right arm and weakened in his leg. A dedicated fiscal conservative, he insisted during his convalescence that he be carried onto the Senate floor so that he could vote to sustain President CALVIN COOLIDGE's veto of the soldiers' bonus bill. Greene died in 1930 as a result of complications from a hernia operation.

Greene, Stephen (1914–1979)

A journalist and co-founder of the West Dover publishing house bearing his name, Stephen Greene was born in Boston and educated at Harvard, graduating in 1937. Interested in writing and journalism, he travelled in Asia after graduation, working briefly for the Japan *Advertiser*, an English language publication. As World War II approached, he worked in Paris for the *Herald Tribune*. When the war erupted, he returned to the United States to work with the West Coast and Pacific offices of the Foreign Broadcast Intelligence Service, where he met and married Janet Gould of Portland, Oregon, in 1944. She, too, was a journalist and had worked for the United Press and the Associated Press in the Pacific Northwest. The Greenes settled in West Dover in 1948, where Stephen served on the Dover school board. He was also a member of the state Forest Festival Commission and the Vermont Educational Television Commission. He represented West Dover in the Vermont House (1953–1954) and was for many years associate editor of *VERMONT LIFE*. Stephen and Janet Greene established Stephen Greene Press in Brattleboro in 1957, specializing in Vermontiana, regional Americana, and country life. They sold the press in 1978. En route to the American Book Sellers Association meeting in Los Angeles in May 1979, Stephen Greene was killed in the crash of an American Airlines jet at O'Hare Airport in Chicago.

Greene, Wallace M., Jr. (1907–2003)

A Waterbury native, Wallace M. Greene, Jr., attained the rank of general, U.S. Marine Corps, becoming the highest ranking Marine officer ever produced by Vermont. He attended Burlington High School and graduated from the U.S Naval Academy in 1930. After several peacetime billets, he was sent to China in 1937, where he was commended for his role in defending the International Settlement during the Sino-Japanese conflict. Early in World War II, Greene was awarded his first Legion of Merit for his role in planning and executing the Marshall Islands invasion, and a second award for similar leadership on Saipan and Tinian. In the post war years, he served as staff special assistant to the Joint Chiefs of Staff at the National Security Council, commanding officer at Parris Island Recruit Depot, and commanding general at Camp Lejeune. In 1960, Greene was named chief of staff of the Marine Corps. Three years later, President Kennedy selected Lieutenant General Greene to be the twenty-third commandant of the Marine Corps and promoted him to four-star rank. He served the customary four-year term as commandant, and retired at the end of 1967. General Greene was awarded two Distinguished Service Medals, one for his service as chief of staff and one as commandant. Not known as a combat leader, General Greene was a skillful organizer, planner, manager, and negotiator who did his best work strengthening the Marine Corps in the nation's capital.   *John McClaughry*

Green Mountain Boys

In the late 1760s, some of the early settlers of Bennington, Arlington, and other towns west of the GREEN MOUNTAINS who held land under pre-1764 grants from New Hampshire's Governor BENNING WENTWORTH formed armed bands to resist court-enforced claims to their land made by holders of New York titles to the same lands. In 1770, a large group of the resisting New Hampshire grantees convened and elected ETHAN ALLEN their "commandant colonel." Responding to the governor of New York's threat to "chase them into the Green Mountains," this loosely organized extra-legal force of the New Hampshire grants assumed the name Green Mountain Boys. With several members of the extended Allen family serving as captains, including brothers LEVI and IRA and cousins EBENEZER ALLEN, SETH WARNER and REMEMBER BAKER, as many as sixty Green Mountain Boys could be called on to block ejectment executions against New Hampshire grantees by the sheriff of Albany County or themselves eject new settlers with conflicting New York titles. In one incident in 1771, Ethan Allen, Remember Baker, Robert Cochran, and six others drove a small group of new settlers from land they claimed with a New York title and burned their cabins, causing Governor William Tryon to proclaim a reward of £20 for Allen and each member of the band. Allen responded by proclaiming a £15 reward for New York's attorney general John Kemp and lawyer JAMES DUANE, both conspicuously active in pressing New York claims. In the same year, Allen and a small group of his men blackened their faces, dressed as Indians, and drove New York surveyor William Cockburn out of Pittsford with threats to kill him. On another occasion, they were reported to the sheriff in Albany for marauding at night dressed as women, tearing down fences, burning hay, and dispersing or hocking the cattle of New York title owners who spoke against them. Unwisely vocal in his support of New York, Dr. Samuel Adams of Bennington was tied to a chair and suspended from a pole in front of the CATAMOUNT TAVERN. In the summer of 1771, Albany County's sheriff, Henry Ten Eyck, led 150 men to Bennington in a third attempt to eject James Breakenridge from his farm on the overlapping Walloomsac grant in Bennington, but nearly three hundred men, many armed and recognizable as part of "Allen's mob," gathered on Breakenridge's land to resist the New York officers, who returned to Albany without firing a shot. In March 1772, New York justice of the peace John Munro and a posse attempted to take Remember Baker to the Albany court, but an armed band rescued him before Munro and his posse could reach the county jail. Later, a cutlass blow to Munro's head balked his efforts to seize Seth Warner. Other incidents included Allen and sixty men driving off a group of Scots settlers in Panton and burning their buildings, as well as a raid on Durham and Socialborough, New York grants in conflict with the New Hampshire grant of Clarendon. New York placed a larger reward on Allen and the other leaders and in March 1774 the New York Provincial Assembly passed the Bloody Acts by which Governor Tryon declared Ethan Allen and several others to be outlaws subject to capital punishment if they refused to surrender. After Cumberland County's delegates to the New York Provincial Assembly, CREAN BRUSH of Westminster and SAMUEL WELLS of Brattleboro, participated in drafting the Bloody Acts, Allen threatened to cross the Green Mountains with his men to put the "beech seal" on Wells and Brush, in other words to flog them with a limb of beech wood. As the American conflict with the Crown turned to violent conflict in April 1775, Allen and BENEDICT ARNOLD led one hundred Green Mountain Boys and some Connecticut men in taking FORT TICONDEROGA on May 10, and Seth Warner and a smaller force swept up the few British troops at a post on Crown Point. SAMUEL HERRICK and NOAH LEE at the same time led a third group to take Skenesborough at the head of the lake. After encouraging an American advance against Canada, Allen and Warner persuaded the Congress in Philadelphia to establish a Green Mountain regiment in the Continental Army. Without a treasury, however, the Congress ordered New York's revolutionary Congress to pay for the new regiment. Though still an outlaw in New York, Allen in July 1775 persuaded the New York Congress to support the Green Mountain regiment. Almost simultaneously, back on the New Hampshire grants, the men who had been Green Mountain Boys but were now a New York ranger regiment of the Continental Army passed over Ethan Allen and elected Seth Warner for their colonel, a command he held until 1781. Allen joined New York General Philip Schuyler's staff as a Continental lieutenant colonel without troops to command. As an armed force on the New Hampshire grants, the Green Mountain Boys dissolved two years before Vermont was organized as a state in 1777. At least seventy of them continued to serve under Seth Warner in New York's GREEN MOUNTAIN CONTINENTAL RANGERS regiment until the end of hostilities in 1781, acquitting themselves well at the BATTLES OF HUBBARDTON, BENNINGTON and Saratoga. When Allen returned in 1778 from nearly three years as a prisoner of the British, Governor Chittenden and the Council appointed him commanding general of Vermont's regulated militia. At the peak of their defense of the New Hampshire grants against New York title claims, concluding with the seizure of Ticonderoga in 1775, the tactics and the loose organization of the Green Mountain Boys were similar to those of other agrarian mobs (most also calling themselves "boys") with grievances against the government in other corners of the eighteenth-century British Empire, including several American colonies. As subsequent generations constructed the story of Vermont's origins, however, the Green Mountain Boys came to symbolize the strong sense of independence and grassroots resistance to threats from the outside formulated in the Vermont motto of "Freedom and Unity."

Green Mountain Club

JAMES P. TAYLOR founded the Green Mountain Club in Burlington on March 11, 1910. The club's purpose was to make "the Vermont mountains play a larger part in the life of the people" by building a hiking trail the length of the state. The LONG TRAIL was completed in 1930, and the club's main focus remains the maintenance and protection of the Trail. A 1971 legislative resolution recognized the trail club as "the founder, sponsor, defender, and protector" of the Long Trail System. The Green Mountain Club, which relies heavily on volunteer labor, has eight thousand members divided between at-large and section members. Section members belong to sections (chapters) that maintain stretches of the Trail and serve as local outing clubs. The club, with headquarters in Waterbury Center, employs permanent staff and seasonal field staff.

Reidun Nuquist

Green Mountain College

Green Mountain College in Poultney was originally founded in 1834 as Troy Conference Academy by the Troy Conference of the United Methodist Church for the education of its young people. The SLATE-VALLEY village of Poultney was chosen quite intentionally by the school's founders as an ideal setting for learning, surrounded by green rolling hills and clean air. As the college grew and evolved, it became a women's college in the mid 1800s. In 1866, Sarah Cutler Mason was the first woman to earn a B.A. from a Vermont college. Also during this period, pioneering mystery writer Anna Katharine Green earned her degree and went on to write a million-selling novel entitled *The Leavenworth Case*. The college returned to co-educational status during the early part of the twentieth century, then became a two-year college for women in 1943 when

World War II altered the composition of the student body. In 1974, it again returned to co-educational status, offering four-year baccalaureate degrees to both men and women. Though historically related to the United Methodist Church, the campus community now reflects a vital respect for broad spiritual values, social responsibility, and interfaith dialogue. Green Mountain College entered the new millennium with a new mission focused on the environmental liberal arts. The college grants B.A., B.S., or B.F.A. degrees in nearly thirty majors and academic programs. Pre-professional studies such as business, education, and resort management are offered in addition to a full complement of traditional liberal arts programs. Every student completes the thirty-seven-credit Environmental Liberal Arts Program, which forms the core of the college's environmental mission. Through this sequence of courses, all students, regardless of major, receive a thorough grounding in modern and historical environmental thought. The college's 165-acre campus is distinguished by its classic Georgian architecture. Most of the 650 students live on campus. Students are drawn from approximately thirty-five states and twenty foreign countries with a nearly equal mix of men and women. The college is perhaps best defined by its strong sense of community, intimate classes, and a spirit of intellectual, physical, and spiritual adventure.   *Stephen Diehl*

Green Mountain Continental Rangers

In early June of 1775, ETHAN ALLEN and SETH WARNER persuaded the Continental Congress in Philadelphia to levy a ranger regiment for the Continental Army from the New Hampshire grants. Congress agreed, but sent Allen and Warner to New York's revolutionary government for money to pay the regiment's expenses. After persuading the New York Congress to pass a resolution on July 4, 1775, to form and fund a regiment on the New Hampshire grants, Allen and Warner learned later in Bennington that a convention of volunteers for the new regiment had elected Warner to be its colonel. While four of the Allen brothers were elected officers, Ethan was given no position. Later, New York's General Philip Schuyler attached Allen to his staff as a lieutenant colonel of the Northern Army for the Canadian campaign. Recruited largely from the GREEN MOUNTAIN BOYS who had

participated in the captures of FORT TICONDEROGA, Crown Point, and Skenesboro, five hundred rangers were mustered as a New York militia unit and joined the Northern Army under General Richard Montgomery at Isle aux Noix on the Richelieu River in September 1775 in the invasion of Canada. During the siege of the fort at St. Johns, Warner's regiment was stationed at La Prairie and Longueuil. The regiment's service in the fall of 1775 was marked by lack of discipline, especially during the harvest, when many of the rangers left the army to return to their farms. Leading a detachment of twenty-five Green Mountain Rangers on an intelligence and recruiting mission for Montgomery among the French-Canadians in late September, Ethan Allen attempted to take Montreal, failed, and was instead captured with forty-five of his men. During and after the siege of St. Johns and Chambly, Green Mountain rangers and Massachusetts militia at positions on the St. Lawrence near Sorel held off British efforts to relieve St. Johns and Montreal. When the Americans took Montreal, however, Montgomery complained that the "rascally Green Mountain Boys have left me in the lurch after promising me to go [to Quebec]." The term of their enlistment was to run out on December 31, but Warner and his men returned to the grants in November. At Quebec in December, IRA ALLEN and Robert Cochran led a remnant of the regiment with other New England troops in a diversionary attack against Cap Diamant on the night of the 31st, when Montgomery was killed in the main assault. Active again in 1777 against BURGOYNE's invasion of the Champlain Valley, the Green Mountain regiment fought well at the BATTLES OF HUBBARDTON—where they suffered heavy casualties—BENNINGTON, and Saratoga. Posted to the Hudson River Valley after Saratoga, the regiment then enrolled men mostly from New York and that state continued to pay the regiment. Between 1777 and 1779, Warner was several times threatened with loss of his command for his pre-war anti–New York activities in the Green Mountain Boys. In 1780, the Vermont General Assembly paid £2,350 in the form of a grant of the town of Eden to seventy volunteers from CUMBERLAND, GLOUCESTER, and Bennington counties who had served in the Green Mountain regiment from 1776 to 1779, to compensate for the depreciation of the Continental dollars they had been paid by New York. The regiment was disbanded in 1779. Seth Warner resigned his commission in 1780 and died in 1782.

Green Mountain Fiddlers

An instructional program for young (kindergarten through twelfth grade) string instrument players, the Green Mountain Fiddlers was founded in 1961 by ALAN CARTER, conductor of the VERMONT SYMPHONY ORCHESTRA, and Stanley Eukers, of Plantsville, Connecticut, a dedicated teacher of young string players who had organized a similar program, the Red Barn Fiddlers, in Connecticut. A demonstration by the Red Barn Fiddlers at Middlebury won the Vermont Symphony Orchestra's sponsorship of a similar program in Vermont. The young players participated in group lessons and junior and senior ensembles. As sponsor, the Vermont Symphony negotiated group rental rates with instrument vendors and provided financial administration for rental and tuition fees. Parental participation, a main tenet of the program's philosophy, was strong in Brattleboro, Middlebury, and Randolph where groups were formed. New player-students were recruited by school concerts. Green Mountain Fiddlers also played with the Vermont Symphony when the orchestra performed in the three groups' home towns. Two-week summer music camps were held at BENNINGTON COLLEGE until 1971 and thereafter at JOHNSON STATE COLLEGE until 1975, when the program disbanded after the death of Alan Carter.   *Doris Severy*

Green Mountain National Forest

The Green Mountain National Forest, established in 1932, is managed by the U.S. Forest Service for multiple uses, including logging, watershed protection, recreation, and habitat preservation. A mix of public and private land, the forest consists of two segments centered on the main spine of the GREEN MOUNTAINS, one running from the Massachusetts border 50 miles north to the area around Wallingford, the other from the vicinity of Rutland 35 miles north almost to Appalachian Gap. The southern section was significantly expanded in 1991 when, at the request of eight towns in Bennington County, the forest was extended from its traditional western border along U.S. Route 7 to the New York state line. This action made it possible to use federal money appropri-

ated for land purchases in the forest to buy sensitive areas in the TACONIC MOUNTAINS. Over 350,000 acres of the forest are federally owned, including six WILDERNESS AREAS and the White Rocks National Recreation Area. The three ranger districts administering the forest are headquartered in Manchester Center, Rochester, and Middlebury.

Green Mountain Parkway

In 1933, Colonel William J. Wilgus, the retired chief engineer of the New York Central Railroad living then in Ascutney, proposed that the state of Vermont seek federal funding for the construction of a "Green Mountain Parkway," a limited-access scenic road running the length of the western crest of the GREEN MOUNTAINS from Massachusetts north to the border with Quebec. The project was meant to capitalize on construction funds made available to the states through the New Deal's National Industrial Recovery Act (NIRA). Despite these benefits, the project engendered enormous controversy in Vermont during the three years it was debated. Several key individuals and organizations played central roles in the controversy. Nationally known for his work on the design of New York's Grand Central Terminal, Wilgus argued that the road would create thousands of jobs for the unemployed, greatly increase tourism, and protect large areas of the Green Mountains from haphazard development. He argued that a project of the parkway's scope would bring to Vermont $7 to $10 million from the NIRA. Wilgus worked closely with JAMES P. TAYLOR, founder of the GREEN MOUNTAIN CLUB and secretary of Vermont's Chamber of Commerce, in promoting the parkway. Taylor believed that the aesthetics of nature had moral effects on viewers so that mountaintop vistas from the parkway and the LONG TRAIL would relieve Vermonters of their narrow and conservative view of the world — their "valley-mindedness." Wilgus won over many members of Vermont's business community. Taylor worked behind the scenes, flooding organizations and individuals with promotional materials on the parkway, and working with a like-minded *BURLINGTON FREE PRESS*, which, despite its general opposition to New Deal programs, believed that the parkway would be an economic boon to the city of Burlington. The Green Mountain Club and the anti–New Deal *RUTLAND HERALD* led

the opposition to the parkway. While the trustees and leaders of the Green Mountain Club opposed the parkway, the club's membership was split. The trustees and their supporters feared the parkway would erode the Long Trail's wilderness value if it were built, and they warned that the trail's hikers would be forced to mingle with hordes of hikers of an "undesirable sort." The *Herald* called the parkway a needless extravagance that would split the state down the middle, give huge amounts of land over to federal control, and siphon money away from Vermont's more pressing needs, particularly the reconstruction of valley roads and bridges wiped out by the devastating FLOOD OF 1927. The *Herald* went so far as to coordinate a huge petition drive to register opposition to the project in Washington. In 1935, the parkway project was debated in the state legislature, where opponents voiced fears about the amount of land Vermont would lose to federal control should the road be built. Finally, on March 3, 1936, Vermont voters in a popular referendum at 248 annual town meetings rejected the proposal to build an $18 million parkway on the spine of the Green Mountains by a vote of 43,176 to 31,101.   *Hal Goldman*

Green Mountains

A range of mountains in the Appalachian chain, the Green Mountains extend the entire length of Vermont from north to south, reaching into Massachusetts to the south and Quebec to the north. They are between 400 and 450 million years old. MOUNT MANSFIELD is the highest point, rising to 4,393 feet on the border between Stowe and Underhill. Other high peaks include Killington Peak (4,241 feet) and CAMEL'S HUMP (4,083 feet). Composed largely of granite, the Green Mountains are heavily forested with stands of pine, spruce, beech, birch, and sugar maple. High-quality granite and MARBLE are quarried in the mountains, and talc and asbestos have been mined in the past. The chief rivers in the Green Mountains are the MISSISQUOI, LAMOILLE, and WINOOSKI, which drain into LAKE CHAMPLAIN, and the WHITE RIVER, which drains into the CONNECTICUT RIVER. Much of the southern and central parts of the range are included in the GREEN MOUNTAIN NATIONAL FOREST. Year-round precipitation in the form of rain and snow provides water sufficient to support substantial recreational opportunities for fishing and skiing. The Appalachian Trail for hikers crosses the southern part of the range, and the LONG TRAIL extends along much of its crest.

Greensboro

Greensboro, population 770, a town in Orleans County, was granted by the Vermont legislature in 1781 to Timothy Green and others. The landscape is primarily hilly and wooded, with several peaks reaching to two thousand feet in elevation. In the southern part of town is 739-acre Caspian Lake, site of a long-established summer colony of professional and academic people that has included journalist John Gunther, author WALLACE STEGNER, U.S. Supreme Court Chief Justice William H. Rehnquist, and others. On its shores is Greensboro village, the town's main settlement.

Green Up Day

Green Up Day was first proclaimed by a joint resolution of the Vermont General Assembly on March 9, 1970, in which Governor DEANE C. DAVIS urged all citizens to observe April 18, 1970, as Green Up Day, and to volunteer two hours of their time to rid the state's highways of litter and to "green up" their neighborhoods. Green Up Day was enthusiastically adopted by Vermonters across the state. Governor Davis participated prominently in the effort to preserve the environment through active citizen involvement as individuals or in conservation groups, and in labor and industrial committees. Black plastic trash bags were issued from publicized locations, filled with roadside trash by "green uppers," and collected later in the day. This Vermont rite of spring continues to be observed in almost all parts of the state.

Lilian Baker Carlisle

Griffith, Silas Lapham (1837–1903)

A lumber baron of Danby, Silas L. Griffith established a GENERAL STORE at that place in 1857, and in 1865 accepted a sawmill as payment for a debt. Over the next thirty years, Griffith acquired more than 50,000 acres in Bennington and Rutland counties, cutting nearly 25 million feet of Vermont spruce per year and employing more than six hundred people in his sawmills, charcoal kilns, and general stores. He served in the Vermont Senate from 1898 to 1900 and directed much of his wealth to philanthropic work in the Danby area. Griffith died at San Diego. *J. Kevin Graffagnino*

Griswold, Rufus Wilmot (1815–1857)

An editor and anthologist, Rufus Wilmot Griswold was born on a farm in Benson, one of fourteen children. His father was a shoemaker, tanner, and farmer who became quite prosperous. When Griswold was seven, the family moved to nearby Hubbardton, where he attended the district school. He learned the printing business at a newspaper in Rutland County, then worked at a number of newspapers in New York State. In 1838 he founded *The Vergennes Vermonter*, a Whig weekly, which he ran for fourteen months. After serving as editor of a literary periodical called the *New-Yorker*, he attained fame with the publication in 1842 of *The Poets and Poetry of America*, an anthology soon followed by others, including *The Prose Writers of America* (1847) and *The Female Poets of America* (1848). He was the editor of more than two dozen works of literature and history, as well as of gift books containing the sentimental poetry of the time. Griswold is best known today for the damage he did to the reputation of Edgar Allan Poe, whose literary executor he was. In addition to writing an uncomplimentary obituary of Poe in the *New York Tribune*, Griswold distorted Poe's career in his edition of the writer's collected works by depicting him as treacherous, ungrateful, and erratic. This view of Poe was influential into the twentieth century, when original scholarship revealed the extent of Griswold's distortions.

Groton

Groton, population 876, a town in Caledonia County, was granted by the Vermont legislature in 1789 and most likely named for Groton in either Massachusetts or Connecticut. Much of the town consists of heavily forested hills and low mountains, which rise to 3,348-foot Signal Mountain in the southwestern quarter. Groton State Forest, a 26,154-acre preserve, was formerly the site of extensive logging operations (the sawmill at Ricker Mills was in operation for a century and a half) but is now a popular summer vacation area centering around picturesque Lake Groton, the source of the Wells River. The only significant settlement, Groton village, is on U.S. Route 302, which crosses the southern part of town from east to west. WILLIAM SCOTT, the Union soldier pardoned by President Lincoln after having been condemned to death for sleeping at his post, was a native of Groton.

Grout, Josiah (1841–1925)

Civil War veteran and governor of Vermont during the Spanish-American War, Josiah Grout was born in Compton, Quebec, educated at Glover and St. Johnsbury Academies, and earned degrees from the UNIVERSITY OF VERMONT and NORWICH UNIVERSITY. He enlisted in the Civil War at the age of nineteen with Company I, First Vermont Cavalry as a second lieutenant, and reached the rank of captain. Wounded in 1863 during a skirmish with Confederate raider John Singleton Mosby and his men, Grout was discharged from the cavalry and returned to Vermont, but after the ST. ALBANS RAID he re-enlisted in the Twenty-sixth New York Cavalry as a major, serving until 1865. Admitted to the Orleans County bar in 1865, he practiced law with his brother WILLIAM WALLACE GROUT in Barton. In 1866, he took the position of deputy collector of customs at Island Pond, where he also had a law office, and worked at the customs station in Newport and St. Albans as well, leaving the service finally in 1872 to open a law office in Newport. He pursued the law until 1875, when he and his wife and son moved to Chicago. He practiced law there until 1878, when he became president and manager of the Moline Scale Company in Moline, Illinois. He left Moline Scale in 1881 to move back to Derby and purchase a farm, which he hired others to manage. In 1905, he resumed his law practice in Newport until his retirement in 1912 and sold the Derby farm in 1916. His political career began in 1873 as representative for Newport in the Vermont House. Re-elected in 1874, Grout was then chosen Speaker of the House. After living in Illinois from 1775 to 1881, Grout returned to Vermont and was elected representative for the town of Derby in 1884, 1886, and 1888. He was also Speaker during the 1886 and 1888 terms. In 1890, he declined to run for the House, but in 1892 he was elected to the Senate from Orleans County. In 1896, he was elected governor on the Republican ticket for one term, serving during the Spanish-American War. His last public office was in 1904, when he returned to Montpelier as representative from Derby. Grout continued as an active lawyer almost until his death in 1925. *Anthony Paré*

Grout, William Wallace (1836–1902)

A United States congressman for eighteen years, William Wallace Grout was born in Compton, Quebec, and moved to Vermont with his family when he was thirteen. He was educated at St. Johnsbury Academy and the Orleans Liberal Institute in Glover and graduated from Norwich University. He taught in a St. Johnsbury district school while still in secondary school. After Norwich, he clerked in O. T. Brown's St. Johnsbury law office and attended Poughkeepsie Law School. He was admitted to the Caledonia bar in December 1857. Soon after, he and George Tucker opened a law practice in Barton. In 1862, Governor Frederick Holbrook authorized Grout to recruit a company at Barton for the Fifteenth Vermont Regiment. Grout was appointed lieutenant colonel, serving with the Fifteenth until 1863, when it was mustered out. After the St. Albans Raid by the Confederates in 1864, he directed defenses of Vermont's frontier from Richford to the Connecticut River. Grout was made a brigadier general of the Vermont militia under the new militia law of 1865. In 1866 to 1867, he served as state's attorney for Orleans County and ran the Orleans *Independent Standard* newspaper for a year until the post interfered with his law practice. From 1868 to 1870, he was representative for the town of Barton in the Vermont House, and also again in 1874. Grout became president pro tempore of the Vermont Senate in 1876. Active in both state and national politics, he was a delegate to the Chicago Republican Convention in 1868 that nominated Ulysses Grant for president. In Vermont, Grout worked at getting Horace Fairbanks nominated for governor, and at the same time promoted Redfield Proctor, Sr., for lieutenant governor. Later, he promoted Proctor's successful bid for secretary of war in Harrison's cabinet. William Grout then spent eighteen years in Congress representing Vermont. During this time, he was also president of the Congressional Temperance Society. Working for Vermonters, he wrote the bill that taxed oleomargarine as a defense of butter producers and secured a pension for the widow of General George Stannard. He was also involved in such projects as the Maple Sugar Bounty,

securing federal funds for the construction of the St. Johnsbury Fish Hatchery and public buildings for Newport and St. Albans, and establishing the Memphremagog Customs District and Fort Ethan Allen in Colchester.   *Anthony Paré*

Guernsey, George H. (1839–1900)

As a builder and later architect, George Guernsey designed bridges, churches, business blocks, homes, and public buildings throughout Vermont and New Hampshire, evolving a robust design style that combined many Victorian elements. Born in Calais, Guernsey started building downtown business blocks using mainly a conservative Italianate style shortly after his service in the Civil War. He settled in Montpelier and shaped the look of the capital with his design of several bridges, including the Three-Mile and Pioneer bridges, six downtown business blocks between 1875 and 1892 including the Walton, Rialto, and French Blocks, as well as several residences and the St. Augustine Catholic Church (1893). At the height of his career in 1892, Guernsey's work ranged from the modified Shingle Style of the Whiting Library in Chester to the High Victorian Gothic style of the Immaculate Heart of Mary church in Rutland. But his most striking designs of that year integrated elements of the Shingle, Stick, Richardsonian Romanesque, and Queen Anne styles in buildings such as the United Baptist Church (Lakeport, New Hampshire), Ludlow Baptist Church, and the South Royalton and Bradford high and graded schools. Guernsey's use of a dramatic corner tower in many of his designs became a trademark of his work. After serving a term as Montpelier's third elected mayor in 1897, for which he was nicknamed "George the III," Guernsey died at his home of tuberculosis in 1900.

Lyssa Papazian

Guildhall

Guildhall (pronounced Gill-hall), population 268, the SHIRE TOWN of Essex County and the smallest shire town in the state,

was granted by Benning Wentworth in 1761. The origin of the name—which is held by no other town in the world—may derive from London's Guildhall, or council hall. The town, which is bounded on the east by the Connecticut River, is mostly wooded and mountainous and has six summits over two thousand feet, the tallest of which is 2,753-foot Stone Mountain near the western border. Except for some farming in the intervale of the Connecticut, lumbering has always been the primary industry. The only settlement is Guildhall village, on Route 102 along the Connecticut in the extreme northeastern part of the town.

Guilford

Guilford, population 2,046, a town in Windham County, was granted by Benning Wentworth in 1754 and probably named for Francis North (1704–1790), first earl of Guilford. The town's rolling terrain culminates in 1,710-foot Governor's Mountain (so named because its topmost 500 acres once belonged to Wentworth) in the extreme northwestern corner. In its earliest days, the town was the scene of intense disputes between residents loyal to New York and those supporting the "republic" of Vermont, and for several years two sets of town officials struggled for control. Eventually, in the summer of 1782, the Vermont legislature sent militia commanded by Ethan Allen to impose martial law and collect taxes. In the end, those Yorkers who could not bring themselves to swear loyalty to Vermont (called the Vermont Sufferers) migrated to New York State. In the first federal census of 1791 and in that of 1800, Guilford had more inhabitants than any other town in Vermont. For most of its history, it has been a supplier of high-quality SLATE for the towns in its region and adjacent areas of New Hampshire and Massachusetts. After a steady population decline for a century and a half, Guilford has rebounded since the end of World War II with the increasing economic activity in the southeastern corner of the state.

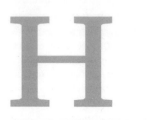

Hackel-Sims, Stella (b. 1926)

Vermont's first woman candidate for governor and director of the U.S. Mint, Stella Hackel was born Stella Bloomberg in Burlington. She attended Burlington schools, the UNIVERSITY OF VERMONT, and received her law degree from Boston University in 1948. Setting up an individual practice in Burlington and then Rutland, in 1956, by then Mrs. Hackel, she was elected Rutland grand juror, a position she held with increasing frequency until 1973 when she was appointed commissioner of the Vermont Department of Employment Security. A Democrat, she was elected state treasurer and served from 1975 to 1977. In November 1976, after winning a hard-fought Democratic primary, she lost the election for governor. Returning to Rutland, she served as city attorney until 1977, when the U.S. Senate confirmed her appointment as director of the Mint. Her tenure as director was highlighted by the issuance of the Susan B. Anthony dollar. After leaving office in 1981, she settled in Arlington, Virginia, and continued to participate in civic affairs.

Hagar, Albert David (1817–1888)

A writer on geography and a Vermont state geologist, Albert D. Hagar was born in Chester. After sales and teaching work outside Vermont, in 1845 he returned to Windsor County as a teacher and carpenter. In 1856, he became assistant state naturalist and the following year joined Edward Hitchcock on the Vermont Geological Survey. When Hitchcock published his two-volume *Report on the Geography of Vermont* in 1861, Hagar contributed the "Economical Geography" section, and he succeeded Hitchcock as state geologist in 1864. He relocated to Missouri in 1869 for a year as state geologist, then moved to Chicago, where his varied career ended with a decade as secretary-librarian of the Chicago Historical Society.   *J. Kevin Graffagnino*

Haldimand, Frederick (1718–1791)

The commander of British forces in Canada during the American Revolution who attempted to negotiate Vermont back into the British Empire, Frederick Haldimand was a native of Neufchâtel, Switzerland. He first served in the Sardinian army against Spain in Italy and then with the Dutch Republic in the Swiss Guards, finally joining the British army in 1756 as an officer in the Earl of Loudon's Sixty-second Regiment of Royal Americans. He distinguished himself in the attack on FORT TICONDEROGA (then called Carillon) in 1758 and at Oswego in 1759 against four thousand French and Indians. He was with Amherst taking Montreal in 1760, after which he was assigned the command at Trois-Rivières until 1766 and then in Florida until 1778. He was British governor and commander-in-chief in Canada from 1778 to 1785, succeeding GUY CARLETON. From 1780 to 1782, Haldimand conducted negotiations with the leaders of Vermont's government through ETHAN and IRA ALLEN under the cover of an exchange of prisoners of war that Haldimand and his superiors in London hoped would lead to the then-independent state of Vermont rejoining the British Empire. The series of meetings and letter exchanges between agents of Vermont, principally Ira Allen, later came to be called the HALDIMAND NEGOTIATIONS. Heavily invested in Canadian land, Haldimand drove Loyalists from their first settlements on Missisquoi Bay near the border, forcing them either to settle on lands he owned near Chaleur Bay in eastern Quebec or return to hostile receptions in Vermont. Considered harsh and arbitrary as an administrator, Haldimand lost several law suits brought against him in England for unlawful imprisonments he had ordered in Canada during the war.

Haldimand Negotiations

In late 1780, the group of Vermont's leaders known as the ARLINGTON JUNTO, including ETHAN and IRA ALLEN, Governor THOMAS CHITTENDEN, JOSEPH FAY, and several others, began secret negotiations with General FREDERICK HALDIMAND, governor of Canada, over terms under which Vermont might rejoin the British Empire. New York and Massachusetts both claimed that Vermont belonged under their jurisdiction, rendering Congress incapable of a decision on Vermont's status. Vermont settlers with New York or Loyalist allegiances, others with grievances against the new Vermont government, and towns along both sides of the CONNECTICUT RIVER sought to control Vermont or form their own state. Vermont also suffered a series of raids on the northern frontier by Loyalists and Indians. Weak defenses, political instability, and failure to secure recognition as a state threatened Vermont's independence and the validity of the land titles deeded under colonial New Hampshire grants and new ones made by Vermont. The British meanwhile schemed either to retain the American colonies or somehow cut their losses. Regaining Vermont would drive a wedge between the New England states and those to the south. The British made overtures to Ethan Allen as early as 1779. The ruling Arlington Junto decided to explore the option following a devastating British raid on Royalton in October that emphasized Vermont's vulnerability. Allen conferred with Haldimand's agent JUSTUS SHERWOOD under the pretext of planning a prisoner exchange. Ira Allen and Joseph Fay subsequently met secretly with Sherwood and agreed to continue discussions in the spring. Talks resumed on Ile aux Noix in Quebec to discuss Vermont's rejoining Britain but retaining its current government. Allen questioned Haldimand's authority to make such a commitment, which Haldimand suspected as duplicity in Allen. In July 1781, after three weeks of fruitless talk, Haldimand declared that he would give the Vermont leaders until October when the General Assembly next met to conclude an agreement or he would send an army and force a decision. Meanwhile, the Junto tried to use persistent rumors of the negotiations to induce Congress to act. The fear of Vermont joining the British prompted a committee of the Continental Congress to recommend admitting Vermont into the Confederation. On that news, Fay, Ira Allen, and BEZALEEL WOODWARD hurried to Philadelphia, where they found Congress astir over captured British documents that revealed intentions to regain Vermont. Congress refused to consider Vermont's status until after it had abandoned the EAST and WEST UNIONS. Failing to move Congress, the Junto assured Haldimand that the general assembly would refuse Congress's conditions for recognition. On the Junto's recommendation, Haldimand issued a proclamation confirming the terms of re-entry, including the recognition of Vermont's government and land titles, free trade with Canada, and the protection of the British army. Pressed by both the impatient British and increasing hostility at home, the Junto was rescued by Cornwallis' surrender to Washington at Yorktown. As the war was ending, opposition to the Junto mounted in a new crop of leaders challenging the old guard. Meanwhile, George Washington told Thomas Chittenden to disband the East and West Unions and perhaps Congress would admit Vermont to the Union, or the Continenal Army would attack Vermont. Vermont complied with Washington's advice, but Congress failed to act. Threatened by its neighbors, with no protection from Congress, and worried that the peace could cut off the commercial access to Canada necessary to maintaining the value of their Champlain Valley land holdings, the Allens re-opened negotiations with Haldimand. Ethan Allen wrote to Sherwood in April 1782 that "I shall do everything in my power to render this State a British Province." The Treaty of Paris ended the Revolutionary War in 1783. With Vermont independent of both Britain and the United States and access to Canadian and British markets denied by Britain's control of the lake's outlet down the Richelieu River, none of the parties' goals in the Haldimand negotiations was achieved.   *H. Nicholas Muller III*

Halifax

Halifax, population 782, a town in Windham County, was granted by BENNING WENTWORTH in 1750 and named for George Montagu-Dunk (1716–1771), second earl of Halifax (after whom Halifax, Nova Scotia, is also named). Mountainous and heavily wooded (five peaks reach from 1,460 to 2,020 feet), the town nevertheless had a substantial population in the early nineteenth century, when farming and then sheep raising were supplemented by lumbering and the building of sawmills and chair-stock mills. Today, the town has only two dairy farms and two beef-cattle farms plus some sheep farms and a woodworking facility that manufactures toys. Most residents work outside of town, especially in the Brattleboro area. Elisha G. Otis, inventor of the safety elevator, was born in Halifax.

Hall, Hiland (1795–1885)

A congressman (1833–1843), associate judge of the Vermont Supreme Court (1847–1850), second comptroller of the United States Treasury, and governor of Vermont (1858–1860), Hiland Hall of Bennington was admitted to the Vermont bar in 1819, subsequently serving as state's attorney and clerk of the county and supreme courts. Already a three-term congressman in 1840, he introduced DANIEL WEBSTER to an audience of ten thousand supporters of William Henry Harrison who had gathered near the top of Stratton Mountain to hear Webster speak for Harrison. In 1851, Hall accepted the office of land commissioner of California, but returned to Bennington in 1854. After two one-year terms as Vermont's governor, Hall pursued his personal interests as a Vermont historian and in 1868 wrote one of the great histories of Vermont, *The History of Vermont from its Discovery to Its Admission to the Union in 1791*, familiarly known as *The Early History of Vermont*. Written largely as a defense of Vermont's legal claims to statehood against revisionist New York historians, Hall's history used original sources to tell the story of Vermont's independence. For most of his last years, he resided at his daughter's home, now the PARK-McCULLOUGH HOUSE, in North Bennington.   *Paul Gillies*

Hall, Lot (1757–1809)

Born in Yarmouth, Massachusetts, Lot Hall settled in Vermont in the 1780s and served in all three branches of state government before his death in Montpelier. In 1775, at the age of eighteen, he joined a party of fifteen sailors on the *Eagle* heading for Charleston, South Carolina, to protect the southern coast from British ships. The *Eagle* captured several British ships on the way south, and gave Hall the charge of one of them. British sailors on board that ship retook command and brought Hall in chains to Glasgow, where he was confined to prison. He later was released in a prisoner exchange, but not given passage back to America. When he did find a friendly ship to take him, he was captured again, and after his final release returned to Yarmouth. There he studied law before moving to Westminster. He served in the General Assembly (1789, 1791, 1792, 1808) and as a member of the Vermont Supreme Court (1794–1801). He was a Federalist, a member of the COUNCIL OF CENSORS in 1799, and one of the incorporators of MIDDLEBURY COLLEGE. In 1795, he defended a woman charged with heresy by the Westminster Church of Christ for believing all persons were saved. Hall's claim that no two members of the church could agree on the doctrine of salvation so as to

"rationally pronounce yourselves upon that score, were you instantly to be called into [God's] immediate presence" failed to convince the congregation, who subsequently expelled the heretical woman from their church.   *Paul Gillies*

Hall, Samuel Read (1795–1877)

A native of Croydon, New Hampshire, a Congregational minister, and an educator, Samuel Read Hall first taught school in Rumford, Maine. He later came to Vermont and opened the Columbian School on March 11, 1823, which in 1825 became the Essex County Grammar School, a public secondary school. He was also Concord's Congregational minister. The town gave him a building at Concord Corners where he opened the first teacher-training school in America in 1823. His book, *Lectures on Schoolkeeping* (1829), was the first book of instruction in pedagogy printed in America. He subsequently taught at Phillips Academy in Andover, Massachusetts, and ran a teacher's seminary in Plymouth, New Hampshire (1837–1840). He returned to Vermont in 1840 and established a teachers' training program in connection with a private academy at Craftsbury (1840–1846).

Hancock

Hancock, population 382, a town in Addison County, was granted by the Vermont legislature in 1780 and named for John Hancock, the Revolutionary patriot. Wooded and mountainous, the town is one of two in Addison County (neighboring Granville is the other) that lie on the eastern slopes of the main spine of the GREEN MOUNTAINS. Except for a small portion in its northeast corner where the single village of Hancock lies along Route 100, the town is entirely within the GREEN MOUNTAIN NATIONAL FOREST. Route 125 heads west out of Hancock village to 2,149-foot Middlebury Gap, the lowest of the four gaps in the central portion of the Green Mountains, near the border with Ripton. Southwest of the gap is the MIDDLEBURY COLLEGE Snow Bowl, a ski area with fifteen trails and a vertical drop of a thousand feet.

Hanrahan, John (1844–1927)

A native of Limerick, Ireland, John Hanrahan was a Civil War veteran and medical graduate of New York University who practiced medicine in Rutland for nearly fifty years and played a large role in shaping a strong Democratic bloc in the city between 1880 and 1900. He was twice elected president of Rutland's Village Council and was a leader of the state DEM-OCRATIC PARTY.   *Vince Feeney*

Hard, Margaret Steel (1886–1974)

Margaret Hard was a member of a family of writers, editors, and booksellers who helped identify and promote Vermont as a special place. Born at her parents' summer home in Manchester and raised in Penn-sylvania and New York, she attended Pratt Institute High School, the Ethical Culture School, and Columbia University's Teach-ers' College. For several years, she taught at the Chapin School and studied under JOHN DEWEY. She returned to her birth-place in 1907, and four years later married Manchester native WALTER HARD, SR. Their children, Ruth and WALTER HARD, JR., (later editor of *VERMONT LIFE*), were born in 1912 and 1915. In 1935, Margaret and Walter Hard assumed ownership of Ruth's increasingly well-known Johnny Appleseed Bookshop and operated it for three decades. The bookstore permitted both Margaret and Walter Hard to devote time to writing. In 1936, they collaborated on an informal guidebook, *This is Vermont*, which was well received by the public if not by critics and reviewers. Margaret Hard's novel, *This is Kate*, about a young girl in a Montreal convent, was published in 1944. In 1967, she completed *A Memory of Vermont*, looking back fondly at the family's thirty-five-year operation of "an open-minded, traditionally independent, Vermont bookshop," as she described it. Some of Hard's many articles on Vermont people and places were collected in *Foot-loose in Vermont* (1969).

Prudence Doherty

Hard, Walter Rice, Jr. (1915–2000)

Editor of *VERMONT LIFE* (1950–1972), Walter Hard, Jr., defined and established the magazine as a nationally recognized voice for Vermont. Succeeding founding editor EARLE NEWTON in 1950, Walter Hard established the magazine's style, for-mat, and high standards of excellence. An unflappable, soft-spoken man with a sharp business sense and a wry turn of phrase, he was born into a long-established Ver-mont family. The son of MARGARET and WALTER HARD, the Manchester poets, Walter Hard, Jr., was educated at Burr and Burton Academy in Manchester and at Dartmouth College. But he once wrote

that his most important educational expe-rience was working summers in his father's Manchester drugstore. His summed up what he learned there in a letter to a Dart-mouth College dean: "1. I have learned to be patient and courteous to impatient and discourteous people. 2. I have learned to carry on a pleasant conversation for as much as 10 minutes about practically nothing. 3. I have learned how many times my father had to walk across the drugstore floor to earn a dollar. (Signed) Walter R. Hard, Jr." Walter brought to *Vermont Life* his sense of a dollar's worth, his skills as a journalist, and his understanding of Ver-mont. He had worked previously as a reporter at the *RUTLAND HERALD*, done a tour of duty with the Tenth Mountain Division in World War II, and was *Vermont Life*'s business manager before becoming editor-in-chief. Almost immediately after his appointment, he began his long battle to establish the magazine's editorial in-dependence from state government. The summer 1950 issue carried a photo of then-Governor HAROLD J. ARTHUR that the governor felt was unflattering. He de-manded to review all material before it was published in the magazine. Walter promptly deluged him with cartons full of manuscripts, proofs, photographs, and type galleys, demanding that they be promptly approved so the magazine could meet its press deadline. Governor Arthur quietly folded. Although freelance pay scales at the magazine were below national norms, Hard was able to inspire well-known Vermont writers and outstanding young photographers such as Hanson Car-roll, Sonya Bullaty, Angelo Lomeo, and Clyde Smith to contribute to the maga-zine. He worked closely with editorial advisors such as historian RALPH NADING HILL, Weston businessman VREST ORTON, and publisher STEPHEN GREENE of Brat-tleboro. With characteristic Vermont fru-gality, he successfully achieved financial independence from the state by selecting color plates from *Vermont Life* photo-graphs to be published in books and scenic calendars. The calendars sold well, and in 1969, *Vermont: A Special World*, the first top-quality pictorial book of color photo-graphs of Vermont, was a best seller. Other publishing projects followed to pro-duce a state-owned magazine that does not require any state funds to operate and as such is unique in the world of regional magazines. After more than twenty years at the magazine's helm, Hard left to be-

come chief editor of Vermont-based Gar-den Way publications. Later he retired to Bakersfield. He was often honored for his work at *Vermont Life*, and in 1982 was given an honorary Doctor of Humane Let-ters degree from the UNIVERSITY OF VER-MONT for "making Vermont, both the land and its people, more widely known." Hard subsequently joked that the honor came to him because "they confused me with my father." He had deep concerns that Ver-mont might be losing its distinctiveness in an era of interstate transportation, elec-tronic communication, mass marketing, and big-box stores. He didn't want Ver-mont to become, as he once put it, "a state of waitresses and busboys." He felt that Vermont—and *Vermont Life*—should do all they could to maintain the small cities, villages, and farmed countryside that have made Vermont distinctive.   *Tom Slayton*

Hard, Walter Rice, Sr. (1882–1966)

Walter Hard, Sr., the popular Vermont poet, was born in Manchester. He attended Burr and Burton Seminary and Williams College, but left the latter in 1903 to take over his ailing father's Manchester drug-store. Unfulfilled by the routines of the store, in the 1920s Hard began writing weekly columns for the *Manchester Jour-nal* and *RUTLAND HERALD*, ending each contribution with a nostalgic local story that he phrased in a free verse based on the oral rhythms and dialects of rural Ver-mont. In 1927, he published his first collec-tion of poetry, *Some Vermonters*, and over the next four decades followed that with an additional eight volumes of verse. Hard's books sold well, making him an influential factor in spreading Vermont's image as a distinctive place that had retained much of the traditional, rural character of a bygone America. In 1935, Hard and his wife Margaret sold the drug-store to become proprietors of the Johnny Appleseed Bookshop in Manchester, and the following year they collaborated on *This Is Vermont*, a popular tourist guide to the state. In addition to his poetry, Hard also published *The Connecticut* in 1947 for the Rivers of America series and repre-sented Manchester for one term in the house and four terms in the senate.

J. Kevin Graffagnino

Hardwick

Hardwick, population 3,174, a town in Caledonia County, was granted by the Ver-mont legislature in 1781 to a group of southern Vermonters including JONAS FAY and MOSES ROBINSON and named for Hardwick, Massachusetts, the town of origin of a number of the investors. The gently rolling countryside, which reaches its highest point at 1,832 feet at Jeudevine Mountain on the boundary with Wolcott to the west, is cut from west to east by the LAMOILLE RIVER. The town was primarily agricultural until the late nineteenth century, when it became one of the country's largest granite centers, using the deposits at Woodbury Mountain in neighboring Woodbury and shipping the finished product all over the United States to be used in monumental public and private buildings. The Woodbury Granite Company, which also had quarries and workshops in Bethel and Northfield, was headed by the dynamic George H. Bickford, who assembled a varied work force and turned the village of Hardwick into a boom town. Bickford's death in 1914, and the declining use of granite for building purposes after the First World War, enfeebled the company, which eventually became a casualty of the Great Depression. Hard times in Hardwick in the 1960s and 1970s as a result of further losses in the granite industry and the reduction in family farms eventually gave way to an ongoing recovery with the construction of an industrial park and the opening of numerous small businesses. Hardwick village, the largest settlement, still has a rough-hewn industrial air, while East Hardwick, a few miles away, retains a more rural atmosphere.

Harmon, Ernest Nason (1894–1979)
Ernest Harmon, athlete, soldier, and educator, was orphaned at an early age and grew up in Newbury. He entered NORWICH UNIVERSITY in 1912 and in the following year accepted an appointment to the U.S. Military Academy where he was an outstanding athlete and from which he graduated in 1917. During World War I, he went to France and fought at St. Mihiel and in the Argonne. In 1924, he participated in the Paris Olympics as a contender in the pentathlon. Returning to Norwich University in the late 1920s, Harmon served as the commandant and professor of military science. In the 1930s, Harmon attended the Army War College and during World War II he served as a formidable combat commander. General Harmon led the First Armored Division in North Africa and Italy and the Second Armored "Hell

on Wheels" Division when it stopped the deepest Nazi penetration during the Battle of the Bulge. After the war, Harmon was the first commander of the U.S. Constabulary in Germany. He served as president of Norwich University from 1950 to 1965, a period of dramatic growth and revitalization of the institution.

Gary T. Lord

Harmon, Reuben D., Jr. (1750–1806)
A silversmith and minter of early Vermont coins, Reuben D. Harmon came with his father from Sandisfield, Massachusetts, to settle in Rupert sometime before 1770. In 1785, the Vermont General Assembly granted Harmon the exclusive right to coin copper money within the state for two years. Harmon established a mint in the northeastern part of Rupert in a small unpainted rough-board building. The east end of this small building contained a furnace and a machine for flat rolling bars of copper. Shears to cut the planchets, the disks from which coin would be cut, filled the middle of the building. A large coin stamp stood in the building's west end. Using a block and tackle method, three men turned the iron screw to imprint the coins. The mint had a maximum production capacity of sixty coins per minute but seldom stamped more than thirty. The coins circulated at first with a value of two coins for a penny. Inflation drove their value down to four coins for a penny, then eight for a penny, then the minting ceased. No coins bear a later date than 1788. Harmon moved to Ohio in 1800.

Lilian Baker Carlisle

Harrington, Theophilus (1762–1813)
A Vermont Supreme Court judge best remembered for refusing to return a fugitive slave for anything less than "a bill of sale signed by God Almighty Himself," Theophilus Harrington served in the Revolutionary War as a fifteen-year-old Rhode Island militiaman and Continental soldier before moving with his family to Shaftsbury in early 1778, finally settling at Clarendon in 1788. A farmer, merchant, and land speculator, his record of public service included selectman (1795–1803), state representative (1795, 1798–1803), Speaker of the House (1803), chief judge of Rutland County (1800–1803), and assistant judge of the supreme court (1803–1813). Harrington had no formal legal training, but in 1804, in his first year on the supreme court, he applied the logic of land title to

the theory that a person may hold a property interest in another when a New York slave owner sued for the return of a fugitive slave in the Middlebury court. The owner's attorney presented a bill of sale for proof of the slave's owner's claim. Accepting the paper as to form, Harrington rejected the owner's claim because the bill did not go back far enough in the chain of title. When the owner's counsel presented a bill of sale for the reputed mother of the slave, Harrington again found that though the document was in order, it too did not go far enough back in time. When the owner's attorney in frustation asked Judge Harrington just what he would accept, Harrington is reported to have said "Nothing short of a bill of sale signed by God Almighty Himself." When chief judge Jonathan Robinson and first assistant judge ROYALL TYLER concurred, the slave was set free. Subsequently, abolitionists in Vermont and elsewhere pointed to Harrington's and the court's actions as a proper expression of the Vermont Constitution's prohibition against slavery. Harrington and his two colleagues on the supreme court were replaced in 1813 when Vermont's Federalists gained control of state government. On July 4, 1886, an anti-slavery Republican-led legislature caused a monument to be erected to honor Harrington in the Chippenhook Cemetery at Clarendon.   *John Lovejoy*

Harrington, William (1756–1814)
In 1784, William Harrington moved from Connecticut to Shelburne and in the mid-1790s to Burlington. He represented Shelburne in the Vermont legislature (1789–1795), and later Burlington (1798, 1802, 1804, and 1806). As state's attorney (1791–1796, 1798–1812, he prosecuted the BLACK SNAKE case in 1808. He also served on the Governor's Council (1812–1813).

Harris, Paul P. (1868–1947)
A co-founder of Rotary International, Paul P. Harris was born in Racine, Wisconsin, and moved to Wallingford at three years of age to live with his maternal grandparents. He graduated from law school in 1891 and for the next five years worked around the United States as a newspaper reporter, college business teacher, cowboy, cattle tender, travelling salesman, and desk clerk. Harris settled in Chicago as an attorney, where he and several friends in 1905 formed the service club now known as Rotary International. The

organization adopted the mottoes "Service Above Self" and "He Profits Most Who Serves Best" as guiding principles. Working from these principles and an unwillingness to discriminate in its mission of service, Rotary International thrived from the start. Today over 29,500 clubs meet in 162 countries. Wallingford and Rotary International recognize Paul Harris's accomplishments by preserving the Paul P. Harris Memorial Building, an 1817 structure that once served the town as a schoolhouse where Harris received his early education. *Donald Wickman*

Hartford

Hartford, population 10,367, a town in Windsor county, was granted by BENNING WENTWORTH in 1761 and presumably named for Hartford in Connecticut, the home colony of a number of the grantees. It lies on the CONNECTICUT RIVER at the point where the WHITE RIVER, which cuts across the town from northwest to southeast, joins the larger stream. Hartford includes five villages, ranging from Quechee and West Hartford, which are relatively small, to Hartford and Wilder, both considerably larger, and White River Junction, the town's major settlement. Quechee, on the Ottauquechee River, which curves through the southern part of town and empties into the Connecticut in the neighboring town of Hartland, was formerly a thriving mill village. Over the past quarter century it has been completely transformed by the Quechee Lakes Corporation, a 5,500-acre second-home and condominium resort community that stirred substantial debate in the late 1960s and 1970s about how Vermont should be developed for leisure and recreation. Nearby is Quechee Gorge, a 165-foot-deep chasm formed by the Ottauquechee and crossed by a highway (formerly a railway) bridge. A wooden railway bridge over the White River between Hartford and West Hartford was the scene of one of Vermont's worst transportation disasters when thirty-one persons died on February 5, 1887, after the bridge caught fire as the result of a train derailment. White River Junction, in the early days of the nineteenth century the site of a canal and locks to facilitate navigation on the Connecticut, later became a significant RAILROAD center and industrial hub at the point where the Vermont Central, the most direct line between Boston and Montreal, crossed the track of the various lines running up the Connecti-

Quechee Gorge in the town of Hartford. Vermont Department of Tourism and Marketing

cut River Valley to link southern New England with Canada's eastern townships and Quebec City. In its heyday, it was the site of mills, lumber yards, manufacturing buildings, and commercial businesses of all sorts. The imposing Junction House, built in 1879, was renamed the Hotel Coolidge (after President CALVIN COOLIDGE's father) in 1924, and, after being rebuilt following a fire the next year, is still in business. Today, White River Junction remains a major hub of transportation and commerce, sitting as it does at the conjunction of Interstates 89 and 91, which provide a modern counterpart to the aforementioned railroad routes. With Lebanon, West Lebanon, and Hanover, New Hampshire, the village is part of the largest urban concentration in the upper Connecticut River valley. It is also the site of Vermont's only U.S. Veterans' Hospital.

Hartland

Hartland, population 3,223, a town in Windsor County, was granted by BENNING WENTWORTH in 1761 as the town of Hertford and renamed Hartland by the Vermont legislature in 1782 to distinguish it from the adjoining town of Hartford to the north. The source of the name is presumably Hartland in Connecticut, the home colony of a number of the grantees. The town rises from the banks of the CONNECTICUT RIVER into a gentle landscape of hills from 1,000 to 1,600 feet high cut by numerous small streams. The main village of Hartland and the smaller settlement of North Hartland both lie on U.S. Route 5, which parallels the course of the Connecticut, the latter at the point where the Ottauquechee River, here backed up into a lake by a U.S. Army Corps of Engineers dam, flows into the larger river.

Hartness, James (1861–1934)

A top executive in the MACHINE-TOOL INDUSTRY and a governor of Vermont, James Hartness was born in Schenectady, New York. When he was two years old, his family moved to Cleveland, Ohio, where his father found work in various machine shops. James was educated in Cleveland's public schools, and then went to work for his father's employer. He apprenticed at the Union Screw Works and at the age of twenty-one took a job as foreman of the Thompson, Stacker Bolt Company of Winstead, Connecticut. Married in 1889 to Lena Sanford Pond of that town, he held a series of different jobs until 1889, when he was hired as shop superintendent at the Jones and Lamson Machine Co. of Springfield. A creative engineer, Hartness, who eventually ascended to the company's presidency, in 1891 had patented the flat turret lathe, a radical improvement on the lathe then in use and which Jones and Lamson elected for a time to market as their only product. Hartness simultaneously cultivated a professional interest in industrial management and was the author of several well-received books and articles. His public career began in 1914 when he was appointed to the State Board of Education. In 1917, he became federal food administrator for Vermont and member of several commissions including the Interallied Aircraft Standardization Commission and the Vermont Committee of Public Safety. He entered the Republican gubernatorial primary in 1920, his first campaign for a public office, and won a comfortable plurality over three rivals. His relative lack of name recognition was overcome by the most expensive and extensive campaign yet seen, incorporating all modern advertising techniques, including a motion picture. His campaign strategy was based on his experience as a business executive who would bring new ideas and new methods to the executive department. Although he succeeded in highlighting the need for greater government efficiency, his lack of political experience handicapped his efforts at securing adoption of his program. He left office frustrated with the system. Hartness remained president of Jones and Lamson until 1930 when he formally retired without breaking all ties. Despite lingering illnesses, he also remained active in professional engineering associations and was issued ten patents in the last three years of his life.

Harvey, Alexander (1747–1809)

A native of the parish of Gargunoch, Stirlingshire, Scotland, Alexander Harvey was appointed in 1774 to act as agent with John Clark for a company of farmers in the shires of Perth and Stirling to search out and purchase a large tract of land in America for the company to settle on. After examining lands between Albany and the New Hampshire grants, Harvey and his group crossed the GREEN MOUNTAINS to the town of Barnet where they selected and negotiated the purchase of 7,000 acres for £408 6s 8d in November 1774. Clearing, planting, and the arrival of additional settlers from Scotland were interrupted in the summer of 1775 by the Revolutionary War. Harvey was colonel of the local militia regiment and served in the Vermont Constitutional Convention of 1777 and for ten years thereafter represented Barnet in the legislature. He was on the COUNCIL OF CENSORS (1791) and assistant judge of Orange County (1781–1794). Harvey's reputation for honesty led John Witherspoon, president of the College of New Jersey in Princeton, to give him and another respected Scot, JAMES WHITELAW, power of attorney to sell his extensive land holdings in Ryegate, Newbury, and Walden to Scots farmers immigrating to Vermont in the 1770s and 1780s.

Haswell, Anthony (1756–1816)

Printers David Russell and Anthony Haswell established the *Vermont Gazette* in June 1783, and in 1784 built the state's first paper mill. Born in Portsmouth, England, Haswell apprenticed with ISAIAH THOMAS, of Worcester, Massachusetts, whose bankrupt printing business Haswell took over in 1777. Haswell remained with Thomas following Thomas's recovery of the business before moving on to Hartford, Connecticut, and Springfield, Massachusetts. In the spring of 1783, Haswell responded to entreaties of a committee of the Vermont legislature and moved to Bennington where, until 1790 when Russell gave up printing and moved to Burlington to become collector of customs, the partners developed a thriving (although fiscally fragile) printing, bookbinding, bookselling, and publishing business as well as the newspaper. In 1784, with some help from a legislatively approved lottery, they built the state's first paper mill on the Walloomsac River. Haswell briefly published the *Herald of Vermont* in 1792 until his office burned down. Attempts to establish other offices in Vergennes and in Litchfield, Connecticut, were unsuccessful. Haswell held the position of postmaster general of the state of Vermont before the state was admitted to the Union in 1791. He was also occasionally appointed state printer. He was some time a member of the COUNCIL OF CENSORS and clerk of the General Assembly. A devoted Jeffersonian Democrat, Haswell was imprisoned for two months in 1800, after having been convicted under the Federal Sedition Act for defending MATTHEW LYON. He died at Bennington.   *Marcus A. McCorison*

Haswell, Nathan (1786–1855)

A leader of the fraternal order of Masons and its staunch defender during the anti-Mason period of the 1830s and 1840s, Nathan Haswell was the second son of the early Vermont printer ANTHONY HASWELL. After learning printing from his father and studying law with JOHN ROBINSON in Bennington, Haswell went to Burlington in 1804 planning to enroll in the UNIVERSITY OF VERMONT, but failed to do so when his father's print shop was destroyed by fire. He pursued a business career instead at Burlington and was also appointed Inspector of Customs for the port of Burlington, serving from 1806 to 1809. He held various other public posts, including clerk of the Chittenden County court (1817–1818) and Burlington representative in the Vermont House of Representatives (1835–1836). His defense of the Masonic Order almost single-handedly kept the Grand Lodge of Vermont alive during the 1830s and 1840s, a time when anti-Masonic feelings ran so high in Vermont and the nation that a majority of Vermonters voted for William Wirt in 1832, the ANTI-MASONIC PARTY candidate for president of the United States. Haswell served as Vermont's grand master (1829–1847) and as grand marshall of the General Grand Royal Arch Chapter of the United States (1841–1853). His official papers as U.S. Customs Inspector for Burlington contain especially interesting documents on the period August to September 1808 pertaining to the *BLACK SNAKE* smuggling affair.

Hay, Udney (d. 1806)

Originally from Pennsylvania, Udney Hay was an Albany, New York, attorney who opposed settlers around Bennington holding land under New Hampshire grant titles in the early 1770s. During the Revolution, he served in Vermont as Continental Army commissary at Bennington, then as quartermaster general and colonel with the Continental army in the southern campaign. He opposed the Washington and Adams administrations and the centralized government of the new constitution. After the war, Hay maintained a home in Underhill. As a leader of Vermont's Jeffersonian Democratic Society, Hay was suspected of collaborating with Vermonters ISAAC CLARK, MATTHEW LYON, IRA ALLEN, and others in a French conspiracy guided by the French ambassador, Citizen Genet, to incite rebellion among French Canadians in the late 1790s.

Hayford, James (1913–1993)

The poet James Hayford was educated at Montpelier High School, Amherst College, and later Columbia University. He is the author of eleven books of poetry including *Star in the Shed Window: Collected Poems* (1989), *Uphill Home* (1992), and *Notes Left Behind* (1997); a novel for children, *Gridley Firing* (1987); and an autobiography, *Recollecting Who I Was* (2001). Hayford followed the poetic tradition of Emily Dickinson and ROBERT FROST while developing his own point of view and voice. At Amherst, Hayford first met his mentor Robert Frost and the two poets developed a relationship that would last until Frost's death in 1963. At various times, Hayford taught English in high school and college and vocal music in grades one through twelve. An inveterate optimist in attempting to apply his philosophical ideals to public life, he helped found GODDARD COLLEGE in the 1930s and a progressive political party in the 1940s. Teaching came naturally to Hayford, and he used every available opportunity to introduce young and old to poetry. Hayford received an honorary degree from the UNIVERSITY OF VERMONT in May 1993.   *Paul Eschholz*

Haynes, Lemuel (1753–1833)

A renowned Congregational divine in early Vermont, Lemuel Haynes is considered the first black man ordained by any religious sect in North America; the first black minister to preach to a white congregation; and the first black minister to supply the pulpit of a Vermont church when in 1788 he was called to what was then known as "the west parish" of Rutland. He was also the first black man to receive an honorary degree from an American college (MIDDLEBURY COLLEGE, 1804).

Named for the family in whose house he was born in West Hartford, Connecticut, to an African-American father and a white mother, both of whom abandoned him, Lemuel Haynes was bound as a servant until he was twenty-one. He received a common school education and in 1774 enlisted as a Minute Man in Roxbury, Massachusetts, then joined the northern army at FORT TICONDEROGA in 1775 to participate in the Canadian campaign. Upon his return in 1776, he resumed farming and began studies for the ministry with the Reverends David Farrand and William Bradford in Connecticut. He supplied the pulpit in Middle Granville and Torrington during the 1780s and travelled through Vermont several times preaching to small communities. In 1805, during his long term at West Rutland, Haynes published his sermon, from the text "Ye shall not surely die," in answer to the Universalist preacher HOSEA BALLOU. Haynes' sermon was reprinted widely and he was consequently much sought after to preach in Congregational churches in Vermont, Massachusetts, and Connecticut. In 1804, the Connecticut and Vermont Missionary societies appointed him to tour and preach in the thinly settled northern regions of Vermont that could not afford resident preachers. In the pulpit, Haynes was impressive, his animated manner marked nonetheless with gravity. His *Liberty Further Extended* is among the first written protests against slavery by an African-American. He was an outspoken Federalist and critic of Thomas Jefferson and the War of 1812. Haynes was spiritual advisor to the defendants in the BOORN MURDER TRIAL and recounted that extraordinary event in his *Brief Sketch of the Indictment, Trial, and Conviction of Stephen and Jesse Boorn for the Murder of Russell Colvin* (1820). He was also noted for his keen wit in repartee when not in the pulpit. Children would bait him for his quick, sharp ripostes. "Father Haynes," one group is said to have inquired, "did you know the Devil is dead?" Haynes extended his hands in blessing and murmured, "Poor, fatherless children!" His West Rutland congregation admired and respected him until 1818 when he was said to have "mixed politics with religion." Having displeased his congregation, he moved on to Manchester and retired finally to Granville, where the debilitations of chronic diabetes seem to have led finally to a gangrenous foot and death.   *Ray Zirblis*

Haynes, Roy (b. 1950)

Roy Haynes, an eccentric resident of Huntington since 1994, has been called the "Cheapest Man in Vermont," "The King of Cheap," and the "epitome of a tightwad" for the extremes to which he will go to save a dollar. A native of Brooklyn, New York, where he grew up in a housing project, Haynes moved to Vermont from Fort Lauderdale, Florida, seeking a simple life with less crime and congestion. Earning his living as a "treasure hunter," he turns others' trash into cash in his business, ROYcycling, which earned him the 1998 Governor's Award for Environmental Excellence in Pollution Prevention. He is the co-author of a book, *The Simple Life* (1998), which shows how his lifestyle is based on a preference for the plain and functional, rather than on over-indulgence. As a guide to his life, he subscribes to Goethe's principle: "He who is plenteous provided for from within needs but little from without." His practice and advocacy of self-imposed frugality earned him a place in *Ripley's Believe It or Not* and appearances on shows hosted by Montel Williams, Joan Rivers, and Sally Jessy Raphael. He has also been featured in newspaper and tabloid stories, as well as WPTZ-TV news programs. Among the extreme measures he takes to save money, Roy Haynes will re-use paper towels by hanging them to dry, "re-gift" items he received for holidays or birthdays, and give his wife flowers he gets from funeral homes. His personal motto is "Just say NO to spending."

Hazeltine, John (fl. 1760–1777)

A grantee and early settler of Townshend, arriving soon after the first settlement in 1761, John Hazeltine was an early opponent of the British Crown's policies toward and treatment of the American colonies. He was chairman of the convention at Westminster, October 19, 1774, which resolved to "assist the people of Boston in defense of their liberties to the utmost of our abilities," and also chairman of the convention of February 7, 1775, which formed a standing committee of correspondence with the friends of independence from Britain in other colonies. Hazeltine was also one of the committee appointed by the convention after the WESTMINSTER MASSACRE in March 1775 to draw up resolutions of indignation and resistance to the Crown's provincial authorities in New York. He procured the signature of every man in Townshend to a

155

pledge to maintain and disseminate the principles of American liberty. In May 1775, he was elected a delegate from CUMBERLAND COUNTY to the revolutionary New York Congress and Convention in New York City, but attended only three days. His leadership among the revolutionary Whigs led a prominent Loyalist, John Grout, to call him "King Hazeltine." A large land speculator in Townshend, he owned about one quarter of the land there when he died in 1777.

Hazen, Moses (1733–1803)

A distinguished soldier with McCurdie's Rangers during the Seven Years' War, Moses Hazen lived at St. Johns, Quebec, in 1775 when the American Revolution erupted. There he owned farms, mills, a forge, and potash works. When the American Northern Army invaded Canada they arrested him, but he joined their leader General Richard Montgomery in the capture of Montreal and the siege of Quebec. In 1776, Hazen returned to the Richelieu Valley to recruit and command the Second Canadian Regiment, "Hazen's Own," leading them at Staten Island, Germantown, Brandywine, and the siege of Yorktown. In 1776, he and JACOB BAYLEY prepared for the retreat of the American army from Canada by supervising the construction of a military road to run from St. Johns to Vermont and there connect to a road to Boston, until it was recognized that the road could have as easily supported a British invasion deep into New England. Hazen spent the last years of his life attempting to develop substantial land holdings in Vermont as well as a grant from New York on the west side of LAKE CHAMPLAIN where he brought many of his veterans to settle.

Healy, Arthur Kelly David (1902–1978)

A painter, architect, and educator, Arthur K. D. Healy served on the MIDDLEBURY COLLEGE faculty from 1943 until 1968, producing memorable landscape paintings of the surrounding countryside. Born in New York City and educated at Princeton University (A.B. and M.F.A. in architecture, 1926), Healy also studied for a year at the École des Beaux-Arts, Paris. After working in architectural offices in New York, where he specialized in hotel interiors, he moved to Rutland in 1929 to pursue his architectural career. Discouraged by the dearth of business during the Depression, Healy turned to painting in

1935. He soon gained membership in a number of prestigious East Coast watercolor societies, including the Boston Society of Watercolor Painters, Baltimore Watercolor Society, American Watercolor Society, Audubon Artists, and the Philadelphia Watercolor Club. In 1941, Healy served as an architectural engineer for the United States Navy in Portsmouth, New Hampshire. Healy was appointed the first artist in residence at Middlebury College in 1943. He became associate professor of fine arts in 1947; chairman of the Department of Fine Arts in 1950; and professor of art in 1958. A colorful, vivid, energetic, and unforgettable presence to both students and colleagues, Healy taught the full range of history of art courses at Middlebury, as well as courses in studio art. The preponderance of Healy's paintings are landscapes and views of Middlebury and its surroundings. His style is broadly realistic, informed by a modernist vocabulary of geometric formal arrangement and, early on, a particularly expressionist moodiness. An avid traveler and horseracing enthusiast, he also produced watercolor views of his travels in France, Florida, and Ireland. In addition to painting and teaching, Healy published book illustrations and numerous exhibition reviews. Among the public collections that include Healy's watercolor paintings are the Addison Gallery of American Art, Andover, Massachusetts; the BENNINGTON MUSEUM; Robert Hull FLEMING MUSEUM, University of Vermont; Harvard University Fogg Museum; Middlebury College Museum of Art; Museum of Fine Arts, Boston; Museum of Fine Arts, Saint Petersburg, Florida; the New Britain Museum of American Art, New Britain, Connecticut; and the Henry SHELDON MUSEUM of Vermont History, Middlebury. Healy was an active trustee of the Sheldon Museum after his retirement from teaching and a member of the Vermont Board of Historic Sites and its successor agency, the Advisory Council on Historic Preservation.

Emmie Donadio

Healy, Eliza:
Sister Mary Magdalen (1846–1918)

An educator noted as the first African-American mother superior of a Roman Catholic convent, Eliza Healy was born to a Georgia slave owner and his mixed-race slave. On her father's death, she and her brother James were sent north and she was reared by the Sisters of Notre Dame in

Quebec from 1851 to 1864. Moving to Boston with her brother in 1864, they bought freedom for their aunt, the surviving member of their mother's family still a slave in Georgia. Eliza Healy then entered the convent of the Sisters of Notre Dame, completing her novitiate in 1874, after which she went on to teach convent schools in Ontario and Quebec. Her brother James, meanwhile, had entered the Sulpician Seminary in Montreal and was ordained a priest. In 1903, Sister Mary Magdalen came to St. Albans as mother superior at the Sisters of Notre Dame convent school in St. Albans, Villa Barlow, a distinguished finishing school for the daughters of wealthy New Englanders. She held this post for fifteen years, revitalizing the school, remodeling the buildings, and stabilizing the institution's budget. Sister Mary Magdalen's leadership abilities were mirrored in the careers of her three brothers. James, the first African-American Catholic bishop, was known as "the children's bishop" for his work on behalf of children throughout New England; Patrick, the first African-American Jesuit, was president of Georgetown University; and Michael, commander of a Coast Guard cutter, was said to be the model for Jack London's "Wolf" Larsen in his novel *The Sea Wolf*. *Ray Zirblis*

Heineberg, Bernard (1809–1878)

Bernard Heineberg was a native of the province of Westphalia, Prussia, who established a medical practice in Burlington in 1834 and was probably the first Jew to settle in Burlington. Educated at the Universities of Bonn and Göttingen, he migrated to Burlington at the suggestion of Willard Wadhams, a UNIVERSITY OF VERMONT graduate then studying in Germany. Heineberg had hoped to secure a teaching post in the UVM Medical Department, but upon finding no openings (whether because he was a Jew, or a German, or because there were too few students), he went into private practice in Burlington, sometimes consulting in Montreal and Albany. He purchased a farm in Colchester on the WINOOSKI RIVER where Richardson's Ferry then provided a link to Burlington's north end. Heineberg was one of the forces behind the erection of a bridge over the Winooski at this point in 1853 and is said to have been the first to cross, rushing to a medical case. His service in promoting the bridge and in medical care was honored by naming the bridge for him. A staunch Democrat, he served as a Colchester selectman and raised volunteers for the Civil War. In his later years, he owned and lived in Burlington's American House Hotel. Heineberg's name is also commemorated by the Heineberg Club, today a Senior Center on Heineberg Road in the "new North End." *Sarah L. Dopp*

Heininger, Alfred H. (1886–1970)

Burlington attorney Alfred H. Heininger was a UNIVERSITY OF VERMONT graduate (Phi Beta Kappa 1908) and a Democrat who served in the Vermont senate (1935–1941) and ran for governor in 1936, losing to GEORGE AIKEN. Heininger served on the Vermont Old Age Assistance Commission (1935–1959) and the Board of Social Welfare and came to be known as the "father of the Vermont social welfare system." Prior to World War II he led the isolationist America First movement in Vermont. He was a partner in Kieslich Construction Company, builders of the first Burlington airport building, the DeGoesbriand Memorial Hospital, and the Centennial Field grandstand. He was married to Erna Neumann, the first woman dentist in Vermont. *Sarah L. Dopp*

Hemenway, Abby Maria (1828–1890)

Chiefly remembered as the editor of the *Vermont Historical Gazetteer*, a five-volume compendium of the state's local history that is still in heavy use today by historians and genealogists, Abby Hemenway was born in Ludlow and educated at Black River Academy. Her studies completed, she moved to Michigan in 1853, where she spent several lonely years teaching school and writing poetry. By 1858, she was back home in Ludlow collecting material for her first published work, *Poets and Poetry of Vermont* (1858), a collection of verse written by known and unknown poets from all across the state. The book's popularity led Hemenway to embark on what would become her life's work, the *Vermont Historical Gazetteer*. Over the course of the next thirty years, Hemenway ran a small publishing empire, engaging hundreds of men and women to write and collect their towns' histories. The work began as the *Vermont Quarterly Gazetteer*. The first issue—covering the towns of Addison County—appeared in 1860. Five more issues were published until printing was suspended in 1863 for lack of funds. During this hiatus, Hemenway, who never married, left the Baptist church of her

Abby Maria Hemenway. Special Collections, Bailey/Howe Library, University of Vermont

childhood to become a Roman Catholic. She was baptized in 1864 and soon after moved to Burlington, where she lived with fellow convert Lydia Clark Meech. Her first volume of poetry, *The Mystical Rose*, a life of the Virgin Mary, which she had begun writing as a young school teacher, was published in 1865. Publication of the *Gazetteer* resumed in 1868, when Hemenway brought out volume 1 of the *Vermont Historical Gazetteer* containing the town histories of five Vermont counties. One third of the histories in this volume had been previously published in the *Quarterly*, the remainder had not. The next ten years would be the most productive of Hemenway's career. Then, in the late 1870s, the chronic indebtedness that plagued the publication of the *Gazetteer* worsened, forcing Hemenway to ask for state aid. But the few hundred dollars she received from the Vermont legislature were not enough to keep the work solvent. By 1884, she was back in Ludlow, where she set up her own printing establishment. Then, within a year, illness and indebtedness induced her to leave Vermont and settle in Chicago. For the next five years, she continued her editing of the *Gazetteer* and supported herself by printing bound copies of individual town histories. Hemenway died of a stroke in 1890. She was sixty-two and had continued working to

the very end. At the time of Hemenway's death, four volumes of the *Gazetteer* had been published. One more appeared in 1892. But the manuscripts destined for volume 6, including the histories of her home county of Windsor, all perished in a fire in North Carolina in 1911.

Deborah P. Clifford

Henderson, George Washington (1850–1936)

Born a slave in Virginia, young George Washington Henderson accompanied Henry Carpenter of Belvidere home to Vermont after the Civil War. Henderson acquired literacy under the tutelage of Oscar Atwood in Underhill. He attended Barre Academy, entered the UNIVERSITY OF VERMONT, graduated first in the class of 1877, and was the second African-American elected to Phi Beta Kappa nationally. After teaching school in Jericho, Craftsbury, and Newport, he enrolled in Yale Divinity School, graduating in 1883, and subsequently earned a graduate degree from the University of Berlin. He returned to America to serve as a Congregational minister in New Orleans (1888–1890). Henderson wrote the first formal protest against lynching in 1894. From 1890 to 1932, he taught theology and classical languages in Straight (now Dillard), Fisk, and Wilberforce Universities. *Ray Zirblis*

Herrick, Samuel (fl. 1740–1790)

A Connecticut man who settled in Bennington in 1768, Samuel Herrick captured Skenesborough (today's Whitehall, New York) allied with NOAH LEE of Castleton on May 10, 1775, with thirty men under his command, but paid by Lee, while ETHAN ALLEN and a larger force seized the fortress at TICONDEROGA. This incident involved the capture of a schooner that the rebellious Americans, led by BENEDICT ARNOLD, quickly armed, allowing them to control LAKE CHAMPLAIN in the crucial early months of the war. Herrick later commanded a company of Vermont militia rangers. At the BATTLE OF BENNINGTON in 1777, he led a militia force totalling three hundred men that attacked the rear of Colonel Baum's right simultaneously with other troops attacking the Brunswickers' front and left. His ranger company later harried and delayed BURGOYNE's movement toward Saratoga. A Continental battalion of six companies under his command was planned for an aborted attack on St. Johns in 1778, as part of a proposed second invasion of Canada to be commanded by the Marquis de Lafayette. After the war, Herrick migrated to New York and disappears from the Vermont record.

Heyde, Charles Louis (1820–1892)

A landscape artist, Charles Heyde (pronounced hy-dee) was born in France, spent his childhood in Pennsylvania, and later lived in Hoboken, New Jersey, and Brooklyn, New York. He painted in New York, New Jersey, Vermont, Massachusetts, and Ontario, and exhibited at the National Academy of Design, the Pennsylvania Academy of Fine Arts, and the Boston Athenaeum. In 1852, he married Hannah Whitman, poet Walt Whitman's sister. Heyde settled permanently in Burlington in 1856 and painted scenes of the GREEN MOUNTAINS, the Adirondacks, and LAKE CHAMPLAIN. In 1861, he redesigned the Vermont coat-of-arms on a commission from the VERMONT HISTORICAL SOCIETY. A prolific artist, he enjoyed early success in the Champlain Valley with "small cabinet pictures, local views selected mainly from the exhaustless resources of Vermont rivers, mountains, and lakes," but by 1880 his sales declined sharply. During the last decade of his life, an alcoholic, destitute Heyde often sold paintings for as little as one dollar to buy food and fuel. He died in the State Hospital in Waterbury. Two exhibits of Heyde's painting with catalogue have been presented at UNIVERSITY OF VERMONT's Robert Hull FLEMING MUSEUM, in 1965 and again in 2000. Many of Heyde's paintings of Vermont landscapes are privately owned.

Barbara K. Hamblett

Highgate

Highgate, population 3,397, a town in Franklin County, was granted by BENNING WENTWORTH in 1763 and named after Highgate in England, a suburb of London. The town is generally flat and devoted primarily to DAIRY FARMING. It is bordered on the north by Canada and is cut in its southern section by the MISSISQUOI RIVER, which forms an extensive delta as it flows into the northernmost reach of LAKE CHAMPLAIN, Missisquoi Bay, which extends into Canada. The delta, partly in the town of Swanton, is a national wildlife refuge. Archeological research shows that humans lived in both towns as long as eight thousand years ago, and members of the ABENAKI nation still

live in the area. Major settlements are Highgate Center, on the Missisquoi, and Highgate Springs, once the site of a spa resort on Missisquoi Bay. JOHN GODFREY SAXE, the poet, and WARREN AUSTIN, the first U.S. delegate to the United Nations, were natives of Highgate. The town is Vermont's main point of entry to Canada.

Hilberg, Raul (b. 1926)

Credited with being the dean of Holocaust studies with his book *The Destruction of the European Jews* (1961), Raul Hilberg was instrumental in focusing research on the Holocaust. The book remains a standard work on the subject. Hilberg was born and spent his early childhood in Vienna, but emigrated with his parents soon after Germany occupied Austria, proclaimed anti-Jewish decrees, and threatened to imprison Raul's father. They reached Cuba September 1, 1939, where Raul spent four months before continuing to the United States. Due to the vagaries of American immigration laws, he was eligible for entry ten months before his parents. He attended high school in New York City, and although he arrived with limited English graduated at sixteen and went on to Brooklyn College. Drafted when eighteen, he served with the army in Europe as an interpreter. After his discharge, he returned to graduate from Brooklyn College and then went on to receive a Ph.D. in public law and government from Columbia University. While researching his dissertation, which eventually was revised

and published as *The Destruction of the European Jews*, he worked on the War Documentation Project in the Federal Records Center at Alexandria, Virginia. He subsequently taught at Hunter College, the University of Puerto Rico, and joined the political science department of the UNIVERSITY OF VERMONT in 1956. He retired in 1991 and continues to reside in Burlington. In addition to an expansion of his major work to three volumes, he is also the author of *Perpetrators Victims Bystanders: The Jewish Catastrophe 1933–1945* (1993) and *Sources of Holocaust Research: An Analysis* (2001). He published a memoir of his career under the title *The Politics of Memory: The Journey of a Holocaust Historian* (1996).

Hildene

The only one of Abraham and Mary Todd Lincoln's four sons to survive past adolescence, Robert Todd Lincoln built a twenty-four-room Georgian Revival mansion in Manchester for his summer home and moved into it in 1905. Set among 400 acres of gardens and meadows, the house was named Hildene, which means "hill and valley," and furnished with possessions and memorabilia of his father. Robert Todd Lincoln's connection to Vermont stemmed from two visits with his mother to the Equinox Hotel in Manchester in 1863 and 1864. He vowed then to build a home in Vermont, but did not buy land until 1902. The Lincolns spent several months each summer in Vermont, travelling from

Hildene, home of Robert Todd Lincoln. Vermont Department of Tourism and Marketing

their winter home in Washington, D.C., in a private railroad car. After his death there in 1926, he was buried at Arlington National Cemetery. Hildene remained in the Lincoln family until the death of Robert's granddaughter Peggy Lincoln Beckwith in 1975, when the house and the 400 acres surrounding it were purchased by a local foundation. It is open to visitors from May to October.

Ann E. Cooper and Sarah L. Dopp

Hill, Ralph Nading (1917–1987)

An author of books on Vermont and LAKE CHAMPLAIN history, Ralph Nading Hall was born in Burlington. He graduated from Dartmouth College in 1939 and served in the Army Counter-Intelligence Corps in Europe during World War II. After returning to Vermont in 1945, he worked briefly at Abernethy's, a department store owned by his grandfather, before pursuing his ambition to become a writer. His first book, *The Winooski*, published as a volume in the Rivers of America series, appeared in 1949 followed in 1950 by *Contrary Country* (1950), a book of popular historical essays about Vermont. Hill published or edited some twenty-five books and wrote numerous articles. Most but by no means all of his works were about Vermont or northern New England. In the early 1950s, Hill spearheaded the preservation of the last sidewheeler on Lake Champlain, the *TICONDEROGA*. With others he formed the Shelburne Steamboat Company in an attempt to keep the *Ticonderoga* afloat as an excursion steamer. That venture proving impracticable, the steamer was transported overland to the SHELBURNE MUSEUM, where it is presently on display as a prime attraction. Hill's other activities included service as a senior editor of *VERMONT LIFE*, chairman of the board of Green Mountain Power Corporation, trustee of the VERMONT HISTORICAL SOCIETY, Vermont Educational Television, and CHAMPLAIN COLLEGE, and member of the Vermont Bicentennial Commission and the Dartmouth College Alumni Council. Perhaps his most personally rewarding accomplishment was the preservation of the ETHAN ALLEN HOMESTEAD. Having documented the authenticity of the site, he was a leading force in restoring it and building an educational center nearby.

Hinesburg

Hinesburg, population 4,340, a town in Chittenden County, was granted by BEN-NING WENTWORTH in 1762 and named for Abel Hine, the original town clerk and presumably one of the grantees. The western part of the town lies in the fertile Champlain Valley and has historically been agricultural, while the eastern half is in the forested foothills of the GREEN MOUNTAINS. The town's location on the edge of the Burlington metropolitan area has resulted in a good deal of recent residential development, both in Hinesburg village and along the country roads.

Hitchcock, John Allen (1894–1944)

The foremost authority on the agricultural economy of Vermont in the pre–World War II era, John Allen Hitchcock produced research reports on land use and economic land classifications still important in Vermont's land-use planning as it relates to the agricultural economy. Hitchcock earned degrees in agriculture from UNIVERSITY OF VERMONT (B.S., 1918; M.S., 1925) and first worked as Vermont's extension dairy specialist and farm management specialist. Further graduate study in agricultural economics at Cornell University (1930–1932) led to the publication by UVM's agricultural experimental station of his research reports on DAIRY FARMING and other economic aspects of the state's agriculture. In the mid-1930s, he came to recognize that Vermont was hindered by the inadequate description and classification of the economic value of agricultural land. Consequently, he launched intensive studies in land utilization practices in nine towns containing some of the state's better agricultural areas. Using a land classification procedure developed at Cornell, Hitchcock sought to identify, first, land areas better adapted to reforestation than agriculture and, second, areas where the agricultural land-use potential could be substantially improved by better approaches to production, marketing, and family farm living. His investigations in Bridport, Fletcher, Hartford, Irasburg, Morristown, Pawlet, Richmond, Rupert, and Swanton provided data that became instrumental in the Nine Towns Reports of ROBERT MCCRILLIS CARTER, JR., that contributed to the development of several progressive public policies in the late 1940s.   *Gerald F. Vaughn*

Hoag, Joseph (1762–1846)

A Quaker minister and visionary, Joseph Hoag was born in Oblong (Pawling), Dutchess County, New York, the son of recommended Quaker minister Elijah and Phebe Hoag of Rochester, New Hampshire. In 1782, he married Hulda Case, moved to Vermont, organized the first Quaker meeting in Monkton, and bought a farm in Charlotte (1790). He was the first settled minister in town, but he refused the free land and served without compensation. For many years, both he and his wife travelled extensively as zealous itinerant preachers, holding their orthodox beliefs against the Hicksite reformers. Hoag had many visions, the most famous in 1803 in a field near his house in which he foresaw the Civil War and the abolition of slavery. He reported this shortly before his death. A successful farmer respected also for his talent in gardening and fruit growing, Joseph Hoag is buried in the Hazard-Friends cemetery in Monkton.

Mary G. Lighthall

Hoagland, Edward (b. 1932)

Called by John Updike "the best essayist of my generation," Edward Hoagland was born in New York City and raised in Connecticut. For many years he has had a seasonal home near Lake Willoughby in Westmore. Educated at Deerfield Academy and Harvard, he began his career by writing novels but then switched to nonfiction. In the latter, Hoagland established a reputation for personal, engaging, skillfully crafted meditations on many subjects, ranging from the street life of New York City to the relations between men and women to the fate of wolves in Texas. His keenly observed nature essays owe much to his intimacy with the lonely fields and woods of his NORTHEAST KINGDOM home, especially those in *The Moose on the Wall: Field Notes from the Vermont Wilderness* (1974). His long essay "Gods, Masks, and Horses," published in 1983, is about Peter Schumann's BREAD AND PUPPET THEATER and its annual (now discontinued) Domestic Resurrection Circus in Glover. As of 2001, Hoagland had published sixteen books, many of them essay collections, and most recently *Compass Points: How I Lived*, a memoir. He has taught at various colleges and universities including Columbia and Brown, and since 1987 at BENNINGTON COLLEGE. His second wife was the late Marion Magid, managing editor of *Commentary* magazine.

Hocquart, Gilles (1694–1783)

The financial commissary (1729–1731) and intendant (administrator) of New France

(1731–1748), Gilles Hocquart ordered a road built from La Prairie near Montreal to Fort Saint-Jean to establish a port on the Richelieu River that opened LAKE CHAMPLAIN for naval transportation. The demand for ships to be built in New France was met in part by timber exploiters from Saint-Jean sending large logging crews of one hundred men or more to the forests of the MISSISQUOI and LAMOILLE RIVER valleys during the 1740s and 1750s. Beginning in the late 1730s, Hocquart enlisted civilians and recently discharged soldiers to settle at POINT À LA CHEVELURE in today's Addison County. Louis XV then granted Hocquart a substantial seigneury on the east shore of Lake Champlain in 1743, which by the 1750s contained a settlement of over thirty houses. By the conclusion of the Seven Years' War and the peace treaty of 1763 between France and England, the settlement at Point à la Chevelure had been abandoned. Today the site is known as CHIMNEY POINT.

Joseph-André Senécal

Hoff, Philip Henderson (b. 1924)

In 1962, Philip Hoff was the first Democrat to be elected governor of Vermont in 108 years. He had represented Burlington in the Vermont House from 1961 to 1963, was governor from 1963 to 1969, and served three terms in the Senate from 1983 to 1989. A native of Turners Falls, Massachusetts, he was educated in local public schools and entered Williams College in 1942. After his freshman year, he enlisted in the United States Navy, where he saw World War II combat action in the South Pacific Theater aboard the USS *Sea Dog*. After the war, Hoff returned to Williams, graduated in 1948, and married Joan Brower. Completing Cornell Law School in 1951, he moved to Burlington to join the law firm of Black and Wilson. Hoff's political career began with an unsuccessful run for the Burlington Board of Aldermen in 1959. In 1960, he was elected as the city's lone member of the Vermont House of Representatives. There he quickly gained influence as part of a bi-partisan freshman caucus known as the "YOUNG TURKS." In 1962, Hoff began an energetic campaign for governor against the incumbent, F. RAY KEYSER, JR. His election was the culmination of a decade of efforts to make the DEMOCRATIC PARTY a competitive force in Vermont elections. At a torchlight victory parade in Winooski, Hoff exclaimed: "One hundred years of Republi-

can rule broken!" He was re-elected in 1964 and 1966. The hallmark of the Hoff administration was the governor's youthful confidence as he reformed Vermont government and thrust the state into the mainstream of modern American life. Hoff opened state government's first planning office, ended the Overseer of the Poor system of administering welfare benefits, and founded the Vermont District Court and the Judicial Nominating Board. He established the Governor's Commission on Women, the Vermont Council on the Arts, and the Vermont Student Assistance Corporation. He promoted regionalization in the delivery of government services, establishing regional airport and library systems. He presided over the REAPPORTIONMENT of the Vermont legislature to comply with the principle of one man, one vote. Hoff suffered defeats as well. His effort to commit the state to an advantageous long-term contract for Canadian electrical power was frustrated, and he was unable to reform school finance. As his administration drew to a close, Hoff grew active on the national political stage. Concerned about the nation's struggle for racial equality, he and New York City Mayor John Lindsay founded the VERMONT–NEW YORK YOUTH PROJECT. The program brought Vermont students together with minority students from the city to work on joint projects at several Vermont colleges. After a Far East tour, Hoff was the first Democratic governor in the nation to split with President Lyndon Johnson over the Vietnam War. Hoff campaigned across the country in Robert Kennedy's effort to obtain the Democratic presidential nomination, and was seriously considered as Hubert Humphrey's vice-presidential running mate in 1968. In 1970, Hoff challenged incumbent WINSTON L. PROUTY for a seat in the United States Senate. Hoff's opposition to the war, his admission that he had drinking problems, and controversy over his efforts to promote racial harmony marked the campaign. Although he mounted a vigorous effort, Hoff was defeated. He returned to the practice of law in Burlington, and after pleading guilty to driving while intoxicated he gave up drinking, thereafter candidly describing himself as a recovering alcoholic. In the 1970s he advised New York City Mayor Abraham Beame in handling the city's financial crisis. In 1982, he returned to elective politics, winning a

seat in the Vermont Senate from Chittenden County. He was re-elected twice (1984 and 1986). In the Senate, he was instrumental in revitalizing the Vermont Human Rights Commission and promoting prevention of social and health problems. Hoff has remained steadfastly committed to the cause of racial justice, serving for many years on the Vermont Advisory Commission to the United States Civil Rights Commission. He has also remained an active supporter of the Vermont Democratic party, serving as its chair in 1972 and 1973.

Richard T. Cassidy

Hoit, Winthrop (fl. 1755–1790)

A Connecticut militiaman during the Seven Years' War, Winthrop Hoit (also spelled Hoyt), was taken prisoner by the Caughnawaga Mohawks and learned to speak their language. Hoit was also taken prisoner by the British in the Canadian campaign of the American Revolution during the summer of 1775, when ETHAN ALLEN sent him and Abraham Nimham, a member of the Wappinger tribe from Stockbridge, Massachusetts, into Canada on a mission to persuade the Mohawks and ABENAKI there to join the Americans against Britain or at least remain neutral. The Caughnawaga leaders convinced the British not to hang Hoit or Nimham, who were released later when the Americans took Montreal. After the war, Hoit settled in Swanton with IRA ALLEN's earliest settlers and seems to have been related by marriage to members of the Missisquoi band of Abenaki who returned to that location after the Revolution.

Holbrook, Frederick (1813–1909)

The twenty-eighth governor of Vermont, from 1861 to 1863, Frederick Holbrook was a native of East Windsor, Connecticut, and a grandson of LUKE KNOULTON, one of the first judges of the Vermont Supreme Court. He spent two years at the Berkshire Gymnasium in Pittsfield, Massachusetts, and then toured Europe. He returned to a Boston apprenticeship in a printing house, but soon rejected the opportunity to become part of his family's prosperous printing business in Connecticut. In January 1835, Holbrook married Harriet Goodhue and settled in Brattleboro on one of the Goodhue farms. He became a lifelong advocate of the improvement of agricultural methods and scientific agricultural education. He was a founding president of the Vermont Agricultural Society (1851–

1861), wrote for Vermont and regional newspapers on agricultural topics, and designed farm tools for Rugges, Nourse & Mason of Boston. His name was well known to Vermont's farmers, who voted heavily for him in 1861. Under his administration, Vermont was the first state to provide hospitals for the Civil War's wounded sent home from the front to recuperate.

T. D. Seymour Bassett

Holbrook, John (1761–1838)

John Holbrook, a native of Weymouth, Massachusetts, was a storekeeper in Newfane prior to moving to Brattleboro in 1795, where he established the successful mercantile business with David Porter of Holbrook & Porter, with a branch in Hartford, Connecticut. Deacon Holbrook was partner from 1805 to 1810 in the Brattleboro publishing firm of Holbrook, Fessenden, & Porter with his son-in-law WILLIAM FESSENDEN, and with the untimely death of Fessenden in January 1815, Holbrook returned to Brattleboro from Connecticut to carry on Fessenden's thriving printing, publishing, papermaking, and bookselling activities. Later he was joined by Joseph Fessenden, William's brother, a papermaker. The firm of Holbrook & Fessenden eventually developed into the Brattleboro Typographic Company, which they incorporated in 1836, and which issued large editions of Bibles and other nationally distributed publications. The company was the foundation of a succession of Brattleboro printing companies that survived well into the twentieth century.

Marcus A. McCorison

Holden, A. John, Jr. (1900–2002)

Educator A. John Holden, Jr., was born in Massachusetts. He received his bachelor's degree in civil engineering and business administration in 1923 and a master's degree in education in 1929 from Harvard, and his doctorate in education in 1943 from Columbia. He taught school in Louisville, Kentucky, and Boston in the 1920s, before coming to Vermont to teach in a small country school and work as a researcher on education for the VERMONT COMMISSION ON COUNTRY LIFE in 1930 and 1931. The Commission report on educational facilities was based in part on his study of general characteristics of Vermont's school system and included his proposal that the system would become economically efficient and educationally effective by reorganizing single-town school districts into larger centralized units. He was a teacher and administrator in the Vermont public schools until his appointment as associate professor of education at MIDDLEBURY COLLEGE in 1943. He was president of Schoolmen of Vermont (1943–1945) and president of the Vermont Society for Mental Hygiene (1944–1946). Leaving Vermont briefly, he was coordinator of field services and public relations at Geneseo State Teachers College in New York from 1947 to 1949. He then returned to Vermont as commissioner of education from 1949 to 1965, during which time he also supervised the teachers' colleges at Lyndon, Johnson, and Castleton and assisted in transforming them into the VERMONT STATE COLLEGES. During his sixteen years as commissioner, he promoted the development of union high school districts, a proposal he had originally made in 1931 in the report of the Vermont Commission on Country Life. He co-authored with William F. Bruce the important college and university textbook *The Teacher's Personal Development: An Introduction to Self-Awareness and Interpersonal Relations* (1957). He was president of the Council of Chief State School Officers (1957–1958), and chairman of the National Education Association's Educational Policies Commission (1962–1963). After retiring in 1965, Holden joined the faculty of JOHNSON STATE COLLEGE, where he taught the course "Man and Nature in Vermont History" and served as vice president of the Education Development Corporation in Newton, Massachusetts.

Gerald F. Vaughn

Holland

Holland, population 588, a town in Orleans County, was granted by the Vermont legislature in 1779 to Timothy Andrews and others. It was probably named for Holland, Massachusetts. Another theory, however, holds that it was named for Samuel Holland, the official New Hampshire surveyor, though this is unlikely as the Loyalist Holland had fled to Canada before the Vermont grant of 1779, where he became Quebec's surveyor general. The town, whose main activity has always been lumbering, is lightly populated and has no true village. In the northeastern corner of the town close to the Canadian border is 334-acre Holland Pond, part of the extensive Bill Sladyk Wildlife Management Area, which extends into the neighboring town of Norton.

Holly, James Theodore (1829–1911), and Joseph Cephas Holly (1825–1855)

Ardent abolitionists, the brothers James and Joseph Holly were born to free black parents in Washington, D.C. About 1849, they moved to Burlington, where they set up a boot-making shop on Church Street with financial assistance from abolitionist Lewis Tappan of New York. They lectured together on the antislavery circuit, but came to opposing views on the question of colonies for ex-slaves in Africa and Haiti. While Joseph was strongly opposed to colonization, James Holly came to believe that blacks would not achieve true freedom in the United States and, with some bitterness, endorsed colonization. Joseph C. wrote verse defending his race, denouncing colonization, championing the right of black Americans to stay in the United States, and celebrating abolition heroes. By 1853, he moved to Rochester, New York, where he published *Freedom's Offerings, a Collection of Poems*. He died there of lung disease in 1855. By 1852, James had moved to Canada to work with Henry Bibb, co-editing *The Voice of the Fugitive*. By 1855, James had again moved to New Haven, Connecticut, and had become involved in the black national convention movement and completed his studies and was ordained as an Episcopal minister. In 1861, he organized a colony of New England and Canadian blacks, which he led to Haiti. He spent the next thirty-seven years founding schools and clinics on the island. James Holly became an ardent anti-imperialist in reaction to the Spanish-American War and advocated the theories of French communitarian Charles Fourier. In 1900, he joined the Pan-African movement.

Ray Zirblis

Holmes, Benjamin (1754–1817)

Called "a scourge of the Loyalists" by the British spy George Smyth, Benjamin Holmes hanged the Loyalists DAVID REDDING in 1778 and Howard in 1781, and in the same year was himself captured by a British scouting party before ETHAN and IRA ALLEN had opened the so-called HALDIMAND NEGOTIATIONS with the British in Quebec that established a prisoner-exchange truce. British General FREDERICK HALDIMAND was reluctant to release Holmes because the rebel had boasted frequently of his record as a hangman to taunt his Loyalist ranger guards. Holmes settled in the town of Georgia after the war.

Holton, Henry Dwight (1838–1917)

An instrumental figure in the establishment of the Vermont State Board of Health and the development of public health regulation in Vermont, Henry Dwight Holton was born in Saxtons River, studied medicine in Boston and New York, and graduated from New York University in 1860. He married Ellen Hoit in 1862. With a practice in Brattleboro, Holton participated actively in state and national medical organizations, serving as president of the Vermont Medical Society in 1873, as vice president of the American Medical Association in 1880, and president of the American Public Health Association in 1901. As a leader in the public health movement in Vermont, Holton worked tirelessly with the legislature from 1873 until 1886 to establish the Vermont State Board of Health. In 1896, he was appointed to the board and assumed the role of secretary from 1900 until 1912. During his tenure, he became a nettling presence among local officials for his condemnations of unsanitary water supplies, sewer systems, and public buildings in the state. Hoping to bring the benefits of preventive medicine to Vermonters, Holton lobbied for a pure food and drug law, school building regulation, and systematic disease reporting. In 1898, he helped initiate the state bacteriological laboratory, which provided the scientific basis for enforcing new state health regulations, and subsequently established an annual school for local health officers to educate them about germ theory, sanitation, and disease prevention methods.

Marilyn Blackwell

Hope, James (1818–1892)

A native of Scotland, James Hope came to Vermont in 1834. He attended Castleton Seminary, apprenticed as a wagon maker, but soon began to make his living as a portrait and landscape artist. After painting for two years in Montreal, Hope returned to Castleton and then in 1852 opened a winter studio in New York City. Hope acquired a reputation as an artist for his landscapes, a fine example of which can be viewed in the reference room of the Rutland Library. A captain of the Second Vermont Regiment in the Civil War, Hope painted several battle and camp scenes that are acclaimed for their detail. His Antietam series is displayed at the Antietam National Battlefield. *Winter Quarters of the Vermont Brigade in Front of Fredericksburg, Virginia, 1862–1863* can be seen in the museum of the VERMONT HISTORICAL SOCIETY. In 1872, he established a studio and gallery in Glens Falls, New York, where he painted until his death.

Donald Wickman

Hope Cemetery

A nationally known treasure house of memorial art, Hope Cemetery in Barre was created in 1895 and is located on a series of gentle knolls on the northern outskirts of town. A Boston landscape architect, Edwin P. Adams, laid out the nonsectarian burial ground in the lawn-park style. Regulations require that all monuments be of Barre granite, lending a uniquely uniform look to the grounds. Today the cemetery encompasses over 125 acres of land, of which approximately 80 are developed. The main interest of the cemetery is the often exquisite detailing of the monuments, especially those that depict in realistic style the individuals they commemorate. The Italian-American sculptors who worked in the granite industry knew many of the deceased as friends and fellow workers, and lavished care on their memorials. Especially noteworthy is the Louis Brusa memorial, which depicts Brusa at the moment of collapse, comforted by his wife, and the contemplative figure nearby of ELIA CORTI, who was killed during an altercation between anarchists and socialists at the SOCIALIST LABOR PARTY HALL in 1903. More recent memorials, such as those depicting a race car and a soccer ball, may be less con-

Elia Corti's memorial, Hope Cemetery, Barre. Ralph H. Orth

ventional. The popularity of the cemetery as a tourist attraction is demonstrated during the summer season, when up to twenty tour buses per day visit the grounds.

Hopkins, John Henry, Jr. (1820–1891)

The son of JOHN HENRY HOPKINS, SR., first bishop of the Episcopal Diocese of Vermont, John Henry Hopkins, Jr., was born in Pittsburgh, Pennsylvania, and, after his family moved to Vermont, graduated from the UNIVERSITY OF VERMONT in 1839. Ordained an Episcopal priest in 1850, he founded and edited the *Church Journal* and served congregations in Plattsburgh, New York, and Williamsport, Pennsylvania. He wrote a lengthy biography of his father, volumes of poetry and theology, and numerous hymns and carols, most notably *The Song of the Magi*, known popularly as *We Three Kings of Orient Are*.

Hopkins, John Henry, Sr. (1792–1868)

A native of Dublin, Ireland, John Henry Hopkins came to America with his parents in 1800 when they settled in Pittsburgh, Pennsylvania. He worked as an ironmaster and lawyer before his ordination as a priest in the Episcopal Church. He first served as rector of Trinity Episcopal Church, Pittsburgh (1823–1830) and then as assistant rector of Trinity Church, Boston. He was named rector of St. Paul's Church, Burlington (1831), and was consecrated first Episcopal bishop of Vermont in 1832. Drawn to the English Tractarians and the Oxford Movement, Hopkins inclined to the polemical, as in his *Christianity Vindicated* (1833). He and his Irish countryman, the Reverend JEREMIAH O'CALLAGHAN, for several years the sole priest serving Vermont's Catholics, disputed doctrinal questions, Hopkins attacking Catholicism in *Primitive Creed* (1834) and *Primitive Church* (1835) and O'Callaghan responding with *The Vagaries and Heresies of John Henry Hopkins* (1837). On a visit to England in 1837 and 1838, Hopkins tempered his High Church affinities after visits to John Henry Newman and other members of the Oxford Movement who seemed too friendly to the Roman Catholic Church. Hopkins's attempts to justify slavery by arguing from scripture failed to win many converts. His treatise *Gothic Architecture* (1836) was an early influence on the development of that style in American church architecture.

Horsford, Frederick H. (1854–1923)

A prominent botanist of Charlotte, Frederick H. Horsford was the founder (1893) and owner of the Horsford Nurseries. Previously he was associated for many years with CYRUS G. PRINGLE in the collection and preparation of botanical specimens for the supply of European herbariums. Horsford also extensively hybridized greens and vegetables. The Horsford Market Garden Pea and the "telephone" pea were among his creations, besides several varieties of barley and oats, among them the beardless barley. *David Blow*

Howard, Oliver Otis (1830–1909)

A decorated Civil War general, commissioner of the Freedman's Bureau, and Indian frontier fighter, O. O. Howard came to Vermont after he retired from the army in 1894. A native of Leeds, Massachusetts, he attended Monmouth Academy and graduated from Bowdoin College before entering West Point in 1850. After graduation, he taught mathematics at the military academy until the outbreak of the Civil War, when he was given command of combat units and rapidly promoted, ultimately commanding the right wing of General William Tecumseh Sherman's army. A veteran of numerous campaigns, Howard lost his right arm at the Battle of Fair Oaks (Seven Pines) and was ultimately awarded the Congressional Medal of Honor for bravery there. Though Howard's personal courage has never been questioned, his military reputation has been a subject of controversy. His administration of the Freedman's Bureau has also drawn criticism, usually charges of "over-enthusiasm" from those unsympathetic with Radical Republican reconstruction policies. Unmoved by this criticism, Howard was instrumental in founding Howard University and served as its president (1869–1874). After retirement and relocation in Burlington, he wrote books and magazine articles and served as a Republican speaker during the presidential campaigns of 1896, 1900, and 1904. He published his autobiography in 1907.

Howe, Harland B. (1873–1946)

Despite early poverty and an attack of poliomyelitis at age sixteen that left him crippled in his right arm and left leg, Harland B. Howe served as a judge in the United States Court for the District of Vermont for thirty years (1915–1945). Born in St. Johnsbury Center, Howe graduated from Lyndon Literary and Biblical Institute and from the University of Michigan Law School (1894). He was immediately admitted to the Vermont bar and established his law office in St Johnsbury. Although St. Johnsbury was a Republican town, Howe entered politics as a Democrat and in 1908 was elected town representative. In 1912, he was his party's gubernatorial candidate and ran second in a three-man campaign in which the Republican candidate failed to gain a majority and was subsequently elected by the legislature. Running again in 1914, Howe was defeated by a larger margin than in 1912. In 1915, on Howe's forty-second birthday, President Woodrow Wilson appointed him U.S. judge for the district of Vermont. A Democrat whose political partisanship was restrained rather than totally abandoned when he served on the court, he continued to contribute financially to Democratic causes while on the bench. A plaintiff's judge, his sympathies were generally with the more vulnerable party. He enjoyed an occasional alcoholic beverage, and in sentencing violators of PROHIBITION laws discriminated between those who had acquired a bottle of liquor for their own use and those in the distribution business. His death in 1946 came soon after his full retirement from the federal bench in 1945.

Howe Scale

In the early 1950s, the Howe Richardson Scale Company of Rutland along with E. & T. FAIRBANKS AND COMPANY of St. Johnsbury accounted for about three-quarters of the industrial scales produced in the United States. The innovation leading to the founding of Howe Scales was an invention patented in 1856 by Thomas Ross and Frank Strong that placed a scale platform on ball bearings resting in cup-shaped depressions over knife-edged pivots, permitting the platform to move freely and absorb jars and vibrations. Numerous improvements were patented in subsequent years, but Strong's ball-bearing principle was at the core of the scale's success. In 1857, John Howe, Jr., a foundry owner in Brandon and financial backer for Strong and Ross, bought out their patents and began to manufacture industrial scales under the name Howe Scale. Acclaimed for its accuracy and durability, the Howe Scale won its first in a series of international prizes at the Paris Exposition in 1867. Hand trucks, developed in 1873 to

Howe Scale Company advertisement. Special Collections, Bailey/Howe Library, University of Vermont

facilitate moving manufactured parts in a factory, subsequently along with trailers, became important company products. In 1873, a fire destroyed the company warehouse and offices, and Howe Scale moved to Rutland to the site it occupied until 1982. At its height, it was among Vermont's major employers and a vital contributor to the Rutland economy. During the second half of the nineteenth and the first half of the twentieth centuries, the company prospered under a succession of owners; two presidents, John B. Page and John Mead, served as Vermont governors. After World War II, with over eight hundred employees, Howe Scale was Rutland's largest manufacturing enterprise. The company adapted new technology and pioneered in scales for aircraft weighing. The largest scale was made to weigh the B-36 bomber and had a capacity of 250 tons accurate to $\frac{1}{40}$ of 1 percent. Computer technology, remote-operating recorders, and tape-drive mechanisms rendered the Rutland foundries obsolete, and they were abandoned in 1982. A year later, the Howe Richardson Scale Company, without the land and buildings it had occupied, was sold to the Mangood Corporation, a Chicago-based scale manufacturer.

Hoyt, William Henry (1813–1883)

A native of Sandwich, New Hampshire, and graduate of the Dartmouth class of 1831, William Hoyt studied divinity at the Andover Theological Seminary, the Vermont Episcopal Institute, and the General Theological Seminary and was ordained an Episcopal priest July 17, 1836. For a brief period, he taught at Bishop Hopkins Seminary in Burlington, then became rector in Middlebury for a year before going to St. Albans in 1838. Influenced by the Oxford Movement, Hoyt resigned his pastorate on December 30, 1845, and renounced his Protestant ministry in 1846, converting to the Roman Catholic Church. Hoyt remained in St. Albans, read law with Benjamin Swift, was admitted to the Franklin County bar in 1852, and was clerk of the U.S. District Court of Vermont. He removed to Burlington in 1860 when he became editor of the *Burlington Sentinel*. In 1868, he helped JOHN LONERGAN found the short-lived *Irish Watchman*, Vermont's only known Irish-American newspaper. A weekly, it first appeared January 1, 1868, and lasted only six months. In 1869, Hoyt removed to New York City, where he was assistant cashier of the Southern Railway. Following his wife's death in 1875, Hoyt, then sixty-three, was encouraged by Bishop DE GOESBRIAND to become a priest. He entered Seton Hall Seminary in December 1876 and was ordained May 26, 1877. For six years, Hoyt labored in several New York City parishes and died while saying mass at St. Anne's.   *David Blow*

Hubbard, Asahel (fl. 1815–1840)

Having obtained a patent on April 28, 1828, for a "Revolving Hydraulic Engine," the first effective rotary pump, Asahel Hubbard of West Windsor acquired financial backing from Jabez Proctor, father of REDFIELD PROCTOR, SR., to form the National Hydraulic Company. With Proctor's influence in Vermont government, Hubbard was appointed warden of the WINDSOR STATE PRISON, where he installed machines to produce his pumps, paying convicts 25 cents per day for their labor. With production and labor under his control, in the spring of 1830 Hubbard personally delivered by wagon a large Windsor pump that he sold to the city of St. Louis, Missouri, where he installed it in

the St. Louis Aqueduct Company's new municipal water works.

Hubbardton

Hubbardton, population 752, a town in Rutland County, was granted by BENNING WENTWORTH in 1764 and named after Thomas Hubbard, a grantee of this and six other towns. The hilly, rocky landscape has always hindered settlement, so that the town has never had even as many as a thousand inhabitants. There are a number of bodies of water, the largest of which are Lake Hortonia (shared with Sudbury to the north) and LAKE BOMOSEEN (most of which is in Castleton to the south). The main settlements are Hubbardton village, East Hubbardton, and Hortonia, which serves the many summer camps on Lake Hortonia. The BATTLE OF HUBBARDTON took place here on July 7, 1777, when SETH WARNER led his GREEN MOUNTAIN CONTINENTAL RANGERS in a rear-guard action to protect a retreating American force that had evacuated FORT TICONDEROGA as the British under General JOHN BURGOYNE advanced up the Champlain Valley.

Hubbardton, Battle of

When British General JOHN BURGOYNE and his army of seven thousand captured MOUNT INDEPENDENCE and FORT TICONDEROGA in July 1777, the Americans had already beaten a hasty retreat, fleeing through Hubbardton. There New Hampshire and Massachussetts troops with SETH WARNER'S GREEN MOUNTAIN CONTINENTAL RANGERS manned a rear guard, hoping to give the main American force time to escape. When the New Hampshire troops withdrew, Warner commanded fewer than eight hundred men against the advance of nearly two thousand Scots and Germans. The Americans withstood Simon Fraser's Scots brigade, but Baron FRIEDRICH VON RIEDESEL'S Brunswickers broke the Yankee line. Warner rallied his men and marched them on to Manchester, where they gathered around General JOHN STARK for the coming BATTLE OF BENNINGTON. The Americans lost 324 killed, wounded, and taken prisoner, including Francis Hale, commander of the Massachusetts troops. Among the British, 183 were killed or wounded. Though a short action involving fewer than three thousand men, the Hubbardton Battle was the beginning of a series of events leading two months later to General Burgoyne's defeat at the Battle of Saratoga.

The Vermont Division of Historic Preservation has established an interpretive center at the Hubbardton battlefield that houses a museum with an exhibit that places this battle into its Revolutionary War context. Strategic points around the battlefield are marked. An annual re-enactment commemorates the anniversary of the battle.   *John Dumville*

Huddle, David (b. 1942)

Born in Ivanhoe, Virginia, and educated at the University of Virginia, Hollins College, and Columbia University, David Huddle, author of fourteen books of poetry, fiction, and essays, has been a member of the English Department of the UNIVERSITY OF VERMONT since 1971 and a full professor since 1982. He has also taught in the undergraduate and graduate writing programs of GODDARD COLLEGE, MIDDLEBURY COLLEGE, the BREAD LOAF WRITERS' CONFERENCE, and the BREAD LOAF SCHOOL OF ENGLISH, where he was the ROBERT FROST Professor of American Literature in 1991. Huddle's work, all of it published during his years in Vermont, originally was set mostly in his home state of Virginia, but in recent years has often dealt with urban and rural Vermont. *La Tour Dreams of the Wolf Girl* (2002), Huddle's second novel, has Burlington as a central locale, and the lake in the title poem of his 1999 poetry collection, *Summer Lake: New and Selected Poems*, is LAKE CHAMPLAIN. *Not: A Trio—A Novella and Two Stories* (2000) is set in Bennington and Ripton and has, as writer George Garrett says in a tribute to Huddle's assimilation to his adopted state, "a wonderful sense of place."   *Ghita M. Orth*

Huden, John C. (1901–1963)

An educator and scholar of Native American history in Vermont, John C. Huden was born in Sag Harbor, New York, and began his career in education as a teacher in Connecticut. He came to Vermont in the 1940s to serve as principal of Bradford Academy and then of Montpelier High School. After serving in the State Department of Education, he was appointed president of Castleton Teachers College (1946–1950) and subsequently joined the education faculty at the UNIVERSITY OF VERMONT, a position he held until his death. A serious student of Native American history in New England since the 1930s, John Huden became the most prolific scholar of that history in Vermont in the 1950s and early 1960s, publishing numerous articles on ABENAKI history and culture in various journals, including especially *Vermont History*. His research on Native American place names in Vermont remains a valuable historical resource. At the time of his death in 1963, Huden was directing Native American–French research for the VERMONT HISTORICAL SOCIETY. *Donald Wickman*

Hudson-Champlain-Richelieu Waterway

The first section of the Hudson-Champlain-Richelieu waterway began as a canal

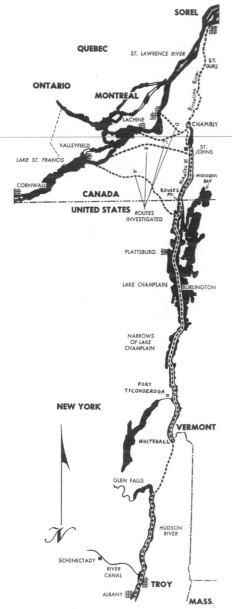

Hudson-Champlain-Richelieu Waterway.
Vermont Life

connecting LAKE CHAMPLAIN to the Hudson River at Troy, New York, completed in 1823 and rebuilt in 1905. The route to the St. Lawrence River proceeds from Whitehall at the south end of Lake Champlain to the mouth of the Richelieu River, approximately 100 miles to the north. A channel 6½ feet deep has been maintained on the Richelieu since 1843, including the nine locks of the Chambly Canal, a part of the Richelieu system that begins 12 miles north of Lake Champlain. The Richelieu reaches the St. Lawrence at Sorel, a 14-mile course with a depth of 12 feet. The shallow draught of the Chambly Canal has been an insuperable barrier to significant commercial use of the full length of the route from Troy to Sorel. The fact that New York City is only 407 miles from the St. Lawrence via this route led to several unsuccessful efforts to deepen the channel. The engineering obstacles are few, but the political and economic difficulties were many. The completion of a fixed-span bridge with a clearance of only 55 feet at Rouses Point in 1987 would seem to have ended forever the prospect of a viable commercial waterway between Lake Champlain and the St. Lawrence. The Hudson-Champlain route is quite another story. Throughout much of the nineteenth century, the Champlain Canal was part of an extensive inland water system centered on the Erie canal. The canal's depth of 12 feet permitted extensive barge traffic, especially in its early history. The SUBCHASERS built at the Shelburne shipyard during World War II passed through the canal on their way to New York. The route has been used commercially until recently. For example, although most oil arrives in northern Vermont by rail or truck, Burlington continued to receive some barge shipments via the canal in the 1990s. While its commercial importance has declined in recent decades, the canal's greatly expanded recreational use led New York State in the 1990s to invest considerable sums in major improvements. *Charles O'Brien*

Hum, The

A little understood aural phenomenon reported to have been heard in Vermont and England, the Hum is a deep sound that those who have experienced it report to be as much "felt" as heard. It is experienced generally at night between ten o'clock and two o'clock, usually when lying in bed. Tests to locate the source in wind-vibrating guide wires on television and radio

antennas have ruled out that possibility. Neighboring dairy farms have been excluded as a source of the Hum, as milking equipment is normally not operated during nighttime hours. Medical examinations have not located a source in internal bodily noises. Not all listeners in the same room might hear the Hum, and rural rather than urban locations seem the best places to hear it. *Mark Hazeltine*

Human Hibernation

A widespread story about Vermont in premodern days concerns the supposed practice of freezing old people in early winter and unfreezing them in spring. Since they could contribute nothing to keeping a farmstead going during the long, cold months yet would consume a portion of the family's precious foodstuffs, it was thought best to put them into a period of hibernation. The usual practice was to get them drunk, then lay them outside unclothed until they lost consciousness and fell into a rigor mortis–like condition. They were then thickly covered with evergreen boughs (or laid in the channel of a brook, or kept in the shed) until warm weather gradually brought them back to consciousness, none the worse for wear. The origin of the story, according to the writer and archeologist Roland Robbins in the Winter 1952–53 issue of *VERMONT LIFE*, was apparently a tall tale first told by dairy farmer Allen Morse of Calais. It appeared in print for the first time, entitled "A Strange Tale," in the Montpelier *Argus & Patriot* for December 21, 1887, and soon passed into Vermont folklore.

Hunt, William Morris (1824–1879)

The son of Judge Jonathan Hunt (1787–1832), who died of cholera while representing Vermont in the U.S. Congress, the artist William Morris Hunt was born and raised in Brattleboro in comfortable circumstances. The eldest of five children (the architect Richard Morris Hunt was his brother), he displayed precocious talent, learning to draw at an early age from an Italian artist, Gambadella, whom his mother, Jane Leavitt, herself an artist noted for her oil paintings, had invited to live with the Hunts in Vermont. William Morris Hunt attended Harvard College, but was expelled in his third year. His mother took him to the south of France and Rome to recover his health, where he began to study painting. Settling in Paris in 1846 to study with Thomas Couture,

Hunt was soon influenced by the French landscape and genre painter Jean François Millet, from whom he learned the principles of the Barbizon school. In 1855, Hunt returned to the United States and introduced the Barbizon school practice of painting in the open air at art schools that he established briefly in Newport, Rhode Island, Brattleboro, Fayal in the Azores, and finally in Boston. He helped establish in America the Parisian method of studying art that he had learned from Couture and Millet, which brought to an end the earlier American fashion of studying art in Rome fostered by the sculptor LARKIN MEAD, a younger contemporary from Brattleboro. Hunt also became a fashionable portrait painter. His importance to American painting, however, lay chiefly in his application of new French methods to landscape—as, for example, in *Bathers* (1877), which can be seen at the Worcester Art Museum, and *American Falls* (1878), at Washington's Corcoran Gallery. He drowned on the Isles of Shoals off New Hampshire, apparently a suicide.

Huntington

A town in Chittenden County with a population of 1,861, Huntington was granted by BENNING WENTWORTH as New Huntington in 1763 to three members of the Hunt family (from whom the town derives its name) and sixty-three others. The "new" in the name was dropped by the Vermont legislature in 1795. The town lies on the western slope of the main spine of the GREEN MOUNTAINS, rising to 4,083 feet at distinctively shaped CAMEL'S HUMP, the state's third-highest peak. The wooded, mountainous terrain has limited settlement to the town's western third, primarily along the north-flowing Huntington River, along which are the three settlements of Huntington village, Huntington Center, and Hanksville. JAMES JOHNS, an eccentric who penprinted a local newspaper for several decades of the nineteenth century, lived in Huntington.

Hyde Log Cabin State Historic Site

On the LAKE CHAMPLAIN island of Grand Isle, life on the northern frontier of early Vermont is exemplified in the restored 1783 Hyde Log Cabin, built by Connecticut native Jedediah Hyde, Jr. After the Revolution, Hyde traveled to northern Vermont to assist in surveying the area with a compass and theodolite he had acquired in the spoils of the BATTLE OF BENNINGTON. The cabin, constructed of 14- to 18-inch diameter cedar logs, consists of one 20-by-25-foot room with a massive fireplace at one end and an overhead loft. It is considered one of the oldest log cabins in the United States. Now restored, it is furnished with items collected by members of the Grand Isle Historical Society.

John Dumville

Hyde Park

Hyde Park, population 2,847, the SHIRE TOWN of Lamoille County, was granted by the Vermont legislature in 1781 to a group of Connecticut Revolutionary War veterans including Captain Jedediah Hyde. The western side of the town, bisected north to south by Route 100, is gently rolling and has a number of dairy farms, while the eastern, wooded side contains 554-acre Green River Reservoir, now a state park, the largest body of water in Vermont closed to motorized watercraft. The main settlement is Hyde Park village, on Route 15 just above the southern border with Morristown. In the late nineteenth century, the village was one of the major tanning centers in the country due to the activity of CARROLL S. "CALF SKIN" PAGE, a dealer in hides and skins who also served terms as Vermont governor and United States senator.

IBM:
International Business Machines

During the second half of the twentieth century, Vermont's greatest economic and population growth occurred in Chittenden County, and a major contributor to that growth was International Business Machines, which in 1957 located a facility in Essex Junction, a community of five thousand. Starting with a work force of two hundred that grew to five hundred before the end of the year and thirty-nine hundred by 1970, employees peaked at eight thousand in the 1980s, but were down to under seven thousand in 1996. With the manufacture of electronic components (the plant began operation manufacturing wire contact relays that stored one bit of information and progressed to semi-conductor microchips that store over one million bits of information) as its major activity, IBM saw its work force fluctuate during the 1990s with the vagaries of the international market, but it has remained since the mid-1960s the largest private enterprise in Vermont. Among the reasons that IBM offered for locating in the state was that it provided a site away from the rush and tangle of great cities and thus would be more attractive to employees. Ironically, the plant's very size inevitably contributed to slower-moving traffic and housing shortages. Other reasons presented were the schools in the area and that the UNIVERSITY OF VERMONT offered a cultural, educational, and recreational resource for employees. Presently UVM and the VERMONT STATE COLLEGES provide technical education programs to IBM employees and a significant number of their graduates are employed at the Essex Junction facility. One of the consequences of IBM's wage and benefit schedules was rising wages among companies competing for labor. When a tight labor supply seemed to hamper struggling small companies, critics charged that IBM was an uncaring outside giant. Though indeed a huge international conglomerate with headquarters outside the state, IBM has attempted to escape the stigma of being solely an economic engine by contributing through grants and other forms of support to a variety of the state's educational and cultural activities and providing incentives for its employees to participate in community affairs. In 1990, the company attempted to downsize through early retirements and in 1994 ordered its first layoffs. In 1999, changes in the company's retirement and pension plan led to calls for union organization.

Independence, Mount

An American fortification constructed in July 1776 to protect the narrow LAKE CHAMPLAIN channel and its companion fortification across the lake at FORT TICONDEROGA, Mount Independence was given its name following receipt of the Declaration of Independence by the Northern Army. Lieutenant Colonel JEDUTHAN BALDWIN was the chief construction engineer. Here the exhausted American Northern Army was stationed after withdrawing from its disastrous Canadian campaign of 1775 to 1776. Built on a rocky plateau and fortified with batteries, redoubts, blockhouses, breastworks, and a substantial picket fort, the post was a natural stronghold facing the British army approaching from the north. Men from New England, New York, New Jersey, and Pennsylvania were garrisoned here. Within its confines, many men suffered greatly from disease and food and clothing shortages and from the brutal winter of 1776 to 1777. The strength of this fort and Ticonderoga, coupled with the lateness of the season, effectively blocked a British advance in 1776, gaining a vital year for the struggling American cause. However, undermanned and ill-prepared for BURGOYNE's advance southward in 1777, the fort was evacuated in the early morning of July 6, 1777. A mixed garrison of British, German, and Loyalist troops garrisoned the fort for the next four months. After Burgoyne's surrender at Saratoga, the fortifications on Mount Independence were determined nonessential and demolished by the British upon their evacuation on November 8, 1777. Presently, the 300-acre site is co-owned by the state of Vermont and the Fort Ticonderoga Association and operated as a state historic site by the Vermont Division for Historic Preservation. *Donald Wickman*

Influenza Epidemic of 1918

Part of a pandemic that killed one hundred million people worldwide, "Spanish Flu" appeared in Vermont in August 1918. It spread quickly throughout the state, reaching its peak in early October. The State Board of Health recorded 35,954 influenza cases in a state population of 356,000, with 1,772 deaths through December 1918 (25.65 percent of all deaths), and 374 deaths in the next year, during a brief resurgence of the epidemic. On October 4, the Board of Health imposed a statewide ban on all public meetings, which lasted until November 3. The virus caused fever and nosebleed, and reduced lungs to a gelatinous mass that suffocated its victims. Pneumonia was a common complication. Spanish Flu was especially fatal for people aged twenty to thirty-five and many children lost one or both parents. A survey in 1919 identified 440 children orphaned, a fact that stimulated creation of the Vermont Children's Aid Society that year. With a shortage of doctors because of World War I recruitment, the Board of Health authorized sending seniors at the UNIVERSITY OF VERMONT medical school into towns to treat patients. In 1919, the state legislature reformed public health administration by eliminating town medical officers and creating ten sanitary districts, each supervised by a "reputable physician." That law was repealed in 1928.
Michael Sherman

Institute for Sustainable Communities

Founded in 1991 by former Vermont Governor MADELEINE M. KUNIN, the Institute for Sustainable Communities (ISC) was incorporated as an independent nonprofit organization to help communities in existing and emerging democracies solve environmental, economic, and social problems through training, advice, and grants that would help them build a better future for themselves and the world. Inspired by the enthusiasm for democratic reform and the role of the environmental movement in those reforms while she was monitoring the first democratic elections in Bulgaria, Kunin created the ISC to assist the countries of Central and Eastern Europe by "providing grassroots examples of how citizens can make the transition from dictatorship and environmental degradation to democracy and sustainable development." She assembled a group to help shape the institute, which sought funds to assist Central and Eastern European (CEE) nations in addressing environmental problems and to promote participatory decision making at the grassroots level. ISC's projects in CEE expanded to Russia and Ukraine. ISC grew from a budget of $400,000 and a staff of seven in 1992 to a budget of $10 million and a staff of eighty in 2001. In 1994 to 1996, ISC established three overseas offices to administer grant programs (Sofia, Bulgaria; Skopje, Macedonia; and Moscow, Russia) that significantly enhanced its presence and capabilities in the region. When Kunin left the ISC board of directors to become U.S. deputy secretary of education in 1993, the board created the Madeleine M. Kunin Special Opportunities Fund to honor Kunin's vision and enhance the organization's effectiveness and originality. With contributions from foundations, corporations, and individuals, funds are allocated upon board approval for projects in need, new project development, and vital institutional development. ISC conducted needs assessments in Japan and the United States in 1997 to explore the applicability of its community-based education and community action programs in countries outside of post-communist Europe. The U.S.-Japan Dialogue on Education for Sustainability was initiated in the fall of 1998 and the Burlington Legacy Project—an effort to develop a community-generated vision, a plan for achieving it, and to make the methods and lessons learned available to other communities—began in cooperation with the city of Burlington in 1999. In 1998, ISC broadened its geographic focus to include countries outside CEE and Eurasia. Over the last nine years, ISC has raised more than $30 million from private foundations, U.S. government programs, corporations, and individuals to support projects in fourteen countries.

Interstate Highways

Three interstate highways totaling 321 miles serve Vermont. Interstate 89 runs south and east from the Canadian border in the northwestern town of Highgate to White River Junction on the CONNECTICUT RIVER and then into New Hampshire; I-91 runs south from northeastern Derby Line on the Canadian border, intersects I-93 at St. Johnsbury and I-89 at White River Junction, and follows the course of the Connecticut River to Vernon at the Massachusetts line; and I-93 runs

Interstate highways I-89, I-91, and I-93 run for 319 miles through Vermont, mostly north to south. Vermont Department of Tourism and Marketing

east from St. Johnsbury to Lower Waterford on the Connecticut River and then into New Hampshire. At the end of World War II, when Congress authorized the National System of Interstate and Defense Highways, only 9 percent of Vermont's roads were paved; 51 percent were gravel and 40 percent were primitive or unimproved. Construction commenced in Vermont at the Massachusetts line in 1957 and finished with the final section of I-93 between St. Johnsbury and New Hampshire in 1982 at a cost of $1 million per mile. A small part of what was hailed as the largest public works project ever attempted on earth, Vermont's sections of the interstate highway system brought 80 percent of the state's population to within thirty miles of an interchange entrance ramp. *Vermont Life* predicted these new roads would "influence the development of the state no less significantly than the coming of the railroad." The new highways erased thousands of acres of wildlife habitat, uprooted farms, detoured traffic and commerce from downtowns, prompted development near interchanges, and eased the immigration of new people, industry, and ideas, as well as the continued emigration of people lured by the world beyond Vermont. Senator GEORGE AIKEN correctly remarked in 1961 at the opening of a section of the highway in Putney that the state was "on the verge of the greatest development Vermont has ever seen."

Ira

Ira, population 455, a town in Rutland County, has an obscure history. It is not clear whether the town was granted by the Vermont legislature in 1780 or 1781, or whether a charter was ever issued for it. What is clear, however, is that by 1790, when it had about three hundred inhabitants, Ira was being treated as a valid entity. It was named after IRA ALLEN, who seemed, however, to take little interest in it, in contrast to the two other towns that bear his name, Irasburg and Alburg. The land, part of the northern TACONIC MOUNTAINS, is rugged, hilly, and largely unsuitable for farming, rising to several peaks over two thousand feet. The town's peculiar shape, which resembles two flat-ended arrowheads pointing in opposite directions, is the result of boundary changes involving the neighboring towns of Castleton, Middletown Springs, and Clarendon. The only settlement is tiny Ira village, on Route 133, linking West Rutland on the north with Middletown Springs on the south.

Irasburg

Irasburg, population 1,077, a town in Orleans County, was granted by the Vermont legislature to IRA ALLEN and, among others, the family of ROGER ENOS. Allen later acquired all the other grantees' rights and, when he married Enos's daughter Jerusha in 1789, gave her the town as a wedding present. Jerusha moved to Irasburg after her husband's death in 1814, along with her mother and her son Ira, and died there in 1838. Primarily agricultural, Irasburg has only one substantial settlement, Irasburg village, on the northern Black River, which bisects the town from south to north. The so-called IRASBURG AFFAIR, in which events following an attack on the home of an African-American Baptist minister eventually led to a board of inquiry into the conduct of the state police, took place in Irasburg in 1968.

Irasburg Affair

The most highly charged event involving race relations in Vermont in recent times, the "Irasburg affair," as it came to be known, began on the night of July 19, 1968. Shots were fired into the home of the Reverend David Lee Johnson, an African-American Baptist minister, who only three weeks before had moved into a house in Irasburg with his wife and children. Slow to investigate, state police eventually arrested twenty-one-year-old Larry Conley, a Glover resident on leave from the army, for the crime and charged him with "breach of the peace." Shortly afterward, however, Johnson and a white woman who had been staying in his house were arrested on charges of adultery, an offense seldom charged and usually associated with divorce suits. Critics, a number of them prominent Vermont clergy, maintained that local prejudice, plus Johnson's statement that one of the investigating officers displayed racist attitudes, was responsible for the arrest. The woman pleaded no contest, was fined $125 and given a suspended prison sentence of six months to a year with probation, and left the state. Conley pleaded no contest also, was fined $500, and given a six- to eighteen-month suspended sentence with probation. Further harassment of the Johnsons continued, however, and police were forced to put a twenty-four-hour guard on their home. In September, the case against the minister was dropped when the main prosecution witness—the woman—refused to return to Vermont to testify. A board of inquiry appointed by Governor PHILIP HOFF and chaired by former governor ERNEST GIBSON, JR., eventually concluded that the state police had acted inappropriately, dragging their feet in solving the shooting but moving with speed to investigate the adultery charge. Public Safety Commissioner E. A. Alexander rebutted the panel's conclusions and refused to discipline any of his troopers. In March 1969, Governor DEANE DAVIS, Hoff's successor, declared the case closed. Johnson and his family, meanwhile, had moved to California. Irasburg resident HOWARD FRANK MOSHER's novel *Stranger in the Kingdom* is a fictionalized version of the events in Irasburg.

Island Pond

See BRIGHTON.

Island Pond Raid

See NORTHEAST KINGDOM COMMUNITY CHURCH.

Isle La Motte

Isle La Motte, population 488, a town in Grand Isle County, was granted by the Vermont legislature in 1779 to BENJAMIN WAIT and ninety-five others. The name derives from PIERRE DE SAINT PAUL, SIEUR DE LA MOTTE, who in 1666 built FORT SAINTE-ANNE, Vermont's first European settlement, on the island's northwestern shore. (From 1802 to 1830, however, the town was officially named Vineyard, perhaps out of the English and Scottish inhabitants' dislike of the French name.) Five and one-half miles long by one and one-half miles wide, the island, whose western shore faces New York State, has a single connection to the mainland, a bridge to the town of Alburg built in 1881. A popular pilgrimage site is STE. ANNE'S SHRINE, built near the site of the old fort and run by the Edmundite fathers; it is the site of daily summertime masses and features an outdoor pavilion, a small indoor chapel, and a path linking the Stations of the Cross on the site of the fort. Nearby is a heroic statue of SAMUEL DE CHAMPLAIN (originally displayed at Expo 67 in Montreal) commemorating his visit to the island in July 1609. Isle La Motte is also noted for the Chazy CORAL REEFS, four-hundred-million-year-old fossils, reputedly the oldest in the world, and for the now-unused Fisk quarry, which once supplied a distinctive MARBLE that can be seen in New York City's Radio City Music Hall and other buildings. The quarry is now part of the Fisk Quarry Preserve and owned by the Isle La Motte Reef Preservation Trust. Vice-President Theodore Roosevelt was staying in the home of NELSON FISK, proprietor of the quarry, in 1901 when he learned that President William McKinley had been shot in Buffalo.

Isle La Motte and *The Stars and Stripes Forever*

A long tradition on Isle La Motte recounts that the great bandmaster and composer John Philip Sousa (1854–1932) wrote his most famous march, *The Stars and Stripes Forever*, in 1897 at "Woody Nook," the summer home of Everett Reynolds on the east shore of the island. But Sousa did not visit Isle La Motte in 1897. Moreover, according to the autograph manuscript in the Library of Congress dated "Christmas '96" in Sousa's own hand, the music was actually composed a year earlier than the island tradition would have it. Sousa arrived in New York City from London on December 23, 1896, having cut short a vacation in Europe to attend the funeral of his manager, David Blakeley, whom Reynolds would succeed. Sousa writes in his autobiography and elsewhere that, while crossing the Atlantic, memories of the Marine Band, of Washington, and thoughts about the prominence of America and its flag stirred a number of patriotic melodies within him. The result, of course, was his most successful and profitable march. Sousa and his family later visited the Reynolds family in Isle La Motte in mid-June, 1898.

James Barickman

J

Jackman, Alonzo (1809–1879)

A distinguished professor of science and mathematics and drill master at NORWICH UNIVERSITY during the middle years of the nineteenth century, Alonzo Jackman of Thetford was forced to leave his home after the death of his father and at age twelve began to shift for himself first as a farm laborer and then as a quarryman and mariner. His great aptitude for mathematics and interest in learning led him to study first at Thetford Academy, next at Franklin Academy in Norwich, and finally at Norwich University, where he received a baccalaureate degree in 1836. For the next four decades, except for a three-year leave to prospect for gold in California, Jackman taught at Norwich University. He was principally a mathematician, but he also taught natural philosophy, civil engineering, and military science. Jackman's published writings and personal papers reveal an inquiring and imaginative mind interested in matters ranging from mathematics and geology to detailed considerations on telescope construction and the laying of a sub-oceanic telegraph cable. His journal of a tour of Canada, including military installations in Montreal and Quebec during the PATRIOTS uprising in 1837, reveals a sharp tactical sense and an advanced understanding of the value of observation balloons for directing artillery fire. Much interested in militia affairs, Jackman rose to the rank of brigadier general in the Vermont militia. During the Civil War, Jackman organized and drilled Vermont recruits with the assistance of Norwich University cadets. The superior performance of Vermont regiments was in no small part due to the training they received under Jackman's direction.

Gary T. Lord

Jackson, Horatio Nelson (1872–1955)

A Burlington physician and entrepreneur, H. Nelson Jackson was the first person to drive an automobile across the United States. Born in Toronto of American parents and raised in Kingston, Ontario, Jackson came to Burlington to attend the UNI-VERSITY OF VERMONT Medical College. Graduating in 1893, he interned at Mary Fletcher Hospital in Burlington and served a year on the staff of the BRATTLEBORO RETREAT. In 1899, he married Bertha Richardson Wells, daughter of the Civil War general WILLIAM WELLS. Jackson wrote a book commemorating General Wells and the First Vermont Cavalry for the dedication of Wells's statue at Gettysburg in 1913. Jackson's adventurous spirit soon led him out of medicine into other pursuits. He made the first-ever cross-country motor journey in 1903, a sixty-four-day trip launched on a $50 wager, accompanied by his mechanic Sewall K. Crocker and a bulldog named Bud. Following the "northern route" from New York City to San Francisco, Jackson crossed unbridged creeks and rivers with the help of a winch and block-and-tackle. He later gave his Winton touring car, *The Vermont*, to the Smithsonian. Jackson's other enterprises included prospecting in Mexico and managing a silver mine there for six years, and serving in France during World War I as a medical officer. In 1936, he lost the Republican gubernatorial primary election to GEORGE AIKEN. He was publisher of the BURLINGTON DAILY NEWS (1921–1939) and owned WCAX-AM radio (1931–1939). Many of his activities were military. He founded the Vermont Chapter of the American Legion and served as its commander, was national vice-commander (1921–1922), organized and was colonel of the Vermont Officers Reserve Corps, and served as a trustee of NORWICH UNIVERSITY. He was president of the board of the Burlington Trust Co. (1925–1952) when it merged with the Howard Bank. His brother, S. Hollister Jackson, was lieutenant governor during the FLOOD OF 1927 and drowned while surveying flood damage in his hometown of Barre.

David Blow and Sarah L. Dopp

Jackson, Shirley (1919–1965)

A writer with an uncommon talent for the bizarre, Shirley Jackson was born in San Francisco and moved with her family to New York state when she was fourteen. After graduation from Syracuse University in 1940, she married fellow student Stanley Edgar Hyman, later a noted literary critic, and in 1945 moved to North Bennington when Hyman became a faculty member at BENNINGTON COLLEGE. Here, apart from brief absences, she lived for the rest of her life. Jackson's fame as a writer was established by the short story "The Lottery," published in *The New Yorker* of June 28, 1948. It tells, in dispassionate prose, of the annual gathering of the inhabitants of a small town for the selection and stoning to death of one of their number, a scapegoat ritual carried out with the neighborliness and casual good humor of a potluck supper. While the locale of the story is not identified, its macabre inversion of the idealized picture of small town life that is part of the Vermont image cannot be overlooked. Among other works by Jackson that may have a Vermont influence are her novels *Hangsaman* (1951), which takes place in an exclusive women's college; and *The Haunting of Hill House* (1959), whose locale is an isolated manor house somewhere in New England; and *We Have Always Lived in the Castle* (1962), about two sisters victimized by their small New England village. She also wrote a series of humorous sketches of domestic life based upon her own family's experiences in Vermont that were published in various women's magazines and collected in *Life Among the Savages* (1953) and *Raising Demons* (1957).

Jamaica

Jamaica, population 946, a town in Windham County, was granted by the Vermont legislature in 1780 to THOMAS CHITTENDEN and a number of others. The name, which also occurs in a section of Boston and in New York City's borough of Queens, supposedly derives from the Natick word for beaver place. The town, much of which lies in the GREEN MOUNTAIN NATIONAL FOREST, has only a few settlements, the most important of which is Jamaica village, near the WEST RIVER where it curves around 1,771-foot Ball Mountain. To some extent the town is in the economic orbit of the Stratton Mountain ski area in the neighboring towns of Stratton and Winhall. A fierce battle between a group of French-allied ABENAKI and an English scouting party on its way to FORT DUMMER near Brattleboro took place in Jamaica in 1748, resulting in fatalities on both sides.

Janes, Henry (1832–1915)

A physician and Civil War surgeon, Henry Janes was the son of a Waterbury lawyer and member of Congress and the grandson, on his mother's side, of the second settler of Waterbury, Governor Ezra Butler. After attending school in Morrisville and St. Johnsbury, Janes studied medicine with a Waterbury doctor and attended medical lectures at the VERMONT MEDICAL COLLEGE in Woodstock before graduating from the College of Physicians and Surgeons in New York City in 1855. After briefly working at Bellevue Hospital and in Chelsea, Massachusetts, he set up practice in Waterbury. In 1861, Janes joined the Third Vermont Regiment as surgeon, two years later becoming surgeon of the U.S. Army and supervising Civil War hospitals in Frederick, Maryland; Gettysburg (where he was on the podium for the Gettysburg Address); Philadelphia; and Sloan Army Hospital in Montpelier 1864 to 1865 (see also CIVIL WAR HOSPITALS). Resuming his Waterbury practice in 1867, Janes was a consulting surgeon to Vermont hospitals, as well as being active in local and state affairs. His wife, Frances (Hall) Janes, died in 1909 and Dr. Janes in 1915, bequeathing the enlarged family homestead on North Main Street to the Waterbury public library, which today shares the building with the Waterbury Historical Society. *Reidun Nuquist*

Jarvis, DeForest Clinton (1881–1966)

Best known for his popular book *Folk Medicine: A Vermont Doctor's Guide to Good Health* (1958), Dr. D. C. Jarvis graduated from the UNIVERSITY OF VERMONT's Medical College and practiced medicine from his Main Street office in Barre for nearly sixty-five years. He was among the first to recognize the threat of granite dust to Barre's granite workers and as early as 1915 started testing for tuberculosis. He also became interested in the effect of diet on the incidence of respiratory disease in the granite industry and collected recipes and cures from his patients and neighbors, which became the basis for his book. In *Folk Medicine*, Dr. Jarvis stressed the healing properties of apple cider vinegar and honey. Vinegar, he explained, "by basically maintaining the body reaction acid instead of alkaline," could relieve a host of health problems from shingles and burns to varicose veins. The benefits of honey included helping to improve athletic performace, controlling muscle cramps, and relieving hangovers. His book was on the best-seller list for one hundred weeks and was the top best-selling book of 1960. Translated into twelve languages and still in demand, Jarvis's *Folk Medicine* is considered a forerunner to the alternative medicine movement. He was also deeply interested in music and sport and organized the Barre Junior Symphony Orchestra in 1925, providing free instruments and instruction, and sponsored several sports teams, including a basketball team, the "Crescents," in the 1920s, that he outfitted and transported to games. In his eighties, he was the trainer for Barre's Spaulding High School football team. Trained on his recipe of grape juice and honey, the team won the state championship in 1961 and contended for the championship in 1964. Barre's police regularly stopped traffic on Main Steet in the 1960s to usher Dr. Jarvis through a street crossing with the announcement that here comes "Barre's number one citizen." *Ann Lyons Fry*

Jarvis, William (1770–1859)

Famed for introducing merino sheep into the United States, William Jarvis was born in Boston and educated in Boston, Bordentown, New Jersey, and Philadelphia schools. Starting in business as a clerk for a mercantile firm, he made and lost a sizable fortune. By 1797, he had recovered sufficiently to own a one-third interest in a brig he commanded and in which capacity he proved a bold and astute trader. His experiences familiarized him with the commercial complexities arising from the war between France and Great Britain and led to his appointment as consul and chargé d'affaires in Lisbon, Portugal. In 1806, after Napoleon conquered Spain and moved on to Portugal, Jarvis purchased 3,500 merino sheep and, although Spain had prohibited their export for centuries, gained a license to export them to the United States. In 1810, he bought a farm in Weathersfield and devoted himself to the care and breeding of merino sheep for the rest of his life. Well before his death, merino sheep breeding became the principal Vermont agricultural activity.

Jay

Jay, population 426, a town in Orleans County, was granted by the Vermont legislature in 1792 to THOMAS CHITTENDEN (the southern section) and John Jay (the northern section). Jay had been instrumental in settling Vermont's land dispute with New York, thus ensuring its entry into the Union. (A previous 1780 grant for the town to sixty officers of a Connecticut line regiment had been invalidated for nonpayment of fees.) The town, which borders on Quebec, has very little land suitable for settlement, most of it being taken up by the northernmost section of the GREEN MOUNTAINS, here culminating in 3,861-foot Jay Peak, which the town shares with Montgomery and Westfield to its south. The Jay Peak ski area (66 trails, 7 lifts, and a vertical drop of 2,153 feet) is popular not only with Americans but with Canadians, the city of Montreal being only seventy miles away.

Jeezum Crow!

A colloquial exclamation frequently heard in Vermont and also in northern New Hampshire and Maine, "Jeezum crow" is a benign alternative to a common profanity. It expresses frustration or emphasis, as in "What, a bunch of hippies are starting a commune in the woods? Jeezum crow, mother, get me my shotgun!"

Jeffords, James (b. 1934)

United States Senator since 1989, James Jeffords is a native of Rutland. His father, Olin M. Jeffords, was chief justice of the Vermont Supreme Court. Jeffords attended Rutland public schools and graduated from Yale University in 1956 and Harvard Law School in 1962. He served with the U.S. Navy (1956–1959), retiring from the Naval Reserve as a captain in 1990. Jeffords served a term (1967–1968) as Rutland County senator and two terms (1969–1973) as Vermont attorney general. In 1972, he lost a bid for the Republican gubernatorial nomination and was then rebuffed in his efforts to secure the party state chairmanship. Intraparty conflicts, exacerbated by Jeffords' candidacies, contributed significantly to the upset victory of Democrat THOMAS SALMON that November. In 1974, after Representative RICHARD MALLARY declared for the U.S. Senate, Jeffords captured the nomination for the House and easily won election despite Democratic successes in most other state contests. In seven congressional terms, Jeffords honed his reputation as a moderate Republican. Ranking member of the House Education and Labor Committee, he also served on the House Agriculture Committee and co-founded the Congressional Arts Caucus. When ROBERT STAFFORD retired in 1988, Jeffords was elected to the Senate. In 2001, with Republicans holding a slim Senate majority, Jeffords served as chairman of the Senate Health Education, Labor and Pensions Committee and on the Senate Finance Committee and Veterans Affairs Committee. A firm supporter of the Northeast Dairy Compact for the increased income it brought to Vermont's dairy farmers, Jeffords urged his Senate colleagues from other major dairy regions to adopt the Northeast Compact model for their state's dairy industries. Often diverging from his party's leadership on such major issues as the size of President George W. Bush's proposed tax cut in 2001, Jeffords demonstrated an ability to harmonize with fellow Republican senators in a high-profile vocal quartet. In May, however, he announced he would leave the Republican party to become an independent. His defection threw control of the Senate to the Democrats, who awarded him chairmanship of the Environment and Public Works Committee. His Senate seat had been held longer by a Republican than any other Senate seat in the nation. A humorous note to Jeffords's "declaration of independence" was sounded when the Magic Hat Brewing Company commemorated the act by producing a special edition of Jeezum Jim ale in a run of fourteen thousand bottles. Adorned with a silver male silhouette and the legend "A celebration of conviction, courage, and the difference one man can make," the 22-ounce bottles sold for $2.50 each. On July 5 at the Magic Hat brewery in South Burlington, Senator Jeffords signed copies for some two hundred people, remarking "I'm not sure Jeezum Jim will threaten Budweiser's market, but I hear they're nervous."

Jenison, Silas H. (1791–1849)

The first native-born Vermonter to serve as governor, Silas H. Jennison of Shoreham was a self-taught surveyor. Jenison was elected lieutenant governor in 1835, but when no gubernatorial candidate received a majority of the popular vote or the legislative vote, he served as governor. He was elected governor, as a Whig, in 1836. During the PATRIOTS uprising in Canada, Jenison ordered Vermonters to comply with President Van Buren's neutrality edict. Jenison was re-elected in 1837 and for the following three years, but declined to run in 1841.

Jericho

Jericho, population 5,015, a town in Chittenden County, was granted by BENNING WENTWORTH in 1763 to THOMAS CHITTENDEN and several others and named for the biblical city of Jericho. The town rises from the lowlands of the WINOOSKI RIVER in its southwestern section to a series of hills one to two thousand feet high in the east, outriders of the GREEN MOUNTAINS. A substantial portion of the eastern part of town is taken up by the government-owned Ethan Allen Firing Range, which extends into neighboring Underhill and Bolton. The town's two major settlements, Jericho village and Underhill Flats (half of which is in the town of Underhill to the north), lie along the Brown's River in the northwestern part of town, while the picturesque upland village of Jericho Center is at an elevation of 800 feet three miles away. Jericho was the home of WILLIAM "SNOWFLAKE" BENTLEY, famous for his glass-plate microphotographs of snowflakes, the largest collection of its kind in the world.

Jogbra

In the 1970s, Burlington residents Hinda Miller and Linda Lindahl became dissatisfied with the inadequate support provided by conventional brassieres when they jogged for exercise. Joined by Polly Smith, Miller and Lindahl sought to design a bra that avoided the persistent problems of chafing and bouncing. Prompted by Lindahl's husband's joking reference to a jockstrap as a jock bra, the three women designed a runner's bra that employed a wide band of cotton, Lycra, and polyester with straps crossed across the back for support. Seams were turned outward and Lycra and salt-resistant swimwear elastic prevented chafing. Hooks were excluded

Governor Silas Jenison. Special Collections, Bailey/Howe Library, University of Vermont

from the final product, which the three women marketed for several years before selling their design to the sportswear company Champion, where it was named Jogbra. The original design is part of the collections of the Smithsonian Institution and the Metropolitan Museum of Art in New York.

Johns, James (1797–1874)

A prolific pen-printer, amateur publisher, and local antiquarian, James Johns was born in Huntington. He received only a rudimentary education in the local schools and for most of his life eked out a meager living as a farmer, but in his early teens he began to issue small quill-and-ink productions designed to resemble printed or published works. Johns maintained his interest in pen-printing from the 1810s to the end of his life, writing out stories, poems, essays, local history and folklore, acrostics, and political commentary in a small, precise lettering that closely resembled a printed typeface. *The Vermont Autograph and Remarker*, a small "newspaper" that Johns began in the 1830s and continued into the 1870s, was his best-known manuscript work, but he also pen-printed broadsides, pamphlets, and small books to send to a circle of Vermont collectors, historians, and writers who occasionally gave him books or nominal sums of money in appreciation of his efforts. Johns also put a few of his writings into published form. In 1828, he had a Burlington printer issue *The Green-Mountain Muse*, a thin volume of poetry. In 1857, he purchased a portable printing press, which he used for the next decade to turn out occasional broadsides, small pamphlets, and other amateurish publications on local subjects. His strong interest in Huntington's early history brought him to the attention of ABBY M. HEMENWAY in the 1860s, and Johns became the author of the Huntington section of her *Vermont Historical Gazetteer*. In 1868, he moved to nearby Starksboro, where he died six years later.

J. Kevin Graffagnino

Johnson

Johnson, population 3,274, a town in Lamoille County, was granted by the Vermont legislature in 1782 to William Samuel Johnson of Stratford, Connecticut, after whom the town was named, and others. The town lies directly on the spine of the GREEN MOUNTAINS where they are cut from east to west by the LAMOILLE

RIVER, giving Johnson great variations in altitude. The valley of the Lamoille is approximately 500 feet above sea level, while Butternut Mountain on the town's northern border is 2,000 feet higher and the slopes of Sterling Mountain on the southern border are more than 2,500 feet higher. Settlement is necessarily concentrated in the valley, the site of the substantial village of Johnson. On a hill above the village is the campus of JOHNSON STATE COLLEGE, one of the five units of the state college system. The college began in 1836 as the Lamoille County Grammar School and later became a State Normal School and then a State Teachers College for the training of teachers. The town's economic base includes agriculture, the production of woolen goods at Johnson Woolen Mills, and the service industry associated with the college. JULIAN SCOTT, the artist whose giant painting of the BATTLE OF CEDAR CREEK hangs in the VERMONT STATE HOUSE in Montpelier, was born in Johnson.

Johnson, Edwin Ferry (1803–1872)

Born in Essex, Edwin Johnson apprenticed as a surveyor with his father before entering the American Literary, Scientific and Military Academy (now NORWICH UNIVERSITY). After graduating in 1825, Johnson served the institution in a succession of teaching positions ranging from mathematics and natural history to engineering. In 1829, he left the academy at Norwich and soon embarked on a long and very successful career as a civil engineer. Early in his career, Johnson was in charge of land surveys for the Erie Canal and the Hudson-Champlain Canal. Subsequently he was involved as the chief engineer or principal assistant for the location of more than a dozen RAILROADS, including the Northern Pacific. Johnson was a prolific writer who published treatises on mathematics and surveying, but his writings dealing with railroad construction were most important. An 1829 pamphlet proposing the construction of a railroad to the Mississippi River attracted considerable attention. Johnson's *Railroad to the Pacific* (1853) was one of the first publications offering a detailed proposal for a transcontinental rail line to the Pacific Ocean.

Gary T. Lord

Johnson, John (1771–1842)

A surveyor and builder of some of Vermont's largest early buildings, John John-son was born in Canterbury, New Hampshire. He moved to Essex in 1790 where he designed and built dams, mills, bridges, and public buildings throughout northwestern Vermont. Among his notable early Vermont structures were the first UNIVERSITY OF VERMONT building, the Grasse Mount mansion in Burlington, the first Chittenden County courthouse, and Burlington's White Street Congregational church. In 1809, Johnson moved to Burlington, where his large home was a training site for many talented young civil engineers and surveyors. Named surveyor general of Vermont in 1813, Johnson led the Anglo-American team that surveyed the eastern end of the U.S.-Canada border in 1817 to 1818. In the 1820s and 1830s, he built UVM's Old Mill and Pomeroy Hall, directed the survey for a proposed canal to connect the CONNECTICUT and WINOOSKI RIVERS, helped design the Burlington breakwater, assisted in the development of the iron industries of Keeseville, New York, and ranged as far as North Carolina to oversee various construction projects. A large collection of his maps and papers at the University of Vermont library documents his career in considerable detail.

J. Kevin Graffagnino

Johnson, Joseph B. (1893–1986)

A two-term governor of Vermont, Joseph Blaine Johnson was born in Helsingborg, Sweden, and came to Springfield in 1902 when his family settled there. Johnson was a mechanical engineer (UNIVERSITY OF VERMONT class of 1915) who rose from draftsman to general manager of Bryant Chucking Gear Company, retiring in 1949. A Republican, he served in the Vermont House of Representatives (1945–1946) and the Senate (1947–1949). He served two terms as lieutenant governor of Vermont (1951–1955) and two terms as a Republican governor (1955–1959). A former UVM trustee, Johnson prompted legislation to increase the state appropriation to the University, shepherded into law a $26 million bond issue to assure Vermont's participation in the federal INTERSTATE HIGHWAY system, and oversaw negotiations with the New York Power Authority for St. Lawrence hydropower, but fought back efforts in the legislature to establish a Vermont Power Authority to negotiate and distribute the power. Instead, he supported the creation of the private Velco distribution system. Johnson retired from public life after his second term as gover-nor, though he continued as a director of Lovejoy Tool Company and an honorary director and president of the First National Bank in Springfield.

Johnson, Oliver (1809–1889)

After finishing his education at Peacham Academy, Oliver Johnson left his father's farm in that town in 1825 to become a newspaperman and anti-slavery activist. While working as editor of the *Christian Soldier* in Boston, he heard WILLIAM LLOYD GARRISON speak, was converted to the cause of immediate emancipation, and became one of the founders of the New England Anti-Slavery Society in 1831. He served throughout the 1830s as a lecturing agent of both the New England (later the Massachusetts) and American Anti-Slavery Societies and was the first agent to lecture in Vermont. Although not well known today as a national abolitionist figure, Johnson dedicated his adult life to the cause and was part of Garrison's inner circle. He was a trusted confidant who could be counted on to handle whatever task needed to be done. He traveled where he was needed as a lecturer and served at various times as editor of *The Liberator*, *The Pennsylvania Freeman*, and *The National Anti-Slavery Standard*. His history of the abolitionist movement, *William Lloyd Garrison and His Times* (1880) extolled the Garrisonian position and held the Protestant churches responsible for the long delay in ending slavery.

Jane Williamson

Johnson, Susannah Willard (b. 1729)

Captured by ABENAKI at Charlestown, New Hampshire, on August 30, 1754, in the earliest days of the Seven Years' War along with six other settlers, Susannah Johnson was pregnant and gave birth en route to Quebec near the settlement of Reading in today's Vermont. The child, Elizabeth Captive Johnson, eventually freed with her mother, later married George Kimball of Woodstock.

Johnson, Thomas (1742–1849)

An early settler of Newbury, Thomas Johnson was an innkeeper, merchant, and farmer. After surveying the BAYLEY-HAZEN ROAD to Hazen's Notch, he blazed a trail from there to Saint Johns, Quebec, in July 1776. He was one of the wealthier men in northeastern Vermont and a militia colonel when he was taken prisoner by a British scouting party at Hanover, New

Hampshire, in March 1781. Taken to Quebec, he helped the British in the unsuccessful plot to capture JACOB BAYLEY. After the Revolution, Johnson represented Newbury in the Vermont General Assembly for eight terms.

Johnson State College

In 1828, John Chesamore, a Johnson cobbler, gave his shoe shop to the town of Johnson for a much-needed elementary and secondary school that served sixteen pupils. Dr. Carpenter, a Chelsea preacher, became the schoolmaster when the school was chartered in 1832 as Johnson Academy. In 1836, five communities incorporated as the Lamoille County Grammar School Association to support the school. In 1866, the state designated Johnson Academy as one of three new normal schools, Vermont's first public institutions specifically for teacher training. The Johnson Normal School offered one-, two-, and three-year teacher training programs until, in 1947, the state approved a four-year teacher training program, and the school became Johnson Teachers College. The college became Johnson State College in 1962 when the VERMONT STATE COLLEGES were established by the legislature. This new name signaled a change in the college's mission from a single-purpose, teacher-training college to a multi-purpose, liberal arts college. Since that time, the college's curriculum in the liberal arts and sciences, its enrollment, and its facilities have expanded dramatically to meet this new mission. The most recent addition is the Library and Learning Center, a 39,000-square-foot library, classroom, and faculty office facility that opened in 1996. Johnson State's twelve buildings and campus spread over 330 hilltop acres to serve nearly seventeen hundred students from Vermont and around the country. The College offers bachelors degrees in the arts, humanities, sciences, environmental studies, business and hotel and hospitality management, as well as bachelors and masters degrees in elementary and secondary education.

Jones, George (1811–1891)

Cofounder with HENRY RAYMOND of the New York Times, George Jones was born in Poultney and taken by his Welsh immigrant parents to Ohio soon afterward. Both parents died when George was very young, and he returned to Poultney. Here he attended school and held jobs at a country store and at the local weekly newspaper, the Northern Spectator, where he met HORACE GREELEY, who also worked there. After the newspaper failed in 1831, Jones entered business in Troy, New York, where he remained until 1841 when he moved to New York City to join Greeley's Tribune in the business department. In 1851, he and Henry Raymond established the New York Daily Times with Raymond as editor and Jones as business manager. After Raymond's sudden death in 1869, Jones assumed editorial responsibilities and his tenure is most distinguished for having successfully conducted the exposé of the Tweed ring, begun by Raymond. Jones's Vermont roots have been prominently celebrated. The Two Editors Inn, a guest house at GREEN MOUNTAIN COLLEGE, is named for Jones and Greeley, and on the seventy-fifth anniversary of the New York Times its editors came to Poultney to dedicate a memorial in front of the house where Jones was born.

Jones, Reuben (1747–1833)

One of the leading figures in Vermont's struggle to declare and maintain its independence between 1775 and 1781, Dr. Reuben Jones was an ardent Whig and resident of Rockingham who appeared at the March 1775 anti-court riot that turned into the WESTMINSTER MASSACRE. He galloped to Dummerston to rouse reinforcements to support the rioters. Jones's Relation of the Proceedings of the People of the COUNTY OF CUMBERLAND and Province of New York provides the best account of the events in Westminster. Jones, along with several others, became the first residents of the eastern side of Vermont to attend the series of conventions beginning in 1775 that culminated in Vermont's independence in 1777. Jones played an active role in the new legislature as a representative from Rockingham (1778–1780) and Chester (1781), and was assistant clerk in 1778. He served on numerous committees dealing with petitions for land grants, the status of Tories, the negotiations concerning the first EAST UNION (1778), and in 1780 helped devise an expression of gratitude to ETHAN ALLEN for his service at the time of his resignation of his commission as brigadier general. Jones sat with the auditors who reviewed IRA ALLEN's performance as treasurer, and took a prominent role in drafting the rules to govern the workings of the General Assembly, the legislation against forcing Vermonters

to contribute to churches, and the oversight of the militia. His attempts to impeach MATTHEW LYON in 1779 and a 1781 suit for trespass against two neighbors in Rockingham suggest a quarrelsome nature. In 1779, the legislature awarded him and co-petitioners land in Concord. Suffering financial reverses, he eventually dropped out of public life, shuttling between Vermont and New Hampshire to escape going to jail for debt. Few traces remain of the last years of his life.

H. Nicholas Muller III

Joyce, Robert F. (1896–1990)

The sixth Roman Catholic Bishop of the Diocese of Burlington, Robert F. Joyce graduated from the UNIVERSITY OF VERMONT (1917), Montreal's Seminary of Philosophy (1919), and Grand Theological Seminary (1923), and was ordained a priest on May 26, 1923. He served several parishes in Vermont and was principal of Burlington's Cathedral High School from 1927 to 1932. During World War II, he served as an army chaplain. From 1946 to 1953, he was pastor of St. Peter's in Rutland, where he helped settle the Rutland Railroad strike of 1953. Named auxiliary bishop of Burlington in 1954, Joyce was installed as the sixth bishop of Burlington in 1957. Bishop Joyce participated in the Second Vatican Council (1962 to 1965) and, following the council's recommendation to develop collegiality in diocesan governance, established an Ecumenical Commission (1964), a Pastoral Council (1966), and Priests' and Sisters' Senates (1967). Responding to the Vatican Council's recommendation on interfaith cooperation, Joyce brought the Diocese of Burlington into the previously Protestant Vermont Ecumenical Council in 1970. A loyal alumnus of UVM, "Pat" Joyce in 1929 was chosen permanent president of his alumni class of 1917 and served several terms on the alumni council. He was the first Roman Catholic priest to serve on the board of trustees of both CHAMPLAIN COLLEGE and UVM, which named him alumnus of the year in 1960. While on the board of UVM in 1954, Bishop Joyce defended Professor ALEX NOVIKOFF against accusations of communist activity, casting the lone vote against Novikoff's dismissal in the board's final vote to remove him from the faculty. During Bishop Joyce's administration of the Diocese of Burlington, demographic and cultural changes led to parochial school enrollments declining by two-thirds, the communities of teaching sisters shrinking by one-half through attrition and the lack of new recruits, and insufficient funds being raised to support lay faculties. Half of the parochial elementary and high schools in the state closed permanently. In 1967, as the crisis in parochial education worsened, Bishop Joyce asked Governor DEANE C. DAVIS for state aid to support parochial schools. Efforts to supply the aid failed in the legislature. Bishop Joyce retired in 1971 when he reached age seventy-five. In 1979, the University of Vermont announced the establishement of the Bishop Robert F. Joyce Distinguished Professorship in Gerontology, which supports a medical faculty member conducting classes in gerontology and provides regular public lectures on the problems of the aging.

David Blow

K

Kake Walk

Kake Walk at the UNIVERSITY OF VERMONT began as an impromptu evening of male student follies on December 19, 1893, and developed, by 1908, into a student-organized weekend of festivities that endured for six more decades. "The biggest event of the students' year," according to the 1940 issue of *Ariel*, the UVM yearbook, Kake Walk consisted of a Grand Peerade of costumes and floats; entertainment stunts performed by fraternity groups and others; and, after 1904, Walkin' Fo' De Kake, or "kakewalking," performed to a rag two-step, *Cotton Babes*, by Percy Wenrich. The ROTC band performed for many years at Kake Walk. Winners in the categories of costumes, stunts, and kakewalking were judged by distinguished UVM alumni and officials and received silver cups. Weekend activities included a masquerade ball, concerts, winter sports competition, an ice-sculpture contest, alumni gatherings, and the election of a king and queen of Kake Walk. The last years of Kake Walk brought jazz stars Duke Ellington, Dizzy Gillespie, Coleman Hawkins, and Cannonball Adderley to campus for Pops night. In its early years, the high-stepping kakewalk dance was performed to the music of *Cotton Babes* by a pair of dancers, usually fraternity brothers (one dressed as a woman), wearing blackface makeup, gaudy outfits, and kinky wigs. By 1950, a formula for kakewalking had developed: the two walkers, both dressed as men, wore identical satin costumes, and the dance became a set of athletic moves that required weeks of training. Vestiges of minstrel show performances cropped up occasionally in the entertainment stunts, as did other ethnic and racial stereotyping, though the stunts usually parodied current events or campus life. In 1923, however, KU KLUX KLAN activity in Vermont seems to have inspired the prize-winning stunt in the "Koon Kut-Ups," entitled "Koon Klux Klan," a skit about lynching in which the persecuted prevail with good humor. In the following decades, yearbook photos suggest, such blatantly offensive stunts were rare, and titles playing on the Ku Klux Klan name disappeared. Yet kakewalking remained a blackface affair until 1963, when the Intrafraternity Council voted to abolish blackface and kinky wigs. Substitute colors were permitted, including light and dark green, gold, and even purple, a compromise that satisfied few. Complaints about kakewalking, which emerged as early as 1950, raised the more fundamental issue of its caricature of African-American behavior. In 1969, black students and faculty, notably Professor Lawrence McCrorey, and sympathizers spoke out against the inherent racism of kakewalking. With civil rights, Vietnam, political assassinations, and the counterculture heating up campus debate, Kake Walk looked not only racist but increasingly frivolous and anachronistic. Although most students and administrators accepted Kake Walk's demise during the 1969 to 1970 academic year, many alumni protested by withholding donations. Attempts to revive Kake Walk off-campus occurred for several years, but students eventually lost interest in it.

James Barickman

Karelia-Vermont Sister States

A program of citizen exchanges between Vermont and the Karelian Republic in the Russian Federation, the sister-states relationship between Vermont and Karelia was initiated by Governor MADELEINE KUNIN in 1988 with the support of the Greeley Foundation. Governor Kunin led a delegation to Karelia that year, and a Karelian delegation headed by then-president Kuzma Filatov came to Vermont in 1989. To carry on the program, Governor Kunin established the Vermont-Karelia Sister State Advisory Committee, which continues to operate by gubernatorial appointment. A counterpart committee was formalized in the Karelian capital of Petrozavodsk in 2000. Exchanges conducted or supported by the program, with federal or private funding, have ranged from schools and colleges to government, law, medical, and business groups. The program is one of only two American sister-state relationships (as distinguished from sister cities) with regions of the former Soviet Union.

Robert V. Daniels

Karme-Choling

A Buddhist meditation community in Barnet formerly known as "Tail of the Tiger," Karme-Choling was established as a center for Buddhist study and practice in 1970 by Chogyam Trungpa Rimpoche (1940–1987), a Tibetan meditation master and scholar. The center features a large, brightly decorated hall for worship. The cluster of attached buildings on 540 acres offers a Tibetan Mahazana experience. Rimpoche is widely regarded as the man who brought Tibetan Buddhism to the western world. Karme-Choling was his first meditation center. He died in Nova Scotia and was cremated at Barnet.

David Blow

Kendall, Burney James (1845–1922)

A patent medicine manufacturer of Enosburg Falls, B. J. Kendall was a graduate of the UNIVERSITY OF VERMONT Medical College (1868). He devised a spavin cure formula in the 1870s and incorporated the Dr. B. J. Kendall Company in 1883. Kendall gradually expanded his product line to treatments for a wide variety of animal and human ailments, and Kendall Company wagons traveled widely to sell medicines and distribute his booklets, *A Treatise on the Horse and His Diseases* and *The Doctor at Home*. Kendall sold his share of the company in 1889 to CARMI MARSH and others and moved to the Midwest, where as his fortunes waned he became bitter and envious of his ex-partners' success. He died in Geneva, Illinois.

J. Kevin Graffagnino

Kent, Louise Andrews (1886–1969)

An author of cookbooks and children's books, Louise Andrews Kent grew up in Brookline, Massachusetts, the daughter of a British father and a New England mother, who died when Kent was three.

Dr. B. J. Kendall's Spavin Cure. John Duffy

After attending the new Simmons College Library School and spending some years as a Boston socialite, she married Ira Rich Kent of Kents Corner in Calais in 1912. They lived in Brookline, Massachusetts, where he was an editor at Houghton Mifflin and where their three children were born. She wrote columns for the *Boston Traveler* and magazine articles for *House Beautiful* and *Ladies Home Journal*. Her first children's book appeared in 1931, followed by the popular *I Went with ...* series. As Mrs. Appleyard, Kent wrote chatty, delightful cookbooks, beginning with *Mrs. Appleyard's Year* (1941). Daughter Elizabeth ("Kenty") co-authored some of Kent's books. The White House at Kents Corner was long the family vacation home, then the permanent home for Kent from 1959. (Her husband had died in 1945.) Kent was instrumental in establishing Kent Tavern in Calais as a house museum under the auspices of the VERMONT HISTORICAL SOCIETY. *Mrs. Appleyard and I* (1968) is her memoir. Kent Tavern is now operated by the Division of Historic Sites.

Reidun Nuquist

Keyes, Frances Parkinson (1885–1970)

A popular writer of novels and magazine articles from 1919 to the 1950s, Frances Parkinson Keyes was a descendant of THOMAS JOHNSON, a prominent early settler of Newbury. Born in Charlottesville, Virginia, where her father, John Wheeler, was professor of Greek at the University of Virginia, she was schooled abroad, spending summers at the Thomas Johnson homestead, the Oxbow, in Newbury. Later she inherited the Oxbow from her mother. In 1904, Frances Parkinson Wheeler married Henry Wilder Keyes (1863–1938), a New Hampshire gentleman-farmer-politician who was elected governor of New Hampshire (1917–1919) and United States Senator (1919–1938). The social life of Washington, D.C., strained the family finances, forcing Keyes to augment their income by writing. She published her first novel, *The Old Gray Homestead*, in 1919. Shortly thereafter, *Good Housekeeping* magazine retained her as a feature writer. Keyes's column, "Letters from a Senator's Wife," appeared regularly for the next fifteen years. She travelled around the world as a foreign correspondent for *Good Housekeeping* and contributed to a number of other popular women's magazines as well. Upon her husband's death in 1938, Frances turned

full-time writer to support her three sons. She published more than fifty books, producing a novel nearly every year as well as poetry, memoirs, cookbooks, and biographies of saints. Many of her novels, including the best seller *Dinner at Antoines* (1948), were set in Louisiana, where she made her home later in life. She founded the Keyes Foundation to support struggling writers and preserve historic homes. Keyes is buried in the Johnson family plot in Newbury and many of her letters and manuscripts are on deposit at the UNIVERSITY OF VERMONT.   *Karen Campbell*

Keyes, Stephen (1754–1804)

After serving in a Connecticut line company during the Revolution, Stephen Keyes moved to Vermont in 1783 where he became the first merchant in Manchester and later built and opened the first regular mercantile store in Burlington in the fall of 1789. Keyes lived and kept a public house on Water (now Battery) Street near GIDEON KING, SR.'s, tavern in the 1790s. He was the first U.S. Customs Collector for the District of Vermont from 1791 to 1797.

Herman Brown

Keyser, F. Ray, Jr. (b. 1927)

F. Ray Keyser, Jr., of Chelsea was the youngest person, at age 34, ever elected governor of Vermont. Keyser graduated from Tufts University (1949) and Boston University Law School (1952) and joined a leading law firm, of which his father was a member. A Navy veteran, he was named one of America's Ten Outstanding Young Men of 1961 by the United States Junior Chamber of Commerce. A Republican, Keyser was elected to the Vermont House in 1954, 1956, and 1958, serving during 1959 to 1960 as House Speaker. Adhering to the single-term speaker tradition, Keyser opted to run for governor in 1960, capturing the Republican primary with 29 percent of the total vote (the lowest victory total on record) and went on to win the general election. His administration was marked by the "longest and costliest" legislative session in state history and intensive intra-party bickering. Critics alleged that Keyser failed to exercise the conciliation skills he had demonstrated as speaker. When new owners of the Rutland Railway precipitated a strike that led to dissolution of the company, Keyser initiated the state's purchase of portions of the railway. The STATE PARK system was expanded and the state budget balanced without new

taxes under Keyser, but he failed to win a second term in 1962, becoming the first Republican gubernatorial candidate to suffer such a defeat when he lost to Democrat PHILIP H. HOFF. Keyser returned to private practice and subsequently succeeded to the presidency and chairmanship of the board of the VERMONT MARBLE COMPANY in Proctor. Retired from Vermont Marble's board since 1979, he continues in his Chelsea law practice.

Kiley, Dan (b. 1912)

Landscape architect and regional planner Dan Kiley of Charlotte was born in Boston, Massachusetts. He began work as an apprentice for Warren H. Manning, a founder of the American Society of Landscape Architects, at the age of eighteen. In 1936, after six years with Manning, Kiley entered Harvard University's Graduate School of Design to study landscape architecture, but left in 1938 before earning a degree. With Garret Eckbo and James Rose, he published the modernist manifesto "Landscape Design" in *Architectural Record* in 1939 and 1940. In 1941, Kiley opened offices in Washington, D.C., and Franconia, New Hampshire. During World War II, he served in the United States Corps of Engineers and later as the director of design to the presentations branch of the Office of Strategic Services. In 1945, Kiley designed the courtroom and offices for the international tribunal in Nuremberg, Germany, for which he was awarded the French Legion of Merit. His post–World War II work included several collaborations with the architect Eero Saarinen, including the winning design for the Jefferson Memorial Competition in St. Louis, Missouri. Kiley settled in Vermont in 1951, opened an office, and continues to work there. He has received numerous awards, including the National Medal of Honor in the Arts in 1997. Kiley's notable landscape designs include the Miller House in Columbus, Indiana; the United States Air Force Academy in Colorado Springs, Colorado; Dulles Airport in Chantilly, Virginia; the John F. Kennedy Library in Boston; Fountain Place in Dallas; the Henry Moore Sculpture Garden in Kansas City; and the Twin Farms Inn in Barnard, Vermont.   *Chris Burns*

Kilgore, Carrie Burnham (1838–1909)

Teacher, lawyer, and crusader for women's rights, Carrie Burnham Kilgore was born in Craftsbury. After receiving a classical education at Craftsbury Academy and

Newbury Seminary, she left Vermont in 1852, eventually settling in Philadelphia. There she taught school and read law with Damon Young Kilgore, a lawyer and women's rights activist. Under his influence, she worked actively for the women's rights movement, and began her long struggle to obtain the right to practice law in Pennsylvania. She married Kilgore in 1876, and in 1883 became the first woman graduate of the Pennsylvania Law School. When her husband died in 1888, she took over his practice. *Deborah P. Clifford*

Killington

Killington, population 1,095, a town in Rutland County, was granted by BENNING WENTWORTH in 1761 under its present name, which was changed to Sherburne by the Vermont legislature in 1800. One hundred and ninety-nine years later, the name was changed back to Killington at the request of the townspeople, who had endured two centuries of confusion with the Chittenden County town of Shelburne. Killington apparently derived from the town of that name in England; Sherburne was named in honor of Colonel Benjamin Sherburne, one of the original grantees. The town is located on the eastern slopes of the main spine of the GREEN MOUNTAINS and contains 4,235-foot Killington Peak, Vermont's second-highest mountain, plus four other summits over 3,500 feet high. One of Vermont's earliest self-promoters, the Loyalist SAMUEL PETERS, claimed after fleeing the Revolution to London that he had stood atop Killington Peak in 1763 (though he believed he was on Mount Pisgah) and dubbed the land he saw "Verdmont," a spelling that never took hold. The town is bisected from north to south by the deep valley of the Ottauquechee River, along whose banks on U.S. Route 4 are some of the inns, restaurants, and shops serving the Killington and Pico ski areas, the largest ski locale in the eastern United States. The two areas have a total of two hundred downhill trails and (at Killington) a maximum vertical drop of 3,150 feet. Extensive development over the last few decades has turned much of Killington town into a major summer resort as well, complete with golf courses, hiking trails, mountain biking trails, and water and skate parks.

King, Gideon, Jr. (fl. 1785–1826)

Known as "Admiral of the Lake," Gideon King, Jr., came to Burlington from New Lebanon, New York, with his father in 1788 and quickly joined with Job Boynton to build two 8-ton cutters on the Burlington lakeshore to carry freight to Essex and Plattsburgh, New York. In 1790, they went to St. Johns, Quebec, and bought two of the British war vessels remaining from the Revolution and fitted them out as schooners to sail between St. Johns and Burlington. King's boat in the pair was called the *Horseboat* because he had fitted out a part of it to carry horses to and from St. Johns. The sloop *Maria* was said to have been built in 1797 by King on the Burlington waterfront, but the name and date of the ship suggest that King went again to St. Johns and bought the armed British sloop *Maria* that had cruised the northern waters of the lake in support of the British posts at Point au Fer and the LOYALIST BLOCKHOUSE until the Jay Treaty retired it from the lake. Richard Fittock, merchant, boatbuilder, publican, and friend of Loyalists in Canada rigged the *Maria* for King's purposes. Between 1793 and 1815, King built eleven boats and acquired or financed most of the boats working from Burlington. By 1800, he was John Jacob Astor's agent in fur buying on the lake and during the War of 1812 was able to maintain a semblance of trade with Canada through an understanding with U.S. Customs Collector CORNELIUS VAN NESS. The war also provided abundant employment for his vessels transporting troops and stores for the government while redirecting his efforts toward the south. At Whitehall his ships would take on passengers and freight from Albany and Troy and sail north to discharge cargo at lake ports. While King was able to maintain a share of the freight trade, the arrival of steamboats—which came to monopolize the passenger trade—offered stiff competition. With the opening of the Champlain and Erie canals in 1823 and 1825, King merged his interests with those of the steamboat line and helped direct its operations until his death in Burlington in 1826.

King, Gideon, Sr. (1743–1804)

A Revolutionary War veteran, Gideon King served as first lieutenant in the Second New York Regiment in 1775 and 1776, and subsequently served as captain in several other regiments. King removed to Burlington in 1788 from New Lebanon, New York, with his second wife, Naomi Hubbel, and the four sons by his first wife, Ruth. He built and operated the first inn in Burlington on the northeast corner of Battery and King streets. Presided over by Naomi "Granny" King, who prepared meals in the "English style and was renowned for her elegant desserts," King's inn was a large two-story building with a kitchen in the rear. Chittenden County Court sat at King's inn from 1790 to 1791. Washington Lodge 3 of the Masons held its first and subsequent meetings here until 1795, when it moved to Court House Square. In front of the inn stood the notorious oak tree used by Sheriff STEPHEN PEARL as a whipping post. After Gideon's death in 1804, the inn was kept by his son, Joseph (1779–1826). Granny King died in 1822 and the old inn burned in 1840. *David Blow*

Kingdom County Productions

Established in 1991 to produce motion pictures rooted in northern New England and to create educational programs in theater and film, Kingdom County Productions (KCP) was started by JAY CRAVEN and Bess O'Brien of Peacham "to cultivate the artistic voice of the region." KCP oversees Craven and O'Brien's narrative film projects, documentary production, and education programs, including school workshops, media arts curriculum development, and the Fledgling Films Institute for high school students. *Kenneth A. Peck*

Kincaid, Jamaica (b. 1949)

Novelist, essayist, and short-story writer, Jamaica Kincaid was born in Antigua as Elaine Potter Richardson. Coming to the United States as an au pair at age seventeen, she soon tired of that role and began taking writing classes at the New School for Social Research, followed by two years at Franconia College in New Hampshire. Taking the pen name Jamaica Kincaid, she became a staff writer for the *New Yorker* in 1976, staying there until 1995 while developing a reputation as an essayist and fiction writer. She and her husband, composer Allen Shawn, moved to Bennington in 1985, where they had been offered jobs at BENNINGTON COLLEGE, and she has lived there ever since. Her works include a short story collection, *At the Bottom of the River* (1984), and the novels *Annie John* (1985), *Lucy* (1990), and *The Autobiography of My Mother* (1996). Her garden in Bennington, about which she has written extensively in short essays, is the subject of *My Garden (Book)* (1999), in which the pleasures and frustrations of gardening frequently lead into depictions of Bennington neighbors and meditations on such subjects as identity, racism, and colonialism.

Kinnell, Galway (b. 1927)

The Pulitzer Prize–winning poet Galway Kinnell settled in Sheffield in 1965. He was born in Providence, Rhode Island, and educated at Princeton and the University of Rochester. VERMONT STATE POET from 1989 to 1993, he has published over thirty books, including poetry collections, novels, translations, and children's books. His *Selected Poems* (1983) won the National Book Award and the Pulitzer Prize; *A New Selected Poems* appeared in 2000. A powerful public reader of his own and other poet's works, he has taught at universities in the United States, France, Iran, and Australia. He currently divides his time between Sheffield and New York City, where he teaches at New York University.

Kipling, Rudyard (1865–1936)

The English poet and novelist Rudyard Kipling and his American wife, Carrie Balestier, lived in Dummerston from 1893 to 1897. The Kiplings engaged Carrie's brother, Beatty Balestier, to supervise construction of a house for them, which they named Naulakha, a Hindi word meaning a treasure house or place of riches. During his years in Vermont, Kipling wrote *The Second Jungle Book* (1895), collections of animal stories that many consider his finest writing. He also wrote many short stories that were collected in *The Day's Work* (1898), and began work on *Captains Courageous* (1897), a story of New England cod fishing that he researched on visits to Gloucester, Massachusetts. Two Kipling children, Josephine and Elsie, were born at Naulakha. The Kiplings led a private and comfortable life in Dummerston. His writing was occasionally interrupted by visits from literary friends such as Charles Eliot Norton and Arthur Conan Doyle, who brought a pair of Nordic skis to Naulakha and left them behind, perhaps the first pair of skis to appear in Vermont. Doyle and Kipling also created a winter golf game by painting their golf balls red to make them retrievable in the snow. Although some in Brattleboro thought the Kiplings to be flaunting their wealth when they rode into Brattleboro covered with furs, including a tigerskin rug, in a sleigh driven by their English coachman, they nonetheless developed close friendships in Brattleboro and Dummerston. These included former Governor FREDERICK HOLBROOK, Walter Childs, and Dr. James Conland, who attended the births of their two daughters and told Kipling of his youthful adventures in the cod-fishing fleet. In 1896, however, a dispute with Beatty Balestier over his use of a field they had bought from him that his sister wished to develop into a formal garden led to Balestier threatening violence against Kipling. A court action followed and subsequently the Kiplings left Brattleboro forever in 1897. Kipling remembered that his years at Naulakha, where he and and his wife started their family in a house he designed, were a special, good time in his life, when some of his best short fiction was written.

Kirby

Kirby, population 456, a town in Caledonia County, was incorporated by the Vermont legislature in 1807 out of the previously granted town of Hopkinsville and a portion of the town of Burke. The specific Kirby after whom the town was named is not known. The landscape, mostly unsuited for settlement, is heavily forested and dominated by Kirby Mountain (2,500 feet), which stretches along the eastern border with Victory, and Sugar Hill (2,040 feet) to its west. The only significant road in the town runs through the valley between them, from Lyndon to Concord. Kirby is one of the few towns in Vermont that has never had either a village or a post office.

Kitchen Junkets

In the early years of the twentieth century, dance events called kitchen junkets, also known as tunks, tunkets, and hops, were common throughout Vermont and the surrounding region. Local, informal, nonpublic events, they took place in neighborhoods and cycled from household to household during the cold-weather months. In the era before the Second World War, farmhouse kitchens were large, relatively empty rooms with a kitchen table, wood cooking range, wood box, and a Morris chair or two; food was prepared and dishes were washed in the pantry. These big kitchen spaces coupled with adjacent rooms on the first floor were emptied of furniture to create a space for dancing. A fiddler, piano player, and a person who could call or "prompt" the dances were the backbone of an evening's entertainment. The dances included contras and quadrilles, which were conservative, old-time dance forms even in the 1920s and 1930s. Junkets were family events: parents, grandparents, and children, all of whom often shared a household, would attend together. Children were spectators and then were bundled off to sleep on the upper floor, with children from various families literally packed together on every available bed. People would start assembling for a junket after supper and the evening chores, which often meant that the dancing would begin as late as nine o'clock. After several hours, the dancers would pause for a "lunch" and then continue past midnight. Junkets appear to have happened on a regular weekly schedule during the depths of the winter although there seems to have been a good deal of variation from neighborhood to neighborhood. Some farmers, for example, report that the dances were always held in a particular household because that family had more space and could accommodate a large group. Whatever the variations, there was a consistent pattern of neighbors banding together to "make their own fun" and dance the evening away with gusto. Kitchen junkets started to die out in the 1930s but persisted in some areas of Vermont into the 1940s. Some farmers credit their demise to an increase in rowdiness as the automobile enabled people to travel greater distances and people from outside a particular neighborhood began showing up at these local gatherings. Alcohol in the form of hard cider, which during the early years of the twentieth century was commonly made throughout rural Vermont, was apparently a routine part of kitchen junkets. But in later years, farmers report that drunken behavior and the destruction of personal property became an issue. Moreover, in the era of big bands, contras and quadrilles were seen as positively antique. In the midst of this change, fiddler Ed Larkin, who played for kitchen dances in Chelsea and Tunbridge, recognized that an important cultural form was vanishing from the rural countryside. Thus he consciously set about preserving the dances and music of the kitchen junket by organizing the ED LARKIN DANCERS.

Greg Sharrow

Knapp, Chauncey Langdon (1809–1898)

A newspaper editor and political insider in Vermont in the 1830s, Chauncey Knapp was also one of the most important early abolitionists in the state. From 1831 to 1836 he published the *State Journal* in Montpelier promoting the ANTI-MASONIC PARTY. Knapp's editorials railed against the secret influence of FREEMASONRY in state government and built significant popular support for the new party, which captured control of the legislature and elected the governor from 1831 until 1836. As early as 1831, Knapp also used the *State Journal* to promote abolition. He was one of the very first public figures to introduce the radical idea of the "immediate emancipation" of slaves to Vermonters. In 1834, he became a founding member of the Vermont Anti-Slavery Society and subsequently served on its executive committee for many years. From 1836 to 1841, as a Whig, Knapp served as secretary of state. From this position, he worked behind the scenes to promote abolitionist ideals within the WHIG PARTY. From 1839 to 1843, he also published the *Voice of Freedom* in Montpelier, a newspaper with the sanction of the Vermont Anti-Slavery Society. Knapp's ardent anti-slavery stance eventually cost him his post as secretary of state when he refused to endorse a pro-slavery Whig for governor and was dropped by the party. Although he remained acting secretary of state until 1843, his political future in Vermont was cloudy, and he moved, in 1844, to Lowell, Massachusetts. There Knapp edited a Liberty party paper (1844–1845), became a founding member of the national FREE-SOIL party (1848), and represented Lowell in Congress (1855 to 1859) for the REPUBLICAN and KNOW-NOTHING parties. *Andrew Barker*

Knickerbacor, John (ca. 1738–1808)

Serving in a New York regiment during the Revolutionary War, John Knickerbacor was wounded at Saratoga in 1777. After the war, IRA ALLEN employed him in his personal land business and as his assistant in his capacity as surveyor general of Vermont. Knickerbacor was clerk of Chittenden County court in 1788 and 1789 and a Burlington selectman from 1789 to 1791.

Knoulton, Luke (1738–1810)

Suspected of British sympathies and spying during the American Revolution, Luke Knoulton (sometimes spelled Knowlton) nonetheless was elected to several important offices in early Vermont. Born in Shrewsbury, Massachusetts, Knoulton

served in the provincial forces stationed at Crown Point in the last French and Indian War. He moved to Newfane Hill in 1773 after purchasing a deed based on a New York patent to that land and was elected town clerk of Newfane in 1774, holding the office for sixteen years. He became a justice of the peace under New York authority, and was present at the WESTMINSTER MASSACRE in 1775, when William French was killed in an anti-court riot. A firm supporter of New York's claims to authority over the grants, Knoulton put forth arguments in 1780 that persuaded Congress not to recognize Vermont statehood, but before he left Philadelphia he met IRA ALLEN and saw the wisdom of the Vermont position. He played an important role in the HALDIMAND NEGOTIATIONS when some of Vermont's leaders negotiated a separate truce with Britain in the middle of the Revolutionary War, for which Congress later ordered Knoulton's arrest for "intriguing" with the enemy. He and SAMUEL WELLS helped transmit correspondence from Quebec to the British in New York. On November 16, 1783, a Yorker Patriot mob carried him across the border to Massachusetts as punishment for British sympathies. The next year, he was elected representative in the Vermont House. He served on the Vermont Supreme Court (1786) and as a county judge of Windham County (1787–1794). He also served eleven years on the Governor's Council (1790–1801). He was at different times regarded as either a traitor or a loyalist to Vermont and the United States, and in 1799 received $249.53 of the $30,000 Vermont paid as reparation for the loss of New York land titles. His grandson FREDERICK HOLBROOK was governor from 1861 to 1863. *Paul Gillies*

Know-Nothings

The Know-Nothings, also referred to as the American party and the Order of the Star-Spangled Banner, were a short-lived phenomenon that thrived in the 1850s. Cloaked in secrecy, members answered questions about the order with the standard reply "I know nothing about it." They were pledged to vote only for native-born Americans and to combat Catholicism. In Vermont, the movement reached its peak in early 1855, when it elected its entire slate to the COUNCIL OF CENSORS and ran a candidate for governor. Later that year, the Know-Nothing candidate received less than 10 percent of the vote, and

in 1857 all the council's proposed amendments, including one that would have imposed house REAPPORTIONMENT down to 150 members, were summarily rejected. By then the movement no longer possessed a formal Vermont presence, having been discredited by a pro-slavery resolution adopted at its 1855 national convention. Nonetheless, Know-Nothing influence is apparent in that early REPUBLICAN PARTY candidates included prominent Know-Nothing leaders. The candidates nominated at the 1856 Know-Nothing state convention were subsequently nominated and elected as Republicans.

Koch, Bill (b. 1955)

The only American ever to win the World Cup overall cross-country ski title, Bill Koch of Brattleboro also won a silver medal at the 1976 Winter Olympic Games. That year in Innsbruck, Austria, Koch became the first American to earn an Olympic medal in Nordic skiing when he finished second in the 30-kilometer race by only twenty-eight seconds. After finishing fifteenth in the 50-kilometer race in the 1980 Winter Games at Lake Placid, New York, Koch developed a technique similar to speed skating. Koch's new technique stirred up considerable controversy in the Nordic skiing world in the early 1980s. When it began to gain wide acceptance among skiers, the sport's officials sought to ban Koch's skating technique. When Koch became the first American to win a medal in world championship competition, finishing third in the 30-kilometer race in Oslo, Norway, officials withdrew their objections to his skating technique. That year, he won the overall Nordic World Cup title on the basis of his season-long results. In 1983, he won the 30-kilometer and 50-kilometer events and finished second in the 15-kilometer competition at the U.S. national championships. Koch led the World Cup standings until the last three races of the season. He narrowly missed another championship, placing third overall. Koch competed in four events at the 1984 Olympics in Sarajevo, Yugoslavia, but won no medals. Briefly retired after 1987, he returned to competition in the 1992 Olympics in Albertville, France. He carried the U.S. flag into the stadium at the head of the American team, but did not win a medal that year. Cross-country skiing leagues and festivals across the country are now named after him.

New Yorker *magazine cartoon by Ed Koren.* New Yorker. © 2001 The New Yorker Collection from cartoonbank.com. All Rights Reserved

Koren, Ed (b. 1935)

A visual social satirist whose cartoons featuring shaggy, long-nosed characters appear regularly in *The New Yorker*, Ed Koren of Brookfield grew up in Mount Vernon, New York, where he began drawing cartoons and other illustrations for the high school newspaper. His satire is based on the tradition of the comedy of manners. Koren traces his interests to many visual satirists from the eighteenth and nineteenth centuries, especially Honoré Daumier and his cartoons of social commentary. A metropolitan New York resident until he was forty-three, Koren was first attracted to Vermont in the 1950s when he attended the McArthur Summer Theater Workshop in Waitsfield, trucking the Workshop's scenery in a Ford Model A to performances around the state. Settling in Brookfield in 1978, he has pursued through visual illustration his longtime interest in the dramatic opportunities often provided by the interactions of rural and urban characters and customs.

Ku Klux Klan

The Ku Klux Klan organized local chapters throughout Vermont in the wave of racism and xenophobic fear sweeping America in the 1920s. Organizers operating out of the northern New England headquarters in Rochester, New Hampshire, canvassed the state in 1922 with propaganda and organized chapters during the summer of 1924. Thousands of Vermonters joined the KKK, conducted cross-burnings on meadows and hillsides, and organized rallies and marches in Vermont cities over the next four years. While the KKK persecuted African-Americans, Asians, and Jews in other states, KKK animosity in Vermont was directed primarily toward Catholics. In Montpelier, crosses were burned in a Catholic cemetery and on the steps of St. Augustine's Catholic Church. A raid on Burlington's St. Mary's Cathedral in 1924 by klansmen brought public censure and led to the demise of the Chittenden County KKK chapter. Opposition to the Klan took the form of city ordinances in Rutland and Burlington banning public meetings of masked or disguised individuals and boycotts of businessmen and professionals alleged to be members of the Klan. Leading Vermont newspapers condemned the Klan as un-American and a desecration of Vermont's traditions of independence and tolerance. *Nancy L. Gallagher*

Kunin, Madeleine May (b.1933)

The first woman elected governor of Vermont, Madeleine Kunin was born Madeleine May in Zurich, Switzerland, and emigrated to the United States in 1940 with her widowed mother and ten-year-old brother Edgar. Jews escaping from the threat of Hitler, they managed to sail on the last ship leaving Italy for New York. After short stays in Forest Hills, New York, and Beverly Hills, California, they moved to Pittsfield, Massachusetts, where Madeleine attended high school and the University of Massachusetts, graduating in 1956. She then enrolled in the Columbia School of Journalism and after receiving a master's degree in 1957, moved to Burlington to work for the BURLINGTON FREE PRESS as an education reporter and editor of the teen page. In 1961, she married Arthur Kunin, a physician and instructor at the UNIVERSITY OF VERMONT. They had four children, and divorced in 1995. In 1967, Madeleine Kunin received a master's degree in English literature and later taught at TRINITY COLLEGE in Burlington. Elected to the Vermont House of Representatives in 1972 as a Democrat from Burlington, she served three two-year terms and became minority whip in 1975 and chair of the House Appropriations Committee in 1977. In 1978, she was elected lieutenant governor and served two terms. In 1982, she ran for governor but lost to Republican incumbent RICHARD SNELLING. Running again in 1984, she was elected to that office. She served three two-year terms and did not run for re-election in 1990. Her administrations are most noted for Act 200, a growth management law designed to streamline the ACT 250 process through establishing land capabil-

Governor Madeleine Kunin, 1986. Special Collections, Bailey/Howe Library, University of Vermont

ity for development in advance of development proposals; creation of a state Human Rights Commission; and expanding a broad range of social welfare benefits. She developed new funding formulas for aid to school districts that increased state aid by 109 percent. Two loan programs for refinancing farm debt were put in place and the current use program was expanded to further reduce the property tax burden on farm and forest land. An increase in state spending without a comparable increase in revenues left a large deficit. After leaving office, Kunin became a Montgomery Fellow at Dartmouth College and Radcliffe College's first Distinguished Visitor in Public Policy. An early supporter of Bill Clinton, she was a member of his team to choose a vice-presidential running mate and a member of his transition team. Appointed deputy secretary of education and in August 1996 ambassador to Switzerland, Kunin served there until 1999, when she returned to Vermont and joined the faculty of MIDDLEBURY COLLEGE to teach political science.

Kurn Hattin

A place where children can find a secure and supportive haven during troubled periods in their families' lives, Kurn Hattin in Westminster was founded in 1894. Encouraged by WILLIAM VAN PATTEN of Burlington, Charles Albert Dickinson, a Westminster native and Boston clergyman,

Boys on the home farm at Kurn Hattin, circa 1902. Kurn Hattin Homes

pursued a personal mission "to improve the lot of the less privileged." Named after two small peaks on a nearby hill that resembled the hill where Christ is said to have recited the Beatitudes, Kurn Hattin today serves about one hundred boys and girls ages six to fifteen who could be at risk of physical, intellectual, and emotional trauma. Children from throughout the northeast are referred to Kurn Hattin by social service workers, guidance counsellors, and members of the clergy, and are placed there voluntarily by a parent or guardian. Boys and girls live in cottages with houseparents. Summer programs augment the school year in a typical three- to five-year stay at Kurn Hattin. After graduation, children may return home, go to a foster placement, or enter private secondary schools. Scholarships are available to Kurn Hattin graduates to help defray tuition costs for high school and college. Kurn Hattin is supported by private benefactors.

la Motte, Pierre de St. Paul, sieur de
(b. 1635)

As a captain in the CARIGNAN-SALIERES REGIMENT of the French army, Pierre de St. Paul, sieur de la Motte came to New France in 1664. He directed the construction of FORT SAINTE-ANNE in the spring of 1666 at a site on the northernmost island of LAKE CHAMPLAIN, which in later years came to be known as Isle La Motte. His soldiers suffering from disease and insufficient supplies in the winter months, la Motte commanded New France's most exposed position for three years. British-allied Iroquois scouts repeatedly threatened la Motte's small force, killing two senior officers on one occasion. When the fort was abandoned in 1669, he was appointed commandant of all forces in New France and returned to France in 1670.

Lake Champlain Committee

The Lake Champlain Committee (LCC), founded in 1963, is a nonprofit citizens group dedicated to protecting and restoring the water quality of LAKE CHAMPLAIN and its basin. The committee supports research on the lake, conducts education and community outreach programs to safeguard the lake's ecosystem, and is a vigorous advocate for the lake to the regulatory agencies of Vermont, New York, and Quebec, as well as the federal governments of the United States and Canada. LCC helped advance the clean-up strategy that removed more than 191,000 cubic yards of PCB-contaminated waste from Plattsburgh's Cumberland Bay and successfully blocked a nuclear power plant proposed for construction on the Charlotte shores of the lake. It helped draft a nationally precedent-setting clean-up agreement for Burlington's Barge Canal Superfund Site and drafted water quality standards to reduce pollution that were adopted by New York, Vermont, and Quebec. LCC has also developed the Lake Champlain Paddler's Trail, an end-to-end water trail currently linking twenty-seven locations on the lake's islands and shoreline.

Lake Champlain Maritime Museum

Dedicated to preserving and telling the story of LAKE CHAMPLAIN through its military, commercial, and recreational periods, the Lake Champlain Maritime Museum at Basin Harbor in Ferrisburgh has preserved or reconstructed a large collection of original small watercraft from the last 150 years. The museum is dedicated to studying Lake Champlain's shipwrecks, the largest collection of wooden shipwrecks in North America, employing archeological conservators in its Nautical Archeology Center. The collection includes a replica of the 54-foot square-rigged Revolutionary War gunboat *Philadelphia*, which is also utilized in presenting the story of citizen soldiers in the Champlain Valley in 1776. Craftsmen continue traditional maritime skills of boatbuilding and blacksmithing in the museum's working shops. Over a dozen exhibit buildings at the Maritime Museum present the maritime history and nautical archeology of the Champlain Valley through hands-on interactive learning stations, video and audio displays, historical artifacts, and images. Long-term exhibitions are enhanced by new research, new acquisitions, and special short-term installations each season. The Lake Champlain Maritime Museum operates daily from May to October.

Lake Champlain Steamboat Company

See CHAMPLAIN TRANSPORTATION COMPANY.

Lamoille River

The Lamoille River, the fourth-longest river in the LAKE CHAMPLAIN Basin, has its headwaters in the uplands to the east of Caspian Lake in the town of Greensboro. It flows through the major villages of Hardwick, Morrisville, and Johnson before opening into a broad intervale after breaking through the barrier of the GREEN MOUNTAINS. At Fairfax, a major falls supplies hydroelectric power, and in Milton the river is dammed to form 732-acre Arrowhead Mountain Lake, also a hydroelectric site. After a distance of 85 miles, the Lamoille empties into Lake Champlain, forming an extensive delta that is the site of both a wildlife management area and SANDBAR State Park, one of Vermont's most popular parks. The ABENAKI name for the Lamoille is *wintegok*, or "narrow river." The present version of the river's name might have resulted from an eighteenth-century English-speaking cartographer's error in reading a French map of the Champlain Valley, mistranscribing as "la moille" the French word for seagull, *la mouette*.

Lampson, Sir Curtis (1806–1885)

Knighted by Queen Victoria for successfully leading the company that laid the first transatlantic telegraph cable, Sir Curtis Lampson was born in New Haven where he received a common school education. At age seventeen, he left Vermont for Canada to work in the fur trade. In these years, Lampson also spent time in New York City employed as an agent for John Jacob Astor, traveling often to England with cargoes of fur. Then, in 1830, he moved permanently to London, where he set up his own fur business and became a British subject. The C. M. Lampson Company flourished, bringing both wealth and power to its youthful owner. In 1870, while serving as deputy governor of the Hudson Bay Company, Lampson helped guide this huge and powerful concern through its crisis with the Canadian and British governments over control of the Dominion of Canada. Firm in his belief that agricultural and industrial development would eventually undercut the fur trading company's power, Lampson was influential in persuading the firm to surrender its territorial rights over 3 million square miles of Canadian wilderness. Lampson was also actively engaged in the laying of the transatlantic cable. In 1856, he was appointed an executive of the company for that purpose, and, despite a decade marked by repeated failures in constructing and laying the cable, Lampson never lost faith that success was possible. Transatlantic telegraph service between England and America was finally achieved by the summer of 1866, and that November, Queen Victoria knighted Lampson for his "resolute support of the project." Sir Curtis Lampson never lost touch with his home town. In 1857, he returned for a last visit to New Haven, and a decade later gave $8,000 for the construction of a school house at New Haven Mills. Recently restored, this elegant Italianate building, complete with bell tower, still stands tall overlooking the New Haven River.

Deborah P. Clifford

Landgrove

Landgrove, population 144, the smallest town in area in Bennington County, was settled by a group of families who believed that they were living in the town of Peru. When surveys showed that the land was actually part of no town, undersized, hatchet-shaped Landgrove was granted to them by the Vermont legislature in 1780. The origin of the name is not known. Always sparsely inhabited, Landgrove was saved from disincorporation in the 1930s by the action of Samuel Ogden, who was instrumental in attracting new residents to the town by buying, restoring, and re-selling many old houses. While the town has several inns and a nondenominational church, it has no store, school, or post office. Much of it lies within the GREEN MOUNTAIN NATIONAL FOREST.

Landmark College

Situated on 125 acres overlooking the town of Putney, Landmark College is the only fully accredited college in the country designed exclusively for students with dyslexia, attention deficit disorder, or other specific learning disabilities. Founded in 1983 on the campus of the former Windham College by Dr. Charles Drake, an innovative educator, it admitted its first 77 students in 1985. Enrollment today is about 360 students, of whom 60 percent are male. The student-faculty ratio is three to one, and the average class consists of eight to twelve students. In addition, each student receives four hours per week of one-on-one tutorial instruction. There are no majors, as the academic program is tailored to individual student needs.

Lane Manufacturing Company

The Lane Manufacturing Company was named for its founder and long-time president Dennis Lane, who was born in Barre in 1818. Eventually settling in Plainfield, Lane in 1858 came into possession of a lumber mill. Dissatisfied with the machinery that moved the log forward and governed the thickness of the cuts of the saw as inaccurate and inconsistent, Lane invented and patented the Lane lever set sawmill that came to be used throughout the country. In 1863, a need for more space prompted Lane to move his business to Mechanics' Street in Montpelier. In 1865, he was joined by General P. P. Pitkin as a partner, and later by James W. Brock, under the company name Lane, Pitkin, and Brock. Incorporated as Lane Manufacturing Company in 1873, the company continued to produce Lane lever set saw-mills. Other company products were clap-board machines, sawmill and dressing machines, and the "monitor" turbine water wheel. Later the company also produced machinery and parts for the granite industry. Lane continued as president of the company until his death in 1888. At that time the company was near the pinnacle of its success, and in 1890 there were major additions. At one point, the eleven-building Lane complex provided employment for one hundred men. However, a gradual decline in the use of portable sawmills produced a corresponding decline in Lane Manufacturing Company fortunes and the foundry was closed around 1935, when some of the buildings were torn down and others acquired by the founder's great-grandson, Dennis Lane. This Lane continued the sawmill business on a small scale until 1973, when he sold the complex to a New England development firm for renovation as housing.

Lane Series

A program of concerts and performing arts events is presented annually by the UNIVERSITY OF VERMONT's George Bishop Lane Series. A memorial to Lane, UVM class of 1883, established and endowed by his family in 1954, the Lane Series has brought distinguished artists to Burlington and the university community under the leadership of three directors. Professor of English Jack Trevithick was the first director and opened the series with a performance of George Bernard Shaw's *Saint Joan*. Members of the Lane family attended the second scheduled event on November 17, 1954, a concert by the London Philharmonic. With artists such as Isaac Stern, John Gielgud, and Benny Goodman appearing in 1958 and 1959, the series grew under Dr. Trevithick, leading to his full-time employment as director during the later years of a twenty-one-year tenure that established the Lane Series' reputation for bringing "the best" to Burlington in all areas of entertainment. In 1968 to 1969, for example, Simon and Garfunkel performed and in 1971 to 1972 Ike and Tina Turner. In 1976, Terry Demas, formerly manager of the Student Association Concert Series, succeeded Trevithick, serving until 1988, sometimes under difficult circumstances as the musical scene changed. Artists' fees escalated, competition for new presenters intensified, and Lane audiences became increasingly dissatisfied with the series' usual venue, the Memorial Auditorium. In 1988, Professor of Music Jane Ambrose was appointed director of the Lane Series and was charged with bringing the series back to campus and to re-identify its educational purpose and its endowment commitment to present artists to the campus and Burlington audiences alike. Most concerts are now held in the UVM Recital Hall, a few are in Ira Allen Chapel, while large presentations like operas and dramatic productions take place in the renovated Flynn Center for the Arts.

Jane Ambrose

Laredo, Jaime (b. 1942)

The fourth and current music director of the VERMONT SYMPHONY ORCHESTRA, Jaime Laredo was born in Cochabamba, Bolivia, and since 1985 has resided in Guilford. In 1947, his family settled in San Francisco, where his father had previously served as Bolivian consul. A gifted young violinist, Laredo was invited at age eleven to solo with the San Francisco Symphony Orchestra conducted by Arthur Fiedler. The family relocated to Philadelphia in 1954, where Laredo studied violin at the Curtis Institute of Music. At age seventeen, he went to Brussels for the Queen of Belgium Competition and won first prize, the youngest violinist to do so. He joined the MARLBORO MUSIC FESTIVAL in 1960. Cellist Sharon Robinson and Laredo married at the Marboro Festival in 1976 and have performed since in the Karlichstein-Laredo-Robinson Trio. Laredo also played in a quartet that included pianist Emanuel Ax, violinist Isaac Stern, and cellist Yo-Yo Ma, a group that won a Grammy Award in 1991 for best chamber music recording for their collaboration on three Brahms pieces. As a soloist, he has performed with more than one hundred orchestras worldwide.

Larkin Dancers

See ED LARKIN DANCERS.

Larrow, Robert W. (1916–1991)

A lawyer, politician, and jurist, Robert W. Larrow was among a small group that led the revitalization of the Vermont DEMOCRATIC PARTY in the 1950s and 1960s, ending the Republican hegemony in Vermont. Larrow was born in Vergennes. After his early education in the Vergennes schools, he graduated from Holy Cross College and, in 1939, from Harvard Law School. He served for nineteen years as Burlington city attorney, and in 1949 was elected to the State house of representatives from Burlington. In 1952, he ran for governor against incumbent LEE E. EMERSON. Known for his diligent work habits and sharp wit, Larrow ran a vigorous campaign, receiving 60,051 votes, then a record for a Democratic gubernatorial candidate. In 1962, he was the Democratic candidate for attorney general on the ticket led by PHILIP H. HOFF. Although Larrow was defeated, Hoff became the first Democrat to be elected governor in 108 years. Larrow chaired the State Liquor Control Board from 1963 to 1966. In 1966, Governor Hoff appointed Larrow to the Vermont superior court. In 1974, he was the last person elevated to the Vermont Supreme Court by legislative election. He served as an associate justice until he retired in 1981.

Richard T. Cassidy

Lawrence, Andrea Mead (b. 1933)

At fifteen years old, Andrea Mead Lawrence of Rutland was the youngest woman on the United States Olympic ski team in 1948. Four years later as a veteran competitor in the 1952 winter games at Oslo, Norway, Lawrence won gold medals in the giant slalom and the Olympic slalom. Her second gold medal was a remarkable victory, for she fell near the top of her first run, but thanks to a swift recovery lost by only 1.2 seconds to the leader. Her winning time on the second run, 1:03.4, made her the first American skier to win two gold Olympic medals in the Winter Games. She resides now in California.

Lawrence, Paul (b. 1944)

The principal figure in modern Vermont's most notorious law enforcement drug scandal, Paul Lawrence, a native of Barrington, Rhode Island, came to Vermont after discharge from the U.S. Army in 1966 for character and behavior disorders. Within a year, he was employed first by the Burlington police department and then the Vermont State Police without background checks. Between 1967 and 1974, while working for the state police and several municipalities, including as an undercover narcotics agent in St. Albans and Burlington in 1973 to 1974, Lawrence accused and caused the arrest of over six hundred people. While inconsistencies in Lawrence's arrest charges and testimony eventually caused some prosecutors—including Windham County's Jerome Diamond, Chittenden County's PATRICK LEAHY, and Addison County's John Depp-

man—to suspect Lawrence of fabricating the crimes and to refuse to prosecute his cases, St. Albans police chief George Hebert and Franklin County prosecutors Michael McGinn and Ronald Kilburn did not suspect his methods. In May 1974, while working with Lawrence as an undercover agent with Burlington's police force, his partner Kevin Bradley began to suspect Lawrence of lying about his arrests. A sting operation managed by Bradley and Officer Dave Demag led to Lawrence's arrest for lying about buying drugs from Burlington police decoys. Fully reflecting the narrow perspectives of Vermont's closed world of law enforcement at the time, prosecutors, judges, police chiefs, the St. Albans city council, the state police administration, and the attorney general of Vermont for seven years resisted believing Lawrence's culpability until his arrest in Burlington. Despite inconsistent evidence and proof of Lawrence's lying, juries convicted many of the St. Albans arrestees, accepting the infallibility of their police. Lawrence was himself finally convicted in St. Albans on a charge of perjury in a drug trial when he claimed that he was honorably discharged from the army. He was also convicted in Burlington for lying in the charges he brought against two decoys set by the chief of police to catch him. In 1976, attorney general Kimberly Cheney, who refused to believe reports of Lawrence's corruption from St. Albans defense attorneys, lost re-election to Jerome Diamond, the first prosecutor to suspect Lawrence's methods. Franklin County prosecutor Ronald Kilburn, despite harsh criticism for believing Lawrence, was promoted to the district court bench. All pending charges against people accused by Lawrence were dropped. Convictions based on Lawrence's charges were pardoned. On January 21, 1999, Paul Lawrence was sentenced to fifteen months in federal prison and fined $5,000 for mail fraud for charging fees when he claimed he had properly disposed of contaminated soil for clients, but had actually illegally dumped it in several locations in New Jersey.

Lawrence, Richard (b. 1817)

A nineteenth-century gun manufacturer of Windsor, Richard Lawrence was born in Chester and moved at an early age to Watertown, New York, where he became an expert gunsmith. He returned to Vermont in 1838 looking for work, which he found with Nicanor Kendall, who was mak-

ing guns at WINDSOR PRISON using prison labor. Lawrence assumed charge of the shop within six months. In 1844, Kendall, Lawrence, and S. F. Robbins won a government contract for ten thousand rifles, which they completed ahead of time and at a profit. Robbins and Lawrence bought out Kendall in 1847 and the new firm won a second large contract on January 5, 1848. In their brief years of glory, Robbins and Lawrence introduced the principle of interchangeable parts in manufacturing, and won a prize for their guns at the Crystal Palace Exhibition in London in 1851. The firm went bankrupt in 1857 as the result of bad business decisions, but Lawrence himself and two other brilliant toolmakers who worked for the company, F. W. Howe and Henry Stone, quickly found work with other companies. It is possible to establish a "genealogical" link between these three inventive Robbins and Lawrence men and most of the larger firms that followed—Jones and Lamson, for example, Brown and Sharpe, Fellows Gear Shaper, and Bryant Chuck Grinding.

John C. Wriston, Jr.

Lawson, John C. (1900–1981)

A resident of Barre, long-time secretary-treasurer of the national granite cutters' unions, John Lawson was a major figure in twentieth-century Vermont organized labor and politics. Born in Aberdeen, Scotland, Lawson moved with his family to Barre when he was twelve. A member of the AFL-affiliated Granite Cutters' National Union, he was among those granite workers locked out by management in 1921 to 1922 when they sought to organize. In 1933 to 1934, as the GCNU's secretary-treasurer, he helped direct a strike in the Barre granite sheds that won the union official recognition and higher wages. When the Congress of Industrial Organizations was founded in 1935, Lawson led the GNWU into it, reforming the union as the United Stone and Allied Products Workers' Union. In the late 1930s, Lawson established a working friendship with Vermont Farm Bureau President ARTHUR PACKARD and Governor GEORGE AIKEN, who was unusually supportive of organized labor. Lawson endorsed Aiken for senator in 1940, and the votes of Vermont workers were a decisive factor in the victory of ERNEST GIBSON, JR., an Aiken ally, in the Republican gubernatorial primary in 1946. Lawson was a union officer well into his seventies.

Paul Searls

League of Vermont Writers

Founded in September 1929 by ARTHUR W. PEACH, JOHN WALTER COATES, and DANIEL CADY, the League of Vermont Writers promotes writing education, expanded opportunities for publication, and communication between writers. The league also sponsors writing conferences and contests. A newsletter, *League Lines*, started in 1942, is published four times each year in different locations around Vermont. Current membership is three hundred writers. LEON DEAN, DOROTHY CANFIELD FISHER, FRANCES FROST, HELEN HARTNESS FLANDERS, FRANCES PARKINSON KEYES, WILLIAM HAZLETT UPSON, and, more recently, LILIAN BAKER CARLISLE and RON ROOD number among past and present members.

Kathleen McKinley Harris

League of Women Voters

The Vermont League of Women Voters was organized in St. Albans in 1920 with the stated goals to promote political responsibility, educate citizens about their government, and encourage their participation in it. The league was expanded over the next three years to include local leagues in twelve other Vermont towns. Annual state conventions began in 1923; a newsletter, *The Green Mountain Citizen*, in 1924. Local leagues have published a series of "Know Your Town" pamphlets. As the league grew, it turned its efforts to active lobbying for issues of concern to the league: child welfare, education, women in the work force, war and peace, and efficiency in government, among many others. These dual goals of voter education and participation, and the exertion of the league's influence on socio-political issues on the local, state, and national levels, still constitute the organization's agenda today. *Sylvia J. Bugbee*

Leahy, Patrick J. (b. 1940)

Patrick Leahy was elected to the U.S. Senate in 1974, edging out Republican Congressman RICHARD MALLARY by 4,400 votes and becoming Vermont's first Democratic senator. Thirty-four years old at the time, Leahy was widely heralded as the only senator too young to be eligible for the presidency. Born in Montpelier, he attended local schools, graduated in 1961 from ST. MICHAEL'S COLLEGE in Winooski, and in 1964 received a law degree from Georgetown University. Locating in Burlington, he was elected Chittenden County state's attorney in 1966, serving through 1974, when he was honored as one of the three outstanding prosecutors in the United States. His election to the U.S. Senate in 1974—a western Vermonter occupying the eastern seat—eliminated the last vestige of the Mountain Rule in Vermont politics. Re-elected to his fifth term in 1998, in the 107th Congress he served on the Agriculture and Appropriations committees and on the Judiciary committee as ranking member. An accomplished legislator adept at attracting national publicity to causes, he has been the leading U.S. officeholder in the international campaign against the production, export, and use of anti-personnel landmines. Actively involved in legislation associated with the Internet, Leahy's efforts to protect privacy rights, copyright, and freedom of speech on this new means of communication helped earn him the 1999 John Peter and Anna Catherine Zenger Award for "outstanding contributions in support of press freedoms and the people's right to know." This was only the second time since 1954 that the award went to a government figure. In June 2001, after Vermont's junior Senator JAMES JEFFORDS left the REPUBLICAN PARTY and the Democrats reorganized the Senate, Leahy was given chairmanship of the Judiciary Committee. Perhaps the most celebrated of Leahy's achievements was helping to secure $25 million in federal funds to clean up LAKE CHAMPLAIN. Initially successful in having Champlain classified as one of the Great Lakes, Leahy later acquiesced in its declassification while the funding was retained.

Leavenworth, Jesse (d. 1824)

A veteran of the battle of Lexington in 1775 and other Continental service, Jesse Leavenworth became a speculator and developer in Vermont lands after the Revolution. Originally from Connecticut, he joined with LUKE KNOULTON, IRA ALLEN, JAMES WHITELAW, and others and purchased the grant of a large parcel of land in Danville from the Vermont General Assembly. His first development at Danville was to erect a mill at Joe's Pond. In the 1790s, he went to France to buy manufactured goods, which he exported to America, and while living in Paris he assisted Ira Allen in an unsuccessful scheme to ship twenty thousand war-surplus guns and cannon to Vermont.

LeClair, John (b. 1969)

Widely considered Vermont's best professional hockey player, John LeClair was born in St. Albans, where he attended local primary and secondary schools. After playing intercollegiate hockey at the UNIVERSITY OF VERMONT (class of 1991), LeClair joined the Montreal Canadiens, helping them to win the Stanley Cup in 1993. Traded in 1995 to the Philadelphia Flyers, LeClair established himself as one of the NHL's premier goal scorers, scoring at least fifty goals in three consecutive seasons between 1995 and 1998. A generous benefactor to Vermont charities, LeClair is president of the John LeClair Foundation, established in 1993 to help poor and needy Vermonters. *Paul Searles*

Leclerc, Agnes Elizabeth Winona Joy, Princess Salm-Salm (1844–1912)

Agnes Elizabeth Winona Joy Leclerc of Swanton met and married a soldier of fortune, Felix Nepomuk, Prince Salm-Salm, a veteran of the Prussian and Austrian armies recently appointed colonel in the Union army, while she was visiting her sister in Washington at the beginning of the Civil War. She followed him through his campaigns as commander of the Sixty-eighth New York German volunteers. Princess Salm-Salm wielded considerable political influence in Washington, at one point blocking the advancement of another German officer who had insulted her husband's unit after they broke and ran at the BATTLE OF GETTYSBURG. After the war, the couple joined Emperor Maximilian in Mexico. When Maximilian's imperial reign ended before a firing squad in 1867, Felix Salm-Salm was imprisoned. Fleeing Mexico to Washington, Princess Salm-Salm persuaded the State Department to intervene for her husband's release. The reunited couple went to Germany at the opening of the Franco-Prussian war in 1870, in which Prince Salm-Salm was killed at the battle of Metz. Princess Salm-Salm returned to America in 1899 to give the Sixty-eighth New York regiment's battle flags to the Bleecker Veterans Association. In 1900, she came to America again to raise funds to equip an ambulance corps for the wounded of the Boer War in South Africa. She figures in several novels written in Germany and England between 1920 and the 1980s and in Franz Werfel's play *Juarez and Maximilian* (Vienna and New York, 1925–1926).

Leddy, Bernard J. (1910–1972)

The leading Democrat in Vermont from the 1940s to the 1960s, Bernard J. Leddy was born in Underhill Center into a family descended from Irish immigrants who settled in Shelburne in the 1840s. His father was a farmer and state legislator. His early education was in the public and parochial schools of Chittenden County. He graduated from ST. MICHAEL'S COLLEGE (1931) and Boston College Law School (1934). A prominent and successful lawyer in Burlington for more than thirty years, Leddy was also extremely active in Democratic politics and was the leading Democratic figure in the state for more than two decades. His political career spans the period from near-total Republican hegemony to great Democratic success. His strong showing in the 1958 gubernatorial campaign (he lost by only 719 votes) paved the way for the Democratic congressional victory that year and for the many victories to follow. He was chairman of the Vermont delegation at the Democratic Convention in 1960 and served as state campaign coordinator in both 1960 and 1964. Leddy was appointed by President Johnson to the new federal judgeship approved by Congress for Vermont in 1966. When ERNEST W. GIBSON, JR., died in 1969, Leddy became chief federal judge, a position he held until his death. His short judicial career was notable. In a case mirroring the cultural conflicts of the era, Leddy ruled in 1970 that athletes with long hair could not be excluded from competing in high school athletics. His 1971 decision striking down major provisions of Vermont's restrictive laws on voter residency was later upheld by the U.S. Supreme Court.   *Charles O'Brien*

Lee, Noah (1745–1840)

While living in Connecticut, Noah Lee served at Crown Point during the Seven Years' War from 1761 to 1762 and on the 1762 expedition of British regulars and American provincials against France's Spanish allies at Havana. In 1771, Lee, Amos Bird, and "a coloured man" surveyed the township of Castleton, where Lee settled shortly thereafter. At his own expense, in May 1775 he raised a company of GREEN MOUNTAIN BOYS, who joined up with SAMUEL HERRICK to take Skenesborough, New York, and captured Andrew Skene, the son of PHILIP SKENE. Lee commanded the American force at Skenesborough most of the summer of 1775. In November 1776, Noah Lee received a commission from the Continental Congress as lieutenant in MOSES HAZEN's Second Canadian Regiment. He was promoted to captain in 1778, served at Yorktown, was discharged in 1783, and then appointed colonel of the Vermont militia. His sixth son, born in 1787, was named after GUY CARLETON, Lord Dorchester, who was governor general of Quebec during the 1775 to 1776 Canadian campaign of the American army. He lived the remainder of his long life in Castleton, where he was a supporter of the Castleton Seminary, a predecessor of CASTLETON STATE COLLEGE.

Leicester

Leicester (pronounced Lester), population 974, a town in Addison County, was granted by BENNING WENTWORTH in 1761 and named for Leicester in either Massachusetts or England. The western half of the town, part of the Champlain Valley, is flat and agricultural, while the eastern half lies in the foothills of the GREEN MOUNTAINS, rising abruptly from the shores of cottage-dotted Lake Dunmore, which is partly in the town of Salisbury to the north, to the long ridge of 1,563-foot Oak Hill. About a quarter of the town is in the GREEN MOUNTAIN NATIONAL FOREST. Leicester village and Leicester Junction, which once served the Rutland and Burlington Railroad, are the town's two settlements.

Leland, Henry (1843–1932)

Designer and engineer of the Cadillac and Lincoln automobiles, Henry Leland was born in Barton and moved to Worcester, Massachusetts, at age seven with his parents who were seeking work. He worked first in a shoe factory and dropped out of school at age eleven to work full time and by fourteen was an accomplished apprentice machinist working for Crompton Loom Works. During the Civil War, he worked in the Springfield armory making machinery used to produce parts for military rifles. Working as a police officer and a machinist in various shops after the war, he eventually went to Detroit, where he opened his own machine factory. Almost accidentally stumbling into automobile manufacturing, he decided he could build a better car than the first one he purchased, and promptly proceeded to do so. He produced the first V-8 engine and in 1902 the first Cadillac, named in honor of Antoine de la Mothe-Cadillac, the French explorer who first settled at Detroit. During the First World War, Leland manufactured airplane engines, and after the war he opened the first Lincoln automobile factory. He remained in contact with his Barton cousins, returning there for regular summer visits to his family's homestead.

Lemington

Lemington, population 107, a town in Essex County, was granted by BENNING WENTWORTH in 1762 to Samuel Averill and others. The name is presumably a variant of Leamington, England. The town, which is bounded on the east by the CONNECTICUT RIVER, is forested and hilly, and lumbering has always been the chief industry. One substantial summit, 3,140-foot Monadnock Mountain, dominates the town's northeastern corner. The town has no post office, school, church, or store. The only settlement is tiny Lemington village, on Route 102 along the Connecticut in the southern part of the town. Colebrook, the largest town in northernmost New Hampshire, lies directly across the river. The journalist, lecturer, and popular historian Stewart Holbrook (1893–1964) spent part of his boyhood in Lemington.

Lemon Fair River

The small Lemon Fair River, which flows northward through the Addison County towns of Orwell, Shoreham, Bridport, Cornwall, and Weybridge to empty into OTTER CREEK, has long attracted attention because of its unusual name. Suggested derivations include "lamentable affair" (circumstances in dispute), "leman fair" (a medieval term meaning "mistress fair"), *les monts verts* (French for "green mountains"), or *limon faire* ("making silt," an apt description of the sluggish stream). Historical evidence for any of these derivations is lacking, and the origin will probably always be in dispute.

Levasseur, René-Nicholas (1705–1784)

Head of royal shipbuilding and inspector of woods and forests in New France during the mid-eighteenth century, René-Nicholas Levasseur established a sawmill at the site of today's Swanton village on the first falls of the MISSISQUOI RIVER in 1749. He sought to exploit the riverine forests of the Champlain Valley for lumber suitable to build ships of 500 to 700 tons burden. Large rafts carried sawed lumber down the river and the lake to Quebec City, a procedure that would continue in the Champlain Valley until the 1840s. As a reward, Louis XV granted Levasseur the seigneury of Saint-Armand, comprising the present town of Swanton and portions of neighboring Quebec in 1748.

Joseph-André Senécal

Lewis

Lewis, population zero, an unorganized township in Essex County, was granted by BENNING WENTWORTH in 1762 to Samuel Averill and others, including Nathan, Sevignior, and Timothy Lewis, for which trio the township was named. Its northern half is heavily wooded, rough, and mountainous, rising to 2,575 feet at Lewis Mountain, while much of its southern half is taken up by a swampy area known as the Yellow Bogs. There are no roads except those used for logging. The highest number of residents Lewis has ever had, presumably all loggers, is eight, in 1900. In 1999, the entire township became part of the CHAMPION LANDS, a public-private project devoted to conservation and sustainable forest harvesting. Lewis is considered the most inaccessible of all Vermont governmental units for those wishing to join the 251 CLUB.

Lewis, John W. (1810–1861)

A Freewill Baptist minister, antislavery and temperance lecturer, denominational historian, and champion of black nationalism and Haitian immigration, John W. Lewis lived in St. Albans during the early 1850s. He was born in Providence, Rhode Island, and taught at the black New England Union Academy in Providence during the 1830s. He lectured on anti-slavery and other reform issues in northern New England, settled in St. Albans about 1850, and became a traveling agent for *Frederick Douglass' Paper* in Vermont, upstate New York, and southern Quebec. His letters to the abolitionist and black press comment keenly on attitudes regarding race and social standing in the U.S-Canada eastern border region. In 1852, he published *The Life, Labors, and Travels of Elder CHARLES BOWLES*. His biography of the black Vermont minister has pronounced anti-slavery overtones. During the 1850s, Lewis served on the National Council of the Colored People, a national coordinating body. By 1860, disillusioned with black prospects in the United States, he led the Lawrence Association colony to Haiti, where he died within a year.   *Ray Zirblis*

Lewis, Sinclair (1885–1951)

The novelist Sinclair Lewis, author of *Main Street* (1920) and *Babbitt* (1922) and winner of the 1929 Nobel Prize, married the journalist DOROTHY THOMPSON in 1928 and in the same year bought a 300-acre farm with two houses in Barnard. The couple named it Twin Farms, and it proved to be, in the words of Lewis's biographer Mark Schorer, "the only real home" he would ever have. Here the peripatetic pair spent many summers, entertaining such visitors as H. L. Mencken, Vincent Sheean, and Louis Untermeyer. When they divorced in 1942, Twin Farms became Thompson's property. One of the less happy incidents during their stay there occurred in 1929, when Lewis was invited to give a lecture at the BREAD LOAF WRITERS' CONFERENCE and, drunk, told the attendees that it was impossible to teach creative writing. Two of Lewis's works have Vermont associations. One was an extended satiric monologue, *The Man Who Knew Coolidge: Being the Soul of Lowell Schmaltz, Constructive and Nordic Citizen*, published in 1928. The other was the novel *It Can't Happen Here* (1935), the story of the rise and establishment of a fascist dictatorship in the United States as experienced by a liberal Vermont newspaper editor and his family and neighbors. Highly successful, the novel was dramatized by Lewis in 1936 and, sponsored by the Federal Theater Project, saw twenty-three productions in eighteen cities. Lewis himself acted the lead role at the summer theater in Cohasset, Massachusetts, in 1938.

Liberty Union

On June 26, 1970, Democratic primary candidates Peter Diamondstone, Dennis Morrisseau, and former congressman WILLIAM MEYER met at Meyer's home. Self-styled populists who believed that American society had become so warped that traditionalist doctrines appeared as dangerous radical dogma and having concluded that the Democratic state organization was systematically excluding them from party forums and debates, they left the party to form the Liberty Union. They described the Liberty Union not as a party, but as a movement that would provide Vermonters with a "real choice" by offering candidates distinguishable from the indistinguishable DEMOCRATIC AND REPUBLICAN PARTIES. Their platform proposed revamping the national economy by the creation of "a flexible 1,000-hour work year" and a "bare minimum" income of $5,000 for a family of four. The Liberty Union's petitions to be placed on the ballot were challenged by Democratic candidate for attorney general THOMAS SALMON, but a Republican secretary of state ruled to validate the petitions despite a number of questionable signatures. The electoral debut was hardly auspicious, with only the congressional candidate, Morrisseau, winning as much as 2 percent of the vote. For a January 1972 special election, recent Vermont arrival BERNARD SANDERS received the party's nomination for the U.S. Senate and became a Liberty Union mainstay until 1977 when he left the party. In the intervening years, Meyer and Morrisseau had drifted back to the Democrats and the Liberty Union had achieved major party status through winning 5 percent of the total governor's vote in 1974. Major party status required a nominating convention, which spawned a contested primary and disputes that promoted the exodus of prominent members. Although the Liberty Union has continued to field slates for state offices and occasionally local candidates, after 1976 it has had little or no impact on election outcomes. By 1980, with the formation of the Citizens Party, it lost its monopoly on Vermont's alternative party movement and has been kept alive largely through the efforts of founder Peter Diamondstone.

Lincoln

Lincoln, population 1,214, a town in Addison County, was granted by the Vermont legislature to Colonel Benjamin Simonds and others, and named for Major General Benjamin Lincoln, who led the Massachusetts militia at the BATTLE OF BENNINGTON. The earliest settlers were Quakers. The town lies on the western slopes of the main spine of the GREEN MOUNTAINS, rising to 4,052-foot Mount Abraham, Vermont's fifth-highest peak, and is largely in the GREEN MOUNTAIN NATIONAL FOREST. The upland settlements of Lincoln, West Lincoln, and South Lincoln, once centers of lumbering, are all along the New Haven River, here a mountain stream occasionally given to sudden floods. The road that runs through the town in an east-west direction from Warren to Bristol rises to a height of 2,424 feet at Lincoln Gap, the highest pass reachable by automobile in the state, and is closed in winter.

Lincoln, Robert Todd (1843–1926)

See HILDENE.

Loeb, William (1905–1981)

A politically conservative newspaper publisher, William Loeb owned three Vermont newspapers in the 1940s and 1950s. With a loan from his mother (his father had been personal secretary to President Theodore Roosevelt), Loeb bought his first newspaper, the *St. Albans Daily Messenger*, in 1941. The next year Loeb purchased the *BURLINGTON DAILY NEWS* and the *Vermont Sunday News*. In the early years of Loeb's tenure as owner, the *Daily News* had a liberal slant, supporting such causes as the Textile Workers Union of America's campaign to organize Winooski's American Woolen Mill in 1943. Loeb resided in Vermont throughout most of the 1940s, and his second wife remained a long-time resident of Windham. He met his third wife, Nackey Scripps Gallowhur, in Burlington and employed her for a time at the *Daily News*. In 1949, Loeb was briefly jailed in Woodstock after an alienation of affections suit was filed against him by Gallowhur's husband. Loeb left Vermont permanently in 1955 to settle in New Hampshire, where he published the *Manchester Union Leader*, which he had purchased in 1946, and often wrote famously vitriolic front-page editorials. Though Loeb continued to publish the unprofitable *Burlington Daily News* until 1961, he never returned to Vermont, thus evading a supreme court order to pay child support payments for his daughter by his second wife. *Paul Searls*

Londonderry

Londonderry, population 1,709, a town in Windham County, was granted by the Vermont legislature in 1780 and originally encompassed the neighboring town of Windham, from which it was separated in 1795. The two towns had previously comprised the New York–patented town of Kent. Londonderry is named after the older town in New Hampshire, from which a number of the first settlers came. The western part of the town lies in the foothills of the main spine of the GREEN MOUNTAINS; the eastern border is largely defined by the long ridge of 2,940-foot Glebe Mountain. The main settlements of Londonderry village and South Londonderry lie on Route 100 along the WEST RIVER, which winds through the center of the town from north to south. To some extent Londonderry is in the economic orbit of the Stratton Mountain ski area in the nearby towns of Stratton and Winhall.

Lonergan, John (1841–1902)

An Irish nationalist and Congressional Medal of Honor winner in the Civil War, John Lonergan was born in county Tipperary, Ireland, and emigrated with his family to settle in Burlington in 1845. In the 1850s, young Lonergan worked as a cooper with his father and helped in a grocery business. His free time was devoted to drilling and training with the local militia. When the Civil War broke out in 1861, Lonergan enlisted and was appointed captain of his own company of mostly Irishmen from Burlington, Westford, and Rutland. Throughout the war, Lonergan's unit, Company A, Thirteenth Regiment Vermont Volunteers, was known as Emmett's Guards, their name taken from Robert Emmet, the Irish patriot. Lonergan's company distinguished themselves at the BATTLE OF GETTYSBURG and he received the Congressional Medal of Honor for his actions at Gettysburg. After the war ended, John Lonergan and many Irish-Vermont veterans of the Union Army joined the Burlington Fenian Club, one of thirteen formed in the state during the war years. Ostensibly social organizations to stimulate Irish pride, the Fenians secretly planned an invasion of Canada to force England into granting independence to Ireland. Lonergan participated in both of the unsuccessful 1866 and 1870 FENIAN RAIDS into Quebec. *Vince Feeney*

Long Trail

The oldest long-distance hiking trail in the United States, the Long Trail was built between 1910 and 1930 by members of the GREEN MOUNTAIN CLUB. The club was founded for the purpose of creating the trail, and remains its steward and protector to this day. The trail follows the ridge of the GREEN MOUNTAINS for 270 miles from the Massachusetts line to the Canadian border. The Long Trail system includes 175 miles of side trails and about seventy overnight shelters to accommodate hikers. Over two thousand hikers have walked the entire Long Trail, sometimes called "the footpath in the wilderness." The official *Long Trail Guide* book is in its twenty-fourth edition (1996). Since 1986, the Green Mountain Club has conducted a fund-raising campaign to purchase land around the trail and protect it from development. *Reidun Nuquist*

Lord, Charles (1902–1997)

One of the original shapers of Vermont's ski industry, Charlie Lord became involved with the industry in 1933 when he came to work in Stowe after being laid off by the state highway department during the Depression. An engineering graduate of the UNIVERSITY OF VERMONT and a skier from his earliest days, Lord was appointed by then State Forester PERRY MERRILL to oversee the CIVILIAN CONSERVATION CORPS' cutting of ski trails on MOUNT MANSFIELD. These trails later served as templates for trails at other mountains to which Lord also contributed his expertise. He designed the first gondola at Sugarbush and the original Mad River chairlift. Lord continued to work at Mount Mansfield until 1974, designing trails, engineering lifts, and generally being involved in every major improvement to that ski area. Three Stowe ski trails bear his name: Upper Lord, Middle Lord, and Lower Lord. The son of a Groton printer and publisher, Lord died in Stowe. *Hilari Farrington*

Low, A. Ritchie (1899–1948)

The founder of the Vermont FRESH AIR PROGRAM, the Reverend A. Ritchie Low was born in New Castle, England, and educated at the University of Aberdeen, where he acquired a Scots burr that still marked his speech when he came to Vermont. A Canadian Army veteran of World War I, Low served Congregational churches in Colchester (1927–1932), Johnson (1932–1948), and Vergennes (1948). His principal work in race relations was to create and execute the Vermont Plan in 1944 under which African-American children from New York City's Harlem were (and continue to be) brought to Vermont for two weeks or longer each summer as guests of white families. Low said his work with the children was based on "aggressive good will [that] has to be more than just talk." At a meeting of the General Council of Congregational Churches at Grinnell, Iowa, in 1946, Low was honored for his contribution to the field of race relations by the Council for Social Action of the Congregational Christian Churches of the United States. *David Blow*

Lowell

Lowell, population 738, a town in Orleans County, was granted by the Vermont legislature in 1791 to New York lawyer John

Kelly and originally called Kellyvale. The name was changed to Lowell in 1831, but whether after the city in Massachusetts or after an individual is not known. The town is hemmed in on the east by the long ridge of Lowell Mountain, which effectively cuts off direct communication with neighboring Albany, and on the east by the main spine of the GREEN MOUNTAINS, culminating in 3,360-foot Belvidere Mountain. For most of the twentieth century, asbestos was mined on the mountain, in the most recent years by the Vermont Asbestos Group, a worker-owned company. The only significant settlement is Lowell village, on Route 100 almost directly in the middle of the town. The last section of the BAYLEY-HAZEN ROAD, built in 1776 to 1779 northwestward from Wells River (in Newbury town) on the CONNECTICUT RIVER as part of a wartime plan for the American army to retreat from Canada in 1776 and then re-invade it in 1780, runs through Lowell and ends in Hazen's Notch a mile further on in the town of Westfield.

Loyalist Blockhouse

In July 1781, JUSTUS SHERWOOD, once a GREEN MOUNTAIN BOY but then serving in the Queens Loyal Rangers, and twenty-five men built a blockhouse on North Hero Island in LAKE CHAMPLAIN at Dutchman's Point (so named for a Dutch man from New York named Tamer who with his wife settled on the spot about 1770). Garrisoned by Loyalist rangers throughout the Revolution, the blockhouse was used as a base for spies to travel into lower New England and New York. Sherwood also supervised the secret meetings here between the British and IRA ALLEN known as the HALDIMAND NEGOTIATIONS. British regulars were stationed there and across the lake at Point au Fer from 1784 until the summer of 1796 at the general evacuation of British posts on American territory under the Jay Treaty. On at least one occasion, in September 1792, the British troops stationed at the blockhouse were fiercely harassed by a large crowd of Champlain islanders seeking their evacuation of the site. No trace remains of the original blockhouse. A marker denoting the site was erected in July 1913. The late Oscar E. Bredenberg of Champlain, New York, purchased the point about 1960 and built a replica of a blockhouse for his home. *David Blow*

Lucia, Rose (1874–1938)

An educator and author of children's books, Rose Lucia and her father, lawyer Daniel Lucia, moved the family from Vergennes to Montpelier to live with maternal grandparents upon her mother's death. She was educated in the capital city and in private schools, graduating from the Allen School in West Newton, Massachusetts, in 1892. The following year, she began teaching in the Montpelier primary school, becoming its principal in 1909. An advocate of Montessori teaching techniques, Lucia was appointed Vermont supervisor of rural schools in 1921; in this capacity she surveyed every rural school building in the state. Lucia wrote four popular children's books, the *Peter and Polly* series, published between 1912 and 1918, which were supplementary reading in the schools. (The books were republished by Montpelier's Kellogg-Hubbard Library in 1983.) The protagonists were modeled on children Lucia knew in East St. Johnsbury, home town of Caroline M. Griswold, Lucia's long-time companion. Active in the Vermont Teachers' Retirement Fund Association and the Young Women's Christian Association, Lucia also found time for her hobbies of gardening and motoring. She died in Santa Rosa, California.

Reidun Nuquist

Lucioni, Luigi (1900–1988)

A native of Milan, Italy, who came to the United States as a child, Luigi Lucioni studied painting at Cooper Union, the National Academy of Design, and during the 1920s in Italy and France supported by a Tiffany Foundation Fellowship. In 1929, ELECTRA HAVEMEYER WEBB, a board member of the Metropolitan Museum of Art, invited him to spend his summers painting at the Webbs' SHELBURNE FARMS. Ten years later, Lucioni bought a house and barn in Manchester and converted the barn into a studio. During his summers in Vermont, Lucioni painted several landscapes that captured a quintessential Vermont mixture of rickety barns, rocky fields, and cloud-shadowed hills. He earned several prizes during the 1930s and 1940s, and at age thirty-two was the youngest painter ever to have his work purchased by the Metropolitan Museum of Art. *Life* magazine called him "Vermont's painter laureate." But with the rise of Abstract Expressionism in the late 1940s and 1950s, Lucioni's work came to be seen as old-fashioned. The SHELBURNE MU-SEUM exhibits two of his paintings and a large collection of his prints.

Ludlow

Ludlow, population 2,449, a town in Windsor County, was granted by BENNING WENTWORTH in 1761 and originally included the eastern half of what is now the town of Mount Holly. It may have been named for the English peer Henry Arthur Herbert (1703–1772), who held, among other titles, that of Viscount Ludlow. The central village of Ludlow, dominated by an old woolen mill now converted into shops and apartments, sits at the junction of Routes 100 and 103 and, with its numerous inns, restaurants, and stores serves as the base for the Okemo Mountain ski resort, which covers the slopes of 3,343-foot Ludlow Mountain just to the west of the village. The resort has ninety-eight trails, thirteen lifts, and a vertical drop of 2,150 feet. The Black River Academy, whose three-story Richardsonian building, now a museum, stands high on a hill over the village, was a premier educational institution during its 104 years from 1835 to 1938. Among its graduates was CALVIN COOLIDGE (1890) of nearby Plymouth. ABBY MARIA HEMENWAY, the indefatigable historian of Vermont, was a native of Ludlow.

Lumière North American Company

A French film manufacturer, A. Lumière et ses Fils purchased Burlington's Howard Park in 1901, demolished the old fair buildings, and built a factory designed by Boston architect Frederick S. Hinds. The firm's founder, Antoine Lumière, and his sons Auguste and Louis had established the business at Lyons in 1882. Having developed color photography in 1900, A. Lumière et ses Fils decided to introduce its products to North America, choosing Burlington because the atmosphere and climate were conducive to processing color plates. In their light- and temperature-controlled factory, the Lumières pioneered the development of color film in America. They employed fifty people and at first produced photographic plates, paper, and chemicals. In the fall of 1907, Auguste Lumière himself came to Burlington to begin mass production of the single plate color process. The Burlington factory lasted from 1902 to 1912, for by 1911 photographic goods could be imported more cheaply from Lyons than made here. The North America end of the business was absorbed by the Eastman Company and moved out of Burlington.   *David Blow*

Lunenburg

Lunenburg, population 1,328, a town in Essex County, was granted by BENNING WENTWORTH in 1763. Like the nearby towns of Brunswick and Ferdinand, it derived its name from Prince Karl Wilhelm Ferdinand of Brunswick-Lüneburg (1735–1806), a German hero of the Seven Years' War with family connections to the British royal house of Hanover. Bounded on the east by the CONNECTICUT RIVER, the town is hilly and forested, with 182-acre Neal Pond lying almost directly in its center. The main settlements are Lunenburg village on U.S. Route 2, which crosses the center of the town from east to west, and Gilman on the Connecticut in the town's southernmost section. The latter was for most of the twentieth century the home of the Gilman Paper Company, founded by Isaac Gilman, an immigrant Jew from Russia. The company was the largest industry in Essex County for many years, employing over five hundred people in its heyday. A reduced work force produced specialty paper for the Simpson Paper Company in recent years, until the plant was purchased by the American Tissue Company in December 1999.

Lung Fever Epidemic of 1812

Immediately after the United States Congress declared war on Great Britain in June 1812, regular army troops were sent to defend Burlington against an anticipated invasion from Canada. They encamped on Pearl Street east of the bluff overlooking LAKE CHAMPLAIN, where a cannon battery was stationed on a site subsequently memorialized as Battery Park. As the encampment expanded with new recruits and activated Vermont militiamen, lung fever erupted among the troops in the fall. Exhibiting chills, cold in the extremities, pain in the chest and head, a weak and fast pulse of 80 to 180 beats per minute, a brown tongue, protruded eyes, and fluid in the lungs, the victims died within twenty-four hours of the onset as their lungs filled with fluid. Hundreds of soldiers died in October and November, but in December only 150 soldiers died from the disease, most in the first two weeks of the month. By January and February, lung fever began to subside among the troops, but Burlington citizens had also started to die from the disease in

late December, and deactivated militia returning home from Burlington's epidemic spread the disease nearly statewide. Civilian deaths in Burlington peaked in February and then the disease spread to other parts of the state, peaking in other regions during March and April. Not all sections of the state were affected to the same extent. Towns in eastern Vermont, where few or no men went to the army in Burlington, saw very few deaths from lung fever. Dr. JOSEPH A. GALLUP in 1815 estimated that 705 soldiers stationed in Burlington and 5,650 residents throughout Vermont died of lung fever, 2.9 percent of the state's population. Modern epidemiologists estimate total deaths from lung fever in 1812 and 1813, including the Burlington garrison's deaths, at 4,350, making the lung fever epidemic the most devastating such event in Vermont's history.   *Jason Roberts*

Luse, Eleanor M. (1904–1997)

A speech pathologist and founder of the UNIVERSITY OF VERMONT's Speech and Hearing Clinic in 1953, Eleanor M. Luse was born in Chicago and earned three degrees from Northwestern University, including a doctorate in voice and speech pathology (1946). Before coming to UVM in 1947 to start a program in voice and speech pathology, she taught at Coe College in Iowa, the Boston School of Physical Education, and Wells College in Aurora, New York. Early in her career in Vermont, Dr. Luse found that the state had a high percentage of babies born with cleft palates. The absence of plastic surgeons in Vermont in the 1940s meant that babies with cleft palates were taken to Boston for surgery or the condition was left uncorrected. By speaking to clubs and schools around the state, Dr. Luse conducted a campaign to educate parents and schools about the need to recognize and treat speech difficulties, an effort that contributed to offering services in schools throughout the state for children with speech and hearing problems. At the Speech and Hearing Clinic, she worked to rehabilitate laryngectomy patients and those with speech disabilities attributed to deafness. Her research in voice rehabilitation produced a therapeutic technique that focuses primarily on the release of tension in the larynx and building breath support for vocalization. Her methods of voice rehabilitation were widely recognized by a Service Award from the American Cancer Society and election as a Fel-

low of the American Speech and Hearing Society. The University of Vermont honored her in 1973 by renaming the Speech and Hearing Clinic the Eleanor M. Luse Center for Communication Disorders, and by awarding her an honorary degree, as did Northwestern University. She retired from UVM in 1975 but continued as a consultant. Eleanor Luse died at her home in Spring Valley, California.

Lydius, John Henry (1694–1791)

A Dutch trader with the Mohawks who claimed a large section of western Vermont, John Henry Lydius lived in Montreal for some years before 1730 when GILLES HOCQUART, the intendant (administrator) of New France, banished him. He then set up a trading post at Wood Creek, New York, the later site of Fort Edward. In 1732, Lydius appeared in Boston exhibiting a deed to land in the Champlain Valley that he claimed to have acquired from the Mohawks. The tract ran 60 miles south of the mouth of OTTER CREEK along LAKE CHAMPLAIN and east 24 miles, including nearly all of modern Addison and Rutland counties. Governor Shirley of Massachusetts confirmed the Indian deed. Hocquart meanwhile acquired a seignieury grant in 1744 from the French Crown for about one-eighth of the Lydius claim, or approximately the full southwestern quarter of today's Addison County. Hocquart sold the seignieury to Michel Chartier de Lotbiniere in 1763. New Hampshire made extensive grants in this tract during the 1760s. The region covered Lydius's plan of thirty-five townships in this tract, of which New York granted several towns, including Durham, which was also granted by New Hampshire as Clarendon, the scene of intense disputes between New Hampshire and New York title holders for the same land. Fleeing to England during the American Revolution, Lydius appeared in London as the Baron de Quade in a military hat, cockade, and a black suit adorned with the Prussian Order of the Eagle, and unsuccessfully sought compensation from the British government.

Lyndon

Lyndon, population 5,448, a town in Caledonia County, was granted by the Vermont legislature in 1780 to JONATHAN ARNOLD of Providence, Rhode Island, and fifty-two associates. It is believed that the town was named for Josias Lyndon, former Rhode Island governor and a friend of

Arnold. The gently rolling countryside, better suited to agriculture than many other towns in the NORTHEAST KINGDOM, is cut by the PASSUMPSIC RIVER and its West and East Branches, which meet north of the contiguous settlements of Lyndon Corner, Lyndon Center, and Lyndonville, the last of which is the major population center. In 1866, after fire had destroyed the St. Johnsbury shops of the Connecticut and Passumpsic Rivers Railroad, a new terminus was built in the town of Lyndon. That was the beginning of Lyndonville, a village created to serve the terminus. The resultant prosperity is still visible in the handsome Victorian architecture along Main Street. Lyndonville retains a substantial manufacturing base today, making products as varied as cutting tools and Bag Balm, an unguent for cows' udders. In Lyndon Center nearby are LYNDON INSTITUTE, a private secondary school serving Lyndon and surrounding communities, and LYNDON STATE COLLEGE, one of the five units of the VERMONT STATE COLLEGES.

Lyndon Institute

An approved comprehensive high school for grades nine through twelve, Lyndon Institute in Lyndonville is a traditional "New England Academy" that enrolls seven hundred students from nearby towns as well as others from across the United States and around the world. Chartered in 1867 as the Lyndon Literary and Biblical Institution by a group of Free Baptist clergymen and Lyndon businessmen, the school was founded in 1869 with the construction of a brick and granite building on a knoll sloping toward the village common. Sumner Shaw Thompson rescued the school from financial difficulty in 1883, purchasing liens on the building and turning it back to the corporation after a $25,000 endowment had been raised and the school's affiliation with the Baptist Church had been dropped. Other benefactors over the years have included ELMER A. DARLING and THEODORE N. VAIL, a president of the board of trustees who established the VAIL SCHOOL OF AGRICULTURE at the Institute in 1910. Known officially as Lyndon Institute since 1923, the school serves Lyndon and several surrounding towns as a high school by annual vote at their town meetings. A teacher training program taught in Lyndon Institute's Normal Department (1911–1938) became the Lyndon Normal School, then Lyndon Teach-

ers' College, and finally LYNDON STATE COLLEGE, one of five VERMONT STATE COLLEGES.   *Harriet F. Fisher*

Lyndon Outing Club

One of Vermont's few surviving COMMUNITY SKI HILLS is operated by the Lyndon Outing Club, the oldest continuing all-volunteer ski club in the state. The Lyndon Outing Club first met formally in February 1937 and elected Milton Kerr, Kermit Grant, and Raymond Russell as its first officers. The club's first ski slope was a pasture near Lyndonville rented for $25. Merchants and other businesses contributed money for lights, and volunteers built a warming cabin, a rope tow, and a 25-meter jump, later replaced by a 40- to 45-meter jump. Membership growth and increasing skills required moving to a larger hill in 1947. The town of Lyndon purchased the second site with federal funds in 1972 and named it Shonyo Park for the original owners, the Shonyo family, who donated the town's share of the purchase back to Lyndon. New buildings have gone up, a 1,600-foot T-bar lift has replaced the rope tow, and trails to serve various skill levels have been constructed. Much of the club's work is accomplished by volunteers, though paid lift operators ensure continuity of service and safe operation. Night skiing on the hill and lighted cross-country skiing have increased usage of the trails. Ticket prices are family affordable. The Lyndon Area Chamber of Commerce's annual Snowflake Festival in February includes the Lyndon Outing Club's Winter Carnival.   *Harriet F. Fisher*

Lyndon State College

Today one of the VERMONT STATE COLLEGES, Lyndon State College traces its origins to 1910, when LYNDON INSTITUTE offered teacher training to senior-year students pursuant to an act of the Vermont General Assembly that sought to meet a shortage of teachers in the state. In 1911, eleven women students were enrolled in a one-year teacher-preparation program offered in a single room at the institute and operated under the auspices of the Vermont Department of Education. Two years later, the legislature provided for teaching training courses in secondary schools for students who had already graduated from approved high schools. In 1923, the first group of students graduated with a two-year degree from the Institute's Normal Department, which by

1933 became a three-year program. In 1938, Lyndon Normal School shared some buildings and teachers with Lyndon Institute, but employed a core teacher-training faculty separate from the institute. In 1944, a four-year program was created. The Vermont state legislature established the school as Lyndon Teachers' College in 1949. Rita Bole, the principal of Lyndon Normal School since 1927, became the first president of Lyndon Teachers' College. In 1951, the college moved up the hill to occupy the Vail mansion. THEODORE VAIL, the founder of AT&T, had left the property to the state to be used for educational purposes. In the late 1950s, Burklyn Manor, the mansion of ELMER DARLING located on the border between Lyndon and Burke, was used as a men's residence hall. In 1960, a two-year liberal arts program was introduced. This was soon followed with four-year degrees in English and history. Lyndon Teachers' College became part of the newly established Vermont State College system in 1962 and its name was changed to Lyndon State College. The 1960s was a period of significant growth in facilities. In 1964, a new library (currently Harvey Academic Center), Wheelock residence hall, and the Stevens dining hall were constructed. In 1967, Arnold, Bailey, Poland, and Rogers residence halls were built. These four are affectionately referred to as "Stonehenge." The SAMUEL READ HALL library was completed in 1972. In 1974, the original Vail Manor was demolished as unsafe and replaced two years later by the T. N. Vail Center. In the late 1970s and early 1980s, several professional programs were added to the curriculum, including communications, business, recreation and resort management, and meteorology. Teacher education remains an important part of the curriculum.

Harriet F. Fisher and Allen Yale

Lyon, Asa (1763–1841)

A pioneer community and spiritual leader in the Champlain islands, Asa Lyon was an honors graduate of Dartmouth College, class of 1781, who came to Vermont after being ordained to the ministry in Sunderland, Massachusetts. He settled in Grand Isle before it was separated from South Hero. Lyon was the first minister of the South Hero Congregational church in 1795, first chief judge of the newly formed Grand Isle county court from 1806 to 1810, and first representative for Grand Isle

County in the Vermont House from 1810 to 1813. He was elected to one term in the United States Congress in 1814. Exceptionally intelligent by all accounts, Lyon was a classical scholar. He gave private lessons in Greek and Latin to prepare young men for the UNIVERSITY OF VERMONT and helped establish Grand Isle's Town Library. In 1799, he officiated at the wedding of Timothy Nightingale and Sally Love, the first wedding in Grand Isle after that town's separation from South Hero. Rigorously frugal, he made his clothes from his own flax crop and wool from his sheep, always dyeing the material with a natural brown vegetable dye he had mixed. He refused to accept any monetary or other reward for his ministerial services and was much revered in the Champlain islands as Father Lyon.   *Donald Tinney*

Lyon, James (ca. 1775–1824)

Born in Wallingford, James Lyon was a printer and newspaper publisher. The son of MATTHEW LYON, he apprenticed to a printer in Philadelphia. Lyon published the Rutland *Farmer's Library* in 1793 and 1794 before moving to Fair Haven, where he and JUDAH PADOCK SPOONER continued the *Farmer's Library* from 1795 to 1798

under the direction of Spooner's father, a papermaker. James Lyon printed Joel Barlow's *Copy of a Letter from an American Diplomatic Character in France* (1798), a letter addressed to Abraham Baldwin that was highly critical of the Jay Treaty and of President John Adams. As such, it was the basis of the third count in Matthew Lyon's indictment under the Sedition Act, for which he was found guilty. A peripatetic but largely unsuccessful printer, James Lyon worked in the South in eleven different cities before settling in Cheraw, South Carolina, where he died at the age of forty-nine.   *Marcus A. McCorison*

Lyon, Matthew (1750–1822)

A printer and politician who was elected to the U.S. Congress from Vermont, Kentucky, and Arkansas, Matthew Lyon was born in county Wicklow, Ireland, and was educated and apprenticed to a printer in Dublin after his father's death in the White Boys uprising. Lyon came to America in 1764, the price of his redeemed fare secured by an indentured contract for his service to Jabez Bacon and Hugh Hamil of Litchfield, Connecticut. By 1773, he had purchased 100 acres in the New Hampshire grants and married Mary Hosford, a

first cousin of ETHAN ALLEN. A member of the GREEN MOUNTAIN BOYS present at the capture of FORT TICONDEROGA in 1775, Lyon continued in the patriot army through the BATTLE OF HUBBARDTON. He then served in the Vermont House of Representatives, as a selectman for Fair Haven, where he operated a successful iron works, and as a Rutland County judge. In 1796, Lyon gained a seat in the U.S. House of Representatives as a Jeffersonian Democrat after several defeats by powerful Vermont Federalist opponents. While in Congress, Lyon fought a brawl with a fellow Congressman on the floor of the House after being insulted. In 1798, he was jailed for defying the Sedition Act by writing harsh criticisms of President John Adams and the Federalist Party. While incarcerated, Lyons was re-elected to his Congressional seat and upon release on bail was able to assist in breaking the tie between Thomas Jefferson and Aaron Burr that allowed Jefferson to become president. Migrating to Kentucky in 1801, Lyon represented his new home state in Congress from 1803 to 1811. He later moved to Arkansas, where he was again elected to Congress, but died before taking his seat there.   *Donald Wickman*

McCullough, Hall Park (1872–1966)

The greatest-ever collector of Vermontiana, Hall Park McCullough was born in San Francisco and named for three distinguished forebears. His father, JOHN G. MCCULLOUGH, was a Philadelphia lawyer who went west for his health before the Civil War and was elected an early California attorney general. He became governor of Vermont in 1902. Hall Park McCullough's mother, Eliza Hall Park, was the daughter of TRENOR W. PARK, a Bennington lawyer who prospered in California after the Gold Rush and returned to Vermont to build the Victorian mansion known today as the PARK-MCCULLOUGH HOUSE. Her grandfather, HILAND HALL, was governor of Vermont from 1858 to 1860. Hall Park McCullough and his wife Edith "Artie" Van Benthuysen preferred to live in the old Hall farmhouse next door to the mansion. Although he could have luxuriated in aristocratic splendor, McCullough practiced law in New York City, where he had a seventy-year affiliation with the firm Davis, Polk & Wardwell. McCullough began collecting Americana at the age of twelve. When he died at the age of ninety-four in 1966, his collection of Vermontiana—maps, paintings, engravings, books, and manuscripts—was displayed over an entire floor of the New-York Historical Society and dispersed among directors and librarians of the society, the UNIVERSITY OF VERMONT, Yale University, BENNINGTON MUSEUM, and the Pierpont Morgan Library. Among McCullough's most impressive intellectual efforts was an extra-illustrated edition of *Early History of Vermont*, originally published in 1868 by his great-grandfather, Hiland Hall. Over a twenty-year period, McCullough almost succeeded in his quest to locate a rare and relevant map, portrait, or signed document to accompany each of the book's 515 pages. The work is now housed at UVM. Hall Park and Artie McCullough were responsible to a large extent for the creation in the late 1920s and early 1930s of BENNINGTON COLLEGE, on a campus near North Bennington donated by family members. Artie McCullough was well connected with prominent educators at Columbia University, Smith College, and elsewhere who favored the launching of a progressive college for women, and Hall Park McCullough had the financial wherewithal to support those efforts. *J. Tyler Resch*

McCullough, John Griffith (1835–1910)

An associate of FREDERICK BILLINGS and TRENOR W. PARK in their San Francisco law firm and later governor of Vermont from 1902 to 1904, John Griffith McCullough was born in Newark, Delaware, and graduated from Delaware College, class of 1855, and the University of Pennsylvania Law School in 1858. After briefly clerking in a Philadelphia law firm, McCullough went to California, settling in Mariposa, where he befriended General John Frémont. He represented Mariposa in the state legislature (1861 and 1863), and prospered in the law business. McCullough moved to San Francisco in 1866, where he associated with Billings's and Park's law firm and was elected attorney general of California in 1867. He followed Park and McCullough east, and in 1873 settled in Vermont to devote his attention to commercial, financial, and railroad interests and marry Eliza Hall, eldest daughter of Trenor Park, who had also settled in North Bennington. Between 1873 and 1910, McCullough was either the chief officer or director of a steel company and eight RAILROADS, including the Erie, which he brought out of receivership to solvency. He served also as a director of seven banks and insurance companies. In Vermont, he served in the senate for Bennington County (1898) as well as governor. In the 1902 gubernatorial race, he failed to win a majority against Local Option candidate PERCIVAL CLEMENT, but was elected by the legislature and served one term.

Macdonough, Thomas (1783–1825)

Commander of the American fleet that defeated British warships on LAKE CHAMPLAIN in the BATTLE OF PLATTSBURGH BAY on September 11, 1814, Lieutenant Thomas Macdonough first faced the daunting task of readying an ill-prepared fleet to challenge the British for supremacy of the Champlain Valley. Macdonough established a shipyard on OTTER CREEK at Vergennes, repaired his makeshift navy, and built the flagship *Saratoga*, the largest military vessel ever launched in Vermont. His efforts were rewarded with a promotion to master-commandant, although he was called commodore out of respect. On the morning of the battle, the American fleet faced a superior British navy in Plattsburgh Bay. Despite heavy gunfire and losses on both sides, Macdonough outmaneuvered the enemy's flagship. Forced to strike her colors, HMS *Confiance* surrendered and the badly mauled remains of the British fleet withdrew down the lake into Canada. *Karen Campbell*

McIntosh, Herbert Miller (1861–1942)

A civil engineer and the first Vermont state engineer (1917–1922), Herbert Miller McIntosh, UNIVERSITY OF VERMONT class of 1890, began practice in Burlington in 1892 and from 1905 to 1927 was associated with Frank H. Crandall in the firm McIntosh and Crandall. He served the city of Burlington as city engineer from 1892 to 1903 and from 1907 to 1914. In 1917, McIntosh was appointed Vermont's first state engineer. For the first two years of McIntosh's tenure, road conservation was the main concern of the state, but engineering service expanded when McIntosh's department was given responsibility to oversee federal road projects under Governor PERCIVAL W. CLEMENT in 1919. By the time of McIntosh's retirement from state service eight years later, the state's engineering department had grown to twenty-seven employees. *David Blow*

McMahon, John (1841–1912)

John McMahon of Bakersfield won the World Championship of Collar and Elbow Wrestling in 1884 when he defeated John Tedford, "The Terrible Welshman," for the title in England. During the mid-1880s, McMahon toured Australia and Argentina, where he also won the national championships of those countries. McMahon started wrestling on the family farm and went on to establish a reputation as a wrestler during the Civil War while serving with the Thirteenth Regiment of Vermont Volunteers. After the war, he developed a professional career. His most famous match was at Boston's Music Hall in 1880, where he fought fellow Vermonter Henry Dunn to a draw before a crowd estimated as the "biggest and most enthusiastic in the sporting history of Boston." *Vince Feeney*

Machine-Tool Industry

The fifteen miles of CONNECTICUT RIVER valley between the towns of Springfield and Windsor have come to be called "Precision Valley" because of their importance in the development of the American machine-tool industry in the 1830s and 1840s. Machine tools shape materials, usually metal, by cutting, grinding, or deforming them, and by doing so precisely time after time allow interchangeability of product parts. Before the development of machine tools, every firearm, for example, was individually made, replacement breeches or barrels not being readily available if such parts failed. The making of identical parts, or the "American system" as it came to be known, foreshadowed modern mass-production methods and made such innovations as Henry Ford's "assembly line" possible. The industry had its start in Windsor when ASAHEL HUBBARD, working from a patent for a rotary pump previously obtained by John Cooper of Guildhall, formed the National Hydraulic Company and, using a convict work force from the local prison, made the pumps, with standardized metal parts, into a nationally available commodity. Hubbard's son-in-law Nicanor Kendall began to produce machine-tooled guns, selling them through the pump company. In the 1840s, the firm transmuted into Robbins and Lawrence and did a booming business selling arms to forty-niners heading for the gold fields of California. In 1851, its rifled guns so impressed the British at the Great Exposition in London that the firm was given a government contract to produce the famous Enfield rifle. Running into difficulties after the end of the Crimean War, the firm was bought by a group of Springfield businessmen and moved to that town, where it eventually became Jones & Lamson. Its superintendent, JAMES HARTNESS, perfected the turret lathe (one having a turret for holding various cutting tools), an important machine for the rapid shaping of materials. Other important figures in the industry were Edwin Fellows of Springfield and Frank Lyman Cone of nearby Weathersfield. In the late nineteenth and early twentieth centuries, various Springfield firms supplied the manufacturers of America with the machines they needed—lathes, grinders, gear shapers, and the like—to make the mass-produced products, from sewing machines to locomotives, that an expanding and prospering country demanded. Despite the almost universal dissemination of machine-tool companies throughout the United States today, the Windsor-

Fish and Game Warden Arnold Magoon. John Hall

Springfield area still retains a portion of its original importance. The American Precision Museum in Windsor, housed in the 1846 Robbins and Lawrence Armory and Machine Shop, a National Historic Landmark, depicts the history of Precision Valley with an extensive display of lathes, grinders, and other machines from the 1830s to the mid-twentieth century.

Magoon, Arnold J. (1930–1978)

The first and only Vermont game warden killed in the line of duty and, as of 2002, the last law enforcement officer killed in Vermont while on duty, Warden Supervisor Arnold Magoon of Brandon heard a gun shot while sitting in his home on the night of April 26, 1978. On call twenty-four hours a day, he immediately went out to investigate. Within one-half mile of his place, Warden Magoon confronted three people in a vehicle who had been previously suspected of taking deer out of season. A struggle ensued with one of the men, Scott Johnson of Brandon, who struck Magoon three times on the head with the warden's own six-cell metal flashlight. Magoon died fourteen hours later. He had been a game warden for fifteen years. The twenty-four-year-old Johnson pleaded guilty to second-degree murder for slaying Arnold Magoon, and was sentenced to prison in 1978 for six to twenty years. *Mark Scott*

Mahady, Frank G. "Skip" (1939–1992)

Dartmouth College class of 1961 and Georgetown University School of Law 1964, Frank Mahady served as deputy attorney general (1968–1969) and Windsor County state's attorney (1969–1972). A liberal Republican, Mahady was an early protegé of Thomas L. Hayes, who was lieutenant governor and supreme court justice and a longtime political opponent of Governor RICHARD SNELLING. In 1984, two years after being appointed district judge by Snelling, Mahady was appointed by Superior Judge Hayes to rule on whether the Snelling administration could retain custody over 112 children that the state had removed from their homes in the NORTHEAST KINGDOM COMMUNITY CHURCH controversy. Mahady mightily embarrassed Snelling by ordering the children released. Later that year, he instructed a jury to find not guilty twenty-six left-wing activists who had trespassed in the office of U.S. Senator ROBERT STAFFORD to protest the government's policies in Central America. In 1987, Governor MADELEINE KUNIN appointed Mahady to the supreme court. His nomination ran into serious difficulty in the Democratic-controlled senate in 1988. In addition to charges that Mahady had made irresponsible trial rulings favoring criminal defendants, it was revealed that he had failed for four years to pay taxes on his legal income, and had presented an explanation at variance with the facts. Mahady was forced to withdraw his nomination, but returned to the district court bench where he served quietly until his death in 1992. *John McClaughry*

Mahicans

The Mahicans (not to be confused with the Mohicans of Connecticut) are indigenous people of southwesternmost Vermont. The homeland of the Mahicans also includes a part of New York State lying to the east of the Hudson River around Albany as well as northwestern Massachusetts. They were culturally related to the other native peoples of southern New England. Also known as Loups (Wolves) to seventeenth-century French writers, the Mahicans were mostly friendly to the British and often so to the Iroquois Confederacy. As their lands became overrun by settlers after King Philips War ended in 1676, the Mahicans congregated at Stockbridge, Massachusetts, along with southern New England natives and became known during the eighteenth century as the Stockbridge Indians. During the American Revolution, the Massachusetts militia company of Stockbridge Mahicans fought in the BATTLE OF BENNINGTON in 1777 and returned later when the General Assembly asked them to help guard the state against British raids during 1780 and 1781. For their services, they were granted the town of Marshfield by the General Assembly in 1782, but they sold it to Amos Marsh in 1789. As settlers demanded Stockbridge landholdings, many Mahicans were forced westward in a series of upheavals similar to the later experience of the Cherokees on the "Trail of Tears." The Mahican tribal government is located in Bowler, Wisconsin, but retains ties to descendants of the Mahicans who remained in Massachusetts and are today scattered throughout their homeland, including in southwestern Vermont.

Frederick Wiseman

Maidstone

Maidstone, population 105, a town in Essex County, was granted by BENNING WENTWORTH in 1761 to Samuel Averill and others and named for Maidstone in England. Bounded on the east by the CONNECTICUT RIVER, the town is hilly, densely forested, and sparsely settled. Logging has always been the only significant industry, and in 1999 much of the town became part of the CHAMPION LANDS, a public-private project devoted to conservation and sustainable forest harvesting. Approximately in the center of town lies glacially formed 796-acre Maidstone Lake, a STATE PARK popular because of its remote, unspoiled location in a mixed hard- and softwood forest and its excellent fishing, which includes lake and rainbow trout.

Mallary, Gertrude Robinson

(1902–2002)

Recognized as the collector of the finest private archive of Vermontiana, print and manuscript, Gertrude Mallary was born in Springfield, Massachusetts, and educated in schools in Springfield, Bennett Junior College in Millbrook, New York, and the University of Connecticut. She first arrived in Fairlee in 1931, shortly after the birth of her two sons, one of whom, RICHARD MALLARY, became prominent in state and national government. Initially a summer resident, she settled permanently in Fairlee in 1942 as a farmer and breeder of Holstein-Friesian cattle, serving as secretary of the New England Holstein-Friesian Association and president of the Vermont Holstein Club. A proponent of public service, she served on national boards of the Community Chests and Councils and Day Nurseries of America. Locally, she was a trustee of the VERMONT HISTORICAL SOCIETY and chairperson of the Fairlee Library Board. She was elected to represent Fairlee for two terms (1953–1957) in the Vermont House of Representatives. From 1957 to 1959, she served as the senator from Orange County and was instrumental in securing legislative approval of Vermont's Little Hoover Commission, which under the chairmanship of DEANE DAVIS provided the blueprint for the state's subsequent administrative reorganization.

Mallary, Richard W. (b. 1929)

Richard W. Mallary was born in Springfield, Massachusetts, and moved with his family to Fairlee in 1942. After graduating from Bradford Academy and Dartmouth College (Phi Beta Kappa and summa cum laude), he purchased and operated a dairy farm in Bradford, developing a herd of Holstein cattle and participating in breeder associations. An active participant in REPUBLICAN PARTY and town politics, he was elected representative from Fairlee in 1960, after his mother GERTRUDE MALLARY retired from distinguished service in the legislature. Once in Montpelier, he joined with other progressive freshmen House members who styled themselves YOUNG TURKS and became a significant force during the 1961 to 1962 sessions. By 1963, the Young Turks, who included PHILIP HOFF and FRANKLIN BILLINGS, JR., had assumed the controls of Vermont government, with Mallary as chairman of the House Appropriations Committee. He served in the House through 1968, the last three years as Speaker. In 1966, he presided over the first House session after REAPPORTIONMENT and, as the highest-ranking elected Republican to hold state office, was in frequent opposition to Democratic Governor Hoff, who disagreed with the Speaker's fiscal conservatism. In 1968, Mallary was elected to the Vermont Senate, where he served one term, and in 1971 was appointed secretary of administration by Governor DEANE DAVIS. In 1972, Mallary won Vermont's seat in the U.S. House in a special election and was re-elected to a full term later that year. In 1974, he sought the Senate seat held by the retiring GEORGE AIKEN, and lost in a close contest with Democrat PATRICK LEAHY. Coming back to Vermont, Mallary served as secretary of administration under Governor RICHARD SNELLING. In 1998, he returned to the Vermont House, but in 2000, believing he would be denied Republican renomination because of his support of the CIVIL UNIONS law that provided same-sex couples benefits similar to marriage, he ran as an independent and was defeated in the general election.

Mallett, Jean Pierre (fl. 1750–1790)

The French man after whom Malletts Bay of LAKE CHAMPLAIN is named, Joseph or Jean Pierre Mallett was said to have died in Vermont in 1790 (or in central France in 1815) leaving vast holdings in the United States. The legend seems as imperishable as that of the UFO. People claiming to be his relatives have been searching for Mallett's wealth ever since. The known facts about Jean Pierre Mallett are quite limited. Practically nothing is known about "Captain" Mallett except that he lived on Malletts Head, a knobby headland jutting into Lake Champlain's Malletts Bay, in the town of Colchester, for a long time during the Revolutionary era, and died an old man in 1789 or 1790. Whether he was a squatter or held a grant from the proprietors of the seigniory of La Moinaudiere or La Perriere has never been ascertained. The cellar hole of his house was still discernible in the 1860s. He is reputed to have welcomed spies and smugglers during the Revolution and in the 1780s, and to have sympathized with the rebels against Great Britain. The legend of Mallett's lost treasure probably developed during the second quarter of the nineteenth century, when a national craze for buried treasure-hunting sent droves of Americans searching for lost or hidden gold. *David Blow*

Mamet, David (b. 1947)

Playwright, screenwriter, and director David Mamet was born in Chicago and attended GODDARD COLLEGE in Plainfield and the Neighborhood Playhouse School of Theatre in New York. In 1972, while teaching acting at Goddard, he formed the St. Nicholas Company with two students, one of them William H. Macy, who has appeared frequently in his plays and films. Moving the company to Chicago, he began his playwriting career with *Sexual Perversity in Chicago* and *American Buffalo* (both 1976), and went on to write such works as *Glengarry Glen Ross* (1984), which won the Pulitzer Prize. The prolific Mamet is responsible for over twenty plays, including the controversial *Oleanna* (1992), about sexual harassment and political correctness on campus. A trademark of his dialogue is its terse, hesitational, elliptical character, often given the name "Mametspeak." In 1981, Mamet began to write for films; his scripts include *The Untouchables* (1987), *Hoffa* (1992), *Wag the Dog* (1997), and *State and Main* (2000). *State and Main*, which Mamet also directed, is a satirical look at the interaction between the inhabitants of a small Vermont town and the Hollywood company that has arrived to use the town as the locale for a film. Mamet and his wife, the actress Rebecca Pidgeon, divide their time between homes in Cambridge, Massachusetts, and Vermont.

Manchester

Manchester, population 4,180, a half-SHIRE TOWN (with Bennington) in Bennington County, was granted by BENNING WENTWORTH in 1761. The specific origin of the name, which occurs in England, Massachusetts, Connecticut, and New Hampshire, is unknown. Settlement is concentrated in the VALLEY OF VERMONT, which runs through the town from southwest to northeast and is here 4 miles wide. To the east are the foothills of the GREEN MOUNTAINS, and to the west the highest portions of the TACONIC MOUNTAINS, rising to 3,816 feet at Equinox Mountain, the summit of which is accessible by a toll road. The main village of Manchester was the site of the first settlement, but a short distance away is Manchester Center, once the manufacturing and industrial center of town and known as Factory Point. Today the two villages continue to play different roles. The first is an idealized version of a New England village, full of large, beautifully preserved early Federal buildings flanked by grassy lawns and sidewalks made of MARBLE slabs; the second is the biggest name-brand discount outlet center in the state, drawing residents and tourists from across New England and New York. Like Bennington and Arlington to the south, Manchester played a substantial role in colonial and Revolutionary times; it was here that the first Council of Safety met, and IRA ALLEN devised the plan for confiscating Tory property to pay for the expenses of newly created Vermont. A thriving marble-cutting industry existed here for much of the nineteenth century, sawing slabs quarried in nearby Dorset. Manchester was one of the earliest resort towns in Vermont, a position exemplified by the Equinox, a sprawling wooden hotel in the middle of Manchester village that first opened in 1853 and subsequently expanded until it dominates the main street. After a period of decline, the Equinox re-opened in 1992 as a year-round resort with its own golf course, tennis courts, conference rooms, and other amenities. In winter, lodging and restaurant facilities in Manchester serve the nearby ski areas of Bromley and Stratton. The Charles F. Orvis Company, which began making bamboo fishing rods in Manchester in 1856, is well represented at the AMERICAN MUSEUM OF FLY FISHING, near the Equinox, and the Southern Vermont Art Center, located in a twenty-eight-room Georgian mansion, displays works of art for sale by local artists. HILDENE, the imposing summer home of Robert Todd Lincoln, Abraham and Mary Todd Lincoln's only son to survive to adulthood, built in 1904, sits in the middle of a 400-acre estate south of Manchester village and is open to visitors.

Mann, Fred (1858–1916)

The first Vermonter to play major league baseball, Fred Mann was born in Sutton and grew up in Windsor in a house that had once housed the DRESDEN PRESS, on which the first Vermont constitution was printed in 1778. A power-hitting center fielder, Fred Mann made his National League debut on May 1, 1882, with the Worcester Ruby Legs against Boston. He played for six years in the National League and the American Association as a member of clubs in Philadelphia, Columbus, Pittsburgh, and Cleveland. An excellent fielding outfielder, Fred was also a reliable clean-up hitter and the all-time major league leader in being hit by pitched balls when he finished his big-league career in 1887. In an era when professional baseball players often made more news through their exploits off the field in show business and barroom brawls than in playing ball, Fred Mann distinguished himself by never appearing in the sports gossip columns of the day. In 1889, when the Hartford club released him in the middle of the season, fan reaction was so great for the popular captain that the team's management was forced to return him to the lineup. Retiring in 1890, Mann settled in Springfield, Massachusetts, and became a bartender.

Richard Leyden

Mansfield, Mount

Vermont's highest peak at 4,393 feet, Mount Mansfield was known as *mozeodebe wadso* ("moose-head mountain") to the ABENAKI. Its English name derives from the town of Mansfield, granted by

Mount Mansfield. Vermont Department of Tourism and Marketing

BENNING WENTWORTH in 1763 and named for Mansfield, Connecticut, the place of origin of some of the grantees. The town, almost completely taken up by the mountain, proved impossible to settle, and in 1839 its western section was annexed to Underhill and its eastern section to Stowe. The mountain's mile-long summit vaguely resembles a human profile and has two peaks, the Nose and the Chin, of which the latter is higher. Mansfield is the centerpiece of 37,000-acre Mount Mansfield State Forest, Vermont's largest. Hiking trails lead to the summit, as does a toll road, and the LONG TRAIL follows the crest. The mountain's elevation has made possible the survival on its top of a 250-acre patch of Arctic tundra, a remnant of the Ice Age and one of only two examples of Arctic tundra in the state (a much smaller one is on CAMEL'S HUMP). Exploitation of Mount Mansfield for recreational purposes began in the 1850s, when a carriage road was built to the top from the Stowe side and a hotel was erected under the Nose. (The last remnant of this hotel, which had been rebuilt several times, was razed in 1964.) In the twentieth century, the mountain became one of the premier ski areas in the east, beginning in the 1930s when downhill trails were cut into its eastern flank. A rope tow was installed in 1936, and a chair lift (the state's first) in 1940. Today, with a gondola car and four chair lifts, Mount Mansfield is one of the state's most popular recreational destinations in both winter and summer, a circumstance that has its downside in the environmental degradation of fragile mountain environments caused by a multitude of visitors. The mountain also suffers, as do other high peaks in the GREEN MOUNTAINS, from acid rain caused largely by coal-burning power plants in the midwestern United States and Canada, with a resultant die-off of vegetation, especially red spruce.

Maple Trees, Maple Research, and Maple Products

Maple (*Acer*) species are distributed worldwide and can be found growing wild in forests and cultivated for roadside planting for their large, beautiful crowns of different shapes and fall leaf color. Hybrid maples are grown for gardens and parks, but the sugar, black, and red wild maples of Vermont are economically the most important for their sweet sap and timber. Sugar and other maples have a unique

Maple sugarhouse near Sheffield. Vermont Department of Tourism and Marketing

sap-flow mechanism that occurs when the trees are still dormant in late winter and early spring before flowerleaf buds begin to open. Tree genetics and specific weather conditions trigger sap flow. Cold nights and days with above-freezing temperatures induce higher than atmospheric pressure that moves from the crown to the roots of maples, impelling sap flow through a tap hole. Though long-lived and resistant to viral and bacterial disease, maples are susceptible to insects, air pollution, road salt, wind storms, and overtapping. Basic research on the sugar maple has been conducted in the laboratories of the botany and agricultural biochemistry department of the UNIVERSITY OF VERMONT for more than a century. Applied research is conducted in the field, in the sugarhouse, in the laboratories of the Proctor Maple Research Center in Underhill, and in producer-owned plots. Research has been ongoing in the entomology lab in the plant and soil science department since 1968. Basic research has been directed at maple tree physiology, sap flow and yield, sugar metabolism, wood anatomy, sap biochemistry and microbiology, and syrup chemistry. Entomology research has been centered on the study and eradication of insects and pathogens that periodically affect the health of the maple tree. Applied research has been devoted to improving techniques for efficient sap collection, sanitation, and evaporation to syrup. The U.S. Department of Agriculture, the U.S. Forest Service, and the maple industry have provided financial support for re-

search. Research reports on maple tree physiology and sap chemistry were first published at UVM in 1892. Since then, more than four hundred papers by UVM researchers have been published in scientific journals and farming magazines. Presently, ongoing research includes long-term meteorological and air pollution monitoring in cooperation with the Vermont Forest Ecosystem Monitoring Program, the State of Vermont, and the U.S. Forest Service. Demonstrations and education for maple producers, students, and visitors continue to be provided by research staff and Agriculture Extension Service personnel. Approximately two thousand Vermont sugarmakers produce about one-half million gallons of maple syrup from about 86 million gallons of harvested 2 percent sap. Excluding the value of timber production and fall foliage tourism, the total value of the maple industry, the largest in the United States, is more than $50 million per year. An agricultural crop, maple syrup is almost exclusively processed from the sap of the sugar maple tree. Gathered by gravity or vacuum systems during the sap-flow season, sap is boiled by both labor-intensive conventional and more efficient advanced techniques of concentrating and evaporating the liquid to produce pure maple syrup. Syrup color and flavor are affected by the biochemical and microbiological quality of the original sap. Following strict state regulations, Vermont maple syrup is graded as Fancy, Grade A Medium Amber, Grade A Dark Amber, and Grade B. State law and regulations of the Agricultural Department also prohibit adulteration or additives, allowing maple syrup to be marketed as a natural, unrefined product. Maple syrup is also reprocessed to produce other products, such as granulated sugar, cream, candies, and taffy fudge.

Mariafranca Morselli

Marble

A crystalline compact variety of metamorphosed limestone, marble consists primarily of calcite, dolomite, or a combination of both minerals. Mostly white, marble mined in Vermont can also be blue, black, or pink and red, depending on other hematite minerals in the limestone. Valued for statuary, building construction, and interior decorations, marble is capable of taking a high polish to visually enhance its mineral composition. Marble has been quarried in Vermont on LAKE CHAMPLAIN's Isle La Motte since the 1660s and in Bennington, Rutland, and Addison counties since the 1780s. Today, marble is extracted mainly from quarries in Rutland County and from the unique blue-marble quarry of Isle La Motte.

Marbleized Slate

Marbleized SLATE was produced in a process known as marbleizing or enameling by floating paint on top of a liquid in large vats. When slate forms were placed on the liquid surface, the marble-like designs of the paint adhered to the slate. Baked in large kilns, sanded, varnished, and baked again, the slate acquired a hard, shiny surface. The ancient process was used in Japan and Persia to marbleize paper. The knowledge spread to Europe and Britain, and Welsh and English workers brought the skill to America in the late 1840s. In Vermont, marbleized slate was produced primarily from the slate quarries around Fair Haven, Poultney, and Castleton, where the secret formulas were applied to produce mantels, table tops, altars, and lamp bases. The nineteenth century's fashion for mantels in parlors passed with the century and its tastes.

Barbara K. Hamblett

Markham, Isaac (1795–1825)

Born to the industrial activity around Middlebury Falls, where his father had a nail factory and a tavern, Isaac Markham worked with mechanics to build the original machinery for Middlebury's first cotton mill in 1811 and power looms for it from designs imported from Scotland in 1817. After working for a year in Waltham, Massachusetts, at the Boston Manufacturing Company, the most advanced textile mill of its time, he returned to Middlebury as superintendent of the cotton factory, before dying of typhoid in 1825. Markham's drawings of textile machines, now in the collections of the SHELDON MUSEUM, are the earliest known of the power looms on which the textile industry in this country was built.

Polly C. Darnell

Marlboro

Marlboro, population 978, a town in Windham County, was granted by BENNING WENTWORTH in 1751 to such famous colonial figures as Timothy Dwight (grandfather of the TIMOTHY DWIGHT who was president of Yale) and Jonathan Edwards, and named after either Charles Spencer (1706–1758), the third duke of Marlborough, or the town of Marlborough in Massachusetts. One major road, Route 9 (the Molly Stark Trail), crosses the hilly, forested town from east to west and passes a short distance north of the only significant settlement, Marlboro village. A predecessor of the trail was the Great Military Road, which was constructed in 1746 to connect FORT DUMMER (near present-day Brattleboro) and Fort Massachusetts (in Williamstown in that state) with Albany, New York. On this road, a fierce four-hour battle was fought on June 26, 1748, between forty English colonial rangers from Fort No. 4 (near present-day Charlestown, New Hampshire) and a much larger band of French-allied ABENAKI, resulting in fatalities on both sides. MARLBORO COLLEGE, a small, innovative liberal arts school founded in 1946, lies in the hills 2 miles south of the village. The campus provides a summer home for the celebrated MARLBORO MUSIC SCHOOL AND FESTIVAL (established in 1950) and the annual October concerts of the New England Bach Festival (founded in 1969).

Marlboro College

Founded in 1946 and located in a rural setting in the town of Marlboro, Marlboro College is recognized far and wide as an innovative liberal arts institution. The cornerstone of the college's education program is the plan of concentration, an in-depth, self-designed exploration of a field or fields designed by each student. The plan culminates in a major independent project involving research, one-on-one faculty tutorials, and an extended oral examination with both faculty and outside examiners of the student's chosen field. The student body numbers approximately three hundred (40 percent male, 60 percent female), and there are thirty-six full-time and nine part-time faculty. The student-faculty ratio is seven to one. The college's community life is inseparable from its academic life, with each student, faculty, and staff member voting equally on issues affecting the college. Marlboro's Graduate Center prepares students to lead the Internet and on-line strategies of companies, nonprofit organizations, and educational institutions, leading to master's of science in internet strategy management and internet engineering and a master of arts in teaching with internet technologies.

Marlboro Music School and Festival

Founded in 1951 at MARLBORO COLLEGE to provide a venue for master concert artists and exceptional young professional musicians to play side-by-side in chamber music ensembles, the Marlboro Music School and Festival meets each summer in a seven-week session that provides extraordinary opportunities to study, rehearse, and play in an original process devised by its founders, Adolf Busch, RUDOLF SERKIN—artistic director from 1952 to 1991—and MARCEL, LOUIS, and BLANCHE MOYSE. Marlboro Music is a pre-eminent American center for advanced musical studies and an important contributor to the development of chamber music performance. Pablo Casals, the world's leading cellist at the time, participated in the festival from 1960 to 1973 as both performer and conductor of the festival orchestra.

Marsh, Carmi (1842–1910)

Carmi Marsh was a Civil War veteran, an officer and later owner of Dr. BURNEY JAMES KENDALL's Spavin Cure Company, and a generous benefactor of Enosburg Falls. He is remembered in Franklin County by the story of his generous support of a Confederate widow in Virginia who in 1863 had nursed him through a near-fatal illness. During the Civil War, Marsh had been elected second lieutenant of Company K, Thirteenth Vermont Volunteers, but soon after arriving in Virginia in late 1862 was stricken with typhoid fever and then cerebrospinal meningitis, during which illness he was received by a Mrs.

Wilcoxon near Fairfax Court House and nursed back to sufficient health to return to Vermont. After many years of searching for Mrs. Wilcoxon, Marsh finally located her in 1893 living in another state in destitute circumstances. Marsh annually visited and financially supported Mrs. Wilcoxon for the rest of her life, paying the expenses of her final illness and funeral in 1902. When Marsh returned from the war, he established a large feed and mill business. In 1879, he purchased a half-interest in Dr. B. J. Kendall's Spavin Cure, Enosburg Falls' largest employer at the time. He soon took in other partners and became president of the business, a position he held until his death. Marsh represented Enosburgh in the Vermont House (1878–1879) and Franklin County in the Senate (1886). He was judge advocate general on the staff of Governor John Barstow (1882) and was customarily addressed thereafter as General Marsh. In 1910, he contributed the Civil War memorial still standing in the center of Enosburg Falls. Franklin Pond in the town of Franklin was renamed Lake Carmi in 1910 in recognition of his generous gifts and in memory of his gallant care for the Confederate widow who nursed him back to health.

Marsh, Charles (1765–1849)

The son of JOSEPH MARSH, Vermont's first lieutenant governor, Charles Marsh, Dartmouth College class of 1786, studied law with Tappan Reeve in Litchfield, Connecticut, and settled in Woodstock after admission to the Connecticut bar in 1788 and the Vermont bar in 1789. Immediately successful partly through the prominence of his family in eastern Vermont, Charles Marsh was appointed Vermont's first United States district attorney by President George Washington in 1791. His manner in court was calm and subtle, but notable for his scathing cross examinations. In politics, he was a Washington Federalist; in theology a Calvinist of the Edwards school. A founder and long-time president of the Vermont Bible Society, he was also trustee of Dartmouth College for forty years and president of trustees for Kimball Union Academy. Elected to Congress in 1814, he did not seek re-election in the eclipse of the Federalists. A highly respected member of the Vermont bar, he was noted for the simplicity and courtliness of his manners and was well known for entertaining the social elite of New England and New York at his large, comfortable home in Woodstock. Charles Marsh's home in Woodstock was subsequently owned by FREDERICK BILLINGS and later by LAURANCE ROCKEFELLER. Today the property is the site of the BILLINGS FARM & MUSEUM and the MARSH-BILLINGS-ROCKEFELLER NATIONAL HISTORICAL PARK. One son, Joseph, became professor of medicine at the UNIVERSITY OF VERMONT. Another was GEORGE PERKINS MARSH, the diplomat and conservationist.

Marsh, George Perkins (1802–1882)

Attorney, diplomat, linguist, and author of *Man and Nature* (1864), the primary text of the American environmental movement, George Perkins Marsh of Woodstock, Dartmouth class of 1820, was the son of CHARLES MARSH, grandson of JOSEPH MARSH (Vermont's first lieutenant governor), and cousin of JAMES MARSH (president of the UNIVERSITY OF VERMONT). George Perkins Marsh practiced law in Burlington after admission to the bar in 1825 and undertook a series of business ventures, most of which fared poorly. He was a Whig in the Congress for Vermont from 1843 to 1849, opposing slavery and the Mexican War. He was appointed U.S. minister to Turkey, 1849 to 1854, and was the first U.S. minister to the kingdom of Italy in 1860, where he served for the rest of his life. Between the two appointments he served Vermont as railroad commissioner, fish commissioner, and state house commissioner (one of three), in the third role guiding the construction of the new state house after a disastrous fire in 1857. A scholar of special accomplishments, G. P. Marsh produced the first American Icelandic grammar, helped found and guide the Smithsonian Institution, shaped the Washington Monument, wrote on fisheries, irrigation, camels, and corporate corruption. According to his biographer, David Lowenthal, Marsh's *Man and Nature* marked the inception of a truly modern way of looking at the world, of taking care lest we irreversibly degrade the fabric of humanized nature we are bound to manage. Marsh's book lies at the base of the continuing efforts at reforestation, watershed management, soil conservation, and nature protection. His birthplace in Woodstock is now the MARSH-BILLINGS-ROCKEFELLER NATIONAL HISTORICAL PARK, which is dedicated to telling the story of American conservation and the global crusade Marsh launched.

Marsh, James (1794–1842)

The sixth president of the UNIVERSITY OF VERMONT (1826–1833) and still notable for his intellectual accomplishments, James Marsh was a talented linguist and scholar of philosophy, literary theory, and criticism. Grandson of JOSEPH MARSH, Vermont's first lieutenant governor, and cousin of GEORGE PERKINS MARSH, he was born in Hartland in his grandfather's house, a landmark building on the Ottauquechee still in use. A Dartmouth College graduate in 1817, Marsh stayed on as a tutor at the college for two years, learning German and reading the German Romantics, the English poets Coleridge, Wordsworth, and Byron, and Madame de Staël, including her famous *De l'Allemagne*. Ordained after ministerial studies at Andover Seminary (1820–1822), Marsh wrote a long article on ancient and modern poetry for the *North American Review* (1822) and translated J. G. von Herder's *The Spirit of Hebrew Poetry* for Princeton's *Biblical Repertory* (1826) while teaching literature and moral philosophy at Hampden-Sydney College in Virginia. Called to the presidency of the University of Vermont in 1826, Marsh revised the college's curriculum to reflect ideas that he had found in the German Idealist philosophers' concepts of the Reason and Understanding. A soft-spoken public speaker, he was loved by his students for his knowledge and supportive attention to their advancement. Marsh's continued study of Coleridge and the Germans, as well as his correspondence with the English poet's literary executor, led to his editions and explications of the writings of the English poet-philosopher Samuel Taylor Coleridge. Marsh's editions of *Aids to Reflection* (1829) and *The Friend* (1831), with long introductory essays and notes by Marsh, influenced the development of the American Transcendentalists Ralph Waldo Emerson, George Ripley, and Frederick Hedge in the 1830s. While his presidency of the university was notable for its intellectual and academic excellence, his leadership failed to improve the institution's finances. He resigned as president in 1833 to continue teaching and writing. Both of his wives—Lucia and Laura Wheelock, nieces of ELEAZAR WHEELOCK—died from tuberculosis, and James Marsh himself died of the disease in Burlington in 1842. Marsh wrote no major treatises on literature or philosophy, but his theory of education, based in Romantic Idealism, was propounded through his lecture notes in several later generations of students. JOHN DEWEY, UVM class of 1879, said on the one hundredth anniversary of the publication of Marsh's edition of Coleridge's *Aids* that it was an influential text in the development of American philosophy and had helped shape his thinking.

Marsh, Joseph (1726–1811)

Vermont's first lieutenant governor, Hartford town representative in the general assembly, and chief judge of Windsor County for twelve years, Joseph Marsh was born in Lebanon, Connecticut, and settled in 1772 on a New York land grant by the south bank of the Ottauquechee River in Hartford, then a town in recently organized CUMBERLAND COUNTY, New York. Prior to the Revolution, Joseph Marsh was allied to the New York faction east of the GREEN MOUNTAINS by virtue of his New York land title and his daughter's marriage into the family of arch-Loyalist Judge SAMUEL WELLS. In 1776, Marsh was twice chosen a delegate from Cumberland County to the revolutionary Provincial Congress of New York and was commissioned colonel of New York's northern militia regiment of Cumberland County. By 1777, however, he had changed his allegiance and served as a delegate to the conventions that declared the independence of the New Hampshire grants, including the putative New York counties, and organized the new state of Vermont. He was a member of the convention that adopted the first Vermont constitution on July 3 to 4, 1777. Despite Vermont's newly independent status, when General Philip Schuyler, commander of New York's military forces, called the Cumberland County militia as a New York regiment into the service of the Continental Congress to oppose the British invasion of the Champlain Valley in mid-1777, Colonel Marsh marched his regiment, including his oldest son Joseph, west to take part in the BATTLES OF BENNINGTON, Whitehall, Fort Ann, Fort Edward, and Sandy Hill. A Loyalist from Vermont with the British Army, probably JOHN PETERS, recognized him on the battlefield and offered a price of £40 for his head. In 1778, Marsh was elected lieutenant governor of Vermont for one term and represented Hartford for the next nine years until he was again elected lieutenant governor in 1787, 1788, and 1789. In 1791, he served on the Vermont convention to ratify the United States Constitution. Opposed to the ARLINGTON JUNTO led by THOMAS CHITTENDEN and ETHAN and IRA ALLEN, Joseph Marsh's political views sometime found him allied with old New York loyalists, such as Samuel Wells, CHARLES PHELPS, and LUKE KNOULTON, from east of the Green Mountains, whom Ethan Allen called "pettifogging scribblers." Joseph Marsh was the patriarch of a family that included his son, CHARLES MARSH of Woodstock, a distinguished lawyer, Charles's son GEORGE PERKINS MARSH, the diplomat and conservationist, and another grandson, JAMES MARSH, a professor of philosophy and president of the UNIVERSITY OF VERMONT.

Marsh-Billings-Rockefeller National Historical Park

The only park in the National Park Service's system of parks to focus on conservation history and the evolving nature of land stewardship in America, the Marsh-Billings-Rockefeller National Historical Park in Woodstock opened in June 1998. Vermont's only national park preserves and interprets the historic Marsh-Billings-Rockefeller property. The park is named for GEORGE PERKINS MARSH, whose book *Man and Nature* (1864) was a seminal text for the environmental movement and who grew up on the site, and for FREDERICK BILLINGS, who established a progressive dairy farm and professionally managed forest on the former Marsh farm, which was designated a National Historic Landmark in 1967. Conservationists LAURANCE S. ROCKEFELLER AND MARY FRENCH ROCKEFELLER, Frederick Billings's granddaughter, continued conservation practices in forestry and farming on the the place through much of the twentieth century. In 1983, they established the BILLINGS FARM & MUSEUM to continue the farm's working dairy and to interpret rural Vermont life and agricultural history. The park was created in 1992, when the Rockefellers gave their residential and forest lands to the federal government. Today, the park interprets the history of conservation with tours of the mansion and the surrounding 550-acre forest.

Marshfield

Marshfield, population 1,496, a town in Washington County, has a complicated early history. It derives from a grant made in 1782 by the Vermont legislature to a group of MAHICANS from Stockbridge, Massachusetts, who had served as militia guarding the state's frontier. The grant was for land in an area of New York State that Vermont was attempting to annex (the WEST UNION). The Mahicans sold the grant to Colonel Amos Marsh, who persuaded the legislature in 1790 to switch the grant to cover land that was indisputably in Vermont and name it after him. The town is wooded and hilly and bisected from northeast to southwest by the fertile valley of the Winooski River. The village of Marshfield lies in the northern part of the town on U.S. Route 2, which follows the course of the river.

Mayo, Henry Thomas (1856–1937)

A native of Burlington, Henry T. Mayo was the son of a LAKE CHAMPLAIN merchant captain, an Annapolis graduate at age nineteen (class of 1876), and commander of the United States Atlantic Fleet in the First World War. He missed the Spanish-American War through service on the survey ship *Bennington*. From 1907 to 1912, he commanded the *Albany*, the cruiser *California*, the Mare Island Navy Yard in California, and served in Washington on personnel matters. Promoted to rear admiral in 1912, he was given command of the Atlantic Fleet in 1913. Mayo precipitated a near-crisis in United States–Mexican relations in 1914 when he insisted on a Mexican twenty-one gun salute of apology for a mistaken arrest of a small-boat crew at Tampico. When the Mexican government refused, President Woodrow Wilson ordered other elements of Mayo's fleet to seize the Mexican Customs House at Vera Cruz. Mayo's snap decision over the apology contributed to the American intervention in Mexico and the subsequent punitive expedition by General John Pershing in 1916. Mayo was promoted to temporary vice-admiral in 1915 and given command of the Atlantic Fleet again in 1916 as temporary full admiral. In 1917, he represented the United States in the London Naval Conference to coordinate allied naval strategy against Germany and its allies. When the United States entered the First World War, Mayo retained command of the Atlantic Fleet during the war. He reverted to his permanent rank of rear admiral and retired in 1920 to become governor of the Philadelphia Naval Home until 1928, when he returned to Burlington, where he lived until his death in the Portsmouth, New Hampshire, naval hospital.

Mead, Larkin (1835–1910)

The sculptor Larkin Mead was born in Chesterfield, New Hampshire, and grew up in Brattleboro, where his father was a prosperous lawyer. His mother was a sister of JOHN HUMPHREY NOYES, founder of the cult of Perfectionism and the Oneida Community. The Mead family's intellectual and creative life was supported by the cultural activities of the guests of Dr. ROBERT WESSELHOEFT's Water Cure. His sister was an artist. A younger brother, WILLIAM RUTHERFORD MEAD, was the central partner in the firm of McKim, Mead and White, the New York architects. Larkin Mead took his early training as a sculptor with Henry Kirke Browne in 1853 to 1855. In 1856, he established a Brattleboro studio and on the night of December 31 built a colossal snow figure called *The Recording Angel* at a crossroads in Brattleboro that astonished town folks and was celebrated in James Russell Lowell's poem "A Good Word for Winter." This exploit brought his first commission from Nicholas Longworth of Cincinnati, Ohio. In 1857, he completed the figure *Agriculture*, based on the Greek goddess Ceres, for the dome of the new VERMONT STATE HOUSE in Montpelier and in 1861 a marble statue of ETHAN ALLEN for the same building, which was replaced by a replica in 1941 due to weather deteriorioration. In 1861, Mead was at the battle front for six weeks at the beginning of the Civil War and sent graphic sketches of camp life to *Harpers Weekly*. In 1862, he went to Italy to study, accompanying his artist sister who was to marry William Dean Howells, the novelist and then consul at Venice. HIRAM POWERS encouraged Mead to establish himself in Florence, where he met and fell in love with Marietta di Benvenuti, whom he married in 1866. Returning to America for a visit, Mead showed three sculptures completed in Florence and gained a $200,000 commission for a giant statue of Abraham Lincoln at Springfield, Illinois, the largest such undertaking attempted in the United States. Mead sculpted the large bust of Lincoln now in the Vermont State House in preparation for the large bronze statue he created for Lincoln's tomb. Another statue of Ethan Allen was commissioned by the state of Vermont in 1876 to be placed in Statuary Hall in the Capitol at Washington. Mead's wood figure of Ceres stood atop the dome of the Vermont State House in Montpelier until 1938 when, rot threatening to topple it, eighty-seven-year-old Sergeant-at-Arms Dwight Dwinell carved a replacement. Mead's Italian-influenced style lost fashion in the 1880s as young sculptors learned their art in Paris rather than Italy. He died in Florence, one of the last of the American expatriate artists who settled there in the nineteenth century.

Mead, William Rutherford (1846–1928)

Born in Brattleboro and a graduate of Amherst College (1867), the architect William Rutherford Mead claimed to have been much influenced toward architecture by the Greek Revival VERMONT STATE HOUSE in Montpelier. In 1868, he entered the office of Russell Sturges, architect, as a paying student. In 1871, Mead went to Florence, Italy, to live with his brother, the sculptor LARKIN MEAD, and to study at the Academy de Belle Arti, where he developed his interest in Renaissance architecture. Back in New York in 1872, he associated with the architect C. F. McKim at 37 Broadway. In 1878, they formed a partnership under the name of McKim, Mead & Bigelow, Stanford White replacing Bigelow in 1879. Mead managed the office and often conceived the plan of a new project. On McKim's death in 1909, Mead took over as president of the American Academy in Rome, an institution founded after the Columbian Exposition of 1893 to give American students of the fine arts an opportunity to study. Mead ran the academy for eighteen years. He died in Paris and is buried in Florence next to his brother.

Memphre

In 1816, Ralph Merry IV first claimed to have seen a large serpent-like creature in LAKE MEMPHREMAGOG. In the middle of the nineteenth century, Uriah Jewett, a New Hampshire settler on the eastern shore of the lake, reported seeing a large serpent that he believed came through an improbable subterranean channel from the Atlantic Ocean. More recently, Barbara Malloy of Newport claims many personal sightings of this creature, has founded the Dracontology Society of Lake Memphremagog to promote faith in its existence, and has copyrighted the name Memphre. Like CHAMP, a similarly fabulous denizen of LAKE CHAMPLAIN, Memphre has acquired many fans despite the absence of verifiable sightings. On March 17, 1987, notwithstanding the skepticism of biologists in the Vermont Fish and Wildlife Department, as well as neglecting to consult the United States Immigration and Naturalization Service or its Canadian counterpart, the Vermont legislature adopted a joint resolution giving Memphre dual American/Canadian citizenship.

Virginia C. Downs

Memphremagog, Lake

Narrow, 24-mile-long Lake Memphremagog extends from Magog, Quebec, southward into Vermont, where its terminus is marked by NEWPORT CITY. (The name is accented on the third syllable.) Only about 6 miles of the lake is actually in Vermont. Three rivers, the Barton, the Clyde, and the northern Black flow into it, and the lake in turn empties via Quebec's St. Francis River into the St. Lawrence. In pre-settlement times, the lake was an important route through the wilderness, and during the heyday of the lumber era provided transportation both for logs and for the milled products into which they were made. Today the lake is used primarily for recreation.

Mendon

Mendon, population 1,028, a town in Rutland County, was granted by the Vermont legislature in 1781 as the town of Medway and changed to Mendon in 1827. Both names presumably derive from neighboring towns in Massachusetts, the home state of a number of the grantees. Mendon lies just east of the city of Rutland on the western slopes of the main spine of the GREEN MOUNTAINS, reaching a height of 3,939 feet at Little Killington Peak. Because of its strategic location on U.S. Route 4 between Rutland and the Killington-Pico ski areas, the town has become largely a tourist service venue featuring motels, restaurants, gift shops, antique stores, and real estate offices. It also plays a role as a suburban extension of Rutland city.

Merrick, Elliott (1906–1997)

A writer best known in Vermont for his enduring novel *Green Mountain Farm* (1948), a tale of farm life in a fictionalized Craftsbury during the Great Depression, Elliott Merrick was born in Montclair, New Jersey, and graduated from Phillips Exeter Academy and Yale University. He tried, but disliked, newspaper and advertising work in New Jersey and Manhattan. In 1929 he went to work for the Grenfell

Medical Mission in northern Labrador as a teacher and later tried trapping for a living. At the Grenfell Mission he met and married an Australian nurse, Kate Austen, the fictionalized subject of his novel *Northern Nurse* (1942), which made the best-seller list for several months. Returning to the United States, they settled on a farm in Craftsbury, where Merrick taught at Craftsbury Academy and then at the UNIVERSITY OF VERMONT. From these years came the experiences behind *Green Mountain Farm* and another novel with a Vermont setting, *From This Hill Look Down* (1934). Merrick drew on the Labrador years for several other books in the 1930s. His first novel, *True North* (1933), and *The Long Crossing and Other Labrador Stories* have been reprinted by university presses. Another novel, *Frost and Fire* (1939), has been translated into several languages and frequently excerpted for anthologies. During World War II he served as an ordinary merchant seaman on Atlantic convoys, from which came a novel, *Passing By* (1947). After the war he taught writing at Black Mountain College, the famous progressive school in North Carolina, and for twenty-two years was a science editor and publications officer for the U.S. Forest Service. In 1985 the Memorial University of Newfoundland awarded him a doctorate in humane letters *in honoris causa* for his writings on Labrador.   *Addison Merrick*

Merrill, Perry Henry (1894–1993)

In a nearly fifty-year career in public service, especially as state forester, director, and then commissioner of forests and parks, Perry H. Merrill of Montpelier was probably the twentieth century's single most important figure in shaping modern Vermont's priorities in forestry use and land preservation, and assuring public spaces for recreation and leisure activities. Born in Westport, New York, Perry Merrill graduated from the New York State College of Forestry at Syracuse University in 1917. He went to France in the First World War with the American Field Service's volunteer ambulance corps, and in 1918 he was appointed inspector general of prisoner of war camps in Germany by the Inter-allied Commission for the Repatriation of Russian Prisoners. On his return from the war in 1919, he was appointed district forester in the Northwest District of the Vermont Forest Service. He studied for a year as a fellow of the American Scandinavian Foundation at the Royal College of Forestry in Stockholm and returned to Vermont to serve as district forester (1921–1924), earn a Yale University master's degree in forestry (1924), and serve as assistant state forester (1924–1929) and state forester in 1929. When the CIVILIAN CONSERVATION CORPS was created by Congress in 1933, Perry Merrill was given the task of supervising the Corps' activities in Vermont. In 1934, he was elected a Montpelier alderman and mayor in 1935. During World War II, he was chairman of the National Association of State Foresters. In 1955, he was named director of Vermont Forests and Parks and MIDDLEBURY COLLEGE awarded him an honorary doctorate. He was appointed commissioner of forests and parks in 1966. After his retirement from forests and parks, Merrill ran for lieutenant governor on the Republican ticket with RICHARD SNELLING, but was not elected. He served in the Vermont House of Representatives from 1969 to 1972, and was vice chair of the Appropriations Committee in his second term. Perry Merrill served through nineteen governors and became a dominant voice in the state's development. He pursued a vision of Vermont founded on Theodore Roosevelt's and Gifford Pinchot's conservation policies. Merrill led efforts in Vermont to purchase and preserve state lands for the wood products industry, wildlife habitat and conservation, and public use of these resources by Vermonters in a STATE PARKS system created for recreational and leisure activities. Beginning with his work with the CCC, Merrill supported the development of ski areas on state-leased land to promote tourism and recreation for Vermonters. Later, in the 1950s and 1960s, he initiated Vermont's efforts to provide conservation education in schools and for the general public.   *Anthony Otis*

Metcalfe, Simon (1735–1794)

In conflict with grants already made to others by the governor of New Hampshire, the governor of New York in 1770 granted the Yorkshireman Simon Metcalfe large tracts of land along northern LAKE CHAMPLAIN for services as deputy surveyor of New York. With the notorious land swindler Simon Sear, Metcalfe acquired 30,000 acres on the MISSISQUOI RIVER called variously Hillsborough or Prattsburg under the New York grant and Swanton under the New Hampshire grant. He settled at the site of today's Swanton near the falls of the Missisquoi and resumed logging where the French colonist RENÉ-NICHOLAS LEVASSEUR had acquired a logging site from the ABENAKI in 1749. Metcalfe supported the Americans in the earliest months of the Revolution, for which he was taken prisoner by the British to Montreal, and in 1781 allowed to return to Swanton to cut logs. JACOB BAYLEY's American rangers suspected Metcalfe's support for the Revolution and took him to headquarters in Peekskill and then Philadelphia. Returning to Swanton after the war in 1784, he found that during the war the British had removed a large supply of logs he had left on the banks of the Missisquoi River and that IRA ALLEN's settlers had taken over his property. When Metcalfe tried to establish ownership under his New York grant, an Allen-dominated freeholders court banished him from Swanton. In 1787, Metcalfe acquired the trading ship *Eleanora* and its cargo of furs from a New York merchant and sailed for China. For nearly seven years, he and his sons traded between China, Hawaii, and the native settlements of the Pacific Northwest. One son was killed by islanders who attacked his ship in Hawaii. In 1794, stopping at Queen Charlotte Island in the Pacific Northwest, Metcalfe and his crew were killed by Indians. As part of the 1791 settlement with New York that allowed Vermont to enter the Union, Metcalfe's widow was awarded $1,417.28 from State of Vermont funds to settle her claim to the New York grant of 30,000 acres in Swanton.

Metzger, Fraser (1872–1954)

Clergyman and 1912 Progressive party candidate for governor, Fraser Metzger was born in Gloversville, New York. He attended St. Johnsville, New York High, School, earned a D.D. degree from Defiance College, and graduated Phi Beta Kappa from Union College in 1902. He came to Vermont as pastor of the Christian Church in Randolph, which after some years joined with the Congregational Church as the Bethany Church. A social activist, Metzger helped organize the Randolph Hospital and led the church to develop facilities that enhanced its importance as a community center. Through the Inter-Church Federation, Metzger worked for improved working conditions for women and children, modernization of farms, and educational improvement. A Roosevelt Republican, in 1912 he was disappointed by the failure of the Vermont Progressive League to secure the Republican nomination of their candidates for state and national office, and after more prominent progressives declined, he accepted the Progressive party nomination for governor. Running third in a three-man race, his candidacy kept the regular Republican candidate from winning a popular majority and the election was decided for Republican Allen Fletcher in the legislature. After Metzger's defeat, he campaigned for Theodore Roosevelt throughout Vermont and in Maine and New Hampshire. In 1914, again as a Progressive, he ran a poor third for Congress and in 1916 was elected as a Republican to represent Randolph in the state house of representatives. Shortly after 1921, he left the state to become dean of men at Rutgers University, where he served for twenty years. From 1945 until his death, he was pastor of the First Congregational Church in South Windsor, Connecticut.

Waybury Inn, East Middlebury, provided the opening shot for a popular television series with Bob Newhart in the 1980s. Vermont Department of Tourism and Marketing

Meyer, William Henry (1914–1983)

The first Democrat elected to a statewide office since before the Civil War, Bill Meyer was elected to Congress in 1958. Born in Philadelphia, Pennsylvania, and educated in the city schools, he graduated from Pennsylvania State University in 1936. A forester-conservationist from 1936 until 1940, he worked as a CIVILIAN CONSERVATION CORPS technician in a number of northeastern states. Moving to Vermont in 1940 and settling in Rupert in 1950, he was employed by the Soil Conservation Service until 1951 when he left government employment for private practice as a consulting forester, becoming executive director of the Vermont Forest and Farmland Foundation. He attended his first Democratic state convention in 1956 and in 1958 received the party's congressional nomination after deferring to veteran Democratic leader Frederick Fayette's claims to the U.S. Senate nomination. The Democrats did well in the 1958 elections, with Meyer leading in total votes and the only one of the party's candidates to win office. The consensus that he had run against an exceptionally weak Republican candidate seemed confirmed in 1960 when he was easily defeated by ROBERT STAFFORD. His highly publicized advocacy of ending nuclear testing, recognizing Red China, and ending the military draft while he was a member of the House foreign affairs committee barred the remotest

chance of his being elected to a second term and made him a pariah among leaders of his own party. In 1960, Meyer was the first Democrat to encounter a primary challenge. In 1962, he lost a primary bid for the U.S. Senate nomination in a campaign orchestrated by party leaders who attacked his foreign policy initiatives. Again failing to secure the Democratic Senate nomination in 1964 and 1970, in 1970 he helped found the LIBERTY UNION party under whose banner he ran for the Senate. He returned to the Democrats in 1972, when he received the party's congressional nomination and lost in the general election to RICHARD MALLARY. A natural-resources consultant, he was president and chairman of the New England United World Federalists from 1962 to 1964, and in 1966 was finance secretary of Farmers and World Affairs.

Middlebury

The SHIRE TOWN of Addison County, Middlebury, population 8,183, received its name as the centermost of three towns (New Haven and Salisbury being the other two) granted in 1761 by BENNING WENTWORTH to a company of proprietors from Salisbury, Connecticut. The core of the town remained agricultural for most of its history, while its two villages developed at peripheral mill sites. East Middlebury, along the southern border, grew along the

Middlebury River. Middlebury village, along the northern border, was formed in the 1780s as twin villages on the Middlebury and Cornwall banks of OTTER CREEK at Middlebury Falls, which were linked physically by the Main Street Bridge in 1787 before they were united politically through annexation in 1796. Under the leadership of town father GAMALIEL PAINTER, Middlebury achieved shire status in 1791 to become the commercial, legal, and educational center of the county. Here were established the Addison County Grammar School (1797), a counterpart female academy (1800), MIDDLEBURY COLLEGE (1800)—the first operative college in Vermont and the first community-founded college in the United States—and EMMA WILLARD's female seminary, the nation's first institution of higher education for women (1814). Village industry included locally significant saw, grist, and paper mills, but also MARBLE and textile manufacturing aimed at national markets. Taking advantage of the town's location atop a vein of white marble likened in quality to that of Carrara, Italy, Eben Judd initiated water-powered marble sawing in Vermont in 1802 to 1803. In 1817, Joseph Gordon constructed what were reputedly the second set of power looms in the United States, serving large-scale cotton mills and (as Addison County became the most productive wool-producing county in the nation) woolen mills. The village, which in the 1830s achieved brief status as the largest municipality in Vermont, ceased its growth and lost most of its industry over the remainder of the nineteenth century. Nevertheless, it displayed a continuing history of prosperity and a taste for the high style in a series of fine homes from all periods. Middlebury village focuses on a large, irregular green surrounded by LAVIUS FILLMORE's Congregational (1806–1809) and Episcopal (1826–1827) churches, marking the height of the Federal and the advent of the Gothic Revival styles in Vermont. Also on the green are the 1827 Middlebury Inn and a series of lively Victorian public and commercial buildings by local architect Clinton Smith. The Henry SHELDON MUSEUM (the nation's oldest incorporated village museum) contains local history collections and archives that make Middlebury one of the most completely documentable communities in the country. Middlebury College, pioneer in intensive language instruction, incorporates on its campus the National Historic Landmark home of Emma Willard and Old Stone Row (1810–1865), modeled on the late eighteenth-century campus of Yale University, as well as a collection of structures by nationally important twentieth-century architects.

Glenn M. Andres

Middlebury College

Founded in 1800, Middlebury College was established and nurtured in its early years by town residents who believed that a college would attract a religious and educated citizenry, and thereby help create a prosperous community. Their efforts bore fruit. By 1836, Middlebury was the largest town in the state, and the college was a major success story. The number of students had increased from seven to 136 (a large minority of whom were poor preministerial students); three large buildings had been constructed, including Painter Hall (1816), the oldest college building in Vermont; an excellent faculty was in place; and a curriculum and extracurriculum modeled on that of Yale had been established by the college's first two presidents, who were Yale graduates. A series of crises resulting from the excitement of extended religious revivals among the students and townspeople, however, rocked the college in the late 1830s and early 1840s, and enrollment plummeted. Between 1840 and 1880, the average

enrollment was about fifty students, and the college nearly closed and considered a merger with the UNIVERSITY OF VERMONT in 1847, 1865, and 1879. The College's decision to admit women in 1883, and a significant increase in the number of Vermont high-school graduates, helped boost enrollment gradually in the late nineteenth and early twentieth centuries. By 1908, when JOHN MARTIN THOMAS assumed the presidency, there were over one hundred students, and the college had constructed new library and science buildings. Under Thomas (1908–1921) and his successor, PAUL DWIGHT MOODY (1921–1942), the college grew much more dramatically: By the eve of World War II, enrollment had increased to eight hundred and the physical plant had expanded exponentially. In addition, pathbreaking programs had been established that would give Middlebury a world-wide reputation: the summer MIDDLEBURY COLLEGE LANGUAGE SCHOOLS (1915), the BREAD LOAF SCHOOL OF ENGLISH (1920), and the BREAD LOAF WRITERS' CONFERENCE (1926). Between 1945 and 2000, the college was transformed again. Enrollment rose to eighteen hundred in the early 1970s, and a plan to increase the size of the student body to twenty-three hundred began to be implemented in the late 1990s. The endowment reached $600 million and the college's outstanding faculty and beautiful, state-of-the-art physical facilities reflected the wealth of the institution. The student body, which before 1945 had been primarily white, Protestant, middle-class, and regional in character, became more diverse as students from a wide variety of religions, economic classes, and national backgrounds enrolled from nearly every state in the union and seventy foreign countries. While its location in the hills of Vermont isolated the college in the nineteenth century, in the twentieth century the college's rural mountain setting was instrumental in establishing exciting summer programs as well as attracting students who wanted to enjoy winter sports while attending one of the outstanding independent residential liberal arts colleges in the nation.

David M. Stameshkin

Middlebury College Language Schools

The Middlebury College Language Schools were the first summer schools in any college in the country that offered only advanced courses concentrated upon single

languages, and which required exclusive use of those languages during the entire school session. The schools were founded in 1915, when Professor Lilian Stroebe moved her innovative two-year-old summer German program, based on isolation, advanced study, and intensiveness, from Pennsylvania to Middlebury. Programs in French (1916), Spanish (1917), Italian (1932), Russian (1945), Chinese (1966), Japanese (1970), and Arabic (1982) followed. Undergraduate courses were established for the first time in the early 1970s and by the 1980s had become more popular than the graduate courses. Enrollment in the schools increased gradually to eight hundred on the eve of World War II, and has remained between nine and thirteen hundred since that time. The French, German, Italian, Russian, and Spanish schools offer graduate programs leading to the master of arts and to Middlebury's unique doctor of modern languages degree. Approximately 150 advanced degrees are conferred each summer; eleven thousand advanced degrees have been awarded since the schools were founded. All language students agree to abide by the Language Pledge, a formal commitment to speak the language of study as the only means of communication for the entire session.

David M. Stameshkin

Middlesex

Middlesex, population 1,729, a town in Washington County, was granted by BENNING WENTWORTH in 1763. The name presumably derives from either of the like-named counties in Massachusetts or Connecticut, or possibly from the former county of Middlesex (now part of Greater London) in England. The town rises from the WINOOSKI RIVER, which forms its southern border, into hilly upland culminating in the Worcester range of the GREEN MOUNTAINS in its western section. Wiped out by the FLOOD OF 1927 was a vibrant commercial area along the Winooski consisting of mills, a creamery, and other enterprises, as were the great mills of Putnamville in the town's northeastern corner. Until recently, the town's economic base was AGRICULTURE, but currently there is only one working dairy farm. Many of the residents commute to jobs in other towns, especially Montpelier to the east and Waterbury to the west. A number of home-based businesses take advantage of computer and communications technology.

Middletown Springs

Middletown Springs, population 823, a town in Rutland County, was incorporated by the Vermont legislature as Middletown in 1784 by taking land from the towns of Ira, Poultney, Tinmouth, and Wells. Residents of those towns who had settled in a fertile, protected valley along the Poultney River felt they had more in common with each other than with their respective towns and requested the change. The name derives from Middletown, Connecticut, the home of the surveyor who laid out the boundaries of the town. A prosperous period in the town's early history ended in 1811 when a flood destroyed most of the saw and grist mills located along the river banks, and like many Vermont towns, Middletown lost population due to emigration in the period leading up to the Civil War. For much of the latter part of the nineteenth century, the town was a center for the manufacture of horse treadmills, which greatly simplified many farm and small-shop tasks. A new era in its history began with the exploitation of the mineral springs along the river, which led to the bottling of the supposedly healthful waters by A. W. Gray & Sons and their distribution throughout New England. The giant Montvert Hotel, built in 1870, which could accommodate 350 guests who had come to "take the waters," was for a time the largest hotel in Vermont. In 1884, the town's name was changed to Middletown Springs in response to a petition by the townspeople. After decades of decline as a health destination, the town saw the springs finally buried under gravel and dirt by the catastrophic FLOOD OF 1927. A vestige, however, is today preserved in a park along the river. The town no longer serves as a local center for commercial and social activities but is essentially a semi-rural residential community, many of whose residents work, shop, and socialize elsewhere. Much of the village of Middletown Springs is a National Register Historic District encompassing sixty-five residences, six public buildings, and six other structures.

Miller, Jonathan Peckham (1796–1847)

A native of Randolph and cousin to JUSTIN MORGAN, Jonathan Peckham Miller completed a common school education in 1813 and went to Woodstock to become a tanner's apprentice, where he joined Captain Libbeus Eggerton's volunteers when they marched off in 1814 to help repel the British invasion of the Champlain Valley. The Woodstock troops arrived too late for the BATTLE OF PLATTSBURGH, but Miller was sufficiently pleased by army life that he enlisted as a regular in 1817. After two years on the northern frontier, he was sent home to Randolph because of ill health. He prepared for college at Nutting's Academy. In 1821, Miller enrolled at Dartmouth College, remaining only a few weeks, and then moved to the UNIVERSITY OF VERMONT, where he studied for three years. Inspired by an international wave of sympathy for the Greek war for independence from the Ottoman Turks and reports of Lord Byron fighting for the Greeks, Miller secured an introduction from Governor CORNELIUS VAN NESS to the Greek Association in Boston, which sent him to join the Greek army at Missolonghi. In 1824, he joined the staff of General George Jarvis with the rank of colonel, arriving after Byron died. His exploits against the Turks during the next two years earned him the title "American Daredevil." Miller was among the last to escape in the final moments before the fall of Missolonghi in 1826. Shortly thereafter, he returned to the United States to lecture and raise funds for Greece. In 1827, he went back to Greece with food and clothing worth $75,000. Returning to America, he published his journal as *The Condition of Greece in 1827 and 1828* (1828). Miller brought back a Greek boy, Luccas Militiades, whom he adopted, and Lord Byron's sword (now in the collections of the VERMONT HISTORICAL SOCIETY) to use as a prop in his fund-raising lectures. Miller finally returned to Vermont in 1829, studied law, and opened a law practice in Montpelier in 1830. He served in the legislature (1831–1833) and initiated the anti-slavery movement by introducing a resolution calling upon Congress to abolish slavery in the District of Columbia. Thereafter, he devoted most of his life and money to the anti-slavery cause. He lectured widely throughout the United States and in 1840 was a prominent participant in the debates of the World Anti-Slavery Convention in London. He died in Montpelier of a spine injury.

Miller, William (1782–1849)

Founder of the "Millerites" and head of the Adventist Church at its founding, William Miller was born in Pittsfield, Massachusetts, and later moved to Hampton, New York, near the Vermont border. In a time of religious revivals across America known as the Second Great Awakening, William Miller preached a message in New York and Vermont that the personal return of Christ, the Second Coming, was imminent. By the 1840s, most Americans saw the future fulfillment of Divine Providence in the nation's destiny. Millerites, however, saw no worldly future at all. For them, Christ was coming and the world would end. William Miller, saying that God had told him, predicted the Coming for "about the year 1843." In Vermont, town histories written in the nineteenth century often recount local episodes of the "Great Disappointment of 1843": in one, a citizen of Castleton, wearing the required white gown, sat for three days in his entrance hallway awaiting the end; in another, after giving away all their earthly goods, a group of Millerites in Calais sat atop the local church in their white gowns, coming down finally to the scoffing laughter of their newly enriched neighbors. Scholars have concluded, however, that the ideas of Miller and his followers, like other dissenters of the time—Mormons, Universalists, JOHN HUMPHREY NOYES' Perfectionists, and other "ultras"—grew out of the booming possibilities opened by independence, religious liberty, Jacksonian democracy, and the Second Great Awakening. Like their fellow dissenters, Millerites became participants—if unwilling ones—in the process of tightening up the acceptable implications of those possibilities as American culture moved from the experimentation of the new nation into the restriction of the Victorian age.

Millis, John S. (1903–1988)

John S. Millis was appointed president of the UNIVERSITY OF VERMONT in 1941 during a period of deep financial crisis. Millis was born in Palo Alto, California, and earned three degrees from the University of Chicago (A.B., 1924; M.S., 1927; Ph.D. in physics, 1931). Before his appointment at UVM, Millis was professor of physics, dean of the college, and dean of administration at Lawrence College, Wisconsin (1929–1939). A Carnegie grant supported his study of higher education management in 1940. At UVM, Millis formulated and implemented a plan to restore the university's financial base. He led the university during World War II through a period of steep declines in student enrollment, and organized a major campus building program to accommodate post-war expansion. Millis reorganized UVM's academic divisions and initiated major reforms, including the adoption of academic freedom and tenure policies for faculty, and retirement and pension programs for university employees. He was appointed president of Case Western Reserve University in 1949, and later named chancellor of Case Western University. He died in Cleveland Heights, Ohio.   *Frank Smallwood*

Mills, Samuel (ca. 1784–1862)

Samuel Mills was an active printer, newspaper publisher, and bookseller in Burlington during the first quarter of the nineteenth century. Born in Worcester County, Massachusetts, Mills apprenticed to ISAIAH THOMAS of Worcester, after which he moved to Burlington. In 1806, Mills and Daniel Greenleaf published the Burlington *Vermont Centinel*. Mills was assisted by his brothers, Ephraim and Thomas, who worked in the printing office that was located in "Mills Row," a commercial building owned by Isaiah Thomas. In late 1817, Mills sold the Burlington business to his brothers, who continued the newspaper as the *Northern Sentinel* until 1834. Earlier in 1808 to 1809, Samuel held an interest in the Middlebury book store of Mills & [Olcott] White. Following the sale of his printing business, Samuel remained in Burlington until about 1826, when he moved across LAKE CHAMPLAIN to Mooers, New York.

Marcus A. McCorison

Milne, George Brown (1857–1916)

One of the leaders of Vermont's granite industry, George Brown Milne was born near Aberdeen, Scotland, and trained as a granite cutter. In 1880, he left for the United States and worked at his trade in Massachusetts, Maine, Alabama, and Missouri before settling in Barre in 1883. He formed a partnership with William S. Wyllie, a fellow Scotsman, and moved from granite cutting to granite quarrying with the purchase of a quarry in 1889. The firm of Milne & Wyllie eventually became Milne & Gray, and later combined with other quarry companies to form Boutwell, Milne & Varnum, the predecessor of the Rock of Ages Corporation. Milne was also a prominent benefactor of many Barre institutions including the city's hospital.

Milton

Milton is a town in Chittenden County with a population of 9,479. Granted by BENNING WENTWORTH in 1763, it is popularly thought to be named after the poet John Milton, although the actual source of the name is probably William Fitzwilliam (1720–1756), Viscount Milton, or his son William Wentworth Fitzwilliam (1748–1833), both relatives of Wentworth. The town is bisected by the gently curving LAMOILLE RIVER, which powers a hydroelectric station in Milton village and backs up the river into 3-mile-long Arrowhead Mountain Lake extending into the town of Georgia to the north. The extensive delta of the Lamoille supports both a wildlife management area and SANDBAR State Park on LAKE CHAMPLAIN, one of Vermont's most popular swimming beaches. The town has a rich history of lumbering, sheep farming, and DAIRY FARMING. Although some of the land is still devoted to dairying, Milton's location on the edge of the Burlington metropolitan area has led to a substantial increase in residential housing and in industry, most notably the recent addition of a Husky plant manufacturing injection-molding machinery.

Minott, Samuel (1714–1786)

Spokesman for advocates for New York jurisdiction in the struggle against those seeking independence for what was to become Vermont, Minott was born in Westford, Massachusetts. In 1752, he relocated in what is now Westmoreland, New Hampshire, where he became an original proprietor, built the first gristmill, helped select the town's first minister, and served as a selectman. In 1755, after the outbreak of the French and Indian War, along with other Westmoreland residents, he crossed the CONNECTICUT RIVER to erect a fort and seek safety on the Great Meadow in what is now the town of Putney. Although most former Westmoreland residents chose to return after the war, Minott remained and erected the first gristmill and later a sawmill in his new location. When in 1770 the town of Putney was organized, he was elected an assessor and overseer of the poor by the town and in 1779 moderator and deacon by the Society of the Gospel. A staunch Yorker, Minott was chosen a representative from Putney to meet with representatives from other towns in CUMBERLAND COUNTY as a committee to determine what action should be taken for the good of the Province of New York against the "pretended State of Vermont." With loyal Yorkers being arrested and others threatened by ETHAN ALLEN, speedy and effectual measures for their relief were imperative. In May 1779, the committee convened in Brattleboro, elected Minott chairman, and petitioned New York Governor George Clinton and Congress for assistance in protecting individuals and property from those intent on the formation of a new state. This was the first in an exchange of letters that elicited assurances but no results. In April 1780, Clinton was informed that unless Congress or New York acted decisively, the petitioners must of necessity throw their fortunes with Vermont. Receiving no effective support, Minott apparently abandoned his resistance. His son Samuel Jr., with the rank of major, served as adjutant in Colonel STEPHEN ROWE BRADLEY's Lower Regiment of Vermont Militia that in 1784 marched on Governor THOMAS CHITTENDEN's orders to Guilford to drive Yorkers to the Massachusetts border.

Addison Minott

Missionaries to Hawaii

In 1819, the Reverend Hiram Bingham of Bennington, a MIDDLEBURY COLLEGE graduate, and his wife Sybil led the first mission band of Congregational ministers and their wives sent by the American Board of Commissioners for Foreign Missions to teach literacy and Christianity to the Hawaiian islanders. Six months later, Bingham preached his first sermon on the island of Oahu on the biblical text, "Fear not, for behold I bring you tidings of great joy." Bingham and his companions on several of the islands lived in grass huts, learned the Hawaiian language, and developed an alphabet of twelve letters, allowing them within four months of their arrival to begin teaching forty men and women to read in their own language. Within two years of their arrival, the mission band printed two hundred copies of a hymnal in Hawaiian on the band's hand press. Quickly acquiring literacy, Hawaiians soon began writing letters to friends and relatives on other islands. Bingham and his band's work was so well respected that in 1829, when he led the construction of a large thatched church, four thousand Hawaiians attended the opening and dedication. In 1842, the Hawaiian royal family and other wealthy Hawaiians raised funds to build a stone church in Honolulu. Hiram and Sybil Bingham worked in the islands for twenty-one years. Levi Chamberlain of Dover went to Oahu in the second company of missionaries in 1822 as business manager and construction supervisor. He also worked in the mission's literacy program and taught reading, arithmetic, and bible classes to Hawaiians. He wrote penmanship manuals and a textbook for the missionaries' literacy campaign. Chamberlain died of tuberculosis in the islands at age thirty-seven. In 1831, Sarah Joiner (b. 1805) of Royalton met the Reverend David Lyman, a recent Andover Seminary graduate headed for the Hawaiian Islands, and was so drawn to his zeal and sincerity that she married him in 1832. They sailed to Hawaii, settling in Hilo, where Lyman conducted his mission and she taught literacy and a sabbath school. They ran a boarding school for sixty boys for twenty years until David built a New England clapboard house. The Hilo Boys Boarding School, a model trade school, graduated eight hundred students in forty-two years. Twelve boatloads of missionaries sailed from New England to the Hawaiian Islands in twenty-eight years. Among them, Dr. Seth Andrews of Putney, a Dartmouth College graduate, became the only medical doctor in the islands when he arrived in 1837. His wife and three of their children died of fever and Dr. Andrews left, but his surviving son returned later. On the same boat was Andalucia Conde (b. 1810) of Jericho, who had ministered to the Seneca of western New York before sailing with her husband the Reverend David Conde for Hawaii. She died on Maui. Other men and women came from St. Johnsbury, Brandon, and Peacham. When the Board for Foreign Missions ran out of funds in 1863, most of the missionaries stayed in Hawaii. Some became businessmen, others served as advisors to the Hawaiian government, others remained as teachers, ministers, and doctors, following the original 1819 instruction to cover "these islands with fruitful fields and pleasant dwellings and schools and churches."

Missisquoi National Wildlife Refuge

This refuge of nearly 6,000 acres in the delta of the MISSISQUOI RIVER in Swanton is part of the Atlantic Flyway and is managed primarily for migratory waterfowl by the U.S. Fish and Wildlife Service of the Department of the Interior. It was established in 1943 under provisions of the Migratory Bird Conservation Act of 1929, and is supported by money from the sale of federal waterfowl hunting permits, also known as duck stamps. It is a major nesting area and refuge for thousands of wildfowl and nearly two hundred species of songbirds, as well as a wide variety of wild animals, fish and vegetation. The delta, a classic "bird's foot" pattern of channels emptying into LAKE CHAMPLAIN, also contains several rare and endangered species. Until quite recently, the refuge has contained one of the largest blue heron rookeries in the eastern United States and Canada. Biologists have not determined what caused the birds to abandon the area in 2001. Recovering from their devastation by the pesticide DDT, osprey resumed nesting in the delta in the 1990s. In spring, the refuge is visited by the endangered lake sturgeon and the river has one of the few remaining populations of muskellunge.

George E. Spear

Missisquoi River

The Missisquoi River is the second longest river in the LAKE CHAMPLAIN Basin. Rising in the Eastern Townships of the province of Quebec, specifically in the region northwest of LAKE MEMPHREMAGOG, the Missisquoi crosses into Vermont in the town of Richford and passes through the major villages of Richford, Enosburg Falls, and Swanton. After a journey of 96 miles, the river empties into Missisquoi Bay, an arm of Lake Champlain, forming an extensive delta that is the site of Vermont's only national wildlife refuge. The name of the river is a corruption of the name of the early ABENAKI settlement in Swanton, *mazipskoik* or "place of the flint." The Abenaki name for the river is actually *wazowategok*, or "crooked river."

Missisquoi Village

Mazipskoik, meaning "place of the flint," is the name of the ancient ABENAKI settlement along the MISSISQUOI RIVER and commemorates outcrops of this important tool-making stone in the Swanton area. Converted to the Francophonic Missisquoi, it appears in many different spellings in early French and later English maps and histories. Missisquoi village was an extensive settlement, and two-thousand-year-old burial sites attest to its continual occupation. The historic village consisted of a series of bark (and later frame) houses, each holding several families, surrounded by a defensive palisade, which some late eighteenth-century maps called GRAY LOCK's Castle after the famous war leader. Surrounding Missisquoi village were numerous cornfields running up and down the river called *wazowategok*, "crooked river." Near the Missisquoi village, the first falls of the river in the spring provided a substantial supply of fish, including walleye, sucker, sturgeon, garfish, and others to be taken and dried for later use. Cartographers gave the village name to the river and also to the northeastern arm of LAKE CHAMPLAIN, Missisquoi Bay. Populations may have peaked at over two thousand residents before 1600, after which new pathogens introduced to Canada and New England by French and English settlers, as well as wars with the English and the Iroquois, reduced and dispersed the Abenaki populations throughout their homeland in the seventeenth and early eighteenth centuries. Missisquoi may have held over two hundred residents before the major dispersions caused by the Seven Years' War (1756–1763) and the American Revolution (1775–1783). Early European settlement by the French included a Roman Catholic chapel in 1700, the first long-term Catholic church in Vermont, and a lumber mill built by RENÉ-NICHOLAS LE-VASSEUR in 1749, which brought in a crew of a hundred loggers. After the Peace of 1763, Abenaki who fled to Canada to avoid the British army began to return to Missisquoi, some of them even leasing a large piece of their riverine farmland to James Robertson, a Scots doctor and trader at St. Johns. SIMON METCALFE, a New York surveyor, settled on a New York land grant along the Missisquoi in the late 1760s and built a sawmill and farm. The Missisquoi Abenaki objected to his presence, however, and complained in 1766 to Quebec's Governor GUY CARLETON and New York's Governor Henry Moore. After the Revolution, in the late 1780s, IRA ALLEN's settlement activities in Swanton at the first falls of the Missisquoi River, which included building a dam and a sawmill, brought him and new settlers into conflict with Abenaki wishing to return to their village and farmlands. The Abenaki population of Swanton increased modestly in peacetime, however, several families of them returning from the St. Regis mission in New York, where they had fled during the war. But as Swanton grew, pressures on the Abenaki settlement drove some families again to Canada, while others stayed, living unobtrusively and retaining elements of Abenaki life in agriculture, healing, and traditional harvests of herbs, fish, and wildlife.

Frederick Wiseman

Mitchell, Robert W. (1910–1993)

A talented newspaper reporter who, by virtue of being in the right places at the right times, became the owner and publisher of his paper, the RUTLAND HERALD, Robert W. Mitchell was born in Randolph and began his reporting career at the BENNINGTON BANNER in the 1930s. Moving on to Rutland, then to Montpelier, he became an authoritative state house writer during the administrations of Governors Charles M. Smith and GEORGE D. AIKEN as he worked for both the BURLINGTON FREE PRESS and Rutland Herald. During World War II, Mitchell agreed to be the Herald's acting publisher while its young publisher, William Field, was in military service. After Field returned and decided he did not want to run the newspaper he had inherited, he arranged to sell the property to Mitchell and Gene Noble, the paper's business manager. Much later, the Mitchell family obtained full control. Mitchell continued to write most of the Herald's editorials—virtually unheard of for a publisher—and became known for an informative style of editorial essay that contained much history and background. After his death in 1993, the Herald published a commemorative anthology of his editorials, The Bob Mitchell Years, which constitutes a kind of political history of twentieth-century Vermont. Mitchell's son, R. John Mitchell, is today the publisher of the Herald and the family's other Vermont property, the Times-Argus of Barre and Montpelier.   J. Tyler Resch

Money, Early Vermont

In February 1781, after exhausting confiscated Tory and Yorkist properties to sell in support of the young independent state of Vermont, the legislature "for the purpose of carrying on the war and the enlargement of the paper currency," issued notes to serve as legal tender until redeemed by June 1, 1782. Past that date, unredeemed paper would no longer serve as legal tender except as payment to the state treasurer. These Vermont notes were extraordinary for their time in that all presented were promptly redeemed in good silver hard money and the issue essentially retired. Some notes continued to circulate beyond their expiration date and a few are preserved in numismatic collections. Vermont was the first of the revolutionary states to strike coins, and Vermont coppers that bear dates from 1785 to 1788 were minted into 1789. In 1785, the legisla-ture conferred upon REUBEN D. HARMON, JR., the exclusive franchise to mint Vermont's copper coins but mandated a greater copper content than was economically feasible. A second act mandated a lower statutory minimum, approximately fifty Vermont coppers to the troy pound. Thirty-nine varieties of Vermont copper coins were minted from available dies. A seated Miss Liberty, complete with shield and staff in one hand and a proffered branch in the other, is plainly copied from the British halfpenny's Britannia. In most, but not all instances, the Union Jack decoration has been removed from the shield. Once Vermont was admitted to the Union as the fourteenth state, it ceased to maintain an independent currency. As many as five thousand Vermont coppers may still exist.

Monkton

Monkton, population 1,759, a town in Addison County, was granted by BENNING WENTWORTH in 1762 and most likely named for General Robert Monckton, General James Wolfe's second in command at the battle of Quebec in 1759 and governor of New York from 1761 to 1763. Located halfway between the fertile lowlands of the Champlain Valley on the west and the foothills of the GREEN MOUNTAINS on the east, Monkton has always been primarily agricultural, although in the nineteenth century iron ore and kaolin were mined in the town. The most prominent physical feature is the long silhouette of 1,500-foot Hogback Mountain, which runs almost the entire length of the town on its eastern border. The main village of Monkton Ridge, founded by Quakers, lies on a height of land in the north central part of town. Below it on the west is 114-acre Cedar Lake, lined with summer cottages.

Montgomery

Montgomery, population 992, a town in Franklin County, was granted by the Vermont legislature in 1780 and named for General Richard Montgomery, the Revolutionary War hero who was killed in the failed attack on Quebec city in 1775. Its eastern border approximates the spine of the northern GREEN MOUNTAINS and includes two of the three summits of Jay Peak: 3,180-foot Little Jay Peak and 3,780-foot Big Jay Peak. (The main summit, at 3,870 feet, is on the border between the neighboring towns of Jay and Westfield.) Economic activity is primarily associated with tourism in the form of bed-and-breakfast inns, restaurants, downhill and cross-county ski trails, bike paths, and hiking trails. The two main settlements of Montgomery village and Montgomery Center both lie along the Trout River. Seven local COVERED BRIDGES built in the lattice truss method, six in the town of Montgomery and one in Enosburgh, were all constructed by local sawmill owners Sheldon and Savannah Jewett.

Montpelier

Vermont's capital city and the SHIRE TOWN of Washington County, Montpelier, population 8,035, was granted by the Vermont legislature in 1781 to Jacob Davis and a number of others. Its name, from Montpellier, France, was inspired by the enthusiasm for France generated by that country's help during the American Revolution. (Calais, directly to the north and also granted to Jacob Davis, derives from the same cause.) Montpelier was selected as the state capital in 1805 because of its central location and the financial support for donating land and erecting state buildings given by its citizens. It originally included what is today the town of East Montpelier, from which it was separated in 1848. The city (awarded that rank in 1895), located at the confluence of the WINOOSKI RIVER and its North Branch, in its early years also became a natural site for mills and a trading center. The VERMONT STATE HOUSE, the center of the Capitol Complex, dates from 1836 and 1859, with two newer additions. Also found within the complex are the Supreme Court building, Department of Agriculture (1891), and Pavilion Office Building (1971). The city's second major employer, after state government, is the National Life Insurance Company, whose headquarters building dominates the plateau to the west; JULIUS Y. DEWEY, one of its founders in 1850, was the father of Admiral GEORGE DEWEY of Manila Bay fame, Montpelier's most famous son. The railroad arrived in Montpelier in 1849. The Vermont Central Railroad built a depot on State Street across from the State House, and the Montpelier and Wells River Railroad had a station on Main Street near the Winooski River. In the 1890s, Montpelier was home to over thirty companies engaged in the granite industry. Other companies that have made Montpelier their home have included LANE MANUFACTURING COMPANY (saws and water wheels),

E. W. Bailey (gristmill), Colton Manufacturing Co. (saddlery hardware), and C. H. Cross & Son Bakery (crackers). During the Civil War, Montpelier was home to the Sloan Army Hospital. The city's own Heaton Hospital was dedicated in 1896 and operated until 1968, when the Central Vermont Hospital was formed. Montpelier's commercial district is centered along Main and State streets, and was devastated by two major fires in 1875, which claimed many older structures. Some landmark buildings today are the Washington County Court House (1844), the Unitarian Church of the Messiah (1865), the Kellogg-Hubbard Library (1895) with a 2001 addition named for native son U.S. Senator PATRICK J. LEAHY, and the City Hall (1911), a distinctive Italian Renaissance building of yellow brick and granite trim. The city is also home to VERMONT COLLEGE, the NEW ENGLAND CULINARY INSTITUTE, the museum of the VERMONT HISTORICAL SOCIETY, the T. W. WOOD GALLERY & ARTS CENTER, the Savoy art cinema, and the Lost Nation Theater. Hubbard Park, donated to the city by John Hubbard in 1900, covers 185 acres on the hillside behind the State House. The capital's location in a narrow river valley offers little room for new building and is prone to flooding, most notably in the FLOOD OF 1927, which resulted in fatalities and extensive damage to property, and in March 1992, when an ice jam blocked the Winooski River and flooded the downtown area. As the smallest state capital in the United States, Montpelier retains a small-town atmosphere but has a high level of cultural sophistication due to the presence of governmental, educational, and business entities. *Paul A. Carnahan and Reidun Nuquist*

Montresor, Frances

See PENNIMAN, FRANCES MONTRESOR BUCHANAN ALLEN.

Montshire Museum of Science

The Montshire Museum of Science, located on a 110-acre site on the CONNECTICUT RIVER in Norwich, is a hands-on museum containing dozens of exhibits relating to the natural and physical sciences, ecology, and technology. The building, opened in 1989, is itself an exhibit, with color-coded ventilation and heating systems and exposed timber trusses to demonstrate construction techniques. Designed to be child-friendly, the museum encourages participation in a wide range of activities, from creating giant soap bubbles to stroking a boa constrictor. A network of trails winds through the property offering further opportunities for observing natural phenomena.

Mooar, John (ca. 1850–1918), and J. Wright Mooar (ca. 1850–1940)

Buffalo hunters in the settlement years of Kansas and Texas, the Mooar brothers of Pownal demonstrated Yankee ingenuity, frugality, and dogged persistence in killing buffalo for their hides in the 1870s. Barely scraping a living as a wood cutter in Fort Hays, Kansas, Wright Mooar saw an opportunity in buying customarily discarded buffalo skins from meat hunters and sent a load back to his brother John in New York. In the Panic of 1873, a growing market for buffalo skins tanned for industrial uses by a new process John had helped to develop brought a rush of hide hunters, each expecting to recoup lost fortunes with a few loads of skins taken from the western plains' herds of over thirty million. Selling at the peak market for $3.50 per skin, over twenty thousand buffalo fell to Wright Mooar's long-range Sharps rifle. In ten years, about ten million buffalo in the southern herd that grazed across Texas and Kansas were exterminated, the last of them killed at Buffalo Springs, Texas, in 1879. When the killing ended, the Mooar brothers settled in West Texas. Still defending the slaughter nearly fifty years later, Wright Mooar said in 1928, "If it had not been for the buffalo hunters, the wild Bison would still graze where Amarillo is now and the Red Man would still reign supreme over the pampas of the Panhandle."

Moody, Paul Dwight (1879–1947)

The tenth president of MIDDLEBURY COLLEGE (1921–1942), Paul Dwight Moody was born in Baltimore, the son of the celebrated revivalist Dwight L. Moody. He received a classical and religious education at Mt. Hermon Academy, Yale (A.B., 1901), Edinburgh's New College and the Glasgow Free Church College in Scotland, and the Hartford Theological Seminary in Connecticut. He taught for six years in the Northfield schools, and worked from 1909 to 1912 for the George Doran publishing house. Ordained as a Congregational minister in 1912, Moody served as pastor of South Church in St. Johnsbury from 1912 to 1917. He was an army chaplain during World War I, serving in 1918 and 1919 as the senior chaplain at General Pershing's headquarters. He was sent on various missions in France and served as a liaison with the French military. For his outstanding work, he was awarded the Academic Palms and in 1924 was made a chevalier of the Legion of Honor. After a brief stint as a minister in New York City, he accepted the Middlebury presidency in 1921. His twenty-one years as president were characterized by critical support of the fledgling Middlebury summer programs, especially the MIDDLEBURY COLLEGE LANGUAGE SCHOOLS and the BREAD LOAF WRITERS CONFERENCE and, until the last several years of his tenure, by strong institutional cohesion. Prexy Moody, as he was called by students, faculty, and townspeople, is widely considered the most popular president in the college's history.

David M. Stameshkin

Moonlight in Vermont

One of the most enduring and oft-recorded ballads ever written since its creation in 1944, *Moonlight in Vermont* was the work of two non-Vermonters, John Blackburn (lyrics) and Karl Suessdorf (music). Blackburn had a brief association with Vermont when he taught drama for two years at BENNINGTON COLLEGE in the 1930s, and teamed up with Suessdorf when they were both working in Los Angeles during the Second World War. They brought the song to popular composer Johnny Mercer, who liked the melody and arranged to have it recorded by Margaret Whiting in 1945. The song's initial popularity was on Armed Forces Radio overseas, where its tranquil, haunting, slightly melancholy character made it a favorite with servicemen far from home. Ten years later, Whiting re-recorded the song and it reached the Top Ten. At least two hundred artists are known to have recorded the song since then. On February 5, 1985, "Moonlight in Vermont Day" in Vermont, Margaret Whiting, on her first trip to the state, sang the song to a joint session of the legislature. Some years later, in the late 1990s, *Moonlight in Vermont* failed to gain approval as the official state song in the legislature, where its commercial origins and complicated vocalizations (considered too difficult for the average person to sing) worked against it.

Moretown

Moretown, population 1,653, a town in Washington County, was granted by BEN-

NING WENTWORTH in 1763. The source of the name is not known, although an apocryphal story maintains that it derives from a surveyor's exclamation as he came across this piece of territory: "My God, more town!" The Mad River flows through it from south to north, bordered on the west by the main spine of the GREEN MOUNTAINS and on the east by a northern extension of the Northfield Mountains before it empties into the WINOOSKI RIVER along the town's northern border. Except for farming along the two rivers, the town's economic base has historically been lumbering. Many residents commute to work in Montpelier, Waterbury, and Chittenden County.

Morey, Samuel (1762–1843)

A native of Hebron, Connecticut, Samuel Morey, an early inventor of steam and internal combustion engines, grew up in Orford, New Hampshire, where his father owned a tavern. Educated in Orford, he showed mechanical ability at an early age. A successful lumberman in Orford, he went on to work in the construction of locks on the CONNECTICUT RIVER between Windsor, Connecticut, and Olcott Falls, working finally as as an engineer in charge of the lock construction at Bellows Falls. Experimenting with heat and light in the 1780s, he received a patent in 1793 for a steam-operated spit and in 1795 for a rotary steam engine. He also obtained patents for a windmill, a steam pump, and a water wheel. He began to experiment with steam boats in 1790, when he operated a bow-mounted small steam engine on a boat launched on the Connecticut River at Orford. A stern wheeler he built in 1794 ran from Hartford, Connecticut, to New York and is reputed to have been the sixth steamboat built in the United States. After 1800, he attempted to persuade Robert Fulton to adopt his model for a steamboat, but failed. Fulton went on to open the era of successful steamboat navigation on a commercial basis. Morey was granted two steam-engine improvements in 1803 and 1815. During the later years of his life he settled in Fairlee, where he worked on internal combustion engines. About 1820, he launched a boat named *Aunt Sally*, which was propelled by a vapor or internal combustion engine, on Fairlee Pond, now known as Lake Morey, and in 1826 received a patent for an internal combustion engine.

Morgan

Morgan, population 669, a town in Orleans County, was granted by the Vermont legislature in 1780 to John and Inneas Calder and others, and originally called Caldersburgh. The name was changed to Morgan in 1801, after John Morgan, another early holder of land in the town. Hilly and heavily wooded, the town has always been sparsely settled. Its main feature is 1,777-acre Seymour Lake, lined with summer camps. Two tiny settlements, Morgan village and Morgan Center, both lie on Route 111 along the lake's northern shore.

Morgan, Justin (1747–1798)

The singing master and horse breeder who established the MORGAN HORSE breed in Vermont, Justin Morgan, a native of Springfield, Massachusetts, lived in Randolph when he acquired the horse Figure, a three-year-old stud, in Hartford, Connecticut, during May 1792. Morgan advertised Figure at stud for the next three years, thereby establishing in Vermont a breed of horse soon called the Morgan. Justin Morgan traded Figure to Samuel Allen of Williston in 1795 for 100 acres of land in Moretown. Morgan was a horse breeder in Massachusetts before migrating to Vermont in 1788. He also was a licensed liquor purveyor, ran a gristmill, taught music, singing, and writing, and composed at least nine songs that were published in Asahel Benham's *Federal Harmony* (1790) and Andrew Adgate's *Philadelphia Harmony* (1791). In Adgate's collection, Morgan's song "Despair," based on a stanza by Alexander Pope, seems to be a eulogy to his wife Martha ("worthy to be loved") who had died that year.

Betty Bandel

Morgan Horse

America's first breed of horse, the Morgan is the only light horse breed to trace its origin to one foundation sire. This horse, called Figure, was foaled about 1789 in West Springfield, Massachusetts, and brought to Randolph by his owner, JUSTIN MORGAN. Figure's strength and stamina were superb; however, his prepotency as a sire set him apart. His get so closely resembled him that they became known as Morgan horses after his owner. Figure was used as a stud extensively throughout the CONNECTICUT RIVER Valley, but Vermont was his home for thirty years until he died in 1821. His three most famous sons were Sherman, Bulrush, and Woodbury. His great grandson, Ethan Allen 50,

Morgan horse. Vermont Department of Tourism and Marketing

held the world trotting record. Over the years, Morgans proved their great versatility by outstanding service as farm and family horses, cavalry mounts in the Civil War, and in opening up the West. They compete successfully in carriage, dressage, hunting, western, trail, jumping, police work, endurance rides, parades, cutting cattle, and many show-ring disciplines. The Morgan contributed to the development of the American Saddlebred, Standardbred, Walking Horse, and Quarterhorse. The breed is distinctive for its energy, willingness, personality, and stamina as well as its style and beauty. It has a high head carriage, bold and kind eye, a ground-covering trot, and stylish canter. Most exhibit great intelligence. Morgans are prized as family horses and are especially good around children. They generally range in height from 14.1 to 15.3 hands and weigh from 950 to 1,150 pounds. Predominant colors are bay, black, and shades of chestnut. The Morgan Registry allows palomino, buckskin, and dun colors, however, no white is allowed above the hocks and knees except in the face. Morgans are now found in all fifty states and many foreign countries. In 1961, the Morgan was designated the Vermont state animal by the legislature. The first volume of the *Morgan Horse Register* was published in 1894 by JOSEPH BATTELL.   *Donald Balch*

Morgan Horse Farm

The UNIVERSITY OF VERMONT's Morgan Horse Farm in Weybridge presently maintains sixty to eighty Registered stallions, mares, and foals at this National Historic Site, a property once owned by JOSEPH BATTELL, who began breeding MORGAN HORSES here on his farm in the late 1800s. His intense interest in preserving and promoting America's first breed of horse undoubtedly saved the Morgan from extinction. Battell spent years of study in tracing out pedigrees that resulted in publication of the first volume of the *Morgan Horse Register* in 1894. In 1906, he gave his farm and Morgans to the United States government. From 1907 until 1951, when the United States government turned the farm over to the University of Vermont, Morgans were bred, trained, sold, and exhibited here. The University Morgan Program is devoted primarily to the continued preservation and improvement of the Morgan through breeding and selection. The objective is to apply scientific knowledge of genetics and animal breeding to the selec-

tion and mating systems employed. UVM Morgans are now among the top in winning at the major Morgan shows throughout the country. They are also highly prized as superb pleasure horses for recreational use and as foundation broodstock. The current UVM Morgan maintains a genetic link to the U.S. Government and Battell bloodlines. The farm is noted for supplying excellent stock to Morgan breeders throughout the United States and abroad. Educational programs are also an important part of the farm's mission.

Morrill, Justin Smith (1810–1898)

Born in Strafford, Justin Morrill became the longest-serving Congressman and United States Senator ever to represent Vermont. The eldest of ten children, Morrill completed his formal education at age fifteen after two terms at grammar school, when he elected to become a clerk in a general store. Demonstrating an extraordinary talent for merchandising, he entered into partnership with a local patron and by 1848 amassed sufficient money to retire. Subsequently, he expanded his efforts for the WHIG PARTY and rose rapidly within the state organization. In 1854, he entered his first elective contest and won a seat in the United States House of Representatives as an anti-slavery Whig and temperance advocate. Converted to Republicanism even before taking his seat, Morrill remained in the House until 1866, when he gained election to the Senate, where he served until his death in 1898. His total of forty-three years in Congress established a record for longevity. He made his most significant contributions as a member of the House, where his adeptness at parliamentary maneuvering assured him a leadership position. Appointed to the Ways and Means Committee in 1858, Morrill relinquished an opportunity to become chairman in favor of THADDEUS STEVENS. He became chairman in 1865, however, and served on the Joint Committee on Reconstruction. An ardent protectionist, Morrill opposed the low tariff bill of 1857 and gained the animosity of the South for the high "Morrill Tariff" of 1861. His most celebrated legislative achievement was the 1862 Land Grant College Act. He had introduced similar legislation three and a half years earlier but southern opposition and, eventually, President Buchanan's veto, kept it from becoming law. As a Senator, Morrill voted President Andrew Johnson "guilty" in the impeachment trial and be-

Justin Smith Morrill. Special Collections, Bailey/ Howe Library, University of Vermont

came the embodiment of the Republican domestic legislative program. As chairman of the Banking and Finance Committee, he opposed inflationary policies, and as a member of the Buildings and Grounds Committee placed his imprint on the Washington Monument, the Library of Congress, and Statuary Hall. Always a stern moralist, his later career was marked by close association with the "Mugwumps" faction of the REPUBLICAN PARTY who rejected their party's presidential candidate, James Blaine, over a railroad graft scandal and voted instead for the Democratic candidate, Grover Cleveland. Later in his career, Morrill gained passage of a second land grant act that assured federal funds would support black as well as white colleges. Morrill died in 1898, while opposing the annexation of the Philippines.   *Gregory Sanford*

Morristown

Morristown, population 5,139, the most populous town in Lamoille County, was granted by the Vermont legislature in 1781 to Moses Morse and others. The name is probably a variation of "Morsetown." The town's landscape is gently rolling and well suited to AGRICULTURE, except for a narrow westward extension that reaches to the main spine of the GREEN MOUNTAINS and includes three summits of the Sterling Range: Morse Mountain (3,380 feet), Madonna Mountain (3,640 feet), and Sterling (or White Face) Mountain (3,715 feet). The main settlement is the substantial village of Morrisville, located at the point where Route 100 crosses the LAMOILLE RIVER, which cuts across the northern part of the town from east to west. North of that village is Cadys Falls, where a dam backs up the Lamoille River into Lake Lamoille, and to the west is the older village of Morristown, now a crossroads hamlet.

Mosher, Howard Frank (b. 1942)

The author of novels and short stories set in the NORTHEAST KINGDOM, Howard Frank Mosher was born in Tannersville, New York, a small town in the Catskills, and graduated from Syracuse University in 1964. He settled in Irasburg with his wife in the 1960s after graduate studies at the UNIVERSITY OF VERMONT and in California. His region of Vermont is usually the setting of his fiction, a place he calls Kingdom County and populates with affectionately imagined independent-minded characters. His early stories were published in a collection called *Where the Rivers Flow North* (1971). His first novel, *Disappearances* (1977), presents a main character who runs whiskey across the Canadian border during PROHIBITION. The novel *Marie Blythe* (1983) is set at the turn of the century and is about a girl who migrates to northern Vermont from Canada, having to cope with the early deaths of her parents. *Stranger in the Kingdom* (1989) is based on the IRASBURG AFFAIR in 1968, the most highly charged event involving race relations in Vermont in recent times. *Northern Borders* (1994) is a novel set in Lost Nation Hollow, again a place near the Canadian border. It combines the past and the present in the life of the protagonist. *North Country: A Personal Journey through the Borderland* (1997) is a nonfiction account of his travels along the U.S.–Canada border from Vermont to the west coast. *Fall of the Year* (1999) Mosher calls an autobiographical novel and is another celebration of the fiercely independent residents of the Northeast Kingdom. Family, community, vocation, and the natural world are all important to this novel. Recently, he collaborated with photographer John M. Miller of Coventry on a book called *Granite and Cedar: The People and Land of Vermont's Northeast Kingdom*, in which selections of his fiction are juxtaposed with Miller's black and white photographs. His short fiction has appeared in *Yankee, Vermont Magazine, Epoch, Colorado Quarterly*, and *Four Quartets*. Some of his fiction has been made into films by JAY CRAVEN, including the short story "High Water" and the novel *Stranger in the Kingdom*. *Disappearances* is scheduled for release in 2003. Leading roles in his films have been filled by actors Martin Sheen, Rip Torn, Tantoo Cardinal, Kris Kristofferson, and RUSTY DEWEES. Governor MADELEINE KUNIN honored Mosher as one of thirty "Extraordinary Vermonters" in 1990. He has been given numerous awards, including the 1991 New England Book Award for Fiction for *Stranger in the Kingdom*. The same book won an ACLU Civil Liberties in the Arts Award the following year. He has also been awarded a National Endowment for the Arts Fellowship in fiction writing, an American Academy of Arts and Letters Literature Award, and a Guggenheim Fellowship. *Addison Merrick*

Mould, Ruth Greene (1894–1979)

A native of Morrisville and graduate of Peoples Academy, the artist Ruth Green Mould attended Johnson Normal School before teaching in a district school. An uncle recognized her ability and sponsored her art studies at the Institute of Art in St. Paul, Minnesota, where she graduated with honors. She went on to study at the Art Students League and became an honorary life member of the league. Ruth Mould taught art students at Johnson Normal School during the 1920s and 1930s, and often tutored others in painting. Mainly a portrait artist, her works are in the BENNINGTON MUSEUM, the FLEMING MUSEUM of the UNIVERSITY OF VERMONT, and the VERMONT HISTORICAL SOCIETY. Her portraits of Chief Justices Percy L. Shangraw, Benjamin N. Hurlburd, and Walter H. Cleary are in the Supreme Court building. Her 1937 posthumous portrait of EDNA BEARD, first female member of both the Vermont House and Senate, hangs in the VERMONT STATE HOUSE. At the 1939 New York World's Fair, Ruth Mould represented Vermont visual arts with her painting *Old Lady Looking for a Bug*. Many portraits of Johnson people, done while she was living there, were in her last exhibit at the Dibden Gallery of JOHNSON STATE COLLEGE in 1978, and some of them are in the permanent Dibden collection. In 2000, many of her paintings were given to the Mary Bryan Memorial Gallery in Jeffersonville. Her work with furniture led to her book, *Refinishing and Decorating Furniture* (1953). *Mary G. Lighthall*

Mount Holly

Mount Holly, population 1,241, a town in Rutland County, was incorporated by the Vermont legislature in 1792 by taking land from the towns of Ludlow and Wallingford (the latter of which included the former Jackson's Gore), probably because the rugged topography made it difficult for inhabitants of the sections concerned to get to their respective town centers. Since the town was settled by Quakers, its name probably derives from the seventeenth-century Quaker settlement of that name in New Jersey. Mount Holly lies on the eastern slopes of the main spine of the GREEN MOUNTAINS and is separated from Ludlow on the east by the bulk of 3,343-foot Okemo Mountain. The upland nature of the land—the town sits on the boundary dividing the headwaters of the CONNECTICUT RIVER from those that flow into LAKE CHAMPLAIN—has made it suitable for dairying but not general cultivation. There are several settlements, of which the most important are Belmont and Mount Holly village. At Summit, the highest point on the former Rutland Railroad, the last spike connecting Boston and Burlington by rail was driven in December 1849.

Mount Tabor

Mount Tabor, population 203, a town in Rutland County, was granted by BENNING WENTWORTH in 1761 as Harwich and named after Wills Hill (1718–1793), Baron Harwich. At the request of the townspeople, the name was changed to Mount Tabor in 1803 in honor of Gideon Tabor, a Revolutionary War veteran who in his lifetime held many town posts and was its representative to the legislature for thirty years. The town, which lies on the main spine of the GREEN MOUNTAINS and is almost totally within the GREEN MOUNTAIN NATIONAL FOREST, is one of the most rugged in the state and has always been sparsely populated. It is crossed by one east-west road, Route 10, which is closed in winter. The only settlement, Mount Tabor village, a mile from the border with Danby, was called Griffith from 1891 to 1905 after SILAS LAPHAM GRIFFITH, a lumber baron and philanthropist whose sawmills exploited the timber wealth of the town for many decades.

Mountain Rule

See REPUBLICAN PARTY.

Moyse, Marcel, Louis Moyse, and Blanche Honegger Moyse

The Moyse family brought the European musical tradition to Vermont in 1949, and has influenced music here perhaps more than any other single group of musicians. They founded the music department at MARLBORO COLLEGE in 1949, co-founded the MARLBORO MUSIC SCHOOL AND FESTIVAL and the Busch-Serkin Trio in 1951, and founded the Brattleboro Music Center in 1951 and the New England Bach Festival in 1969. Born in Saint Amour, Jura, France, flutist Marcel Moyse (1889–1984) was considered the greatest flutist and flute pedagogue of his time, performing in the world premiere of Stravinsky's *Rite of Spring* in 1913, as well as concertos by Jacques Ibert and Jean Francaix, which were written for him. Marcel's son, flutist-pianist-composer Louis Moyse (b. 1912) was born in Scheveningen, the Netherlands, studied composition with Eugene Bigot and Olivier Messiaen, and performed on piano as well as flute, becoming one of the greatest flutists of his generation. Louis's wife, Swiss-born conductor-violinist Blanche Honegger Moyse (b. 1909) debuted with L'Orchestre de la Suisse Romande in the Beethoven Violin Concerto in 1927. Marcel, Louis, and Blanche formed the Moyse Trio, one of the most respected chamber ensembles in Europe. After World War II, they moved to Brattleboro, where they taught and performed at the Marlboro Music Festival and taught at Marlboro College. Marcel also taught privately in New York (his students included James Galway and Paula Robison, among many). Blanche and Louis were divorced in 1974, and Louis left Marlboro to teach for short times at the University of Toronto and Boston University before moving to Montpelier, where he lives with his second wife Janet, and teaches and composes. He also conducts flute master classes in France and Japan, as well as other parts of the world. Louis Moyse is considered to be the world's most prolific composer of flute music, and has been editing flute music for G. Schirmer publishers for most of his career. Remaining in Brattleboro, Blanche Moyse, who gave up the violin in the 1960s, has become one of the world's foremost conductors of the choral works of J. S. Bach, taking her Blanche Moyse Chorale, made up of local amateur singers and professional performers from other parts of New England, to New York's Carnegie Hall, Symphony Space, and Metropolitan Museum of Art, winning rave reviews. She continues to conduct each summer at Marlboro Music Festival, where she is the only remaining founder, and at her New England Bach Festival each October.

James Lowe

Mozart Festival

Beginning in 1974 as a summer series for the UNIVERSITY OF VERMONT'S LANE SERIES and inspired by the many beautiful sites throughout the Vermont countryside, the Mozart Festival was conceived in the European musical festival tradition of performances at a variety of locations and events. This model remains the cornerstone of the summer festival. The first festival visited six locations and consisted of ten concerts, a dressage exhibition, lectures, and a course, "Mozart and His Times." The festival has since grown into a multi-week event featuring eighteen concerts and three "Branching Out" events throughout Vermont. The festival first exclusively performed works by Wolfgang Amadeus Mozart, but by 1976, the music of other composers found its way into the programs. Since then, programs have become increasingly enterprising and eclectic. The festival has now presented music spanning six centuries: over two hundred different compositions by Mozart alone; plus great choral masterpieces, the entire Beethoven Quartet cycle, Gilbert and Sullivan, medieval motets, Baroque dance-opera, jazz, and, of course, chamber music for every conceivable combination of instruments. The festival has performed over twenty-one hundred pieces in thirty-five different locations, including on the lawn of SHELBURNE FARMS and on a hillside meadow in Stowe. The Vermont Mozart Festival was voted a "Top 10 Summer Event" in 1994, 1996, 1997, 1998 and a "Top 10 Winter Event" in 1998 by the Vermont Chamber of Commerce. It was also named "Best of Vermont" Classical Music Festival by editors of *Vermont* magazine, February 1998.

Mundell, William (1912–1997)

Poet William Mundell lived in or near Newfane most of his life. He held a variety of jobs, working as a radar technician, carpenter, stonemason, owner and operator of a ski area, and foreman for the Vermont Highway Department. He published five collections of poems—*Hill Journey* (1970), *Plowman's Earth* (1973), *Mundell Country* (1977), *Finding Home* (1984), and *Book of Common Hours* (1989)—and his poems were published in the *New Yorker*, *Atlantic Monthly*, *Poetry*, and *Yankee* magazines. In 1989, the Poetry Society of Vermont named him Vermont Poet Laureate, a position not to be confused with VERMONT STATE POET.

Murray, Orson S. (1806–1885)

A radical or "ultra-ist" social reformer, Orson Murray was born in Orwell. Little is known of his early life, but as a young man he "accepted Christ" and joined the Baptist Church, the leading religious denomination in western Vermont. In his twenties, Murray also joined the radical wing of Vermont's quickly growing temperance movement, which favored total prohibition of the manufacture, sale, and possession of alcohol. Adopting extreme positions in social reform matters marked Murray's involvement in several other reform movements. In 1835, he bought *The Vermont Telegraph* of Brandon, a Baptist weekly newspaper that he quickly transformed from an uncontroversial journal of religious affairs to an outspoken voice of the reform movement. He published the paper until 1843, filling it with articles advocating temperance, ANTI-MASONISM, ABOLITION, pacifism, nonresistance, diet reform, prison reform, and opposition to capital punishment. Heavily involved in the abolition movement during the 1830s, he worked as a paid agent of the New England (later American) Anti-Slavery Society. In that position, he traveled extensively around the state speaking on abolition and helping to establish many local anti-slavery societies. He was an impassioned but intemperate speaker and received hostile receptions in many Vermont towns. In Burlington, the editor of a local newspaper told another abolitionist agent, OLIVER JOHNSON, that the crowd's hostility was directed more at Murray himself than at the anti-slavery message. His passionate anti-slavery attacks antagonized moderate mainstream abolitionists when he echoed WILLIAM LLOYD GARRISON, who publicly burned the Constitution, exclaiming, "So perish all compromises with tyranny." Moderates hearing Murray's opposition to compromise called him an "anti-government man." His radical steadfastness helped precipitate the dissolution of the Vermont Anti-Slavery Society. Opposition to Murray in his church developed in 1841 as his radicalism was seen to distract from fulfilling his religious duty. He was dismissed from the fellowship of the Baptist Church Association, and the Vermont Baptist Convention withdrew its support from *The Telegraph*. His waning influence in Vermont drove Murray to West Liberty, Ohio, in the mid-1840s, where he briefly belonged to a communitarian group called the Prairie Home Community. This group seems to have lasted only a few months, but Murray remained in Ohio for the rest of his life. During the 1870s, he briefly resumed contact with his reformist associates from New England. His principal crusade at that time was against Henry Ward Beecher, whom he vilified in private letters during and after a notorious sex scandal involving Beecher and a young member of his Brooklyn choir, though it is not known if Murray made this public. He died in Fosters or Fosteria, Ohio.   *Ronald J. Salomon*

N

Nearing, Helen Knothe (1903–1994), and Scott Nearing (1883–1983)

Helen and Scott Nearing came to Vermont in 1932 and settled at Pike's Falls in a remote corner of Winhall to construct an alternative life away from the social and economic ravages of the Great Depression. Convinced that pursuing their ideals of pacifism, vegetarianism, and collectivism were unattainable in mainstream America, the Nearings spent the next twenty years experimenting with and enjoying a life of simplicity in which they took their livelihood from the land while avoiding excess and the money economy. Scott Nearing was an academic economist with radical views—his socialist distrust of big business got him fired from the University of Pennsylvania in 1915—and Helen Knothe was an accomplished violinist. They married in 1948. Resourceful, hardworking, and healthy, the Nearings raised their own food, built their own stone house, and earned the little cash they needed from their sugar bush. Although some urban disciples eventually followed them to settle nearby, by 1952 the Nearings concluded that the example of their simple life had made so little impression on their neighbors that the communitarian social goals they had sought were unattainable among highly individualistic Vermonters. Yet had they remained in Vermont into the 1960s, instead of moving to Maine, they would have seen a wave of new settlers in Vermont—the BACK-TO-THE-LANDERS—many of them inspired by the Nearings' 1954 book, *Living the Good Life*. Their thinking on social justice and their practical advice for simple living remain accessible today in reprints of their many books, including a fiftieth anniversary edition of *The Maple Sugar Book* (1950) by the Chelsea Green Press.

Neshobe Island

In 1924, Alexander Woollcott (1887–1943)—author, *New York Times* drama critic, and famous wit in the group of artists and actors who held forth at the Hotel Algonquin Round Table in Manhattan in the 1920s—joined with six friends in buying a primitive summer camp on Neshobe Island, which lies in LAKE BOMOSEEN in the town of Castleton. In the early 1930s, Woollcott purchased most of the island and built a large stone house where he ruled autocratically and generously over such guests as Dorothy Parker, Charles MacArthur, Heywood Broun, and Harpo Marx. While many of the guests came to Neshobe Island for the relaxation of croquet, chess, word games, swimming, and Woollcott's acerbic wit, others came to work on their current writing projects. Ben Hecht and Charles MacArthur, for example, finished their screenplay of *Wuthering Heights* as Woollcott's guests. Charles Brackett's novel *Entirely Surrounded* (1934) is based upon the characters and activities at Woollcott's house on Neshobe Island; Woollcott, Dorothy Parker, Harpo Marx, and other habitués of the island are clearly recognizable in their fictional counterparts. Woollcott made Neshobe his permanent residence after 1938, at one town meeting running unsuccessfully for a seat on the Castleton library's board of trustees.

Newark

Newark, population 470, a town in Caledonia County, was granted by the Vermont legislature in 1781 to Colonel William Wall and several others. The specific source of the name is not known. The landscape is rough and uneven, suitable for logging and hunting but not for farming, and so the town has always been sparsely populated. Packer Mountain, Walker Mountain, and Hawk Rock, all about two thousand feet high, dominate the eastern part of town. The only significant settlement, though it has no post office, is tiny Newark village, on the north-south road cutting across the town from West Burke to Island Pond.

Newbury

Newbury, population 1,955, a town in Orange County, was granted by BENNING WENTWORTH in 1763 to JACOB BAYLEY (one of the builders of the BAYLEY-HAZEN MILITARY ROAD, which began in Newbury's village of Wells River) and seventy-four others. It was named for Bayley's home town in Massachusetts. Broad fertile meadows along the fish-rich CONNECTICUT RIVER, which forms the eastern border of the town, made the area attractive to the ABENAKI, who had a permanent settlement here. The land rises inland through a series of wooded hills and upland pastures cut by watercourses and culminates in 1,740-foot Woodchuck Mountain near the western border with Topsham. The main village of Newbury was the first colonial settlement on the Connecticut north of Charlestown, New Hampshire, over 60 miles to the south, and contains a number of late-eighteenth-century buildings including the THOMAS JOHNSON house, 1775. The village of Wells River, at the mouth of that river at the extreme northern edge of town, was once the head of navigation on the Connecticut River and later an important railroad junction. On December 31, 1957, the still-unsolved murder of ORVILLE GIBSON, a Newbury farmer whose death even today is a source of controversy, occurred here.

Newell, Graham Stiles (b. 1915)

Educator and legislator born in St. Johnsbury, Graham Newell attended local schools and the University of Chicago, where he received an A.B. in Political Science in 1938 and an A.M. in Latin in 1949. A Latin and history instructor at ST. JOHNSBURY ACADEMY from 1938 to 1947, he also taught at Hatch Preparatory School in Maine and St. Johnsbury Junior High School. From 1959 until 1979, when he retired from full-time teaching, he served as professor and chairman of the Social Science Division of LYNDON STATE COLLEGE. He continued to teach part time at Lyndon and since 1982 has been teaching Latin at St. Johnsbury Academy. His political career began as chairman of the Caledonia County Republican Committee and he was first elected to the Vermont House in 1952. He served four terms in the House and eight in the Senate. While in the legislature, he was chairman of the education committee, a member of the Little Hoover Commission to study state government, and served on the New England Board of Higher Education. Newell was a justice of the peace for twelve years and a member of the town Republican committee for thirty-three years.

New England Culinary Institute

The New England Culinary Institute (NECI, pronounced "nekki") offers training and education programs in the culinary arts and restaurant management to more than seven hundred students per year at its headquarters in Montpelier and its centers in Burlington and Essex Junction. The most popular program is the two-year associates degree in culinary arts, which prepares graduates for employment as chefs. A one-and-one-half-year associates degree in food and beverage management prepares graduates to manage a restaurant, and an upper-level one-and-one-half-year bachelor's degree prepares for restaurant ownership. A ten-month certificate program in basic cooking is also offered. Programs are enhanced by paid, personalized internships at a restaurant or hotel.

Newfane

Newfane, population 1,680, a town in Windham County, was granted by BENNING WENTWORTH in 1753 as the town of Fane and renamed New Fane in 1761. It honors John Fane, seventh earl of Westmoreland and one of Wentworth's relatives, and has been the SHIRE TOWN of Windham County since 1787. The rugged nature of the landscape has limited settlement largely to the valleys of the Rock River, in the southern part of town, and the WEST RIVER, which sweeps in gentle arcs along the eastern boundary. The main population center is Newfane village, an impeccably preserved collection of early nineteenth-century buildings that is on the National Register of Historic Places. Antique stores, upscale inns and restaurants, and one of Vermont's largest

summertime flea markets make the town a tourist destination.

New Hampshire Grants

See WENTWORTH, BENNING.

New Haven

New Haven, population 1,666, a town in Addison County, was granted by BENNING WENTWORTH in 1761 and named for New Haven, Connecticut, the co-capital of the home colony of the grantees. Located in the fertile lowlands of the Champlain Valley just west of the foothills of the GREEN MOUNTAINS, New Haven has always been primarily agricultural, although in the nineteenth century two centers of local industry were at New Haven Mills and Brooksfield along the New Haven River, a tributary of OTTER CREEK. The latter was home to the Brooks Edge Tool Company, a firm that for half a century made axes renowned for their high quality. The Union Church of New Haven Mills, constructed in 1852, is on the National Register of Historic Places. In the late 1850s, New Haven Methodists organized a summer camp meeting in Spring Grove, near the railroad, where every August for nearly half a century crowds came from miles around for two weeks of revivalist excitement. After the decline of Brooksville and New Haven Mills at the turn of the twenti-

eth century, the village of New Haven, on Route 17, became the town center and remains so today.

Newport City

The city of Newport, population 5,005, the SHIRE TOWN of Orleans County, was incorporated by the Vermont legislature in 1917 out of portions of Newport and Derby towns, with Newport village forming the nucleus of the city. (For the early history of Newport town, see its entry.) Located at the southern end of LAKE MEMPHREMAGOG, which extends 20 miles into Canada, the city has long been the focus of cross-border travel. By the 1870s, visitors to Newport from Canada or the United States could come via lake boat or railroad and be accommodated at several large hotels, including the four-hundred-room Memphremagog House on the waterfront, which was destroyed by fire in 1907. An image of Newport's best-known lake steamer of that era, the *Lady of the Lake*, is incorporated into the seal of the city. For much of the nineteenth century, Newport was a leading lumber milling center and shipping port, drawing on the vast forests of the NORTHEAST KINGDOM. Its firm of Prouty and Miller was one of the biggest timber companies in the East, and the lake's South Bay was choked with logs awaiting the sawmills. The long decline that followed the end of the lumber era led to a loss of economic vitality and of population that has only recently been reversed. Today, the city's two largest industries are Columbia Forest Products, which specializes in hardwood veneer, and Bogner of America, makers of skiwear and sportswear. The buildings of present-day Newport retain some of their Victorian character, which blends smoothly with renovated Main Street. On a hill above the downtown area stands the twin-towered St. Mary Star of the Sea Roman Catholic church, an edifice in the French-Canadian style. The restored lakefront includes an office complex housing the courts and offices of state agencies, along with walking and bike paths. Docking facilities on the waterfront allow boaters to tie up and walk to stores and restaurants, and a replica stern wheeler provides tours of the lake.   *Anthony Paré*

Newport Town

The town of Newport, population 1,511, in Orleans County, was granted by the Vermont legislature in 1802 to George Dun-

Windham County court house in Newfane. Vermont Department of Tourism and Marketing

can and others, and originally called Duncansborough. The name was changed to Newport in 1816, probably because it was a "new port" on LAKE MEMPHREMAGOG. Originally, the town included what is today Newport city until that was incorporated by the legislature in 1917. Despite its proximity to the city, Newport town, with a landscape made up of low rolling hills interspersed with streams, has remained almost entirely agricultural. Its 3-mile shoreline along Lake Memphremagog, once lined with summer camps, now has mostly year-round homes.

Newton, Earle Williams (b. 1917)

Historian, educator, and editor, Earle Newton was born in Cortland, New York, and resides in Brookfield. He graduated magna cum laude from Amherst College in 1938 and in 1939 received an M.A. and in 1974 a Ph.D. from Columbia University. From 1941 until 1950, he served as director of the VERMONT HISTORICAL SOCIETY, moving then to Sturbridge Village, in Sturbridge, Massachusetts, where he served as director until 1954, leaving for a Fulbright fellowship at the University of London. Continuing active in history and historical preservation organizations, he also served as president of the College of the Americas. Newton is the author of many volumes on United States and Vermont history and the recipient of numerous awards. He is most noted for his entrepreneurial and editing skills, having been a founding editor of *American Heritage* and *VERMONT LIFE*.

Nichols, Clarina Howard (1810–1885)

A Townshend native, Clarina Howard Nichols was raised to value the freedoms on which the young American nation had been founded. After an unhappy first marriage, Clarina left her husband, finding work as a journalist for the *Windham County Democrat*. Divorced in 1843, she married the paper's editor, George Nichols. When George became too ill to work, Clarina took control, gradually transforming this conventional political weekly into a literary and reformist journal. In 1847, she published a series of articles on women's lack of legal rights that influenced the state legislature to pass a law giving married women the right to own, inherit, and bequeath property. Additional laws in 1849 and 1850 further expanded married women's legal rights. Then, in 1852, Nichols submitted a petition to the General As-

Clarina Howard Nichols. Special Collections, Bailey/Howe Library, University of Vermont

sembly asking that women be allowed to vote in school meetings. In support of that petition, she became the first woman ever to address the legislature. Although the lawmakers extolled her speech, they refused to give Vermont women even partial suffrage. In 1854, Nichols left Vermont for Kansas. There, in 1859, she mounted a successful campaign to include several women's rights provisions, including school suffrage, in the new state's constitution. In 1871, after joining Susan B. Anthony and others in a fruitless struggle to obtain full suffrage for women in Kansas, Nichols moved to California and remained there until her death.   *Deborah P. Clifford*

Northeast Kingdom

Initially used to designate the far northeastern section of Vermont comprised of Orleans, Caledonia, and Essex counties, the location of the Northeast Kingdom today is sometimes expanded to include the most eastern portions of Franklin, Lamoille, and Washington counties. Three men played important roles in originating the idea of a distinctive northeastern section of Vermont. W. ARTHUR SIMPSON of Lyndon and Newport newspaper publisher Wallace Gilpin referred to their region as "the northeast kingdom" in the 1940s. GEORGE AIKEN, who enjoyed fishing in the region, also popularized the phrase in a 1949 address to a newly formed three-county development commission meeting in Lyndonville, referring to its area of responsibility as the "Northeast Kingdom," a phrase he used repeatedly during his long political career. He

employed the label while criticizing outside economic exploitation of Vermont's forest and water resources, and encouraging locally financed and managed development and the preservation of the area's recreational attractiveness. Although the phrase "Northeast Kingdom" quickly became popular, during the next twenty-five years the region experienced little of the change that Aiken promoted in his Lyndonville speech while the rest of Vermont prospered from a mixture of tourism, SKIING, industrial growth, second-home construction, and in-migration by often affluent urbanites attracted by the state's natural beauty. Failure to share significantly in these developments left Orleans, Caledonia, and Essex counties with not much more than a label and a reputation for backwardness. Moreover, REAPPORTIONMENT of the legislature reduced the counties' influence in state politics. By the mid-1970s, the term "Northeast Kingdom" symbolized—except to many of those living in it—unemployment, educational and cultural decay, and desecration of the environment by corporate interests. A *Yankee* magazine article emphasizing poverty in the region reflected that unflattering image and may have even prompted state government to become involved in a controversy over what the outside world labeled the NORTHEAST KINGDOM COMMUNITY CHURCH in the early 1980s. Since 1980, however, developments more in keeping with the hopes of those who coined the phrase "Northeast Kingdom" have predominated. A heavily forested landscape and sparse population attracted the attention of environmental groups who saw opportunity, not backwardness, in the lack of economic progress. STERLING COLLEGE, in Craftsbury, became a center for training in skilled environmentalism. The three-county area drew poets, novelists, artists, and actors who celebrated the region's history, ethnic diversity, and general ambience. Most visible within the group is novelist HOWARD FRANK MOSHER, whose narratives are based in a fictional Northeast Kingdom. The CATAMOUNT FILM AND ARTS CENTER, CIRCUS SMIRKUS, and the BREAD AND PUPPET THEATER entertain locals and tourists alike. Promoters have discovered much in the region—the life of ALEXANDER TWILIGHT and the richness of Franco-Vermont culture, for examples— to publicize and celebrate. While the ski industry has not expanded into the region as widely as it has through central and southern Vermont, long-term deep snow cover has attracted large numbers of snowmobilers to a large trail system throughout the kingdom. In 1998, the Conservation Trust Fund of Virginia, the VERMONT LAND TRUST, and the State of Vermont acquired 133,000 acres of heavily forested land in the Northeast Kingdom from Champion International, a logging company. Much of that acquisition is now part of the Silvio O. Conte National Wildlife Refuge, which guarantees that the area will never be clear-cut and that it will be forever open to the public for recreation. The area's most populous town, St. Johnsbury, began advertising itself as the "gateway" to the Northeast Kingdom. Local businesses created a Northeast Kingdom Chamber of Commerce and a Northeast Kingdom Travel and Tourism Association. The latter organization, through its maps and proposed tour routes, expanded the geographical territory of the kingdom to include towns outside the original three counties. The ideas generated by Arthur Simpson, Wallace Gilpin, and George Aiken have taken hold.   *Jere Daniell*

Northeast Kingdom Community Church

A community of faith located in the village of Island Pond in the town of Brighton and based on a strict, literal interpretation of the bible, the Northeast Kingdom Community Church was formed in 1978. At least forty local residents joined the church, but opposition to the group soon developed, finding expression in vandalism of the church's restaurant and citations from the town for a series of zoning violations, as well as the state charging church leaders with contributing to truancy when the church's children stayed home from school. A father in the church was convicted of removing the body of his stillborn child before state officials could autopsy it. Fire-code violations closed down several church buildings. The Internal Revenue Service was called in for an audit of the church's books when state police alleged tax fraud by the church. Unofficial opposition continued with gunshots fired at church buildings. When church members refused to answer questions about corporal punishment used to discipline children, they were briefly jailed. Finally, Chris Braithwaite, a reporter with the Barton *Chronicle* who had followed the church since its arrival in Island Pond, filed an affidavit with the Vermont Social and Rehabilitative Services Department (SRS), saying that, based on his interviews at the church, the state should intervene. Regional director of SRS William Young, John Burchard, then head of SRS in Montpelier, and Attorney General John Easton convinced Governor RICHARD SNELLING that the children had to be taken from the church. On June 22, 1984, in what has become known as the Island Pond Raid, ninety Vermont State Police officers and forty state social workers, with a warrant from Judge Joseph Wolchik based on the state's claim that children of the Northeast Kingdom Community Church were being physically abused by elders of the church, took 112 children from church buildings so they could be examined for signs of abuse. Later that day, District Judge FRANK MAHADY ruled that the state's action was unconstitutional because the warrant was not based on specific allegations about specific children and ordered the children released. The state did not pursue any further action. The incident was seen as a clash between modern and traditional attitudes toward child-rearing and as demonstrating the difficulty of accommodating the values of "closed" communities with those of society at large. Known today as the Twelve Tribes, the community church in Island Pond and twenty-five other communes it has established in various parts of the world continue to conduct religious services and their congregations pursue the communal ideas they find in biblical texts.

Northern League

Organized big-league caliber baseball came to Vermont, northern New York, and Canada in the first Northern League (1901–1906). Playing in central Vermont towns such as Barre-Montpelier and Rutland and to the west in Plattsburgh and Malone, New York, and Ottawa, Ontario, the league featured over one hundred future major leaguers who played in a schedule running from July 4 to Labor Day. Mostly the best collegiate players of the time, some of them aspiring major leaguers and others just hoping to earn enough to pay for college, they included Columbia's Eddie Collins, a future Hall of Famer; "Colby" Jack Coombs; Notre Dame and UVM pitcher "Big" Ed Reulbach; Harvard's Eddie Grant; and UVM's WILLIAM "LARRY" GARDNER. William Clarence Matthews broke the "color barrier" in professional baseball in 1905 with Burlington and was poised to join Boston, but major league baseball refused to integrate. Considered an "outlaw league" by the national sports press, the Northern League was created and financed by community leaders and businesses without financial or other assistance from organized baseball. The league's organizers recognized that no town in the region had a sufficient fan base to fund an advanced level of play, so each town hosting a team needed to attract tourists. Town rivalries were developed between teams, such as St. Albans vs. Plattsburgh and Burlington vs. Barre-Montpelier, and the mass transportation systems of railroad, trolley, and steamboats connecting league towns in Vermont, New York, and Canada sold reduced fares for groups of fans travelling to another town's "baseball grounds" for the game. Frequent changes in lineups kept the teams competitive and their fans travelling to watch them play. The league disbanded in 1918 when its players were lost to the military in World War I. The second Northern League (1935–1952) was also conceived as a "collegiate" summer league. The Adirondack resort towns of Tupper Lake and Saranac Lake had brought college teams to play for their guests since at least 1910. Industrial and mill towns such as Bennington and Brattleboro and Glens Falls, New York, had long histories of independent semi-pro baseball. Those towns combined with the nucleus of the first Northern League—Burlington, Barre-Montpelier, Rutland, and St. Albans—to form a popular and highly competitive short-season league. Also like the first Northern League, the new league was unaffiliated with the major leagues. Nonetheless, in its twelve years of play, the Northern League developed many collegiate and other players who went on to the majors, such as Hall of Famer Robin Roberts; American League batting champion and New York Yankee "Snuffy" Stirnweiss; Boston Red Sox and 1945 Rookie of the Year "Boo" Ferris; famous umpire Jim Honochick; Chuck "The Rifleman" Connors, post-baseball a star of a TV western series; Brooklyn Dodger Johnny Podres; Brave and Giant Johnny Antonelli; Washington's Chuck Stobbs; and forty other future major leaguers. World War II interrupted the league from 1942 to 1945, but its post-war continuance suffered greater difficulties when the National Collegiate Athletic Association and the East Coast Athletic Conference in 1947 adopted stringent codes of amateurism for their athletes. Failing to bar "pros" or acknowledge professionalism in its players, the Northern League soon lost its character as a collegiate summer program. Yet some of the best baseball in Vermont was played by the "pros" in the Northern League from 1947 to 1952. In the end, however, the rise of televised major league baseball and the Northern League's failure to integrate or abandon the pretense of being a collegiate league, as well as the economic decline of member cities, particularly those dependent on railroad yards and textile mills, combined to bring an end to Vermont's longest-lived professional athletic league.

Richard Leyden

Northfield

Northfield, population 5,791, a town in Washington County, was granted by the Vermont legislature in 1781 and named for Northfield, Massachusetts, the home state of a number of the grantees. The main settlements of Northfield village, Northfield Falls, and Northfield Center all lie in the valley of the Dog River, which cuts across the town from south to north. On the eastern border is the elongated form of 2,405-foot Paine Mountain, and on the western the long range of the Northfield Mountains, rising to 2,911 feet at Scrag Mountain just over the line in the town of Waitsfield. Through the years, the town's economy has been variously based on AGRICULTURE, lumbering, wood products, textiles, granite working, and, in the nineteenth century, railroading, when the town's location on the line of the Central Vermont Railroad (engineered by Governor CHARLES PAINE, a native son) led to the construction of railroad shops. NORWICH UNIVERSITY, the nation's oldest private military college, moved to Northfield Center from Norwich in Windsor County in 1867.

North Hero

North Hero, population 810, the SHIRE TOWN of Grand Isle County, was granted by the Vermont legislature in 1779 as part of the grant of Two Heroes to ETHAN ALLEN and 364 others, mostly Revolutionary War veterans, and made a fully independent town in 1798. (See the entry for Grand Isle town for information on Two Heroes.) During the Revolution, a LOYALIST BLOCKHOUSE was constructed on the island, which the British continued to occupy as a military post until it was vacated in 1796 under the terms of the Jay Treaty of 1794. The island is 11 miles long from north to south and 1 mile wide at its widest point; at its narrowest point it is not much wider than U.S. Route 2, the road that runs its full length and connects it to Alburg on the north and Grand Isle on the south. The landscape is uniformly flat and in spots swampy. Three dairy farms, a boat livery, three marinas, a general store, and a country inn constitute the main economic activities. The only significant settlement is North Hero village, although many camps and year-round homes line the shores of the island. STATE PARKS are located at its northern and southern tips and on Knight's Island, an island off the eastern shore.

Norton

Norton, population 214, a town in Essex County, was granted by the Vermont legislature in 1779 to Timothy Andrews and others, including four members of the Norton family, after whom the town was named. Because of its remoteness and wild character, Norton was one of the last towns settled in Vermont, just before the Civil War, and the first town meeting did not take place until 1885. Lumbering has always been the main activity. Norton village lies directly on the Canadian border, which forms the northern boundary of the town. The settlement of Averill, on the eastern border, serves the sparsely settled neighboring township of the same name. The tip of Norton Pond, 583 acres, juts across the southern border, while the major portion of the pond lies in Warren Gore.

Norwich

Norwich, population 3,544, a town in Windsor County, was granted by BENNING WENTWORTH in 1761 and named for Norwich in Connecticut, the home colony of a number of the grantees. The town rises from the banks of the CONNECTICUT RIVER into a varied landscape of hills, meadows, and small streams, culminating in 1,873-foot Gile Mountain on the western border with Sharon. The town's main settlement, attractive, well-preserved Norwich village, lies directly across the Connecticut from Hanover, New Hampshire, site of Dartmouth College, many of whose faculty have chosen to live in the town. Norwich Military Academy, today NORWICH UNIVERSITY, was founded here in 1820 but in 1867, after a disastrous fire, moved to Northfield in response to an invitation from residents there. Norwich and Hanover are partners in the Dresden School District, the first dual-state arrangement of its kind in Vermont. The MONTSHIRE MUSEUM OF SCIENCE, on the Connecticut River, with its interactive, hands-on exhibits, is largely directed toward children. Norwich also hosts the Northern Spy contradance band, which recently celebrated its twentieth year and was honored by the Smithsonian Institution in a folklife arts center recording.

Norwich University

Established in 1819 at Norwich as the American Literary, Scientific and Military Academy by Captain ALDEN PARTRIDGE, the institution became the embodiment of the founder's highly innovative "American System of Education." Partridge sought to reform the traditional curriculum by making it more practical, scientific, and liberal in its scope. Additionally, military instruction was seen as a necessary "appendage" to civil education in order to prepare youth for leadership roles in a citizen army. Partridge's school was the first to offer instruction in civil engineering and pioneered in offering physical education as well as courses in AGRICULTURE. The classical curriculum was expanded to include modern languages, political economy, and history. The school was perhaps the first to offer experiential education in the form of field trips and rigorous pedestrian excursions that were precursors of the present-day "outward bound" programs. Moreover, Partridge's institution encouraged the attendance of nontraditional, adult learners and offered an early version of an elective system that left much latitude for students to design their academic programs. In 1825, the academy at Norwich was relocated to Middletown, Connecticut, where it remained for four years until it moved back to its original location in Vermont. The Middletown property was sold to form the nucleus of what is now Wesleyan University. Unsuccessful attempts were made in 1834 to establish a female seminary as a satellite school. At Norwich, the school was chartered by the State of Vermont as Norwich University in 1834 and remained in place until 1866, when the institution moved to its present location, Northfield, after the destruction by fire of one of the principal buildings. In 1898, the Vermont legislature accorded Norwich the status of the Military College of Vermont. In 1972, Norwich merged with VERMONT COLLEGE in Montpelier, a woman's college, and two years later the Military College of Vermont became the first senior military college in the United States to admit women into a corps of cadets. Norwich conveyed ownership of Vermont College to Union Institute & University of Ohio in 2001. Consonant with Alden Partridge's thinking was the acquisition of four adult-centered programs from GODDARD COLLEGE in 1981. The creation, in 1987, of the nation's first Peace Corps Preparatory Program, the encouragement of volunteer community service, and more recently the launching of a Leadership Development Program that engages all undergradutes, represent an extension of those aspects of the university mission that relate to experiential learning and social service. The system of education articulated by Alden Partridge in 1819 was so broad, flexible, and visionary that it continues to have extraordinary currency.

Gary T. Lord

Novikoff, Alex Benjamin (1913–1987)

A distinguished biochemist who was dismissed from the UNIVERSITY OF VERMONT in the anti-communist purges of the 1950s, Alex Novikoff was born in Chernigov, Russia, and came to New York with his parents in that same year. Educated in New York City public schools, he earned bachelor's, master's, and doctoral degrees from Columbia University and was appointed to the biology faculty of Brooklyn College, where he was recognized as an excellent teacher and scholar. In 1946 to 1947, he spent a sabbatical year at the McArdle Research Institute of the University of Wisconsin in Madison, where he studied the biochemical changes associated with the origins of cancers, a subject that became his major interest in later experimental work. In 1948, he was appointed to UVM's College of Medicine in the departments of pathology and biochemistry. His primary research interests were in the young field of cytochemistry, employing techniques of macerating tissue and separating cellular components that could then be fractionally analyzed to determine their role in cancer development. With his research assistant Lorraine Korson, Novikoff developed a transmissible tumor, the N-K Hepatoma, which could be maintained in culture, a process

for which he earned wide professional notice. In 1953, Novikoff was cited by the U.S. Senate Internal Security Subcommittee as a member of the Communist Party while at Brooklyn College and called to testify about his colleagues and associates from there in the 1930s and early 1940s. Novikoff refused to testify about his colleagues and others, citing his constitutional rights under the Fifth Amendment. UVM held its own investigation and a committee of faculty and board members chaired by the Most Reverend ROBERT JOYCE, an alumnus trustee from Burlington, exonerated Novikoff. But the board of trustees, urged mainly by Governor LEE EMERSON and the editorial writers of the *BURLINGTON FREE PRESS* and the *BURLINGTON DAILY NEWS*, after a second review, dismissed Novikoff from the faculty on a motion by Governor Emerson. Forced to leave Vermont in 1954, Novikoff worked for a while at Waldemar Laboratories on Long Island and then was appointed professor of pathology at the new Albert Einstein College of Medicine in New York. A re-invigorated research career led him to work on subcellular particles, notably the complex of Golgi-endoplasmic reticulum-lysosomes with the acronym "GERL." In 1983, UVM's President Lattie Coor named him doctor of science *in honoris causa* to right what was by then considered a miscarriage of justice in Novikoff's dismissal. He continued his research until shortly before his death.

Roy Korson

Noyes, John Humphrey (1811–1886)

Born in Brattleboro and educated at Dartmouth and Yale Divinity School, John Humphrey Noyes was licensed as a Congregational minister in 1833 but the following year lost his license to preach because of his "perfectionist" doctrine that attributed a dual sexual nature to God and taught that no one was bound by any moral code because Jesus Christ saved the human race from sin. Noyes established the Perfectionist Community in Putney in the late 1830s. In 1846, public condemnation of his tenet of "complex marriage," the practice of free sexual sharing within a community, forced him to disband his community and leave Vermont; two years later he re-established it in Oneida, New York. Faced with adultery charges, Noyes fled to Canada in 1880. He wrote a number of religious treatises,

including *Bible Communism* (1848) and *Scientific Propagation* (circa 1873).

Nudism

Nudism, or naturism as it is also called, has its adherents in Vermont as it does in other states and countries. Beginning in Germany in the early twentieth century, nudism came to the United States in the 1930s. The National Nudist Conference (later to become the American Sunbathing Association) was founded in 1933, and by the end of the decade there were approximately eighty nudist camps in the country. The oldest in Vermont, the Forest City Lodge in Milton, was established in 1956 on the shores of LAKE CHAMPLAIN by George Fletcher, formerly of Montreal. A secluded property of 50 acres on the Milton-Georgia Road, it provides the usual amenities of a Vermont summer campground: camps and trailers for rent, a tenting area, and an RV park. Activities include swimming, volleyball, and an old-time French bowling game called *petanque*. Only couples and families are welcome to the park. Organized nudism is specifically non-erotic and family-oriented, and governed by strict rules of conduct. Much informal nudism, or "skinny dipping," takes place in Vermont in a variety of locations, including secluded lake beaches, forest ponds, and traditional swimming holes along rivers and streams.

Nuquist, Andrew E. (1905–1975)

A political scientist and expert on Vermont state and local government, Andrew Nuquist was born in Osceola, Nebraska. After graduating from Doane College, he spent 1927 to 1930 teaching at a missionary school in China. He received his M.A. and Ph.D. from the University of Wisconsin at Madison before being hired by the UNIVERSITY OF VERMONT, where he taught from 1938 to 1973, becoming McCullough Professor of Political Science. In 1958 and 1959, he was visiting professor of political studies and public administration at the American University of Beirut, Lebanon. Nuquist ran in the 1946 Republican primary for Vermont's single seat in the United States House of Representatives, but lost to the incumbent. He held numerous offices on state boards and committees, including director of the Town Officers Educational Conferences (1945–1969); advisor to the Vermont "Little

Hoover" Commission (1957–1959); acting executive director of the Vermont League of Cities and Towns (1967–1969); president of the VERMONT CHILDREN'S AID SOCIETY (1970–1976); and member of the Vermont Legislative Reapportionment Board (1972–1980). Nuquist wrote *Town Government in Vermont* (1964) and *Vermont State Government and Administration* (1966), the latter with his wife Edith Wilson Nuquist, a teacher and prominent civic leader. *Reidun Nuquist*

O'Callaghan, Jeremiah (ca. 1780–1861)

The first resident priest to serve Vermont's Catholics, Father Jeremiah O'Callaghan was born, one of seventeen children, at Dooneens, county Cork, Ireland. Ordained priest at Cork in 1805, he ministered for nearly twenty years in Ireland before becoming embroiled in a controversy with his local bishop over the common practice of the loaning of money at interest, which he bitterly condemned as usury. His attacks on the banks led his bishop to dismiss him in 1819, and he left Ireland, travelling in Europe, Canada, and the United States looking for another assignment. Finally, in 1830, Bishop Benedict Fenwick of Boston sent him to serve the entire state of Vermont with its growing population of French-Canadians and Irish. In 1834, Father O'Callaghan again attacked usury, roundly criticizing the opening of the Burlington Savings Bank and publishing several anti-usury tracts. He and JOHN HENRY HOPKINS, the Episcopal Bishop of Vermont, carried on a short pamphlet war in which they attacked each other's views on various doctrinal issues. Father O'Callaghan, known as "The Apostle of Vermont," persevered for nearly twenty-five years in the state, saying the first mass in many communities, until the establishment of the statewide diocese of Burlington in 1853. Unaccustomed to a resident bishop supervising him, Father O'Callaghan left Vermont in 1854. Moving to Massachusetts, in his mid-seventies he established a new parish, St. Jerome, in Holyoke, where he served until his death. A monument stands in his memory in St. Jerome's churchyard.   *William W. Goss*

Old Consititution House

Built in the mid-1770s in the middle of Windsor and today located on U.S. Route 5 in Windsor, Elijah West's large tavern, known as West's Hall, was a place where townsmen met and argued town politics. Efforts to establish a new, independent state in a region where both New York and New Hampshire had claimed jurisdiction led on July 2, 1777, to a convention of dele-gates from the length and breadth of the newly declared state of Vermont to meet at West's tavern. Convened to write a constitution, the delegates continued working despite news of the British capture of FORT TICONDEROGA and MOUNT INDE-PENDENCE. Tradition has it that a violent thunderstorm delayed their adjourning long enough for them to vote and sign the constitution amid "a baptism of thunder, lightning and rain." Often called the "birthplace of Vermont," the Old Constitution House has been restored and has an exhibit on the writing and meaning of Vermont's Constitution.   *John Dumville*

Old First Church of Bennington

The first Protestant church in Vermont, the Old First Church of Bennington (Congregational) was gathered in 1762. Much of the early history of Bennington and of Vermont took place in and around the original Meeting House, built in 1763, and the present church, designed and built by LAVIUS FILLMORE and dedicated in 1806. The Vermont legislature in 1935 designated the church a "Colonial Shrine." The cemetery adjacent to the church contains the graves of many of the citizens who contributed to the founding of Bennington and Vermont. It also contains the graves of ROBERT FROST and approximately seventy-five Revolutionary War patriots as well as British and Hessian soldiers killed in the BATTLE OF BENNINGTON. The site of one of ETHAN ALLEN's homes is on the border of the cemetery. The Old First Church greets visitors to Bennington as they enter the town from the west on Route 9.

Old Stone Store

A well-preserved and still very functional commercial property on the northwest corner of Battery and Maple streets in Burlington, the Old Stone Store is a waterfront landmark built soon after the War of 1812. It was originally the headquarters of TIM-OTHY FOLLETT and Henry Mayo's mercantile firm, Follett & Mayo (1818–1835), and then Follett & Bradley's wholesale and forwarding empire (1835–1857). The north half of the building was built by Mayo & Follett in about 1818, and the southern part in 1827 to 1828. Over the years, a total of eight firms or changes of partnership have

Old First Church of Bennington. Vermont Department of Tourism and Marketing

occupied the building. Here, in 1850 to 1852, Edwin P. Johnson and THOMAS H. CANFIELD planned the route of the Northern Pacific Railroad.   *David Blow*

O'Malley, Margaret:
Mother Stanislaus (1846–1921)

Mother Stanislaus O'Malley was the founder and first Mother Superior of the Vermont Sisters of Mercy. Born in Galway, Ireland, Margaret O'Malley was the only child of wealthy iron industrialist Martin O'Malley and his wife, Anne, and received her education through private tutors and in one of Ireland's National Schools. After coming to America, she entered the Sisters of Mercy in Manchester, New Hampshire, professing her vows on August 19, 1871, and taking the religious name Sister Stanislaus. She and three other sisters accepted Bishop LOUIS DE GOESBRIAND's invitation to come to Vermont to take charge of the schools in Burlington. The first Mother Superior of the Sisters of Mercy in Vermont, she held the office for twenty-four years with brief intervals between her terms of office. During the pioneer days when trials and hardships were many and sickness among the sisters was common, she proved to be a woman of vision, courage, endurance, and financial acumen as she led the community in purchasing about 35 acres of land on Mansfield Avenue in Burlington, some of which was sold to provide money for such ambitious building projects as the construction of the first Mt. St. Mary Academy, 1885–1886; the major wing of Mt. St.

Mother Stanislaus O'Malley. Sisters of Mercy of Vermont

Mary (the current mother house); and the original chapel in 1890. For many years, Mother Stanislaus labored to educate and serve her religious community and the people of Vermont. While in office, she established branch houses in Montpelier in 1889 and in Barre in 1890, and provided the staffing of the Sancta Maria Home for the Aged in 1914. In the 1880s, schools were not graded and the curriculum in both public and private schools generally consisted simply of reading, writing, and arithmetic. Mother Stanislaus and Ella Baird developed a grading system for the elementary school and expanded elementary and high school curricula at Mt. St. Mary Academy and other schools in Vermont operated by the Sisters of Mercy. By 1890, several diploma courses were offered, including a classical course. Mother Stanislaus O'Malley died in Burlington in 1921.   *Gertrude Myrick*

Onion River Land Company

Founded in January 1773 by IRA ALLEN, his brothers ETHAN, HEMAN, and Zimri, and their cousin REMEMBER BAKER, the Onion River Land Company (ORLC) speculated in New Hampshire titles to lands in the Champlain and WINOOSKI RIVER valleys. By the summer of 1775, the company owned 65,000 acres, but the American Revolution postponed development of the ORLC properties. After the war, Ira Allen absorbed his partners' holdings and bought tens of thousands of additional acres, established a base at Colchester, and actively promoted settlement in northwestern Vermont. When Allen's dreams of a commercial and real-estate empire foundered in the late 1790s and early 1800s, his brothers' and cousin's heirs instituted a series of lawsuits claiming inheritance of lands held by the pre-1776 ORLC partnership that helped drive him into bankruptcy and exile from Vermont.
J. Kevin Graffagnino

Opera Houses

Vermont's historic theaters, called opera houses to distinguish them from more modest venues of entertainment, were largely the product of the Gilded Age of the late 1800s and early 1900s. Some, like the Barre Opera House, were large and free-standing buildings, while others were more modest and often found on the second floor of a town hall, library, or commercial structure. The interior arrangements could range from that of a standard

theater, with a raked floor, proscenium arch, orchestra pit, balconies, and side boxes, to a flat floor with a simple raised stage at one end and movable chairs for the audience. Whatever their level of sophistication, the opera houses were constantly in use for musical and dramatic productions, lectures, political rallies, minstrel shows, exhibitions, town meetings, and high school graduations. They marked a town as having achieved a certain level of cultural awareness and often served not only a local but a regional audience. With the growth of other forms of entertainment such as radio and motion pictures, opera houses gradually fell into disuse in the 1930s and were either boarded up, turned into storage space, abandoned, or torn down. For an extended period of time many of them were civic eyesores. In the 1970s, however, an awareness of the historic character of opera houses and their potential for use gradually developed, and one by one many of them were restored by volunteer groups who raised money—often many hundreds of thousands of dollars—to bring them back to their former glory. Today, many of these renovated opera houses are once again a living part of their communities and a contributor to downtown regeneration. A representative example of the rise, fall, and resurrection of opera houses is provided by the Enosburg Falls Opera House. Built by Dr. BURNEY JAMES KENDALL, whose Spavin Cure factory was the town's leading employer, for $10,000 in 1892 (when the town's population was 2,300), it was in use until the early 1950s, after which it underwent two decades of neglect. In the 1970s, a private group calling itself the Enosburg Opera House Association was founded and the building, still in considerable disrepair, was opened for sporadic use. In 1993, the town selectboard appointed a restoration committee, which was able to begin significant restoration with a grant from the Vermont Historic Preservation Trust. The committee grew into the nonprofit Friends of the Opera House, which in 1998 began a capital campaign that eventually raised $750,000, due to a large grant received from the U.S. Department of Housing and Urban Development through the efforts of Senator JAMES JEFFORDS. Today the Enosburg Falls Opera House, still undergoing rehabilitation, is once again a center of town activity. Among other noteworthy opera houses in Vermont that have been renovated and are currently in use are the Briggs Opera House in White River Junction (opened as the Gates Opera House in 1890), the Vergennes Opera House in Vergennes (1897), the Barre Opera House in Barre (1899), the Haskell Opera House in Derby Line (1904, standing astride the border with Canada), the Chandler Music Hall in Randolph (1907), and the Paramount Theater in Rutland (opened as the Playhouse Theater in 1913). Burlington's grand Howard Opera House, opened in 1879 and located above a row of shops on Church Street, operated for twenty-five years before closing and being turned into commercial space. The city is served by the cavernous, rehabilitated FLYNN THEATER, opened in 1930 as an art deco movie palace. In various parts of Vermont where opera houses are lacking, town halls, churches, and college auditoriums and theaters serve in their place.

Orange

Orange, population 965, a town in Orange County, was granted by the Vermont legislature in 1781 and takes its name from the House of Orange, which included the prince who became King William III of England in 1689. Despite its proximity to Barre city and Barre town directly to the west, Orange remains primarily rural. It reached its top population in the 1830s, when there were approximately a thousand people and five times as many sheep. After a century and a half of gradual decline, the population began to grow again beginning in the 1980s due to residential sprawl from its western neighbors. Much of the land lies above 1,500 feet, rising to 3,062-foot Knox Mountain and 3,166-foot Butterfield Mountain in Groton State Forest in the town's northeastern corner. The village of Orange lies on U.S. Route 302, which cuts across the town from east to west, and the smaller settlement of East Orange is in the southeast corner where Orange, Topsham, Corinth, and Washington join. At the beginning of the twenty-first century, the town had four dairy farms, two small market gardens, a sheep farm, and several small home businesses.

Orton, Vrest (1897–1986)

"Writer, publicist, merchant" was the way Vrest Orton described himself. He was born in Hardwick and spent his childhood in East Calais. His family subsequently moved to Massachusetts, where he graduated from Athol High School. After service in World War I as a sergeant in the medical corps in France, he attended Harvard and Brown universities and in 1925 moved to New York City, where he worked for a time at H. L. Mencken's *American Mercury* magazine. In 1934, Orton returned to Vermont, writing a column for the RUTLAND HERALD and for weeklies published by the Belknap family in Bellows Falls. He also wrote articles for national magazines, helped set up the STEPHEN GREENE Press in Brattleboro, and founded the Countryside Press in Weston. In 1946, he opened a country store (modeled after the one his grandfather had run in East Calais) in Weston and issued a small catalogue of its wares. Trading on the widespread nostalgia for the simpler way of life of times gone by, the store became hugely successful, and developed into an international mail-order business (the Vermont Country Store) operated today by his son Lyman Orton. Its catalogue now runs to ninety-six pages and features hundreds of items ranging from rocking chairs to Bag Balm. Vrest Orton was also a co-founder of the Vermont Guild of Old Time Crafts and Industries, a chairman of the Vermont Historic Sites Commission, an officer of the VERMONT HISTORICAL SOCIETY, and an associate editor of VERMONT LIFE magazine. A conservative Republican, his salty comments on American life in his catalogues were eventually published as *The Voice of the Green Mountains*, aptly subtitled *A Collection of Philippics, Admonitions and Imponderables*.

Orvis, Franklin Henry (1824–1900)

"Father" of Manchester's summer business and older brother of Charles Orvis of fly fishing equipment fame, Franklin was schooled at Burr and Burton Seminary and Union Village Academy in Greenwich, New York. After graduation, having had some business experience in his father's store, he followed mercantile pursuits in Illinois and Wisconsin and then moved to New York, where in partnership with E. M. Carrington, formerly of Poultney, he established the wholesale dry goods house of Carrington and Orvis in 1846. After his father's death, Franklin purchased his father's elegant Manchester home, expanded it, and in 1853 opened it as the Equinox House, a summer hotel. In 1860, he retired from the dry goods business to devote more attention to hotel management, subsequently purchasing hotels in Jacksonville and Palatka, Florida. A Republican and ardent protectionist, in 1869 and again in 1892 to 1893, he represented Bennington County in the Vermont senate. In 1871, he purchased the Manchester *Journal*, which for some time he published and edited. His obituary credited him with taking the lead in and bearing a good share of the expense of Manchester's public improvements.

Orwell

Orwell, population 1,185, a town in Addison county, was granted by BENNING WENTWORTH in 1763 and named for Francis Vernon (1715–1783), first Baron Orwell. Bordered by LAKE CHAMPLAIN on the west, the town's gently rolling countryside is largely devoted to orchards and DAIRY FARMING. In the nineteenth century, it was a leading lake-trade and sheep-raising center in the Champlain Valley. A promontory on the lake, named MOUNT INDEPENDENCE when word of the signing of the Declaration of Independence reached the area, was the site of a fort built by the Americans in the summer and fall of 1776 as a companion to FORT TICONDEROGA across the lake in New York state. It is now a state historic site, with a museum. The town's main settlement is Orwell village, a short distance east of Route 22A, the main north-south road.

O'Shea, Bernard G. (1921–1988)

Publisher, peace activist, and Democratic political figure, "Bun" O'Shea was born in Northampton, Massachussetts, served in the U.S. Navy in World War II, and in 1949 settled in Swanton as publisher of the *Swanton Courier*. In 1956, he moved to Enosburg Falls, acquired the *Enosburg Standard* and the *Richford Gazette*, and founded the *St. Albans Leader*, ultimately combining the four weeklies into the *County Courier*. O'Shea entered politics in 1956 as the unsuccessful Democratic candidate against Senator GEORGE D. AIKEN. He served in the state senate by appointment of Governor PHILIP H. HOFF in 1963 to 1964, and then in 1964 and again in 1970 ran unsuccessfully against Representative ROBERT T. STAFFORD for Vermont's seat in the U.S. House. He was defeated in the 1978 Democratic primary for governor. He held numerous appointive positions, including on the State Board of Education, and was active in the peace movement along with other civic causes. He was New England peace education secretary for the American Friends Service

Committee, and died in New York City of a heart attack while participating in a conference of the Mobilization for Survival.

Robert V. Daniels

Otter Creek

Otter Creek, Vermont's longest river at 102 miles, rises in the town of Dorset in northernmost Bennington County, then flows north through the VALLEY OF VERMONT and, after skirting the city of Rutland, enters the Champlain lowlands in the town of Brandon. For the next 16 miles it moves sluggishly through a broad, flat area in which it forms a succession of wetlands known, in order, as Brandon, Whiting, Cornwall, and Middlebury swamps. It flows over a falls in the heart of Middlebury village and several smaller falls in Weybridge/New Haven, then finally over one in the city of Vergennes, in the early nineteenth century one of the most important industrial sites in Vermont. During the War of 1812, the U.S. Navy's fleet for LAKE CHAMPLAIN was built in Vergennes on Otter Creek. From this point, the river runs placidly for several more miles until it enters Lake Champlain at Fort Cassin Point. The Lower Otter Creek Wildlife Management Area is a prime viewing spot for migratory waterfowl in the spring and fall. In ABENAKI, "Otter creek or river" is *onegigwizibok*.

Packard, Arthur (1885–1976)

The president of the Vermont FARM BU-
REAU from 1928 to 1953 and a highly influential political figure, Arthur Packard was
born in Jericho and schooled at the Essex
Classical Institute. A dairy farmer, he was
associated with Mt. Mansfield Maple Products and served as the president of the
Chittenden County Farm Bureau from 1922
to 1924, before being elected to the Vermont House in 1922. Chosen president of
the Vermont Farm Bureau, he led it to become a major force in state politics during
the 1930s and 1940s and was acknowledged as the state's most powerful lobby-
ist. A liberal Republican openly allied with
the wing of the Republican Party led by
GEORGE AIKEN and ERNEST GIBSON,
JR., he championed farmer and electric
cooperatives, soil conservation programs,
price supports for farm products, and an
income tax to reduce the property tax
burden on farmers. Another feature of his
leadership was entering agreements with
insurance companies to provide lower
cost insurance for Farm Bureau members,
which also created income for the bureau
treasury. After Governor MORTIMER
PROCTOR replaced ELLSWORTH CORN-
WALL, an Aiken appointee to the Public
Service Commission and Packard's predecessor as Farm Bureau president, Packard
retaliated in 1946 by recruiting Farm
Bureau members to campaign for Ernest
Gibson, Jr., and thus helped defeat Proctor in the 1946 Republican primary. After
his retirement from the Farm Bureau,
Packard wrote a column of agricultural
news for the *New England Homestead* and
continued to campaign for candidates for
appointment to state agricultural offices.

Paul Searles

Packard, Lambert (1832–1906)

An architect whose surviving work can be
seen in many private homes and public
buildings across central and eastern Vermont, Lambert Packard was born in Coventry where, like all of his many brothers
(he had eleven siblings), he was trained by
his father as a carpenter. At eighteen, he
left his home in Waterford for Lowell and
then Lawrence, Massachusetts, to apprentice to an engineer and later to an architect. In 1866, St. Johnsbury's E. & T. FAIR-
BANKS AND COMPANY employed him as
foreman of the carpenter shop and company architect, a position he held until
1891. He soon developed a friendship with
FRANKLIN FAIRBANKS, a partner in the
firm since 1856 and president from 1881 to
1895, a relationship that resulted in some
of the finest Victorian architecture in Vermont. Especially in St. Johnsbury, Packard's skill as an architect and planner and
the Fairbanks family's sense of *richesse
oblige* prevented a turn-of-the-century
"company town" from being a bleak industrial slum, as many New England company
towns were. The two friends produced a
well-planned and laid-out "garden city,"
which had parks, municipal water, gas,
and electricity, commodious worker housing, and significant benefactions such as
an academy, a museum, a library and art
gallery, a YMCA, and churches. Influenced by ideas on architecture found in
The Stones of Venice and other books by
John Ruskin, the English art and architecture critic, Fairbanks and Packard believed
that well-proportioned, well-built, and visually delightful architecture had an en-
nobling effect on society by lifting the spirits and inspiring the imagination. The
Fairbanks' patronage aimed for those effects and Packard sought to realize them
in such buildings as South (1870) and
North (1872) halls at ST. JOHNSBURY
ACADEMY, North Congregational Church
(1877), the St. Johnsbury YMCA (1883),
Pinkerton Academy in Derry, New Hampshire (1885), and Bartlett Hall at Dartmouth College (1890). The Fairbanks scale
plant was perhaps Packard's greatest accomplishment. On the banks of the Sleepers River on Western Avenue, Packard designed and supervised the construction of
the company store (1877), the COVERED
BRIDGE shipping depot which, until it
burned in 1972, was the only example in
the United States of a two-story, two-aisle
lattice truss bridge, the brick-veneered
scale shops (1876), the boiler house (1870),
the carpenters' shop (1867), the castings
shop (1867), the foundry (1866), the brass
foundry (1867), and what was at the time
the tallest chimney in Vermont, rising 152
feet above the factory (1891). Most of
Packard's commissions, however, were for
private dwellings, included Underclyffe
(1871), the Second Empire home of Franklin Fairbanks; Sheepcote (1874), the Italianate-style home of Edward T. Fairbanks;
and the Queen-Anne style C. H. Stevens
house on Main Street, St. Johnsbury.
Packard also designed an entire housing
development for Julia Pettigrew of Lyndonville. His commercial designs included
the Second Empire–style Odd Fellows
Block (1874) on Railroad Street, St. Johnsbury; the Hanover Inn (1888); and the
Lyndonville Savings Bank (1895). In the
1890s, he designed the Lisbon Public
School (1890); the Spaulding Graded
School (1890) in Barre; the Wood Free Library (1894); the Richardsonian Romanesque Judevine Memorial Library (1895)
in Hardwick; the Passumpsic Baptist
Church (1895) in Passumpsic; and the Universalist Church (1898) in Lyndonville.
His last known commission was for a
round barn in Waterford in 1903. Many of
his privately commissioned residential and
commercial buildings, as well as churches
and libraries, remain in use today. Not
only an architect in the traditional sense,
Lambert Packard was also an engineer,
contractor, finisher and furnisher, landscape designer, craftsman, and astute
businessman. *Allen D. Hodgdon*

Page, Carroll Smalley "Calf Skin" (1843–1925)

Governor, U.S. Senator, and the nation's
largest calfskin dealer, Carroll Page's advertising methods revolutionized Vermont
business and political environments. Born
in Westfield, he attended People's Academy in Morrisville, Lamoille County Grammar School in Johnson, and Lamoille Central Academy in Hyde Park. Although
president and director of banks and corporations, Page's most noted business affiliation was as a dealer in raw calfskins,
with interests reaching into Canada and
Europe. Relying on extensive publicity,
Page adapted organizational and publicity
techniques to politics. He had used his picture on calfskin advertisements and was
the first Vermonter to use his picture in
political advertisements. In 1890, political
opponents denounced his self-promotion
as unseemly, lamenting that "practically
every farm house in the state had [Page's]
picture on the wall or in the window," and
charging his use of paid publicists would
make it too expensive for most Vermonters to run for office. His political career
began in 1869 when he was elected to represent Hyde Park in the state legislature.
He served until 1872 and in 1874 was

elected Lamoille County state senator. From 1872 through 1890, he was a member of the Republican State Committee and for the last four of those years served as chairman. In 1890, he was elected governor after having been nominated by a passionately contentious convention. In 1908, he was elected to the U.S. Senate to fill the vacancy created by the death of REDFIELD PROCTOR, SR., and was re-elected to a full term in 1910 and again in 1916. In 1916, the first year for a Vermont primary, Page triumphed over his opponents, two former governors, with 62% of the vote. Among his principal interests was national legislation to advance the cause of vocational education. He did not run for re-election.

Paine, Charles (1799–1853)

After serving as governor for two terms (1841 and 1842), Charles Paine played a leading role in bringing the state into the RAILROAD age. Born in Williamstown, he was a son of ELIJAH PAINE, an eminent figure in the early years of statehood. Charles graduated from Harvard College in 1820 and settled in Northfield, where the Paine family had extensive land holdings. He and his father built a large hotel on the village square, provided a meeting house for the Congregational Church and land for an academy. The Paine family also built and operated the town's woolen mill, which under Charles's management became one of the three largest in the state. Paine developed his political skills in Northfield, serving as selectman and town representative and, for a decade, as town moderator. As a leader in the state's new WHIG PARTY, he made a failed bid for the governorship in 1835. Six years later, at age forty-one, Charles Paine became the youngest governor until then. He was re-elected in 1842. After leaving the governorship, Paine led a group of investors who financed construction of the state's first railroad, the Vermont Central, intending to provide a Vermont rail link to Atlantic ports, Montreal, and markets in the West. His initiative opened the way to two decades of sometimes frenzied railroad construction in the state. Work was completed on the Vermont Central's route from Windsor to Burlington in December 1849. In a controversial decision concerning the road's location, Paine, as Vermont Central's president, brought the rails up the WHITE RIVER valley but bypassed the easier eastern path north through the

towns of Barre and Montpelier and instead directed the road to be built over high ridges to the Dog River Valley, thus bringing the rails through his home village of Northfield but at a significantly greater expense than an eastern route. In 1852, the Vermont Central faced a financial crisis, brought on, according to his critics, by Paine's unsound leadership. The road fell into receivership and stockholders forced Paine to resign as its president. Soon after the Vermont Central fiasco, Paine became involved with a group of New York and Boston promoters in a venture to construct the nation's first rail line to the Pacific Ocean. While on an exploratory expedition in the summer of 1853, planning and surveying for a route across the southwestern United States, Paine died of an acute case of dysentery at the Texas frontier village of Waco.

Gene Sessions

Paine, Elijah (1757–1842)

A prominent political leader in the formative years of statehood, Elijah Paine was born in Brooklyn, Connecticut, and graduated from Harvard College in 1781, his studies interrupted by a term of service in the Continental Army. After studying law, he bought land in Windsor in 1784 and acquired land in Northfield, Montpelier, Berlin, and Williamstown in the following year. After establishing a large farm at Williamstown, Paine built the area's first sawmills and gristmills and constructed the state's first turnpike, completed in 1803 from Brookfield to Montpelier. Paine also participated in the state's SHEEP BOOM, at one time owning fifteen thousand merinos. Exploiting opportunities presented by the British blockade during the War of 1812, he constructed a five-story brick woolen mill on the Dog River in Northfield that produced high-quality broadcloth and employed approximately two hundred workers. Paine supported the development of educational institutions, donating land for an academy in Northfield and money to the UNIVERSITY OF VERMONT and Dartmouth College. Intellectually vigorous, he presented the initial address of Harvard's Phi Beta Kappa Society in 1782, and in 1789 the society elected him as its president. In 1812, he was elected a fellow of the American Academy of Arts and Sciences. Paine occupied many positions of public trust during the state's crucial early years. He served as a Vermont delegate to the 1786 Constitutional Convention and in 1789

acted as one of the commissioners who negotiated Vermont's boundary with New York. From 1791 to 1793, he served as a judge on the Vermont Supreme Court. In 1795 and 1801, the legislature elected Paine, an ardent Federalist and friend of George Washington, as a United States Senator, and in that capacity he drew intense criticism in Vermont for supporting the unpopular Jay Treaty with England. In 1805, after the legislature designated Montpelier as the permanent seat of state government, he served on the committee that chose the site and laid the plans for construction of the buildings to accommodate the legislature. Paine was also active in the national debate over slavery, serving for a number of years as president of the Vermont Colonization Society, an organization devoted to persuading free blacks to emigrate to Liberia. In 1801, President John Adams appointed Paine to the position of United States judge for the district of Vermont. The designation earned him notoriety as one of Adams's "midnight judges," a group of federal court appointments made by the president with the help of a lame-duck Federalist-controlled United States Senate in the period after his defeat by Thomas Jefferson for re-election. Paine held the judgeship for forty-one years, resigning only months before his death, at age eighty-five, brought on by an attack of gout. A son, CHARLES PAINE, served as Vermont governor from 1841 to 1843.   *Gene Sessions*

Painter, Gamaliel (1743–1819)

Entrepreneur, Revolutionary War officer, and Middlebury town father, Gamaliel Painter first settled with his young family in Middlebury in 1773. Arriving in the grants from Salisbury, Connecticut, after having purchased a New Hampshire title to 200 acres, he was almost immediately drawn into conflict with New York Province as a member of the GREEN MOUNTAIN BOYS. He participated in the capture of FORT TICONDEROGA and subsequently served under SETH WARNER as a lieutenant in the GREEN MOUNTAIN CONTINENTAL RANGERS. In 1777, with the recapture of Ticonderoga by British forces and their occupation of the Champlain Valley, Painter fled with his family back to Connecticut where he became a captain in a Continental Army regiment of artificers. Discharged in 1782, by early 1783 he was among the first to return to Middlebury, where he found a chimney and charred remains where his cabin had been. Painter restored his farm while acquiring large tracts of land, principally along the Middlebury Falls, which due largely to his promotional efforts would become the center of Middlebury village. There he built a gristmill and a sawmill, and engaged in real estate dealings that advanced Middlebury's commercial and industrial development along with Painter's personal gain. Combining business activities with public service, Painter attended the January and September 1776 Dorset Conventions and the June 1777 Windsor Convention, served as town representative for fourteen intermittent years, 1786 through 1793, and again in 1796, 1801, 1803, 1805, 1809, and 1810. He was elected Addison County sheriff (1786–1787); assistant judge (1785–1786 and 1787–1795); and was a member of the Governor's Council (1813 and 1814). Neither he nor his sons received more than a common school education and Painter's awareness of their educational deficiencies along with his passion for his town's development drove him to assume the leadership role in a drive to charter MIDDLEBURY COLLEGE. As a principal founder and benefactor, he was named a college trustee in its 1800 charter and remained a trustee until his death.

Palmedo, Roland (1893–1977)

A New York City investment banker and a ski industry pioneer, Roland Palmedo was one of the founders of the ski areas at Stowe and Mad River Glen. In 1940, Palmedo's company, Mount Mansfield Lift, Inc., built what was then the longest chairlift in the world on MOUNT MANSFIELD, with CHARLES LORD as the first manager. Disenchanted with the commercial growth at Stowe in 1949, Palmedo sold out his interests on Mount Mansfield and developed another area, Mad River Glen. A respected alpine ski official both at home and abroad, he organized the Ski Teachers Certification Program and was one of the founders of the National Ski Patrol System. Palmedo was inducted into the National Ski Hall of Fame in 1968. After his death, his family donated his extensive ski-sport library to the National Ski Hall of Fame in Ishpeming, Michigan, and the collection became the nucleus of the Roland Palmedo Memorial Library.

Hilari Farrington

Panton

Panton, population 682, a town in Addison County, was granted by BENNING WENTWORTH in 1761 and probably derives its name from Panton, England, or Francis Panton, a grantee of other Wentworth towns. Bordered by LAKE CHAMPLAIN on the west and the city of Vergennes on the northeast, the town's gently rolling landscape, bisected north and south by Dead Creek, has at different times been devoted to general agriculture, sheep raising, and DAIRY FARMING. Arnold Bay, on the lake, is the place where BENEDICT ARNOLD burned his boats after the BATTLE OF VALCOUR ISLAND in 1778. The tiny crossroads village of Panton is located in the town's northwestern corner.

Park, Trenor William (1823–1882)

Lawyer, financier, son-in-law and father-in-law to Vermont governors, Trenor Park was born in Woodford. His family soon relocated to nearby Bennington, where, living under impoverished conditions, Park saw his educational opportunities sorely limited. At sixteen, he began clerking at a local law office and at twenty-one was admitted to the Vermont bar. When his wife's father, HILAND HALL, was appointed to the federal commission to settle land claims in California in 1852, the Park family followed him to that state, where Trenor became a junior partner in a law firm that included Henry Halleck and FREDERICK BILLINGS. Park was credited with doing a very large share of the business generated by land-title controversies, and a major factor in building his personal fortune was his connection with General John C. Frémont's Mariposa Estate, upon which gold mines were located. In 1863, after narrowly losing a contest for U.S. Senator from California, Park sold out his Mariposa interests and returned to Bennington, where he commissioned architects to design a "summer home," a thirty-five-room house in the French Second Empire style completed in 1865. The mansion became his permanent home, and today, as the PARK-McCULLOUGH HOUSE, is operated as a museum. Continuing to engage in business activities, Park established the First National Bank of Bennington and acquired interests in Vermont RAILROADS. An effort to create a rail system centered in Bennington failed at considerable personal expense. His persisting interest in mining operations included the Emma mine, a silver mine in Utah, from which he made a huge profit after selling his interest under dubious circumstances. Park was sued for fraud but was acquitted with a reprimand from the judge. He subsequently acquired control of the Panama Railroad, was its president from 1875 until his death, selling out to the De Lesseps Panama Canal Company in 1881. He was a Ulysses S. Grant delegate to the 1868 Republican National Convention and served four terms (1865–1868) in the Vermont state legislature. During the Civil War, he contributed to the outfitting of Vermont troops. He donated an art gallery to the UNIVERSITY OF VERMONT, for which he served as a trustee, and contributed $5,000 to establish the Bennington Public Library. His son-in-law, JOHN G. McCULLOUGH, was elected governor in 1902.

Park-McCullough House

Since 1967, after the death of the last member of the McCullough family to reside in it, the Park-McCullough House in North Bennington has been in the hands of a nonprofit community association. The house is the setting for concerts, lectures, croquet contests, holiday festivities, and other community gatherings, and its use for weddings and special events brings in extra revenue. TRENOR W. PARK, a lawyer and speculator who made a fortune in the aftermath of the California Gold Rush, built the handsome three-story Second Empire Victorian "cottage" when he returned home to North Bennington in 1865. The site was on the old farm of Park's father-in-law, HILAND HALL, whose grandfather had settled these North Bennington acres in the 1770s, having migrated to Vermont from Guilford, Connecticut. Two Vermont governors, Hiland Hall (elected in 1858 and 1859) and Park's son-in-law JOHN G. McCULLOUGH (1902), made their homes in this house. With wide support from the greater Bennington community as well as the family, the Park-McCullough House Association operates as a community-based house museum. Personnel and missions have changed somewhat, but the basic idea has always been to utilize the house and grounds, including the handsome carriage barn. Unlike many "white elephants," the mansion's major assets include its original contents of furniture and art, a rich collection of wearing apparel, and an extraordinary archive of documents and photographs.

J. Tyler Resch

Parmalee, Annette Watson (1865–1924)

A native of the town of Washington, Annette Parmalee was a noted crusader for

WOMEN'S SUFFRAGE. In 1889, she married Edward Jones Parmalee and moved to Enosburg Falls. Like other Vermont suffragists, Parmalee was originally drawn to the temperance crusade. Then, in 1907, she joined the Vermont Equal Suffrage Association (VESA), and a year later began lobbying the legislature to give women the vote. For nearly a decade this "Suffragette Hornet," as she was called, badgered the lawmakers with her witty and convincing arguments in support of the question. Parmalee was one of the few leaders of VESA who understood that vaguely worded suffrage measures giving women the same rights as men had little chance of becoming law. She also recognized that before women could obtain further voting rights they would have to show evidence of taxable property or goods. Her efforts were finally rewarded in 1917 when the legislators passed a law giving tax-paying women the right to vote in municipal elections. *The Vergennes Enterprise* noted in 1920, "Mrs. Annette Parmalee has done more to bring the suffrage cause before the public in three years than have all her predecessors." After American women achieved full suffrage in 1920, Parmalee continued to speak and work for the rights of her sex in Vermont. When the LEAGUE OF WOMEN VOTERS was formed in 1920, her legal expertise led to Parmalee's appointment as chairman of the research committee. She spent the last four years of her life as the league's watchdog, uncovering injustices suffered by Vermont women.   *Deborah P. Clifford*

Partridge, Alden (1785–1854)

A military educator, Alden Partridge was born in Norwich and attended Dartmouth (1802) and the United States Military Academy at West Point (1805–1806). Commissioned first lieutenant of engineers, Partridge stayed at West Point as an instructor, rising to professor in 1813 and acting superintendent from then until 1815, when he was superseded by Sylvanus Thayer. Conflicts between Thayer and Partridge over curricular issues led to his court martial and a sentence to be cashiered for neglect of duty. After President Monroe remitted the sentence, Partridge resigned from the army in 1818. The following year, he established the American Literary, Scientific and Military Academy at Norwich. Six years later, the school moved to Middletown, Connecticut, where it functioned for four years, returning to

Norwich in 1829, where it was chartered as NORWICH UNIVERSITY in 1834. Between 1839 and 1853, Partridge established short-lived elementary and secondary military schools in several eastern states, thereby launching the American tradition of precollegiate military education. Vermont, like other states, counted all able-bodied male citizens as members of the state's militia. The training Partridge instilled at Norwich, though simple, was valuable for a nation of citizen soldiers. Norwich also provided engineering and agricultural education when both were considered easily learned on the job. Partridge originated a novel system of education that combined civilian and military studies in order to produce enlightened and useful citizen-soldiers. For more than four decades, the innovative and energetic educator worked to promote his "American System of Education." In 1841, Partridge unsuccessfully advanced to Congress what was the first detailed plan for large-scale aid to the states to support institutions of higher education that would offer a broad curriculum, including courses in agriculture, engineering, physical education, and military science; essentially, the curriculum that was offered at Norwich University. The Morrill Land-Grant Act of 1862 and the 1916 legislation that created the Reserve Officers Training Corps can be viewed as logical extensions of Partridge's ideas. Partridge served as surveyor general of Vermont (1822–1823), in the legislature (1833, 1834, 1837, 1839), and three times ran unsuccessfully for governor.

Gene Sessions and Gary T. Lord

Passumpsic River

The Passumpsic River, the major river of Caledonia County, has two main branches, the West and the East, which begin in the hilly terrain to the southeast of LAKE WILLOUGHBY. They join just to the north of the village of Lyndonville, after which the river runs due south through St. Johnsbury and eventually empties into the CONNECTICUT RIVER in the town of Barnet. The total length of the river, with its branches, is approximately 27 miles.

Patriots or *les Patriotes*

A French-Canadian nationalist and leader of the *Parti Canadien*, Louis-Joseph Papineau (1786–1871) in 1826 led his party as it transformed into *les Patriotes*. LUDGER DUVERNAY's Montreal newspaper, *La Minerve*, soon became the Patriots' voice for

governmental reform, calling especially for a responsible executive, a strengthened legislature, and the preservation of French language and culture in Quebec. Framed as ninety-two resolutions, the Patriots' demands for reforms were rejected by the Crown in 1837, propelling Papineau and the radical wing of the party into armed rebellion. When British regulars and Canadian militia defeated the Patriots at St. Charles in the Richelieu River Valley on November 25, 1837, Papineau and other leaders, including CYRILLE CÔTÉ and THOMAS STORROW BROWN, escaped to New York and then Vermont where Patriot exiles and American sympathizers formed irregular militia, calling themselves Freres Chaussers or Hunters Lodges. Public meetings were called throughout western Vermont to show support for the Patriots. At Middlebury in early January 1838, for example, over two thousand Patriots and their Vermont sympathizers gathered to hear Patriot leader T. S. Brown, cheer for Louis-Joseph Papineau, and resolve to support Canadian liberties against the British. Large illuminated silhouettes of Papineau and Brown were hung from the Addison County court house. Similar meetings, with resolutions and cheers of support, convened in St. Albans, Royalton, Barre, Northfield, Swanton, and Westford. Stowe's militia company lent their cannon to the Patriots. Americans, including many Vermonters, joined the Patriots army that formed in the Champlain Valley in 1838, but the invasion stalled at Lacolle and St. Denis a few miles above the border near Alburg. Once south of the border, the retreating Patriots surrendered to an American army under Colonel John Wool. Papineau fled to Paris, where he wrote *Histoire de l'insurrection du Canada. En refutation du rapport de Lord Durham* (Paris, 1839), the first North American printing of which was issued one month later by Ludger Duvernay from his press in Burlington, where he had taken refuge in 1837. The governor general of Canada, Lord Durham, in his *Report on the Affairs of British North America* (1839), advised the British parliament to grant the self-government and other reforms sought by *les Patriotes*, but opposed French nationalism in Canada. The parliament's North American Act of 1867 granted most of those reforms.

Pavilion Hotel

Known in its heyday as "Vermont's Third House," the Pavilion Hotel, located next door to the VERMONT STATE HOUSE in Montpelier, was a popular tourist destination and residence for Vermont's part-time legislators during the nineteenth and first half of the twentieth century. In 1970, the hotel was rebuilt as a state office building. The hotel's history has been linked to changes in transportation patterns and the growth of the largest employer in Montpelier—the state government. Thomas Davis, son of Montpelier's most prominent early settler, Jacob Davis, built the first hotel on the Pavilion site in 1807 in anticipation of the completion of the State House on land he donated for that purpose. Mahlon Cottrill, who had an interest in all nine stage lines that then converged in Montpelier, purchased the "Davis Tavern" in 1827. He enlarged the building to twice its former size, added covered piazzas, and renamed the building the "Pavilion Hotel." Theron O. Bailey acquired the property in 1874 and tore down the building to make room for a modern, ninety-room luxury hotel designed by Boston architect George Ropes. This distinctive structure featured a wrap-around two-story verandah in the "steamboat gothic" style. The hotel became a popular destination for tourists who arrived by train at the elegant train depot built across the street in 1880. In 1886, Jesse Sumner Viles, Jr., purchased the hotel and enlarged it further. He updated the structure in 1888 with an elevator, new plumbing, and thirty-five additional rooms under a new mansard roof. The Pavilion enjoyed a reputation as one of the finest hotels in New England, hosting Presidents Theodore Roosevelt, Herbert Hoover, William Howard Taft, and native-son CALVIN COOLIDGE. The growth of Vermont's INTERSTATE HIGHWAY system and changes in vacation preferences in the mid-twentieth century rendered the structure obsolete as a hotel. In 1966, the Pavilion Hotel closed. A four-year battle ensued pitting preservationists against advocates of a new office structure, even attracting the attention of Ada Louise Huxtable, architecture critic of the *New York Times*. By the end of the 1969 legislative session, a compromise had been forged: the Pizzagalli Construction Company of South Burlington would demolish the original structure and reconstruct the exterior façade around a modern interior providing 60,000 square feet of office space for state government. The old building was dismantled in 1969 and rebuilt out of modern materials and techniques with a large wing to the north designed by Robert Burley of Waitsfield. The building received a second addition in the mid-1980s, also designed by Burley. Today, the building houses the working offices of the governor, attorney general, the tax department, and the interpretive center of the VERMONT HISTORICAL SOCIETY.

Paul A. Carnahan

Pawlet

Pawlet, population 1,394, a town in Rutland County, was granted by BENNING WENTWORTH in 1761 and probably named after Charles Paulet (1718–1765), fifth duke of Bolton. The town, which abuts the town of Granville in New York State, lies on the western slopes of the TACONIC MOUNTAINS and has numerous summits in the 1,000- to 2,000-foot range. It is cut from south to north by the Mettawee River, which flows into New York in the town's northwesternmost corner. The main settlements are North Pawlet, West Pawlet, and Pawlet village, which is built around the gorge of Flower Brook, a tributary of the Mettawee. As early as 1768, a gristmill operated in Pawlet village, and in the nineteenth century it became a substantial industrial center, manufacturing, among other items, Philo Stewart's cast iron cookstoves. Today, it is a popular tourist spot whose main street is lined with art galleries and craft studios. In addition to a flourishing dairy industry in the town, numerous SLATE quarries dot the western section of Pawlet, as they do other towns along the New York border as far north as Castleton.

Payant dit St-Onge, Joseph
(ca. 1700–1777)
As captain of a 45-ton sloop built at Quebec by the Corbin brothers, Joseph Payant from 1742 to 1759 carried passengers and freight between a supply center at Sainte-Therese on the Richelieu River and the settlement on the lake's east shore at POINT À LA CHEVELURE (today's CHIMNEY POINT) and the fortifications on the west shore at Forts Carillon and Saint-Frédéric. Called "Admiral of LAKE CHAMPLAIN" by the French commander at Ile aux Noix during the Seven Years' War (known as the French and Indian War in New England), Payant cruised the lake off Isle La Motte in 1759 and 1760 to defend the river route into the Quebec heartland against the English in a sloop with four 10-pound guns leading a fleet of eight heavily armed double-masted *xebecs* and a single-masted tartan and crews totalling fifty regular navy officers and men. In one encounter with the British fleet north of the Four Brothers Islands, the French captured a bark and twenty prisoners, but lost several of their own boats. In August 1760, however, the British took Ile aux Noix, and New Hampshire militia captured Payant when a west wind blew his boat onto a sand bar in front of the entrenched British artillery. Paroled, Payant later settled in Chambly.

Peace & Justice Center

Founded in 1979 as the Burlington Peace Coalition, the Peace & Justice Center originally had as its primary mission opposing nuclear power and nuclear arms proliferation. It did so through nonviolent protests and educational events involving speakers, films, and discussion groups. As the group evolved, it turned its attention to other international issues, for example, protesting U.S. involvement in Central America and apartheid in South Africa, as well as to more local issues such as the manufacture of armaments at the General Electric plant in Burlington. Today, the center believes that local action toward a more just society is a vital component of the quest for international peace and states that it is "Dedicated to Community Building, Inclusion, Tolerance and Justice." It concentrates its activities in three program areas: racial justice and equity; Vermont economic justice; and peace and human rights. The center, which has a paid staff, dozens of volunteers, and twelve hundred members, has an annual budget of about $300,000 and is located on Church Street in downtown Burlington.

Peach, Arthur Wallace (1886–1956)
A graduate of MIDDLEBURY COLLEGE, Arthur Wallace Peach taught English literature at NORWICH UNIVERSITY for many years and was chairman of the department. He was an original member of the VERMONT COUNTRY LIFE COMMISSION and chairman of its Committee on Vermont Traditions and Ideals for which he and HAROLD RUGG edited *The Green Mountain Series* (1931–1932), a four-volume collection of Vermont poetry, prose, folk songs, and biographies. In 1936, Peach was a leading opponent of the GREEN MOUNTAIN PARKWAY. Arthur Wallace Peach was the founding president of the Poetry Society of Vermont and the 251

CLUB and executive director of the VER-
MONT HISTORICAL SOCIETY from 1952
to 1956.

Peacham

Peacham, population 665, a town in Caledonia County, was granted by BENNING
WENTWORTH in 1763. The source of the
name is not known, although one fanciful
theory suggests that it was Polly Peachum,
a character in John Gay's popular work
The Beggar's Opera (1726). The eastern side
of town has most of the arable land and all
of the settlements, the chief of which is
often-photographed Peacham village; the
western side is dominated by a number of
low mountains, culminating in 2,566-foot
Cow Hill. The town's largest body of water
is 331-acre Peacham Pond. Groton State
Forest, in the southwestern corner, contains Peacham Bog and a number of recreational sites associated with the summer
vacation area in the town of Groton to the
south. While Peacham still has five farms
that maintain its rural appearance, it is
increasingly a bedroom town, primarily
for St. Johnsbury. THADDEUS STEVENS,
the leader of the Radical Republicans during the Civil War and Reconstruction, was
raised in Peacham although he was born
in Danville, and OLIVER JOHNSON, one
of the twelve organizers of the American
Anti-Slavery Society, was born in Peacham
and educated at Peacham Academy.

Pearl, Stephen (1747–1819)

An early Burlington settler, Stephen Pearl
served at Bunker Hill as a captain and
came out of the war a major. He came to
Vermont after the Revolution, settling first
at Pawlet, where he failed to prosper as a
merchant. He was colonel of the Rutland
county militia during the Vermont phase
of SHAYS' REBELLION in 1786. Moving to
Grand Isle in the late 1780s, he continued
as a merchant, but again had no success in
business. He finally settled in Burlington
in 1794, moved into a house at the head of
today's Pearl Street, and was elected sheriff of Chittenden County, an office he held
for many years. Pearl acquired 50 acres in
the Burlington intervale from IRA ALLEN,
a friend since Pawlet, and successfully
farmed them for many years. In Burlington, Pearl was elected justice of the peace
and earned a reputation for good sense
and fair judgments as a magistrate, often
ignoring the legal opinions of contending
lawyers. He again tried to be a merchant,
but once more failed. Selectman and town

clerk of Burlington, large and portly
Stephen Pearl was generally admired for
his good sense, wit, and benevolence.

Pecor, Ray (b. 1939)

Owner of the CHAMPLAIN TRANSPORTA-
TION COMPANY and the Vermont Expos,
the state's only professional baseball team,
Ray Pecor grew up in Burlington and was
educated in the city's public schools and
the UNIVERSITY OF VERMONT. His first
business venture was a mobile-home sales
agency in Plattsburgh, New York, that
grew into a large operation with sales outlets from Canada to Florida. In the fall of
1975, Pecor acquired the Lake Champlain
Transportation Company (LCTC) from
Lewis Evans, Richard Wadhams, and
James Wolcott. Remembering his frustrations as a winter commuter to business in
Plattsburgh when the frozen lake kept ferries at the dock, Pecor authorized an experiment to extend the Grand Isle–Cumberland Head ferry crossing to a year-
round operation by employing an air bub-
bling system at the docks that would give
the boats room to build up enough speed
to open a channel through the ice during
the winter. The success of this experiment
changed the transportation patterns of
the region and "built a bridge" across the
lake. Pecor credits this decision for the
growth in LCTC service and the revenues
that provided the financial foundation
for his subsequent community-supportive
business opportunities. These include the
renovation and conversion of the Champlain Mill in Winooski into a retail shopping mall and office complex, the construction of the Courthouse Plaza office
complex in downtown Burlington, and the
return of professional baseball to Burlington in 1994 when the Vermont Expos
began to "play ball" to the delight of
regional baseball fans.   *Arthur Cohn*

Penniman, Frances Montresor
Buchanan Allen (1760–1834)

Thought to be the illegitimate daughter of
John Montresor (1736–1799), a prominent
British military engineer in America dur-
ing both the French and Indian War and
the Revolution, and Anna Schoolcraft of
Schoharie, New York, Frances Montresor
was raised in New York City by her aunt
Margaret Schoolcraft after her mother's
death in childbirth. Margaret married the
Loyalist CREAN BRUSH in 1766. In 1770,
the family moved from New York City to
Westminster, where Brush had several

large New York land grants. A member of
the New York Assembly, Brush and his
family were in New York when the Revolution erupted. At age sixteen, Frances married John Buchanan, a British army officer
on half-pay, who was killed shortly thereafter serving with the King's Loyal Rangers. Their child died before 1784. At the
conclusion of the war, Frances and her
aunt, who had married Patrick Wall after
Brush's death, returned to Westminster as
heirs to Brush's large land holdings. Probably the wealthiest young woman in the
state at the time by virtue of inheriting
20,000 acres of Brush's land in Vermont
and New Hampshire, she married ETHAN
ALLEN in 1784, and settled finally in Burlington on Allen's land by the WINOOSKI
RIVER. Frances bore Ethan three children:
two boys, Hannibal Montresor and Ethan
Voltaire, who attended West Point and
served as Army officers, and FRANCES
MARGARET (Fanny), who converted to
Catholicism and became a nun. Able to
realize very little money from the Brush
estate, and that only by selling her interest
in it to Brush's daughter Elizabeth Norman in Ireland, Frances Allen was financially straitened after Ethan's death in
1789 and left Burlington to live in Westminster with her aunt. She married Dr.
JABEZ PENNIMAN in 1793, and they
moved back into the house Ethan had
built. Here they lived for five years, while
Frances gave birth to three children. Supported by Penniman's medical practice,
they were able to improve the farm, but
debts and disputed land titles led them to
abandon it again for Westminster. After
Penniman was appointed U.S. Collector
of Customs in 1803, the family moved to
Swanton. Strangely, during the Burlington trial of the smugglers in the BLACK
SNAKE AFFAIR for killing three of Penniman's officers in 1808, Frances's son Ethan
Voltaire Allen was excused from serving
on the jury when he declared to the court
that the smugglers were heroes. During
the War of 1812, the family returned to
Burlington, where Penniman's business
successes enabled Frances to live out her
final decades in comfort. She was noted
for her gardening and botanical knowledge.   *David Bryan*

Penniman, Jabez (1764–1841)

A physician in Burlington in the 1790s,
Jabez Penniman married Frances Montresor Buchanan Allen, ETHAN ALLEN's
widow, on October 28, 1793. The couple

resided first in Burlington at the Allen farm, where Penniman assumed financial responsibility for the three Allen children. They moved to Westminster, and in 1803 he was appointed U.S. Collector of Customs for Vermont, stationed at Swanton, an office he held until 1811. Penniman's efforts to implement President Jefferson's EMBARGO ACT OF 1808 led to smugglers killing three of his customs officers in the notorious *BLACK SNAKE* AFFAIR that coincidentally occurred on a section of the Allen farm in Colchester. The Pennimans moved to Burlington after 1811, where he was elected probate judge. *David Bryan*

Perkins, Henry Farnham (1877–1956)
Henry F. Perkins was born in 1877 in Burlington, the only son of George Henry Perkins, professor of natural sciences and dean of arts and sciences at the UNIVERSITY OF VERMONT. Harry followed in his father's footsteps to carry on the family tradition of civic and scientific leadership in Vermont. He graduated Phi Beta Kappa from UVM in 1898 and received a Ph.D. in zoology at Johns Hopkins University in 1902, after which he began teaching zoology at UVM. He advanced to full professor in 1911 and served as chairman of the zoology department as more faculty were added. His sporadic research projects included field studies on birds, game fish, and marine invertebrates. Harry Perkins's interest in human affairs and civic improvement gradually overshadowed zoological research. In 1922, Perkins began teaching courses specifically on heredity and evolution. His heredity course provided the first known venue for eugenics education at UVM and the inspiration for a "Eugenics Survey"—a field station to study Vermonters. As director of the EUGENICS SURVEY OF VERMONT, Harry Perkins emerged as Vermont's resident eugenicist and dedicated the second half of his career to preserving the Yankee Protestant hold on the identity, the heritage, and the future of Vermont. In 1927 and 1928, Perkins organized a state-wide survey of all aspects of rural life that might explain the causes and effects of rural decline in the state. The resulting VERMONT COMMISSION ON COUNTRY LIFE permitted Perkins to incorporate eugenic agendas into a comprehensive plan for community development in the state. He served as VCCL secretary until 1931 and as executive vice president of the commission thereafter. As president of the American Eugenics Society (1931–1934), Perkins publicized the accomplishments of the Eugenics Survey and the Vermont Commission on Country Life to national audiences. Perkins succeeded his father as director of the University Museum in 1930 and served as curator of the Robert Hull FLEMING MUSEUM from 1931 to 1945, where he developed programs to preserve Vermont's cultural heritage. When the Eugenics Survey office closed in 1936, Perkins moved the archives of the Eugenics Survey and the Commission on Country Life to the museum to be catalogued and preserved for posterity with WPA funds. Perkins continued to teach eugenics and genetics at UVM until his retirement in 1945 and remained active in the UVM Alumni Association until his death in 1956. *Nancy L. Gallagher*

Peru
Peru, population 416, a town in Bennington County, was granted by BENNING WENTWORTH in 1761 as the town of Brumley or Bromley (probably after Bromley, a municipal borough southeast of London) and changed at the request of the residents in 1804 to Peru, probably because the name, with its suggestion of Andean-type topography, would attract more settlers. The town sits astride the main spine of the GREEN MOUNTAINS, which here rise to 3,429 feet at Peru Peak, and lies completely within the GREEN MOUNTAIN NATIONAL FOREST. The only significant road is Route 11, along which lies not only Peru village but also the Bromley ski area, on the slopes of Bromley Mountain, which has thirty-nine trails and a vertical drop of 1,334 feet.

Peters, John (1740–1788)
An early settler of Bradford and commander of the Queen's Loyal Rangers with General JOHN BURGOYNE's invasion of the Champlain Valley in 1777, John Peters was born in Hebron, Connecticut, and graduated from Yale in 1757. He settled in Piedmont, New Hampshire, in 1763, where Governor BENNING WENTWORTH appointed him captain of the local militia company and deputy surveyor of the King's Woods. In 1770, Peters moved across the CONNECTICUT RIVER to the New York patent of Mooretown, which was renamed Bradford in 1788 by the Vermont General Assembly. New York Governor Tryon appointed him colonel of the Gloucester county militia, justice of the peace, judge of probate, clerk of the court, and judge of the court of common pleas. CUMBERLAND AND GLOUCESTER COUNTIES sent him to the Continental Congress in 1774, where he refused to take the oath of secrecy. He was mobbed as a Loyalist on his journey to the congress and returning home. Upon his return to Mooretown in the spring of 1775, a mob took him before JACOB BAYLEY and the local committee of safety under charges of spying for the British. Harassment, threats, and looting of his property by patriot mobs led Peters to feign loyalty and join the American army in Montreal. There, he gathered information for the British that ensured a series of American defeats in the Montreal area. While still undetected as a spy, Peters was arrested on accusations of aiding the enemy by Jacob Bayley in a letter sent from Newbury. During the American retreat from Canada, Peters escaped, joined the British at Quebec, and served as a guide for General GUY CARLETON's aborted invasion of the Champlain Valley. In the meantime, the committee of safety for the New Hampshire Grants outlawed Peters on penalty of death and Bayley seized Peters's land in Mooretown and deported his wife and children to TICONDEROGA. The family was reunited in Montreal, where Carleton appointed Peters colonel commandant of the Queen's Loyal Rangers. There Peters mustered 290 men, most from the grants, and in 1777 joined Burgoyne's army. At the BATTLE OF BENNINGTON, he lost nearly half his force, took a gunshot wound to his foot, and was stuck in the chest with a bayonet by his wife's cousin, a childhood playmate, whom he shot dead. By 1778, under the command of FREDERICK HALDIMAND, he had sufficiently recovered from his wounds to organize a raid on Newbury. Left with only thirty-four of the original three hundred men when they reached the upper LAMOILLE RIVER, Peters returned to LAKE CHAMPLAIN by way of the WINOOSKI RIVER, burning blockhouses and other buildings along the river for about 30 miles. Haldimand having denied Peters pay for serving with Burgoyne, he complained to his uncle SAMUEL PETERS, who in turn brought the issue to Colonial Secretary Lord George Germaine. In retaliation, Haldimand demoted Peters to captain of invalids and inflicted other economic damages. Peters went to London in 1785, where he unsuccessfully sought compensation from the Loyalist Claims Commission and died in 1788 from a chest

disease perhaps attributable to the lingering effects of the Bennington bayonet wound.

Peters, Samuel A. (1735–1826)

A Connecticut Loyalist ordained in the Church of England, Samuel Peters claimed authorship of the name "Verdmont," which he devised in the 1760s while standing, whiskey bottle in hand, atop Mount Pisgah (later renamed Killington Peak). Peters fled America early in the Revolution, leaving a motherless twelve-year-old daughter, an infant son, and twenty slaves. In London, he received a small Crown pension until 1804. John Trumbull's satirical poem "M'Fingal" includes him in a list of people to be avoided: "From priests of all degrees and metres, / t'our fag-end man, poor Parson Peters." After he left for England, the Vermont Court of Confiscation took more than 30,000 acres of the land in Westminster and other eastern Vermont towns granted to Peters by New Hampshire's Governor BENNING WENTWORTH. The British Loyalist Claims Commission granted him only a small fraction of the £40,000 he claimed as losses in Vermont and Connecticut.

Pettingill, Samuel Barrett (1886–1974)

A Democratic Congressman from Indiana who led the opposition to President Franklin Roosevelt's attempt to pack the Supreme Court in 1937, Samuel Pettingill was born in Oregon and returned to the ancestral Pettingill home in Grafton at age six after his mother died. A graduate of Vermont Academy (1904), MIDDLEBURY COLLEGE (1908), and Yale Law School (1911), Pettingill relocated to South Bend, Indiana, to practice law with a friend from Yale. In 1930, he was elected to the first of four terms in Congress from Indiana, where he was the primary author of the important Interstate Oil Compact of 1935. A Jeffersonian states'-rights, free-enterprise, sound-money Democrat, he parted ways with President Franklin D. Roosevelt when the latter abrogated the gold clause in 1934. In 1937, Pettingill made the first speech against Roosevelt's plan to pack the Supreme Court, and won national attention for his successful fight to stop it. This political defeat, administered by an overwhelmingly Democratic Congress, was the most serious that Roosevelt ever suffered. Rather than face Roosevelt's wrath in the 1938 election, Pettingill chose

to retire from Congress. Four years later, he was chosen to be national finance chairman of the REPUBLICAN PARTY. In 1948, he purchased the family home, "Robin Lawn," in Grafton and resettled there. In his years in public life, Pettingill was an extraordinarily handsome and charismatic man, imbued with great political courage. His principled opposition to Roosevelt's centralization of power and "federal socialism" undoubtedly cost him a far more memorable career in national elective office. A prolific author, his *Jefferson the Forgotten Man* (1938) developed the principles of Jeffersonianism and related them to the political issues of the day. *Yankee Pioneers* (1971), described the hardships of the early settlers of rural New England. His autobiographical notes, edited and supplemented by his wife Helen Pettingill, were published as *My Story* (1979).   *John McClaughry*

Phelps, Charles (1717–1789)

The first lawyer to live in the New Hampshire grants when he settled at Marlborough in 1764, Charles Phelps was a native of Northampton, Massachusetts. He was a leader in organizing CUMBERLAND COUNTY under New York after the Crown proclamation of 1764 limited New Hampshire's authority to the west bank of the CONNECTICUT RIVER, but was unsuccessful in petitioning New York to confirm his town's New Hampshire charter. After the WESTMINSTER MASSACRE in 1775, he opposed New York provincial and Crown authority. He intrigued for Massachusetts to annex the territory of the New Hampshire and New York grants and appeared before the Continental Congress in 1779 and 1782 as a delegate from Cumberland County to oppose recognition of Vermont by Congress. His opposition to the government of Vermont sent him to jail in 1784 and his property was sold for the benefit of the state. His law books were given to NATHANIEL CHIPMAN and MICAH TOWNSHEND to pay for their services in rewriting the laws of the state. Phelps petitioned for a pardon and took an oath of allegiance to Vermont in October 1784. The state restored such property as had not been sold. Yet he remained to the end intensely opposed to the new state, dating his last will at "New Marlborough, in the county of Cumberland, state of New York." His great grandson was Civil War General JOHN WOLCOTT PHELPS.   *J. Kevin Graffagnino*

Phelps, Edward John (1822–1900)

A remarkable public speaker and arguably the greatest advocate Vermont ever produced, Edward John Phelps, of Middlebury, was the eldest son of Frances Shurtleff and SAMUEL SHELTAR PHELPS. He graduated from MIDDLEBURY COLLEGE at eighteen in 1840. After an extended journey to Virginia, where he taught at a family school on a plantation, he attended lectures at the New Haven (later Yale) Law School, and studied law with Horatio Seymour in Middlebury. Phelps was admitted to the bar in 1843 and opened an office in Middlebury, but soon moved to Burlington to practice law. For forty years, he was involved in nearly every major decision that came before the Vermont Supreme Court. His later years were dedicated to federal practice, including a number of cases before the U.S. Supreme Court. Phelps's practice took him to other states and countries. He argued before the Alabama Supreme Court in 1892 on behalf of the Mobile and Ohio Railroad Company. The following year, he argued the United States position at the Fur-Seal Arbitration in Paris. His political appointments included a term as second comptroller of the U.S. Treasury under President Millard Fillmore (1851–1853), and, at the end of his career, as President Cleveland's minister to the Court of St. James (1885–1889), leaving a strong impression on the English as a diplomat and a public speaker. During that period, he was considered for appointment as chief justice of the U.S. Supreme Court. His 1891 speech at the dedication of the BENNINGTON BATTLE MONUMENT impressed everyone present, including President Benjamin Harrison. Biographer Frank Fish wrote, "He would not hesitate to say that he loved some things simply because they were old and because the things that were old and had survived are likely to be the best. He loved to find the good in ancient institutions and laws. He loved the old-time manners, old courtesies and reverences." Phelps is best remembered, perhaps, as the author of "The Lay of the Lost Traveler," satirical verses lamenting the inadequacies of nineteenth-century Vermont rail travel.   *Paul Gillies*

Phelps, John Wolcott (1813–1885)

Graduated from West Point in 1836 and embarked on a career in the U.S Army, John W. Phelps of Guilford was promoted to captain (after initially declining the honor) for conspicuous bravery in the

Mexican War. In 1859, he resigned from the Army, but was called back to service as colonel of the First Vermont Regiment in 1861. Arriving at Ship Island, Mississippi, in December 1861, the slavery-hating Phelps, by then a brigadier general, announced what came to be called "Phelps' Emancipation Proclamation," an essay on the baneful consequences of the slave-holding system. This premature declaration caused considerable political embarrassment for President Lincoln, who was forced to countermand it. Phelps again resigned his commission in 1862, objecting to the employment of freed slaves as camp laborers as a reconstitution of slavery. Phelps returned to Brattleboro, where he pursued a career of letters and studies. He became president of the Vermont Teachers Association, vice president of the VERMONT HISTORICAL SOCIETY, and a member of the Vermont bar, and carried on publication and correspondence on such topics as secret societies, Madagascar, fossil whales, the metric system, artillery practice, and manumission. At home in Brattleboro, Phelps was notified in 1880 that he had been chosen as the presidential nominee of the "American Party," a Christian-oriented party opposed to Masonry and secret societies, alcohol, tobacco, socialism, and communism. This made Phelps the only person ever to become a party's presidential candidate while a resident of Vermont. He did not campaign, and his national vote total was reported as 707. A long-time bachelor, Phelps married a widow and, at age seventy, fathered his one child.

John McClaughry

Phelps, Samuel Sheltar (1793–1855)

Samuel S. Phelps was an unrepentant Whig and, according to biographer Frank Fish, the "most powerful and gifted man" ever to serve on the Vermont Supreme Court. Phelps was born in Litchfield, Connecticut, and died in Middlebury. He attended Yale and Litchfield Law School, and fought in the War of 1812. Subsequently, he became a Middlebury lawyer, state representative (1821–1832), an associate judge on the Vermont Supreme Court (1831–1838), Addison County senator (1838–1839), and United States Senator (1838–1851). He was the foremost advocate in southwestern Vermont before his election to the bench. He argued the WEST RIVER Bridge case against Daniel Webster in the United States Supreme

Court and won. While he was in the U.S. Senate, Webster himself pronounced Phelps one of the ablest lawyers in that body. Chief Justice Chase, who also served in the Senate with him, said "that in power of clear, convincing statement he had no peer in that body." During the election of 1844, running for his second U.S. Senate term, Phelps waged a bitter battle with WILLIAM SLADE, also from Middlebury and a U.S. Representative from Vermont. The fight engendered a series of malicious pamphlets from Slade and Phelps, and stands as the dirtiest campaign for public office in Vermont political history. He was the father of eleven children, among them EDWARD J. PHELPS.

Paul Gillies

Phish

Playing mostly their own songs and instrumental compositions, Phish, Vermont's leading performers of popular music and a nationally known ensemble, consists of lead guitarist Trey Anastasio, who is the quartet's principal composer, bassist Mike Gordon, who also provides original material for the group, drummer Jonathan "Fish" Fishman, and keyboardist Page McConnell. Their performances are distinguished by a complex personal style, influenced by rock, jazz, swing, bluegrass, reggae, and classical music, which spotlights the group's improvisational skills. The complexity of their music has required a group discipline that they have developed through exhaustive rehearsals. They played for seven uninterrupted hours in their Millenium Concert before an audience of seventy-five thousand fans at the Big Cyprus Seminole Reservation in Florida. Phish has performed over fifteen hundred concerts worldwide, where they invited audiences to audiotape their performances. This extraordinary noncommercial policy has not diluted the sales of Phish's recordings, which have exceeded four million and earned them several gold and platinum records from their recording companies. They also release albums through Phish Dry Goods, their mail-order sales outlet in Burlington.

Ernest Stires

Pitkin, Royce S. (1901–1986)

Royce Pitkin grew up in a Marshfield family that was Democratic in politics and Universalist and Congregational in religion to become a progressive educator and the founding president of GODDARD COLLEGE in Plainfield from 1938 to 1969. He was educated in Marshfield schools,

graduated from Goddard Seminary in Barre in 1919, attended Cornell University, graduated from the UNIVERSITY OF VERMONT in 1923, taught and was principal in high schools in Plymouth and Groveton, New Hampshire, and in Hyde Park and Wallingford, Vermont. He married Helen McKelvey in 1924, the first woman enrolled in the UVM College of Agriculture. With her assistance, he earned master's and doctoral degrees at Columbia University's Teachers College, studying with leading proponents of progressive education including HAROLD RUGG. At Teachers College, Pitkin studied the works of JOHN DEWEY, and in a Yale summer school met Boyd Bode and John W. Studebaker. In 1932, he became principal of the elementary school operated by the New London School, a two-year college in New Hampshire later renamed Colby-Sawyer College. Always sensitive to educational needs of young people of limited means, Pitkin saw an opportunity for a new kind of junior college at Goddard Seminary in Barre, then struggling with its educational role among burgeoning community high schools. During his first years in Barre (1935–1938), he gathered a group of thoughtful Vermont community leaders, among them GEORGE D. AIKEN, DOROTHY CANFIELD FISHER, RALPH E. FLANDERS, ALFRED H. HEININGER, MARY JEAN SIMPSON, and Stanley C. Wilson, to assist the faculty of Goddard Seminary in developing an educational plan for Goddard College, which soon (1938) moved to the Martin estate at Greatwood Farms in Plainfield. There, for thirty-one years, he led the two- and four-year programs of Goddard in a series of major educational experiments centering on the ability of students to assume responsibility for their own study programs. With faculty, staff, and students, he evolved a community-centered, democratic college, and the general and educational philosophies expressed in action to support it. Retiring in 1969, he continued his active involvement in educational affairs. Goddard's model of the low-residency undergraduate adult degree program has been copied and adapted in various forms among hundreds of higher education institutions. A fifth major educational experiment—articulated small campuses each developing independently in individual ways—was never developed by Pitkin's successors.

Forest Davis

Pittsfield

Pittsfield, population 427, a town in Rutland County, was granted by the Vermont legislature in 1781 and is named after Pittsfield, Massachusetts, the home town of some of the grantees. The town, roughly triangular in shape, is about half the size of most Vermont towns and lies on the eastern slopes of the main spine of the GREEN MOUNTAINS. Its rugged topography, which rises to 3,230 feet at an unnamed peak near the border with Chittenden, has always limited settlement to the extreme eastern edge of the town, where the single village of Pittsfield, in the valley of the Tweed River, is located. Approximately 54 percent of the town is owned by the U.S. Forest Service as part of the GREEN MOUNTAIN NATIONAL FOREST. Charles W. Emerson, founder of Emerson College in Boston, was born in Pittsfield.

Pittsford

Pittsford, population 3,140, a town in Rutland County, was granted by BENNING WENTWORTH in 1761 and named after William Pitt (1708–1788), first earl of Chatham, a staunch supporter of the American colonists in their quarrels with the Crown. The town lies in the northern reaches of the VALLEY OF VERMONT, with the foothills of the GREEN MOUNTAINS on the east and the TACONIC MOUNTAINS to the west, and is bisected by northward-flowing OTTER CREEK. The main settlement is Pittsford village, approximately in the center of the town. During the Revolution, Pittsford was the site of Fort Mott (1777) and Fort Vengeance (1779), built to protect the settlers in the area from British incursions. Nicholas M. Powers, who built lattice-type covered bridges throughout Vermont and New Hampshire, was born here. In the late nineteenth century, the hamlet of Florence served a MARBLE quarry nearby, one of many established to exploit the deposits of the West Rutland marble belt. The Swiss firm OMYA, owner of the former VERMONT MARBLE COMPANY since 1979, extracts and refines large quantities of calcium carbonate at its Florence production facilities for the paper, paint, and plastics industries.

Plainfield

Plainfield, population 1,286, a town in Washington County, was created by the Vermont legislature in 1797 out of land from St. Andrews Gore, part of a 1788 land parcel known as the Whitelaw, Savage, and Coit Grant. The name apparently derives from Plainfield, Connecticut. The landscape is largely hilly and wooded, rising to 3,037 feet at Spruce Mountain along the eastern border. Agriculture has historically been the town's economic base, although in recent decades a commuter overlay has developed because of the proximity of Barre. The only significant settlement is Plainfield village, along the WINOOSKI RIVER in the extreme northwestern section of the town. GODDARD COLLEGE lies just outside the village.

Plattsburgh Bay, Battle of

September 11, 1814, has been called "the proudest day" for, against all odds, the Americans defeated the British in a decisive victory of the War of 1812. Following three years of petty skirmishes for control of LAKE CHAMPLAIN and the Champlain Valley, the British assembled an army of eleven thousand soldiers, mostly veterans of the Peninsular campaign against Napoleon, and a superior fleet for a two-prong assault by land and lake through the Champlain Valley to attack Albany, and ultimately capture New York City. Under the command of Sir George Prevost, the British marched down the west side of the lake, accompanied by a heavily armed lake flotilla, attacking Plattsburgh, New York, on September 6. A badly outnumbered American force of fifteen hundred regulars and several thousand New York and Vermont volunteers under Brigadier General Alexander Macomb withdrew to a position on the Saranac River, waiting for the appearance of the United States fleet commanded by THOMAS MACDONOUGH. The fleet had been built hastily by Macdonough at Vergennes on OTTER CREEK. By the morning of the eleventh, Macdonough's four ships and ten gunboats had come down the lake from the mouth of the Otter and swung around Cumberland Head into Plattsburgh Bay. With the tactical advantage of riding at anchor, Macdonough waited for the British fleet. In the first minutes of the engagement, the British commander George Downie was killed. At a critical moment during the two hours of heavy fire, Macdonough ordered his flagship *Saratoga* to kedge anchor, a turning maneuver to bring fresh portside guns into action against Downie's flagship, HMS *Confiance*, which shortly surrendered. Losing both their commander and their flagship, the British soon surrendered. On land, Prevost with-drew his troops and retreated back to Canada. Macdonough's "signal victory on Lake Champlain" was one of the most decisive battles of the War of 1812. Naval victories on the Chesapeake and Lake Champlain induced the Duke of Wellington to advise his prime minister against demanding concessions at the peace negotiations at Ghent. Thus the British withdrew their claims to the Great Lakes, including Lake Champlain, conceded conquered territory, and brought the hostilities to a close.   *Karen Campbell*

Plymouth

Plymouth, population 555, a town in Windsor County, was granted by BENNING WENTWORTH in 1762 as the town of Saltash and had its name changed to Plymouth by the Vermont legislature in 1797. The origin of the new name is usually assumed to be Plymouth in Massachusetts, not England, although it is worth noting that the English city is directly across the Tamar Estuary from the borough of Saltash. The town is located on the rugged eastern slopes of the GREEN MOUNTAINS, rising to 3,286 feet at Salt Ash Mountain in its southwestern corner. Running through the town from north to south is the deep valley of the southern Black River, which forms a series of small lakes dotted with summer cabins along its course. Before the Civil War, the TYSON IRON COMPANY, just above the southern border with Ludlow, was one of the busiest iron-producing facilities in New England. Today Plymouth is best known as the birthplace, childhood home, and burial site of CALVIN COOLIDGE, who was administered the oath of office as president of the United States here by his own father at 2:47 A.M. on August 3, 1923. Much of the village of Plymouth Notch is now part of the President COOLIDGE STATE HISTORIC SITE and retains many of the buildings and the appearance of earlier days. The Plymouth Cheese Factory, for example, was built in 1890 by Colonel John Coolidge, James S. Brown, and two other local farmers. It served as a convenient outlet for the milk produced on their farms. The plant closed in the 1930s, but was reopened by the president's son, John, in the 1960s. The original formula is still used for the "granular curd" type cheese, which can be purchased at the factory.

Point à la Chevelure

Today called CHIMNEY POINT on LAKE CHAMPLAIN, Point à la Chevelure ("Scalp

Point") in the present Addison County was part of the domain of King Louis XV of France from the 1730s until its abandonment in 1758. Military installations and dependencies included Fort Saint-Frédéric across the lake on Crown Point, and various shops, barns, stables, and a stone gristmill on the east shore. On the west shore, farms stretched southward from Fort Saint-Frédéric to Carillon, the stone fortress later to be renamed TICONDER-OGA by the British. The King's domain on the east side of the lake included thirty lots surveyed south to Doctor's Creek in Addison. Twenty-five lots had been sold and occupied by 1758 when the French withdrew to Quebec. Among the earliest settlers in 1741 to 1742 were François and Marguerite Breilly, Jean-Guillaume and Marie Françoise Darabi, François and Marie Motier, Jean-Baptiste and Marie Anne Prudhomme, and their slave, Marguerite Charlotte, who had been captured from the ABENAKI in the region of Pike River near Missisquoi Bay.

Joseph-André Senécal

Poland, Luke (1815–1887)

A chief judge of the Vermont Supreme Court and both senator and representative in Congress, Luke Poland was born in Westford and attended a town school and the Jericho academy. Before he was twenty, he taught school and began to read the law in the Morristown office of Samuel A. Willard. Admitted to the bar when he was twenty-one years old, he served as probate register in Lamoille County in 1839 to 1840; as a member of the state constitutional convention in 1843; and as Lamoille County state's attorney in 1844 and 1845. As a Democrat with FREE-SOIL sympathies, he was elected judge on the Supreme Court by a Whig legislature in 1848. A Republican by 1860, he was chosen chief judge of the Supreme Court. His opinion on the power of the state to permit absentee voting for active duty troops during the Civil War was followed by several states, thus assuring President Lincoln a large bloc of votes from the Union army. Upon the death of JACOB COL-LAMER, the legislature chose Luke Poland to fill out the unexpired Senate term. In 1866, he was elected to the House of Representatives and JUSTIN MORRILL was elected to succeed him in the Senate. While in the Senate, Poland served on the judiciary committee and directed a bankruptcy bill to enactment. During that short Senate term, he also initiated what has been called the greatest work of his congressional career, the revisions and consolidation of the statutes of the United States. While in the House, he directed subsequent action on the revisions of the statutes, which became law in 1874. He also chaired the House committees to investigate the KU KLUX KLAN and the Credit Mobilier affair. His report criticizing military interference in Arkansas state elections and state government did not please President Grant. In 1873 to 1875, Poland's national prominence from his committee chairmanships led to suggestions that he might be a Republican presidential candidate. But the passage of a notorious "salary grab" bill, so called for increasing House members salary by $7,500, retroactive to the beginning of that Congress, brought sharp popular attacks on the House. Poland had voted against the bill, but refused to give back the pay raise. Seen as arrogant, he was defeated for re-election in 1874 in one of the staunchest Republican districts of Vermont. In 1876, however, he was rumored to be a possible vice-presidential candidate at the Republican National Convention. St. Johnsbury sent him to the legislature in 1878; and in 1882 he nearly defeated Justin Morrill for the latter's seat in the United States Senate. When a new Second Congressional district was organized in 1884, he was elected to the House again, but served only one term.

Pomeroy, John (1764–1844)

Dr. John Pomeroy was the organizer and first faculty member of the UNIVERSITY OF VERMONT's College of Medicine, a founding member of the Vermont Medical Society, and a highly respected citizen of Burlington. He was born in Middleboro, Massachusetts. At the age of sixteen, he joined the militia and served for some months at West Point. Returning to Middleboro, he apprenticed to Dr. James Bradish of nearby Cummington, performing the customary physician's apprentice duties of caring for the doctor's horse, helping to prepare the medicines, participating in care of patients, and studying the doctor's medical books. After two years, Pomeroy called himself doctor and went to Vermont to set up his own practice in Cambridge. In 1792, he moved his young family to Burlington. The town's population grew rapidly during the next few decades and Pomeroy prospered along with the town. In 1797, he built a home and office on the waterfront, the first brick house in Burlington. He became the pre-eminent practitioner in the area, respected by colleagues and patients alike. A bold surgeon, he was said to have boarded a canal boat in the harbor to save the life of a choking sailor by inserting a goose quill in his windpipe, an operation he had never seen performed. By 1800, Pomeroy was taking pupils for medical instruction. Recognizing a need for more formal training of physicians in Vermont, Pomeroy petitioned the recently founded and struggling University of Vermont to give a course of medical lectures. In 1804, he was appointed lecturer in anatomy and surgery and in 1809, when he was still the only medical member of the university faculty, as professor of physic and surgery. In that same year, though Pomeroy himself had never attended college, the University of Vermont awarded him an honorary M.D. degree. The lectures were held in his home and office on Battery Street. Students paid him directly. During the War of 1812, the university suspended services when its one building was taken over by the military, but Pomeroy continued his medical instruction on Battery Street. When the college building was returned to the university in 1815, two rooms were made available to Pomeroy, who began to assemble a faculty and expand the curriculum. The university awarded its first degree of doctor of medicine in 1823. Pomeroy served as a member of UVM's corporation intermittently between 1817 and 1822. Pomeroy took an active part in organizing a medical society in the Burlington area in order to improve professional standards of practice and to examine and certify the qualifications of new practitioners. He also served as one of the founding officers of the statewide Vermont Medical Society. A prominent figure in the community affairs, Pomeroy was one of the organizers in 1805 of the First Unitarian Society. *Lester Wallman*

Pomfret

Pomfret (pronounced "Pumfrit"), population 997, a town in Windsor County, was granted by BENNING WENTWORTH in 1761 and named for Pomfret, Connecticut, the home town of a number of the grantees. Despite its nearness to bustling Woodstock directly to the south, Pomfret remains a quiet upland region of wooded hills cut by small watercourses. The highest elevation is 1,964-foot Thistle Hill. The several small settlements include North Pomfret, Pomfret village, and South Pomfret, the last two on the road cutting across the town from Woodstock to Sharon. One of Vermont's smallest ski areas, Suicide Six, with only nineteen trails, three lifts, and a drop of 650 feet, lies near the southern border of the town.

Pond, Arlington (1872–1930)

A successful pitcher for the Baltimore Orioles during the 1890s while completing his medical studies, Arlington Pond of Rutland graduated from Rutland High School, studied at NORWICH UNIVERSITY from 1888 to 1890, and graduated from the UNIVERSITY OF VERMONT in 1893. He played center field for UVM's 1891 baseball team and in 1892 played second base and pitched to help UVM's "Wonder Team" finish its season with a 21–9 record. He pitched a no-hitter against Yale. In 1893, while Pond was enrolled in the Medical School, UVM was invited to play in a tournament against seven other college teams at the 1893 Chicago World's Fair, where the Vermonters finished second. UVM was the only team to beat Yale, the tournament's eventual champion. After Medical School, Pond went to Baltimore's College of Physicians and Surgeons for a post-graduate surgical course. During his internship at Baltimore City Hospital and a residency at St. Joseph Hospital, Pond pitched for the Orioles. In his first season, he pitched in only six games, but in the 1896 season he started twenty-six games and compiled a 16–8 record with a 3.49 ERA, providing substantial help toward the Oriole's second consecutive National League pennant. In 1897, he had his best season, going 18–9 with a 3.52 ERA, but the Orioles finished second behind the Boston Beaneaters. In the early months of the 1898 season, Pond was used sparingly until July, when he left baseball at the outbreak of the Spanish-American War to become acting assistant surgeon in the United States Army headed for service with the Tenth Pennsylvania Regiment in the Philippine Islands. After the defeat of Spain and the subsequent suppression of a nationalist Filipino insurrection against American rule, Pond stayed in the islands to work in the humanitarian effort to improve public health by stopping the spread of cholera, smallpox, and leprosy, diseases previously unchecked. In 1902, he was detached from the Army to cholera duty with the Philippine Islands

Board of Health in a public health project in Manila City funded by the Rockefeller Foundation. In 1906, he was appointed first chief of the Southern Islands Hospital on the island of Cebu, 400 miles south of Manila, where he founded a hospital for lepers and successfully led a campaign to vaccinate the island's entire population. He found time to develop a high school baseball team on Cebu that won the Philippines interscholastic championships of 1910, 1912, and 1913. In World War I, he was recalled to military service as post surgeon at Camp Stotsenburg with the Ninth United States Cavalry and the Philippine Field Artillery and later at Fort Santiago, Manila. Near the end of the war, he was assigned to the American Expedition sent to Vladivostok, Siberia, to assist the White Russian Army, but the war's conclusion on November 11, 1918, sent him back to the Philippines. Arlie Pond spent the rest of his life on Cebu working at his hospital. In 1930, he died at Cebu of peritonitis associated with an appendectomy.

Poor Farms

Until the second half of the twentieth century, the responsibility to care for the poor in Vermont was administered at the local level. A 1797 law stated "that every town and place in this state, shall relieve, support and maintain their own poor." Different communities met this responsibility in different ways, with varying degrees of compassion and success. One policy followed by many towns was that of "hiring out," a procedure in which paupers were, in effect, auctioned off to the lowest bidder. Another was "warning out," in which poor residents, or residents thought likely to become a burden on the town, were "warned" that the town would not support them, and sent back to their earlier places of residence. This procedure led to frequent lawsuits between Vermont towns over what constituted residency. The overseer of the poor, a town officer who was expected to be well acquainted with the circumstances of the town's poor and unfortunate, was authorized to provide assistance when warranted. There were problems with these approaches, however, especially in larger towns, and starting in the second quarter of the nineteenth century, many towns established "poor farms." None of these, even the best, could have been pleasant places to live in. The residents were a mixture of "transients" (people temporarily out of work or

homeless) and "permanents." The latter would include not only the chronically poor, but the lame and the halt as well, usually elderly and often with mental illnesses but with no one to turn to for help. The farms were usually operated by a farmer and his wife, hired by the town, and hired hands as needed, but able-bodied residents, both men and women, were expected to help with the work of the place. The role of the poor farms began to shrink in the 1930s with the advent of new programs and institutions and expansion of the role of state government in caring for the poor and the mentally and physically ill. New Deal programs such as Social Security that provided some financial assistance to the elderly and disabled, as well as the poor, accelerated the trend in the 1930s and 1940s. There were sixty-two poor farms in Vermont in 1916, and only thirty-seven by 1928. Burlington's poor farm was sold in 1958, and Rutland closed its town farm in 1966. The Sheldon Poor Farm, by all accounts, might have been the best in a not very good system of caring for the poor, and was the one that lasted the longest. It was established on April 24, 1834, when four Franklin County towns bought a farm in the western part of Sheldon. It moved twelve years later, on March 12, 1846, to a bigger farm in Sheldon Springs, where it stayed until it closed on October 1, 1968. Towns withdrew or joined from time to time, but for most of its existence from 1846 on, nine towns (Fairfield, Sheldon, Swanton, Highgate, Enosburgh, Franklin, Berkshire, and St. Albans, both town and city) belonged to the association, which was formally incorporated in 1906. The state's Social Welfare Act of 1967 repealed town authority to operate poor farms, assigned legal responsibility for the poor to the state, and abolished the office of overseer of the poor.

John C. Wriston, Jr.

Postal Service in Early Vermont

Prior to 1784, Vermont had no regular or official postal service. ANTHONY HASWELL, the publisher of the *Vermont Gazette*, persuaded the General Assembly in 1784 to establish postal service for letter mail and newspapers between Albany (New York), Bennington, Brattleboro, Windsor, Newbury, and Rutland. Samuel Sherman, Governor THOMAS CHITTENDEN's personal post rider, hired additional weekly post riders to carry mail at 2 pence per mile on regular routes and 3 pence per mile over the mountains between Bennington and Brattleboro. The governor and council appointed Haswell postmaster general. David Russell in Bennington, Frederick Hill in Rutland, John Arms in Brattleboro, ALDEN SPOONER in Windsor, and David Haseltine in Newbury were appointed postmasters in their towns. In 1791, the Congress in Philadelphia authorized Postmaster General Pickering to extend mail service from Albany to Bennington. Within Vermont, state postal service lasted until an Act of Congress in 1792 created four post routes. East of the GREEN MOUNTAINS, a weekly route ran from Springfield, Massachusetts, to Brattleboro. A second weekly route ran from Brattleboro via Westminster to Windsor. The third weekly route ran west of the mountains from Albany via Bennington and Manchester to Rutland. A fourth biweekly route ran from Rutland via Vergennes to Burlington. Although Burlington's population in 1792 (332) was smaller than Shelburne's and Charlotte's along the route, this northward mail route was created to comply with the first United States and Canada postal convention of March 1792. To avoid the long overland trip to Halifax, Nova Scotia, in the winter, Canadian mail to Europe travelled the shorter route through Burlington to New York City. John Fay was appointed Burlington's postmaster. Postal rates in 1792 for letters were based on the number of sheets of paper and distance. Single-sheet rates for distances less than 30 miles were 6 cents and increased incrementally to 25 cents for more than 450 miles. Double sheets paid double rates and three sheets paid triple the rate. Recipients paid the postage for most letters. Local or drop letters were 1 cent. Rates were modified in 1799, and increased by 50 percent in 1815 for a year to help pay for the War of 1812. Rates remained much the same until rate reductions in 1845 and 1851 brought in 3-cent prepaid letters for 3,000 miles. After 1792, additional post offices were established in Vermont, reaching twenty-eight by 1800 and 118 by 1810, when thirteen different postal routes crisscrossed Vermont. Postmasters were paid on the basis of total postage collected. Like members of Congress, they also had a franking privilege, which permitted them to send and receive mail free of postage charges. Post offices in early Vermont were located in GENERAL STORES or newspaper offices until the post office department began constructing post offices after 1850. Burlington's first post office building went up in 1857. Carriers transported mail over post roads under advertised and regulated term contracts. Frequency of mail conveyance increased from the very early weekly trip to three days per week to daily in the first quarter of the nineteenth century. Mode of transport also changed as LAKE CHAMPLAIN steamboats and then RAILROADS won mail contracts. As population increased, even very small communities were often able to enjoy the convenience of a local post office. The United States Post Office Directory for 1856 listed 387 post offices in Vermont. *Donald B. Johnstone*

Potter, Henry L. (1891–1986)

Henry Potter was for most of the twentieth century Vermont's foremost naturalist, with a great knowledge of the state's birds and plants. A self-taught naturalist and unassuming farmer, Potter lived all his life on the family farm in the Chippenhook section of North Clarendon. His formal education ended with the completion of the eighth grade in the local one-room schoolhouse. A life-long conservationist, he was a member of the original National Audubon Society, one of the first bird-banders in the United States (1909 member of the American Bird Banding Association), and joined the newly formed Vermont Botanical and Bird Society in 1910, remaining an active member all his life. His excellent nature photography included films of peregrine falcons nesting at White Rocks in the mid-1950s, one of the last nestings before DDT decimated the population. He was active with the newly founded VERMONT INSTITUTE OF NATURAL SCIENCE from 1974 on, imparting his knowledge by leading field trips on birds and ferns. The *Atlas of Breeding Birds of Vermont* (1984) quotes him extensively, drawing on his near-century of first-hand knowledge. In his eighty-ninth year, he was awarded an honorary doctor of science degree by the UNIVERSITY OF VERMONT, in part for his extensive work on hybrid ferns. *Henry Potter's Field Guide to the Hybrid Ferns of the Northeast* (Vermont Institute of Natural Science, 1989) was completed after his death by Frank and Libby Thorne. *Sarah B. Laughlin*

Poultney

Poultney, population 3,633, a town in Rutland County, was granted by BENNING WENTWORTH in 1761 and settled by, among others, ETHAN and IRA ALLEN's brother HEBER and their cousin EBENEZER ALLEN. It was named for William Pulteney or Poultney (1684–1764), first earl of Bath, one-time secretary of war and member of the British parliament for fifty years. The town, which abuts the towns of Granville and Hampton in New York State, lies on the low western slopes of the TACONIC MOUNTAINS and is bisected from east to west by the Poultney River. It contains the northern half of 852-acre Lake St. Catherine, a popular resort area, the southern half of which is in the town of Wells. The town has two major settlements, East Poultney and Poultney village. The first was the vital center of town during the town's earliest years and contains, among other old buildings, the Eagle Tavern, built as a stagecoach stop in 1790 and now a private home. HORACE GREELEY, founder of the *New York Tribune*, and GEORGE JONES, a native of Poultney and co-founder of the *New York Times*, apprenticed together at the East Poultney *Northern Spectator*. The second settlement, Poultney village, whose business district is on the National Register of Historic Places, is the home of GREEN MOUNTAIN COLLEGE, founded in 1836 as the Troy Conference Academy of the Methodist Episcopal Church. Numerous SLATE quarries dot the western section of Poultney, as they do other towns along the New York border from Castleton to Pawlet. The first Jewish community in Vermont came into existence in Poultney around the time of the Civil War, its members drawn to the town as merchants serving the active slate quarrying industry. Congregation B'nai Israel was founded in 1873 and acquired a cemetery, which eventually held twenty-five graves.

Powers, H. Henry (1835–1913)

Congressman, judge, and state legislator, H. Henry Powers was the son of a Lamoille County sheriff and father of a Vermont Supreme Court chief justice. Born in Morristown, he attended People's Academy and graduated from the UNIVERSITY OF VERMONT in 1855. After teaching for a short time in Canada, he returned to Vermont to serve as the first principal of the Lamoille Central Academy at Hyde Park. The following year, 1858, he was elected as a Republican to the legislature from Morristown, the youngest member of that body, and having simultaneously been studying law was admitted to the Vermont bar. In 1861 and again in 1862, he was elected state's attorney for Lamoille County and during the latter year formed a law partnership with Thomas Gleed that they maintained until Powers was elected to the bench. In 1869, Powers was elected to what became the last COUNCIL OF CENSORS and then to the Constitutional Convention that considered the council's proposed amendments. He exercised leadership roles in both bodies. In 1872, he was elected to the state senate and in 1874 to the house, where he served as speaker until the waning days of the session, when he was elected to the state supreme court. He served until 1890, when he was elected to Congress. After five consecutive terms, he was defeated for renomination in 1900. Although Powers and WILLIAM GROUT, the other member of Vermont's House delegation, publicly disputed about Powers' insistence upon the sanctity of contract, his defeat is generally attributed to the Republican convention's invoking rotation-in-office principles. Upon return to private life, Powers established a successful law practice, primarily in corporation law, serving as general counsel for the Rutland Railroad and other corporate clients.

Powers, Hiram (1805–1873)

The sculptor Hiram Powers of Woodstock was drawn to sculpting after moving to Cincinnati, Ohio, about 1829, where his skill in making wax figures for a local "chamber of horrors" attracted attention and several commissions for portrait busts. In 1834, Powers moved to Washington, D.C., where he made busts from life of prominent national figures such as Andrew Jackson and Daniel Webster. Nicholas Longworth, a wealthy patron in Cincinnati who had already helped LARKIN MEAD of Brattleboro advance his career as a sculptor, with other benefactors lent Powers the money to go to Italy in 1837, where he spent the rest of his life. In 1843, he completed his famous *Greek Slave*, a marble figure of a nude woman in chains leaning against a draped pillar. It was the most celebrated statue of its time. Nathaniel Hawthorne and others wrote about it and it was exhibited at the Crystal Palace, London, in 1851. The *Greek Slave* remains historically important as the first American sculpture to gain broad public recognition. Powers also sculpted statues of American statesmen, including Benjamin Franklin and Thomas Jefferson, for the Capitol in Washington, D.C. Powers

Hiram Powers. Special Collections, Bailey/Howe Library, University of Vermont

was a lifelong friend of diplomat and environmentalist GEORGE PERKINS MARSH, a fellow native of Woodstock, with whom he carried on an extensive correspondence preserved in the Special Collections at the Bailey-Howe Library of the UNIVERSITY OF VERMONT. Powers did a bust of Marsh's wife, Caroline Crane Marsh, in 1862, that is now in the university's FLEMING MUSEUM.

Pownal

Pownal, population 3,560, in Bennington County, is the southwesternmost town in Vermont. It was granted by BENNING WENTWORTH in 1760 and derives its name from Thomas and John Pownall, two of the grantees. The town is cut north to south by the VALLEY OF VERMONT, and in the western section by the Hoosic River running into New York State. In the southeastern part of the town rises the Dome, 2,748 feet high, the first significant peak of the GREEN MOUNTAINS. The main settlement is Pownal village, near the Massachusetts border; two other settlements are North Pownal and Pownal Center. Two U.S. presidents, James Garfield and CHESTER ALAN ARTHUR, Republican candidates for president and vice president in the election of 1880, in their youth taught (separately) at the North Pownal Academy.

President Coolidge, S. S.

On October 6, 1942, the U.S. Army's 172nd Regimental Combat Team, originally the 172nd Infantry Regiment of the Vermont National Guard but now a unit of the Forty-third Division, sailed from San Francisco for the New Hebrides islands in the South Pacific on the U.S. Presidents Line's *President Coolidge*. Entering the harbor of the island of Espiritu Santo on October 26, the *Coolidge* accidentally struck and detonated friendly anti-submarine mines and sank. Commander of the combat team Colonel James A. Lewis led four thousand men to safety from the sinking ship in less than one hour. Most of the men swam the nearly one thousand yards to shore, while a few life boats picked up others who could not swim or panicked. Only one casualty resulted from this accident. All of their equipment lost with the *Coolidge*, the 172nd remained in New Zealand until late 1942, when it was finally able to follow the Forty-third Division to Guadalcanal, where the combat team prepared for the invasion of Rendova and their first front-line combat. At that time, the original Vermont National Guardsmen made up 30 percent of the 172nd's strength.

Preservation Trust of Vermont

Founded in 1980, the Preservation Trust of Vermont is a nonprofit, statewide organization that works with local groups, businesses, local governments, and interested citizens to save and use Vermont's historic, architectural, and cultural resources. Current programs focus mainly on strengthening downtowns and village centers and protecting the character of Vermont. Funded by the Freeman Foundation, the trust provides preservation grants for nonprofit organizations and municipalities to rehabilitate historic buildings. Projects include affordable housing, libraries, community meeting places, art spaces, educational facilities, and churches. A partnership of the Preservation Trust of Vermont and the National Trust for Historic Preservation, the field service program provides assistance to local groups who are undertaking a preservation project. Through the Robert Sincerbeaux Fund, the Preservation Trust offers seed grants to help communities and organizations take the initial step in saving and using historic places. The Preservation Trust works with other nonprofit partners to ensure public policies that strengthen downtowns and curb commercial sprawl. In partnership with the Vermont Country Store of Weston, they help support existing village stores and work with communities to start up new stores where none existed. The Grand Isle Lake House, a restored Victorian summer resort owned by the Preservation Trust, is used for weddings, private gatherings, meetings, and retreats. Preservation awards by the trust recognize communities and organizations that have achieved great successes. The trust's educational programs include an on-line newsletter, an annual Preservation Conference, and a Web site.

Ann S. Cousins

Prince, Lucy Terry (c. 1732–1821), and Abijiah Prince (1706–1794)

A slave, free woman, and early settler, Lucy Terry Prince was born in Africa, kidnapped, and taken to Deerfield, Massachusetts, where she became the slave of Captain Ebenezer Wells by 1738. At age sixteen, she achieved local fame for a vivid verse account of a Native American ambush of local white settlers. She married Abijiah Prince, a freed slave who worked for her owner, when he purchased her freedom in 1756. They had six children, two of whom served in the American Revolution. They settled first in Guilford and finally in Sunderland on the New Hampshire grants in 1764. Prince was by all accounts a remarkable woman, and a sense of her dignity and courage come through in the sparse record of her life. Along with the typical hard labor and privation of pioneer life, the Prince family faced harrassment and vandalism of their property, leading Lucy to petition the town's selectmen for protection. Later, the family's Guilford land title was contested and they went to court against their neighbor, Eli Bronson, in 1785. A nineteenth-century town history has it that Lucy Terry Prince appeared before the Vermont Supreme Court and argued the case laid out by her counsel, ISAAC TICHENOR, against Bronson's co-counsels, ROYALL TYLER and STEPHEN R. BRADLEY. She is said to have received praise from presiding judge Samuel Chase for her conduct of the case, though she did not prevail against Bronson. She is also said to have made an articulate, though unsuccessful, three-hour appeal to the dean and faculty of Williams College on behalf of a son refused admission on account of race. She was widowed in 1794, and tradition has her faithfully visiting her husband's grave

in her last decades. She died in Sunderland. Lucy Prince is frequently cited as the first African-American female poet on the strength of her single poem. In recent decades, researchers imbued with the spirit of the civil rights and women's movements have adopted Prince as a symbol of the struggle for race and gender equity.

Ray Zirblis

Prindle, Almira E. Green "Mother" (1837–1914)

Almira Green Prindle, a social worker in several large American cities, came to be known as Mother Prindle for her work with homeless women and boys. Born in South Starksboro, she was a life-long Orthodox Quaker, a talented speaker, and, before marriage, a school teacher. She was much influenced by the Quaker prophet JOSEPH HOAG of Charlotte and followed his example to become a Public Quaker, speaking often on the plight of homeless women and children. In 1863, she married the conscientious objector and botanist CYRUS G. PRINGLE (then "Prindle"), whom she had helped to become a Quaker the previous year. She divorced in 1877 and left Vermont to become a social worker. Most of her work was with the Florence Crittenden Homes in Buffalo, Chicago, New York City, Philadelphia, Boston and Watertown, Massachusetts, and Little Rock. She founded the Newark, Ohio, Florence Crittenden Home. From a large family, she had three brothers who graduated from medical college and practiced medicine, and her eldest brother, Joseph, had the Lord's Prayer carved into a large boulder still accessible to view in Bristol.

Kathleen McKinley Harris

Pringle, Cyrus Guernsey (1838–1911)

A self-taught hybridizer, nurseryman, botanist, and plant collector, Cyrus Pringle was born in Charlotte as Cyrus Prindle. He matriculated at the UNIVERSITY OF VERMONT in 1859 but did not graduate. Married to ALMIRA E. GREENE PRINDLE of South Starksboro, an Orthodox Quaker, he joined the Society of Friends in 1862. Among the few Vermonters drafted into (rather than volunteering for) the Union Army, Pringle and two other Vermont Quakers professed conscientious objections to war, refused hospital duty, and were imprisoned. At President Lincoln's request in November 1863, Secretary of War Stanton released Pringle after four

months' internment. *The Atlantic Monthly* published part of his diary of his pacifism and prison experience in 1913. A pioneer plant breeder, Pringle started his first nursery in 1858. During the years 1864 to 1880, he concentrated on breeding plants in East Charlotte, benefitting farmers with improved varieties of wheat, oats, grapes, and potatoes. He also raised and experimented with ornamentals. After his divorce in 1877, Pringle focused on plant collecting, travelling to gather specimens from the northeastern United States, Canada, the Pacific coastal states, and Mexico. From 1881 to 1909, he made annual and often more frequent trips to the Southwest to gather specimens for Harvard, the Smithsonian, and other major herbaria throughout the world. His personal collection is now housed in the Pringle Herbarium at UVM. Botanist Asa Gray called him "Prince of Plant Collectors." During his lifetime, he collected over five hundred thousand specimens from twenty thousand species, 12 percent of them previously unknown to botanists. For many years, Pringle contributed articles to *Country Gentleman* and *Garden and Forest*.

Kathleen McKinley Harris

Printing in Vermont, 1778–1800

At the request of ELEAZAR WHEELOCK, president of Dartmouth College, ALDEN SPOONER in 1778 brought press and types to Dresden, a precinct of Hanover, New Hampshire, that had incorporated itself as a town in the first EAST UNION with Vermont. Wheelock's College Party and their opponents, led by ETHAN and IRA ALLEN, used the DRESDEN PRESS to publish their sides of the controversy. JUDAH SPOONER, Alden's brother and official printer for the state of Vermont, produced numerous pamphlets on the Dresden Press for the state and published the *Dresden Mercury* from May to September 1779. After the dissolution of the East Union and Dartmouth College's failure to make Dresden the capitol of Vermont, Judah Spooner moved across the CONNECTICUT RIVER to Westminster. Timothy Green III of Norwich, Connecticut, who owned the Dresden printing types, and probably even the press, sent his son Timothy IV to Westminster to assist the unreliable Judah in publishing the *Vermont Gazette* in Westminster from June to December 1780. They also printed all of Vermont's official documents and several important publications pertaining to the on-going controversies between the ARLINGTON JUNTO and Connecticut Valley towns on both sides of the river. The Spooner-Green press closed in early 1782. Still needing a printer, the Vermont General Assembly induced ANTHONY HASWELL of Springfield, Massachusetts, to establish his press at Bennington in early 1783. Haswell and David Russell, his partner until 1790, began publication of the *Vermont Gazette* on June 5 of that year. Haswell's state printing work declined with the waning influence of his close friend Ethan Allen in 1784. Alden Spooner, meanwhile, had moved to Windsor in 1783, the thriving SHIRE TOWN of Windsor County, where he and George Hough set up shop with Timothy Green III's printing types and began to publish the *Vermont Journal* on August 7, 1783. Hough left the business in 1788, but Spooner continued as a very active and successful printer in Windsor until he retired in 1817. As a Federalist, Spooner was frequently awarded state government printing jobs when his party controlled Vermont politics during the 1790s. After Vermont became the fourteenth state in 1791, the printing work required by busy state and federal courts and attendant lawyers in Rutland led Anthony Haswell to establish a press there and issue the short-lived *Herald of Vermont, or, Rutland Courier* (June–September 1792). Also in Rutland in 1793, James Lyon, the son of the political firebrand MATTHEW LYON of Fair Haven, began printing the *Farmer's Library*. In 1794, Judge SAMUEL WILLIAMS and the Reverend SAMUEL WILLIAMS purchased the business from Lyon and brought printers Josiah Fay and WILLIAM FAY to produce the *Herald of Vermont*. Later renamed the *RUTLAND HERALD*, it continues to this day. By the end of the eighteenth century, printers worked in Fair Haven (1795, Judah P. Spooner and James Lyon for Matthew Lyon); Burlington (March 1796, Donnelly & Hill); Newbury (May 1796, Nathaniel Coverly, Jr.); Brattleboro (January 1997, Dickman & Smead); Putney (January 1797, Cornelius Sturtevant & Co.); Vergennes (August 1798, G. & R. Waite); Peacham (February 1798, Samuel Goss); and Randolph (December 1800, Sereno Wright). A printer opened for business in Middlebury in 1801, a year after the founding of the college there. Brown & Parks began printing in Montpelier in November 1806. Some of these establishments were short lived but the printing businesses in Bennington, Windsor, Rutland, Burlington, and Brattleboro were forerunners of enterprises that have lasted to the present day.

Marcus A. McCorison

Proctor

Proctor, population 1,877, the smallest town in area in Rutland County and once the self-styled "MARBLE Capital of the World," was incorporated by the Vermont legislature in 1886 out of portions of the towns of Rutland and Pittsford. The name derives from REDFIELD PROCTOR, SR., a former governor and founder of the state's leading family dynasty, who created the VERMONT MARBLE COMPANY in 1880 and made sure that the town's boundaries almost exactly matched the Proctor family's holdings. The town's high-quality marble, first quarried in 1836, has been used in many imposing structures, including the U.S. Supreme Court building in Washington and the United Nations Secretariat in New York, and in more humble fashion for sidewalks, walls, and house foundations throughout Proctor village, the town's only settlement. The Vermont Marble Company strike in 1935 led to a classic confrontation between capital and labor that was only resolved by arbitration in the spring of 1936. Eventually, a decline in the use of marble led to a contraction in the company's business, and in 1976 it was sold to a European concern. An extensive exhibit on the history and uses of Vermont marble is located in one of the company's finishing sheds.

Proctor, Fletcher Dutton (1860–1911)

Governor and president of the VERMONT MARBLE COMPANY, Fletcher D. Proctor was the elder son of REDFIELD PROCTOR, SR. Born in Proctorsville in the town of Cavendish, he studied at the Rutland Military Institute, Middlebury High School, and Amherst College, graduating in the class of 1882. He began working in the Vermont Marble Company as a machinist to learn all the processes of the marble industry and in 1885 he was made superintendent of the company. In 1889, when his father was named secretary of war, Fletcher Proctor succeeded him as president, a position he held for the rest of his life. He entered public service as a selectman and schoolboard member in the early 1880s. He served as secretary of civil and military affairs for Governor Ormsbee from 1886 to 1888. In 1890, 1900, and 1904, he served in the Vermont house of representatives, in 1900 as house speaker. In 1892, he represented Rutland County in the senate. Elected governor in 1906 for one term, Fletcher D. Proctor rejected his father's emphasis on fiscal conservatism to proclaim that Vermont had "a higher duty than to live cheaply," and enuciated one of the more ambitious legislative agendas in state history. His administration succeeded in reorganizing the state judiciary into separate trial and appeals benches, applying managerial systems to state institutions, imposing closer supervision over school districts, and mandating weekly wage payments to employees of Vermont corporations. He died unexpectedly in 1911. Fletcher D. Proctor was the second of four Proctors to serve as governor, the others being his father Redfield Sr. (1878–1880), his brother REDFIELD JR. (1923–1925), and his son MORTIMER (1945–47).

Proctor, Mortimer Robinson
(1889–1968)

The fourth Proctor elected governor, Mortimer Robinson Proctor was son of FLETCHER PROCTOR. He was born in the town of Proctor and attended Proctor schools, the Hill School in Pottstown, Pennsylvania, and Yale University, graduating in 1912. During World War I, he served in the artillery in France from April 1918 to February 1919. Associated with the VERMONT MARBLE COMPANY his entire life, he was elected a director upon graduating from Yale, a vice president in 1935, president in 1952, and chairman of the board in 1958, a position he held until shortly before his death. Following the family path into politics, he was president of Proctor village in 1930 and chairman of the Republican town committee in 1932. He was elected to the Vermont house from Proctor in 1932, 1934, and 1936 and served his last term as speaker. In 1938, he was elected to represent Rutland County in the Vermont senate. In 1940 and 1942, he was elected lieutenant governor. His election broke a long-standing tradition known as the Mountain Rule under which the lieutenant governor's home town was on the opposite side of the state from the governor's. Proctor further broke this tradition with his election as governor in 1944; a western Vermonter, he succeeded another western Vermonter. In 1946, Proctor was defeated in the Republican gubernatorial primary by war hero ERNEST W. GIBSON, JR. Proctor was the first Republican gubernatorial incumbent to be denied renomination in the primary. He secured a measure of revenge by helping block Gibson from gaining control of the state party organization but declined subsequent opportunities to run for office. After his defeat, he devoted his attention to his business interests.

Proctor, Redfield, Jr. (1879–1957)

The youngest child and younger son of REDFIELD PROCTOR, SR., was born in the village of Proctor, in Rutland town, where he attended the public school, and went on to the Hill School at Pottstown, Pennsylvania, and the Friends School in Washington, D.C., during his father's second elected term as United States Senator. Graduating from the Massachusetts Institute of Technology with a degree in mechanical engineering in 1902, he followed the family career track by assuming a position in the lower levels of the VERMONT MARBLE COMPANY and advancing through the ranks, assuming the presidency in 1935 and serving until 1952, when he became chairman of the board of directors. Entering politics, he was elected to the town of Proctor's selectboard, to two terms in the Vermont house (1912–1916), and a term in the Senate (1916–1918). During World War I, he served as a captain in the Army Corps of Engineers. In 1922, he was elected governor, becoming the third Proctor to hold that office following his father and elder brother. As governor, he instituted an executive budget that the governor was then responsible for proposing to the legislature. Other administrative reforms included instituting a director of budget responsible to the governor and establishing the governor's authority to fill house vacancies and to remove commission members appointed by the senate. After leaving office, Proctor maintained leadership of the Vermont Marble Company and served as a trustee and benefactor of universities and philanthropic societies.

Proctor, Redfield, Sr. (1831–1908)

Governor, secretary of war, and United States senator, Redfield Proctor, Sr., was born in the village of Proctorsville in the town of Cavendish. He attended local schools and graduated from Dartmouth, class of 1851, and Albany Law School in 1859. That same year, he was admitted to the Vermont and New York bars. He enlisted in the Third Vermont Volunteers in

Redfield Proctor, Sr. Special Collections, Bailey/Howe Library, University of Vermont

1861 and was soon promoted to major of the Fifth Regiment, serving with them for twelve months in the Washington defenses and on the Virginia Peninsula. In 1862, he commanded the Fifteenth Vermont at Gettysburg and helped quell the draft riots in New York City. Mustered out in August 1863, Proctor returned to Vermont and settled in Rutland, entering into a law practice with WHEELOCK G. VEAZEY, with whom he organized the politically potent Reunion Society of Vermont Officers. Six years later, he gave up the law to manage the Sutherland Falls Marble Company near Rutland. The marble company's business grew with the nation's post-war prosperity and consolidated with the Rutland Marble Company as the VERMONT MARBLE COMPANY, with Proctor as president. Drawing from quarries in the Rutland-Pittsford area, the company employed two hundred and fifty gangs of saws continuously from Monday morning to Saturday night, shipping product to distribution centers as far distant as St. Louis and San Francisco. Entering public service as a selectman, Proctor served in the Vermont general assembly as representative from Rutland in 1867 and 1868, and in 1888 from Proctor, a town carved out in 1886 from the towns of Rutland and Pittsford. He was elected a senator from Rutland County in 1874, lieutenant governor in 1876, and governor in 1878. A fiscal conservative, he gloried in Vermont being the first state to pay off its Civil War debt while

laboring with little success to reduce state expenses, especially court expenses between 1860 and 1876, which had become the largest cost of state government. He struggled also to eliminate substantial town debts. President Benjamin Harrison appointed Proctor secretary of war in 1889, in which office he worked to improve coastal defenses, reduce corruption by instituting more rigorous record keeping and procurement procedures, and professionalize the officer corps. When he refused to fly the flag at half mast for thirty days before the War Department on the death of the Confederacy's President Jefferson Davis in 1889, thus denying Davis the traditional honor given former secretaries of war, citizens of Tupelo, Mississippi, hanged Proctor in effigy. He resigned the cabinet post to fill a vacant Vermont seat in the United States Senate, first by appointment in 1891 and then by election in 1892 and re-election in 1898 and 1904. During the Cuban revolution of 1897 to 1898, Proctor was instrumental in securing the appointment of GEORGE DEWEY as commander of the Asian Fleet. He went to Cuba to observe the effects of Spanish rule at first hand and returned to report in a Senate speech that Spain was responsible for half a million Cubans starving to death "at our very doors." Some contemporaries credited Proctor's speech, not the sinking of the USS *Maine*, as "America's highest and best justification for going to war," and the major influence in persuading Congress to demand Spain's departure from Cuba. Influential at the national level of the REPUBLICAN PARTY, he framed the gold plank of the 1896 Republican platform. The Republican National Committee also sent Proctor to California and Oregon in 1896 to revive a badly divided Republican effort to elect William McKinley to the presidency. Presidents Harrison, McKinley, and Theodore Roosevelt, all personal friends of Proctor, accepted his invitations to visit Vermont. Proctor was reported to be the wealthiest member of Congress during his terms in the Senate. The Vermont Marble Company that he organized in 1880 is today owned by a foreign corporation, but it continues to own quarries and extract marble from several locations in Vermont. *Donald Wickman*

Prohibition

Vermont struggled to control the sale and abuse of alcohol as early as 1853, when the state followed Maine in passing a temperance law. Despite the obvious damage to individuals and society resulting from alcohol abuse, the temperance law never won broad public support. Additionally, the police force during the nineteenth century consisted only of the town constable and the county sheriff, who provided limited or no government control of alcohol consumption. In 1918, the U.S. Congress finally prohibited the manufacture and consumption of alcohol by the Eighteenth Amendment to the Constitution and the Volstead Act to enforce the prohibitions. During the fifteen years of Prohibition, Vermonters traveled by car and boat to acquire alcohol from whiskey warehouses conveniently located above the Canadian border. Occasionally intercepted by U.S. Customs agents upon returning to Vermont, a small state where smugglers and customs agents had often grown up together and even married each other's sisters, the interception rate was not high. Nonetheless, at least three federal agents and several civilians were killed in Vermont during police efforts to prevent smuggling.

Prouty, Charles Azro (1853–1921)
An attorney, lumber merchant, and longtime member of the Federal Interstate Commerce Commission, Charles Azro Prouty of Newport graduated from Dartmouth College at the head of his class in 1875. He spent a year at the Allegheny City Observatory in Pennsylvania, but ill health forced his return to Newport. Prouty then read the law under Theophilus Grout and was admitted to the bar in Vermont in 1877. In addition to practicing law, Prouty was the principal of Newport Academy for two years, was elected state's attorney in 1882 and 1884, and to the Vermont house of representatives in 1888. From 1888 to 1896, Prouty was reporter of decisions for the Vermont Supreme Court. He helped to found both the Newport Electric Company and the Orleans Trust Company, the latter of which he also served as president. Prouty was appointed to the Interstate Commerce Commission (ICC) in 1896 by President Grover Cleveland, and served as a commissioner until 1914. Having been counsel for both the Central Vermont Railroad and the Rutland Railroad, Prouty was well prepared for the role the ICC played in regulating RAILROAD commerce. Prouty helped to make the ICC the regulatory agency for railroad rates and encouraged Congress to grant the ICC the

power to valuate railroad property. When Congress did authorize the ICC to valuate railroad property, Prouty became the first director of valuation in 1914. In Vermont's first popular election of a United States senator on November 3, 1914, Prouty lost to WILLIAM DILLINGHAM.   *Chris Burns*

Prouty, Winston (1906–1971)
A native of Newport and educated in local schools, Winston Prouty attended the Bordentown (New Jersey) Military Institute and graduated from Lafayette College in Easton, Pennsylvania. After college, he entered the family lumber and building supplies business, Prouty and Miller, and quickly became active in civic affairs consistent with being a member of a distinguished political family. Uncle CHARLES PROUTY had been chairman of the Interstate Commerce Commission and uncle George Prouty had been governor of Vermont. A founder, in the 1930s, of the Young Republicans of Vermont, Winston Prouty served as alderman in Newport from 1933 to 1937 and 1941 to 1943, and as mayor from 1938 until 1941. In 1936, he was a supporter of GEORGE D. AIKEN for governor. He was elected to the Vermont house of representatives in 1941, 1945, and 1947, and was speaker of the house in 1948. After a term as chairman of the Water Conservation Board (1948–1950), he served four terms in the United States House of Representatives (1951–1958), and then succeeded RALPH FLANDERS in the United States Senate, where he served until his death, winning re-election in the 1964 Goldwater debacle and in 1970 against the popular Democrat and former governor PHILIP HOFF. A moderate Republican, Prouty was known for his support of health care, education, worker training, programs for the elderly, and the expansion of Social Security coverage and benefits. He was also an early backer of Amtrak and the construction of the St. Lawrence Seaway. Although he rose to become ranking minority member of important committees, he was continually overshadowed by his senior Senate colleague George D. Aiken.   *Ann E. Cooper*

Prouville de Tracy, Alexandre de
(ca. 1596–1670)
When the Iroquois threatened to obliterate New France in the 1660s, attacking settlements and even massacring Algonquins under the walls of Quebec, Louis XIV ordered lieutenant governor of New France

Alexandre de Prouville de Tracy to carry the war to the Iroquois' homeland, sending him the CARIGNAN-SALIERES REGIMENT to lead the attack. In 1665, de Tracy built forts on the Richelieu River at Chambly and Sainte-Therese and then sent PIERRE DE ST. PAUL, SIEUR DE LA MOTTE in the same year to construct FORT SAINTE-ANNE on an island in LAKE CHAMPLAIN that later was named for him. Manned by a detachment from the Carignan-Salieres regiment, the fort on Isle La Motte was finally abandoned by the French in 1669.
          Joseph-André Senécal

Putney
Putney, population 2,634, a town in Windham County, was granted by BENNING WENTWORTH in 1753 and presumably named for Putney in England, now part of greater London. The landscape rises from the broad meadows of the CONNECTICUT RIVER, which forms the town's eastern boundary, through a series of hills and valleys to 1,660-foot Putney Mountain on the western border with Brookline. The main settlement is Putney village. Craft shops and studios, bed and breakfasts, and a variety of eating establishments cater to a well-developed tourist trade. The Putney School (which includes a working farm), Greenwood School and LANDMARK COLLEGE (both for dyslexic students), and the Oak Meadow School (devoted to home-schooling support) provide educational opportunities. In the 1840s, Putney was the site of an experiment in bible communism led by JOHN HUMPHREY NOYES, who later founded the Oneida Community in New York State. GEORGE AIKEN, Vermont's governor and later U.S. Senator, lived in Putney, as did JODY WILLIAMS, winner of the 1997 Nobel Peace Prize. Novelist John Irving, who has won several awards for his fiction, including an Oscar for the screenplay of the movie made from his novel *The Cider House Rules*, maintains a part-time residence in Putney.

R

Railroads

Railroads came late to Vermont. In 1840, there were almost 3,000 miles of railroad track laid in the United States, two-thirds of it in the New England and Middle Atlantic states. By 1848, travelers and goods could move by rail between the East Coast and large portions of the Old Northwest, almost to Chicago. But Vermont did not get its first railroad until December 1849, with the completion of the Rutland and Burlington, followed a few weeks later by the opening of the Vermont Central linking White River Junction and Essex Junction. By 1869, nine railroad lines snaked north and south through the state connecting Boston and Montreal, and one—the Grand Trunk—connecting Portland, Maine, and Montreal with a loop through the NORTHEAST KINGDOM and an important depot at Island Pond. For the next thirty years, railroad building flourished, with over twenty lines constructed to link Vermont's interior with the main north-south routes serving Boston, New York, and Montreal, bringing opportunities to some and making fortunes for others. Governors CHARLES PAINE, JOHN GREGORY SMITH, ERASTUS FAIRBANKS, and PERCIVAL CLEMENT were all railroad owners or deeply invested in them. So was WILLIAM SEWARD WEBB of Shelburne, who was related to the Vanderbilts of the New York Central Railroad and wanted to be governor but never received the nomination. The railroads brought Irish workers for construction, and Welsh, Scandinavian, Italian, and other European artisans to the burgeoning SLATE, MARBLE, and granite industries. The railroads opened Vermont's lumber, dairy, and extractive resources to large eastern markets, and its industries, such as the HOWE SCALE Works in Rutland, Fairbanks Scales in St. Johnsbury, and the MACHINE-TOOL INDUSTRY in Springfield and Windsor to national markets. The railroads also promoted Vermont's potential as a tourist attraction. They brought summer tourists from eastern seaboard cities to spas and resorts, which the companies frequently built or owned, and promoted tour packages using lavishly illustrated publications. Railroads were a troubled industry, however. Despite the fortunes they made for their owners, the companies struggled financially with expensive construction and maintenance costs and a relatively low volume of freight. They changed hands often and suffered from the opportunism of owners, a lack of continuity in management, and bad reputations. Many acquired derogatory nicknames: the Ogdensburg and LAKE CHAMPLAIN (O&LC) was known as the Old and Late Coming; the Hoosac Tunnel and Wilmington became Hold Tight and Worry; the WEST RIVER Railroad was called Thirty-Six Miles of Trouble. In the twentieth century, Vermont's railroads eventually lost out to trucks and cars for transporting Vermonters and most of what they imported and exported. The single event most destructive to railroads in the twentieth century was the FLOOD OF 1927 when floodwaters destroyed hundreds of miles of tracks and dozens of bridges. When the state failed to provide major assistance to railroad restoration, several lines and many miles of tracks were abandoned. By the early 1960s, a strike by workers on the Rutland Railroad brought an end to rail transport along the western side of the state. Soon after the Rutland's demise, passenger traffic over the Central Vermont ceased. Since the early 1970s, however, Amtrak has restored limited passenger service to Vermont.   *Michael Sherman*

Randolph

Randolph, population 4,853, a town in Orange County, was granted by the Vermont legislature in 1780 and most likely named after one of the Randolphs of Virginia, probably either Peyton Randolph (1721?–1775), first president of the Continental Congress, or Edmund Randolph (1753–1813), who was part of a committee to examine Vermont's request to be admitted to the federal union. The landscape consists of a height of land running north and south through the town, encompassed by the Second Branch of the WHITE RIVER on the east and the Third Branch on the west. The original settlement of Randolph Center, located on the height of land, was eventually superseded in size by Randolph village in the valley of the Third Branch, where water power for mills was available and where the railroad eventually was built. The village, which contains the handsome Chandler Music Hall, serves as a regional shopping, dining, and entertainment center. At one time, Randolph hoped to be the capital of Vermont because of its central location in the state, but Montpelier was chosen instead. VERMONT TECHNICAL COLLEGE, one of the five state colleges, is located in Randolph Center. JUSTIN MORGAN, musician, schoolmaster, and developer of the MORGAN HORSE, lived in Randolph from 1788 until his death in 1798.

Ransom, Truman Bishop (1802–1847)

Born in Woodstock, Truman Ransom worked as a chairmaker and musician in order to pay for his education while attending the American Literary, Scientific and Military Academy (later NORWICH UNIVERSITY). After completing his course of studies in 1825, Ransom taught mathematics and music at the academy before establishing short-lived schools on the Norwich model in New Jersey and North Carolina. From 1832 to 1834, Ransom served as acting president of Jefferson College in Mississippi, which also adopted the educational philosophy of his mentor ALDEN PARTRIDGE. Ransom joined the Norwich University faculty in 1834 and taught natural philosophy, political economy, civil engineering, and military science. He served as president from 1844 to 1847 when he resigned to join the New England Ninth Regiment during the Mexican War. Ransom had been active in the Vermont militia, rising to the rank of major general. He also published a book on tactics for the militia of the United States in 1838. After Franklin Pierce left the command of the Ninth Regiment, Truman Ransom replaced him. Ransom was killed while leading his regiment in a charge at the fortress of Chapultepec located near Mexico City.   *Gary T. Lord*

Raymond, Henry Jarvis (1820–1869)

Co-founder of the *New York Times* and among the founders of the REPUBLICAN PARTY, Henry J. Raymond was born in Lima, New York, and graduated from the UNIVERSITY OF VERMONT in 1840 with high honors, a distinction one biographer thought "more than they were worth" since while at UVM he contracted the habit of overwork that led to his early death. Influenced by JAMES MARSH, his favorite professor at UVM, he taught several terms in country schools before going to New York City where he found work with HORACE GREELEY on the *New*

Yorker, a weekly he had contributed to while in college. Raymond subsequently became Greeley's chief assistant on the *New York Tribune*, and was elected as a Whig to the New York Assembly in 1849 and speaker in 1851. That year, in association with GEORGE JONES, who had worked in the *Tribune*'s business office, he established the *New York Daily Times* with himself as editor and Jones as business manager. Breaking with the WHIG PARTY over slavery, he wrote the statement of principles for the founding of the Republican party and assumed a leadership role in the party organization. A loyal supporter of President Lincoln, Raymond was credited with managing the nomination of Andrew Johnson as vice president at Lincoln's request. His subsequent support for President Johnson led to clashes with radical Republicans, particularly THADDEUS STEVENS after 1866 when Raymond was elected to Congress. By 1868, however, he and the *Times* were back in the Republican fold. Among the most-respected newspaper editors of his era, at the time of his death he had begun the *Times* campaign to expose William Marcy "Boss" Tweed and his followers that Jones completed.

Reading

Reading (pronounced Redding), population 707, a town in Windsor County, was granted by BENNING WENTWORTH in 1761 and named for Reading, Massachusetts, the home town of a number of the grantees. Located in the eastern foothills of the GREEN MOUNTAINS, Reading is marked by a number of summits over 2,000 feet, the highest of which is 2,478-foot Mount Tom, in the Coolidge State Forest. The several small settlements include Felchville (Reading post office), Hammondsville, and South Reading, the first two on Route 106, which crosses the eastern section of the town from north to south. Probably the single most photographed site in Vermont, the Jenne farm, which has appeared on magazine covers, posters, calendars, advertisements, jigsaw puzzles, and in at least two films (*Funny Farm* and *Forrest Gump*), and has a Web site devoted to the best way to photograph it, is in Reading.

Readsboro

A town in Bennington County with a population of 809, Readsboro derives from a New York patent of 1770 to John Reade. Although Governor BENNING WENT-WORTH of New Hampshire also granted land in the same area, the Vermont legislature eventually recognized the primacy of the New York patent in resolving land title disputes. Rugged and heavily forested, the town is bounded on the south by the Massachusetts border and is approximately halfway between Bennington and Brattleboro. Cutting southeast to northwest across it is Route 100, on which lies the main settlement of Readsboro village. Approximately a third of the town's 23,000 acres is federally owned as part of the GREEN MOUNTAIN NATIONAL FOREST. From the beginning, industries using wood played a major part in the town's economic history. The Readsboro Chair Company, founded in 1874, operated into the 1980s, when it was known as Vermont Hardwoods. A narrow-gauge RAILROAD from the Hoosac Tunnel in Massachusetts to Readsboro was built in 1884, and later extended to Wilmington as the Hoosac Tunnel and Wilmington Railroad, popularly called the Hold Tight and Worry. The town now has about thirty small businesses, including several cottage industries and at-home computer workers.

Reapportionment

After the 1964 Vermont Supreme Court decision in *Buckley v. Hoff*, which was based on the decision of the U.S. Supreme Court in *Baker v. Carr* and *Reynolds v. Sims*, the Vermont General Assembly in May 1965 voted to reapportion its house and senate. The state senate, the chamber initially reflecting population, was kept at thirty members but each county was no longer granted at least one senator. Instead, senate districts were created to meet the "one person, one vote" principle. The Vermont house, like the United States Senate, had been apportioned on the basis of political geography and each town or city had elected one representative. Before reapportionment, Stratton, population 24, had the same representation as Burlington, population 35,000, and 200,000 rural Vermonters elected 225 representatives while their 190,000 urban neighbors elected only 21. The new plan reduced the house to 150 representatives apportioned according to the "one person, one vote" principle.

Redding, David (d. 1778)

In an incident more like a lynching than a legal procedure, New Yorker David Redding was the first person to be tried and hanged in the state of Vermont. Redding had been a Loyalist with BURGOYNE's army at Saratoga, stolen horses, shot, and powder in New York, and eluded arrest there by riding into Vermont, where he was caught and tried in Bennington for theft and treason and convicted. When it appeared that Redding would go free because of an improperly empanelled jury, ETHAN ALLEN, back in Vermont only a few days after nearly three years as a British prisoner, arranged with Governor THOMAS CHITTENDEN to serve as prosecutor in a new trial on June 6, 1778. Allen ignored the threshold issue of jurisdiction, which the Bennington court lacked for crimes committed in New York. Moreover, as Vermont was independent from the thirteen states, the United States' cause against Redding was also not in the court's jurisdiction. Nonetheless, Allen's empassioned anti-Loyalist rhetoric swung the jury away from the legal question to the patriotic requirement of hanging a Loyalist and Redding was hanged in the afternoon of the trial before a large crowd on Bennington green.

Redfield, Isaac Fletcher (1804–1876)

Isaac Fletcher Redfield, a native of Weathersfield, was elected to the Vermont Supreme Court in 1834 and spent the next twenty-four years on the court, the last twelve as chief judge, finally retiring in 1860. Of him, EDWARD J. PHELPS wrote, "No man was ever more capable of appreciating and profiting by good argument or was more candidly open to its influence." Redfield graduated from Dartmouth College in 1825, studied law, and was admitted to practice in 1827, opening an office in Derby. He served as state's attorney (1832–1835), and in 1835 was appointed to the Vermont Supreme Court. While on the court he wrote *The Law of Railways* (1857), which quickly earned international acclaim as the first treatise on the subject. After retiring from the Vermont Supreme Court, he moved to Boston to write and publish treatises on wills and equity. He edited the *American Law Register* while practicing law and consulting on law suits. He served as special counsel for the United States in England, sorting out claims to Confederate property in that country. His brother Timothy Redfield also served on the Vermont Supreme Court (1870–1884).
Paul Gillies

Remy de Courçelle, Daniel, sieur de Montigny (1626–1698)

Appointed governor of New France in 1665, Daniel de Remy de Courçelle was instrumental in subduing the Iroquois, the long-time enemies of New France. Following his predecessor ALEXANDRE DE PROUVILLE DE TRACY's plan, Remy de Courçelle hastened the construction of new forts along the Richelieu River and LAKE CHAMPLAIN, the traditional Mohawk invasion route into New France. The CARIGNAN-SALIERES REGIMENT was sent from France to garrison the forts and crush the Mohawks. In January 1666, de Courçelle led six hundred men to the northernmost island in Lake Champlain where they were to join a party of Algonquin guides. When the guides failed to appear, Remy de Courçelle marched his force south on the ice toward the Mohawk settlements near Albany. Wandering without guides, the French stumbled upon settlements in which they learned that the Dutch had ceded New Netherlands to England. Eventually, settlers aided the French force, which returned to Montreal without engaging the Mohawk. In September 1666, Remy de Courçelle gathered at the recently completed FORT SAINTE-ANNE on Isle La Motte the largest army ever seen in that part of the world, fourteen hundred French and one hundred Huron and Algonquin who went on to burn and pillage four Mohawk villages close to Albany. The Iroquois were pacified by this powerful attack until the 1690s, when the Oneida and Onondaga assaulted settlements along the St. Lawrence from Montreal to Trois Rivières.   *Joseph-André Senécal*

Republican Party

In July 1854, anticipating the collapse of the national WHIG PARTY, Vermont political managers, fusing anti-slavery, nativist, temperance, and pro-tariff sentiment, coalesced Whigs and FREE-SOILERS into a Republican party. In the years immediately prior to 1853, the Whigs had succeeded in organizing the legislature and electing the governor. That year, however, despite Whig legislative and gubernatorial pluralities, Free-Soil and DEMOCRATIC legislators united to organize the house and elect a Democratic governor and subject the Whigs to a defeat from which they never recovered. In July 1854, in combination with Free-Soilers and free Democrats, Whigs collaborated on a joint slate and platform, the latter calling for the non-extension of slavery and a protective tariff. Referring to themselves as Republicans, their candidates were swept into office. The exception was a congressional race in which Whig JUSTIN MORRILL faced a Republican opponent. Morrill emerged the only candidate for a major state office to win without Republican support, but he cast his first vote in Congress as a Republican. It would be 1958 before any Republican would lose a race for Congress and 1962 before the GOP would lose a governor's contest. The antebellum years were marked by continuing anti-slavery agitation, ardent nativism— the most-popular Republican candidates were often drawn from the state's KNOW-NOTHING leadership—and uncompromising pro-Union sentiment. At the outbreak of the Civil War, pro-Union Democrats defected to the Republicans and were accepted into leadership positions. By 1870, candidates were routinely attracting 70 percent of the statewide vote. Republicans frequently claimed over 200 of the 240 or so house members and all 30 senators. The first genuine threat to Republican hegemony occurred in 1902, when PERCIVAL CLEMENT challenged the prohibition law in effect since 1853 and succeeded in having it replaced with a local option law. In the process, he defected from the party and ran in the general election as a Local Option candidate. In the three-man race, the Republican candidate, JOHN G. McCULLOUGH, won a plurality but was denied a popular majority and was subsequently elected by the legislature. Legislative elections for constitutional officers were a common phenomenon before the party's founding, but this marked the first time the Republican party was forced into a legislative election for a constitutional officer. A second occasion occurred in September 1912, when a Progressive candidate along with a Democrat denied Republican Allen Fletcher a popular majority and again necessitated an election by the legislature. That November, with Bull Moose candidate Theodore Roosevelt drawing large numbers of Republican voters elsewhere, William Howard Taft captured the state in the presidential election, giving Vermont the distinction of being the only state with Utah to vote Republican. Vermont added another such distinction in 1936, when along with Maine, it voted for Alf Landon against Franklin Roosevelt. In the course of its long dominion over state politics, the party utilized informal understandings that helped sustain an orderly transfer of office and have since been abandoned. Chief among them were rotation in office and the "mountain rule." Separate in principle, they were linked in practice. Governors were initially limited to two years in office and, after 1928, to two two-year terms. The mountain rule circumscribed a candidate's eligibility by whether he resided on the east or west side of the GREEN MOUNTAINS. A governor from the west was succeeded by a governor from the east and served with a lieutenant governor from the opposite side of the mountains. Since 1791, when Vermont became the fourteenth state, until 1946, there was an eastern and a western U.S. Senate seat. Nineteen forty-six was also memorable as the only time an incumbent governor was defeated in a primary contest. ERNEST W. GIBSON, JR., who along with Senator GEORGE AIKEN led the more liberal faction of the party, defeated MORTIMER PROCTOR, heir to the Proctor or more conservative wing. Gibson was re-elected in 1948 but resigned in 1949 after President Harry Truman nominated him to become Vermont's Federal District Court Judge. In the 1960s, rotation and mountain-rule strictures crumbled under the force of Democratic electoral successes. Although the state continued to lead the nation in percentage voting for Republican presidential candidates, by 1952, growing Democratic minorities for lesser offices were a harbinger of changing party fortunes. In 1958, the GOP lost the state's sole seat in the U.S. House to Democrat WILLIAM H. MEYER, recaptured it in 1960, and lost it again in 1990, this time to Independent BERNARD SANDERS, who proved invulnerable to over a decade of challenges. In 1962, a party split proved a luxury Republicans could no longer afford in the face of increased Democratic strength, and PHILIP HOFF was elected governor. The Republican incumbent, F. RAY KEYSER, JR., managed to garner more Republican votes than Hoff did Democratic, and the election was decided by third-party support. The 1964 Goldwater-Johnson presidential campaign led to mass defections, proving a disaster from which the state Republican party has yet to recover fully. Democrats captured all statewide offices and for the first time in history Vermonters cast their electoral votes for a Democratic presidential candidate. By 1992, Vermont ranked among the most reliable Democratic presidential states in the nation. It was also losing its Republican senators. In 1975, when George Aiken retired, he was replaced by Democrat PATRICK

LEAHY; in 2001, Senator JAMES JEFFORDS left the Republican Party to become an Independent. His seat had been a Republican seat longer than any Senate seat in the nation. Despite Vermont's quintessential conservative image, the state Republican party long enjoyed a livelier reform tradition than that of its Democratic counterpart. The overwhelmingly rural Republican legislature was among the first in the nation to institute electoral reforms, apply state aid formulas, and frequently adopted progressive and even occasional New Deal reforms in advance of other states. After court-ordered REAPPORTIONMENT in 1965, Republican legislative majorities were gradually reduced until the party lost its house majority in 1983 and its senate majority in 1985. A testimony to the state party's historic defiance of political orthodoxy (or lack of party discipline) is that even before losing its Republican majority, the house elected Democratic speakers. Although more recently Republicans have been a minority in both houses, in 2000 they were able to recapture the house in protest against recently enacted social and economic legislation.

Rice, Howard Crosby (1878–1965)

Owner and publisher of the *BRATTLE-BORO REFORMER* for more than fifty years, Howard C. Rice was born in Worcester, Massachusetts, but returned with his parents to their hometown of Brattleboro when he was an infant. After graduating from Brattleboro High School and a European grand tour in 1896, he went to work as a reporter for a year on the *Vermont Phoenix* and from 1898 to 1901 on the *Daily Sentinel* in Ansonia, Connecticut. Returning to Vermont in late 1901, he worked first as a reporter for the *Windham County Reformer* and in 1903 acquired an interest in the Vermont Printing Company, which bought the *Reformer* in that year. The *Reformer* and the *Phoenix* were consolidated in 1913 and the *Reformer* issued as a daily newspaper. Howard Rice was business manager of the two papers until 1918, when he became editor and publisher, a position he held until the 1960s. Rice served six consecutive terms in the Vermont General Assembly, 1933 to 1944, as either town representative for Brattleboro or senator for Windham County. He professed a simple political philosophy: "I made it my point to get as many people as possible under obligation to me and to get under obligation to as few as possible."

During both world wars, Rice was chairman of Brattleboro's War Chest. He was president of the Brattleboro Memorial Hospital and president of the board of trustees of KURN HATTIN for many years.

Rice, Joseph John (1871–1938)

The third Roman Catholic bishop of Vermont, Joseph John Rice was educated at Holy Cross College in Massachusetts (1891), Laval University, Quebec (1894), and the Urban College of the Propaganda, Rome (1896), and ordained a priest in 1896 in Springfield, Massachusetts. After pastoral work in the Springfield Diocese and among the Penobscot Indians of Maine, he was appointed bishop of Burlington in 1910. Bishop Rice almost immediately initiated reforms in Catholic secondary education. Recognizing that two-year secondary academies provided inadequate educations, he expanded high schools to four years, built six new high schools (in Burlington, Brattleboro, Montpelier, Swanton, and Rutland), opened St. Albans' all-girls Villa Barlow to boys, and started eight new elementary schools. He established the policy of opening schools to students from surrounding parishes, with home parishes paying tuition to the receiving school. To improve the quality of education offered in Catholic schools, in 1913 he authorized Vermont's religious communities to send teaching sisters to the UNIVERSITY OF VERMONT to pursue degrees. Ten sisters attended that first summer, and by the 1920s, increasing numbers of teaching sisters were completing college degrees each year. In response to a request from Burlington authorities during the INFLUENZA EPIDEMIC OF 1918, Bishop Rice opened an emergency hospital in Burlington High School under the direction of the Religious Hospitalers of St. Joseph from the nearby Fanny Allen Hospital. Rice also requested religious sisters throughout Vermont to care for the sick in their homes and several hundred victims of the Spanish flu received their only care from the visiting sisters. In 1919, a bill was proposed in the Vermont legislature that purported to "Promote Americanism in Schools" by abolishing the teaching of foreign languages in the state's schools. Vermont's Catholic high schools taught Latin and French, and sometimes Spanish and German. Especially in parishes of Francophonic Vermonters, French was often taught and commonly used in the elementary school

and in parts of the church service on Sunday. In a letter to house member Ira La-Fleur, Bishop Rice publicly opposed the bill for its suspect motives and likely anti-educational effects. The bill died in committee. Bishop Rice also oversaw the construction of the Bishop DeGoesbriand Hospital in Burlington in 1925.

David Blow

Richford

Richford, population 2,321, a town in Franklin County, was granted by the Vermont legislature in 1780. No specific origin for the name is known, and it may have been created to imply the potential value of the location. The substantial village of Richford, for many years a RAILROAD and woodworking center, lies on both banks of the MISSISQUOI RIVER a mile from the Canadian border in the northwestern part of the town. The town's former prosperity began to decline in the 1960s as businesses closed, until today when many residents commute to jobs in surrounding towns. Recent projects both public and private, however, have sparked a modest economic upswing. The eastern part of Richford is largely unsettled, lying as it does along the western flank of the northernmost GREEN MOUNTAINS, which rise to 3,870-foot Jay Peak just across the border in the town of Westfield.

Richmond

Richmond, population 4,090, a town in Chittenden County, was created by an act of the Vermont legislature in 1794 out of segments of the neighboring towns of Jericho, Williston, Huntington, and (in 1804) Bolton. The origin of the name is obscure. Richmond sits at a prime location, where the WINOOSKI RIVER emerges from the forested foothills of the GREEN MOUNTAINS into the fertile lowlands of the Champlain Valley. The main settlement is Richmond village, although Jonesville, near the eastern border with Bolton, was in the past the site of a large lumber mill. Across the river from Richmond village is a National Historic Landmark, the ROUND CHURCH (actually sixteen-sided), built in 1813 by the village's five Protestant sects for common use. It also served as the town hall for 160 years, until 1974. Richmond's proximity to the Burlington metropolitan area has led to an increase in large-lot residential building, although the main impression is still small-town and rural.

Riedesel, Friedrich Adolphus Baron von (1738–1800)

Born in Lauterbach in the Rhineland, Baron von Riedesel served bravely in the Seven Years' War as an aide to Duke Ferdinand of Brunswick, achieving the rank of colonel of hussars by 1757. By a treaty of 1776 between Britain and several petty sovereigns of German states, four thousand Brunswick troops under the command of Major General Riedesel were taken into the regular British army to fight the rebels in America. Riedesel and his troops joined the British army in Quebec on June 1, 1776. In Guy CARLETON's autumn campaign that year into the Champlain Valley, Riedesel had moved his troops up the lake only as far as Point au Fer when Carleton, after his victory at the BATTLE OF VALCOUR ISLAND, withdrew north for the winter. The British invasion in the following spring brought Riedesel's German brigade on the British left wing to the east shore of LAKE CHAMPLAIN at CHIMNEY POINT nearly in sight of four to five thousand Americans on MOUNT INDEPENDENCE in Vermont and at FORT TICONDEROGA across the lake in New York. On July 2, Riedesel had moved his troops to the north bank of East Creek. On the fifth, the Americans set fire to Fort Independence and withdrew during the night. After taking the fort, Riedesel went on in daylight to support General Simon Fraser's pursuit of the Americans retreating toward Hubbardton. The British had engaged the American rear guard, which, though taking heavy losses, was hurting Fraser's men. Before rushing into the battle, Riedesel ordered his small band of musicians to precede the company of jägers (rangers) that he sent against the Americans, who were threatening to get the better of Fraser, making the rebel rear guard think Riedesel's force was greater than it really was. The Americans retreated, leaving twelve cannon to Riedesel's men. During the next week, SETH WARNER grouped a force of four to five thousand men around Manchester, while urging local men to strengthen his force. After Riedesel went to Castleton with Loyalist PHILIP SKENE and took loyalty oaths from four hundred inhabitants, Warner quickly attacked and plundered the newly sworn Loyalists. Riedesel sent seventy men toward Tinmouth to discourage Warner and another detachment to Wells, while he personally led a force toward Rutland. Riedesel counselled General BURGOYNE against attacking Bennington for the Continental Army stores there. Subsequently, Riedesel's Brunswickers under Lieutenant Colonel Frederick Baum and the relief column under Colonel Breymann suffered over two hundred casualties in the August 16 engagement with the Americans at the Walloomsac River, an event called thereafter the BATTLE OF BENNINGTON. Riedesel's wife travelled with her husband through this campaign and kept a personal journal of her experiences that gives detailed and interesting insights into a British army at war.

Ripton

Ripton, population 556, a town in Addison County, was granted by the Vermont legislature in 1781 and named after Ripton Society (or parish), Connecticut, the birthplace of several of the original grantees. Wooded and mountainous, with its eastern border approximating the main spine of the GREEN MOUNTAINS, the town lies entirely within the GREEN MOUNTAIN NATIONAL FOREST. The highest peak is 3,823-foot Breadloaf Mountain. The tiny village of Ripton, once the site of twelve sawmills, is located on Route 125, the single road cutting across the town from east to west. Also on this road is the site of MIDDLEBURY COLLEGE'S BREAD LOAF WRITERS' CONFERENCE, founded in 1926 and held every August in an old Victorian summer resort. ROBERT FROST bought a summer home in Ripton in 1939 and later made the town his legal residence.

Riverside Women's Reformatory

Originally constructed in the nineteenth century as a prison for both men and women, the Rutland prison, complete with stone floors, heavy bars, and painted-over windows, was transformed into a women's prison in 1921 after standing unused for three years. Director of State Institutions JOHN E. WEEKS and Lena Ross, the new director of the women's prison, oversaw the construction of new facilities and amenities that included a recreation room, kitchen, dining room, and chapel. Renamed the Riverside Women's Reformatory, the institution was a change in Vermont's practice of imprisoning men and women in the same building. Women served prison terms at the Riverside Reformatory for illegal sales of whiskey and drugs, counterfeiting, theft, adultery, prostitution, and murder. The Riverside Reformatory was operated with a rehabilitative policy that claimed a low 6 percent recidivist rate for its released inmates, an accomplishment for which it gained national attention. In the 1940s, the number of Vermont women in prison began to decline, leading the state to accept prisoners from other state and federal prisons to help meet the cost of operating the Riverside Reformatory. As prison construction increased in other jurisdictions and Vermont decriminalized adultery, the Reformatory's inmate numbers declined to a handful. Some of the buildings were converted to other state functions, including probation offices and the Rutland municipal court. In 1967, the Riverside Reformatory for Women was closed and in 1970 the buildings were demolished.

Robinson, David (1754–1843)

Born in Hardwick, Massachusetts, David Robinson was the third son of SAMUEL ROBINSON, SR., of Bennington and a long-time public servant of Vermont and the United States. He fought as a private in the Vermont militia at the BATTLE OF BENNINGTON and continued on the militia rolls until 1817, rising to major general. He was sheriff of Bennington County from 1789 to 1811, and United States marshal from 1810 to 1818. Like his oldest brother MOSES ROBINSON, David married a daughter of STEPHEN FAY of Bennington, Sarah, by whom he fathered three sons, of whom Stephen (1781–1852) was a member of the General Assembly, a judge of the county court, and a member of the COUNCIL OF CENSORS.

Robinson, John S. (1804–1860)

Vermont's only Democratic governor since before the Civil War until 1963, John S. Robinson, the grandson of former governor, chief judge, and U.S. Senator MOSES ROBINSON, was heir to Bennington's most distinguished family name. An 1824 graduate of Williams College, he was admitted to the Vermont bar in 1827. Elected to the Vermont house in 1832 and 1833 and the senate in 1838 and 1839, his ambitions for higher office were thwarted by splits within the DEMOCRATIC PARTY over slavery. Unsuccessful in an 1836 congressional race, he also failed in his first two attempts for the governor's office. In 1851, as the candidate of the Free-Soil Democrats he managed barely 15 percent of the popular vote. Gaining the regular Democratic nomination in 1852, Robinson captured over

39 percent. Significantly, the Whig candidate, ERASTUS FAIRBANKS, fell just short of a popular majority and was elected by the legislature. Whig support of prohibition eroded both party and Fairbanks support and in the 1853 election, Fairbanks' plurality over Robinson significantly diminished as the Whigs lost control of the legislature. An anti-Whig legislative coalition elected Robinson and organized the legislature but their subsequent efforts at cooperation failed and the administration floundered. The following year, the Vermont REPUBLICAN PARTY formed and fielded its first gubernatorial candidate. Robinson did not run. Caught in the wake of a decaying Democratic party, Robinson nonetheless remained loyal. He died in 1860 after an apoplectic stroke while attending the Democratic National Convention in Charleston, South Carolina.

Robinson, Lewis (1793–1871)

Lewis Robinson, a.k.a. Roberson, of South Reading, was a successful publisher of engraved regional maps. He apprenticed at ISAAC EDDY's Weathersfield printing shop, where he published pamphlets, prints, and maps from 1816 to 1822, when he set up on his own in South Reading in the early 1820s. Robinson specialized in engraved maps of Vermont and New Hampshire, utilizing an extensive network of itinerant peddlers to sell his maps and prints, including the work of Eddy and Moody M. Peabody, throughout the North and Northeast. In 1836, he established a branch office in Akron, Ohio, and in 1844 he set up a shop in Stanstead, Quebec, publishing regional maps at each. Robinson remained working in South Reading until his death.   *J. Kevin Graffagnino and Marcus A. McCorison*

Robinson, Moses (1741–1813)

The first chief judge, a governor, and one of Vermont's first two United States senators, Moses Robinson was the second son of SAMUEL ROBINSON, SR., of Bennington. He was born at Hardwick, Massachusetts, and studied at Dartmouth College. He was elected Bennington's first town clerk, serving from 1762 to 1781. A colonel in the Vermont militia in early 1777, Robinson led his regiment in evacuating MOUNT INDEPENDENCE. He was a member of the Council of Safety in 1777 and the Governor's Council from 1778 to 1785. Upon the organization of Vermont in 1777, Robinson was appointed its chief judge, a position

he held until 1789, when he was elected governor for one year. Robinson was a confidential advisor to the Chittenden-Allen faction during the HALDIMAND NEGOTIATIONS and signed the certificate in 1781 that was drawn up to protect THOMAS CHITTENDEN, ETHAN and IRA ALLEN, and JONAS FAY during that affair. Sent to the Continental Congress in 1782 as an agent of Vermont, he was subsequently chosen one of the commissioners to adjust the controversy with New York over land claims and the states' mutual boundary. In 1791, he was chosen United States senator with STEPHEN R. BRADLEY by the General Assembly. Robinson was very active during the 1790s with the new Democratic Republicans, opposing the Jay Treaty and working against the Federalists. Robinson was warmly sympathetic to the French Revolution, unfriendly to Britain, and an ardent supporter of Thomas Jefferson and James Madison, who visited him in Bennington in 1791. While a faithful Democrat in civil affairs, in religious matters he strongly preferred a Congregationalist community, even to the point of refusing to sell his lands in Bennington to new settlers with differing religious views, steering them instead to land he owned in Pownal or Shaftsbury. His influence ensured that Bennington supported only one house of public worship until 1830. Moses Robinson's first wife, by whom he had six sons, was Mary Fay, daughter of STEPHEN FAY. Moses, the eldest, was a member of the Governor's Council in 1814 and represented Bennington in the General Assembly from 1819 to 1823. Unlike the rest of his family, he was a Federalist. The only time he was defeated in an election was when he omitted "Jr." from his name on the ballot.

Robinson, Rowland Evans (1833–1900)

Born at ROKEBY, his family's farm in Ferrisburgh, the artist and writer Rowland E. Robinson was the youngest of Rachel G. and ROWLAND T. ROBINSON's four children. Indifferently educated in the local schools and the Ferrisburgh Academy (operated by his father) until age thirteen, he read widely in the extensive library in his own home. An early artistic talent was indulged when he was sent to New York City to study engraving and drafting in his late teens. Robinson was to make numerous forays to New York over the next twenty years in search of work and markets for his illustrations, which he found in the agri-

cultural and sportsman's press of the day. His career in visual art was cut short by failing eyesight, but by the turn of the twentieth century he had become Vermont's most beloved author. His work falls into two main categories: the folk stories based on "Danvis," his imagined Vermont hill town, and nature essays. Written in scrupulously, if not painfully, accurate dialect, the Danvis stories provide a wonderfully vivid, if romanticized, picture of life in nineteenth-century Vermont. They are almost unknown outside of Vermont today and certainly under-appreciated. The nature essays were collected in several anthologies and express his deep sadness over the destruction of Vermont's woods, waters, and wildlife in the second half of the nineteenth century. Although much of his writing was composed after he was blind, it is marked by a sharpness of observation that can only come from the eye of an artist. Whether working in pictures or words, however, Robinson expressed his love of the Vermont landscape and the people who worked it. Robinson married Ann Stevens of Montpelier in 1870 and they had four children, including the artist RACHEL ROBINSON ELMER. He did not leave home again after 1873 and ran the farm with his brother George G. Robinson until his death in 1900.   *Jane Williamson*

Robinson, Rowland Thomas (1796–1879)

One of two children of Thomas and Jemima Robinson, Quakers from Newport, Rhode Island, who settled early in Ferrisburgh, Rowland T. Robinson received the "guarded education" many Friends sought for their children at this time, studying at a Quaker boarding school in Nine Partners, Dutchess County, New York. Here he met his future wife Rachel Gilpin and their lifelong friend Ann King. When the great split in the Religious Society of Friends came in 1828, Rowland and Rachel joined the reformist Hicksites, both serving as clerks of the Ferrisburgh Meeting. Radical reformers and religious perfectionists, the Robinsons were among the earliest and most outspoken opponents of slavery. He worked actively in anti-slavery societies from the local to the national, while she kept their home free of slave-made goods. Together they sheltered dozens of fugitive slaves, often offering them both a home and work on the farm for extended periods. Rowland T. Robinson was a lifelong believer in the ideas of WILLIAM LLOYD

GARRISON and followed the trajectory from abolition to nonresistance to spiritualism traveled by so many, particularly Hicksite Friends. He operated a school on his own property that was run on nonresistant principles and educated black and white children together, a practice unheard of at the time. Robinson knew and corresponded with many of the great reformers of the day—Garrison, Lucretia Mott, Charles C. Burleigh, Isaac T. Hopper, and Henry C. Wright, among others. His commitment to full equality for African-Americans never wavered; he offered work for freedmen after the Civil War and funds for black colleges as late as 1878. He lived his entire life at ROKEBY, the family farm and one of the largest merino sheep farms of the period. Among his four children was Vermont author ROWLAND EVANS ROBINSON. *Jane Williamson*

Robinson, Samuel, Jr. (b. 1738)

The oldest son of SAMUEL ROBINSON, SR., of Bennington, Samuel Robinson, Jr., was active in the New Hampshire grants controversy and after his father's death in 1767 was elected to succeed him on the town committee dealing with that issue. During the Revolution, he commanded a militia company at the BATTLE OF BENNINGTON and rose to colonel. In 1777 to 1778, he was in charge of Loyalist prisoners, and in 1779 to 1780, represented Bennington in the Vermont General Assembly and was a member of the Board of War. He was the first justice of the peace appointed in the town under Vermont authority and was one of the judges of the court for the south shire of Bennington County in 1778, when he presided at the trial of the Loyalist DAVID REDDING who was prosecuted by ETHAN ALLEN. Recently released from British captivity, Allen won a conviction against Redding on a charge of stealing a horse in New York State. BENJAMIN HOLMES, "the scourge of the Loyalists," carried out Robinson's sentence on the day of the trail, hanging Redding on the Bennington green.

Robinson, Samuel, Sr. (1705–1767)

The leader of the pioneer settlers of Bennington in 1761, Samuel Robinson, Sr., was born in Cambridge, Massachusetts, and was a resident of Hardwick in that state when he moved to Bennington. He knew the TACONIC MOUNTAINS and the territory west of the GREEN MOUNTAINS from his service as a captain of Massachu-

setts militia in several campaigns around Lake George and LAKE CHAMPLAIN during the final French and Indian War of 1754 to 1763. Governor BENNING WENTWORTH appointed him the first justice of the peace on the New Hampshire grants. When two settlers with New York and New Hampshire titles to the same land in Pownal came before Justice Robinson, he found for the New Hampshire title holder. After Samuel Ashley, a New Hampshire–appointed deputy sheriff, attempted to enforce Robinson's ruling and eject the New York title claimant, Robinson and Ashley were both arrested by a New York deputy, taken to the Albany jail, and indicted for resisting New York's officers, but released without a trial. Subsequent hostile correspondence between the governors of New York and New Hampshire heated up the controversy over conflicting land titles. In 1765, Robinson was sent by the Bennington landowners to negotiate a settlement with New York City land speculators who were acquiring grants from Lieutenant Governor Cadwallader Colden that overlapped New Hampshire grants, but he was unsuccessful. The next year, Bennington settlers and Connecticut speculators sent Robinson to England to present their case to the Crown, but Robinson died in London in 1767. Samuel Robinson was the progenitor of a Vermont family remarkable for its generations of public service. During the eighteenth and nineteenth centuries, his descendants included two governors, two United States senators, six judges of one degree or another, leaders of the Vermont DEMOCRATIC PARTY in three different generations, United States marshals, generals and colonels of the Vermont militia, state's attorneys, and town clerks.

Rochester

Rochester, population 1,171, a town in Windsor County, was granted by the Vermont legislature in 1781 and probably named for Rochester, Massachusetts. Located directly on the eastern slopes of the main spine of the GREEN MOUNTAINS and hemmed in on the east by a southern extension of Braintree Mountain, the town contains many summits in the 2,000- to 3,000-foot range, culminating in 3,366-foot Gillespie Peak in the extreme western section. The town's highly irregular shape, the most unusual aspect of which is a 6-mile-long spade-shaped area projecting deep into Addison and Rutland counties,

was caused by the accretion at various times of segments of the surrounding towns of Braintree, Goshen, Hancock, and Pittsfield. Inhabitants of the added segments had been cut off from the main villages of their respective towns by the mountainous topography. Rochester is bisected from north to south by the valley of the WHITE RIVER, on whose banks lies the main settlement of Rochester village on Route 100. Almost all of the town west of the highway is in the GREEN MOUNTAIN NATIONAL FOREST, through which runs Route 73 westward toward Brandon Gap in Goshen. Just south of Rochester village, the name Talcville marks the spot where a flourishing talc-mining operation existed in the early twentieth century. Verde antique MARBLE has also been quarried in the town. In recent decades, the number of dairy farms has dwindled to a handful, and the number of businesses taking advantage of computer and communications technology has grown.

Rock Point

An interesting geologic feature in Burlington, Rock Point has been the administrative center of the Protestant Episcopal Church in Vermont (Diocese of Vermont). In 1841, the Right Reverend JOHN H. HOPKINS, first Episcopal bishop of Vermont, established Rock Point as the bishop's home and eventually as the educational and administrative center of the diocese. On the rise known as Hemlock Hill, Hopkins erected a house where, until his death in 1868, he raised his family and administered the diocese and the school that he founded in 1860. A large Celtic cross marks his grave in a private cemetery on the Point. The Vermont Episcopal Institute opened at Rock Point in 1860 as a boys' school and theological seminary, but closed in 1899. From then until it was destroyed by fire in 1979, it housed conferences and retreats. Bishop Hopkins Hall opened in 1889 as a girls' school but closed in 1899. It reopened in 1928 as a school for boys and girls. A new bishop's house was built on Hemlock Hill in 1894. The Bishop Booth Conference Center, erected on the site of the Institute, opened in 1980. At the end of Rock Point is found the Lone Rock Thrust Fault, also known as Rock Point Overthrust, the most famous geological formation in the Burlington area. The fault occurred when ancient forces toppled dolomite—older, whitish limestone-like rocks—on top of younger, dark grey SHALE. *David Blow*

Rockefeller, Laurance S. (b. 1910), and **Mary French Rockefeller** (1910–1997)
Generous benefactors to Woodstock and dedicated stewards of the conservationist heritages of GEORGE PERKINS MARSH and FREDERICK BILLINGS, Mary F. and Laurance S. Rockefeller created the BILLINGS FARM & MUSEUM and the MARSH-BILLINGS-ROCKEFELLER NATIONAL HISTORICAL PARK from the land and buildings originally occupied by Marsh and Billings. Mary Rockefeller was the grand-daughter of Frederick Billings, and Laurance Rockefeller is the son of John D. Rockefeller, Jr. In 1954, following the death of her mother, Mary Montagu Billings French (1869–1951), Mary came to own the Marsh-Billings mansion and much of the adjoining Mount Tom forest. The Rockefellers made the mansion their principal summer residence, rehabilitating and preserving the character of the historic Queen Anne house. In 1967, fellow conservationist Lady Bird Johnson dedicated the mansion as a National Historic Landmark, emphasizing its importance as the boyhood home of George Perkins Marsh. The following year, the Rockefellers established the Woodstock Foundation, Inc., to further their preservation, civic, and philanthropic efforts. Laurance purchased, razed, and rebuilt the Woodstock Inn as a first-class resort that would anchor Woodstock's growing tourist economy. Through the 1970s and 1980s, the Woodstock Foundation and the Woodstock Resort Corporation undertook and supported numerous projects to enhance the community's quality of life, attractiveness, historic preservation, environmental quality, and economic sustainability. In 1974, Laurance acquired the Billings Farm, revitalizing the historic model farm of Frederick Billings and setting the stage for the creation of the Billings Farm & Museum in 1983. In 1992, Congress established the National Historical Park in anticipation of the Rockefellers' donation to the United States of the mansion, its historic artwork and furnishings, and the 555-acre Mount Tom forest. They also established a dedicated endowment, held by the Woodstock Foundation, to ensure the ongoing preservation of the park. Vermont's first unit of the National Park system, the park preserves and interprets the heritage of Marsh, Billings, and the Rockefellers as nationally significant conservationists and furthers appreciation of conservation stewardship in America. The park opened in 1998, operating in partnership with the Farm & Museum as a model of public-private partnership.   *David Donath*

Rockingham

Rockingham, population 5,309, a town in Windham County, was granted by BENNING WENTWORTH in 1752 and named for one of his relatives, Charles Watson–Wentworth (1730–1782), second marquis of Rockingham. The town lies on the CONNECTICUT RIVER and is cut by two of its tributaries, the Williams and Saxtons rivers. The original village of Rockingham, on a hillside above the Williams River, contains the Old Rockingham Meeting House, built in 1787, Vermont's oldest unchanged public building. The village was displaced early as the town's major settlement by Bellows Falls on the Connecticut, named after Colonel BENJAMIN BELLOWS, one of the original grantees. Bellows Falls sits at the spot where the river narrowed to the 50-foot Great Falls, effectively ending river transportation northward. A favorite fishing spot for Native Americans, who caught salmon, shad, and eel and left petroglyphs on the rocks, the falls were bypassed after the Revolution by one of the earliest canals in the United States. Nine locks lifted barges, rafts, and small steamers around the falls. The canal remained in operation for several decades until rendered obsolete by the RAILROADS, which turned Bellows Falls into a prime transportation hub. The falls also provided power for industry, not only the usual sawmills and gristmills but, in the nineteenth century, mills that produced paper (made from wood pulp, an innovation) and even silk, and for the Vermont Farm Machine Company, in its day one of the largest concerns of its kind in the world. Today a power plant at the lower end of the canal still generates electricity. Bellows Falls's long history as a center of transportation, commerce, and industry was responsible for the creation of separate neighborhoods of elegant mansions and sturdy workers' houses on glacial terraces rising steeply from the river and of a main street of imposing brick and granite buildings. Like so many older, middle-sized villages in Vermont, however, Bellows Falls entered a long period of economic decline in the 1960s, a situation from which the village has begun to recover in recent years, especially with the growth of citizens' initiatives in the arts and tourism. Rockingham's second-largest village, Saxtons River, is the home of Vermont Academy, founded 1876, a private co-educational college preparatory school. A noteworthy event in the town's history occurred in the pre-settlement era, when the first Protestant sermon preached in what was to become Vermont was delivered by the Reverend John Williams in 1704. The event took place at the mouth of the Williams River as he and over one hundred settlers captured in a raid on Greenfield, Massachusetts, were being taken northward to Canada. Bellows Falls's most famous, or notorious, citizen, was HETTY GREEN (1834–1916), "the Witch of Wall Street," whose astute financial manipulations were matched only by her legendary stinginess.

Rockwell, Eli Barnum (1830–1923)

Captain Eli Barnum Rockwell came from the region's most prolific family of LAKE CHAMPLAIN mariners. At age twelve he began his career as a cabin boy on the schooner *Cynthia*. During his more than eighty years on the lake, Captain Rockwell piloted or captained almost every steamer to come on the lake after 1850. In 1875, he was second pilot on the steamer *Champlain II* when she was driven up on the shore outside of Westport. Just prior to the accident, first pilot John Eldredge had taken over the wheel. A subsequent investigation revealed that John was addicted to morphine, and consequently had fallen asleep at the wheel. In 1881, Rockwell was hired by the Grand Isle Steamboat Company to build a steamboat for them, which he did on the beach of Ransom Bay near his home in Alburg Center. Named the *Reindeer*, she was the only major steamboat not to be owned by the CHAMPLAIN TRANSPORTATION COMPANY. Rockwell was still the active captain of the *Vermont III*, the CTC's flagship, when he died at age ninety-three. Captain Rockwell's brothers Jabez, William W., Edwin R., and Sumner J. were all pilots and captains of steamboats.   *Arthur Cohn*

Rockwell, Norman (1894–1978)

One of America's most popular illustrators, famous for his scenes of American small-town life on numerous *Saturday Evening Post* covers, Norman Rockwell lived in Arlington from 1939 until 1953. His first residence there was an 1860s house on the River Road in West Arlington, then, after his studio on the property burned, he and his wife Mary moved to a late-eighteenth-century house on the West Arlington green. Painters Rockwell Kent and Mead Schaeffer also lived in Arlington, as did DOROTHY CANFIELD FISHER and her husband, all providing intellectual and artistic companionship for the Rockwells. The couple took full part in the life of the small town, joining local organizations, going to covered-dish suppers, and attending town and school board meetings. As many as two hundred residents of Arlington served as models for Rockwell's magazine covers and other paintings, including, during the Second World War, the Willie Gillis series (depicting the adventures of a young army recruit) and the Four Freedoms, Rockwell's most noteworthy contribution to the war effort. Eventually the Rockwells moved to Stockbridge, Massachusetts, their home for the rest of the artist's life. The Arlington Gallery and Norman Rockwell Exhibition, in a converted church on Route 7A in Arlington village, contains reproductions of Rockwell's paintings and memorabilia from his time in the town, plus reminiscences of people who posed for his paintings.

Rogers, Mary (d. 1905)

The last woman put to death by the state of Vermont for the capital crime of homicide and only the second woman to be executed by the state, Mary Rogers was hanged on December 8, 1905, for the 1902 murder of her husband, Marcus Rogers. "To all appearances," the BURLINGTON FREE PRESS reported, "Mrs. Rogers was the calmest person in the chamber of death."

Rogers, Robert (1731–1795)

Best known in regional lore for leading his New Hampshire rangers to raid the ABENAKI settlement at St. François, Quebec, in 1759, Robert Rogers has been immortalized in the novel *Northwest Passage* by Kenneth Roberts, a motion picture by the same name based on the novel, and a television series. Born in Methuen, Massachusetts, Rogers grew to manhood in Rumford, New Hampshire, where he acquired frontiersman skills. As a militia officer his lack of personal discipline made him an ineffective field commander, though he especially relished the dangers of scouting enemy positions, for which the British gave him command of nine companies of rangers. After the fall of FORT TICONDEROGA in 1759, General Amherst ordered

him from Crown Point to destroy the Abenaki base at St. François. Rogers' account of the raid was published in the *Journals of Major Robert Rogers*, which was the source of Roberts's novel. The widely read *Journals* earned him a reputation as the most romantic figure of the French and Indian Wars, yet an oral tradition among the Abenaki recounting the raid on St. François and the report of a French priest who arrived at the village immediately after the raid significantly deflate Rogers's claims for the tactical effectiveness of the attack. It was a strategic waste as well, for Wolfe had already taken Quebec. In peace, Rogers's unprincipled business dealings led to failures and huge debts. Imprisoned as a spy by George Washington in 1776, Rogers soon escaped to British lines, where he formed the Queen's Rangers, but lost the command for his feckless leadership. After undistinguished military service, Rogers fled to England in 1780, where he unsuccessfully tried to stage a play he had written earlier on Pontiac's uprising, *Ponteach: or, The Savages of America* (London, 1766). He died impoverished in a cheap London lodging house. The story of Rogers's men plundering sacred silver artifacts from the Catholic church at St. François and hiding them in the forest as they retreated south toward the CONNECTICUT RIVER drew treasure hunters well into the nineteenth century to the supposed route through the region that later became northeastern Vermont. Rogers self-dramatizing *Journals* and Hollywood's version of him seem to have prompted groups recently to dress and arm themselves as Rogers Rangers for simulated eighteenth-century militia encampments and skirmishes at annual reenactments of episodes in the history of Fort Ticonderoga.

Rokeby Museum

A National Historic Landmark in Ferrisburgh, Rokeby provides an intimate glimpse into two centuries of Vermont family life and agriculture. The house and 90-acre farm were home to four generations of Robinsons, a Quaker family of farmers, millers, abolitionists, authors, and artists. Rokeby was settled in the early years of Vermont's statehood by Thomas and Jemima Robinson, emigrés from Newport, Rhode Island, who ran mills and imported merino sheep. Frugal Yankees, the Robinsons saved anything and everything of value. Today, the eleven-room

house displays two hundred years of the family's personal and domestic belongings—furniture, clothing, textiles, and a large collection of art. It contains the family's immense library of books, pamphlets, and periodicals. Agricultural implements and artifacts relating to wool, butter, and fruit production are on view in the eight outbuildings. Interpretation of the site is supported by an impressive archive of letters, diaries, account books, and photographs. Rokeby Museum was established in 1961 at the death of Elizabeth Robinson, the last member of the family to live on the site, and is open to the public.

Jane Williamson

Rood, Ronald (1919–2001)

Born in Connecticut, naturalist and writer Ronald Rood moved with his wife to Lincoln in 1953, and at first taught biology at Vergennes Union High School and MIDDLEBURY COLLEGE. By the late 1950s, he was writing nature articles and books full time, eventually producing such popular works as *How Do You Spank a Porcupine?* (1983), *Loon in My Bathtub and Other Adventures with Wildlife* (1985), *Animals Nobody Loves* (1987), *Ron Rood's Vermont: A Nature Guide* (1988), and *A Land Alive* (1992). He contributed over four dozen articles to VERMONT LIFE and was a commentator for Vermont Public Radio. Many of his books were illustrated by Reed Prescott, an artist who also lived in Lincoln.

Rosenberg, Israel (1875–1956)

Vermont's first ordained rabbi, Israel Rosenberg was born in Kovno and ordained at the theological seminary in Vilno, both then in Russia but presently in Lithuania. Rabbi Rosenberg came to the United States in 1902 upon receiving a call from a congregation in Poughkeepsie, New York, where he served for two and a half years while also attending Hebrew Union College. His eloquence in Yiddish gained him a wide reputation and he became a member of many rabbinical associations. In 1904, he received a call from the Jewish community in Bayonne, New Jersey, and came to Burlington from there in 1909 to serve until 1911. During his tenure in Burlington, he served as community rabbi, filling the pulpits of Burlington's three synagogues, and was responsible for building the Hebrew Free School. Rosenberg became vice president of the Associated Rabbis of America in 1908 and also vice president of the Board of Education of Isaac

Elchanan Seminary of New York City. In 1925, he was elected chairman of the presidium of the Union of Orthodox Rabbis in the United States and Canada. Later he became president of the union and was a director and founder of the Joint Distribution Committee. He subsequently was honored as the union's first honorary president.   *David Blow*

Ross, Charles R. (1920–2003)

A holder of numerous public service positions, Charles R. Ross was born in Middlebury, where he attended primary and secondary schools before going to the University of Michigan, graduating with a B.A. in 1941. After military service in 1942 to 1946, he received a master's in business administration and a law degree from Michigan in 1948. He practiced law in Kentucky for several years, then was admitted to the Vermont bar and began to build a reputation as a specialist in environmental and regulatory fields. He served on the Vermont Public Service Commission from 1959 to 1961, on the Federal Power Commission from 1961 to 1968, and as a member of the United States Section of the International Joint Commission (charged with resolving environmental border disputes) from 1962 to 1981. As an IJC Commissioner during the mid-1970s, he resisted Canadian efforts to secure approval from the IJC Commission to remove the St. Jean shoals in the Richelieu River in order to relieve spring flooding along the upper river, a project that threatened to alter the flow of LAKE CHAMPLAIN and damage Vermont lakeshore property. In the early 1970s, he was president of Public Resources, Incorporated, which held a national conference on energy policy in the town of Johnson, and a member of the Ford Foundation Energy Policy Project. He also served as a trustee of the Environmental Defense Trust Fund. A Republican, he ran for the Republican nomination to the U.S. Senate in 1974 but was defeated in the primary. His reputation as a consumer advocate is derived from his staunch defense of the public interest during his career.

Round Church of Richmond

Between 1812 and 1814, the five religious denominations of Richmond—Baptists, Congregationalists, Methodists, Universalists, and Christians—built a sixteen-sided polygonal church with an octagonal belfry. The five sects mutually agreed

Round Church in Richmond. Ralph H. Orth

upon separate times to conduct their services and at first the building functioned as a community church, probably the first such church building in America. But when disputes arose between the various sects over using the church, separate buildings for their congregations were built. In 1880, the town of Richmond secured ownership of the Round Church and used it as a town hall. In the 1920s, Henry Ford offered to buy the building and move it to Dearborn, Michigan, where he was collecting Americana for a museum. The town refused to sell. Later in the twentieth century, the Round Church was restored and preserved. While no congregation uses it today for religious services, the handsome building has become a popular place for weddings.

Router Bit Affair

In 1978, during Governor RICHARD SNELLING's administration, the discovery was made that Nelson Charron, an employee at the Northeast Tool Company in Lyndonville and an auxiliary for the state police on snowmobile patrol, was distributing free router bits to state troopers. Ostensibly seconds, they were found to be first quality bits stolen by Charron. The handling of the internal investigation and alleged coverup by St. Johnsbury Police Sergeant David Reed and other state police officers was but one of a number of incidents that led to a wider allegation of improper behavior within the state police. Governor Snelling eventually demanded the resignation of State Police Commissioner Francis Lynch in 1979. In July of that year, Corporal Howard Gould, one of

the troopers named in the router bit investigation, committed suicide at the VERMONT STATE HOUSE, protesting the publicity and the resulting ruin of his career. In August 1979, Snelling created the so-called "Keyser Commission," led by Justice F. Ray Keyser, Sr., to investigate state police conduct. The commission's April 1980 report criticized the handling of the internal investigation and recommended changes in procedure within the Department of Public Safety. Additionally, a Vermont State Police Advisory Committee now advises the Commissioner of Public Safety and reviews internal affairs investigations.   *Sylvia J. Bugbee*

Rowley, Thomas (1721–1796)

The poet of the GREEN MOUNTAIN BOYS, Thomas Rowley was born in Hebron, Connecticut. At the age of forty-seven, Rowley helped found the town of Danby. Elected the first town clerk in 1769, an office he held until 1782, Rowley taught himself surveying and became active in the separatist movement against New York. At the urging of ETHAN ALLEN, Rowley turned his skill at improvised versifying to political topics, becoming the bard of the Green Mountain Boys. While most of Rowley's verses fail to inflame modern sensibilities, contemporaries credited Rowley with "setting the mountains on fire" with his poetry, and his poems were reprinted in most American newspapers. Rowley took part in the capture of FORT TICONDEROGA in 1775, served as chair of the region's committee of safety, played a key role at the Vermont constitutional convention, led the more radical faction within the state's assembly, and served as a judge on the court for the confiscation of Loyalist lands. With the war's end, Rowley moved to Shoreham, where he became the first town clerk and justice of the peace, positions he held from 1783 until his death.

Michael A. Bellesiles

Roxbury

Roxbury, population 576, a town in Washington County, was granted by the Vermont legislature in 1781. The name probably derives from Roxbury, Massachusetts, now a part of Boston. The land is wooded and mountainous, rising to 3,086 feet at Rice Mountain in the Northfield range of the GREEN MOUNTAINS along the town's western border. The town, which lies in the exact center of the state, straddles the headwaters of the Dog and WHITE RIVERS. The Dog flows north into the WINOOSKI RIVER, which empties into LAKE CHAMPLAIN, and the White flows south into the CONNECTICUT RIVER, which empties into Long Island Sound. The small village of Roxbury lies on Route 12A, which cuts through the town from north to south. Historically, Roxbury's main industry has been logging. Today, some residents commute to work in Montpelier and Barre.

Royalton

Royalton, population 2,603, a town in Windsor County, was originally a New York patent of 1769 whose legitimacy was subsequently confirmed by the Vermont legislature in 1781. The name reflects the impulse toward monarchial flattery, a common trait among colonial governors, in this case New York's acting governor, Cadwallader Colden. The town's rolling topography, made up of gentle hills interspersed with meadows cut by watercourses, is divided roughly in half by the WHITE RIVER, which flows through the town from west to east. The settlements of Royalton, North Royalton (Foxville), and South Royalton (the major village) are all on Route 14 along the river. During a series of British attacks into central Vermont and the Champlain Valley during the last year of the Revolution, the town was the site of the ROYALTON RAID, the most calamitous event of that war for civilians in Vermont. Among noteworthy individuals born in Royalton were FREDERICK BILLINGS, railroad magnate and philanthropist, and HENRY TRUMAN SAFFORD, JR., a mathematical prodigy who performed amazing mental feats as a child and later became a professor of mathematics and astronomy. The VERMONT LAW SCHOOL, founded in 1972, one of twelve independent private law schools in the United States and the only law school in Vermont, is located in South Royalton.

Royalton Raid

On October 16, 1780, a British attack force of regimental strength, including nearly three hundred Kahnawake Mohawks, descended upon the widely scattered homesteads along the WHITE RIVER as part of a series of British raids into central Vermont and the Champlain Valley. In addition to destroying dozens of dwellings and barns and killing much livestock, the attackers killed four settlers, two of whom were speared in revenge for their killing two

Mohawks before the war, and took twenty-seven prisoners with them on their retreat into Canada, most of whom were allowed to return home the following summer as a result of the peace truce between the British and Vermont negotiated by IRA ALLEN in the so-called HALDIMAND NEGOTIATIONS.

Royce, Stephen (1787–1868)

The first Republican and last Whig governor of Vermont, Stephen Royce was born in Tinmouth and raised in Berkshire. He earned money for college as a fur trapper and trader, graduated from MIDDLEBURY COLLEGE (1807), and studied law in Sheldon, where he was admitted to the bar, opened his first law office, and served two terms, 1815 and 1816, as state representative. He was state's attorney from 1816 to 1818. Moving to St. Albans in 1817, he represented that town in the legislature (1822–1824) and was elected to the Vermont Supreme Court in 1825 and 1826. He left the court to return to the private practice of law, but was elected to the court again in 1829 and served until 1852, the last five years as chief judge. In 1854, receiving the Whig nomination for governor and shortly thereafter the endorsement of the newly organized REPUBLICAN PARTY, he was elected overwhelmingly and re-elected in 1855 as a Republican. His administrations were most noted for an act protecting married women's property rights and appropriating funds for a monument over ETHAN ALLEN's grave. As a lawyer, he was incapable of arguing a case he did not believe in personally, and if he discovered during the course of a trial that he was on the "wrong side," he would accept no fee for his services. As a jurist, he was known as the "doubter," reflecting the difficulties he had in reaching some decisions. He refused to publish decisions he felt were wrong, explaining that it was bad enough to have done an injustice without having to send it out as a precedent. The General Assembly consequently withheld some of his pay as a judge in reaction to this practice.   *Paul Gillies*

Rugg, Harold Goddard (1883–1957)

Harold Rugg, associate librarian of Dartmouth College, was a preeminent twentieth-century collector of Vermont imprints. Born in Hartland, Dartmouth class of 1906, Rugg spent his entire career at Dartmouth College, where he greatly increased and improved the college's research collections

through significant purchases and personal gifts. Vermontiana and modern English and American literature were his primary interests. Rugg introduced Dartmouth students to the art of the book in a class that he taught for twenty years which, in 1940, transformed itself into the Graphic Arts Workshop led by Ray Nash. In 1941, Rugg and Nash published a history of the press in Hanover, New Hampshire, entitled *Pioneer Printing at Dartmouth* that delineated the work of the press that JUDAH P. and ALDEN SPOONER established at Dresden, a precinct of Hanover, during the period of the EAST UNION. Despite his commitment to Dartmouth and the town of Hanover, however, Rugg was always a Vermonter. His personal collections of Vermont printed and manuscript matter, Vermont glass, and Bennington ware, as well as other antiques, were noteworthy. He worked for years to revise *The Bibliography of Vermont* by MARCUS D. GILMAN. He bequeathed his large Vermont collections to the VERMONT HISTORICAL SOCIETY. He was also an inveterate mountain climber, gardener, world traveler, and botanist. A fern he identified, *Osmunda ruggii*, is named for him.
Marcus A. McCorison

Ruggles, Carl (1876–1971)

Born in Marion, Massachusetts, Carl Ruggles was a composer of highly original, often mystical music. After classes in literature and studying with the composer John Knowles Paine at Harvard, he moved to Winona, Minnesota (where he founded the Winona Symphony), and New York City. Ruggles first contact with Vermont came in 1921, when he was invited to share a house in Sunderland with Rockwell Kent, for whom he posed as the model for Captain Ahab in a Random House edition of Herman Melville's *Moby-Dick*. While there, Ruggles also produced his first painting, a landscape of Mount Anthony. He returned to Vermont the next summer as a guest of DOROTHY CANFIELD FISHER and in the spring of 1923, he and his wife bought a schoolhouse in Arlington, where he lived and worked for the rest of his life. His compositions are dissonant, with long, angular melodic lines. Critics have found his work uncompromising, confrontational, dismissive, untraditional, stubborn, and Emersonian in its refusal to imitate. His most famous work is *Sun-Treader* (1932), for orchestra. A perfectionist, he destroyed all but a few of his works. Ruggles devoted himself to painting as well as music after 1950.   *Jane Ambrose*

Runaway Pond

On June 10, 1810, some residents of the town of Glover began to dig a channel from Mud Pond to connect with and send water down the Barton River to power mills during a period of low water. Rushing water quickly eroded the channel deeper than it could be controlled, with the result that the entire pond emptied into the river, scouring the valley of the Barton clean of mills and houses for 15 miles to LAKE MEMPHREMAGOG. A boggy wetland along Route 16 is a vestige of Runaway Pond.

Rupert

Rupert, population 704, a town in Bennington County, was granted by BENNING WENTWORTH in 1761 and almost certainly named for Prince Rupert (1619–1682), duke of Cumberland and earl of Holderness, a leader of Royalist forces in the English Civil War. The heavily forested town, which lies in the TACONIC MOUNTAINS along the New York border, consists of a series of disparate valleys and hills, rising to 2,803 feet at Spruce Peak. The small settlements of Rupert village and West Rupert lie on Route 315, the major road crossing the town from east to west. REUBEN HARMON, JR., an original settler, was granted the right to mint coins at East Rupert for the new republic of Vermont in 1785.

Ruschp, Sepp (1903–1990)

An engineer and competitive skier who won the 1936 Upper Austrian National Combined Champion, Sepp Ruschp of Linz, Austria, was invited by the MOUNT MANSFIELD Ski Club to Stowe in 1936 to be a ski instructor and to coach the ski teams at the UNIVERSITY OF VERMONT and NORWICH UNIVERSITY. He founded the Sepp Ruschp Ski School, which became a leading United States ski school. After service in World War II as a pilot and flight instructor in the United States Army Air Corps, he played a key role, along with CRAIG O. BURT and CORNELIUS VANDER STARR, in the growth of the ski industry in Stowe and Vermont. He was president and general manager of the Mount Mansfield Company (now Stowe Mountain Resort) from 1949 to 1977. He was responsible for the first television coverage of the Winter Olympics and for helping to bring the 1960 Winter Olympics to Squaw Valley, California. Sepp Ruschp received honorary doctorates from both the University of Vermont and Norwich University and was elected to the United States Ski Hall of Fame in 1978.

                    Kathleen McKinley Harris

Rutland City

The city of Rutland, population 17,292, was created out of the town of Rutland in 1892. It began as a frontier settlement in the southeastern part of the town after the Revolution, helped by its strategic location at the center of Rutland County, where major north-south and east-west pathways met, and by a dependable source of waterpower in OTTER CREEK. In its early years, it was known as Mill Village for its numerous saw- and gristmills. Businesses soon grew along the main street, today's U.S. Route 7. The discovery of MARBLE in the vicinity produced a new industrial base in the 1800s, as marble mills dotted Otter Creek's banks. In 1852, the RAILROAD came to the region and a major rail yard and depot added to Rutland's importance. The depot's location west of Main Street soon shifted Rutland's marketplace as stores moved closer to the railroad. In 1886, the marble-producing communities of Proctor and West Rutland were split off from Rutland town, and in 1892, Rutland city was formally chartered. Industry continued to thrive until after World War II, when the demand for marble products slackened. In 1954, rail passenger service ended and the expansive rail yard was reduced in size, nearly disappearing after the Rutland Railroad ceased operations. Since the 1970s, business has diversified and a renewed downtown marketplace exemplifies the city's revival. Rail passenger service to New York City also returned in 1996. The *RUTLAND HERALD*, the state's oldest newspaper, founded in 1794, is still one of Vermont's most influential news sources. The Rutland County Agricultural Society has held its annual late summer agricultural fair at the fairgrounds in the southern section of the city since 1860. Rutland has a well-preserved residential base, which in its architectural styles captures the social and economic history of the community. Nineteenth- and early-twentieth-century commercial buildings along Merchants Row comprise one of the best-preserved downtown districts in the state. The city, in addition to remaining one of the state's most important industrial locales, also profits from its proximity to year-round recreational opportunities in the surrounding mountains, especially the Killington-Pico ski resort complex 15 miles to the east. Rutland lost its title as Vermont's second-largest population center when the 2000 census showed that the town of Essex, in the Burlington metropolitan area, had moved into second place.   *Donald Wickman*

Rutland Fair

Also known as the Vermont State Fair, the annual Rutland Fair began in 1846 with the formation of the Rutland County Agricultural Society to present an annual late-summer agricultural fair. First held in Castleton, the fair moved to Rutland in 1852. Since 1860, the fair has been held in its present location in the southern section of the city, where it remains a seasonal entertainment highlight. The early emphasis of the fair was agricultural, but soon harness racing was added, providing a major attraction for many years until it was discontinued in the late 1990s. In 1937, fire destroyed the grandstand just over two months prior to the fair opening. A new structure was quickly erected, the fair successfully opened, and the grandstand is still in use. As the agriculture base of Vermont grew smaller after World War II and attendance declined at the fair's agricultural exhibits, it began to offer entertainment for broadly based audiences. A midway with carnival rides and other entertainment was added and still serves as a major feature of the fair.

                    Donald Wickman

Rutland Herald

Vermont's *Rutland Herald* is one of the oldest daily newspapers in the nation in continuous publication from the same city of origin and that remains in the hands of a single family. Nearly all others have been absorbed by "chains," which in turn tend to be owned by large corporations. The *Herald* today, with a daily and Sunday audited circulation of twenty-two thousand, provides the best and fullest coverage of the central and southern regions of the state, including Montpelier for state politics, but unfortunately provides no competitive coverage in the populous northwest sector. The *Herald* was launched as a weekly on December 8, 1794, by two cousins who shared the name SAMUEL WILLIAMS. This newspaper's two centuries can be divided into eight distinctive eras of publishers or owners. Among the finest of these was during the Civil War, when the public's thirst for news from the front justified going from weekly to daily. The *Herald* engaged local soldiers to submit reportage—usually anonymously— on what was happening in the war. Rutland's Tuttle family was in charge at the time. The Herald's least admirable era was probably under the leadership of the politically ambitious PERCIVAL W. CLEMENT, who had served in numerous political offices and was elected governor in 1920 after several attempts. Clement used the paper to promote his own business and political agendas. After his death, the *Herald* came into the hands of William Field, a Rutland native who had been one of the founders of the successful *New York Daily News*. Since the end of World War II, ROBERT W. MITCHELL and his family have controlled the *Herald* and adamantly retained one-family ownership in an era dominated by chain acquisitions. The Mitchell family also publishes the *Times-Argus* in Barre and Montpelier. The *Herald* won a Pulitzer Prize in 2001—first ever for a Vermont newspaper—for its series of thoughtful editorials by David Moats on the politically explosive issue of the CIVIL UNIONS law. *J. Tyler Resch*

Rutland Town

Rutland, population 4,038, a town in Rutland County, was granted by BENNING WENTWORTH in 1761 to a group of individuals headed by John Murray of Rutland, Massachusetts, the source of the new town's name. Originally, it included what is today the town of West Rutland and most of the town of Proctor, both of which were incorporated by the Vermont legislature in 1886, and the city of Rutland, incorporated in 1892. What was left was good agricultural land and the village of Center Rutland, at the junction of the Castleton River with OTTER CREEK. The village lies at the point where the CROWN POINT MILITARY ROAD crossed Otter Creek, and it was also the site of Fort Ranger, built during the Revolution. An early resident was the Reverend SAMUEL WILLIAMS, author of the first (1794) history of the state (*Natural and Civil History of Vermont*) and co-founder of the *RUTLAND HERALD*, 1794. The mining and working of MARBLE was a major industry in the town before it was divided, as was transportation after the RAILROAD arrived in 1852. Rutland strongly supported the Civil War, raising whole companies for seven different regiments and supplying recruits for additional units. Two regiments mustered within the town's boundaries. JOHN DEERE, the inventor of the steel plow, was born in the town. On the West Proctor Road is Wilson Castle, a thirty-two room Gilded Age mansion open to visitors. Much of Rutland town today serves as a suburban extension of Rutland city.

Ryan, Thomas (1790–1849)

Thomas Ryan came to Burlington from county Tipperary, Ireland, shortly after 1816, stayed a few years working as a tailor, then moved to Fairfield, bought a farm, and prospered. Writing back to Ireland, he encouraged others to join him, and through his efforts a strong Irish community composed of Denivers, O'Neills, Rooneys, and Collinses was established in Fairfield by 1830. This group was later augmented by a number of families escaping the Irish Famine of the 1840s, including the Branons, Howrigans, and Branigans, many of whose descendants, along with several of Thomas Ryan's, continue to farm in Fairfield, a town where herds of Holsteins and low, rolling green hills visually echo the rural countryside of modern Ireland.

Ryegate

Ryegate, population 1,150, a town in Caledonia County, was granted by BENNING WENTWORTH in 1763 to a group of nincty-four persons headed by Richard Jennes, whose family originated in Reigate, England. It was later sold to John Witherspoon, president of the College of New Jersey and formerly of Paisley, Scotland, from whom it was purchased in 1773 by JAMES WHITELAW for the Scotch American Company of Inchinnan. It was one of two Vermont towns settled from "across the water" (neighboring Barnet was the other). The landscape is gently rolling, culminating in 2,363-foot Blue Mountain, once the site of several large granite quarries. There are three villages, Ryegate Corner in the center, East Ryegate on U.S. Route 5 along the CONNECTICUT RIVER, and South Ryegate on U.S. Route 302 along the Wells River. Ticklenaked Pond, a 225-acre lake famous out of all proportion to its size, probably derives its name from some similar sounding Native American word for that body of water.

S

Sabin, Noah (1715–1811)

Settled in Putney with a New York title to his land, Noah Sabin, a native of Rehoboth, Massachusetts, in 1771 was appointed judge in New York's CUMBERLAND COUNTY court. In March 1775, Sabin insisted on holding the court that led to the WESTMINSTER MASSACRE. He was seized by New Hampshire militia and jailed in Massachusetts for his role in that affair. After he returned to Putney, the Committee of Safety on the grants ordered him confined to his farm for his Loyalist sympathies, with permission given to anybody to shoot him if he was seen beyond its limits, and he was refused communion in church. He soon became an earnest Patriot and was elected judge of probate for Windham County in 1781.

Safford, Henry Truman, Jr. (1836–1901)

Growing up in Royalton, Henry Truman Safford, Jr., showed extraordinary mathematical prowess as a boy. At several public examinations, he astonished learned panels with his rapid ability to answer complex problems in multiplication and division, and he published several almanacs featuring his astronomical calculations in the mid-1840s. Safford graduated from Harvard University in 1854 and worked at the Harvard Observatory for twelve years. After serving as director of the Dearborn Observatory and working on United States geographical surveys, in 1876 he became professor of astronomy at Williams College. Safford died at Newark, New Jersey.

J. Kevin Graffagnino

Safford, Samuel (1737–1813)

A Revolutionary soldier, judge, and member of the Governor's Council, Samuel Safford of Norwich, Connecticut, was among the earliest Bennington settlers. Actively opposing New York in the land controversy over the New Hampshire grants in Bennington, he represented his town at several of the conventions that settlers held and early on supported the idea of a new province or state. Chosen major and second in command to SETH WARNER in the regiment of New Hampshire grants settlers authorized by the Continental Congress in July 1775 and funded as a New York militia regiment, Safford served in the Canadian expedition of 1775 to 1776, and when Warner's unit was elevated to a regiment of the Continental line, he was promoted to lieutenant colonel, serving at the BATTLES OF HUBBARDTON and BENNINGTON. He was appointed by the Vermont General Assembly to succeed ETHAN ALLEN as brigadier general in command of the Vermont militia on June 20, 1781. He represented Bennington in the legislature in 1781 and 1782 and was in the Governor's Council for nineteen years. Safford was also chief judge of Bennington county court from 1781 to 1807. Safford was privy to the HALDIMAND NEGOTIATIONS but, unlike Ethan and IRA ALLEN, his patriotism was never questioned.

St. Albans City

Incorporated as a village in 1859 and a city in 1897, the city of St. Albans, population 7,650, lies at the center of the town of the same name in Franklin County and is the SHIRE TOWN. The city is laid out around tree-shaded Taylor Park, bordered on the west by 90-foot-wide Main Street with its busy commercial blocks, and on the east by churches, a court house, and a historical museum. The city is the center of a major trading and economic area that reaches from St. Jean, Quebec, on the north almost to Burlington on the south. For over one hundred years, St. Albans depended heavily on the Central Vermont Railway for its economic well-being. The railroad, founded in the 1850s as the Vermont and Canada Railroad by local entrepreneurs John Smith, his son JOHN GREGORY SMITH, and LAWRENCE BRAINERD, later merged with the Vermont Central Railroad and was renamed and run by the Smiths as the Central Vermont Railway (CVR). It was the largest railway system in New England in the late nineteenth century, with headquarters and shops in the city employing seventeen hundred people. St. Albans became known as the "Railroad City," a name that was use for the product of a local microbrewery. Owned by the Canadian National Railroad in the late twentieth century, the CVR was sold to a Texas firm and operates today as the New England Central. With the decline of the once-vital railroad industry, the city's economy diversified. The St. Albans Cooperative Creamery, founded in 1919, today enrolls over five hundred farmer-members from ten of Vermont's counties. It annually receives and markets roughly a billion pounds of milk, most of it going to the plant of BEN & JERRY'S HOMEMADE ICE CREAM in St. Albans town, Lucille Foods cheese factory in Swanton, and several other dairy-product manufacturers in Vermont and elsewhere. An important international breakthrough for the creamery came recently when Montreal's Liberté Yogourt began importing the creamery's milk for yogurt production at a Quebec plant and export to their U.S. distributors. *Vermont Business Magazine* ranks the creamery as tenth among the top one hundred businesses in the state and third among the state's hundred largest manufacturers. While the railway shops, iron foundries, and manufacturers of clothing and wood products that dominated here in the late nineteenth and early twentieth centuries are mostly gone, other businesses have developed to take their place. Leader Evaporator, for instance, manufactures equipment to produce maple syrup, a major agricultural product of Franklin County. The St. Albans *Messenger*, founded by ENOCH B. WHITING in 1861, continues daily publication. A fixture of St. Albans for more than one hundred years, the Fonda Group's paper-products factory operates with modern technology. The international border a dozen miles north of the city is important to St. Albans, as the old county jail behind the court house has been renovated to provide holding cells for illegal aliens detained by the U.S. Border Patrol and the Immigration and Naturalization Service, which also operates a large regional center on the west side of Taylor Park to process thousands of citizenship applications monthly. St. Albans hosts a Vermont Maple Festival every April, and, in a throwback to earlier times, residents enjoy free skiing four nights a week at Hard'ack in Aldis Park, one of Vermont's few surviving COMMUNITY SKI HILLS.

St. Albans Raid

On October 10, 1864, twenty mounted Confederate soldiers in civilian clothes led by Lieutenant Bennett Young rode into the border town of St. Albans, killed one man and wounded two others as they robbed the St. Albans Bank, the Franklin County Bank, and the First National Bank of St. Albans of more than $200,000. The raid lasted less than half an hour and created a panic in towns all along the northern border of the United States, nearly precipitating an international incident between the United States, Canada, and Great Britain. Confederate Senator Clement Clay of Richmond, Virginia, sent Young to Canada to scout the border for a target of opportunity that would cause havoc and possibly raise some money for the cash-poor South. Learning in Montreal that Union horse buyers would be in St. Albans to purchase MORGAN HORSES, Young waited until the horse money was deposited in the St. Albans bank. The Confederate soldiers filtered into town in separate groups, raising no suspicions among the inhabitants. Young planned to rob the banks and then fire the town using hand-thrown incendiary bombs filled with Greek fire, an inflammable substance ignited by contact with the air, but the bombs failed to ignite. Three small groups of four or five men separately struck the banks, while the remainder seized horses for their escape. Inexperienced bank robbers, the raiders netted about $208,000, overlooking an estimated additional $350,000. Townsmen offered resistance on the streets, several were wounded, and one man was killed, a New Hampshire contractor in St. Albans on a building construction job. On the way out of town, one raider was shot but survived. The raiders escaped into Canada, trying to burn a bridge on the way, while armed posses pursued them, nearly creating an international incident when they rode into Canada. Eventually, Canadian authorities captured eighteen of the raiders along with $80,000; only a single raider made it back south with some money. After a Montreal court ruled that Canada had no jurisdiction to hold the Confederates, they were released and given back the $80,000. Vermonters were outraged, and amidst threats of international consequences, the Canadian government repaid the banks about $88,000. The St. Albans and First National Banks never recovered from their losses and eventually went out of business. The U.S. Army's Invalid Corps, a unit of recuperated wounded troops, were stationed at Fort Montgomery on LAKE CHAMPLAIN to guard against a Confederate invasion, and militia units, including Vermont's Frontier Cavalry under General GEORGE STANNARD, were called to patrol the northern border from Maine to the Midwest. Bennett Young and his men were welcomed as heroes in the South.   *Anthony Paré*

St. Albans Town

St. Albans, population 5,086, a town in Franklin County, was granted by BENNING WENTWORTH in 1763 to sixty-four investors and named for St. Albans in England. Originally it included the area that became the city of St. Albans, incorporated as a village by the Vermont legislature in 1859 and as a city in 1897. It has a long shoreline on LAKE CHAMPLAIN and includes Burton and Woods islands, both state parks. The earliest settler was Jesse Welden, who built a house at St. Albans Bay before the outbreak of the Revolution in 1775, but withdrew until the peace of 1783. IRA and LEVI ALLEN acquired a large part of the town in 1773 to 1774 from some of the original Boston investors and encouraged settlement after the peace. The first town meeting was held in 1788. Although earliest settlement occurred at the bay, a committee of the town in 1794 determined the town center (for purposes of posting notices and establishing a pound) to be at the present site of St. Albans city. Franklin County was organized in 1792 and St. Albans was named SHIRE TOWN in 1793. By virtue of its location on the lake and the growing legal business generated by the court house, St. Albans became an important trading community for northwestern Vermont early in the nineteenth century. The embargo on trade with Britain and Canada in 1808 to 1810 imposed sufficient hardships to encourage widespread and effective smuggling in a wide range of products by land and over the lake. Schooners, sloops, and steamboats were built at the bay after the War of 1812, including *The Gleaner*, the first boat to sail from Lake Champlain to New York City after the Hudson-Champlain Canal was opened in 1823. The PATRIOTS uprising of 1837–1838 in Canada sent some of the first French-Canadian settlers to St. Albans. One out of every eight St. Albans town citizens served in the Civil War. A major dairy center by 1861, the town contributed a 100-pound Cheddar cheese to feed the Ransom Guards, the town's militia unit that enlisted as Company C of the First Vermont Volunteers. The ST. ALBANS RAID, the northernmost incident of the war, occurred on October 19, 1864, when a band of twenty-one Confederate soldiers in civilian clothes robbed three of the banks in St. Albans village of more than $200,000 and killed one man before escaping into Canada. Twice in the 1860s, the FENIAN Brotherhood, an Irish-American society devoted to the liberation of Ireland from British rule, launched invasion attempts into Canada from the town. Beginning in the 1850s, St. Albans village (later city) became the headquarters of the Vermont and Canada railroad and later the Central Vermont railroad, with extensive offices and shops. As improved railroad refrigeration developed for shipping milk, the region's major agricultural product, to major eastern markets, the town flourished. Although milk transporting today is carried out by trucks operating over the INTERSTATE HIGHWAYS, continued high volume milk production in St. Albans and surrounding towns has drawn BEN & JERRY'S HOMEMADE ICE CREAM to open a plant in the town's industrial park. Other service and supply businesses in the industrial park support the dairy industry of Franklin County, and yet other firms make such diverse products as storage batteries and ceramic components for industrial electronics.

St. Francis, Homer (1935–2001)

Chief of the Missisquoi ABENAKI (1974–1980, 1986–1995, and grand chief, 1995–2001), Homer St. Francis was born in the "Back Bay" section of Swanton. After serving in the U.S. Marine Corps in the late 1950s and early 1960s, including duty in President Eisenhower's Honor Guard, St. Francis became involved with the organizing efforts of the Abenaki community in the late 1960s and early 1970s, and was elected chief of the St. Francis-Sokoki band of the Abenaki Nation in 1974. He immediately began a series of political and social actions to, as he said, "put the Abenaki on the map." Very blunt and highly confrontational, his oratory and activities, such as the MISSISQUOI RIVER "Fish-Ins," polarized other Vermonters. However, his outspoken leadership and subsequent media attention in the 1970s attracted the attention of scholars such as Marjorie Power, William Haviland, and John Moody, who began serious inquiries into the origins and culture of Vermont's Abenaki. Their research and writing eventually led to a general recognition that Vermont's Abenaki community has survived and persisted into the present. Initiatives during St. Francis's tenure as chief included the ABENAKI HERITAGE DAYS celebration, an unsuccessful petition for federal recognition, and a two-year state recognition that was rescinded soon after

the election of Governor RICHARD SNEL-
LING in 1976. His most important legacy
was that Vermont had to recognize that
the Abenaki were here to stay.

Frederick Wiseman

St. George

St. George, population 698, the smallest
town in area in Vermont (2,304 acres),
was granted by BENNING WENTWORTH
in 1763 and is no doubt named for the
patron saint of England, with an oblique
allusion to King George III. Why a parcel
of land so small and gore-shaped was not
originally granted as part of the neighboring towns of Shelburne or Williston is
not known. St. George has always been
sparsely populated and rural, even in its
prime sheep-raising years, but its location
on the inner edge of the Burlington metropolitan area has led to an increase in residential building in the last few decades.
There is no village, store, school, church,
or post office, although a golf course is
located in the extreme southwestern section of town.

St. Johnsbury

St. Johnsbury, population 7,571, the SHIRE
TOWN of Caledonia County, was granted
to JONATHAN ARNOLD and others by the
Vermont legislature in 1786. It is the most
populous town in the NORTHEAST KING-
DOM and was named for Hector St. John
de Crèvecoeur, author of *Letters from an
American Farmer* (1782) and French consul to the United States from 1783 to 1790.
The PASSUMPSIC, Moose, and Sleepers
rivers run through the town and provided
the power for early industries, among
them the Fairbanks mills and hemp works.
In 1830, THADDEUS FAIRBANKS invented
a platform scale to facilitate the weighing of hemp by the wagon load. Within
four years, brothers Thaddeus, Joseph,
and ERASTUS FAIRBANKS had formed
the E. & T. FAIRBANKS AND COMPANY
to manufacture and distribute scales. The
success of their endeavor played a significant role in the development and prosperity of St. Johnsbury. As workers came to
the area from far and wide, the town's
population soared and diversified. In
1856, the Caledonia County seat was relocated from neighboring Danville to
St. Johnsbury. RAILROAD lines developed
by the Fairbanks brothers and brought to
the area in 1850 and 1877 ensured the
town's status as a center of commerce and
industry. As Fairbanks family members

experienced burgeoning wealth, they endowed the town with numerous cultural
and educational facilities, among them
the ST. JOHNSBURY ATHENAEUM, the
Y.M.C.A., the FAIRBANKS MUSEUM AND
PLANETARIUM, and the ST. JOHNSBURY
ACADEMY. With the exception of the
Y.M.C.A., which was destroyed by fire in
1984, these institutions continue to play a
vital role in the community. At the height
of the scale works' success, in the late
nineteenth century, St. Johnsbury was
lauded as a model of enlightened indus-
trialism and was studied by critics here
and abroad. As central operations for the
Fairbanks Scale Company shifted to larger
urban centers, new owners came in and
the Fairbanks family's influence, which
lasted well into the twentieth century,
slowly diminished. Many other businesses, among them Maple Grove Farms
(syrups, sauces, confections), Lydall Wes-
tex (automobile thermal insulation products), and E.H.V. Weidmann Industries
(paperboard) operate out of St. Johnsbury, which has continued as a regional
center in the Northeast Kingdom, offering a concentration of both locally and
nationally based businesses and services.
Located amidst rolling hills along Interstates 91 and 93, with its Victorian legacy
evidenced by its active cultural institutions and its architectural landmarks
(many designed by architect LAMBERT
PACKARD), St. Johnsbury has aptly been
characterized as the "capital" of the north
country.

Selene Colburn

St. Johnsbury Academy

The St. Johnsbury Academy, a private
high school, was established in 1842 by the
founders of E. & T. FAIRBANKS AND COM-
PANY, with continued support from THAD-
DEUS FAIRBANKS as the school expanded.
In 1874, arrangements were made with the
town of St. Johnsbury taxpayers to send
area students to the academy, a tradition
that continues to this day. In addition to its
750 local day students, the academy is
home to approximately 160 boarding students from across the United States and
around the world. The school offers a
post-graduate year, which in 1891 was
attended by future President CALVIN
COOLIDGE.

Selene Colburn

St. Johnsbury Athenaeum

The St. Johnsbury Athenaeum, a public
library in St. Johnsbury, was endowed by
HORACE FAIRBANKS in 1871. The build-

ing, a National Historic Landmark, was
designed by architect John Davis Hatch
III. In 1873, an art gallery wing was added
to house works from Fairbanks's collection, including paintings by the Hudson
River School and Albert Bierstadt's magnificent work *The Domes of the Yosemite*.
In addition to its circulating materials, the
Athenaeum maintains its original nine-
thousand-volume book collection, which
was assembled under the guidance of the
noted bibliographer William F. Poole.

Selene Colburn

St. Joseph's Church

The largest church structure in Vermont
and the oldest French-Canadian national
parish in New England (founded in 1850),
St. Joseph's Church serves Burlington's
original Roman Catholic parish. The large
Romanesque church was built between
1883 and 1887 according to a design by
Quebec architect Reverend Joseph Michaud, C.S.V., who also designed the Ba-
silica of Mary Queen of the World in Montreal. The Burlington church is 200 feet
long, 80 feet wide, and has a 55-foot-high
interior. The tall landmark spire is 6 inches
less than 200 feet high. Although the
French language is no longer used in regular services, the complex of buildings
continues the typically Quebec parish tradition with a church, presbytere (built in
1904–1905), school (1929), and convent
(1956–1957) in one location.   *David Blow*

St. Michael's College

The first Catholic institution of higher
education in Vermont, St. Michael's College was founded by the Society of St.
Edmund, a religious order for men established in Pontigny, France, in 1843. The
school, located in Winooski Park, Colchester, opened its doors to thirty-five male
students, ages eleven to twenty-three, and
a faculty of seven Edmundites and one layman on September 14, 1904. Classes were
held in a farmhouse the Fathers had purchased in 1902 and in a new four-story, all-
purpose building. Classical, commercial,
and religious courses were accompanied
by multiple extracurricular activities practiced in a highly disciplined ambience for
a total cost of approximately $150 per year.
The college incorporated in 1913, and in
1928 discontinued its high school department. On the college's twenty-fifth anniversary in 1929, enrollment had reached
126 students and a faculty of nine Edmundites and four laymen offered Bachelor of

Arts and Philosophy degrees with pre-medical, pre-dental, and science majors. Master's degrees were also offered. A physical education program with many popular sports had been established. Enrollment increases following World War II required additional classroom and dormitory space. Eighteen buildings were moved from neighboring FORT ETHAN ALLEN, adding a military character to a campus that also included Cheray Science Hall, Jeanmarie Hall, and Founders Hall. On St. Michael's golden anniversary in 1955, the college employed fifty-four faculty, fourteen administrative officers, and support staff to serve over eight hundred students enrolled in under- and post-graduate, nursing, international, and ESL programs. It was also educating Korean War veterans and conducting a successful summer session that had begun admitting women in 1939. An expanding sports program and an Air Force Reserve Officers Training Corps benefitted from good enrollments and Saint Michael's Playhouse boasted a flourishing summer theatre. At the jubilee seventy-fifth anniversary in 1979, St. Michael's College enrolled two thousand students. It had become co-educational in 1970, the president was a layman, and the army barracks had been replaced by four brick residence halls, the Alliot Student Center, Ross Sports Center, Durick Library, McCarthy Arts Center, Holcomb Observatory, and the Chapel of St. Michael the Archangel. A second and new "North Campus" functioned at the nearby former Fort Ethan Allen. Today, the college campus also contains Saint Edmund's Hall, multiple town-house residences, a library addition, and expanded sports facilities. A major fund-raising campaign has been launched to help celebrate the centennial in 2004. This is intended to secure the school's future with an enhanced endowment, restore Founders' Hall, and construct a welcome center. Although St. Michael's continues to emphasize the liberal arts and sciences, it also offers programs in undergraduate professional training, international studies, and graduate studies, all supplemented by appropriate extracurricular activities. The college supports an enrollment of eighteen hundred undergraduates and plans to expand to seven hundred graduate students in a future-oriented, technologically advanced, and international academic setting.

Thomas H. Geno

Sainte-Anne, Fort

Isle La Motte, the northernmost island in LAKE CHAMPLAIN, lying approximately 8 miles from the Canadian border, was the site of Fort Sainte-Anne. Intended to block advances of the Iroquois and British against New France, the fort was built on the western shore of the island by a company of the CARIGNAN-SALIERES REGIMENT of the French army in the spring of 1666. Under the command of Captain PIERRE DE ST. PAUL, SIEUR DE LA MOTTE, a fort 144 feet long and 96 feet wide was built of earthworks and a double log palisade 15 feet high. Four bastions stood at the corners. It contained a forge, a well, and fourteen interior buildings ranging in size from 16 by 32 feet to 16 by 12 feet, including fireplaces. Severe winter conditions in the first year of the fort's service cost the lives of thirty men out of a company of sixty. Nearly three hundred men served at the fort from 1666 to 1669, when it was abandoned.

Sainte-Anne's Shrine

The Shrine of Sainte-Anne on Isle La Motte stands on the site of the old French FORT SAINTE-ANNE built in 1666 by a company of soldiers from the CARIGNAN-SALIERES REGIMENT commanded by Captain PIERRE DE ST. PAUL, SIEUR DE LA MOTTE. The site is believed to be the first European occupation of the region now known as Vermont. A priest accompanying the French soldiers who manned the fort celebrated the first Catholic mass in what later became Vermont. The Catholic Church acquired the site in 1892, erected a small shrine in honor of Sainte-Anne— the patron saint of Canada who is also much revered by Catholic Vermonters— and in 1893 the first organized pilgrimage to the shrine brought nearly two thousand people from Vermont, New York, and Canada to celebrate the Feast of Sainte-Anne. By 1900, day-long steamboat excursions for the feast had become regular summer events. In 1904, Bishop John Michaud asked the Fathers of St. Edmund to take over the administration of the facility. After World War I, the popularity of the shrine declined. Seldom visited during the Depression of the 1930s, the site served mainly as a summer residence for the Edmundite Fathers. A resurgence of devotional activities began under Bishop Edward F. Ryan, who presided annually at ceremonies at the shrine and encouraged pilgrimages. Today, the shrine includes a

chapel, grotto, cafeteria, gift shop, and outdoor devotional Way of the Cross on the actual site of the fort. Eucharistic celebrations are offered daily. Huge crowds gather on Sundays and Feast days in the summer to participate in devotions culminating in the Solemn Triduum marking Sainte-Anne's Feast Day, July 26. During the diocesan celebration of the United States Bicentennial in 1976, an estimated seven thousand persons participated in the three-day observance at the shrine. Best independent estimates of the number of visitors at the shrine during the summer seasons of recent years are fifty thousand to sixty thousand. About 30 percent are French-speaking. *David Blow*

Salisbury

Salisbury, population 1,090, a town in Addison County, was granted by BENNING WENTWORTH in 1761 and named after Salisbury, Connecticut, the home colony of many of the grantees. It lies on the dividing line between the Champlain lowlands and the foothills of the GREEN MOUNTAINS, with its eastern third lying in the GREEN MOUNTAIN NATIONAL FOREST. Its western section is primarily agricultural, although much of the land is taken up by an extensive swamp that extends into six neighboring towns from Brandon to Middlebury. Salisbury shares Lake Dunmore, a summer resort area, with the town of Leicester to the south. The main settlement of Salisbury village, on the border with Leicester, was once a regionally important industrial center. ANN STORY, the Revolutionary War heroine, had her home in Salisbury.

Salmon, Thomas P. (b. 1932)

The second popularly elected Democratic governor of Vermont, Thomas P. Salmon was born in Cleveland, Ohio, and grew up in Stow, Massachusetts. He graduated from Boston College (B.A., 1954; J.D., 1957), with further legal study at New York University, and came to Vermont in 1958 to practice law in Bellows Falls. He settled in Rockingham and became active in community life, serving as municipal judge in Bellows Falls from 1963 to 1965 and in the Vermont House of Representatives from 1965 to 1971, the last two years as minority leader. The successful tenure of Governor DEANE DAVIS and a probable Richard Nixon landslide re-election as president seemed to promise an invincible Vermont Republican ticket in 1972. With only PHILIP

HOFF having won a modern gubernatorial election, Vermont's Democrats had difficulty locating a candidate to run against such odds. Though relatively unknown outside of Windham County and despite no opposition in the Democratic primary to raise his statewide visibility, Salmon ran a vigorous campaign on the theme "Vermont for Vermonters," declaring "Vermont is not for sale." He promised property tax relief on income criteria through federal revenue sharing and a land gains tax. Even Governor Davis recognized that Salmon was an effective campaigner, writing later that Salmon "presented himself as an extremely intelligent, articulate, handsome individual with loads of charm." The Republican candidate, Luther F. Hackett of South Burlington, conducted a lackluster campaign after a divisive primary battle with Attorney General JAMES JEFFORDS, and fifty-five thousand Vermonters who voted to re-elect Richard Nixon also voted for Salmon, who beat Hackett by a decisive 56 to 43 percent in one of the biggest upsets in Vermont electoral history. The Salmon administration was faced with growing inflation, a stagnant economy, Nixon's domestic cuts, and the OPEC-created fuel crisis. Yet he persuaded a firmly Republican legislature to pass a land gains tax and a property tax refund, renew a bottle deposit law, and prohibit phosphates in Vermont's lakes and streams. He also achieved a consolidation in state government with the formation of the Agency of Transportation. The economy and high inflation forced Salmon to be fiscally conservative, though he failed to convince the legislature to raise the sales tax by 1 percent, which led to budget cutting in his second term. Drawn to mediating and building coalitions rather than partisan conflict, Salmon helped heal the break in the DEMOCRATIC PARTY between old-line conservative Democrats in Chittenden and Franklin counties and the liberal wing of the party opposed to the war in Vietnam and supportive of environmentalism and human rights. But when he won the 1976 Democratic nomination to run against U.S. Senator ROBERT STAFFORD in a harshly fought primary campaign against Scott Skinner, director of the Vermont Public Interest Research Group, some of the Democratic party's liberal wing sat out the general election and Salmon lost by 3.3 percent, a strong showing in a state that had never turned out an incumbent U.S.

Senator. Salmon returned to his law practice in Bellows Falls, served as a mediator in labor disputes, and as a director of several corporations, including National Life Insurance Company and Green Mountain Power Company, where he was chairman. In 1991, he was named interim president of the UNIVERSITY OF VERMONT to succeed a president who had been forced to resign after one year in the office. Salmon served UVM for six years, five as president, attempting to restore fiscal stability and convince the state to increase its funding to Vermont's state university. While he led UVM to a balanced budget, a successful $108 million capital campaign, several new buildings, and better relations with the state, funding from state government actually declined during his tenure and tuition costs continued to rise. He continued to teach in UVM's master's degree program in public administration after he retired from the presidency in 1997.

H. Nicholas Muller III and Vince Feeney

Sandbar, The

The Sandbar is a natural sand bank in LAKE CHAMPLAIN stretching between the town of South Hero on Grand Isle and the mainland town of Milton. The sandy shoal hampered boats traveling the eastern length of the Hero Islands during summer. A ferry operated next to the bar from early settlement of the islands in the 1780s and 1790s until 1850, when a toll bridge and causeway were constructed. Benajah Phelps of South Hero oversaw the Sandbar causeway and collected tolls for bridge crossings from the early 1890s, adding an inn to his toll house in 1899. Son George bought the Phelps House in 1923, making renovations prompted by the two-lane improvements to the bridge. The inn continues to operate as the Sand Bar Inn. Paving of the causeway came in 1930, though high lake levels in the spring could shut down highway travel to the mainland for as much as three weeks in some years. In 1933, the state of Vermont opened the Sandbar State Park on the east end of the causeway, and later in that decade the CIVILIAN CONSERVATION CORPS constructed several stone buildings for park amenities. Today the Sandbar is Vermont's most popular STATE PARK. In the 1950s, the roadbed was reconstructed and raised above the highest water levels. Additional improvements in the 1990s were required to manage increased traffic over U.S. Route 2, the main transportation artery of

Grand Isle County. During that construction project, a grass roots movement persuaded public utility companies to remove a series of power transmission poles standing in the lake and bury the lines in the causeway, a move that opened a clear, splendid southern view of outer Malletts Bay and the distant Adirondack Mountains.   *Donald Wickman*

Sanders, Bernard (b. 1941)

Vermont's representative in the U.S. House of Representatives since 1991 and before that mayor of Burlington, Bernard ("Bernie") Sanders is a self-professed socialist who has had a remarkable career in state and national politics. Born in Brooklyn, New York, the son of a paint salesman and his wife, Sanders attended public elementary and high schools, went to Brooklyn College for a year, and then transferred to the University of Chicago. Here he developed a social philosophy critical of capitalism and a commitment to political activism. Following graduation in 1964 with a degree in political science, he moved to Vermont, where he made a meager living as a freelance writer and educational-film maker. His first run for public office was in 1972 as a LIBERTY UNION candidate in a special election for the U.S. Senate, where he garnered a mere 2 percent of the vote. Two runs for governor in 1972 and 1976 and another run for the Senate in 1974 resulted in similar low support. In 1981, however, having left the Liberty Union, he surprised everyone by being elected mayor of Burlington as an independent by a ten-vote margin, defeating a Democratic incumbent. Despite initial antagonism from the board of aldermen and members of the business community, he went on to win re-election three times, always by a solid majority. Eventually, like-minded allies gained several aldermanic seats, making the implementation of his goals easier. His administration was marked by successes such as competitive bidding on city insurance contracts, amicable contract settlements with the police and fire unions, an increase in commercial property taxes and utility rates, the imposition of special fees on utilities for excavation projects on the city's streets, the establishment of a municipal day-care center and an arts council, and other "sewer socialist" victories. He was not successful, however, in other matters, such as repealing the tax exemption of the Medical Center Hospital or reforming the city housing code, and his repeated criticisms of the Reagan administration's support of the Nicaraguan contras did not sit well with many citizens. In 1986, he set his sights on the governorship, capturing 14 percent of the vote and denying the incumbent, MADELEINE KUNIN, an outright majority (she was later elected by the legislature). In 1988, he ran for Vermont's house seat, losing narrowly to Republican PETER SMITH. Two years later he challenged Smith again, and this time, helped by the fact that Smith had angered gun owners by voting for the Brady bill and in the absence of a credible Democratic alternative, he won with 56 percent of the vote. Despite his extra-party standing, Sanders was able to gain committee assignments from the Democrats, and as the years passed—he was re-elected for the sixth time in 2002—has acquired seniority rights as well. He is a member of the Committee on Banking and Financial Services and the Committee on Government Reform and Oversight, and the ranking member of the latter committee's Subcommittee on International Monetary Policy and Trade. He is a founding member of the Progressive Caucus, a group of like-minded representatives mostly from urban districts. His agenda includes tax reform that will shift the burden of taxation to wealthier Americans, the elimination of corporate subsidies ("corporate welfare"), a universal health care plan patterned after the Canadian model, major reductions in military spending, an affordable housing program, support for family farms, and adherence to positions held by organized labor such as opposition to the North American Free Trade Agreement (NAFTA) and the Free Trade Area of the Americas (FTAA).

Sanders, Daniel Clark (1768–1850)

Daniel Clark Sanders was the first president of the UNIVERSITY OF VERMONT. Born in Sturbridge, Massachusetts, he graduated in Harvard's class of 1788, and earned a master's degree in 1791. He served the next nine years as pastor of the Vergennes Congregational Church and in 1800 was appointed the first president of the University of Vermont. He nurtured the university through its formative years, serving as administrator, faculty member, and librarian. Sanders raised funds for the first major building, the College Edifice (1806), which cost over $24,000. He was involved in ongoing disputes with some orthodox ministers on the board of trustees over the liberal religious views he expressed while continuing to serve as the pastor of the Congregational Church in Burlington. Sanders published a major scholarly study, *A History of the Indian Wars* (1812). During the War of 1812, five of his children died in the LUNG FEVER EPIDEMIC, and the federal government seized the College Edifice as an army barracks. UVM's enrollment grew from four students in 1800 to 120 students when he resigned from the university in 1814. After leaving Burlington, he ended his professional career by serving as a Congregational pastor in Medford, Massachusetts, and as a member of the Massachusetts state legislature.

Frank Smallwood

Sandgate

Sandgate, population 353, a town in Bennington County, was granted by BENNING WENTWORTH in 1761 and named for Sandgate, England. The heavily forested town, which lies in the TACONIC MOUNTAINS, consists of a series of picturesque valleys and hills, rising to 3,301 feet at Bear Mountain. It is cut off from neighboring Manchester to the east by the bulk of Equinox Mountain and has sparse connections with Rupert to the north, Arlington to the south, and New York State to the west. Its seclusion has led to the construction of numerous vacation homes by people attracted to privacy and the outdoor life. The small village of Sandgate lies on the Green River, a tributary of the BATTEN KILL, and the CHARTERHOUSE OF THE TRANSFIGURATION, a Carthusian monastery, is located on the side of Equinox Mountain. After Daniel SHAYS' REBELLION against Massachusetts taxes failed in 1787, Shays escaped to Sandgate with some of his followers and lived in hermit fashion until moving to New York State.

Saunders, Prince (ca. 1780–1839)

An educator, author, Mason, abolitionist, early Pan-Africanist, and advisor to the Haitian government, Prince Saunders (Sanders), the son of African-born Cuff and Phyliss Saunders, was born in Lebanon, Connecticut, and when the man who owned his parents' service by an indenture contract settled in Thetford, young Saunders was brought along. He received his early schooling in the town. He taught in a colored school in Connecticut, studied at Moor's Charity School at Dartmouth College in 1807, and began teaching at the African school in Boston by 1808. In Boston, he became secretary of the African Masonic Lodge (1811), taught at the Negro Baptist Church, and founded the Belles Lettres Society, a literary group. In 1815, he traveled to England as a delegate to the Masonic Lodge of Africans, intent on missionary work in Africa. He was received into society and began a life-long friendship with abolitionists Thomas Clarkson and William Wilberforce. Instead of Africa, Saunders traveled to Haiti in 1816. He became a confidant of King Henri Christophe, set up schools under the Lancastrian system, and introduced public vaccination to the island. While back in London in the same year to recruit teachers, he published *Haytian Papers*, his translation of the Haitian legal code, which led to a falling out with Christophe. He continued to teach in Haiti until 1818, when he returned to the United States. He settled in the black community in Philadelphia and joined the Pennsylvania Society for Abolition, where he championed the colonization of the Caribbean by free United States blacks. He published *An Address Delivered . . . before the Pennsylvania Augustine Society for the Education of People of Color and A Memoir . . . for Promoting the Abolition of Slavery* (1818). In August 1820, he was back in Haiti negotiating a major colonization project, which collapsed when the Haitian army rebelled and Christophe's regime ended. Saunders attempted to rekindle the project with Boyer, the new leader, but was distrusted for past associations. Between 1823 and 1839, Sanders was in Haiti, lobbying for colonization and advising the government. He is said to have filled the post of attorney general in Haiti during these years, but this is unlikely given his association with the Christophe government, and Haitian history records no such cabinet appointment. Saunders died in Port-au-Prince, Haiti, in 1839. His particular importance today lies in the international perspective he brought to issues facing African-Americans.

Ray Zirblis

Saxe, John Godfrey (1816–1887)

A lawyer, politician, and poet, John Godfrey Saxe was born in Highgate, attended St. Albans grammar school, graduated from MIDDLEBURY COLLEGE, read the law in St. Albans, and practiced law there from 1843 to 1850, though not very effectively. He was superintendent of Franklin County common schools and wrote humorous verse for several magazines, including New York's *Knickerbocker*. He published his first book of verse, *Progress, A Satire*, in 1846. Moving to Burlington in 1850, he was elected Chittenden County state's attorney as a Democrat and in 1851 became editor of the Burlington *Sentinel*, the state's leading Democratic paper. Political patronage gave Saxe an appointment as deputy collector of customs for the port of Burlington. He twice ran unsuccessfully for governor as a Democrat in 1859 and 1860. Leaving the *Sentinel*, he returned to St. Albans, where he continued to write popular humorous verse. *The Atlantic Monthly* and *Harpers* published his verses from the 1850s to the 1870s. Several collections were very popular, including *The Money King and Other Poems* (1860) and *Leisure-Day Rhymes* (1875). His collected *Poems* (1850) went through forty reprints. In 1872, he moved to Brooklyn, New York, but as his family died off he became a recluse, returning alone to St. Albans where he died.

Schmitt, George (1892–1913)

Aviation pioneer George Schmitt was born in New York City and moved with his family to Rutland. After Rutland High School, he briefly attended a New York City electrical trade school and then a flying school in Mineola, Long Island. An unsuccessful rival for the distinction of making the first airplane flight in Vermont, in 1911 he formed with Henry Thor the Thor-Schmitt Aviation Company and appeared at state fairs to give flying exhibitions and carry passengers. In the process he set the speed record for biplanes, flying 24 miles in 16 minutes. In 1913, he conducted a triumphal tour of the Caribbean, Central America, and northern South America, and at the time became the first to fly from the Atlantic to the Pacific oceans by crossing the Isthmus of Panama. Returning to Vermont, he performed at the Addison County Fair and then at the RUTLAND FAIR, where in the course of an exhibition flight his engine misfired and his plane fell 500 feet into a nearby field. His passenger survived, but Schmitt died four hours later in a nearby hospital, becoming Vermont's first aviation casualty.

Scott, Julian (1846–1901)

Julian Scott of Johnson was a fifteen-year-old fifer with the Third Vermont Regiment when he acquired the Civil War experience that led to his vivid post-war paintings of

The Vermont Brigade at White Oak Swamp near Richmond, June 30, 1862, *by Julian Scott. Robert Titterton*

battlefield scenes. Scott was awarded a Congressional Medal of Honor for rescuing wounded under enemy fire at the Battle of Lee's Mill, Virginia. After the war, he studied art under Emanuel Leutze at the National Academy of Design and in 1870 was elected an associate member of the Academy. *The BATTLE OF CEDAR CREEK*, his monumental 1874 painting, was commissioned as a memorial for Vermont troops. This painting and three others by Scott, including *Rear Guard at White Oak Swamp* with its portraits of twenty Vermonters, can be seen in the Cedar Creek Room at the VERMONT STATE HOUSE. In 1890, Scott was appointed special agent to the Eleventh Census to work in the first assessment of the condition of Native Americans. Scott surveyed Indian communities in Oklahoma, New Mexico, and Arizona territories at the time for their acculturation and assimilation, producing nearly 70 percent of the illustrative material and twenty-five pages of written reports. The full report has been called, "One of the most exhaustive sources of information on the American Indian ever published."   *Robert Titterton*

Scott, William, the "Sleeping Sentinel"

The incident of the "sleeping sentinel" occurred early in the Civil War and was widely regarded as an example of the humanity of President Lincoln. William Scott, a farmboy from Groton, answered the President's call for volunteers in the summer of 1861, joining Company K of the Third Vermont Regiment. The regiment

was detailed to guard a bridge across the Potomac near Washington, a potential Confederate invasion route into the capital. In the early morning hours of August 31, after a hard day of marching and drilling, Scott was found asleep at his post, arrested, quickly court-martialed, and sentenced to be shot on September 9. The motive for the draconian sentence was to instill discipline into raw Union troops by making Scott an example of those guilty of dereliction of duty. Several of Scott's comrades, convinced the sentence was too harsh, were taken to see the president by LUCIUS E. CHITTENDEN, a Treasury Department official from Burlington, and Lincoln personally interceded with Major General George B. McClellan to issue a pardon. Returned to duty, Scott was killed the following April at a battle of the Peninsular Campaign near Lee's Mill, Virginia. A popular poem of the day, "The Sleeping Sentinel" by Francis De Haes Janvier, romanticized the incident by having Lincoln race up in a coach just in time to halt Scott's execution. A section of U.S. Route 302 in Groton is designated the William Scott Memorial Highway, and a granite shaft on the road near the site of the family farm commemorates the "sleeping sentinel." Five Scott sons served in the Civil War; only one returned alive.

Searsburg

Searsburg, population 96, a town in Bennington County, was created by the Vermont legislature in 1781 from the northern part of the town of Readsboro. The origin of the name is obscure, although it may have been derived from Isaac Sears, a New York merchant and ship owner whose name was listed in a number of other Vermont-granted towns. Remote, rugged, and heavily wooded, the town lies completely within the GREEN MOUNTAIN NATIONAL FOREST. Lumbering has been the only industry. Route 9, the Molly Stark Trail, one of only three roads crossing the GREEN MOUNTAINS in southern Vermont (of which one is closed in winter), cuts across the town from west to east, following the course of the Deerfield River part of the way.

Serkin, Rudolf (1903–1991)

World famous pianist, co-founder and long-time musical director of the MARLBORO MUSIC FESTIVAL, Rudolph Serkin was born in Eger, Austria-Hungary (now Cheb, Czech Republic), and was first taught music by his father, a singer. The family moved to Vienna when he was nine, where he studied piano and composition and was soon hailed as a child prodigy, playing Mendelssohn's concerto with the Vienna Philharmonic at twelve. His regular concert career began in 1920. In Vienna, he came to know Adolf Busch and the many musicians of the Busch family, one of the most famous music performance families of the twentieth century. Serkin became known for his chamber music performances, which began during his association with Busch in the 1920s. His playing was characterized by faithfulness to the text and classical clarity. Driven from Austria by the Nazi regime in 1939, Serkin and the Busch family fled to America. Serkin settled at Guilford, and took a position at the Curtis Music Institute in Philadelphia, serving on the piano faculty until 1975. He co-founded the Marlboro Music Festival with Adolf Busch and MARCEL, LOUIS, AND BLANCHE MOYSE in 1949, becoming musical director after Busch's death in 1952. With Serkin as director until 1991, the Marlboro Festival became one of the most famous music festivals in America. His extensive discograpy includes many records made at Marlboro, including with his pianist son Peter Serkin and cellist Pablo Casals. He died of cancer in 1991 at his Guilford home.

Shaftsbury

Shaftsbury, population 3,767, a town in Bennington County, was granted by BENNING WENTWORTH in 1761 and probably named for Anthony Ashley Cooper (1671–1713), third earl of Shaftesbury, a highly regarded moral philosopher. The central portion of the town lies in the VALLEY OF VERMONT, with the TACONIC MOUNTAINS rising to the west (to 2,401 feet at West Mountain) and the GREEN MOUNTAINS to the east. Route 7A bisects the main settlement, Shaftsbury village, near the south end of town, as well as a small historic district called Center Shaftsbury. The EAGLE SQUARE COMPANY, maker of the original carpenter's square, had its beginnings in 1817 and became the town's principal industry between 1916 and 2001 as a subsidiary of Stanley Tools of New Britain, Connecticut. ROBERT FROST resided for many years in Shaftsbury, first in a house on Route 7A near the Bennington line and then at the Gulley Farm, now owned by television producer Norman Lear. The town abuts New York State to the west, and the unorganized town of Glastenbury to the east.

Sharon

Sharon, population 1,411, a town in Windsor County, was granted by BENNING WENTWORTH in 1761 and named for Sharon in Connecticut, the home colony of most of the town's grantees. The deep valley of the WHITE RIVER cuts across the town from northwest to southeast and contains most of its good farming land. The single village of Sharon lies on the river approximately in the center of the town and is surrounded by steep hills, the highest of which is 1,630-foot Quimby Mountain. The Mormon prophet JOSEPH SMITH was born on a remote hill farm in Sharon and lived there for the first ten years of his life. A memorial encompassing the area is maintained by the Church of Jesus Christ of Latter-Day Saints.

Shattuck, Ira (1804–1886)

Hotelier and stagecoach-line operator Ira Shattuck, a native of Weathersfield, moved from Windsor to Burlington in 1836 to run the American Hotel on Court House Square. In 1842, he formed a partnership with Mahlon Cottrill (owner of Montpelier's PAVILION HOTEL) to establish a line of stagecoaches from Montreal to Boston. Shattuck and Cottrill operated coaches over the stretch from Burlington to Montpelier. Two Concord coaches made the daily trip, employing 134 horses on 12-mile relays, stopping only so passengers could eat. The stagecoach line linking Montreal to Boston was an alliance of linked routes operated by regular consultation and contracts. The lines employed common agents, divided the proceeds on a mileage basis and fought off competition. Revenues for carrying the U.S. mails met the lines' operating expenses, while mailcoach passengers provided the profit. The completion of two RAILROADS through Vermont in 1849 and the loss of the mail contract to the Vermont Central Railroad put Shattuck and Cottrill out of business.

David Blow

Shays' Rebellion

Vermont experienced civil disturbances in 1786 when the strains of scarce money, increasing costs for credit, and legal actions brought out protestors and rioters against the courts and lawyers. The militia firmly suppressed riots in Rutland County, and the legislature responded by a voter survey on such questions as whether to accept cattle as legal tender. Subsequent legislative acts also seemed to meet the people's demands for relief. In Massachusetts, however, in early 1787, Daniel Shays, Luke Day, Adam Wheeler, and Eli Parsons led a similarly motivated rebellious army against the courthouses and other civil institutions of western Massachusetts, which a sympathetic militia could not be trusted to suppress. A private army led by Benjamin Lincoln routed Shays, but some of his followers fled into Vermont, where they sought reinforcements and invited ETHAN ALLEN to lead them. While Shays and other rebels were hiding in a neighboring farm, on February 27, 1787, Governor THOMAS CHITTENDEN, under pressure from a slim majority of the General Assembly, issued a proclamation forbidding Vermonters to harbor Shays or his followers and ordering his arrest and deportation to Massachusetts with any of his known supporters. Nonetheless, Shays seems to have remained in Vermont for two more years, quiet, unmolested, and impoverished.

Sheep Boom

The first merino sheep arrived in the United States in 1810 when WILLIAM JARVIS, former U.S. consul to Portugal, imported several hundred from Spain for his farm in Weathersfield. Between 1820 and 1840, a peaceful and prosperous America increased its demand for wool clothing that in turn increased the numbers of sheep needed for the rising market. Vermont's central role in the growth of

wool production more than tripled the
state's sheep population between 1824 and
1840 from 475,000 to 1,680,000. Addison
and Rutland counties were the leaders,
but most regions of the state had substantial sheep flocks. Addison County's Shoreham in 1840 had 41,000 merino sheep that
produced over 95,000 pounds of wool.
The town could boast an average of one
and a fraction sheep per acre, including
the unimproved land. When the supply
surpassed demand, prices fell, federal tariff protections were repealed, and whole
flocks were slaughtered for meat and
hides. Then cheaper western wool flooded
the eastern markets, and from the mid-
1850s sheep raising in Vermont was limited to a few farms producing breeding
stock for the west, Australia, and New
Zealand. During the sheep boom, fewer
than 150,000 dairy cattle, by contrast,
browsed Vermont's farms.

Sheffield

Sheffield, population 727, a town in Caledonia County, granted by the Vermont legislature in 1780 but not chartered until
1793, was probably named for Sheffield,
Massachusetts. Always sparsely settled
(the maximum population was 884 in
1880), the town has a number of low mountains in the 2,000-foot range and only one
settlement, Sheffield village, in the southernmost part of town. Although Interstate
91 cuts through the town from north to
south, there is no exit for Sheffield.

Shelburne

Shelburne, population 6,944, a town in
Chittenden County, was granted by BEN-
NING WENTWORTH in 1763 and named
after William Fitzmaurice Petty (1737–
1805), second earl of Shelburne, who was
president of the board of trade and planta-
tions of the British government. The gently rolling, well-watered landscape soon
attracted settlers, whose farms lined the
shores of LAKE CHAMPLAIN. In 1785, as
settlement progressed inland, IRA ALLEN
set up a sawmill at the falls of the La Platte
River, which runs through the town from
south to north and drains into Shelburne
Bay. On the flats a mile north of the falls,
on what became the stage road to Burlington, the village of Shelburne developed
into the town's population center. The
Shelburne Shipyard began to build steamboats in its yards on the bay in the 1820s,
and continues as a major boat service and
supply operation today. The town took

Sycamore tree in Shelburne. Ralph H. Orth

part in the merino sheep boom of the
1840s and somewhat later saw the development of apple orchards in favorable
locations along the lake. Much of Shelburne's later history has been connected
with SHELBURNE FARMS, the large, rambling estate of railroad magnate WILLIAM
SEWARD WEBB and his wife Lila Vanderbilt Webb, who in the 1880s bought several thousand acres of prime land along
Lake Champlain and turned them into a
magnificent retreat landscaped by Frederick Law Olmsted. The estate today, reduced in size but with its main residence
and large, architecturally significant barns
intact, is maintained by the Webb family
as a model farm, agricultural research
center, and locus for small enterprises
such as a vineyard and a cheese-making
facility. Near the center of Shelburne village is the SHELBURNE MUSEUM, a 45-
acre complex containing thirty-five historic buildings, many of them moved to
the site from around Vermont. It owes its
existence to ELECTRA HAVEMEYER WEBB,
whose vast trove of Americana was the
basis for the folk and fine art collections
that fill the buildings. The centerpiece of
the museum is the landlocked steamboat
TICONDEROGA, the last of the side-wheel
steamboats that used to operate on Lake
Champlain. In the last few decades, housing pressures from the Burlington urban
area to the north have led to the creation

of numerous small neighborhoods of middle-class and upper-middle-class homes,
many on cul de sacs, but so far no large
tract developments such as exist in South
Burlington and Williston have been built.
The southeastern section of town, which
includes 450-acre Shelburne Pond, whose
protected shores remain in a natural state,
retains the rural aspect of an earlier era.

Shelburne Farms

Founded in 1886 by Dr. WILLIAM SEWARD
WEBB and Eliza (Lila) Vanderbilt Webb,
Shelburne Farms is located along LAKE
CHAMPLAIN in Shelburne. An ambitious
country estate property, Shelburne Farms
was designed by architect Robert H. Robertson with the assistance of landscape
architect Frederick Law Olmsted, using
much of Lila Webb's $10 million Vander-
bilt inheritance. By 1900, the estate encompassed 3,800 acres and four major
buildings housing a country manor home,
a model farm, and an English Hackney
horse-breeding service intended to improve Vermont farmers' horse stock. The
estate employed approximately three hundred people in its heyday between 1890
and 1905. In 1972, after almost a hundred
years of private-family ownership, the
Webbs' great-grandchildren founded
Shelburne Farms Resources, a nonprofit
educational organization that currently
owns the core section of the estate. Dedi-

cated to the stewardship of agricultural and natural resources, the organization has rehabilitated several historic structures for use in its educational programs, public tours, cheesemaking operations, an inn and restaurant, and continues to operate the estate as a working farm, managing a herd of Brown Swiss dairy cattle.

Erica H. Donnis

Shelburne Museum

Located on 45 landscaped acres just south of the center of Shelburne village, the Shelburne Museum contains thirty-five structures, most deriving from the eighteenth and nineteenth centuries, that have been transported from their original locations and arranged about the grounds in a rough imitation of an early Vermont village. They are filled largely with exhibits designed, in the words of the museum's founder, ELECTRA HAVEMEYER WEBB, "to show the craftsmanship and ingenuity of our forebears." Founded in 1947, the museum was closely overseen by Mrs. Webb until her death in 1960, and further structures and exhibits have been added since then. Highlights of the museum include a double-lane covered bridge, originally erected in Cambridge in 1840 and used for many years as the museum's entrance; a stagecoach inn (Charlotte, 1783) containing tobacconist's figures, trade signs, weathervanes, and the like; the Dutton house (Cavendish, 1782), with an exhibit of eighteenth- and nineteenth-century decorative arts; a meeting house (Charlotte, 1840) with a pipe organ and trompe l'oeil wall panels; a GENERAL STORE (Shelburne, 1840), with a barber shop, taproom, and post office; a furnished one-room schoolhouse (Vergennes, 1840); a round barn (East Passumpsic, 1901), used as a visitor center; a jail and jailer's quarters (Castleton, 1890); and the COLCHESTER REEF LIGHTHOUSE (1871), with an exhibit on LAKE CHAMPLAIN and lighthouse keeping. The most unusual item in the museum is the steamboat *TICONDEROGA*, built in 1906 and transported a full mile overland to its present site in 1954. A recently opened exhibit is the 1950s house, furnished as a young family's home in post–World War II Vermont. The museum is open from late May to late October.

Polly C. Darnell

Sheldon

Sheldon, population 1,990, a town in Franklin County, was granted by BENNING WENTWORTH in 1763 and originally named Hungerford for the chief grantee, Samuel Hungerford. The name was changed to Sheldon in 1792 after Hungerford's interest had been sold and Colonel Elisha Sheldon and his sons had become prominent residents. The gently rolling countryside, largely devoted to DAIRY FARMING, is divided in two by the MISSISQUOI RIVER as it flows across the town from east to west. The main settlements are Sheldon village, on Black Creek, a tributary of the Missisquoi, and Sheldon Springs, once a thriving resort exploiting mineral springs reputed to have medicinal value. In October 1864, Confederate soldiers retreating towards Canada after the ST. ALBANS RAID set fire to the covered bridge at Sheldon Junction, and in 1866 members of the FENIANS, a group intent on invading Canada in a bid for Irish independence, were dispersed peacefully here by Federal troops.

Sheldon, Harold Pearl (1887–1951)

A native of Fair Haven, Harold Pearl Sheldon attended Georgetown and George Washington universities and received an honorary master of science from NORWICH UNIVERSITY "in recognition of his services as soldier, author, and conservationist." In 1910, he enlisted in the Vermont National Guard as a private. A captain by 1914, he saw service in World War I with the 102nd Machinegun Battalion of the Yankee Division, and was wounded at the Meuse-Argonne. Invalided home, Sheldon served as post-commandant of FORT ETHAN ALLEN in Colchester, retiring as lieutenant colonel in 1919. On a commission from the Vermont General Assembly in 1920, Sheldon wrote and John Cushing was statistical editor of *Vermont in the War, 1917–1919*. A dedicated conservationist, in 1921 Sheldon was appointed Vermont Commissioner of Fish and Game, a position he held until 1926 when he was appointed chief conservation officer of the United States Bureau of Biological Survey, the predecessor agency to the Fish and Wildlife Service of the United States Department of the Interior. With the establishment of the Fish and Wildlife Service, Colonel Sheldon was named its chief of public relations, retiring in 1943. Through the 1930s and 1940s, Sheldon wrote prolifically for a wide range of conservation and outdoors journals. Published collections of his pieces from *Country Life, Field and Stream*, and *Outdoor Life* on camping, fishing, hunting, and the rural life employing scenes from the Sheldon family farm and its environs in Fair Haven were published as *Tranquility* (1936), *Tranquility Revisited* (1945), and *Tranquility Regained* (1945). Although in the 1920s and 1930s GEORGE PERKINS MARSH's *Man and Nature* (1864) was hardly known outside a group of writers on environmental topics such as Wisconsin's Aldo Leopold, Harold Sheldon demonstrated his grasp of Marsh's message in a speech he wrote for Secretary of Agriculture Henry A. Wallace to deliver at the 1937 North American Wildlife Conference. "As a people we have been intensively engaged in developing and using machinery to subdue nature," Sheldon wrote. "It is necessary to readjust our perspective and devote a much larger proportion of our interest to the subject of life itself. Every form of life has value and interest of some sort; even the most insignificant creatures may be found to exercise the most profound influences upon mankind."

Sheldon, Henry (1821–1907)

Founder of Middlebury's SHELDON MUSEUM, Henry Sheldon was born in Salisbury, the youngest of four sons of Samuel and Sarah Weeks Sheldon. For his first twenty years he lived and worked on his father's farm. In 1841, he moved to Middlebury, where he worked for a time in the post office and his brother Harmon's store, investing his earnings in downtown real estate and various short-lived business ventures, such as a MARBLE quarry and an oyster saloon. After a year in Nebraska, he returned to Middlebury and concentrated on real estate, a piano business, and community activities. He was Middlebury village clerk from 1870 to 1895 and organist at St. Stephen's Episcopal Church from 1842 until 1876, when he gave it up because of increasing deafness. In 1882, he founded the Sheldon Art Museum, Archaeological and Historical Society "to benefit future generations by preserving the handiwork of the early settlers of Middlebury: books, all printed matter, manufactured articles representing all the different occupations of the early pioneers," as he wrote in his diary. Sheldon spent the rest of his life gathering a comprehensive collection of artifacts and documents, researching local history, and showing his collections to visitors.

Polly C. Darnell

Sheldon Museum

The Henry Sheldon Museum of Vermont History was founded in 1802 by HENRY SHELDON as the Sheldon Art Museum, Archaeological and Historical Society. The oldest community museum in the country, it is located in downtown Middlebury in a brick house built in 1829 by MARBLE merchants Eben Judd and Lebeus Harris. Sheldon purchased it to house his artifacts and documents relating to the history of Middlebury and Addison County, as well as the history of Vermont, the United States, and beyond. The Stewart-Swift Research Center was added in 1972. The Fletcher Community History Center, completed in 1990, houses a gallery and museum shop. The collections have grown, reflecting Addison County in the twentieth century and expanding Sheldon's collections from the eighteenth and nineteenth centuries. Highlights include furniture, portraits, tools, textiles and clothing, as well as documents relating to Addison County families, businesses, organizations, towns, and villages. The museum has also collected photographs, ephemera, and local publications, including almost all of Middlebury's newspapers from 1810 to the present. Changing exhibits and an active education program draw on these resources. The museum serves the public by preserving the historic memory of Addison County and its connections to the broader story of Vermont.

Nancy Rucker

Sherwood, Justus (1747–1798)

A GREEN MOUNTAIN BOY who remained loyal to the Crown during the Revolution and actively opposed American independence as an officer in the Loyalist Queen's Rangers, Justus Sherwood was born in Newton, Connecticut, but virtually nothing is known of his childhood. He migrated to the New Hampshire grants in the early 1770s, where he joined the Green Mountain Boys against New York in defense of New Hampshire titles. He would not follow ETHAN ALLEN into rebellion against the Crown, however, and fled to British lines at Crown Point in October 1776. There he joined the Queen's Rangers and participated in BURGOYNE's campaign as a scout and forager. He saw action at the BATTLE OF BENNINGTON, where he lost most of his company, and escaped with the remnant of his rangers to Fort George and FORT TICONDEROGA. For the next three years, he worked in the

secret service, and in June 1781 was placed in charge of all secret service activities on the northern frontier. From the LOYALIST BLOCKHOUSE he built at Dutchman's Point on North Hero Island in LAKE CHAMPLAIN, Sherwood sent Loyalist rangers and Indian allies to gather intelligence in the northern colonies, contact Loyalist informants behind rebel lines, and kidnap prominent Patriots. In October 1780, Sherwood was sent to Castleton to open discussions with Ethan Allen over Vermont rejoining the British Empire. Sherwood was the chief British agent in the subsequent protracted HALDIMAND NEGOTIATIONS, which ultimately failed. By October 1781, Sherwood believed that he was on the verge of success, but the defeat of Lord Cornwallis at Yorktown derailed negotiations. In an attempt to keep reconciliation an issue, Sherwood maintained a correspondence with Ethan and IRA ALLEN until the end of the war. After the war, he unsuccessfully requested a grant of Dutchman's Point from the British, who occupied it until 1796. He also filed a claim for compensation from the state of Vermont for the loss of his New Haven farm and lands in Poultney taken from him by the Vermont Court of Confiscation. In 1784, he moved to Cataraqui, later Kingston, on the upper St. Lawrence River, and in 1794 he and twenty-two Loyalist families from Vermont settled on a Crown grant in Leeds County, Upper Canada (Ontario). Acquiring land became a major interest and he remained prominent locally until his death by drowning in 1798, when he fell from a log raft headed down the St. Lawrence River to Montreal.

Shire Town

Shire was a term for an administrative district in England prior to the Norman Conquest. With the adoption of Norman law in the eleventh century, the Anglo-French word *counte* (i.e., "county"), replaced *shire*. Following eighteenth-century English and colonial American practice, Vermont's early legislatures established counties as administrative districts with tax levying authority to support trial courts of general jurisdiction. In recent years, the legislature has shifted most costs for county court houses to the state budget. Statutory descriptions of each Vermont county designate the town containing county court houses as the shire town (what in other states is called a county seat), a status towns sought competitively in the settlement period for the economic

benefits resulting from a court. While county court houses today can contain superior, family, probate, and sometimes district and traffic courts, the benefits of commerce unrelated to the administration of justice in most of Vermont's shire towns far exceed the economic value of the courts for that town.

Shoreham

Shoreham, population 1,222, a town in Addison County, was granted by BENNING WENTWORTH in 1761 and probably named for Shoreham-by-the-Sea, England. The land was acquired by Colonel Ephraim Doolittle and a number of his soldiers, who were impressed with the area's fertile soil and prime location on LAKE CHAMPLAIN when they were building the CROWN POINT ROAD in 1759. Today the land is devoted to dairying and apple orchards, although during the sheep-raising boom of the 1830s and 1840s the town supported up to forty thousand sheep. The main settlement is Shoreham village, just west of Route 22A, which crosses the town from north to south. Hands Cove is the spot from which ETHAN ALLEN and the GREEN MOUNTAIN BOYS crossed the lake to capture the British fortress at FORT TICONDEROGA in May, 1775. A cable-driven ferry at Larrabee's Point provides a six-minute ride to the town of Ticonderoga in New York State. It is the oldest continuously operating ferry crossing in the United States, having been in constant service since 1759. LEVI P. MORTON, U.S. vice president under Benjamin Harrison and later governor of New York, was born and raised in Shoreham. The Shoreham Covered Railroad Bridge State Historic Site lies on the LEMON FAIR RIVER in the extreme southeastern corner of the town.

Shrewsbury

Shrewsbury, population 1,108, a town in Rutland County, was granted by BENNING WENTWORTH in 1761 and named for the earldom of Shrewsbury, which was held by the Talbot family. It lies on the western slopes of the main spine of the GREEN MOUNTAINS, rising to 3,700 feet at Shrewsbury Peak on the border with Mendon to the north. Despite the mountainous terrain, Shrewsbury was fairly well populated in the mid-nineteenth century and had a number of settlements, including Shrewsbury village and Cuttingsville. Copperas (ferrous sulfate) was once mined near the latter village, and dairying takes

The John P. Bowman Memorial in Shrewsbury. Ralph H. Orth

place in the town's gentler stream valleys. In the Cuttingsville cemetery is the striking Bowman Memorial, a marble and granite Greek temple outside of which is a granite statue of John P. Bowman in deep mourning.

Simpson, Jean Walker (1897–1980)

A generous benefactor and for many years one of Craftsbury's notable residents, Jean Walker Simpson (known as "Miss Jean," to distinguish her from her likewise notable next-door neighbor and first cousin MARY JEAN SIMPSON), was born in New York City. Her education was acquired by private tutoring and extensive travelling, from which she acquired fluency in several modern languages, as well as reading ability in Greek and Latin. Her efforts to promote the appreciation of Shakespeare's plays in performances by Craftsbury's East Hill Players for over fifty years were applauded with degrees *in honoris causa* from MIDDLEBURY COLLEGE and the UNIVERSITY OF VERMONT. She also served her community as a two-term legislator, a school board member, a founding leader of the Craftsbury Girl Scouts, and an animal rights advocate. She was a generous, discreet philanthropist, benefitting a wide range of individuals and organizations. Her most visible legacy is the John Woodruff Simpson Memorial Library, which she founded, stocked, operated, and endowed in what had been her grandfather's East Craftsbury GENERAL STORE. Since 1921, surrounding communities have profited

from its twenty thousand books and its eclectic museum and costume collection.

Sherry Urie

Simpson, Mary Jean (1888–1977)

A long-time public servant in Vermont and Washington, D.C., and an influential dean of women at the UNIVERSITY OF VERMONT (1937–1955), Mary Jean Simpson was born in East Craftsbury and attended Craftsbury Academy, ST. JOHNSBURY ACADEMY, Wheaton Seminary, Mount Holyoke College, and the University of Vermont, where she received a Ph.B. in 1913. Later she did graduate work at Columbia University (1923–1924). Upon graduating from UVM, she taught at People's Academy in Morrisville (1913–1916) and Montpelier High School (1916–1918) and was principal at People's Academy (1918–1920). She returned to Montpelier to teach again at the high school for one year and then went to New York City, where she taught in the 1921 to 1922 school year. She ran for the Vermont legislature as a Republican and represented Craftsbury in 1924, serving on the Fish and Game and the Military Committees. From 1926 to 1933, Mary Jean Simpson was bill clerk of the United States Senate, the first woman ever to have been appointed to the staff of the secretary of the Senate. Later she served the YWCA as financial secretary, then headed the Women's Division of the Civil Works Administration and of the WPA, from which she resigned to become UVM's dean of women in 1937. She served in that position for seventeen years, retiring in 1955. Though this position was her most visible and influential, she was also a leader in dozens of other organizations—the WPA, boards of Craftsbury Academy, East Craftsbury's John Woodruff Simpson Library, and GODDARD COLLEGE, State Commission on Alcohol Education, YWCA, NEA, Vermont Rural Rehabilitation Commission, Vermont Council of Church Women, Vermont CCC, and the Republican State Committee, among many others. She was an elder of the Presbyterian Church. During and after World War II she established the Mary Jean Simpson Scholarship Fund, which was used for loans and a tutoring program for veterans. Simpson was characterized as a "Liberal Republican" who supported progressive reforms within the political establishment, yet remained conservative in the areas of religion, personal responsibility, and educational standards. A friend later wrote of her "keen mind,

sparkling wit and tremendous energy." When new women's residence halls were built at UVM in 1955, the central building was named in her honor. Retiring to East Craftsbury, she remained active in state and civic affairs for another twenty years.

Sarah L. Dopp

Simpson, W. Arthur (1887–1971)

A prominent Vermont political figure for nearly fifty years, W. Arthur Simpson was born in Lyndon, where he graduated from LYNDON INSTITUTE in 1905. Between 1912 and 1923, he served as a Lyndon school director (1914–1920), selectman (1921–1935), and town moderator for forty-three years. He served two terms in the Vermont House (1923–1927) and one in the Senate (1927–1929). His appointments included the state Highway Board (1927–1933) and the Vermont Old Age Assistance Commission as chairman and director (1935–1944). He resigned in 1944 to run as a Republican for governor, one of four unsuccessful bids he made for that office beginning in 1930. In 1947, he was again elected to the House and re-appointed as director of the Old Age Assistance Commission, which soon became the Department of Social Welfare. Simpson was commissioner of social welfare until his forced retirement in 1959 at age seventy-two. During his years as commissioner of social welfare, he was indicted under the Hatch Act for political activity while holding an office subsidized by federal funds. Unable to stay out of politics after his retirement, he served three terms in the house (1963–1968). From the age of eighteen, he was involved in improving the milking shorthorn breed of cattle, joining with breeders in Pennsylvania to improve the milking qualities of the breed. He became president of the New England and the American Milking Shorthorn Societies and a prominent judge of the breed. A charter member of the New England Milk Producer Association (1914) and the Caledonia County Farm Bureau, Simpson remained active in agricultural affairs and continued to run his farm and write articles on AGRICULTURE until his death at eighty-four. *Harriet F. Fisher*

Skene, Philip (1725–1810)

A veteran Scots officer of the British Army in the Seven Years' War, Philip Skene acquired by grant, military patent, and purchase 54,350 acres in the Province of New York at the head of LAKE CHAMPLAIN, including land on the east shore of the lake where New York claimed jurisdiction against New Hampshire. Skene built a large stone house at the head of the lake and presided over the region, including the settlement called Skenesborough (today's Whitehall, New York). During the dispute between New York and the New Hampshire grantees in the early 1770s, Skene, the Allen brothers, and other prominent New Hampshire grantees developed a proposal for the Crown to organize a new province beginning at the backbone of the GREEN MOUNTAINS and running west to Lake Ontario, bounded on the south by the Mohawk River and on the north by the forty-fifth parallel, with Skene as royal governor. Carrying the petition to London in 1774, Skene won appointment as lieutenant governor of the crumbling fortifications at FORT TICONDEROGA and Crown Point and an order to poll inhabitants of the region for their sentiments on creating a new province. Officers of the Continental Congress arrested him at the dock in Philadelphia when he returned to America in June. Ticonderoga and Crown Point had in the meantime been taken from the British by ETHAN ALLEN and the GREEN MOUNTAIN BOYS. After the Americans occupied Skenesborough, they stripped the lead from Skene's late wife's crypt to be molded into bullets for their new army. Exchanged in late 1776, Skene went to Canada and joined JOHN BURGOYNE's army on the march up the Champlain Valley in 1777. Burgoyne sent him on an unsuccessful mission to Castleton in mid-July to coerce the settlers into seeking British protection against the American rebels. Returning to England after the war, Skene was well known in the former American Loyalist community when LEVI ALLEN visited and borrowed money from him in 1790. At Allen's request, Skene lobbied the Crown for a free-trade agreement between Canada and Vermont, an arrangement Allen finally achieved when he returned to Vermont. Levi told his brother Ira that he had dined with and benefitted from the experience and politial influence of "Our first governor."   *Herman Brown*

Skiing

Skiing in Vermont, today the state's most important recreational industry, can be said to have begun in earnest in Stowe and other locales in the 1930s. Before that time, crude skis allowed cross-country travel and also downhill runs for those willing to make the arduous climb up hills or, for true enthusiasts, mountains. (The first known ascent of MOUNT MANSFIELD on skis was made via the Toll Road in January 1914.) But starting in 1933, a number of trails were cut on state land on Mansfield by the CIVILIAN CONSERVATION CORPS under the direction of State Forester PERRY MERRILL. A rope tow was installed in 1935. (The actual first ski tow in the United States, powered by an old Model T Ford engine, began operation in Woodstock the previous year.) The nation's first ski patrol followed in 1936. In 1940, the Mount Mansfield Company leased state forest land on Mount Mansfield, and by the next year had built a chairlift most of the way up the mountain. Other ski areas that opened in the 1930s were Bromley in Manchester, Hogback in Marlboro, and Pico in Killington. Special overnight ski trains from New York City to Waterbury allowed skiers to get to the Stowe slopes by Saturday morning, and also contributed to the growth of the Stowe lodging industry, which in its earliest phase utilized barns, attics, and spare rooms for visitors. After World War II, the modern era of skiing in Vermont came into existence with the construction of large resorts covering whole mountains, among which were Mount Snow in Dover (1954), Okemo in Ludlow (1956), Killington in Killington (1958), and Stratton Mountain in Stratton and Winhall (1960). Many of these are in the southern part of the state within a few hour's drive of population centers in Massachusetts, Connecticut, New York, and New Jersey. The largest, Killington, is representative of

Skiing at Okemo Mountain. Okemo Mountain Resort

the scope of these resorts: it has 77 miles of alpine ski trails on seven mountains, a maximum vertical drop of 3,150 feet, and thirty-two lifts of various kinds to hurry skiers up the slopes. With its subsidiary Pico Peak, the resort employs five hundred people and is the nucleus of a widespread area of lodges, motels, condo developments, restaurants, shops, pubs, and other places largely designed for an out-of-state clientele. Trail grooming has reached a fine art, and snowmaking, which is now standard at most ski areas, allows continuous skiing in low-snow periods and can create a ski season lasting up to six months. Many resort areas have also developed a summer season with hiking trails, tennis courts, swimming pools, alpine slides, and the like. Smaller ski areas, which attract a larger proportion of Vermont skiers, tend to be in the northern part of the state and often have highly loyal customers. Among these are Bolton Valley (Bolton), Mad River Glen (Waitsfield), Burke Mountain (Burke), and Jay Peak (Jay), the last of which also attracts many skiers from Quebec. Many ski areas have developed cross-country trail networks, and in recent years have had to accommodate themselves to SNOWBOARDERS, who now make up a significant number of customers at some places. The eighty-one ski areas that existed in Vermont in the mid-1960s have been reduced to two dozen or so today, largely through the disappearance of smaller COMMUNITY SKI AREAS that could not provide the range of services customers demanded or through the amalgamation of resorts under corporate ownership. One skiing industry giant, the American Skiing Company, currently owns two of the state's largest areas (Killington and Mount Snow) and formerly also owned Sugarbush, in addition to resorts in Maine, Colorado, Utah, and California. Given Vermont's modern-day vigilance in protecting its environment through ACT 250 and other legislation, it is unlikely that any further large- or even small-scale ski areas will be developed in the state, although those that already exist should provide continued enjoyment and healthy outdoor activity for Vermonters and out-of-staters alike.

Slade, William (1786–1859)

Lawyer, congressman and governor, William Slade, a native of Cornwall, graduated from MIDDLEBURY COLLEGE in 1807 and was admitted to the bar in 1810.

Slade practiced law in Middlebury but attracted few clients and edited the *Columbia Patriot* (1814–1816), a political but not financial success that burdened him with a lifelong debt. He compiled the *Vermont State Papers* (1823), the *Statutes of Vermont* (1825), and volume 15 of *Vermont Reports*. In 1812, Slade was a Democratic-Republican presidential elector for James Madison in the Madison versus Gerry presidential elections. He served as secretary of state (1815 to 1822), judge of Addison County court, and state's attorney. Briefly, in the late 1820s, he worked as a clerk in the United States Department of State in Washington. In 1831, Slade was elected as a Whig to the Twenty-second Congress and was reelected five times. In Congress, he fiercely opposed gag rules and the Southern "slavocracy," supported protective tariffs, and initiated a resolution to instruct the committee on the District of Columbia to report a bill abolishing slavery in the District. He was elected governor of Vermont in 1844. Governor Slade led a reorganization of the public school system of Vermont, opposed the admission of Texas to the Union, and harshly criticized national policy that led to the war with Mexico. His second administration was marred by a "War of Pamphlets" between him and U.S. Senator SAMUEL S. PHELPS, a conflict that quickly descended to personal insults. Slade lost the support of the Whig party and withdrew from public life after 1846. He later served as secretary of the Board of National Popular Education, an agency devoted to sending female teachers from the east to new western settlements. Slade's *Vermont State Papers*, a collection of early Vermont documents, remains a valuable source for Vermont historians.

Slate Valley and Slate

The slate-quarrying region of Vermont, known as the Slate Valley, extends from Benson to Salem, New York, and includes Fair Haven, Castleton, Poultney, Wells, and Pawlet in Vermont and Salem, Granville, and Hampton in New York. The first quarrying in this region was done by Alonson Allen in 1839 in the town of Fair Haven. Allen spent several years in experimenting with and developing the quarrying and manufacture of slate products, and in 1845 went extensively into the manufacture of school slates. In 1847 to 1848, he abandoned that and commenced the manufacture of roofing slate. Allen was

the pioneer in slate quarrying and manufacture. F. W. Whitlock of Castleton opened a quarry in that town as early as 1848. The first slate quarry in the town of Poultney was made by Daniel and S. E. Hooker, in 1851, about three miles north of Poultney village. Hooker & Sons were the third party to enter the slate business in Vermont, acquiring several quarries that they and their successor Hugh G. Hughes worked through most of the century. Hughes manufactured mainly roofing slate, some of which found a market in England. Many of the quarries are actively working today, their product used to manufacture roofing and flooring tiles. Beginning in the early nineteenth century immigrants from Wales came in steady numbers to work in the industry. Welsh culture continues to be fostered in the Slate Valley, as in Middle Granville, New York, where the volunteer fire department still carries the name Penrhyn Hose Company, named for the many workers of the Penrhyn quarries of North Wales who emigrated here. Today, Hilltop Slate Company in Wells and Middle Granville is owned by McAlpine, the current owner of the huge Bethesda, North Wales, quarry. The valley has an active St. David's Society with over six hundred members. It sponsors many annual Welsh heritage events and has twice sponsored the Penrhyn Choir of Bethesda, North Wales, to come to the valley, the members and hosts renewing many family relationships and close friendships each time. A slate museum opened in 1996 and is located just 10 miles from Poultney in the village of Granville, New York. It commemorates all of the heritages that shaped this valley's slate industry including the Welsh, the Italians, the Irish, and the Slovaks.

Slavery in Vermont

In the eighteenth century, African-Americans, whites, and Native Americans were enslaved in all of the American colonies of France and England. In 1705, New York enacted fugitive slave laws to interdict fugitives to the French and their Indian allies. A 1745 royal French decree declared slaves escaping from British territory to Quebec to be the property of Louis XV. New England captives from French and Indian raids were sometimes sold into slavery in Quebec. Marguerite Charlotte, an ABENAKI captured on Missisquoi Bay, was a slave among the French settlers at POINT À LA CHEVELURE in 1741 to 1742.

After the British conquest of New France opened the GREEN MOUNTAINS and the LAKE CHAMPLAIN region to settlement, whites from southern New England and New York brought slaves to Vermont. The early presence of African-American slaves is documented in probate papers, census records, bills of sale, town and church records, family histories, obituaries, newspaper advertisements, and town histories and gazetteers as follows: Middlebury, 1766; Castleton, 1767; Pawlet, 1770 to 1771; Springfield, 1770, 1785, 1790; Pomfret, 1772; Ryegate, 1774; Woodstock, 1774; Bennington, ca. 1776, 1780 to 1783, 1800; Bridport, ca. 1776; Windsor, 1783; Manchester, ca. 1785; Poultney, ca. 1785; Hungerford, 1790; Ferrisburgh, 1791; Cabot, 1796; Killington, ca. 1800; Burlington, 1806; Leicester, 1810; Salisbury, 1810. Well-to-do settlers brought African slaves, indentured servants from the British Isles, and hired hands to clear land and raise buildings. Typical owners were lawyers, doctors, ministers, businessmen, and militia officers. In 1784, LEVI ALLEN purchased a slave in New York, probably Prince Robinson, an African-American veteran of the Continental Army, who gained his freedom by 1795 and settled in Windsor. Slaves functioned as status symbols and, in performing domestic and farm labor, freed professionals to follow their business or profession. African-American children were contracted—"bound out"—as servants to white families. Under this custom, PRINCE SAUNDERS and ALEXANDER TWILIGHT received education important to their advancement. However, coerced indenture and contracting out children's labor as they reached a useful age could also turn into a form of legal kidnapping, as in the case of the children of ex-slaves JEFFREY and Susannah BRACE of Poultney, ca. 1790. Caught up in the ideological battle of the American Revolution, some Vermonters saw slavery as a symbol of aristocracy. They might also have sought to protect their premium labor advantage. The nature of small-scale farming and lack of hard cash on the Vermont frontier also limited slavery. Townspeople are said to have enticed slave Dinah Mason to leave her Windsor owner in the 1790s. About 1780, a female slave owned by Congregational minister David Avery of Bennington was encouraged by ETHAN ALLEN to sue for her freedom. The Vermont Constitution abolished adult slavery in 1777, strengthening this with a law prohibiting the sale of slaves out of state in 1786. The latter provision would seem to indicate that the former was not completely in force. Some continued as slaves, some as servants, but the precise nature of servitude after 1777 remains unclear, though it must have had the force of custom as well as strong economic compulsion behind it. Federal census records for Vermont suggest some 50 percent of African-Americans lived in white households from 1791 to the Civil War. From the 1790s to the early 1800s, slaves from New York State and other northern areas sought liberty in Vermont. During the ante-bellum period, a new generation of southern slaves settled in the state or passed through to Canada on the UNDERGROUND RAILROAD—often aided by Vermonters. During the Civil War, fugitives and resident African-Americans in Vermont served in segregated units of the Union army. Town and family histories record Civil War veterans bringing home escaped slaves, among them, Thorton Jackson Kenny, who settled in Rutland. Until the late twentieth century, the state's historians have been silent on slavery in Vermont. Ignorance of the record of slavery in Vermont probably supported a self-congratulatory view of Vermont's past, which reinforced the racist attitudes still evident in the twentieth century, most notably in the formation of the Vermont KU KLUX KLAN in the 1920s and the IRASBURG AFFAIR in 1966.

Ray Zirblis

Slayton, Ronald Alfred (1910–1992)

A painter and teacher, Ronald Slayton was born in Barre, studied at the Pratt Institute and the UNIVERSITY OF VERMONT in the early 1930s, and then painted with the Works Progress Administration (WPA). After completing a B.S. at Columbia in 1945, Slayton taught at the University of Tennessee from 1947 to 1957, and toured the Appalachian Mountains to organize local craftsmen. He taught school in Northfield and Montpelier until the mid-1960s and was curator of Montpelier's T. W. WOOD GALLERY AND ART CENTER until 1986. A self-described "social realist," his early work in oils and ideas about the artist's responsibility for advancing social change were influenced by Ben Shahn, John Sloan, and especially by Edward Steichen and Mexican muralist José Clemente Orozco. While teaching during the summers of the 1950s and 1960s at the Fletcher Farm Craft School in Ludlow, Slayton began painting in a richly colored, naturalistic watercolor style he employed for many years. Influential in promoting the arts, he received the VERMONT ARTS COUNCIL Award of Merit in 1971. Becoming active in politics and peace movements during the 1970s and 1980s, he chaired a section of an international conference in Florence, ran for the Vermont Senate, and traveled to Germany and the Soviet Union with Parents and Teachers for Social Responsibility in 1988. His works in this period included both overtly political statements on war and economic inequality and lyrical landscapes. Major exhibitions of Ron Slayton's work were presented at UVM in 1939 and the T. W. Wood Gallery in 1989, the latter with catalogue, and his paintings are in the permanent collection of UVM's FLEMING MUSEUM as well as private collections.

William Steinhurst

Smith, Edward Curtis (1854–1935)

President of the Central Vermont Railroad and governor of Vermont, Edward Curtis Smith was the son of JOHN GREGORY SMITH. He was born in St. Albans, attended St. Albans and Phillips academies and graduated from Yale in 1875. After studying at Columbia Law School, he was admitted to the Vermont bar in 1879 and practiced in St. Albans until 1881, when he became vice president of the Central Vermont Railroad, serving as president from 1892 to 1895 and as its receiver until 1898. In 1899, when the Central Vermont was reorganized as the Central Vermont Railway, he was again named president and served until World War I. He remained a director until his death. Other business interests included the presidency of Peoples Trust Company, Welden National Bank of St. Albans, and the Sherman National Bank of New York City. Gold mining in South Dakota was also among his investments. He served in the legislature from St. Albans in 1891 to 1892 and was elected governor in 1898. An economic and political conservative, Smith was among the state's most vehement opponents of the corporation tax that from 1881 until the adoption of the income tax in 1931 was the principal source of state revenues.

Smith, Israel (1759–1810)

Born in Suffield, Connecticut, Israel Smith graduated from Yale in 1781 and moved to Vermont in 1783, following his brother NOAH SMITH. He represented the town of Rupert in the General Assembly (1785, 1788–1790) and also served as one of the commissioners who resolved New York's claims to Vermont land, a condition of statehood in 1789. He was elected one of Vermont's first two representatives to Congress in 1791, serving until 1797. Elected to represent the town of Rutland in 1797, he was elected chief judge of the Supreme Court, a position he held for one year. In 1798, he was replaced by his brother Noah in a political purge by the Federalists known as the Vergennes Slaughter. Losing the governor's race to ISAAC TICHENOR in 1801, Smith was elected chief judge, but he refused to accept the position. He was elected to Congress again (1801–1803) and then to the United States Senate in 1803, defeating NATHANIEL CHIPMAN. In 1807, he was elected governor, resigning his seat in the Senate to take the position.

Paul Gillies

Smith, John Gregory (1818–1891)

A member of a prominent St. Albans family, John Gregory Smith was the twenty-ninth governor of Vermont (1863–1865). After college (UNIVERSITY OF VERMONT 1838) and Yale Law School (1841), Smith entered his father's law practice and assumed an interest in his father's substantial railroad holdings as trustee and manager of the Vermont Central and the Vermont and Canada railroads, a connecting link between New England and the Great Lakes region. He represented Franklin County in the Vermont Senate from 1858 to 1862, and in 1862 was elected to the House, where he was chosen Speaker. He assisted Governor ERASTUS FAIRBANKS in organizing troops for the Civil War before his own election to governor in 1863. He was re-elected in 1864. His most notable efforts as the last of Vermont's three war governors were recruiting troops and providing care for the wounded. He was frequently with the Vermont troops at the front. In 1864, after consolidating Vermont's RAILROADS, he became involved in the construction and management of the Northern Pacific Railroad, serving as its first president from 1866 until 1872. Although never holding elective office after 1865, he remained a dominant force in state politics and active in national REPUBLICAN PARTY affairs until his death. The large fountain in the middle of St. Albans' city park was a gift from John Gregory Smith.

Smith, Joseph (1805–1844)

The founding prophet of Mormonism, Joseph Smith was born in Sharon. The family moved near the town of Palmyra, in upstate New York, where between the ages of fourteen and twenty-five Smith experienced visions calling him to restore the true Christian religion. According to his account, an angel guided him to a set of golden plates buried in a hill near the Smith farm; these contained a narrative written in a hieroglyphic script, which he translated "by the gift and power of God." The result was published in 1830 as the Book of Mormon, which he believed to be a religious record of the ancient inhabitants of North America. The church that Smith founded on April 6, 1830, soon known officially as the Church of Jesus Christ of Latter-day Saints, quickly attracted followers. He was killed by a mob in Carthage, Illinois, an event that led to the Mormon migration to Utah under BRIGHAM YOUNG. Smith's birthplace in Sharon is a memorial landmark maintained by the Church of Jesus Christ of Latter-day Saints.

Smith, Noah (1755–1812)

One of the first two lawyers admitted to the Vermont bar, Noah Smith was a native of Suffield, Connecticut, Yale class of 1778. He settled in Bennington the year he left Yale, and was admitted to the Vermont bar in 1779 with STEPHEN R. BRADLEY. He was a prosecutor against Loyalists (1779) and was county court judge in the early 1780s and mid-1790s and a Vermont supreme court judge in 1789 to 1791 and 1798 to 1801. He moved to Milton in 1801, where he engaged in lengthy legal disputes with IRA ALLEN over property he claimed against Allen. In 1810, he was confined to a Burlington debtor's cell until the legislature passed an act of relief that freed him shortly before he died.

Smith, Peter (b. 1945)

Congressman, lieutenant governor, and the founding president of the COMMUNITY COLLEGE OF VERMONT (CCV), Peter Smith attended public school in Burlington, secondary school at Phillips Academy in Andover, Massachusetts, and graduated from Princeton University in 1968. He earned a master of arts in teaching (1970) and a doctor of education (1984) from Harvard University. He served as president of CCV from 1970 to 1978 and oversaw the design and implementation of a statewide community college system. In 1975, the VER-MONT STATE COLLEGES Board of Trustees established the CCV as the fifth unit of the state college system. In 1975 to 1976, Smith also led the state colleges' efforts to establish an external degree program for nontraditional students and a portfolio assessment program for evaluating students' experiential learning accomplishments outside the college. Smith served one term in the Vermont Senate (1980–1982) and two terms as lieutenant governor (1982–1986). He was vice president for development at NORWICH UNIVERSITY during 1986 to 1988, when he designed and managed the school's first capital fund drive, which exceeded its $12 million goal by $4 million. In 1988, he was elected to the U.S. House of Representatives, but was defeated for a second term by Burlington's Mayor BERNARD SANDERS, largely by a bloc of voters who objected to Smith voting for the federal gun control measures provided in the Brady law. Remaining in Washington after the term in Congress, Smith was a senior fellow at the American Council on Education and executive director of the Commission on Responsibilities for Financing Post-Secondary Education during much of 1991. From September 1991 to 1994, he was dean of the School of Education and Human Development at George Washington University. Since 1995, he has been the president of California State University at Monterey Bay.

Smith, Preston Leete (b. 1930)

A SKIING enthusiast who became a ski industry mogul, Preston Smith developed Killington Peak in Killington (then Sherburne) in 1958 and then went on to acquire other ski properties. Born in New York City, Smith attended school in West Hartford, Connecticut, and Oakwood Preparatory School in Poughkeepsie, New York. He graduated from Earlham College (a Quaker-affiliated institution), where he studied agriculture, in 1952 and in lieu of military service worked for Good Will Industries. Although Smith had been a ski patrol member as early as 1947, he maintained it was not until after college that he really learned to ski and by the 1950s was scouting Vermont for a place suitable for his own operation. PERRY MERRILL was then encouraging private development of state land through rental agreements, and with very limited capital Smith acquired the rights to Killington. He led the crews that did the initial trail cutting and helped build the lifts, but it was his pioneering innovations, particularly snow making, that contributed most to building the Killington region into the largest ski area in the east. Snow making proved controversial, arousing opposition among environmentalist groups and forcing Smith to use purer water than he had originally proposed. In 1996, his S-K-I Ltd., a nearly $100 million resort holding company he headed that included Killington Ltd., merged with American Skiing Company, and Smith has since retired as CEO.

Smith, Robert Holbrook (1879–1950)

The co-founder of Alcoholics Anonymous (AA), Robert Holbrook Smith was born in St. Johnsbury in 1880. After graduating from the ST. JOHNSBURY ACADEMY in 1898, he received a bachelor's degree from Dartmouth College, completed premedical studies at the University of Michigan, and graduated from Rush Medical College in 1910. Rebelling against the early religious demands of his family, Smith had ceased attending church and begun to drink. After he had a prestigious internship at the Akron City Hospital, Smith opened a private practice in 1912, but by 1935 alcoholism had so consumed him that he was dropped by the hospital. Henrietta Sieberling, a friend of Smith's wife, convinced him to participate in a local chapter of the Oxford Group, a loosely organized religious fellowship. Through Sieberling, a friend of Smith's wife, Anne Robinson Ripley, whom he had married in 1915, Smith met WILLIAM GRIFFITH WILSON, another alcoholic and native Vermonter, who had achieved sobriety. Drawing on the principles of the Oxford Group, the two began to develop a program that would assist alcoholics with their recovery. After forming successful groups in Akron, Cleveland, and New York, Smith and Wilson co-authored Alcoholics Anonymous, commonly referred to as the "Big Book," which was published in April 1939 and outlined the twelve steps of recovery. In keeping with the principles of anonymity expressed in AA, Smith was known during his lifetime as "Dr. Bob." The AA movement continued to expand, so that by 1950 its first convention was held in Cleveland, Ohio. Smith died a few months later, a victim of colon cancer.
Selene Colburn

Smith, William Farrar "Baldy" (1824–1903)

An 1845 graduate of West Point, William Farrar "Baldy" Smith of St. Albans was commissioned colonel of the Third Vermont Volunteer Infantry regiment in July 1861, and soon won approval to form and command a brigade consisting of his own regiment plus the Second, Fourth, Fifth, and Sixth Vermont regiments. Before Smith could take command of the brigade, however, General George B. McClellan promoted him to lead a division. Smith led his division, which included the Vermont Brigade, with competence through the Peninsula and Antietam campaigns. Late in 1862, he was appointed to lead the Sixth Corps. Though popular with the troops, Smith's habit of maligning fellow officers, culminating with his involvement in a political intrigue against General Ambrose Burnside, led to his dismissal from corps command in March 1863. Later appointed chief engineer in the Army of the Cumberland, Smith designed a successful plan to establish a supply route to relieve the beleaguered Union army in Chattanooga, Tennessee, in the fall of 1863. Impressed, General Ulysses S. Grant restored Smith to the command of a corps in the Army of the James in March 1864. Smith soon resumed his criticism of other army officers, including his superior officer, General Benjamin Butler, and Army of the Potomac commander George G. Meade. In mid-June 1864, his Eighteenth Corps led an assault on the massive but thinly defended fortifications around Petersburg, Virginia, but Smith halted the attack before he could exploit what seemed, in retrospect, a golden opportunity to force the evacuation of Richmond. Whether the blame lay with a lack of cooperation among commanders, Smith's horror at the frontal assault massacre at Cold Harbor the month before, or an untimely bout with malaria, the missed opportunity at Petersburg doomed Smith's career in the army. Weary of the general's continuing criticisms, Grant dismissed Smith in July. He would not serve on active duty for the rest of the war. After the war, Baldy Smith led a successful career in business and wrote several books and articles in which he tried to vindicate his controversial military career.   *Jeffrey D. Marshall*

Smuggling

See EMBARGO ACT OF 1808 and PROHIBITION.

Snelling, Barbara Weil (b. 1928)

Barbara Weil Snelling of Shelburne has pursued a distinguished career in business, education, government, and community service. She was a member and chair of the Shelburne School Board and the first chair of the board of Champlain Valley Union High School. She served on the State Board of Education and as President of the Vermont School Boards Association. She was a trustee of Radcliffe College, from which she graduated magna cum laude and was elected to Phi Beta Kappa, and CHAMPLAIN COLLEGE. Snelling has received honorary degrees from NORWICH UNIVERSITY and MIDDLEBURY COLLEGE. After raising four children, she served eight years as vice president for development and external affairs at the UNIVERSITY OF VERMONT. In 1982, Snelling launched her own firm of Snelling and Kolb, an international company that provided fundraising and public relations counsel to major nonprofit organizations. She authored several publications on fundraising and was a frequent speaker at professional seminars. She served for twenty-six years as a director of the Chittenden Bank and chaired the board for eight. She served on the board of the Lake Champlain Regional Chamber of Commerce, as a corporator of the Burlington Savings Bank, and as a director of a temporary employment agency. While her husband, the late RICHARD A. SNELLING, was governor of Vermont, Barbara Snelling became founding chair of the Friends of the VERMONT STATE HOUSE, an organization that has restored the capitol building to its nineteenth-century splendor. Following the sudden death of her husband in 1991, many urged Barbara Snelling to launch a political career in her own right and to seek the governorship—which had switched to Democratic control through the elevation of the lieutenant governor, HOWARD DEAN—in order to finish the fiscal task begun by her husband. She opted instead to run for lieutenant governor, an office she held for two terms beginning in 1993. She planned to seek the governorship in 1996, but was stricken that spring by a near-fatal cerebral hemorrhage. Although given only a 5 percent chance of survival, Snelling recovered completely. It was then too late to launch a major statewide campaign, so she chose to seek a Chittenden County seat in the state senate and was overwhelmingly elected. She narrowly lost a bid to reclaim her position as lieutenant governor in 1998 and in 2000 regained her Chittenden County senate seat, but by a smaller margin than in 1996 because of her support for the CIVIL UNIONS law. In January 2002 she resigned from the legislature for health reasons.

James H. Douglas

Snelling, Richard A. (1927–1991)

Richard A. Snelling was born in Allentown, Pennsylvania, and settled in Shelburne in 1953. He served as Vermont's governor from 1977 to 1985 and was returned to office in 1991, serving until his death in August of that year. His tenure was marked by restraint in state spending, an income tax cut, the attraction of new industries, and an increased attention to state-federal relations known at the time as the New Federalism. He brought the perspective of a business executive to government, having founded Shelburne Industries, a manufacturer of hardware and ski products. His spouse, BARBARA WEIL SNELLING, pursued a career in business and government. Elected to the Vermont house in 1958, he advocated a sales tax and a right-to-work law, neither of which was popular at the time, though their advocacy earned him statewide recognition. In 1964, as his party's nominee for lieutenant governor, he was defeated along with the entire Republican ticket. In 1966, he was defeated in the governor's race against PHILIP HOFF. In 1973, Snelling returned to the Vermont house and in 1975 was elected majority leader, paving the way for his successful 1976 race for governor. He served as chairman of both the Republican and National Governors Association and as a member of the Advisory Commission on Intergovernmental Relations and continued to serve as spokesman for reforming federal-state relations after he left office in 1984. In 1986, he made an unsuccessful attempt to unseat U.S. Senator PATRICK LEAHY, and in 1990 he announced he would again seek election as governor. Democratic incumbent MADELEINE KUNIN stepped down and Snelling won the open seat. When he took office in 1991, the economy had weakened, the state budget was in deficit, and a Wall Street bond agency had lowered the state's credit rating. Snelling persuaded the General Assembly to enact a package of spending cuts, temporary tax increases, and short-term debt authorizations. Struck down by a heart attack seven months into the term, he died before the onset of the economic recovery of the 1990s restored financial health to the state's budget.   *James H. Douglas*

Snowboarding

Snowboarding has been around since before the 1930s, but only in the 1990s did it develop into a winter sport included in the Olympic games. Initially banned at most ski resorts for its unorthodox style, snowboarding slowly gained popularity as smaller ski areas that needed to sell lift tickets accepted snowboarders on their slopes. A major breakthrough came when Stratton Mountain agreed to permit snowboarders. In 1985, only 7 percent of U.S. ski resorts permitted snowboarding, but 97 percent allowed their use by 2000. The world's leading snowboard manufacturer, Burton Snowboards, was founded in Londonderry in 1977 by Jake Burton Carpenter, who is recognized for first incorporating high-back bindings, metal edges, and boots into his snowboards. Burton (who adopted his middle name as his last) actively promoted the sport in the 1980s and his lobbying efforts helped to increase acceptance of the sport, which became a winter Olympic event in 1998. In 1996, Burton located his national headquarters in South Burlington. In 2000, Burton Snowboards claimed a payroll of 375 employees in the United States and did business in over thirty countries, selling boots made in China, bindings from Italy, and snowboards manufactured in the company's Vermont factory. At the 2002 Winter Olympics in Salt Lake City, eighteen-year-old Kelly Clark of West Dover won the gold medal in women's half-pipe snowboarding, and twenty-three-year-old Ross Powers of South Londonderry won the

Snowboarding at Mount Snow. Burton Snowboards

gold medal in men's half-pipe on the following day.

Snowmobiling

See VAST.

Socialist Labor Party Hall

Designated a National Historic Landmark in 2000, the Socialist Labor Party Hall on Granite Street in Barre was erected in 1900 by Italian graniteworkers. The hall embodied their radical ideals and the strength of working-class movements in the United States during the early years of the twentieth century. Socialists, anarchists, and union leaders gathered at the hall to vigorously debate the future direction of America's labor movement. The building served as a social and political center for Barre's large Italian colony, housing a large meeting space with mirrored chandelier, plus classrooms, office space, a co-operative grocery store, bottling works, bakery, butcher shop, laundry, and coal and firewood depot. May Day (*Primo Maggio*) was celebrated at the hall annually, and social activities included Italian-language opera and theater, masquerade balls, weddings, funerals, and dances. The hall was an incubator for local unions and Italian cultural groups such as the Italian Pleasure Club and the *SOCIETA MUTUO SOCCORSO*. In 1903, sculptor ELIA CORTI was fatally wounded inside the hall during a dispute between anarchists and socialists, and thirty-five children from Lawrence, Massachusetts, found refuge at the hall during the Bread and Roses textile strike of 1912. Closed to the community since 1936, the Labor Hall is being restored as a community center and interpretive history site. The hall's proud heritage is represented by the granite medallion above the building's entrance that depicts the arm and hammer and initials of the Socialist Labor party. *Karen Lane*

Socialist Mayors

In the twentieth century, Vermont cities elected three socialist mayors. Robert Gordon (1865–1921) was mayor of Barre from 1916 to 1917. A native of Aberdeen, Scotland, he came to Barre as an apprentice granite cutter when he was twenty-two. Politically and socially active in the city where he resided for thirty-one years, he served one term as mayor. He died in a Lynn, Massachusetts, tuberculosis sanatorium. Fred Suitor (1879–1934) was mayor of Barre for two terms, from 1929 to 1931.

Born in Leeds, Quebec, he started working in a copper mine in Quebec at the age of eight. When his family moved to Barre, he became a tool boy in the granite quarries and later a quarry blacksmith until 1908, when he became a union organizer and official. He was elected secretary-treasurer of the Quarry Workers International Union of North America in 1910 and held that office until his death in 1934 and was succeeded by JOHN LAWSON. BERNARD SANDERS (b. 1941) was mayor of Burlington from 1981 to 1989. Both Suitor and Sanders ran for governor. Suitor received 1,210 votes in 1912. After losing in a special election for a U.S. House seat in 1972, Sanders ran later that year for governor and again in 1976 as a LIBERTY UNION candidate and registered few votes. In 1986, he tallied 14 percent of the gubernatorial vote, which denied a majority to Democrat MADELEINE KUNIN, who was elected by the legislature. He was first elected to Congress in 1990.

Ann Lyons Fry

Social Security, first check

The first Social Security check issued in the United States went to Ida May Fuller, a native of Ludlow. Born in 1874, Miss Fuller, who worked as a school teacher and later a legal secretary, contributed to Social Security for just under three years. Her first check, which she received in January 1940, was for $22.54. She continued to receive monthly Social Security checks until her death at the age of one hundred in January 1975.

Societa Mutuo Soccorso

Societa Mutuo Soccorso (Mutual Aid Society) was organized in Barre, March 6, 1906, by Italian residents of the city who had been drawn there to work in the granite industry since the 1880s. *Mutuo Soccorso* was founded as a benefit society that would provide weekly compensation to members disabled from work in the granite quarries and cutting sheds. With three hundred members today, the society continues to meet monthly at the headquarters in Barre and provide benevolent aid, mostly in the form of scholarships.

William Doyle

Soirées

Among Franco-American families in Vermont, the soirée was an evening social gathering in the kitchen. In contrast with KITCHEN JUNKETS, they appear more often to have been family events that were planned to celebrate birthdays, anniversaries, and holidays. They included food, alcohol, and music, but in addition to an informal dance ensemble that might be made up of fiddle, piano, accordion, harmonica, spoons, and bones—or in place of an ensemble—there was often a great deal of a capella singing. This commonly included *tutelutte* (mouth music), *les pieds* (rhythmic foot tapping), and *les chansons à repondre* (response songs). Response songs featured a lead singer who would sing a phrase that was then echoed by the group. Particular songs were associated with specific family members who always sang them at family events. Everyone within a family recognized these songs as belonging to certain people and others would only sing them in their absence. Songs were passed orally from generation to generation so that individual families often had their own particular repertoire. Although the music was never written down, people sometimes created their own personal songbooks by writing lyrics on the backs of calendars or in notebooks. However, not all Franco-American families were musical, and although response-song singing at soirées was common, it was by no means universal. The soirée tradition appears to have persisted in rural Quebec into the 1970s, but like kitchen junkets seems to have died out much earlier in Vermont.   *Greg Sharrow*

Solzhenitsin, Alexander Isayevich
(b. 1918)
The Nobel Prize–winning Russian author, dissident, and exile, Alexander Isayevich Solzhenitsin resided in Vermont from 1976 to 1994. Deported from the Soviet Union in 1974, Solzhenitsin first visited Vermont in 1975 (at the NORWICH UNIVERSITY Summer Russian School), and returned the following year to establish his residence in the town of Cavendish, together with his wife Natalia and three sons (plus an older stepson). He had a fenced-off compound of several buildings constructed in a wooded area, but he established his popularity with the townspeople by addressing Town Meeting in March 1977. Rebuffed by most American opinion after his Harvard University speech of June 1978 criticizing Western individualism, Solzhenitsin concentrated on his writing projects of historical novels about the Russian Revolution (*The Red Wheel*, 1972–1999) and polemics against the

Soviet leadership. In 1985, he applied for American citizenship but declined to finalize it, and in 1994 he returned to post-Communist Russia, where he remains a critic of the new regime as he was of the old.   *Robert V. Daniels*

Solzhenitsin, Ignat Alexandrovich
(b. 1972)
A concert pianist and the son of the writer ALEXANDER SOLZHENITSIN, Ignat Alexandrovich Solzhenitsin resided in Vermont with his family from 1976 to 1994. He began performing at the age of eleven with the Windham Community Orchestra, then studied at the Curtis School of Music in Philadelphia, and has subsequently pursued a successful musical career, extensively touring the United States and Europe, including Russia.   *Robert V. Daniels*

Somerset
Somerset, a town in Windham County with five residents, was, like neighboring Glastenbury, disincorporated as a town by the Vermont legislature in 1937. It was originally granted by BENNING WENTWORTH in 1761 and named for either the county in England or the town of Somerset in Massachusetts. The rugged, remote location of the town, between the main spine of the GREEN MOUNTAINS on the west and the long ridge of 3,556-foot Mount Snow on the east, has always severely limited population, which attained a high of 321 in 1850 but shrank to zero by 1970. All of the town is in the GREEN MOUNTAIN NATIONAL FOREST. It shares 1,597-acre Somerset Reservoir, the fifth-largest body of water entirely within Vermont, with the town of Stratton to the north.

Sorrell, Esther Hartigan (1920–1990)
Democratic legislator and party leader, Esther Sorrell grew up with a passion for politics and a deep appreciation for detail and organization. Born in Burlington, she attended Cathedral High School and TRINITY COLLEGE, graduating magna cum laude in 1942. While she and her husband raised a family of five children, and well before Democratic candidates had reasonable chances for election, Sorrell participated in party politics. By stuffing envelopes and working check lists, she helped lay the ground work for the party's eventual success. For years, her power base was her dining room table, and she built her political reputation working

behind the scenes to get other people elected. In 1972, she and a group of other women aligned themselves with the new women's movement that encouraged women not only to work for male candidates but to run for office themselves. She and her friends were at the center of an organization called the Women's Political Caucus. Always bothered by gender discrimination, she was particularly effective in encouraging women to run. Among her legislative recruits were two future governors, MADELEINE KUNIN and HOWARD DEAN. Sorrell's life changed after a women's caucus meeting when she was persuaded to run for the state senate. She was elected in 1972, and re-elected to four subsequent terms, at times serving as the only woman senator. A strong advocate of women's causes and a deeply religious person, she was personally opposed to abortion but believed the decision to have an abortion was a personal one. Sorrell was a strong advocate of increased welfare benefits, and her "Good Friday Speech" is remembered as a major force in securing legislative approval of an increase in the state's Aid to Needy Families with Children Program. She was a passionate supporter of Jimmy Carter in 1976, carried his banner in the national convention, and served as his Vermont coordinator.
     Madeleine M. Kunin

South Burlington
South Burlington, population 14,879, a city in Chittenden County, was created in 1864 when the state legislature approved the town of Burlington's request to be split into two entities. The built-up area on LAKE CHAMPLAIN became the city of Burlington, and the rural hinterland became the town of South Burlington. Its northern boundary is the WINOOSKI RIVER, and there are 4 miles of shoreline on Lake Champlain. The landscape is flat or gently rolling, suitable for AGRICULTURE in times past but today primarily devoted to industrial buildings, shopping centers, and residential housing. South Burlington remained predominantly rural until after World War II, when it became one of the first towns to feel the effects of the rapid suburbanization of the Burlington area. Its population in 1940 was 1,736, which by 1970 had risen to 10,032, leading to its incorporation as a city in 1971. Today it is the fifth-largest population center in Vermont, after Burlington, Essex, Rutland, and Colchester. South Burlington is the

site of Burlington International Airport (owned by the city of Burlington), and of University Mall, the state's largest shopping center. It also has the largest concentration of the Burlington area's lodging facilities in the Williston Road-Dorset Street area. The city has attempted, with only partial success, to retain by zoning a rural atmosphere in its Southeast Quadrant. Lacking a true urban core, South Burlington has for many years had a plan for a city center in one of its oldest, most densely populated neighborhoods.

Southern Vermont College

A career-oriented, liberal arts college in Bennington, Southern Vermont College has its roots in Saint Joseph College, which was established in downtown Bennington by the Sisters of Saint Joseph in 1926. In 1974, the Sisters of Saint Joseph turned the college over to an independent board of trustees, who changed the college name and moved to its current location on the Everett estate as a private, independent college without a religious affiliation. Southern Vermont College places an emphasis on serving students who have yet to fulfill their potential. Within its financial resources, the college provides institutional aid to support the unmet financial needs of students who are motivated to achieve their academic goals and demonstrate continued, satisfactory academic progress. Accredited by the New England Association of Schools and Colleges, the college offers fifteen bachelor and ten associate degrees.

South Hero

South Hero, population 1,696, a town in Grand Isle County, was granted by the Vermont legislature in 1779 as part of the grant of Two Heroes to ETHAN ALLEN and 364 other Revolutionary War veterans, made a semi-independent town in 1798, and a fully independent one in 1810. (See the entry for Grand Isle town for information on Two Heroes.) It occupies the lower half of 12-mile-long South Hero island and is connected to the Vermont mainland by the SANDBAR bridge. The landscape is gently rolling, with several swampy areas. Several dairy farms and apple orchards dot the town, but leisure activities—especially camping and fishing with their attendant services—form the main economic base. Most of the town's employable residents work in Chittenden County. South Hero village and Keeler's Bay are

the town's two settlements, although many camps and year-round homes line the shores of the island. It was at Allen Point, on the southernmost tip of the island, that Ethan Allen stayed with his cousin EBENEZER ALLEN in February 1789, the night before he had his fatal stroke on his way home across the ice to Burlington.

Spargo, John (1876–1966)

Born in Stithians, Cornwall, England, John Spargo as a child went down to work in a tin mine, an experience that led to an active role in the British trade union movement. He came to America in 1901 and became a leading pre–World War I spokesman for socialism in the United States. In later life, he became an important contributor to the preservation of Vermont history. A leader in the American Socialist party's moderate or reform wing for fifteen years after coming to the United States, he along with several other prominent members quit the party in 1917 after it adopted a resolution against American involvement in the European war. Disillusioned with socialism, he turned his energies to the civic affairs of Bennington, where he had taken residence in 1909. His strong interest in history led him in 1926 to found the BENNINGTON MUSEUM, which he served as curator and director until his retirement in 1954. He was president of the VERMONT HISTORICAL SOCIETY for twelve years, beginning in 1927, and wrote a number of books on Vermont topics.

Gene Sessions

Spooner, Alden (1757–1827)

Alden Spooner, an early Vermont printer, was born at New London, Connecticut. He apprenticed as a printer in New London before serving in the American Revolution. In 1778, he moved to the Dresden district of Hanover, New Hampshire, and established a printing press on the campus of Dartmouth College. In sporadic partnership with his brother Judah, Alden Spooner operated the DRESDEN PRESS for more than a year as official printer to the new state of Vermont, while also printing political materials promoting the Dresden party's goal of a CONNECTICUT RIVER Valley state independent of both Vermont and New Hampshire. He suspended operations at Dresden late in 1779, after which JUDAH P. SPOONER set up shop at Westminster, Vermont. When the Westminster press failed in 1783, Alden Spooner moved its equipment to Windsor,

where he printed for the next thirty-five years. Throughout that period, Spooner and his Bennington counterpart ANTHONY HASWELL handled much of the state's printing work during Vermont's formative decades. Spooner represented Windsor five times in the state legislature and served as the town's first postmaster. His Dresden Press imprints survive as an important set of primary sources for the political struggles attending independent Vermont's first years. *J. Kevin Graffagnino and Marcus A. McCorison*

Spooner, Judah Padock (1748–1807)

When Timothy Green III was engaged by ELEAZAR WHEELOCK of Dartmouth College to send a printer to Hanover, New Hampshire, Green sent his brother-in-law, Judah P. Spooner, a permanently injured Revolutionary War veteran of New London. ALDEN SPOONER, Judah's brother, however, preceded Judah on the mission to Dresden, the new name of Hanover under the first EAST UNION. Although Judah was the senior member of the enterprise and was the official printer of Vermont, brother Alden was the active one. When Dresden returned to its former condition as Hanover, New Hampshire, in 1780, the Vermont state printer, Judah, removed himself to the west side of the CONNECTICUT RIVER. Timothy Green IV joined him to form J. P. Spooner & T. Green and publish the *Vermont Gazette* in Westminster until early 1782. Judah's next brief stop was in Windsor, where he went to work for Hough & Spooner before disappearing from the record for more than a decade. He reappeared in Fair Haven in the printing office of MATTHEW LYON, where he was the publisher of the *Farmer's Library* (1795–1798). It is possible that Judah Padock Spooner accompanied Lyon to Louisville, Kentucky, in 1799. It is certain that he died, aged 59, in Rutland at the home of his daughter.

Marcus A. McCorison

Sprague, Achsa W. (1827–1862)

A spiritualist, evangelist, social reformer, and poet, Achsa W. Sprague was born in Plymouth Notch and, a precocious child, began work as a teacher at the age of twelve. When barely into her twenties, she was crippled by a "scrofulous disease of the joints," possibly a form of arthritis. Her condition worsened and she became housebound and then bedridden. When she was twenty-seven, she had a spiritual experience that persuaded her she was surrounded by guardian angels whose message of eternal life and the "Progression of the Soul" she was destined to proclaim. Gradually restored to comparative health, she embarked upon a lecture career as the best way to carry out her mission, travelling throughout New England and into the Midwest as far as Missouri. In addition to her role as a spiritual missionary, she was a reformer on such topics as the position of women and conditions in slums and prisons, as well as an advocate of temperance and the abolition of slavery. Her poems, many of them still unpublished, were written in both illness and health, and had a strong emotional and spiritual cast. One of them, "The Poet," written shortly before her death, contains over forty-six hundred lines and was reportedly written in only seventy-two hours. Worn out by the intensity of her mission, Achsa Sprague died of a severe illness, designated as a brain fever, at the age of thirty-four.

Springfield

Springfield, population 9,078, a town in Windsor County, was granted by BENNING WENTWORTH in 1761 and derives its name from Springfield, Massachusetts, the home town of many of the grantees. It rises from the CONNECTICUT RIVER, which forms its eastern boundary, into a hilly landscape cut from northwest to southeast by the southern Black River. The earliest settlements developed along the route of the CROWN POINT ROAD, built by the British in 1759 to connect Fort Number 4 on the Connecticut River near present-day Charlestown, New Hampshire, with Crown Point on LAKE CHAMPLAIN. Beginning in the 1770s, dams on a constricted section of the Black River— now the site of the village of Springfield— powered grist mills, sawmills, and other early industries. By the closing decades of the nineteenth century, the development of the MACHINE-TOOL INDUSTRY, which had begun in the town of Windsor ten miles to the north, made Springfield one of the major industrial sites in the United States. Its importance lasted well into the twentieth century, but eventually the dissemination of the industry throughout the country brought an inevitable decline. The succession of deserted factory buildings along the Black River and in the downtown area, with their acres of empty floor space, stand today as a reminder of

the town's vibrant past, as do the Victorian mansions on the hillsides above the commercial area. Despite a drop in population of over a thousand inhabitants in the last twenty years, Springfield still contains a number of firms employing large numbers of people, among them Dufresne-Henry, Inc. (consulting engineers), Fellows Corporation (lathes and grinders), and Goldman Industrial Group (precision grinding machines, gear shapers, lathes). South of Springfield village, the EUREKA SCHOOLHOUSE State Historic Site preserves a relic of the town's earliest days, a one-room schoolhouse completed in 1790 and one of the few surviving eighteenth-century buildings in Vermont.

Stafford, Robert T. (b. 1913)

Robert Stafford was born in Rutland and served as Rutland city grand juror (1939–1942), Rutland County state's attorney (1947–1951), deputy attorney general (1953–1955), attorney general (1955–1957), lieutenant governor (1957–1961), Congressman (1961–1971) and U.S. Senator (1971–1989). Despite a number of hard-fought contests —in 1958 he beat Democrat BERNARD LEDDY for governor by a margin of only 619 votes, up to that time the closest a Republican gubernatorial candidate had ever come to defeat—Stafford never lost an election. A graduate of MIDDLEBURY COLLEGE (1935) where he was a football star, and Boston University Law School (1938), he served in the navy in World War II, attaining the rank of lieutenant commander, and in the Korean War (1951–1953). As a gubernatorial candidate in 1958 he opposed elements in his party who supported right-to-work laws and a sales tax. As governor, Stafford promoted implementation of the recommendations of the Little Hoover Commission for efficiency reforms in government, and established the Department of Administration. Stafford promoted ski area development and restricted state promotion to accommodations without racial or religious restrictions. In 1960, Stafford ran for Congress, stressing national defense issues and defeating incumbent Democrat WILLIAM H. MEYER. Assigned to the House Armed Services Committee, over time he became less supportive of Southeast Asian military interventions and an advocate of an all-volunteer army. In 1971, shortly before Senator WINSTON PROUTY's death, Stafford voted for a Nixon-supported abbreviated draft bill as preface to an all-vol-

unteer army. Uncertain as to the bill's fate in the Senate, President Nixon pressured Governor DEANE DAVIS to appoint Stafford to the vacant seat, enabling Stafford to vote in both houses on the same bill. Stafford's Senate reputation, however, was built on his contributions to the Superfund Cleanup Act, his key role during the Reagan administration in maintaining provisions of the Clean Air Act, and in blunting efforts to restrict education funding. Upon his retirement in 1989, major environmental groups praised his efforts and a student loan program was named after him.

Stafford, Wendell Phillips (1861–1953)

A jurist and poet, Wendell Stafford of St. Johnsbury was a member of the Vermont Supreme Court from 1900 to 1904, and of the Supreme Court of the District of Columbia, 1904 to 1931. He published three books of poetry and numerous pamphlets and was a popular public speaker in Vermont and Washington. Stafford was born in Barre and educated at the Barre Academy, ST. JOHNSBURY ACADEMY, and Boston University Law School. He practiced law in St. Johnsbury from 1883 until 1900, a portion of that time in partnership with Henry C. Ide. Stafford represented St. Johnsbury in the Vermont legislature for one term, 1892 to 1893, during which time he was a member of the Judiciary Committee and advocated municipal suffrage for women. He was reporter of decisions for the Vermont Supreme Court from 1896 to 1900, and was president of the Vermont Bar Association in 1898 and 1899. Stafford spent twenty-seven years on the Supreme Court of the District of Columbia, a court of general jurisdiction. While in Washington, Stafford worked for the civil rights of residents of that city and of African-Americans. He participated in the effort to increase the self-governance power of the nation's capital, while keeping it accountable to Congress. He was one of the first white members of the Washington branch of the National Association for the Advancement of Colored People and spoke out in support of black soldiers during a time of racial tension in Washington in 1919. In a 1909 address entitled "The Negro and the Nation" delivered at the Cooper Union in New York, he argued that every citizen was obliged to insure the constitutional rights of all citizens throughout the country. Stafford's published books of poetry include *North Flowers: A Few Poems*

(1902), *Dorian Days* (1909), and *The Land We Love: Poems, Chiefly Patriotic* (1916). His speeches were collected and published in 1913. Stafford died at his home in Washington, D.C., and is buried in Mt. Pleasant Cemetery in St. Johnsbury.   *Paul A. Carnahan*

Stamford

Stamford, population 813, a town in Bennington County, was granted by BENNING WENTWORTH in 1753, then re-granted in 1761 after the French and Indian War intervened, and finally once again in 1764 to a new set of grantees. The town was named either for Stamford in Connecticut or England or possibly for Harry Grey (1715–68), fourth earl of Stamford. Settlement in the heavily forested town lies primarily in the valley of the North Branch of the Hoosic River, which flows southward into Massachusetts between the Hoosac Range on the east and the main spine of the GREEN MOUNTAINS on the west. The isolation of Stamford—it is connected to the rest of Vermont by only one main road, the combined Routes 8 and 100—means that historically its major links, commercially and industrially, have been with the city of North Adams, Massachusetts, a few miles across the state line.

Stannard

Stannard, population 185, the smallest town in area in Caledonia County, was originally granted by the Vermont legislature as Goshen Gore Number 1 in 1798 as part of the town of Goshen in Addison County, sixty miles away. After almost seventy years of inconvenience to the settlers of the little territory, the legislature incorporated it as the town of Stannard in 1867, naming it after Brigadier General GEORGE STANNARD, a native of the town of Georgia who had served throughout the Civil War. The town has always been sparsely settled and has not had its own post office since 1912. The eastern half is forested and roadless, while all 18 miles of road in the western half are unpaved. There is no village, and residents go to neighboring Greensboro, Hardwick, or Lyndon for shopping and other services. Stannard Mountain, 2,572 feet high, and Round Mountain, 10 feet lower in elevation, straddle the southern border with the town of Walden.

Stannard, George Jennison

(1820–1886)
Brigadier general of United States volunteers in the Civil War, George Jennison Stannard was born in the town of Georgia. Although he received no formal military training, Stannard was active in the state militia, and helped organize the Ransom Guards in St. Albans in 1856. He claimed the honor of being the first Vermonter to offer his services as a soldier after the bombardment of Fort Sumter in April, 1861. Governor ERASTUS FAIRBANKS appointed him lieutenant colonel of the Second Vermont Infantry Regiment, a position he held until his promotion to colonel of the Ninth Vermont Infantry in the spring of 1862. During the Antietam campaign in September, 1862, the Ninth was part of a ten-thousand-man force at Harpers Ferry that surrendered to Confederate general Stonewall Jackson, virtually without a fight. The Southern general paroled his captives, and the Ninth began a long journey that ended in a Chicago prison camp, where the parolees awaited exchange. After his exchange in March 1863, Stannard received a commission as brigadier general of the Second Vermont Brigade, five regiments of nine-month volunteers then nearly half-way through their terms of enlistment. The brigade served most of its nine months in the Washington defenses, but in June was transferred to the First Army Corps for combat service. Stannard drove his men on a severe, week-long march to catch up with the First Corps, an ordeal they completed at the end of the first day of the BATTLE OF GETTYSBURG. On the third day of the battle, Stannard ordered a flank attack on Confederate general George Pickett's division that helped to shatter the Confederate assault. Stannard was seriously wounded, but remained on the field until the battle was nearly over. With the mustering out of the brigade, Stannard was placed in charge of harbor defenses in New York City while he recovered from his wound. In the spring of 1864, he took command of a brigade in the Tenth Corps, but soon was transferred to an Eighteenth Corps brigade. He was wounded at Cold Harbor and again at Petersburg in June, 1864. During the initial siege of Petersburg, he was promoted to the command of a division, but his wounds subsequently necessitated a leave of absence for several months. When he returned to his division in September, he led the successful assault on Fort Harrison, and held it against a determined counterattack the next day. Here, however, he received his most serious wound, requiring the amputation of his right arm. He was awarded the brevet rank of major general for his leadership at Fort Harrison. By December 1864, in response to the ST. ALBANS RAID in October, Stannard was back in service as the commander of Vermont's newly formed Frontier Cavalry. His last military assignment, under General OLIVER O. HOWARD, was with the Freedmen's Bureau in Baltimore. After his retirement from the military in 1866, Stannard served as Collector of Customs for Vermont until 1872. The Vermont legislature named a newly incorporated town in Caledonia County after Stannard in 1867. Among the general officers who hailed from the Green Mountain State, none surpassed George J. Stannard for military competence and sheer courage. He was a plain, no-nonsense officer who worked his men hard but gained their respect and loyalty.

Jeffrey D. Marshall

Stark, John (1728–1822)

John Stark distinguished himself with New Hampshire rangers at FORT TICONDEROGA and Crown Point in 1759. In the earliest days of the Revolution, Stark commanded a regiment of New Hampshire volunteers at Bunker Hill, fighting from behind a hay and rail fence on the American left. Despite distinguishing himself again at Trenton and Princeton with Washington, he was not promoted by the Continental Congress, so he resigned his commission and returned to New Hampshire in time to respond to Vermont's call to New Hampshire for help against BURGOYNE's invasion of the Champlain Valley. Stark marched his militia to join SETH WARNER's GREEN MOUNTAIN CONTINENTAL RANGERS, Vermont militia, and Benjamin Simmonds's militia from Massachusetts to defeat Baum's Hessians, Loyalists, and Indians at the BATTLE OF BENNINGTON on August 16, 1777. According to tradition, Stark is said to have urged the New Hampshire, Massachusetts, and Vermont militia in the final crushing charge on the forces opposing them with the shout: "Those redcoats are ours today, or Molly Stark's a widow!"

Starksboro

Starksboro, population 1,898, a town in Addison County, was granted by the Vermont legislature in 1780 and named after General JOHN STARK, who led the New Hampshire militia in the BATTLE OF BENNINGTON. Many of the early settlers were Quakers. Lying in the foothills of the

GREEN MOUNTAINS, the town is largely hilly and wooded and was at one time a center of the lumbering industry. Today some dairying still takes place in the broad valley of Lewis Creek in the western part of town. Starksboro village, the major settlement, lies on Route 116, which runs through the valley from north to south. An easy commuter's drive up Route 116 to South Burlington and the commercial centers of Chittenden County contributed to a 26 percent population increase since 1990.

Starr, Cornelius Vander (1892–1968)

"Neil" Starr was an insurance entrepreneur who founded the American International family of insurance companies, now known as American International Group (AIG) Inc. At the age of forty-seven, Starr became an avid skier. He made his first ski trip to Stowe in the 1943 to 1944 season, and during a subsequent visit in 1945 offered to put up 51 percent of the money needed to construct a new ski lift to alleviate the long wait at the existing chairlift built in 1940. The new lift, a T-bar, was installed in 1946. In rapid succession, Starr acquired majority interests in the mountain highway, the Toll House, the MOUNT MANSFIELD chairlift (which belonged to a corporation headed by New York investment banker ROLAND PALMEDO), the luxury hotel owned by the Mount Mansfield Hotel Company, and a substantial part of the mountain outside the State Forest owned by CRAIG BURT. By 1951, the hotel company was renamed the Mt. Mansfield Company, Inc. and reorganized with Starr as president. It was under his ownership that Stowe became the "Ski Capital of the East." In 1953, Starr stepped down as president and personally nominated SEPP RUSCHP, founder of the Sepp Ruschp Ski School and director of the Mount Mansfield Hotel Company, to succeed him. He remained as director and chairman of the board.   *Hilari Farrington*

State Parks

Vermont's fifty-one state parks, which today encompass more than 40,000 acres, began with the 1924 donation by Frances Humphreys of Massachusetts of 974-foot Mount Philo in the town of Charlotte. Acquisition of other parks was slow until the 1930s, when a dozen were added as a result of the activities of the federal CIVILIAN CONSERVATION CORPS, whose crews cut roads and trails, erected cabins, and built campsites and fireplaces. Other sites have been acquired on a regular basis ever since. PERRY H. MERRILL, first as state forester and later as commissioner of forests and parks, was the guiding spirit behind the development of the state park system from 1929 to 1966. The parks today provide opportunities for hiking, biking, picnicking, camping, fishing, swimming, boating, cross-country skiing, and snowmobiling. Over two thousand campsites, either rustic or suitable for trailers and RVs, are available at many parks. Total yearly attendance is estimated at eight hundred thousand, composed of both Vermonters and out-of-staters. With tourism as Vermont's second largest industry, the parks contribute as much as $60 million per year to the state economy.

Stearns, Howard G., Jr. (1925–1999)

Clergyman and social activist, Reverend Howard Stearns came to Vermont in 1969 as the executive minister of the Vermont Ecumenical Council and Bible Society, a position he held until the society was dissolved in 1981. Born in Newton, Massachusetts, he graduated from Wellesley High School and then served as an aviation cadet in the Army Air Force until 1946. He received a B.A. degree from Boston University in 1949 and a Bachelor of Divinity degree from Yale Divinity School in 1952. After serving Congregational ministries in Connecticut and Massachusetts, he was called to Vermont. Among the many causes he championed were the Joint Urban Ministry Project, which aided low-income families in the Burlington area, and the Howard Mental Health Service and the Chittenden County Housing Assistance Program, both of which he served as president. He also helped found Vermont Public Radio and wrote a column for the BURLINGTON FREE PRESS. For a time after his retirement, Stearns served as interim minister for the First Congregational Church of St. Albans.

Stegner, Wallace (1909–1993)

A novelist and long-time director of the writing program at Stanford University, Wallace Stegner was born in Iowa, raised in Saskatchewan, and educated in Utah and Iowa. Usually considered a writer of the West, beginning in 1938 he maintained a home in Greensboro, where he and his family spent their summers for the rest of his life. Stegner first won fame with his novel *The Big Rock Candy Mountain* (1943), and received the Pulitzer Prize for *Angle of Repose* in 1972. Two of his novels had direct links to Vermont. *Second Growth* (1946) is set in the fictional town of Westwick, New Hampshire, but its principal characters and geography were inspired by Greensboro. One of his last novels, *Crossing to Safety* (1987) recounts the friendship between two academic couples who vacation each year in Vermont.

Vince Feeney

Sterling College

Founded in 1958 in Craftsbury as a preparatory school, Sterling became a college in the late 1970s. Its educational philosophy is rooted in the precepts developed by Kurt Hahn, the founder of Outward Bound, and emphasizes learning through a combination of academics, physical challenge, craftsmanship, and service to others. An integral part of education at Sterling is the Winter Expedition, which was introduced in 1963 when students and faculty bivouacked at the base of West Mountain near the Canadian border. This four-day experience in the Lowell Mountains still defines the fall semester for all first-year students. The first associate of arts degree was awarded in 1982. The New England Association of Schools and Colleges granted full accreditation to Sterling College in 1987. A baccalaureate program was accredited in 1997. Majors are offered in wildland ecology and management, sustainable agriculture, and outdoor education and leadership, as well as self-designed majors. The hundred-plus acre campus includes twelve buildings. Among them are newly renovated residential, administrative, and classroom facilities, as well as a wood shop and library. Outdoor teaching facilities include a managed woodlot, a climbing wall, an organic garden, a moveable hoop-house, a glass greenhouse, and a working livestock farm with two barns. Food harvested from Sterling's organic farm is served in the dining hall. On-campus programs are augmented by the off-campus internships, which allow students to gain valuable work experiences and provide service to others while earning college credits. Overseas programs are conducted in Scandinavia, Nepal, and Japan. Sterling is a member of the national Work Colleges Consortium, which stipulates that every student engage in chores and work for all aspects of campus life in return for a reduction in tuition. The college attracts faculty dedicated to undergraduate teaching, an interdisciplinary and experiential curriculum, and diverse learning modes.

Jed Williamson

Stevens, Henry, Jr. (1819–1887)

The son of HENRY STEVENS, SR., of Barnet, the great collector of early manuscript and print Vermontiana, Henry Stevens, Jr., was also a book collector and seller who helped form major book collections at several of the great research libraries in the United States and England. He received his early education in Barnet, Peacham, and Newbury Seminary in New Hampshire. After a brief career at MIDDLEBURY COLLEGE, Stevens transferred to Yale and then studied for one year at Harvard Law School, which he left to concentrate on his already-growing business in manuscript transcriptions and book dealing. With his book-selling firm established by 1843, he left for Europe in 1845 intending a two-year stay but, except for occasional visits home to see his family and secure books for his European clients, remained there the rest of his life. Nourished by life and opportunities in London, he helped form some of the valuable book and manuscript collections now held at major American libraries, including the John Carter Brown collection at Brown University and the James Lenox Collection at the New York Public Library. He was also largely responsible for the Americana collection at the British Library, then the library of the British Museum. His firm still operates in the United States as Henry Stevens, Son & Stiles. Stevens is buried in Hampstead Cemetery, London, where his grave is marked by a monument of Barre granite.

Stevens, Henry, Sr. (1791–1867)

An avid collector of books, manuscripts, and newspapers, Henry Stevens, Sr., of Barnet, was the premier Vermont antiquarian in the ante-bellum period. He attended district schools until 1807 when he left to assist his ailing father in running the family farm, inn, and mills. After his father's death the following year, he helped his mother manage the family businesses. In addition to family affairs, Henry was an organizer of the Passumpsic Turnpike Corporation, which ran between Barnet and Wells River, and operated a section of the stage line on the Quebec to Boston run. He was elected Barnet town representative in 1826 and a justice of the peace the following year. An incurable antiquarian, his great love was buying and selling old books and documents. Described as very much a man of business but not a businessman, Stevens was more interested in his antiquarian pursuits than in remaining solvent and in his later years his sons, particularly HENRY STEVENS, JR., came to his financial aid. Henry Sr.'s most enduring contribution was as a principal founder in 1838 of the VERMONT HISTORICAL and Antiquarian SOCIETY. The society's first president, he served eighteen years while also performing the duties of librarian and cabinet keeper or curator before the society was relocated with its collections from Barnet to the VERMONT STATE HOUSE in Montpelier. For a time, Stevens's historical collection was the sole holding of the society, about twenty-five hundred items of which were lost when in 1857 the state house was destroyed by fire. Stevens resumed collecting but did little to promote the society. The organization became more broadly based only after he left the presidency in 1859. The trustees also sought unsuccessfully to obtain from him documents and artifacts that were given the society but which he had apparently added to his own collections. Stevens died in Barnet after a long illness.

Stevens, Roger (1743–1793), and Abel Stevens (1750–1816)

Originally from Quaker Hill, Dutchess County, New York, the brothers Roger and Abel Stevens of Pittsford fled Vermont to join the Loyalist King's Rangers in Quebec during the Revolution, becoming spies and couriers in Vermont and New Hampshire disguised as hunters and trappers. At the LOYALIST BLOCKHOUSE on LAKE CHAMPLAIN's North Hero Island, spymaster JUSTUS SHERWOOD suspected the Stevens brothers of falsifying expenses for furs bought to cover their missions. Sherwood warned them to work harder and stop "dancing and frolicking with girls" in Vermont. After the war, Abel was ordained a Baptist minister and in 1789 with Roger took forty Baptist families to settle on the Rideau River in Bastard Township, Upper Canada (Ontario), on land granted for the brothers' war service and for bringing Loyalists to Canada after the war. Roger died four years later while duck shooting.

Stevens, Thaddeus (1792–1868)

One of the first political leaders to urge President Abraham Lincoln to emancipate slaves in territory occupied by the Union army, Thaddeus Stevens was born in Danville, attended Caledonia County Grammar School in Peacham, and entered Dartmouth College as a sophomore in 1811. He transferred to the UNIVERSITY OF VERMONT in 1813, attending for only a few months in the spring and summer when his play, *The Fall of Helvetic Liberty*, was performed in the Junior Exhibitions, but then returned to Dartmouth to graduate in 1814. In 1816, he began the practice of law in Gettysburg, Pennsylvania, subsequently serving in the Pennsylvania legislature, and was a U.S. congressman from 1849 to 1853 and again from 1859 until his death. As a leading Radical Republican, he urged President Lincoln to decree the emancipation of slaves and proposed to enlist them in the Union army. After the war, he favored strict federal control of the South in order to ensure the full enfranchisement of the liberated slaves as a necessary condition for the region's reintegration into the Union. He also advocated and sponsored the legislation that later, as the fourteenth Amendment to the U.S. Constitution, affirmed the political and civil rights of black Americans. Stevens played the leading role in the impeachment of President Andrew Johnson.

Stinehour, Roderick (b. 1925)

Founder and president of the Stinehour Press of Lunenburg, Roderick Stinehour was born in Canada and raised in Whitefield, New Hampshire. After serving four years as a naval aviator in World War II, he ventured 12 miles across the CONNECTICUT RIVER to Lunenburg in 1947 in search of a job to support himself and his new wife, Elizabeth Maguire, in their beloved northern rural homeland. He was taken on by Ernest Bisbee, mastered the work of an apprentice job printer during summers and vacations away from Dartmouth College, and purchased Bisbee's shop after his death in 1950. "Rocky" was a member of Ray Nash's Graphic Arts Workshop at Dartmouth, and it was here that he learned the intellectual side of his craft, a hallmark of Stinehour Press. His motto from the beginning was to do "common things uncommonly well," and the press has achieved this goal, as reflected in the numerous awards it has won for its books from the American Institute of Graphic Arts. In 1977, Stinehour acquired the old and distinguished Meriden Gravure Press of Meriden, Connecticut, and formed the Meriden-Stinehour Press. In 1998, the press was acquired by James Crean of Dublin, Ireland, but it retains the name Stinehour Press as it continues to produce the fine books, in editions ranging from fifty to five thousand copies, that have been its mainstay from the beginning. Stinehour has received numerous personal awards for his printing and scholarship, and was elected as a Fellow in the American Academy of Arts and Sciences in 1966.

Connell Gallagher

Stockbridge

Stockbridge, population 674, a town in Windsor County, was granted by BENNING WENTWORTH in 1761 and named after Stockbridge in Massachusetts, the home colony of most of the grantees. It lies in the eastern foothills of the GREEN MOUNTAINS and contains a number of summits above two thousand feet, the most prominent of which is 2,625-foot Sable Mountain. The town is cut in its northern portion by the deep valley of the WHITE RIVER, along whose banks lie the two significant settlements, Stockbridge village and Gaysville. During the FLOOD OF 1927, terrible destruction was wrought here by the raging waters of the White River, and many structures in the valley and most of the village of Gaysville disappeared. ORESTES A. BROWNSON, the noted nineteenth-century writer on religion and philosophy, was born in Stockbridge.

Stone Chambers

One-room stone chambers shaped like beehives are scattered throughout Vermont. Various experts disagree on the origins and dating of these structures. They have been identified as lime kilns, root cellars, burial tombs, and various kinds of shelters. Archaeologists interested in the earliest native peoples of this region have proposed that these structures were once associated with celestial calendars and seasonal solstices. Another theory on the origins of these structures claims that the markings on stones at the entrances resemble letters in the Ogham alphabet associated with ancient Celts, but that theory has very few adherents. The origins of the beehive-shaped chambers remain a mystery.

Donald Wickman

Story, Ann Reynolds (1735–1815)

A patriot of the Revolution, Ann Story left Preston, Connecticut, in 1755 with Amos, her husband of twenty years, and their five children, to become the second family to settle in the New Hampshire grant town of Salisbury. After building a cabin with son Solomon, Amos was killed by a falling tree. Ann became a spy and courier for Vermont's militia during the Revolution. Traditional stories of her life recount how she bravely faced down Loyalist neighbor Ephraim Jenny who, musket in hand, threatened to kill her as a rebel spy: "I have no fear of being shot by so consummate a coward as you." Salisbury citizens have constructed a garrison-type cabin on the site of her original log home. On a simple monument nearby are the words: "In grateful memory of her service in the struggle of the GREEN MOUNTAIN BOYS for independence."

Virginia C. Downs

Stowe

Stowe, population 4,339, a town in Lamoille County, was granted by BENNING WENTWORTH in 1763 and originally spelled Stow, the "e" having been added in the nineteenth century. The name derives from Stow, Massachusetts, the home colony of a number of the grantees. At 47,808 acres, Stowe has the largest area of any town or city in the state, a result of the absorption in 1839 of the eastern half of the town of Mansfield, which straddled the main ridge of the GREEN MOUNTAINS at its highest point and proved impractical as a cohesive unit. Although Stowe shares the summit of 4,393-foot MOUNT MANSFIELD, the highest point in the Green Mountains, with Underhill to the west and reaches to the foothills of the Worcester range in the east,

it has a substantial lowland area along the Waterbury River as it runs through the town southward toward the WINOOSKI RIVER. At first the town was primarily agricultural, but beginning in the mid-nineteenth century, Mount Mansfield began to attract visitors and resort hotels sprang up, including one on top of the mountain. After the advent of SKIING in the 1930s, the town began its long run as the "ski capital of the east," and today it remains one of Vermont's major winter (and summer) tourist destinations, devoted to the lodging, feeding, and entertaining of thousands of visitors per day. The combined number of downhill ski trails on Mount Mansfield and Spruce Peak is forty-seven, with a vertical drop of 2,360 feet on the first mountain and 1,550 feet on the second; there are also four major cross-country trail systems in the area. The summer provides opportunity for golfing, biking, fishing, and other outdoor activities. The "mountain road" (Route 108), which follows the West Branch of the Waterbury River to the foot of the ski lifts, is lined with hotels, motels, restaurants, antique stores, and other tourist venues. The well-preserved village of Stowe retains the look, if not the feel, of its historic role as a market town. The TRAPP FAMILY SINGERS of *Sound of Music* fame settled in Stowe in 1941, and members of the younger generation still run a lodge there.

Strafford

Strafford, population 1,045, a town in Orange County, was granted by BENNING

Justin Smith Morrill Homestead in Strafford. Vermont Department of Tourism and Marketing

WENTWORTH in 1761 and named for one of the titles held by the Wentworth family; at the time the fourth earl of Strafford was his cousin, William Wentworth (1722–1791). The landscape is a typical central Vermont mixture of forested hills and upland pastures cut by watercourses. The highest points are Whitcomb Hill and Tug Mountain, both of which are 1,866 feet tall. The two main settlements of Strafford and South Strafford both lie on the banks of the West Branch of the Ompompanoosuc River, which cuts across the town in a southeasterly direction. The first copper mine in the United States was opened in Strafford in 1793, and remained in operation until 1957. Cleaning up the environmental devastation wrought by the mining—about a ton of heavy metals leaches out of the mine site daily—remains a priority. JUSTIN SMITH MORRILL, the author of the Land Grant College Act, was born in Strafford, and his home here, a State Historic Site, is one of Vermont's best surviving examples of high Victorian architecture.

Stratton

Stratton, population 136, a town in Windham County, was granted by BENNING WENTWORTH in 1761 and probably named for Stratton, England. The remote, rugged location of the town, directly on the main spine of the GREEN MOUNTAINS and entirely within the GREEN MOUNTAIN NATIONAL FOREST, has always severely limited population, which attained a high of 366 in 1860 but shrank to 24 by 1960. The town was probably kept from suffering the fate of Glastenbury and Somerset, its neighbors to the south, which were disincorporated by the legislature in 1937, by having one of the three roads that cross the Green Mountains in southern Vermont (it is closed in winter). The town's most noteworthy physical feature is 3,936-foot Stratton Mountain, site of a ski area with ninety trails and a vertical drop of 2,003 feet, the lodging and service area for which extends into the town of Winhall to the north. In the election campaign of 1840, a Whig rally held in Stratton heard DANIEL WEBSTER speak before a crowd reported to number fifteen thousand; the spot is today a State Historical Site.

Subchasers

To support the war effort between 1942 and 1944, the Shelburne Shipyard built a total of five 110-foot-long wooden "sub-chasers" for the Navy. The Shelburne Shipyard was one of LAKE CHAMPLAIN's most active and oldest boat-building facilities. The Lake Champlain Steamboat Company moved its boat operations there in 1820, and later the CHAMPLAIN TRANSPORTATION COMPANY (CTC) used the shipyard to build and repair its steamboats. At the outbreak of World War II, the fortunes of the CTC, the shipyard, and the greater Burlington area were declining. HORACE CORBIN, SR., the owner of the CTC since 1937, leased the shipyard to the Donovan Company, a rural electrification company from Minnesota whose work had been interrupted by the war. After initial setbacks in their bid to construct warships at Shelburne, their efforts were successful and the keels of the SC 1029 and SC 1030 were laid down on the shipyard's 1,200-ton capacity marine railway. The success of these two ships led to contracts for the SC 1504, 1505, and 1506, all launched in 1944. The SC 1029 and SC 1030 were actively engaged in the European theater and in 1944 were given to France. The subchasers built at Shelburne were the first warships built on Lake Champlain since the American and British fleets were constructed during the War of 1812. *Arthur Cohn*

Sudbury

Sudbury, population 583, a town in Rutland County, was granted by BENNING WENTWORTH in 1763 and named for Sudbury in either Massachusetts or England, or possibly for Augustus Henry Fitzroy (1735–1811), Baron Sudbury. The town lies at the spot where the VALLEY OF VERMONT and the TACONIC MOUNTAINS give way to the Champlain lowlands, and thus contains both hills over a thousand feet high and flat land suitable for DAIRY FARMING. On its eastern border, Sudbury shares with Brandon an extensive swamp that extends as far north as Middlebury, and on its southern boundary is 449-acre Lake Hortonia, part of which is in Hubbardton. The only settlement is Sudbury village, near the western border with Orwell.

Summer Camps

Vermont has been a popular location for summer camps for children and adults for over a century. Some of the pioneering ventures were St. Anne's at Isle La Motte and Camp Champlain on Malletts Bay, both founded in 1892; Eagle Camp on LAKE CHAMPLAIN, founded about 1893 and operated today as a family camp; Kee-waydin on Lake Dunmore, founded 1894; and Camp Iroquois, also on Malletts Bay, founded in 1899. By the turn of the century, summer camps dotted the landscape along the shores of Lake Champlain and the CONNECTICUT RIVER or nestled into the forests elsewhere around the state. In 1924, one annual directory of camps said of the Connecticut River region, "There is no more important center for summer camps for girls than the Thetford-Fairlee section." That year, nine camps operated on Lake Fairlee, including boys' camps like Billings (1907) and Passumpsic (1914). Many of these camps are still in operation. Most, however, have changed from eight-week sessions to shorter ones of two or four weeks, offering today's more mobile populations a greater range of options for their summer vacations. Contemporary summer camps for children continue the traditional camp activities, especially at waterfront camps where boating, sailing, and swimming are available. In the Champlain Islands, the YMCA Camp Abnaki, which celebrated its centennial anniversary in 2001, and the YWCA Camp Hochelaga offer full water programs, including long-distance canoe trips from the headwaters of western Vermont rivers to the lake and camp. A camp to learn French, *l'école Champlain* in Ferrisburgh, for many years provided total-immersion language learning, but is today Kingsland Bay State Park. Sports and weight-loss camps have developed in the past twenty years. Equestrian camps and computer camps can also be found in Vermont. The 4-H of Vermont runs a summer camp for its members, and the Vermont Department of Fish and Wildlife operates Camp Buck, an environmental education camp. *Michael Sherman*

Sunderland

Sunderland, population 850, is a town in Bennington County granted by BENNING WENTWORTH in 1761 and probably named after George Spencer (1739–1817), sixth earl of Sunderland. Most of the heavily forested town lies up against the main spine of the GREEN MOUNTAINS in its eastern section and is cut by only one east-west road, the Kelley Stand Road, which is closed in winter. Settlement is concentrated in the lowlands (the VALLEY OF VERMONT) running north-south along the town's western border with Arlington. All of the town lies in the GREEN MOUNTAIN NATIONAL FOREST. It shares the extensive Lye Brook Wilderness Area with the town of Manchester to the north.

Susap, Joseph (fl. 1739–1819)

Thought to be a Micmac from Cape Breton Island, Nova Scotia, Joseph Susap, known as Indian Joe, was famous for his generosity to early Vermont settlers. His parents were killed when the Massachusetts militia under William Pepperell captured the French fortress of Louisbourg (1745). Raised by an ABENAKI family at Odanak (St-François), Quebec, Joe and his Abenaki wife Mali (pronounced Molly) escaped ROBERT ROGERS' attack on Odanak in 1759, and spent the remainder of their lives south of LAKE MEMPHREMAGOG. Newbury, Peacham, Cabot, Danville, Derby, Walden, Morrisville, and Hyde Park are among northern Vermont towns that preserve stories about an Indian Joe. Because Joseph and Mali (the Abenaki for Mary or Marie) were names often taken by the Catholic Abenaki, stories about other Joes and Malies arose in other parts of early Vermont. An "Indian Joe" who is probably Joseph Susap is credited as the guide who showed his friend JACOB BAYLEY the Native American route followed by the BAYLEY-HAZEN ROAD. He also served as a scout, one of forty Abenaki in Captain JOHN VINCENT's ranger company, during the American Revolution. Joe and Mali are said to have traveled to Newburgh, New York, to meet George Washington, a highlight of their lives. In nineteenth-century Vermont variants of the earlier Massachusetts stories of Squanto the "friendly Indian," Joe was a renowned hunter and fisherman who often fed early settlers food when their first crops failed. In 1792, the Vermont General Assembly provided Joe and Mali with a pension. Joe spent his final years in Newbury, where he died after a hunt. A monument in his honor was raised there. Across northern Vermont, several ponds were named after the couple, though their exact connections with the sites remains obscure. Modern historians have observed that many accounts of Joe and Mali's kindnesses could have arisen from nineteenth-century Vermonters needing "good Indians" in the story of early Vermont. While such stories probably originate in real events involving other native people as well as Joseph and Mali Susap, the story of "Indian Joe and Molly" epitomizes the Native American experience in early New England of loss and accommodation to overpowering colonizing forces.

Kathleen McKinley Harris

Sutton

Sutton, population 1,001, a town in Caledonia County, was granted by the Vermont legislature in 1782 as the town of Billymead after William, the son of Dr. JONATHAN ARNOLD, one of the grantees. After William became the town drunkard (so the story goes), the inhabitants petitioned for a name change and in 1812 the town became Sutton after Sutton, Massachusetts, the home town of the man who initially proposed the change. The valley of the Sutton River, a tributary of the PASSUMPSIC RIVER, cuts across the gently rolling terrain from northwest to southeast, while on the northern border 2,648-foot Mount Hor looms over the shore of LAKE WILLOUGHBY in the neighboring town of Westmore. Henry O. Houghton, who established the publishing firm that later became Houghton Mifflin, was born in Sutton in 1823.

Swanton

Swanton, population 6,203, a town in Franklin County, was granted by BENNING WENTWORTH in 1763 and probably named for Thomas Swanton, a British naval officer and later owner of a shipyard in Maine. The popular impression that the name has something to do with swans prompted Queen Elizabeth II to send a pair of the birds to the town for its bicentenary in 1963, where they (and their successors) have been a fixture ever since. Bordered on the west by LAKE CHAMPLAIN, the town is generally flat and devoted primarily to DAIRY FARMING. The substantial village of Swanton, a major trading center for northwestern Franklin and northern Grand Isle counties, lies on the banks of the MISSISQUOI RIVER, which makes a broad curve through the northern part of the town. Swanton shares the broad delta of the Missisquoi, a national wildlife refuge, with the town of Highgate to the north. Archeological research shows that humans lived in both towns as long as eight thousand years ago, and members of the ABENAKI nation still live in the area. Because of its location on Lake Champlain just a few miles below the Canadian border, Swanton was the scene of much smuggling activity in the nineteenth century and during PROHIBITION. Militiary munitions were manufactured in Swanton during the First World War.

Swift, Samuel (1782–1875)

A long-time attorney and the first historian of Addison County, Samuel Swift was born in Amenia, New York, graduated from Dartmouth College in the class of 1800, and served as a tutor at MIDDLEBURY COLLEGE from 1801 to 1803. One of fourteen children of Reverend Job and Mary Sedgwick Swift and one of seven sons, of whom four became lawyers, Samuel read the law and was admitted to the Vermont bar in 1808. A lawyer in Middlebury for nearly seventy years, he served also as county clerk for thirty-two years, judge of probate for twenty-two years, treasurer of a glass factory, a turnpike, and the Rutland and Burlington Railroad, which was the predecessor to the Rutland Railroad. During the War of 1812, he was secretary to Federalist Governor MARTIN CHITTENDEN and his council, and served two terms as a Whig state senator (1838–1839). Swift's histories of Middlebury and Addison County remain useful. The records of his business affairs and legal work have survived in crushing detail, but Swift twice burned large caches of his personal letters, thus leaving us no access to his personal and private life.

T. D. Seymour Bassett

Taconic Mountains

A range of the Appalachian Mountains straddling the border between New York and Massachusetts, the Taconics extend into the southwestern corner of Vermont and run as far north as the town of Brandon. To their east, separated by only a few miles, are the GREEN MOUNTAINS, and the gap between them is known as the VALLEY OF VERMONT. Although they are as old as the Green Mountains, the Taconics are geologically quite different, and generally lower in elevation. The highest peak is Mount Equinox, 3,816 feet, in the town of Manchester.

Taggard, Genevieve (1894–1948)

Poet, biographer, and socialist writer Genevieve Taggard settled in East Jamaica in 1935, where as a contributing editor she wrote for *The Masses*, the leading American Marxist magazine of the decade. Originally from Waitsburg, Washington, Taggard grew up in Hawaii, graduated from the University of California at Berkeley in 1919, and went to New York, where she founded a poetry and social commentary magazine, *The Measure*, in 1920. Later, while teaching at Mount Holyoke College, she wrote a critical biography of Emily Dickinson that earned her a Guggenheim Fellowship. Her full conversion to socialism came in 1930. In 1936, she published *Calling Western Union*, a collection of poems that responded to the degraded social conditions widely experienced during the Depression. She also taught at BENNINGTON COLLEGE and Sarah Lawrence. Her activist interest in social issues led to her joining the Committee for the Protection of the Foreign Born, the United Committee to Aid VERMONT MARBLE COMPANY Workers during the Vermont Marble Company strike, and the New York Teachers Union, and serving on the executive committee of the League of American Writers. She published thirteen collections of her poetry. *A Part of Vermont* (1945) celebrates her love for the state. Some of her poems were set to music by Aaron Copland and William Schuman.

Take Back Vermont

During the general elections of 2000, the slogan "Take Back Vermont" appeared on signs across the state. Initially a populist protest against state environmental controls, particularly the thirty-year old Land Use and Development Act (ACT 250) and those that prohibited clear-cutting forest lands, the movement grew after the enactment of Act 200 in 1988, which had been adopted to improve the Act 250 regulatory process. Property holders organized as "Landowners United," fiercely attacked Act 200, posted their lands with "no trespassing" signs, and urged fellow Vermonters to fight the loss of local control, claiming they had "lost property rights" to the "growing bureaucracy in Montpelier." The movement did not peak, however, until after the legislature passed ACT 60 in 1997, creating a statewide property tax pool to fund education, and a CIVIL UNIONS law (Act 91) in 2000 that extended marriage benefits to same-sex couples. A favorite slogan of conservative Republicans during the 2000 gubernatorial candidacy of Ruth Dwyer, "Take Back Vermont" appeared on signs throughout the state, particularly in Orange County. Although Take Back Vermonters attributed the loss of many of their traditional rights to the large out-of-state population influx and the economic growth of Chittenden County, many Chittenden County front lawns displayed Take Back Vermont signs. The movement did not achieve Dwyer's election but did succeed in defeating a number of legislative candidates who had supported the Civil Unions Act and captured a Republican house majority for the first time in a decade. In the subsequent legislative session, however, none of the offending legislation was repealed or amended.

Taplin, John (1727–1803)

An early settler of the upper Connecticut Valley and the first judge to preside in northern Vermont, John Taplin was born as John Tapley in Charlestown, Massachusetts. He changed his name to Taplin at an early age, a reversion to its French Huguenot form, which had been Anglicized when his family fled France following the revocation of the Edict of Nantes in 1685. Beginning in 1755, as a Massachusetts militia officer he commanded troops in the Champlain and Hudson valleys and probably Nova Scotia in the war against the French. A grantee of the town of Corinth, he settled in 1764 in nearby Newbury, where he became a town official. In 1770, he was appointed chief judge of Gloucester County, a New York colonial jurisdiction that was created for what is now northeastern Vermont. A few years later, he moved to East Corinth, where he developed grist- and sawmills. During the Revolution, Taplin was believed by many to be loyal to the British Crown, and in actuality by 1780 he had become an informant (codenamed "Tanner") for the British Secret Service's Canadian contingent working in Vermont out of the LOYALIST BLOCKHOUSE on North Hero Island. His most critical test came in 1782 when the British called on him to assist in the capture of his friend, Colonel JACOB BAYLEY of Newbury, a staunch supporter of independence. Taplin sent a son to guide the British team to Newbury by a circuitous route while he rode directly there, and through an intermediary he warned Bayley, who narrowly avoided capture. Because of his double role during the Revolution, Taplin narrowly avoided retribution from each side. For twenty years following the war, he lived quietly in East Corinth, the only town grantee who actually settled in Corinth.   *Winn L. Taplin*

Taylor, James P. (1872–1949)

"Father of the LONG TRAIL," educator, environmentalist, and promoter of Vermont, James P. Taylor was born in Hamilton, New York. He earned an A.B. from Colgate University, class of 1895, and did graduate work at Harvard and Columbia. For several years, he was a faculty member at Colgate. In 1908, he arrived in Vermont as assistant principal of Vermont Academy in Saxton's River, never again to leave the state. Finding a lack of hiking trails, Taylor conceived of a Long Trail along the spine of the GREEN MOUNTAINS from Massachusetts to Canada. To make the dream a reality, he founded the GREEN MOUNTAIN CLUB in Burlington in 1910 with the sole purpose of building the trail, and became the club's first president. In 1912, he was hired by the Greater Vermont Association, predecessor of the Vermont State Chamber of Commerce, which he served as executive secretary until his death. Besides campaigning for the Long Trail, he was an advocate for improved roads, the

GREEN MOUNTAIN PARKWAY, clean water and pollution abatement, better town reports, and was an all-round booster for Vermont. Taylor drowned off the SANDBAR in LAKE CHAMPLAIN in September 1949. *Reidun Nuquist*

Teal, John Jerome, Jr. (1921–1982)

A pioneer ecologist and decorated bomber pilot in World War II, John Teal was born in New York City, raised in Connecticut, attended Dartmouth College, and graduated from Harvard College in 1944. He received a Master's Degree from Yale University and went on to further study at McGill University. The recipient of fellowships to pursue arctic studies in human ecology and animal husbandry, he taught briefly at a number of universities, including the University of Alaska and the UNIVERSITY OF VERMONT. Teal's concern for both the Arctic's impoverished peoples and threatened animal species gave rise to his project to domesticate the musk ox. Teal saw in the underwool shed each spring by the musk ox (qiviut) a resource that could supply a crucial year-round supplementary income for arctic inhabitants. Unable to locate a suitable arctic site, in 1952 he bought a hill farm in Huntington where he established the Vermont Institute of Northern Agricultural Research. In 1954, he received permission from the Canadian government of the Northwest Territories to capture seven musk ox calves in the Canadian Barrens. He brought these calves to Huntington, where he began a ten-year study on the feasibility of domes-

John Teal's musk ox. Nuna Teal

tication. His success resulted in the establishment of a large breeding farm in Alaska. The Vermont musk oxen were allowed to live out their natural lives. Two records were established in Huntington, the largest musk ox bull ever known at 1,200 pounds, and the longest-lived musk ox at twenty-three years. Teal eventually established five arctic musk ox farms. The Palmer, Alaska, farm provides wool for approximately 250 Inuit and Upik families who earn a significant portion of their income through knitting qiviut garments.

Tennien, William Albert (1895–1964)

A native of Pittsford who was ordained a priest in 1923, Monsignor Tennien was an influential designer of church architecture and one of the Roman Catholic Church's chief spokesmen for labor in the 1940s. After serving small parishes in northern Vermont, Tennien was appointed pastor of St. Patrick's parish in Fairfield and of two mission churches, St. George in Bakersfield and St. Anthony in East Fairfield, serving from 1935 to 1941. He drew the plans for and supervised the construction of a new fieldstone church in East Fairfield. In 1941, he was appointed the first pastor of a new parish on North Avenue in Burlington, where he designed and built the modernist St. Mark's Church. A forerunner in liturgical reform, Tennien designed the altar of St. Mark's in the center of the church instead of against the gable wall of the nave. He was the first priest in Vermont to seek and receive permission to say mass facing the congregation. His innovations in church architecture gained national attention and were influential in subsequent church construction beyond the borders of Vermont. Father Tennien had already been involved in the Vermont labor movement when a second attempt was made in 1943 to unionize the American Woolen Mills in Winooski. He preached in favor of labor and joined workers on the picket line. Father Tennien presented Bishop MATTHEW BRADY's historic message to a War Labor Board hearing in Burlington in 1943 that put the Church on the side of unions in Vermont. *David Blow*

Tenth Mountain Division

After a day of skiing at Manchester in February 1940, Charles Minot Dole and several other then-prominent skiers discussed the surprising success of highly mobile Finnish ski troopers against larger Red Army forces in the previous November's

Soviet invasion of Finland. Minot and other members of the National Ski Patrol System subsequently urged the United States Army to form, train, and equip a unit capable of operation in winter conditions and over mountainous terrain. The Army did establish such a force of ski troopers, which eventually became the Tenth Mountain Division, with a primary training center at Camp Hale, Colorado. The division served well in Italy, breaking through the last German defense lines, racing across the Po Valley and on into the Alps, where the German surrender in Italy took place in early May 1945. Vermont was well represented in the Tenth Mountain Division, with 165 troopers joining the force from seventy-nine towns. Of that total, 114 served in Italy. Seven were killed, 15 wounded, and 67 were awarded Bronze or Silver Stars for bravery. Today, Vermont's Army National Guard maintains a training school on the west flank of MOUNT MANSFIELD in the town of Jericho where the Army and other services send troops to acquire skills in mountain and winter operations. A museum at the mountain training school displays exhibits and photographs presenting the experiences of the Tenth Mountain Division in World War II. *William E. Osgood*

Thetford

Thetford, population 2,617, a town in Orange County, was granted by BENNING WENTWORTH in 1761 and probably named for one of his distant relatives, Augustus Henry Fitzroy (1735–1811), among whose titles was Viscount Thetford. The landscape contains four distinct regions running north and south. The first consists of the fertile meadows along the CONNECTICUT RIVER, which forms the town's eastern boundary, the second by a series of forested summits rising to 1,765 feet at Bald Top, the third by the valley of the Ompompanoosuc River, and the fourth by low mountains in the 13- to 17-hundred-foot range on the western border with Strafford. On the town's northern border is 463-acre Lake Fairlee, which lies partly in Fairlee and West Fairlee. The main settlements are North Thetford and East Thetford (on the Connecticut), Thetford Center and Union Village (on the Ompompanoosuc), Thetford Hill, Post Mills, and Rices Mills. Thetford Academy is the oldest secondary school in Vermont, and Thetford Hill Congregational Church is the oldest Congregational church in continuous use in the state. George Peabody, the merchant and philanthropist who endowed museums at Harvard and Yale, spent part of his boyhood in Thetford, and Henry Wells, founder of American Express and Wells Fargo, was born in the town. The award-winning fiction writer and current VERMONT STATE POET Grace Paley, who has also been actively involved in anti-war and anti-nuclear movements, resides in Thetford Hill.

Thomas, Isaiah (1749–1831)

A native of Boston who settled in Worcester, Massachusetts, in 1775, Isaiah Thomas became a major printer, publisher, and bookseller of his day. He was the senior partner in many business arrangements in the eastern United States including that of Thomas and Carlisle in Walpole, New Hampshire, and of Thomas & Merrifield of Windsor (1808–1809). In Rutland, he was partner with Anson Whipple in the firm of Isaiah Thomas & Co. (1812–1813) and in the firm of Peter Brown & Co. (1813–1817) (in which Anson Whipple was also involved). In addition, Isaiah Thomas had considerable business and personal dealings with the SAMUEL MILLS family, printers of Burlington. Thomas, who wrote *The History of Printing in America* (1810), founded the American Antiquarian Society in 1812 and died in Worcester at the age of eighty-two.   *Marcus A. McCorison*

Thomas, John Martin (1869–1952)

The ninth president of MIDDLEBURY COLLEGE (1908–1921), John Martin Thomas was born in Fort Covington, New York. His father, the Reverend Chandler N. Thomas, sent John to his alma mater, Middlebury College, where he graduated first in his class in 1890. Thomas then attended Union Theological Seminary, was ordained in 1893, and called that year to the pulpit of the Arlington Avenue Presbyterian Church in East Orange, New Jersey. Over the next fifteen years, he built a small congregation into one of the largest and most active in the greater New York area. Appointed president of Middlebury in 1908, he was an indefatigable builder and fund-raiser. During his tenure, the college experienced the most dramatic growth in its history in student enrollment, physical facilities, and faculty. In addition, the MIDDLEBURY SUMMER LANGUAGE SCHOOLS and the BREAD LOAF SCHOOL OF ENGLISH were first organized. After leaving Middlebury, he served as president of Pennsylvania State University (1921–1925), Rutgers University (1925–1931), and NORWICH UNIVERSITY (1939–1944). From 1931 to 1938, he was also vice president of the National Life Insurance Company in Montpelier, helped found Rutland Junior College, and served several terms in the Vermont state legislature.   *David M. Stameshkin*

Thompson, Daniel Pierce (1795–1868)

Called by his biographer "The Novelist of Vermont," Daniel Pierce Thompson of Montpelier was a lawyer, man of letters, and public servant. A native of Charlestown, Massachusetts, "at the foot of Bunker Hill," Thompson was five years old when his family moved to Berlin. Graduating from MIDDLEBURY COLLEGE in the class of 1820, he went to Virginia, where he read law and worked as a tutor for a wealthy family, returning to Vermont to open a practice in Montpelier in 1823. He was active in Vermont politics, serving two years as secretary of state and holding consecutive memberships in the DEMOCRATIC, Liberty, and REPUBLICAN PARTIES. He was appointed clerk of the legislature in 1830 and a few years later compiled the *Laws of Vermont* (1835). He was a probate judge (1837–1840), clerk of the Washington County court and the Supreme Court (1843–1845), secretary of the state Education Society (1846–1849), and secretary of the state of Vermont (1853–1855). He is best known as an author of historical fiction, in which he employed his large fund of local legends and lore about Vermont in the Revolutionary era. In 1838, Thompson was a principal figure in the founding of the VERMONT HISTORICAL SOCIETY, remaining active in the affairs of the society for the rest of his life, serving as its vice president from 1860 to 1862 and as its corresponding secretary for many years. In 1849, he became editor and owner of a newspaper, *The Green Mountain Freeman*, which he published until 1856. He was an ardent anti-slavery advocate and used his paper to promote that cause. Thompson's most popular romantic adventure novels, *The Green Mountain Boys* (1839) and *Locke Amsden* (1847), were reprinted well into the twentieth century. He also wrote a history of Montpelier, another of Vermont, and one on the 1777 northern campaign of the Revolutionary War.

Thompson, Dorothy (1894–1961)

One of the most respected journalists of her time, Dorothy Thompson had an international reputation as a reporter and commentator when she married the novelist SINCLAIR LEWIS in 1928. They bought a 300-acre farm in Barnard that they named Twin Farms where, for the fourteen years of their marriage, they spent many summers working and entertaining literary notables such as H. L. Mencken and Vincent Sheean. When they divorced in 1942, Twin Farms became Thompson's property. During the war years, she found time to participate in community projects such as the Volunteer Land Corps, which brought several hundred young men and women to work on Vermont farms. In 1943, she married the painter Maxim Kopf, and they are both buried in a Barnard cemetery. Twin Farms is today an upscale resort.

Thompson, Zadock (1796–1856)

Historian, naturalist, and mathematician, Zadock Thompson was born in Bridgewater. A member of the UNIVERSITY OF VERMONT Class of 1823, he was appointed tutor at the university in 1825, during which time he edited the magazines *Iris* and *Green Mountain Repository*. He taught school in Burlington and Hatley and Sherbrooke, Quebec, from the late 1820s until 1837, during which years he published his *History of the State of Vermont from its Earliest Settlement to the Close of the Year 1832* (1833) and *Geography and History of Lower Canada* (1835). In 1837, he taught at a boys' school at Rock Point in Burlington and began writing his most important work, the *History of Vermont, Natural, Civil and Statistical* (1842). Thompson's history remains very useful on the early years of Vermont, as well as providing an interesting view of how nineteenth-century Vermonters understood and utilized their natural resources, including fish and wildlife. He was named assistant state geologist in 1845, professor of chemistry and natural history at UVM in 1851, and state naturalist in 1853. He also was author of a popular school book, *The Youth's Assistant in Practical Arithmetic* (1825), which went through fourteen editions.

Thunder Road International Speedway

Operating since 1949 on Quarry Hill in Barre, Thunder Road is a stock-car raceway that features both professional and amateur races on a high-banked, quarter-mile oval track. Weekly Thursday night races are offered from June until September, when the season ends with a two-day Milk Bowl race, after which the winner kisses a cow.

Tichenor, Isaac (1754–1838)

The fourth governor of Vermont, serving from 1797 to 1807 and 1808 to 1809, Isaac Tichenor was born in Newark, New Jersey, and graduated from Princeton, then known as the College of New Jersey. While studying law in Schenectady, New York, he was appointed assistant commissary-general for the northern department of the Continental army and stationed at Bennington in August 1777 to collect supplies in the region. He subsequently settled in Bennington. As commissary general buying supplies for the army, he incurred large debts that were never reimbursed by Congress. He began to practice law in Bennington in 1783, served as town representative from 1781 to 1784, and speaker of the Vermont House in 1783. As an agent to Congress seeking Vermont's admission to the Union in 1782, Tichenor was sent in that same year by the legislature to Windham County to quell disturbances there by residents who wished New York's jurisdiction to be restored to Vermont. His persuasive powers earned him the nickname "Jersey Slick" and aided his rise to prominence. He was a judge of the Vermont supreme court from 1791 to 1796 and chief justice the last two years. During the legislative session of 1793, IRA ALLEN challenged Tichenor to a duel in consequence of an altercation arising over Allen's alleged misuse of funds during the Revolutionary War. The duel was aborted only after friends disarmed the combatants on the field of honor. In October 1796, Tichenor resigned from the court to fill MOSES ROBINSON's unexpired term in the United States Senate and was elected in 1797 to the full six-year term. He resigned from the Senate that fall, however, when he was elected governor. A leading Federalist by then, Tichenor failed to win a majority of the popular vote, but the Federalist-dominated legislature then chose him by a large majority. He was re-elected every year until 1809, except 1807, when he lost to Jeffersonian Democrat ISRAEL SMITH. Tichenor was elected even after the Federalist party became a minority, and in 1814 he was again sent to the United States Senate for one term. In the 1820s, however, the Federalist party effectively disappeared from American politics and Tichenor returned to private life in Bennington.

Ticonderoga

The steamboat *Ticonderoga* was built in 1906 at the Shelburne Shipyard on LAKE

Steamboat Ticonderoga *at the Shelburne Museum. Vermont Department of Tourism and Marketing*

CHAMPLAIN for the CHAMPLAIN TRANSPORTATION COMPANY (CTC). Capable of running at nearly 25 miles per hour, the coal-fired steamboat was 220 feet long, with a 58-foot beam, and drew 11 feet of water. Her initial route ran daily from Westport, New York, where she met the New York City evening train and carried travelers and freight northward to St. Albans. Besides passengers, the *Ti* transported farm produce, livestock, and dry goods, and during both World Wars ferried U.S. troops between Plattsburgh and Burlington. Under HORACE CORBIN's ownership of the CTC in the late 1930s and 1940s, the *Ti* steamed on the east-west run from Burlington to Port Kent, New York, and had a brief career as a floating casino. When more modern ferries made her obsolete, the *Ti* was operated as an excursion boat by new owners for several seasons, but by 1950 a steady decline in business threatened the boat's future. The *Ti* was saved from the scrap heap by RALPH NADING HILL, who persuaded ELECTRA HAVEMEYER WEBB to buy her for the Webbs' SHELBURNE MUSEUM in 1950. In 1954, the *Ti* was hauled out of the lake and moved overland to its present exhibition site at the museum. Declared a National Historic Landmark in 1960, the *Ticonderoga* is the last remaining side-paddlewheel passenger steamer with a vertical or walking beam engine.

Ticonderoga, Fort

In 1755, the army of France in North America built a large star fort on the west shore of LAKE CHAMPLAIN overlooking the river outlet from Lake George and large stretches of Champlain. The Iroquois called the place *ticonderoga*, falling water, but the French named the fort Carillon. Controlling a strategically important narrow stretch of Champlain from the lake's western shore with a garrison of three thousand soldiers, Carillon was the largest French fortification on the lake. In 1758, an army of fifteen thousand British regulars and American provincial militia under General Abercromby failed to take Carillon from the French, suffering two thousand casualties in the loss. Under General Jeffrey Amherst in 1759, however, an equally large British and American army captured the fort, renaming it Ticonderoga. Lightly manned by the British over the following sixteen years, its stone walls crumbling from frost and neglect, Ticonderoga remained a symbol of Britain's control of the Champlain Valley, the best transportation route between Quebec and New York. On May 10, 1775, prompted by the Connecticut General Assembly, a force of mostly GREEN MOUNTAIN BOYS from the New Hampshire Grants, as well as some agents of the Connecticut Assembly, took possession of Ticonderoga from a British garrison of less than fifty men. The attacking force was led by ETHAN ALLEN, commander of the Green Mountain Boys, and BENEDICT ARNOLD, who had been sent by the Massachusetts Provincial Congress with a militia force to take the old fort, though he had outridden his men to join Allen's group. After this first Patriot victory of the Revolution, the Americans held the fort until 1777, using it first as a base to form the Continental Congress's Northern Army for a campaign against Canada in 1775, and in 1776 as a garrison for the retreating army after its failure before the heavily fortified walls of Quebec. Patriot Colonel Henry Knox transported cannon from the fort to strengthen George Washington's siege of Boston in the winter of 1776. Later that year, a British army and fleet invaded the valley and defeated Arnold's fleet at the BATTLE OF VALCOUR ISLAND, but failed to press its attack on Ticonderoga. Then, in July 1777, the Americans abandoned their bases at Ticonderoga and across the lake on MOUNT INDEPENDENCE before General JOHN BURGOYNE's army as it advanced up the valley. Within days of the American victory over Burgoyne at Saratoga, the Americans reoccupied Ticonderoga. By 1780, the old fort was no longer a military post, except for a brief occupation that year by a British force under Major CHRISTOPHER CARLETON, who invited some of Vermont's leaders, including Ethan and IRA ALLEN, to enter the so-called HALDIMAND NEGOTIATIONS. By 1800, Ticonderoga was effectively a stone quarry supplying material for building local houses and other structures. The Pell family acquired the ruined fort in 1820, and in the early years of the twentieth century reconstructed and restored it to a close approximation of its original condition. In 1931, the Pells deeded the fort and its adjacent lands to the Fort Ticonderoga Association, a nonprofit educational corporation, which has ever since run it as a museum offering a picture of everyday military life on the eighteenth-century frontier.

Tinmouth

Tinmouth, population 567, a town in Rutland County, was granted by BENNING WENTWORTH in 1761 and probably derives its name from either Tynemouth or Teignmouth (both pronounced "Tinmuth") in England. The town consists primarily of a broad river valley, that of the Tinmouth Channel of the Clarendon River, lying between the elongated summits of 2,835-foot Tinmouth Mountain on the west and 1,965-foot Clark Mountain on the east. Beginning in the 1780s, iron was produced in Tinmouth and, by the early nineteenth century, furnaces and forges dotted the town. After iron production ceased in the 1830s, AGRICULTURE and DAIRY FARMING

became the town's economic base. The only settlement is Tinmouth village, on Route 140 in the exact center of the town.

Tomasi, Mari (1907–1965)

A native of Montpelier, Mari Tomasi attended Wheaton College in Illinois and graduated from TRINITY COLLEGE in Burlington in 1938. She wrote for newspapers and magazines after college, becoming city editor of the Montpelier *Evening Argus* and participating in the federal Vermont Writers Project. Her first book, *Deep Grow the Roots* (1940), is a novel about a farm family in Italy and their deep attachment to the land. It was well received and the following year she was awarded a BREAD LOAF WRITER'S CONFERENCE Fellowship. Tomasi's next novel, *Like Lesser Gods* (1949), dealt with life in a Barre community of Italian granite workers. Her short stories are also concerned with the Italian immigrant community in Vermont. She continued to write for the *Argus* during and after World War II, edited three volumes of *Vermont, Its Government*, and served one term in the Vermont House of Representatives. Her death came after a brief illness.

Topsham

Topsham (pronounced Tops'm), population 1,142, a town in Orange County, was granted by BENNING WENTWORTH in 1763 and named for Topsham, Maine, the home town of some of the first settlers. Much of the land lies above fifteen hundred feet, leading to a landscape of forested hills, upland pastures, and stream-cut valleys. The highest point is 2,340-foot Fuller Hill, on the northern border with Groton. The lowest land lies along the Waits River in the southwestern part of town, where are the settlements of West Topsham and Waits River, and along the Tabor Branch of the same river to its east, the site of East Topsham and Topsham Four Corners.

Town Bands

Band concerts on the town green or in the town band shell are part of the rituals of summer in Vermont. Their unmistakable sound is one of the gifts of New England to American culture. A descendant of the military bands of the eighteenth and nineteenth centuries and of small ensembles of brasses and woodwinds that performed for dances, holidays, and other celebrations throughout the nineteenth century,

community bands continue to play an important part in the social and cultural life of Vermont towns. Some of the earliest Vermont town bands were organized in the first decades of the nineteenth century. Subscription lists dating from 1811 in Strafford and 1839 in Cambridge show that individual citizens contributed amounts from a few cents to several dollars to help purchase instruments and music that were loaned to anyone who would play them. Often the board of selectmen could require performances by the band on specific holidays and other occasions. Town bands were the training ground for many young musicians, some of whom eventually made their livelihood touring with dance bands and small orchestras. David Blakely, who taught at the Bradford Academy from 1854 to 1857, went on to be the manager of John Philip Sousa's band. On at least one occasion, Sousa brought his band to Bradford for rehearsals. George Clark of Cavendish pursued a career in music that included directing one of the most popular touring bands in New England. During the Civil War, many town bands played at recruiting ceremonies, accompanied troops to the local train depot and sometimes to the battle field, and greeted the returning veterans. In Grafton, the town band still plays an important role in the annual Memorial Day celebrations that began just after the Civil War. During World War I, the Montpelier town band played at a gathering of citizens to promote the sale of war bonds. An Italian band in Barre helped send off the young men from that city who were going to the war. Town bands continue to be democratic institutions. Youngsters with only a few years of training sit among the old hands who have long since memorized parts to classic marches and popular tunes. Once the exclusive domain of the men and boys of the community, town bands used to have an unsavory reputation for teaching their members as much about drinking as about playing a cornet. Present-day bands are tamer and include women. Mary Sanders Mitchell was the first woman to play with the Morrisville band. She joined in 1946, chaperoned by her father, brother, and husband. Several Vermont bands claim long histories. The Rutland band is said to have the longest continuous existence in the nation as a town-supported ensemble. Grafton has had an active band since 1867. The Enosburg Falls band is also over 130 years old.

The Morrisville band celebrated its centennial in 1995.   *Michael Sherman*

Town Meeting

The town meeting is the legislative branch of town government in Vermont. All the citizens of a town are in effect legislators and possess the inherent powers of lawmakers in a democracy. Meetings are held at least once a year on dates approved by the state. The "warning" (public notice) of these meetings, the dates they may be held, various procedural arrangements, and questions such as how "special" town meetings may be called are all prescribed by state law. Typically, the town's voters approve tax levies to pay for such services as local law enforcement, town highway maintenance, cemetery and library expenses, and fire protection, and to approve proposed town ordinances. Town and city school districts normally meet as separate municipalities to determine annual school budgets. Attendance at town meetings is closely tied to a town's population. Towns with less than five hundred registered voters average from 25 to 40 percent attendance, while towns with over twenty-five hundred voters average under 10 percent. Responding to population growth since the 1960s, towns have attempted to enhance attendance by offering flexible voting opportunities with the Australian or secret ballot (which is often employed for significantly contentious questions) during day and night polling hours and scheduling night meetings to accommodate voters in Vermont's large commuting workforce. But these measures may themselves contribute to a decline in town meeting attendance. Some observers attribute the decline in attendance simply to a sense of loss of decision-making power to state government. Nevertheless, the town meeting remains a significant element of citizen governance in Vermont and a vital part of the state's self-image.   *Frank Bryan*

Townshend

Townshend, population 1,149, a town in Windham County, was granted by BENNING WENTWORTH in 1753 and probably named for Charles Townshend, a member of the British Ministry, who was later responsible for the repressive Townshend Acts that led to the Boston Tea Party. Early settlement was on the hills above the West Village, now West Townshend, then shifted gradually to the East Village, now Townshend. The first town meeting was held in 1771. Principal industries in the early years were, as elsewhere, farming, lumbering, potash making, with the attendant sawmills, gristmills, tanneries, blacksmith shops, and the like. Today, the economic base includes furniture manufacturing, optical manufacturing for high-tech satellites, a hand-painted glass and ceramics studio, plus a health services complex with a small hospital and extensive outpatient services. The WEST RIVER, which flows through the town from northwest to southeast, is the site of Townshend Dam, built by the U.S. Corps of Engineers in 1960 to 1961. Alphonso Taft, who served in President Grant's cabinet and was the father of president William Howard Taft, was born in Townshend.

Townshend, Micah (1749–1832)

A native of Oyster Bay, Long Island, Micah Townshend was a lawyer at Brattleboro for twenty-four years and Vermont Secretary of State from 1781 to 1788. He graduated from Princeton in 1767, studied law in New York City, and settled in practice at White Plains, New York. A Patriot and militia officer during the early years of the Revolution, Townshend left White Plains after a fire destroyed the village in 1778 and settled in Brattleboro, where he married Mary Wells, daughter of the Loyalist SAMUEL WELLS. At first loyal to New York, Townshend honored its jurisdiction in CUMBERLAND COUNTY and was selected as county delegate to the New York Assembly. There, he opposed the proposal to divide the recently self-proclaimed state of Vermont at the ridge of the GREEN MOUNTAINS between New York and New Hampshire. He finally recognized that New York could not maintain its claim to jurisdiction over the land of Vermont and declared his loyalty to Vermont, in whose government he then served in various capacities. Besides secretary of state, he was judge and register of probate for Windham County from 1781 to 1787 and secretary of the COUNCIL OF CENSORS for the first revision of the constitution. He had a large and successful practice as a lawyer when he decided to leave Vermont, selling his Brattleboro property to ROYALL TYLER, and settling in Farnham, Quebec, on lands that the British government had granted his Loyalist father-in-law.

Trapp Family Singers

Refugees from Hitler's takeover of Austria in 1938, the family of Maria and Georg von Trapp made their way to Stowe in 1939, where they purchased a 600-acre farm as a home. The family made its living for the next twenty years as a touring choral group, and in 1950 opened a guest lodge on their Stowe property that today remains family managed. The musical play and movie *The Sound of Music* were based on the story of Maria, Georg, and their singing children as presented in her book *The Story of the Trapp Family Singers* (1949). Maria Augusta Kutschera, born in 1905, was a member of a religious convent in Austria when she was sent to the home of retired naval captain Georg von Trapp to care for his sick daughter. She soon left the convent and married von Trapp in 1927, assuming the responsibility for his nine children. Expecting their tenth child in 1938, the family, which had begun to acquire fame as a singing group, fled Austria for America, supporting themselves by their choral performances. By the time the Trapp Family Singers ended their twenty years of performing and touring, most of the children were married, although Maria and three of her children, Maria, Rosemarie, and Johannes, travelled to the South Pacific on missionary service, visiting New Guinea and other islands. Maria von Trapp continued to take part in the operations of the lodge in Stowe until her death in 1987. The youngest of her sons, Johannes von Trapp, is currently the president of the Trapp Family Lodge.

Trees, Largest in Vermont

A record of Vermont's largest trees of different species may be found in the Vermont Big Tree Survey, maintained by the Green Mountain Division of the Society of American Foresters. Trees are scored by the sum of three factors: trunk circumference in inches, height in feet, and one-quarter of the average crown spread in feet. This total determines a tree's standing and allows comparison among ninety species of trees in the state. (The national Big Tree Survey compares four hundred species.) As of 2001, the Vermont tree with the largest total is a cottonwood below a railroad embankment north of the Colchester depot with a total of 403 in 2002. Among other record specimens with readings over 300 are a red oak in Shaftsbury (363), a white pine in Londonderry (355), a sycamore on Route 30 in Harmonyville in the town of Townshend (341), a black willow in Plainfield (329), a sugar maple in Guilford (322), a bur oak in New Haven (319), a white ash in Bennington (319), a white oak in Rupert (304), and a black locust in Pittsford (303).

Trinity College

Founded in Burlington in 1926 by the Sisters of Mercy of Vermont, Trinity College began as an undergraduate college for women offering degrees in education and the liberal arts. In the 1970s, the college enrolled men in some of its courses and developed degree affiliations with the UNIVERSITY OF VERMONT and ST. MICHAEL'S COLLEGE. Continuing its mission to serve Vermont's women, Trinity added graduate programs in education in the 1980s, as well as in community mental health and women's small businesses. Peak enrollments in the 1980s and 1990s supported 125 faculty members. In the late 1990s, however, women seeking higher education turned increasingly to coeducational institutions rather than single-sex colleges, and Trinity experienced significant declines in enrollments. The college closed in September 2000. Trinity College alumnae exceed five thousand.

Trombly, Daniel T. "Baptiste"
(1849–1940)

A resident of Isle La Motte, a railroad worker, farmer, host to city boarders at "Trombly's Lake View Cottage," detective, and high sheriff of Grand Isle County (1912), Daniel T. Trombly recounted in a distorted Anglo-French dialect the misadventures of Baptiste of Isle La Motte. Trombly published his local-color stories and "Poems of Baptiste" in pamphlets for more than twenty years, often selling over two thousand copies in a summer for twenty-five cents each. Some of his stories were collected as *Baptiste of Isle La Motte and His Trubbles* (1915). Writer and radio commentator Lowell Thomas so enjoyed "Baptiste's Tall Tales" that he enrolled Trombly as a "Grand Giraffe" in Thomas's "Tall Story Club."

Troy

Troy, population 1,564, a town in Orleans County, was incorporated by the Vermont legislature in 1801 out of two equal-size parcels of land, Averys Grant and Kellys Grant. Its original name was Missiskouie, after the MISSISQUOI RIVER that flows through the town, but that was changed to Troy in 1803, probably after the town of the same name in New York rather than the classical locale. The landscape is made up of low hills and streams that lead into the Missisquoi. Iron was mined in the town in the middle of the nineteenth century, although AGRICULTURE has always formed the main economic base. There are two settlements, the hamlet of Troy and the incorporated village of North Troy, which is only a mile from the Canadian border.

Tunbridge

Tunbridge, population 1,309, a town in Orange County, was granted by BENNING WENTWORTH in 1761 and named for one of the most prominent members of the British establishment, William Henry Nassau du Zuylestein (1717–1781), among whose titles was Viscount Tunbridge. The town is cut through the center from north to south by the First Branch of the WHITE RIVER, along whose banks are the settlements of North Tunbridge, Tunbridge village, and South Tunbridge. To the east is a typical central Vermont landscape of forested hills and upland pastures, while to the west, near the border with Randolph, the land rises to a long ridge between 1,400 and 1,900 feet high. In October 1780, during the Revolution, a British military force, including nearly three hundred Kahnawake Mohawks from Canada, attacked Tunbridge and killed two villagers before heading south to plunder and burn Royalton. The Tunbridge World's Fair, the town's most famous attraction, has been held every September since 1867. Its once-lurid reputation, based upon its games of chance, burlesque shows, and excessive drinking—it was said that all sober persons were thrown off the grounds at three in the afternoon—has long since disappeared. FRED TUTTLE, who played himself in the 1996 film *Man with a Plan* and later was a quixotic Republican candidate for U.S. Senator, lives in Tunbridge.

Turkey Drives

For over fifty years of the nineteenth century, the largest annual migration in Vermont was that of turkeys to out-of-state markets. In the days before RAILROADS, the birds, in flocks several thousand strong, were driven overland to Boston and other cities, where they were sold for the Thanksgiving and Christmas holidays. At the rate of 10 to 12 miles per day, the journey took several weeks. Numerous obstacles along the route—foxes and other predators, deep watercourses, the natural attrition of straying or enfeebled birds—normally led to a loss of 10 percent or more of the animals, but enough survived to make the arduous trip profitable for the turkeys' owners. In October 1824, it is estimated that seven thousand turkeys from more than forty homesteads in three Vermont counties constituted one of the largest flocks ever to make its way to Boston. After the arrival of railroads in Vermont in the 1850s, the drives terminated at the local depot. When the Rutland Railroad put refrigerator cars (using ice) in service in 1857, the shipment of live turkeys ceased in favor of slaughtered and dressed ones, an interstate commercial activity that ended in the 1960s when Vermont's few poultry processors could no longer meet federal public health standards.

Turner, Bates (1760–1847)

State Supreme Court judge and law-school proprietor, Bates Turner was born in Canaan, Connecticut, and graduated from Litchfield Law School in 1780. He moved to Fairfield in 1796, assuming that it would become the SHIRE TOWN of Franklin County. When St. Albans was chosen instead, he relocated there. A law practice with Asa Aldis did not work out and Turner returned to Fairfield, where he opened Vermont's first school devoted specifically to the preparation of lawyers. An early success, the school attracted approximately 175 students but was closed in 1812, largely in consequence of debts Turner had assumed in ambitious preparations for expanding his school facilities. Turner represented Fairfield in the 1813 legislature, served two terms as a Supreme Court judge (1827 and 1828), and was a member of the 1827 COUNCIL OF CENSORS. His most enduring contribution was his law school which, although short-lived, provided the state with able lawyers.

Turner, Jessie "Daisy" (1884–1988)

Born in Grafton, Daisy Turner was the daughter of Alexander and Sally Turner. Her father was a slave on the Goulden plantation in eastern Virginia who fled the South at the outbreak of the Civil War and eventually joined the First New Jersey Cavalry. After the war, he worked for the Freedmen's Bureau, helping resettle former slaves along the eastern seaboard. In Boston, Alec met Vestus Wilbur and Charles White, operators of a Grafton lumber operation, who enticed him to move to Vermont and work for them as a logger. Alec, Sally, and three children settled in Vermont in 1872. A powerful and industrious man, he eventually purchased 150 acres of land in Grafton. Besides logging the property for himself, Alec built a home for his growing family, naming the homestead "Journey's End." In addition to logging and selling timber, the Turners raised produce, turkeys, sheep, and chickens for the Boston markets. In time, they built other accommodations on their land and rented them out to Boston gentlemen and hunters, who were entertained in the evening with folk ballads and music-hall songs, skits and Civil War tableaus. The latter were accompanied with recitations of popular poems describing various battle scenes. Into this vibrant oral performance culture, Daisy was born in 1884. She attended the Grafton elementary school, but when she was old enough, she helped Alec with his logging and farming. As a child and teenager, she heard repeatedly the tales of her father and was encouraged by her parents to compose her own poetry. Around 1902, she left Grafton to become a housemaid in Boston, remaining there until 1923, when her father died and she returned to Journey's End. Although she occasionally worked as a maid for Grafton residents, Daisy remained at the family homestead, growing her own food and developing an independent life. When Journey's End burned in 1962, she moved into a smaller house on her land. At age 103, failing health forced her to move to the convalescent center in Springfield. Daisy died from a heart attack in 1988. In her own life, she continued the storytelling and singing tradition of her family. She composed poems about family life on Turner's Hill and continued to recite the extended narrations she had heard from her father. Some of her own stories dealt with her earliest encounters with racism, Boston business dealings in which shop owners sought unsuccessfully to outwit her father, and her suing and winning a case against an unfaithful fiancé. She composed poems that document important events in her family's history, and she passed along the stories her father had told her about his experiences in the Civil War. Although Daisy won a local reputation for her outspoken independence, her fame as a raconteur spread beyond Grafton. She was featured in the video *On My Own: The Traditions of Daisy Turner* (UNIVERSITY OF VERMONT and the Vermont Folklife Center, 1986), which was a finalist in the American Film and Video Festival. She also appeared in Ken Burns's television documentary *The Civil War* (1990) and a compilation of her stories, entitled *Journey's End* (Vermont Folklife Center), was broadcast as a series on public radio and won a 1990 George Peabody Award for Documentary Programming. None of these productions were made until Daisy was over one hundred years old, completely blind, yet living independently. Until the last months of her life, Daisy's mind remained sharp; her wit, tart; her ability to sing and recite extended narratives, active. Her legacy, captured on tape and film and preserved in the archives of the Vermont Folklife Center in Middlebury, will continue to document a small portion of Vermont's ethnic diversity and the rich traditions of a vibrant African-American family.   *Richard Sweterlitsch*

Tuttle, Fred (b. 1920)
A modern folk hero for his starring role in John O'Brien's 1996 independent film, *Man with a Plan*, in which he played a retired dairy farmer (which he is) who runs for Congress on a shoestring budget, Fred Tuttle of Tunbridge in 1998 became a real Republican candidate for the U.S. Senate. Comical primary debates attracted national media attention, culminating in a *New York Times* story and a Tuttle appearance on *The Tonight Show*. "Spread Fred" bumper stickers distributed to advertise O'Brien's film may still be seen on Vermont cars. O'Brien, who managed Tuttle's primary campaign against Massachusetts businessman Jack McMullen, admitted that Tuttle's run for the Senate was a publicity stunt, but said it was also a protest against millionaire out-of-stater McMullen coming to Vermont to seek a national office. After winning the Republican primary, calling McMullen a carpetbagger, and spending only $16 on his campaign, Tuttle faced Senator PATRICK LEAHY, a man he admired, in the general election. "I hope I don't get too many votes today," Tuttle said on Election Day. Leahy was re-elected with 72 percent of the vote, while Tuttle received 23 percent.
Kenneth A. Peck

Twilight, Alexander (1795–1857)
The first African-American to graduate from an American college, MIDDLEBURY COLLEGE class of 1825, Alexander Twilight was born in Bradford, the son of Ichabod Twilight, an African-American who served in the Revolutionary War, and his wife Mary, a white woman. After graduating from Middlebury, Twilight taught school in Peru, New York, where he also studied for the ministry, then moved back across LAKE CHAMPLAIN to teach and preach for four years in Vergennes. In Peru, he also met and married Mercy Ladd Merrill in 1826. In 1829, he was called to Brownington, where he took up the duties of pastor of the Congregational Church and headmaster of the Orleans County Grammar School. Faced with a growing enrollment in his school and a school board reluctant to invest in a new building, Twilight designed and built Athenian Hall to provide both classrooms and a school dormitory (1834–1836). He paid with his own funds and private subscriptions, erecting the first public building in Vermont made of granite. In 1836, Twilight was elected to the Vermont General Assembly, becoming the first African-American to serve as a representative in the Vermont legislature and possibly in any state legislature. In 1847, after a falling out with the school directors, Twilight moved to Quebec and taught there for five years, then returned to Brownington to resume his old role. Twilight devoted most of his remaining years to supervising the education of pupils at his academy. In October 1855, he suffered a debilitating stroke and died on June 19, 1857. His wife died July 29, 1878. They are both buried in the churchyard at Brownington, in sight of the stone school house Twilight built and directed. He is memorialized by the Alexander Twilight Theater at LYNDON STATE COLLEGE, and in 1986 Middlebury College named a newly renovated academic building for their noted alumnus. Today, Athenian Hall is called the Old Stone House, and contains a museum and the headquarters of the Orleans County Historical Society. The Old Stone House with the surrounding buildings and fields are listed on the National Register of Historic Districts.
John Lovejoy

Twitchell, Amos (1781–1850)
A graduate of the Dartmouth class of 1802, where he studied medicine under Nathan Smith, Amos Twitchell resided in Keene, New Hampshire, and practiced medicine on both sides of the CONNECTICUT RIVER, becoming the most prominent physician in eastern Vermont and New Hampshire during the second quarter of

the nineteenth century. A skillful surgeon, Twitchell in 1807 successfully tied off the carotid artery of a patient. He was among the first American surgeons to perform tracheotomies and amputations for malignant disease.

251 Club

The 251 Club is an organization whose members have as their goal visiting all of the 242 towns and 9 cities in Vermont. (Visiting the three gores and one grant is not necessary). The club, founded by AR-THUR W. PEACH, director of the VER-MONT HISTORICAL SOCIETY, held its first meeting in Montpelier on July 18, 1955. Currently there are 4,500 members, 910 of whom are from out of state. The first year's dues are seven dollars, four dollars a year thereafter. Membership includes a subscription to *The Wayfarer*, the organization's newsletter, published three times annually. Meetings are held in various locations around the state twice a year, in summer and fall. It is generally agreed that Lewis in Essex County is the most difficult of the towns to visit, since it is an unpopulated wilderness with no public roads.

T. W. Wood Gallery & Art Center

The T. W. Wood Gallery & Art Center in Montpelier began in 1895 with a gift by THOMAS W. WOOD of forty-two of his paintings to the city where he was born. First housed with the public library at the Young Men's Christian Association on State Street, it moved to the Kellogg-Hubbard Library, where it remained until 1986, when it was relocated to VERMONT COLLEGE. The gallery's collection includes nearly eight hundred nineteenth- and twentieth-century works by Wood and several of his contemporaries, including William Beard, J. G. Brown, Frederick Church, and Asher B. Durand. The gallery also serves as the repository for Vermont's allotment of the Works Progress Administration's Federal Art Project work of the 1930s, including works by Joseph Stella, Reginald Marsh, Jerome Meyers, and Raphael Soyer. Also in the collection are works by Jacob Lawrence, Stanford Stevens, and Isabela Bishop. From the late 1960s, under the leadership of curator RONALD SLAYTON, the Gallery has produced frequent exhibits by contemporary artists.

Tyler, Mary Palmer (1775–1866)

Born in Watertown, Massachusetts, Mary Palmer Tyler moved to Vermont in 1796 with her husband, lawyer and playwright ROYALL TYLER. The daughter of Elizabeth Hunt and Joseph Pearse Palmer, Tyler received no formal education but learned the value of reading and the skills of housewifery from her parents. She put those skills to good use after her marriage to Royall Tyler, her father's friend, who was eighteen years her senior. After five years in Guilford, the Tylers moved to a farm in Brattleboro, where Mary supervised her growing family of eleven children while Royall served on the Vermont Supreme Court. During those years, she developed the ideas that informed *The Maternal Physician* (1811), a book of advice to mothers about infant problems of feeding, teething, disease, and discipline. With an emphasis on rational but affectionate child rearing, Tyler argued that mothers' authority in the physical care and mental development of children is superior to that of physicians or fathers. Tyler's book claimed an elevated cultural role for mothers more than a decade before American books on practical child health care became popular. Facing poverty after her husband's death in 1826, Mary struggled to educate her sons and to maintain her status in the family and community. She helped her daughter run a local school in the Tyler house in Brattleboro and sought to extend her maternal influence through leadership in religious and benevolent activities in the town. As an anonymous author, Tyler did not receive recognition for her child care manual at the time, nor did she mention the work in her memoir, *Grandmother Tyler's Book*, first published by her great-granddaughter Helen Tyler Brown in 1925.   *Marilyn Blackwell*

Tyler, Royall (1757–1826)

The author of *The Contrast* (1787), considered the first American comedy produced professionally, Royall Tyler was a novelist, poet, and lawyer who became chief judge of the Vermont Supreme Court. Originator of the rural Yankee as a literary figure and a skilled parodist of British manners and literary forms, Tyler was both wit and moralist. Born in Boston, he served briefly as a military aide during the Revolution and assisted in suppressing SHAYS' REBELLION, which first brought him to Vermont in 1786 in pursuit of Daniel Shays and his followers. By the time he settled in Vermont in 1791, he was famous not only for his success as a playwright but also for his brilliant wit and youthful escapades at Harvard, and an ill-fated engagement to John Adams's daughter Abigail. Moving with his youthful wife MARY PALMER TYLER to Guilford, Tyler divided his time between a career as state's attorney for Windham County and literary pursuits. He continued to write satirical plays, witty poetry, and a novel, *The Algerine Captive* (1797), until his election to the Vermont Supreme Court in 1801, when he and Mary moved to a farm in Brattleboro. Celebrated for his skill as an orator and his compassion as a jurist, Tyler was also appointed a trustee of the UNIVERSITY OF VERMONT in 1802 and professor of jurisprudence from 1811 to 1814. After becoming chief judge in 1807, Tyler's shift from Federalist to Republican politics and his support for the War of 1812 eventually resulted in his replacement in 1813. Meanwhile, he had elevated the status of Vermont jurisprudence by publishing two volumes of *Reports of Cases Argued and Determined in the Supreme Court of Judicature of the State of Vermont* (1809–1810), the only record of court opinions for 1800 to 1803. Retiring to Brattleboro, Tyler served briefly as register of probate but became increasingly reclusive until his death from cancer in 1826.   *Marilyn Blackwell*

Tyson Iron Company

The Tyson Iron Company, originally incorporated as the Windsor and Plymouth Ascutney Iron Company, was founded in 1837 by the noted metallurgist Isaac Tyson, Jr. (1792–1861) of Baltimore, Maryland, who discovered an outcrop of iron near the southern Black River while prospecting for minerals in the GREEN MOUNTAINS in 1835. When Tyson sent Joseph Martin, foreman of his copper mine in Strafford, to prospect for ore in the Plymouth area, Martin found three deposits of workable ore and in 1837 Tyson began to erect his blast furnace on the southern edge of the town. In its peak years, Tyson Furnace employed 175 men in the smelting of pig iron, part of which was recast into stoves, hollow ware, machinery parts, and water pipe. To fuel the furnace, Tyson purchased 2,500 acres of woodland to provide timber for charcoal. He erected a dam to supply a constant flow of water to power the furnace, and a post office, tavern, school, and reading room with books and newspapers for his employees. According to John W. Stickney, Tyson's long-time agent in Vermont, the furnace produced between 600 and 1,000 tons of iron annually. The company ceased the manufacture of ironware in 1844 and sold only pig iron thereafter. In 1855, the works closed down due to Tyson's failing health, and remained closed until the Civil War, when they were re-opened under new ownership to produce iron for the building of the Monitor class gunboats. After the war, the works were taken over by Spathic Iron Company of Hartford, Connecticut, which manufactured steel cutlery. In 1872, the furnace closed down for good.

U

Underground Railroad

During the ante-bellum era, an undetermined but probably small number of Vermonters—Quakers, clergymen, free African-Americans, reformers, and Liberty party members prominent among them—provided food and shelter, clothing, work, transportation, and contacts for runaway slaves attempting to find safety and establish free lives in the northeastern United States and Canada. Beginning in the 1830s, these activities, whether premeditated and organized or random, were popularized in the press as the Underground Railroad. The amount of organization, number of fugitives and activists, and the degree of risk involved in passage along the Vermont branch of the Underground Railroad are hotly debated topics. The value of cubby holes, attic spaces, knee-wall recesses, and other purported hiding places as credible evidence linking Underground Railroad activity to a particular building or its ante-bellum inhabitants has also been questioned by modern scholars. Among those activitists whose involvement is documented are Reverend Kiah Bailey, Hardwick; Lemuel Bottom, Shaftsbury; William Davis and LAWRENCE BRAINERD, St. Albans; Samuel Chalker, New Haven; Zenas C. Ellis, Fair Haven; Erastus and Hervey Higley, Castleton; Nathan C. Hoag, Charlotte; ROWLAND T. ROBINSON, Ferrisburgh; Howard Griswold, Randolph; Charles Hicks, Bennington; CHAUNCEY L. KNAPP, Montpelier; Louden Langley, Hinesburg; JONATHAN P. MILLER and Steven F. Stevens, East Montpelier; GEORGE W. BENEDICT, Lucius H. Bigelow, Joshua Young, and John K. Converse, Burlington. Shadrach Minkins, Moses Roper, and Milton Clark were fugitives known to have associations with the Vermont Underground Railroad. Former Vermonters THADDEUS STEVENS, OLIVER JOHNSON, and DELIA WEBSTER aided fugitives elsewhere.

Ray Zirblis

Underhill

The largest town in area in Chittenden County, Underhill, population 2,980, was granted by BENNING WENTWORTH in 1763 and named for members of the Underhill family, who were among the original grantees. Its physical size is the result of the absorption in 1839 of the western half of the town of Mansfield, which straddled the main ridge of the GREEN MOUNTAINS at its highest point and proved impractical as a cohesive unit. Although Underhill shares the summit of 4,393-foot MOUNT MANSFIELD, the highest point in the Green Mountains, with Stowe to the east and has much hilly terrain, it also has a fertile lowland area along the Brown's River in the southern part of town. Here are located the two main settlements, Underhill Center and Underhill Flats, the latter of which is partly in neighboring Jericho. The summit of Mount Mansfield is easily accessible by trails from Underhill State Park on the mountain's flank. In the southeastern corner of the town is the government-owned Ethan Allen Firing Range, which extends into Jericho and Bolton. Although much of Underhill is still rural, its location on the edge of the Burlington metropolitan area has resulted in an increase in residential development in recent years.

Underwood, Levi (1821–1902)

Lawyer and lieutenant governor of Vermont, Levi Underwood was born in Hardwick, studied law in Morrisville with LUKE POLAND, and settled in Burlington in 1842 to specialize in RAILROAD law. He became counsel and a director of the Vermont Central Railway (later the Central Vermont). An ardent opponent of slavery, Underwood entered politics as a Free-Soil Democrat, chaired the convention of the Vermont REPUBLICAN PARTY in June 1856, and was a delegate to the Philadelphia convention that nominated John C. Frémont for president. After serving a term in the Vermont senate, he was elected lieutenant governor in 1860 with Governor ERASTUS FAIRBANKS, and re-elected in 1861 with Governor FREDERICK HOLBROOK. Governor Fairbanks appointed him a delegate to the futile Washington peace conference of February 1861. Active in the mobilization of Vermont troops for the Civil War, Underwood headed the state's program of aid to soldiers' families, and Camp Underwood in Burlington was named for him.

Robert V. Daniels

Unitarian-Universalist Church

Burlington's landmark church building, the Unitarian-Universalist Church stands at the head of Church Street, the city's main shopping street. Designed by Boston architect Peter Banner, it was completed in 1817 and remodeled inside and out several times since. In 1845, the structure was "Greek Revivalized" with the addition of a massive cornice, bricked-in shortened façade windows, and brick pilasters at the corners. Lightning struck the tower in 1955, exposing structural weakness caused by dry rot. Donors from the entire Burlington community provided funds to rebuild the tower from measured drawings that had been transcribed as a WPA project in the 1930s.

David Blow

University of Vermont

The largest institution of higher learning in the state, the University of Vermont was chartered by the state legislature in 1791 on the initiative of IRA ALLEN. "UVM" (the Latin initials for *Universitas Viridis Montis*) actually opened in Burlington in 1800 with President DANIEL CLARKE SANDERS and a handful of students. Its slow growth was interrupted by the War of 1812, when its premises were commandeered for military use. It progressed gradually through the following century under a number of notable presidents, including JAMES MARSH, John Wheeler, Joseph Torrey, and MATTHEW BUCKHAM. Under their leadership, enrollment grew past three hundred, and the curriculum expanded from its original basis in classics and mathematics toward the modern panoply of departments. Medical instruction was begun by Dr. JOHN POMEROY in 1804. Agricultural education pursuant to the Morrill Act began in 1865 when the legislature reorganized the institution into the "University of Vermont and State Agricultural College" under a part-state, part-self-perpetuating board of trustees, thus initiating the unique public-private character of the institution. The Agricultural Experiment Station was established in 1891, and the Extension Service was formalized in 1914. UVM was a pioneer in coeducation, admitting women for the first time in 1872. It was the first university anywhere to admit women to Phi Beta Kappa, in 1875. The first female professor was Bertha Terrill, appointed in 1909 to create the Department of Home Economics. In the first half of the twentieth century, UVM was academically static relative to other institutions of its vintage, although enrollment jumped to nearly a thousand after World War I, and to over two thou-

Ira Allen Chapel at the University of Vermont. Special Collections, Bailey/Howe Library, University of Vermont

sand after World War II. In 1954, President CARL W. BORGMAN secured regular state funding to reduce tuition for Vermont students, and in 1960 President John T. Fey broke the provision of the James B. Wilbur scholarship trust that had limited the College of Arts and Sciences to one thousand students. During the 1960s and early 1970s, the university more than tripled its faculty and student body while expanding its physical plant, and reached the size and complexity that prevail at the present time. Since the early 1970s, several proposals to merge UVM with the VERMONT STATE COLLEGES failed to gain sufficient support. National controversies roiled the university in the 1950s and 1960s. Concerns for academic freedom were aroused in 1953 when the board of trustees fired a

professor of biochemistry, ALEX NOVI-KOFF, for refusing to testify to the U.S. Senate Internal Security Subcommittee about his prior Communist affiliation. The nation-wide student ferment of the 1960s was echoed at UVM, where the most emotional issue was the abolition of the minstrel-type dance competition known as KAKE WALK. In the 1980s, under President Lattie F. Coor, the university initiated sustained efforts to achieve racial and cultural diversity in its admissions and programs. The present organization of the university into colleges, dating from 1911, includes the College of Arts and Sciences, the largest unit with twenty-one academic departments, and professional colleges of Agriculture and Life Sciences (including the School of Natural Resources and the

Extension Service), Business Administration, Education and Social Services, Engineering and Mathematics, and Medicine (with the schools of Nursing and Allied Health Sciences making up the Division of Health Sciences). The teaching hospital is Fletcher Allen Health Care (formerly the Medical Center Hospital of Vermont and before that the MARY FLETCHER Hospital) in Burlington. Ph.D. programs are offered in education, the physical and biological sciences, engineering, and psychology, along with over seventy M.A. and M.S. programs. The Division of Continuing Education administers evening, summer, and extension courses. Interdisciplinary programs include Area and International Studies, the Environmental Program, Women's Studies, and the African–Latin American–Native American ("ALANA") program. Major intercollegiate athletic programs include hockey and basketball; football was dropped in 1974. The board of trustees now numbers twenty five members, including nine elected by the legislature for six-year terms, nine self-perpetuating members, three members appointed by the governor, two student trustees, and the governor and the president of the university ex-officio. The university administration is headed by the president, the provost, and vice presidents for university relations and operations, development and alumni relations, and student affairs. President Judith A. Ramaley resigned in 2001, and was succeeded by Daniel M. Fogel in 2002. As of 2001, there were 928 full-time faculty members, including the clinical medical faculty. The faculty voted in April 2001 to unionize in affiliation with the American Federation of Teachers and the American Association of University Professors. The student body totaled 8,961 degree students (7,472 undergraduate, 1,103 graduate, and 386 medical) and 1,120 nondegree students. Undergraduates included 38 percent Vermont residents and 62 percent out-of-staters. Resident tuition was $8,040, and nonresident $20,100. Fraternities and sororities enrolled about 15 percent of the undergraduates. For the fiscal year 2002, the university budgeted general fund revenues and expenditures of $167 million, including a state appropriation of $35,055,595 or 21 percent. Research grants, the residence system, and other restricted and self-supporting accounts brought the total budget to $348 million.

Robert V. Daniels

Upson, William Hazlett (1891–1975)
A writer whose short stories amused and enlightened American readers for more than four decades, William Hazlett Upson settled in Middlebury in 1928. His series of Earthworm Tractor tales, published in *The* *Saturday Evening Post* between 1927 and 1967, featured the irrepressible Alexander Botts, tractor salesman par excellence, who was capable of overcoming all manner of adversity by outsmarting his opponents and adversaries. Upson's deft use of humor to highlight old-fashioned common sense and practical flexibiltiy touched a sympathetic chord with the American public and gained him thousands of loyal readers.

Vail, Theodore Newton (1845–1920)

Born in Carroll County, Ohio, self-educated Theodore Newton Vail rapidly rose to head the U.S. Railway Mail Service. He was a pioneer in America's telecommunications industry and in 1907 became the first president of the American Telephone and Telegraph Company. He bought land in Lyndon in 1883 for summer vacations, built a mansion, and eventually owned 2,500 acres, where he raised blooded cattle and horses that he entered in county fairs. After Vail became a legal resident, he was a major influence on the town's agricultural and business development. When the Lyndon Literary and Biblical Institution floundered, he put it on its feet financially. He served as president of its board of trustees for a quarter of a century as it evolved into LYNDON INSTITUTE, the town's high school. He founded the VAIL SCHOOL OF AGRICULTURE in 1910, open to Vermont boys for training in progressive farm practices. He was a major donor in the building of Lyndon's Cobleigh Public Library, a president of the Lyndonville Savings Bank and Trust Company, and co-founder of the Lyndonville Creamery, which provided a market for area dairy farmers. His Speedwell Farms estate became a center for community events such as Christmas parties for children and family clambakes. Noted financier J. Pierpont Morgan visited in the summers and William Howard Taft was a guest during his Vermont campaign for the presidency. The Vail and Speedwell names are prevalent in Lyndon today. LYNDON STATE COLLEGE is located on his former estate, where an annual summer clambake is held in his memory.   *Virginia C. Downs*

Vail School of Agriculture

In 1910, THEODORE N. VAIL organized and funded his school of agriculture at LYNDON INSTITUTE as the first agricultural high school in Vermont. Tuition-free to Vermont boys, the institute provided classes in AGRICULTURE conducted in Thompson Hall and also practical experience at Vail's Speedwell Farm on the hill above the institute. While Vail's school and the institute were separate institutions, they shared building space and some teachers, and students could enroll in courses offered by both schools. In 1913, agricultural students built a large barn and a creamery on the lower campus at the institute. In 1915, Vail gave the school to the state, which led to the Vermont Boards of Agriculture and Education managing it as the Theodore N. Vail Agricultural School and Farms. The school enrolled both out-of-state and Vermont resident students. In 1918, the Departments of Agriculture and Education also established Camp Vail at the agricultural school, a two-week program to train 150 boys from large towns and cities in Vermont in farm work to help meet Vermont's farm labor shortage during World War I. After Vail's death in 1920, the state turned the agricultural school over to Lyndon Institute, which initiated a vocational agricultural and forestry program. With the decline of farming in Vermont after 1970, low enrollment in the institute's agricultural program led to its discontinuance in 1990.   *Harriet F. Fisher*

Valcour Island, Battle of

Charged in 1776 with resisting the British advance south through LAKE CHAMPLAIN —the strategic key to North America— BENEDICT ARNOLD built a fleet of fifteen ships manned by eight hundred mostly untrained soldiers and armed with cannon that could throw a combined weight of 703 pounds. The fleet jeopardized the advance of the British forces, but the Royal Navy, under the command of Captain Charles Douglas, managed in less than ninety days to put together a fleet of twenty gunboats and five big sailing vessels that threw a combined weight of more than 1,300 pounds from guns better manned than those of the American fleet. After creating a vastly superior fleet in a very short time, the British were prepared to take control of the lake. The fleets clashed on October 11, and the outcome of the battle was never in doubt. Positioned at the south end of a channel west of Valcour Island, the British took five American ships out of action while only one of their vessels came under heavy fire. Darkness fell with American ammunition almost gone, and Arnold slipped his remaining ships past the British line. A shift in the wind doomed the weary rebels after twenty-four hours at their sweeps and their pursuers were able to catch up with them. One ship surrendered and the others, while under fire, were deliberately run aground at Button Mold Bay in Ferrisburgh. The crews set the ships afire before escaping to Crown Point on foot, just ahead of pursuing Indians. Valcour is the only naval battle of the War for Independence involving American ships that had any significance for its outcome. Ironically, historians are generally agreed that though the Americans lost the battle, the strategic victory was theirs even before the battle began. By denying the British control of Lake Champlain throughout the summer of 1776, the Americans delayed General JOHN BURGOYNE's army an entire year before he could invade the Champlain Valley.   *Neil Stout*

Vallee, Rudy (1901–1986)

A nationally popular band leader and singer who also enjoyed a long career in films, Rudy Vallee was born Hubert Pryor Vallee in Island Pond, the son of Charles Alphonse Vallee, a pharmacist and drugstore owner, and Kathryn Lynch. The family moved to Westbrook, Maine, when he was a small child. His musical career began while he was attending the University of Maine, where he changed his name to Rudy as a tribute to saxophonist Rudy Wiedoeft. Later, at Yale, he formed a dance band, the Yale Collegians, which, renamed the Connecticut Yankees, became famous via radio and records in the late 1920s and early 1930s. Vallee's thin, pleasant singing voice, ideally suited for intimacy, made him the king of crooners in an era that also saw the rise of rivals such as Bing Crosby and Russ Columbo. He also had a long career in Hollywood, appearing in dozens of movies from 1929 to 1967, first as a singer and then as a comic actor, and had a great success in the Broadway musical comedy *How to Succeed in Business Without Really Trying* (1961). Island Pond fans still celebrate his birthday with a musical and dramatic performance that in recent years has featured appearances by his widow.

Valley of Vermont

The gap between the GREEN MOUNTAINS on the east and the TACONIC MOUNTAINS on the west in southwestern Vermont is known as the Valley of Vermont. It is only a few miles wide (shrinking to half a mile at its narrowest point) and extends as far north as the town of Brandon, where it disappears into the LAKE CHAMPLAIN lowlands. In its southern section, its streams, including the BATTEN KILL and the Walloomsac River, feed into the Hudson, while in its northern section it is drained by OTTER CREEK, which empties into Lake Champlain. A prime route in early settlement times, the Valley of Vermont includes the towns of Bennington, Arlington, Manchester, Wallingford, Rutland, Pittsford, and Brandon.

Van de Water, Frederic F. (1890–1968)

After a first career in journalism in New York City with the *American, Evening Post*, and *Tribune*, during which he published several mysteries and a revisionist volume on General Custer, Frederic F. Van de Water purchased a small farm in Dummerston in 1932. Two years later, he moved there permanently. Situated close to RUDYARD KIPLING's former home Naulakha, Van de Water came to know Beatty Balestier, Kipling's eccentric brother-in-law, whose intense family fight with Kipling had driven the popular British writer out of Vermont in 1896. The result was a small monograph, *Rudyard Kipling's Vermont Feud*, published in 1937. Van de Water developed a deep affection for his adopted state, and between 1938 and 1949 published six volumes of what amounted to extended essays on his and his family's encounter with life in Vermont. Increasingly, he turned to history, and *Lake Champlain and Lake George* (in the American Lake Series) and *The Reluctant Republic: Vermont, 1724–1791* both appeared in 1941. Two pieces of his on the Champlain Valley appeared in 1949 in the first volume of *American Heritage*. Between 1949 and 1958, Van de Water published four historical novels set in revolutionary Vermont. *The Reluctant Republic* stands as his most important contribution to the literature of the state. Van de Water untangled the complex events of early Vermont history and developed its colorful characters in strong, bold prose. He believed that Vermonters were "a peculiar folk whom the very word Freedom and its implications made a little drunk. In a strange way, the climate, the soil, the contours of the land itself, had nurtured—still preserves—that disconcerting passion."

H. Nicholas Muller III

Van Dyke, George (1846–1908)

A logger and lumberman who ran some of the last of the long log drives on the CONNECTICUT RIVER, George Van Dyke rose from teenage axeman to millionaire. Born in Stanbridge, Quebec, one of eight children of a subsistence farmer and logger from Highgate, Van Dyke left home at age fourteen to support himself as an axeman in the logging industry on Maine's Androscoggin River. By age twenty-six, he was part-owner of a sawmill in Guildhall, and in 1878 bought a timber lot in Hereford, Quebec, for $100, from which he cut a million log feet. When the prospective buyer went bankrupt, Van Dyke ran the logs down the Connecticut to South Lancaster, New Hampshire, where he took over a mill and put his rivermen to work sawing his logs. An upmarket in lumber gave him sufficient profit to begin buying timber stands in Vermont and New Hampshire. In 1886, he bought into the Connecticut River Lumber Company, and even though he still owned sawmills at Guildhall and McIndoes Falls, sent his logs downriver to Mount Tom above Holyoke, Massachusetts. In 1902, Connecticut River Lumber became Connecticut Valley Lumber with new partners, but Van Dyke continued to run the company's logs down the river to Massachusetts. Driving along beside the Connecticut in his car to accompany a run of 53 million feet of log, Van Dyke died when his car fell off a bluff from which he had been watching his wealth float by. The largest long log drive after Van Dyke's, and the last such drive on the Connecticut, was a 65-million-log-feet drive in 1915. After that event, only pulpwood went to mills by floating down the Connecticut.

Van Ness, Cornelius (1782–1852)

A lawyer from Kinderhook, New York, Cornelius Van Ness moved to St. Albans in 1806 with an inheritance of $40,000. He joined nine other practicing attorneys in Franklin County's SHIRE TOWN. A Jeffersonian Republican, he assisted in the enforcement and prosecution of the BLACK SNAKE AFFAIR, the most notorious anti-embargo smuggling case in Vermont. Van Ness was appointed United States attorney in 1810 and customs collector of Burlington in 1813. Also in 1813, he was named a director of the Lake Champlain Steamboat Company, which launched the ill-fated *Phoenix* in 1815. He obtained a twenty-three-year monopoly for steam navigation on the lake in 1816. Van Ness served four terms in the Vermont General Assembly (1818–1821), led the effort to obtain a charter for the Bank of Burlington, was elected chief judge of the Vermont Supreme Court in 1821, and governor in 1823 and 1824. The Van Ness House, a popular hotel at the southwest corner of Main and St. Paul Streets in Burlington that was erected in 1870 and burned in 1951, was named in his honor.

Van Patten, William J. (1848–1920)

An industrialist, mayor, and benefactor of Burlington, William J. Van Patten was born in Wauwatosa, Wisconsin, but removed to Vermont with his family, where he attended the public school and academy in Bristol. Leaving school at age sixteen, he went to Burlington with one dollar in his pocket to work in A. C. Spear's drugstore, then at Henry & Company, and within eight years was a partner at Wells, Richardson & Company, a drug manufacturer and chemical compounder. With this firm, he developed several products for both retail sales and other manufacturers, obtaining patents for Diamond Dyes, analine compounds that produced vivid colors; Paine's Celery Compound, a tonic of vegetable ingredients to "take away all desire for intoxicants"; and Improved Butter Colors, a yellow dye approved by the Vermont Dairy Association to enhance butter color during winter months when cows were kept indoors from grazing. A growing export trade in these and other Wells, Richardson products led to offices in Montreal, London, and Sydney, Australia. In 1891, Van Patten took over the Champlain Manufacturing Company, a producer of chairs, toboggans, packing boxes, fine cabinets, and decorative woodwork, running it until it failed in 1915. As mayor of Burlington from 1894 to 1895, Van Patten improved the city's water system, extended the sewer system to new housing developments, built S. W. Thayer and IRA ALLEN schools, established the Parks Department and undertook extensive shade-tree street plantings. In 1902, he purchased a portion of the 1,200-acre farm once owned by ETHAN ALLEN and developed carriage drives and trails through the scenic area. He donated 15 acres of this parcel for the erection of the ETHAN ALLEN TOWER. As president of the Young Men's Christian Association, he led a campaign to build a new building for the YMCA at Church and College Streets, for which he contributed $20,000 and extensive furnishings. Van Patten's service to the community included nine years as president of the Fletcher Library, president and director of the MARY FLETCHER Hospital, a founding member of KURN HATTIN Home in Westminster, and a director of the Burlington Building and Loan Association. He also represented Chittenden County in the Vermont Senate. He died in 1920 of a respiratory infection acquired during the INFLUENZA EPIDEMIC after World War I.

Lilian Baker Carlisle

Van Vliet, Claire (b. 1933)

Artist, printer, publisher, and proprietor of the Janus Press of Newark, Claire Van Vliet is Canadian by birth. She came to the United States in 1947, graduated from San Diego State College (1952) and the Claremont Graduate Schools (1954), founded Janus Press in 1955, and settled in Vermont in 1966. She has published over a hundrd handmade books in editions of fifty to three hundred copies, all printed on a Vandercook SP15 proofing press, and sometimes in collaboration with other artists. Many of her earlier books illustrate stories by Franz Kafka, but in the 1970s, she pioneered the use of color pulp paintings to capture Vermont landscapes in books and prints. More recently she has experimented with nonadhesive book structures to give her books archival permanence, and to add another dimension to the art of the book. In 1989, she was awarded a John D. and Catherine T. MacArthur Prize Fellowship Award in recognition of her accomplishments.   *Connell Gallagher*

VAST

The Vermont Association of Snow Travelers, Inc., was founded over thirty years ago and is responsible for the organization of the sport of snowmobiling and maintaining and grooming trails. One of the oldest snowmobiling organizations in the country, VAST is a nonprofit, private group that includes over 145 clubs statewide, with over thirty-three thousand members combined. The association is run by fourteen directors, who are elected by the clubs in each of Vermont's fourteen counties, and by four officers also elected by the members. The VAST office in Berlin operates with five full-time and two seasonal employees. The snowmobiling season, when 150 to 250 inches of snow might fall, usually starts in mid-December and ends in early April. Because 80 percent of Vermont's trail system is on private land, some of the best snowmobiling in New England is permitted only through the traditional generosity of thousands of property owners whose permission is required

Snowmobiling in East Montpelier. Vermont Department of Tourism and Marketing

to ride on their land. Local clubs obtain landowner permission for trails on private property. All riders in Vermont must belong to VAST and a local club to ride legally in the state. The fine for riding unlicensed is $110. Permission to use snowmobile trails does not extend to their use by ATVs, four-wheelers, motor or mountain bikes, or hikers, unless specifically authorized. A VAST trail is a trail only during the snow season; landowners may consider any other use as unlawful trespassing.

Veazey, Wheelock G. (1835–1898)

A prominent attorney, political figure, and Congressional Medal of Honor winner for his service at the BATTLE OF GETTYSBURG, Wheelock Veazey of Rutland was appointed to important Vermont and federal offices. Born in Brentwood, New Hampshire, Veazey graduated from Phillips Academy in Exeter, New Hampshire, Dartmouth College (class of 1859), and Albany Law School (1860), and was admitted to the Vermont bar in the same year. He opened a law practice in Springfield, but enlisted as a private in Company A, Third Vermont Volunteers in 1862, was elected captain, and then promoted to lieutenant colonel, serving for a time on the staff of General WILLIAM F. "BALDY" SMITH. In September 1862, Veazey was promoted to colonel of the Sixteenth Vermont Volunteers, and took part in several imporant battles of the Army of the Potomac. After the Battle of Gettysburg on July 3, 1863, General GEORGE JENNISON STANNARD later reported, "I saw another rebel col-

umn charge immediately upon our left. Colonel Veazey of the Sixteenth was at once ordered to attack it upon the flank. . . . The rebel forces were scooped en masse into our lines. The Sixteenth took in this charge the regimental colors of the Second Florida and Eighth Virginia Regiment, and the battle flag of another regiment." Medically discharged from the army in 1863, he returned to Vermont where in 1864 he was appointed Supreme Court reporter, the first of his many public positions, and prepared nine volumes of the *Vermont Reports* (1864–1873). After the war, he formed a law practice with REDFIELD PROCTOR, SR., served in the Vermont Senate from Rutland County (1872–1874), as register of bankruptcy (1874–1878), as a commissioner to revise the laws of the state (1878), and as a Vermont Supreme Court judge (1878–1879). He resigned the last post to accept appointment as a member of the Interstate Commerce Commission, a position that he held until his death. Veazey was a cofounder with Proctor of the Reunion Society of Vermont Officers. He was a delegate to the Republican National Convention in 1876, a trustee of Dartmouth College from 1879 to 1891, and national commander of the Grand Army of the Republic in 1891.

Donald Wickman

Vergennes

Vergennes (pronounced ver-jenz), population 2,741, a city in Addison County, was chartered by the Vermont legislature in 1788 and formed from adjoining portions of the towns of Ferrisburgh, Panton, and New Haven. The main reason for its creation was to provide a political unit for the existing settlement at the main falls of OTTER CREEK, which soon grew into a thriving manufacturing and trading center. At the suggestion of Michel Guillaume Jean de Crèvecoeur as relayed to ETHAN ALLEN, the city was named for Charles Gravier (1717–1787), comte de Vergennes, who as France's minister of foreign affairs had given the Americans vital assistance during the Revolution. Vergennes is one of the oldest cities in New England, only Hartford and New Haven, Connecticut, being older. Its early history is marked by rapid industrial growth, and by 1812 forges, blast furnaces, a wire factory, and other facilities operated by the Monkton Iron Company, at the time the largest iron works in the United States, were grouped around the falls. During the War of 1812, Commander THOMAS MACDONOUGH built a fleet of ships at the foot of the falls that later defeated the British at the BATTLE OF PLATTSBURGH BAY in September 1814. During the same era, the Lake Champlain Steamship Company was chartered and over a period of ten years built four lake steamers at the shipyard. The opening of the Champlain Canal in 1824, connecting LAKE CHAMPLAIN with the Hudson River, led to a period of new prosperity as freight and passenger traffic grew rapidly on the lake. The coming of the RAILROAD in 1855 enhanced the possibilities for the transportation of lumber, leading to the expansion of a wood-products industry. An imposing main street and block after block of elaborate homes were visible signs of commercial success, with the result that Vergennes today has an unusually large number of architecturally significant structures in a wide variety of building styles. The central business and residential district is listed in the National Register of Historic Places. Beginning in 1875, the state Reform School for Troubled Youth—later renamed the Vermont Industrial School and again the WEEKS SCHOOL—was located in Vergennes and housed on a campus with buildings dating from 1828 (the old U.S. Arsenal) to the 1960s. The federally supported Job Corps now provides residential vocational training programs on the site. After the decline of the lake trade in the late nineteenth century, Vergennes continued to serve as a regionally important commercial center for the surrounding agricultural area, a

position it still holds. It also maintains a strong industrial base, the most important element of which are two major electronic equipment companies: B. F. Goodrich and Nathaniel Electronics.

Vermont Academy of Arts and Sciences

Founded in 1965 on the initiative of Lucien M. Hanks, a professor of anthropology at BENNINGTON COLLEGE, the Vermont Academy of Arts and Sciences has as its purpose "to foster wiser and more intensive participation in the arts, humanities, and basic and applied sciences" in Vermont through lectures, occasional papers, an annual fall conference on some significant subject, and intercollegiate student symposia. Every year several individuals who have made "outstanding contributions in the arts, humanities, sciences, or teaching" in Vermont are elected by the academy's board of trustees as fellows of the academy. As of 2000 almost one hundred fellows have been created since the academy was founded, including RONALD ROOD, BLANCHE MOYSE, ROYCE S. PITKIN, A. JOHN HOLDEN, JR., RALPH NADING HILL, GEORGE D. AIKEN, BETTY BANDEL, NOEL PERRIN, T. D. S. BASSETT, and JAMAICA KINCAID. The academy's newsletter is sent to members four times a year.

Vermont Academy of Medicine

Chartered by the general assembly in 1818, the Vermont Academy of Medicine was located in Castleton. Before moving into a Greek Revival building constructed in 1821, the academy presented a first set of lectures in 1818 to 1819 in an old law office. In 1819, the academy became the first independent degree-granting medical school in New England with legislative authorization to confer degrees. Dr. Selah Gridley was a co-founder with Drs. Thomas Woodward and John Cazier. During the school's existence (1818–1861), over fourteen hundred degrees were conferred. The Academy of Medicine proved vital to the town and in 1841 changed its name to Castleton Medical College. Twenty years later, internal problems prompted closure of the college. The academy's building has been restored and moved to the grounds of CASTLETON STATE COLLEGE.

Donald Wickman

Vermont Arts Council

Founded in 1964, the Vermont Arts Council has as its mission the enhancement of

all forms of artistic expression throughout the state. It does this by collecting and disseminating arts information; offering advice, development opportunities, and funding to individual artists, art organizations, schools, and communities; and generally acting as an arts advocate in public and private forums. Its funding comes from the state of Vermont, the National Endowment for the Arts, membership dues, and private contributions. The council annually recognizes individual and organizational contributions to the arts through a series of awards including the Governor's Award for Excellence in the Arts (established 1967), the Walter Cerf Award for Lifetime Achievement in the Arts (1992), and the Chair's Business Awards (1968), presented by the chair of the board of trustees to "a Vermont business for outstanding support of the arts." The council also recommends to the governor the individual who serves a four-year term as VERMONT STATE POET.

Vermont Breeding Bird Atlas Project

The first survey of breeding birds completed and published in North America, the Vermont Breeding Bird Atlas Project (1975–1981) is a map-based survey of the birds nesting in a geographical area based on a protocol developed in Europe. Similar surveys have since been conducted in most of the United States and Canada. The breeding bird atlas is a powerful tool that uses hundreds of volunteers to conduct thousands of hours of field work, collecting data on the avifauna of a region that documents bird distribution and establishes the location of rare and endangered species and habitat. The Vermont Atlas Project was led by the VERMONT INSTITUTE OF NATURAL SCIENCE with the assistance of Vermont's seven chapters of the National Audubon Society, and 250 volunteers. Sarah B. Laughlin directed the project and with Douglas P. Kibbe edited *The Atlas of Breeding Birds of Vermont* (University Press of New England, 1985). Bird atlases should be repeated every twenty-five years, and plans for the state's second atlas are now underway.

Sarah B. Laughlin

Vermont Children's Aid Society

The privately funded Vermont Children's Aid Society was founded in 1919 in response to the concerns of social reformers, charity workers, and public welfare officials over the alarming findings of children living in poverty. A 1918 state-wide survey of the needs of Vermont children orphaned by the INFLUENZA EPIDEMIC and the First World War had confirmed suspicions of pervasive child welfare problems in rural Vermont. For the first fifteen years, Vermont Children's Aid officers and social workers assumed a leading role in developing a state-wide network of child-helping services, collaborating with state and local authorities to locate and rescue children from unhealthy or unwholesome family surroundings and place them in foster homes, state institutions, or for adoption. During the Depression, the VCAS was instrumental in implementing New Deal programs in Vermont: the Child Welfare Service, Aid to Dependent Children, and the state-wide Central Index, a file on dependent, delinquent, or handicapped Vermonters requiring public assistance. These state programs signaled a shift in the function of the VCAS from its proactive role in child welfare investigation and intervention to its current programs in child adoption and family support. Today, the Vermont Children's Aid Society offers adoption and post-adoption counseling and support services.

Nancy L. Gallagher

Vermont Children's Theater

A community theater project conducted in a red barn on Darling Hill in Lyndonville, the Vermont Children's Theatre has given some fifteen hundred NORTHEAST KINGDOM youngsters the opportunity to learn the art of acting during the ten years of its existence. The barn was once part of the ELMER A. DARLING agricultural estate in the early 1900s. North country natives and tourists gather there on summer evenings to watch the children perform in Broadway musicals. Founded by Nancy Huling Hartswick, it offers children professional acting, singing, and dancing instruction. Nine- and ten-year-olds take workshops, while eleven- through eighteen-year-olds are auditioned and assigned roles. The orchestra for the children's theater features community musicians and includes Hartswick at the piano, her father and a sister, Dale Camara, on the French horn, her mother on the trumpet, and her brother, Brian Huling, on the trombone. In late 2000, the Hulings and Nancy Hartswick left the Children's Theatre to pursue other interests, but the show goes on.

Virginia C. Downs

Vermont College

Grounded in JOHN DEWEY's theory of progressive education, Vermont College in Montpelier awards bachelor's degrees in liberal studies, master's degrees, and master of fine arts degrees through its non-residential Adult Degree Program (ADP). Vermont College merged with NORWICH UNIVERSITY in 1972 and the college in 1981 began offering the ADP, which it had acquired from GODDARD COLLEGE. In 2001, the college and its programs were acquired by the Union Institute & University of Cincinnati, Ohio, a national leader in experiential-based and distance education. All courses of study at the college continue to follow the original ADP model and feature brief on-campus stays, after which students return home to work in consultation with a faculty advisor. Each student designs a semester-long fifteen-credit interdisciplinary project that reflects his or her own questions, interests, and concerns. A study plan and bibliography, generated with the advisor's assistance, guide the work. Students submit critical book reviews and essays. Central to the learning is written dialogue between student and advisor emphasizing critical reflection and close questioning. Most students enter with transfer credits and about two-thirds are adult women. They may enroll in the weekend model (six weekends over eighteen weeks) or the "cycle" model (residencies of eight days every six months). Approximately fifteen full-time faculty members and a pool of adjuncts currently serve one thousand students. The ADP pedagogical model stimulated creation of other programs now offered at Vermont College, including the M.F.A. in Visual Arts, the Masters in Education, and New College for traditional-aged students.

Ann Stanton

Vermont Commission on Country Life

The Vermont Commission on Country Life (1928–1931) was organized by Prof. HENRY F. PERKINS, director of the EUGENICS SURVEY OF VERMONT. Funded by grants from the Social Science Research Council and the Laura Spelman Rockefeller Memorial Fund, the commission's purpose was to study the cultural, sociological, and demographic factors influencing the apparent economic decline in rural Vermont. Former Governor JOHN E. WEEKS chaired the commission's executive committee and work was directed by agricultural economist Henry C. Taylor as execu-

tive director coordinating projects for sixteen study committees of two hundred Vermont academic, civic, and cultural leaders. Their final reports, published in *Rural Vermont: A Program for the Future by Two Hundred Vermonters* (1931), presented a comprehensive program of progressive reforms in public administration and land utilization that promised to improve the quality of life in the country. Unlike most contemporary agricultural commissions, the VCCL subordinated economic and material considerations to its focus on the "Human Factor," the social, cultural, and demographic trends that had shaped "Vermonters," and placed its recommendations within the larger context of restoring pride in the historic relationship between the land and the people of Vermont. Subsequent critics have pointed to VCCL's origins in the Vermont Eugenic Survey and charged that the commission's vision of the human factor was biased by its implicit aim to preserve Vermont as an Anglo-Saxon community nurtured by rural values. While many of the programs encompassed in *Rural Vermont* had been urged by Vermont progressives for two decades, the VCCL provided a vehicle to advance progressive agendas within a unified program for rural development through regional and state-wide planning. The effort to replace the traditional town-based administration of public health, education, and poor relief with a regional and state-wide system was gradually realized beginning in the 1930s through New Deal programs and expansion of state programs. In the domain of AGRICULTURE and land utilization, the commission recommended that mountain and hillside subsistence-farming communities marked by depopulation, abandoned farms, and economic decline be developed for forestry, recreation, and tourism. This goal inspired subsequent projects, including a study and economic classification of Vermont's agricultural regions by JOHN ALLEN HITCHCOCK and ROBERT MCCRILLIS CARTER, JR., the ill-fated Sub-marginal Lands Project (1934–1936), and the GREEN MOUNTAIN PARKWAY. Drawing on research by A. JOHN HOLDEN, JR., the commission's report on public education recommended reducing the number of school districts and organizing secondary education into centralized schools serving several communities, a concept that Holden eventually led to completion in the development of union school districts throughout the state in the 1950s and 1960s after he became commissioner of education. Other VCCL initiatives met with immediate success. The Committee on Vermont Traditions and Ideals, chaired by Professor ARTHUR WALLACE PEACH, published the *Green Mountain Series* (1931), a four-volume collection of Vermont literature, biography, and folklore. The VCCL committees continued to meet throughout the 1930s to promote their vision, sponsor reforms in public health, education, and welfare, and initiate cultural and historic preservation projects.

Nancy L. Gallagher and Gerald F. Vaughn

Vermont Conference of Social Work

In 1916, a socially minded group of Vermont civic leaders led by WILLIAM J. VAN PATTEN of Burlington founded the Vermont Conference of Charities and Corrections (renamed the Vermont Conference of Social Work in 1918, the Vermont Conference of Social Welfare in 1945). Its mission, "to unite the voluntary efforts of all who are interested in the charitable, correctional, and social welfare work of the state," took the form of annual conferences where social workers, government officials, philanthropists, and college professors heard lectures from national experts, shared their research and experiences, and developed reforms in social legislation. Since its inception, VCSW leaders focused on the problems of rural poverty and urged the state to assume a larger role in protecting "its greatest asset, its children." Many state reforms concerning poor relief and child welfare of the inter-war years can be attributed to the political activism of the VCSW. After World War II, the VCSW gradually evolved into a predominantly professional organization of social workers and agencies working in study committees on specific policies or problems. *Nancy L. Gallagher*

Vermont Copper Company

Copper was discovered in Strafford in 1793 and copper mining began there soon after. In subsequent years, mines were also developed in Corinth and Vershire (Ely), the latter the most celebrated. The property was purchased in 1853 and developed by Henry Barnard, who as the major investor organized and directed operations until 1865, when Smith Ely, another original investor, became president. Initially prosperous, Vershire became a thriv-

ing town of two thousand and its grateful residents temporarily renamed it Ely. Copper mining prospered in Ely through 1880, when the combined production of the Vermont mines amounted to three-fifths of the nation's copper output. After the market for copper collapsed in 1883, a financial crisis exacerbated by a depletion in the Ely mine's lode precipitated a strike accompanied by a week-long riot, during which the unpaid workers took over the mine and the town. This most famous of Vermont's early labor incidents was suppressed by the National Guard, and the company closed the mines, abandoning them in 1893. Interest in Vermont's copper mines revived at the turn of the century and out-of-state backers, led by August Hecksch at Strafford and George Westinghouse at Ely, invested millions of dollars in equipment, but the venture proved unprofitable and the mines were again abandoned. A demand for metals stimulated by World War I brought on another revival that lasted into the 1920s. The final revival came in 1942 when the mines, which had been operating independently until then, were merged into the Vermont Copper Company. Under the guidance and direction of a board that included former Governor Stanley C. Wilson, who served as secretary and later president, together with government aid, the mines operated until 1958, when they closed for the last time. Environmental degradation and continuing pollution by mine drainage constitute the ambiguous heritage of Vermont's copper mines.

Vermont Council on the Humanities

A private, nonprofit organization, the Vermont Council on the Humanities was established in 1974 as an affiliate of the National Endowment for the Humanities. Its mission is "to strengthen the humanities in the educational system and in the discussion of public issues, and to foster an appreciation of the richness and diversity of our cultural heritages." It does this through a range of free activities. In 2001, the council sponsored 202 book discussions at libraries and other public venues; offered public lectures by 77 speakers on a wide range of subjects; and invited applications for grants up to $15,000 to organizations offering programs that have a strong humanities content. The council has tried to end the cycle of illiteracy in the state by encouraging reading in adults and has blanketed the state with literacy

programs, devoting nearly half the council's budget to the project. About five thousand adults are signed up to learn to read at any given moment in Vermont. The council designed "Creating Communities of Readers," to provide grants of up to $5,000 to community groups who have started book wagons that travel to playgrounds, and programs in which parents receive home visits from volunteers, who give away books and talk about the importance of reading to young children. The executive director of the council from its inception to 2002 was Victor Swenson; its current director is Peter A. Gilbert.

Vermont Federation of Sportsmen's Clubs

Responding to the disappearance of many wild species from the landscape by the mid-nineteenth century, returning Union Army officers successfully lobbied the Vermont General Assembly in 1868 to prohibit the hunting of wild deer at any time. Continuing efforts to protect wildlife and limit the method of taking fish to angling led in 1875 to the founding of the Vermont Fish & Game League, which in 1878 reintroduced to Rutland County a small herd of deer that had been trapped in the Adirondacks. Vermont's first successful wildlife restoration project led to the regulated hunting of deer again in 1897. Between 1878 and 1920, the league lobbied and worked with the general assembly to establish most of the basic legislation now regulating hunting and fishing, encouraged the imposition of fees to support the enforcement of those laws, and assisted the state in fish-stocking programs. The league was instrumental in convincing the general assembly to establish the Vermont Fish and Game Department in 1920. Renamed the Federation of Sportsmen's Clubs in 1950, the association of thirty-nine clubs remains dedicated to its original objectives of protecting, restoring, and improving the environment and fish and wildlife. Additionally, it monitors and lobbies state and local governments on issues important to Vermont's sportswomen and men, including firearm ownership and access to public lands.

Vermont Fish & Game League

See VERMONT FEDERATION OF SPORTSMEN'S CLUBS.

Vermont Historical Gazetteer

See HEMENWAY, ABBY MARIA.

Vermont Historical Society

The youngest of New England's state historical societies, the Vermont Historical Society was founded in 1838 by HENRY STEVENS, SR., an antiquarian and collector from Barnet. The society moved to Montpelier in 1848 when the Vermont General Assembly gave it a room in the VERMONT STATE HOUSE, and the society has ever since been dependent on the state for housing as well as financial support. Today, exhibitions and displays from VHS's collections, the Vermont Museum, are presented in an interpretive center dedicated to Vermont's history in the PAVILION BUILDING on the state house green. The society's staff offices, education facilities, and library—one of the major history collections in Vermont, which includes books, ephemera, maps, photographs, and manuscripts—moved to new quarters in the former Spaulding Graded School in Barre in 2002. The genealogy section of the library is the largest in the state. The headquarters and library in Barre and the interpretive center in Montpelier are visited by thousands each year. The society has active education and publication programs and has published the scholarly *Vermont History* under different titles since 1870.   *Reidun Nuquist*

Vermont in Mississippi, Inc.

Vermont in Mississippi (VIM) was a civil rights project organized in June 1965 under the auspices of the Vermont Civil Rights Union with honorary directors that included Governor PHILIP HOFF and distinguished clergy from throughout the state. The organization promoted community advocacy projects for African-Americans in Jackson, Mississippi, to develop voter education classes, voter registration drives, a cooperative day care center, a community center, and the Medgar Evers Neighborhood Guild. Montpelier High School English teacher Edward (Ted) Seaver and his wife, Carol, directed the activities of VIM in Jackson. Ted Seaver applied for a one-year leave of absence from his teaching position, but in January 1965 the Montpelier Board of School Commissioners voted not to extend Seaver's teaching contract for "attitudes unbecoming a teacher." This action created a controversy over whether the decision of the board was related to Seaver's civil rights activities. The goal to have Jackson community members assume leadership roles in the struggle to gain constitutional rights

for African-Americans was achieved when the Reverend Jesse Montgomery took over the Seavers' responsibilities. Funded primarily through private contributions with the assistance of the Schwerner Memorial Fund as well as the Taconic Foundation, VIM was self-supporting. Vermont in Mississippi, Inc. was dissolved in 1967 partly because Vermont's civil rights activities were redirected to securing fair housing legislation in Vermont.

Vermont Institute of Natural Science

The Vermont Institute of Natural Science (VINS) is Vermont's largest environmental education and natural history research organization. A private nonprofit membership organization, VINS was founded in 1972 and has been headquartered in Woodstock since, with statewide outreach programs and nature centers in Montpelier and Manchester. Currently, a major new museum headquarters near Quechee Gorge in Hartford is being developed. VINS is best known for the ELF (environmental learning for the future) program that reaches thousands of elementary school children yearly; the Raptor Center, a living museum of birds of prey unable to be released back to the wild (and a hospital for injured birds); and on-going ornithological research from bird banding to work with endangered species.

Sarah B. Laughlin

Vermont Land Trust

Recognizing that, despite ACT 250 and local zoning and subdivision regulations, productive farm and forest land was continuing to be fragmented and converted to other uses, a group of concerned citizens in the Woodstock region founded the Ottauquechee Regional Land Trust to assist land owners in preserving the rural character of the region by a program of voluntary conservation agreements. By 1980, the land trust worked on easement and conservation agreements that lay outside of the Ottauquechee region. Early accomplishments included the purchase and protection of the former Woodstock Country School property in South Woodstock, the conversion of the Boy Scouts' Camp Plymouth to a state park, and the acquisition of a conservation easement on 1,000 acres in Tinmouth. It also assisted the National Park Service in negotiating the purchase of easements for the Appalachian Trail from Killington to Norwich. By the mid-1980s, it had conserved 6,650

acres of land and the organization had changed its name to the Vermont Land Trust (VLT). One of VLT's most significant accomplishments was its leading role in the creation of the Vermont Housing and Conservation Trust Fund. Bringing together a coalition of land conservation and affordable housing organizations, VLT and its public and private partners succeeded in creating a public funding source for both objectives. The trust fund has been instrumental in conserving more than 130,000 acres of land and creating over 4,500 units of perpetually affordable housing throughout Vermont. From 1994 through 1998, the Freeman Foundation of Stowe granted $36 million for land conservation and historic preservation efforts in Vermont. Nearly two-thirds of those funds were administered by the Vermont Land Trust. By 2001, VLT had helped protect over 350,000 acres throughout Vermont, including 250 operating farms. VLT seeks to build public-private partnerships and coalitions with other interests that influence land use decisions. For example, VLT actively works with groups involved with AGRICULTURE, forestry, tourism, outdoor recreation, historic preservation, and affordable housing. VLT is also an advocate for land protection and promotes environmentally sound and sustainable land use.

Vermont Law School

Founded in 1972, Vermont Law School is located in South Royalton on a 13-acre campus comprised of nineteen buildings, including a new library and new classroom building. The state's only law school, it has been ranked first or second in the field of environmental law in each of the last nine years and named one of the best law schools for women by *The National Jurist*. It enrolls 538 full-time students and offers four degree programs: Juris Doctor (J.D.), Master of Studies in Environmental Law (M.S.E.L.), Joint J.D. and M.S.E.L., and Master of Laws in Environmental Law (LL.M.). The Vermont Law School is accredited by the American Bar Association, the Association of American Law Schools, and the New England Association of Schools and Colleges. Ninety percent of the school's students come from outside Vermont. A traditional core legal curriculum and experiential programs with a specialty in environmental law prepare graduates to practice law in all fifty states.

Vermont Leadership Center

Founded by Bill Manning in East Charleston in 1989, the Vermont Leadership Center was designed to provide Vermonters of all ages with opportunities for experiential learning about the environment of the NORTHEAST KINGDOM. The center's staff works with students and teachers in twenty-two Vermont schools from Derby to Cabot and two in New Hampshire. The Freedom Foundation and other funding organizations help support programs ranging from eight-week daylong sessions identifying traces of animal and bird life to a "Kingdom Corps" experience intended to develop both leadership and team skills for youth from twelve to fifteen who learn conservation practices and trail building. Speakers address such issues as the make-up and management of Northeast Kingdom forests, the conservation and utilization of natural resources in the region, and wilderness travel using a compass and U.S. Geodetic Survey maps.

Virginia C. Downs

Vermont Life

The first issue of the state's premier magazine, price 25 cents, appeared in the fall of 1946, largely the inspiration of EARLE W. NEWTON, former director of the VERMONT HISTORICAL SOCIETY and *Vermont Life*'s first editor. Its contents were those that still characterize the magazine, a mix of color photographs and articles about various aspects of life in the state. Supported by a state subvention of $2,000, the publication was instantly popular and saw its circulation rise in its first year from twelve to forty thousand copies. In 1950, Newton turned the editorship over to WALTER R. HARD, JR., who remained in the post for twenty years. Among regular contributors to the magazine in its early period were NORWICH UNIVERSITY Professor ARTHUR WALLACE PEACH, Weston entrepreneur VREST ORTON, historian RALPH NADING HILL, and Brattleboro publisher STEPHEN GREENE. Its quality reproduction of photographs increasingly attracted both young photographers and established professionals. Editors after Hard were Brian Vachon (1972–1981), Charles T. Morrissey (1981–1983), Nancy Price Graff (1983–1985), and, since 1985, Tom Slayton. Up until 1970, *Vermont Life* operated with a slight deficit, which was made up annually by a state appropriation, but beginning in that year the sale of calendars, maps, and coffee table books

A controversial early cover of Vermont Life.
Ralph H. Orth

such as *Vermont: A Special World* made the magazine financially independent. By the early 1990s, however, expenditures once again exceeded income, and the magazine began to accept advertising with the winter 1991 issue. Since then, *Vermont Life* has remained modestly profitable, requiring no direct expenditure of state funds. The magazine's traditionally upbeat tone and positive view of the Vermont scene have in recent years been tempered by recognition of the challenges the state faces as major social and technological changes affect the Green Mountain State. *Vermont Life*'s average circulation is currently about one hundred thousand.

Vermont Marble Company

In 1869, REDFIELD PROCTOR, SR., a Civil War veteran and lawyer in Rutland, took over as receiver a small MARBLE-sawing firm at Sunderland Falls. Proctor reorganized the company to handle both quarrying and sawing and in 1880 merged with the failing Rutland Marble Company to form the Vermont Marble Company. By 1922, from headquarters in the town of Proctor, the company owned and operated seventy-five different quarries across the country, employing three thousand workers. It produced one million cubic feet of marble annually and was recognized as the largest marble works in the world. Skilled marble workers immigrated from Europe to work for Vermont Marble. Monuments and buildings in Washington, D.C., are evidence of the Vermont Marble era, including the Supreme Court building, Jefferson Memorial, and

Senate Office building. The Proctor family remained in control of the company until 1976, when it was purchased by Pluess-Staufer, a Swiss-based company. After forming the company OMYA to conduct its Vermont operations, Pluess-Stauffer turned to mining and processing fine and ultrafine calcium carbonate from former Vermont Marble holdings in a plant built in Florence in 1980. They also acquired Vermont Talc in Chester, another Vermont Marble operation. The firm annually extracts at least 500,000 tons of calcium carbonate from its Vermont quarries. The Vermont Marble Company strike, 1935–1936, Vermont's most infamous industrial dispute, took place in the Rutland area over efforts to unionize the Vermont Marble Company. The strike was part of the long series of management-labor battles in America that, over a period of fifty years, involved many industries such as mining and automobile production. The company countered declining revenues during the Great Depression by cutting working hours and distributing the available work without dismissing employees. The employees, already subjected to a low wage rate, struck the company to secure organization by a national union, and details of the strike were reported in the national press. Reports that the strikers enjoyed Communist support were countered by disclosures that the company had maintained its stock dividend levels and had hired special deputies under the Rutland County's sheriff's authority to break the strike and had supplemented them with additional deputies at state expense. The latter revelations engendered out-of-state sympathy for the strikers and a fund-raising committee to assist destitute strikers was started at Dartmouth College and joined by groups at BENNINGTON COLLEGE, Skidmore College, and the University of Wisconsin. An umbrella organization, the United Committee to Aid the Vermont Marble Workers, was established in New York City and conducted well-publicized anti-Proctor meetings in West Rutland. These activities had no influence on the outcome of the strike, which ended in a complete victory for management. In 1945, while MORTIMER PROCTOR was governor, Vermont Marble was unionized.

Vermont Medical College

Founded in Woodstock by Dr. JOSEPH A. GALLUP, the Vermont Medical College offered its first course of instruction in the autumn of 1827 as a "clinical school of medicine." Students for several years received degrees from Colby College in Waterville, Maine. In 1830, the medical school affiliated with MIDDLEBURY COLLEGE, which thereafter conferred degrees on graduates of the school. The school was incorporated in 1835, by which time 207 doctors of medicine had completed the course of study. The college closed in 1856.

Vermont Music Festival

Launched in 1927 by Adrian Holmes, supervisor of music at Burlington High School, the Vermont Music Festival brought 175 music students from around Vermont to Burlington for a one-day event. Originally modelled on a state-wide basketball tournament, the performance contest format continued until 1931, when the event was reorganized to become "a glorious Music Festival, from which each school and each student would return a winner, richer in never forgotten musical memories." The first music festival parade was held in 1932. The festival grew to a two-day affair in 1936, when the All-State Orchestra and Chorus were formed, and participation increased: in 1938 nine bands, twenty-one orchestras, and twenty-eight glee clubs performed. An All-State Band was added in 1938. By 1947, the festival had expanded to three days. The Burlington Lions Club has co-sponsored the event since 1930 and arranges for overnight accommodations for students from distant corners of Vermont.   *David Blow*

Vermont–New York Youth Project

Governor PHILIP HOFF conceived the Vermont–New York Youth Project in 1968 after reading the advance text of a report by a special presidential commission that attributed recent urban riots to white racism and separate and unequal black and white societies. Determined that Vermont, "the whitest state in the union," attempt something to bring the races together, Hoff called on New York City Mayor John V. Lindsay, who had served as vice-chairman of the riot commission, and together they framed the Vermont–New York Youth Project. With the assistance of the Youth Service Agency of New York City, three hundred black teenagers were brought to Vermont to join three hundred Vermonters in various summer programs throughout the state. Sites included the

UNIVERSITY OF VERMONT, Windham College, CASTLETON STATE COLLEGE, Putney School, and Vermont Academy. Programs varied from academic classes to performing arts and camping. The program lasted two summers and generated considerable controversy. It was discontinued by Governor DEANE DAVIS because of lack of popular support.

Vermont Old Cemetery Association

Founded in 1958 by LEON W. DEAN, the Vermont Old Cemetery Association has as its mission to preserve, restore, and protect abandoned and neglected cemeteries. The association offers workshops and modest grants to community organizations willing to restore cemeteries both public and private. The four hundred all-volunteer members of the association have mapped known cemeteries in each of Vermont's towns and published their findings as *Burial Grounds of Vermont* (1991, revised editions 1992 and 1998), edited by Arthur and Frances Hyde. The *VOCA Newsletter* appears four times a year. The association's motto is "Graveyard Preservation is our Business." Officers are called Headstones; members of the board of directors are Footstones.   *Lilian Baker Carlisle*

Vermont Sanatorium and Caverly Preventorium

The state's only residential facility for tuberculosis patients, the Vermont Sanatorium and Caverly Preventorium operated in Pittsford from 1907 to 1966. It was founded as a private hospital by the Proctor family, owners of the VERMONT MARBLE COMPANY. Lung disease had been recognized as a major occupational hazard in the mineral extractive industry beginning in the 1870s. The Proctors transferred ownership of the sanatorium to the state in 1921. Prior to World War II, therapy at the sanatorium followed the conventional treatment for tuberculosis patients, who were provided with plenty of fresh air, nutritional meals, exercise, and rest during their stays. The sanatorium was closed when antibiotic medical treatment of the disease obviated the need for a long-term resident facility. The original sanatorium buildings are now the site of the Vermont Police Academy.
            Donald Wickman

Vermont State Colleges

Established as a public corporation in 1961 by an act of the Vermont General Assem-

bly, the Vermont State Colleges (VSCs) is Vermont's system of public colleges, which consists of four public colleges with histories as teachers' colleges from at least the mid-nineteenth century and the COMMUNITY COLLEGE OF VERMONT, which became a Vermont State College in 1975 and offers programs at regional locations throughout the state. The other VSCs are CASTLETON STATE COLLEGE, LYNDON STATE COLLEGE, JOHNSON STATE COLLEGE, and VERMONT TECHNICAL COLLEGE in Randolph. Together, the Vermont State Colleges are the highest enrolled higher education institutions in the state, with over 10,300 students from Vermont, other parts of the United States, and other countries. The VSCs offer 120 academic programs at the associate, baccalaureate, and master levels. All of the colleges offer small classes and individualized attention for students. The Vermont State Colleges provide affordable, high quality, student centered and accessible education, fully integrating professional, liberal, and career study. The central office of the VSCs is located in the Vermont Government Office Complex in Waterbury.

Vermont State Hospital

The Vermont State Hospital for the Insane was built in 1890 in Waterbury in response to overcrowded conditions at the Vermont Asylum for the Insane in Brattleboro (BRATTLEBORO RETREAT). Originally built for "the care, custody, and treatment of insane criminals of the state," the Waterbury State Hospital eventually became the temporary or permanent shelter for Vermonters with mild to severe mental disabilities, including epilepsy, depression, alcoholism, or senility. Throughout its history, methods of patient diagnosis and treatment varied according to medical opinion and the philosophy of the superintendents. Early twentieth-century efforts among reformers to reduce the stigma of mental illness and hospital confinement yielded to the pessimism of the eugenics thinking of 1920s and 1930s, when Dr. Eugene A. Stanley directed affairs at Waterbury. An advocate of eugenics, Dr. Stanley promoted sexual sterilization of the insane and convinced the state to construct a new three-story building for the growing number of "acutely disturbed female patients." The patient population grew, peaking at 1,728 in the mid-1930s. By today's standards, treatment of patients before 1950 was primitive, at times barbaric. Disruptive patients and severe epileptic patients were tied to wooden benches with "camisoles," which secured their arms in back of them. "Hydrotherapy," where patients were immersed in continuous cold-water baths or wet packs, and "colonic irrigation" were standard treatments for disruptive patients, eventually replaced by electro-shock treatments and drug therapy in the 1950s. More able patients contributed to the support of the institution, as custodians, laborers on the institution-run farm in Duxbury, and industrial workers in shoe repair and manufacture of clothespins, chairs, rugs, and baskets. The 1970s brought a shift from institutional care to community-based outpatient mental health services and residences, reducing the patient population from over one thousand to less than two hundred in the 1980s.   *Nancy L. Gallagher*

Vermont State House

Vermont has had three state houses since it joined the union in 1791. The first, completed in 1808, three years after Montpelier became the state capital, cost $9,000. It was a three-story wood-frame structure similar to many meetinghouses throughout New England. Within two decades it had become too small for the rapidly growing general assembly and, as one observer noted, "The dry pine benches [being] too strong temptations for whittling . . . this old house was literally whittled out of use." In 1838, a new state house was completed at a cost of $132,000. The architect was AMMI YOUNG, a thirty-two-year-old architect from Lebanon, New Hampshire, who had recently moved to Burlington. Young's building was a masterpiece of the Greek Revival style. Constructed of Barre granite on an elevated site well back from the WINOOSKI RIVER, it was 72 feet high from the base of its six Doric columns on the portico to the top of its dome. This second state house was badly damaged by a fire on the night of January 6, 1857, and eventually replaced by a new and larger building designed by the architect Thomas W. Silloway. Built on the same site, its ornamental scheme is in the Renaissance Revival style popular at the time. The only portion of its predecessor retained in its design is the Grecian portico. This third state house cost $150,000 and was dedicated in 1859. Its gold dome is capped by a wooden statue of Agriculture based on the Greek goddess Ceres, a 1938 replica of the weathered original carved by the sculptor

The Vermont State House on the bicentennial celebration of the state's founding, 1991. Vermont Department of Tourism and Marketing

LARKIN G. MEAD of Brattleboro. Three additions made to the rear of the state house date from 1888, 1900, and 1987. In recent years, extensive renovations of the interior of the building have returned most of the corridors, rooms, and legislative chambers to their 1859 appearance.
     Michael Sherman

Vermont State Poet

In June 1961, the state legislature named ROBERT FROST the Poet Laureate of Vermont, a post he held until his death in January 1963. Twenty-eight years later, the idea of a similar position, to be given the name of Vermont State Poet, arose, with the individual selected being recommended by the VERMONT ARTS COUNCIL and appointed by the governor. He or she serves for four years. The criterion states

that the Vermont State Poet must be "a person whose primary residence is in Vermont; whose poetry manifests a high degree of excellence; who has produced a critically acclaimed body of work; and who has a long association with Vermont." The four poets chosen so far are GALWAY KINNELL (appointed 1989), LOUISE GLÜCK (1994), ELLEN BRYANT VOIGT (1999), and Grace Paley (2003).

Vermont Studio Center

Founded in 1984 in Johnson, the Studio Center is an international creative community dedicated to serving artists and writers in a stimulating, supportive work environment free of judgment, hierarchy, and competition. VSC residencies provide artists with working time free from the interruptions of their usual activities. A residency also offers encounters with fellow professional peers in the country's largest artists' community, with fifty artists and writers in residence each month, representing an intentional mix of ages, cultures, experience, and media. In addition, the Studio Center provides the support of prominent visiting artists/writers presenting their own work and offering individual studio visits and writing conferences to those residents who wish them. VSC awards full and partial fellowships.

Vermont Sufferers

The Vermont Sufferers were petitioners from Guilford and nearby towns whose property was confiscated by Vermont between 1777 and 1781 for actively opposing the legitimacy of Vermont's self-declared statehood during its struggles with New York. In 1786, the state of New York granted land to 134 sufferers in a tract previously purchased from the Oneida and Tuscarora Indians. The 8 mile square grant was formally organized as a township in 1791, and took the name of Bainbridge in 1814.

Jeffrey D. Marshall

Vermont Symphony Orchestra

The oldest state-supported symphony orchestra in the United States, the Vermont Symphony Orchestra (VSO) was organized in Woodstock in the fall of 1934 by ALAN CARTER, who was fresh from musical studies in Cologne and Paris, and a small group of musicians and supporters. Except while he was in the army during World War II, Carter served as the orchestra's music director for nearly forty years. While most other orchestras perform in one concert hall and tour only occasionally, the Vermont Symphony Orchestra from the start traveled to any school gymnasium, armory, town hall, or church where an audience could be found. The musicians, who included barbers, accountants, mail carriers, doctors, and farmers, came from across the state to rehearse and perform. Important events of the VSO's early years included an invitation in 1939 to perform at the New York World's Fair, the formation of a Vermont Festival of the Arts two years later, and, at the conclusion of World War II, the founding of a COMPOSERS' CONFERENCE for contemporary music. In observance of its fiftieth birthday, the VSO and Efrain Guigui, its second music director (1974–1990), conceived a plan for a two-year series of concerts to commemorate a half-century of

music-making and to emphasize that the VSO belonged to all of the people of Vermont. Between 1984 and 1986, the "251 Project" sent the VSO's small ensembles as well as the full orchestra to locales large and small in every corner of the state, giving many Vermonters a chance to hear their own orchestra for the first time. Kate Tamarkin was named the VSO's third music director in 1991. Public and critical acclaim for her work with the orchestra caused concert attendance to grow to record numbers. Programs were both accessible and challenging, featuring Vermont artists as well as world-class performers. Tamarkin also launched the VSO's statewide volunteer chorus. In 1999, JAIME LAREDO was named music director. Known worldwide as a violinist, conductor, recitalist, and chamber musician, Laredo has performed with orchestras in Boston, Chicago, Cleveland, New York, and Philadelphia, and with such conductors as Barenboim, Mehta, Ozawa, Slatkin, and Colin Davis. He makes his home in Guilford and has appeared with the VSO on a regular basis since the 1991 to 1992 season, when he and his wife, cellist Sharon Robinson, performed the Brahms Double Concerto with the orchestra. While the VSO has grown over the years, it pursues its original goals. Beginning with the Vermont legislature's 1939 grant of $1,000 for the orchestra to perform at the New York World's Fair, the legislature has continued to be a major source of funding. Volunteer committees still provide the necessary support functions of fund raising, ticket sales, and publicity, and tend to many details behind the production of concerts across the state, as well as finding accommodations in private homes for musicians, who still travel many hours, often in bad weather, to get to rehearsals and concerts. During the 2000 to 2001 season, the VSO performed fifty concerts in more than twenty communities around Vermont. The Symphony Kids educational program set a new record of 217 performances in 114 different towns, reaching over twenty-six thousand schoolchildren. The orchestra's season begins with the annual Made in Vermont Music Festival, which brings a chamber orchestra to smaller venues in ten different towns during the peak foliage season. Two five-concert subscription series take place at the FLYNN THEATER in Burlington and other locations between October and May. The pops festival tours the state from late June to

mid-July to perform in some of Vermont's most beautiful outdoor settings. The VSO's summer season includes a series of concerts at the Hunter Park pavilion in Manchester. The VSO has been a major attraction at Burlington's First Night Celebration.

Vermont Technical College

One of the five VERMONT STATE COLLEGES, Vermont Technical College in Randolph Center is a two-year public college offering associate and bachelor's degrees in a variety of technical and professional fields. Founded in 1866 as one of Vermont's first public teacher-training schools, the Randolph State Normal School served this function until 1910, when the legislature transformed it into the Vermont School of Agriculture. In response to evolving educational needs in the state, the school was reorganized as Vermont Agricultural and Technical Institute (VATI) in 1957 and technical courses were added to the school's offerings, initially serving seventy-five students. The establishment of the Vermont State Colleges in 1961 included VATI under the new name of Vermont Technical College and the college was authorized to grant the degree of associate in applied science. The degree of associate in engineering was first granted in 1965, while the first one-year certificate was awarded in 1986. The first baccalaureate-level degree program—the bachelor of science with a major in architectural engineering technology—was first offered in 1993. A second baccalaureate curriculum—the bachelor of science with a major in electromechanical engineering technology—was offered in 1995. Nursing programs were added to the college curriculum in 1994, when Vermont's three schools of practical nursing were allied with VTC. Beginning in the fall of 1996, the diploma in practical nursing became a credit-bearing program that can also be applied toward a two-year associate's degree in nursing from VTC.

Vernon

Vernon, population 2,141, a town in Windham County, was granted by BENNING WENTWORTH in 1753 as part of the town of Hinsdale, New Hampshire, and made a separate town when the CONNECTICUT RIVER was established as the boundary between that colony and the New Hampshire grants as a result of a 1764 ruling of the British Privy Council. It was renamed

Vernon by the Vermont legislature in 1802, possibly after Mount Vernon, George Washington's home. The town's location on the Connecticut in the extreme southeastern corner of Vermont and its low, gently rolling terrain (the highest elevation is 837 feet) made it one of the earliest settled areas in the state, and as early as 1724 it was the site of FORT DUMMER, the first permanent English structure in Vermont. Today, it retains its rural appearance despite its proximity to much-larger Brattleboro directly to its north. The Vernon Dam on the Connecticut, which forms a lake several miles long, serves the Vermont Yankee nuclear power plant, one of the main sources of electricity in the state.

Vershire

Vershire (pronounced Ver'shr), population 629, a town in Orange County, was granted by the Vermont legislature in 1781 and got its name by combining "Vermont" with "New Hampshire." Mainly agricultural in its early years, the town saw its fortunes change with the development of its copper deposits beginning in 1854. By 1881, the VERMONT COPPER COMPANY was producing 60 percent of the entire United States' output of the metal, employing 851 workers, many of them foreign. The town's name was changed to Ely in 1878 after Smith Ely, who held a controlling interest in the company, but was changed back to Vershire in 1882 after the mines ran into such production and financial difficulties that there was no money to pay miners' back wages. This led in 1883 to the civil disturbances known as the "Ely War," which ended only when the governor sent in the state militia to restore order. The town's population dropped drastically thereafter, from a high of 1,875 in 1880 to 236 in 1960. Topographically, Vershire is a collection of hills in the 1,500- to 2,400-foot range cut by watercourses, the major one being the Ompompanoosuc River, which flows eastward into the town of West Fairlee and eventually empties into the CONNECTICUT RIVER. The major settlement is Vershire village, which lies on

Route 113 cutting across the town from east to west. The environmental devastation produced by copper mining over a century ago is still severe, and the mine locale is a Superfund site.

Victory

Victory, population 97, a town in Essex County, was granted by the Vermont legislature in 1780 to Captain Ebenezer Fisk and others. The name presumably derives from the anticipated American success in separating from Great Britain. Sparsely settled today, in the late nineteenth century Victory had seven villages serving the extensive lumbering industry and a resident population of over five hundred. The only settlements today are Victory village, in the southern part of town, and Gallup Mills, in the northern part. The western section of town is dominated by 3,020-foot Umpire Mountain, while the eastern section is part of the 4,970-acre Victory Basin Wildlife Management Area. Victory, along with neighboring Granby, was one of the last two towns in the state to get electricity, in 1963.

Vincent, John (1715–1810)

A Mohawk war leader on the French side in the first French and Indian War (1754–1755), Captain John Vincent scouted the country around the French *fort du Quesne*, near today's Pittsburgh, and on July 9, 1754, led over six hundred native allies of the French in their devastating ambush of British General Edward Braddock's one thousand regulars and militia. With Braddock dead, Vincent's warriors turned their fire on the Virginia militia and directly on its commander, George Washington, whom Vincent had known from the Virginian's command of an unsuccessful attack on the French and Indians at Great Meadows in 1754. At the conclusion of the conflict that expanded into the Seven Years' War, Vincent returned to the Mohawk settlement at Kahnawake, remaining there until 1775, when envoys from ETHAN ALLEN and a later meeting with George Washington at Boston convinced him to leave the Mohawks in Quebec and

ally himself with the newly forming Continental Army. He was one of the guides with BENEDICT ARNOLD's expedition across Maine to join the Northern Army before Quebec in 1776, and was with Richard Montgomery in the unsuccessful attack on the walled city. Settling at Newbury with nearly two hundred Odanak and Missisquoi ABENAKI, Vincent in 1779 was commissioned captain of a company of rangers on the recommendation of MOSES HAZEN to George Washington as part of a later aborted plan to attack Canada. His rangers included JOSEPH SUSAP, who was memorialized in nineteenth-century Newbury as Indian Joe. After the war, Vincent settled permanently in Vermont, living for nearly thirty years in the town of Killington. A devout Roman Catholic educated by Jesuits in Quebec, John Vincent was an avid Bible reader and was considered a pious man by his neighbors. For many years he proudly wore the Continental Army officer's coat that George Washington had given him. The Vermont General Assembly granted him a veteran's pension in the 1790s and annual assistance grants to his guardians for his care during the last decade of his life. He died in Mendon.

Voigt, Ellen Bryant (b. 1943)

Poet and founder in 1976 of the GODDARD COLLEGE M.F.A. in writing program, Ellen Bryant Voigt was nominated for the National Book Critics Circle Award in poetry for her book *Kyrie* (1995). Born in Virginia, Voigt taught writing at Iowa Wesleyan College before coming to Goddard in 1969. The Goddard M.F.A. program was a model later adopted at BENNINGTON COLLEGE and VERMONT COLLEGE. Voigt has published six collections of poetry and a book of criticism, *The Flexible Lyric* (1999). Her collection of poems in *Kyrie* takes as its subject the INFLUENZA EPIDEMIC OF 1918 and is written in the voices of people variously affected by it. Voigt lives in Marshfield and teaches in the M.F.A. program for writers at Warren Wilson College. She was named VERMONT STATE POET for a four-year term in 1999.

W

Wait, Benjamin (1737–1822)

Benjamin Wait had many adventures in the wars of the northern frontier. He was taken prisoner at Lake George in the Seven Years' War, carried to France, and later exchanged, returning to America in 1757. He served in the Louisbourg campaign, the conquest of Canada, and a winter march to Detroit and Illinois to bring in the French garrisons in that region. By age twenty-five, he had served in forty battles and skirmishes but had not been wounded. He was the third settler of Windsor in 1767 and was appointed protector of the King's timber under New York authority, but in 1770 allied himself with the GREEN MOUNTAIN BOYS. In June 1775, he joined the call for a regiment to be raised by New York east of the GREEN MOUNTAINS to protect the region against British regulars, "Roman Catholicks, and the savages at the northward." By 1776, he was a captain in Jacob Hoisington's militia rangers and after Vermont declared independence in 1777 joined SAMUEL HERRICK's Vermont militia rangers as a major. He was active throughout the remainder of the war and during many of the most interesting moments of Vermont's early history. On October 26, 1779, Wait was appointed sheriff of CUMBERLAND COUNTY by the governor and council. On the 27th, the General Assembly granted the Two Heroes Islands in LAKE CHAMPLAIN to Wait, Samuel Herrick, ETHAN ALLEN, and their associates for the price of £10,000. On November 11, Wait and ninety-four associates were also granted Isle La Motte, containing approximately eight thousand acres, for £3,276. After the Revolution in 1782, the general assembly granted Wait and a group of associates the town named after him in the Mad River Valley, Waitsfield, where he finally settled and built a handsome house still in use today.

Waitsfield

Waitsfield, population 1,659, a town in Washington County, was granted by the Vermont legislature in 1782 to General BENJAMIN WAIT, a hero of the French and Indian Wars and the Revolution, and others. It lies in the Mad River Valley between the main spine of the GREEN MOUNTAINS on the west and the Northfield range on its eastern border. Although it contains no ski area of its own, it is the commercial center of the ski-oriented valley, servicing Sugarbush in Warren to its south and Mad River Glen in Fayston to its west. The historic village of Waitsfield is a well-preserved collection of early nineteenth-century buildings clustered around the General Wait House (1793). A number of the buildings now house craft studios, retail shops, and restaurants. To the south of the village, continuing along Route 100, are two small shopping malls with additional stores and, along the roads in the surrounding hills, numbers of both year-round and vacation homes. The Waitsfield-Fayston Telephone Company, incorporated in 1904, is one of the few surviving local telephone companies of the sort that were once common in rural and small town areas.

Wakefield, James (1829–1912)

Born in England, James Wakefield left home at age thirteen to follow the sea. He experienced an extraordinary series of adventures, shipwrecks, and mutiny before visiting a brother in Whitehall, New York, and resolving to make a living on dry land. In 1857, he settled in the active seaport of Burlington and established a business as a ship chandler, providing sails, rigging, anchors, blocks, and other marine supplies to the many vessels then working on LAKE CHAMPLAIN. In December 1876, Captain Wakefield's maritime experience and skill were brought to bear in the heroic rescue of the passengers and crew of the General Butler. The General Butler was on her way to Burlington with a load of Isle La Motte MARBLE when she encountered a tremendous storm. Her steering mechanism broke and she drifted helplessly toward the Burlington breakwater. On board were Captain William Montgomery, an unnamed crewman, Elisha Goodsell of Isle La Motte (an injured man being transported to the hospital), and the captain's daughter Cora and her friend. As the Butler struck the breakwater, each person jumped or fell to the rough ice-covered stones. By all accounts, after Captain Montgomery abandoned the ship, she immediately sank in 40 feet of water. As each new wave covered them with icy water, the survivors faced the real possibility of dying from exposure. At this critical moment, James Wakefield and his son rowed out from the harbor in a 14-foot boat and saved all their lives. Captain Wakefield continued his career in a changing world. As the commercial use of Lake Champlain began to decline, his company, which included several sons, diversified into tents, awnings, and flags. The General Butler was rediscovered in 1980 and is one of Vermont's Underwater Historic Preserves. *Arthur Cohn*

Walden

Walden, population 782, a town in Caledonia County, was granted by the Vermont legislature in 1781 and supposedly named after a Major Walden who was commander of a blockhouse on the BAYLEY-HAZEN ROAD. Except for the northeastern corner of town—which is heavily wooded, nearly roadless, and marked by two 2,500-foot peaks, Stannard Mountain and Round Mountain, which are on the border with Stannard—the landscape is gently rolling and cut by watercourses. The settlements of Walden village, Walden Station, and South Walden lie on Route 15 cutting across the southern part of town from east to west.

Waldron, Clarence H. (b. 1885)

A Baptist minister in Windsor from 1915 to 1918, Clarence H. Waldron was the central figure in the nation's first important criminal court case during World War I involving religious opposition to the war. Born in New Jersey and educated at a Pentecostal Training School in Nashville, Tennessee, Waldron held Quaker-like convictions against war that became controversial after the United States entered the war in April 1917. Waldron made statements to his parishoners that led to his indictment in December 1917 for violations of the Federal Espionage Act. A Burlington jury found Waldron guilty, and he was sentenced to fifteen years in a federal prison in Atlanta, Georgia. After the European fighting ended, President Woodrow Wilson commuted Waldron's sentence, and he was released from prison on April 1, 1919.

Gene Sessions

Wall, Max (b. 1915)

Rabbi Max Wall's family emigrated from Poland to Denver, Colorado, when Max was six years old and then when he was twelve to New York City, where he completed his public school education. He graduated from Yeshiva University with an A.B. in 1938, and received a master's degree and was ordained a rabbi at graduation from the Jewish Theological Seminary. His first pulpit was in Woodbury, New Jersey, where he served from October 1942 until October 1943, when he entered the U.S. Army as a chaplain. In 1944, he joined the Ninth Infantry Division in Europe and witnessed heavy fighting, particularly at the Battle of the Bulge. With the cessation of hostilities, he directed his efforts toward relieving the plight of survivors of the Buchenwald and Dachau concentration camps. Rabbi Wall was invited to Burlington in 1946 to fill the pulpit of Ohavi Zedek, the city's conservative synagogue, and preached his first sermon while still in uniform. Regarding community service as a function of religious leadership, his tireless efforts in behalf of such causes as ecumenism earned him honorary degrees from the UNIVERSITY OF VERMONT, ST. MICHAEL'S COLLEGE, and the Jewish Theological Seminary of America. He taught for twenty-five years at St. Michael's and CHAMPLAIN COLLEGES, and St. Michael's instituted a lecture series in Rabbi Wall's name. In 1987 he became Rabbi Emeritus.

Wallingford

Wallingford, population 2,274, a town in Rutland County, was granted by BENNING WENTWORTH in 1761 and named after Wallingford, Connecticut, the home town of Captain Eliakim Hall, the first named grantee. The eastern three-quarters of the town lies on the main spine of the GREEN MOUNTAINS and is largely in the GREEN MOUNTAIN NATIONAL FOREST, rising to 2,784-foot Wilder Mountain on the southern border with Mount Tabor. The western one-quarter consists of the broadening valley of north-flowing OTTER CREEK, and beyond that is the bulk of Clark Mountain, a segment of the TACONIC MOUNTAINS whose summit is in the town of Tinmouth. The main settlement is the substantial village of Wallingford, a tool-manufacturing center. PAUL P. HARRIS, founder of Rotary International, spent his boyhood in Wallingford, and the town was also well known in the nineteenth century for the farm implements sold nationally and internationally by Lyman Batcheller, whose sons sold the business to AMERICAN FORK & HOE COMPANY in 1902. Another village, South Wallingford, lies near the Mount Tabor border, and a third,

East Wallingford, on the eastern border with Mount Holly, is connected to the rest of town by Route 140, the only east-west road.

Walsh, M. Emmett (b. 1935)

M. Emmett Walsh is a native of Swanton who graduated from Clarkson College with a degree in business administration but afterwards went on to study acting at the Academy of Dramatic Arts. His theatrical career runs from Broadway shows through off-off Broadway ensembles to summer stock. He has performed at Ford's Theater in Washington and has Broadway credits for *That Championship Season* and *Does a Tiger Wear a Necktie?* He has appeared in over one hundred films, starting with *Alice's Restaurant* in 1969 and including *Little Big Man*, *Serpico*, *Reds*, *Blade Runner*, *Raising Arizona*, and *My Best Friend's Wedding*. On television, he has appeared in *The Waltons*, *Bonanza*, *Baretta*, *Starsky and Hutch*, *Cheers*, and *The Bob Newhart Show*. Walsh has endowed a scholarship for theater students at the UNIVERSITY OF VERMONT.

Waltham

Waltham, population 479, the smallest town in area in Addison County, was established by a Vermont act of incorporation in 1796, before which it had been part of New Haven and then of Vergennes. The name derives from Waltham, Massachusetts, the home town of the first town moderator, Phineas Brown. Lightly populated and devoted largely to DAIRY FARMING, the town has never had a village or a post office; residents do their shopping in nearby Vergennes.

Walton, Eliakim Persons (1812–1890)

A Congressman, newspaperman, and editor, Eliakim Persons Walton was born in Montpelier. His father, EZEKIEL PARKER WALTON, was a major-general in the Vermont militia, prominent in Whig and Republican politics, and editor and proprietor of the *Vermont Watchman*. Eliakim attended Washington County common schools and, after an early apprenticeship to a printer, took up the study of law in the office of United States Senator Samuel Prentiss (Vermont), to whom he was distantly related. Walton never practiced law, however, and in 1833 became a partner in his father's paper. He became sole owner in 1853 and served as its editor/owner until 1868. Walton also edited Vermont's

first legislative newspaper and, at the beginning of the Civil War, published a daily based on his extensive correspondence with the Vermont troops. Walton was active in Vermont Whig politics and represented Montpelier in the state House of Representatives in 1853. He was active in the state's opposition to the Kansas-Nebraska Act and was a major architect of the Vermont REPUBLICAN PARTY. In 1856, at the urging of Senator SOLOMON FOOT, he ran for, and was elected to, the U.S. House of Representatives, where he served until 1863, when he declined renomination. During 1858, he urged the admission of Kansas as a free state and in 1864 was a delegate to the Republican National Convention. In 1860 and 1870, he successfully marshalled opposition to Vermont losing one seat in the House of Representatives, a feat that is frequently cited as his greatest service to Vermont. Walton was a member of the Vermont Senate from 1875 to 1879 and was active in the VERMONT HISTORICAL SOCIETY, for which he edited and published several volumes. He was also editor of *Walton's Register and Farmer's Almanac*. His most valuable editing work was *The Records of the Council of Safety and Governor and Council of the State of Vermont*, in eight volumes (1873–1880), which covered the documentary history of the state from its origins until 1836.

Walton, Ezekiel Parker (1789–1855)

Ezekiel Parker Walton was publisher and editor of the *Vermont Watchman* and a founder of the Vermont REPUBLICAN PARTY. Walton was born in Canterbury, New Hampshire, and moved to Peacham, where he attended the academy apprenticed as a printer to SAMUEL GOSS. He started the *Green Mountain Patriot* with Samuel Goss, moving the paper to Montpelier in 1807 with a new name, the *Vermont Watchman*. Walton became sole proprietor in 1816, and continued as editor for twenty years. Over the years, General Walton (a title earned by service in the Vermont militia) prospered in the paper-making business in Berlin and with the *Watchman*, located in a large building on the site of the present Montpelier City Hall. He became the printer of the state of Vermont, issuing hundreds of reports and other official publications. Beginning in 1817, he issued for many years *Walton's Vermont Register and Almanac*, a publication that became the bible of Vermont information. He was a Whig until 1854, when he helped found the Vermont Republican party. He was a strong writer, who modeled his style on Benjamin Franklin, and a dedicated member of the Congregational Church. He was the father of ELIAKIM PERSONS WALTON, who succeeded him as editor of the *Vermont Watchman*.

Paul Gillies and Marcus A. McCorison

Wardner, Henry Steele (b. 1867)

Henry Steele Wardner of Windsor prepared for college at St. Paul's School in Concord, New Hampshire. Harvard College class of 1888 and Harvard law 1891, he was admitted to the New York bar in 1892 and served for ten years as assistant United States Attorney for the southern district of New York, keeping his close connections with Windsor by maintaining a home there. After 1901, he was general counsel for the New Jersey Zinc Company. Wardner and his cousin attorney Maxwell Evarts challenged the constitutionality of the federal corporate tax in *Flint v. Stone-Tracy Company*. He was the president and a founding member of the MORGAN HORSE Club and wrote on Morgans for *Vermonter* magazine. Wardner was the author of *The Birthplace of Vermont: A History of Windsor to 1781* (Scribners, 1927), based on the Windsor town records from 1765 to 1785, documents he salvaged from beneath a pile of rotting wood in the basement of the town's office. Wardner with Charles Downer actively promoted the GREEN MOUNTAIN NATIONAL FOREST, which was approved by the federal government in 1927 to 1928.

Wardsboro

Wardsboro, population 854, a town in Windham County, was granted by the Vermont legislature in 1780 to William Ward and others, and until 1810 included the area that is now the town of Dover. The hilly, heavily wooded land, which rises to 2,700-foot White's Hill on the town's southern border, has always discouraged intensive settlement, and today most of the town lies in the GREEN MOUNTAIN NATIONAL FOREST. The main villages are Wardsboro and West Wardsboro, from the last of which begins one of the three roads that cross the GREEN MOUNTAINS in southern Vermont (closed in winter). The microscopic settlement of Podunk (a Natick word supposedly meaning "a boggy place") is as remote as its name implies.

Warner, Seth (1743–1784)

A prominent leader of the paramilitary GREEN MOUNTAIN BOYS in the conflict with New York over the validity of New Hampshire land grants and commander of the GREEN MOUNTAIN CONTINENTAL RANGERS regiment during the Revolution, Seth Warner was born in Woodbury, Connecticut. He moved to Bennington to settle on a New Hampshire grant with his family in 1763. Warner had a common school education but was accomplished as a botanist, woodsman, hunter, and horseman. A warrior and a natural leader of men, he was a captain under his cousin ETHAN ALLEN in the Green Mountain Boys. He drove a party of New York surveyors out of Bennington in 1771, and later that year rescued REMEMBER BAKER from a New York sheriff's posse taking him to the Albany jail. A force led by Warner captured Crown Point on the day that Allen took FORT TICONDEROGA. In July 1775, after the capture of Ticonderoga, Warner and Allen persuaded the Continental Congress to authorize a Green Mountain regiment. Congress left the funding to the New York Congress, which agreed to assume the cost. Meanwhile, on the grants, a convention of settlers elected Warner to command the rangers instead of Allen, whose badly botched attack on St. Johns, Quebec, in June probably cost him the settlers' confidence. Warner led his ranger regiment in the Canadian campaign of 1775. He led elements of his regiment at the BATTLE OF HUBBARDTON (July 1777) and again at the BATTLE OF BENNINGTON (August 1777). Though commissioned by the Continental Congress, Warner actually commanded a New York militia unit, rather than a line regiment of the Continental Army. He was threatened with the loss of his command by influential New Yorkers because of his pre-war hostility to New York authority in the grants and promotion to general was probably denied him by influential New Yorkers with continued land interests in Vermont. Ill health and exhaustion caused Warner to retire from the Continental service in 1780. He returned to Connecticut in 1782, where he died two years later. In 1859, a granite shaft commemorating him was erected in Woodbury, his birthplace, and in 1910 a statue of him by Olin Scott was set in front of the BENNINGTON BATTLE MONUMENT in Bennington. *Sarah L. Dopp*

Warner's Grant

Warner's Grant, population zero, in Essex County, was granted by the Vermont legislature in 1791 to Hester Warner, widow of SETH WARNER, one of the most prominent of the GREEN MOUNTAIN BOYS and commander of the GREEN MOUNTAIN CONTINENTAL RANGERS of the Continental Army. Three years after Warner's death in 1784, the destitute Mrs. Warner petitioned the legislature for a grant of land to help support her and her three children. What was eventually found was 2,000 acres of the most remote and rugged land in the state which, in all of its history, has never had any roads or permanent residents. Except for the nearby town of Lewis, Warner's Grant is considered the most inaccessible of all Vermont governmental units.

Warren

Warren, population 1,681, a town in Washington County, was granted by the Vermont legislature in 1780. The name may be an attempt to honor the memory of Dr. Joseph Warren of Boston, who died at the battle of Bunker Hill. The town is bisected from south to north by the Mad River, with the main spine of the GREEN MOUNTAINS on the west and the Northfield range on its eastern border. The town's economic mainstay is the Sugarbush ski resort (115 trails and a vertical drop of 2,650 feet), which is spread out across the slopes of two mountains: 3,812-foot Nancy Hanks Peak and 3,975-foot Lincoln Peak. Lodging, eating, and service facilities cluster along Route 100, centering in the village of Warren and extending into the town of Waitsfield to the north. One road out of Warren (closed in winter) crosses the Green Mountains through Lincoln Gap in the neighboring town of Lincoln in Addison County.

Warren Gore

Granted by the Vermont legislature in 1789, Warren Gore, population ten, in Essex County, was part of the previously granted (in 1780) town of Warren in Washington County, an action designed to compensate for the fact that Warren was somewhat below the usual town size of 23,000 acres. The name of both entities probably derives from Doctor Joseph Warren, a major general in the Massachusetts militia who was killed at the battle of Bunker Hill in 1775. Unlike Avery's Gore and the town of Lewis on the east and

Warner's Grant on the west, which have no residents, Warren Gore has residents because it is bisected by Route 114, one of only four numbered routes in Essex County. The road passes by 583-acre Norton Pond, a small portion of which is in the town of Norton to the north.

Washburn, Peter (1814–1870)

The thirty-second governor of Vermont, Peter Washburn was a native of Lynn, Massachusetts. His parents moved to Vermont in 1817, finally settling in Ludlow. Washburn, Dartmouth class of 1835, practiced law in Woodstock and was prominent in Vermont's political affairs by 1860, when as a delegate to the Republican National Convention he cast his vote for Abraham Lincoln. Washburn commanded the Woodstock light infantry militia company, leading them to the muster camp at Rutland in May 1861, where they joined the First Vermont Regiment of Volunteers. When the ninety-day enlistment of the First Vermont expired, Washburn was elected adjutant and inspector general of Vermont. For his work bringing Vermont's enlistees and conscripts into regiments, the RUTLAND HERALD compared him to the French Revolution's Lazare Carnot, "the organizer of victory." He was elected governor in September 1869 and inaugurated in October, but he died in office less than four months later.

Washington

Washington, population 1,047, a town in Orange County, was granted by the Vermont legislature in 1781. Previously, in 1770, it had been part of a New York patent called Kingsland, a name that the legislature probably found highly inappropriate and remedied by naming the town after George Washington. The town sits on the height of land separating streams that flow into the CONNECTICUT RIVER from those that flow into the WINOOSKI RIVER, resulting in a landscape of forested hills cut by small watercourses. The single village of Washington lies on Route 110, which cuts across the town from north to south.

Wasp, the

The only automobile to have been produced in Vermont (not counting the single steam wagon built by the Lane, Daley company in 1900 and sold to a Boston company for its use) was the Wasp, assembled between 1920 and 1925 by coach

Karl Martin and his 1921 Wasp Phaeton. Vermont Life

craftsman Karl Martin and his workers in his plant in Bennington from parts largely made elsewhere. Eighteen Wasps were made in six years, in models ranging from phaetons to touring cars to sports runabouts. High-quality items with innovative styling and hand-finished bodies, Wasps were expensive and affordable only by the well-to-do. Movie starts Mary Pickford and her husband Douglas Fairbanks, Sr., each owned one. Two Wasps are known to still exist, one of which is in the BENNINGTON MUSEUM. *David Blow*

Waterbury

Waterbury, population 4,915, a town in Washington County, was granted by BENNING WENTWORTH in 1763 and named for Waterbury, Connecticut, the home colony of many of the grantees. The landscape consists of a broad, fertile north-south valley flanked on either side by a mountain range: the Worcester Mountains on the east, with summits rising to 2,700 feet, and the GREEN MOUNTAINS on the west, topping out at 3,401 feet at Ricker Mountain on the border with the town of Bolton. Running through the valley is the Waterbury River and a number of smaller streams, all draining into the WINOOSKI RIVER on the town's southern border. The main settlements are the substantial village of Waterbury, spread out over a flat area along the Winooski, and Waterbury Center, on the road to Stowe. The residual settlement of Colbyville was once the home of the Colby Brothers factory, which made baby carriages that were shipped around the world. A large complex of brick buildings in the center of Waterbury village was once the VERMONT STATE HOSPITAL for mental patients, and today contains various state agencies formerly housed in Montpelier, including the Agency of Human Services and the Departments of Corrections and Public Safety. The FLOOD OF 1927 did enormous damage to the village, killing several people and destroying many buildings. Several dams were built on the Winooski's tributaries to control future flooding in its basin, including a large one in the northern part of town built by the U.S. Army Corps of Engineers in 1935 to 1938. The dam, an earth-fill type with stone rip-rap facing, is 2,130 feet long and has a maximum height of 158 feet; the reservoir behind it is a popular recreation area and the site of a state park. Because of Waterbury's proximity to Stowe on the north, the town has developed a substantial tourist trade on Route 100, including one of Vermont's most popular attractions, the main plant of BEN & JERRY'S HOMEMADE ICE CREAM.

Waterford

Waterford, population 1,104, a town in Caledonia County, was granted by the Vermont legislature in 1780 and originally named Littleton in honor of Moses Little, a prominent New Hampshire landowner who had fought as an officer at the BATTLE OF BENNINGTON. After the town of Littleton in New Hampshire was incorporated four years later, the Vermont town became Waterford, possibly after the town of that name in Ireland. Although the bustling urban center of St. Johnsbury is less than a mile from its northern border and Interstate 93 makes a long loop through its territory, Waterford remains overwhelmingly rural. Five peaks approaching two thousand feet dominate the landscape, which falls away southward to the CONNECTICUT RIVER, here backed up into a miles-long reservoir behind Moore Dam and one of the largest hydroelectric stations in New England. Since the inundation of Waterford village beneath the waters of the reservoir, the town center has been Lower Waterford a few miles to the east.

Waterman, Sterry R. (1901–1984)

An attorney and federal appellate judge, Sterry R. Waterman was born in Taunton, Massachusetts, graduated from Dartmouth College, and attended Harvard and George Washington University Law Schools. In 1931, he opened a law office in St. Johnsbury and subsequently served as Caledonia County state's attorney (1933–1937), as a member of the Vermont Board of Commissioners for Promotion of Uniformity of Legislation in the United States (1928–1958), and on the United States Second Circuit Court of Appeals (1958–1972). He was president of the Vermont Bar Association (1957–1958) and the American Judicature Society (1962–1964), and president of the Board of Trustees of the VERMONT LAW SCHOOL (1974–1983). In the 1930s and 1940s, Waterman was a prominent member of the Aiken-Gibson wing of the REPUBLICAN PARTY. A founder and president of the Vermont Young Republicans, Waterman was GEORGE AIKEN's campaign manager in the gubernatorial election of 1936. He was assistant secretary of the Vermont Senate when ERNEST W. GIBSON, JR., was secretary (1933–1940). When Senator George Aiken recommended Sterry Waterman for the vacant seat on the federal appellate court in 1957, President Dwight Eisenhower asked for another recommendation. Aiken and Senator RALPH FLANDERS persisted in support for Waterman. He was eventually appointed and enjoyed a distinguished judicial career.

Virginia C. Downs

Waterville

Waterville, population 697, the smallest town in area in Lamoille County, was incorporated by the Vermont legislature in 1824 out of Coits Gore and parts of Belvidere and Bakersfield. The reason, as the legislature noted, was "that it is inconvenient for the inhabitants of [those regions] to attend town meetings and transact town business in their respective towns." Mountainous and wooded, Waterville is bisected from north to south by Route 109, which follows the North Branch of the LAMOILLE RIVER, possibly the source of the town's name. Waterville village is the only significant settlement.

WCAX-TV

Vermont's first television station when it went on the air in 1954, WCAX was founded at the UNIVERSITY OF VERMONT in 1924 as a student-run AM radio station. Its call letters were derived from the College of Agriculture Extension Service. In 1931, Dr. HORATIO NELSON JACKSON purchased WCAX-AM, converting it into a commercial station. WCAX-AM was sold again in 1939 to Charles Hasbrook and became a CBS affiliate in 1940. When Hasbrook co-founded WCAX-TV with his son-in-law, Stuart "Red" Martin, Vermont was the last state to have its own television station. Martin was appointed WCAX-TV's first president and general manager, positions he still occupied in 2000. In 1963, WCAX-AM was sold and renamed WVMT. WCAX-TV's "Across the Fence," a weekday program on Vermont issues started by UVM's Extension Service in 1956, is reputed to be the longest-running show of its kind in the United States.   *Paul Searls*

We Americans

Initiated in 1932 by the EUGENICS SURVEY OF VERMONT and directed by Elin L. Anderson, an ethnic study of Burlington was originally conceived to compare the contributions of various immigrant communities to the civic life of the city. Anderson, a native of Winnipeg, Manitoba, with a degree in social work from the New York School of Social Work, transformed the project into a four-year sociological study of the prejudices and divisive forces at work in schools, social life, city government, neighborhoods, and industry and commerce. Anderson and her assistants, each representing Burlington's ethnic communities (French-Canadian, Irish, Italian, German, Jewish, and Yankee Protestant), interviewed over 450 Burlington residents concerning their attitudes toward other ethnic groups and the obstacles ethnic minorities encountered in their quest for opportunity and acceptance. Published as *We Americans: A Study of Cleavage in an American City* (Harvard University Press, 1937), Anderson's book captured the sentiments and realities of life in Burlington in the 1930s with startling clarity and set the problem of race and class prejudice in Vermont within the context of the larger national and international turmoil of the inter-war years. *We Americans* received the John Anisfield Award for its outstanding contribution to promoting inter-racial understanding and endures as a testimony to the value of cultural diversity and an indictment of the social forces that work to suppress it.   *Nancy L. Gallagher*

Weathersfield

Weathersfield, population 2,788, a town in Windsor County, was granted by BENNING WENTWORTH in 1761 and presumably named for Wethersfield (so spelled) in Connecticut, the home colony of many of the grantees. The town rises from the broad intervales of the CONNECTICUT RIVER into a hilly landscape marked on the north by the broad flank of Mount Ascutney, whose summit lies in the neighboring town of Windsor, and on the west by a spur of Hawk's Mountain, most of which lies in neighboring Cavendish and Baltimore. The highest summit in Weathersfield itself is 1,709-foot Little Ascutney Mountain. The main village is Perkinsville, located in the western section of town, and the hamlet of Ascutney, along the Connecticut. It was at the little settlement of Weathersfield Bow, so named for the land formed by a sweeping arc of the Connecticut River, that WILLIAM JARVIS first pastured the merino sheep that he had imported from Spain, an act that led to Vermont's SHEEP BOOM of the 1830s and 1840s.

Webb, Electra Havemeyer (1888–1960)

The founder of the SHELBURNE MUSEUM in 1947, who wished to share with the public the folk art, decorative arts, and fine art that she had been collecting most of her life, Electra Havemeyer Webb was the daughter of H. O. and Louisine Havemeyer, leading collectors of French Impressionist art. In 1910, Electra married J. Watson Webb (1884–1960), son of Lila Vanderbilt and WILLIAM SEWARD WEBB, founders of SHELBURNE FARMS. They had five children and maintained homes on Long Island, in New York City, and in Shelburne. Throughout her adult life, Mrs. Webb collected folk art and antiques, focusing on the unexpected beauty of utilitarian objects. She moved historic structures such as houses, barns, an inn, a covered bridge, a lighthouse, and the steamboat TICONDEROGA to the museum to display her collections and for their own interest. Until her death in 1960, she directed all facets of the museum. A Greek Revival–style building at the museum reconstructs six rooms of her New York apartment at 740 Park Avenue, completely furnished, and displays sculptures and paintings by artists including Rembrandt, Degas, Corot, Manet, and Monet.

Erica H. Donnis

Webb, William Seward (1851–1926)

A RAILROAD businessman and founder of SHELBURNE FARMS, William Seward Webb was a native of New York City. He was trained as a surgeon (Columbia, class of 1875) but entered the Vanderbilt family railway business after marrying Eliza (Lila) Vanderbilt (1860–1936) in 1881. He was president of the Wagner Palace Car Company, the Pullman Company's main competitor in the making of railway cars, and built the Adirondack and St. Lawrence Railroad in upstate New York. In 1886, Dr. and Lila Webb founded Shelburne Farms, an ambitious country estate in Shelburne. Here Dr. Webb established a model farm, importing English Hackney horses with the hope of improving the horse stock of Vermont farmers. In addition to his estate activities, he held a controlling interest in the Rutland Railroad for several years, served on the UNIVERSITY OF VERMONT's Board of Trustees, was the inspector-general of rifle practice for the Vermont militia, and was a state representative for the town of Shelburne. Although favored to be the Republican candidate for Vermont governor in 1902, Dr. Webb eventually decided not to run. He died at Shelburne Farms.

Erica H. Donnis

Webster, Daniel, at Stratton

In 1840, Daniel Webster came to Vermont for the Whig presidential campaign of William Henry Harrison and John Tyler. The major event of his tour through Vermont came when he spoke on the west side of Stratton Mountain to the largest political crowd gathered in Vermont during the nineteenth century. Billed as the Log Cabin Convention, the remote site was said to have been chosen by Webster for the favorable acoustics of the mountainside as compared to three other more convenient locations. A log cabin "100 feet long from north to south, by 50 feet wide, cut in two width-wise by a drive for teams" was erected at Kelley Stand in Stratton. A reporter described the scene: "a clearing of about 300 acres in the midst of a magnificent amphitheater of hills, of at least five miles diameter. From the verge of the clearing to the summit of the mountains, there was a deep and unbroken fringe of foliage, which added greatly to the beauty of the scene. It was far from the haunts of men, scarcely a house being visible." Webster's opening words were: "Fellow citizens, we meet today among the clouds . . ." Over ten thousand people came to hear Webster's famous oratory.

Weed's Imperial Orchestra

Conducted by Sterling Weed (b. 1901) of St. Albans, Weed's Imperial Orchestra may be the oldest still-active dance band in the country. Sterling Weed continues to lead his dance band at Franklin County weddings and performed at Governor HOWARD DEAN's 1998 Inaugural Ball. As a talented young performer on the piano, piccolo, and flute, Weed had his first musical job as flute accompaniest for silent movies at the Empire Theatre in St. Albans. In 1922, he played saxophone with Harold Sault's orchestra and was introduced to the world of dance music. In 1928, he joined his brothers Ora and Lorenzo in a dance band that they had formed in Enosburgh, which he quickly renamed Weed's Imperial Orchestra. The band played at dance halls, summer camps, grange halls, and other venues across northern Vermont and Quebec. By the 1940s, when big band swing was at the peak of its national popularity, Weed's Imperial Orchestra played to as many as three thousand dancers in a night at the dance pavilion in Malletts Bay. Sterling Weed also taught music for over sixty years to thousands of students in Franklin County schools and in private lessons, and led St. Albans high school bands in the VERMONT MUSIC FESTIVAL for many years. In addition to the Imperial Orchestra, he conducted the St. Albans boys' band, the Enosburgh band, and the St. Albans City Orchestra. Most of the original members of Weed's Imperial Orchestra are dead, but some of their grandchildren now perform with the group.

Weeks, John Eliakim (1854–1949)

A two-term governor and one-term congressman, John Weeks was born in Salisbury, his home until 1896 when he moved to Middlebury, where he resided until his death. Educated in the Salisbury common schools and Middlebury High School, he had numerous occupations, including farmer, insurance agent, and bank officer. A Republican, in 1884 he was named assistant doorkeeper for the Vermont Senate and in 1888, 1912, and 1915 served in the Vermont House, the last year as Speaker. Other elective offices included state senator and assistant judge of the county court. A student of penal reform, Weeks served as a director of the Vermont Industrial School (subsequently renamed the WEEKS SCHOOL) and for eleven years as chairman of the state penal board. In 1917, he was named director of state institutions and served until 1923, when he was named Vermont's first commissioner of public welfare. In 1926, he was elected governor and the following year presided over the state's reconstruction after the FLOOD OF 1927, the worst disaster in the state's history. Maintaining that recovery dictated the need for administrative continuity that could best be provided by the governor retaining office, Weeks sought and won re-election, becoming the first governor re-elected since 1870, when Vermont adopted a two-year term. His handling of flood recovery measures was regarded as exemplary, and in 1930 he was rewarded by election to Congress. In 1932, Vermont was reapportioned down from two congressional districts to one and Weeks retired from public life.

Weeks School

The Vermont Reform School in Vergennes was built in 1874 to provide separate facilities for "the discipline, correction, and rehabilitation" of youthful offenders, who were previously incarcerated with adults. In 1900, the Reform School was renamed Vermont Industrial School, and in 1937 it was named "Weeks School" in honor of Governor JOHN E. WEEKS, a former trustee and supervisor of state institutions. Throughout its history, VIS superintendents struggled with the challenges of meeting the needs of a mixed population. Not only did the severity of offenses committed by inmates vary, but the school also served as a temporary shelter for children who were not delinquent, but were dependent or neglected children from poor families unable to care for them in towns that wished to be rid of them. During the progressive era, jurisdiction over juvenile cases broadened, so that municipal courts, county courts, and justices of the peace could commit children to VIS. In 1915, "juvenile delinquency" was legally defined to include such offenses as school truancy, associating with "disreputable persons," using vulgar language, and "wandering around the streets at night." Superintendents of the Vermont Industrial School advocated rehabilitation of youthful offenders through vocational education, supervised parole programs, and eliminating the "reform school" stigma. In the early 1920s, social workers began pedigree studies of families of children at the Vermont Industrial School, which inspired subsequent studies of so-called "degenerate families" by the EUGENICS SURVEY OF VERMONT in the late 1920s and further stigmatized VIS inmates. In 1937, a state Probation and Parole Division in the Department of Public Welfare enlarged the authority of probation officers over community supervision of juvenile delinquents, a trend that continued over the next three decades. Weeks School was closed in 1979 and today the federally funded Job Corps operates a residential training program in its buildings.

Nancy L. Gallagher

Wells

Wells, population 1,121, a town in Rutland County, was granted by BENNING WENTWORTH in 1761 and named for the small cathedral town of Wells, England. The town, which abuts the town of Granville in New York State, lies on the low western slopes of the TACONIC MOUNTAINS and contains the southern half of 852-acre Lake St. Catherine, a popular summer resort area, the northern half of which is in the town of Poultney. The only settlement is Wells village, on Wells Brook, a tributary of the Mettawee River, and lies at the base of Pond Mountain, a shear fault that rises 800 feet. Numerous slate quarries dot the western section of town, as they do other towns along the New York border from Castleton to Pawlet in the region known as SLATE VALLEY.

Wells, Samuel (1730–1786)

In 1762, Samuel Wells settled on a 600-acre farm in Brattleboro that was part of a New York grant. New York Governor Tryon appointed Wells judge of the court of common pleas and justice of the peace for CUMBERLAND COUNTY in 1766. Wells and CREAN BRUSH were elected from Cumberland County to the New York Provincial Assembly in 1773, where they opposed New Hampshire's claim to jurisdiction on land matters west of the CONNECTICUT RIVER and also opposed the Revolution. Wells served on the assembly's committee chaired by Brush that drafted the infamous Bloody Acts of 1774 that imposed a death penalty for failing to surrender ETHAN ALLEN and other leaders of the GREEN MOUNTAIN BOYS. Unlike Brush and many other Loyalists and New York supporters, Wells somehow escaped banishment and confiscation of his land by Vermont during the war, though he was confined to his farm in 1777 by the Committee for Conduct and was warned that he would be shot if found outside the bounds of his land. During the so-called HALDIMAND NEGOTIATIONS between Vermont and Quebec's Governor General FREDERICK HALDIMAND in the summer of 1781, Wells managed the movement of letters from British-occupied New York to authorities in Canada. Although the Continental Congress ordered him arrested for "intercourse with the enemy," Wells remained free, later receiving 1,200 acres in Canada as compensation for his loyalty, land on which many of his eleven surviving children settled. He is buried in Brattleboro.

Wells, William (1837–1892)

A native of Waterbury, where he worked in his father's mercantile firm until the opening of the Civil War, William Wells was largely instrumental in raising Company C of the First Vermont Cavalry regiment in the late summer of 1861. Chosen first lieutenant of the regiment when it was formed, he rose to brigadier general in 1865. He led his troops in battles and raids in Virginia and Maryland during 1862 to 1863, distinguishing himself in the fight at Orange Court House, Virginia, and in the repulse of J. E. B. Stuart's cavalry at Hanover, Pennsylvania. In the desperate cavalry charge on Round Top at the BATTLE OF GETTYSBURG, July 3, 1863, Wells commanded the second battalion of the First Vermont Cavalry, penetrating the enemy's lines about three-quarters of a mile and coming out unharmed almost by a miracle, while his commander was killed by Confederate infantry. Five days later, Wells was wounded by a sabre thrust at Boonsboro, Maryland, and in September at Culpepper Court House, Virginia, he was wounded again by a shell burst. He temporarily commanded the Seventh Michigan Cavalry and then accompanied Sheridan in his raid on Richmond and in a famous cavalry fight at Yellow Tavern, where his regiment killed Confederate General Stuart. At the BATTLE OF CEDAR CREEK, Wells commanded a brigade, of which the Vermont cavalry formed a part. The Vermont and the Fifth New York cavalry captured forty-five pieces of artillery at Cedar Creek, which helped turn a near rout into a decisive victory before nightfall. After the Battle of Winchester, September 19, 1864, he commanded the Second Brigade, Third Cavalry Division, and several times commanded the division. He was with Sheridan through the Shenandoah Valley and James River campaigns, finally joining in a raid on the rear of Richmond in June 1864. On the morning of the Confederate surrender at Appomattox, his brigade had started on its last charge when it was stopped by General Custer in person. Wells participated in seventy cavalry engagements, in eighteen of which he led a brigade or division, and his service in the field was continuous from the date of his muster to the close of the war. He was awarded the Congressional Medal of Honor for "distinguished gallantry at the Battle of Gettysburg." After the war, he became a partner in a wholesale drug company in Waterbury, Henry & Company, which later moved to Burlington and in 1872 became Wells, Richardson & Company. President Grant appointed Wells collector of customs for the District of Vermont in 1872, in which capacity he served for thirteen years. A popular figure in Vermont when he returned from the war, he represented Waterbury in the Vermont House in 1865 to 1866, and Chittenden County in the Senate from 1886 to 1888. He served as a director or trustees of several businesses and banks, as well as charitable institutions. A bronze statue of Wells, a replica of the one erected by the state of Vermont at Gettysburg, stands in Burlington's Battery Park.

Welsh Immigrants

From the 1850s through the 1920s, Welsh immigrants settled in the SLATE VALLEY, a border region located in Rutland County, Vermont, and Washington County, New York, that includes such Vermont towns as Fair Haven, Castleton, Poultney, and West Pawlet. Fleeing the low pay, feudal nature, and industrial strife of the slate industry in Wales, they came to work the rich slate

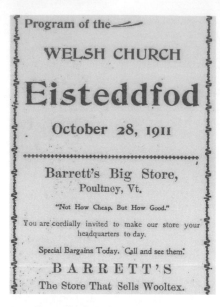

Program of the

WELSH CHURCH

Eisteddfod

October 28, 1911

Barrett's Big Store,
Poultney, Vt.

"Not How Cheap, But How Good."

You are cordially invited to make our store your
headquarters to day.

Special Bargains Today. Call and see them.

BARRETT'S
The Store That Sells Wooltex.

Poster for a Welsh festival, 1911. Stephen Diehl

seams of the valley. As experienced and knowledgeable quarrymen, the Welsh often enjoyed a privileged position in this difficult and hazardous industry and some of them became wealthy quarry owner-operators. The census records 1,645 immigrants from Wales in the valley in 1900, 979 of them located in Vermont. The size of this Welsh-American community, including American-born children and grandchildren, was significantly larger. Regularly spoken in the valley as late as the 1950s, the Welsh language was the medium of community life. Worshipping in the "old language," fifteen Welsh congregations were established in the region as a whole, nine of them in Vermont. The main denominations were Congregationalist and Welsh Calvinistic Methodist, a distinctly Welsh sect that eventually merged with the Presbyterian Church USA in 1920. Central to Welsh worship was the tradition of four-part congregational singing of Welsh hymns, and the region became known for its many outstanding choral groups and choirs. The center of much of cultural life, the churches regularly held traditional events such as the *gymanfa ganu* (hymn-singing festival) and *gymanfa pregethu* (preaching festivals). The *eisteddfod*, a musical and literary competition devoted to poetry and song, was another important cultural institution, the largest of which was held annually on Christmas day over the border in Granville, New York. Welsh immigration declined after the First World War and the Welsh-American community was hard hit

by the collapse of the slate industry during the Depression. The Welsh presence, however, remains a strong element in the character of the region. Welsh cultural events continue to be sponsored by the Welsh Presbyterian Church of Poultney, the Poultney Area St. David's Society, the Slate Valley Museum, and GREEN MOUNTAIN COLLEGE, which runs a Welsh Heritage Program and maintains an archive related to the history of Welsh-American life.   *John S. Ellis*

Welsh Male Chorus

At the peak of slate production and Welsh settlement in SLATE VALLEY in Rutland County, the area boasted fifteen Welsh chapels, and traditions long esteemed in Wales were brought here. *Eisteddfods* (music, art, and literary contests) were regular events, as were *gymanfa ganu* (hymn-singing) festivals. The longest-lived Welsh male chorus in the northeastern United States, the twenty-five man Poultney Welsh Male Chorus, performed regionally from 1930 to 1955. About half of the original members had been born in Wales. Untutored musicians, but skilled in the Welsh tradition of church singing as youths, choir singing, *gymanfa ganu*, and *eisteddfodau,* many of the members also played musical instruments and were soloists in the area's churches and community organizations. The chorus travelled throughout New England and New York, averaging thirty radio and concert performances annually of traditional music sung in Welsh. State funds and private donations supported a notable performance of the Welsh Male Chorus for the British War Relief Fund in New York City's Town Hall Auditorium on March 15, 1941. Non-Welsh singers joined the chorus in later years, but the repertoire of nearly sixty songs continued to be sung in Welsh and English. At their concerts, the men sang without sheet music, and were dressed in choir robes with a red-fringed white stole decorated with the Welsh flag's red dragons. Directors were Ezra Roberts (1930–1937), Hugh Lewis (1937–1940), and Evan Glyn Williams (1940–1955). The accompanists were Marion McDonald Ripley (1930–1938) and Gladys M. Jones (1938–1955). Welsh choral music is still performed in the Slate Valley through yearly *gymanfa ganu* held by the Poultney St. David's Society and the Poultney Welsh Presbyterian Church, as well as by visiting Welsh musical artists. In 1995, the

GREEN MOUNTAIN COLLEGE Choir began a program including Welsh music in their repertoire.   *Janice B. Edwards*

Wentworth, Benning (1696–1770)

The first royal governor of New Hampshire, Benning Wentworth was born in Portsmouth, New Hampshire, the eldest son of John Wentworth, lieutenant governor of Massachusetts with administrative responsibility for the province of New Hampshire. He graduated from Harvard College in 1715 and joined his uncle's mercantile business in Boston. His rise to ultimate power in the province included service in the New Hampshire Assembly and the governor's council. He worked hard to gain New Hampshire's independence from Massachusetts, which was accomplished in 1741, and he became the province's first royal governor, serving twenty-five years, the longest tenure of any royal governor in the colonies. Consistent with corrupt British political practices of the eighteenth century both at home and in the colonies, Wentworth enriched himself by appointing friends and family to lucrative offices and by his policy of granting for high fees wild land on both sides of the CONNECTICUT RIVER to settlers and speculators, reserving for himself 500 acres in each grant. By 1764, after the French and Indian War, he had granted 138 townships totalling 3 million acres in what was to become Vermont. With the end of the war with France, settlers began to move in earnest into the New Hampshire grants lands west of the Connecticut River, soon attracting the attention of the New York governors, who claimed the land as New York's, issued conflicting land grants, and made efforts to force New Hampshire settlers to leave the land or to purchase title confirmations from New York. Settlers and speculators with large holdings in New Hampshire grants west of the GREEN MOUNTAINS instead resisted New York's attempts to dispossess them by organizing the GREEN MOUNTAIN BOYS, an irregular militia led by ETHAN ALLEN. Although New Hampshire grew in population and wealth during his tenure, Wentworth aroused opposition because of his self-enrichment and nepotism. He was allowed to resign in 1767 and was succeeded by John Wentworth, his nephew. Bankrupt at the beginning of his term as governor, Wentworth left his widow a fortune at the end. Bennington, one of his earliest grants, is named for him.   *Ann E. Cooper*

Wesselhoeft, Robert (1797–1852)

A native of Chemnitz, Saxony, Robert Wesselhoeft operated a popular water-cure, the Brattleboro Hydropathic Institution, from 1845 to 1851. Before coming to America, he practiced law in the duchy of Saxe-Weimar, but was jailed for seven years for political activity and left Germany in 1840. Wesselhoeft studied medicine under his brother Wilhelm in Allentown, Pennsylvania, and in 1845 opened the water-cure establishment in Brattleboro. Wesselhoeft's Hydropathic Institution drew such notable guests as Harriet Beecher Stowe, James Russell Lowell, Martin Van Buren, and Francis Parkman for treatment that included hot and cold baths, simple diets, and regular exercise. Wesselhoeft became ill in 1851 and returned to Germany, where he died. The Hydropathic Institution continued to function until 1871.   *J. Kevin Graffagnino*

West Fairlee

West Fairlee, population 726, a town in Orange County, was created by the Vermont legislature in 1797 out of the previously granted town of Fairlee. The reason for the division was the difficulty of communicating between the low-lying lands along the CONNECTICUT RIVER and the upland region inland, separated as they are by a series of hills ranging from 1,200 to 1,700 feet high. The town's landscape, composed of forested hills cut by small streams, has always limited settlement. The main village of West Fairlee, on the banks of the Ompompanoosuc River, lies on Route 113 in the extreme southwestern corner of town. Summer camps line the shores of 463-acre Lake Fairlee, which the town shares with Fairlee and Thetford.

Westfield

Westfield, population 503, a town in Orleans County, was granted by the Vermont legislature in 1780 to William West and others. The town has very little land suitable for settlement, its entire western half being taken up by the northernmost section of the GREEN MOUNTAINS, here culminating in 3,861-foot Jay Peak, which the town shares with Jay to its north and Montgomery to its west. The single village of Westfield is on Route 100 in the town's eastern section. In the extreme southwestern corner of the town is Hazen's Notch, the northern terminus of the Revolutionary-era BAYLEY-HAZEN ROAD.

Westford

Westford, population 2,086, a town in Chittenden County, was granted by BENNING WENTWORTH in 1763 and may derive its name from the fact that it was the most westerly of the seven towns granted that day. Although a few hills in the eastern section of town rise from 1,000 to 1,600 feet, the countryside is mostly gently rolling and well watered, and has historically been devoted to AGRICULTURE and DAIRY FARMING. The main settlement, Westford village, lies on the banks of the Brown's River almost directly in the middle of the town. Although Westford is still primarily rural, its location on the northern edge of the Burlington metropolitan area has resulted in an increase in single-lot housing in recent years.

West Haven

West Haven, population 278, a town in Rutland County, was incorporated by the Vermont legislature in 1792 out of the western three-fifths of Fair Haven, which had been chartered in 1779. The southern border of the town is defined by the long curve of the Poultney River, which enters the beginning of LAKE CHAMPLAIN just north of the village of Whitehall, New York, after which point the lake becomes the town's western border. Tucked into the pocket created by the two bodies of water is the town's only eminence, 1,080-foot Bald Mountain, part of the TACONIC MOUNTAINS and home to Vermont's only known rattlesnake den. The single settlement is West Haven village, in the rolling hills and pastures of the northern part of town. A geographical curiosity is that, because of the winding course of the Poultney, West Haven is the only place in Vermont where it is possible to drive eastward into New York state.

Westminster

Westminster, population 3,210, a town in Windham County, was granted by BENNING WENTWORTH in 1752 and named for Westminster, England, now a borough of London. (Before that, in 1736, it had been granted by Massachusetts as Township Number 1 and the next year named New Taunton by its proprietors. When the boundary line between Massachusetts and the newly created province of New Hampshire was drawn in 1740, New Taunton fell north of it, encouraging Wentworth eventually to issue new grants.) The town rises from broad fertile meadows along the CONNECTICUT RIVER on the east through a series of low wooded hills to the long ridge of 1,680-foot Windmill Hill on the western border with Brookline and Athens. The bulk of the hill effectively prevents a direct road connection with either town. Westminster village, along the Connecticut, is the main settlement, while North Westminster shades imperceptibly into the large village of Bellows Falls in the neighboring town of Rockingham. New York established its CUMBERLAND COUNTY court there in 1770. On March 13, 1775, occurred the "WESTMINSTER MASSACRE," when farmers protesting impending foreclosure and eviction actions occupied the courthouse in an attempt to stop the court from sitting. In the ensuing melee, two dissidents were killed and ten wounded. The following month, a convention in Westminster voted to renounce all New York claims to authority, one of a series of steps that eventually led, on January 15, 1777, to the declaration (again at a convention in Westminster) of the "new and separate" state of New Connecticut, later renamed Vermont. The first printing office in Vermont was set up in Westminster in 1778, and the first newspaper, *The Vermont Gazette*, or *The Green Mountain Post Boy*, issued in 1781.

Westminster Massacre

In an event similar to several others in corners of the eighteenth-century British Empire, an agrarian protest riot over court foreclosures on land debts in March 1775 erupted into gunfire and two deaths in Westminster outside the CUMBERLAND COUNTY court house. ETHAN ALLEN later rhetorically escalated the event into the "Westminster Massacre," and early historians of Vermont claimed it was a pivotal event in the sequence that culminated in Vermont's independence. In an economy short on cash and dependent on good harvests to acquire it, farmer-debtors on the east side of the GREEN MOUNTAINS sought to postpone the New York court's foreclosures for debt by petitioning chief judge Thomas Chandler to defer the debtors' cases until after the harvest. Chandler agreed to limit the spring session to a murder case. When a rumor spread that hardline judges would insist on hearing the original docket, an angry crowd of settlers descended on Westminster on March 13, 1775, seizing the courthouse. In response, Cumberland County Sheriff William Paterson took a posse to the courthouse and exchanged noisy threats and insults with the insurgents. Chandler convinced a number of settlers to leave, but a remnant occupied the courthouse. In the meantime, Paterson and his posse retired to John Norton's tavern. Primed with rum, a little before midnight Paterson and his men returned to the courthouse to evict the protestors, who twice repelled Paterson's men. Court clerk SAMUEL GALE threatened the mob with his pistol, prompting the posse to open fire, fatally wounding William French and David Houghton, and, according to Dr. REUBEN JONES, "did most cruelly mammoc [wound] several more." The posse then jailed ten of the settlers. When the court prepared to sit on March 14, 1775, word of the tumult quickly spread, and a crowd of angry settlers gathered at Westminster. The court prudently adjourned, unaware that it would not convene again once the provincial government in New York adjourned permanently in April. The mob freed the prisoners. When militia from New Hampshire and Massachusetts came on the scene, they took Paterson and his men into custody and marched them off to Northhampton, Massachusetts. On March 15, Robert Cochran led a group of westside GREEN MOUNTAIN BOYS to Westminster in support of the rioters. Cochran's men lifted the spirits of the settlers who that day buried William French, whom anti-British supporters of independence soon memorialized as a victim of "Cruel Ministerial tools of George Ye 3rd," in an effort to elevate the event beyond a common anti-court riot and the failure of a sheriff to control his posse.   *H. Nicholas Muller III*

Westmore

Westmore, population 306, a town in Orleans County, was granted by the Vermont legislature in 1781 as the town of Westford and changed to Westmore in 1787. (Vermont already had a town of Westford, granted by BENNING WENTWORTH in 1763.) The mountainous nature of the landscape—at least six peaks reach well over 2,000 feet—has always limited settlement. The town's most striking feature is 5-mile-long LAKE WILLOUGHBY, a fjord-like body of water formed more than twelve thousand years ago. The southern end of the lake is bracketed by the steep cliffs of biblically named Mount Pisgah and Mount Hor, which provide a somber backdrop to the lake's deep-blue waters.

Weston

Weston, population 630, a town in Windsor County, was created by the Vermont legislature in 1799 out of the western half (or West Town) of the town of Andover. The difficulty of crossing from one side of town to the other, separated as they are by a series of summits culminating in 2,882-foot Terrible Mountain and 2,509-foot Markham Mountain, was the cause of the separation. Directly below these summits is the long valley of the south-flowing WEST RIVER, on the banks of which is the village of Weston, and beyond that are the foothills of the GREEN MOUNTAINS, part of the GREEN MOUNTAIN NATIONAL FOREST. Despite its isolation, the well-preserved and restored village, which is listed on the National Register of Historic Places, is one of the most popular tourist destinations in Vermont. It is the home of the enormously successful Vermont Country Store, founded by VREST ORTON in 1946 in imitation of the practical, homespun village emporiums of former times (although now much of its business is mail order), and other shops devoted to crafts, pottery, toys, and Christmas collectibles. The WESTON PLAYHOUSE, founded in 1933, Vermont's oldest professional theater company, presents a summer season of plays and musicals in a modern white-columned building on the village green. Two museums, the Farrar-Mansur house and the Old Mill, display artifacts of nineteenth-century life. Several miles north of the village is the WESTON PRIORY, a Benedictine monastery known for its schedule of daily prayers and its recordings of inspirational music by the monks.

Weston Playhouse

The longest-running professional theatre in Vermont, the Weston Playhouse was built in 1935 by Weston-born architect Raymond Austin in a converted Congregational church facing onto the town green. Renovations of the handsome Greek Revival building were supported through a generous donation from Mrs. Herbert Otis Bailey. WPA Federal Artist Roy Williams painted four large theatrical murals for the playhouse walls. The beauty of the town and its theatre building led Boston Conservatory teacher Harlan Grant to assemble a professional summer stock company there in 1937, and the first professional summer season opened with Noel Coward's *Hay Fever*, featuring Lloyd Bridges. Through the 1940s and 1950s, the company offered a schedule of ten new productions each summer, and in several summers ran "overnight tours" to Woodstock, Rutland, Manchester, and Burlington. In 1962, a fire destroyed the playhouse and its stock of props, settings, costumes, and lights. The Weston community raised $150,000 to build a combined theatre and community center, replicating the Greek Revival facade of the original playhouse. Raymond Austin was again the architect. The new Weston Playhouse opened the 1963 season with *The Fantasticks*. Harlan Grant continued to direct productions until his retirement in 1971 after thirty-four seasons. In 1972, Walter Boughton, chair of Amherst College's drama department, became the second director of the playhouse company and expanded the repertory to include musical theatre and added an after-hours revue, the Act IV Cabaret. Rain storms in 1973 and 1976 flooded the WEST RIVER and inundated the playhouse's storage area, destroying most of the theatre's stock. By 1980, the playhouse had added a restaurant. Boughton died in 1988, but three of his colleagues, Malcolm Ewen, Tim Fort, and Steve Stettler, formed a management team to succeed him and reorganized the Weston Playhouse Theater Company as a not-for-profit organization in 1989. Today the company performs year-round in an air-conditioned playhouse utilizing an infrared listening system.

Weston Priory

The Weston Priory, in Weston, is a Benedictine monastery, established in 1953 as dependent on the Dormition Abbey in Jerusalem. In 1968, it became an independent Conventual Priory. Music, work, social activism, and the welcoming of guests for varying lengths of time are vital aspects of priory life. In their concern for the war-ravaged countries of Central America, the Weston Priory monks established a sanctuary for refugees fleeing violence and conflict in that region. In the 1970s, the Weston Priory became especially known for its recordings of religious music, which are sold nationally. Many visitors have been attracted to the community by their music ministry.   *David Blow*

West River

The West River, the major river of Windham County, has its source in the sparsely populated area of the GREEN MOUNTAINS where Windham, Bennington, and Rutland counties come together. It cuts its way through hilly terrain southeastward, passing through the towns of Weston, Londonderry, Jamaica, Townshend, Newfane, and Dummerston until it empties into the CONNECTICUT RIVER just to the north of Brattleboro village. The total length of the river is approximately 38 miles.

West Rutland

West Rutland, population 2,535, a town in Rutland County, was incorporated by the Vermont legislature in 1886 out of the western part of Rutland town. The single settlement is the village of West Rutland, which lies on a plain separating the west-flowing Castleton River from the east-flowing Clarendon River. The town is dominated on its western edge by an elongated ridge 1,500 feet high, a part of the TACONIC MOUNTAINS, which extends into the town of Pittsford to the north and can be crossed only at the point where the Castleton River cuts through it. West Rutland both before and after its incorporation was the center of the MARBLE belt that lies to the west of Rutland city and reaches into the the towns of Proctor and Pittsford to its north.

West Union

On July 18, 1781, Vermont's first governor, THOMAS CHITTENDEN, issued a proclamation announcing the annexation of ten New York towns between Vermont's western border and the Hudson River. IRA ALLEN, in his history of Vermont (1798), and subsequent historians have characterized this West Union as a clever counterweight to the recently formed EAST UNION. The annexation of sixteen New Hampshire towns in the CONNECTICUT RIVER valley threatened the hold of the Allen-Chittenden faction on the Vermont legislature. Historians have also characterized the West and East Unions as bargaining chips in Vermont's effort to win the recognition of Congress as an independent state, or to make "greater" Vermont more attractive to the British, with whom the faction had begun the HALDIMAND NEGOTIATIONS. Beyond any Vermont political strategy, conditions in these towns on New York's northeastern frontier made many settlers eager to seek an arrangement with it. In their view, New York had utterly failed to protect them from the British and their Indian allies operating from FORT TICONDEROGA. Nor did the stoutly democratic settlers like the high

property qualifications to vote, plural office holding, official corruption, and downstate control of the New York government. Consequently, in February 1781, some residents of the New York towns presented a petition to the Vermont legislature requesting union. The legislature encouraged them, and in March Ira Allen toured the towns drumming up support and suggesting the Vermont negotiations with Haldimand could forestall the threat of the British army. At its April session in Windsor, the legislature recommended that the New York towns hold a convention at Cambridge in May, to which it would dispatch a committee. The convention worked out the terms of union with Vermont, and in June the towns presented their credentials to the receptive legislature meeting in Bennington, and Governor Chittenden proclaimed the West Union. New York's Governor Clinton took strong exception to the Union. In August, when the U.S. Congress accepted a recommendation that it recognize Vermont as a state should it dissolve the West and East Unions, Clinton denied its authority. In October, he ordered General Peter Gansevoort to reclaim the lost territory. As Gansevoort entered the West Union with a force of eighty men, he encountered a group of Vermont militia. After an exchange of shots, the opposing groups took positions across the Walloomsac River from each other, and the Battle of Walloomsac settled into a war of invective. On Ira Allen's advice to make a show of force, Colonel Ebenezer Walbridge with five hundred men and ETHAN ALLEN in full military regalia intimidated the Yorkers, who retreated to Albany, ending the "war." With the British surrender at Yorktown that same month, the Haldimand Negotiations collapsed and the British threat to the frontier ended. The Vermont legislature, currying favor with Congress, disbanded the West and East Unions in February 1782.   *H. Nicholas Muller III*

West Windsor

West Windsor, population 1,067, a town in Windsor County, has the distinction of having been created twice by the Vermont legislature. The first time was in 1814, when it was formed out of the western half of the town of Windsor, an act that was rescinded the following year when the inhabitants of the two towns thought better of the move. The second was in 1848, when separation sentiment proved strong enough to be per-

manent. The landscape consists of a series of ridges and valleys except in the southeastern corner, where the imposing bulk of 3,144-foot Mount Ascutney, which the town shares with Windsor and Weathersfield, dominates the landscape. The main village is Brownsville, serving the Ascutney Mountain Resort, which has forty-seven ski trails and a vertical drop of 1,530 feet.

Weybridge

Weybridge, population 824, a town in Addison County, was granted by BENNING WENTWORTH in 1761. The source of the name would seem to be Weybridge in either Massachusetts or England. The town's gently rolling landscape, used for extensive sheep raising in the nineteenth century, is today devoted to AGRICULTURE and DAIRY FARMING. In recent decades, the proximity of Middlebury has resulted in some residential development along the town's roads. The two main settlements are Weybridge Hill and Weybridge village, the latter on OTTER CREEK as it curves through the northern section of town. There are two noteworthy geographical features: Snake Mountain (elevation 1,287 feet) on the western border with Addison, and Weybridge Cave, the largest cave in Vermont. The town is the site of the University of Vermont's MORGAN HORSE FARM.

Wheelock

Wheelock, population 621, a town in Caledonia County, was granted by the Vermont legislature in 1785 to John Wheelock and the trustees of Dartmouth College and named for both Wheelock, the college's second president, and ELEAZAR WHEELOCK, its founder and John's father. For some time after the town was settled, the rentals paid by its tenants provided a substantial part of Dartmouth's permanent funds, and to this day a Dartmouth scholarship is available to residents of Wheelock. The eastern part of town is gently rolling and contains the two settlements of Wheelock village (in a prong of territory jutting up between the towns of Sheffield and Lyndon) and South Wheelock. The western part of town is heavily wooded, largely roadless, and culminates in 2,783-foot Wheelock Mountain and its companion Ide Mountain, about 50 feet lower.

Wheelock, Eleazar (1711–1779)

Congregational minister and founder and first president of Dartmouth College,

Eleazar Wheelock was born in Windham, Connecticut. He graduated with distinction from Yale College in 1733 and continued his studies an additional year, when he was licensed to preach and named pastor of the Second Society in Lebanon, Connecticut. During the Great Awakening, although charged with stimulating an excess of fervor, he opposed Separatists. In addition to his ministerial duties, Wheelock prepared white students for college and then took on the task of training Indians who were to return to their tribes as missionaries and teachers. Difficulties with his parishioners, disappointment over the project's progress, and Superintendent of Indian Affairs Sir William Johnson's withdrawal of support led Wheelock to obtain a charter in December 1769 from Governor John Wentworth of New Hampshire for Dartmouth College to be located in that colony. Wheelock fund-raisers had succeeded in raising £12,000 in England, and Wheelock was determined to build Dartmouth into a preparatory school as well as a college. Without the consent of the trustees of the fund or of the earl of Dartmouth, after whom the college had been named without his knowledge, or the governor and others who wanted the college sited elsewhere, Wheelock located it in Hanover. As president of Dartmouth and Moor's Charity School, Wheelock performed all manner of functions, including preaching, teaching, arranging recruiting parties to Canada for Indian students, and raising money. By 1775, the fund raised in England was exhausted and the American Revolution precluded England as a source of further capital. Wheelock's search for additional finances eventually drew him, along with his son-in-law BEZALEEL WOODWARD, into active leadership of the first EAST UNION, joining sixteen New Hampshire CONNECTICUT RIVER towns to Vermont. One of the anticipated advantages of union was that, since Vermont then had no colleges, it would assume financial responsibility for Dartmouth. The first East Union was formally agreed to in June 1778 and then dissolved in February 1779. Eleazar died very shortly thereafter and his son John succeeded him as president of the college.

Whig Party

The American Whigs were a political party formed in the early 1830s in opposition to the administration of President Andrew Jackson and promoted as a challenge to the tyranny of King Andrew. From its inception until after 1852, it functioned as the principal national rival of the DEMOCRATIC PARTY. After that date, it disintegrated under the pressures of sectional discord. It was indisputably Vermont's preeminent political party after 1837 when, having absorbed the ANTI-MASONS, it exercised a virtual monopoly over the state's office holding. For sixteen consecutive years, from 1837 through 1852, Whigs never failed to elect Vermont's governor, although on eight occasions its candidate won a plurality but failed to gain a popular majority and was subsequently elected by a Whig legislature. The multiplicity of political parties made it equally difficult to win a majority in congressional races, yet from 1834 through 1852 Whigs lost only six of forty-five contests for House seats. Except for 1836, when it cast its electoral votes for the Anti-Mason presidential candidate, Vermont supported Whigs through 1852. The party's breakdown in Vermont was apparent soon after the September 1853 state elections. Incumbent Whig Governor ERASTUS FAIRBANKS won the accustomed Whig plurality, but the party—rent by anti-slavery agitation and temperance advocacy—failed to return its accustomed Whig legislative majority. An alliance of Democrats and FREE-SOILERS took this opportunity to organize the legislature and elect Democrat JOHN ROBINSON governor. Anticipating the Whig party's imminent collapse, by March 1854 Whig and Free-Soil party political managers organized a movement for a new party. By July, they had agreed upon a common slate and platform and were calling themselves REPUBLICANS.

White, George (1797–1873)

A native of Cavendish, George White was an engraver, who learned printing and copper-plate engraving in ISAAC EDDY's Weathersfield shop and worked in several Windsor County print shops in the 1810s and early 1820s. In 1826, White took over Eddy's establishment and thereafter eked out a marginal living as printer, engraver, and manufacturer of paint and ink. He published several engraved prints and around 1850 issued small matching wall-maps of Vermont and New Hampshire.

J. Kevin Graffagnino

White, Lavater Sprout (1799–1876)

A shipbuilder for himself and the CHAMPLAIN TRANSPORTATION COMPANY, Lavater White was a steamboat inspector for the U.S. government for twenty-five years. On LAKE CHAMPLAIN, he built the steamboats *General Greene* (1825), *Winooski* (1832), *Burlington* (1838), *Saranac* (1842), *Ethan Allen* (1847), *Boston* (1851), *Adirondack* (1867), and *Vermont* (1871). White was also noted for his steamship models, some of which can be seen at the SHELBURNE MUSEUM. He also built steamships on Lake Ontario. *David Blow*

White, Pliny (1822–1869)

Lawyer, clergyman, and author, Pliny White was born in Springfield. His father died when he was three and he attended local schools until age fifteen, when he clerked in a local store. Studying law under WILLIAM CZAR BRADLEY, he was admitted to the bar in 1843. Restless in the profession, he practiced in a number of communities and edited the *Brattleboro Eagle* and other newspapers. In 1852, he became a clerk for E. & T. FAIRBANKS AND COMPANY and served as secretary of civil and military affairs for Governor ERASTUS FAIRBANKS. Other public offices included representative to and clerk of the Vermont House. In 1859, he was licensed to preach, ordained a minister of the Congregational church, and moved to Coventry, where he spent the rest of his life. He served as chaplain of the state senate and contributed numerous historical and biographical articles to Vermont publications. He died while president of the VERMONT HISTORICAL SOCIETY.

Whitelaw, James (1748–1829)

A native of Old Monkland, Lanarkshire, Scotland, James Whitelaw was Vermont's second surveyor general, succeeding IRA ALLEN in 1787. He came to America in 1773 as agent for the Scots-American Company of Farmers and purchased the southern half of Ryegate for Scottish settlement. An accomplished land surveyor, Whitelaw became deputy surveyor of Vermont in 1783 and, upon succeeding Allen as surveyor general, cleared up much of the confusion over boundaries and property lines that had arisen during Allen's tenure. His Ryegate land office became the main clearinghouse for information on Vermont real estate. In 1796, Whitelaw published a large wall-map of the state that in several revised editions served as the model for Vermont maps into the 1830s. The VERMONT HISTORICAL SOCIETY and Vermont State Archives have substantial collections of his papers and surveys.   *J. Kevin Graffagnino*

White River

The White River, the major river of east-central Vermont, rises in the town of Granville on the eastern flank of the GREEN MOUNTAINS and cuts its way through hilly terrain across Windsor County. It is joined by its Third Branch in the town of Bethel and its Second and First branches in the town of Rochester. A number of small and medium-sized villages line its banks, including Rochester, Stockbridge, Bethel, South Royalton, and Sharon, until it enters the CONNECTICUT RIVER at White River Junction, a major highway and rail transportation center. The total length of the river is approximately 46 miles. The ABENAKI name for the White River is *wasabastegok*, or "clear stream."

White River Junction

See HARTFORD.

Whiting

Whiting, population 380, a town in Addison County, was granted by BENNING WENTWORTH in 1763 and named for the Whiting family, five members of whom were among the grantees. Much of its eastern section, along OTTER CREEK, is taken up by a large swamp that extends into six neighboring towns from Brandon to Middlebury. The rest of the town is devoted to AGRICULTURE and DAIRY FARMING. The single settlement of Whiting village lies on Route 30, which runs through the town from north to south.

Whiting, Enoch B. (1816–1898)

A native of Amherst, Massachusetts, Enoch B. Whiting worked for the *Hampshire Gazette* in Northampton and the Boston *Journal* before moving to St. Albans to join his brother and, in 1837, buying the local paper and founding a weekly, *The Messenger*. At the outbreak of the Civil War in 1861, Whiting established *The Daily Messenger* and a bookbindery and bookstore. In 1873, he purchased the equipment of the defunct Burlington Brush Company and with his son Alfred Catlin Whiting established a business in Burlington that machine-dressed brush fibre for brushmakers under the name of E.B. & A.C. Whiting. Their first factory was on Battery Street at the foot of Cherry Street. In 1891, the firm moved to a large new factory on the northeast corner of Pine and Howard Streets in Burlington. Today the site is occupied by Specialty Filaments, Inc., which produces synthetic filaments for brushes and brooms.

Whitingham

Whitingham, population 1,298, a town in Windham County, derives from a New York patent of 1770 made to Nathan Whiting and others and enlarged by the Vermont legislature several times in later years. Despite its isolated location as one of the tier of hilly, heavily forested towns along the Massachusetts border, Whitingham had a substantial population ranging from fifteen hundred to two thousand in the first half of the nineteenth century. Today, the westernmost quarter of the town lies within the GREEN MOUNTAIN NATIONAL FOREST. The main settlements are Whitingham village and Jacksonville, both on Route 100, which cuts through the town in large arcs. Lake Whitingham, at 2,157 acres the second-largest body of water entirely within Vermont, is formed by Harriman Dam on the Deerfield River and extends into the town of Wilmington to the north. The dam was created as part of a hydroelectric project that remains Whitingham's largest industry and tax base. BRIGHAM YOUNG, the Mormon leader, was born in Whitingham.

Wilbur, James B. (1856–1929)

Born in Cleveland, Ohio, James B. Wilbur was a banker, philanthropist, Vermont historian, and founder of the Wilbur Collection at the UNIVERSITY OF VERMONT. After receiving a public school education, he served as cashier of the New York, New Haven and Hartford Railroad from 1876 to 1882 and spent several years as a rancher and banker in Colorado. In 1891, Wilbur organized the Royal Trust Company of Chicago, serving as its president for the next eighteen years. At his retirement in 1909, he moved to Manchester, where he built a large farm and country estate. Wilbur's considerable interest in early Vermont history resulted in the two-volume biography *Ira Allen: Founder of Vermont* (1928), as well as in the donation of a statue of IRA ALLEN to the University of Vermont and $200,000 to the University to build the Ira Allen Chapel. In addition, he established the Wilbur Trust in 1919 as a gift to UVM, and gave his library and $150,000 to the University to found the Wilbur Collection of Vermontiana, with a further donation to build a wing on the FLEMING MUSEUM to house the collection. Wilbur's generosity to UVM totaled $3 million, the largest single gift in the university's history when adjusted for inflation. UVM's continuing benefit from the Wilbur grant was contingent on limiting enrollment to 1,000 students, a restriction that was lifted by the United States Supreme Court in 1960.

Wilderness Areas

Six areas in the GREEN MOUNTAIN NATIONAL FOREST have been designated Wilderness Areas by the U.S. Congress. Administered by the Forest Service, these areas total 59,421 acres. The northernmost, Bristol Cliffs Wilderness, in Bristol and Lincoln (3,738 acres), designated in 1975, is the smallest of the areas. It takes its name from the cliffs on the rocky western slopes of 2,300-foot South Mountain, from which a vista taking in the Champlain Valley and the Adirondacks is obtained. A bulge of quartzite called Devil's Pulpit dominates the cliff face, which is considered unsafe for climbing. A state program to restore peregrine falcons has been very successful on these cliffs. Bristol Cliffs has no established trails. Breadloaf Wilderness, in Ripton, Hancock, Lincoln, Granville, and Warren (21,480 acres), designated in 1984, is the largest of the areas. Named for 3,823-foot Breadloaf Mountain, it lies directly on the main spine of the GREEN MOUNTAINS and is crossed by the LONG TRAIL. Once heavily logged, the forest has now regenerated and harbors moose and black bear in substantial numbers. The headwaters of the New Haven and WHITE RIVERS offer good brook-trout fishing. Big Branch Wilderness, in Mount Tabor, Peru, and Dorset (6,720 acres), designated in 1984, is part of the White Rocks National Recreation Area. The forest is largely maple, beech, and birch, interspersed with red spruce, balsam fir, and hemlock. Elbow Swamp is a large wetland on the eastern edge of this area. Hunting, trout fishing, and cross-country skiing are allowed. The Long Trail crosses the wilderness for approximately 5 miles. Peru Peak Wilderness, in Peru and Mount Tabor (6,920 acres), designated in 1984, is located in the White Rocks National Recreation Area immediately east of the Big Branch Wilderness. Beaver ponds in the remote northern section offer excellent trout fishing, and hunting opportunities for bear and deer are many. Deep snow cover attracts cross-country skiing enthusiasts. The Long Trail crosses the southern end of the Peru Peak Wilderness, taking in the summits of Peru and Styles Peak. Lye Brook Wilderness, in Manchester, Winhall, Sunderland, and Stratton (15,503 acres), was designated in 1975. The forest is primarily northern hardwoods interspersed with spruce. Lye Brook Falls is a principal feature of the area, as is Prospect Rock, which allows a wide view of the terrain. Fishing, hunting, snow-shoeing, and cross-country skiing are permitted. A long-abandoned railroad bed crosses the wilderness. GEORGE D. AIKEN Wilderness, in Woodford (5,060 acres), designated in 1984, was named after Vermont's U.S. Senator who was a leader in securing the Eastern Wilderness Act of 1975. Situated in the southern Green Mountains on a remote plateau rising as high as 2,300 feet, the terrain is one of ponds, meadows, and forest without trails or maintained roads, and is home to bear, moose, deer, otter, beaver, and other wildlife.

Wildlife Game Species

Populations of Vermont's four major big animals—white-tailed deer, black bear, moose, and wild turkey—reached record high numbers by the year 2000. White-tailed deer were so rare in the early 1900s that animals were trapped in other states and brought into Vermont by railway cars to be released. Today, the population stands at 150 thousand, with the greatest densities in agricultural areas with substantial secondary growth forests and fewer (but larger) deer in mountainous terrain and in the northeastern part of the state. The state manages deer numbers through hunting seasons (on males and females) in order to continue the tradition of deer hunting and to reduce the conflicts—whether on highways or in vegetable gardens—between humans and deer, particularly in the state's growing suburban areas. The moose is Vermont's largest living wild animal, reaching weights up to 1,400 pounds. Prior to the 1970s, they were found only in the NORTH-EAST KINGDOM, but today moose can be found throughout Vermont, with the state herd numbering more than three thousand animals. The surge in the moose herd during the 1970s and 1980s may have been caused by a declining deer population, which likely reduced the chance of moose contracting fatal brain-worm infections from deer. At the same time, forest cutting

increased as landowners harvested maturing timber, resulting in an abundance of browse for moose. The Vermont Fish and Wildlife Department manages moose in Vermont through regulated hunting of cows (females) and bulls (males) in northeast, central, and southern Vermont. Whereas moose are often visible from roadsides, the black bear, one of Vermont's common game animals, manages a rather secretive existence. Bears rarely approach populated areas, unless natural food supplies are low. Then they will be attracted to bird feeders, garbage cans, and beehives, creating a potential danger to people. Natural bear habitat is a mixture of coniferous and hardwood trees, wetlands, and variation in terrain. Vermont's current bear management focuses on four areas: educating the public; protecting critical habitat such as beechnut and acorn stands, forest wetlands, and travel corridors; regulating hunting; and responding to animal damage and public safety concerns. The best chance for seeing one of Vermont's estimated three thousand bears is to spend some quiet time in a remote beechnut stand in September and October. Even then, the observer may have to be satisfied with seeing their telltale claws marks left behind on mature apple, cherry, or beech trees. After a 120-year absence, thirty-one wild turkeys were re-introduced to the state during the winters of 1969 and 1970 in Pawlet and Hubbardton. Today, their numbers fluctuate widely, ranging from twenty to thirty-five thousand, and they range throughout the state. Spring turkey hunting is a popular outdoor pastime. Vermont is home to twelve fur-bearing species: coyote, red fox, gray fox, bobcat, fisher, otter, beaver, raccoon, mink, muskrat, striped skunk, and weasel. All of these species are trapped for their fur in Vermont, and they all are abundant, existing statewide. Major small game animals include ruffed grouse, American woodcock, snowshoe hare, eastern cottontail rabbit, and gray squirrel. The numbers of these species fluctuate in cycles ranging from three to five years for rabbits and hare, to ten-year cycles for grouse. Woodcock numbers continue to decline gradually as the woods grow up. Grouse, rabbits, and woodcock are most abundant in early stages of forest regrowth created from both logging and farmland abandonment. Higher densities of hare are found in young coniferous stands located in the mountains or in northern Vermont.

Gray squirrels depend heavily upon the state's nut-producing trees, such as oak, hickory, and beechnut and are most common in the Champlain Valley. Up to twenty species of waterfowl nest or migrate through Vermont each spring and fall. The most abundant ducks include the mallards, black ducks, wood ducks, green-winged teal, blue-winged teal, goldeneyes, buffleheads, scaups, and mergansers. Canada geese now nest throughout the state. Snow geese, sometimes numbering more than ten thousand, can be seen in October and again in March at the Dead Creek Wildlife Management Area in Addison, where they stop to feed and rest during their biannual migration.

Mark Scott and Will Ryan

Willard, Emma (1787–1870)

Born Emma Hart in Berlin, Connecticut, Emma Willard was self-educated. She became a school teacher in 1803 and was appointed principal of the Female Academy in Middlebury, serving from 1807 to 1809. Willard established a boarding school for girls in Middlebury in 1814. Contrary to the standards of education for women in her time, she offered a curriculum that included mathematics and history, subjects customarily offered only in schools for boys. Her *Plan for Improving Female Education* (1818), which proposed additional innovations, won the approval of New York's Governor DeWitt Clinton, and in 1819 she left Middlebury to open a girls' seminary in Waterford, New York. This was the first school in the United States to offer a college-level education for women. In 1821, she founded the Troy Female Seminary, today's Emma Willard School, in Troy, New York, which she managed until 1838. In later years, Willard traveled extensively, lecturing on public and female education. She wrote several textbooks and a volume of verse, *The Fulfillment of a Promise* (1831), remembered today for the poem "Rocked in the Cradle of the Deep."

Williams, Charles Kilbourn (1782–1853)

A native of Cambridge, Massachusetts, and son of the Reverend SAMUEL WILLIAMS, the historian and a founder of the *RUTLAND HERALD*, Chief Judge of the Vermont Supreme Court Charles K. Williams was considered one of the most eloquent writers ever to serve on the high court. As a young boy, he moved with his family to Rutland in 1790, graduated from Williams

College in 1800 at eighteen, studied law at Middlebury, and was admitted to the bar in 1803. After service in the War of 1812, Williams settled in Middlebury and served as representative in the General Assembly and as state's attorney for Addison County. Williams was first elected to the Vermont Supreme Court in 1822 and 1823, but then served as collector of customs for the next four years, and in 1829 was re-elected to the court. He served until 1846, the last twelve years as chief judge. After one more year in the Vermont House, he was elected governor for two one-year terms (1850–1852). Chief Judge Williams, a forceful and persuasive writer, was a judicial conservative, a viewpoint shown in his unwillingness to question legislation and his respect for the common law. He believed that the court should avoid extremes at all costs. His more than three hundred reported decisions reflect the clarity and forthrightness of his mind.

Paul Gillies

Williams, Jody (b. 1950)

Born in Poultney and now a resident of Putney, Jody Williams received the Nobel Peace Prize in 1997 for her efforts to ban the use of landmines worldwide. An anti–Vietnam War activist in the 1970s, in 1992 she aligned herself with the Vietnam Veterans of America, which was deeply committed to ending the use of landmines. By the mid-1990s, Williams was the international coordinator of the campaign to ban landmines, and for this work she received the Peace Prize.

Williams, Samuel (1743–1817), and Samuel Williams (1756–1800)

Two persons with identical names founded the *RUTLAND HERALD* in December 1794, so it is not surprising to find that over the years many accounts of that newspaper's origins have been confused. Partners in the venture were a clergyman—clearly the more dominant—the Reverend Samuel Williams, and his lawyer friend (and distant cousin) Judge Samuel Williams. Reverend Williams belonged to the American Philosophical Society, was a surveyor, astronomer, weather observer, historian, and writer with a literary bent. In the same year that he launched the *Herald* in Rutland, he also wrote and published the first history of Vermont when the state was only three years old. *The Natural and Civil History of Vermont*, printed at Walpole, New Hampshire, remains remarkable for its substantive and diverse content. A graduate of Harvard, where he held the position of Hollis Professor of Mathematics and Natural Philosophy, Reverend Williams was believed to be a candidate for president of Harvard. Instead, accusations of misusing Harvard funds drove him to Vermont in 1788. One reason for that destination was said to be its status as an independent republic, from which he could not be extradited; another was that Rutland was where his cousin, Judge Williams, owned considerable property and had been residing since 1777. Reverend Williams preached for about seven years at Rutland's East Parish church, though he was never formally installed as pastor. He was instrumental in the establishment of the UNIVERSITY OF VERMONT in 1791, but was never elected to the board of trustees. He gave up the pulpit the Sunday before he launched the weekly *Herald* on December 8, 1794. Judge Samuel Williams was judge of the Rutland County Court from 1790 to 1798, and in 1794 was named official state printer west of the GREEN MOUNTAINS. The partnership of the two Samuel Williamses at the *Herald* did not last long, for they had parted by 1796 when Judge Williams ran a losing race for Congress against MATTHEW LYON. Two years later, the same opponents faced each other but this time Lyon won re-election while serving a four-month term in jail at Vergennes for his violation of the anti-Federalist Alien and Sedition Acts. Judge Williams was killed at age forty-three in a logging accident in the winter of 1800, the same season in which Reverend Williams turned the *Herald* over to WILLIAM FAY, who would run it, on and off, for the next four decades. Reverend Williams also produced a monthly *Rural Magazine* in 1795 and 1796, and in 1799 published *The Vermont Register and Almanac*.

J. Tyler Resch

Williamstown

Williamstown, population 3,225, a town in Orange County, was granted by the Vermont legislature in 1781 and probably named for Williamstown, Massachusetts, the home colony of many of the grantees. Topographically the landscape consists of the valley of the Stevens Branch of the WINOOSKI RIVER running south to north through the center of town, with a range of hills rising to 1,500 feet and more on either side. On the southern border with Brookfield is the narrow defile of Williamstown Gulf, out of which flows the Second Branch of the WHITE RIVER heading southward to join the White and in turn the CONNECTICUT RIVER. Despite its proximity to the city of Barre one town to the north, Williamstown remains predominantly rural. The main village of Williamstown lies on Route 14 in the valley of the Stevens Branch. THOMAS DAVENPORT, the inventor of the first electric motor, who later lived in Brandon, was born in Williamstown.

Willoughby, Lake

Probably Vermont's most dramatic body of water, Lake Willoughby in the town of Westmore stretches its narrow length almost 5 miles from its low-lying northern shore to the narrow defile at its southern end formed by the looming bulks of Mounts Pisgah and Hor, both about 1,600 feet above lake level. With a surface area of 1,653 acres, Willoughby is the fourth-largest lake entirely within the borders of Vermont. Cut by a glacier 12,000 years ago from an already-existing valley, the lake is one of the deepest in New England, with a maximum death of about 310 feet. The rugged nature of the terrain has limited lakeside development largely to the lake's northeastern shore. Anglers value the lake for its rainbow trout, lake trout, brook trout, and landlocked salmon.

Williston

Williston, population 7,650, a town in Chittenden County, was granted by BENNING WENTWORTH in 1763 and named for Samuel Willis, whose name led the list of grantees. The first settler is generally regarded to have been THOMAS CHITTENDEN, later Vermont's first governor, who arrived in 1774 but withdrew for ten years until the conclusion of the Revolution. Ideally situated on a fertile, well-watered plateau rising from the WINOOSKI RIVER, which forms its northern boundary, Williston has prospered as an agricultural community, as the main route between Burlington and points east, and, in recent times, as one of the primary commercial, industrial, and residential sites of the Burlington metropolitan area. Although parts of the town are still rural, especially in the lowlands flanking the Winooski River (where Chittenden had his homestead) and along the eastern and southern borders, the area known as Taft Corners contains more "big box" stores than anywhere else in Vermont, and extensive housing developments have sprouted rapidly in the area north of Interstate 89, which cuts across the town from east to west. The old town center, Williston village, has, however, largely retained its nineteenth-century appearance.

Wilmington

Wilmington, population 2,225, a town in Windham County, was granted by BENNING WENTWORTH in 1751 and named for Spencer Compton (1673–1743), first earl of Wilmington, Wentworth's patron. Located high on the eastern slopes of the main spine of the GREEN MOUNTAINS, the town was relatively isolated for most of its history. Today it is part of the extensive ski and resort area that extends from Wilmington village, at the junction of Routes 100 and 9 (the Molly Stark Trail) in the center of town, to the Mount Snow complex in Dover to the north. Lake Whitingham, at 2,157 acres the second-largest body of water entirely within Vermont, extends into the southern part of Wilmington from Harriman Dam on the Deerfield River in nearby Whitingham.

Wilson, James (1763–1855)

A pioneer American globe maker, James Wilson, a farmer and blacksmith with little formal education, was born in Londonderry, New Hampshire, and moved to Bradford in 1796. He developed his interest in geography, astronomy, engraving, and cartography by reading the *Encyclopaedia Britannica*. In 1810, he sold his first "New Terrestrial Globe" and subsequently became the first American to market terrestrial and celestial globes on a commercial basis. In 1817, Wilson's sons opened a second factory in Albany, New York, while he remained in charge of the Bradford shop, where in his eighties he expanded production into model planetariums. His globes were first displayed at the Library of Congress in 1827 and can be seen today at the Bradford Historical Society building in Bradford and in the VERMONT HISTORICAL SOCIETY's exhibits in Montpelier.

J. Kevin Graffagnino

Wilson, William Griffith (1895–1971)

Co-founder of Alcoholics Anonymous with ROBERT SMITH, another Vermont native, William Griffith Wilson was born in East Dorset. His parents divorced when he was eleven. He attended Burr and Burton Academy in Manchester and there fell in love with Bertha Bamford, whose unexpected death in 1912 at the age of eighteen propelled Wilson into a deep depression. He attended NORWICH UNIVERSITY. In 1918, he married Lois Burnham, and served in France in the dwindling days of World War I. By this time, he had begun to seek solace in drinking. His alcoholism progressed for many years, eventually affecting his career as a stock analyst on Wall Street. Through a childhood friend, Wilson was exposed to the principles of the Oxford Group, a religious fellowship that had begun to develop a program for working with alcoholics. Drawing on their precepts, he was able to stop drinking. Through members of the group, he met and assisted in the recovery of Dr. Robert Smith, a fellow Vermonter who came to be known in the movement as Dr. Bob. The two collaborated in the development of a program specifically designed to help alcoholics achieve sobriety. After forming successful groups in Akron, Cleveland, and New York City, Smith and Wilson coauthored *Alcoholics Anonymous,* commonly referred to as the "Big Book," which was published in April of 1939 and outlined the twelve steps of recovery. Wilson, known anonymously as Bill W., continued to oversee the growth and development of Alcoholics Anonymous until his death on January 24, 1971. His birthplace, the Wilson House in East Dorset, functions as a hotel and site for local Alcoholics Anonymous meetings.

Selene Colburn

Winans, John (1766–1829), and James Winans (1768–1830)

The first steamboat on LAKE CHAMPLAIN was built and operated by John and James Winans. After building the hull for Robert Fulton's steamboat *Clermont* at their shipyard in Poughkeepsie, New York, in 1807, and drawing on James's knowledge of the Champlain Valley from his work there as a government surveyor, the Winans developed a plan to apply steam power to transportation between New York City and Canada. In 1808, they came to Burlington to organize a company with Joseph Lough to finance a shipyard at the southwest corner of Battery and King Streets. The brothers built the *Vermont I* and launched her in June 1809, making her the second successful steamboat in the world. At 120 feet long, 20 feet wide, and 167 tons burden, the *Vermont* was considerably larger than the *Clermont*. She had a 20-horsepower engine and cost $20,000 to construct. The *Vermont*'s conformation was similar to the canal boats of the day except for her sidewheels. In June 1809, she began regular trips from Burlington to Whitehall and St. Johns, Quebec, with HIRAM FERRIS as pilot, until the latter stage of her route was interrupted by the War of 1812. The boat carried both passengers and freight. During the War of 1812, the *Vermont* was used as a transport for troops and supplies serving the American fleet. After the peace, she started again on her regular route. The *Vermont*'s short career ended on October 15, 1815, when an accident in her steamroom caused her to sink in the Richelieu River near Ash Island, south of Ile aux Noix. The owners removed the engine and boiler and sold them to the Lake Champlain Steamboat Company. John Winans was an incorporator of the Lake George Steamboat Company in 1817 and was also master of the *James Caldwell*, that lake's first steamboat. John lived several years in Ticonderoga, New York, but returned to Poughkeepsie where he died. James resettled at Basin Harbor in Ferrisburgh, where he died a year after his brother.

David Blow

Windham

Windham, population 328, a town in Windham County, was originally part of Londonderry but was separated from it by the Vermont legislature in 1795. The name most likely derives from the county name although, by curious coincidence, the town of Windham, New Hampshire, had been similarly separated from the town of Londonderry in that state in 1742. One of the highest occupied towns in the state— Windham village, the main settlement, lies at an altitude of 2,000 feet—its highest point is 2,940-foot Glebe Mountain, on the border with Londonderry to the west. Logging and the mining of talc, asbestos, and a species of MARBLE known as verde antique have been economically important to the town at various times.

Windsor

Windsor, population 3,756, a town in Windsor County, was granted by BENNING WENTWORTH in 1761 and originally included what later became the town of West Windsor. The origin of the name is presumably Windsor in Connecticut, the home colony of some of the grantees. The town rises from the lowlands along the CONNECTICUT RIVER into a gently rolling landscape dominated by 3,144-foot Mount Ascutney, an imposing monadnock

Old Constitution House, Windsor. Vermont Department of Tourism and Marketing

The Robbins and Lawrence Machine Shop and Armory, Windsor, circa 1851. Special Collections, Bailey/Howe Library, University of Vermont

along the southern border that extends into the neighboring towns of Weathersfield and West Windsor. On its slopes is the Ascutney Mountain ski resort, which has forty-nine trails, four lifts, and a vertical drop of 1,530 feet. The substantial village of Windsor has a number of claims to fame. Here, in a tavern on July 8, 1777, was adopted the constitution of the "Free and Independent State of Vermont," the sovereignty of which had been declared the previous January in Westminster. The tavern, now known as the OLD CONSTITUTION HOUSE and moved from its original location, is a State Historic Site and features period rooms and an interpretation center. Windsor is also the site of the American Precision Museum, a National Historic Landmark housed in the 1846 Robbins and Lawrence Armory. Like nearby Springfield, Windsor was a center of the MACHINE-TOOL INDUSTRY in the mid-nineteenth century. Here were developed, among other inventions, the breech-loading rifle, the band saw, glaziers' points, the first use of interchangeable parts (known as the "American System"), and many other techniques vital to the expansion of the Industrial Revolution. A less inviting institution that had its home in the town was the WINDSOR PRISON, which was built in 1809 and closed in 1975; the last execution in Vermont occurred in it in 1952. Two other noteworthy sites are the Vermont State Craft Center at the 1840 Windsor House, which exhibits and sells the work of artists and craftspeople, and the 1866 Windsor-Cornish (New Hampshire) COVERED BRIDGE over the CONNECTICUT RIVER, at 460 feet the longest covered bridge in the United States.

Windsor Prison

From 1809 until it was closed in 1975 as the oldest state prison in continuous operation, Windsor prison served as Vermont's maximum-security prison and from 1921 until 1975 doubled as a house of correction. Originally built with stone quarried from nearby Mount Ascutney, it had walls 3 feet thick and 14 feet high topped with implanted iron spikes. The structure contained thirty-five cells on three floors. Enlarged in 1830, 1882, and 1928, it grew into a compound of several buildings with 352 cells averaging 3 feet by 7 feet in length and width and 6½ feet in height. Windsor townspeople accommodated themselves to the prison's presence; there was a school playground adjoining the prison millyard and the athletic teams from Windsor High School were often referred to as the Prisontowners. In 1936, penologists concluded that with some additions Windsor prison could be made into one of the most effective institutions in the country, but by 1944 they were recommending that Vermont build an entirely new maximum-security institution. A 1954 legislative committee concluded that "the physical facilities make it difficult and at times impossible to operate a good institution." By the mid-1960s, conditions had deteriorated to the point where many regarded them as intolerable and, in 1970, the legislature voted funds for a new prison, but contract bids were all in excess of the amount appropriated. By then, Windsor prison was a physical anachronism, and the dominant correctional philosophy promoted the view that traditional prisons failed to rehabilitate and instead promoted recidivism. The state responded by creating a medium-security youthful offender facility and regional correctional centers under the umbrella of the corrections department that would determine appropriate rehabilitation programs for those imprisoned. By November 1974, it had been decided to close Windsor prison at an estimated savings of $1,500,000 annually and $1,000,000 in repairs over the next five years. From December 1974 to June 1975, the corrections department distributed the prison population to community correctional centers and the youthful offender facility. Maximum-security prisoners were transferred out-of-state to the custody of the Federal Bureau of Prisons. On August 7, the formal closing of Windsor prison was marked by ceremonies celebrating "going on a different and better approach to corrections."

Wing, Leonard (1893–1945)

Born in Ira, Leonard Wing graduated from Rutland High School and in the same year began reading law in the office of Lawrence, Lawrence and Stafford of Rutland. He passed the bar exam after he enlisted in the army for World War I service in May 1917. Discharged from the regular army as a first lieutenant in 1918, he established a law practice in Rutland and joined the Vermont National Guard. He served as Rutland city attorney (1919–1921) and city judge (1921–1925). By 1933, he was commander of the 172nd Infantry Regiment of the Vermont National Guard. Five years later, he commanded a regional brigade as

a brigadier general. At the outbreak of World War II, this brigade became part of the Forty-third Infantry Division and Wing received an appointment as its assistant commander. The division saw action at Guadalcanal and on other Pacific islands. At New Georgia in October 1943, he was promoted to major general and assumed division command. The Forty-third participated in the New Guinea campaign and landed at Luzon at the opening of the Philippine invasion, where the division fought in several major engagements. After Japan's capitulation, the Forty-third Division served in the occupation army before returning to the United States. During his World War II service, Wing was awarded the Bronze Star, Silver Star, Legion of Merit, and Distinguished Service Medal. He was the only National Guard officer to reach divisional command in World War II.   *Donald Wickman*

Winhall

Winhall, population 702, a town in Bennington County, was granted by BENNING WENTWORTH in 1761. The origin of the name is not known. The town lies directly on the spine of the GREEN MOUNTAINS, resulting in two widely separated areas of settlement, in the VALLEY OF VERMONT in the town's extreme northwestern section and along the headwaters of the Winhall River (which flows into the WEST RIVER) in the eastern section. Only one road, Route 30, connects the two sections. Most of the town lies in the GREEN MOUNTAIN NATIONAL FOREST. Historically a lumbering town, Winhall today has an economic base derived from the Stratton Mountain ski area, which it shares with the town of Stratton to the south.

Winooski

Winooski, population 6,561, a city in Chittenden County, is located on the north bank of the river of the same name across from the city of Burlington. While the city supports a number of small businesses, a thriving industrial park, several large nineteenth-century mills converted into apartment complexes, and a retail mall, it is principally a residential community, most of its inhabitants travelling elsewhere in the county for work. The site of the present-day city at the head of navigation at the river's last falls eight miles upstream from LAKE CHAMPLAIN drew Native American foragers and travelers here as early as five thousand years ago,

and recent archeological discoveries indicate aboriginal settlements at least as early as 600 A.D. An ABENAKI word, *WINOOSKIK* means "onion place." IRA ALLEN was the first colonial American to recognize the importance of the falls while exploring the area in 1772. He convinced his family to form a development company—the ONION RIVER LAND COMPANY—and bought up almost all the land in the lower Winooski Valley, including the uninhabited township of Colchester in which the falls were located. Subsequently, Allen built FORT FREDERICK, a stockade fort, his home, an iron forge and a sawmill at the falls. Until his financial problems forced Allen to leave Vermont in 1803, his place at the falls was often referred to as "the Allen Settlement." In the SHEEP BOOM of the 1830s, a group of Burlington entrepreneurs built a large textile mill at Winooski Falls, beginning a tradition of textile manufacturing at the site that lasted down to the 1950s. An important industrial center in an agricultural state in the nineteenth century, Winooski as early as the 1840s attracted numerous immigrants from Ireland, followed by waves of French-Canadians beginning in the 1850s, and by the end of the century also Italians, Armenians, Lebanese, and Poles. By 1900, however, French-Canadians were by far the largest single ethnic group in the community, and came to dominate its political and cultural life. In 1866, Winooski was chartered as a village in Colchester town, a change that recognized that Winooski's urban interests did not coincide with those of the agricultural township. Finally, in 1922, the industrial settlement at the falls was chartered by the state as the city of Winooski. During the First and Second World Wars, Winooski's textile mills prospered, but were forced to close down in 1954 when American textile businesses moved to the South to take advantage of inexpensive labor, sending the city into a period of economic decline. In 1967, however, Winooski was named a Model City by the U.S. Department of Housing and Urban Development, after which much of its deteriorating downtown was razed and it reinvented itself as a centrally located residential community.   *Vince Feeney*

Winooski River

The Winooski River, the third-longest river in Vermont, has its headwaters in the streams feeding into Molly's Falls Pond in the town of Cabot. It joins its two main tributaries, the North Branch and the Stevens Branch, in Montpelier, after which it breaks through the great barrier of the GREEN MOUNTAINS in the town of Bolton and winds its way westward through the heart of Chittenden County. Three major falls, at Bolton, Essex Junction, and Burlington/Winooski, provide electric power, after which the river enters a broad intervale and eventually reaches LAKE CHAMPLAIN after a total journey of 88 miles. The river's valley has historically been the main route through the Green Mountains, but it has also been the scene of terrible natural disasters, especially the FLOOD OF 1927 and, on a smaller scale, the inundation of Montpelier in 1992. The name derives from the ABENAKI word *WINOOSKIK* or "onion place," and the river was known in the earliest days of settlement as Onion River.

Winooski Valley Park District

Created in 1972, the Winooski Valley Park District has as its mission to preserve and clean up the WINOOSKI RIVER in its lower reaches and to promote regional conservation and recreational parkland along its banks. The district, a regional municipal corporation, is supported by Burlington, South Burlington, Colchester, Winooski, Essex, Jericho, and Williston. The first regional park district in Vermont, it is now steward of 1,722 acres with 15 miles of developed trails and 11.4 miles of river shoreline. It provides a string of parks along the Winooski River's winding path to LAKE CHAMPLAIN, including the historic ETHAN ALLEN HOMESTEAD.

David Blow

Winooskik

An ABENAKI term meaning "onion place," Winooskik was an important Abenaki fishing station and village, comparable to their settlement at Missisquoi. The falls of the WINOOSKI RIVER and the celebrated "Salmon Hole" immediately downstream from the falls provided easy access to a substantial fish supply. In the spring, fish could be speared or trapped in large numbers, then dried for later storage and use. This abundant resource attracted large numbers of people to settle in the area and then use the fertile floodplain of the river for AGRICULTURE. In time, villages sprang up, the latest of which was historically known as Winooskik. According to linguist-ethnohistorian GORDON DAY, in early historic times Winooskik had a cos-

mopolitan population of local people and even people from what is now New Hampshire and elsewhere. Settlement pressure in and around Burlington in the late eighteenth and early nineteenth centuries led to the abandonment of Winooskik as a coherent village center and the villagers dispersed. As late as the early twentieth century, there was a distinctive persistent Abenaki community in the Burlington intervale. Subsequently, as settlement in the intervale was restricted and then not permitted, the community dispersed into the multi-ethnic community of Winooski and the "Old North End" of Burlington.

Frederick Wiseman

Wolcott

Wolcott, population 1,456, a town in Lamoille County, was granted by the Vermont legislature in 1781 to a group of Connecticut Revolutionary War veterans including General Oliver Wolcott, who had been an advisor to Vermont's founders at the earliest period. The town's gently rolling countryside reaches its highest point at 1,832-foot Jeudevine Mountain on the border with Hardwick. The village of Wolcott is on Route 15 as it follows the course of the LAMOILLE RIVER, which bisects the town from east to west. One of Vermont's two COVERED railroad BRIDGES (the other is in Shoreham), a State Historic Site, is two miles to the east of the village.

Woman Bishop

At a special convention in Burlington on June 5, 1993, Vermont Episcopalians chose Reverend Mary Adelia R. McLeod of West Virginia as their new bishop. The rules of the diocese require that a majority of both clergy and laity, voting separately, elect the same person on the same ballot; Reverend McLeod was chosen on the third ballot. She is the first woman in the country to become a diocesan bishop, and the second in the world. She was installed 1993, and retired in 2001.

John C. Wriston, Jr.

Women's Christian Temperance Union

In the pre–Civil War years, large numbers of Vermont women were attracted to the temperance crusade. But the idea of exclusively female temperance organizations did not take hold until a crusade to close down saloons in Ohio led to the formation of the Women's Christian Temperance Union (WCTU) in 1873. The following February, a Vermont WCTU was organized as

an auxiliary to the national union. The WCTU held that intemperance, the excessive drinking of alcohol, was responsible for many of society's ills. Vermont members accused immigrants from Canada and Ireland as particularly guilty of intemperance. By encouraging these newcomers to lead temperate lives, the WCTU hoped to eliminate poverty, crime, and other social evils. The Vermont Union's major contribution to the national WCTU's program was the inauguration of "county institutes." These regional conventions of temperance women aimed at developing effective field-work skills. Prominent WCTU workers from both inside and outside the state participated in these meetings, exposing rural women to a range of female talent and experience. When, in 1876, Frances Willard, the national WCTU president, came out in favor of WOMEN'S SUFFRAGE, the Vermont WCTU was sharply divided over the issue. But members did work together to petition the Vermont legislature for school suffrage. A law allowing tax-paying women to vote in school meetings was passed in 1880. Lobbying efforts by Vermont WCTU members also led to the enactment in 1882 of the first temperance education law in the country. Within a decade, similar measures requiring public schools to teach physiology and hygiene had been adopted nationwide. By the late 1880s, Vermont WCTU avoided political questions and returned to single-issue temperance reform. The state union continued to attract a sizeable membership well into the twentieth century, emphasizing gospel temperance (prayer and moral suasion) to achieve its goal.

Deborah P. Clifford

Women's Suffrage

The first Vermonter to publicly advocate woman suffrage was CLARINA HOWARD NICHOLS, a native of Townshend and editor of the *Windham County Democrat*. In 1852, she submitted a petition to the Vermont legislature asking for the right of women to vote in school district elections. In support of that petition, she became the first woman ever to address the legislature. Although the lawmakers extolled her speech, her appeal was denied. In 1870, the COUNCIL OF CENSORS submitted a woman suffrage amendment to the Vermont Constitution to a constitutional convention. In support of this effort, the Vermont Woman Suffrage Association (VWSA) was organized and representatives of the American Woman Suffrage Association (AWSA) — the moderate wing of the national movement—attended a convention in Montpelier in February 1870. Despite these pro-suffrage efforts, the consitutional convention voted the amendment down 233 to 1. During the 1870s, various suffrage measures were brought before the legislature. Then, in 1880, with the help of the Vermont Women's Christian Temperance Union (WCTU), tax-paying women obtained the right to vote and hold office in school districts. Encouraged by the passage of the school suffrage measure, AWSA renewed its efforts in support of further suffrage legislation in Vermont. VWSA was reorganized in 1884 with a progressive member of the WCTU as its president. The focus again was on partial suffrage, giving women the right to vote in municipal elections. For the next thirty-three years, VWSA saw to it that at least one suffrage bill was introduced at each session of the legislature. Finally, in 1917, the lawmakers passed a municipal suffrage measure, making Vermont the first New England state to give women more than school suffrage. Anti-suffrage sentiment was still strong in 1919, however, when Governor PERCIVAL CLEMENT refused to sign a presidential suffrage bill, claiming that it was unconstitutional. A year later, he also refused to call a special session of the legislature to ratify the Nineteenth Amendment to the U.S. Constitution giving women full voting rights. Vermont ceded to other states the final ratification of a woman's right to vote.

Deborah P. Clifford

Wood, Thomas Waterman (1823–1903)

A portrait and genre painter, Thomas Waterman Wood was inspired to paint by a travelling artist who visited Wood's home town, Montpelier. Following self-study and instruction in Boston, he spent two decades painting portraits in Washington, D.C., Baltimore, Quebec City, Nashville, Tennessee, and Louisville, Kentucky. He also spent two years in Europe studying art and copying old masters. In 1866, he set up a studio in New York City, gradually turning to genre painting depicting nineteenth-century everyday life. Wood gained attention in 1867 when he exhibited his paintings of freed slaves, a subject he returned to several times. He was honored by his fellow artists, who elected him president of the American

Water Color Society (1878) and of the National Academy of Design (1891). Wood died in New York in 1903. The T. W. WOOD GALLERY & ART CENTER in Montpelier, founded by the artist, houses a large collection of his oils and watercolors, many of which show local scenes and townspeople. His summer home, Athenwood, a picturesque Gothic cottage and city landmark, was originally built as a home for Wood and his bride, Minerva Robinson of Waterbury.

Reidun Nuquist

Woodbury

Woodbury, population 809, a town in Washington County, was granted by the Vermont legislature in 1781. The name may derive from Woodbury, Connecticut, or from Colonel Ebenezer Wood, who was the second-named of the grantees. The two small settlements of Woodbury village and South Woodbury are both on Route 14, which crosses the town from north to south. The landscape is rugged and dotted with more lakes than any other town in Vermont—twenty-three in all. Woodbury Mountain, which spreads its elongated shape along the town's western border, rises to a height of 2,483 feet. For many years, in the late nineteenth and early twentieth centuries, it was the source of superior building granite, which was transported to the neighboring town of Hardwick and worked in the mills there for shipment all over the world. Quarrying continues today on a smaller scale.

The village of South Woodbury. Vermont Department of Tourism and Marketing)

Woodbury College

Located in Montpelier, Woodbury College provides career-focused education for adults. The average student age is thirty-five, and eight out of ten students work while taking classes. Seventy-five percent of the 150 enrollees are women. There are fourteen core faculty and fifty teaching faculty. Programs offered by Woodbury include paralegal studies, mediation and conflict management, prevention and community development, and essential career skills. Each program includes individual mentoring and internships in law offices, courts, state agencies, and community organizations.

Woodchuck

Two species of woodchuck are native to Vermont. The first, *Marmota monax*, is a small burrowing rodent with coarse red-brown fur. Its burrows are commonly found in meadows and farm fields. Also known as the groundhog, the woodchuck can be found throughout much of North America. Although it is sometimes considered a pest and has been the prey for generations of casual teenage hunters, the woodchuck is a harmless creature that feeds on grass and the occasional garden vegetable, hibernating in its burrow through the winter. The second species, *Homo vermontis*, like its distant cousin *M. monax*, often inhabits otherwise abandoned farmsteads, typically those littered with derelict automobiles and appliances, but has been spotted in such exotic locations as the VERMONT STATE HOUSE. *H. vermontis* is capable of bipedal locomotion but usually moves about in an old pickup truck. This endangered species of woodchuck—not found anywhere outside of the state—will eat anything *M. monax* eats, but is fond of beer, chips, and deer meat, and has been known to eat *M. monax* itself. Some consider *H. vermontis* a pest, but those who get to know the species usually find them harmless and indeed charming denizens of the Green Mountain State.

Jeffrey D. Marshall

Woodford

A town in Bennington County, Woodford, population 414, was granted by BENNING WENTWORTH in 1762 and probably named for Woodford in England. The town lies directly on the spine of the GREEN MOUNTAINS, rising to 2,857 feet at Bald Mountain in its extreme northwestern corner. It is crossed from east to west by Route 9 (the Molly Stark Trail), one of only three roads (one closed in winter) crossing the Green Mountains in southern Vermont. Settlement has always been sparse (there is no true village) and lumbering has historically been the main economic activity. Woodford lies in the GREEN MOUNTAIN NATIONAL FOREST, which includes the George D. Aiken Wilderness in the town's southeastern corner.

Woodruff, Caroline (1866–1949)

A native of West Burke, Caroline Woodruff attended ST. JOHNSBURY ACADEMY and graduated from Johnson Normal School. She first taught in the Little Red Schoolhouse on the east side of Stannard Mountain in Wheelock, and later for many years was a teacher and principal of the Union School in St. Johnsbury. Meanwhile, she studied in summer courses at the UNIVERSITY OF VERMONT, MIDDLEBURY COLLEGE, and Teachers College of Columbia University. Between 1914 and 1921, she consecutively served as a training teacher for the State Department of Education, superintendent of schools for Essex County, and principal of the junior high school at the Johnson Normal School. In 1920 to 1921, she earned a master's degree at Columbia Teachers College and was named principal of Castleton Normal School, a position she held until her retirement at the age of seventy-five in 1941. In 1909, Caroline Woodruff was instrumental in convincing the legislature to establish the Vermont State Retirement Fund for Teachers. She was also a leader in the efforts to establish the McConnell Home for Retired Teachers in 1926, thus making Vermont the first state to have such an institution. She served on the board of managers of the Teachers Retirement Fund and was the first woman elected to serve as the president of the Vermont Teachers Association in 1915. She was vice president of the Vermont chapter of the National Education Association in 1928 to 1929 and president in 1937. In 1925, Middlebury College awarded her an honorary Master of Arts degree for "conspicuous service in the cause of public education." She was also the first woman to be awarded an honorary degree by NORWICH UNIVERSITY.

Donald Wickman

Woodstock

Woodstock, population 3,232, the SHIRE TOWN of Windsor County, was granted by BENNING WENTWORTH in 1761 and most likely derives its name from Woodstock, Connecticut. Situated in hilly country cut from southwest to northeast by the Ottauquechee River, it has several small settlements (West Woodstock, South Woodstock, and Taftsville) and the major village of Woodstock, a historic locale noted for its elegant and harmonious character. Substantial nineteenth-century houses, public buildings, craft shops, and the Colonial-style Woodstock Inn surround the elongated green under the wooded slopes of Mount Tom and Mount Peg. The early gristmills and sawmills that developed around a dam on the Ottauquechee gave way to a later era of prosperity as an educated elite of lawyers, doctors, bankers, and merchants who were attracted by Woodstock's status as a shire town served the needs of the surrounding region. Woodstock was an early publishing center and had a medical school from 1827 to 1856. Summer visitors began arriving in the 1890s with the development of mineral springs, and by the 1930s Woodstock was also a locus of early skiing. The first rope tow in the United States, powered by an old Model T Ford engine, began operating on Mount Tom in 1934. A determined effort to retain Woodstock village's character has led to its current reputation as one of the most historically authentic of Vermont's small population centers. The town's two most famous native sons were GEORGE PERKINS MARSH, the diplomat and conservationist, and HIRAM POWERS, the internationally renowned sculptor. Marsh's family home was purchased in 1869 and rebuilt by railroad magnate FREDERICK BILLINGS, who developed the property as a model dairy farm based on the most advanced scientific principles. The farm is maintained today as the BILLINGS FARM & MUSEUM and is open daily to visitors. The Billings house and grounds were later owned by MARY ROCKEFELLER (Billings' granddaughter) and her husband, LAURANCE, who were active in the preservation of Woodstock village and eventually donated the Billings property to the National Park Service, which maintains it as the MARSH-BILLINGS-ROCKEFELLER NATIONAL HISTORIC PARK devoted to conservation. A mile and a half south of the village is the VERMONT INSTITUTE OF NATURAL SCIENCE, which has exhibits of local flora and fauna, nature trails, and a raptor center.

Woodward, Bezaleel (d. 1804)

A member of the Yale class of 1764, Bezaleel Woodward was professor of mathematics and natural philosophy at Dartmouth College and son-in-law of ELEAZAR WHEELOCK, the college's president. An active promoter of the union of New Hampshire towns with Vermont in both 1778 and 1781, he served as clerk of the Vermont House of Representatives, represented Dresden (the section of Hanover, New Hampshire, where Dartmouth College was located) in the Vermont House, and was secretary pro tempore of the governor's council during the EAST UNION and in 1781 was elected by the General Assembly to join JONAS FAY and IRA ALLEN as agents to the Continental Congress to negotiate Vermont's joining the Union and, if successful, to take seats in Congress.

Worcester

Worcester, population 902, a town in Washington County, was granted by BENNING WENTWORTH in 1763 and presumably named for Worcester, Massachusetts. The landscape is rugged and hilly, dominated in the western section by the elongated Worcester Mountains, which lie in the C. C. Putnam State Forest and rise to a height of 3,539 feet at Mount Hunger, effectively preventing a road connection with the neighboring town of Stowe. The population lives in single-family homes along Route 12, which follows the North Branch of the WINOOSKI RIVER as it cuts across the town from north to south, or on side roads that branch off on either side.

World Learning

One of the first international educational exchange organizations in the United States, World Learning in Brattleboro, formerly known as the Experiment in International Living, was founded in 1932 by Donald and Leslie Watt in Syracuse, New York. The Watts's goal was to promote international and intercultural understanding through citizen exchange programs, primarily by homestay experiences. The Experiment operated in Putney from 1937 to 1962, when its new training program for Peace Corps volunteers led to the purchase of the 233-acre farm in Brattleboro where English author RUDYARD KIPLING had lived in the mid-1890s and written many of his Jungle Book stories and the novel *Captains Courageous*. The Experiment's work as the charter training institution for the Peace Corps helped launch the School for International Training (SIT) in 1964, which offers master's degrees in teaching and several aspects of international and intercultural relations. A national leader in academic study abroad, with fifty-seven programs in more than forty countries, the school's total enrollment in all programs at fall 2000 was 1,236 students. It has awarded undergraduate credits to twenty thousand students from over two hundred colleges and universities in the United States. Nobel Peace Prize winner JODY WILLIAMS is one of the school's four thousand graduates. The Experiment in International Living, World Learning's original program, carries on the Watts's tradition of international student exchanges with forty-one summer abroad programs for high school students located in twenty-three countries. Over fifty thousand students have been enrolled in this program since its inception. World Learning also provides language and intercultural training for global companies such as Exxon and Procter & Gamble. The Projects in International Development and Training division of World Learning, based in Washington, D.C., administers social and economic projects worldwide under U.S. government and international contracts and grants.

Wright, Ralph (b.1935)
Armed with a flair for camaraderie and a super-sincere manner accented with the intonations of an old-fashioned Boston politician, Ralph G. Wright dominated politics in Montpelier for much of the final decade he served as a representative from Bennington. A teacher at Mt. Anthony Union High School, his first elective office was as a selectman in 1965 to 1966, representing his home village, North Bennington. A Democrat, Wright was first elected to the Vermont House in 1978 and served eight consecutive terms, serving as minority leader in 1983. He was chosen Speaker in 1985 when the Democrats organized the house, though the Republicans had a five-member majority, and he held that position through the 1994 session. His political priorities focused heavily on improvements in education and social services. Wright was born in Arlington, Massachusetts, where he graduated from local schools, and served in the U.S. Marine Corps for two years. He received a bachelor's degree from Boston University in 1961 and a master's in education from Massachusetts State College at Framingham (now Framingham State College) in 1963. At Mt. Anthony Union High School, he became well known for his vigorous Bennington Program, designed to boost

skills and self-esteem for youths who seemed headed on a pre-delinquent course. For several summers, the program was known for its character-building hikes the length of Vermont's LONG TRAIL.   *J. Tyler Resch*

Wriston, Hildreth Tyler (1899–1969)
Born in Enosburg Falls, where her father was editor of the *Enosburg Standard*, Hildreth Tyler Wriston graduated from Enosburg High School in 1917 and from the UNIVERSITY OF VERMONT in 1921. She wrote ten children's books, which were published by well-known New York publishing houses. Best known were three Junior Literary Guild selections: *Camping Down at Highgate* (1939), *Open Water* (1942), and *Susan's Secret* (1957). Thorough and accurate research are earmarks of her work, which remain a good source for young students of Vermont history. Several of her articles appeared in popular magazines, including *VERMONT LIFE*. Hildreth and her husband John C. Wriston managed or owned hotels and inns in Vermont, Maryland, and Florida for forty years, the last eight as owners of the Tavern in Grafton. Special Collections in the Bailey-Howe Library at UVM contains a collection of her correspondence and personal papers.

Yankee Division

Mobilized during World War I in line with army reorganization plans for larger combat units, the Yankee Division was formed out of National Guard troops from throughout New England and formally designated the Twenty-sixth Division. Twenty-seven officers and over seventeen hundred enlisted men were transferred from the First Vermont Regiment. The Yankee Division was transported to France and underwent training in trench warfare while stationed at Neufchâteau. Early in February 1918, it was sent to the front at Chemin des Dames, a "quiet sector," where the soldiers received their baptism of fire. Subsequent engagements were at Toul, Château Thierry, St. Mihiel, and the Meuse-Argonne. Four and one-half months after Armistice Day, March 29, 1919, troops began boarding homebound ships and were accorded tumultuous stateside welcomes. A review at Fort Devens reportedly attracted three hundred thousand viewers and a parade through Boston an even larger number. Although Vermonters fought in every combat division of the United States Army, more served in or were wounded and killed in action in the Yankee Division than in any other unit.

Young, Ammi Burnham (1798–1874)

Born in Lebanon, New Hampshire, Ammi Burnham Young was the architect of the second VERMONT STATE HOUSE (constructed 1830 to 1836), which was destroyed by fire in 1857. Prior to his work on the state house, Young had designed Dartmouth College's Thornton and Wentworth Halls (1828 to 1829). He designed several churches in Vermont (Norwich, 1817) and New Hampshire (Lebanon, 1828) that obviously relied on the copy books of ASHER BENJAMIN, the first Kimball Union Academy in Meriden, New Hampshire (1824–1825), St. Paul's Episcopal church, and the United States Bank in Burlington (1830). The TIMOTHY FOLLETT and John Wheeler houses in Burlington were also Young designs. The red-brick city hall of Winooski was originally designed by Young as the Winooski Congregational church (1837–1838). He designed railroad depots at Burlington and Bellows Falls for the Burlington and Rutland Railroad in 1849. He served as supervising architect of the U.S. Treasury Department in Washington from 1850 to 1862 and designed several additional buildings in Vermont in the classic-revival style, including the Customs House and Marine Hospital at Burlington. His federal court house in Rutland is now the Rutland Public Library. All of his works are variants of the Greek Revival, with some Italianate detailing. He also employed cast-iron construction, employing cast-iron columns for vertical internal supports and cast-iron beams for floor supports. Most of his work for the federal government outside Vermont is gone, but designs by Young can still be seen in Vermont and along the coast of Maine in former government and domestic residential buildings.

Young, Brigham (1801–1877)

Successor to JOSEPH SMITH as leader of the Church of Jesus Christ of Latter-Day Saints, Brigham Young, the ninth of eleven children, was born in Whitingham, seventy miles south of Smith's birthplace in Sharon. Belonging to the same impoverished frontier class as Smith, Young's family resettled in western New York's "burnt-over district." In 1832, after studying the Book of Mormon, Young converted from Methodism and quickly climbed to the top ranks of Mormon leadership. After Smith's murder in Carthage, Illinois, Young rallied the church membership and organized and led the migration to Utah, then under Mexican jurisdiction. His vigorous promotion of economic and social policies enriched and strengthened the Mormon community. Appointed territorial governor under United States jurisdiction, he was displaced only to continue in authority with his successors serving as figureheads. Young reportedly had as many as twenty-seven wives and fifty-six children.

Young Turks

The Young Turks were an informal bipartisan association of freshman members of the Vermont House who exercised influence disproportionate to their numbers during the 1961 to 1962 sessions. Perceived as particularly articulate and progressive, the Young Turk roster included FRANKLIN BILLINGS, JR. (R), PHILIP HOFF (D), RICHARD MALLARY (R), John Downs (R), Ernest Gibson III (R), Sanborn Partridge (R), Byron Hathorn (R), Anthony Farrell (R), Stanton Lazarus (D), and William Jay Smith (D). Some of the above consider Daulton Mann (R) and state senator James B. Oakes (R) to have also been members. All of them were well under fifty years of age, while the average age for house members was fifty-nine. By 1963, the Young Turks were in control of state government. Hoff had captured the governor's office and Billings, elected House Speaker, promptly appointed Young Turks to the chairmanships of the major house committees. Over time, however, the membership dispersed and, Hoff and Mallary particularly, came to divide on important issues.

Z

Zebra Mussels

A freshwater bivalve introduced to the Great Lakes during the 1980s in the dumped ballast water of Russian freighters, the zebra mussel has made its way to LAKE CHAMPLAIN, where it can be found in almost all regions of the lake attached to any hard surface including boats, docks, stones, and even other mollusks. While they can grow up to 2 inches long, most zebra mussels are under an inch. They feed by filtering microscopic algae from the water, processing as much as a half gallon of water per day. Their filter-feeding clarifies water to the point where native aquatic plants threatened by pollution receive more sunlight and begin to thrive. However, because zebra mussels rapidly reproduce, their dense clusters can clog municipal and industrial water supply lines. Labor-intensive steam and high-pressure water blasting, hand-scraping, poisons, and electrocution may control them. Exceptionally fine filters are required to prevent them in their microscopic larval stage from blocking domestic water systems that draw from the lake. Zebra mussels concentrate heavy metals as they filter feed, which may have an adverse effect on the reproductive systems of some fish and ducks, especially scaup, that feed on them.

Zuckmayer, Carl (1896–1977)

German dramatist Carl Zuckmayer, famous for his play *Der Hauptmann von Köpenick* (*The Captain of Köpenick*), 1931, was forced to flee Austria for the United States after the Nazi takeover in 1938. Unable to make a living in New York or Hollywood, in 1941 he settled with his family on a remote farm in Barnard, where he raised poultry, goats, and pigs. He and his wife little by little became members of the community, going so far as to join the Grange. While on the farm, he wrote an anti-Nazi play, *Des Teufels General* (*The Devil's General*), which had its world premiere in Zurich in 1946. Eventually he and his wife returned to Europe, where he took part in re-establishing a free German theater. He wrote of his Vermont experiences in an autobiography, *Als Wär's Ein Stück von Mir* (published as *A Part of Myself*), 1966. His wife, Alice Herdan-Zuckmayer, published an extended memoir, *Die Farm in den Grünen Bergen* (published as *The Farm in the Green Mountains*), 1968.